MIG
4 [[]]

W9-CZM-412

THE
American Nation

A HISTORY OF THE UNITED STATES
★ FROM 1865 TO THE PRESENT ★

BY JOHN D. HICKS

A. F. and May T. Morrison Professor of History
University of California, Berkeley

SECOND EDITION

53517

HOUGHTON MIFFLIN COMPANY
BOSTON · NEW YORK · CHICAGO · DALLAS · ATLANTA · SAN FRANCISCO
The Riverside Press Cambridge

The Riverside Press
CAMBRIDGE · MASSACHUSETTS
PRINTED IN THE U.S.A.

★

TO
J. H., C., AND M.

★

PREFACE

HISTORY is so alive and growing that it is hard to see how anyone can think of it as dead and dry. It is, in reality, little more than a study of the present, explained in terms of the past. History looks forward, not backward; it is dynamic, not static. Those who condemn history as a mere rattling of ancient skeletons only betray their unfamiliarity with the subject. Out of the world of yesterday the world of today has grown; out of the world of today will come the world of tomorrow. It is impossible to understand our times without a knowledge of the conditions which brought them about; and it is equally impossible to make intelligent decisions for the future if we have only an uncomprehending view of the age in which we live. At least for a democracy, history is the most practical of subjects. One overstates but little to say that any democracy will function smoothly only in proportion as its history is well-taught and well-understood.

The field of history has long since been redefined to include social and economic as well as political development, and I have done my best in this volume to give a well-rounded picture of the American nation during the last seventy-five years. I have not yielded, however, to those pedagogical faddists who insist that political history should be stripped of its garments and consigned bare and meaningless to occasional thin chapters of names and dates. Just who is responsible for such a trend in an age when democracy is fighting for its life I do not know; it is hard to believe that this pernicious idea is the product merely of ignorance. Politics in a democracy is of obvious importance, and past politics throws much light on the evolving political scene. If the young people of our colleges are ever made to believe that the political life of their nation is unimportant, then our democracy will be in a sorry way indeed.

Nor have I yielded to that other group of faddists who insist that recent history is too complex to be integrated, but must be considered as a set of more or less unrelated problems, each to be pursued after the hop, skip, and jump method through a long period of time. The task of integration is indeed difficult, and I may not have done it well. But I have at least tried to recognize two important truths: first, that all history is interrelated; and second, that chronology is of profound importance. The task of the historian is not merely to spin out fine threads of knowledge; he must weave these threads together into a pattern which, however complicated, will have meaning as a whole.

In this book as in its predecessor, *The Federal Union*, references for further reading are suggested in footnotes scattered throughout the text rather than in formal bibliographies following each chapter. This is done with the hope that students will be induced to read further in subjects that particularly interest them. "The trouble with textbooks," according to one college president, "is that they take the sport out of learning. Their authors have had all the excitement of the chase . . . and leave the student only the dead quarry." This might be true if the textbook were regarded as the end rather than the beginning of wisdom. The wise teacher will assure his students that there is plenty of game still untaught, and that the textbook merely points the way to the chase.

I would be ungracious indeed not to acknowledge the very great debt I owe to the men whose single volumes on recent American history have preceded my own. I have borrowed freely from all of them. In the main, however, this book reproduces the organization and content of a course in the subject it covers that I have given for many years past. Introduced to this field first by Professor Frederic L. Paxson, now of the University of California, my debt to him is greater than to any other scholar. It was only with his definite encouragement that I presumed to parallel his *Recent History* with a book of my own.

Acknowledgments are also due to two of my colleagues, Professor William B. Hesseltine, who read and criticized the whole manuscript, and Professor Chester V. Easum, who gave me the benefit of his advice on the section pertaining to American entrance into the World War; to Professor George E. Mowry of the University of North Carolina for information gleaned from the Theodore Roosevelt papers; to Mr. Mannel Hahn of Winnetka, Illinois, who supplied essential data concerning the stamps reproduced on pages 680–81; to Dr. Theodore Saloutos, my research assistant, whose suggestions with reference to recent agricultural history were particularly valuable; to two of my graduate students, Miss Anne Cochrane and Mr. James Bringe, who cheerfully performed many time-consuming tasks; and to my wife, Lucile Curtis Hicks, who took time out from her already well-filled schedule to type a large part of the manuscript.

JOHN D. HICKS

MADISON, WISCONSIN

CONTENTS

Chapter One

THE PROBLEM OF THE SOUTH

Post-war Problems — Conditions in the South — National Policy — The Freedmen's Bureau — "Forty acres and a mule" — The army of occupation — Private benevolence — Cotton culture — The tenant system — Lincoln's plan of reconstruction — The Wade-Davis Bill — Andrew Johnson — Johnson's plan of reconstruction.

Pages 1–18

Chapter Two

RADICAL RECONSTRUCTION

Johnson's first message — Thaddeus Stevens — Charles Sumner — The black codes — Spirit of the South — Johnson and Congress — The Joint Committee on Reconstruction — The Fourteenth Amendment — Elections of 1866 — Impeachment of Johnson — The process of reconstruction — Negro suffrage — The Union League — The Fifteenth Amendment — Carpetbag rule

Pages 19–39

Chapter Three

THE GRANT RÉGIME

Grant and Colfax — The ambitions of Chase — Election of 1868 — Grant, the politician — Civil service reform — The Ohio idea — Legal-tender cases — Taxation reform — The Ku Klux Klan — The Solid South — Liberal Republicanism — Election of 1872 — The Grant scandals — Grant's foreign policy — Treaty of Washington

Pages 40–58

Chapter Four

A BUSINESS CYCLE

Failure of Jay Cooke and Company — Post-war prosperity — Rise of big business — The romance of steel — Andrew Carnegie — The petroleum industry — Rockefeller — The packing industry — Flour-milling — Other industries — Immigrant labor — Railroad expansion — The Union Pacific — The railroads and the panic

Pages 59–81

[vii]

CONTENTS

Chapter Five

AMERICAN SOCIETY DURING THE DEPRESSION

American cities — The newly rich — Business ethics — Corporation finance — Political scandals — The Tweed ring — A brighter side — Godkin, Curtis, and Schurz — The Patrons of Husbandry — Granger contributions — Educational changes — Technical and professional schools — Negro education — American literature — Religion and reform — The Centennial Exposition

Pages 82–114

Chapter Six

THE FAR WESTERN FRONTIER

The Far West — California prospectors — Mining booms — Colorado — Nevada — the Northwest — the Southwest — Staging and freighting — Evolution of law and order — The Indians wars — The new Indian policy — The killing of the buffalo — The cow country — The "long drive" — The range cattle industry — The passing of the cattleman

Pages 115–138

Chapter Seven

THE HAYES ADMINISTRATION

Elections of 1874 — The disputed election of 1876 — Rutherford B. Hayes — Restoration of white rule — Civil service reform — Resumption — Greenbackism — The "crime of 1873" — Bland-Allison Act — Labor unrest — The "Molly Maguires" — Railway strikes of 1877 — Kearneyism in California — The return of prosperity — Election of 1880

Pages 139–163

Chapter Eight

CAPITAL AND LABOR

Railroad building — The Transcontinentals — James J. Hill — Railroad regulation — Interstate Commerce Commission — The telephone — Tendencies toward monopoly — Sherman Anti-Trust Act — Labor organization — The Knights of Labor — Terence V. Powderly — Strikes of 1886 — The Haymarket riot — American Federation of Labor — Samuel Gompers — Immigration and labor

Pages 164–190

Chapter Nine

FROM GARFIELD TO HARRISON

The tragedy of Garfield — James G. Blaine — Chester A. Arthur — The "star-route" frauds — Civil service reform — The tariff argument — Tariff of 1883 — Campaign of 1884 — The Mugwumps — Grover Cleveland — Cleveland's tariff message — Campaign of 1888 — Benjamin Harrison — Admission of new states — Reed's rules — Republican legislation

Pages 191–220

CONTENTS

Chapter Ten

THE NEW SOUTH AND THE NEW WEST

Industrial beginnings in the South — Southern mill workers — Southern agriculture — The crop-lien system — The one-crop evil — The one-party system — The railroads and the West — Federal land policy — The western real estate boom — Drouth — The "end of free land" — Common interests of West and South

Pages 221–244

Chapter Eleven

THE POPULIST REVOLT

Third-party movements in American history — The Farmers' Alliance — The Alliance in politics — Elections of 1890 — Alliance successes — The People's Party — Election of 1892 — Cleveland and the gold reserve — Condition of the Treasury — Repeal of the Silver Purchase Act — Purchases of gold — Tariff legislation — Populist reactions

Pages 245–259

Chapter Twelve

THE SILVER CRUSADE

Labor disorders — The Homestead strike — The Pullman strike — Railroad tie-ups — Use of federal troops — The labor injunction — Coxey's army — Rise of the silver issue — Elections of 1894 — The "battle of the standards" — William Jennings Bryan — Plight of the Populists — Election of McKinley — The return of prosperity

Pages 260–278

Chapter Thirteen

THE OLD AMERICAN WAY

The Chicago World's Fair — Frederick Jackson Turner — The frontier influence — Uniformity of American society — Immigrant influences — Passing of the frontier — Business on a national scale — Rise of the city — Rural America — Town life — Religion — The conflict between science and religion — Public education — Sports

Pages 279–298

Chapter Fourteen

THE DIPLOMATIC FRONT

American isolation — Blaine's foreign policy — The fur-seal controversy — Hawaii — Samoa — Pan-Americanism — Relations with Chile — The Venezuelan controversy — Cuba — Nature of the Cuban revolt — American opinion on Cuba — The de Lôme letter — The *Maine* — American negotiations with Spain — A "needless war"

Pages 299–313

[ix]

CONTENTS

Chapter Fifteen

THE SPANISH–AMERICAN WAR

Admiral Mahan — The new navy — Theodore Roosevelt — Preparations for war — The American army — War legislation — Dewey at Manila — The Spanish fleet reaches Santiago — Sampson's strategy — Confusion at Tampa — The expedition to Santiago — Shafter's campaign — Naval battle of Santiago — An army of convalescents — Treaty of Paris

Pages 314–332

Chapter Sixteen

THE AMERICAN EMPIRE

The United States as a World Power — Alaska — The new possessions — Revolt in the Philippines — Election of 1900 — Imperialism the paramount issue — Death of McKinley — Occupation of Cuba — The Platt Amendment — Status of the dependencies — The insular cases — Government of the Philippines — Puerto Rico — Decline of imperialism

Pages 333–350

Chapter Seventeen

WORLD POLITICS

Theodore Roosevelt — Europe and America — The open-door policy — The Boxer uprising — Hay's diplomacy — Japan's ambitions — Russo-Japanese War — Japan and America — The Alaskan boundary — Panama Canal diplomacy — Building the canal — The "Big Stick" policy — The Drago doctrine — Caribbean control — The Hague Conferences

Pages 351–379

Chapter Eighteen

"MY POLICIES"

Roosevelt's interpretation of the Presidency — Integration in industry — The "Muckrakers" — Roosevelt and the trusts — The Northern Securities Case — Other prosecutions — Railroad regulation — The "square deal" — The Anthracite Coal Strike — Conservation — State reforms — The direct primary — Initiative and referendum — Labor legislation — Prohibition — Woman suffrage

Pages 380–409

Chapter Nineteen

ROOSEVELT AND TAFT

Roosevelt's popularity — Roosevelt and the Negro problem — Election of 1904 — Panic of 1907 — Roosevelt chooses Taft — Election of 1908 — Payne-Aldrich tariff — The Ballinger-Pinchot controversy — The fight on Cannonism — Roosevelt's return from Africa — Elections of 1910 — La Follette's candidacy — Roosevelt's "hat in the ring" — Election of 1912

Pages 410–439

CONTENTS

Chapter Twenty

WOODROW WILSON

Woodrow Wilson — Wilson as governor — Wilson and Bryan — Wilson to Congress — The Underwood-Simmons Tariff — Banking and currency reform — The Federal Reserve System — The trust problem — Party pledges on the trusts — Trust legislation — Administration of the Anti-Trust Acts — A "Magna Charta" for Labor — The Department of Labor — The I.W.W. — Mooney and Billings — Movement for immigration restriction — Rural credits — "Dollar-matching" — Federal Highways Act — Wilsonian *vs.* Jeffersonian democracy

Pages 440–462

Chapter Twenty-One

WILSON'S FOREIGN POLICY

Mexico — The fall of Huerta — Carranza — Constitution of 1917 — War in Europe — The balance-of-power system — Imperial rivalry — The Balkans — Nationalism — House's "great adventure" — Immediate causes of the war — American neutrality — Sympathy for the Allies — German-Americans — International law and the war — Relations with Great Britain — Relations with Germany — Submarine warfare — The *Lusitania* — Germany Backs Down — Preparedness — Election of 1916 — The Adamson Act — Wilson's narrow victory — Wilson's bid for peace — The submarine again — Congress declares war — Why America fought — Economic factors — Fear of a German victory — The defense of the Atlantic

Pages 463–486

Chapter Twenty-Two

THE FIRST WORLD WAR

The American army — Officer training — Financing the war — Private benevolence — War risk insurance — Public opinion on the war — The Creel Committee — Restrictions on civil liberties — Council of National Defense — The wartime government — Labor and the war — The "home front" — The navy in the war — The A.E.F. — The Saint-Mihiel salient — The Meuse-Argonne — The Russian Revolution — America's contribution to victory — The will to win — Unity of command and supply — The debate on war aims — German aspirations — Defeat of Germany — The armistice — Military terms of the armistice — Election of 1918 — The Paris Peace Conference — The Treaty of Versailles — The League of Nations — The Peace of Paris — The Senate and the treaty — Wilson's collapse

Pages 487–514

CONTENTS

Chapter Twenty-Three

THE SEARCH FOR NORMALCY

The Election of 1920 — Nomination of Harding — Cox and
Roosevelt — The "solemn referendum" — Harding — The
"best minds" — Separate peace with Germany — The Washington Conference — The Four-Power Pact — The Nine-
Power Pact — The World Court — Demobilization — Railway legislation — The merchant marine — The veterans'
bonus — Budget reform — Financial legislation — Restrictions on immigration — The Harding scandals — Daugherty
and Miller — Fall and the oil men — Death of Harding

Pages 515–534

Chapter Twenty-Four

THE ROAD TO PROSPERITY

Post-war prosperity — The real estate boom — Strikes of
1919 — "Red" baiting — The Ku Klux Klan — A business
decline — The depression in agriculture — Bank failures —
Farmer organizations — The Non-Partisan League — Co-
operative marketing — The Farm Bloc in Congress — Calvin
Coolidge — The recovery program; economy — Reduction
of taxes — Government withdrawal from business — Restraints on regulation — Government aids to business — The
disciplining of labor — Business recovery — The automobile
industry — Installment buying — Farmer and labor discontent — The "left wing" — Conference for Progressive Political Action — The La Follette candidacy — Democratic dissensions — Davis and Bryan — Coolidge and Dawes — The
Coolidge landslide

Pages 535–564

Chapter Twenty-Five

THE ROAD TO DEPRESSION

America and the world — Reparations — The quest for peace
— The Kellogg-Briand Pact — American agriculture — The
McNary-Haugen Bill — The export debenture plan — Nomination of Hoover — Smith and Robinson — Hoover — Smith
— Hoover's victory — The Federal Farm Board — Stabilization activities — The Hawley-Smoot Tariff — Background
of the Great Depression — Stock speculation — Panic of 1929
— Causes of the depression — Agricultural overexpansion —
Industrial overexpansion — Labor-saving machines — Capital surpluses — Overexpansion of credit — Decline of international trade — Political unrest

Pages 565–588

CONTENTS

Chapter Twenty-Six

THE NEW AMERICAN WAY

The automobile — Henry Ford — The "movies" — Talking pictures — Influence of the movies — Radio — The airplane — Air mail — Passenger travel by airplane — A mechanized age — Prohibition — Problems of enforcement — The bootleggers — The Wickersham Commission — Racketeering — Educational trends — Colleges and universities — Scientific achievements — American literature — Sinclair Lewis — Poetry — Plays and playwrights — Architecture — Century of Progress Exposition — World's Fairs of 1939

Pages 589–616

Chapter Twenty-Seven

THE NEW DEAL BEGINS

Hoover begins the New Deal — Public works — Relief policies — The RFC — The Home Loan Banks — The Bonus Bill — Relief for agriculture — Hoover's moratorium — Elections of 1930 — Presidential nominations of 1932 — Franklin D. Roosevelt — The campaign — The Democratic landslide — The "lame-duck" amendment — Hoover and Roosevelt — The banking crisis — Roosevelt's cabinet — The Emergency Banking Act — The Economy Act — The Beer Act — The CCC — Presidential leadership — Direction of the New Deal — The London Economics Conference

Pages 617–636

Chapter Twenty-Eight

THE NEW DEAL IN OPERATION

The three R's — Relief; FERA — The CWA — Work relief; WPA — WPA results — Recovery; RFC loans — Public Works; PWA — The NRA — NRA codes — End of NRA — The labor split; CIO — The "sit-down" — The AAA — Cotton control — Wheat, corn, and hogs — The AAA invalidated — Rural credits; FCA — The RA and FSA — The new AAA — Wheat surpluses — The plight of cotton — Social changes in the South — Reform; The currency — Roosevelt opposes inflation — The Glass-Steagall Act — The SEC — Railroad co-ordination — The merchant marine — The housing problem — National Housing Act of 1937 — The TVA — Opposition to TVA — Varieties of TVA endeavor — Social security — Unemployment compensation — Old-age insurance

Pages 637–670

Chapter Twenty-Nine

POLITICS, AT HOME AND ABROAD

The "Roosevelt Revolution" — The national debt — Roosevelt haters — Elections of 1934 — Campaign of 1936 — The new political division — Straw votes — Election results — Roosevelt attacks the Court — The new Supreme Court — The recession of 1937 — Party politics — Third-party misfortunes — The Hull trade pacts — The "good neighbor" policy — Cuba — Canada — The Philippines

Pages 671–685

Chapter Thirty

THE DISINTEGRATION OF PEACE

The Russian Revolution — Mussolini's rise in Italy — Fascism — Hitler's rise in Germany — Naziism — The rise of Fascism in Japan — Manchukuo — The Chinese "incident" — Ethiopia — The Spanish Civil War — Appeasement — Rome-Berlin Axis — End of appeasement — The Russian-German accord — The Second World War — The fall of France — England — "Collective security" — A quarantine of aggressors? — Naval expansion — Neutrality legislation — Roosevelt urges changes — "Continental solidarity" — Act of Havana — The Far East — American fears

Pages 686–708

Chapter Thirty-One

THE UNITED STATES IN THE SECOND WORLD WAR

Amendments to the Neutrality Act — Isolationists *vs.* Interventionists — Preparedness — Lessons from the Nazi victories — The defense program — Measures "short of war" — The presidential campaign — The Lend-Lease Act — Hitler attacks Russia — The Atlantic Charter — Pearl Harbor — Invasion of North Africa — Tunisia — Italy — The second front — On the sea and in the air — The eastern front — The German counter-attack — Conquest of Germany — "V–E Day" — The Pacific — Iwo Jima — Okinawa — MacArthur's return to the Philippines — The Asiatic mainland — The atomic bomb — Japanese surrender — The "Home Front" — The Japanese in Hawaii — The Japanese in California — Cost of the war

Pages 709–736

CONTENTS

Chapter Thirty-Two

POST-WAR PROBLEMS

Election of 1944 — Death of Roosevelt — Truman — Allied unity — The Yalta decisions — Concessions by Roosevelt — Concessions by Stalin — Military considerations — Dismemberment of Germany — Dumbarton Oaks — The San Francisco Conference — Other Conferences — The Potsdam Conference — Demobilization — G.I. benefits — The peace-time draft — Reconversion — Labor troubles — Inflation — Elections of 1946 — The Eightieth Congress — The Taft-Hartley Act — The pursuit of peace — Soviet policy — Minor peace treaties — Germany and Austria — Occupation of Germany — Trials of war criminals — Russian intransigence — China — Marshall's mission to China — Korea — Japan — Japanese war trials — Reforms in Japan — The Philippines — The Hukbalahap — India, Burma, Malaya — Indo-China and Indonesia — Latin America — The Argentine — Truman to Mexico

Pages 737–768

Chapter Thirty-Three

ONE WORLD — OR TWO?

The United Nations — Organization — The Security Council — Economic and Security Council — The Trusteeship Council — International Court of Justice — Military Staff Committee — The "Little Assembly" — Iran, Indonesia — Greece — Spain, Trieste — Palestine — The new State of Israel — The control of atomic energy — The Cominform — The "iron curtain" — The Truman Doctrine — The bipartisan foreign policy — The Marshall Plan; ERP — Background of ERP — UNRRA — Dissatisfaction with UNRRA — Russia rejects ERP — Congress supports ERP — European reaction — The North Atlantic Treaty — Russian aggressions — The Air-Lift — Divided Berlin — Efforts to compromise — End of the Air-Lift — Election of 1948 — Conventions and candidates — Democratic discouragement — The truce on foreign policy — The Dixiecrats — Truman — Another Democratic landslide

Pages 769–791

List of Books Cited   *Pages i–xxxii*

Index   *Pages xxxiii–lxv*

[xv]

ILLUSTRATIONS

ULYSSES S. GRANT; ANDREW JOHNSON ... 29

"CARPET-BAG RULE" ... 35

PRODUCTION OF STEEL IN THE UNITED STATES, 1863-76 ... 61

"DRAKE'S FOLLY" ... 64

A MODERN OIL FIELD ... 65

TWO PIONEER INDUSTRIALISTS: ANDREW CARNEGIE, JOHN D. ROCKEFELLER ... 67

BUILDING THE TRANSCONTINENTAL RAILROAD ... 76

CARTOON: "WHO STOLE THE PEOPLE'S MONEY?" ... 88

FOUR LEADERS AMONG WOMEN: FRANCES E. WILLARD, SUSAN B. ANTHONY, JANE ADDAMS, IDA M. TARBELL ... 111

EARLY TYPES OF REVOLVERS ... 133

THE EVOLUTION OF BARBED WIRE ... 135

WILLIAM F. CODY ... 137

THE APPRECIATING DOLLAR, 1865-95 ... 148

SAMUEL GOMPERS ... 187

FOUR REPUBLICANS: CHESTER A. ARTHUR, JAMES G. BLAINE, ROSCOE CONKLING, JAMES A. GARFIELD ... 193

FOUR DEMOCRATS: GROVER CLEVELAND, SAMUEL J. TILDEN, WILLIAM JENNINGS BRYAN, JOHN P. ALTGELD ... 206

CARTOON: THE BOSSES OF THE SENATE ... 210

CARTOON: CZAR REED ... 215

FOUR NONCONFORMISTS: HENRY GEORGE, CARL SCHURZ, GEORGE WILLIAM CURTIS, JAMES B. WEAVER ... 240

FREDERICK JACKSON TURNER ... 281

THEODORE ROOSEVELT ... 353

CARTOON: "THE DEAD RETURNED TO LIFE" ... 383

FOUNDERS OF THE NORTHERN SECURITIES COMPANY, J. PIERPONT MORGAN AND JAMES J. HILL ... 387

CARTOON: THE MISSISSIPPI BEAR HUNT ... 412

CHARLES EVANS HUGHES ... 416

ILLUSTRATIONS

ELIHU ROOT   418

WILLIAM HOWARD TAFT; ROBERT M. LA FOLLETTE   423

CARTOON: "PLEASE, MR. ALDRICH"   425

CARTOON: THE COMMON PEOPLE AWAITING T. R.'S RETURN   429

WOODROW WILSON   443

CARTOON: HARDING'S PLATFORM ON THE LEAGUE   518

CARTOON: THE USELESS MIDDLEMAN   545

CALVIN COOLIDGE; HERBERT HOOVER   573

CARTOON: WHAT A GRAND AND GLORIOUS FEELING!   576

HENRY FORD   583

AUTOMOBILES IN USE, 1900–39   590

EVOLUTION OF THE AUTOMOBILE   591

EVOLUTION OF THE AIRPLANE   597

PREDICTED CHANGES IN AGE COMPOSITION OF THE AMERICAN POPULATION   608

FOUR MEN OF LETTERS: WILLIAM DEAN HOWELLS, MARK TWAIN, SINCLAIR LEWIS, EUGENE O'NEILL   611

THE NEW YORK SKYLINE   613

TWO EXAMPLES OF MODERN ARCHITECTURE: THE NEBRASKA STATE CAPITOL, THE SEATTLE ART MUSEUM   615

FRANKLIN D. ROOSEVELT   625

THE SEAT OF GOVERNMENT   634

HISTORIC POSTAGE STAMPS   650–51

CARTOON: "IT'S ALL PART OF A GREAT BIG PLAN"   673

CARTOON: WARMONGER!   698

CARTOON: RENDEZVOUS   699

CARTOON: "IT'S A LIE, WE'RE NOT RETREATING — JUST ADVANCING BACKWARD!"   720

CARTOON: "LOOK, NO HANDS!"   789

MAPS

WESTERN HEMISPHERE *between* pp. 28 and 29

THE PROCESS OF RECONSTRUCTION 49

THE AMERICAN RAILROAD SYSTEM, 1870 79

THE GREAT PLAINS ENVIRONMENT, 1870 116

INDIAN RESERVATIONS IN THE UNITED STATES, 1883 129

PRESIDENTIAL ELECTION OF 1876, BY STATES AND COUNTIES 144

GROWTH OF THE WESTERN RAILROADS, 1830–1920 167

THE UNITED STATES IN 1940 *between* pp. 220 and 221

THE BLACK BELT 230

THE COTTON BELT 230

FEDERAL LAND GRANTS FOR TRANSPORTATION, 1823–71 232

AVERAGE ANNUAL RAINFALL IN THE UNITED STATES 234

AVERAGE ANNUAL TEMPERATURE IN THE UNITED STATES 235

DISTRIBUTION OF PUBLIC LANDS IN THE UNITED STATES, 1929 243

PRESIDENTIAL ELECTION OF 1892, BY STATES AND COUNTIES 253

PRESIDENTIAL ELECTION OF 1896, BY STATES AND COUNTIES 275

DENSITY OF POPULATION, 1870–1930 286–287

RELATIVE IMPORTANCE OF CITY AND COUNTRY POPULATION 292

MANILA BAY 320

SANTIAGO DE CUBA 320

THE PACIFIC OCEAN *between* pp. 332 and 333

SOUTH AMERICA *between* pp. 332 and 333

THE ALASKAN BOUNDARY DISPUTE 363

THE CARIBBEAN ZONE *between* pp. 364 and 365

THE DOMINION OF CANADA *between* pp. 364 and 365

TWO TYPICAL RAILROAD SYSTEMS, 1914 389

NATIONAL FORESTS AND NATIONAL PARKS 399

PRESIDENTIAL ELECTION OF 1912, BY STATES AND COUNTIES 439

TARIFF LEGISLATION, 1909–13 447

THE FEDERAL RESERVE DISTRICTS 448

THE FEDERAL HIGHWAYS SYSTEM 461

PRINCIPAL FRENCH PORTS AND RAILROADS USED BY THE
AMERICAN EXPEDITIONARY FORCES 499

FOREIGN-BORN POPULATION IN THE UNITED STATES, 1900–30 530

DISTRIBUTION OF FACTORY OUTPUT, 1919 536

AGRICULTURAL PRODUCTION IN THE UNITED STATES, 1919 541

INCREASE IN FARM TENANCY 543

FEDERAL INCOME AND PROFITS TAXES, 1928 551

GEOGRAPHICAL DISTRIBUTION OF PRODUCTS IN THE UNITED
STATES 555

CONCENTRATION OF WEALTH, 1922 557

PRESIDENTIAL ELECTION OF 1924, BY STATES AND COUNTIES 563

SELF–SUFFICING FARMS IN THE UNITED STATES 570

PRESIDENTIAL ELECTION OF 1928, BY STATES AND COUNTIES 579

RADIO BROADCASTING STATIONS IN THE UNITED STATES 595

AMERICAN AIRWAYS 600

RATES OF TRAVEL 601

IRRIGATION AND POWER DEVELOPMENT IN THE UNITED
STATES 664

THE TENNESSEE VALLEY AUTHORITY 665

RATES OF NATURAL INCREASE IN THE AMERICAN POPULATION 669

AIR LINE OR GREAT CIRCLE DISTANCES IN THE PACIFIC 722

ZONES OF OCCUPATION: GERMANY, AUSTRIA, BERLIN 755

INTERNATIONAL AIR ROUTES 764

THE DEMOCRATIC SWEEP 790

CHAPTER I

THE PROBLEM OF THE SOUTH

THE generation that has grown up in the United States since the first World War will not need to be told that the end of hostilities may precipitate problems quite as perplexing as those which mark *Post-war* the progress of a war itself. With the spring of 1865 the *problems* American Civil War had worn itself out, but the tardy arrival of peace introduced other difficulties more appalling, perhaps, than the nation had ever faced before. The South, after four years of warfare within its borders, was not only defeated; its whole pattern of social organization lay in hopeless ruins. How were the people of the New South to live? What was to be the status of the freedmen? When and how were the normal processes of government to be resumed? Nor were the problems of the day confined wholly, or even mainly, to the South. The government of the United States, and, indeed, the governments of the northern states also, had become accustomed to the exercise of unusual wartime prerogatives. Were these practices to become permanent, or were they to be trimmed to fit the needs of peace? A million men were under arms. How could their speedy absorption into the ordinary walks of life be best facilitated? A huge national debt, an inflated currency, an overgrown system of taxation were parts of the inevitable legacy of war. What should the new financial picture be like? Manufactures of many sorts and kinds, stimulated by war orders and war profits, had reached a phenomenal development. Could their prosperity be preserved with the nation at peace? Agriculture, too, particularly in the Northwest, had expanded abnormally. How were the farmers to find markets for their produce? Less tangible, but no less important, the peoples of North and South for full four years had unbridled their prejudices, each against the other, and had carefully nourished their hatreds. How were the two parts of the restored Union ever to become one again in spirit? How could they learn to forgive and forget?

"Reconstruction" is the label that historians have generally applied to these post-war years. The word gained currency on the eve of the

Civil War, when a "reconstruction of the Union" that would satisfy *Reconstruc-* the South was often suggested as an alternative to seces-*tion* sion. It was applied during and immediately after the war to the "reconstruction" of loyal governments in states from which secessionist officials had fled. As a descriptive term it leaves much to be desired. Neither the pre-war South nor the pre-war Union could ever be rebuilt or restored. Out of the ordeal of war and its aftermath there emerged a new nation, a nation so different from the old that the term "revolution" would scarcely overstate. But "reconstruction" has the sanction of long usage, and, properly redefined, it may still be permitted to serve. In a narrow sense, "reconstruction" means the process by which state government was revived in the South; broadly speaking, it must include all the drastic transformations of the period, both North and South.

Four years of warfare had left their marks upon the South.[1] Armies had marched, camped, foraged, and fought in practically every southern *Conditions* state, and in some of them almost continuously. Sherman's *in the South* exultant report of the desolation wrought by his column on the way from Atlanta to the sea speaks for itself:

> We have consumed the corn and fodder in the region of country thirty miles on either side of a line from Atlanta to Savannah as also the sweet potatoes, cattle, hogs, sheep and poultry, and have carried away more than 10,000 horses and mules as well as a countless number of slaves. I estimate the damage done to the State of Georgia and its military resources at $100,000,-000; at least $20,000,000 of which has inured to our advantage and the remainder is simple waste and destruction.

As Sherman's army turned northward into South Carolina, it vented its fury upon the state that most Northerners held responsible for starting the war. Carl Schurz reported, from observations made six months later, that the countryside along the "track of Sherman's march"

> looked for many miles like a broad black streak of ruin and desolation — the fences all gone; lonesome smoke stacks, surrounded by dark heaps of ashes and cinders, marking the spots where human habitations had stood; the fields along the road wildly overgrown by weeds, with here and there a sickly looking patch of cotton or corn cultivated by negro squatters.

Traveling through Virginia in October, 1865, Alexander H. Stephens

---

[1] An excellent picture of post-war conditions in the South is contained in W. L. Fleming, *The Sequel of Appomattox* (1919). E. P. Oberholtzer, *A History of the United States since the Civil War* (5 vols., 1917–37), begins at this point to be useful. W. A. Dunning, *Reconstruction, Political and Economic* (1907), set a pattern for historical thinking on the problem that has only recently been challenged. J. G. Randall, *The Civil War and Reconstruction* (1937), is a useful summary of the latest opinions on the subject.

wrote in his diary: "The desolation of the country from Alexandria to near Charlottesville was horrible to behold." Around Petersburg, where the forces of Grant and Lee had fought under conditions resembling modern trench warfare, farmers were stopped in their plowing by the quantity of metal they found in the ground, and the stench of death ended only with the autumn frosts. The Shenandoah Valley was so thoroughly denuded that, in accordance with Sheridan's promise "a crow could not fly over it without carrying his rations with him." Several years after the war an English traveler in America found the Valley of the Tennessee little better:

> It consists for the most part of plantations in a state of semi-ruin, and planta-tions of which the ruin is total and complete. . . . The trail of war is visible throughout the valley in burnt-up gin-houses, ruined bridges, mills, and factories, of which latter the gable walls only are left standing, and in large tracts of once cultivated land stripped of every vestige of fencing. The roads, long neglected, are in disorder, and having in many places become impassable, new tracks have been made through the woods and fields with-out much respect to boundaries. Borne down by losses, debts, and accumu-lating taxes, many who were once the richest among their fellows have dis-appeared from the scene, and few have yet risen to take their places.[1]

The sight of Charleston, once the proudest city of the South, moved the war-hardened Schurz to rhetoric:

> There was no shipping in the harbor except a few quartermaster's vessels and two or three small steamers. We made fast to a decaying pier con-structed of palmetto-logs. There was not a human being visible on the wharf. The warehouses seemed to be completely deserted. There was no wall and no roof that did not bear eloquent marks of having been under the fire of siege guns. . . . Nothing could be more desolate and melancholy than the appearance of the lower part of the city immediately adjoining the harbor. Although the military authorities had caused the streets to be "policed" as well as possible, abundant grass had still grown up between the paving stones. The first living object that struck my view . . . was a dilap-idated United States cavalry horse bearing the mark I.C. — inspected and condemned — now peacefully browsing on the grass in a Charleston street. A few cows were feeding in a vacant lot near by, surrounded by buildings gashed and shattered by shell and solid shot. The crests of the roofs and the chimneys were covered with turkey-buzzards, who evidently felt at home, and who from time to time lazily flapped their wings and stretched their hideous necks. Proceeding higher up into the city, we passed through a part of the "burned district," looking like a vast graveyard with broken walls and tall blackened chimneys for monuments, overtopped by the pic-turesque ruins of the cathedral.[2]

---

[1] Robert Somers, *The Southern States Since the War, 1870–71* (1871), p. 114.   This is typical of the great mass of travel literature on the South.
[2] *The Reminiscences of Carl Schurz* (1908), iii, 165.

Many another southern city had been similarly despoiled. Columbia, the thriving pre-war capital of South Carolina, was the customary "mass of blackened chimneys and crumbling walls." The fire that destroyed it had swept eighty-four blocks, and had consumed every building for "three-fourths of a mile on each of twelve streets." Atlanta was a riot of tangled brick and mortar, charred timbers, and rubbish. "Hell has laid her egg," one Georgian observed, "and right here it hatched." Mobile, too, had suffered from fire and had fallen into "torpor and decay." Galveston was described as "a city of dogs and desolation."

The havoc that the war had wrought on the South's transportation system was one of the worst of the calamities from which it suffered. *Transpor-* Columbia, South Carolina, had been a railway center before *tation* the war, with five lines converging upon it. By the time Sherman's troops had departed, the tracks had been torn up for thirty miles in every direction. Rolling stock was left standing in the fields to be used by the homeless as dwellings. Rails were heated in the middle and twisted fantastically around trees. Similar thoroughness had characterized railroad destruction in Georgia, Mississippi, and various other parts of the South, while the wear and tear of wartime usage without adequate repairs had made the railroads outside the devastated regions almost as worthless as those within. Before the war river traffic had played a large part in moving the produce of the South. Now river channels were blocked, steamboats were destroyed, and wharves were missing. Seaports, so essential to the trade of the pre-war South, were in similar disarray. Country roads were non-existent or worse; bridges were gone; horses, mules, oxen, carriages, wagons, and carts had all too frequently been commandeered by the troops of North or South.

Property losses suffered in the states of the former Confederacy should include numerous other items. The Confederate bonds, both *Southern* state and national, into which much southern capital had *losses from* gone, had ceased altogether to be of value. So also had Con-*war* federate currency. Banks were closed; factories were idle; land values had toppled to nearly nothing; business in general was shattered. Property in slaves, which before the war accounted for so much of the South's wealth, was completely wiped out. Worse still, confiscation, contrary to a common opinion, took a heavy toll from the scanty resources of the defeated states. President Johnson tried to prevent this by ordering, in an amnesty proclamation issued May 29, 1865, that no further seizures of private property be made, and his Attorney-General helped still more by ruling that private property already seized must be restored to anyone who had received a presidential pardon. But it was generally agreed that the property of the Confederate government was now the property of the United States, and that all such property must be located and attached.

It was from the attempt to seize this public property that the South came to know what confiscation might mean. Agents of the Treasury Department, sent South on a twenty-five per cent commis- *Confiscation* sion basis to locate the 150,000 bales of cotton that the Confederate government was supposed to have had on hand at the close of the war, developed a tendency to take whatever cotton they happened to find, and to turn over to the United States only such of their takings as they saw fit. "I am sure I sent some honest cotton agents South," Secretary of the Treasury McCulloch admitted ruefully, "but it sometimes seems doubtful whether any of them remained honest for long." Not only cotton, but livestock, tobacco, rice, sugar, or anything of value was seized by individuals who represented themselves as agents of the United States. The total sum realized by the Treasury from seizures was $34,000,000, a considerable part of which was later returned. But this sum represents only a fraction of the damage done. With laudable candor Secretary McCulloch reported in 1866:

> Contractors, anxious for gain, were sometimes guilty of bad faith and peculation, and frequently took possession of cotton and delivered it under contracts as captured or abandoned, when in fact it was not such and they had no right to touch it. . . . Residents and others in the districts where these peculations were going on took advantage of the unsettled condition of the country, and representing themselves as agents of this department, went about robbing under such pretended authority, and thus added to the difficulties of the situation by causing unjust opprobrium and suspicion to rest upon officers engaged in the faithful discharge of their duties. Agents, . . . frequently received or collected property, and sent it forward which the law did not authorize them to take. . . . Lawless men, singly and in organized bands, engaged in general plunder; every species of intrigue and peculation and theft were resorted to.

In assessing the damage done the South by the war, the personal element must not be ignored. Perhaps a quarter of a million soldiers and an untold number of civilians lost their lives because of the *The southern* clash of arms. Among those who perished were a large *people* portion of the natural leaders of the South — men who, had they lived, could have helped most during the trials of the reconstruction era. Many of the survivors were themselves immeasurably the worse for their experiences; even when they were not maimed or broken in body, men trained in the school of war could never be quite the same as if trained in the normal pursuits of peace. As for the Negroes, the boon of freedom

[5]

was not without its unfortunate consequences. Before the end of the war about 180,000 of them had been enrolled as free soldiers in the United States armies, others were merely camp-followers and refugees. The downfall of the Confederacy plunged all the rest into freedom — a state of society for which they were almost totally unprepared. As slaves, they had looked to their masters for food, shelter, and protection. As free men they had little idea how to provide such things for themselves. Freedom meant freedom from work, and the right to leave the plantation at will; that it might carry with it unpleasant responsibilities few of the Negroes were able to understand. Some stayed with the old masters and worked on as if nothing had happened; others wandered away to places they had never seen before. During the spring and summer of 1865 they could be found in bands like gypsies, roving the country, and emulating Sherman's "bummers" in their search for food. From one point of view the abolition of slavery had cost the South nothing. The Negroes were still there, and they could do as much work as ever before — if only they would. But the evidence compounded that most of the ex-slaves, temporarily at least, had no will to work. And with the blacks constituting nearly forty per cent of the total population, this was a frightfully serious matter.[1]

At the present time the people of the United States, or of any other great power, if confronted with such a condition as existed in the South *National policy* of 1865, would take it for granted that the government must play the principal part in restoring the economic life of the war-stricken section. In the middle of the nineteenth century, however, there were few who would have thought of such a thing. The "less government the better" was still the dominant philosophy, not only of the Democrats, but also of the great majority of the Republicans; indeed, the doctrine of rugged individualism, whether derived from the experience of the American frontier, or from the writings of European savants, or from both, was never more universally accepted. In the main, therefore, the economic problems of the South were regarded as the concern of individuals, rather than of the government, and in their solution the government gave only incidental assistance.

The necessity of direct aid for the freedmen, however, was something that could not easily be overlooked. The power of the national government had been used to free the slaves; hence the Negroes, now that they were free, had become in a sense the wards of the nation. The

[1] W. E. B. DuBois, *Black Reconstruction* (1935), and A. A. Taylor, *The Negro in South Carolina During the Reconstruction* (1924), present the problem from the Negro's point of view. See also B. G. Brawley, *Social History of the American Negro* (1921), and G. W. Williams, *History of the Negro Race in America* (2 vols., 1882).

freedmen themselves were by no means unaware of this obligation. Just as their masters had cared for them in the past, so now they expected their "deliverers" to look after them. That Congress was ready to accept such responsibility, at least for a limited time, was shown by the passage in March, 1865, of an act creating the Freedmen's Bureau. This organization, which was to last for a year after the close of the war, was to be set up in the War Department under a commissioner appointed by the President, and an assistant commissioner for each of the insurrectionary states. It was authorized to distribute "such issues of provisions, clothing, and fuel" as might be necessary to relieve the "destitute and suffering refugees and freedmen and their wives and children." It had also the right to take over any land within the designated states that had been abandoned by its owners or confiscated by the United States, and to distribute it in tracts of forty acres or less, on a three-year rental basis, to "loyal refugees and freedmen." *The Freedmen's Bureau*

Under the leadership of General Oliver O. Howard, an able and conscientious man, the Freedmen's Bureau went promptly to work.[1] Its agents soon penetrated to every portion of the South, and were kept busy, for a time, distributing the bare necessities of life to hundreds of thousands of needy, white as well as black. Without this assistance there can be no doubt that many of both races would have starved to death; or, one might properly say, many more might have starved than did. The Bureau also made a laudable effort to provide its dependents with medical care and hospitalization, but among the Negroes, who knew so little about how to take care of themselves, illness took a frightful toll. The mortality among Negro children, who in slavery times would often have been nursed through their illnesses by the plantation mistress herself, but now had to depend upon the pitifully inadequate ministrations of their parents, was particularly appalling.

The plan to distribute abandoned land to the freedmen led to an unfortunate misunderstanding. It was inferred at first that all land "abandoned" because its owners had left it for Confederate service would be available for distribution, but President Johnson's policy permitted the pardoned owners of such property to recover it. The result was that the Bureau had comparatively little land of value to give away. The Negro, however, got the impression, often deliberately spread by unscrupulous agents, that each freedman *"Forty acres and a mule"*

[1] The Freedmen's Bureau has been the subject of many historical studies. Among the best are Paul S. Peirce, *The Freedmen's Bureau* (1904), and Laura J. Webster, *The Operation of the Freedmen's Bureau in South Carolina* (1916).

[7]

would soon be given "forty acres of land and a mule." Some included, for good measure, a white man to do the work. With so rosy a prospect for the future, and an abundance of free rations for the present, many of the Negroes found it difficult to see why they should do more than await the day of "jubilee." For some of them this day was dated. On January 1, 1866, they believed, the redistribution of land would take place.

In noting the governmental assistance given to the South after the war, one should remember the army of occupation. For several years de-
The army of occupation tachments of Federal troops were not far away in any part of the South; and there were regions in which the hated "blue-bellies," as they were inelegantly termed, were very numerous. The northern army, always abundantly provided with rations, clothing, and other supplies, shared its plenty with the destitute. This was the more natural because some of the Federal troops were themselves Negroes. When the war ended, most of the whites in the Federal army had taken the first opportunity to be "mustered out," but the Negroes had shown no such eagerness, and many of them were allowed to remain in the service. The soldiers, whether white or black, had money to spend, and the government spent still larger sums for their maintenance. Directly or indirectly, the army thus contributed an appreciable amount to the economic rehabilitation of the South.

One other item of governmental aid to the South deserves mention, and that, curiously, was given to the southern railroads.[1] While northern troops accounted for an enormous amount of railroad destruction, it is also a fact that wherever the operations of the Federal army required the reconditioning of the railroads, that, too, was done. In those portions of the upper South that the North had long held, the railroads were actually left in better condition than they were found. At the end of the war the United States War Department even went so far as to take over and reorganize some of the bankrupt railroad companies, and then, with "loyal" boards of directors assured, to return them to their owners.

Private benevolence added a little to the aid given by the government. The Negroes, naturally, were the recipients of much such attention.
Private benevolence Even before the end of the war the American Missionary Association, for example, had begun a work among them that led to expenditures after the return of peace of about $100,000 annually, mostly on Negro education. Also, the churches of the North sent a sizable army of missionaries, preachers, and teachers into the South. At first many such individuals assumed that the collapse of the Confederacy meant that the separate southern churches would also cease

[1] Carl Russell Fish, *The Restoration of the Southern Railroads* (1919).

[8]

to exist, and that reunion under northern domination would follow immediately, with themselves in prominent positions. This failed to happen, but the missionary zeal of the northern workers found a ready outlet in helping the Negroes adjust themselves to freedom. They induced most of the ex-slaves to separate from the churches of their former masters, and to form new churches of their own. They used northern missionary money to build and maintain Negro churches and schools, and to care for the needy. Among the most active in this respect were the agents of the Freedmen's Aid Society of the Methodist Episcopal Church, but similar work was supported by the Baptists, the Presbyterians, and many other denominations.

Philanthropy, although then in its infancy, furnished another source of outside income to the South. The most notable donation of this kind came from George Peabody, who gave the income from a *Philanthropy* fund of two million dollars, or more, "to the suffering South for the good of the whole country." The Peabody Education Fund was wisely administered, and proved to be an effective aid to the establishment of better common schools in the South. The Negroes themselves were pathetically eager for book-learning, and flocked into whatever schools were provided for them. Most of them, however, showed no great proficiency beyond the elementary stages, and the wisest of their advisers were soon counseling them to seek vocational training rather than the higher learning, including Greek and Latin, that altogether too many of them craved.

Southerners were at first hopeful that a great outpouring of northern capital would aid in the rehabilitation of the South, but in this they were to be sadly disappointed. Northern investors did, indeed, *Scarcity of* buy southern railway securities in sufficient amounts to *capital* make possible a rapid recovery on the part of the southern railroads, and they also purchased, to their later regret, the new bond issues of the southern states. But their southern investments went little further. The North, with its own fields of endeavor to look after — industrial expansion, agricultural extension, the building of transcontinental railroads, the development of the mining and ranching West — had little left to risk in a region where political conditions were disturbed and a racial conflict was in the making. Thrown back upon its own meager resources, the South made numerous small beginnings in the lumbering industry, in the manufacture of tobacco, in the establishment of cotton mills, in the exploitation of its resources in coal and iron, as well as in the restoration of its agricultural activities, particularly the growing of cotton, which became again, as before the war, its chief concern.

Fortunately for the South the world had need of cotton, but to restore production was no easy matter. Seed was lacking, tools and machinery *Cotton* were worn out, horses and mules were scarce, and the labor *culture* supply was an unknown quantity. Many Southerners, convinced that without slavery the Negroes could never be induced to work, hoped to devise some scheme for sending them back to Africa or to the West Indies; and still more believed that the salvation of the South lay in replacing or supplementing Negro labor with that of immigrants from Europe or elsewhere. But the Negroes would not go and the immigrants would not come. Some of the planters attempted to revive the old plantation system on the basis of free labor. Backed with whatever money the promise of cotton enabled them to borrow in Europe or in the North, they offered the Negroes wages to return to their former duties. Such a transaction was apt to be carefully watched by the Freedmen's Bureau, which usually insisted on a written contract, with the amount of wages and the conditions of labor carefully set down. It was not the planter, however, who broke the contract, but the freedman, who rarely saw point to working after he had earned a few dollars. Delayed wages were sometimes tried, but with equally indifferent results. Other planters offered laborers a share in the annual proceeds of the plantation, but this system, likewise, proved defective. The freedmen resented the necessity of working in gangs, as in slavery times, and even more, the existence of anything bordering on oversight.

In the end the plantation system had to go, and in a sense the promise of "forty acres and a mule" was realized. The planters found by experi- *The southern* ence that only when they split up their land into small plots, *tenant* with a Negro, or it might be a white tenant, in charge of *system* each, could they obtain satisfactory results. Each tenant had usually to be supplied with not only his mule, but his seed, his tools, and his living until the crop was harvested; all this the landlord either furnished directly, or by obtaining credit for his tenants at one of the numerous "country stores" that sprang up all over the South. A crop lien secured both the landlord and the storekeeper against loss. As a rule the tenant turned over from a third to a half of his produce to the landlord as rental, and all the rest went to repay his debts; but by working along on his own time in his own way he at least produced a part of a crop. His status, bound as he was by his crop lien, lay somewhere between slavery and freedom, but it amounted, perhaps, to as great a change as his limited experience would permit. The first few crops after the war, with the Negroes unsettled and the Freedmen's Bureau at hand to back them up in fantastic demands, were miserable failures, but by

1869 a cotton crop worth a quarter of a billion dollars was marketed. From that time forward the acute poverty of the South began to abate.[1] So much attention has been focused upon the Negroes, whether slave or free, that the rôle of the small white farmer of the South has rarely received the prominence that it deserves. Even before the *The white* Civil War white labor accounted for a considerable part of *farmer* the South's crop of cotton, and after the war the proportion tended to increase. In general the land worked by the whites in the time of slavery was inferior to that included in the great plantations and worked by slaves. But after the war the planters were glad to obtain tenants, white as well as black, and they often found it necessary to sell a part, or even all, of their holdings. Independent ownership was greatly stimulated by the low prices that landowners were obliged to accept. Land that had been worth from twenty to thirty dollars an acre before the war sold for from three to five dollars an acre after the war, and sometimes for less. Many of the whites who had owned poor land before, or no land at all, took advantage of this remarkable opportunity to buy. In ten years, according to the census of 1870, the number of farms in South Carolina had increased from 33,000 to 52,000; in Mississippi, from 43,000 to 68,000; in Louisiana, from 17,000 to 28,000. In the other southern states the figures, while not so striking, show the same general trend. Some of the new landowners were Negroes, but their holdings were generally very small, and most of the land that changed hands went to whites. A considerable number of Northerners were attracted into the South by the low prices of land, but most of them were unable to adjust themselves satisfactorily to the new environment.

While cotton was the best money crop of the South, it must not be forgotten that southern agriculture, both before and after the war, produced some of nearly everything that can be grown on *Rice, sugar* farms. Rice culture, which had been an important activity *and tobacco* in South Carolina and Georgia before the war, showed in those states few symptoms of revival, but in Louisiana the production of both rice and sugar-cane was successfully undertaken. Tobacco-growing in the upper South made rapid headway, particularly in Kentucky, where the crop increased from 54,000,000 pounds in 1865 to 103,000,000 pounds in 1871.[2] In the states where cotton had never been "king," and where in consequence the concentration of Negroes had been less marked, the problem

---

[1] M. B. Hammond, *The Cotton Industry* (1897), is a book of enduring merit. Consult also R. P. Brooks, *The Agrarian Revolution in Georgia, 1865–1912* (1914).

[2] Meyer Jacobstein, *The Tobacco Industry in the United States* (1907); B. W. Arnold, *History of the Tobacco Industry in Virginia from 1860 to 1894* (1897).

of restoring normal production was far more easily solved. After the first two or three hard years, livestock and foodstuffs could be found practically anywhere in abundance.

Unfortunately, the valiant efforts of the South to work out a new economic system proved to be of far less concern to the national government *Lincoln's* than the strictly political problem. Early in the war Presi*plan of re-* dent Lincoln had faced the necessity of deciding what to do *construction* with a seceded state after the armies of the North had conquered it. He was not much interested in theorizing about whether such a state was still in the Union, or had by the act of secession lost its legal life. He wished merely to promote the establishment within its borders of a loyal state government, and the resumption as speedily as possible of a normal relationship to the nation as a whole. As early as 1862 he appointed for each of the seceded states then occupied in considerable part by northern troops a military governor, who was expressly charged with the responsibility of reviving loyal sentiment among the state's inhabitants. Then, in December, 1863, he set forth in a presidential proclamation his plan for the re-establishment of state governments.[1] Pardons were promised, with a few exceptions aimed mainly at high civil and military officers of the Confederacy, to all who would take a prescribed oath of allegiance to the United States, and, whenever in any state as many as one tenth of the number of persons who had voted in 1860 should take the oath, a civil government was to be inaugurated which the President bound himself to recognize "as the true government of the state." Operating under this plan, three states, Tennessee, Louisiana, and Arkansas, succeeded during the year 1864 in re-creating state governments, and were accorded presidential recognition. The President also recognized a loyal, although decidedly impotent, government in Virginia that throughout the war had maintained a precarious existence at Alexandria. From these acts, and from his various utterances, it was evident that he intended to use the full power of his high office to make the "road to reunion" as short and straight as possible.

Lincoln's magnanimous attitude toward the vanquished foe was not *The Wade-* shared, however, by the majority of his party in Congress. *Davis Bill* Few of them understood as clearly as did he, the difficulties that the South had to face, and fewer still were able to view the

---

[1] C. H. McCarthy, *Lincoln's Plan of Reconstruction* (1901). On the political side of reconstruction the bibliography is enormous. Still useful among the older histories are James Ford Rhodes, *History of the United States from the Compromise of 1850*, VI, VII (1906); Peter J. Hamilton, *The Reconstruction Period* (1906); W. L. Fleming, *Documentary History of Reconstruction* (2 vols., 1906–07); J. W. Burgess, *Reconstruction and the Constitution, 1866–1876* (1902); and William A. Dunning, *Essays on the Civil War and Reconstruction* (1904).

scene with a like sense of detachment. It was natural for Northerners, more especially, northern Republicans, to hold the South responsible for the war, and to raise doubts as to whether an enemy, only recently under arms against the Union, could so speedily be trusted to maintain it. More to the point, many leading Republicans were fearful lest the return of the southern states to the fold should pave the way for the rise of the Democratic Party to power, and they were particularly aggrieved that the President should have taken into his own hands a matter so important. Congress, they maintained, should have been consulted, and a law rather than a presidential proclamation should have charted his course. As a fitting answer to his act of "executive usurpation," all senators and representatives chosen by the states that he had "reconstructed" were denied admission to Congress, and in July, 1864, by the so-called Wade-Davis Bill, a congressional substitute for the presidential plan of reconstruction was proposed.

The provisions of this bill, as a matter of fact, differed from the President's plan less than might have been expected. It provided for the appointment of a provisional governor in each conquered state, but the duties assigned him were not unlike those that the President had expected of his military governors. Each provisional governor was to take a census of the white male citizens under his jurisdiction, and to request each citizen to take an oath in support of the Constitution of the United States. In case a majority (rather than ten per cent) of those so enrolled complied with this request, the governor was to call upon the oath-bound citizens, as voters, to elect delegates to a convention, which must pledge the state (1) to deny political rights to all high-ranking civil and military officers of the Confederacy, (2) to abolish slavery, and (3) to outlaw all debts, state or Confederate, "created by or under the sanction of the usurping power." The convention might then draw up a constitution in which the three pledges were to be included, and in case this document should be approved by a majority of the voters at the polls the President, *after obtaining the consent of Congress*, was to "recognize the government so established, and none other, as the constitutional government of the state."

The fact that this measure was passed by Congress during the closing day of a session gave Lincoln the chance to defeat it by a pocket veto. He was far too clever a politician, however, to allow him- *Lincoln and* self to be placed in the position of outright opposition to its *Congress* more reasonable provisions. In a formal proclamation on the subject he declared himself unwilling as yet "to be inflexibly committed to any single plan of restoration," but he recommended the congressional plan to the people for their consideration, and described it as "one very proper plan for the loyal people of any State choosing to adopt it." What terms he might have had to make with Congress, had he lived, will never be known, but when the next session adjourned without further action on reconstruction he was not displeased. At his last cabinet meeting he spoke with regret of the tendency to treat the southern people as if they were not fellow citizens, and promised to "reanimate the States" before Congress should meet again.

It was difficult for the more radical members in Congress to conceal the relief they felt at the death of Lincoln. His "tenderheartedness" toward the South, and his determination to use the executive power to indulge it, had been their chief concern, for they feared his strength with the country at large. Now, with a new President in office, a man relatively unknown and lacking as yet in a strong personal following, they felt certain that they could have their way. They hoped by wholesale arrests and confiscations to insure that the leaders of the Old South should not become the leaders of the New; they proposed to maintain military rule until such a time as the party they represented could be made the dominant political party of the South; and as a means to this latter end they were determined to give the freedmen the right to vote. After Lincoln's death they believed that they could count on public support for the most drastic action. They could blame the South for the assassination, and fan once more to a flame the wartime passions that Lincoln had tried to allay.

Strangely enough, Andrew Johnson (1808–1875), whose accidental succession to the Presidency so heartened the northern Radicals, was *Andrew Johnson* both a Southerner and a Democrat.[1] He was not, however, of the southern ruling caste, for his North Carolina parents were as humble as the Kentucky parents of Abraham Lincoln; and Johnson, quite as much as Lincoln, was a self-made man. Unable to forget the hard and unhappy youth that poverty in the slaveholders' South had meant for him, he became a belligerent champion of the rights of the common people and a bitter enemy of the whole favored fraternity of southern aristocrats. Migrating at an early age to Greeneville, Tennessee, he worked at his trade as a tailor, and ultimately became the proprietor of a moderately prosperous tailor shop. From his youth up he was interested in oratory, and his love of argumentation seems to

---

[1] The career of Andrew Johnson has been generously re-estimated. Claude G. Bowers, *The Tragic Era* (1929), is extremely readable but somewhat overdrawn. George Fort Milton, *The Age of Hate* (1930), is eminently fair. Less satisfactory in the order mentioned are R. W. Winston, *Andrew Johnson, Plebeian and Patriot* (1928), and L. P. Stryker, *Andrew Johnson* (1929).

have furnished the stimulus that drove him persistently forward in his quest for learning. As a highly effective rough-and-tumble debater, he drifted easily into politics — a Democratic denouncer of the aristocratic Whigs — and for ten years, beginning in 1843, he represented his district in the national House of Representatives. Twice during the fifties he was elected governor of Tennessee, and the outbreak of the Civil War found him in the midst of his first term as a United States Senator.

Although Johnson had voted for Breckinridge in 1860, he was an ardent advocate of compromise and conciliation, and he utterly refused to become a party to the destruction of the Union. Alone among the senators from the seceding states, he remained at his desk in the Senate when his state left the Union, and gave his full support to the Union cause. While still a senator he accepted Lincoln's commission to become military governor of Tennessee, and in that capacity he worked with courage and with moderate success toward the carrying-out of Lincoln's plan of restoration.[1] When the National Union Convention of 1864, composed of many Republicans and a few War Democrats, looked about for means of emphasizing its bipartisan character, the choice of Johnson for second place on the ticket with Lincoln seemed natural and logical. Lincoln himself insisted upon it. Had the delegates foreseen Johnson's accession to the Presidency, no doubt they would have acted differently. His obstinacy and tactlessness were not unknown, and, with the exception of his devotion to the Union, his political principles differed markedly from those of the great majority of the men who worked for him.

Probably it was Johnson's well-known dislike of the southern aristocrats that commended him most to the Republican Radicals. Given to intemperate utterances, he had repeatedly denounced the *Johnson and* "slavocracy" as responsible for the chief woes of the South, *the Radicals* including the war, and as President he ordered the arrest of many high Confederate officials whom Lincoln had been minded to leave alone. "Johnson, we have faith in you," Senator Benjamin Wade of Ohio, a leading Radical, told the President. "By the gods, there will be no trouble now in running the Government." To this remark Johnson is said to have replied: "Treason is a crime and crime must be punished. Treason must be made infamous and traitors must be impoverished."

But, as matters turned out, Johnson's vindictiveness was short-lived. Undoubtedly he planned to rebuild the South with the long-neglected lower-class whites in control, but he was soon to learn that, whatever the status of the southern aristocrat before the war, he was at the moment as penniless and as powerless as his humblest neighbor. Further-

[1] C. R. Hall, *Andrew Johnson, Military Governor of Tennessee* (1916).

more, Johnson as a Southerner was under no delusion as to the unpreparedness of the ex-slave for the full responsibilities of citizenship. For a time he may have toyed with the idea of Negro suffrage, but, if so, his common sense and his southern background soon led him to give it up. More important still, he was at heart as much a states' rights southern Democrat as he had ever been. Like Jackson, he was willing to go to any length to preserve the Union, but he wished to keep the powers of the national government at a minimum. To him the southern states were still states, and with them, rather than with the national government, the solution of their principal problems must lie.

Thus it soon transpired that Johnson, from the Radical point of view, was quite as untrustworthy as Lincoln. For the time being he kept *Johnson's* Lincoln's cabinet intact, and inclined more and more to the *plan of re-* advice of its more moderate members. He gradually re- *construction* laxed the orders he had given for the arrest and prosecution of southern officials. He accepted as legal the loyal governments that Lincoln had recognized in Tennessee, Louisiana, Arkansas, and Virginia.[1] And, for the seven other states of the Confederacy, he prescribed during the summer of 1865 a process of reconstruction quite as breathtaking in its generosity as Lincoln himself could have devised. For each state he appointed as provisional governor a local man, not an outsider; and, although every such official had at some time been an active opponent of secession, not one of them had fought for the North, while most of them had passively supported the Confederacy. It was the duty of each provisional governor to call a constitutional convention, the delegates to which were to be chosen by such members of the old white electorate as were now ready, and were permitted, to take the oath of allegiance to the United States. Johnson did, indeed, add a few new classes, including the owners of more than twenty thousand dollars' worth of property, to those whom Lincoln had disqualified from taking the oath, but he promised liberal pardons to those who chose to apply for them, and he did nothing to insure that even so small a number as ten per cent of the former voters must take part in the work of restoration. The constitutional conventions, so selected, were required (1) to invalidate their old ordinances of secession, (2) to abolish slavery, and (3) to repudiate all debts contracted in order to aid the Confederacy in its prosecution of the war; but otherwise they were as free as any other such conventions to write into their constitutions whatever they chose.

---

[1] J. W. Patton, *Unionism and Reconstruction in Tennessee* (1934); J. R. Ficklen, *History of Reconstruction in Louisiana* (1910); T. S. Staples, *Reconstruction in Arkansas* (1923); H. J. Eckenrode, *Political History of Virginia During Reconstruction* (1904).

Johnson specifically acknowledged that it was their privilege to decide who should vote and who should hold office, but he let it be known privately that, for the effect such action would have upon the northern Radicals, he hoped that Negroes who could read and write, or who owned a small amount of real estate, would be permitted to vote. With their constitutions rewritten, the states might elect their own governors, legislators, and other officers, and resume their place in the Union.

Johnson foresaw that for several months he could proceed with his plan unhampered by Congress, which, to the distress of the Radicals, could not convene without the President's call until the following December. By this time he hoped to have state governments restored throughout the South. He knew that the Radical leaders of Congress would resent deeply whatever he did, but he believed that they would find it difficult to undo a series of accomplished facts. Furthermore, he counted upon the approval of a majority of the people both in the South and in the North for what he was doing. In the former section, the easy terms he had prescribed should insure him a strong following, while in the latter he hoped to rally to his standard most of the Democrats as well as the more moderate Republicans. He took seriously the name and implications of the Union Party, which had elected him, and expected it to become, with himself at its head, a kind of party of the center, opposed only by the northern Radicals at one extreme and the southern irreconcilables at the other.

When Congress met in December, Johnson's work of restoration was far along. The provisional governors had revived the old county and municipal governments sometimes with little change of per- *Johnson's* sonnel. They had called constitutional conventions, and in *plan in effect* every state but Texas the conventions had met. Unfortunately, perhaps, none of them had accepted the President's advice about allowing exceptional Negroes to vote; nor did they show any disposition to place restrictions upon the political rights of the former enemies of the Union. Furthermore, the first elections that were held showed that, for the most part, the leaders of the Confederacy were still regarded by the voters as the leaders of the South. In Mississippi, for example, an ex-Confederate brigadier-general who had not even been pardoned as yet by the President, was chosen governor; in Alabama three fourths of the members of the legislature had at one time or another fought for the Confederacy; and in Georgia the legislature chose Alexander H. Stephens, late Vice-President of the Confederate States of America, to be United States Senator. Every legislature, however, except that of Mississippi, had promptly ratified the Thirteenth Amendment, and before the end of the year the President was able to tell Congress that only in Florida and Texas was the work of restoration incomplete, and that in those states it would be finished soon.

The President's defense of what he had done was presented in an able message to Congress, the happy phraseology of which was due to the skillful pen of George Bancroft, the historian. The meaning of the message, however, was the President's own. In it he maintained, more insistently than Lincoln had thought advisable, that the southern states, as such, had never ceased to exist, but had merely been in a state of suspended vitality. It had been his duty to assist in restoring them to their rightful energy, and this duty he had performed as "gradually and quietly" as possible. Inasmuch as he had found no constitutional warrant to do otherwise, he had left with the states themselves the problem of enfranchisement of the freedmen. As for the delegations that the restored states had sent to Congress, he believed that the adoption of the Thirteenth Amendment warranted their reception, but of this each house of Congress must judge for itself.[1]

[1] Henry Lee Swint, *The Northern Teacher in the South, 1862–1870* (1941), describes an interesting phase of carpetbag history. Vernon Lane Wharton, *The Negro in Mississippi, 1865–1890* (1947), is a modern re-interpretation. Willie Malvin Caskey, *Secession and Restoration in Louisiana* (1938), is primarily political.

CHAPTER II

RADICAL RECONSTRUCTION

THE straightforwardness and good temper of Johnson's first message to Congress won much acclaim, and his Radical opponents were greatly embarrassed. It was more than could reasonably be ex- *Johnson's* pected, however, that Congress would permit the President *first message* to complete the process of reconstruction without legislative interference. Indeed, on the first day of the session, before the President's message had been received, the House had voted to establish a joint committee of nine representatives and six senators to inquire into the condition of the former Confederate states, and to inquire into whether they were "entitled to be represented in either House of Congress." A few days later the Senate concurred in this action, and the southern delegations were required to stand aside while this "Joint Committee on Reconstruction" conducted its investigations.

Thaddeus Stevens (1792–1868), a representative from Pennsylvania, was the elder statesman who sponsored the House resolution.[1] A New Englander by birth and training, he had practiced law and *Thaddeus* politics in Pennsylvania, first at Gettysburg and then at *Stevens* Lancaster, for half a century. Early in his political career he won wide recognition for his leadership in the Anti-Masonic Party, his courageous and successful fight to save from repeal the public-school system of his state, and his opposition to a new state constitution because it limited the suffrage to whites. Meantime he had conceived, in part, perhaps, from his New England background, but in larger part, no doubt, from the unhappy experiences of such runaway slaves as chanced to cross his path, an intense dislike of slavery. As a member of the national House of Representatives during the framing of the compromise measures of 1850, and later while the secession movement was under way, he opposed with the utmost violence all concessions to the slaveholders; and after

[1] James A. Woodburn, *The Life of Thaddeus Stevens* (1913), is more satisfactory than the earlier Samuel W. McCall, *Thaddeus Stevens* (1899). T. F. Woodley, *Thaddeus Stevens* (1934), presents some new material, but the definitive life of Stevens has not yet appeared.

1861, as one of the most powerful of the Republican leaders, his counsel was ever for the sternest possible prosecution of the war. His ill-temper toward the South was not bettered when in 1863 Lee's troops destroyed some ironworks near Chambersburg, Pennsylvania, in which he was financially interested, and well before the end of the war he had broken with Lincoln over reconstruction. The southern states, he held, were no longer states, but only "conquered provinces" with which Congress might deal as it chose; Lincoln's pocket veto of the Wade-Davis Bill was nothing less than "infamous." Lame from his birth, old and perilously ill, unmarried and cared for only by a faithful colored housekeeper, his one passion became the ruthless punishment of the South. Congressmen had already learned to fear his lashing tongue, and he proposed to destroy Johnson, whose easy terms of reconstruction he despised.

No less the enemy of Johnson than Stevens was Charles Sumner (1811–1874), the Republican senator from Massachusetts whose body *Charles* still bore the marks of Preston Brooks's assault.[1] From *Sumner* his youth up Sumner had been a favored member of the Boston intelligentsia. He was a graduate of Harvard, a student of history and the classics, a friend of nearly every New Englander who had won distinction in the realm of literature, and a European traveler whose *entrée* into the highest political and intellectual circles was never denied. The soul of honor, and upright to a fault, he was vain of his own abilities, and utterly contemptuous of lesser mortals. He had always opposed slavery — the first newspaper to which he subscribed was Garrison's *Liberator* — and his scorn for all who practiced or condoned it was complete. Trained for the law, he had preferred politics, and in 1851 he was chosen by a coalition of Free-Soilers and Democrats to take the seat in the United States Senate that Webster vacated to become Fillmore's Secretary of State. From the time of his first election to the day of his death he remained a senator, although the injuries that he suffered from the Brooks assault necessitated his absence from duty for many years. Measurably recovered, but never again quite the same, he was on hand in 1863 to oppose Lincoln's plan of reconstruction, and to advance his "state-suicide" theory, that the seceding states, by their treasonous act, had ceased to exist, and that Congress had therefore precisely the same power over them that it had always exercised over the territories. A philosophic defender of the doctrine of political equality,

---

[1] Moorfield Storey, *Charles Sumner* (1900), is a satisfactory biography, but see also E. L. Pierce, *Memoir and Letters of Charles Sumner* (4 vols., 1877–93). Excellent short sketches of the leading participants in American history are to be found in the *Dictionary of American Biography* (20 vols., 1928–36), edited by Allen Johnson and Dumas Malone.

he insisted from the beginning that Congress should make Negro suffrage a condition of reconstruction for the seceded states; and when Johnson, like Lincoln, failed to urge such a policy, he allied himself with Stevens to wreck the presidential program. His views were not shared by every member of his party in the Senate, nor were Stevens's in the House, but a less obstinate man than Johnson would have hastened to make terms with an opposition so powerful.

Unfortunately for the President, the Radical case was greatly strengthened by the action that the southern legislatures were taking with reference to the status of the freedmen. Realizing far *The black* better than the Northerners the great gap that lay between *codes* slavery and freedom, the restored states had sought to bridge that gap by laws especially designed to fit the needs of the Negroes. "Persons of color" were invariably subjected to various regulations not required of whites. In some states, for example, they might not carry arms unless licensed to do so; they might not testify in court except in cases involving their own race; they must make annual written contracts for their labor, and if they ran away from their "masters" they must forfeit a year's wages; they must be apprenticed, if minors, to some white person, who might discipline them by means of such corporal punishment as a father might inflict upon a child; they might, if convicted of vagrancy, be assessed heavy fines, which, if unpaid, could be collected by selling the services of the vagrant for a period long enough to satisfy the claim. These "black codes," or "black laws," which at best were meant mainly to protect the Negroes from their own ignorance and helplessness, and at worst were meant to circumscribe their freedom as much as possible, were deeply resented at the North.[1] The Thirteenth Amendment had just been adopted, and yet some of the very legislatures that had voted for it were seemingly taking steps to undermine it. Of what avail to abolish slavery if Johnson's newly established southern governments retained it in fact if not in name?

There were certain other disquieting factors about the southern situation that Radical politicians were quick to exploit. While Johnson's plan of reconstruction was carried through without the *The spirit of* complete withdrawal of northern troops from the South, *the South* enough troops were withdrawn to give some of the southern states a pretext for establishing militia of their own. It was easy to say that all such actions were designed to make possible the complete subjugation of the Negro, and perhaps to lead the way in a new revolt. Radicals

[1] Samples of the southern codes are given in H. S. Commager, *Documents of American History* (1934), items 246–47. This collection of sources is invaluable for handy reference.

could point also to the prevalence of racial conflicts, particularly between the lower-class southern whites and the Negroes, whose long-standing hatred for one another was greatly aggravated by the fact of emancipation. Moreover, the South did not fear to show that in spirit it was neither broken nor contrite. Cordial hatred of the North, and particularly of the northern Radicals, was freely expressed; and regret that the South had failed to win was rarely well concealed. Carl Schurz, whom the President himself had sent to study conditions in the South, seemed exasperated at the failure of Southerners to recognize the "criminality" of their recent treason, and deplored their "utter absence of national feeling." Schurz's report, which throughout was most unfavorable to the South, gained wide currency, whereas a short but favorable statement on the same subject by General Grant was scarcely noticed.[1]

The first real test of strength between the forces led by the President and those led by Stevens and Sumner came over the so-called Freedmen's Bureau Bill. The ground for this conflict had been *The Freedmen's Bureau Bill* carefully chosen. The Freedmen's Bureau was not a new thing, for it had been created by an act of Congress signed shortly before Lincoln's death. Hence the Radicals were proposing merely to continue an existing institution. Also, the apparent purpose of the Freedmen's Bureau was humanitarian — to provide a kind of guardianship for the Negro during the period of transition from slave labor to free labor. Its agents, with full military backing, for the Bureau was attached to the War Department and headed by an army officer, supervised the relief work carried on among the Negroes and whites; watched over the labor arrangements that freedmen made with their employers; assigned abandoned land to the freedmen, and helped them to acquire other land; in general, made sure that the work of emancipation should not be halted halfway. But the original Freedmen's Bureau Bill had provided that the Bureau should cease to exist one year after the end of the war, whereas the measure that Congress presented to President Johnson in February, 1866, proposed that the existing organization, with greatly amplified powers, should be continued for an indefinite period. In other words, Congress raised the issue: Should the Negro remain the ward of the national government working through the Freedmen's Bureau, or should he be left to the tender mercies of

[1] Schurz's "Report on Conditions in the South" is published in Frederic Bancroft (editor), *Speeches, Correspondence and Political Papers of Carl Schurz* (6 vols., 1913), I. 279–374. Paul H. Buck, *The Road to Reunion, 1865–1900* (1937), traces with impartial hand the slow process of reconciliation between the victorious North and the defeated South.

whatever "black laws" Johnson's restored state governments chose to pass?

Johnson met this challenge with a courageous veto. The bill, he said, proposed to maintain in time of peace a military jurisdiction that could ignore at will such ordinary guaranties of the civil *Johnson's* law as trial by jury and the right of appeal. It assumed *veto* that wartime conditions still existed, whereas in fact the country had all returned, or was returning, "to a state of peace and industry." It overstepped constitutional bounds by making the government of the United States, rather than the state governments, responsible for the care of indigents, and a favored class of indigents at that. Furthermore, it was the work of a Congress that denied representation to the eleven states most concerned, whereas in the judgment of the President those states had been "fully restored," and were "entitled to enjoy their constitutional rights as members of the Union." If American traditions of democracy were to be maintained, then majorities, to have the right to rule, must be majorities of the whole people, not merely a part of it.

While both houses of Congress had passed the Freedmen's Bureau Bill by overwhelming majorities, the President's veto was sustained, with only a few votes to spare, in the Senate. On Washington's Birthday following, the President was serenaded at the White House, in accordance with a custom of the time, by a group of his admirers, and asked to speak. Unfortunately, he not only spoke, but let himself go in a manner not wholly becoming to the office he held. Much of what he told the crowd was strictly to the point, but he indulged also in unnecessary personalities, and asserted that such men as Thaddeus Stevens, Charles Sumner, and Wendell Phillips were as much opposed to the Union as "the Davises, the Toombses, and the Slidells."

Johnson's conduct won enthusiastic support throughout the South and among the Democrats of the North, but, when abundantly exaggerated by the press, it tended to solidify the Republicans *The Civil* behind their Radical leaders. Before long Congress pre- *Rights Bill* sented him with an unpalatable Civil Rights Bill, which declared the freedmen to be citizens of the United States, guaranteed them the same civil status that was enjoyed by the whites, and prescribed severe penalties for all who, under state law, might discriminate against them. If Johnson could not sign the Freedmen's Bureau Bill, clearly he could not sign the Civil Rights Bill; nor did he. But this time both the Senate and the House repassed the measure by the two-thirds majorities necessary to make it a law. Congress had thus won the ascendancy. It could, if it would, take the whole policy of reconstruction out of Johnson's hands, and direct him to do whatever it wanted done. The Radicals, conscious of their advantage, presently revived in slightly different form the Freedmen's Bureau Bill, and on second trial passed it, too, over the President's veto. The new bill provided, however, that the Freedmen's Bureau should be assured of only two years' existence.

Meanwhile the joint committee that Congress had set up in December, 1865, had been hard at work on a congressional plan of reconstruction that could be substituted for the President's plan. Of the *The Joint Committee on Reconstruction* fifteen members who comprised this committee, only one senator and two representatives were Democrats, while nearly all of the remaining members, Stevens among them, were extreme Radicals. The committee soon began a spectacular sequence of hearings, in which it collected an enormous quantity of evidence, much of which was intended to prove that the loyalty of the South was far too tenuous to permit of such generous treatment as the President had accorded it. By the early summer of 1866 its deliberations had resulted in the formulation of a proposed Fourteenth Amendment to the Constitution, which, after some revision in the Senate, was duly submitted to the states for adoption.[1]

The first section of the amendment virtually restated the terms of the Civil Rights Bill. It declared that all persons born or naturalized in the *The Fourteenth Amendment* United States were citizens of the United States and of the state in which they resided, and that no state might abridge in any way the "privileges or immunities" of such citizens, nor "deprive any person of life, liberty, or property, without due process of law." This clause of the amendment became in later years a matter of the greatest importance. For a time the courts showed a disposition to restrict its application to ex-slaves whose civil rights were endangered; but ultimately they held that all persons, corporations no less than individuals, were subject to its protection. One member of the committee, John A. Bingham of Ohio, explained eventually that he had formulated the statement with this later interpretation in mind, for he believed that the restriction of the Fifth Amendment to the Constitution, which denied to the national government the right to interfere with the rights of private property, should be extended also to the states, and that responsibility for its enforcement should, accordingly, be lodged with the national courts. Roscoe Conkling of New York, another member of

[1] B. B. Kendrick, *The Journal of the Joint Committee of Fifteen on Reconstruction* (1914), and H. E. Flack, *The Adoption of the Fourteenth Amendment* (1908), shed much light on this subject.

the joint committee, confirmed Bingham's words in an argument he made before the Supreme Court in 1882:

> At the time the Fourteenth Amendment was ratified, individuals and joint stock companies were appealing for congressional and administrative protection against invidious and discriminating state and local taxes. . . . That complaints of oppression in respect of property and other rights made by citizens of northern states who took up residence in the South were rife in and out of Congress, none of us can forget. . . . Those who devised the Fourteenth Amendment wrought in grave sincerity. . . . They planted in the Constitution a monumental truth to stand four square to whatever wind might blow. That truth is but the golden rule, so entrenched as to curb the many who would do to the few as they would not have the few do to them.[1]

A second section of the Amendment dealt with the problem of Negro suffrage. This innovation, to the regret of the more extreme Radicals, was not required; instead, a state that denied the suffrage *Negro* to any of its male inhabitants over twenty-one years of age, *suffrage* "except for participation in rebellion or other crime," would merely have its basis of representation in Congress and in the Electoral College correspondingly reduced. This was not an unreasonable position. The old "three-fifths" compromise of the Constitution, which for such purposes counted five slaves as equal to three whites, had lost its meaning, for slavery had been abolished. But with freedmen counted exactly the same as whites, the number of representatives from the southern states in Congress and the number of southern votes in the Electoral College would be materially increased. If, therefore, the Negroes were denied the vote and the southern whites were not, the curious result would be to give the latter a greater weight in the Union than they had had before the war. Thus the Amendment held out an inducement to the South to permit the Negroes to vote, but the penalty for failure to do so was slight.

The third section of the amendment was designed to make ineligible for officeholding all the ex-Confederate leaders, regardless of whatever presidential pardons they might have received. Anyone *Disabilities* who, after taking an oath of office under the United States, had aided the Confederacy might not again hold office unless Congress by a two-thirds vote of each house should remove the disability. Thaddeus Stevens was bitterly disappointed that the right to vote was not included in the disability, but, although the House dare not disagree

---

[1] Quoted in Charles A. and Mary R. Beard, *The Rise of American Civilization* (1927), II, 113. This work presents a brilliant case for the economic interpretation of American history.

with him, the Senate refused to take so extreme a position, and he was forced to yield the point.

A fourth section provided that the debt of the United States, incurred to preserve the Union, should never be questioned, and that the debt of the southern states and the Confederacy, incurred to destroy it, should never be paid. This portion of the amendment was meant to allay the fear that the Democrats, if ever they should regain control of the government, would use their power to repudiate the national debt; also, to insure that the provisions in the southern state constitutions against the payment of the Confederate debt must be observed.

A fifth section of the amendment gave Congress the power to enforce its provisions by appropriate legislation.

By the time the amendment was offered, the mid-term congressional elections of 1866 were close at hand, and Congress refused to proceed *Elections* further with its work until the people had been heard from. *of 1866* While in general the effective portion of the press seemed to favor the Radicals, there were mutterings of discontent at the long-continued exclusion of the South from representation in Congress, and Johnson's appeals to moderate sentiment had not been wholly in vain. As a discreet gesture of friendliness toward the South, more apparent than real, the State of Tennessee, which in July, 1866, reiterated its loyalty to the Union by ratifying the Fourteenth Amendment, was declared by act of Congress fully restored. As for the other ten states, every one of which rejected the Fourteenth Amendment as promptly as possible, all depended upon the outcome of the election. In case the Radicals were able to retain control of Congress, the President's plan would be completely overthrown; but, if the supporters of the President could only increase their numbers enough to prevent the overriding of presidential vetoes, then the President's plan might yet succeed.

A part of the President's strategy in the campaign was to emphasize the name and the history of the Union Party that had elected him to *The Union* the Vice-Presidency in 1864. His friends in Congress took *Party* the lead in calling a "National Union Convention" to meet at Philadelphia in August in order to endorse his program. When the convention met, however, it was apparent that Republicans were far less in evidence than Democrats, both northern and southern. The main body of the Republicans, including many who had once been Democrats, followed the congressional leaders rather than the President. Because the President's enemies wished also to retain the Union label, there was much confusion as to party names during the election, but it was not difficult to see that the President would have to look mainly to the Democrats for his support, and that the terms "Radical" and "Republican" were rapidly becoming synonymous.

Johnson opened his campaign with great hope of success, but the trend of events soon turned against him. Among his most effective, but usually unseen, enemies were the northeastern indus- *Opposition* trialists who had come to identify their growing prosperity *to the* with a continuance of Radical control of the government. *President* They feared that the return of Southerners to the national councils might result in a revival of the old alliance between the agricultural South and the agricultural West that would imperil their interests. The agreeably high rates of the Morrill Tariff, for example, had been an impossibility until the South seceded; would the return of the South bring them down? Holders of United States bonds were frightened by the bugaboo that a revived Democracy, composed largely of northern ex-Copperheads and southern ex-Confederates, might, if it won control of the government, repudiate the war debt, or, quite as bad, pay it off in depreciated paper currency. The Radicals in Congress had also taken a benevolent attitude toward governmental assistance to railroad building, toward the rapid elimination of the income taxes and internal taxes levied during the war, and toward corporation prosperity generally. Could these policies be maintained with the South back in the Union? [1]

Supported by such powerful vested interests, the opponents of the President made rapid headway. A congressional campaign commit- tee, well supplied with funds, spread endless propaganda *Johnson's* throughout the North about the "outrages" that southern *"swing* whites were perpetrating upon the freedmen. Two race *around the* riots, one at Memphis in May and another at New Orleans *circle"* in July, in both of which many more Negroes than whites were killed, were seized upon as evidence of what would surely happen if Johnson's plan of reconstruction were permitted to stand. When the President made a "swing around the circle" to Chicago, where he laid the corner- stone of a monument to Stephen A. Douglas, and back again by a different route to Washington, anti-Johnson demonstrations were sys- tematically organized, which in some instances actually prevented the President from speaking, and in others goaded him into the intemperate utterances for which he was famous. The Radical press made the most of his mistakes, and burlesqued his speeches so successfully that many of his former supporters were deceived and deserted him. He was

[1] This thesis is strongly stated in Howard K. Beale, *The Critical Year; A Study of Andrew Johnson and Reconstruction* (1930).

[27]

repeatedly charged with drunkenness, and although all such charges were demonstrably false, such a well-known person as John Sherman complained that Johnson had "sunk the Presidential office to the level of the grog-house." [1] Thomas Nast, the cartoonist, and Petroleum V. Nasby, the favorite wit of the time, did their able best to make the President appear ridiculous. By the time the election was held, the outcome was no longer in doubt. The Radicals carried both houses of Congress by staggering majorities, and the total defeat of the President's program was assured.

When Congress reassembled in December, 1866, the triumphant Radicals took quick advantage of their victory. Confirmed in their *The Radicals* power to pass laws over the President's veto, they meant *in control* to set up a congressional dictatorship that would reduce the President to the rôle of a well-disciplined clerk, if, indeed, it did not dispense with his services altogether. To insure that he should have no "breathing-spell" between Congresses, a new law set the fourth of March instead of the first Monday in December as the beginning date for a session of Congress. Thus, when, on the third of March next, the existing, or Thirty-Ninth, Congress should come to an end, it could rest assured that on the next day its successor, the Fortieth Congress, would be on hand to carry on. By another law, the Tenure of Office Act, Congress made it a misdemeanor, punishable by fine and imprisonment, for the President to remove civil officeholders without the consent of the Senate. The purpose of this law was to save from dismissal such Radical officials as the President had not already removed from office, and perhaps to lay a trap that might at length remove the President himself from the scene. Still another law, in utter defiance of the Constitution, sought to destroy the President's power as Commander-in-Chief of the Army. Believing that Grant, who now held the exalted rank of General, would bow to their will, the Radicals induced Congress to forbid the President to issue military orders, except through the General of the Army, or to relieve the General of his command, or assign him to duty elsewhere than in Washington, unless by his own consent or by consent of the Senate. All contrary orders were declared void, and officers who obeyed them were made subject to heavy penalties. By the same act, such militia as had been organized in any of the seceded states was declared disbanded, and its organization or use without the

---

[1] At the time he was inaugurated Vice-President Johnson was so ill that only the insistence of Lincoln brought him to Washington. To help himself through the ordeal he took more liquor than in his weakened condition was wise, and cut a sorry spectacle. He was deeply humiliated by this incident, and although he did not become an abstainer he was never again publicly drunk.

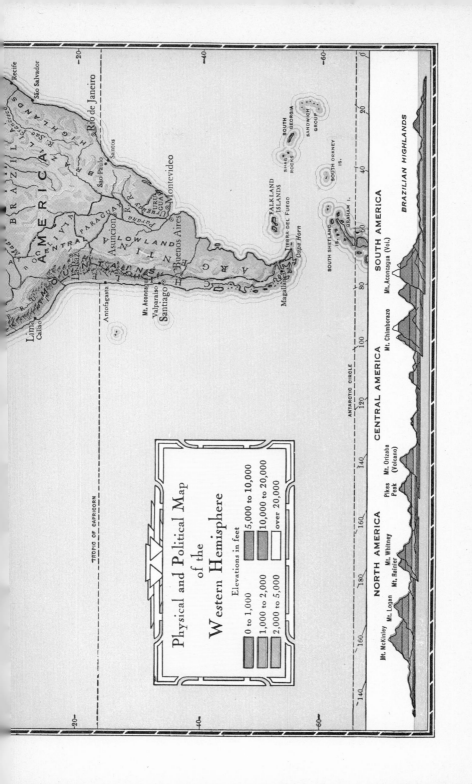

Physical and Political Map
of the
Western Hemisphere

Elevations in feet

0 to 1,000
1,000 to 2,000
2,000 to 5,000
5,000 to 10,000
10,000 to 20,000
over 20,000

NORTH AMERICA

Mt. McKinley   Mt. Whitney
    Mt. Logan   Mt. Rainier   Pikes   Mt. Orizaba
                                 Peak   (Volcano)

CENTRAL AMERICA

Mt. Chimborazo

SOUTH AMERICA

Mt. Aconcagua (Vol.)

BRAZILIAN HIGHLANDS

BRAZILIAN HIGHLANDS

B R A Z I L I A N   H I G H L A N D S

A M E R I C A

BOLIVIA

CENTRAL

PARAGUA

Asunción

Paraná

URUGUAY

LOWLANDS

Montevideo

Buenos Aires

A R G E N T I N A

PAMPAS

PATAGONIA

Magallanes

TIERRA DEL FUEGO

Cape Horn

FALKLAND ISLANDS

SOUTH GEORGIA

SHAG ROCKS

SANDWICH GROUP

SOUTH ORKNEY IS.

SOUTH SHETLAND IS.

GRAHAM I.

ANTARCTIC CIRCLE

Recife
São Salvador

Rio de Janeiro
Santos

São Paulo

Lima
Callao

Antofagasta

Mt. Aconcagua
Valparaíso
Santiago

TROPIC OF CAPRICORN

-20-

-40-

-60-

0

20

40

60

80

100

120

140

160

180

160

140

-20

-40

-60

ULYSSES S. GRANT

ANDREW JOHNSON

consent of Congress was forbidden. The scene was thus set for an era of ruthless legislative usurpation of executive prerogatives.[1]

Even before the fourth of March the Radicals persuaded Congress to enact a new plan of reconstruction far more drastic than the plan *Congressional* they had embodied in the Fourteenth Amendment; and a *reconstruction* supplementary act passed after the fourth of March showed the new Congress to be in thorough accord with the old. These laws, in spite of the fact that two years had elapsed since the end of the war, were designed to undo completely all that Lincoln and Johnson had done to restore normal civil government in the ten southern states unrecognized by Congress. Military rule was to be resumed, with the South divided into five military districts and an officer of the United States Army not below the rank of brigadier-general in charge of each. Each general, duly supported by an adequate military force, must register all the legal voters, excluding all who had ever been disfranchised for disloyalty, and admitting Negroes on the same basis as whites. He must then call upon these voters to elect a constitutional convention, which should draw up a new constitution providing for Negro suffrage. If, on submission to the voters, this constitution should receive a popular majority, the general in charge should order the necessary elections to put it into effect; whereupon, if Congress should approve the new constitution, and if the legislature of the state should adopt the Fourteenth Amendment, and if as many as three-fourths of all the states should ratify the Fourteenth Amendment and so make it a part of the national Constitution, then and not until then should the representatives and senators of each restored state be considered eligible for admission to the two houses of Congress; and then, and not until then, should Federal troops be withdrawn from the state's borders. Furthermore, each of the newly chosen representatives and senators must be able to take the so-called "ironclad oath" that he had never given voluntary aid to the Confederacy.

The key to this plan of reconstruction was of course Negro suffrage. By giving the blacks the vote and by denying it to many whites the *Negro* Radicals hoped to make sure that the southern states would *suffrage* long remain true to the Republican Party. They feared *again* that, without such a provision, the Democratic Party might not only win the ascendancy in the South, but in the national government as well. Education of the Negroes in the belief that their freedom depended upon the preservation of Republican rule was well along,

[1] C. E. Chadsey, *The Struggle Between President Johnson and Congress over Reconstruction* (1896), is still useful.

and the new scheme would give abundant time to complete the process.

These measures were passed over the presidential vetoes, but the President took good care to enforce their provisions as painstakingly as if he believed in them. The Radical Congress thus found *The* it impossible to impeach him for non-enforcement of the *President* Reconstruction Acts, as they had hoped to do, so for a case *and Stanton* against him they turned to the Tenure of Office Act which he seemingly had violated. Edwin M. Stanton, whom Lincoln had appointed Secretary of War, continued under Johnson to hold that office even after he had deserted the President in all but name, and had made common cause with the Radicals. Several of Lincoln's cabinet appointees, more scrupulous than Stanton, had resigned when they could no longer support Johnson's policies, but Stanton seems to have stayed on precisely in order to act as a kind of spy, or informer. Of his close relations with the President's enemies there can be no doubt. Irritated at length beyond endurance, Johnson in August, 1867, asked Stanton to resign, and when Stanton refused, suspended him from office and named the popular General Grant as his *ad interim* successor.

When Congress met again in December, 1867, the President explained to the Senate his reasons for the suspension of Stanton, and asked that what he had done be confirmed. This action, however, the *Attempt to* Senate promptly refused to take, whereupon Grant, in vio- *remove* lation of an agreement he had made with Johnson, turned *Stanton* over his office to Stanton. Johnson had supposed that Grant would refuse to make way for Stanton, and had hoped that a court case, *Stanton vs. Grant*, would ultimately result in the Tenure of Office Act being held unconstitutional. The President did not hesitate to berate Grant roundly for his failure to live up to the bargain he had made, a course which drove the somewhat bewildered General directly into the arms of the Radicals. Thereupon the President, in defiance of the Tenure of Office Act, which all along he had regarded as unconstitutional, attempted to remove Stanton from office, but the Secretary of War in turn defied the President and kept possession.

Immensely pleased with so excellent an opening, the Radicals in the House of Representatives, led by the now infirm but still indomitable Stevens, brought impeachment charges to the Senate. Nine *Impeach-* of the charges dealt with the President's violation of the *ment of* Tenure of Office Act, the tenth charged the President with *Johnson* attacking Congress in his addresses, and the eleventh served as a kind of catch-all for all sorts of presidential misdeeds.

In March, 1868, the trial of the President began, with Chief Justice Chase presiding, and the Senate acting as jury. It was soon evident that the prosecution was out to "get" Johnson, regardless of the law, and that it thought that it had the necessary two-thirds vote for that purpose in sight. Johnson, however, was represented by an able panel of lawyers, who pointed out, among other things, that such a contingency as the removal of Stanton, an appointee of Lincoln's, had been considered when the law was passed, and that many prominent members of Congress had at that time assumed that the Tenure of Office Act would not be applicable to such a case. Moreover, inasmuch as the President believed the act to be unconstitutional, he was taking the only possible course, in dismissing Stanton, to get it before the courts for final decision — a procedure on his part that could hardly be regarded as a "high crime and misdemeanor."

Faced by these arguments, and fully aware of the purely political nature of the attack on the President, seven Republican senators voted *Acquittal by one vote* with twelve Democrats for acquittal, and by the narrow margin of one vote (35 to 19) the President was left in possession of his office. The seven Republicans who voted for the President were soon made to feel the full weight of party discipline, for not one of them was permitted to remain in politics, but the correctness of their position was attested years later when the Tenure of Office Act, in spite of certain congressional modifications, was held unconstitutional by the Supreme Court. Stanton, after the failure of the impeachment proceedings, retired from office, and General J. M. Schofield took his place.[1]

Meanwhile the President, following as he felt he must the recommendations of General Grant, had placed an army officer in charge of *Radical reconstruction begins* each of the five reconstruction districts of the South. The generals so chosen lacked nothing in authority, for the law set them above existing state governments, and empowered them to make arrests, to conduct military trials, and to carry on as they saw fit the ordinary processes of civil government. Specifically authorized by a "third reconstruction act," passed in the summer of 1867, to remove such state officials of the Johnson régimes as were in any way obstructing their efforts, they made various uses of their prerogatives. General Sheridan, in charge of Louisiana and Texas, gave proof of his radicalism by removing from office the governors of both

[1] On the struggle between Johnson and Congress, see, in addition to the Johnson biographies, already cited, D. M. Dewitt, *The Impeachment and Trial of Andrew Johnson* (1903); Frederic Bancroft, *William H. Seward* (1900); Horace White, *Lyman Trumbull* (1913); and the *Diary of Gideon Welles* (3 vols., 1911).

states, the attorney-general of Louisiana, the mayor of New Orleans, and numerous other officials, all of whom he replaced with his own appointees. On the other hand, General Schofield, in charge of Virginia, made comparatively few removals and interfered as little as possible with the existing civil government of the state. Protests, both from the northern Radicals, who resented any appearance of softness on the part of the "brigadiers," and from the southern victims of their misrule, resulted in repeated and disconcerting changes in personnel. Sheridan, for example, was succeeded by General Winfield S. Hancock, whose honorable behavior led to his being superseded by General J. J. Reynolds, who in turn gave way to General R. C. Buchanan.

The main business of these military overlords was, of course, to organize new state governments according to the plan laid down in the Reconstruction Acts. The first step in the process was to register the voters, a task that presented many difficulties. *Registration of voters* Army officers, Freedmen's Bureau agents, and loyal citizens generally, among them many Negroes, were made members of the registration boards. Eligible whites, although admonished by many of the best-beloved southern leaders to roll up the largest possible majorities for their race, were reluctant to register, but the Negroes presented themselves gladly.

Immediately at the close of the war, many Southerners had had no very great fear of Negro suffrage, believing that the blacks could be persuaded to vote as their former masters directed. Indeed, one of the most telling of the arguments made against giving the freedmen the vote was based on precisely this premise. *Southern opinion on Negro suffrage* It was a well-known fact that the Negro population was concentrated in the best cotton-growing areas where before the war the great planters had held sway. Sometimes in these "black counties" the number of Negroes far exceeded the number of whites, although in the less favored "white counties" of the interior the exact reverse was true. And so it could be maintained that, in case the few favored whites of the "black counties" were aided by Negro votes, they could control the various state governments in complete disregard of the far larger number of whites in the back-country. Negro suffrage was thus feared, not so much for itself as for the danger it might involve of turning the South back to the rule of the old pre-war plantation aristocracy.

The northern Radicals, however, had taken great pains to wean the Negroes away from their natural allegiance to their former masters. Working mainly through the Union League, a *The Union League* private organization that during the war had existed to disseminate northern propaganda, but that after the war had turned its attention to the Negro problem, they taught the freedmen that their former masters were not to be trusted, and that in all political matters they must rely strictly upon Republican advisers. To make the League the more appealing to the blacks, it was converted into a kind of lodge, with an elaborate ritual and much ostentatious ceremony. Soon, with the aid of the northern soldiers stationed in the South and the agents of the Freedmen's Bureau, the League organizers had most of the Negroes under their control, so that when the time came for registering them as voters there was no question but what they would both register and vote as the Radicals desired.

Slowly and painfully the reconstruction process worked itself out. When the eligible voters were duly registered, it was found that in five *The new* of the ten states the number of Negro voters exceeded the *electorates* number of whites, while in all the other states, with the possible exception of North Carolina, the white majorities were very slender indeed. Late in 1867 or early in 1868 these electors, or such of them as were permitted to vote, chose delegates to constitutional conventions, which with a minimum of delay, began their deliberations. In every such convention there was a large block of Negro delegates and a considerable sprinkling of southern whites, mostly of the less-favored classes, but the leaders turned out to be Northerners rather than Southerners — men who had come South with the army or with the Freedmen's Bureau, or perhaps merely to fish in troubled waters.[1] These "carpet-baggers," as they were called, were thoroughgoing Radicals, almost to the last man, and they saw to it that such constitutions were adopted as the Radicals in Congress would favor. Those southern whites who were willing to follow the lead of the "carpet-baggers" were generally termed "scalawags."

The new constitutions, as a matter of fact, contained some admirable provisions. They looked forward to the establishment of far better *New state* public-school systems than the South had ever known be- *constitutions* fore — an end eagerly sought by the Negroes, who regarded their lack of education as the most serious obstacle they confronted in their struggle for racial equality. These documents also copied the latest reforms in systems of taxation and finance, of local government, and of judicial organization that had found their way into northern state constitutions, but had not previously been current in the South.

[1] The number of Negroes in each of the southern conventions was approximately as follows: South Carolina, 76 (out of 124); Louisiana, 49 (out of 98); Georgia, 37; Virginia, 25; Alabama, 18; Florida, 18; Mississippi, 17; North Carolina, 13; Texas, 9; Arkansas, 8.

Culver Service

"CARPET-BAG RULE"

Such reforms, however, were small compensations to the dispossessed Southerners for the prospect of "carpet-bag rule" that the suffrage provisions of every constitution seemed to make certain. Some of these provisions were even more drastic than those which Congress had prescribed. Nor could the various attempts to insure social as well as civil and political equality between the races be viewed with equanimity.

When the newly drawn constitutions were submitted for adoption or rejection at the polls, the tendency was for the whites of every class, whatever their previous political connections, to unite in opposition. Sometimes these opponents of adoption called *Ratification* themselves Conservatives; more and more frequently they came to be called Democrats, and to accept that designation. The Negroes, "carpet-baggers," and some of the "scalawags" remained steadfastly Republican, supported the new documents, and in most cases were able to command majorities for them. In Mississippi, however, the proposed constitution was rejected at the polls, while in Alabama ratification was defeated temporarily by a ruse. The law required that for a constitution to be adopted the total vote cast in the election must constitute a majority of the whole number of registered voters. The whites, by

[35]

systematically abstaining from voting, succeeded in keeping down the number of votes cast to a minority of the registered voters, and so in defeating the constitution in spite of the fact that a large majority of those who voted were for it. But their rejoicing was short-lived, for the Radicals in Congress promptly pushed through a "fourth reconstruction act" which asserted that a majority of the votes actually cast, regardless of the size of the total vote, would be sufficient for ratification. Furthermore, to stop real or fancied discriminations against itinerant Negroes, who tended to forget where they had registered and even the names they had adopted for the purpose, residence for ten days preceding an election was declared sufficient to entitle such a person to vote "upon presentation of his certificate of registration, his affidavit, or other satisfactory evidence."

Between June, 1868, when Congress consented to the readmission of Arkansas under its new constitution, and July, 1870, when Georgia, *The* after much tribulation, was finally reinstated, each of the *Fifteenth* ten southern states, including Mississippi whose constitu- *Amendment* tion after some amendment was accepted by the voters, completed the process of reconstruction that Congress had prescribed.[1] All but three of these states were rushed through to admission in time to vote for Grant in the election of 1868. As a culminating act each newly elected legislature ratified the Fourteenth Amendment to the Constitution of the United States, which in July, 1868, was declared in force. For those states that had not been readmitted before 1869, when the Fifteenth or Negro Suffrage Amendment was submitted, that addition to the Constitution (in effect, February, 1870) had also to be approved. Senators and representatives from the readmitted states, most of whom were Republicans and many of whom were Negroes, were at length permitted to take their seats in Congress, and reconstruction, technically speaking, was over. But the promise of withdrawal of northern troops was not always fulfilled, for throughout the South opposition to "carpetbag" rule mounted so rapidly that its continuance was everywhere recognized as wholly dependent upon military support.

In carrying through this program of reconstruction, Congress had

[1] Of the many state histories of reconstruction the least biased and best is F. B. Simkins and R. H. Woody, *South Carolina During Reconstruction* (1932). Others of merit, most of them reflecting a more or less official "southern white man's" point of view, are J. W. Garner, *Reconstruction in Mississippi* (1901); J. G. de R. Hamilton, *Reconstruction in North Carolina* (1914); W. W. Davis, *The Civil War and Reconstruction in Florida* (1913); W. L. Fleming, *Civil War and Reconstruction in Alabama* (1905); E. M. Coulter, *Civil War and Readjustment in Kentucky* (1926); C. Mildred Thompson, *Reconstruction in Georgia, Economic, Social, Political, 1866–1872* (1915); C. W. Ramsdell, *Reconstruction in Texas* (1910); Ella Lonn, *Reconstruction in Louisiana after 1868* (1918).

consistently shown the finest disregard of constitutional niceties. It had not only ridden roughshod over the executive branch of the government; it had also defied the judiciary. In 1866 a decision of the Supreme Court, *Ex parte Milligan,* read by Justice David Davis, condemned as illegal the trial *The Supreme Court and reconstruction* of civilians by military courts in regions where the civil courts were open for business. Although this case came up with reference to the action of a military tribunal in Indiana during the war, the decision seemed to cast serious doubt upon the legality of any such structure of military rule as that which Congress, notwithstanding, soon proceeded to establish in the South. Furthermore, if this decision held, numerous important verdicts of military commissions had been illegal, among them the one that had resulted in the execution of four persons, including the innocent Mrs. Surratt, for conspiring to bring about the death of Abraham Lincoln, and another that had cost Henry Wirz, a Confederate official at Andersonville Prison, his life.

After the Milligan decision Radical denunciation of the Supreme Court went to violent extremes, and leading Republicans in Congress took thought as to how they might most effectively destroy its power. In July, 1866, they pushed through a law reducing the number of judges from nine to seven. By providing that the next two vacancies among the associate justices should not be filled, they not only, in effect, reprimanded the court, but they also diminished the danger that President Johnson might appoint any liberals to sit upon it. Two years later another measure, providing that a two-thirds majority of the justices should be required to set aside a law of Congress, passed the House, but was not brought to a vote in the Senate. Although Thaddeus Stevens favored legislation to deny the Court any jurisdiction whatever over the enforcement of the Reconstruction Acts, Congress provided only that the Court might not hear appeals from the lower courts in cases involving the right of *habeas corpus.* Reeling under these blows, the Court took pains to avoid as completely as possible all decisions that might offend Congress, although in the case of *Texas vs. White* (1869) it went on record as favoring the Johnson theory that the southern states, in spite of their acts of secession, had never legally ceased to exist.

The first elections in the reconstructed states resulted in the choice of a dubious array of officials. The highest places went mainly to Northerners who had not become residents of the South until after the war, and who had frequently seen it for the *Elections in the South* first time as members of the Union army. Lesser offices were held almost exclusively by Negroes, scalawags, and carpet-baggers. One

Negro became lieutenant-governor of Louisiana, another secretary of state in South Carolina. Negroes were numerous in every legislature, and in South Carolina they outnumbered the whites eighty-eight to sixty-seven. Most of the office-holders were men of little property. In Louisiana only ten members of the legislature were taxpayers; in South Carolina the total taxes paid by the members of both houses were less than seven hundred dollars; in Georgia, they were less than one hundred dollars. Most of the Negroes and many of the whites chosen to office, including even judicial positions, were utterly illiterate.

The inevitable result of entrusting the powers of government to such persons was an orgy of corruption.[1] Private enterprises, such as railroad and canal companies, were expected to pay sizable bribes in order to secure charters, and, indeed, in order to carry on their legitimate business. If any enterprise happened to be thoroughly dubious, however, the chances were good that public money or public credit would be generously voted toward its support. Contracts were let to favorites at ridiculously high figures, and the public servants responsible took a cut of the profits. Public printing in Louisiana during a three-year period cost approximately a million and a half dollars a year, about seven hundred thousand of which was paid in two of these years to a newspaper belonging to the governor of the state, H. C. Warmoth, whose private fortune, incidentally, rose to a tidy sum before he left office. Worthless real estate, acquired for next to nothing, was sold by connivance to states or municipalities for prodigious figures. A single session of the carpet-bag legislature in Louisiana cost nearly a million dollars, whereas before the war the cost of a session had never been more than one tenth that amount. What happened to this money was explained by a governor who had good reason to know the facts:

"Carpet-bag rule"

> It was squandered in paying extra mileage and per diem of the members for services never rendered; for an enormous corps of useless clerks and pages, for publishing the journals of each house in fifteen obscure parish newspapers, some of which never existed, while some never did the work; in paying extra committees authorized to sit during the vacation and to travel throughout the state and into Texas; and in an elegant stationery bill which included ham, champagne, etc.

The rule of the carpet-baggers raised tax-rates to figures never known

---

[1] James Pike, *The Prostrate State: South Carolina Under Negro Government* (1874; new edition, 1935), is a classic picture. Another excellent contemporary account is Charles Nordhoff, *The Cotton States in the Spring and Summer of 1875* (1876). For later opinions see W. F. Nowlin, *The Negro in American National Politics* (1931); Charles S. Johnson, *The Negro in American Civilization* (1930); and A. A. Taylor, *The Negro in the Reconstruction of Virginia* (1926).

before, and piled up debts which most of the southern states felt obliged later on to repudiate; but it must not be forgotten that such political depravity was no monopoly of the South. In New York, for example, during this same period, the Tweed Ring reduced graft to a science that the carpet-baggers might well have envied, while the word "racketeering," with all of its relevant connotations, was the product of a much later age. Of all those who participated in the work of Radical reconstruction the Negroes were the least to blame for its excesses. Only a few of them understood what was being done, and only a few of those who did were shrewd enough to line their pockets with plunder. For the most part they were but helpless victims of the conscienceless rogues who controlled them.

Strange as it may seem, there was a brighter side to the rule of the carpet-baggers. They and their allies represented, however crudely, the underprivileged classes in southern society, and they inaugurated many policies that were designed to better the lot of the ordinary man. Free public schools for the children of both races were generously supported, although with little regard for available taxation resources.[1] The tax burden itself, unreasonable as it became, was distributed with better regard for ability to pay than formerly. Poor relief had never been less neglected, and the rebuilding of roads, bridges, and public buildings that had been damaged or destroyed during the war was carried forward with little regard for expense. Most of all, the taste of democracy that the lowly of both races obtained was not soon forgotten. The rights of the Negroes were soon curtailed, but the incentive remained, at least with some of them, to win back by merit privileges that they had lost because they had been given them too soon. As for the poorer whites, from whose ranks many of the "scalawags" had been recruited, they were never again quite so inarticulate as they had been in the days before their kind had sat in the seats of power.[2]

[1] E. W. Knight, *The Influence of Reconstruction on Education in the South* (1913).

[2] R. N. Current, *Old Thad Stevens: A Story of Ambition* (1942), is objective and critical, and does much to rehabilitate Stevens' reputation, especially in his earlier years. John H. Franklin, *From Slavery To Freedom* (1947), is a comprehensive treatment of the history of the Negroes. E. M. Coulter, *The South During Reconstruction, 1865-77* (1947), is a recent re-evaluation. F. B. Simkins, *The South Old and New: A History, 1820-1947* (1947), follows the main currents of southern history.

CHAPTER III

THE GRANT RÉGIME

THE impeachment proceedings that ultimately failed by so narrow a margin to make Andrew Johnson a private citizen were still in progress *The Election* when the Republicans, no longer under the necessity of *of 1868* disguising themselves as Unionists, met in convention at Chicago to make General Grant their standard-bearer in the campaign of 1868. From the time the war ended it had been quite apparent that, when the next election year rolled around, Grant could have whichever nomination he wished, Democratic or Republican. The course of events had given him to the Republicans. Before the war, to be sure, he had been a Democrat if he had been anything, and he had never yet voted the Republican ticket. But his quarrel with Johnson had endeared him to the Radicals, who, on that account, according to Thaddeus Stevens, were ready to "let him into the Church." Also, as General of the Army he, rather than the President, had had command of military reconstruction, and his ready compliance with Radical desires had made for mutual trust and admiration. Most of all, the rank and file of the Republican Party, among whom could be counted an overwhelming majority of the men who had fought in the Union armies, were determined to have him; they were certain that they had the votes to elect him; and their active insistence was more than one so unaccustomed to political pressure could be expected to resist. On the first ballot every one of the six hundred and fifty [1] delegates to the Republican Convention voted for Grant.

The other business of the convention was also quickly done. For the Vice-Presidency, after a short but exciting contest, it named Schuyler *Grant and* Colfax of Indiana, the amiable, albeit Radical, Speaker of *Colfax* the House, whom one observer had likened to "a good-tempered, chirping, warbling, real canary bird." It congratulated the country on the "assured success of the reconstruction policy of Congress"; defended Negro suffrage as a necessity in the South, although

[1] C. H. Coleman, *The Election of 1868* (1933).

[40]

timidly conceding it to be a matter for each state to decide for itself in the North;[1] urged the payment of the national debt in the "spirit of the laws under which it was contracted," the reduction of taxation, the strictest economy in national administration, the most liberal encouragement to immigration; and finally, exhausted its vocabulary of vituperation upon Andrew Johnson, whose acquittal of the crimes charged against him was already clearly foreshadowed.

To Salmon P. Chase (1808–1873), Chief Justice of the United States Supreme Court, the Republican determination to select Grant came as a bitter disappointment. Chase was a New Englander by *The* birth and ancestry, and a graduate of Dartmouth College, *ambitions* who as a legal practitioner in Ohio had early commanded *of Chase* attention for his able arguments in defense of fugitive slaves. Always prominent in the anti-slavery crusade, he became United States Senator from Ohio in 1849, governor of Ohio in 1855, and Secretary of the Treasury under Lincoln in 1861. Handsome and impressive in appearance, scholarly and proud of his scholarship, he was not one to hide his light under a bushel. He cherished deeply the customary ambition to achieve the Presidency, and while still a member of Lincoln's cabinet did not hesitate to allow his name to be urged by Lincoln's opponents as one more fitting than the President for the Republican nomination in 1864. This lack of loyalty Lincoln overlooked with his customary magnanimity. "If he becomes President," he told his private secretary, "all right. I hope we may never have a worse man." But when shortly after Lincoln's renomination, Chase, because of a fancied slight, presented his resignation, Lincoln accepted it. Nevertheless, a few months later, on the death of Chief Justice Taney, Lincoln unhesitatingly redeemed an outstanding promise to Charles Sumner to make Chase Chief Justice.[2]

When Johnson became President, Chase, whom Lincoln had described as "a little insane" on the subject of the Presidency, soon had his eyes fixed on 1868. He made an extensive trip through the South in 1865, and from time to time sent back public reports on conditions as he saw them. When he maintained, with much argument as to the superior qualities of the freedmen, that Negro suffrage was a prime necessity, he won the hearty approval of the Radicals, whose candidate he hoped to be.

---

[1] The Fifteenth Amendment was not submitted until after the election. Then, in spite of this plank in the Republican platform, the Radical leaders maintained that the election of Grant amounted to a mandate to write Negro suffrage into the Constitution.

[2] A. B. Hart, *Salmon Portland Chase* (1899), is inadequate, but still the best biography of Chase available. See also Mary M. Phelps, *Kate Chase, Dominant Daughter; the Life Story of a Brilliant Woman and Her Famous Father* (1935), and Hugh McCulloch, *Men and Measures of Half a Century* (1888).

Aided socially by his daughter, Kate Chase Sprague, the most charming hostess in Washington, he had good reason to believe that his dreams might come true. But the Johnson trial, over which he presided so impartially as to make the Radicals boil with rage, was his undoing. Indeed, the whole-hearted way in which his former friends deserted him for Grant commended him to the Democrats, who talked enough of naming him to arouse his hopes once more. That he earnestly desired the Democratic nomination and would have accepted it had it been tendered him, there can be no doubt.

Logically the Democrats should have nominated President Johnson, and this they seriously considered. But Johnson's record of political *The Demo-* ineptitude, together with the fact that he had made no *crats name* practical move to secure the nomination, told against him. *Seymour* The Democratic Convention, meeting in July at Tammany Hall in New York City, gave him sixty-five votes on the first ballot, and extravagant praise for "exercising the powers of his high office in resisting the aggressions of Congress upon the constitutional rights of the States and the people"; but, after much fruitless balloting, it passed by both the President and the Chief Justice in order to give the nomination to Horatio Seymour, the Democratic war governor of New York, who as chairman of the convention had supposedly favored the nomination of Chase. Seymour's views on reconstruction were moderate, but for the Vice-Presidency the Democrats chose Francis P. Blair, Jr., of Missouri, perhaps the most violent critic of Radical reconstruction in the party.[1]

The Democratic platform, by its scathing denunciation of the congressional plan of reconstruction, made opposition to that policy the chief *Issues of the* issue in the campaign. Congress, it declared, instead of *campaign* restoring the Union, had, "so far as in its power, dissolved it, and subjected ten states, in the time of profound peace, to military despotism and Negro supremacy." But there was a definite undercurrent of interest in the money question. So far, Republican policy had shown every disposition to befriend the holders of United States bonds, and in general to protect the interest of the creditor class. In protest against this, George H. Pendleton, a prominent Ohio Democrat, had some time before advanced the theory that the Civil War bond issues should be paid off in greenbacks, whenever the letter of the law would permit, instead of gold, as "hard-money" men were wont to advocate. Pendleton's "Ohio idea" was incorporated in the Democratic platform, but the nomination of Seymour, whose views on the money question were

---

[1] The surface facts concerning this and subsequent presidential campaigns are set forth in Edward Stanwood, *A History of the Presidency* (2 vols., new edition, 1916).

regarded as "sound," did much to eliminate this issue from the consideration it probably deserved.[1]

The campaign was more vigorous than the one-sided result would seem to indicate. Radical reconstruction still excluded three southern states from voting, and made certain that several others would vote *A Republi-* for Grant. A generous campaign chest, contributed by *can victory* businessmen who were unwilling to take any chances on the Democratic "soft-money" platform, was also useful. Nor were voters allowed to forget the historic connection of the Democratic Party with secession and Copperheadism. Nevertheless, the outrageous character of the Radical usurpation of power, both in the national government and in the South, was so courageously exposed by Democratic campaigners that eight states, including New York and New Jersey, voted for Seymour, while in most of the twenty-six that voted for Grant the Democratic minorities were far too large for Republican comfort. In a total popular vote of nearly six millions, Grant's majority was only about three hundred thousand, and far more than that many Negroes had voted! Of the total white electorate, therefore, clearly Grant was a minority choice. The electoral returns gave Grant 214 votes to Seymour's 80. Both houses of Congress remained in the hands of the Radicals, but the death of Stevens, late in the summer of 1868, had deprived them of their most competent leader.

Some of the very qualities that had made Grant the soldier a success, made Grant the politician a sore trial to his colleagues and to his country.[2] In the army most of the men he liked he trusted, and because *Grant the* the men he felt drawn to instinctively were generally good *politician* soldiers, they rarely betrayed his trust. In politics he met a different breed. Those he liked he trusted, but his instincts often played him false. In the army, Grant had learned to stand loyally behind his subordinates, regardless of popular criticism. In politics, this trait sometimes made him the last to recognize that one of his appointees was a rogue. In the army, when counsels were divided, he had often been compelled to think things out for himself, and to follow his own course. In politics, where his counsels were usually divided, his lack of expert knowledge sometimes made his independent judgments ridiculous. Years of political experience taught him something, and he left office a better politician

---

[1] M. S. Wildman, *Money Inflation in the United States* (1905); W. C. Mitchell, *History of the Greenbacks* (1903).

[2] W. B. Hesseltine, *Ulysses S. Grant, Politician* (1935), traces with a sure hand the progress of Grant's political career. L. A. Coolidge, *Ulysses S. Grant* (1917), is also useful, but W. E. Woodward, *Meet General Grant* (1928), is more interesting than important. Helen Todd, *A Man Named Grant* (1940), is the newest study of Grant's career.

than when he entered it; but there may be some significance in the fact that, ever since his time, the people of the United States have steadfastly refused to elevate a professional soldier to the Presidency.

Grant's extraordinary capacity for political bungling was at once apparent when his nominations for cabinet positions were announced; some *Grant's* of those named he had not so much as consulted in advance. *cabinet* For Secretary of State he chose Elihu B. Washburne, the congressman from his home district in Illinois who, early in the Civil War, had urged Grant's appointment as brigadier-general. For Secretary of War, he at first made no nomination, but presently chose his most trusted staff officer and personal friend, John A. Rawlins, also a neighbor from Illinois. For Secretary of the Treasury he chose a millionaire New York merchant named A. T. Stewart, who, according to law, was ineligible for the post because he was "concerned in trade or commerce." For Secretary of the Navy he further indulged his growing fondness for rich men by selecting a Philadelphia merchant, Adolph E. Borie, who had contributed generously to the Republican campaign chest, but had no desire to serve. The other appointments were not so unusual, but the whole cabinet had been constructed without regard to political consequences, and was no sooner made than the process of remaking had to be begun. According to a prearranged plan Washburne resigned after a week to become Minister to France, and Hamilton Fish of New York, an excellent choice, became Secretary of State. At the insistence of the politicians George S. Boutwell, one of the Radical impeachment managers at the trial of Johnson, became Secretary of the Treasury. Borie was replaced within a few months, and as time went on numerous other changes were made.

Many people had acclaimed Grant's independent essay at cabinet-making as the beginning of the end for the spoils system, but it turned out *Civil service* that, as soon as the President had taken care of his personal *reform* friends and indigent relatives, he fell easily into the hands of the Radical leaders, and followed their advice almost exclusively. Similarly, most of his cabinet, notably Boutwell, found the spoils system a satisfactory way of making appointments. His Attorney-General, E. Rockwood Hoar, and his Secretary of the Interior, Jacob D. Cox, however, sometimes refused to do as the politicians bade, and mainly on this account Grant soon forced them out of office. All this led to a violent outcry from a small but influential group of civil service reformers. Led by such men as E. L. Godkin of the New York *Nation*, George William Curtis of *Harper's Weekly*, Thomas A. Jenckes, a representative from Rhode Island whose study of the English civil service had made him an ardent advocate of reform, and Carl Schurz, now United States Senator from Missouri, the agitation went to such lengths that Grant, in his second annual message to Congress, urged the passage of a law to govern "the manner of making appointments." In 1871 Congress, not unwilling to cultivate the reform vote on the eve of a presidential election, actually authorized the appointment of a commission to inquire into the matter. When George William Curtis was made head of the commission and promptly reported a set of rules to be followed in making appointments, the hopes of the reformers ran high, but after the election was over Congress failed to supply the funds necessary to keep the commission alive, and all its work came to nothing.

The "sound-money" men who hoped for help from the Grant administration fared far better than the civil service reformers. They claimed that the election of 1868 constituted a mandate to save the country from the "Ohio idea," according to which billions *The "Ohio idea"* of greenback dollars might conceivably be printed to pay off the national debt. One of the first measures to pass Congress, in March, 1869, pledged the United States to redeem its bonds "in coin or its equivalent," a phrase which Grant's and successive administrations interpreted to mean "in gold." Thus bonds that had been paid for in depreciated greenbacks were to be redeemed in dollars that were worth up to twice as much as the dollars originally lent the government. A refunding act, passed in July, 1870, provided for the systematic refinancing of the national debt on a long-term basis. Quite properly, in view of the friendly attitude the government had taken toward its creditors, the new bonds carried a much lower rate of interest.

What to do with the greenbacks that had been so freely issued during the Civil War, and that were still in circulation, was another serious problem. In Johnson's administration the expedient of reducing them in quantity, in order ultimately to raise their value to a parity with gold, had been tried, but the outcry from the country when prices began to drop was so great that Congress in 1868 called a halt. At the time Grant became President the greenback circulation stood at $356,000,000, far more than the government had, or could easily get, the gold to redeem. For the moment it seemed inexpedient to work for the resumption of specie payments, but "sound-money" men looked forward anxiously to the time when a greenback dollar should be equal in value to a gold dollar.

In February, 1870, the Supreme Court became involved in the matter. In the case *Hepburn vs. Griswold*, it reached the unexpected conclusion that the "legal-tender" quality with which Congress had *The Legal-* endowed the greenbacks was unconstitutional to the extent *tender cases* that it applied to debts contracted before the passage of the acts in question. The opinion of the Court, delivered by Chief Justice Chase, was reached by a four-to-three vote. Had this decision been allowed to stand, it would have added merely one more element of instability to the already unsatisfactory monetary situation, but a combination of circumstances enabled the Court to reverse itself the following year. With Johnson out of the way, Congress had again raised the number of justices to nine, and on the very day that the Hepburn case was decided, President Grant had sent to the Senate the names of two new justices, who, shortly after their confirmation, joined with the minority of the Hepburn decision to affirm by a five-to-four vote the constitutionality of the legal-tender clause. It has often been argued that the Court was deliberately packed to bring about this reversal, but the general consensus of opinion among historians seems to be that Grant had decided on his nominations without particular reference to the greenback decision. That the prestige of the Court suffered considerably from the proceedings, however, can hardly be denied.[1]

In the campaign of 1868 the Republicans had definitely committed themselves to the reduction of taxation, a policy which, in fact, was *Reduction of taxes* already under way. Just before the end of the war, Congress had authorized the appointment of a special commission to study how new revenues might be obtained, but by the time the appointments were made the war was over. The commission, therefore, turned its attention to the problem of how the tax burden might best be reduced, and so impressed the Secretary of the Treasury with its diligence that when its term had expired he kept on its able chief, David A. Wells, as "special commissioner of the revenue." Both the commission and the special commissioner advised the gradual reduction of tariffs and excises, and on the latter subject Congress responded willingly. When Grant became President, however, many of the war taxes were still in force, so in July, 1870, an act was passed which eliminated most of the "nuisance" taxes, restricted the internal revenues to a small number of articles, such as liquor and tobacco, and greatly reduced the income tax, which, two years later, was abolished entirely.

For a long time efforts to lower the tariff met with successful opposition from those who profited from the high rates, and during Johnson's term *Tariff legislation* Congress was actually persuaded to raise the duties on raw wool, woolen goods, copper, and copper ore. Not until 1872 were the first real reductions made. At that time many non-protective duties, such as those on tea, coffee, spices, and various raw materials,

---

[1] Charles Warren, *The Supreme Court in United States History* (2 vols., new edition, 1937), is extremely useful throughout the whole period of recent American history.

were lowered or abolished, and a ten per cent cut was reluctantly conceded for a few carefully chosen duties on manufactured articles.

Grant at the end of the Civil War had shown his thorough sympathy for the prostrate South, and perhaps at that time he could have been counted on to help it. By the time he became President, he *Grant and* was ready to act as the willing agent of the Radicals, and it *the Radicals* was during his administration that the worst excesses of carpet-bag rule occurred. With the co-operation of the army assured, detachments of soldiers were always available to put down revolts, real or fancied, and to sustain the carpet-baggers. States that showed signs of going over to the Democrats were apt to be subjected to a congressional investigation, and then dealt with most drastically. On several occasions, for example, military officers deliberately purged southern legislatures of undependable members. Some of the carpet-bag governors also made use of Negro militia, whose chief duty, apparently, was to terrorize "disloyal" whites.

It was inevitable that violence of this sort would beget similar violence. As early as 1866 a group of young men who had lately been soldiers in the Confederate army organized, at Pulaski, Tennessee, a secret *The Ku* society, which, from the Greek word κύκλος, meaning *Klux Klan* circle, they called the Ku Klux Klan.[1] The society at first spread slowly, and seemed as barren of any real reason for existence as most such societies; but the mysterious name, and the equally mysterious letters, K. K. K., that stood for it, were soon utilized to frighten the Negroes. Before long night riders in various disguises, such as ghostly gowns, false faces, and tails, were visiting the cabins of bothersome Negroes, breaking up meetings of the Union League, beating up Negro militiamen, frightening black Republicans away from the polls, and occasionally attacking both scalawags and carpet-baggers. As soon as the vigilante possibilities of the Klan were realized, it grew like wildfire, and was paralleled by numerous similar organizations such as the Knights of the White Camellia, the Constitutional Guards, the Pale Faces, and the Knights of the Rising Sun. By the year 1869 these various orders had covered the South with their activities, and had attracted to membership, or to imitation, which amounted to much the same thing, men who would stop at nothing. Murders now replaced whippings as a common proceeding, and the most fiendish acts of torture were by no means rare. Horrified at the turn events had taken, and certain that such an opportunity for reprisals would not long be neglected, the responsible heads of the various

[1] J. C. Lester and D. L. Wilson, *Ku Klux Klan, Its Origin, Growth and Disbandment* (new edition, 1905); Susan L. Davis, *Authentic History, Ku Klux Klan, 1865–1877* (1924); W. G. Brown, *The Lower South in American History* (1902); W. A. Sinclair, *The Aftermath of Slavery* (1905); S. F. Horn, *Invisible Empire: the Story of the Ku Klux Klan* (1939).

orders, as early as the spring of 1869, did everything they could to disband them. But the worst of the "midnight banditti" continued their activities unabated.

Congress replied to the Ku Klux challenge with a series of three drastic Enforcement Acts. The first, passed in May, 1870, laid down heavy *The En-* penalties for all found guilty of using force, bribery, or in- *forcement* timidation to prevent citizens from voting. All such cases *Acts* were to be tried in the federal courts, and the President was authorized, in case of necessity, to use the army and the navy to enforce court decisions. In spite of this law, the Democrats in the South won many substantial victories in the elections of 1870, so in February, 1871, Congress passed a second Enforcement Act along the same lines as the first, but more drastic in its provisions.[1] The third Enforcement Act, passed in April, 1871, was aimed directly at the Klan, and was sometimes known as the Ku Klux Act. It listed as high crimes subject to severe penalties the various activities of the Klan, such as forming conspiracies, wearing disguises, resisting officers, and intimidating witnesses, and it authorized the President to suspend the writ of *habeas corpus* wherever he deemed such action necessary to suppress "armed combinations" in rebellion against the authority of the United States. Grant knew precisely how to enforce such a law, and did it thoroughly. He singled out for an example nine counties in South Carolina where the lawlessness had been most marked, suspended the writ of *habeas corpus* within their borders, and brought hundreds of law-breakers to trial. Federal troops stood by to see that the courts were left free to do their work, and in less than two years United States judges in South Carolina imposed heavy sentences upon eighty-two persons for violation of the act. The example proved effective, and in part on this account the number of outrages attributed to the Klan declined sharply from this time on.

Congress, at the time the Ku Klux Act was passed, had also appointed a committee to investigate "affairs in the late insurrectionary states." *The Ku* The committee began at once to take testimony on the Klan, *Klux Klan* and sent subcommittees into the South to find out more *Committee* definitely what the situation there was like. Reputable Southerners did not hesitate to denounce the Klan, and to reveal its atrocities, but they shrewdly took advantage of the opportunity to read into the record the incompetence of Negro voters, the excesses of the carpet-baggers, the misconduct of Federal soldiers, and the generally

[1] These laws, which gave the United States government control over state and congressional elections, were made use of, not only in the South, but also in the northern cities, to restrain the tendency of immigrants to vote the Democratic ticket. They were repealed in part during the Hayes administration and in full under Cleveland.

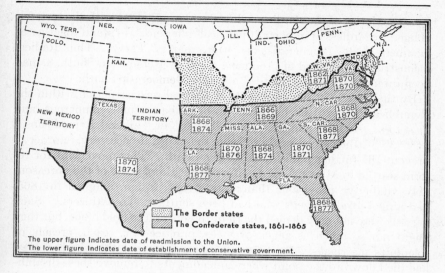

The upper figure indicates date of readmission to the Union.
The lower figure indicates date of establishment of conservative government.

THE PROCESS OF RECONSTRUCTION

deplorable conditions that Radical reconstruction had wrought. Their testimony, published in northern as well as southern newspapers, and ultimately set forth in twelve large volumes of congressional documents, brought home for the first time to many Northerners the disabilities under which the South was laboring. Southerners, likewise, were impressed with the sum total of Ku Klux violence, and realized the necessity of using less dubious methods if ever their efforts to rid themselves of alien rule were to succeed.

Ultimately the attempts of Grant and the Radicals to maintain Republican majorities in the South came to nought. Southerners, bent on the restoration of home rule in the South, learned to stop short of violence in their efforts to restrain the Negroes from the exercise of their newly acquired political rights, but they *Emergence of the "Solid South"* often found more peaceable means quite as potent. Also, the pressure of northern opinion for greater leniency toward the South forced Congress to pass an Amnesty Act, in May, 1872, that reduced the number of ex-Confederates excluded from the suffrage to about five hundred. Gradually, in state after state, Democratic majorities took over the administration of government, carpet-baggers were expelled, and great numbers of Negroes ceased to vote. The chief legacy of reconstruction, from the party point of view, was the emergence of the "Solid South." Thereafter a vast majority of the southern whites, scalawags along with the rest, felt obliged, regardless of important political differences, to stand together as members of the Democratic, or "white man's," Party. Thus Radical reconstruction, instead of producing a solidly Republican South, as had been intended, produced instead a solidly Democratic South.

By the year 1872 the opponents of Radical reconstruction within the Republican Party itself had come to be embarrassingly numerous, and *Liberal Re-* to have a name. As "Liberals," or "Liberal Republicans," *publicanism* they stood ready to leave the party, if necessary, in order to prevent the further punishment of the South. This movement for reform started in Missouri, as an effort to get rid of some of the unreasonably vindictive provisions that a state constitution, adopted in 1865, had aimed at all citizens who had been southern sympathizers.[1] Such persons were not only denied the right to vote and to hold office, but they might not so much as act as trustees, practice law, teach, preach, or solemnize marriages. By 1870 the animosities that the war had bred had died down to the point where amendments to remove these disabilities could be submitted for ratification, but the Radical ring that ruled the state, fearful that their adoption might drive it from power, determined on their defeat. This led to a split in the party, with the Liberals supporting the amendments and a ticket of their own, headed by B. Gratz Brown for governor. In the election, with the aid of such Democrats as were permitted to vote, the Liberal ticket won and the amendments were adopted. Schurz, an outstanding Liberal, was already a member of the United States Senate.

The spirit of revolt that had thus manifested itself in Missouri soon became national in scope, and swept into its ranks many prominent *Opposition to* citizens, among them Horace Greeley, who brought to the *"Grantism"* movement the powerful support of the *New York Tribune*.[2] Opposition to "Grantism" went much farther with some Liberals than mere denunciation of the southern policy. Grant's administration of the civil service, and the excesses of the spoils system generally, led most of those who hoped for a day when appointments would be made on merit to denounce him. Tariff reformers within the Republican Party, of whom there were many, particularly in the West, likewise found little consolation in the Grant régime. When the Radicals, in spite of this growing volume of criticism, made known their determination to bring

[1] E. D. Ross, *The Liberal Republican Movement* (1919), and T. S. Barclay, *The Liberal Republican Movement in Missouri, 1865–1871* (1926), trace the revolt against "Grantism" from its origins.

[2] Horace Greeley, *Recollections of a Busy Life* (new edition, 1930), is a fuller revelation of Greeley's character than is found in any other work.

about the President's renomination, a split in the party became inevitable. Finally the Missouri Liberals took matters into their own hands, and called a national convention of all who shared their views to meet in Cincinnati, May 1, 1872.

The Cincinnati Convention turned out to be a comedy of errors. It could, and did, condemn the administration heartily on every aspect of its southern policy, and it could even agree to the inclusion in *The Liberals* its platform of a demand for civil service reform. But on the *nominate* matter of the tariff, which so many Liberals wished to see *Greeley* lowered, the convention collided with the views of Horace Greeley, who threatened to desert the cause if a low tariff plank were adopted. The platform committee therefore determined upon an undignified evasion, and voted to refer the tariff question to the people in their congressional districts, and to Congress. This was bad enough, for the Liberals intended to seek Democratic support for their ticket, and the historic position of the Democratic Party favored a low tariff. But the crowning calamity came with the naming of a presidential candidate. The longest-headed of the Liberal leaders wished to nominate Charles Francis Adams, the distinguished son of one President and grandson of another, who had so ably represented his country as Minister to England during the war. But Adams suffered acutely from an oversupply of New England frigidity; Greeley wanted the place for himself; Justice David Davis of the United States Supreme Court, already the candidate of a National Labor Reform Convention, was equally determined to have it; Chief Justice Chase, as ever, was ready and willing; and numerous minor candidates, such as Governor B. Gratz Brown of Missouri and Senator Lyman Trumbull of Illinois, had their adherents. In spite of the best efforts of Schurz, who presided over the convention, and to the dismay of most of the leaders, a "stampede" to Greeley gave the New York editor the nomination he so much craved. For second place on the ticket, B. Gratz Brown was chosen.

Could the Democratic Party support such a ticket? If not, the Liberals had no chance whatever to win. Greeley had been anti-slavery and anti-southern before the war, and had been an ardent *The South* Republican from the time the party was founded. After *supports* the war, however, he had endeared himself to Southerners by *Greeley* signing the bail-bond of Jefferson Davis when, in 1867, the Confederate ex-President was being held under an indictment for treason. Davis, it turned out, was never brought to trial, and Greeley's part in freeing him was not forgotten. This fact, together with the telling attacks of the *Tribune* on the Radical program, made the New York editor far more palatable to the South than might have been expected, and northern Democrats had little choice but to forgive and forget. When the Democratic Convention met, it accepted both the ticket and the platform.

In the campaign that followed the Liberal-Democratic coalition proved to be no match for the realistic Radicals. The latter saw to it that in the *Election of 1872* South the administration tightened up on its prosecutions of southern violators of the Ku Klux Act, so that on election day the intimidation of Negro voters could be held at a minimum. With the Union League hard at work to get out the full Republican vote, the Negroes came to the polls in sufficient numbers to carry all of the lately reconstructed states except Georgia and Texas for Grant. In the North appeals to party loyalty and to patriotism — "vote as you fought" — were ably reinforced by ridicule of the Liberal ticket and platform. Thomas Nast, the cartoonist, heaped insults upon the eccentric Greeley, whose moon-shaped, bespectacled face, surrounded by a ludicrous border of beard, made him a veritable cartoonist's delight. George William Curtis of *Harper's Weekly*, still suffering from the delusion that Grant meant business about civil service reform, not only printed Nast's cartoons, but also editorialized in similar vein. Greeley toured the country, an unusual procedure then for a presidential candidate, and did what he could to spread the gospel of better understanding between North and South. But he never had a chance. In addition to Georgia and Texas, Greeley carried four border states, Missouri, Tennessee, Maryland, and Kentucky, but Grant won all the rest. Worn out by the strenuous campaign he had made, deeply disappointed at its result, and saddened by the death of his wife, Greeley fell ill and died three weeks after his defeat was accomplished.

Most of the scandals that are associated with the Grant administration occurred during the second term, but an unsavory beginning was *The "gold conspiracy"* made in the first term. The infamous "gold conspiracy," engineered in 1869 by two speculators, Jay Gould and James Fisk, was actually accomplished with the effective, although unintended, assistance of the President himself. While gold did not then circulate as money, it was constantly in demand for such needs as the payment of customs duties and the adjustment of international trade balances. The government of the United States, although not on the gold standard, constantly received large quantities of gold into the Treasury, and from time to time the Secretary of the Treasury was accustomed to sell enough gold to satisfy the normal demands of trade. It occurred to Gould, who already controlled large stores of gold, that if the government would only stop its sales of gold for a while he might "corner" the country's supply drive the price to a fancy figure, and so make a huge profit. Gould therefore managed, through one of Grant's numerous brood of unsavory relatives, to meet the President from time to time, and even to win his confidence. On one such occasion he set forth at length a fine-spun theory to the effect that it would be a great help for western farm prices if the government should cease its sales of gold. Grant naïvely fell for this talk, and presently, even before the order had been given, Gould learned through his confederate, Grant's relative, that the President was about to stop the Treasury from selling gold. Immediately Gould began his activities, but, finding his own resources inadequate for the undertaking, he invited into the speculation his ally, Fisk, who not only bought heavily, but, in order to induce others to buy, spread the false story that the President himself and all his political friends were in on the deal. Between Monday, September 20, and "Black Friday," September 24, the price of gold rose from 140 to 163½. Then the Secretary of the Treasury, under emergency orders from the President, announced the sale of government gold, and the price came down. In the meantime, however, many legitimate businesses had been disastrously affected, and the stock exchange had experienced a violent panic. The investigation of the whole matter by Congress exonerated the President from any intentional wrongdoing, but his bad judgment was hard to explain away.

In 1872 came the revelation of another precious scandal which, while it had occurred before Grant took office, nevertheless touched closely many of the men who were associated with his administra- *The Crédit Mobilier* tion. The Crédit Mobilier was a joint-stock company, organized in Pennsylvania ostensibly for the purpose of assisting in the building of the Union Pacific Railroad.[1] Its real purpose, however, was to enable a few of the Union Pacific stockholders, who were also stockholders in the Crédit Mobilier, to drain off huge profits from construction contracts. Inasmuch as the funds of the Union Pacific came in considerable part from a subsidy granted by Congress, it was deemed wise to forestall trouble from that quarter by offering blocks of Crédit Mobilier stock to members of Congress at a generous discount, and on the understanding that the purchase price need not be paid until earned by profits from the stocks. The agent of the Crédit Mobilier in this brazen attempt to buy good-will was Oakes Ames, a congressman from Massachusetts, who was able to induce such prominent politicians as Vice-President Schuyler Colfax, Senator James W. Patterson of New Hampshire, and Representative James Brooks of New York to accept the favors he of-

[1] J. B. Crawford, *The Crédit Mobilier of America* (1880).

fered. Many others were involved, some quite innocently, some not so clearly so. A congressional investigation got well toward the bottom of the matter, and a number of individuals, including all those mentioned, had their reputations badly smirched. In general, the frank admission of speculation in Crédit Mobilier stock was regarded by the public as far less reprehensible than any attempt at concealment.

During Grant's second administration one unpalatable revelation succeeded another with disheartening regularity. The Forty-Second *The "Salary* Congress, on the day before its final adjournment in March, *Grab" Act* 1873, voted to increase the salaries of Senators and Representatives from $5000 a year to $7500 a year, with back pay for two years. This "Salary Grab" Act was mainly the work of Benjamin F. Butler of Massachusetts, who aspired to fill the position of leadership in the House left vacant by the death of Stevens, and who in fact had far more influence than was good for Congress or the country. The measure drew such hearty public criticism that it was repealed by the next Congress, and many of those who accepted the back pay were speedily retired from public life by the voters.

In May, 1874, the House Ways and Means Committee brought to light a scandal in the Treasury Department. It appeared that one John *The Sanborn* D. Sanborn, under contract with the department, had col- *contract* lected some $427,000 of overdue revenue, and had received for his services a commission of fifty per cent. This fact in itself was bad enough, and was even of doubtful legality; but Sanborn, as everyone in politics knew, was only the political henchman of the notorious Ben Butler. When Sanborn swore that he paid most of his earnings to his assistants, the public was not slow to conclude that the money was really used to maintain Butler's political machine. William A. Richardson, Grant's second Secretary of the Treasury, resigned to escape the formal censure of Congress for allowing the contracts.

Before another year was up Grant's third Secretary of the Treasury, Benjamin H. Bristow, had uncovered a "Whiskey Ring," composed of *The* revenue officers and distillers who made a business of de- *"Whiskey* frauding the government out of a part of its excise on liquor. *Ring"* Grant at first seemed sympathetic, and commanded; "Let no guilty man escape!" But when the scandal involved John McDonald, a prominent Missouri Republican from whom Grant had received marked favors, and even Grant's private secretary, General Orville E. Babcock, the President's attitude underwent a change. He actually helped his guilty secretary to escape, rewarded him with another office, and seemed somehow to blame Bristow for stirring up so much trouble. Finally, in the summer of 1876, Bristow, in disgust, resigned, and the President paid him no compliments.

Already another major scandal had broken, this time out of the Indian country, where graft at the expense of the red men and the government had become the rule rather than the exception. A House committee found that William W. Belknap, Grant's current Secretary of War, was deeply involved. Belknap in 1869 *Graft in the Indian service* was an obscure collector of revenue out in Iowa, but because of a favor he had done for one of Grant's relatives the President, following the death that year of Secretary Rawlins, had brought him into the cabinet. It now developed that Belknap, as the price of keeping in office a post-trader at Fort Sill, in the Indian Territory, had since 1870 received annual payments, through his wife as intermediary, amounting in all to $24,450. The House by a unanimous vote promptly brought impeachment charges against him, and the Senate refused to convict only because Grant, in the meantime, had accepted Belknap's resignation, and by so doing, according to many senators, had placed the offender outside the jurisdiction of the Senate.

It is a relief, after this sordid recital to turn to the foreign policy of the Grant administration, which, while in part misguided, was in the main highly creditable.[1] The misguided part was almost wholly the fault of Grant himself, who became obsessed with the *Grant's foreign policy* strange desire to add the republic of Santo Domingo to the United States. A few Americans, hoping to profit from speculative investments on the island, doubtless connived at this end, and the Dominican government, what there was of it, was ready to accept annexation as preferable to the revolution it might normally expect at any time. Ignoring his State Department, Grant sent his private secretary, General Babcock, to investigate conditions in Santo Domingo, and on receiving a favorable report authorized Babcock to negotiate a treaty of annexation. This was done, and Grant immediately began to exert every effort to secure its ratification. In spite of the President's pressure, the Senate refused to concur unless another investigation should be made, and after the second investigation it still refused. Charles Sumner, chairman since 1861 of the Senate Committee on Foreign Relations, led the fight against the treaty, and won the undying enmity of Grant, who succeeded in having Sumner's chairmanship taken away from him, but not in obtaining ratification of the treaty.

Probably the most creditable performance of the Grant administra-

[1] Allan Nevins, *Hamilton Fish; The Inner History of the Grant Administration* (1936), gives a satisfactory account of Grant's diplomacy.

tion was the settlement of all outstanding diplomatic differences between
The Fenian the United States and Great Britain.[1] The most serious of
movement these troubles came from the lax interpretation of neutral
duties that, to the great grief of northern shipping interests, had characterized British policy during the Civil War. It soon became apparent
that a similar laxity on the part of the United States could be equally
unpleasant to the British. In 1866 the Fenian Brotherhood, an organization composed mainly of Irish-Americans who were interested in securing
freedom for Ireland, planned as a part of its program an invasion of
Canada from the soil of the United States. Recruiting went on openly
and actively, and many veterans of the Civil War, including some who
were not Irish but were enthusiastically anti-British, agreed to serve.
Troops and supplies were concentrated along the Canadian border, and
although American authorities seized most of the supplies, several hundred Fenian soldiers actually crossed into Canada, captured Fort Erie,
fought a battle with some Canadian volunteers, and retreated to the
United States. Although Johnson acted somewhat belatedly, he properly denounced the whole scheme in a presidential proclamation, and
sent General Meade, with a detachment of the United States Army, to
prevent any further misconduct by the Fenians. When the British
government raised the question of compensation by the United States for
the damage the Fenian invaders had done, however, the American government was not impressed. Several years later President Grant nipped
in the bud another Fenian project for the invasion of Canada.

Whether because of the Fenian incidents or not, the British government showed an increasing disposition to accept responsibility for the
The Ala- depredations of the *Alabama,* and such other Confederate
bama claims cruisers as had operated from British ports during the war.
In 1869 Reverdy Johnson, Adams's successor as Minister to England,
negotiated a "convention" with Lord Clarendon to submit the *Alabama*
claims to arbitration, but early in Grant's administration the agreement
was rejected by the United States Senate, 54 to 1. Charles Sumner, in
opposing ratification, argued that the unneutral conduct of Great Britain
had prolonged the war by two years, and that the United States was
therefore entitled to damages amounting to half the cost of the war, or
approximately two billion dollars. He even had the temerity to suggest
that Great Britain, in lieu of cash, should turn over Canada to the United
States. This ended, for the moment, all possibility of agreement, but

---

[1] E. D. Adams, *Great Britain and the American Civil War* (1925), continues through
these episodes. See also S. F. Bemis, *A Diplomatic History of the United States* (1936):
and T. A. Bailey, *A Diplomatic History of the American People* (1940).

Grant's Secretary of State, Hamilton Fish, worked tactfully toward a settlement, and representatives of the two countries at length affixed their signatures to the Treaty of Washington (1871), which provided the means for its achievement. In the treaty the British government definitely expressed its regret for the "escape" of the Confederate cruisers, accepted as binding a set of rules that amounted to a clear confession of unneutral action, and agreed to submit the matter of damages to an arbitration tribunal of five, one each to be chosen by the United States, Great Britain, Italy, Brazil, and Switzerland. Meeting at Geneva the *Alabama* Tribunal, as it was often called, awarded to the United States damages of $15,500,000, a sum so large as to arouse indignant protests in England. Nevertheless, full payment was made, and the United States did the best it could to reimburse the individuals who had suffered the losses.[1]

The Treaty of Washington arranged also for the settlement of several other disputes between the two countries. One had to do with the claims of British subjects for damages they had suffered from the *Minor* United States during the Civil War, such, for example, as the *disputes* destruction of British-owned cotton, and the illegal detention or capture of British merchantmen. This subject also was referred to an arbitration commission, which assessed damages of nearly $2,000,000 against the United States. Another problem that claimed attention was the perennial disagreement over the North-Atlantic fisheries. A satisfactory *modus vivendi* was worked out, but the British negotiators held that the privileges granted Americans were more generous than those granted the subjects of Great Britain. To settle this matter another commission was created, which encountered many difficulties, but ultimately, in 1877, ordered the United States to pay Great Britain $5,500,000 in gold for the advantages its citizens enjoyed. Still another problem considered in the treaty had to do with the exact boundary between the United States and British Columbia in Puget Sound. The German Emperor, to whom this dispute was referred for settlement, decided in favor of the United States, and so cleared the American title to the island of San Juan and several lesser islands.

The numerous settlements reached under the terms of the Treaty of Washington emphasized once more to the two English-speaking nations, and for that matter to many others, the advantage of peaceful over warlike methods in adjusting international disputes. For the third time,

[1] C. F. Adams, *Charles Francis Adams* (1900), is useful in this connection. See also S. F. Bemis (editor), *The American Secretaries of State and their Diplomacy* (10 vols., 1927–29), VII, 165 ff. The articles in this series are of unequal merit, but the work as a whole is the most complete study of American diplomacy yet undertaken.

once soon after the War of 1812, once in the forties under the leadership of Webster and Ashburton, and now once again during the seventies, Great Britain and the United States had made differences of far greater consequence than those which often resulted in war the subjects of successful negotiation. Such a succession of precedents, as subsequent events have proved, could not easily be broken.[1]

[1] H. R. Ferleger, *David A. Wells and the American Revenue System, 1865–1870* (1942), covers a significant problem of the post-war period in the North.

G. W. McGinty, *Louisiana Redeemed; The Overthrow of Carpetbag Rule, 1876–1880* (1941), continues the reconstruction story beyond the end of carpetbag rule.

CHAPTER IV

A BUSINESS CYCLE

ON THURSDAY, September 18, 1873, the banking firm of Jay Cooke and Company closed its doors in New York, Philadelphia, and Washington. Cooke's fame had risen during the Civil War with his successful flotation of the bond issues by which the North financed its operations. After the war he turned his attention to railway securities, and again demonstrated his ability to win the confidence of investors. In attempting to back the Northern Pacific Railroad, however, he met with disaster. The huge sums needed for this undertaking could not be obtained without European assistance, and after the outbreak of the Franco-Prussian War in 1870 foreign capital became harder and harder to get. The result was that Cooke tied up so much of his firm's resources in advances to the railroad that his partners, without his knowledge or consent, finally took the drastic step of closing. Already a number of bankruptcies had made the business world nervous, and on the day before Cooke's failure there had been a ruinous decline in values on the New York Stock Exchange. But no one dreamed that the firm of Jay Cooke and Company, long regarded as the last word in financial solvency, was in danger. Hence, when the suspension was announced, the Exchange was immediately thrown into a panic so severe that, in comparison, the disturbance of the preceding day looked like nothing at all. Two days later, with the price of stocks still going down, the Exchange was closed, and it remained closed for ten days. Bankruptcies followed thick and fast, factories shut down, business came to a standstill; a depression that was to last for nearly six years had begun. Thus dramatically did the "boom" that the Civil War unleashed come to its inexorable end.[1]

The era of prosperity that began for the North during the war con-

Failure of Jay Cooke and Company

---

[1] E. P. Oberholtzer, *Jay Cooke, Financier of the Civil War* (2 vols., 1907), continues useful through this episode. Henrietta M. Larson, *Jay Cooke: Private Banker* (1936), is a later but more limited study. D. R. Dewey, *Financial History of the United States* (new edition, 1936), was first published in 1903, but for a short account has not yet been surpassed.

tinued without abatement on the return of peace. There were many
Post-war reasons why this should be so. The greenbacks, despite
prosperity Secretary McCulloch's efforts to reduce them in quantity
and so raise their value, remained in circulation, and thus the cutting of
prices and wages that would certainly have occurred had they been withdrawn was avoided. Capital was abundant. War profits had been
handsome, and graft at the expense of the government so common as
scarcely to excite comment. About two billion dollars' worth of United
States bonds were outstanding, and regardless of how cheap the money
with which they had been purchased, both interest and principal were
payable in gold. Capital so invested multiplied with startling rapidity.
Gold and silver poured in from the western mines. European investors
readily purchased large blocks of American securities. Banks, with
credit so inflated, flourished as never before. Not until 1864 had the
national banking system, created during the war, really begun to function, but by 1865 there were more than fifteen hundred national banks
scattered throughout the country, with a bank-note circulation that was
soon almost to equal that of the greenbacks.

Under these circumstances it is not surprising that manufacturing
lost none of the momentum it had accumulated during the war. The
Rise of big United States, indeed, became a sort of paradise for in-
business dustrialists. A dependably high tariff assured them of the
right to exploit the steadily growing American market, while soldiers
returning from the war and immigrants streaming in from Europe supplied a comfortable abundance of labor. One by one the high records
of production set up during the war fell below the higher records that
came with the first five years of peace. "More cotton spindles were set
revolving, more iron furnaces were lighted, more steel was made, more
coal and copper was mined, more lumber was sawed and hewed, more
houses and shops were constructed and more manufactories of different
kinds were established, than during any equal term in our earlier history." [1] The economic transformation of the United States that had
begun with some deliberation before the war had thus reached the
crescendo of revolution. Agricultural America had no chance to keep
up the pace being set by industrial America; Jefferson's dream of a nation composed mainly of small free farmers had faded before the realities
of the machine age. The America of the future was to be less rural than
urban, more factory than farm. The black belt of the cotton kingdom
was to recede in importance before a northern black belt, traced by the

---

[1] Allan Nevins, *The Emergence of Modern America, 1865–1878* (1927), p. 32. This work
furnishes a well-balanced account of the social readjustments made during the machine age.

PRODUCTION OF STEEL IN THE UNITED STATES, 1863–76

smoke of factory chimneys, a belt that ultimately was to extend far into the South itself.

Closely identified with almost every aspect of these revolutionary changes was the production of steel.[1] Before the Civil War the high cost of steel confined its use to the manufacture of such *The romance* small articles as tools and cutlery in which quality was *of steel* demanded regardless of price. That anything so bulky as railroad rails, or the heavy locomotives that ran on the rails, should ever be made of steel rather than of iron seemed utterly fantastic. All this was changed as the result of a remarkable discovery made independently and at about the same time by an American, William Kelly, and an Englishman, Henry Bessemer. Kelly, a resident of Eddyville, Kentucky, who made wrought-iron sugar kettles for his neighbors, observed one day that the effect of an air-blast on molten iron was to make it white-hot. From this he readily deduced that the molten metal itself contained enough carbon to burn out its impurities, if only a strong blast of air could be directed against it. Plainly this "air-boiling" process, if only it could

[1] J. R. Smith, *The Story of Iron and Steel* (1908), gives the essential points of this development.

[61]

be made practicable, would tend to eliminate the expensive use of charcoal, and so greatly reduce the cost of refinement. In a series of experiments, carried on between 1851 and 1856, Kelly demonstrated the soundness of his idea, although his patrons obstinately insisted upon wrought-iron kettles made in the old-fashioned way.

In 1856 the Englishman, Bessemer, who had been carrying on similar experiments, announced the successful application of a "fuel-less" *The Besse-* process, and obtained a United States patent upon it. *mer process* Kelly, however, soon convinced the Patent Office that he was the original inventor, and it was some time before the conflicting interests could be reconciled. Before the Civil War ended, successful efforts were being made within the United States to make commercial use of the "Bessemer process," as it was generally called, and in 1866 one Alexander Lyman Holley, by obtaining the right to use both the Bessemer and the Kelly patents, paved the way for a phenomenal development. Within a few years the number of Bessemer steel works in the country could be counted by the dozen, and the price of steel had dropped to a figure that made its use instead of iron entirely practicable. Another new method of producing steel, known as the "open-hearth" process, was introduced into the United States from Europe in 1868 by Abram S. Hewitt, who shared with his father-in-law, Peter Cooper, control of the New Jersey Steel and Iron Company at Trenton.[1] Ultimately far more open-hearth than Bessemer steel was to be made, but until well toward the end of the century Bessemer steel cost less to produce, and so enjoyed a great advantage. Naturally the steel industry, like the iron industry, tended to concentrate in Pennsylvania, where both iron ore and coal were found in great abundance; but by 1873 the Michigan iron mines, little used before the Civil War, were furnishing more than half of the ore supply.

The steel industry was to produce many great names, but none more glamorous than that of Andrew Carnegie (1835–1919), the Scottish *Andrew* immigrant lad whose career became an almost perfect *Carnegie* pattern for the typical American success story. The son of a humble, but by no means unintelligent, Dunfermline weaver, young Carnegie was brought to America in 1848 by his parents in the proverbial quest of opportunity. He found it, first as a bobbin-boy at a dollar and twenty cents a week in a western Pennsylvania cotton factory, then as a messenger at two dollars and a half a week in a Pittsburgh telegraph

[1] Allan Nevins, *Selected Writings of Abram S. Hewitt* (1937), contains an illuminating report by Hewitt, as commissioner to the Paris Exposition in 1867, on "The Production of Iron and Steel in Its Economic and Social Relations." See also by the same author, *Abram S. Hewitt, with Some Account of Peter Cooper* (1935).

office. Soon he was a telegraph operator, one of the first to learn to read "by sound" the messages that came over the wire, and a little later, as much because of his personal charm as because of his outstanding proficiency, the private secretary of Thomas A. Scott, a Pennsylvania Railroad official. From that position to railroading was an easy transition; and then from railroading to bridge-building, where he made a specialty of supplanting outmoded wooden construction with iron. Astoundingly versatile, he pursued many side lines, nearly all of which turned out well. He built bridges, made money out of oil, and sold railway bonds in Europe — all at the same time. On one of his trips to England he saw steel being made by the Bessemer process, and returned to the United States determined to put "all of his eggs in one basket," the manufacture of steel. By 1873, the date when he opened the J. Edgar Thomson Steel Mills — named after a powerful partner in the enterprise — his career as a steel magnate had begun.[1]

No less startlingly new than the steel industry, and almost as revolutionary in its possibilities, was the production and refinement of oil. For centuries petroleum, by seeping to the surface in various parts of the earth, had advertised its existence to mankind, *"Rock oil"* but, strangely enough, no one had seemed to realize that it was of any particular value; much less that, by sinking wells, great pools of it could be tapped. Years before the Civil War enterprising farmers in Venango County, Pennsylvania, were accustomed to skim the substance from Oil Creek, a branch of the Allegheny, and use it to grease their wagons. Some even bottled it and sold it as a medicine "guaranteed," when externally applied, to cure rheumatism, and good for almost anything, if taken internally. A Pennsylvania manufacturer, Samuel M. Kier, whose wells persisted in pumping up petroleum as well as salt water, resolved this dilemma by putting "Kier's Rock Oil," a medicine for which he made the most extravagant claims, upon the market. The chief contribution of the salt producers to the oil industry, however, was to be the methods of boring deep wells and of pumping that they had worked out. These methods the early oil men were able to take over almost without modification.

The possibility that petroleum could be refined into a practical illuminant was not unrealized by the versatile Kier, who made some significant experiments along that line, but the chief credit for *Oil for* this epochal discovery belongs to a graduate of Dartmouth *illumination* College, named George H. Bissell, who remembered, curiously, some of

[1] In his *Autobiography of Andrew Carnegie* (1920), the author has told his life-story with few reservations. See also J. K. Winkler, *Incredible Carnegie: the Life of Andrew Carnegie* (1931).

"DRAKE'S FOLLY"

the experiments with crude oil that one of his teachers had made. Convinced that ultimately he could supplant the old-fashioned tallow candles and whale-oil lamps with something far superior, Bissell leased some land in western Pennsylvania, and sent a sample of the oil it produced to Benjamin Silliman, Jr., professor of chemistry in Yale College, for analysis. In a memorable document, written in 1855, Silliman reported that an excellent illuminant could be made from petroleum, that the cost of refinement would be slight, and that from it a number of important by-products, such as naphtha and paraffin, could also be recovered. Bissell now turned promoter, won sufficient support from capitalists to begin operations, and sent Edwin Drake with the standard equipment for opening a salt-well out to Titusville, Pennsylvania, to drill for oil. In August, 1859, "Drake's folly," as the incredulous natives called this venture, was producing oil at the rate of twenty barrels a day.

What followed was hardly less tumultuous than a gold rush. That fabulous sums were to be made from oil, few could deny, and the venture-

The petroleum industry

some flocked to western Pennsylvania by the thousands. Farmers who had known only the extreme of poverty sold their land for fantastic prices, or, by good luck, sometimes became part owners in oil wells that speedily made them rich. Oil

[64]

derricks dotted the landscape; crossroads became towns, and towns became cities, almost overnight. Pittsburgh, and other strategic centers, found a new source of wealth in the business of oil refining, while the whole country bought the new "coal-oil" lamps, and began to sit up nights. Inasmuch as almost anyone with a little capital could make a start in the oil business, competition for a while was utterly unrestrained. On this account, and also because of the unpredictable nature of both the supply and the demand, the prices of crude oil and of kerosene varied from year to year, from month to month, and even from day to day. Fortunes were lost as well as made. Nevertheless, by 1864 the oil fields around Titusville had expanded to four hundred square miles, and by 1872 not only western Pennsylvania, but parts of West Virginia and Ohio also, were included within the two thousand square miles in the United States devoted to the production of oil. With a total output to date of nearly forty million barrels, the petroleum industry had in a dozen years climbed to a place of high prominence in the nation's business. In a single year, 1871, foreign purchasers took over one hundred and fifty thousand gallons of American oil, making this commodity the fourth largest item among the country's exports.

A MODERN OIL FIELD

[65]

Inextricably intertwined with the history of oil refining in the United States is the name of John D. Rockefeller (1839–1937), a native of *John D.* Richford, New York, who had moved with his parents to *Rockefeller* Cleveland, Ohio, when he was thirteen years old. Young Rockefeller had only a common-school education, but he early exhibited extraordinary business talent. Before he had reached his majority he had become a partner in a produce commission firm that took excellent profits, particularly after the outbreak of the Civil War. Shrewd, calculating, and thrifty, he made up his mind in 1862, while other young men of his age were patriotically going off to war, that the "coal-oil" business had a future worth sharing. With characteristic good judgment he first backed a refinery that the inventive genius of one Samuel Andrews had provided with a highly improved process; then, at the end of the war, when it was apparent that he had made no mistake, he gave up his commission business, formed a partnership with Andrews, and started out as an oil refiner on his own. By this time the two chief western centers for the refining of oil were Pittsburgh and Cleveland, but the advantage, as Rockefeller sensed, lay with Cleveland, which had easy access, both by water and rail, to the East no less than to the West, whereas Pittsburgh, for its eastern market, was wholly dependent upon the Pennsylvania Railroad. Five years later, reinforced by two new allies, H. M. Flagler and S. V. Harkness, Rockefeller had founded the Standard Oil Company of Ohio, which that year refined four per cent of the nation's total output.[1] By 1872, with monopoly as his goal, he had acquired twenty out of the twenty-five refineries in Cleveland and was laying plans for further conquests that within a decade were to bring him control over ninety per cent of the oil refineries of the country.

It would be difficult to maintain the thesis that the Civil War was in any fashion responsible for the steel or oil industries. Indeed, the de- *The Civil* velopment of steel manufacturing in the United States was *War and* doubtless retarded because of the necessity of keeping up *American* the flow of the standard iron products demanded by the *industry* war, and it is quite possible that the uses found for oil might have been greater had the nation been at peace. Wartime necessities, however, acted as a powerful stimulus to many other industries, such, for example, as meat-packing, flour-milling, and the manufacture of prepared foods, textiles, and leather goods. And yet it is impossible

[1] Ida M. Tarbell, *The History of the Standard Oil Company* (2 vols., 1904) was an early attempt at muckraking, but of commendable accuracy. Less satisfactory is G. H. Montague, *Rise and progress of the Standard Oil Company* (1903). The rise of the great industrialists is told in journalistic style by Matthew Josephson, *The Robber Barons* (1934).

ANDREW CARNEGIE

Brown Brothers

JOHN D. ROCKEFELLER

Brown Brothers

TWO PIONEER INDUSTRIALISTS

to believe that these developments would not have come, more slowly, to be sure, but quite as certainly, had there been no war. Undoubtedly the Civil War greatly accelerated the economic revolution in the United States, and greatly promoted the change of emphasis in the nation's business from agriculture to industry. But this transformation only accompanied and followed the war; it was not caused by it. Furthermore, such evidence as is sometimes adduced to prove that the Civil War was primarily the result of a conspiracy of industrialists bent on obtaining longer profits is not convincing. The industrialists made much of the advantage that the war offered them, and after the war was over they enjoyed a tremendous prosperity; but there is no reason to suppose that the war was essential to their triumph, or that they thought of the struggle in any such light.

Probably the meat-packers owed as much as any of the industrialists to the war, and yet the causes of their phenomenal success are more *The meat-packers* closely associated with railroads and refrigeration than with civil strife. Early Americans thought of the meat business as a strictly local affair. The "butcher" who supplied a village or a community bought his stock from near-by farmers, slaughtered it at night, and hurried its sale next day. His offerings, especially in the smaller communities, were apt to be monotonous and, particularly in the summer months, undependable. The advent of railroads made it possible to ship live animals considerable distances, and well before the Civil War large consignments of livestock from the Ohio and Mississippi valleys were being shipped regularly to eastern slaughter-houses. Such a system, however, was uneconomical, for freight had to be paid on the whole animal when only a part of it could be turned into meat; also, the losses from shrinkage and deterioration were heavy. As a partial remedy for this situation, pork was often salted down, packed in barrels, and shipped long distances — an age-old process that gave the "packing industry" its now inappropriate name.

Cincinnati, as the first city to gain a reputation for its pork-packing, was often referred to as "Porkopolis," but other western cities, especially Milwaukee and Chicago, were quick to follow its example.[1] Late in the Civil War, Philip Armour, of a Milwaukee firm, Plankinton, Armour, and Company, laid the basis for his subsequent great fortune by contracting for future deliveries of pork in New York at about forty dollars a barrel. Armour foresaw more clearly than most the speedy collapse of the Confederacy, and the consequent drop in prices that the cessation of

[1] Institute of American Meat Packers, *The Packing Industry* (1924); R. A. Clemen, *The American Livestock and Meat Industry* (1923).

war orders would insure. When the time came for him to make deliveries he was able to buy pork at about half the price he received for it. The result was a profit of about two million dollars for Armour, and ruin for many of the traders who bought from him. Shortly after the war, Armour began to concentrate his activities in Chicago, where in 1865 the Union Stockyards had been incorporated to furnish better facilities to the shippers and buyers of livestock. Under the firm name of Armour and Company, he and his brothers soon made the Armour brand known all over the world. No less successful was another Chicago packer, Nelson Morris, who had made a good thing of supplying livestock to the Union army during the war, and was one of the first to experiment in the transporting of dressed beef from Chicago to the Atlantic seaboard. The earnings of Morris's company by 1873 had reached the startling total of eleven million dollars a year. Lively competition for the Armour and Morris firms was soon furnished by Gustavus F. Swift, an eastern buyer of western livestock, who finally located in Chicago. By perfecting the refrigerator car to a degree that would permit of warm-weather as well as cold-weather shipments, Swift contributed to the packing industry a development of incalculable significance.

Added impetus came when, shortly after the Civil War, the "long drive" of Texas cattle to the western railroads furnished a cheap source of supply for livestock. This supply, soon heavily rein- *Western* forced by the range-cattle industry of the Great Plains, led *cattle* to the establishment of packing centers even farther west than Chicago, particularly at Kansas City, which became, next to Chicago, the greatest packing center in the country. Other towns along the bend of the Missouri, such as St. Joseph, Omaha, and Sioux City, also shared in this new source of prosperity. The time was not far distant when throughout the country meat from the local slaughter-house was to be almost entirely supplanted by a standardized product shipped from one of the great packing centers.

Another notable group of industrialists, the flour-millers, like the packers, found it necessary, if they were to take full advantage of their opportunities, to follow the producers into the West. *The flour-* During the eighteen-forties the center of the wheat belt *millers* crossed the Alleghenies, and before the outbreak of the Civil War more than sixty per cent of the flour that the nation consumed was made in the West. The work was still done, however, by thousands of grist-mills scattered throughout the country, and the methods of manufacture were not materially different from those in use during the early years of the republic when Oliver Evans first perfected a strictly mechanized flour-milling process. Given an immense lift by the war, the milling industry showed unmistakable signs at its close of concentrating in the upper Mississippi Valley, where thousands of acres of new wheat land were being opened up each year. By 1870 Minnesota ranked fourth among the states of the Union in the manufacture of flour, and Minneapolis, located at the Falls of St. Anthony, had begun the forward march that was to make it within twenty years the leading flour-milling center in the country.

During the early eighteen-seventies those "revolutionary changes," so characteristic of the times, began to transform the manufacture of *The "new* flour. Edmond N. La Croix, a Frenchman who had come *process"* to Minnesota by way of Canada, contributed the first startling innovation when he installed in the Minneapolis mill of George H. Christian a process newer to American than to French millers, whereby the hard spring wheat of the Northwest could be turned into as good a grade of flour as could be made from winter wheat. Soon not only Christian, but other Minneapolis millers also, notably Cadwallader C. Washburn and Charles A. Pillsbury, were making effective use of the "new process," and were seeking earnestly for other improvements. When a delegation sent abroad to investigate European methods reported favorably upon the Hungarian "high-milling" or gradual-roller process, all the millers who could afford to do so promptly installed the chilled-iron rollers it required, and began to produce at low cost a fine white "patent" flour of high gluten content. Other ingenious improvements, mostly of American invention,[1] made the changes that took place in the flour-milling industry during these few eventful years quite as significant as all the changes of the preceding two hundred years put together; while the wisdom of the northwestern millers in picking Minneapolis as the proper site for their activities was amply attested by the fact that within half a century the mills of Minnesota were producing each year more than twice as much flour as the mills of any other state in the Union. Other important milling centers tended to develop wherever grain was grown near-by in great quantity or the cost of shipping it in was not prohibitive. New York, Pennsylvania, Ohio, Illinois, and presently Kansas, all manufactured great quantities of flour. The small flour-mill did not at once disappear, but as time went on the local miller found himself fighting a losing battle against the same forces that were putting his neighbor, the "butcher," out of business.

[1] The original American inventor of the roller mill is generally conceded to be John Stevens of Neenah, Wisconsin, who made his invention about 1870, but did not receive a patent upon it until 1880. For a detailed account consult C. B. Kuhlmann, *The Development of the Flour-milling Industry in the United States* (1929).

It would be impossible even to list all of the industries that underwent in the years following the Civil War the same type of startling transformation that revolutionized meat-packing and flour- *Other* milling.[1] The manufacture of boots and shoes by machine *industries* rather than by hand labor became common during the war, and was expanded at its close until practically all the footwear of the country was factory made. The use of newly invented machinery, such, for example, as the McKay sole-sewing machine, greatly cheapened the price, and made for increased comfort as well. Lynn, Massachusetts, became the leading city of the country in the manufacture of shoes. Tanneries, with a new source of supply from the western cattle ranges, expanded to meet the new demands. Readymade clothing became as much a necessity as readymade shoes, and was as effectively supplied. In 1872 the installation of cloth-cutting machines by a Staten Island establishment registered the first significant advance in this industry since the invention of the sewing-machine. Meanwhile, the manufacture of textiles brought handsome profits to the industrialists of New England and the North Atlantic states. By 1870 the United States was making about one fifth of the world's output of machine-spun cotton goods, and was using weaving machinery of unexcelled excellence. Woolens and silks, carpets, blankets, and flannels, knit goods and linens, of nearly every sort and kind, poured in increasing abundance from American factories. Among the numerous other businesses that developed along factory lines in the post-war period, mention should be made of refined sugar; prepared foods; intoxicating beverages, particularly whiskey and beer; pottery, glass, and enameled wares; clocks and watches; organs and pianos; stoves and hardware; farm machinery; and building materials. All these expanding activities widened the base of industrial operations to include the meat-packers of Kansas City, the millers of Minneapolis, the watch-makers of Elgin, Illinois, and the farm-implement manufacturers of Moline, in the same state. No longer could it be said, without ample qualification, that the West was merely an agricultural section.

Labor for the new factories was recruited both at home and abroad. As the war ended, an occasional ill-starred prophet arose to predict that the great armies of the North could never be peacefully *Ex-soldiers* disbanded; either they must remain in service to lay the *as workers* basis of a military dictatorship, or they must dissolve into an army of the

---

[1] Nearly every industry has attracted its historian; for example: F. J. Allen, *The Shoe Industry* (1916); A. H. Cole, *The American Wool Manufacture* (2 vols., 1926); M. T. Copeland, *The Cotton Manufacturing Industry of the United States* (1912).

unemployed to spread disorder throughout the land. Both guesses were wrong. The soldiers, as fast as they could be mustered out, rejoiced to abandon military for civilian life. Many returned to the pursuits they had left when they went to war, many followed the frontier into the West, and many found work in some department of the rapidly expanding industrial life of the times.

Employers could count also upon a steady influx of immigrants from Europe who were conditioned to a lower wage scale and lower standards

Immigrants of living than most native Americans were willing to tolerate. So economical was it to employ these immigrants that manufacturers sometimes combined to send agents abroad to recruit the supply. Such urging, however, was of far less consequence than the general dislocations in Europe resulting from the economic revolution. Men thrown out of work, or unable to find it, looked longingly toward the greater opportunities of America, which the diminishing cost of ocean transportation brought more and more frequently within their grasp. During the first two years of the Civil War immigration had fallen off precipitately, but by 1863 confidence in the future of America had revived, and the number of newcomers had swelled to a figure greater than had crossed the Atlantic in any one of the three years preceding the war. Official stimulation came from the American side, both by way of liberal bounties for those who would volunteer to serve in the army, and by an immigration act, passed in 1864, which allowed the importation of laborers under contracts not particularly different in principle from the contracts that in colonial times had brought so many indentured servants to America. In 1865 a quarter of a million immigrants landed on American shores, and three years later the annual total had reached 326,000, well above the average for the eighteen-fifties. By 1873 when more than 460,000 aliens entered the country, the immigrant tide broke all preceding records. The census of 1870, which counted 38,558,371 people in the United States, described 2,314,000 of them as immigrants who had arrived during the sixties; while five years later the total number of foreign-born in the population was set at 7,500,000.

The great bulk of this immigration came, as before the war, from the British Isles and from Germany, but some notable new trends were in evidence. Immigration from Ireland, although still heavy, never again reached the startling totals of the forties and fifties, and was even exceeded during the seventies by the numbers coming from England. From Norway, Sweden, and Denmark came also a Scandinavian migration that in the first half of the seventies averaged not less than

European Immigration into the United States, 1841–1930

From Statistical Abstract of the United States (1931)

Country	1841–50	1851–60	1861–70	1871–80	1881–90	1891–1900	1901–10	1911–20	1921–30
Austria }			7,800	72,969	353,719	592,707	2,145,266	453,649	32,868
Hungary }								442,693	30,680
Belgium	5,074	4,738	6,734	7,211	20,177	18,167	41,635	33,746	15,846
Bulgaria						160	39,280	22,533	2,945
Czechoslovakia								3,426	102,194
Denmark	539	3,749	17,094	31,771	88,132	50,231	65,285	41,983	32,430
Finland								756	16,691
France	77,262	76,358	35,986	72,206	50,464	30,770	73,379	61,897	49,610
Germany	434,626	951,667	787,468	718,182	1,452,970	505,152	341,498	143,945	412,202
Greece	16	31	72	210	2,308	15,979	167,519	184,201	51,084
Italy	1,870	9,231	11,725	55,759	307,309	651,893	2,045,877	1,109,524	455,315
Netherlands	8,251	10,789	9,102	16,541	53,701	26,758	48,262	43,718	26,948
Norway }	13,903	20,931	109,298	95,333	176,586	95,015	190,505	66,395	68,531
Sweden }				115,922	391,776	226,266	249,534	95,074	97,249
Poland	105	1,164	2,027	12,970	51,806	96,720		4,813	227,734
Rumania				11	6,348	12,750	53,008	13,311	67,646
Russia	551	457	2,512	39,284	213,282	505,290	1,597,306	921,201	61,742
Spain	2,209	9,298	6,697	5,266	4,419	8,731	27,935	68,611	28,958
Portugal	550	1,055	2,658	14,082	16,978	27,508	69,149	89,732	29,994
Switzerland	4,644	25,011	23,286	28,293	81,988	31,179	34,922	23,091	29,676
Turkey (in Europe)	59	83	129	337	1,562	3,626	79,976	54,677	14,659
United Kingdom	1,047,763	1,338,093	1,042,674	984,914	1,462,839	659,954	865,015	487,589	550,804
England	32,092	247,125	222,277	437,706	644,680	216,726	388,017	249,944	157,420
Ireland	780,719	914,119	435,778	436,871	655,482	388,416	339,065	146,181	220,591
Scotland	3,712	38,331	38,769	87,564	149,869	44,188	120,469	78,357	159,781
Wales	1,261	6,319	4,313	6,631	12,640	10,557	17,464	13,107	13,012
Not Specified	229,979	132,199	341,537	16,142	168	67			
Yugo Slavia								1,888	49,064
Other Europe	79	5	8	1,001	682	122	665	8,111	22,983
Total Europe	1,597,501	2,452,660	2,065,270	2,272,262	4,737,046	3,558,978	8,136,016	4,376,564	2,477,853

twenty-five thousand a year. Most of the Scandinavians went to Illinois, Wisconsin, and the states of the new Northwest, particularly Minnesota. By no means less significant was the arrival of smaller numbers of Slavs and Italians from eastern and southern Europe, the vanguard of a mighty host.[1]

It is not too much to say that the common denominator for all these remarkable transformations was to be found in the rapidly expanding railroad system of the country. The steel manufacturers found their greatest market in supplying steel rails and other new equipment for the railroads; the oil men at first depended upon the railroads for the transportation of the crude oil that they refined no less than for the refined oil that they sold; the packers owed their very existence to the facilities that the railroads provided them; industrialists of every kind saw their establishments grow in direct ratio as the railroads grew.

Railroads

Greatly overbuilt before the Civil War, the railroads of the country enjoyed a tremendous prosperity while the war was on. Rates soared, except where the competition of the Great Lakes and the Erie Canal kept them down, and companies that had never made profits before now felt obliged to disguise their heavy earnings by issuing stock dividends. Railroad managers, as long as they could count on a wartime abundance of traffic, showed little interest either in new construction or the improvement of their equipment. Indeed, by 1865 the number of railroad accidents due to avoidable defects in roadbeds and rolling stock had reached the point where the public would no longer have tolerated such neglect except for the immunity to tragedy that accompanies war. With the return of peace the time was ripe for the renovation of the old roads and the building of new ones. Capital for the purpose was easily obtained by Jay Cooke and other promoters, who convinced the public that railroad securities were among the safest as well as the most profitable of investments.

The government itself, particularly by its generous subsidies to the

---

[1] The literature of this subject is voluminous. The most recent and best of the single-volume studies is Carl Wittke, *We Who Built America, the Saga of the Immigrant* (1940), but G. M. Stephenson, *A History of American Immigration, 1820–1924* (1926), is also a convenient summary. Samuel P. Orth, *Our Foreigners* (1920), is more popular than scholarly. John R. Commons, *Races and Immigrants in America* (1907), is a pioneer work that has not been entirely superseded. Racial groups have nearly all drawn their historians, among the best of which are Kendrick C. Babcock, *The Scandinavian Element in the United States* (1914); Theodore C. Blegen, *Norwegian Migration to America, 1825–1860* (1931); C. C. Qualey, *Norwegian Settlement in the United States* (1938); and Emily Greene Balch, *Our Slavic Fellow Citizens* (1910). A different and effective approach to the subject is to be found in Theodore C. Blegen and Martin B. Ruud, *Norwegian Emigrant Songs and Ballads* (1936).

building of transcontinentals, did much to stimulate the railroad boom.
This policy, contemplated for many years before the war *The first*
broke out but postponed because of southern opposition, *transconti-*
was inaugurated in 1862 when Congress chartered the *nental*
Union and the Central Pacific Railroads. In addition to the original
reasons for building a transcontinental road, proponents could now
cite the necessity of connecting California closely enough to the Union
to insure its loyalty for all time to come. The Union Pacific was to
build westward from Omaha, Nebraska; the Central Pacific, eastward
from Sacramento, California. Each company, after the completion of
an initial forty miles of track, was eligible to receive from the government, for each mile of track laid, ten square miles of land in alternate
sections, checkerboard fashion, along the right of way; and also, for each
mile of track laid, the loan of sixteen, thirty-two, or forty-eight thousand
dollars (for plains, foothills, or mountain country, respectively) in government bonds. Generous as these offers seemed, they proved to be
inadequate to attract the modest sums necessary to build the first essential divisions of forty miles each, so in 1864 Congress amended the
original terms. The government now doubled the land grant, accepted
a second mortgage for the loans it made, and permitted the companies
to borrow private capital, up to the amount of the government loans, on
first-mortgage bonds. The prospect of title to nearly twenty million
acres of land and loans amounting to about sixty million dollars proved
to be a sufficient inducement to moneylenders, and building soon began
in earnest. At first it was stipulated that the eastern boundary of California should be the dividing line between the two roads, but ultimately
they were permitted to race for distance, and in 1869, when they met
near Ogden, Utah, the Union Pacific had laid 1086 miles of track and
the Central Pacific 689.[1]

To complete the road the two companies had had to solve problems
that in some respects were quite similar, in others vastly different.
Both operated at great distances from their source of supply. *Problems of*
When the Union Pacific began construction at Omaha, the *construction*
nearest railhead to the east was far away on the Iowa plains, and until
late in 1867, when the Chicago and Northwestern reached the Missouri
River, all supplies had to be brought overland by freight wagons, or up
the river by steamboat from St. Joseph. The Central Pacific was little

[1] The building of the Union Pacific has attracted many historians, among them; G. M.
Dodge, *How We Built the Union Pacific Railway* (1910); John P. Davis, *The Union Pacific
Railway* (1894); E. L. Sabin, *Building the Pacific Railway* (1919). On the Central Pacific
see the extremely lively and interesting Oscar Lewis, *The Big Four; the Story of Huntington,
Stanford, Hopkins, and Crocker* (1938).

Bettmann

BUILDING THE TRANSCONTINENTAL RAILROAD

better off, for many of the materials it used had to be sent by sea, a ten months' voyage from Philadelphia or New York. On this account the first years of construction, before the builders were able to make accurate predictions of their needs, witnessed a succession of disappointments and delays. Much credit for the ultimate solution of these vexatious problems belongs to Theodore D. Judah, the able engineer and original promoter of the Central Pacific. The Union Pacific, building out over the plains, met a minimum of construction difficulties, although the lack of timber and stone was keenly felt, and materials of this sort often had to be brought long distances. The Central Pacific had no lack of timber or stone, but it was confronted with the difficult engineering feat of crossing the Sierra Nevada. In a single stretch of sixty miles fifteen tunnels had to be bored. Neither road was built according to specifications that would be regarded as tolerable today, although in this respect the Central Pacific was far superior to the Union Pacific. Curves and grades were regularly taken with the greatest unconcern.

The labor problem was about as perplexing for one company as for the other. The builders of the Union Pacific solved it by employing, among others, thousands of Irish immigrants, many of them ex-soldiers, who, under the efficient direction of General Grenville M. Dodge, not only built the road, but on occasion fought off the attacks of hostile Indians besides. Terminal towns on the Union Pacific, which moved westward as the road advanced, often had a population of as many as ten or twelve thousand people, and a type of life by night or day that led the pungently accurate Samuel Bowles, editor of the *Springfield Republican*, to name the town he visited in 1868 "Hell on Wheels." The Central Pacific, after many initial difficulties, finally resorted to the use of some ten thousand Chinese coolies, who excelled the Irish in tractability, if not in versatility. On the matter of food, for example, the bulk of which both roads had to import, the Chinese were far more easily pacified than the Irish, although hunting parties from the Union Pacific insured the latter a fair supply of fresh meat.

Unfortunately the building of both roads was accompanied by the most shameless profiteering. In each case the device of a construction company, controlled by the leading stockholders of the *Profiteering* railroads concerned, was utilized to drain off through unreasonably high contracts all possible profit from the building of the road. The Crédit Mobilier of America [1] served this purpose so well for the Union Pacific that it received, according to a congressional committee, a total of $73,000,000 for construction that cost about $50,000,-000. In one year, 1868, the favored holder of Crédit Mobilier stock took dividends amounting to 230 per cent in first-mortgage bonds, 515 per cent in Union Pacific stock, and 60 per cent in cash. The construction companies that did the work for the Central Pacific were two in number. At first the firm of Charles Crocker and Company received the contracts, but Crocker's close connection with the Central Pacific was so well known that in 1867 a new firm, the Contract and Finance Company, was formed. The two Central Pacific construction companies did even better for their stockholders than the Crédit Mobilier was able to do for its, for their profits on an investment of $121,000,000 amounted to $63,000,000. Most of this sum went to the four leading officials of the Central Pacific, Leland Stanford, Collis P. Huntington, Charles Crocker, and Mark Hopkins. Unlike the original owners of Union Pacific stock, most of whom sold out their holdings as soon as the road was built, the original Central Pacific group operated their road for many years, and took excellent profits from it. Each of the four mentioned left a fortune at his death of forty million dollars, or more.[2]

[1] See *ante*, p. 53.

[2] Among the best books on the railroad expansion of this period are John Moody, *The Railroad Builders* (1919); Robert E. Riegel, *The Story of the Western Railroads* (1926); and Glenn Chesney Quiett, *They Built the West* (1934).

When the Union Pacific engine "No. 119" touched noses with the Central Pacific's "Jupiter," a celebration was staged, not only at the meeting-place, where speeches were made and gold and silver spikes were driven, but throughout the country. The excitement over the completion of the first transcontinental, however, was doubtless accentuated by the fact that railroad progress was by no means confined to this one project, but was general. Everywhere new rails were being laid, new lines were being planned. The United States itself had chartered two other transcontinentals on terms almost as generous as it had given the Union and the Central Pacific, and was soon to charter a third. These roads received no sub- sidy in bonds, but they were allowed a double portion of land — twenty sections per mile in the states, and forty in the territories. The Northern Pacific (1864) was designed to connect the head of Lake Superior with Puget Sound; the Atlantic and Pacific (1866), to build southwestward from Springfield, Missouri; the Texas and Pacific (1871), to cross the continent still farther to the south through Texas, New Mexico, and Arizona.

Other railroad construction

National assistance to state-chartered railroads, after the pattern set by the Illinois Central grant of 1850, also continued unabated. The Chicago and Northwestern, the Chicago, Rock Island and Pacific, the Burlington and Missouri River, the Chicago, Milwaukee and St. Paul, the Missouri Pacific, the Atchison, Topeka and Santa Fe, the Kansas Pacific, and a host of minor western lines all profited, directly or indirectly, from government aid, and built feverishly. In the East and the South there was not only much new building, but, even more important, the consolidation of many lesser lines into systems that rivaled in their magnificent reaches the projected transcontinentals of the West. By 1873 Commodore Vanderbilt, the ruthless ruler of the New York Central, had extended his control from New York City to Chicago, J. Edgar Thomson, the associate of Andrew Carnegie, had done much the same thing for the Pennsylvania; and Jay Gould, for the Erie, had found a way through Cleveland and Cincinnati to St. Louis. In the South the Chesapeake and Ohio connected Norfolk with Cincinnati, and easy communication through Tennessee linked both Charleston and Norfolk with Memphis. Within five years after the Civil War the South had twenty-five hundred more miles of railroad than ever existed in the old Confederacy, while in the single year, 1873, new construction for this area reached a total of thirteen hundred miles. For the country as a whole, the eight years following the Civil War saw the laying of about thirty-five thousand miles of new track, an increase during the period of almost exactly one hundred per cent.

THE AMERICAN RAILROAD SYSTEM, 1870

A great variety of improvements kept pace with the new construction. In 1864 George M. Pullman built his first sleeping-car, the "Pioneer A," *Railroad improvements* at a cost of twenty thousand dollars, and a few years later he was actively at work on separate dining-, drawing-room, and reclining-chair cars.[1] In 1868 George Westinghouse demonstrated on a Pennsylvania passenger train his epoch-making airbrake, a device which by 1872 became an automatic appliance. During these years steel rails were introduced, although a heated debate continued for some time as to the relative merits of iron and steel for this purpose, and it was not until 1877 that the rapid replacement of iron by steel began. As the roadbeds were improved, heavier locomotives and rolling stock were built and a uniform gauge of four feet, eight and one half inches — the gauge used by the Union Pacific — came into general use. Terminal facilities were greatly improved, union stations made easier the transfer of passengers, and extensive freight yards expedited the traffic in "through freight." Long bridges, after the beginning of work on the Brooklyn Bridge in 1866, became a sort of passion. In 1869 the Missouri River was bridged at Kansas City, and in 1872 at Omaha. Between 1867 and 1874 James B. Eads built the famous bridge that bears his name across the Mississippi at St. Louis. John A. Roebling, the man who planned the Brooklyn Bridge, had first spanned the Ohio River at Cincinnati. These great bridges, and numerous lesser ones, enormously enhanced the speed and ease of railroad transportation.

Overinvestment in railroads, many of which, especially in the West, were built into unpopulated regions where for years operations could be *The railroads and the panic* carried on only at a loss, together with the wildest sort of speculation in railroad securities, had much to do with bringing on the panic of 1873. During these years the amount of capital invested in railroads alone had reached a billion dollars, while other huge sums had gone into the development of the new American industries. Capital from abroad amounting to over a billion and a half dollars had been borrowed to carry on the expansion, and interest charges of eighty million dollars annually had to be met. To pay these charges, and to remedy an adverse balance of trade, more gold had to be sent abroad each year than the United States could well spare. The new national banks yielded to the temptation to overextend their loans, and in the five years preceding the panic let out many times as much money as they took in by way of new deposits. Insurance companies were hard hit by the Chicago Fire of 1871, which cost them $200,000,000, and the Boston Fire of 1872, which added another $73,000,000 to the bill

[1] Joseph Husband, *The Story of the Pullman Car* (1917).

they had to pay. Conditions in Europe were similarly gloomy, and a sharp panic on the Vienna Bourse in May, 1873, inaugurated a general European depression that could not long be kept from America. It was the unloading by European investors of their American holdings that so depressed the New York Stock Exchange during the summer of 1873, and prepared the way for the crash that the failure of Jay Cooke and Company precipitated.[1]

[1] Thomas C. Cochran and William Miller, *The Age of Enterprise: A Social History of Industrial America* (1942), is a left-wing view of the development of big business. Allan Nevins, *John D. Rockefeller* (2 vols., 1940), does much to rehabilitate the oil magnate's reputation. Paul H. Giddens, *The Birth of the Oil Industry* (1938), a useful attempt at synthesis, is supplemented by the same author's *The Beginnings of the Petroleum Industry: Sources and Bibliography* (1941). The rise of typical industrialists is featured in H. O. Evans, *Iron Pioneer: Henry W. Oliver* (1942); J. K. Winkler, *Tobacco Tycoon: The Story of James Buchanan Duke* (1942); and Harper Leech and John Carroll, *Armour and His Times* (1938). D. B. Steinman, *The Builders of the Bridge* (1945), is the story of John Roebling and his son.

CHAPTER V

AMERICAN SOCIETY DURING
THE DEPRESSION

THE sudden descent from post-war prosperity to post-panic adversity plunged the American people into an atmosphere of the deepest gloom. Critics of American society had not been lacking while times were good, but their comments, all too frequently, had fallen on deaf ears. Now, with each succeeding year a little harder than the one that had gone before, the apostles of pessimism reigned supreme. Long and earnestly they dwelt upon the sins of society, the wickedness of business, and the total depravity of the politicians. Could the United States hope to survive the moral collapse it had suffered? [1]

There was reason for the gloom. America had long been regarded as the land of opportunity, but a trip through the slum district of any
American great American city seemed to show rather that it was the
slums land of want. In New York City, out of a hundred thousand slum-dwellers, twenty thousand lived in cellars; in Boston, one fifth of the total population lived in flimsy, overcrowded tenements. Unemployment estimates for the country at large revealed that from two to three million people were out of work, and for most of these the long, expensive trip to the "free lands" of the West completely closed that "safety-valve." Wages dropped precipitately, woman and child labor were ruthlessly exploited, actual starvation was by no means unknown. Everywhere, but most of all in the crowded city centers where ignorance of the simplest sanitary precautions was rivaled only by indifference to those that were known, preventable diseases, such as smallpox, typhoid, and typhus, took a heavy toll. Always such suffering fell heaviest upon the poor. At any given time three fourths of the sickness and death in New York City was furnished by the less-favored half of the population.

Hardly less distressing than the plight of the poor was the vulgar

[1] Don C. Seitz, *The Dreadful Decade* (1926), makes no effort to avoid overstatement.

ostentation of a small army of *parvenu* rich.[1] War profiteers, successful speculators, oil men and miners who had "struck it rich" *The newly rich* flocked to the cities to display their wealth. Few of them could approximate the extravagances of the notorious Jim Fisk, but many of them tried. Fisk, at the height of his glory, had sumptuous offices in "Castle Erie," a huge marble building on Eighth Avenue in New York that also housed his privately owned and operated Grand Opera House. From his theatrical stars and dancers, many of whom were imported, he recruited a harem that might well have been the envy of an Oriental potentate. The chief recipients of his favor lived in palaces, and fared forth in handsome carriages, drawn sometimes, when Fisk went along, by three teams of fine horses, whites to the left and blacks to the right. Among Fisk's other fancies were canary birds, hundreds of which, in gilded cages, adorned his rooms, and the well-appointed steamboats that he also owned and loved. On occasion he would dress himself up in the gold lace of an admiral's uniform, and once, when so arrayed, he contrived to receive President Grant. The colonelcy of the Ninth Regiment of the New York National Guard, a position he obtained by means of generous gifts, furnished him another opportunity to indulge his penchant for gaudy pageantry. During the summer of 1871 he took the entire regiment to Boston at his own expense to celebrate the anniversary of the battle of Bunker Hill. He died on January 7, 1872, from bullet wounds inflicted by one of his own kind, Edward S. Stokes, a "business and amatory rival." Stokes, for his crime, was sentenced to four years in the penitentiary at Sing Sing, but there he received many special privileges, such, for example, as being permitted to drive about after night with the span of horses he kept for the purpose at a local livery stable. On his release he became the proprietor of the Hoffman House at Broadway and Twenty-Sixth Street, New York, a hotel chiefly noted for the daring paintings on its barroom walls.[2]

While the loose living of a Jim Fisk could hardly be said to reflect against the character of the American people as a whole, there was an abundance of other evidence at hand for the use of alarmists *Moral laxity* who held that morality "to a fatal extent" had broken down. It was disheartening to have the name of the leading preacher of the time, Henry Ward Beecher, bandied about among the unregenerate because of an affair he was alleged to have carried on with a woman of

---

[1] Gustavus Myers, *History of the Great American Fortunes* (3 vols., 1910), shows little sympathy for its subject.
[2] R. H. Fuller, *Jubilee Jim; the Life of Colonel James Fisk, Jr.* (1928).

his congregation. Beecher was probably innocent, but in any event the conspiracy to disgrace him and the long trial it involved were ugly enough. Conventional citizens were shocked, in a day when divorce had not yet become a national pastime, at the ease and frequency with which marriages were annulled under the lax laws of two offending states, Connecticut and Indiana. From West Virginia to Arkansas, the region over which the Civil War had been fought, bands of ruffians continued their wartime habits, and for years escaped arrest. Most noted of these outlaws was Jesse James, who in 1872 robbed the Kansas City Fair of ten thousand dollars, and until the time of his death a decade later kept the Kansas-Missouri border in a state of frightened expectancy. City gangs likewise defied the law, and committed depredations that would have taxed the talents of twentieth-century racketeers.[1] Gambling, particularly in the cities and along the frontier, flourished covertly or openly as the taste of the community perferred. The State of Louisiana raised money by a lottery. Prostitution was railed at and preached against, but flaunted itself in every sizable town. Intemperance was the commonest vice of all, and since the Civil War had seemingly been definitely on the increase. During the war most of the state prohibition laws had been repealed, while the national government, by placing a tax on intoxicants, had, in a sense, given the liquor traffic its blessing. Saloons, as the places where liquor was sold came universally to be called, were outfitted with clublike attractiveness and their popularity is attested by the fact that the total capital invested in the liquor business grew from \$29,000,000 in 1860 to \$193,000,000 in 1880. Most of the immigrant groups gave the liquor interests their enthusiastic support.

The sordidness of business during the post-war years was another subject that aroused the anxiety of thoughtful critics. The well-nigh *Business* universal devotion of Americans to the pursuit of wealth *ethics* was in itself a heavy curse, but the devious means that men used to gain their ends hit at the very foundations of society. In part this alarming laxity of conduct could be blamed upon the war itself, which, for literally millions of young Americans, had stood in lieu of a college education. As students of war they had been taught to deceive the enemy, to take his property, to destroy, and to kill; as graduates of such a course they sometimes failed to perceive that the virtues of war were not also the virtues of peace. Furthermore, with business expanding so rapidly, executive experience of any kind was in great demand. American capitalists had not often gone to war themselves, but when

[1] Herbert Asbury, *The Gangs of New York; an Informal History of the Underworld* (1928).

peace was restored they made good use of the war-trained heroes. Army officers were, after all, trained executives, and the high-ranking officer who was not promptly solicited to accept a "business opening" was rare indeed.

It would be a mistake, however, to blame the war for every evil practice of the business world. Far more important was the utter novelty of large-scale business operations. Before the Civil War most American businesses were relatively small, and their fields of activity were local. Standards of conduct existed which the prudent business man, to retain the good-will of his customers and the public, felt obliged to recognize. But for large-scale business no code of ethics had yet been evolved. With monopoly, or at least near-monopoly, as the goal, the struggle for survival among competitors was intense, and as a rule only the ruthless had a chance to win. The law offered no restraint, for, since similar problems had never before been faced, laws to meet them had never been devised; furthermore, as business organizations grew in size and power they found that they could, when they chose, have a hand in both the making and the enforcement of laws. The situation was not unlike that on the high seas in the days when piracy and buccaneering, unchallenged by international law, amounted almost to legitimate occupations.[1]

Corporation methods of finance offered an opportunity, never long neglected, for astounding frauds in the issuance and manipulation of stocks and bonds. "Wildcat" or "blue-sky" securities *Corporation* were easily sold to a public made gullible by the unprece- *Finance* dented number of fortunes that the "boom" times actually produced. Oil companies were organized that never drilled a well, mining companies that never sunk a shaft, railroad companies that never laid a rail, all for the sole purpose of separating careless investors from their savings. General Robert C. Schenck, an ex-congressman from Ohio whom Grant sent as Minister to England, gave his support to the promoters of a mining venture that sold fifty thousand dollars' worth of worthless stock to British investors.[2] General George B. McClellan, more innocently, backed a ten-million-dollar corporation that proposed to exploit a mythical diamond and ruby field in California.

Even the more substantial corporations were frequently led to "water" their stock and to incur bonded indebtedness altogether out of proportion to their assets. Daniel Drew, a pious old fraud who hoped to purchase pardon for his sins by making generous pledges, mostly

[1] F. C. Sharp and P. G. Fox, *Business Ethics; Studies in Fair Competition* (1937).
[2] Schenck further distinguished himself by writing a treatise on poker-playing.

never paid, to Drew Theological Seminary, wormed his way into the directorate of the Erie Railway, became its treasurer, and for years manipulated the price of its stock in such a way as to enhance his private fortune. According to a current Wall Street saying: "Dan'l says up — Erie goes up. Dan'l says down — Erie goes down. Dan'l says wiggle-waggle — Erie bobs both ways." In 1868 Cornelius Vanderbilt, who already controlled the New York Central and the Hudson River Railroad, proposed to add the badly wrecked Erie to his domain. A battle royal followed in which Drew, supported by his apt "pupils," Jay Gould and Jim Fisk, finally won. To do so, however, Drew and his associates found it necessary to issue fifty thousand shares of fraudulent stock, to flee to New Jersey to escape arrest, and to bribe the New Jersey legislature to legalize their transaction. But Drew's luck did not last. His two "pupils" raised the price of Erie stock by sales abroad, thanklessly cornered their teacher, and trimmed him of a million and a half. The Panic of 1873 also hit him hard, and by 1876 he was bankrupt with liabilities of over a million dollars and no assets to speak of. Long a target of reproach, he died three years later with none to mourn his passing.[1]

Not many types of sizable business enterprise came through the cycle of boom and depression with clean records. Three New York *Bank failures* savings banks failed in 1872 under the most scandalous circumstances; while small investors suffered acutely, the former bank officials continued to live in luxury. During the first eight years of the seventies, twenty-eight New York life insurance companies either failed outright, or avoided failure by amalgamation with some stronger concern. Losses to policy-holders amounted to a nominal total of $159,000,000 insurance. Even the solvent companies unblushingly "froze out" aged and undesirable policy-holders, usually by increasing rates. "The whole chapter," said the *Commercial and Financial Chronicle*,[2] "is so dark a record of betrayal of corporate trust — incapacity being so blended with dishonesty that it is impossible to separate them — that if we had the space and the data, we should not have the desire to expose its details."

Whatever the shortcomings of business may have been, they met their *Political* match in politics. The Grant administration was known, *scandals* even before it had ended, as the most corrupt that the Republic had yet experienced. Reconstruction, with its attempt to per-

[1] Bouck White, *The Book of Daniel Drew* (1910), and A. D. H. Smith, *Commodore Vander-bilt* (1927), are true in the picture if not in every detail.

[2] April 19, 1879.

petuate the rule of the northern Radicals by forcing Negro rule upon the South, would have been a scandal even if honestly carried out, but the number of honest officials in the "carpet-bag" South seems to have been negligible. And yet the scandals that rocked the country were as frequently associated with the North or the West as with the South. The Crédit Mobilier, the Whiskey Ring, the frauds in the Indian service, and the Salary Grab Act [1] had no southern or reconstruction connotation whatever. In the fields of state and local government political degradation reached its lowest depths. The spoils system, everywhere deeply entrenched, had produced an unsavory set of petty party "bosses," each presiding over his county or city or state because, by fair means or foul, he had gathered into his hands the disposal of the "patronage." Working together as a party "machine," the bosses could levy assessments, win elections, reward the faithful, punish the disobedient, and, if they chose, line their pockets with public money and exact a heavy toll from business.

As befitted its size and prominence, New York City furnished the country with the outstanding example of municipal corruption. There the Tammany Society, a political organization that dated back to the eighteenth century, controlled the local machinery of the Democratic Party, and regularly rolled up huge majorities for the Democratic ticket. Tammany Hall, as the society was usually called (after its meeting-place on Fourteenth Street), won the support of the masses by providing them with a kind of unofficial social insurance. Tammany leaders in each ward made it their business to find jobs for the unemployed, to relieve the needy, to care for the sick, to aid the newly arrived immigrants in their efforts to become adjusted. In return for all this, Tammany chiefs expected and obtained unquestioning political support. When extra votes were needed, wholesale frauds were easily possible, for the election machinery was in Tammany hands. In the election of 1868, for example, it was generally believed that the returns from New York City and Brooklyn were held back until the rest of the state could be heard from so that enough votes could be cast for John T. Hoffman, the Tammany candidate for governor, to insure his election.

When Grant became President of the United States the "Grand Sachem" of Tammany Hall was William M. Tweed, a thoroughgoing corruptionist who had worked his way up in politics from *The Tweed* membership in a volunteer fire department. Tweed's op- *Ring* portunity for wholesale graft came after he and his associates by the most barefaced bribery had secured from the state legislature a city

[1] See *ante*, pp. 53–55.

"WHO STOLE THE PEOPLE'S MONEY ?"

THE TWEED RING

charter that was specifically designed to enable them to avoid responsibility for their crimes. The principals of the "Tweed Ring" were "Boss" Tweed himself, whose presidency of the board of supervisors of New York County (coterminous with New York City) had obvious possibilities; A. Oakey Hall, the mayor, an aspirant for social recognition whose fastidious appearance won him the sobriquet, "Elegant Oakey"; Peter B. Sweeny, treasurer of both city and county, useful not only because of his position, but also because of his unquestioned ability as a lawyer; and Richard B. Connolly, the controller, otherwise and appropriately known as "Slippery Dick." In 1869 this disgusting crew began a series of peculations that mounted year by year until at the height of their power they were dividing among themselves and their confederates eighty-five per cent of the total expenditures made by the city and county. Tweed received as his share twenty-four per cent of the "take," and the rest was apportioned out according to a prearranged plan. The actual cost of maintaining the city's armories, for example, totaled for a given period $250,000, but the amount paid out allegedly for that purpose was $3,200,000. A courthouse was built that cost about three million dollars, but the county's books showed expenditures for that purpose of about eleven millions. The plastering of this building alone cost the taxpayers $2,870,464.06, and its carpeting $350,000, "enough to cover the whole City Park three times." During a period of thirty months the city and county printing bill ran to over seven million dollars. Probably the total loot taken by the Tweed Ring reached a hundred million dollars.[1]

At last, scathing editorials in the *New York Times*, and cartoons by Thomas Nast in *Harper's Weekly*, began to take effect, and the public was aroused. George Jones, the owner of the *Times*, was *The ring* offered a million dollars to quiet his paper; Nast, a half *broken up* million to go to Europe and cease his campaign of caricature.[2] Long baffled for lack of direct evidence, the *Times* finally had the proofs it wanted put into its hands by an insider with a grievance. The exposure that followed was complete and devastating; the more so when the efforts of Tweed, Hall, and Sweeny to lay the entire blame on Connolly drove the latter to open his records to the reformers. Under the brilliant leadership of Samuel J. Tilden and Charles O'Conor, they were able by the end of 1872 to drive every member of the "ring" out of office. Tweed himself died in jail.[3]

The national rejoicing that Tweed had at last been brought to bay was tempered by the reflection that his misconduct differed only in degree from what went on almost everywhere. James Russell Lowell well expressed the national sense of humiliation when he wrote, apropos of the opening of the Centennial Exposition at Philadelphia:

> Columbia, puzzled what she should display
> Of true home-make on her Centennial Day,
> Asked Brother Jonathan; he scratched his head
> Whittled awhile reflectively, and said,
> . . . .
> Show your State Legislatures; show your Rings;
> And challenge Europe to produce such things
> As high officials sitting half in sight
> To share the plunder and to fix things right;
> If that don't fetch her, why you only need
> To show your latest style in martyrs — Tweed.
> She'll find it hard to hide her spiteful tears
> At such advance in one poor hundred years.

[1] Rhodes, vii, and Oberholtzer, ii, cover this subject with generous detail.

[2] A. B. Paine, *Thomas Nast, His Period and His Pictures* (1904), reproduces many of these cartoons.

[3] Further details on this unsavory story may be found in D. T. Lynch, *"Boss" Tweed* (1927), and M. R. Werner, *Tammany Hall* (1928).

Lowell's bitter sarcasm well expressed the feeling of hopelessness that overcame so many Americans when they saw depression added to the *A brighter* lengthening list of their nation's woes. Nevertheless, there *side* was a brighter side to the picture, even if most men failed to see it. The United States could not have been wholly bad; if so it would have produced fewer Jeremiahs. There is an element of hope in the recognition of an existing evil, and the number of Americans who now sprang forward to denounce the shortcomings of their nation and their fellow citizens was so great as to constitute in itself good evidence that the times were not altogether out of joint. Three of these unconscious optimists, Edwin Lawrence Godkin, George William Curtis, and Carl Schurz, deserve particular mention. A nation that could list such men among its leaders of thought had no reason to despair. There was yet "balm in Gilead."

E. L. Godkin (1831–1902) was Irish-born but of English stock, the son of a distinguished Protestant clergyman and journalist.[1] Educated *E. L. Godkin* for the law, young Godkin chose instead to make journalism his career, and, after a brief connection with the London *Daily News* and the Belfast *Northern Whig*, he emigrated in 1856 to America. Here he at once made friends, and forged ahead so rapidly that in 1865, when he was not yet thirty-four years of age, forty interested stockholders subscribed one hundred thousand dollars with which he was to start a weekly newspaper, the *Nation*. Despite many early financial embarrassments, the venture succeeded beyond its founders' highest hopes, and the *Nation* came to exercise an influence upon American life second to none. According to James Bryce, it was "the best weekly not only in America but in the world." Its pronouncements were awaited eagerly by ministers, editors, and minor publicists who pushed the radius of its influence far beyond the number of its readers. Godkin fearlessly attacked every evil that he saw, and aimed his most barbed shafts at the venal politicians whom the spoils system had foisted on the country. He stood steadfastly for a sound-money policy, but he denounced scornfully the business rascality that the age produced. He saw, far more clearly than if he had been a native American, the elemental flaws in American society, and bitingly headed an editorial on the Beecher trial "Chromo Civilization." Ruefully he pointed out what the witnesses revealed about American "ways of living, standards of right and wrong, traits of manners, codes of propriety, religious and social ideas." Floral tributes sent by Beecher's

---

[1] Rollo Ogden (editor), *Life and Letters of Edwin Lawrence Godkin* (2 vols., 1907).

congregation to grace the trial he likened to "wreaths round the manhole of a sewer."

George William Curtis (1824–1892) was a New Englander by birth who had come to New York City as a boy.[1] He maintained the best traditions of Puritan New England: read Emerson, lived *George William Curtis* for a while at Brook Farm, and before the Civil War wrote several books of travel and criticism. Stirred deeply by the war, he became in 1863 editor of the strongly pro-northern *Harper's Weekly*, which, in the ascendancy it soon gained over men's minds, was rivaled only by its more strictly intellectual contemporary, the *Nation*. Allotting generous space to pictorial representation of current events, frequently drawn on the spot, and featuring the cartoons of Thomas Nast, *Harper's Weekly* appealed to a far wider audience than the *Nation;* nor was it, out of deference possibly to the publishers' profits, so avowedly militant in its advocacy of reform. Curtis's influence, however, was exerted from the lecture platform almost as actively as from the editor's desk. Scores of audiences heard his lecture on "Political Infidelity," but he did not always deal exclusively with politics. Concerned because American materialism was deadening the moral sensibilities of the people, he once cried out:

> Are we satisfied that America should have no other excuse for independent national existence than a superior facility of money-making? Why, if we are unfaithful as a nation, though our population were to double in a year, and the roar and rush of our vast machinery were to silence the music of the spheres, and our wealth were enough to buy all the world, our population could not bully history, nor all our riches bribe the eternal justice not to write upon us: "Ichabod, Ichabod, thy glory is departed."

Carl Schurz (1829–1906), like Godkin, was alien-born. His father, a small-town German schoolmaster, made every sacrifice in order to permit young Carl to work for a doctor's degree in history *Carl Schurz* at the University of Bonn. Here the boy was caught up, along with many other student liberals, in the revolutionary movements of 1848–49, joined the rebel forces, and escaped capture only by fleeing to France. Later he went to Switzerland, where many other German refugees had gathered, and where he might have remained but for his determination to rescue one of his Bonn professors, Gottfried Kinkel, who was under sentence of imprisonment for life at Spandau, near Berlin. The exciting story of Kinkel's rescue by Schurz, and of their joint flight to England, is not often paralleled except in fiction, but much of the rest of Schurz's life also reads like a romance. He tried

[1] Edward Cary, *George William Curtis* (1894).

living in France, only to be expelled as a dangerous radical, and at last sailed for America where, naturally, he joined the German colony in Wisconsin. Because of his intense interest in liberal democracy, he was soon drawn into politics, and his anti-slavery sentiments made him a Republican. A born orator, he spoke not only in German, but had soon acquired such facility in the use of English that his assistance in campaigns was in great demand. He fought loyally in the Civil War, from which he emerged a major-general, and after the war made an official tour of the South at the behest of President Johnson.[1] In 1867 he became part owner and editor of a German-language newspaper, published at St. Louis, and was soon in the thick of the fight for Liberal Republicanism. By the time he went to the United States Senate in 1869 his Americanization was thoroughgoing and complete. Like Lincoln, he was intensely interested in proving that democracy as a form of government was fit to survive, and the venality of the spoilsmen who stood ready to betray it for a price drove him to the highest invective. When he spoke in the Senate the galleries were packed, and when he took to the lecture platform, as he often did, great crowds came out to hear him.[2]

In the political world the work of such men as Godkin, Curtis, and Schurz was not wholly without effect. Scandals were ruthlessly exposed, and sometimes, as in the case of Tweed, the guilty parties were punished. A governor in Nebraska and a state treasurer in Minnesota were impeached and removed from office. A member of the Kansas legislature laid on the speaker's desk seven thousand dollars that he had been paid to vote for the re-election of Samuel C. Pomeroy to the United States Senate, and Pomeroy was not re-elected. The Whiskey Ring was put out of business; thievery in the Indian service was restrained; wholesale attempts to bribe Congress, as in the Crédit Mobilier, were not again attempted; alien rule in the South and the corruption it bred were soon overthrown.

Far more difficult to deal with were the problems presented by the business world, but even here a beginning was made. The brunt of
Railroad the first attack was borne by the railroads. These were not
extortions particularly worse in their conduct than other big businesses, but their public nature made their behavior more easily observable; moreover, with the railroads, sooner than with most other enterprises, the breakdown of the competitive system was fully apparent. Among

[1] See *ante*, p. 22.
[2] C. V. Easum, *The Americanization of Carl Schurz* (1929), treats of his pre-Civil War career; Joseph Schafer, *Carl Schurz, Militant Liberal* (1930), of his whole life.

the first to protest against railroad extortions were the grain-growers of the upper Mississippi Valley, whose dependence upon the railroads was well-nigh complete. Only by means of the railroads could they ship their produce to market; only in the same fashion could they obtain from the outside world the manufactured articles they had to have. Inasmuch as the number of regions served by competitive lines was few indeed, the ordinary farmer had no choice but to use the road that ran nearest his farm. Competition was a myth; the railroads regularly charged "all the traffic would bear," and dictated at will the terms on which they chose to serve their patrons. Elevators and warehouses, often owned or controlled in turn by the railroads, did likewise; and middlemen, themselves compelled to pay a heavy toll in freight to the roads, were not far behind. Efforts to "get another railroad" so as to restore competition rarely availed; more frequently companies that had once been competitive joined forces and ceased to compete.

Ripe for an organized revolt, the farmers of the Northwest found in the Patrons of Husbandry, or the Grange, as it was more frequently called, the tool they needed. The founder of this order, Oliver Hudson Kelley, a government clerk at Washington, had intended it to be a farmers' lodge with an attractive secret ritual that might induce the farmer and the farmer's wife, who was also eligible to membership, to listen to expositions of the latest ideas on scientific farming. Founded in 1867, the order began to grow only in the early seventies when the northwestern farmers seized upon it as a means of attacking the railroads. Then Granger orators inflamed public opinion against the railroads, and the Granger organization cleared the way for action.[1]

The Granger idea — that the state should regulate the railroads, if necessary to the point of fixing maximum rates — was older than the movement. Toyed with gingerly in Massachusetts, its real beginning was in Illinois, where during the late sixties laws were passed to restrain both the elevators and the railroads. These early measures proved unavailing, but a new state constitution, adopted in 1870, specifically stated:

> *Section* 15. The General Assembly shall pass laws to correct abuses and to prevent unjust discrimination and extortion in the rates of freight and passenger traffics on the different railroads in this state, and enforce such laws by adequate penalties, to the extent, if necessary for that purpose, of forfeiture of their property and franchises.

With a similarly strong mandate to regulate warehouses, the Illinois

---

[1] This movement is fully covered by Solon J. Buck, *The Granger Movement* (1913), and less extensively by his *The Agrarian Crusade* (1921).

legislature of 1871 promptly established maximum rates for the transportation of passengers, required that freight charges should be based entirely upon distance traversed, provided regulations for the storing and shipping of grain, and created a state board of railroad and warehouse commissioners charged with the duty of enforcing the laws. Against these measures the railroads made a determined, and at first a successful, fight, for on the first test case the Supreme Court of Illinois held the laws to be unconstitutional. But the Grangers, now thoroughly aroused, promptly voted one of the judges who had held against them out of office, and replaced him with a judge who shared their views. The result was that in 1873 a new law, better drawn but designed to effect the same ends, was sustained.

Meantime the Grangers, bent on using the power of the state to curb the railroads, had gone into politics throughout the Northwest. Some-*The Granger* times they were content merely to vote for Republicans or *movement* Democrats who shared their views, but frequently they chose third-party candidates on separate "Anti-Monopoly" or "Independent" or "Reform" tickets. Independence Day, 1873, was long remembered as the "Farmers' Fourth of July," for on that day hundreds of Granger audiences gave their approval to a *Farmers' Declaration of Independence*, which repeated in well-worn phraseology the grievances from which farmers suffered, and announced in no uncertain way their determination to find relief. Presently Granger legislatures had enacted, not only in Illinois, but also in Wisconsin, Minnesota, and Iowa, measures of drastic regulation for railroads and warehouses. In each instance litigation followed, and the railroads, despairing of aid from the Granger-minded state courts, at length took their cases to the federal courts. The Granger laws, railroad attorneys claimed, were impairments of contracts that the states had already made in granting charters to the railroads, and they provided for the taking of private property without due process of law. But in the spring of 1877, the United States Supreme Court ruled against the railroads in a series of decisions, the most important of which were *Munn vs. Illinois* and *Peik vs. the Chicago and Northwestern Railroad.* Thus the "right of a state to regulate a business that is public in nature though privately owned and managed" won striking vindication, and a weapon was forged with which, it was hoped, not only the railroads but other monopolistic enterprises also could be attacked. Most of the early Granger laws were defective and had to be repealed, but the principle on which they were founded endured, and before long railroad and warehouse commissions were hard at work in nearly every state.

The Granger movement, although short-lived, left other important legacies besides the point of law it had made. Convinced that they were being robbed by manufacturers and middlemen, the Grang- *Granger* ers made strenuous efforts to establish co-operative farm- *contributions* implement factories, elevators, creameries, and general stores. They experimented with purchasing agencies, and tried out co-operative selling. Many of these ventures were unsuccessful, not so much because they were wrong in principle as because of the inexperience and mismanagement of the men who were placed in charge. These business failures, more than anything else, account for the sudden decline in Granger popularity about 1876, and the relegation of the Patrons of Husbandry once more to the inconspicuous rôle of a farmers' lodge. But the farmers who had participated in the movement did not soon forget the fright they had given the politicians by their independence, the victory they had won over the railroads, and the good times they had had at lodge meetings and picnics. Also, the occasional surviving co-operatives paved the way for an important development later on.

Even more noteworthy than all these efforts to purify politics and to regulate business were the spiritual strivings of a people, now acutely conscious of its shortcomings. The success of the American experiment in democracy depended in the last analysis upon the character of the individual citizens who made up the population. If the citizens were honest, capable, and intelligent, the future of the nation, however much it might be temporarily eclipsed by the depression, was bright; but if the citizens were unworthy, prosperity itself could not dispel the gloom. Out of such heart-searchings there came a significant educational renaissance, a renewed interest in literary activity, and a wholesome enthusiasm for humanitarian reform.

With respect to public elementary education, the Civil War, at least so far as the North was concerned, merely interrupted a trend of development that had begun long before. After the war, as *Educational* before, the "little red schoolhouse," or its equivalent, con- *advances* tinued to be the chief citadel of rural education, and from its lowly rostrum young men and maidens, only a little older than the "scholars" they taught, dispensed knowledge of the "three R's" — reading, writing, and arithmetic. In the towns and villages, buildings of several "rooms" could be found, and the process of separating the various "grades" from one another, with a teacher for each, was an ideal more and more frequently attained. Most rapid progress, however, was made in the cities, where new ideas in education did not put so severe a strain upon taxable resources. In 1873, for example, St. Louis, following the lead of Mrs. Carl Schurz, whose efforts to introduce the European kindergarten idea into America antedated the Civil War, accepted the innovation, and so began a movement that was soon to spread to the whole country. The rapid multiplication of tax-supported normal schools (of which there were only twelve when Lincoln was inaugurated) served greatly to improve the quality of instruction: teachers who themselves had no opportunity to attend such schools learned the latest methods at summer "institutes," locally provided for the purpose.[1] The spell cast by the Webster spellers and by the McGuffey readers had not yet been broken, but new and better books were being written. Publishers did not long neglect this opportunity for profit, and the means they used to secure "adoptions" sometimes failed to square with the precepts so generously sprinkled through the books they sold. The fact that the several states, operating through local school districts set up by state law, had complete control of educational policy accounts for the wide variety of educational practice in the different parts of the country, but in 1867 the national government took a hand by creating the office of the United States Commissioner of Education, whose business it was "to collect statistics and facts concerning the conditions and progress of education in the several states and territories and to diffuse information respecting the organization and management of schools and school systems and methods of teaching."

Even more striking than the rapid development of the elementary schools was the movement for free public high schools that swept the country during the post-war period, and persisted throughout the dark days of depression.[2] Before the Civil War *High schools* private academies had generally carried forward the education of such students as intended to enter college; indeed, when the war broke out, there were only about one hundred public high schools in the whole United States. The next few decades, however, witnessed the almost complete elimination of the old-fashioned academy and the substitution in its place of secondary instruction at state expense. By 1870 the country had about five hundred public high schools; by 1880 the number had risen to eight hundred; by the end of the century, to six thousand. With the state so thoroughly committed to expenditures for high schools, insistence upon better qualified teachers was inevitable, and systems of certification were devised for the purpose of weeding out the unfit. As

[1] A comparison of Edward Eggleston, *The Hoosier Schoolmaster* (1871), with Herbert Quick, *One Man's Life* (1925), shows how rapidly conditions were changing.

[2] Two excellent manuals on the general subject of education are E. P. Cubberley, *Public Education in the United States* (1934), and E. G. Dexter, *A History of Education in the United States* (1904).

the children of the masses pushed on into the high schools, revision of the curriculum to meet the needs of those who had no thought of entering college began to be made, although an undue emphasis upon mathematics and the classical languages long persisted. From shorter beginnings the high-school term generally lengthened out to four years, which, together with the eight years usually assigned to the elementary school, provided a total of twelve years' instruction. Eight or nine months of school per year was the customary goal toward which educators worked, but frequently, especially in the country districts, the school year was much shorter. Many of the northern states enacted compulsory education laws of varying terms and efficacy.

In these significant developments the South, necessarily, lagged far behind. What little there was of free public education in the South before the war had vanished during the conflict, and the *Education in* freeing of the slaves now placed upon the limited financial *the South* resources of the reconstructed states a double burden, schools for the children of the freedmen, and schools for the children of the whites. As already noted, most of the carpet-bag governments made generous legal provisions for education, although the distance between promise and performance was often very great. Nevertheless, to cite a single example, South Carolina by 1876 had a public-school population of fifty thousand whites and seventy thousand colored children as against a total of only twenty thousand in 1860.[1]

Quite the most striking educational development of the times, however, appeared in the field of higher education. It would seem, almost, that from this source Americans expected to draw the inspiration and the information that would confound the critics of democracy and make of the United States a kind of Utopia. Even the uneducated masses showed a touching faith in the power of learning. Education, especially higher education, they tended to regard as an unfailing panacea for all of the ills that beset both the nation as a whole and the individuals that composed it.

The remarkable transformation that came over higher education in the United States during the generation that followed the Civil War owed much to the statesmanship of a small group of uni- *American* versity presidents. Chief among these, no doubt, was *universities* Charles W. Eliot, the brilliant young chemist, who in 1869, when only thirty-five years of age, took the helm at Harvard. Much older, but fully alive to the currents of the age and destined to serve for many years, was Frederick A. P. Barnard, the president after 1864 at Co-

[1] E. W. Knight, *Public Education in the South* (1922).

lumbia. Almost equally noteworthy were such other newly chosen presidents as Andrew D. White of Cornell (1868), James McCosh of Princeton (1868), Noah Porter of Yale (1871), James B. Angell of Michigan (1871), John Bascom of Wisconsin (1874), and Daniel Coit Gilman of Johns Hopkins (1876).[1] Six of these eight men were of New England birth, and all but one of them, McCosh, a Scot from the University of Edinburgh, were graduates of New England colleges. Most of them, according to the prevailing custom of American scholars, had traveled or studied abroad, and possessed a fair familiarity with European university methods. Their concern, however, was neither to preserve the traditional New England college nor to imitate what was being done in Europe. Rather, what they set out to do was to revise the American system of higher education in such a way as to make it fit the needs of a rapidly changing America.

The best efforts of educators would have been in vain but for the liberal financial resources they were able to tap. The profits of the new *Philan-* industrial age were not all put back into business; millions of *throphy* dollars were poured by philanthropists into education. Before the Civil War such a gift as that of Stephen Girard, who at his death in 1831 left two million dollars to found a school for boys in Philadelphia, was so rare as to brand its donor as an eccentric. After the war such gifts became increasingly common, in fact, they were both sought after and expected. In 1865, Ezra Cornell, whose fortune had been made from the electric telegraph, gave a half-million dollars to found Cornell University in Ithaca, New York. In 1873, a similar gift from Cornelius Vanderbilt, the railroad magnate, made possible the establishment of Vanderbilt University in Nashville, Tennessee. Three years later, Johns Hopkins University opened its doors because a rich merchant, banker, and railroad director of Baltimore had endowed it with property worth four and one half million dollars, and his name. Supplemented presently by the outpourings of such philanthropists as John D. Rockefeller, Andrew Carnegie, and Edward Stephen Harkness the total endowment of colleges and universities in the United States ultimately reached enormous figures. The resources of Harvard, for example, amounted to only two and one half million dollars when Eliot became its president in 1869; two thirds of a century later this sum had grown to one hundred and thirty millions.[2]

A powerful stimulus to higher education at public expense came from

---

[1] Fabian Franklin, *The Life of Daniel Coit Gilman* (1910), furnishes an excellent insight into the way in which a great university was built.

[3] C. F. Thwing, *A History of Higher Education in America* (1906).

the generous gifts of land made by the federal government to the states under the terms of the Morrill Act of 1862. Each state, in *Federal land* return for a land subsidy of as many times thirty thousand *grants* acres as it had senators and representatives, was required within five years to establish at least one college which, "without excluding other scientific and classical studies," would "teach such branches of learning as are related to agriculture and the mechanic arts." The law provided also that whenever any of the land so given should be sold, the principal must be kept intact, and only the interest used; furthermore, depletions in the fund must be made good by legislative appropriation. Unfortunately the original law failed to specify a minimum price per acre below which lands might not be sold, and the correction made in 1889 that fixed a minimum of ten dollars per acre came too late to do much good. Nevertheless, the sums realized by the states were considerable, and in a few instances they were about all that could have been expected. Ezra Cornell, for example, so successfully located and sold the lands handed over by New York to the university that bore his name that he was able to pile up for it an endowment of five and one half million dollars.

Hardly less important than the financial aspect of the Morrill Act was the obligation it laid upon the states to support a greatly extended program of higher education. The intent of the law was *State-* clearly to place a college course within the reach of anyone *supported* who wanted it, and to make this privilege a charge on gov- *universities* ernment. Nevertheless, state after state revised its educational system in order to meet the terms of the act. Many states used their grant to help along, or sometimes to found, a single state university; others showed a preference for separate colleges of agriculture and engineering; only a few attempted in any way to dodge the issue. Once a college or university was accepted as a financial responsibility of the state, it could almost certainly count upon annual legislative appropriations to keep it alive and growing. Many of the western state universities, notably Wisconsin, Illinois, Minnesota, and California, rose to prominence as a result of the Morrill Act, and ultimately not less than sixty-nine "land-grant colleges" profited from its terms.

But the changes that came over higher education during these years went far deeper than mere size and numbers; no less in the endowed than in the state institutions there came a determined *Changes in* break from the traditional idea of what a college course *the* should be. The backbone of the old curriculum had been *curriculum* the classical languages and mathematics, with somewhat less attention to such subjects as ethics and rhetoric. Courses in the modern languages and history were occasionally tolerated, and a little science, with the laboratory work confined to what experiments the professor could do in the presence of the class. Most of the teachers were all-around scholars who were as much at home with one subject as with another. Indeed the "chairs" that some of them occupied were veritable benches of learning; one heroic Columbia professor taught mental and moral philosophy, English literature, history, political economy, and logic. But the old curriculum bore scant resemblance to the new civilization that was growing up outside the college walls. Its drill on the classics and its moralistic, theological bent were designed at best only to fit the needs of the few — most of whom expected to enter some "learned" profession — rather than the many, most of whom in the new age were destined for decidedly materialistic careers. If higher education was to be opened to the masses, then its content must be such as would have meaning for them. There was, moreover, an infinite quantity of new data to be evaluated and assimilated into the scholar's store of knowledge. An economic revolution was in process that the colleges and universities had all but ignored, while every field of science cried out for further exploration and investigation.

Under the leadership of President Eliot, Harvard University began to emphasize the right of a student to have some voice in the selection of his course of study. In most colleges the studies were *The elective system* rigidly prescribed, but Harvard's experiments with "electives" during the sixties convinced Eliot that the elective principle was the correct one upon which to build a new curriculum. Year after year the number of "prescribed" courses was cut down and the number of "electives" was lengthened. This process served a double purpose. On the one hand, it permitted the student to escape from subjects for which he lacked interest or aptitude; on the other, it permitted the indefinite expansion of the number of "subjects" that a given institution might offer. Once more, as in the Middle Ages, the totality of knowledge became the university's goal, rather than merely the set pattern of disciplines that tradition had developed; and an infinite number of subjects that previously had been regarded as well beyond the pale of educational respectability — some of them frankly "bread-and-butter" courses — began to enter the curriculum. The elective idea spread like wildfire all over the country, and awakened both enthusiastic approval and fierce denunciation. President McCosh of Princeton was among the skeptics, and on one occasion he met President Eliot in a public debate on the topic. Critics of the new system complained, as Henry Cabot Lodge said later, that it permitted students "to escape without learning anything at all by a judicious selection of unrelated subjects taken up only because they were easy or because the burden imposed by those who taught them was light." But, for good or for ill, electives had come to stay, although most institutions ultimately insisted upon a central core of "required" subjects.[1]

Quite as revolutionary as the elective system was the equally determined insistence upon technical and professional training. The Morrill Act gave a great stimulus to agricultural education, and as time went on more and more students who were primarily interested in the problems of farming began to put in their appearance. For a long time, however, the agricultural *Technical and professional schools* colleges were decidedly on the defensive because of their low enrollment. The University of Wisconsin, for example, had only one graduate in agriculture by 1880. Nevertheless, the building up of a staff of experts went on, and ultimately the public realized that the agricultural colleges reached a far wider field than the small number of students who attended them. Remarkable progress was made in the investigation of such subjects as the diseases of plants and animals, the proper treatment of soils, and the selection of seeds. All this information was passed along in one fashion or another to the farm population, and the schools themselves became headquarters not so much for the training of farmers as for the training of experts to advise the farmers. The Morrill Act did a similarly important service for engineering, particularly with respect to the more practical aspects of the subject. Courses in mechanical and civil engineering, mining and metallurgy, and architecture were established which presently produced sufficiently well-trained graduates that the business world was eager to obtain their services.

Perhaps the most astonishing development of all began in the medical schools, which before the Civil War had been nothing less, according to one authority, than a "social disgrace." Most of these early institutions existed to make what little money they could out of the students who patronized them, and the so-called "doctors" they turned out were quite definitely a liability to society. *Medical education* Even at Harvard, which possessed one of the best of the medical schools in the country, the student who took two lecture courses for a term less than four months in length was entitled to his degree if he could prove that his total medical experience ran to three years, and could pass a simple examination. Written examinations were said by the head of

[1] Charles W. Eliot, *A Late Harvest* (1924). Many of the great universities have produced their historians, among them F. P. Keppel, *Columbia* (1914); J. H. Gardiner, *Harvard* (1915); Elizabeth H. Haight and J. M. Taylor, *Vassar* (1915); J. F. A. Pyre, *Wisconsin* (1920); Jonas Viles, *The University of Missouri* (1939).

the school, as late as 1870, to be out of the question, because "a majority of the students cannot write well enough." President Eliot had much to do with the progress that Harvard made in medical education, and that was soon communicated to other colleges. Supported by Oliver Wendell Holmes, whose service to American medicine ranks parallel to his service to American literature, Eliot insisted upon actual attendance for the three-year period, together with laboratory and clinical training. Drawing freely upon the superior knowledge and techniques of European scientists, American medical scholarship was soon to be fully abreast of the times.

What was being done for the teaching of medicine was also being done for the law. Instead of a few months' cramming, law students were now introduced by Dean C. C. Langdell of the Harvard Law School to the "case method," by which they were required to dig out for themselves the rules of law that had grown out of judicial decisions. Here again, as with the colleges of arts and sciences when the elective system was introduced, there arose from conservative sources a great outcry of opposition, but the new method had come to stay, and in the course of time was adopted by practically every reputable law school in the country. As with medicine, the course was lengthened, standards were raised, and competent scholars were engaged to devote their full time to teaching.

Perhaps the best evidence that American scholarship was reaching maturity was supplied by the establishment of a considerable number of *Graduate* graduate schools. Prior to this time the determined devotee *schools* of learning had little recourse from the requirement of study abroad. American scholars were European made. Some obtained their training in England, but an apparent disdain on the part of English savants for Americans who pretended to scholarship led the latter to prefer the Continent, especially Germany, where they were more cordially received.[1] When the time came for the establishment of American graduate schools, therefore, it was the German, not the English, model that was followed; and presently the Ph.D. (Doctor of Philosophy) degree, virtually unknown in England, was to become in America, as in Germany, the heart's desire of every budding young scholar. The first Ph.D. ever conferred in America was given by Yale in 1861, but it was not until ten years later that the Yale graduate school was organized. By 1872 Harvard had established a graduate school, and in 1876 Johns Hopkins University sought to set a new precedent by making graduate

[1] C. F. Thwing, *The American and the German University* (1928), shows the Teutonic influence upon American educational development.

work its main concern. Before long even the new state universities of the West were emphasizing the importance of research and the training of scholars, and the day had passed when the only possible place to do advanced work was in Europe. According to President Ira Remsen, Gilman's successor at Johns Hopkins, there had been in 1850 only eight graduate students in the whole United States; by 1875 this number had risen to 399; by the end of the century it was 5668.

The new emphasis on intellectual achievement was revealed also in the activities of a small but able group of scholars. Major J. W. Powell, a war veteran who served for a time as a professor in Illinois *Science and* Wesleyan University, established his reputation as a geolo- *philosophy* gist by an exploration in 1869 of the Grand Canyon of the Colorado that led presently to its systematic survey under the auspices of the Smithsonian Institution. In 1879 Powell became director of the United States Bureau of Ethnology, and a year later of the United States Geological Survey. During the same period Lewis Henry Morgan, who had won fame even before the Civil War for his studies of the Iroquois Indians, brought out two notable works, *Consanguinity and Affinity* (1868) and *Ancient Society* (1877), which still rank among the most distinguished of the writings of American anthropologists. During these years also Othniel Charles Marsh, professor of paleontology at Yale after 1866, made a number of dangerous but fruitful expeditions into the Rocky Mountain region, and as vertebrate paleontologist for the United States Geological Survey discovered more than a thousand new fossil vertebrates. Other names of note were Simon Newcomb, the astronomer, Benjamin Peirce, the mathematician, and John Fiske, the philosopher. Fiske, as an ardent disciple of Herbert Spencer, did much to popularize in America the Darwinian views on which Spencer's *Synthetic Philosophy* was based; and when, years later, he turned to the writing of American history he treated that subject as a strictly evolutionary process.[1] At best, however, the list of American scholars was not a long one. According to one authority, for every work of research published in the United States during this period not less than fifty appeared in Europe. What interested Americans more than research was the widening of educational opportunity so that everyone might have his chance at learning. The deepening process could wait.

Even the women shared in the new opportunity. Their right to equal treatment in elementary and secondary schools was fairly well acknowledged before the Civil War, but their chance of obtaining instruction on the college level remained slight. In 1865, however, Vassar opened

[1] J. S. Clark, *The Life and Letters of John Fiske* (2 vols., 1917).

its doors at Poughkeepsie, New York, as a strictly women's college, only to be followed a decade later by Wellesley, not far from Boston. *Education* Both institutions struggled along for years without adequate *for women* endowments and without adequately prepared students — "between the devil of bankruptcy and the deep sea of the young ladies' seminary." [1] In 1875, Smith College, with a gift of $365,000 from Sophia Smith of Hatfield, Massachusetts, to found an institution that would provide educational opportunities for young women equal to those available for young men, opened at Northampton, Massachusetts, with only fourteen freshmen. Each year it admitted a new class, but continued to insist on adequate preparation, however small the numbers. When Bryn Mawr was established in the eighties, near Philadelphia, enough young women were being fitted for college work that the battle for high standards had no need to be fought over again. The beginnings of Radcliffe College go back to 1879 when the "Annex" at Harvard offered its first courses for women.

It was not through women's colleges, however, but through co-education that most American women were to get their chance at a college *Co-education* course. The demand for co-education antedated the Civil War and was for a long time closely connected with the movement for women's rights. After the war it grew mainly as an economical and common-sense western idea. Reassured by the experiments of Oberlin, Antioch, and Iowa, all of which had admitted women along with men before the Civil War, the University of Wisconsin set up a special normal department for women in 1863, and was presently drawing no distinction between men and women students. Ohio State University admitted women from its beginning in 1870. Other western universities fell into line, and with them the small denominational colleges, not only in the West, but to a considerable extent also in the East and even in the South. While co-education thus promptly became the rule in the West, the number of skeptics in the older sections of the country was great, and in the South separate state institutions for women were often established as a lesser evil.

Higher education for the Negro made progress in 1867 with the incorporation of Howard University in Washington, named after one of its *Negro* most active promoters, General O. O. Howard of the Freed-*education* men's Bureau; and in quick succession such other institutions as Fisk University in Nashville, Straight University in New Orleans, and Shaw University in Raleigh began to function. For these and similar

---

[1] F. L. Paxson, *Recent History of the United States* (new edition, 1937), p. 52. See also A. C. Cole, *A Hundred Years of Mount Holyoke College* (1940).

schools northern philanthropy retained for a time a certain fondness, born of the abolitionist crusade. The Peabody Fund, already mentioned,[1] was administered mainly with a view to the improvement of common schools for Negroes, but the Peabody Normal College in Nashville, which it aided generously, also served notably the cause of education among the whites. Unfortunately the Negroes at first thought of education, particularly higher education, primarily as a means of escape from manual labor, and showed little interest in substituting for Latin and Greek the more "practical" subjects that were crowding into the curriculums of the northern colleges and universities. Nevertheless, the Hampton Normal and Agricultural Institute, which opened at Hampton, Virginia, in 1870 with funds provided by the American Missionary Association, struck out along new and bold lines. Its purpose was to emphasize the dignity and importance of skill in labor with the hands, and to prepare its students as well as might be for the type of work that was actually available to them in the South. Means were provided at the Institute whereby the poorer students might "work their way through," and in 1872 Hampton's most distinguished student, Booker T. Washington, walking and begging rides to make a five-hundred-mile journey from his home in West Virginia, arrived with fifty cents in his pocket to take advantage of the opportunities that the Institute offered. Less than ten years later, Washington was chosen to head a school for Negroes at Tuskegee, Alabama, that under his leadership was soon to rival Hampton in its success with the same type of instruction.[2] Critics of so much emphasis upon industrial education for the Negroes complained that such training was designed merely to keep the colored race in a permanently inferior status, but in the main the aims and efforts of Hampton, Tuskegee, and their imitators were applauded by both Negroes and whites. Probably the gradual easing of the tension between the two races owed much to the activities of these institutions.

The Civil War dealt harshly with American literary talent. The old generation of American writers — Emerson, Longfellow, Lowell, Whittier, Bryant, Holmes — lived on and continued to write, but the roar and bustle of the new age had passed them by. The *American letters* America they represented was dead and gone. This was not true of Walt Whitman, perhaps, whose *Leaves of Grass* was presently to become, according to one opinion, the "Bible of democracy," but the hiatus between the old generation and the new was nevertheless well marked. The

[1] *Ante*, p. 9.

[2] Booker T. Washington, *Up From Slavery* (new edition, 1937), is one of the most significant of Negro autobiographies.

period represented politically by the Civil War and reconstruction was one of stalemate for American letters. Whether this was because too many men of potential literary genius perished on the battlefield, or because the martial spirit dulled the interest of Americans in bookish pursuits, will never be known. "For ten years," said a discouraged observer, "the new generation read nothing but newspapers."

That a new day was soon to dawn became evident when the literary world discovered that Samuel Langhorne Clemens (1835–1910), better known by his pen-name, Mark Twain, had more to his credit than an irreverent, western sense of humor.[1] Definitely out of line with the American literary tradition was Mark Twain's birthplace, the western town of Florida, Missouri. Quite as unorthodox was his education, which, to begin with, was derived less from the ungraded school which he attended than from the Mississippi River, which flowed by the town of Hannibal, Missouri, where he spent his boyhood. Always fascinated by the river, and curious about the unknown world from which its steamboats came and into which they went, young Clemens, after spending a few years as an itinerant printer, apprenticed himself to a river pilot, and learned the river "by heart" from St. Louis to New Orleans.

Mark Twain

> In that brief, sharp schooling [he wrote later] I got personally and familiarly acquainted with all the different types of human nature that are to be found in fiction, biography, or history. When I find a well-drawn character in fiction or biography, I generally take a warm personal interest in him, for the reason that I have known him before — met him on the river.

Clemens's career as a river pilot was cut short by the Civil War in which he fought for two full weeks as a Confederate bushwhacker. His heart was not in the fray, and his sympathies ultimately turned to the North. Before the summer of 1861 had ended, he was on his way to Nevada, and by the time the war was over, he had seen most of the mining West, making his way about by reporting for various newspapers. A visit to Hawaii in 1866 gave him the material for a story published in *Harper's Magazine* that same year, and set him to lecturing. Immensely successful with Pacific Coast audiences, he soon had the means to return by way of New York and Panama for a visit to his old home, to make a trip to Europe, and to establish himself in a new home at Hartford, Connecticut.

His writings, based upon his varied experiences and interpreted by the

[1] A. B. Paine, *Mark Twain: A Biography* (3 vols., 1912), and *A Short Life of Mark Twain* (1920), are the best works to consult, but Bernard De Voto, *Mark Twain's America* (1932), is also useful.

lore he had learned on the river, came thick and fast. *The Celebrated Jumping Frog of Calaveras County, and Other Sketches* (1867), was sheer hilarity; *Innocents Abroad* (1869) became immediately a best-seller because of the fun it poked at the tourist's Europe; *Roughing It* (1872) introduced Easterners to a Far West that was immensely interesting and vital, although in writing it Mark Twain undoubtedly followed the advice he later gave to Rudyard Kipling, "Young man, first get your facts; then distort them as you please"; *The Gilded Age* (1874), written in collaboration with Charles Dudley Warner, satirized skillfully the corrupt politics, ruthless fortune-chasing, and social bankruptcy of the reconstruction era; *Life on the Mississippi*, published first as a series of articles in the *Atlantic Monthly* for 1875, preserved for all time what Mark Twain knew so well about the fast-ebbing civilization that had centered about the river; *Tom Sawyer* (1876) recovered the scenes of the author's childhood in what William Dean Howells called "the best boy story ever written"; and for a generation longer the list continued to grow. Europeans sooner than Americans recognized that Mark Twain's books had literary merit as well as humor; that in a manner quite at variance with respectable tradition they set forth themes that were equally new. Brahmin Boston, still the self-confessed literary capital of America, was slow to acknowledge that this upstart Westerner was a man of parts, but on December 17, 1877, when the *Atlantic* gave a dinner in honor of Whittier's birthday, Mark Twain was invited to make one of the main addresses. Unfortunately, he resorted to a type of burlesque better suited to the West than to his hearers, who were definitely unamused. But the recognition he had at last received was not recalled.

Mark Twain was not so much the founder of a new school of American writers as he was the ablest representative of a considerable group of Westerners who exploited the frontier theme in literature *Other western* well before Frederick Jackson Turner had introduced it to *writers* the historians. Far-famed also was Bret Harte, who, although a New Yorker by birth, grew up in California while the spirit of lawlessness was still strong in the mining camps, and with a vividness that has seldom been surpassed described that West in such stories as "The Luck of Roaring Camp" and "The Outcasts of Poker Flat," both of which were published in the *Overland Monthly* during 1868. Harte also stooped sometimes to the writing of charming doggerel, such as the tale of the "Heathen Chinee" whom two white men tried unsuccessfully to cheat at cards:

Which is why I remark,
And my language is plain,

That for ways that are dark
And for tricks that are vain,
The Heathen Chinee is peculiar.

Joaquin Miller, born a Hoosier, was taken to Oregon as a child, saw life as a gold miner, soldier, journalist, lawyer, and judge, but won distinction mainly as a minor poet of the West.

The period of the seventies witnessed the rise of numerous "local-color" writers from other sections of the country also. William Dean Howells, an Ohioan, went East instead of West, and from the *William Dean Howells* time of the Civil War to the end of the century he was connected in an editorial capacity successively with the *Nation*, the *Atlantic*, and *Harper's*.[1] While he wrote of the East, he never forgot the experiences of his youth, and he featured in his writings the problems of adjustment that confronted one who came from a primitive to a cultured environment. Howells's fame rests mainly upon a long and distinguished sequence of novels, beginning with *Their Wedding Journey* (1871), *A Chance Acquaintance* (1873), and *A Foregone Conclusion* (1875). Edward Eggleston, a Methodist "circuit-rider" who had experienced much of what he wrote, portrayed in his first and best novel, *The Hoosier Schoolmaster* (1871), the quaint country life of southern Indiana. Mention also should be made of George W. Cable of New Orleans, whose *Old Creole Days* appeared in 1879, and Sarah Orne Jewett of Maine, whose exquisite delineations of New England character were printed first as stories in the *Atlantic*, and were later collected into books, *Deephaven* (1877) and *Country Byways* (1881). In these years, too, Henry James, who "was born an American and died an Englishman," began with his *Roderick Hudson* (1875) and *The American* (1876) to write finely spun novels dealing with the contacts of Americans with European sophistication.

Paralleling the educational and literary achievements of the post-war period came a definite upsurge of humanitarian reform. To a great *Humanitarian reform* extent this can be accounted for on the ground that exactly such an interest had preceded the Civil War, and that with the war and the immediate problems it raised out of the way, the old desire to better the lot of the unfortunate reasserted itself. It should not be forgotten, however, that the work of such organizations as the United States Sanitary Commission and the United States Christian Commission had done much to keep alive the humanitarian spirit, even while the war was on; and that the crying needs of the freedmen had made for an aware-

[1] W. D. Howells, *Years of My Youth* (1916). For a general survey see F. L. Pattee, *A History of American Literature Since 1870* (1915).

ness of the problems that confronted downtrodden humanity, whether white or black.

Among the many factors that contributed to the popular interest in humanitarianism doubtless the religious revival that swept through Protestant America during these years was one of the most *Moody and* important. Poured forth from thousands of pulpits, the *Sankey* doctrine that the depression was but a just judgment upon men for their sins produced a multitude of penitents. Rivalry with the Catholics and the Jews, whose numbers were being enormously increased by immigration, and rivalry among the various Protestant denominations themselves spurred on religious workers to greater and greater activity. Leadership was furnished, less by the great preachers of the day, such as Henry Ward Beecher and Phillips Brooks, than by the evangelists, among whom Dwight L. Moody, the exhorter, and Ira D. Sankey, the singer, were pre-eminent.[1] In 1875 Moody and Sankey, just returned from a series of successful revivals in the British Isles, began a meeting in Philadelphia that lasted three months, and then went on to New York, Chicago, Boston, and other great cities; in Chicago for four months their "tabernacle" was crowded daily by an audience of from five to ten thousand persons. The narrow and traditional doctrines of these evangelists, and of the host of lesser lights who imitated them, had but little direct bearing upon the social problems of the current age, but they at least extolled the Christian virtues and filled "converts" with an earnest if unguided desire to better the lot of their fellowmen.

Far more conscious than the churches of the needs of the time were the Young Men's and Young Women's Christian Associations, both of which dated back to the middle of the century, but began to be *Practical* really effective only during the seventies. Religion, for *Christianity* them, meant wholesome recreation, study classes, and even musicales, far more than the inculcation of Christian theology. Immediately effective among the submerged classes was the Salvation Army, which invaded the United States from England in 1879, and soon extended its interest from saving the souls of the down-and-out to an extensive program of social activity. Quite at the other extreme of society was Christian Science, a new religious sect that took its tenets from *Science and Health*, a book published by Mrs. Mary Baker G. Eddy in 1875. Rejecting medicine, and claiming for the mind a complete superiority over matter, the Christian Scientists preached a doctrine that wrought many cures among those whose nerves were unstrung by the increasing tempo of

---

[1] Gamaliel Bradford, *D. L. Moody* (1927), is an understanding study. See also F. G. Beardsley, *A History of American Revivals* (1912).

civilized life; its influence, also, reached over into other denominations and into medicine itself. More and more, at least in sophisticated circles, people were prone to admit that a vigorous will had much to do with the attainment of happiness and health.[1]

One shocking cause of unhappiness and ill-health was intemperance, a vice that the Civil War, as already noted, had done much to promote. *The W.C.T.U.* At the end of that struggle only two states, Maine and Massachusetts, remained true to their earlier stand for prohibition, and in 1868 Massachusetts voted in favor of the licensing system. Representatives of the old school of temperance reformers, such as John B. Gough, were still at work, but it was clear that their efforts alone would avail little against the effective organization that the liquor interests were able to achieve. In 1867, a National Brewers' Congress openly went on record against the election of any candidate to office, whatever his party, in case he showed himself favorable to the cause of total abstinence, and very generally the cause of one liquor dealer became the cause of all. Faced by this situation the evangelical churches, especially the Methodists, the Baptists, and the Presbyterians, presented a united front against the "Demon Rum," and began to urge such measures as the raising of license fees to liquor dealers, local option for towns and counties, and the revival of state-wide prohibition. A few gave their votes to the Prohibition Party, which was founded in 1869, but by far the greater number stood steadfastly by their old party affiliations regardless of their interest in the temperance cause. Outside the churches, the most effective organization of temperance advocates was the Women's Christian Temperance Union, which, founded in 1874, campaigned energetically, with Frances E. Willard of Evanston, Illinois, as its leader, for temperance instruction in the schools and the better awakening of the public to the evils of intemperance. By the end of the seventies the temperance forces could point to only a few victories, but their confidence in the future was complete.[2]

Because women seemed to be more easily aroused against intemperance than men, temperance advocates very generally favored the *Woman* "emancipation of women," particularly with respect to con-*Suffrage* ferring upon them the right to vote. The woman suffrage movement, like the temperance movement, had attracted attention long before the Civil War, but the attainment of suffrage by the illiterate

[1] For a favorable view, see Sibyl Wilbur, *The Life of Mary Baker Eddy* (1929). More critical are E. F. Dakin, *Mrs. Eddy* (1930), and L. P. Powell, *Mary Baker Eddy* (1930).

[2] Frances E. Willard, *Glimpses of Fifty Years* (1889); Ray Strachey, *Frances Willard: Her Life and Work* (1912).

FRANCES E. WILLARD

SUSAN B. ANTHONY

JANE ADDAMS

IDA M. TARBELL

FOUR LEADERS AMONG WOMEN

freedmen of the South had spurred the women reformers on to renewed activity. Surely women were as fit to cast their ballot as ex-slaves. Led by such intrepid workers as Susan B. Anthony and Elizabeth Cady Stanton, and joined by a host of professional reformers who before the Civil War had centered their attack upon slavery, the suffragists made a little progress. A few states reluctantly conceded to women the right to vote in school elections, and far out in the West the two territories of Utah and Wyoming established complete political equality. Eventual victory for the suffragists was forecast by the increasing freedom with which women attended college, entered such professions as the ministry, the law, and medicine, and organized Women's Clubs.[1]

That the zeal for reform, so characteristic of Americans during the generation preceding the Civil War, had been eclipsed rather than de-
Other reformers stroyed by that struggle was apparent in a multitude of ways. Dorothea L. Dix, to mention a single name, laid down her war work only to resume her earlier efforts for the improvement of conditions among criminals, paupers, and the insane. In state after state boards of charities were set up to deal with the problem of relief. State schools for the deaf and the blind were established, and occasional efforts were made to deal separately with the problem of juvenile delinquency. In Massachusetts, for example, an industrial school for delinquent girls was opened during the seventies at Lancaster. Even the humane treatment of animals was demanded, and an American Society for the Prevention of Cruelty to Animals, founded in 1866 by Henry Bergh on the model of the British Royal Society for the same purpose, made rapid progress. Through its efforts American children by the million read the well-told tale, *Black Beauty* (1877), by Anna Sewell, an English writer; more important still, the Society interested itself in the well-being of children as well as animals, and did much to rescue the unfortunate from conditions that were sure to drag them down. All such efforts, however, were at best only piecemeal, and comparatively little thought was given to the underlying causes of insanity, poverty, and crime. Some light was shed on the subject by the work of R. L. Dugdale, *The Jukes: A Study in Crime, Pauperism, Heredity, and Disease* (1877), which traced the history of a feeble-minded and diseased family that had cost the state of New York a million dollars since 1800.

Probably only a few Americans were able to take comfort during the dismal years of depression from the fact that an educational and literary renaissance seemed imminent, or that their humanitarian instincts were

[1] Elizabeth Cady Stanton and others, *History of Woman Suffrage* (6 vols., 1881–1922), neglects few aspects of the movement.

still alive, but a great many had their faith in their country restored by a visit to the Centennial Exposition, held in Philadelphia *The* from May to October, 1876. Similar "world's fairs" had *Centennial* recently been staged in Europe, notably at London, Paris, and *Exposition* Vienna, but the Philadelphia Exposition was the first ever to be undertaken in the United States. Preparations for it had been begun before 1873, and in spite of bad business conditions the project was not abandoned. Interested individuals gave heavily of their time and money, the city of Philadelphia contributed generously, and still further assistance was obtained from the various states and from the government of the United States. The railroads, famishing for lack of business, offered greatly reduced rates to Philadelphia, and from all over the country the people came. By the time the Exposition closed, more than nine million visitors had entered its gates, and on a single day as many as 275,000. With total receipts of $3,000,000 the fair was a brilliant financial success.

Compared with later exhibitions, the Philadelphia Centennial had little to offer. Its architecture was mediocre, and its art exhibits, while representative of the best that the United States could then supply, suffered from the unwillingness of foreign nations to send their treasures to America. England, however, was more generous than her Continental neighbors, and for the first time thousands of Americans were able to view the works of such masters as Gainsborough and Reynolds. English furniture and household decorations, German porcelain, French textiles, Japanese bronzes and lacquer wares, and Indian shawls and jewels were also freely displayed. These foreign exhibits greatly impressed the common run of visitors, whose provincialism had always made them slow to recognize that Americans in some ways might possibly be excelled by foreigners. Such exhibits also definitely stimulated interest in foreign lands, and more than ever before Americans began to find opportunity for travel abroad.

The greatest success of the fair was along materialistic rather than artistic lines. Its very size was impressive. The Main Building, covering twenty acres of land, was reputed to be the largest build- *Successes of* ing in the world. Numerous other buildings, four of them *the fair* also of large dimensions, occupied an enclosure of two hundred and thirty-six acres in Fairmount Park, overlooking the Schuylkill River. Machinery Hall housed a magnificent Corliss engine and numerous other symbols of the triumphs of American industry. When it came to commercial and industrial exhibits, European nations, eager to advance their trade in America, vied with the United States in the richness of their offerings, but Americans were able to feel pleasantly elated as they observed that in such matters as these their own country was more often than otherwise in the lead. The agricultural exhibit opened the eyes of farmer visitors to the possibilities of scientific agriculture; the educational exhibit forced the attention of educators to the progress that was being made in educational methods both at home and abroad; the Woman's Pavilion presented in a full acre the products of feminine industry; the mining and mineral exhibit revealed effectively the tremendous resources of the Far West.

Americans who visited the fair returned home with far more faith in the future than they had had before. After all, the depression could hardly be so dark as it seemed if so many persons could afford the trip to Philadelphia. Nor could an America that in a hundred years had made such marked advances be forever arrested in its progress by a single unfavorable turn of the business cycle. As for the mediocrity of American painting, sculpture, and architecture, most Americans were not aware of any shortcomings in what they saw and were surprised and pleased, rather, that so much was being done by their fellow countrymen along these lines. The years that followed 1876 saw a veritable rash of centennial celebrations, as one important anniversary after another recalled the times in which the foundations of the Republic had been laid. It might not be flattering to compare Grant, Blaine, and Ben Butler with Franklin, Jefferson, and Washington, but it was true, nevertheless, that since the time of the "founding fathers" the United States had conquered a continent, had exchanged economic dependence upon Europe for a remarkable degree of self-sufficiency, and had at least begun to create a civilization of its own. The cloud of depression was still dark, but the silver lining was in sight.[1]

[1] Van Wyck Brooks, *New England: Indian Summer, 1865–1915* (1940), pictures entertainingly the twilight of literary New England. John C. French, *A History of the University Founded by Johns Hopkins* (1946), and Ferris Greenslet, *The Lowells and Their Seven Worlds* (1946), throw light on the development of two great American Universities. E. D. Ross, *Democracy's College: The Land-Grant Movement in The Formative Stage* (1942), describes the Morrill Act and its results. It is supplemented by John Ise, *United States Forest Policy* (1920); Carl L. Becker, *Cornell University: Founders and the Founding* (1943); and Paul W. Gates, *The Wisconsin Pine Lands of Cornell University: A Study in Land Policy and Absentee Ownership* (1943).

On women's suffrage and temperance, see Mary Gray Peck, *Carrie Chapman Catt: A Biography* (1944); and Mary Earhart, *Frances Willard: From Prayers to Politics* (1944). On the Y.M.C.A., Sherwood Eddy, *A Century with Youth: A History of the Y.M.C.A. from 1844 to 1944* (1944). For the life story of a Negro who became one of America's greatest scientists, see Rackham Holt, *George Washington Carver: An American Biography* (1943).

CHAPTER VI

THE FAR WESTERN FRONTIER

THE exciting events of the Civil War and reconstruction, followed as they were by the manifold calamities of depression, served somewhat to obscure the importance of what was happening far out *The Far* on the western frontier. Americans were accustomed to *West* an advancing frontier — there had always been one; but this last American frontier differed markedly from all the rest. As Professor Webb so aptly points out, civilization east of the Mississippi proceeded comfortably into the West on three legs — land, water, and timber. But beyond the Mississippi on the Great Plains, two of these legs, water and timber, gave out, and thereafter civilization limped along as best it could on only one leg — land.[1] This newest West was a frontier of miners and cattlemen rather than of farmers, a frontier where mounted Indians fought desperately and sometimes successfully to hold back the tide of white invasion. Moreover, it was all that was left of the area within the national boundaries for civilization to conquer. The end of the frontier process, which from the beginning had been a kind of common denominator of American history, was in sight.

Within a few years after the "forty-niners" had invaded California, they and their successors had exhausted practically all of the free gold that that region had to offer. California mining then be- *California* came a capitalistic enterprise; expensive machinery was *prospectors* required to do the work that formerly anyone with a shovel and a "washbowl" felt himself adequately equipped to do. As this situation unfolded, some of the adventurers turned to agriculture for a livelihood, others went back to the "States," and still others became "prospectors," men who searched the mountains for signs of gold, and sometimes made a "strike." These prospectors went everywhere, for gold had a way of appearing in the most unlikely places. Not content with having pros-

[1] W. P. Webb, *The Great Plains* (new edition, 1936). Webb perhaps overemphasizes the contrasts between the plains and the earlier frontiers, but many marked differences did exist.

[115]

THE GREAT PLAINS ENVIRONMENT (1870)
(Based on a map from W. P. Webb, *The Great Plains*, Ginn and Company)

[118]

pected every bleak plateau and every hidden valley of the Rocky Mountains, they found their way to such distant regions as South Africa and Australia, and there, too, they discovered gold. Only rarely did one of them acquire wealth, but thanks to their efforts the world's supply of gold was soon to be doubled.[1]

The Pike's Peak gold rush, which occurred just a decade after the rush to California, laid the basis of Colorado. As compared with the forty-niners, the fifty-niners had an easy time of it. Those who came from the East had less than half as far to go, *Colorado* they had no mountains to cross, and the trail which they followed was well supplied with ferries, merchants, and even stage-coaches. Denver arrived full-grown almost overnight, and within a matter of weeks other mining camps in the "hills," such as Central City and Idaho Springs, achieved sizable proportions. Horace Greeley, of the New York *Tribune*, who went out merely to see what a gold rush was like, vividly described one of these early camps:

> As yet the entire population of the valley sleeps in tents or under booths of pine boughs, cooking and eating in the open air. I doubt that there is ... a table or chair in these diggings, eating being done on a cloth spread on the ground, while each one sits or reclines on mother earth.

Far sooner than in California the free gold of Colorado gave out, and for a time it even seemed as if no permanent settlement might result. Covered wagons that had gone west displaying the hopeful legend, "Pike's Peak or Bust," returned east by the same route with the label changed to read, "Busted, by gosh." Some, however, stayed on, as in California, to farm; as early as the summer of 1859 radishes, lettuce, onions, and peas brought high prices on the Denver market. Native grasses were cut for hay; claims were staked out and claims clubs formed; irrigation, after the manner of the Mormons in Utah, was introduced. Soon capitalistic mining replaced the crude efforts of the first comers, and such "valley" towns as Golden, Colorado City, and Pueblo showed sure signs of permanence. Efforts to follow the example of California in making a new state without going through the customary territorial stage came to nought, although an unauthorized Territory of Jefferson existed for a few months. In 1861 Congress made Colorado a territory, and a few years later, in order to obtain more Unionist senators and representatives in Washington, would have admitted it as a state. This offer, however, was wisely declined, for as late as 1870 the popula-

[1] The advancing frontier is the theme of several excellent one-volume texts, including F. L. Paxson, *History of the American Frontier, 1763–1893* (1924); E. D. Branch, *Westward, the Romance of the American Frontier* (1930); R. E. Riegel, *America Moves West* (1930).

tion of Colorado was only 40,000. Admission as the "Centennial State" came finally in 1876. Shortly afterward the exploitation of silver mines around Leadville inaugurated an era of prosperity that the region had not known before.[1]

While the rest of the country resounded to the din of Civil War, the mineral empire of the West expanded with unconcerned rapidity. Close *Nevada* on the heels of the Pike's Peak gold rush came a similar rush to the western part of what is now Nevada, where gold had been discovered along the main trail to California. The famous Comstock Lode, discovered in the spring of 1859, brought in no less than fifteen million dollars' worth of gold and silver in a single year. Located in the heart of a desert, a less auspicious place for the development of a new area of settlement could hardly have been imagined, but such was the richness of the mines that adventurers by the thousand flocked in from California and Oregon to the West, as well as from the settled regions of the East. Such towns as Carson City and Virginia City fantastically flaunted their wealth in the face of a desert where water was almost as dear as the other liquid refreshments the miners so liberally consumed. In 1861 Congress made Nevada a territory, and three years later, with a population probably greater than it possesses at the present time, Nevada accepted the same hasty offer of statehood that Colorado rejected. Unlike most of the mining regions, the opportunities for agriculture in Nevada were negligible, and the prosperity of the new state was limited almost exclusively to the exploitation of its mineral resources.[2]

After the opening of Nevada, mining booms came thick and fast. In the vicinity of Lewiston, Idaho, then a part of Washington Territory, *Mining* gold was found in 1860, and next year the inevitable boom *booms in the* occurred. As news of new strikes came in, the miners *Northwest* rushed from place to place founding, as they went, such permanent settlements as Florence and Boise City, but leaving often as suddenly as they had come. "The Idaho miners," said H. H. Bancroft, "were like quicksilver. A mass of them dropped in any locality, broke up into individual globules, and ran off after any atom of gold in their vicinity. They stayed nowhere longer than the gold attracted them." In 1863 the Territory of Idaho was created, but by that time the miners

[1] LeRoy R. Hafen, *Colorado — The Story of a Western Commonwealth* (1933). Ina Faye Woestemeyer and J. M. Gambrill, *The Westward Movement* (1939), contains many excellent readings on the history of the West.

[2] Mark Twain, *Roughing It* (1872), gives a classic picture of early days in Nevada; William M. Stewart, *Reminiscences* (1908), is more interesting than accurate; H. H. Bancroft, *History of Nevada, Colorado and Wyoming* (1890), supplies much useful information; C. H. Shinn, *The Story of the Mine* (1901), is mainly the story of the Comstock Lode, which is also described vividly in C. B. Glasscock, *The Big Bonanza* (1931).

had crossed the Bitter Root Mountains to lay the foundations of Montana. Such mining centers as Bannack City, Virginia City, Deer Lodge, and Missoula not only drew population away from the farther western camps, but also attracted newcomers from the East, many of whom came up the Missouri River to Fort Benton, which in high water could be reached by steamboats. Among those who came were a number of refugees from the guerrilla warfare that raged along the Kansas-Missouri border during the Civil War, and others who preferred the hazards of the mines to the prospect of being drafted into the army. In 1864 Montana was separated off from Idaho as an independent territory.[1]

During this same period the Far Southwest, too, had its mining booms. The mineral resources of New Mexico, twin territory with Utah, had long been known, but the Spanish-Mexican *The Far* population, located mainly in the upper Rio Grande Valley, *Southwest* subsisted upon agriculture and ignored the mines. The Americans, however, reopened the ancient diggings near Tucson and Tubac, and found placer gold in considerable quantities in the valley of the lower Colorado. When in 1862 Colonel James H. Carleton attempted to lead a column of eighteen hundred Californian volunteers to the aid of the Union forces in New Mexico, he was plagued by desertions to what he described as "one of the richest gold countries in the world." Thus another mining boom got under way, and in 1863 Congress, as usual, obliged by creating out of the western half of New Mexico the new Territory of Arizona.

The prosperity of these new mountain territories varied markedly in the years that followed the war. As long as the Comstock Lode continued to yield up its riches, Nevada fared best, but by 1880 this magnificent deposit had been worked out, and the desert cities faded as rapidly as they had bloomed. Stocks in Nevada mines valued at $393,000,000 in 1875 could be bought five years later for $7,000,000. The fate of the mines in Colorado, where the quartz lodes could be reached and reduced only with the aid of heavy financial outlays, fluctuated according to the availability of capital and the intelligence with which it was utilized. In Idaho and Montana the fortune hunters of 1866 numbered probably thirty and forty thousand respectively, but the census of 1870 found that only half that many had seen fit to remain. A dozen years later, the opening of rich copper mines near Butte, Montana, ushered in an era of unprecedented prosperity for that region

[1] W. J. Trimble, *The Mining Advance into the Inland Empire* (1914), is a work of dependable scholarship.

which the exploitation of other base metals, such as lead and zinc, handsomely reinforced. Ultimately the world's largest copper smelters were to be located at Anaconda, Montana. In the Southwest the exhaustion of placer gold brought the Civil War boom to a quick conclusion, and, in the years that followed, the warlike nature of the Apache Indians tended to discourage even the prospectors. Here, as in Montana, copper presently became a more important product than gold. None of the other mountain territories achieved the prosperity that came to Utah, where the Mormon leader, Brigham Young, urged the saints to eschew mining and devote themselves to agriculture. Indeed, hard as was the lot of the farmer in these regions of inadequate rainfall, Indian raids, and grasshopper plagues, the prosperity of any territory could almost be measured by the number of its inhabitants who forsook the mines for the farms.[1]

Social conditions on the mining frontier differed little from place to place. Most mining towns consisted of a single long crooked street *The mining* that followed, and occasionally crossed, a mountain stream. *towns* Horses hitched along the street testified to the almost universal dependence upon horseback means of communication, and no other criminal was so utterly despised or so certainly punished as the horse-thief. Most of the houses were hastily improvised, one-roomed, one-storied structures, the kind that frequently appear near city dump heaps. Invariably the most pretentious buildings were occupied by saloons and gambling-houses, to which the men turned for amusement after the hard and lonely labor of the mines. Few women reached the early mining camps, and those who came were usually of easy virtue. Drunkenness and debauchery were too common to attract much notice, and for a long time individual vengeance provided almost the only punishment that was meted out for crime. Medical help for the sick and injured was of the crudest sort, or, more likely, was altogether missing, and the death rate was high. The romance of the mines, so dear to the heart of the fictionist, was built on the slenderest possible basis of fact.[2]

The business of supplying the mining camps with the necessities of life and of transporting to the East the product of the mines soon *Staging and* reached formidable proportions. Stage-coaches and freight-*freighting* wagons made their appearance on the western plains during the fifties, and by the time the Civil War ended there were few places

[1] An interesting popular account of the mines is G. C. Quiett, *Pay Dirt, a Panorama of American Gold Rushes* (1936).

[2] C. H. Shinn, *Mining Camps: A Study in American Frontier Government* (1885).

too remote for them to reach.   As early as 1857, when the United States government asked for bids to carry the mail to California, there was no dearth of plains express companies ready to do the work.   The contract went to John Butterfield, whose "Overland Mail" operated until 1861 along the southern route, and thereafter by the central route.   During the years 1860–61 the firm of Russell, Majors, and Waddell, without a government subsidy, relayed light mail by "pony express" from St. Joseph, Missouri, to Sacramento, California, in less than two weeks. The pony express and the company that backed it were put out of business by the completion of a telegraph line to the Pacific in 1861, but stage-coach connections, with the aid of generous mail contracts, continued to be multiplied so that by 1866 Ben Holladay, into whose monopolistic grasp most of the western routes had fallen, could claim a total of five thousand miles of stage-lines.   That same year Holladay sold out to Wells, Fargo, and Company.[1]

Travel by western stage was an experience not to be forgotten.   The stage itself, with its high, heavy wheels, its wide, thick tires, and its sturdy leather thorough-braces instead of springs, was no western invention, but rather the product of centuries of experience.   It was equipped with three inside seats for passengers, an outside front seat for the driver, and a rear container for baggage.   Painted a bright red or green, and drawn by two or more teams of horses, it bowled along the prairies, forded bridgeless streams, ignored wind, sand, and dirt. Dangers abounded from the charges of angry buffaloes, from attacks by hostile Indians, from robberies in a region that long knew no law. Passage through these hazards from the Mississippi to the Pacific cost about two hundred dollars, with corresponding charges for shorter distances.   One articulate traveler, a certain Demas Barnes, who took the stage to Denver in 1865, described his trip as follows:

It is not a *pleasant*, but it is an *interesting* trip.   The conditions of one man's running stages to make money, while another seeks to ride in them for pleasure, are not in harmony to produce comfort.   Coaches will be overloaded, it will rain, the dust will drive, baggage will be left to the storm, passengers will get sick, a gentleman of gallantry will hold the baby, children will cry, nature demands sleep, passengers will get angry, the drivers will swear, the sensitive will shrink, rations will give out, potatoes become worth a gold dollar each, and not to be had at that, the water brackish, the whiskey abominable, and the dirt almost unendurable.   I have just finished six days and nights of this thing; and I am free to say, until I forget a great many things now visible to me, I shall not undertake it again.[2]

---

[1] F. L. Paxson, *The Last American Frontier* (1910), contains much interesting detail. See also Emerson Hough, *The Passing of the Frontier* (1921).

[2] D. E. Clark, *The West in American History* (1937), p. 517.

Freighting on the western plains was no less important than staging. Little of this went through to the Pacific coast, for water transportation served that purpose better, but the great interior region opened up by the mines was served, for the most part, by slow-moving freight-wagons, drawn by ox teams from such Missouri River towns as Independence, Leavenworth, Nebraska City, and Omaha. After the building of the Union Pacific the freight-wagons, and the stages also, took off into the interior from such railroad stations as lay nearest the desired destinations, but in any event huge freight charges had to be paid. According to a reliable estimate the total freight bill of the mountain towns for one year, 1866, was $31,000,000. High prices gave merchants a chance for long profits, and laid the basis for many pioneer fortunes, such, for example, as those amassed by the Creighton brothers of Omaha, and William A. Clark of Montana. Demas Barnes was much impressed with the freighting activities he witnessed:

> The great feature of the Plains is the transportation trains, usually consisting of thirty to fifty wagons, five yoke each.... As they wind their slow course over the serpentine roads and undulating surface in the distance, a mile in extent (I saw one train five miles long), the effect is poetic, grand, beautiful. They select a high position for camping, draw the wagons in a circle, enclosing say a quarter, half, or full acre, the exterior serving as a fort, the inside as a camp, and a place wherein to drive the animals in case of danger, and to yoke or harness them for the next trip. One of these camps, seen at sundown, with night fires kindled, and from five hundred to a thousand head of animals feeding near by, is well worth a long visit to behold.

The traffic of the plains, particularly the cargoes of gold that the stage-coaches took out, led inevitably to many robberies. Gangs of *Lawlessness* "bad men," drawn together to live by their wits rather than by their labor, terrorized the stage-routes, and took a heavy toll, not only in gold but also in lives. The gang led by Henry Plummer of Montana during the sixties was guilty of over a hundred known murders and an untold number of robberies. In Montana, as in California, vigilantes, administering lynch law, finally put the disorderly elements of society out of business. One might note, indeed, four stages of development on any given mining frontier: (1) peaceful exploitation by the original prospectors; (2) the mining "boom," with its full quota of violence and crime; (3) the establishment of vigilance committees to punish the worst criminals and to introduce a reign of law; and (4) the creation of regular legal governments. In many instances, however, the third and fourth stages were reversed. Legal government in Montana, for example, preceded the work of the vigilantes; Plummer himself was a sheriff, and local government throughout the territory was in the hands of the "bad men" until the vigilantes broke their power.[1]

In 1876, the last great mining boom of the West broke forth in the Black Hills region of southwestern Dakota Territory — a wild, barren region, long suspected of harboring gold. Deadwood, the *The Black* principal city, lay in the heart of a wilderness, and depended *Hills* for the necessities of life upon stage-coaches and freighters from Bismarck to the east and Cheyenne to the south. Bandits and Indians were plentiful, but Wells, Fargo, and Company carried out the gold in steel-lined, heavily guarded coaches that were not lightly attacked. In a single trip, July, 1877, $350,000 in gold was taken out, and before the stage-line surrendered its business to the railroad, the grand total of such shipments had reached $60,000,000.[2] Deadwood, as the chief supply station for the various mining camps near-by, built up a lively prosperity. Here, too, gathered a notable array of gamblers and out-laws, the backwash of all the mining booms; among them, "Wild Bill" Hickok, who shot from the hip and rarely missed his mark, and "Calam-ity Jane" Canary, a colossal sinner whose fame spread far and wide. Deadwood was more sophisticated than most of the early mining towns, and boasted, along with its gambling-houses and saloons, several theaters, particularly the *Gem*, which provided living quarters for its players, and produced numerous plays of merit. During one season, before street-carnivals, dance-halls, and bar-room singers put the theater out of business, the *Mikado* had a run of one hundred and thirty nights.

For all its seeming tumult, life in the mining camps was founded upon a sound substratum of common sense. Lawlessness eventually was curbed, and the normal institutions of government were *Evolution of* evolved. Agriculture, even under the most adverse circum- *law and order* stances, was speedily introduced. Rule-of-thumb arrangements — such, for example, as those which enabled the discoverer of a mine to "stake out his claim," or the first farmer to use the waters of a given stream for irrigation purposes to have a "priority right" over all others — presently received the sanction of law. More women came in, and with them schools, churches, and the amenities of life. Frontier characteristics gradually gave way before the advance of civilization: the individualism of the early miners to the co-operative, capitalistic enterprises that were

[1] N. P. Langford, *Vigilante Days and Ways* (1912), is a vivid first-hand account.
[2] Total output of all the western mines, 1860 to 1890, has been set at $1,241,827,032 in gold, and $901,160,660 in silver.

[123]

required to carry on their work; the actual democracy of the boom days to the astounding inequalities between those who "struck it rich," and those whose poverty endured; the radicalism of a new society to the conservatism of one that approached middle age. And yet, the social inheritance from the mining frontier could hardly be called negligible. Throughout the region first opened by the mines, the tendency to paint an overbright picture still reflects the chronic optimism of the prospector, and the ease with which the speculative spirit is fanned into a flame shows that the gambling instinct is not yet quite dead. Here, too, where unruly elements from all over the world broke the "cake of custom" most thoroughly, the old willingness to try anything new remains a hardy perennial. Widely separated from the rest of the country, and for a long time a law unto itself, the Far West to this day retains to a degree its aloofness — a part of the United States, and yet at the same time apart from it. Californians still speak, as the miners did before them, of going back to the "States."

Among the inevitable complications that resulted from the opening of the mining West was the necessity of developing a new Indian policy *The Indians* for the United States. The old policy of leaving the region west of the "bend of the Missouri" for the exclusive use of the Indians had broken down badly in the decade before the Civil War. Thousands of emigrants, crossing the plains to Oregon, to Santa Fe, to Utah, and to California, came into contact and often into conflict with the Indians. Demands for protection of the trails led to the establishment of army posts in the Indian country at such strategic centers as Fort Kearney and Fort Laramie, and to treaties between the United States and most of the Indian tribes, describing the tribal boundaries, and authorizing the government to build both roads and posts wherever it wished. While the Indians received annuities as compensation for the losses they sustained from the white intrusion, they found the new agreements far from satisfactory, and frequently forgot their promises not to molest the emigrants. The requirement of new cessions in Minnesota, in Iowa, in Kansas, and in Nebraska added still further to the unrest, both on the part of the tribes that had to find new homes, and on the part of those who had to make room for unwanted newcomers. Altogether, the time was ripe for trouble from the Indians when the Civil War broke out, while the combing of the mountains for gold that accompanied the conflict furnished still further cause for alarm.

In 1862 came the first uprising. The Sioux of Minnesota, reduced by land cessions to a narrow and indefensible reserve along the Minnesota River, had long suffered from the dishonesty of traders and government

agents. With the regular army garrisons withdrawn, and their places
taken by unsuspecting volunteers, the Indians' temptation   *The Sioux*
to seek revenge was great. Nevertheless, the trouble, when   *outbreak in*
it came, was precipitated by the unauthorized action of a   *Minnesota*
few irresponsible braves who on August 18, 1862, murdered five whites
near New Ulm, Minnesota. The white population of the vicinity,
sure that a general attack was impending, fled for their lives, while the
Indians, no less frightened, divided into two groups, one of which made a
hasty retreat to the west, while the other under Little Crow, knowing
that the whites would never forgive the murders, took the warpath,
burning farmhouses and villages, and killing men, women, and children
by the hundreds.   In due time the Indians were met by overwhelming numbers of state militia, decisively defeated, and many of them
captured.   Of the captives some four hundred were tried by court-
martial in St. Paul, and over three hundred were sentenced to death.
All but thirty-eight of those sentenced were pardoned by President
Lincoln, but these unfortunates paid the full penalty for their crime at a
great hanging-bee, held at Mankato, Minnesota, the day after Christmas, 1862.   Settlers came from far and near to witness the executions,
which were made the more weird by the fact that the unhappy Indians
during their imprisonment had been converted to Christianity, and had
come to be known as the "praying Indians."   In 1863 the remnants of
the Sioux were harassed by an expedition into Minnesota and Dakota,
and the entire Sioux holding in Minnesota was confiscated.   Little Crow
himself was killed in July, 1863, and his tanned scalp, his skull, and his
wrist bones presently became prized exhibits of the Minnesota Historical Society.[1]

The rigorous punishment meted out to the Minnesota Sioux failed
to deter the plains Indians from following their example.   Among the
tribes most affected by the coming of the miners were the   *The Arapaho*
Arapaho and Cheyenne, who were persuaded in 1861 to make   *and*
way for the white advance into Colorado by withdrawing   *Cheyenne*
into what was generally known as the Sand Creek Reserve, a barren
and gameless tract in the southeastern part of the territory.   Sullen
and resentful, they began by the spring of 1864 to raid the trails along
the South Platte, and to push on down into Nebraska.   Companies
engaged in staging and freighting were put out of business, settlers and
travelers were killed, and the whole frontier as far east as the Blue River

---

[1] W. W. Folwell, *A History of Minnesota* (4 vols., 1921–30), presents faithfully the·story
of this uprising.   See also T. C. Blegen, *Building Minnesota* (1938), a brilliantly written
and scholarly textbook.

was thrown into a panic. Promptly Governor John Evans called out the Colorado militia, but before ordering an attack he urged all peaceable Indians to concentrate in certain designated posts where they would be safe from harm. Not until fall, when the best fighting weather was over, did any considerable number of Indians choose to accept this invitation, but by that time about five hundred of them, including Black Kettle, their leading chief, had reported to Fort Lyon on Sand Creek, and were encamped near-by. As evidence of their peaceful intentions they flew both a white flag and the Stars and Stripes above their camp.

Meanwhile, however, Major-General Curtis of the United States Army, in command of the West, had telegraphed, "I want no peace till the Indians suffer more," and Colonel J. M. Chivington in command of the Colorado militia made ready to oblige him. Although there were bands of Indians still on the warpath, Chivington chose to ignore them, and instead to make a surprise attack upon the camp at Sand Creek. At the break of day, November 29, 1864, with about nine hundred men he fell upon the unsuspecting camp and murdered in cold blood about one hundred men, women, and children. Following the practice of the savages, the soldiers indulged in indescribable mutilations of the dead bodies, the mildest of which was scalping. Next year the government made a new treaty with the Arapaho and Cheyenne, pushing them farther to the southeast, but the Senate failed to confirm it, and the homeless Indians were sometimes guilty of attacks on settlers and travelers. Expeditions against them in 1867 and 1868 culminated in another massacre, this time on the Washita, near the Texas border, where Major-General George A. Custer with a detachment of regulars duplicated Chivington's unsavory exploit (November 27, 1868). Black Kettle himself was slain, and his people at length accepted lands assigned to them in the Indian Territory.[1]

The western Sioux, who ranged north of the Platte and east of the mountains, were deeply disturbed, both by the fate that had overtaken *The western Sioux* the Arapaho and Cheyenne, and by the advent of mining activities in Montana. When, in 1865, the government decided to open a road along the Bozeman Trail, from Cheyenne northwestward to the mouth of the Rosebud in Montana, the Sioux determined to resist this invasion of their finest hunting-grounds with all their might. That year General P. E. Connor in command of sixteen hundred men,

[1] G. B. Grinnell, *The Fighting Cheyennes* (1915), is among the best of the books on the Indian wars of the plains. See also his more elaborate *The Cheyenne Indians: Their History and Ways of Life* (2 vols., 1923).

and guided by Jim Bridger, the noted plainsman,[1] marched over part of the route, but was turned back by the Sioux; and in 1866 a second expedition under Colonel H. B. Carrington succeeded only with the greatest difficulty in building Fort Phil Kearny and Fort C. F. Smith to the east of the Big Horn Mountains. Red Cloud, the Indian leader, and his Sioux warriors risked no open fighting, but they continually harassed wood-trains sent out from the forts, and otherwise hampered the operations. On one occasion, a brash young officer, Captain W. J. Fetterman, was dispatched from Fort Phil Kearny to the aid of a wood-train with definite orders not to take the aggressive. New to western fighting and disdainful of Indians, he disobeyed orders, was ambushed, and in the resulting combat (December 21, 1866) every member of his party was slain. Two years later, when the government made peace with Red Cloud and his warriors, it was on condition that the "country north of the North Platte River and east of the summits of the Big Horn Mountains shall be held and considered to be unceded Indian Territory," and that the forts on the Bozeman Trail should be abandoned. This was one of the few instances in American history in which an Indian treaty registered a white retreat.

Meanwhile the government had taken steps toward the formation of a new Indian policy. A congressional Committee on the Condition of the Indian Tribes, created in 1865, visited the West, took *The new* full testimony on such gruesome events as the Chivington *Indian* massacre, and revealed how utterly untenable the status of *policy* the Indians had become. Its illuminating *Report on the Condition of the Indian Tribes*, made in 1867, led to the creation of an Indian Peace Commission, composed of three generals and four civilians, whose duty it was not only to stop the Indian wars, but also to work out a permanent solution of the Indian problem. The commission planned two great meetings, one for the southern tribes at Medicine Lodge Creek, near the southern border of Kansas, held in 1867, and one for the northern tribes at Fort Laramie, held in 1868. At these councils treaties were concluded that definitely foreshadowed the reservation system. Confiscation of the western half of the holdings of the Five Civilized Tribes in the Indian Territory, on the ground that the tribes had sided with the Confederacy during the Civil War, made possible the resettlement in that region of the Arapaho and Cheyenne and other plains Indians. In the North the Sioux were left in peaceable possession of southwestern Dakota, and such minor tribes as the Utes, Shoshonis, and Bannocks

[1] J. C. Alter, *James Bridger* (1925), tells the life-story of this typical plainsman. Useful also are the two volumes by Stanley Vestal, *Mountain Men* (1937) and *Kit Carson* (1928).

were concentrated within appropriate narrow limits. Subsidies in the form of annuities, payments for lands, and outright doles helped the dispossessed Indians to eke out a precarious existence, and unconsciously introduced pauperization as a means of insuring docility. A new Board of Indian Commissioners, composed of civilians, was created in 1869 to advise with the Bureau of Indian Affairs, which, since 1849, had been a part of the Department of the Interior. Believing that the Indians could eventually be made over into peaceful and contented farmers, the civilian commissions tried to break down tribal autonomy, and in 1871 they induced Congress to abolish the legal fiction of dealing with the tribes by treaty as if they were foreign nations. This was a definite improvement, but the road to civilization for the Indian was long and hard.[1]

By this time most of the Indian fighting was at an end, although occasional outbreaks occurred until as late as 1890. The worst of these *Later Indian uprisings* was precipitated by the Black Hills gold rush, which brought thousands of whites into the heart of the region reserved for the Sioux. Even before the rush started, military maneuvers, designed merely to check up on the rumors of gold, and wholesale frauds, perpetrated systematically at the Red Cloud Indian Agency, had alarmed the Sioux, and many of them had left the reservation. Led by two able braves, Sitting Bull and Crazy Horse, the fugitives ignored all orders to return, and fought bravely when troops were sent to herd them in. During this campaign General George A. Custer and his command of over two hundred cavalrymen met the same fate that Custer had meted out to the Indians on the Washita eight years before. Lured into an ambush that he should have known enough to avoid, Custer and his entire command lost their lives. The campaign, however, could have but one end, and within a short time General Nelson A. Miles had restored order.[2] Crazy Horse was captured, and Sitting Bull fled to Canada. In 1877, a somewhat similar uprising among the Nez Percés of Idaho came to the same inexorable end. Chief Joseph, the Indian leader, gave a good account of himself, but at length surrendered. "I am tired of fighting," he told his chiefs, "My heart is sick and sad. From where the sun now stands I will fight no more forever." Down in New Mexico the Apaches repeatedly gave trouble, and the campaigns against them amounted almost to wars of extermination. Not until

[1] Among the best of the many popular books on the Indians are Flora W. Seymour, *The Story of the Red Man* (1929), and F. E. Leupp, *The Indian and His Problem* (1910).

[2] N. A. Miles, *Serving the Republic* (1911), and G. A. Custer, *My Life on the Plains* (1874), tell of army life in the Far West, but consult also P. E. Byrne, *Soldiers of the Plains* (1926), and Stanley Vestal, *Sitting Bull* (1932). The Custer Massacre occurred June 25, 1876.

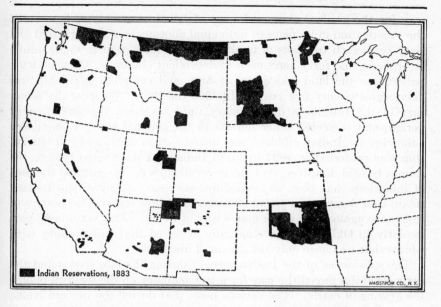

Indian Reservations, 1883

HAGSTROM CO., N.Y.

INDIAN RESERVATIONS IN THE UNITED STATES, 1883

1885, when Geronimo, their principal chief, was captured and exiled to Florida, was a lasting peace established. Trouble broke out again about 1889 with the Sioux in Dakota. A religious frenzy, based upon hope for an Indian Messiah, led to demonstrations by Indian "ghost dancers" that frightened the Indian agents into calling for troops. Fearful of soldiers' vengeance, many Indians left the reservation, only to be massacred at the so-called battle of Wounded Knee (December 29, 1890). Two weeks before, Sitting Bull, who in 1881 had returned to the United States and had been allowed to live with his people, had lost his life while resisting, or seeming to resist, arrest.

The wars against the Indians, conducted after 1865 exclusively by regular army detachments, were far from popular with the American people, and protests against the inhuman treatment that *Lands in* the tribes received grew more and more insistent. The *severalty* publication in 1881 of Helen Hunt Jackson's *A Century of Dishonor*, with its stinging indictment of the American Indian policy, brought public opinion strongly behind all efforts to alleviate the lot of the Indians. Their retention upon reservations, however, was an obvious necessity, and was long continued. In 1887 the Dawes Act paved the way for the gradual extinguishment of tribal ownership of lands, and the substitution in its place of individual allotments of one hundred and sixty acres each to heads of families, eighty acres each to single adults or orphans, and forty acres each to dependent children. Only a "trust patent" to the land was given at first, and complete ownership was delayed for twenty-five years. In 1906 the Burke Act gave the Secretary of the Interior a discretionary right to lessen the probationary period, and corrected other defects in the original law. Compulsory education for Indian children was introduced in 1891, and full citizenship was conferred in 1924 upon all Indians in the United States. It cannot be said, however, that the government's policy, granted the best of intentions, has been an unqualified success. Many of the Indians retain to a degree their tribal identity, and show remarkable powers of resistance against the white man's way of living. And yet others, particularly in Oklahoma, have actually achieved that full equality with whites that was once only the dream of idealists.[1]

The subsidence of the Indian menace during the late sixties and the early seventies paved the way for a new industry on the western plains, the grazing of cattle. The various posts that dotted the western trails, some wholly private, and others centered about a garrisoned fort or an Indian agency, got an early start in cattle from the emigrants, who were frequently only too willing to exchange for urgent necessities any livestock they happened to have brought along. It was soon discovered that cattle could fend for themselves on the plains the whole year through, for the wiry "buffalo grass" cured on the ground and remained all winter long as nutritious as hay. There was no temptation, however, to increase these herds beyond immediate needs, for the plains still swarmed with buffalo, and outside markets were too distant to be considered.

Shortly after the Civil War the killing of the buffalo began. Organized hunting parties equipped with repeating rifles killed them by the *The killing* tens of thousands to obtain "buffalo robes," soon regarded *of the buffalo* as almost a necessity in the average American home. Others were killed, by Indians and whites alike, for their meat, but often only the tongue and a few choice cuts would be taken, and the rest of the carcass left to rot. Hunters killed them just for the sport of it, although one English sportsman who came to America primarily to hunt buffalo refused to take part in a game that he described about as exciting as shooting cows in a pasture. The building of the Union Pacific Railroad aided the hunters greatly, and divided the buffalo into two herds,

[1] E. E. Dale, *Cherokee Cavaliers; Forty Years of Cherokee History* (1939).

one to the north and the other to the south. By 1870 from five to seven million buffalo still existed, but in the succeeding years the slaughter was terrific. The southern herd was gone by 1875, and in 1883 Sitting Bull and his braves destroyed the last sizable remnant of the northern herd. Probably not more than a thousand head were left alive. For years buffalo bones were gathered for shipment by the trainload to eastern factories, where they were turned into fertilizers, or into carbon for the use of sugar refineries.[1]

The passing of the buffalo, unpleasant as it is to contemplate, was not an unmixed evil. The government purposely did nothing to prevent the tragedy, for as long as the herds remained intact the Indians had a sure food supply, and could the more easily defy governmental control. Some of the later Indian uprisings were caused in part by the Indians' concern at the threatened destruction of their herds, but once the buffalo were gone the end of Indian resistance had been reached. Furthermore, the disappearance of the buffalo, together with the building of the western railroads and the pacification of the Indians, gave the cattle industry the chance it needed to grow.

In a sense, however, the western cattle industry was already full grown. Its real beginnings were Mexican, rather than American, and dated back for centuries. Both the cattle themselves, and the horses without which the industry would have been vastly different (to say the least), were the descendants of European stock brought over by the Spaniards in the sixteenth century, and allowed to go wild. Survival of the fittest produced by the nineteenth-century cattle that were more noted for their speed and endurance than for tender cuts of beef, each blessed also with an incredible spread of horns. The horses, sprung no doubt from noble Arabian forebears, had developed into sure-footed, quick-witted, wiry broncos, well under a thousand pounds in weight, but ideally suited for riding purposes.[2] The technique of cattle-raising, to the last detail, was worked out in Mexico long before it was introduced into the United States, and was practiced for years in New Mexico, Texas, and California before it was known on the western plains. The cowboy's saddle, bridle, bit, lariat, and spurs were adaptations, for the most part, of equipment used by Spanish cavalrymen, while the "round-up" and the

Beginnings of the cattle industry

[1] E. D. Branch, *The Hunting of the Buffalo* (1929), possesses literary as well as historical merit.

[2] The western Indians early found this out, became expert horsemen, and as such, with their bows and arrows, were more than a match for white cavalrymen with carbines. Only when the six-shooter was invented could the white horseman meet the mounted Indian on equal terms. W. P. Webb, *The Texas Rangers* (1935).

use of "brands" to indicate ownership were early invented to meet obvious needs. The unimportance of the cattle industry for so many years was not due to inability to produce cattle. Anyone in the Southwest with a little ambition could have all the cattle he wanted. What the industry needed was a market for its produce, and until that could be found it remained insignificant.[1]

Attempts to drive Texas cattle to an outside market were made from the time of the Mexican War on, but all such ventures amounted *The long* to little until the railroads began to push out across the *drive* western plains. Then the idea of the "long drive" from somewhere in Texas to a shipping point in Kansas or Nebraska immediately took hold. Abilene, Kansas, a station on the Kansas Pacific, became noted as early as 1867 as a "cow-town." Here untold numbers of Texas cattle, driven northward through the Indian Territory, or the "Nation," as cowboys called it, were purchased for the use of the newly established packing-houses. Early each year drovers assembled herds for the "drive," or else individual ranchers rounded up their cattle and threw them upon the trail — a route generally known as the "Chisholm Trail," regardless of where it ran. Grazing the cattle as they went, cowboys moved them slowly northward in herds of two or three thousand head. Such a group required the services of sixteen or eighteen cowboys, a cook with a "chuck-wagon," and a "wrangler" with extra cow-ponies. Trials on the march included the danger of stampedes due to lightning, buffalo, or Indians.

On the "long drive" the cowboy developed those peculiar characteristics that made him, like the fur-trader, the lumberjack, and the prospec-*The cowboy* tor, a unique specimen of the American frontier. He found the revolver indispensable to the protection of his herd, and of great advantage in the actual business of herding. Naturally he became a fair marksman. He sang to the cattle, whether to help him bear the loneliness, or to keep the cattle aware of his presence, or to prevent or promote a stampede. The verses he invented were colorful, they told of the life he led, and they became as authentic a part of the American folklore as the songs of slavery and freedom that the southern Negroes sang. In reality, just a "plain everyday bow-legged human," the cowboy's occasional excesses after periods of long riding and lack of sport caught the eye of the fictionist, and were romanticized out of all proportion to the facts. A wanderer, an adventurer, and sometimes a

[1] P. A. Rollins, *The Cowboy* (1922), and J. H. Cook, *Fifty Years on the Old Frontier* (1923), give excellent accounts of the origins of the plains cattle industry. Much valuable information is contained also in Emerson Hough, *The Story of the Cowboy* (1897), and in E. D. Branch, *The Cowboy and His Interpreters* (1926).

Texas Paterson

Walker-Colt, 1838–1842

Dragoon, 1848

Civil War dragoon
with fluted cylinder

Frontier six-shooter

EARLY TYPES OF REVOLVERS

Courtesy of Colt's Patent Fire Arms Manufacturing Company

refugee, the cowboy's actual exploits did make good stories, but most of his life was given over to hard and monotonous labor.[1]

The advance of the frontier into Kansas and Nebraska drove the "Chisholm Trail" farther and farther west, and determined the location of new cow-towns to take the place of those enclosed in settled areas. Dodge City, Kansas, for example, soon replaced Abilene as the leading shipping-point for Texas cattle. Settlement interfered with grazing; moreover, the Texas cattle brought with them the germs of the dreaded "Texas fever" to which they themselves had become immune, but which brought almost certain death to other cattle that caught it. Quarantine laws were passed that pushed the drive still farther into the west. Also, a new market was discovered when the northern plains had been cleared of buffalo. Northern ranchers, eager to expand their herds, paid good prices for the Texas longhorns, bred them up rapidly by the introduction of blooded cattle from the East, and laid the basis for a short, but spectacular, prosperity. Points on the Union Pacific such as Ogallala and Sidney, Nebraska, were visited by western as well as eastern buyers, and Cheyenne, Wyoming, which had once had no other excuse for existence than the railroad, now found itself the center of an exciting cattle industry. Texas cattle were driven northward as far as Dakota and Montana, and even westward into New Mexico, Arizona, Colorado, and Utah.

The profits of cattle-growing on a well-policed range, for the use of which the government made no charge, and to which, thanks to the railroads, markets were now easily accessible, did not fail to attract capital, not only from the American East, but also from Europe, particularly England. Ranchers, or "cattlemen," as they were called to distinguish them from their employees, the "cowboys," figured that an original investment of five thousand dollars should pay profits of from forty to fifty thousand dollars in four years' time. Ranching companies, some of them with capital investments well up into the millions, were formed to crowd more and more cattle upon the range. Access to water was, of course, essential, and each individual or company engaged in the cattle business took care to

The range-cattle industry

---

[1] The following lines are inscribed on a tombstone in the Cemetery at Douglas, Wyoming:
'Underneath this stone in eternal rest
Sleeps the wildest one of the Wayward West.
He was gambler and sport and cowboy too,
And he led the pace in an outlaw crew.
He was sure on the trigger and staid to the end,
But he was never known to quit on a friend.
In the relations of death all mankind is alike,
But in life there was only one George W. Pike.'

PRE-GLIDDEN PATENTS

L. B. Smith, June 25, 1867, Ohio

William D. Hunt, July 23, 1867,
New York

M. Kelly, February 11, 1868,
New York

THE HAISH-GLIDDEN GROUP
(IMPRACTICAL)

Henry M. Rose, May 13, 1873, Illinois

Jacob Haish, February 17, 1874,
Illinois

I. L. Ellwood, February 24, 1874,
Illinois

THE EVOLUTION OF BARBED WIRE
Courtesy of American Steel and Wire Company

obtain title to some land so situated. Here the ranch house and other necessary buildings were located, and from this headquarters operations were carried on over a range bounded by the distance the cattle were willing to travel to water. Large "outfits," as the companies were called, sometimes had access to water at many different places, and companies existed that claimed the grazing rights to strips of land no less than a hundred miles long and fifty miles wide.[1]

The law of the range, like the law of the mining camp, was to a great extent invented to meet the needs of the situation. Stock-growers' associations were formed, at first for mutual protection, but later to work out rules for users of the range that actually had the effect of law. Indeed, the Wyoming Stock-Growers' Association, formed in 1873, came to have more power than the territorial government of Wyoming, which, as a matter of fact, it controlled. The Association promoted community rather than individual round-ups, regulated the use of brands and recorded them, required that "mavericks" (unbranded calves that no longer followed their mothers) should be sold to the highest bidder and the proceeds paid into the Association treasury, discouraged overstocking of the range by refusing membership to outsiders, and made relentless warfare upon all who were suspected of "rustling" (stealing) cattle. Punishment for defiance of the Association might or might not await court action.

The day of the cattleman soon passed. Trouble with rustlers who branded mavericks and "worked" (altered) brands cost the ranchers *The passing* heavy losses, both in cattle stolen and in fees paid to de-*of the* tectives and inspectors. Trouble with "nesters" (farmers) *cattleman* whose fences interfered with the free access of cattle to water-holes not only caused heavy losses in property, but frequently resulted also in loss of life. Cowboys learned to carry wire-cutters as part of their equipment; and finally, in self-defense, the cattlemen themselves began to fence the land they used but did not own, only to have their fences branded as illegal by the United States government, and ordered down. But the greatest calamity that befell the cattlemen was the overstocking of the range. By the middle eighties so many millions of cattle had been turned loose to pick up a living from the plains that one severe winter was sure to bring disaster, and instead of one such winter most of the range country saw two, 1885–86, and 1886–87. The result was wholesale ruin and bankruptcy, and a complete change in the nature of the cattle industry. After this time, ranchers tended more

---

[1] The best works on the cow country are E. S. Osgood, *The Day of the Cattleman* (1929), and E. E. Dale, *The Range Cattle Industry* (1930).

Keystone

WILLIAM F. CODY

and more to raise hay for winter feed, and in general to carry on farming as well as ranching activities.   On many ranges sheep replaced cattle, although not without resort to actual warfare between sheepmen and cattlemen.   The close-grazing sheep left the range stripped of grass, so when sheepmen came to stay cattlemen had to fight or leave.   In some of these conflicts, sheep-herders were slain, the wagons that carried their supplies were burned, and the herds themselves were destroyed.[1]

Short-lived as it was, the range-cattle industry left its mark upon the

[1] The story of a typical mountain region which passed through every stage of the frontier process is told in Charles Lindsay, *The Big Horn Basin* (1932).

West and upon the country as a whole. It did its share to promote the growth of the meat-packing industry. It made clear the absurdity for the Far West of land legislation devised to meet the needs of the eastern half of the continent, and paved the way for important changes, such as the Desert Land Act of 1877, and the Timber and Stone Act of 1878.[1] It bequeathed to the residents of the plains a breezy, slangy language, cowboy costumes, "dude" ranches, and rodeos. It lived persistently in stories of the "Wild West" such as Owen Wister's *The Virginian*, and the multitudinous works of Zane Grey; in the infinite number of scenarios derived from them for the use of the motion-picture industry; in the "Wild West" shows first popularized by "Buffalo Bill" Cody; in the solemn melodies and bungling rhymes of the cowboy songs.[2]

> Oh, beat the drum slowly and play the fife lowly;
> Play the dead march as you carry me along.
> Take me to the green valley and lay the sod o'er me.
> I'm just a poor cowboy and I know I've done wrong.

---

[1] See *post*, p. 234.

[2] Several collections of these interesting songs exist: John A. Lomax, *Cowboy Songs and Other Frontier Ballads* (1910), and *Songs of the Cattle Trail and Cow Camp* (1920); Badger Clark, *Sun and Saddle Leather* (1936).

LeRoy R. Hafen and Carl Coke Rister, *Western America* (1941), describes the exploration, settlement, and development of the region west of the Mississippi. Dorothy Gardiner, *West of the River* (1941), features trails and transportation in the same region. J. V. Frederick, *Ben Holladay, the Stagecoach King* (1940), concentrates on the period 1862–1866. Everett Dick, *Vanguards of the Frontier* (1941), is a social history of the traders, trappers, and others who preceded the settlers on the Great Plains.

On recent state and regional history, see Oscar O. Winther, *The Great Northwest* (1947); P. S. Fritz, *Colorado, the Centennial State* (1941); Effie M. Mack, *Nevada: A History of the State from Earliest Times Through the Civil War* (1936); Merrill G. Burlingame, *The Montana Frontier* (1942); and J. K. Howard, *Montana: High, Wide, and Handsome* (1943).

On the Great Plains livestock industry, see J. W. Thompson, *A History of Livestock Raising in the United States* (1942); Louis Pelzer, *The Cattlemen's Frontier* (1938); and Ora Brooks Peake, *The Colorado Range Cattle Industry* (1937).

On the Indian Wars, see Martin F. Schmitt (ed.), *General George Crook: His Autobiography* (1946); Ralph H. Ogle, *Federal Control of the Western Apaches, 1848–1886* (1940); and C. C. Rister, *Border Command: General Phil Sheridan in the West* (1944).

CHAPTER VII

THE HAYES ADMINISTRATION

THE ascendancy of the Republicans in the years that followed the Civil War, already shaken by the excesses of reconstruction and the scandals of the Grant régime, tottered almost to a fall with the advent *Elections of* of depression. For the customary two-thirds Republican *1874* majority in the national House of Representatives, the congressional elections of 1874 substituted a Democratic majority of more than seventy. The Senate remained Republican, although by a greatly reduced majority, and the signs of the times could be further read in the fact that among the minority members were many ex-Confederates, many former "Copperheads," and even the hated Andrew Johnson himself, who, until the time of his death, July 31, 1875, again represented the State of Tennessee. North as well as South, state after state had passed to the control of the Democrats, and Republican leaders were unable to disguise their presentiments that unless something drastic were done the Presidency would soon be in Democratic hands. To loyal Republicans, many of whom had marched in the Union armies, such a calamity must be prevented at whatever cost. What sensible person could wish to entrust the safety of the United States to a man who drew his support from one-time enemies and traitors? [1]

As the election of 1876 approached, the nervousness of the Republicans was intense. With the Grant scandals ruthlessly exposed by Democratic investigating committees, all thought of a third term *Hayes and* for the General was given up; a Democratic resolution con- *Wheeler* demning any departure from the two-term tradition passed the House of Representatives with a bipartisan majority of 234 to 18. Search for an "available" candidate to draw back into the party the discontented Liberals who had voted for Greeley in 1872 was seriously handicapped by the determination with which several of the least liberal of the Republican leaders sought the presidential prize for themselves. James G.

[1] An excellent popular account of the political life of this period is Matthew Josephson, *The Politicos, 1865–1896* (1938).

Blaine of Maine, the last Republican Speaker of the House, won an earl;
lead on all the rest by frantically "waving the bloody shirt," an exercis
that immensely pleased the regulars, but was ill-calculated to bring man;
of the straying Liberals back home.   No less unbending on the Souther
question was Oliver P. Morton of Indiana, whose soft-money proclivi
ties, however, had a strong appeal for the debtor farmers of the Middl
West.   Regular of the regulars was Roscoe Conkling, Republican "boss"
of New York, who would have preferred to keep Grant in office, but wa
not unwilling to run when Grant was eliminated.   More palatable to the
Liberals were Benjamin H. Bristow of Kentucky, who as Secretary of the
Treasury had helped expose the "Whiskey Ring," and Rutherford B
Hayes of Ohio, whose upright character and devotion to civil service
reform had not prevented him from being thrice chosen governor of his
state.   Fortunately for his opponents, Blaine, whose reputation hac
already been smirched by the publication of the famous "Mulligan letters," fell ill from a sunstroke during the time when the Republican Convention met, and after seven ballots Hayes was accorded an unenthusiastic nomination.   Second place on the ticket went to William A.
Wheeler, a Radical Republican from New York.   The platform charged
the Democratic Party with "being the same in character and spirit as
when it sympathized with treason," and warned the country against
trusting a party that had proved itself "unworthy, recreant, and incapable."

The Democrats had their candidate, and knew it.   Samuel J. Tilden
(1814–1886),[1] elected governor of New York in the "tidal wave" of 1874,
Tilden and had first won national recognition by the part he played in
Hendricks the overthrow of the Tweed Ring, and as governor had still
further endeared himself to reformers by his vigorous and successful
attack upon the "Canal Ring," another organization of grafters.   Educated at Yale and New York universities and possessed of a first-rate
mind, Tilden had long been a close student of the law, and had made a
fortune in the service of corporations.   Half the railroads between the
Hudson and the Missouri Rivers, he claimed, had made use of his talents.
Shrewd and calculating, conservative by training and habit, a strict
"party man" whose father had been intimately associated with the Albany regency, sixty-two years of age and of uncertain health, a cultured
"old bachelor," he was not exactly the type ordinarily favored by reformers, but circumstances had cast him in the reform rôle, and he willingly
accepted it.   On the first ballot the Democratic Convention gave him a

[1] A. C. Flick, *Samuel Jones Tilden* (1939), has a degree of objectivity lacking in the older
John Bigelow, *The Life of Samuel J. Tilden* (2 vols., 1895).

clear majority, and on the second, the two-thirds vote necessary to a nomination. For Vice-President the Democrats chose Thomas A. Hendricks of Indiana, a soft-money man who had been Tilden's only serious contender for first place on the ticket. As for the Democratic platform, its tone was set by a continuous reiteration of the words, "Reform is necessary..." Preliminary to every other reform, however, was "the people's choice of honest men from another party."

The circumstances that had shaped the results of the election of 1874 applied equally in 1876, and for a time it seemed that the Democrats must surely win. The depression was still on, the Grant scandals had multiplied, Radical reconstruction was as bad as ever. Democratic orators made the most of their opportunities, and the country rang with their denunciations. The Republicans fought back quite as bitterly, and in the Civil War record of the Democratic Party they found ample ammunition. As for live issues between the parties, there were none. Both candidates were hard-money men, both of them favored civil service reform, both admitted that the time for home rule in the South had come. Tilden enjoyed a decided advantage from the fact that the supremacy of the carpet-baggers had been overthrown in all but three of the southern states, South Carolina, Louisiana, and Florida. The consequent certainty of an almost solidly Democratic vote from the South was noted in the Republican platform "with deep solicitude." On the other hand, Hayes's unimpeachable record as governor of Ohio satisfied most of the former Liberals that reform could be achieved within the Republican Party, and they generally preferred that course to an alliance with the Democrats. Soft-money men found little consolation in either candidate, and a few of them gave their votes to a new Independent, or "Greenback," Party, which favored expansion of the currency by the issue of more paper money, and supported the candidacies of Peter Cooper of New York for President and Samuel F. Cary of Ohio for Vice-President. Most voters, however, even if they held soft-money views, were too enthralled by the main contest to take the Greenbackers seriously.

Early in the evening of election day, November 7, the news came out that Tilden had carried New York, New Jersey, Connecticut, and Indiana. These states, together with the "solid South," would apparently account for enough votes to insure a Democratic victory. Next day nearly every newspaper in the country conceded Tilden's election, but the *New York Times* and the *New York Herald* claimed that the election was in doubt. Tilden had for a certainty 184 electoral votes, but 185 were necessary for a choice, and if the three

Prospects of Democratic victory

The disputed election returns

carpet-bag states, South Carolina, Louisiana, and Florida, could only be counted for Hayes the Republicans would win. Zachariah Chandler, chairman of the Republican National Committee, unhesitatingly claimed the election for Hayes, and for weeks the country was in a turmoil. Complete returns seemed to show that South Carolina, with its preponderance of Negro voters, had probably gone Republican by a small majority, but in Louisiana and Florida the Democrats were in the lead. In every case, however, the returning boards, charged with the duty of certifying the results of the election, were under Republican control. That wholesale frauds had been committed by both sides in each of the disputed states was a matter of general knowledge. Why, then, should not the returning boards throw out enough allegedly fraudulent votes to give the election to the Republicans? "Visiting statesmen" from the North speedily descended upon the doubtful states, particularly Louisiana, where the Democratic majority ran to six or seven thousand, and where the difficulty of altering the result was deemed greatest. Here the Republican returning board, while doubtless ready at all times to sell out to any satisfactory bidder, finally certified the choice of the Hayes electors. The same result was achieved with less difficulty and better reason in South Carolina and Florida, where the vote was closer and room for an honest difference of opinion existed.

The matter did not end at this point, however, for the Democratic electors in each of the three states refused to concede their defeat, and met on the appointed day in December to cast their votes for Tilden and Hendricks. A fourth contest occurred in Oregon, where one of the three Republican electors turned out to be ineligible. According to the Democratic contention his place must go to the elector with the next highest number of votes — a Democrat; but according to the Republican contention, well sustained by the law, the two legally chosen Republican electors were entitled to fill the vacancy. Thus, when Congress should meet to count the vote, it would be confronted by two sets of returns from four different states. As to the method of counting the vote, the Constitution, unfortunately, was ambiguous. "The President of the Senate," it said, "shall, in the presence of the Senate and House of Representatives, open all the certificates and the votes shall then be counted." But how? If the President of the Senate, a Republican, should count them, then Hayes and Wheeler would be elected. If the two houses should vote separately on the results, there would be a deadlock. If they should vote jointly, each member having one vote, Tilden and Hendricks would win. If each house might at will throw out contested votes, as an old rule provided, no candidate would have a majority.

Faced by this dilemma, a compromise plan was devised whereby all disputed returns were to be referred to an electoral commission of fifteen, five senators, five representatives, and five justices of the *The Electoral* Supreme Court. Care was taken to insure the selection of *Commission* seven Democrats and seven Republicans to serve on the commission, while the deciding vote, it was originally intended, should go to Justice David Davis of Illinois, a man of independent views. But Davis, it chanced, was unexpectedly elected to the United States Senate by a combination of Greenbackers and Democrats in the Illinois legislature, and resigned from the Court to accept his new office. As all the remaining justices were Republicans, the disappointment of the Democrats was extreme. Nevertheless, the law was carried out to the letter, and by a strict party vote of eight to seven every dispute was resolved in favor of Hayes and Wheeler, who were declared elected by a majority of one vote, 185 to 184, only two days before Grant's term expired.[1]

The right and wrong of the "disputed election" is a hard matter to decide. By any reckoning Tilden had a popular majority of more than a quarter of a million votes, and the fact that the lower house of Congress remained decisively Democratic is also significant. The best argument in favor of the Republicans was made by Hayes himself, who pointed to the intimidation of Negro voters throughout the South as the chief reason for his poor showing. "A fair election," he said, "would have given us about forty electoral votes at the South — at least that many." Nevertheless, Hayes had declared himself opposed to any effort to "defeat one outrage and fraud by another. There must be nothing crooked on our part." That this advice was taken in Louisiana, few would try to maintain. But the Republicans probably did nothing worse than the Democrats would have delighted to do had they had the opportunity. Indeed, some "cipher dispatches," discovered and deciphered by the Republicans, seemed to indicate that offers of bribery from a Democratic source had not been lacking. The real victory of the election rested less with either party than with the American people as a whole, who, in spite of the tenseness of the situation, kept their tempers, and accepted in good faith the decision that had been reached.

Rutherford B. Hayes (1822–1893), the new President, was Ohio born and educated.[2] Like Tilden he was a lawyer, but he had never counted many of the country's great corporations among his clients. Unlike

---

[1] The most thorough study of this election is P. L. Haworth, *The Hayes-Tilden Disputed Presidential Election of 1876* (1906).

[2] Hayes has had two excellent biographers, C. R. Williams, *The Life of Rutherford Burchard Hayes* (2 vols., 1914), and H. J. Eckenrode, *Rutherford B. Hayes, Statesman of Reunion* (1930).

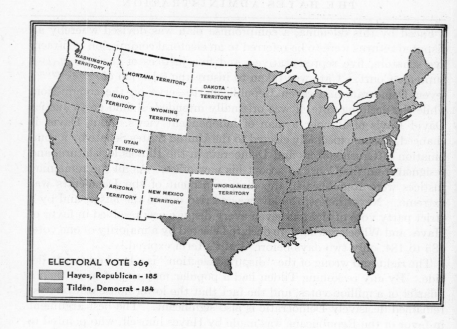

ELECTORAL VOTE 369

Hayes, Republican - 185
Tilden, Democrat - 184

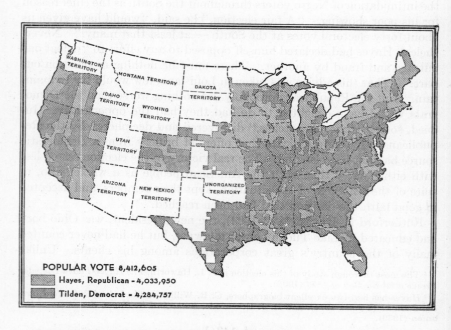

POPULAR VOTE 8,412,605

Hayes, Republican - 4,033,950
Tilden, Democrat - 4,284,757

PRESIDENTIAL ELECTION OF 1876 BY STATES AND BY COUNTIES

Tilden, who had avoided as nearly as possible any stand on the Civil War Hayes had served loyally, if without distinction, as a volun- *Rutheford* teer officer in the Union army, and at the close of the war had *B. Hayes* been brevetted major-general. As governor of Ohio he had made an excellent record: he took his duties seriously, his judgment was good, his word could be trusted, he made appointments for merit even to the extent of naming Democrats to office. During the campaign he astonished reformers by the earnestness with which he denounced the spoils system, and he irritated party regulars by the assertion that "he serves his party best who serves his country best." Utterly unable to bend to expediency, he confided to his diary during the campaign that "if elected, the firmest adherence to principle, against all opposition and temptations, is my purpose. I shall show a *grit* that will astonish those who predict weakness." As President, however, his good intentions frequently betrayed him into bad politics. His cabinet, for example, which was called by some the ablest since Washington's, contained four men who had voted for Greeley in 1872. One of them, the Postmaster-General, was an out-and-out Tilden Democrat from Tennessee, and Hayes had even considered naming General Joseph E. Johnston, the ex-Confederate, as Secretary of War. A man so unversed in political finesse could never become the successful leader of a party, however great his integrity. His wife, a strong temperance advocate, did her husband no good with the politicians and socialites by refusing to serve wine at White House functions.

The first concern of the Hayes administration was to end the scandal of reconstruction. In Florida, although its vote was counted for Hayes, carpet-bag rule came to an end with the inauguration of a *Restoration* Democratic governor on January 2, 1877. In the two other *of home rule* southern states that were counted for Hayes, South Carolina and Louisiana, Republican state administrations retained power only because they were supported in each instance by small detachments of federal troops. On all sides it was conceded that if these troops were withdrawn, the rival Democratic candidates, whom nearly every white voter had preferred, would promptly seize the reins of power. Should Hayes continue to support carpet-bag rule in these two states by ordering the troops to remain, or should he withdraw the troops and permit the southern whites to have things their own way? Knowing full well that his course would greatly strengthen the case for those who claimed he had no right to the Presidency, and that he would assuredly be accused of having bargained with the Southerners to give them "home rule" in return for the necessary votes to put himself into the White House,

Hayes ordered the removal of the troops. The reaction in Columbia and New Orleans was instantaneous; Democratic officials moved in as Republicans moved out. The "solid South" had become a fact; military reconstruction had broken down. Six years later, when the Supreme Court of the United States ruled in the Civil Rights cases that the Fourteenth Amendment could not be used to restrain individuals from conduct designed to enforce social discriminations against the Negroes, civil reconstruction may be said to have broken down. Within another decade, as one southern state after another began to devise laws that made the Fifteenth Amendment a mockery, the last remnant of political reconstruction faded away.

"Now for civil service reform!" Hayes wrote in his diary, April 22, 1877, after he had decided on his southern policy. Until Congress should *Civil service* provide him with a really effective civil service commission, *reform* however, the best he could do was to issue orders, and to hope that they would be obeyed. To John Sherman, Secretary of the Treasury, upon whose action rested the fate of many thousands of federal employees, he wrote:

> It is my wish that the collection of revenue should be free from partisan control and organized on a strictly business basis with the same guaranties for efficiency and fidelity in the selection of the chief and subordinate officers that would be required by a prudent merchant. Party leaders should have no more influence in appointments than other equally respectable citizens. No assessments for political purposes on officers or subordinates should be allowed. No useless officer or employee should be retained. No officer should be required or permitted to take part in the management of political organizations, caucuses, conventions or election campaigns. Their right to vote and to express their views on public questions, either orally or through the press, is not denied, provided it does not interfere with the discharge of their official duties.

These statements, backed up by official orders to all federal officers, went as far as words could go toward redeeming Hayes's pledge during the campaign that civil service reform must be "thorough, radical, and complete." But more was needed than mere words. Some of the President's advisers, Carl Schurz, for example, Secretary of the Interior, and to a lesser extent, John Sherman, Secretary of the Treasury, took the President seriously, but most of them were highly indifferent to reform, and winked at the very practices their leader had condemned. Congress showed no disposition whatever to co-operate. Not only did it refuse to set up a commission that could give examinations and award offices on merit, but it also fought tenaciously the efforts of the President himself to make appointments independently of politics. Congressmen preferred the old system, by which they advised the President to appoint their political friends. A test case came when the President removed from office Chester Alan Arthur, collector of the port of New York, who was a political henchman of Roscoe Conkling, senator from New York, and chose in his place Theodore Roosevelt, father of the President by the same name, a man notably independent of politics. Conkling invoked the rule of "senatorial courtesy," according to which, as Hayes put it, "no officer should be appointed in New York without his consent, obtained previously to the nomination." The fitness of Roosevelt for the place was not questioned, but enough other senators, hoping for the same "courtesy" when they should need it, voted against his confirmation to defeat it. The President waited until Congress adjourned, then gave the place to General E. A. Merritt, who on the reassembling of Congress was confirmed (with the help of Democratic votes) only after Sherman had threatened to resign if it were not done. Hayes did what he could to make good appointments, and his record in this respect was the best of any President's since John Quincy Adams. But his occasional mistakes annoyed the reformers, who spoke slightingly of his "opportunities and failures," and declared that "his course has provoked the laughter of his enemies and the profound sorrow of his friends," while his successes won him the undying hostility of the most powerful of the Republican leaders. Hayes was the only man that the Republican Party ever nominated and elected to the Presidency, and then refused to accord the honor of renomination.

Hayes's tenacious adherence to hard-money views, even in the face of persistent depression, was in keeping with his character.[1] On this issue he saw eye to eye with the leading men of his party, and he approved cordially the action taken by Congress during Grant's *Resumption* administration to bring about the resumption of specie payments. By a law passed early in 1875, before the Democrats took control of the House of Representatives, Congress had authorized the Secretary of the Treasury to prepare for resumption on the first of January, 1879, by building up a gold reserve. John Sherman was chiefly responsible for this measure, and as a member of Hayes's cabinet it fell to his lot to carry it into effect.[2] Backed steadfastly by the President, he sold bonds for gold, and ultimately accumulated a gold reserve of $100,000,000. As this fund grew, confidence that the government would be able to exchange gold dollars

---

[1] A good running account of the money question is A. D. Noyes, *Forty Years of American Finance* (1909).

[2] The active part taken by Sherman in many phases of American politics is told by himself. John Sherman, *Recollections of Forty Years* (2 vols., 1895).

THE APPRECIATING DOLLAR, 1865–95

Based on weigted averages of commodity values   From A. M. Arnett,
The Populist Movement in Georgia, p. 69 (1922)

for greenbacks on the appointed day grew with it, and the value of the greenback dollar, expressed in terms of gold, also grew. Worth only sixty-seven cents in 1865, the greenback dollars had risen to eighty-nine cents in 1875, to ninety-six cents in 1877, and well before January 1, 1879, to one hundred cents. In 1878 Congress decided that $346,681,016 in greenbacks should remain a permanent part of the national currency, but the existence of the gold reserve made every greenback dollar "as good as gold." Accustomed by long usage to a paper currency, no one cared to make the exchange, and the greenbacks continued to circulate.

The steadily appreciating value of the dollar insured comfortable profits to money lenders, particularly those who made long-term loans.
Soft-money For borrowers, however, the situation was far different.
ideas The farmer who mortgaged his farm as security for a five-year loan found to his sorrow when the time for payment came that the dollars he had borrowed were worth far less than the dollars with which he must repay. Dearer dollars meant lower prices for the wheat, or corn, or livestock he had to sell. He must therefore in effect pay back not only principal and interest, but enough more to cover the amount which the dollar had appreciated. When he borrowed, a thousand bushels of wheat might equal in value the amount of his loan; when he repaid, it took from twelve to fifteen hundred bushels of wheat to raise the money he needed, and more for interest. Protests against dearer dollars and lower prices came thick and fast as one depression year after another compounded the gloom, and in the West and the South, where debtors were numerous and creditors were few, soft-money ideas, such as Pendle-

ton's "Ohio idea," found much favor. In general the Democratic Party was more hospitable to soft-money views than the Republican, but in both parties hard-money men, representing the point of view of eastern creditors rather than of southern or western debtors, were in the ascendancy. With resumption imminent, the Greenback Party, founded in 1876, won more and more adherents. In the elections of 1878, it polled a million votes, as against its eighty thousand of two years before, and elected fifteen members of Congress.[1] Disappointed western Grangers in search of a new panacea accounted in considerable part for the increasing strength of the Greenbackers, and for the Republican loss of the Senate as well as the House. The "rag baby," as the greenback dollar was fondly called, came to have a sentimental place in the hearts of its advocates:

> Thou, Greenback, 'tis of thee,
> Fair money of the free,
> Of thee we sing.
> And through all coming time
> Great bards in every clime
> Will sing with joyful rhyme,
> Gold is not king.
>
> Then smash old Shylock's bonds,
> With all his gold coupons,
> The banks and rings.
> Monopolies must fail,
> Rich paupers work in jail,
> The right will then prevail,
> Not money kings.

The success of resumption, and the return of prosperity in 1879, tended to discredit Greenbackism, and the high-water mark of 1878 was never attained again. In the meantime, however, a new soft-money panacea had been discovered in what was popularly *Free silver* known as "free silver."[2] For ages the two precious metals used as money, gold and silver, had depended for their value, not upon the fiat of government, but upon commercial demand. By a curious and long-sustained coincidence the relative value of the two metals had been almost constant; and it took fifteen or sixteen times as much silver to equal in value a given unit of gold. In early times the slight fluctuation in the ratio of value between the two metals had been of small concern.

[1] F. E. Haynes, *Third Party Movements Since the Civil War, with Special Reference to Iowa* (1916), contains a good account of the Greenbackers. See also D. C. Barrett, *The Greenbacks and Resumption of Specie Payments* (1931).

[2] An excellent account of the rise of the silver issue is given in J. L. Laughlin, *History of Bimetallism in the United States* (1892).

Methods of refinement and of measurement were too crude to make the variations noticeable, and governments themselves were not above deceiving the public all they could. With the progress of modern science, however, the exact amount of silver and of gold in a coin could be easily ascertained, and nations made an effort to establish coinage ratios that would harmonize with the existing commercial ratio. Always this was difficult, or even impossible, for the commercial ratio was inevitably a variable, while the coinage ratio established by law was a constant. Human nature being what it is, people who knew the difference hoarded the overvalued coins, and spent those undervalued; or, as the ancient Gresham Law expressed it, the cheap money drove the dear money out of circulation. Paper issues, being as a rule less valuable than either gold or silver, rarely had much difficulty in driving both out of circulation. Such had been the case in the United States during most of its history, while during and after the Civil War the rule of the greenbacks and the national bank notes had been supreme.

Because of the prevalence of a cheap paper currency, efforts in the United States to set a proper coinage ratio for gold and silver had been of little importance. In Hamilton's time the ratio had been set at about fifteen to one, that is, fifteen units of silver in the silver dollar to one unit of gold in the gold dollar. Experience proved that this ratio put too little silver in the silver dollar, and too much gold in the gold dollar, so that silver circulated in preference to gold. In Jackson's time, with the President hopeful that a hard-money currency could be established to take the place of the existing bank-note issues, the coinage ratio was corrected to sixteen to one. But the correction proved to be an overcorrection, and now the gold coins circulated in preference to silver. In order to keep fractional silver currency (dimes, quarters, etc.) in circulation, these coins were greatly debased, but by the time of the Civil War the overvalued silver dollars were so rarely seen as to amount to curiosities. When free-silver advocates came later to demand the "dollar of our daddies," they were demanding something that many of their "daddies" had never even seen.

All hard money, including for a time fractional currency, was driven out of use by paper money during the Civil War, but by 1873 plans were *The "crime of 1873"* being laid for the return of coins to circulation. At the request of the Secretary of the Treasury a new coinage law was passed in February, 1873, which dropped the overweight silver dollar from the coinage lists altogether. This was the famous "crime of 1873," which according to a generation of silver orators was committed as the result of an "international conspiracy to demonetize silver." The fact of the matter was that European nations, confronted by the difficulties of maintaining a double standard, were beginning to adopt gold as their sole standard of monetary measurement. The framers of the law of 1873 did not go this far, for existing silver dollars were not "demonetized," but the law at least acknowledged the futility of minting a coin that had not circulated as money for nearly forty years. The measure was given only the most perfunctory consideration by Congress, and was passed as a routine matter.[1]

Had there been no drop in the price of silver no one would have thought of branding this coinage law of 1873 as a crime. But almost immediately after its passage the ratio of value between gold and silver began to change. The huge outpourings of the Comstock Lode in Nevada and the generally increased productivity of silver mines throughout the West added a disproportionate quantity of silver to the world's supply. The cost of extracting silver from the ore in which it was found was lessened by scientific discoveries. Probably, also, there was less use for silver as money. Bank checks and bills of exchange took the place of actual transfers of money to a greater extent than formerly, while gold, because of its smaller bulk, was preferred to silver for large transactions. Whatever the causes, the trend in the price of silver was steadily downward for the next twenty-five years. By 1875 it was no longer true that the silver in the silver dollar was worth more than the gold in the gold dollar, as silver miners learned to their sorrow when they sought to take advantage of the old privilege of having their silver minted into dollars at the coinage ratio of sixteen to one. A quarter of a century later the amount of silver required to make an old-fashioned silver dollar was worth only about fifty cents in gold.

This steady drop in the price of silver was a nightmare to the silver miners, who professed to believe that the cause of their distress was the "demonetization" policy of the government, and demanded *"Sixteen* as a remedy the "free and unlimited coinage of silver at the *to one"* ratio of sixteen to one." They hoped that "remonetization" would bring the price of silver up. They were soon joined in their demand by the debtor farmers of the Middle West, and to a lesser extent by those of the South, who had no interest in a higher price for silver, but believed that "free coinage," or "free silver," as they termed the desired policy, would mean a cheaper dollar. Former Greenbackers altered their paper-money arguments to fit this new demand. If the government would only

---

[1] Evidence of the increasing interest of European historians in American affairs is seen in a recent scholarly study by Jean Paul Hütter, *La Question de la Monnaie d'Argent aux États-Unis des Origines à 1900* (1938).

take silver from all who offered it, as it still took gold, coin the silver into silver dollars at the rate of sixteen to one, and put the new silver dollars into circulation, the country would have more money and cheaper money, just as surely as if more greenbacks had been issued. Free silver thus became the adopted child of the Greenbackers.

During the last half of Hayes's administration the advocates of free silver, with a clear majority in the House of Representatives, forced *Bland-* through a measure sponsored by Representative Richard *Allison Act* P. Bland of Missouri that would have required the resumption of unlimited silver coinage at the old ratio of sixteen to one.[1] In the Senate, however, the hard-money men were able to alter the bill in such a way as to change its nature materially. An amendment offered by Senator W. B. Allison of Iowa provided that the Secretary of the Treasury should purchase each month from two to four million dollars' worth of silver at the market price, and should coin it into silver dollars at the old coinage ratio of sixteen to one. This meant limited coinage, however, instead of unlimited coinage, and while the new silver dollars were to be legal tender Secretary Sherman and others saw clearly that if only they could be backed by gold, as was the case with the greenbacks, they would be "as good as gold." The measure, as amended, passed the Senate and the House. Hayes promptly vetoed it, but it was passed over his veto by a two-thirds majority of both houses, and so became a law. As administered it failed completely to cheapen the dollar. Sherman and his successors at the Treasury Department bought always only the minimum amount of silver required, and without sanction of law stood ready at all times to exchange gold dollars for silver, regardless of the fact that the silver in the silver dollar was worth far less than one hundred cents in gold. The free-silver forces, finding themselves thus outgeneraled, began a campaign of protest that lasted on until the Democrats made free silver their major issue in the campaign of 1896.

Not among the least of the problems that confronted the country during the Hayes administration was the increasing confidence with *Labor unrest* which labor undertook to marshal its strength against capital.[2] Hard times meant an unmeasured amount of unemployment, frequent reductions of wages, and a growing feeling on the part of labor that employers had little or no regard for the welfare of their employees. Labor organizations were particularly frowned upon

---

[1] W. V. Byars, *An American Commoner, the Life and Times of Richard Parker Bland* (1900), recounts the successive failures of "Silver Dick."

[2] On this subject the monumental work of John R. Commons and associates, *History of Labor in the United States* (4 vols., 1918–35), is indispensable.

by the great corporations, and industrialists were known to circulate among themselves "blacklists" containing the names of agitators who tried to form labor unions. As a matter of fact, the American public, still wedded to the frontier ideal of individualism, had little sympathy for the unions, and believed that an employer might rightfully "hire and fire at will." The workers themselves were surprisingly lacking in class consciousness. Most of them had come from the farm, and many of them expected to return to it. Others hoped to rise from the status of employee to the status of employer, and frequently saw their dreams come true. Nevertheless, the Civil War, with its attendant rise of industrialism, had greatly stimulated labor co-operation. Many strikes occurred during the war, and at its close, with the ex-soldiers home in search of work, and the immigrant tide beginning, the need of organization was more marked than ever before.

Local labor unions had existed in the United States since the early nineteenth century, and the Jacksonian period had witnessed the development of a well-defined labor movement; but the depression *Trades* that began in 1837 had been disastrous for labor, and not *unions* until the time of the Civil War was any considerable part of the ground lost regained. During the fifties and sixties a few national organizations, formed by such groups as the printers, the locomotive engineers, and the bricklayers, came into existence, but for a long time none of them succeeded in drawing into its ranks any large percentage of those eligible, while attempts at all-labor organizations were even less satisfactory. In August, 1866, a National Labor Union was formed at Baltimore by a group of seventy-seven delegates, representing a great variety of labor interests. This organization lasted for half a dozen years, sponsored annual labor congresses that were well attended, and at one time claimed a membership of 640,000. It was soon drawn off into politics, however, and by 1872 had assisted in the formation of the Labor Reform Party, which survived only one presidential election. What little was left of the National Labor Union crashed with the Panic of 1873, but, while it lasted, it had given the movement for an eight-hour day a good start, and had promoted in a variety of ways the study of labor problems. It furnished, also, an example of concerted action by labor that was not forgotten.

The labor troubles of the seventies came in spite of the fact that labor was imperfectly organized, and some of them might actually have been averted had the unions been strong enough to bargain *The "Molly* successfully with employers. One of the worst outbreaks *Maguires"* came in the anthracite coal mining region of Pennsylvania, where the

"Molly Maguires," a secret society of terrorists, had for a decade carried on their depredations. Conditions in the mining towns were bad enough to justify the firmest protests, but the "Mollies" depended primarily upon murder for results. The name of the order, together with its methods of operation, were imported from Ireland, and membership was confined to Irish immigrants and their sons. By 1865 the "Mollies" were beginning to make their influence felt. "Bosses" who refused special privileges to a member were murdered. "Scabs" were notified in writing that they might have a week in which to go, but if they dared stay, "on next Saturday you will die." Superintendents who were carrying money to pay the miners were set upon and robbed, and sometimes murdered. Members of the society became policemen, and gave protection to their friends. Others went into politics, stuffed ballot-boxes, won local elections, and grafted generously. Finally, when the terror could no longer be tolerated, a former district attorney of Schuylkill County hired a Chicago detective named James McParlan to gather the evidence necessary to crush the "Mollies." McParlan worked his way into the order, and two years later emerged with the evidence he had been commissioned to obtain. In a series of spectacular trials nearly a dozen death sentences were obtained, and many long prison terms. The first executions occurred in June, 1877.[1]

Less than a month later the country was startled by the news that a series of strikes, accompanied by much violence and disorder, was sweeping over the eastern railroads. The railroad unions were not very strong, and a strike on the Philadelphia and Reading only a few weeks before had been easily defeated by the employment of non-union workers. But the strikes that broke out in July, 1877, were supported by non-union as well as union men. All employees felt keenly the injustice of a ten per cent cut in wages that four great systems had decreed, and in many of the railroad towns sentiment in support of the strikers was so intense that to the faint-hearted it looked as if the day of revolution had come. During the early years of the depression the four systems in question, the New York Central, the Erie, the Pennsylvania, and the Baltimore and Ohio, had competed ruthlessly for what little business there was, and on the long hauls from St. Louis or Chicago to the Atlantic seaboard had quoted ruinously low rates. At one time cattle were hauled from Chicago to New York for a dollar a carload, and the low passenger fares that the "rate wars" promoted had had much to do with the success of the Centennial Exposition at Philadelphia. After many unavailing efforts, the presidents of

Railway strikes of 1877

---

[1] The best study of this subject is J. W. Coleman, *The Molly Maguire Riots* (1936).

the competing roads finally reached an agreement in April, 1877, to call off the rate wars, and to recover some of the losses they had suffered by a ten per cent reduction in wages. The pay cuts were announced without warning, and without consultation with minor officials who might have foretold the result. They came, too, after a long period of depression during which few trainmen had had anything like full-time work. The punishment that they inflicted was simply more than the men were able to take without protest.

The trouble began, July 16, at Martinsburg, West Virginia, on the Baltimore and Ohio, when railroad firemen, just apprised of the cuts, began to abandon their engines, and succeeded in persuading other workers to join them.[1] Enthusiastically supported by the unemployed and by many mere roisterers, the strikers stopped all trains, destroyed railroad property, and staged a general riot. The governor promptly called out the state militia, three companies strong, but the state troops were no match for the rioters, so on July 18 he appealed to President Hayes for help. The two hundred and fifty regulars that Hayes sent to the scene restored order, but it took several days to break the strike. Trains that went through Martinsburg were stopped elsewhere, and even with the promise of protection it was difficult to find men to handle them.

Meantime the excitement had spread to the neighboring State of Maryland. Disorder at Cumberland, far out in the western panhandle, led the governor, on July 20, to summon the Baltimore militia to strike duty. They never went, for an angry mob intervened, and Baltimore itself became the scene of determined street fighting. Again the President had to be importuned for aid, and again detachments of United States regulars had to be sent to the rescue. Order was restored on July 22.

Three days earlier the strike had opened in Pittsburgh, where an order to run double-headers over the mountains, and so to cut down on the number of trainmen employed, was resented even more than *Disorders in* the wage cut. Here the mayor and the police seemed to *Pittsburgh* sympathize with the strikers, and the Pittsburgh militia fraternized freely with the mob. State troops from Philadelphia, however, opened fire on the rioters, an action that seemed to add fuel to the flames. For days the city was in the grip of terrorists. Railroad buildings and rolling stock were burned, freight cars were pillaged, stolen barrels of liquor were opened and drunk. When federal troops arrived on July 23 at least nineteen rioters and several militiamen had lost their lives. Not until July 29, after more than a week of confusion, was the first freight train permitted to leave the city, and either it or the next one after it was

[1] Rhodes, VIII, and Oberholtzer, III, treat fully of these events.

wrecked. But by the end of the month the strike was completely broken and the men were back at work.

Elsewhere, in New York, New Jersey, Ohio, Indiana, Michigan, and Illinois, similar incidents occurred. In every instance, the power of the state, reinforced by federal troops, was used to break the strike. For two weeks the whole country was in a fever of excitement. Even when the railroad strikes were ended, and the trainmen went back to work at the lowered wages, anxious citizens wondered if the danger was over. In Scranton, Pennsylvania, the rolling-mill men of the Lackawanna Coal and Iron Company had struck for a thirty-five per cent increase in wages, and the miners for twenty-five per cent, both in a sense sympathetic strikes. Here, as in the railroad strikes, violence was the order of the day, and federal troops were required to stand guard for a month. Could the government really govern, or would the next such outbreak mean revolution?

News that began to come through from California was far from reassuring. On July 23, 1877, a mass meeting of workingmen in San Francisco, *Unrest in California* called to express sympathy for the Pittsburgh strikers, got out of hand and turned into a prolonged riot. California was seemingly the ideal place in the United States for revolutionary sentiment to grow. Its people were descended, lineally or spiritually, from the "forty-niners," and Californians, ever since the days of the mining camps, had shown a tolerance of lawlessness and a resentment of constraint rarely met with elsewhere in like degree. Speculation, too, was in the very air that they breathed, and it seemed reasonable to suppose that individuals who were ready at all times to take a chance on mining stock might be willing also to take a chance on something different in government. Isolation from the rest of the United States added to the danger. Only one transcontinental railroad connected the Pacific coast with the East, and the conservative influence of the older states was too far away to have much effect. Added to all this was a unique and perplexing problem, the Chinese.[1] Welcomed in the days when the whites were interested primarily in the mines, and used freely in building the Central Pacific Railroad, their popularity ebbed away when times grew hard and jobs were scarce. In 1870 California had about fifty thousand Chinese, and by the end of the seventies about seventy-five thousand. They constituted approximately nine per cent of the total population of the state, and, since practically all of them were men, at least twice as

[1] Oberholtzer, IV, treats this subject in great detail, but see also Mary R. Coolidge, *Chinese Immigration* (1909), and G. F. Seward, *Chinese Immigration in its Social and Economical Aspects* (1881).

large a percentage of the total number of laborers. They worked for "coolie wages," on which a white man would starve, and their presence was held responsible for the large number of California's unemployed. They made no attempt to accept American ways, and the Chinese quarter of any city was sure to be a plague spot of vice and disease. This was particularly true of San Francisco, the greatest center of Chinese concentration.

The full effects of the Panic of 1873 arrived late in California, for out on the coast the depression was scarcely felt until 1876. The year before that Californians, hypnotized by stories of some great new "bonanza" finds, had indulged in a veritable orgy of speculation. When the bubble broke, thousands had lost their savings. Agriculture, too, suffered acutely from the light snowfall during the winter of 1876–77. Streams essential for irrigation dried up, and crops were sure to be short. Distressed farmers, as in the Middle West, blamed the railroads as well as the weather for their calamities, and not without some reason. In California the Southern Pacific had monopolized the railroad opportunities of the state. It had received the customary rich land grants; it charged all the traffic would bear; it had gone deeply into politics to obtain taxation favors and other valuable privileges; its word was law with most of the state's officials. The farmers of the coast, still enthusiastic Grangers, demanded the greater taxation of wealth, control of the railroads by a really representative state government, and an end to the railroad monopoly on land. For good measure, they held that something must be done about the Chinese.

By the summer of 1877 San Francisco had become a city of job-hunters — miners, farmhands, laborers of every kind, including the hated Chinese. Feeling was keen against the upper classes, partic- *"Kearney-*
ularly the newly rich, who lived ostentatiously on "Nob *ism"*
Hill," and were accused of employing Chinese in preference to whites. Self-appointed orators who addressed the meeting of July 23 did not confine themselves to expressions of sympathy for the Pittsburgh strikers, but took full advantage of the opportunity to denounce the capitalists and the Chinese in fervid language. More meetings followed, and because they were held on the vacant sand-lot opposite the city hall those who attended them were called "Sand-Lotters." The idol of the crowd was Denis Kearney, an eloquent but ungrammatical Irishman, who had seen the seamy side of life as a sailor and a drayman, and now made it a practice to wind up each of his harangues with the words, "The Chinese must go!' Soon a Workingmen's Party had taken form, through which the Sand-Lotters hoped to "cinch" capital, and drive out the hated

[157]

Chinese. Kearney sometimes threatened direct action. "A little judicious hanging right here and now," he told one meeting, "will be the best course to pursue with the capitalists and stock sharps who are all the time robbing us." Again, at a meeting held on Nob Hill itself, he told the railroad owners that they had but three months in which to discharge all Chinese laborers. "Remember Judge Lynch," he warned.[1]

Curiously, however, it was to regular legal procedure rather than to lynch law that the Sand-Lotters appealed. By chance a proposal for *California* a state constitutional convention had already been sub-*constitution* mitted to the people at the polls, and in September, 1877, *of 1879* the voters gave their consent to the project. Instead of going on with the idea of revolution, the Workingmen's Party now set out, with the assistance of the discontented Grangers, to capture a majority of the delegates to be elected in June, 1878. So successful were their efforts that when the votes were counted it was apparent that the farmers and laborers together had won a clear majority of the seats in the convention. Continuing their co-operation, the Workingmen and the Grangers wrote a new constitution for the state that embodied most of their radical ideas. The Chinese were forbidden to hold property and to engage in certain occupations; taxation was shifted to the "wealthy," with "bonds, notes, and evidence of indebtedness" called upon to bear a heavy burden; a railroad commission was set up with full authority to regulate the railroads; home rule, which meant rule by the Workingmen's Party, was granted to San Francisco in generous measure; and the state judicial system was radically reformed in order to enforce more effectively the new provisions. Conservative delegates, certain that some of the more fantastic provisions would insure the defeat of the document, made little effort to eliminate them. They realized their mistake, however, when in May, 1879, the constitution was adopted by a majority of about 10,000.

Nevertheless, the victory of the radicals was short-lived. Many of the new clauses, including the anti-Chinese provision, were held by the courts to be in conflict with the Constitution of the United States or treaties with a foreign power, and so became null and void. The railroads quickly captured the commission set up to regulate them. Prosperity returned, and both Grangers and Workingmen thought less about politics. Amendment after amendment was submitted and adopted until the difference between the California constitution of 1879 and other state constitutions

---

[1] James Bryce, *The American Commonwealth* (2 vols., new edition, 1924), contains an illuminating account of this subject.

was comparatively insignificant. In San Francisco the labor forces long ruled, but unfortunately not without permitting the same type of scandals that characterized city government elsewhere. Kearney went East to popularize the Workingmen's Party there, but failed to win support, and soon dropped back into the obscurity from which he had so suddenly emerged. And yet the movement was not without a certain deep significance. Revolution in the United States, even in so hospitable an environment as California, came hard. Peaceful and orderly means of protest were preferred, often by the most radical. Violent departures from long-established precedents failed to endure. Few could deny that the workingmen's movement in California and the strikes on the eastern railroads presaged an era of conflict between labor and capital, but the average American, reassured that his government could really govern, soon gave up worrying about the danger of revolution.

The hatred on the coast for the Chinese, however, did not fail to awaken an echo in national politics. Strongly supported by representatives from the Far West, a law passed both houses of Con- *Chinese* gress in 1879 that prohibited any ship from bringing to the *immigration* United States more than fifteen Chinese passengers on a single voyage. This measure was obviously meant to stop the stream of Chinese migration across the Pacific, an end generally regarded as desirable. But unfortunately the United States had signed a treaty with China in 1868 — the Burlingame Treaty — that gave the two powers mutual rights of immigration and emigration. While action by a single state would have no effect on such a treaty, a law of Congress, passed subsequent to its negotiation, would nullify it. Should the United States so insult a friendly power? President Hayes thought not, and votes enough to override his veto were not forthcoming. The remedy, he maintained, lay in negotiation with China, not in the passing of a law. Hayes's unpopularity on the coast as a result of this veto was intense, although he promptly dispatched a commission to China to secure a change in the offensive treaty. Ultimately the Chinese government agreed to give the United States the right to "regulate, limit or suspend but not absolutely prohibit" the immigration of Chinese laborers, and in 1882 a Chinese Exclusion Act, based on this principle, went into effect.

As the time approached for the election of 1880, it began to appear that the Republicans could count upon that most valuable of all political allies, prosperity. Foreign trade had increased. In 1880 the total value of imports into the United States reached $667,954,746, while the total value of exports reached a still higher figure, $823,946,353. Thus the United States enjoyed, not only a greater volume of trade than had ever been recorded in any previous year, but also a favorable balance of trade. The government itself was rich, for its revenues each year for a long period averaged annually about $100,000,000 more than its expenditures. Business was generally good. The year 1880 saw a phenomenal wheat crop, and, what was the more remarkable, fairly satisfactory farm prices. Railway earnings were up; cotton-growers had regained the volume of productivity to which they had been accustomed before the Civil War; manufacturers, with a total population for the United States of about fifty million (an increase of sixty per cent in two decades), had begun at last to realize the possibilities of the American market, and to seek to capitalize upon it. A feeling of confidence replaced the feeling of gloom that had characterized the depression years. After all, the United States had survived a great civil war and a great depression. It had triumphed over labor difficulties that might have wrecked less favored nations. It had turned its back upon the mistakes of reconstruction. Blessed as it was with almost limitless resources, it could afford to forget sectionalism and give itself over to the enjoyment of its riches.

Comforting as these thoughts were, the Republican leaders were not so sure that they could count upon a Republican victory. The Grand *The* Old Party, soon generally to be known as the "G. O. P.," *"G. O. P."* was badly torn by dissension. At one extreme (the "right," a later generation would have said) were the "Stalwarts," hard-boiled realists who believed in practical politics and scoffed at reform. At their head was Roscoe Conkling, the able and unscrupulous senior senator from New York. Only a little less conservative were the "Half-Breeds," who regarded James G. Blaine, the "man from Maine," as their leader, and sometimes gave lip-service, although little else, to reform. Indeed, there is reason to suppose that Blaine and Conkling would never have headed separate factions but for the undying personal enmity that existed between them. Years before, when both were members of the national House of Representatives, Blaine had raised a laugh at Conkling's expense by referring to the New Yorker's "haughty disdain, his grandiloquent swell, his majestic, supereminent, overpowering, turkey-gobbler strut." Blaine's description was too apt for a man of Conkling's disposition ever to forgive it, and thereafter the Republican Party was barely large enough to contain them both. In addition to the Stalwarts and the Half-Breeds were many Independents, or reformers, most of whom were more friendly to Blaine than to Conkling, but had very little use for either. For a time the Independents had regarded Hayes as one of them, but the querulous nature of reformers made it impossible for him to please them all, so that in effect the President and his friends constituted a fourth Republican faction. Could a party so divided ever hope to win an election?

The choice of a presidential candidate proved to be difficult enough. Conkling was determined to nominate Grant, and the General, after a triumphant journey around the world, was nothing loath. *Garfield and* But Blaine wished the nomination for himself, and the *Arthur* friends of John Sherman were sure that the Secretary of the Treasury was entitled to the honor on his record. Among the minor contenders were George F. Edmunds of Vermont and Elihu B. Washburne of Illinois. By the time the convention met, Conkling had garnered in enough votes to renominate Grant, if only the unit rule, requiring each state to cast its vote as a solid block for the candidate favored by a majority of the delegation, could be enforced. But the opponents of Grant combined to defeat the unit rule, and on each of the thirty-six ballots taken the General received only a few more than three hundred votes, some seventy short of the necessary majority. While the Grant phalanx could not be broken, the anti-Grant delegates finally united upon a dark-horse candidate, James A. Garfield of Ohio, who had served several terms in the House of Representatives and had just been elected to the United States Senate. Garfield, as the leader of the Sherman forces and a close friend of Blaine's, was eminently satisfactory to the Half-Breeds, so, to appease the Stalwarts, Chester Alan Arthur, Conkling's obedient servant in New York, was chosen for Vice-President. The ticket was as strong as compromise could make it. Even the Independents thought well of Garfield, and many of them gave him cordial support.

The Democrats, quite as badly divided as the Republicans, were less successful in achieving a united front. The northern wing of the party was extremely suspicious, and not a little ashamed, of the *Hancock and* southern wing; and *vice versa*. Moreover, in both sections *English* there was internal strife that dated at least as far back as the Civil War. Northern Democrats who had been loyal to the Union during the war had not yet forgiven the "Copperheads" whose desire for peace had almost led them to support the South. Southern Democrats whose devotion to the party stemmed from the leadership of Andrew Jackson had little use for the ex-Whigs and conservative "Bourbons," who now, under the necessity of maintaining white supremacy, called themselves Democrats and sought to monopolize party leadership. Native Americans generally, of whatever section, regretted the dire necessity of cultivating the immigrant vote, particularly the Irish vote, which in many American cities had become a factor to be reckoned with. So long out of power as to have lost its personality, bereft of intelligent leaders, tainted with treason and with pacifism, the Democratic Party floundered help-lessly through the campaign. Tilden was too old and too ill to be a candidate, and the nomination went, almost by default, to General Win-field S. Hancock of Pennsylvania, who had won distinction as a Union officer at Gettysburg, and had later pleased the South by the way he con-ducted himself as military commander of Louisiana during reconstruc-tion. In politics, however, he was only, as one wag expressed it, "a good man, weighing two hundred and fifty pounds." For Vice-President the Democrats named William H. English of Indiana, a political anachro-nism whose last significant deed had been to promote the admission of Kansas as a slave state during the Buchanan administration. Such a ticket amounted almost to an open confession of political bankruptcy.

As a matter of fact, both parties were completely bankrupt. The issues that divided them were historical merely. The Republican Party *Lack of* had come into existence because of the stand it had taken on *party issues* slavery, and it had lived on because of its determination to free the slaves, to save the Union, and to punish the South. Its program was now finished and its excuse for existence had disappeared. The Democrats, likewise, had so long centered their attention upon the issues of slavery, the Civil War, and reconstruction that they failed to observe that the era in which these issues meant anything had rolled by. The platforms of the two parties in 1880 revealed few real differences of opinion as to policies and no real awareness of the problems that con-fronted the nation. Neither Democrats nor Republicans seemed to sense the significance of the vast transformation that was coming over business, nor the critical nature of the relationship between labor and capital, nor even the necessity of doing something definite about civil service reform, the money problem, and the tariff. The Republican Party existed to oppose the Democratic Party; the Democratic Party ex-isted to oppose the Republican Party. Real issues cut across both parties, and even when recognized, which was rare, had to be evaded or ignored. When the Republican Convention prepared to adopt the customary meaningless platitudes about civil service reform, a delegate from Texas named Flanagan protested in plain language: "What are we up here for?" What, indeed, if not for the offices?

With issues lacking, the campaign turned on personalities. The Republicans, in rejecting the candidacy of General Grant, had freed *Campaign of* themselves of the charge of "Bonapartism." Their nominee *1880* was, to be sure, a Union officer in the Civil War, but he had been, like Hayes, a volunteer officer, and had won distinction in politics rather than in the army. The Democrats, on the other hand, in their effort to shake off the charge of treason, had nominated a professional soldier. If anyone was prepared to play the rôle of "the man on horseback," it was Hancock, not Garfield. Efforts were made to prove that Hancock, whose exploits on the battlefield had won him the sobriquet, "the Superb," was in reality a coward, and that Garfield, whose record was far cleaner than that of most politicians, had been deeply involved in the Crédit Mobilier and other scandals. Neither charge carried much weight. Garfield, as a matter of fact, was satisfactory enough to the reform element in the Republican Party and most Independents gave his candidacy their warm support. The Democratic platform, written by Colonel Henry Watterson of Kentucky, called for "a tariff for revenue only." When the Republicans showed a disposition to press this issue, Hancock declared that it was unimportant because the tariff was a "local affair." For this statement he was roundly ridiculed, but he spoke far more truly than he knew. Tariff rates must be levied by Congress, but they have generally been fixed, item by item, because of some local demand.

Fought with fury, and as if the result would really be important, the campaign settled nothing much except that Garfield, not Hancock, was to be the next President of the United States. The Repub- *Election* lican plurality, out of a total vote amounting to over nine *results* million, was about nine thousand. Neither of the two leading candidates had a majority of all the votes cast, for James B. Weaver of Iowa, the Greenback candidate, polled over three hundred thousand votes. The Republicans, however, won enough local victories to enable them to recapture the Senate, and, although the membership of the House was so evenly divided as to leave its control in doubt until Congress actually met, the Republicans were finally able to organize it also. For the first time in six years the Presidency and both houses of Congress were under the control of a single party.[1]

[1] Two useful studies of Hayes' Secretary of State are C. L. Barrows, *William M. Evarts, Lawyer, Diplomat, Statesman* (1941); and Brainerd Dyer, *The Public Career of William M. Evarts* (1933). L. B. Richardson, *William E. Chandler, Republican* (1940), throws light on elections and politics from the disputed election of 1876 to the end of the century. Ira B. Cross, *A History of the Labor Movement in California* (1935), is confined principally to the Nineteenth Century when the movement was new.

CHAPTER VIII

CAPITAL AND LABOR

WHILE the depression years of the seventies had called a halt to the rapid expansion of industry in the United States, it was only a temporary halt. Indeed, businesses that escaped annihilation were often the better off for the restraints that the depression imposed upon them. In flush times comfortable profits were too easily achieved; in hard times even small profits were won, more than likely, only as the reward of efficiency. In flush times American manufacturers had depended all too exclusively upon the American market; in hard times they sought to adapt their products to the needs of other lands, and began to sell abroad. Solvent organizations bettered their positions by absorbing their weaker rivals, and by devising trade agreements with their stronger rivals to forestall the menace of cut-throat competition. When, at last, the depression was over, business, particularly big business, was in position to begin another era of spectacular expansion.

As had happened before, the railroads led the way in the new development. Sure signs of life appeared as early as 1878 when the Northern *Railroad* Pacific, the misfortunes of which had plunged Jay Cooke and *building* Company into bankruptcy, again prepared to build. Under the leadership of Frederick Billings, a conservative Vermont capitalist, investors were persuaded to put their money once more into Northern Pacific securities, and for three years the westward march of Billings's railroad builders went forward without incident. In 1881, however, Billings's plans came into conflict with those of Henry Villard, a hard-headed German-American whose Oregon Railroad and Navigation Company controlled the railroad and steamboat lines of the Pacific Northwest.[1] Villard had long sought to induce Billings to agree to some traffic arrangement that would prevent competition between the two systems when the Northern Pacific should be finished, but Billings received all

[1] Villard's spectacular career is best followed in his own *Memoirs of Henry Villard* (2 vols., 1904). Also useful are E. V. Smalley, *History of the Northern Pacific Railroad* (1883), and J. B. Hedges, *Henry Villard and the Railways of the Northwest* (1930).

such overtures with cold refusals. Thereupon Villard induced his financial backers in New York to put money into a "blind pool" upon which, for an unrevealed purpose, he might draw at will. With this money he bought up enough stock to secure complete control of both the "N. P." and the "O.R. and N.," and organized a holding company, the Oregon and Transcontinental, through which to manage them. He then deposed Billings as president of the Northern Pacific, took the place for himself, and as president of all three corporations achieved the harmony he desired. On the completion of the Northern Pacific in 1883, by way of celebration he ran a "Golden Spike Special," filled with the most distinguished company of American notables that he could assemble, the entire length of the line.

By this time, however, the American public could no longer be thrilled by news that another transcontinental railroad had been finished. In addition to the Union Pacific, completed in 1869, the South- *The* ern Pacific was now running trains to the western coast. *Transcon-* The Southern Pacific was a California corporation which had *tinentals* shrewdly acquired the right to build within the borders of that state to meet any eastern land-grant railroad. Owned and managed by the same able group that had built the Central Pacific, it had pushed its lines southward through the state, and was prepared to receive all newcomers at Fort Yuma and the Needles, the two points on the border of southern California where the canyon of the Colorado could be crossed. With the aid of territorial charters from Arizona and New Mexico and a state charter from Texas, the Southern Pacific built eastward from Fort Yuma to meet the old Texas Pacific,[1] which it presently absorbed. By January, 1882, it had through trains running over this route from San Francisco to St. Louis, and by February of the next year it had opened up an alternative route through southern Texas to New Orleans. Alert to every opportunity, the Southern Pacific also connected at the Needles with the Atchison, Topeka, and Santa Fe, which had built westward through Kansas on a state land grant, and from Albuquerque to the Needles on the federal grant of the defunct Atlantic and Pacific. Trains were running the entire length of this route shortly after Villard's "Golden Spike Special" made its much-advertised tour. In 1884 the owners of the Southern Pacific, who were now in a position to monopolize the railroad business of the Southwest, followed the example of Villard and created a holding company, the Southern Pacific of Kentucky, through which to administer their extensive properties. The Southern Pacific owned no railroads in Kentucky, but the laws of that state were friendly

¹ See *ante*, p. 78.

to its purposes, while incorporation in a state far removed from the scene of the road's activities seemed likely to reduce to a minimum the danger of investigation and regulation.[1]

Other western railroads extended their lines during these years with the same feverish speed. The Burlington, the Rock Island, the Northwestern, and the Missouri Pacific competed with the transcontinentals and their branches for the exploitation of the Great Plains. The Denver and Rio Grande built heroically around the Colorado mountains, by way of the Royal Gorge of the Arkansas, to connect with the Union Pacific at Ogden. James J. Hill of Minnesota advanced the fortunes of the St. Paul, Minneapolis and Manitoba slowly but surely until by the time the next panic broke, in 1893, it had become, under a new name, the Great Northern, another transcontinental. North of the United States, in Canada, Donald A. Smith, later known as Lord Strathcona and Mount Royal, brought the Canadian Pacific to completion in 1885, while south of the United States, in Mexico, the Mexican Central, an affiliate of the Santa Fe, had reached Mexico City the year before.

While the most spectacular railroad activities of the period occurred in the trans-Mississippi West, the southern and eastern roads were by *Southern* no means idle. In the South the Richmond and West Point *and eastern* Terminal Railway and Warehouse Company, a holding com- *roads* pany formed in 1881, laid the foundations for what later became the Southern Railway system. In the East the great systems that had taken form before the Civil War — the New York Central, the Pennsylvania, the Erie, and the Baltimore and Ohio — built or acquired branch lines, consolidated their holdings, and, when well-managed, made money. Everywhere the substitution of steel for iron rails, together with an equally revolutionary improvement of rolling stock and equipment, called for enormous expenditures, funds for which, in spite of much cut-throat competition, the railroads somehow managed to find. Because of these expensive innovations, statistics on mileage fail to give a complete picture of the railroad development of the period. Nevertheless the statistics are impressive. From 52,000 miles of railroad in 1870 the total mileage in the United States had risen by 1880 to 93,000 and by 1890 to 163,000 — an increase of 70,000 miles in ten years. Construction more than kept pace with the expansion of population. In 1870 the United States had 1380 miles of railroad per million inhabitants; in 1880 it had 1858 miles, and in 1890 it had 2625 miles. By the last-mentioned date the main outlines of the American railroad map were complete; after that date the mileage continued to increase, but such new tracks as were laid

---

[1] Stuart Daggett, *Chapters on the History of the Southern Pacific* (1922).

WESTERN RAILROADS
1930

WESTERN RAILROADS
1880

GROWTH OF THE WESTERN RAILROADS

served mainly as feeders for existing lines. The age of railroad pioneering was over.

Typical of the railroad builders was James J. Hill (1838–1916), the creator of the Great Northern. Hill was born in a log cabin near Rock-*James J.* wood, Ontario, the third child of a hard-working Scotch-*Hill* Irish farm couple. His father died when James was only fourteen, and the boy quit school to go to work in a village store. Four years of this was enough, and at eighteen the lad made his way to St. Paul, Minnesota, then a town of only four or five thousand, to grow up with the new country. He was not slow to see that the future of the Northwest was intimately bound up with transportation, and the opening in the early sixties of a ten-mile stretch of railroad between St. Paul and Minneapolis fired his imagination. Successful, seemingly, at everything he undertook, he soon had a contract to supply the rapidly growing "St. Paul and Pacific" with the fuel for its wood-burning engines, and he took advantage of the opportunity to find out more about the affairs of the road than most of its officials ever knew. Overexpanded in its haste to acquire title to a land grant, and in chronic trouble with the stronger Northern Pacific, the St. Paul and Pacific went into bankruptcy when the panic broke in 1873. For years its later-built portions were described as "Two streaks of rust and a right of way," but in 1878 Hill and three associates, including Donald A. Smith, with borrowed money bought themselves into its control. Reorganized as the St. Paul, Minneapolis, and Manitoba, Hill soon had the road earning good profits out of the rich trade of the Red River Valley. Unlike some railroad builders, he was not interested primarily in acquiring a land grant or making money out of road construction. What he hoped to do was to build up the country as he advanced his lines so that the settlers would support the road through the business they made for it. Time proved that his faith in the future of the Northwest was justified. Within fifteen years after he assumed its management, his little local road had been transformed into the Great Northern system, with lines that really reached the Pacific, and an income that had made its builder rich.[1]

The creation of these great railroad systems was not usually accomplished without the elimination of a multitude of lesser lines. Back in *Railway* the pre-Civil War era more or less accidental connections had *consolida-* played a considerable part in railroad consolidation. In *tions* this way the work of Cornelius Vanderbilt in welding together the New York Central had been greatly facilitated. Panics and periods of depression had also done their bit. During the years following

[1] J. G. Pyle, *The Life of James J. Hill* (2 vols., 1917), is an appreciative biography.

1857, and even more after 1873, the weaker roads had gone into bankruptcy only to emerge as parts of some stronger, and usually much larger, system. During the depression years of the seventies no less than four hundred and fifty railroads, fully two fifths of the roads of the country, had suffered this experience. The holding company idea, well exemplified by the Oregon and Transcontinental in the Northwest, the Southern Pacific of Kentucky in the Southwest, and the Richmond Terminal Company in the South, also greatly facilitated consolidation. Great sectional systems were thus created that could monopolize the business of the region they covered. Within these areas competition was stifled, and only the interposition of governmental authority could prevent railroad monopolies from charging for their services "all the traffic would bear." [1]

Competing systems, however, could not always be united, and wherever competition existed it tended to become both ruthless and costly. Rebates were given to favored shippers, particularly to those who shipped large quantities of goods long distances. Regions or cities that were served by more than one railroad were granted cut rates, while those dependent upon the services of a single road were overcharged in an effort to make up the losses from the competing rates. More was charged for a short haul where there was no competition than for a longer haul over the same line when competition between the terminal points existed. Efforts on the part of the roads to eliminate competition usually came to nought. Sometimes competing roads, after a disastrous "rate war," made rate agreements, but the temptation to break such self-imposed promises when to do so meant good profits was always more than some managers could resist. Pools were tried through which a common treasurer collected all earnings and paid out profits according to a ratio agreed upon, but these, too, led mainly to wrangling and non-observance. From the railroad point of view consolidation into large non-competitive systems seemed the only ideal solution.

Public criticism of the railroads, common during Granger times, had diminished somewhat during the later seventies. For a time, perhaps, there was less to criticize. Railroad managers, remembering *Criticisms of* the effective protests of the Grangers, took care when they *the railroads* could do so not to revive them. Even more to the point, many of the worst of the railroad offenses were associated primarily with a period of expansion, whereas contraction, not expansion, had been the watchword of the depression. During the eighties, with an unprecedented amount

[1] C. F. Adams, Jr., *Railroads: Their Origin and Problems* (new edition, 1893), is the work of an acute contemporary, and is still valuable.

of railroad building going on, most of the old abuses reappeared, and with them a new wave of protests. The way in which the railroads, as corporations, enjoyed privileges not accorded to the ordinary individual came in for heated denunciations. Their charters, obtained by fair means or foul, endowed the fortunate possessors with "eternal life," and yet gave them rights and privileges before the law designed originally for natural persons whose life-span was limited. By right of eminent domain a road might take whatever land it wanted, and pay a price for it that to the dispossessed owner seemed unfair and inadequate. Special privileges of taxation enabled the roads to be taxed only on their gross or net earnings, whereas the ordinary individual had to pay taxes on whatever property he possessed, whether it brought him an income or not. Railroads went into politics, determined who should and who should not be nominated to office, and by distributing free passes to legislators, governors, judges, and other office-holders put all those who had authority to restrain them in their debt.

Critics of the railroads could multiply their charges at will. Communities in dire need of a railroad connection were forced to subscribe heavy subsidies under threat of being left off a projected line. When the railroad came, the outraged citizens found themselves obliged to pay a double tribute — high taxes because of the subsidy they had voted, and high rates because the railroad now had them at its mercy. Western railroads, thanks to the land-grant policy of the United States government, were usually the owners of great tracts of land that otherwise might have been available for settlers to take as homesteads. Thus the charge of land monopoly could be hurled. Stock-watering and stock-manipulation were the rule rather than the exception, and most railroads, in addition to paying dividends on a capitalization far in excess of their value, were also bonded for all they were worth. High freight and passenger rates to keep such overcapitalized, debt-ridden structures from collapse could not be avoided. Graft and dishonesty in railroad administration were all too common. Printed schedules of rates were deliberately kept out of shippers' hands so that rebates and other special favors might the more easily be granted favored shippers. Small stockholders were "frozen out" when large stockholders found such an operation to their advantage. Roads were built — often roads that were not needed — for the benefit of the contractors, who presently unloaded a bankrupt company upon unsuspecting stockholders and unappreciative communities.[1]

[1] Among the many books on railroad history the following may be noted: E. R. Johnson, *American Railway Transportation* (1912); Slason Thompson, *A Short History of American Railways* (1925); L. H. Haney, *A Congressional History of Railways in the United States, 1850–1887* (2 vols., 1908–10).

The Granger movement had called attention to many such grievances, and had led to the creation in most of the states of governmental commissions for the regulation of the railroads. These com- *Railroad* missions, ill-informed as to the problems that confronted *regulation* them, and often subservient to the corporations they were supposed to regulate, accomplished comparatively little. Knowledge, to be sure, came with the years, but it added nothing to the effectiveness of state regulation; by the time a railroad was large enough to need regulation, it was too large for a state commission to regulate it. Local intrastate roads that the commissions could handle were being quietly absorbed into powerful interstate systems that were beyond them. "The number of separate railroad companies operating distinct roads in Minnesota was as high as twenty, three years ago," wrote a perplexed Minnesota commissioner in 1881. "Now the number is reduced to substantially one third that number." Other state commissions reported the same trend toward consolidation, and the census of 1880 proclaimed it eloquently. While, according to the Granger decisions, the regulatory authority of a state did not necessarily stop at the state's borders, the fact of the matter was that increasingly it did. Finally, in 1886, the Supreme Court of the United States admitted the inadvisability of its earlier ruling, and in a case involving the Wabash Railroad and the State of Illinois held in effect that Congress alone had authority to regulate interstate commerce.

Meantime one investigating committee after another had studied the railroad problem. As far back as Granger times a Senate committee, headed by William Windom of Minnesota, had urged that *Investiga-* a federal bureau of commerce be created, and twice during *tions* the seventies the national House of Representatives had passed bills to that effect. Another of Windom's proposals, that trunk lines should be built by the government to compete with private lines, and so reduce rates, won less approval. In 1879 the Hepburn committee in New York State submitted a wealth of evidence on the misconduct of the railroads, and inferentially pointed to national regulation as the proper way out. In 1885, after both the House and the Senate had passed measures looking toward railroad regulation, but had failed to agree on details, the Senate appointed a new investigating committee with a larger range of powers than had been accorded the Windom committee. Headed by Shelby M. Cullom of Illinois, this committee traveled widely and investigated carefully the regulatory efforts of the state commissions. It reported in 1886 that three fourths of the railroad business of the country was interstate in character, hence, under the rule of law laid down in the

Wabash decision, beyond the control of state regulation.[1] Four possible methods of dealing with the situation were listed: (1) the continuance of private ownership and management, but with more effective governmental regulation; (2) government ownership and management; (3) government ownership and private management under public regulations; and (4) government ownership and management in competition with private companies. Noting the widespread opposition throughout the country to government ownership, the committee recommended regulation by the national government as the preferable alternative.

Congress was now ready to act, and in 1887 it established an Interstate Commerce Commission to consist of five members, of whom not *The I.C.C.* more than three might belong to the same political party, to be appointed by the President for six-year terms. The law forbade most of the evil practices uncovered by the various investigating committees, and in a sense made national the current trends in state regulation. Rebates, pools, and discriminations were branded as illegal, and the rule that more could not be charged for a short haul than for a longer one over the same line was established. The commission was authorized to investigate complaints against the railroads, and to make decisions which, however, it could enforce only through court action. This provision for a judicial review of its rulings proved to be the undoing of the early commission. Although headed by an eminent ex-judge, Thomas M. Cooley of Michigan, it failed to obtain the judicial backing through which, alone, its decisions could be made effective. Delays and reversals permitted the railroads to operate about as they had operated before. Not until the Presidency of Theodore Roosevelt did the Interstate Commerce Commission become a really effective body.[2]

The trend toward consolidation, so evident in the history of the railroads, was equally apparent elsewhere in the business world. This was due in large part to the transportation revolution that the completion of the railroad system had worked, but a number of other newly devised means of communication were available by the eighties that facilitated almost as much as the railroads themselves the operation of large business units. One of these was the electric telegraph, used for years before the Civil War, but now extended to parallel every railroad right of way and to serve practically every hamlet in the nation. Cable service also had steadily improved. The first transoceanic cable, laid in 1858, had

[1] An immense amount of miscellaneous information is contained in the report of the Cullom committee, Forty-Ninth Congress, first session, *Senate Report*, number 46 (serial 2356).

[2] The two treatises by W. Z. Ripley, *Railroads: Rates and Regulation* (1912), and *Railroads: Finance and Organization* (1915), best cover these subjects.

soon been destroyed by the use of too strong electric currents, but by 1866, through the persistent labors of Cyrus W. Field, a better one had been laid, and soon thereafter many others. American businessmen were thus able to keep in as close touch with London as with New York quotations, and to make their plans with a fuller knowledge of world affairs than had ever been possible before.

Of incalculable importance also was the telephone, the invention of Alexander Graham Bell, an American Scot who taught deaf mutes, and had interested himself in acoustics. At the Centennial *The* Exposition of 1876 Bell exhibited his instruments, and made *telephone* a deep impression on the American public. He was not the first to study the problem of transmitting human speech by electricity, nor the only one to find a solution, but he did develop the first practicable telephone.[1] Even so, it was not easy to induce capital to invest in so fantastic an enterprise, and the successful launching of the telephone owed much to the organizing genius of Theodore N. Vail, later president of the American Telephone and Telegraph Company. During the eighties telephone systems were introduced into virtually every American city, and by the end of the decade no less than 440,000 instruments were in use. Well before the turn of the century successful long-distance connections had been generally established.

The significance of the telephone in the business world can hardly be overestimated. Among other things, it enabled business executives to keep in close touch with a veritable army of subordinates, and thus tremendously facilitated the process of consolidation. A natural monopoly, it soon furnished in its own tightly woven business organization an example that other businesses strove earnestly to follow. Incidentally, it provided at its switchboards a new occupation for women, and through its rural extensions another effective weapon against social isolation.

The telephone was only one of the many new uses which electricity was being made to serve. Wizard of electrical inventors was Thomas A. Edison (1847–1931), an Ohioan by birth whose formal schooling had been limited to three months, but whose natural ingenuity has probably never been surpassed. At fifteen he had learned to send and receive telegraph messages, but his fondness for experimentation doomed him to frequent dismissals by irritated employers. In 1879 he made his first really revolutionary invention, a practicable incandescent light. Others had already devised the arc light, which served well enough for street-

[1] H. N. Casson, *The History of the Telephone* (1910); Catherine Mackenzie. *Alexander Graham Bell, the Man Who Contracted Space* (1928).

lighting, but was wholly unsatisfactory for indoor use. By January, 1880, Edison had taken out a patent on his light bulb, which before long he was able to manufacture, in quantities for commercial use, at a factory in Harrison, New Jersey. Improvements in generators followed, and soon business houses and even dwellings were depending for illumination on the new device. The next need was for central electric power stations, an opportunity for business expansion so fully appreciated that the number of such stations increased from eight in 1881 to 2774 in 1898.[1] While Edison, with his numerous inventions, including among others the phonograph, motion pictures, automatic telegraphy, the stock-ticker, and the microphone, ranks as the leading electrical engineer of his time, he was by no means the only one. Soon electric railway systems were banishing horse cars from the city streets, electric elevators were adding innumerable stories to the height of skyscrapers, and electric power was being used to turn a larger and larger proportion of the wheels of industry.

The typewriter met another business need. Its inventor was a Milwaukee printer, Charles Latham Sholes, who as early as 1867 had devised *The* a machine that would write with fair rapidity. Fortu-*typewriter* nately, a letter written on one of Sholes's typewriters fell into the hands of James Densmore, a Pennsylvania businessman, and led him to come to the aid of the inventor with money and ideas. Within a decade the collaborators had sufficiently perfected their machine that it was finding its way into business offices, and within another decade it had become a business necessity. Sholes's machine, which was first manufactured commercially by the firm of E. Remington and Son, had many imitators, and by the end of the century nearly a hundred different models were on the market. Like the telephone, the typewriter provided a new gainful occupation for women. Women operators, it transpired, were not only quite as efficient as men, but they could also be hired for less. Soon it was generally assumed that the noun stenographer was feminine gender, and that it referred to any member of the vast army of young women whose skill at shorthand and typewriting made their services indispensable to the smooth functioning of business offices.

A number of other circumstances promoted also the widening of busi-*Nation-wide* ness horizons. Advertising took on new life with the inven-*advertising* tion of the half-tone process, through which the image recorded by the camera could be inexpensively transferred to print paper.

---

[1] Ida M. Tarbell, *The Nationalizing of Business, 1878–1898* (1936), reviews admirably these and similar transformations. On Edison himself see F. L. Dyer and T. C. Martin *Edison, His Life and Inventions* (1929).

Improvements in photography served the same useful end. The cost of job printing was reduced by the invention of the linotype and the monotype, and at the same time the quality was greatly improved.[1] Meantime the United States Post-Office, regardless of deficits, cheapened its rates, and amplified its service. Railroad extensions were followed everywhere by postal extensions. Mail delivery at the door was inaugurated in a few American cities as early as 1871, and thereafter was rapidly bestowed upon smaller and smaller communities. Catalogues and printed circulars were accorded special rates to facilitate general distribution. The penny postal card, introduced into the United States from Europe in 1873, brought the cost of personal mail service to an irreducible minimum; but the two-cent letter rate, inaugurated in 1883, was not far behind.

It is not difficult to see why business, with all these aids, became increasingly national rather than local in scope. With nation-wide competition at work only the ablest, the most selfish, and the *Tendencies* most unscrupulous of the competitors could survive. Great *toward* producers tended to become the cheapest producers, and *monopoly* little companies tended to disappear. Close observers of business trends during the eighties noted that the current formula of business evolution called for a greatly increased output from a steadily diminishing number of plants. In 1880, for example, the nation had 1990 woolen mills, in 1890, only 1311; in 1880 it had 1934 factories that made agricultural implements, in 1890, only 910. During the same decade the number of iron and steel mills decreased by one third, and the number of leather establishments by three fourths. In every case, however, the total capital investment and the total output of the industry had vastly increased, while ownership, or at least management, had been concentrated far more rapidly than even the reduced number of plants would indicate. What the nation was witnessing was the emergence of a large number of near-monopolies, each of which aspired to the complete control of some important national necessity.[2]

Public awareness of the situation began with the appearance of an article, "The Story of a Great Monopoly," by Henry Demarest Lloyd, in the *Atlantic Monthly* for March, 1881. Lloyd's article was a scathing

---

[1] Ottmar Mergenthaler, a naturalized American of German birth, invented the linotype in 1885, and Talbot Lanston, a clerk in the Pension Office in Washington, D.C., invented the monotype in 1887. On the general subject of inventions two short treatises are available: Holland Thompson, *The Age of Invention* (1921); and George Iles, *Leading American Inventors* (1912).

[2] J. W. Jenks and W. E. Clark, *The Trust Problem* (new edition, 1929). Other interesting surveys are Burton J. Hendrick, *The Age of Big Business* (1920), and John Moody, *The Masters of Capital* (1921).

attack on the Standard Oil Company, and the deep impression it made was fully attested by the fact that that particular number of the *Atlantic* sold out seven editions. John D. Rockefeller, the guiding genius of Standard Oil, had planned monopoly from the start. The first important step toward this goal, control of the oil-refining business of Cleveland, Ohio, he had accomplished by the time the Panic of 1873 broke. This gave him perhaps one third of the oil-refining business of the country, and undismayed by the depression he set out to get the rest. Skillful at obtaining financial backing, and always equipped with a large cash balance of his own, he bought up whatever refineries would sell, induced others to join forces with him, and drove still others out of business. By the time the depression was over, the Rockefeller interests, with control over all the greatest refineries in New York, Philadelphia, Pittsburgh, Baltimore, and Titusville, had approximated the complete monopoly their leader had sought.[1]

Rockefeller's ruthless methods left him a rich legacy of hatred. The railroads, hard-pressed for business during the depression, had little *The Standard Oil Company* choice but to give him the rebates he demanded. Shippers less favored either were ruined by the unfair competition or sold out to Standard Oil. When it came to the marketing of oil, Rockefeller gave no quarter. The United States was divided up into convenient sections, each with its agent and subagents, with every agent under instructions to "sell all the oil that is sold in your district." Agents who succeeded in this undertaking were rewarded with higher salaries and promotions; agents who failed were summarily dismissed. Railroad records were spied upon by Standard Oil men so that the business of competitive refineries could be stolen. Price-cutting was carried to any extreme necessary to put a competitor out of business, and as soon as his defeat was assured the price of oil was set again at a figure as high as or higher than before the price-war began. Pipeline companies that carried the crude oil to railway centers, and even hundreds of miles to the refineries, were gathered up by Standard Oil, one by one, usually at its own price. Determined to pay no man profits, Rockefeller built terminal warehouses of his own, established factories to make barrels and other necessary articles, and eliminated hundreds of wholesalers and middlemen. Finally, in order to facilitate centralized control and to insure against unintentional competition among the various Standard properties, the Standard Oil Trust was formed. This device, first adopted in 1879, but revised and more completely applied in 1882, con-

[1] J. T. Flynn, *God's Gold; the Story of Rockefeller and His Times* (1932), is exciting and colorful.

sisted merely of a group of nine trustees to whom was surrendered all the stock of the Standard Oil Company and its various affiliates. Trust certificates were then issued to each Standard stockholder in the proportion of twenty trust certificates for each share of Standard stock. For several years the nine trustees, with John D. Rockefeller at their head, made the decisions for all of the stockholders and all of the companies that were dominated by Standard Oil.

"This is the original trust," declared a New York committee that in 1888 began the investigation of Standard Oil. "Its success has been the incentive to the formation of all other trusts or combina- *The "trusts"* tions. It is the type of a system which has spread like a disease through the commercial system of this country." What the committee charged was fully borne out by the facts. One after another "an incredible number of the necessaries and luxuries of life, from meat to tombstones," had fallen into the hands of some tightly organized little group that frequently only by the most unscrupulous and underhand methods had achieved control. Sugar, salt, whiskey, matches, crackers, lead, cottonseed oil, linseed oil, wire and nails, agricultural machinery, electrical supplies, and a host of other items could be obtained only by paying tribute to some such trust or combine. The exact pattern of the Standard Oil Trust was not always followed, but the results were generally about the same. Sometimes the possession of exclusive patent rights promoted the cause of monopoly, and thus made of the liberal patent laws of the United States a kind of subsidy to big business.[1]

The evils of the "trusts," as the public without much discrimination described all big businesses, became increasingly apparent. Prices were fixed without benefit of competition, and sometimes at higher levels than before the trust was formed. Raw producers were compelled to take what the trust chose to pay, for there was no one else to whom to sell. Labor was forced into line by the closing of troublesome plants, and by the circulation of "blacklists" that made it difficult for agitators to obtain employment. Politicians were influenced by free passes from the railroads, by campaign contributions, and by outright bribes. Oliver H. Payne, treasurer of the Standard Oil Company, was reputed to have spent one hundred thousand dollars to secure the election of his father, H. B. Payne, to the United States Senate in 1886. Powerful lobbies appeared in Washington and in the several state capitals charged with the duty of winning favors from lawmakers and law-enforcers. The Washington lobbyists were sometimes described as the "third house" of

---

[1] An admirable history of a developing "big business" is W. T. Hutchinson, *Cyrus Hall McCormick: Harvest, 1856–1884* (1935).

Congress. Plants that experience had shown to be well located were enlarged, and others less ideally situated were closed down, without regard to the inevitable unemployment involved or the municipal problems that arose from the concentration of vast numbers of people at whatever centers business leaders deemed strategic. Individual freedom suffered blow after blow as the owners of small establishments became the employees of larger ones, and as the chance to enter business independently grew less and less. Employees were pushed farther and farther from the sight and hearing of employers, and fewer occasions existed for emotions of the "heart" to influence the conduct of businessmen who prided themselves upon their "hard-headedness."

And yet the "trusts" were by no means without their good points. Much of the competition that they eliminated was sheer waste, and with-*Advantages of the trusts* out it prices could be, and often were, reduced. Large-scale businesses were usually far more efficient than the small concerns they supplanted, and were able to make money out of by-products that the smaller operators were forced to throw away. The packers, for example, claimed that they paid more for a live steer than they received for the dressed meat it yielded. Their profits came from the use they made of horns, hoofs, and other materials that the local slaughter-house wasted. Big business could afford to take heavy initial losses while waiting for ultimate profits. It could bear the cost of advertising and of the slow enlargement of markets. Usually, too, it was better managed, better located, better equipped. Small establishments could not so easily afford to scrap expensive machinery because new inventions made better equipment possible. They could not compete with big businesses in paying salaries to the ablest managers. Even without the cut-throat competition to which they were subjected, many of them would have lost out anyway because of their inefficiency.[1]

As public awareness of the trust problem grew, an insistent demand set in that something should be done about it. This meant, to most *Legal status of the trusts* Americans, that the government should take action against the trusts, but unfortunately governmental action under the existing system was not easily attainable. The Constitution gave the central government only definitely specified powers, and left all others to the states. Since the "founding fathers" had never heard of a trust, the only power to control such organizations that they had lodged with the central government was whatever might be inferred from the right to control interstate commerce. Obviously, the extent to which

[1] John Moody, *The Truth About the Trusts* (1904); W. Z. Ripley, *Trusts, Pools, and Corporations* (new edition, 1916); Eliot Jones, *The Trust Problem in the United States* (1921).

any such implied power might be exercised would have to be determined by the courts after extensive litigation. The states, on the other hand, had ample power within their several jurisdictions, but their boundaries were too small, for the activities of any important trust extended through many states. Moreover, the requirement of the national Constitution that each state must give "full faith and credit... to the public acts, records, and judicial proceedings of every other state" had embarrassing possibilities. Under the terms of this clause special favors obtained in one state might easily be interpreted to mean special favors in every state. Another constitutional advantage enjoyed by corporations flowed from the Fourteenth Amendment which required that the states might not "deprive any person of life, liberty, or property, without due process of law." In 1886 the Supreme Court, reversing an earlier ruling, held that the use of the word person in this clause was meant to apply to corporations as well as to individuals.[1] Thus the states, themselves the creators of the corporations, were restrained by the federal government from any measures of taxation or regulation that the courts chose to regard as depriving the corporations of property "without due process of law."

Attempts to restrain the trusts were made nevertheless. Just as the Grangers had invoked to good advantage the old rule of common law that a common carrier was subject to regulation because it was quasi-public in nature, so now the states fell back upon the common-law prohibition of conspiracy in restraint of *The Sherman Anti-Trust Act* trade. During the later eighties state after state passed statutes based on this principle. Finally, Congress also fell into line, and on July 2, 1890, the Sherman Anti-Trust Act received the President's signature. This measure, named after Senator Sherman, for no other reason, according to Senator Hoar, "except that Mr. Sherman had nothing to do with framing it whatever," lacked nothing in vigor of language. It branded as illegal "every contract, combination in the form of trust or otherwise, or conspiracy in restraint of trade or commerce among the several states, or with foreign nations." It defined as a misdemeanor any "attempt to monopolize, or combine or conspire with any other person or persons to monopolize, any part of the trade or commerce among the several states or with foreign nations." Penalties for persons held guilty of violating the act were set at a fine not to exceed five thousand dollars, and imprisonment not to exceed a year, one or both, as the court might pre-

---

[1] *Santa Clara County vs. Southern Pacific Railroad*, 118 United States Reports, 396. W. P. Webb, *Divided We Stand* (1937), vigorously attacks this extension to corporations of immunities intended, as he believes, only for individuals.

scribe. Furthermore, any person injured by means that the act declared unlawful might recover in court "threefold the damages by him sustained."

Enforcement of these acts was quite another matter. A number of suits were lodged by the states, and a few decisions unfavorable to the *Difficulties in* corporations were obtained. In New York State, for ex-*enforcement* ample, the North River Sugar Refining Company, a part of the sugar trust, lost its charter; and in Ohio, the Standard Oil Company was held guilty of attempting "to establish a virtual monopoly." Since the technical trust was so clear-cut a violation of both the common law and the statutes, that type of organization was generally discontinued, but in its place new devices to accomplish the same end were speedily invented. Chief among these was the holding company, through which a controlling fraction of the stocks in a great number of enterprises were owned and voted by a single corporation, but many of the trusts chose instead to incorporate as a single great company in the most friendly state they could find. As for the Sherman Anti-Trust Act, for all its brave language, it proved to be unenforceable. Seven out of the first eight attempts to invoke its penalties went against the government, and in the Knight case (1895) the Supreme Court of the United States held that the mere purchase of property, even if it made for monopoly and the restraint of trade, was not in itself illegal; further, that manufacture and production (in this case the refining of sugar) were no part of interstate commerce. Confronted by this rebuff, the government made little further effort to enforce the Sherman Act, and lawyers felt free to advise their clients that the Supreme Court of the United States had conceded the legality of private monopoly.

The increasing concentration of capital that characterized the eighties was accompanied by a steady growth in labor organization. This de-*Labor* velopment was well-nigh inevitable. As the corporations *organization* grew in size and strength, the bargaining power of the individual laborer became correspondingly less effective. Concentration gave the employer greater power to oppress, whether by way of low wages, long hours, or bad working conditions. But concentration meant also a diminishing number of employers, and a proportionately larger number of employees. By acting together and bargaining collectively laborers might hope to protect themselves against undue exploitation. This they attempted to do by means of more and stronger trade unions, but even more significantly, by efforts to unite all laborers, of whatever crafts, under one leadership.[1]

[1] Selig Perlman, *A History of Trade Unionism in the United States* (1922), is compact

The National Labor Union, formed in August, 1866, by fifty trade-union representatives, was intended to serve this purpose. It was built upon the federative principle, and included among its affiliates a motley array of organizations, some of which could hardly be regarded as labor unions. It held seven annual congresses, and advocated such important reforms as the eight-hour day, the use of arbitration in labor disputes, the establishment of profit-sharing co-operatives, and the improvement of factory laws. By 1868 it claimed to represent through its member unions a total of 640,000 workers. Numerous flirtations with reforms that were not directly the concern of labor brought the organization to an untimely end. Its leaders showed interest, at one time or another, in women's rights, civil service reform, money inflation, and even the repudiation of the national debt. Half converted to socialist doctrines and intent on separate political action, they backed the abortive Labor Reform Party of 1872, only to be thoroughly discredited by its dismal failure. What little was left of the National Labor Union after this fiasco disappeared with the advent of hard times.

The Noble Order of the Knights of Labor had a more distinguished history. This organization was founded in 1869 by Uriah S. Stephens, a Philadelphia garment-cutter, who provided it with a *The Knights* secret ritual, a password, and a grip. Since the name of the *of Labor* order was at first represented in public notices by five asterisks, it was long known to the uninitiated as "the five stars." Unlike its predecessor, the Knights of Labor built directly upon the individual, rather than upon existing trade unions. "One big union," to which all workers, skilled or unskilled, should belong, was the ideal; indeed, practically anyone, regardless of race, color, or occupation, could become a "Knight." Under these circumstances members of the more exclusive trade unions, who took pride in their craft skills, tended to hold aloof, and for a decade the growth of the Knights was only moderate. After 1878, however, when Terence V. Powderly (1849–1924) of Scranton, Pennsylvania, became its "Grand Master Workman," the order took on new life.[1] Powderly, as his name would indicate, was of Irish origin, but he was a native American, not an immigrant, born in Carbondale, Pennsylvania. At thirteen years of age he joined the ranks of labor as a switch-tender; later as a Scranton machinist he took so prominent a part in the work of the Machinists' and Blacksmiths' Union that he not only lost his job,

and dependable. Also useful are Mary R. Beard, *The American Labor Movement: A Short History* (1924), and S. P. Orth, *The Armies of Labor* (1919).

[1] Terence V. Powderly, *Thirty Years of Labor* (1889), recounts the history of the Knights of Labor, as does also somewhat more objectively, N. J. Ware, *The Labor Movement in the United States, 1860–1895* (1929).

but also won a place for his name on an employers' blacklist. This happened in 1873, after which he worked for a time in Ohio and western Pennsylvania, but on returning to Scranton won election as mayor of the city in 1878 on the Greenback-Labor ticket. When later a meeting was held at Reading, Pennsylvania, to reorganize the Knights, Powderly dominated the proceedings, and for the next fifteen years his name and the Knights of Labor were almost synonymous terms. Secrecy was done away with, the name of the order was publicly proclaimed, and Powderly, with only the barest apology of a salary, traveled at his own expense wherever he felt he could gain more recruits for the Knights. From a membership of only 28,000 in 1880 the organization shot forward to 52,000 in 1883, 104,000 in 1885, and perhaps as many as 700,000 by 1886.

The ideals of the Knights were by no means new. They believed, with Edmund Burke, that "When bad men combine, the good must associate, else they will fall, one by one, an unpitied sacrifice in a contemptible struggle." Like the National Labor Union they favored the eight-hour day, the "establishment of co-operative institutions productive and distributive," the use of arbitration as a substitute for strikes, and such legal innovations as were calculated to improve the status of labor. Powderly saw especial virtue in the co-operative idea, and under his urging not less than one hundred and thirty-five such ventures were undertaken, some of which for a time seemed destined to endure. But bad management, internal dissensions, insufficient funds, and cutthroat competition accounted for the undoing of most of them. Labor co-operatives proved to be no less difficult to inaugurate than farmer co-operatives.

In spite of their insistence upon arbitration the Knights became embroiled in a series of violent strikes. In 1884 a business recession set in, accompanied by the inevitable increase in unemployment and in labor unrest. Companies that took advantage of the opportunity to discharge union men, particularly Knights, were sometimes fought successfully by boycotts, but the chief weapon of labor proved to be the strike. By use of it, for example, the Missouri Pacific, early in 1885, was forced to restore a wage-cut made without warning and without even the excuse of declining earnings. Public sympathy was almost unanimously with the strikers, and the company in yielding felt obliged to grant its employees time and one half for overtime, something the strikers had not even asked. In many minor instances during the middle eighties the Knights helped to win such victories.

Sometimes, however, the outcome was far different. In March, 1886, when a foreman in the Texas and Pacific car shops at Marshall, Texas, was dismissed apparently because he was a member of the Knights of Labor, another important strike occurred. Under the *Strikes of 1886* leadership of Martin Irons, some nine thousand shopmen employed on the Gould system (of which the Texas and Pacific was a part) quit work, and attempted by sabotage to make all freight-hauling locomotives unfit for duty. So successful were their efforts that along five thousand miles of railroad in the Southwest freight traffic was at a standstill; only passenger trains carrying United States mails were permitted to move. At first popular hatred for Jay Gould worked in favor of the strikers, but when food shortages began to be felt and factories had to close down for lack of coal, the public had had strike enough. Four state governors, strongly backed by public opinion, ordered the strikers to cease interfering with trains, and Powderly himself, hoping for arbitration, intervened to call a temporary halt. When Gould refused to arbitrate, the strike was resumed with renewed violence, but the public was now so definitely against the strikers that their cause was soon lost.

Excitement over the southwestern railroad strike had scarcely subsided when the May Day strikes of 1886 claimed the attention of the country.[1] The purpose of these strikes, in which perhaps *The Haymarket riot* 340,000 men participated, was to promote the cause of the eight-hour day. Although the claim was made that half the strikers won a reduced work day, an episode that occurred in Chicago, the storm-center of the strike, gave organized labor the most severe set-back it had yet received. Chicago happened to be the headquarters of a small group of foreign-born anarchists who welcomed the opportunity to expound to the strikers, both orally and in print, their principal tenet, the abolition of the state. To promote this end they were ready to advocate, although far less ready to perform, deeds of violence and terror. On the afternoon of May 3, August Spies, anarchist editor of the *Arbeiter Zeitung*, was addressing a meeting of strikers and strike sympathizers on a vacant lot not far from the McCormick Harvester Works, when the police attempted to disperse the assembly. In the ensuing mêlée several strikers were killed, and about twenty were wounded. That night a circular, printed in English and German, called lustily for "Revenge! Revenge! Workmen to arms!" Next day many meetings of protest occurred, the most notable being set for the evening at Haymarket Square, where a crowd of fifteen hundred assembled to listen to speeches by three leading anarchists. Although the crowd was orderly, the police again appeared

---

[1] Samuel Yellen, *American Labor Struggles* (1936), covers all the important strikes after the Civil War.

and attempted to disperse it. This time, however, the officers of the law were met with a bomb that exploded with terrific violence, killing one policeman and wounding many more. Hard fighting followed, and when the casualties were reckoned it was found that of the policemen seven had lost their lives and over sixty had been seriously wounded, while of the civilians, four were dead and about fifty wounded.

The feeling of blind rage with which the public reacted to the "Haymarket riot" demanded victims. Efforts to find the guilty culprits, however, proved singularly unavailing. "For days," wrote one observer, "the police stations were filled with suspected persons, rigorously examined in the method of the third degree; persons for the most part that had no knowledge of the bomb nor of the meeting, nor of anything connected with either, and could not have." At length, for lack of better scapegoats, eight well-known anarchists, including Spies, were marked for trial. Evidence that any one of the eight had had anything to do either with the making or the throwing of the bomb was never produced, but seven of the men were given death sentences, and the eighth, imprisonment for fifteen years. The convictions were made on the assumption that these men, by advocating violence, had influenced some unknown person to throw the bomb, but this was merely an assumption utterly unbuttressed by evidence. It was clear that the men were convicted because of the opinions they held. In general, the public applauded the sentences, and rejoiced when four of the convicted men were hanged. One of the others had managed to blow out his brains with a bomb, and two had had their sentences commuted to life imprisonment. A few hardy souls condemned the whole proceedings as a miscarriage of justice, and in 1893, Governor John P. Altgeld, by pardoning the two men who were serving life sentences, classed himself with this number, an act of courage that wrecked his political career.[1]

It was the irony of fate that the public saw in the Haymarket riot occasion for further condemnation of the Knights of Labor. Actually *Decline of* the strike for the eight-hour day had been promoted mainly *the Knights* through local trade unions, and Powderly had counseled against it on the ground that the weapon of the strike should not be invoked until all other means of protest had been exhausted. Nevertheless, the Knights had already won a reputation for violence and they received the blame. Anarchists and other advocates of revolution had found it easy to obtain membership in the order and had used its forums to propagate their views. Powderly even charged that an attorney for one group of employers confessed that anarchists had been paid to

[1] Henry David, *The History of the Haymarket Affair* (1936).

become Knights so that "they might stir up the devil and bring discredit upon your whole movement." As the control of the central organization over the behavior of the locals disintegrated, strikes were often undertaken "against the advice of the General Executive Board." The result was that skilled workers, alienated by the ruthless way in which the unskilled precipitated conflicts, tended to withdraw from the Knights in order to build up their own trade unions. By 1888 the membership of the Knights of Labor had declined to less than 260,000, and by 1890 to about 100,000. Within a short time the order had disappeared entirely.

Meantime a rival organization, which discarded the "one big union" idea in favor of the older federative plan, had begun to make headway. The American Federation of Labor, which was founded in 1881 at Pittsburgh as the "Federation of Organized Trades *The A.F. of L.* and Labor Unions of the United States and Canada," shortened its name in 1886, and at about the same time began to lengthen its membership list. While individuals, as such, were excluded from membership, almost any kind of labor organization, whether national, state, or local, might belong. The intent of the new order was no less to protect skilled labor from competition by the unskilled than to protect labor as such from the oppression of capital. It had, in fact, no real quarrel with capitalism as an economic system. Its mission, rather, was to insure that labor should share generously in the profits of capitalistic enterprise. To this end it set for itself such definite goals as an eight-hour work day, a six-day work week, a high wage level, greater security of job tenure, and the elimination of child labor. It showed little interest in the establishment of labor co-operatives, and it convincingly resisted all efforts to make the Federation over into a separate political party. Instead of going directly into politics, it supported candidates and platforms, of whatever party, provided only that they were favorable to the program of the Federation. While it hoped to see labor win most of its victories peacefully, either by obtaining favorable legislation or by collective bargaining with employers, the Federation, like the Knights, was willing in case of necessity to rely on the strike and the boycott. Its organization lent itself admirably to the use of the sympathetic strike, by means of which workers in a related craft, although lacking a grievance of their own, might come to the aid of a striking union. A sizable "war chest," supported by a per capita tax levied on members, enabled the Federation's central board of control to aid unemployed strikers and to prolong any conflict it chose to support.

What Terence V. Powderly was to the Knights of Labor, Samuel

Gompers (1850–1924) was to the American Federation.[1] Gompers was
Samuel Gompers born in London, the son of a cigarmaker. At ten years of
age he began to learn the shoemakers' trade, but he soon
gave that up in favor of his father's trade, because the latter was organized and the former was not. In 1863 he came with his parents to
America, and a year later he joined the first cigarmakers' union ever
organized in New York City. Always an enthusiastic member, when
he grew to manhood he became first the union's secretary and later its
president. The training that he thus received was of great significance,
for in many ways this local New York cigarmakers' union was a model
organization. It followed the British system of benefit payments in
case of unemployment, sickness, or death; it tried to encourage skill and
intelligence among its members; it gained many of its victories by collective bargaining, by arbitration, and by retaining the good-will and
respect of employers. Gompers never forgot this early training, and
much of the conservatism of his later career may properly be attributed
to it. He was one of the original group of delegates that founded the
Federation in 1881, and was even more active in the reorganization of
1886. From 1885 to the time of his death, with the exception of a single
year, 1895, he was regularly elected president of the Federation.

Under Gompers's devoted leadership, the Federation scored many
successes.[2] It backed the strike for the eight-hour day in 1886, and
claimed substantial gains in spite of the unfavorable reaction to the
Haymarket riot. It conducted another strike for the eight-hour day
in 1890, this time in the carpenters' union, with fairly satisfactory results. It supported innumerable movements, both in the states and in
the nation as a whole, that resulted in the enactment of laws favorable
to labor. In part through its activities practically every state in the
Union was soon equipped with a bureau of labor statistics, and in 1903
Congress went so far as to establish the Department of Commerce and
Labor, with a seat in the cabinet. The Federation encouraged member
unions to set up their own systems for sickness and unemployment benefits, and could soon point to many instances in which its advice had been
followed. Its assistance could be counted upon, also, in efforts to secure
adoption by employers of the "closed shop," which meant that only
union labor might be employed in a given plant, and to eliminate
"yellow dog" contracts, by which workers were obliged to agree in
advance of employment that they would not join labor unions. From a

[1] Samuel Gompers, *Seventy Years of Life and Labor* (2 vols., 1925), is an excellent autobiography. See also R. H. Harvey, *Samuel Gompers* (1935).

[2] The most satisfactory history of the Federation is L. L. Lorwin, *The American Federation of Labor* (1933).

Keystone

SAMUEL GOMPERS

membership of about one hundred and fifty thousand in 1886 the Federation by 1900 had grown to more than half a million, by 1905 to a million and a half, by the outbreak of the World War to two million. The greatest weakness of the American Federation lay in the fact that it represented only a favored minority of labor. All unskilled workers were excluded from membership, together with all skilled workers who did not belong to a union. Moreover, a number of labor organizations, including the four great railway unions, refused to affiliate with the Federation on the ground that they were able to take care of themselves, and were not eager to accept responsibility for others. The railway unions, however, ordinarily could be counted on to co-operate fully with the Federation.

[187]

Closely connected with the labor problem was the new immigration which came to the United States from Europe in an increasing tide from *The new* 1880 on.[1] Easier means of communication had much to do *immigration* with the acceleration of this long-established migration. The effort that had once been involved in making the trip to America had become for many by the last quarter of the nineteenth century a mere following of the line of least resistance. Steamship companies that wished to fill their holds with immigrants quoted low rates and joined with the American railroads that had land to sell in describing the boundless opportunities awaiting the newcomer on American shores. American industrialists in need of unskilled labor sent recruiting agents abroad to offer wages that to Europeans seemed high, but that to Americans seemed ridiculously low. Immigrants who had come to America wrote back to their relatives in glowing terms of the success they had achieved in the New World, and in many such letters the passage money was included to bring more immigrants across the Atlantic. The oppression of minorities in central and eastern Europe, the desire to escape military service, the official encouragement of emigration as a means of alleviating poverty and unemployment, all sent their quotas to America. In the decade of the sixties, 2,314,824 immigrants landed at American ports; in the decade of the seventies, in spite of the depression, the number rose to 2,812,191; and in the decade of the eighties all previous records were broken by an influx of 5,246,613, an average of more than half a million immigrants a year. By 1905 the million mark had been reached, and until the outbreak of the World War in 1914 the avalanche continued.

Far more significant than the actual number of immigrants was their racial origin. During the first half of the eighties Germany furnished *Nationalities* about one third of the newcomers, the British Isles and the *of the* Scandinavian countries another third, with most of the *newcomers* rest, the really "new" immigration, coming from southern and eastern Europe. In the last half of the eighties the proportion began to change; from that time on the numbers coming from southern and eastern Europe rose as those coming from northern and western Europe fell. By the later nineties the former exceeded the latter in the proportion of three to two. The descendants of colonial Americans had long been familiar with immigrants from the British Isles and from Germany, and they found little difficulty in accustoming themselves to

[1] In addition to the works cited on page 74, J. W. Jenks and W. J. Lauck, *The Immigration Problem* (1912), and M. R. Davie, *World Immigration with Special Reference to the United States* (1936), will be found useful.

the Scandinavians. All of these peoples took on American ways with a minimum of difficulty, and were soon in process of absorption into the native population. But Italians and Poles, Rumanians and Ruthenians, Magyars and Bulgars, Czechs and Croats, Slovaks and Slovenes, Jews and Greeks seemed somehow vastly different.[1] Most of them went to work at once in the factories, in the mines, or on railroad construction gangs. They clung together in racial groups and retained tenaciously their Old-World languages and customs. They reproduced in American cities the living conditions of European slums, ideal breeding-grounds for disease. They fell in easily with city machines, and complicated the already difficult problem of good city government. They shocked the dominantly Protestant native Americans with their devotion to Catholicism, whether Roman or Greek Orthodox, or to Judaism. They often refused to send their children to the public schools, and established instead foreign-language parochial schools. In short, they put every obstacle in the way of the traditional process of amalgamation by means of which, ever since America began, the perpetual problem of immigration had been solved.

Organized labor in the United States was at first hostile to the new immigrants, and attempted to keep them out of the unions. Skilled workmen, however, soon won recognition, and in due time the foreign element began to play an important rôle in the labor world. Unversed in American ways, the newcomers *Labor and the immigrant* sometimes employed in their adopted land the methods of violence they had used against European tyrannies. Each such outbreak increased the dislike of the so-called "native American" for the immigrants, and tended to discredit the labor organizations to which they belonged. From the unions themselves, in self-protection, and from the public in general a demand for the restriction of immigration set in. In the nineteenth century, however, the restrictionists gained only modest victories. A law of 1882 excluded paupers, criminals, convicts, and the insane. Steamship companies found guilty of bringing such immigrants to the United States were required to take them back again free of charge. More important was the prohibition of the importation of laborers under contract. A more comprehensive law, passed in 1891, added to the proscribed lists prostitutes, idiots, polygamists, and persons suffering from certain types of diseases; prohibited under penalty of fine the recruitment of foreign laborers by advertising or solicitation; made

[1] R. F. Foerster, *The Italian Emigration of Our Times* (1919); William I. Thomas and Florian Znaniecki, *The Polish Peasant in Europe and America* (5 vols., 1918–1920); Samuel Joseph, *Jewish Immigration to the United States from 1881 to 1910* (1914); Jerome Davis, *The Russian Immigrant* (1922).

a charge of fifty cents against each immigrant admitted; and placed the administration of the law in the hands of a federal superintendent of immigration. Efforts to secure a literacy test, which would have excluded great numbers of immigrants from southern and eastern Europe, but comparatively few from northern and western Europe, culminated in a law that passed Congress in 1897, only to be vetoed by President Cleveland.[1]

[1] Carl Brent Swisher, *American Constitutional Development* (1943), is particularly good on problems arising from the issues of government versus capital. R. C. Overton, *Burlington West: A Colonization History of the Burlington Railroad* (1941), throws much light on the motives and methods of a single railroad. More general in scope is James Marshall, *Santa Fé: The Railroad that Built an Empire* (1945). Malcolm MacLaren, *The Rise of Electrical Industry During the Nineteenth Century* (1943), is an excellent guide book. On labor, see Marjorie R. Clark and S. Fanny Simon, *The Labor Movement in America* (1938); and H. J. Carman, Henry David, and Paul N. Guthrie (eds.), *The Path I Trod: The Autobiography of Terence V. Powderly* (1940).

CHAPTER IX

FROM GARFIELD TO HARRISON

FROM almost any point of view, the Garfield administration turned out to be a tragedy. The speed with which an assassin's bullet cut short the career of the young President was, of course, the greatest *The tragedy* tragedy. James A. Garfield (1831–1881), like Abraham *of Garfield* Lincoln, was a typical product of the American frontier.[1] Born in an Ohio log cabin, Garfield as a boy learned the meaning of hard work on the farm, and as a youth tried his hand at mule-driving along the towpath of the Ohio Canal. Fired with an ambition to become a teacher, he earned his way through the Eclectic Institute at Hiram, Ohio (later known as Hiram College), and set off for Williams College, in Massachusetts, where he was graduated in 1856. Of Mark Hopkins, who was then president of Williams, he used to say, "A log with a student at one end and Mark Hopkins at the other is my ideal college." After his graduation, Garfield returned to the Institute at Hiram, where he remained, first as an instructor and later as principal, until the outbreak of the Civil War. On the side, he read law and in 1859 was admitted to the bar; preached to congregations of the Disciples Church, of which he was a devout member; and served for a time as a member of the Ohio state senate. As a volunteer officer in the Union army he won rapid promotion, and after the battle of Chickamauga, in which he distinguished himself by his gallant conduct, he was commissioned major-general. Meantime, in the critical election of 1862, Garfield had stood as the Union candidate from his Ohio district to Congress, and had won. So in December, 1863, possibly at Lincoln's insistence, he resigned his commission in order to take his seat as a member of the House, a position he retained until the time of his nomination for the Presidency. In Congress he proved to be a finished debater, a tireless committeeman, and a dependable party regular. None could doubt that a brilliant future lay before him, and had he not achieved the Presidency when he

[1] T. C. Smith, *Life and Letters of James Abram Garfield* (1925); R. G. Caldwell. *James A. Garfield* (1931).

did, the honor might well have been his later on. Four months after his inauguration as President he was shot by a disappointed office-seeker. For weeks he lingered between life and death, but finally on September 19, 1881, he died. It cannot be said that with his passing the country lost a great man, but it can perhaps be said that it lost one who was potentially great at a time when great men in politics were rare.

The Garfield administration was a tragedy, also, from the point of view of Garfield's Secretary of State, James G. Blaine (1830–1893). *James G.* Blaine was born in Pennsylvania, was graduated from *Blaine* Washington (later Washington and Jefferson) College, and after a short period of teaching, had become a journalist in Maine, where he was connected with the Kennebec *Journal* and the Portland *Advertiser*. He was deep in state politics before the Civil War, and after 1858 served three terms as a member of the state legislature. When war broke out, he did not join the army, but in 1863 entered the national House of Representatives, and remained there until 1876, when he went to the Senate. During Grant's administration he emerged as the outstanding leader of the Republican Party. A firm believer in the righteousness of Radical reconstruction, and a veritable incarnation of Republican prejudice, he appealed strongly to a party-loving age. Both on and off the platform he possessed great personal charm, a quality which he used, no less than Henry Clay, to excite the worshipful support of his followers. Both in 1876 and in 1880 far more sentiment had existed for Blaine than for the men the Republicans had nominated, and Garfield showed himself a good politician when he made Blaine his Secretary of State.[1]

In his new office, Blaine revealed a disposition to mark out new policies.[2] American diplomacy had long been a routine case-by-case *Blaine's* affair, but Blaine hoped to make it a potent force in the *diplomacy* whole of the western hemisphere. He believed that he could induce the other American republics to renounce war as a means of settling their disputes with one another, and to turn instead for advice and mediation to the United States. He wished, like Henry Clay, whom he admired and imitated, to expand American trade in Latin America. He shared with many others the desire to obtain for the United States the right to construct a strictly American canal across the Isthmus of Panama, and to this end he sought to persuade Great

[1] The best biography of Blaine is D. S. Muzzey, *James G. Blaine* (1934). Those written by Blaine's contemporaries are too prejudiced to be of value. Blaine's own *Twenty Years in Congress* (2 vols., 1884–86) treats only of his earlier career.

[2] Every aspect of Blaine's career as a diplomat is treated admirably in Alice F. Tyler, *The Foreign Policy of James G. Blaine* (1927).

CHESTER A. ARTHUR

JAMES G. BLAINE

ROSCOE CONKLING

JAMES A. GARFIELD

FOUR REPUBLICANS
(Pictures from Brown Brothers)

Britain to modify the Clayton-Bulwer Treaty of 1850, which provided that any such canal must be international in character and not exclusively either British or American. In most of these ambitions he would have been doomed to disappointment, even if he had remained in office. He was abysmally ignorant of international law, and in his dealings with foreign powers he sometimes adopted the same disdainful tone that he habitually directed toward Democrats. He was wedded to the spoils system, and was ill-served by the politically minded subordinates that he selected. Had his time been longer, however, the congress of Pan-American nations that he had called would have been held, whereas his successor promptly withdrew the invitations. The death of Garfield and the succession of Arthur meant the resignation of Blaine and a tragic end for his Pan-American dreams. It amounted also to a personal tragedy for Blaine. The real leader of his party, he found himself out of office. A poor man, who needed his salary, he was unemployed. He turned for consolation to the writing of his memoirs, *Twenty Years in Congress*, a document which he meant to serve as effective campaign literature in his bid for the Presidency in 1884.

Garfield's death was also a tragedy, or at least it seemed to be a tragedy, to the reform element in the Republican Party. They had hoped for much from him, and he was now to be replaced by a Stalwart of the deepest hue. Indeed, Garfield's assassin had openly boasted that he had shot Garfield to make Arthur President, and during the trial he had had the effrontery to call upon those who had "come into fat offices through him, to send in their contributions" to his defense. Civil service reformers, in particular, had little to hope for from Arthur's record. As collector of the port of New York, he had used his position to serve the best interests of the Republican machine in New York. Even as Vice-President his conduct had been unseemly. When Garfield, like Hayes, ignored Conkling in choosing a collector for the port of New York, Conkling had fought viciously to prevent confirmation, and, on discovering that he would probably fail, had resigned as senator in order to prove, by obtaining re-election, that his state was with him, and against the President. In this dramatic gesture the junior senator from New York, Thomas C. Platt (ever after known as "Me-too" Platt), had joined him. When re-election proved to be more difficult than the resigning senators had anticipated, Vice-President Arthur appeared at Albany to work for his two political friends. His mission proved futile, for to their chagrin both senators were left at home; but the Vice-President by supporting them had openly arrayed himself against the President. What good could come of such a man?

Chester Alan Arthur (1830–1886), the new President, proved to be a far better man than the skeptics feared.[1] He was born in Vermont, of Scotch-Irish ancestry, and, in conformity with the best *Chester A.* biographic pattern of the period, attended college (Union *Arthur* College, Schenectady, New York), taught school, and studied law. From his youth up an organization Republican, he held important administrative posts during the Civil War, but saw no military service. His code of ethics, while calling for the strictest personal honesty, tolerated freely the time-honored custom of rewarding the faithful with the spoils of office. As collector of the port of New York he had, as a matter of course, overstaffed his force with party workers, and he never hesitated to call upon the men who held their positions through his favor to do their full political duty during campaigns and on election days. As President, however, he was scrupulously on guard against criticism. He bore himself with becoming dignity, refused to indulge in a wholesale proscription of Garfield's appointees, and took up the cudgels in favor of civil service reform,[2] and even tariff revision, with wholly unexpected zeal.

Public opinion, never deeply concerned about civil service reform until after the death of Garfield, was aroused at last to the necessity of action. A newly uncovered scandal in the Post-Office De- *The "star-* partment, the "star-route" frauds, gave added strength to *route"* the arguments of the reformers. The "star routes," so- *frauds* called because they were designated on the post-office lists by stars, were those over which the mail was carried by stage or rider rather than in the customary way, by rail or by boat. The western plains were dotted with such routes, and because population in the mining area was subject to numerous sudden shifts, the law permitted an elasticity in the alteration of star-route contracts that was not tolerated elsewhere. If at any time a contractor could show cause for an increase in his contract because he had to carry more mail or expedite the service, then his compensation might be readjusted without readvertising for bids. Suspicion was rife as early as 1880 that the Second Assistant Postmaster-General, Thomas J. Brady, to whom fell this task of readjustment, was acting in collusion with star-route contractors, and in April, 1881, Garfield forced Brady out of office. It developed that Stephen W. Dorsey, a former senator from Arkansas, and a few others, had regularly been awarded star-

---

[1] G. F. Howe, *Chester A. Arthur* (1934), is an excellent political biography.

[2] C. R. Fish, *The Civil Service and the Patronage* (1905), is the definitive work on this subject. For the later period it is admirably supplemented by A. B. Sageser, *The First Two Decades of the Pendleton Act* (1935).

route contracts, and that these contracts had then, quite consistently, been raised out of all proportion to the service rendered. Dorsey and his friends actually had nothing whatever to do with carrying the mails, but sublet that work to others. Matters were made worse by the fact that Dorsey had served as secretary of the Republican National Committee in 1880, while Brady had been solicited indirectly by Garfield himself for campaign funds. Arthur nevertheless pushed the prosecution of the star-route grafters to the best of his ability, and, although they escaped punishment, they stood fully convicted in the eyes of public opinion. Here was another important reason why civil service reform ought no longer to be delayed.

Congress, however, made haste slowly. Both parties had pledged action on the subject in their platforms, and President Arthur in his first message to Congress had laid down the principle that "original appointments should be based upon ascertained fitness." Nevertheless, not until the mid-term congressional election of 1882 had returned a Democratic majority in the House of Representatives was the needed law forthcoming. Then the Republicans, in a somewhat unconvincing "death-bed repentance," joined with the Democrats to redeem the promise that both parties had long evaded. Congress had barely reconvened for the "lame-duck" session following the election, when George H. Pendleton, Democratic Senator from Ohio, introduced the long-awaited measure. In January, 1883, an overwhelming bipartisan majority enacted it into law.

The Pendleton Act authorized the President to appoint three civil service commissioners, not more than two of whom should belong to the *Civil service reform* same political party, whose duty it should be to provide "open competitive examinations for testing the fitness of applicants for the public service now classified, or to be classified." Only the lowest offices were at first classified, but the law provided that the President might extend the classified lists at will to include other executive appointees. President Arthur administered the law in complete good faith. He appointed as the first chairman of the commission Dorman B. Eaton, who as secretary of the Civil Service Reform Association had been an ardent advocate of reform. During the first year of its existence the commission was given jurisdiction over about fourteen thousand offices out of a total of one hundred and ten thousand, or about twelve and one half per cent. In contrast with the British system, which examines a candidate upon what fields he happens to know, the American system is based upon strictly practical tests.

Changes of national administration from Arthur's time on worked to the advantage of civil service reform. It happened that Arthur was succeeded by a Democrat, Cleveland; then Cleveland was succeeded by a Republican, Harrison; Harrison in turn was succeeded by a Democrat, Cleveland; and Cleveland, by a Republican, McKinley. Each President, as he was about to retire from office, tended to protect his own appointees by extending the classified lists. Men thus "blanketed" into the civil service were not required to take examinations, but when they died or resigned, their successors received appointments only on recommendation of the commission. By 1893 the number of civil servants under the merit system had reached forty-five thousand; by the turn of the century it was about one hundred thousand; by the time of the World War nearly half a million — over sixty per cent. The multiplication of offices by the "New Deal" under Franklin D. Roosevelt lowered for a time the percentage of civil servants selected for merit, but before the end of his administration, Roosevelt, like many of his predecessors, very generously extended the lists.

One of the chief obstacles to the greater extension of the activities of the commission is the fact that constitutional offices, involving appointments that require confirmation by the Senate, cannot be transferred to the classified lists by the President. He may bind himself (as Wilson did, for example, in the choice of first-, second-, and third-class postmasters), but he may not bind his successors; nor may he neglect to consult the Senate.

Tariff revision was another major effort of the Arthur administration, and if the achievement fell far short of the promise it was no fault of the President's. As already noted,[1] the high tariff rates of the Civil War period could be reduced only with the greatest difficulty. Indeed, the slight reductions obtained in 1872 were practically annulled by the Revenue Act of March 3, 1875, which added twenty-five per cent to the duties on molasses and sugar, and repealed the ten per cent reductions of three years before on manufactured goods. The net result was to leave virtually intact the old Civil War schedules, which had been made especially high to offset income and manufacturing taxes long since repealed. *Tariff reform*

Criticism of the unreasonably high tariff rates had grown with the years. David A. Wells, once a protectionist and for many years special commissioner of the revenue, came out strongly for a low-tariff policy in a series of articles published in the *Atlantic Monthly* during the year 1875. William Graham Sumner, professor of political and social science at Yale after 1872, began about the same time to expound his

[1] See p. 46.

gospel of the "forgotten man," not the poor man, who never allows himself to be forgotten, but the ordinary citizen whose pockets are picked by the tariff. Frank W. Taussig, graduated from Harvard in 1879, was soon back at a professor's desk, rivaling Sumner in his denunciations of protection. High tariffs, the economists observed, embarrassed foreign trade, for American raw products, increasingly in need of foreign markets, met discriminations abroad because of the duties the United States charged on foreign manufactures. The American citizen paid far too much for the tariff-protected articles he had to buy. The government of the United States actually collected, mainly from the tariff, about $100,000,000 more revenue each year than Congress could find ways to spend.

Over against these arguments the believers in a protective tariff system had a good deal to say in favor of high duties as a means of *The pro-* stimulating American manufactures. Repeating the argu-
tectionist ments of Henry Clay, they maintained that the trouble
argument with the United States was that it still devoted too much energy to producing raw materials, and too little to manufacturing. Horace Greeley, while he lived, had hammered home this view:

> If I had my way — if I were king of this country, I would put a duty of $100 a ton on pig-iron and a proportionate duty on everything else that can be produced in America. The result would be that our people would be obliged to supply their own wants, manufactures would spring up, competition would finally reduce prices, and we should live wholly within ourselves.

Most protectionists, however, did not go so far. The Republican platform of 1880 stated merely that "the duties for the purpose of revenue should so discriminate as to favor American labor." H. L. Dawes of Massachusetts, whose views were fairly typical of protectionist opinion, admitted freely that he favored "revision and reform."

> Great inconsistencies and incongruities exist in the tariff. A great many excessive duties remain upon the statute-book. Many dutiable articles should be on the free list and many of the provisions of the tariff have become obsolete and inoperative. The present is a favorable time for such revision owing to the increased prosperity of the country.

It was one thing, however, to favor revision, and quite another to put it into effect. As long as Hayes was President it was easy to evade *Divided* action because neither party had full control of the govern-
party ment. After the election of 1880 the Republicans were in
counsels control of both legislative and executive branches, and so were free to act, if only they could be sure what they wished to do. But tariff reform, like civil service reform, cut across party lines. The

Republicans, while more friendly to a high tariff than the Democrats, had many outspoken tariff reformers in their ranks; the Democrats, while nominally in favor of a tariff for revenue only, were led in the House of Representatives by Samuel J. Randall of Pennsylvania, an arch-protectionist who was by no means the only Democrat to hold such views. Not until 1882 was any action taken, and then it was only to set up a citizen's tariff commission empowered to study the question and report back to Congress. President Arthur, who had urged that such a commission be created, was embarrassed by the unwillingness of able men to serve upon it, and finally, almost as a last resort, chose John L. Hayes of Massachusetts, secretary of the National Association of Wool Manufacturers, to head it. Every member of the commission was an avowed protectionist, and four out of the nine members had a financial stake in protection. Even so, the commission reported back a "scheme of tariff duties in which substantial reduction" was meant to be the "distinguishing feature," with specific recommendations that would have brought the rates down by an average of twenty per cent.

The report of the commission was made in December, 1882, immediately following the congressional elections that had cost the Republicans their majority in the House of Representatives. It *The "Mongrel Tariff"* was decided, therefore, to speed along the passage of a tariff bill before March 4, during the short session of Congress, so that the Republicans could take the credit for what was done. To expedite matters, both houses of Congress worked on the measure at the same time, the Senate, to avoid the constitutional requirement that money bills should originate in the House, attaching its rates to a bill for the reduction of internal revenues that had already passed the House. The results were far from satisfactory. The House bill lowered the rates, but by much less than the twenty per cent the commission had advocated; the Senate bill attached rates still lower; a conference committee on which leading Democrats refused to serve revised both sets of rates upward to a level not far different from those already in force. As Senator Sherman admitted, the action of the committee "restored nearly all the inequalities and incongruities of the old tariff and yielded to local demands and local interests to an extent that destroyed all symmetry and harmony." Lobbyists representing the leading tariff-protected industries descended upon Washington while the bill was pending, and had much to do with the result; "log-rolling" did most of the rest. Least important of all the influences that operated in the shaping of the rates was their probable effect on government finances. As the measure finally passed Congress in March, 1883, it deserved the name that Ida M. Tarbell has given it, the "Mongrel Tariff." [1] Meant to achieve revision downward, it served rather to commit the Republican Party more definitely than ever before to the principle of tariff protection, and at the same time to hand over to the Democrats full responsibility for promoting tariff reform.

The drift of the Democratic Party toward an out-and-out low-tariff policy was unmistakable. When in 1883 the Democratic majority in *Defeat of* the House of Representatives was faced with the necessity *Randall* of choosing a Speaker, it ignored the claims of Samuel J. Randall, a Pennsylvania protectionist who before 1881 had three times been elected to the office, in order to support John G. Carlisle of Kentucky, a low-tariff advocate.[2] Most of the Democrats in the House wished also to take legislative action to record their opposition to the existing high tariff, although they knew that the Republican Senate would prevent any such measure from becoming a law. In May, 1884, Representative W. R. Morrison of Illinois tried to push through a flat twenty per cent reduction in tariff rates, and failed only because forty-one Democrats led by Randall voted with the Republicans against it. When the time came for drawing up the Democratic platform of 1884, the strongly low-tariff delegations from the South and West felt obliged to compromise with the Randall group from the Northeast, and a noncommittal tariff plank was the result. The Republicans chose similarly to placate the tariff-reform group within their party. Thus, while the great majority of the Democrats appeared to favor a low tariff and the great majority of Republicans a high tariff, the issue was not clearly drawn during the presidential campaign of 1884.

With the credit for civil service reform divided between the two parties, and with the tariff issue in abeyance, the result of the election was sure to hinge mainly upon the personal appeal of the men nominated. The Republicans with perfect propriety might have nominated Arthur. His record on reform was respectable in spite of his antecedents; he had even broken with Conkling. He had vetoed in 1882 an $18,000,000 rivers and harbors ("pork-barrel") bill that was designed primarily to aid the congressmen in whose districts the money was to be expended.

---

[1] Ida M. Tarbell, *The Tariff in Our Times* (1911), is popular and dependable. It may be supplemented by F. W. Taussig, *Tariff History of the United States* (revised edition, 1931), which adds a new chapter for each new tariff bill, and by Edward Stanwood, *American Tariff Controversies in the Nineteenth Century* (2 vols., 1903), which shows sympathy for the protectionist point of view.

[2] One of the best biographies on a man of this period is J. A. Barnes. *John G. Carlisle* (1931).

These actions, however, displeased the regulars without entirely winning the Liberals. Most damaging to the President's prestige was the defeat in 1882 of his Secretary of the Treasury, William J. Folger, for the governorship of the State of New York. It was well known that Arthur had used his utmost influence to secure both the nomination and the election of Folger, and the victory of Folger's opponent, Grover Cleveland, seemed to indicate that the President's influence in his own home state was of no very great avail. With the probability strong that Cleveland would head the Democratic ticket, the Republicans simply could not afford to nominate Arthur.

They turned instead to their glamorous leader, James G. Blaine. Arthur would have been glad to obtain the nomination, although his health was as precarious as his political support. George F. *Campaign* Edmunds of Vermont, described by his opponents as a *of 1884* "presidential glacier," was favored by the Republican independents, but Blaine had the enthusiasm and the votes. Mindful of the fact that their leader had fought Democrats on the floor of Congress but never on the field of battle, the convention chose John A. Logan of Illinois, an ex-Union soldier and an ex-Democrat, for second place on the ticket.

The nomination of Blaine was totally unacceptable to the Liberal wing of the Republican Party. Such men as Carl Schurz, George William Curtis, Henry Ward Beecher, Charles William Eliot, Theodore Roosevelt, and Henry Cabot Lodge had been numbered among his opponents. To them he was not the "plumed knight" that Robert G. Ingersoll had so eloquently acclaimed him in his nominating speech before the Republican Convention of 1876. Rather, he was an old-fashioned politician with his eyes glued firmly to the past, and his reputation slightly tarnished. Ingersoll's well-remembered speech had revealed Blaine's weakness no less than his strength.

> The people [cried Ingersoll] called for the nomination of the man who has torn from the throat of treason the tongue of slander — for the man who has snatched the mask of Democracy from the hideous face of rebellion . . . Like an armed warrior, like a plumed knight, James G. Blaine marched down the halls of the American Congress and threw his shining lance full and fair against the brazen forehead of the defamers of his country and maligners of his honor.

The "tongue of slander" referred to the famed "Mulligan letters," and the "maligners of his honor" were those who found in these letters evidence that Blaine's influence had at one time been for sale.[1]

[1] C. E. Russell, *Blaine of Maine: His Life and Times* (1931).

Known since 1876, the "Mulligan letters" revealed that Blaine as congressman had helped obtain a land grant for an Arkansas railroad, *The "Mulli* the Little Rock and Fort Smith. As a return favor he was *gan letters"* given the privilege of selling the bonds of this railroad on a generous commission. These bonds, he claimed, fell in value, and because he had to indemnify his friends for their losses, he himself lost money on the transaction. However this might be, Blaine had been sufficiently exercised about the letters to obtain them from James Mulligan, their possessor, on a ruse, and then to refuse to return them. Blaine also refused to submit the letters to the inspection of a congressional investigating committee on the ground that they were purely personal and not relevant to the investigation; but when his conduct seemed to be turning public opinion against him, he read them into the *Congressional Record* in "one of the most extraordinary exhibitions of histrionic skill, one of the most consummate pieces of acting that ever occurred upon any stage on earth." Actually, he had edited the letters freely to secure the effect he desired, and they seemed far less damaging as he presented them than they really were.

The "Mulligan letters" had doubtless had something to do with Blaine's failure to achieve the Republican nomination in 1876, and they arose again to plague him in 1884. *Harper's Weekly* reprinted them in regular installments, beginning May 10 and continuing until September 27, 1884. Without Blaine's careful shading they appeared far more questionable than when he read them into the *Congressional Record.* New letters, even more embarrassing than the first set, turned up at Democratic headquarters, and were released shortly before the election. They emphasized the fact that Blaine as Speaker of the House had been on extremely friendly terms with railroad interests that stood a good chance to profit from his friendship. Did Blaine profit from theirs? It transpired, also, that Blaine himself had drafted one of the statements he had used in 1876 to clear his record. Unfortunately the business associate whom he had asked to sign the document had kept Blaine's covering letter, which now appeared in print with its concluding admonition, "*Burn this letter.*" Could the word of such a man be trusted?

The reform element within the Republican Party definitely thought not, and many of them — nicknamed "Mugwumps" — prepared to *The "Mug* bolt the ticket. This they could do with a clear conscience *wumps"* because of the impeccable public record of the Democratic nominee, Grover Cleveland. Cleveland's nomination was made, in fact, practically at the insistence of the Mugwumps, and to the considerable anguish of many long-time Democratic leaders who had counted on the place for themselves. But the Democratic Convention had little choice. It was Cleveland and a chance to win the Mugwump vote, or someone else and the risk of losing the election. For the Vice-Presidency, however, the Democrats turned to a party wheel-horse, Thomas A. Hendricks of Indiana, whose soft-money views might be of some help during the campaign and would do no harm afterward.

Grover Cleveland (1837–1908) was born in Caldwell, New Jersey, one of the many children of a small-town Presbyterian minister.[1] Soon afterward the Cleveland family removed to Fayetteville, *Grover* New York, and from there to Clinton. At the time he *Cleveland* should have been going to college young Cleveland, because of his father's death, felt obliged to seek employment, and got a job as clerk in a Buffalo law office. By 1859 he was admitted to the bar. During the Civil War, when other young men were joining the army, he borrowed money to hire a substitute because his meager earnings were needed for the support of his mother and sisters. In 1863 he received a welcome appointment as assistant district attorney, and in 1870 he was not above accepting a nomination as sheriff of Erie County. Elected, he revealed qualities of scrupulous honesty and unflinching courage that soon made him a marked man. He refused to hire a hangman when two murderers were to be executed, and sprang the trap himself. He made life consistently uncomfortable for local crooks and grafters. In 1881, nominated and elected mayor of Buffalo to placate the "better element," he reorganized the city administration, purged it of venal politicians, vetoed dubious measures, and in general endeared himself to reformers. The fame of the "veto mayor" spread, and when in 1882 the New York Democrats needed a candidate for governor with an unimpeachable record to oppose Secretary Folger, they turned to Cleveland and elected him by a majority of nearly 200,000 votes. As governor, he struggled irritably against a bewildering accumulation of governmental inefficiency or worse, made some progress and many enemies, particularly among the Tammany leaders of New York City. "We love him most for the enemies he has made," General E. S. Bragg told the Democratic Convention of 1884, mindful of Tammany's earnest desire to prevent Cleveland's nomination for the Presidency.

"The paramount issue this year," George William Curtis told an audience of New York Mugwumps, "is moral rather than political." No sooner had this keynote been sounded than the Republicans countered

---

[1] Allan Nevins, *Grover Cleveland: a Study in Courage* (1932), is in reality a well-rounded history of the period. Useful also is Allan Nevins (editor), *Letters of Grover Cleveland* (1933). These works completely supplant the earlier lives of Cleveland.

with the charge that Cleveland, far from being the paragon of virtue
Issues of the he seemed, was the father of an eight-year-old illegitimate
campaign child. Cleveland was a bachelor, he had supported the child,
and he did not deny paternity. When asked by his campaign managers
what to say about the matter, he replied simply, "Tell the truth." Not
since the trial of Henry Ward Beecher had the scandal-loving American
public had such a thrill. Blaine's private life was blameless; he was a devoted husband and father, and Cleveland bluntly forbade the spreading
of false rumors to the contrary. The Republicans, he said, could "have
a monopoly of all the dirt in this campaign." Undoubtedly this serious
indiscretion cost Cleveland many votes, but the sober second thought
of most Americans seemed to coincide with that of a philosophical Mugwump who held that "we should elect Mr. Cleveland to the public office
he is so admirably qualified to fill and remand Mr. Blaine to the private
life which he is so eminently fitted to adorn." The Democrats, as a
matter of fact, did their full share of mud-slinging. Their parades
marched to the rhythm of the words:

> Blaine! Blaine! James G. Blaine!
> The con-ti-nen-tal liar from the State of Maine,

or

> Burn this letter! Burn this letter!
> Burn, burn, oh, burn this letter!

To which the Republican marching clubs replied somewhat lamely,

> Ma! Ma! Where's my Pa?
> Gone to the White House. Ha! Ha! Ha!

Blaine's defeat is sometimes ascribed to an incident that happened
close to the end of his campaign. When a delegation of Protestant
"Rum, ministers paid him a visit at the Republican headquarters
Romanism, in New York City, their spokesman, Doctor Samuel Burch-
and re- ard, referred to the Democratic Party as one "whose an-
bellion" tecedents have been rum, Romanism, and rebellion."
Blaine failed to note the implied insult to the Roman Catholic voters,
strong support from whom he had counted on, partly because his mother
was a Catholic and partly because his own anti-British sentiments appealed to the Catholic Irish. As a result, the Democrats were soon
spreading the gossip that Blaine had allowed a slander on the Catholics
to pass unrebuked, and even that he himself was the author of the fateful words. His denial was vigorous and convincing, but in the few remaining days of the campaign it did not always succeed in catching up
with the charge. Cleveland carried the State of New York, without

which he could not have been elected, by a plurality of only 1149 votes; hence, it is reasonable to suppose that, except for the Burchard speech, Blaine rather than Cleveland might have won.[1]

The decision in 1884 was almost as close as in 1880. Cleveland's plurality over Blaine in the country as a whole was only 23,000, and the electoral vote stood 219 to 182. Cleveland carried the *Election of* solid South, Delaware, Indiana, Connecticut, New Jersey, *Cleveland* and New York. All the rest of the states voted for Blaine. The Democrats won control of the House of Representatives by a comfortable margin, but the Republicans retained their majority in the Senate. Benjamin F. Butler, the Greenback candidate, received a total of 175,370 popular votes, and John P. St. John of Kansas, Prohibitionist, 150,369. The Prohibitionist vote in New York State alone ran to over 25,000, another factor in the defeat of Blaine. Had the temperance forces not had a candidate of their own, undoubtedly most of them would have voted for Blaine and against Cleveland, whose bibulous habits were well known. And yet, as the *Nation* aptly explained, "the real force which defeated Blaine was Blaine himself. He had created during his twenty years of public life a public distrust too deep to be overcome by even the most formidable combination of political wiles, money, and treachery ever organized in this country."[2]

"A public office is a public trust." So an enterprising reporter had translated Cleveland's more prosaic statement that "public officials are trustees of the people." As President, Grover Cleveland *Cleveland* strove earnestly to live up to this principle. He appointed *and the* a competent cabinet, headed by Thomas F. Bayard of *civil service* Delaware, and methodically set about the business of proving that the Democratic Party, although it had been out of power for twenty-four years, could still administer the government. As was natural after so many lean years, he was immediately beset by throngs of Democratic office-seekers to whom civil service reform had meant only "the turning-out of office of Republicans and putting honest Democrats in their places." Cleveland thought otherwise, but he could not entirely resist the demands of the spoilsmen. He protected the Civil Service Commission in its work, and extended the classified lists by the addition of some twelve thousand offices. But among the non-classified office-holders the changes he made or approved, if somewhat gradual, were

[1] H. C. Thomas, *The Return of the Democratic Party to Power in 1884* (1919), is a work of competent scholarship.

[2] Two entertaining popular histories, written without much perspective, are H. T. Peck, *Twenty Years of the Republic, 1885–1905* (1907), and E. B. Andrews, *The United States in Our Own Time* (1903).

GROVER CLEVELAND

SAMUEL·J. TILDEN

WILLIAM JENNINGS BRYAN

JOHN P. ALTGELD

FOUR DEMOCRATS

(Pictures from Brown Brothers)

fairly thorough. By the end of his administration probably two thirds of the federal office-holders were newly appointed Democrats. Cleveland's yielding to the politicians on so many appointments cost him the support of many reformers, but it was no doubt the only way in which he could head off a revolt within his own party that would nullify his every effort to lead.

Also susceptible of a partisan interpretation was Cleveland's attitude toward pensions. Well before his term began, the aging veterans of the Union army had begun to flock into the Grand Army of the Republic, a benevolent and patriotic order that dated *Pensions* back to 1866. Whatever the original purpose of this organization, its ultimate goal came to be more and larger pensions. In 1879 it scored its first great victory. The original pension policy of the United States had been based upon the principle that only disability incurred in service entitled an ex-soldier to a pension, but the Arrears of Pension Act of 1879 provided that all pensioners might recover back payments for the period between the time of mustering-out and the time a given pension was granted.[1] As a result many pensioners collected a lump sum of hundreds, or even thousands, of dollars, and many veterans who had scorned to apply for pensions before sought eagerly to place their names on the pension rolls. Pension attorneys who helped the veterans win their awards took fat fees out of the arrears bonuses, and searched diligently for unpensioned veterans whom they could prove to have suffered some disability from the war. For those who had come through unscathed there was always the chance of inducing some lenient congressman to present to Congress a private pension bill, and few such bills failed of passage. Cleveland was the first President to examine these private pension bills critically, and the frauds he uncovered aroused his wrath. Before his term ended he had vetoed hundreds of them. He also vetoed a so-called "pauper" pension bill that would have given a pension to all who stood in need of it, regardless of disability. These vetoes were deeply offensive to the G.A.R., most of whose members were Republicans and professed to believe that it was for political reasons only that the President denied them their due.

The "old soldiers," by this time thoroughly antagonized, soon had a chance to charge the President with treason. More to solve a difficult storage problem than to give offense, Cleveland ordered the return of the captured Confederate battle-flags to their respective states. "May

---

[1] There are two revealing monographs on this subject: J. W. Oliver, *History of the Civil War Military Pensions* (1917); W. H. Glasson, *Federal Military Pensions in the United States* (1918).

God palsy the hand that wrote that order! May God palsy the brain that conceived it! May God palsy the tongue that dictated it!" was the fervent prayer of the current commander of the G.A.R. Cleveland was notably stubborn, and he might have persisted in his course, but careful examination of the law showed that to legalize his action he should have obtained a prior act of Congress. Accordingly, he withdrew the order. Not many years later, during the Presidency of Theodore Roosevelt, Congress restored the flags, and there was no uproar, but the Congress that restored them was a Republican Congress.

Cleveland was not elected as a tariff reformer, and in his annual messages of 1885 and 1886 he had little to say on the tariff. Evidence that *Cleveland's tariff message* his party was still divided on the subject was supplied in April, 1886, when the House refused to consider a new Morrison bill, lacking the objectionable horizontal feature of the first, by a vote of 140 yeas to 157 nays. Thirty-five Randall Democrats voted with the Republicans to defeat revision. By 1887, however, Cleveland's methodical study of government finance had led him to the conviction that tariff reduction was imperative, and he made up his mind to force the issue. Heretofore his annual message to Congress had followed the traditional pattern of including every good thing that entered the presidential mind. In the message of 1887 he dealt exclusively with the tariff, and presented a well-reasoned, hard-hitting argument against the existing high rates. He did not ignore the way in which the tariff increased the cost of living for the many in order to pile up fortunes for the favored few, but he based his argument mainly upon the fact that the Tariff of 1883 was bringing into the Treasury each year a heavy surplus — on an average about $100,000,000 more revenue each year than the government needed. Business stagnation, he predicted, must be the inevitable result of such a short-sighted policy. "It is a condition which confronts us, not a theory."

Cleveland was not the only one to recognize the risk involved in the government's collecting more money than it could spend. Students of the money question pointed out that the appreciating value of the dollar was due in part to the way in which the United States Treasury was taking money out of circulation. The old sub-Treasury system was still in force, and under its terms the government was still legally obliged to keep its money in its own vaults and not in banks. While Treasury officials made it a point to take their time about withdrawing currency from use, eventually, extremists argued, the government would have all the money and the people would have none. Efforts to pay off the national debt incurred during the Civil War had long been fruitless.

Bonds of the United States were legally required as a part of the capital of national banks, and could be purchased back only at a high premium. Furthermore, if the government should use its surplus to retire the last dollar of its bonded debt, it would by so doing put the national banks out of business, and would at one stroke remove from circulation all the currency they had issued.

It seems incredible to Americans of a later generation that any difficulty should have been experienced in finding a way to expend the excess revenue, however great, but such seems to have been the case. Cleveland did his stubborn best to prevent Civil War *Problems of the revenue* pensions from eating up the surplus, as they could so easily have done. He also followed Arthur's precedent in vetoing a wasteful "pork-barrel" bill, and thus closed another avenue of expenditure. About the only extravagance in which he was willing to permit Congress to indulge was the building-up of the new steel navy that Garfield's Secretary of the Navy, William H. Hunt, had dreamed of and begun. Four steel vessels were already authorized before Cleveland took office, but during the next four years Congress appropriated funds for no less than twenty more, including two second-class battleships, the *Maine* and the *Texas*, and an armored cruiser, the *New York*. To Cleveland's Secretary of the Navy, William C. Whitney, goes much of the credit for making the new navy a success.

Cleveland was under no illusions as to the result of his tariff message. The mid-term elections of 1886 had left the party line-up in Congress about where it had been before, with the Republicans in control of the Senate and the Democrats in control of the House. Cleveland knew that he could not persuade the Republican Senate to accept a low tariff, and that therefore, regardless of what the House did, no tariff legislation would immediately result. But he did believe that he could force the Democrats in Congress to go on record as favoring tariff reduction. The issue could then be clearly drawn in the election of 1888, with the Democrats definitely lined up on one side and the Republicans on the other.

All worked out as the President had planned. Roger Q. Mills of Texas, as chairman of the House Ways and Means Committee, promptly reported a bill calling for reductions from an average level *The Mills* of about forty-seven per cent to an average level of about *Bill* forty per cent. Wool, flax, hemp, salt, lumber, and tinplate were placed on the free list, but it is an open question whether the bill, had it become a law, would have reduced the revenue. Increased importations due to the lower rates might actually have added to the total revenue collected. The Mills Bill was framed in secret to avoid the interference of lobbyists,

THE BOSSES OF THE SENATE

and it did not neglect the special interests of the Democratic South. With the aid of a little presidential pressure and the confident assurance that it could not possibly become a law, it commanded the support of all Democrats to an extent never possible before. Only four Democratic congressmen voted against it. Meantime the Republicans in the Senate had joyfully accepted the challenge. Accusing the House of attempting to frame a "dark lantern bill," the Senate Committee on Finance, under the leadership of Senator Allison, held open hearings to which all lobbyists who wished to come were invited. When the proper time came, the Senate was able to set over against the Mills Bill an example of Republican tariff revision in which the generally high level of duties was maintained; but a smaller revenue was insured by prohibitive duties, by the lowering of excises, and by a cut in the duty on sugar. As anticipated, the House would not accept the Senate bill, and the Senate would not accept the House bill. Compromise was not desired by either side. What both parties wished was to draw the issue.[1]

The season for nominating presidential candidates arrived in 1888 before the two houses of Congress had completed their tariff proposals, but there was already no doubt as to where each stood. The Republicans

[1] W. D. Orcutt, *Burrows of Michigan and the Republican Party* (2 vols., 1917), reveals clearly the mind of a typical protectionist.

would declare for a high tariff, the Democrats for revision downward. As for candidates, Cleveland was the inevitable choice of his party for President, and in place of Vice-President Hendricks, who had died in office, the Democrats nominated Allen G. Thurman of Ohio. Among the Republicans sentiment for the renomination of Blaine was almost too strong to withstand, but seasoned politicians, including Blaine himself, doubted the advisability of tempting fate by presenting the same candidate that Cleveland had defeated four years before. After a long-drawn-out session, and on the eighth ballot, the Republican Convention finally followed without enthusiasm the advice of Blaine to "take Harrison" — Benjamin Harrison of Indiana — who had the triple advantage of a presidential grandfather, residence in a close state, and a clean, if almost empty, political record. For Vice-President they "took" Levi P. Morton, a New York banker.

The campaign of 1888 was a revelation to the Republicans. They found out, for the first time, how advantageous an issue the tariff could be. Senator Matthew Quay, Republican "boss" of Penn- *Campaign* sylvania and chairman of the Republican campaign com- *of* 1888 mittee, cheerfully accepted the advice of a friend to "put the manufacturers of Pennsylvania under the fire and fry all the fat out of them." Campaign contributions as insurance against Democratic tariff reductions poured into Republican coffers in a flood. The funds thus collected were used both to carry on an extensive campaign of education and to "get out the vote." The latter process was at its brazen worst in Indiana where "floaters," who made it a practice to sell their votes to the highest bidder, held the balance of power. Party workers within the state, well supplied with funds from the national campaign chest, were told by the national treasurer just how to proceed: "Divide the floaters into blocks of five and put a trusted man in charge of these five, with the necessary funds, and make him responsible that none get away, and that all vote our ticket." Democratic watchers claimed that the floaters were sometimes paid as high as fifteen or twenty dollars each for their votes. Even so, Harrison carried the state by only 2300 votes. What happened in Indiana happened also in Connecticut, West Virginia, and other "doubtful" states. The scandals of the election were so open and notorious as to give great impetus to the movement for the "Australian" system of secret voting, which down to this time had made little headway in the United States.[1]

Harrison's election was made possible by the use of ample funds, but

[1] S. P. Orth, *The Boss and the Machine* (1919), and H. J. Ford, *The Cleveland Era* (1921), are interesting and accurate, but somewhat superficial.

there were other factors that told heavily against Cleveland. The British Minister to the United States, Sir Lionel Sackville-West, with curious ineptitude, fell into a carefully baited trap when he answered a letter asking how the British government would wish an ex-British naturalized American to vote. Marking his reply "private," Sackville-West plumped for Cleveland, only to read his letter in the newspapers when Quay saw fit to publish it. Cleveland promptly and angrily dismissed the blundering Britisher, but the damage had already been done. If the British favored Cleveland, many Americans, especially those of Irish descent, knew that they were against him. If the British were for free trade, then the Americans must be against it. The G.A.R. also took a prominent part in the campaign, and everywhere turned out the "old soldier vote" against the President. Labor, too, was generally persuaded that its interests lay with the protectionists, who claimed that their chief purpose was not so much to feather the nest of the American industrialist as to insure that the American wage-earner would continue to receive higher wages than were customarily paid in Europe. Gossip played only a minor rôle in the campaign, as compared with 1884, although Cleveland, who had married a young wife during his term of office, was constantly accused of drunkenness and wife-beating. Mrs. Cleveland herself felt obliged to deny the accusation, and to extol the domestic virtues of her husband. Cleveland's failure to serve in the Union army could also be raised against him, now that the Republicans had a candidate in Harrison who had seen hard fighting as the commander of an Indiana regiment of volunteers, and had been brevetted brigadier-general at the close of the war.

Harrison won the election by a slender margin. In the popular vote Cleveland led by more than 100,000 votes, but Harrison carried the cru-
Closeness of the contest cial states of New York and Indiana, and amassed 233 electoral votes to Cleveland's 168. In New York State Harrison's plurality over Cleveland was only 12,000, while David B. Hill, the Democratic candidate for governor, won by 19,000 votes. Hill was the bitter rival of Cleveland, and as devoted to machine politics as Cleveland was to his independence.[1] Cleveland's followers always thought that the Republican organization in New York had bargained with the Hill forces to trade Republican votes for Hill in return for Democratic votes for Harrison. Both houses of Congress were to be Republican by thin margins, and Harrison in jubilation proclaimed that "Providence has given us the victory." "Think of the man," protested Chairman Quay,

[1] D. S. Alexander, *Four Famous New Yorkers; the Political Careers of Cleveland, Platt, Hill, and Roosevelt* (1923), is an excellent and comprehensive study.

who knew better than anyone else just how the victory had been achieved. "He ought to know that Providence hadn't a damn thing to do with it."

Benjamin Harrison (1833–1901) was designed to be, and as President became, a "dignified figurehead." He was at the time of his nomination a successful lawyer of great party regularity who had served *Benjamin* one term in the United States Senate. He was in no sense *Harrison* the leader of his party, and James G. Blaine, whom he made his Secretary of State, completely overshadowed him. Harrison was a good platform orator, but cold in his personal relationships. "Harrison can make a speech to ten thousand men," said one of his associates, "and every man of them will go away his friend. Let him meet the same ten thousand in private, and every one will go away his enemy." His honesty was probably as unimpeachable as Cleveland's, but he lacked Cleveland's forceful nature. During Cleveland's administration the Democratic Party leaders, one by one, acknowledged the President's supremacy, whereas Harrison from the beginning of his administration to its end, had far less to do with charting his party's course than many another of lesser rank.[1]

Harrison had aroused hopes during the campaign that he would do well by the cause of civil service reform. "In appointments of every grade and department," he maintained, "fitness and not party service should be the essential and discriminating test, and fidelity and efficiency the only sure tenure of office." His action belied his words. His cabinet, except for Blaine, was composed of mediocre men, and his appointment of John Wanamaker, the Philadelphia merchant, as Postmaster-General was regarded as mainly a reward for Wanamaker's large campaign contribution. Like President Grant, he also saw fit to allot many minor offices to his indigent friends and relatives. In making other appointments he leaned on the advice of the politicians, and did what they wanted if he could. "Corporal" James Tanner, for example, Harrison's commissioner of pensions, took office with the prayer, "God help the surplus," and J. S. Clarkson of Iowa, his first assistant postmaster-general, boasted less than a year after his appointment: "I have changed 31,000 out of 55,000 fourth-class postmasters and I expect to change 10,000 more before I finally quit." Harrison's chief contribution to civil service reform was his appointment of Theodore Roosevelt to membership on the Civil Service Commission, an appointment which Roosevelt earned as a reward for serving his party faithfully during the campaign of 1888. As civil service commissioner, however, Roosevelt made it his

---

[1] D. R. Dewey, *National Problems, 1885–1897* (1907), is good political history. A journalist's survey of the period is A. W. Dunn, *From Harrison to Harding* (2 vols., 1922).

business to see that no such rewards as he had received were made through the agency of the commission. In the pursuit of this course he soon fell afoul of the President, whom he came to dislike, and of many of the President's friends, but Harrison was nonetheless obliged to retain the obstreperous commissioner in office, and when in 1893 Cleveland became President again he also retained Roosevelt.

The Republicans had never hoped for much from Harrison, but it was legislation that they desired, and they put their faith in Congress. For-
Admission of new states tunately for their program the election of 1888 had given them small majorities in both houses, although in the House of Representatives the margin was far too slender to be dependable. This situation was somewhat improved by the admission of six new Republican states, North and South Dakota, Montana, Washington, Idaho, and Wyoming. Shortly before Harrison's inauguration, the "lame-duck" session of the preceding Congress, anticipating an action that the next session was likely to take if it did not, had passed an "omnibus bill" for the admission of the first four of these embryo states, while the last two, confident that they would be accorded admission when the Republicans came into power, drew up constitutions without formal authorization. When the new Congress met in December, 1889, eight senators and five representatives were on hand from the "omnibus states" to bolster up the Republican majorities, and six months later the admission of Idaho and Wyoming brought still further assistance. One of the four remaining territories, New Mexico, also earnestly desired admission and had a constitution ready, but the Republican majorities in Congress were not interested in creating potentially Democratic states.

Even with the assistance of the new northwestern representatives, the Republican majority in the House required discipline if it were to prove
Thomas B. Reed effective. As Speaker, Thomas B. Reed (1839–1902), a member from Maine, undertook to play the rôle of disciplinarian.[1] A powerful man physically, with a stentorian voice, he led an attack on the traditional interpretation of parliamentary rules by which a strong minority had long enjoyed the right to interfere with the smooth functioning of a slender majority. One of these traditions maintained that a member could be counted as present only in case he chose to vote. If, instead of voting, he merely sat silent in his seat when his name was called, then he was technically absent; and if a majority of all the

[1] S W. McCall, *Life of Thomas Brackett Reed* (1914), gives a good picture of the Reed personality, but W. A. Robinson, *Thomas B. Reed, Parliamentarian* (1930), is the more scholarly.

CZAR REED

members of the House failed to respond to a roll-call, then there was no quorum. Repeatedly, on controversial questions, every member of the minority party refused to vote, and so compelled the majority to get out a full quorum from its own members to enable business to proceed. Speaker Reed, with a majority that never exceeded twenty out of a total membership of three hundred and thirty, found it next to impossible to keep enough Republicans present and voting to constitute a quorum. Accordingly, he decided to defy tradition, and to count a quorum from the members he saw in attendance, whether they chose to vote or not. After a fruitless roll-call, in which the Democrats sat silent, Reed announced: "The Chair directs the clerk to record the names of the following members present and refusing to vote." After a period of pandemonium in which only his calm demeanor saved the Speaker from assault, a minority member obtained the floor to protest against the ruling, only to be met by Reed's retort: "The Chair is making a statement of fact that the gentleman from Kentucky is present. Does he deny it?"

In the end Reed's view of this matter was written into the House rules, along with other amendments that enabled the majority to have its way. The House had long before limited its freedom of debate, but now, under "Reed's rules," it put an end to dilatory motions, and accepted without much protest whatever special orders the powerful Committee on Rules, of which Reed was chairman, chose to bring in. But for the reign of "Czar Reed," as his critics called him, the House could never have passed the long program of legislation that it had promised during the campaign. "The caucus, the lash, and the gag," so the disgruntled Democrats maintained, had been "substituted for debate and deliberation."

First in order on the Republican calendar, if not in importance, was the Dependents' Pension Act, by which the Grand Army of the Republic

The Depend- was to be duly rewarded for its faithful party service. This
ents' Pen- measure followed in the main the principles laid down in the
sion Bill "pauper" pension bill that Cleveland had vetoed. All veterans of the Civil War who had served for as long as ninety days, and who suffered from any mental or physical disability that made them incapable of making a living, were to receive pensions of from six to twelve dollars a month, according to the degree of disability from which they suffered. Widows of veterans, if dependent upon their own labor for support, were awarded pensions of eight dollars a month, and minor children, two dollars a month. As a result of this law the number of pensions rose from 489,725 in 1889 to 966,012 in 1893, and the amount of money appropriated for pensions in the same period from $89,000,000 to $157,000,000. Harrison had said before he was nominated that this "was no time to be weighing the claims of old soldiers with apothecary's scales," and his signature to the Dependents' Pension Bill proved that, in this matter at least, he was as good as his word. For a long time this measure was regarded, even by the Grand Army of the Republic, as the last word in pension legislation, but in 1904 a presidential order placed all veterans over sixty-two years of age on the pension rolls, while a few years later a Service Pension Act gave legislative sanction to the new policy. By 1911 the total expenditure of the United States for Civil War pensions had exceeded four billion dollars, a sum far in excess of the original cost of the war itself, with the end not yet in sight.

The main business of the Fifty-First Congress was to pass a high protective tariff law, but before that desired end could be accomplished the

Sherman Republican leaders felt obliged to push through the Sherman
Silver Pur- Anti-Trust Act as a more or less meaningless gesture against
chase Act the industries that the tariff was designed to help, and the
Sherman Silver Purchase Act as a sop to the silver mining states of the West whose representatives refused to boost the tariff until something had been done for silver. Throughout the eighties the price of silver had continued to drop, so that by 1890 the ratio of value between silver and gold had reached twenty to one. By this time it was clear that the limited coinage of silver required by the Bland-Allison Act had neither ar-

rested the decline in price of silver nor cheapened the value of the circulating dollar. Secretaries of the Treasury habitually purchased only the minimum of two million dollars' worth of silver each month, and quite as habitually backed up the silver dollars with gold. Westerners insisted that the time had come to pass a straight-out free-coinage act, and it was only with the greatest of difficulty that the hard-money men of the East persuaded them to accept another compromise. The Sherman Silver Purchase Act, which became a law in July, 1890, required the Treasury to buy 4,500,000 ounces of silver a month, or 54,000,000 ounces a year, the estimated annual output of all the silver mines of the United States. Not all the silver need be coined, but it was to be paid for in Treasury notes redeemable "in gold or silver coin," a substantial addition to the amount of money in circulation. The Act further declared, in words practically devoid of meaning, that it was "the established policy of the United States to maintain the two metals on a parity with each other upon the present legal ratio or such ratio as may be provided by law." What actually happened was that the Treasury continued to maintain the gold standard, as formerly, by redeeming all issues of paper or silver in gold. But the strain on the gold reserve, accumulated in the seventies to carry through resumption, was sure to grow, and the bare possibility of its ultimate exhaustion struck terror to the hearts of conservative businessmen.[1]

For the moment, however, they were abundantly consoled by the tariff bill which William McKinley of Ohio, chairman of the House Ways and Means Committee, had framed. To McKinley and his *The McKinley Tariff* associates high protection was both a gospel and an obligation. They believed in it on principle, and they had promised it to heavy campaign contributors before the election. The House Ways and Means Committee gave full hearings to all who wished to appear before it, and few important industries failed to take advantage of their opportunity. Piloted by McKinley through the House, and by Nelson W. Aldrich of Rhode Island through the Senate, the McKinley Bill became a law on October 1, 1890.[2] It provided first and foremost a set of duties on manufactured articles higher than the American government had ever levied before. Some of these duties turned out to be, as their authors had intended, actually prohibitive; others went to the length of offering protection to non-existent industries, provided only that responsible per-

---

[1] Jean Paul Hütter, *L'Incidence Économique de la Frappe de Monnaie d'Argent aux États-Unis de 1878 à 1893* (1938), is an interesting statistical study of the inflationary efforts of the period.

[2] C. S. Olcott, *The Life of William McKinley* (2 vols., 1916), is highly partisan, but contains much useful material.

sons could demonstrate their intent to begin manufacture. The law also embodied an impressive list of agricultural duties, charged against such imports as eggs, butter, potatoes, wheat, and barley. These items were included primarily for their psychological effect upon the farmer vote. Duties levied upon commodities of which the United States had an excess for export, and the price of which was fixed on the world market, amounted, as was well known, to little more than empty gestures.

The reduction of the revenue, deemed imperative by both Democrats and Republicans, was accomplished in part by the discouraging effect on importation of the high duties, but in greater part by placing raw sugar on the free list. Seven-eighths of the unrefined sugar used in the United States had to be imported, and from the substantial tariff rates it carried the Treasury had realized each year over $50,000,000. Thus, at one stroke, the McKinley Bill accounted for a reduction of the annual surplus by one half. McKinley's protectionist principles, however, were in no wise violated by the removal of the duty on raw sugar. The Havemeyer sugar interests, which had a virtual monopoly on the production of man-- ufactured sugar in the United States, could now purchase raw sugar at a lower rate than ever before, while a tariff of one half cent a pound on refined sugar guarded the monopoly adequately against the competition of foreign manufacturers. Generous to a fault, the McKinley Bill even took care of the American producers of raw sugar (although most of them were Louisiana Democrats) by authorizing the payment of a bounty of two cents a pound on all raw sugar produced in the United States. Thus the sugar schedule, figuratively speaking, succeeded in taking money out of the Treasury with both hands.

James G. Blaine, as Secretary of State, was eager to see included in the tariff revision some plan of reciprocity that he could use to advantage *Reciprocity* in opening markets for American goods in Latin America. The elimination of the duty on sugar, however, together with the free admission of certain other items produced in Latin America, such as molasses, coffee, tea, and hides, seemed to destroy any bargaining power that the United States might otherwise have possessed. In defer- ence to Blaine's desires the Senate finally attached as an amendment, and the House accepted, a somewhat back-handed provision for reci- procity. The President was authorized to enforce a specified schedule of tariff rates on items listed as free in case the nations that produced them failed to grant equivalent advantages to American exports, on or before the first of January, 1892. Blaine was deeply disappointed that his hands were so closely tied, but under these provisions he succeeded in obtaining reductions in duties on American commodities entering Cuba,

[218]

Puerto Rico, and many other Latin-American countries, as well as small concessions from Germany and France.

One further measure, a Federal Elections Bill, the Republicans sought in vain to add to their program of legislative achievement. The closeness of the decision in 1888 made many of the party leaders long *Federal* for a return to the times during reconstruction when south- *Elections* ern states were dependably Republican; if only the federal *Bill* government might resume control of southern elections, then the intimidation of Negro voters could be stopped, and the "solid South" would disappear. Strongly championed by the youthful Henry Cabot Lodge, a representative from Massachusetts, the "Force Bill," as the public called the measure, passed the House, but failed in the Senate, where it became involved in an intricate pattern of vote-trading on the more pressing issues of free silver and the tariff. Thereafter, the southern states, far from showing any repentance for their discrimination against the Negroes, proceeded as rapidly as possible to fortify themselves behind skillfully drawn legal provisions. Long terms of residence in the same locality, the payment of a heavy poll tax, and ability to read, write, and understand any section of the state or federal Constitution were among the qualifications for voting that were laid down. To make sure, however, that indigent and illiterate white voters were not prevented from voting, some of the southern states made use of the famous "grandfather clause," which exempted the descendants of anyone who could vote in 1867, or earlier, from the tests otherwise applied. Not until 1915, when the Supreme Court of the United States invalidated a "grandfather clause" in the constitution of Oklahoma, was there any serious interference with this method of restricting Negro voting.

Public reaction to the behavior of the Fifty-First Congress was far from cordial. Each of its measures made a generous quota of enemies, and the grand total of accumulated grievances grew with each succeeding month. To the effect of the McKinley Bill on the revenue, which was sure to be disastrous, was added the orgy of spending in which Congress permitted itself to indulge. Its lavish appropriations for pensions, river and harbor improvements, federal buildings, coast defenses, and other extravagances led the newspapers to refer to it as the "billion-dollar Congress," a description strikingly lacking in political appeal. Unfortunate as a Treasury surplus might have been, a deficit, even less desirable, appeared to be in sight. Consumers found that the higher rates of the McKinley Tariff meant higher prices for what they had to buy; when its rates were made known, John Wanamaker, the storekeeper Postmaster-General, with more business than political acumen, openly urged his customers to "buy now, before prices go up." The Force Bill, based as it was upon an attempt to revive sectional antagonisms, was unpopular, North as well as South. As Elihu Root phrased it a little later, the whole country was ready to concede "the failure of the plan formulated at the close of the war to elevate the black man by conferring the suffrage upon him."

Held only a few weeks after the passage of the McKinley Bill, the congressional elections of 1890 showed how unpopular that measure, and *Elections* the Congress that passed it, had become. Democratic cam- *of 1890* paigners did not fail to take full advantage of the opportunity to denounce "Bill McKinley and the McKinley Bill." Peddlers were sent through the country, so the Republicans claimed, to offer tin cups at twenty-five cents each and tin pails at a dollar apiece in order to show the rural voters how much the McKinley duties had increased the cost of living. Merchants and salesmen apologized for high prices, whatever the truth might be, on the ground that the new tariff law had made them necessary. The Republicans, with tea, coffee, and sugar on the free list, had hoped to make much of the "free breakfast table," but the fact that the sugar duties were retained for six months after the passage of the bill made this battle-cry seem decidedly premature. When the votes were counted, the Republicans discovered that they had received the most emphatic rebuke in the history of their party. In the Senate the Republican majority was narrowed to eight, and would have been wiped out altogether but for the hold-over senators from the newly admitted states of the Northwest. In the House the Democrats had 235 seats, and the Republicans 88, while nine Farmers' Alliance men, or Populists, refused to vote with either of the older parties. The appearance of this group of independents in Congress marked the beginning of an agrarian revolt in the Middle West and the South, which, with the assistance it received from the silver mining states of the Far West, threatened for a time to bring about a complete realignment of political parties in the United States.[1]

[1] Wilfred E. Binkley, *American Political Parties: Their Natural History* (1943), is an excellent synthesis. Frank H. Heck, *The Civil War Veteran in Minnesota Life and Politics* (1941), throws much light on the political activites of the G.A.R. On Cleveland's first Secretary of State, there are two admirable books by C. C. Tansill, *The Congressional Career of Thomas Francis Bayard, 1869–1885* (1946), and *The Foreign Policy of Thomas F. Bayard, 1885–1897* (1940).

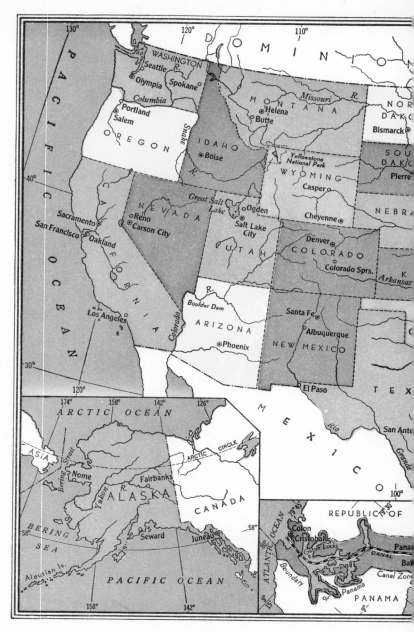

THE UNITED STATES IN 1940

CHAPTER X

THE NEW SOUTH AND THE NEW WEST

THE South that raised its voice in protest against the Force Bill of 1890 was a very different land from the South that had submitted helplessly to the Force Bills of the Grant administration. Its leading citizens called it pridefully the "New South." Much that *The New South* it had to offer was not so new as enthusiasts stated, for the roots of the New South lay deep in the Old. But beyond a doubt, "times had changed." Particularly was this true of the long tongue of piedmont and mountain country extending southward from the border of Pennsylvania through western Maryland, the Virginias and Kentucky, the Carolinas and Tennessee, into Georgia and Alabama. Throughout this region a new and startling devotion to industry had taken hold. Here, if anywhere, the New South was really new.[1]

Before the Civil War the South had made beginnings in manufacturing, but almost everywhere the complete supremacy of agriculture had gone unchallenged. How great a mistake this had been the results of the war seemed only too clearly to indicate. The industrial North had triumphed; the agricultural South had lost. Even before the war was over, with the southern armies paralyzed for lack of equipment that the northern armies possessed in abundance, this lesson had been brought home. The almost inevitable reaction, once the war was over, was that the South must imitate its conquerors. If the North had cities and factories and wealth, then the South, too, must find some way to have them.

It was a hard struggle. Impoverished by the war and handicapped by reconstruction, the builders of the New South had next to wait out the depression of the seventies. Outside capital was reluctant to come in, so Southerners who had "caught the vision" pooled their own meager resources and made the best start they could. They had a few important advantages. The world still needed southern cotton and the price it

---

[1] W. B. Hesseltine, *A History of the South, 1607–1936* (1936), contains a significant chapter on this subject. Holland Thompson, *The New South* (1919), and P. A. Bruce, *Rise of the New South* (1905), are sympathetic studies.

brought was high. As southern agriculture came back, its profits, slender as they were, could be tapped to expand the southern infant industries. Southern land was cheap and the cost of factory sites was negligible. The labor supply was inexhaustible, utterly unorganized, and willing to work at any price. Cotton mills, the chief industrial hope of the South, could be located so close to the cotton-fields as to hold at a minimum the cost of freight-handling. Water-power was abundant, if only it could be harnessed, and the mountains were known to harbor formidable quantities of coal. The politicians, once the "black and tan" governments of reconstruction times had been eliminated, were friendly and helpful. Indeed, the so-called "Bourbon" Democrats who succeeded the carpet-baggers in the rule of the South were little more than agents of the new industrialists. They kept the cost of government at a minimum, and sometimes even exempted new industries from taxation. They leased out convicts, most of whom were ex-slaves, at ridiculously low rates, to all who wished to use them, and gave the employers whatever disciplinary powers they needed. Eventually, as the southern manufacturers began to make money, northern capital sensed the opportunity for profits and came to the southerners' aid.

By the eighties the industrial road to wealth had become almost a religion in the South. Henry W. Grady, able editor of the influential *Industrial beginnings* Atlanta *Constitution*, radiated enthusiasm for it in his editorials.[1] "He did not tamely promote enterprise and encourage industry," wrote one of his contemporaries, "he vehemently fomented enterprise and provoked industry until they stalked through the land like armed conquerors." Others preached the same gospel, among them Benjamin H. Hill, senator from Georgia, who wrote, after one of the annual cotton expositions held in Atlanta during the eighties:

> Factories are springing up in all directions. Our industries are being multiplied as never before. Thousands of the best men of the North have gone home from the exposition enthused with the brightening prospects of all business in the State. Our taxes were scarcely ever so low. Our credit was never so high. Capital and people and machinery are flowing in, and everybody is brushing away the tears of war, and laughing with a new hope in a new era!

The manufacture of cotton in the South before the Civil War had achieved more prominence than is generally supposed. By 1860 the South had one hundred and sixty cotton mills, with 300,000 spindles, and a total output valued at $8,000,000. During the war many of the mills

---

[1] Also in a book, H. W. Grady, *The New South* (1890).

were worn out and many others destroyed, so that in 1870 there were fewer southern mills in operation than in 1860. By 1880, however, the pre-war level had been passed, and from that time forward progress was rapid. By 1890 there were about 1,750,000 spindles in the South, and every mill, seemingly, paid excellent profits. At the end of the century the South had nearly half the cotton mills of the country, and accounted for about the same proportion of the cotton goods manufactured. Most of the mills were located along the piedmont in North Carolina, South Carolina, Georgia, and Alabama, usually in small towns and villages, or adjacent to, rather than actually within, some of the larger cities. At first the southern mills produced mainly the coarser grades of cotton, such as denim, leaving to New England the manufacture of the finer grades, but as time went on the variety of southern-made textiles was steadily expanded. The allied knitting industry also made rapid headway, no less in Tennessee and Virginia than in the lower South.[1]

Quite as natural as the development of the textile industry in the South was the utilization of cotton-seed, long regarded as little more than a nuisance. Before the Civil War, and for some time *Cotton-seed* after, cotton-seed at best was rotted in barnyard manure to *products* be used as fertilizer, and at worst was dumped into the streams along which, for power purposes, so many of the cotton-gins were located. A little cotton-seed was fed to livestock, great quantities of it were burned. Realization that the cotton-seeds were saturated with an oil which, when extracted, was both digestible and inoffensive in taste, opened the way to innumerable possibilities. With the help of the chemists cotton-seed oil was made available as a cheap substitute for such expensive items as olive oil, lard, and butter; it was used also for making soap, cosmetics, and numerous other oil products. The crushed seeds, after the oil was removed, were still rich in nitrogen and could be turned into fertilizer, or pressed into oilcake and fed to cattle. From the seeds, too, great quantities of "linters," or short, close-clinging cotton fibers, were recovered, to be used, again with the help of the chemists, in making celluloid, collodion, and a great variety of other commodities. Not every use to which cotton-seed products are now put was known in the nineteenth century, but the beginnings had been made in an industry that by the time of the World War was adding annually over $200,000,000 to the income of the South.

Almost as significant as the cotton and cotton-seed industries of the

[1] Broadus Mitchell and G. S. Mitchell, *The Industrial Revolution in the South* (1930), Broadus Mitchell, *The Rise of the Cotton Mills in the South* (1921); Holland Thompson; *From the Cotton Field to the Cotton Mill* (1906).

New South were its mining industries. The existence of rich coal and
Coal and iron deposits in the southern mountains was known long
iron before the Civil War, but with comparatively little effort at
exploitation. The coal-fields of West Virginia, Maryland, Kentucky,
and Virginia, however, were in too easy reach of the great industrial
cities of the North to be long ignored. Partly to satisfy the needs of
northern industry the output of southern coal mines was speeded up from
six million tons in 1880 to fifty million tons in 1900. Meanwhile, the iron
mines of eastern Tennessee and northern Alabama began to attract
attention.[1] Located, as they were, adjacent to inexhaustible fields of
bituminous coal, and in the Birmingham area close to limestone as well,
they furnished an ideal setting for the development of the iron and steel
industry. Birmingham, named after Birmingham, England, and soon
called "the Pittsburgh of the South," was not incorporated as a city
until 1871, but by 1900 it had 38,000 inhabitants, by 1910, 132,000, and
by 1930, nearly 260,000. Its growth may be taken as a kind of barometer of southern iron and steel, although the city became an important
center for nearly every type of industry represented in the South.

More and more the industrial diversification of the South approached
that of the North. The manufacture of tobacco was helped rather than
Tobacco and hindered as a result of the war. Northern soldiers who had
lumber grown accustomed to southern makes of tobacco wrote back
for more to the southern towns where they had been quartered, and such
enterprising Southerners as the Dukes of North Carolina took advantage
of the opportunity to expand their markets. Small tobacco factories
grew into larger ones, or, as the inevitable concentration in industry proceeded, were eliminated; but the total output of tobacco manufactured in
the South steadily increased.[2] Lumbering opened another opportunity
for wealth, and southern yellow pine was soon competing strongly with
the white pine and hemlock of the Northwest. Southern hardwoods also
proved to be easily adaptable for use in all sorts of woodwork, particularly furniture, and by the opening of the twentieth century, High Point,
North Carolina, was becoming to the furniture industry of the South
what Grand Rapids, Michigan, was to the furniture industry of the
North. In the making of fertilizer the South took advantage of another
natural opportunity. Rich phosphate deposits in the Southeast, together with the abundance of cotton-seed, gave the southern states a long
lead in this industry over the states of any other section. Other types of

---

[1] Ethel Armes, *The Story of Coal and Iron in Alabama* (1910).

[2] B. W. Arnold, *History of the Tobacco Industry in Virginia from 1860 to 1894* (1897);
W. K. Boyd, *The Story of Durham* (1925); J. W. Jenkins, *James B. Duke* (1927).

industry that came to be well represented in the South were corn- and wheat-milling, meat-packing, the making of cement and cement products, brick, pottery, turpentine, and coal-tar derivatives.

Labor conditions in the South differed markedly from labor conditions in the North. For one thing, until well after the beginning of the twentieth century the South failed to attract immigrant labor, *Southern* or even the children of the immigrants. Whites from the *mill workers* poorer lands of the Piedmont and from the mountains furnished the bulk of the labor supply for the textile mills and such others as required skilled operatives, while a preponderance of blacks did the harder work of the mines, the blast furnaces, and the lumber industry. Only in the rarest instances were the two races employed to work side by side at the same tasks; industries that used both whites and blacks took care that there was a division of labor that separated the races, with the inferior position being regularly assigned to the blacks. In the textile mills the employment of women and children was practically universal, although the extent to which small children were exploited has doubtless been exaggerated. Nevertheless, one of the chief attractions of the mills to the rural whites was the opportunity they furnished for the whole family to be gainfully employed. Wages were low, at first far lower than wages paid in the northern mills, but with the wife and children at work as well as the head of the house the total income realized was so much larger than could be wrested from a rundown southern farm that the temptation to leave the farm for the factory was well-nigh irresistible. It often turned out that women and children kept their jobs, while the men, less easily adaptable to the new type of work, lost theirs. Not every husband who stayed home while the rest of the family went to work did so of his own volition. Hours of labor were long, sometimes as much as seventy-two hours per week.[1]

Most of the southern mills and factories developed along definitely paternalistic lines. Someone had to provide houses for the workers, and the "company" made it its business to provide them. The company likewise opened stores, and in many instances paid the workers in scrip, good at any time for payments to the company, but redeemable in cash only at infrequent intervals. The company also provided such schools and churches as it deemed desirable, and hired both the teachers and the preachers. To the country people who flocked to the mills these acts of forethought were accepted without suspicion. The houses of the mill villages were better than the houses of the farms, the company stores were easy of access, and charged little more, if any, than other stores;

[1] M. A. Potwin, *Cotton Mill People of the Piedmont* (1927).

while the schools, the churches, and the factories themselves furnished such an opportunity for community life as the workers had never known before. At first labor unions were virtually unknown, and throughout the nineteenth century labor agitators were given little encouragement either by employers or by employees. In the twentieth century, however, unionism took strong hold in the South and worked many changes.

For all the vast transformation wrought by industrialism in southern life, the South at the end of the nineties, as before the war, was still a *Southern* dominantly agricultural region. In every southern state *agriculture* far more people were engaged in agriculture than in any other occupation, while most of the business and professional classes were dependent upon farm income for their support. The New South, like the Old, had few large cities, and its annual output of manufactured goods actually accounted for only about one eighth of the nation's total output. Southern cotton was still grown after much the same fashion, by nearly the same types of laborers, in approximately the same regions as before the war. The yield had steadily increased. By 1894 the production of cotton in the South exceeded ten million bales, nearly twice that of the pre-war years. Much the same could be said of tobacco, sugar-cane, cereals, and livestock, but if the total produce of the South had increased, so also had its population. For the great majority of the southern people, the industrial frenzy of the New South was of no direct or immediate consequence.

The southern farmer, whether white or black, had little of the restless energy that had characterized the pioneer farmer of the North. The climate was easy, survival after some fashion was reasonably well assured, and with farm prices ever falling the reward of ambition was slight. The rural South also suffered acutely from disease. The hookworm, an intestinal parasite common to most warm countries, was probably brought to the South by the Negroes, but it was far less disastrous in its effects upon them than upon the whites. Fortunately the disease it breeds yields easily to medical treatment, and in the twentieth century the Rockefeller Foundation, after a persistent and expensive campaign, succeeded in almost entirely eradicating it. In the nineteenth century, however, it was still sapping the vitality of a countless number of the lower classes; as was also the pellagra, a disease that resulted from their too restricted diet. The Negroes, especially after they had escaped from the care and supervision of their masters, showed themselves to be particularly susceptible to pulmonary diseases and tuberculosis. Physical unfitness was thus by no means least among the reasons for the backwardness of the rural South.

Seventy per cent of the farmers of the South, a generation after Appomattox, were tenants. The Negroes, starting as ex-slaves with nothing but their labor to sell, could hardly have been expected to *Tenancy* do better; but they had made almost as much progress toward individual ownership as the lower-class southern whites. For both races the tenant system, once it was well established, tended to become self-perpetuating. In general there were three types of tenants in the South: (1) the cash tenant, who paid rent in money or a specified number of bales of cotton, and was otherwise no different from a landowner; (2) the share tenant, who in lieu of rent paid for the use of his land from one fourth to one third of his crop, but furnished his own stock, tools, and foodstuffs; and (3) the share-cropper, who paid a larger proportion of his crop to his landlord, but furnished nothing whatever for himself. Some of the cash and share tenants, who were usually white, were fairly thrifty; the "croppers," on the other hand, among whom most of the country Negroes were numbered, were barely one degree removed from slavery.[1]

One of the many unhappy results of the Civil War, and an important cause of southern tenancy, was the inadequate credit system from which the South long suffered. After the war the national banking *The crop-* system advanced so slowly into the impoverished South that *lien system* by 1895 the ten cotton states had only four hundred and seventeen national banks among them, and of these more than one half were located in Texas. The dearth of local capital kept down likewise the number of state and private banking institutions; in Georgia, for example, more than a hundred counties lacked banking facilities altogether. Such money as was available for loans went in a disproportionate amount to industry rather than to agriculture; money to lend to farmers, even landowners, was simply not available. Faced by these circumstances the South developed a unique institution, the country store. Such a store was not necessarily located in the country; it took its name from the fact that it catered to the country trade. The country storekeeper did not expect to sell for cash, for most of the country people had no cash. He sold on credit, and to insure himself against loss took a lien on the farmer's crop and, if possible, a chattel mortgage also. If the farmer chanced to be a tenant, as might normally be expected, then the merchant's lien was taken only on the tenant's share of the crop. Landlords sometimes attempted to supervise these contracts, but the competition for tenants was so keen that independent crop liens to the storekeeper were generally

[1] R. B. Vance, *Human Geography of the South* (1932), and by the same author, *Human Factors in Cotton Culture* (1929), are unsurpassed as studies of the conditions of southern life.

the privilege of the humblest share-cropper. The storekeeper for his own credit needs was often compelled to rely in large part upon advances from cotton-buyers, whom he would pay off ultimately not in cash but in cotton.

While the landlord from whom the tenant rented his land and the storekeeper from whom he bought his goods were likely in the years immediately following the war to be two different persons, they tended as time went on to become one and the same person. Landlords themselves sometimes moved to town and went into the store business, not only for the profit involved, but also as a means of insuring that too much of their tenants' produce was not used up in trade. Merchants, at the same time, purchased land, or more likely took it over from unsuccessful landlords on mortgages. In general the merchant-landlord who lived in town and made only occasional tours of inspection into the country was preferred by the tenant over the landlord-neighbor, with his constantly exhibited interest in the tenants' industry. To the easygoing share-cropper of the South, absentee landlordism was regarded as a blessing rather than a curse.

Legal sanction for the crop-lien system was readily provided by the "Bourbon" legislators of the post-reconstruction South. To the mer-

Plight of the share-cropper chant, in return for the promise of a year's supply of necessities in advance, the farmer was permitted to sign over title to as much of his future crop as might be necessary to settle his store bill. Furthermore, in case his purchases during the year exceeded the amount he owed at the store he was legally bound to trade the next year with the same merchant, or, as was so often the case, the same merchant-landlord, with whom he had contracted the previous year, and to whom he still owed money. Thus the way was opened for the establishment of a system of virtual peonage, for the number of farmers who could so plan their expenditures as to break even at the end of the year was few indeed. For many of them, the only means of escape from this new bondage was flight to a community so far distant that the law would not be likely to follow them.[1]

The plight of the farmer who found himself ensnared by the crop-lien system was always hard. He might not purchase more goods than the merchant thought he needed; he must pay whatever prices the merchant asked, usually not less than double the prices asked of cash customers; he had little or no recourse against the merchant who chose to cheat him. Fully convinced of the hopelessness of his situation, the ordinary share-cropper rarely tried seriously to get cash ahead; if he raised more

[1] E. M. Banks, *Economics of Land Tenure in Georgia* (1905).

cotton than he needed to pay his store bill, he frequently picked only enough to discharge his obligation and left the rest unharvested. But the merchant, for all his long profits, had no sure road to wealth. A season of crop failures or low prices, when matched by the all too characteristic shiftlessness, illnesses, and jail sentences among his customers, might mean that the merchant would receive for his heavy outlays next to nothing in return. Storekeepers occasionally became rich, but they also more than occasionally went bankrupt.

In much of the lower South a tragic accompaniment of the crop-lien system was the one-crop evil, for merchants in the cotton-growing areas strongly preferred that their credit-customers plant cotton *The one-crop evil* to the exclusion of other crops. Cotton could always be marketed at some price; it did not deteriorate with age; it could not, like corn, for example, be fed to livestock or consumed as "roasting-ears" by the farm family; its value in comparison to its bulk made it easy to handle. Furthermore, the farmer who raised cotton only was a far better customer than the farmer who supplied his table and fed his mule from his own garden and fields; all such supplies he had to purchase at the store, together with such quantities of fertilizer as were necessary to produce cotton on his worn-out soil. Merchants rarely admitted that these were the reasons which led them to insist on cotton-growing. The Negro farmer, they said, and many of the whites also, knew how to grow cotton, and but little else; if permitted to try other crops, the returns were sure to be meager. Nor did the cotton-growers show much interest in emancipating themselves from the one-crop system. "Cotton-planting has been a mania," wrote one observer. "The neglected corn-field with all its consequences is a part of Southern history." [1]

The one-party system which the reconstruction period had left as a legacy to the South made it extremely difficult for the farmers of that section, whether black or white, to seek through political *The one-party system* action the amelioration of their ills. The blacks were virtually disfranchised, and, because of the peculiar distribution of the white population, the power of the lower-class rural whites in politics was far less than their numbers would have justified. The best cotton lands lay along the river valleys and close to the sea, precisely the same lands that had grown the cotton of the pre-war plantation South. Here the Negroes were concentrated, no longer as slaves but as tenants of a favored few of the whites. In these "black belts" the landlords and the merchants, supported by the votes of the towns-

---

[1] C. H. Otken, *The Ills of the South* (1894), is an old but extremely revealing study. See also Hammond, *The Cotton Industry*, already cited.

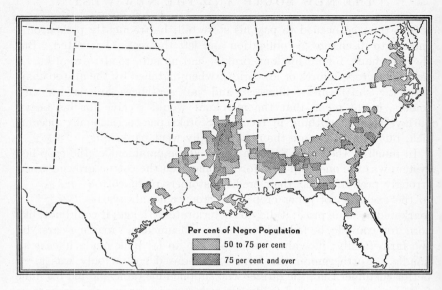

Per cent of Negro Population

50 to 75 per cent

75 per cent and over

THE BLACK BELT
(Based on Census of 1910)

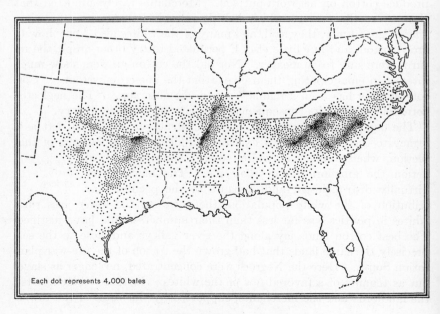

Each dot represents 4,000 bales

THE COTTON BELT
(Based on Census of 1910)

people, not only ruled supreme over a population predominantly Negro and non-voting, but exercised also a disproportionate influence in the politics of any given state. Since the assignment of membership in the legislature and of delegates in nominating conventions was according to population, the representatives of the "black counties" could practically always outvote the representatives of the "white counties." And, since white solidarity demanded unfailing support of whatever Democratic candidates were nominated, the "Bourbons" of the "black belt," eager servants of the industrialists, the landlords, and the merchants, maintained their uninterrupted sway. Hardly less than before the Civil War the South remained in the hands of a favored ruling caste. Discontent with such a system, followed by an open revolt against it, was sure to come.

During the same period that the New South was emerging from the rigors of reconstruction a New West was also taking form. The New West differed from the New South, however, in that it had *A New* no past; the region in which it had been created had been *West* little more than wilderness before the Civil War. Sometimes called the "Middle Border," this newly settled region stretched from the bend of the Missouri to the Rockies. It included Kansas, Nebraska, the Dakotas, and parts of Colorado, Wyoming, and Montana. Much of western Missouri, Iowa, and Minnesota was similarly new, and belonged, at least in spirit, with the New West. The Indian Territory, into which after 1889 white population was legally permitted to go, was soon to become, as Oklahoma, its newest portion.[1]

The New West was the product of the railroads. Without them to bring in the population and to take out the produce, it could never have been. But the railroads were responsible for the develop- *The rail-* ment of this section in an even more literal sense, for they *roads and* owned, advertised, and sold directly to settlers a good *the West* share of its lands. Only the great transcontinentals had received land grants directly from the United States, but many of the other roads had been recipients of state grants. Every land-grant railroad had at once set up a land department, and had begun an active campaign for settlers. Railroad agents, both in the United States and in Europe, distributed pamphlets which demolished the "myth" of the "Great American Desert," and proclaimed the boundless resources of the New West. Land was offered at prices as low as $2.50 per acre, and sometimes lower, with attractive credit features that stretched out almost

---

[1] Two extremely colorful narratives of this last frontier are Everett Dick, *The Sod House Frontier, 1854–1890* (1937), and H. E. Briggs, *Frontiers of the Northwest* (1940).

See note at foot of page 233.

FEDERAL LAND GRANTS FOR TRANSPORTATION, 1823–71

NORTHERN PACIFIC R.R.

UNION PACIFIC R.R.

CENTRAL PACIFIC R.R.

KANSAS PACIFIC R.R.

ATCHISON, TOPEKA AND SANTA FE R.R.

SOUTHERN PACIFIC R.R.

ATLANTIC AND PACIFIC R.R.

TEXAS AND PACIFIC R.R.

indefinitely the period of payment. Land-seekers' excursion tickets were sold on the understanding that the price paid for the ticket might be counted as a down payment on any purchase of railroad land. Most railroads made little money out of the disposal of their lands. What they did, and what they meant to do, was to bring in the population and "build up" the country. Only by so doing could they hope for a volume of business adequate to maintain their lines; without people to pay freights and passenger fares a railroad could not long survive.

Indeed, the railroads did not much care whether the incoming settlers bought railroad land, or acquired lands from the government by purchase or homestead. In the numerous pamphlets that their land offices brought out, they pointed out that through the Homestead Act there existed a cheaper way of obtaining land than they themselves could provide. For a few dollars in fees any American citizen, or any alien who had declared his intention of becoming a citizen, could obtain by living on it for five years one hundred and sixty acres of unoccupied government land if located outside the radius of a railroad grant, or eighty acres if located within such an area. This latter proviso was included on the assumption that lands close to a railroad were worth twice as much as lands at a distance from a railroad. An Act of 1870 extended special privileges to soldiers who had fought in the Union army. Any such veteran might count his time of service toward the five-year period required for "proving up" on a homestead, and any widow of a soldier might count the full term of her dead husband's enlistment in the same way.

Railway pamphlets often pointed out methods of obtaining from the United States more land than the homestead laws offered. The Preemption Act of 1841, which remained on the statute books *Federal land* until 1891, allowed the settler to locate a claim of one hun- *policy* dred and sixty acres, and after six months' residence to buy it from the government at the minimum price, $1.25 an acre under ordinary circumstances, or $2.50 an acre if located in a railroad grant area. In its effort to adapt the national land policy to conditions of life on the Great Plains, the government soon went to even more generous lengths. The size of the original homestead — one hundred and sixty acres — was based upon farming experience east of the bend of the Missouri, where

Note to map on page 232: This map shows the total area from which lands were granted. The shaded portions include (1) both the non-railroad sections and the alternate sections actually taken by the railroads; (2) "indemnity lands" from which the railroads selected grants in case lands near their tracks had already been taken; and (3) lands granted for wagon roads (mostly in Michigan and Oregon). The state of Texas, which owned its own lands, also made extensive grants to railroads.

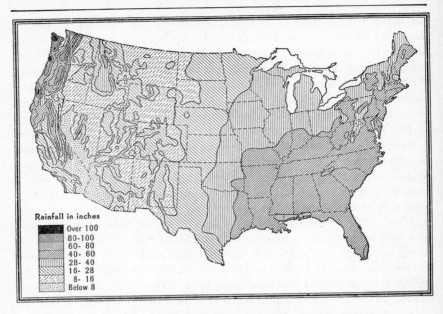

Rainfall in inches

■	Over 100
	80-100
	60- 80
	40- 60
	28- 40
	16- 28
	8- 16
	Below 8

AVERAGE ANNUAL RAINFALL IN THE UNITED STATES

a quarter-section of land made as large a farm as any one family could conveniently work. On the treeless plains of the West where rainfall was generally inadequate, the farming experience of the East was more or less inapplicable. The Timber Culture Act of 1873 was the first of a series of laws designed to meet the needs of the farther West. Under its terms the settler who would plant forty acres (later reduced to ten) in trees, and keep them in a growing condition for ten years, could obtain title to a quarter-section of land. The Desert Land Act of 1877 contemplated still larger holdings. In eleven states and territories a person might buy an entire section of land — six hundred and forty acres — at the minimum price of $1.25 an acre, provided that he would irrigate it within a period of three years after filing his claim. Only twenty-five cents an acre need be paid at the time of filing, and the rest when the proof of irrigation was submitted. Under the terms of this law many cattle and sheep ranchers got title to the land they needed for headquarters, and a few individuals, mostly speculators, opened up irrigation projects. Finally, by the Timber and Stone Act of 1878, the ambitious pioneer might purchase at not less than $2.50 an acre a quarter-section of land valuable chiefly for timber and stone. Thus it became possible

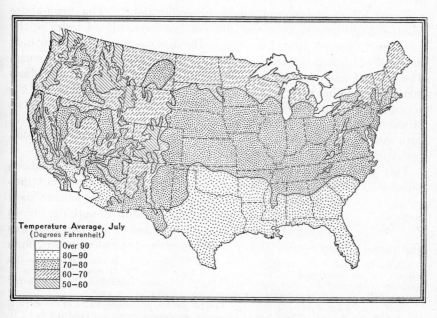

AVERAGE ANNUAL TEMPERATURE IN THE UNITED STATES

for the man with a little capital at his disposal to obtain in all two full sections of government land — 1280 acres — at an average cost per acre of $1.12½. Although the railroad advertisers could not print such facts, it was known to most Americans that by a little perjury and fraud, not highly condemned in the frontier region, disagreeable requirements could be evaded.[1]

The result of the railroad propaganda was such a wholesale migration of population as the nation had never known before. Veterans of the

The west-ward movement

Civil War flocked to Kansas and Nebraska in such numbers as to give those states for a generation, or even longer, top-heavy Republican majorities. Substantial farmers through-out the North, but more especially those of the upper Mississippi Valley, sold their high-priced holdings to buy the cheaper lands of the West. Farm boys lately grown to manhood, small businessmen who had seen, or who hoped to see, better days, and not a few unemployed artisans joined the procession to the West. Europeans, persuaded by railroad and steamship agents to leave their Old-World homes, were herded aboard ship, and having reached America were sent by special trains from the port of entry to some prearranged location on railroad lands. Within a single generation a region that started as wilderness had achieved all of the paraphernalia of civilization.[2] The "sod-house frontier," spectacular as it was, did not last long. Hard times in the East during the seventies led many of the discontented to try their luck in the West, but the good times of the eighties led even more to come. The area of adequate rainfall seemed surely, if slowly, to be pushing farther and farther west. Grasshopper plagues, so destructive during the seventies, were not repeated in the eighties. With good crops western farmers prospered, or thought they prospered, even when the price of corn and wheat was low. What had happened in the New West can perhaps best be told in figures. (See table on page 237.)

This rapid expansion of the western frontier would not have been possible, however, without easy credit. The farmers who went into

Eastern credit to the West

the new region rarely had enough capital to finance their venture, and many of them had almost nothing at all. The kind of farming that they wished to do, however, was expensive. They needed heavy breaking-plows to deal with the tough

[1] B. H. Hibbard, *A History of the Public Land Policies* (1924), is the best book on this subject, but see also appropriate sections in L. B. Schmidt and E. D. Ross, *Readings in the Economic History of American Agriculture* (1925). Thomas Donaldson, *The Public Do-main* (1884), contains large quantities of undigested material.

[2] S. K. Humphrey, *Following the Prairie Frontier* (1931), recaptures much of the spirit of this headlong advance. The trials of a pioneer immigrant group are recorded in C. H. Smith, *The Coming of the Russian Mennonites* (1927).

GROWTH OF POPULATION IN THE NEW WEST

	1860	1870	1880	1890
Kansas	107,206	364,399	996,096	1,428,108
Nebraska	28,841	122,993	452,402	1,062,656
Dakota	4,837	14,181	135,177	539,583
Iowa	674,913	1,194,020	1,624,615	1,912,297
Minnesota	172,023	439,706	780,773	1,310,283
Colorado	34,277	39,864	194,327	413,249
Montana		20,595	39,159	142,924
Wyoming		9,118	20,789	62,555

prairie sod, and high-priced oxen or horses to draw them. They needed planters, cultivators, mowing machines, reapers, and threshing machines. They needed houses and barns, cattle and hogs. For good or ill the New West, unlike the New South, could have what it wanted, or at least much that it wanted, on credit. Easterners with money to lend had a settled conviction that there was no security so safe as a western farm mortgage, and a long record of rising land values seemed to bear out their judgment. Interest rates were high. Farm mortgages brought from six to eight per cent, while loans secured by town property often brought even more. Chattel mortgages brought still higher interest rates, from ten to eighteen per cent and more. With plenty of eastern money to lend and plenty of western borrowers to borrow, the little banks of the West were unable to handle the traffic, and loan companies were organized to help them out. By 1890 Kansas statistics showed only 350 farms unmortgaged out of a total of 3107 that were tabulated, and the total mortgage indebtedness of the state was estimated at $146,563,000.

Western borrowing went much further than the mere outfitting of farmers. The new western communities made haste to reproduce as nearly as possible the conditions their citizens had been *The western* used to farther east. City dwellers went in for better homes *boom* and gardens. Counties needed and obtained courthouses and jails, roads and bridges. School districts put up school buildings, towns pledged their futures for city halls, waterworks, electric light plants, and, if they could find the slightest justification for it, streetcar systems as well. As the population increased, demands were voiced for more railroads, and companies to build them were promptly founded and financed. The New West itself furnished for all this "development" next to nothing by way of capital, but the steady faith of eastern investors showed no signs of abatement. Western securities, railroad stocks and municipal bonds no less than farm mortgages, were regarded as "gilt-edged," and what the New West wished to borrow it could have, provided only that it would promise high interest rates. So the New West, also sure of its future, borrowed and promised. During the middle eighties, with all this easy credit, it became the scene of a veritable "boom." Each sizable town was convinced that it was soon to become a metropolis. Around such strategic centers as Omaha, Yankton, Atchison, Topeka and Kansas City new additions were platted into lots that were sold, borrowed upon, and sold again, only to be returned in the end to the cornfields from which they had been taken.[1]

The collapse of the western boom began with the summer of 1887, the first of a long series of dry seasons. Time proved that the myth of *Collapse of* the Great American Desert was no less groundless than the *the boom* myth that the region of adequate rainfall was advancing steadily into the West. Settlers who had gone hopefully into western Dakota, Kansas, or Nebraska, and even out into eastern Montana or Colorado, learned to their sorrow that they had gone much too far.

> Week after week [wrote one observer] the hot burning sun glared down from a cloudless steel-blue sky. The dread hot winds blew in from the south. Day after day they continued. All fodder, small grain and corn were cut short. Where farming had been carried on extensively rather than intensively the yield amounted to preciously near nothing. The careful expert got some returns for his work, though small.

The same covered wagons that had taken the settlers to the West were now turned toward the East, sometimes decorated with legends such as "Going home to the wife's folks," or "In God we trusted, in Kansas we busted," or

> Fifty miles to water,
> A hundred miles to wood,
> To hell with this damned country,
> I'm going home for good.

How many people left the drouth-stricken states during these hard years will never be known, but so many went that the census-takers of 1890 felt obliged to pad their records generously. It is not unlikely, however, that the New West had as many people in 1887 as the census claimed for 1890, and in some regions it probably had many more.

With the advent of the drouth, eastern moneylenders promptly

---

[1] Tarbell, *The Nationalizing of Business*, already cited, contains an illuminating account on the "peopling" of the West and the results that followed.

changed their minds about the future of the West. Not only was the
flow of new money to the West abruptly stopped, but at- *Drouth*
tempts to collect that which had already been lent became
also more and more insistent. Foreclosures followed thick and fast.
Hundreds of western bankers, unable to make collections, closed their
doors. Loan companies disappeared overnight. As if to make the
disaster doubly complete, farm prices showed a steadily declining curve,
for the crop shortage of the New West, great as it was, failed to produce
a similar shortage in the world market, or, for that matter, even in the
United States. Moreover, the opportunity of flight to a new frontier,
for generations the standard American formula for escape from economic
distress, was no longer of much avail. The wholesale assault of railroads and individuals upon the lands of the West had all but used them
up. The era of good cheap lands was coming to a close. Commenting
on the recklessness with which the government had squandered its
resources, an indignant Nebraska editor complained:

> Only a little while ago the people owned this princely domain. Now they
> are *starving for land* — starving for the right to create from the soil a sub-
> sistence for their wives and little children. . . . They would gladly buy land if
> they could. But the merciless contraction of money and fearful shrinkage
> of values and prices have put it out of their power to buy land, even though
> it may be offered at reduced prices. They want *free land* — the land that
> Congress squandered . . . the land that should have formed the patrimony
> of unborn generations.

The importance of the alienation of the national domain was not lost
upon other and more sophisticated observers. In 1887 Professor A. B.
Hart of Harvard University published an article on "The *The "end of*
Disposition of the Public Lands" in the first volume of the *free land"*
Quarterly Journal of Economics, and the year before Shosuke Sato, a Japanese student at Johns Hopkins University, had written a monograph on
the *History of the Land Question in the United States*. The government, so
these critics of its policy observed, had treated its lands as if the supply
were inexhaustible, only to discover when it was too late that they were
nearly gone. Of mountains and deserts and arid plains the government
still possessed an abundance, but of lands suitable for the traditional
types of agriculture perhaps less than two million acres remained. More
philosophic than either Hart or Sato was Henry George, whose *Progress
and Poverty* had appeared in 1879. George's ideas, although actually
published as early as 1871 in a forty-eight-page pamphlet, *Our Land and
Land Policy*, and widely heralded abroad, were slow to attract attention
in America. By the middle eighties, however, his writings were being

HENRY GEORGE

CARL SCHURZ

GEORGE WILLIAM CURTIS

JAMES B. WEAVER

FOUR NONCONFORMISTS
(Pictures from Brown Brothers)

extensively circulated on both sides of the Atlantic. "All who do not possess land," he argued, "are toiling for those who do, and this is the reason why progress and poverty go hand in hand." To remedy the situation there need be no redistribution of land. Instead, landowners should pay the equivalent of economic rent in taxation. From the proceeds of this "single tax" George believed that enough revenue would be realized to make possible the elimination of all other forms of taxation. Of particular interest to the agricultural classes was his assumption that growing crops, houses, and all other improvements upon the land should be exempted from taxation. With the abolition of customary taxes, because of which labor, capital, and enterprise alike were robbed, George held that economic laws would work with a smoothness never known before. Monopolies would disappear, wealth would be equitably shared, and the fear of recurring depressions would cease to be the nightmare of business.[1]

Whether the reasoning of George was right or wrong, Americans of his generation felt that the "passing of free land" was an extremely serious matter. Probably they were wrong in their assumption that free land, up to their time, had been a perfect safety-valve for farmer and labor discontent. Only since the passage of the Homestead Act in 1862 had the government really given away land to settlers, and, as already noted, the policy of land sales had not even then been discontinued. As a matter of fact more free land was to be distributed in the twentieth century than in the nineteenth. It was not so much the high cost of land that hampered the pioneer as the high cost of farming with expensive machinery, the uncertainty of rainfall, and the low price of farm produce. Furthermore, the existence of free lands in the West was always of uncertain benefit to laborers of the industrialized regions. Such lands might draw away farm families from regions adjacent to the factories, and so reduce the number of rural competitors for city jobs, but underpaid or unemployed laborers were rarely able to raise the funds necessary to transport themselves to the West to make a new start. The New West was mostly the work of men who had been farmers before, and of these the great majority came from near-by states. Nevertheless, the tradition persisted that the frontier should furnish a haven of refuge for all the distressed of the United States and of Europe, and information which tended to show that the West was no longer able to fulfill this rôle was received with deep apprehension. Someone was to blame. Denied the opportunity of flight to another frontier, and convinced that the ills from which they suffered were not

[1] G. R. Geiger, *The Philosophy of Henry George* (1933).

of their own making, the farmers of the New West and the farmers of the New South were alike ripe for revolt.[1]

In spite of their common problems, however, there were many obstacles in the way of the two sections working together. The New West *Common interests of West and South* and the New South had come into existence while the rancors of reconstruction were at their worst, and each had accepted as a matter of course the dominant sectional bias of the times. Many of the pioneers of the Middle Border had fought under Grant and Sherman; they were honored members of the Grand Army of the Republic; they had not yet forgiven the South for precipitating the Civil War. Likewise, the builders of the New South had marched with Lee and Johnston; they, too, had formed their military orders, only lately merged as the United Confederate Veterans; they held their tongues about the North, but thought what they had always thought. But even these historic political antagonisms could not prevent the development of a bond of sympathy between the impoverished farmers of the two sections. While industry flourished, agriculture, whether western or southern, tended to languish. The downward trend of cotton prices was matched only by the downward trend of prices paid for wheat, corn, and livestock. Railroads made money, banks made money, factories made money; but the farmers barely made a living, and sometimes not even that. The suspicion grew, in both the South and the West, that some sinister force restrained agriculture, while industry climbed steadily to the mountain-tops of prosperity. Before the Civil War the agricultural South and the agricultural West, to their own considerable advantage, had stood together and ruled the country; now industry, with the forces of agriculture divided and ignored, reigned supreme. Could the old agricultural alliance be revived and the political advantages from which industry had fattened be restrained?

Few people asked themselves that question directly, but common grievances acted powerfully to draw the farmers of the two sections closer together. The western wheat-grower who was convinced that, unless the price of wheat was as much as a dollar a bushel, he could not make money, talked the same language as the southern cotton-grower, who held that any price less than ten cents a pound for cotton meant disaster. The northern farm-owner who was chronically on the verge of losing his property to the mortgage-holder was only a trifle better off than the southern tenant who each year turned over his entire crop to the storekeeper, only to learn, when the books were balanced, that he

[1] Mark Sullivan, *Our Times*, I, *The Turn of the Century* (1926), chapter 8, discusses this subject understandingly. The whole volume is useful as a social history of the nineties.

Per Cent of Total Area

Less than 0.5	30 - 44	
0.5 - 4	45 - 59	
5 - 14	60 - 74	
15 - 29	75 and Over	

DISTRIBUTION OF PUBLIC LANDS IN THE UNITED STATES, 1929

was still in debt. The West had by far the greater grievance against the railroads.[1] The railroads had built the West, but they had built it for a price. Debts for lands purchased from them were hard to wipe out, and the high cost of transporting bulky western crops to distant markets ate away an alarming proportion of western farm receipts. But the South, no less than the West, knew how railroad companies watered their stock, granted rebates, evaded taxation, bought favors with free passes, and mixed business with politics. Southern farmers, who sold abroad and would have preferred to buy cheap foreign manufactured goods in return, could see more clearly the disadvantages of the high-tariff system than the farmers of the Northwest, but even the Westerners registered their objections to buying in a tariff-protected market and selling against the competition of the whole wide world. Both sections recorded heated protests against the tolls paid to trusts and middlemen, the high taxes that for farmlands seeemed inescapable, and the steadily appreciating value of the dollar. And, although the West knew it best, both sections were seriously affected by the fact that good cheap lands were rapidly disappearing. The prospect of a new alliance between the dominantly agricultural sections of the country was by no means an idle dream.[2]

[1] See ante, p. 170.

[2] Books on the "New South" are increasingly plentiful. W. J. Cash, *The Mind of the South* (1941), shows the antebellum roots of southern society. R. B. Nixon, *Henry W. Grady, Spokesman of the New South* (1943), portrays well the part played by one of the prime movers in the southern economic revolution. A. F. Raper and Ira DeA. Reid, *Sharecroppers All* (1941), is a new study of the "ills of the South." Virginius Dabney, *Below the Potomac* (1942), is another book about the New South. Jonathan Daniels, *A Southerner Discovers the South* (1938), is illuminating on later developments. Thomas D. Clark, *Pills, Petticoats, and Plows: The Southern Country Store* (1944), is as colorful as its title implies.

On the West there is also much new writing. John Carl Parish, *The Persistence of the Westward Movement and Other Essays* (1943), is fertile in re-interpretations. Angie Debo, *Prairie City: The Story of an American Community* (1944), attempts a synthetic picture of the growth of the western prairie town. James C. Olson, *J. Sterling Morton* (1942), is the biography of a prominent Nebraska pioneer and Democrat. James C. Malin, *Winter Wheat in the Golden Belt of Kansas: A Study in Adaptation to Subhumid Geographical Environment* (1944), is what its title implies. Earl S. Pomeroy, *The Territories and the United States, 1861–1890: Studies in Colonial Administration* (1947), throws light on the political growth of the West. Alfred N. Chandler, *Land Title Origins: A Tale of Force and Fraud* (1945), reveals the weaknesses of the land system. Glenn S. Dumke, *The Boom of the Eighties in Southern California* (1944), brings the farther West into the picture.

There are several good books on Oklahoma and the Southwest. Carl Coke Rister, *Land Hunger: David L. Payne and the Oklahoma Boomers* (1942), tells the story of white penetration of the Indian country, and by the same author, *Southern Plainsman* (1938), studies the folk-ways of the region. Angie Debo, *Tulsa: From Creek Town to Oil Capital* (1943), gives the life story of an Oklahoma boom town.

CHAPTER XI

THE POPULIST REVOLT

THIRD-PARTY movements are more nearly the rule than the exception in American political history. From the time when the "Quiddists" or "Quids," led by John Randolph of Roanoke, broke away *Third-party* from the leadership of Thomas Jefferson on the ground that *movements* the President had abandoned the original tenets of Jeffersonian democracy, such revolts have been common. Before the Civil War the Anti-masons, the Abolitionists, the Free-Soilers, and the Know-Nothings aroused in turn the anxiety of all "right-thinking" citizens. After the war the Liberal Republicans, the Anti-monopolists, the Greenbackers, and finally the Populists caused the same concern. None of these third parties ever became really a first party, but the hope that some such movement might achieve success lasted on into the twentieth century. The Populist Party was almost exclusively a farmers' affair. Its roots lay in the acute agricultural distress that overtook both the New West and the New South toward the end of the eighties. Impressed with the occasional effectiveness of labor unions and eager to win comparable victories for agriculture, the farmers of both sections began to band themselves together into farm orders of various names and natures. Most important of these organizations were two great sectional "Alliances," the National Farmers' Alliance representing the Northwest, and the Farmers' Alliance and Industrial Union representing the South. Some of the smaller orders, such as the Grange, which had lasted on in spite of the collapse of the Granger movement, the Farmers' Mutual Benefit Association, and the Patrons of Industry, continued to exist; others were absorbed into one or the other of the two dominant organizations, which, commonly called the "Northern" or "Northwestern" Alliance and the "Southern" Alliance, became the authoritative spokesmen of agricultural discontent.[1]

---

[1] The changing point of view with respect to Populism may be noted by comparing F. L. McVey, *The Populist Movement* (1896), with J. D. Hicks, *The Populist Revolt* (1931).

The Northern Alliance was founded in 1880 by Milton George, editor of the *Western Rural*, a Chicago farm paper. George's paper made a *The Farmers' Alliance* specialty of denouncing the railroads, especially for the political favors they purchased by means of free passes, and the "Farmers' Transportation Convention," that George called together to launch the Alliance, branded the order from its beginning as an anti-railroad affair. Local alliances were multiplied throughout the Northwest, and, as soon as a state could count enough locals to warrant the step, a state alliance was formed. Each state alliance, as it gathered strength, tended to become autonomous, so that in the end the Northern Alliance turned out to be a loose confederation of state orders bound together by only the faintest of ties. The growth of the order was tremendously accelerated by the collapse of the western boom in 1887 and the hard times that followed. By 1890 it was fully organized in ten northwestern states, but the bulk of its strength lay in the wheat-raising sections of Kansas, Nebraska, the Dakotas, and Minnesota, where low prices, high freight-rates, oppressive mortgages, and, as a final crushing blow, the drouth had driven the long-suffering farmers to despair.

The origins of the Southern Alliance can be traced back to an organization that some frontier farmers in Lampasas County, Texas, formed in the middle seventies to catch horse-thieves, round up estrays, purchase supplies co-operatively, and defend their rights against land sharks and cattle kings. Armed with a pretentious secret ritual, the order expanded into a few neighboring counties, but mixed too freely in politics and died out. Revived at the close of the decade in Parker County, it kept clear of politics, and by 1885 it could claim fifty thousand members. Next year a new president, Doctor C. W. Macune, furnished the leadership necessary to make the Alliance a really important factor in the life of the South. Macune was a born promoter, and as president he dazzled his associates with the vision of transforming the Alliance into a money-saving business venture that every southern cotton-farmer would wish to join. Macune promptly established an Alliance Exchange through which the farmers of Texas were urged to buy and sell co-operatively, and, pointing to the temporary success of the Texas Exchange, he began to spread his gospel of business co-operation throughout the South. With amazing rapidity Macune's organizers captured state after state. Sometimes they found local farm orders in operation and induced them to join forces with the Alliance; sometimes they had little to begin with but the presence of smouldering discontent. But invariably their doctrines won converts, and soon exchanges patterned after the Texas model appeared in nearly every southern state. Unlike the Northern Alliance, the Southern Alliance was a closely knit national organization in which the state alliances played definitely subordinate rôles. For Negro farmers a separate, but affiliated, Colored Alliance was established.[1]

Circumstances conspired to drive both Alliances, contrary to their expressed intentions, into politics. The Northern Alliance, like the Southern Alliance, made numerous and sometimes success- *The Alliance* ful ventures into co-operative buying and selling, and both *in politics* orders earnestly stimulated among their members a wide variety of social and educational activities. But in spite of all such efforts farm prosperity failed to put in its appearance. More and more the conviction grew that the real trouble with agriculture lay in the unfair discriminations from which it suffered. Some sinister force restrained the farmers from the prosperity that their hard labor should have earned. The railroads, the bankers, the manufacturers, and the merchants were somehow robbing the farmers. Only through the power of government could these evil practices be brought to light and corrected, and to influence the government, whether in state or nation, political action was essential.

The Northern Alliance from its beginning had not hesitated to mix its business with politics. Northwestern Alliance men, on the assumption that what they did as individuals in no way involved the order to which they belonged, made it almost a point of honor to vote for farmers or farmer-minded politicians whenever opportunity offered. Through farmer-controlled legislatures they secured laws to insure the fair grading of grain, to impede the foreclosure of mortgages, and to curb the unfair practices of railroads. Most of this legislation, however, failed of its purpose, whether because of the indifference of administrative officials, the hostility of the courts, or the inability of state laws to deal effectively with nation-wide problems. By the year 1890, with the pressure of hard times growing ever more acute, most western Alliance men were convinced that the only hope of the farmers lay in turning their organization into an out-and-out political party — a party which, at first in the states, and later in the nation, could drive both of the older parties from power. Accordingly, third-party tickets were nominated in every state where the Alliance was strong. As yet the name of the new party varied from state to state, but the Kansans, seeking to dramatize the battle between the people and the "plutocrats," called their organization the

---

[1] The development of Populism in the South can best be followed through the several excellent state studies that have appeared: F. B. Simkins, *The Tillman Movement in South Carolina* (1926); J. B. Clark, *Populism in Alabama* (1927); A. M. Arnett, *The Populist Movement in Georgia* (1922); R. C. Martin, *The People's Party in Texas* (1933); W. D. Sheldon, *Populism in the Old Dominion* (1935).

People's Party, a name that won increasing acclaim. "Populist" and "Populism" were natural derivatives.

In the picturesque campaign that the northwestern Alliance men waged in 1890, a surprising number of really magnificent orators took *Elections* up the farmers' cause. Ignatius Donnelly of Minnesota *of 1890* delighted hundreds of audiences with his inimitable wit and his biting sarcasm; James B. Weaver of Iowa hammered home his points with a degree of resourcefulness that suggested comparison with James G. Blaine; "Sockless" Jerry Simpson of Kansas combined the oddities of James Whitcomb Riley with the skill of the trained dialectician; Mrs. Mary Elizabeth Lease, also of Kansas, a hard-bitten pioneer mother who had experienced most of the tragedies of frontier life, discovered in herself a rare gift of words that thrilled her hearers to their finger-tips. "What you farmers need to do," she is said to have told a Kansas audience, "is to raise less corn and more *Hell.*"

But the professional politicians and the oratorical head-liners were not the only spokesmen of Populism:

> It was a religious revival, a crusade, a pentecost of politics in which a tongue of flame sat upon every man, and each spake as the spirit gave him utterance. . . . The farmers, the country merchants, the cattle-herders, they of the long chin-whiskers, and they of the broad-brimmed hats and heavy boots, had also heard the word and could preach the gospel of Populism. . . . Women with skins tanned to parchment by the hot winds, with bony hands of toil and clad in faded calico, could talk in meeting, and could talk right straight to the point.

They not only talked, they picnicked, they marched, they sang for their cause. One of their favorite songs, "Good-bye, My Party, Good-bye," which celebrated in forthright verse the break that so many of them had made with a beloved old party, certainly had much to do with the success of Populism in Kansas.

Meantime in the South events had taken a somewhat different course. Macune's effort to solve the problem of the cotton-farmer by a policy of business co-operation received a fatal blow with the collapse of the Texas Exchange some eighteen months after it was founded. Discouraged with economic methods, Macune now turned to politics. Laws would have to be passed to improve the status of the southern farmer, the strangle-hold of the "Bourbon aristocrats" on state government would have to be broken, a debt-paying system of finance would have to be evolved. Other Southerners, too, had similar ideas, among them Colonel L. L. Polk, editor of a North Carolina farm journal, Benjamin R. Tillman, a hard-hitting back-country South Carolinian, and Thomas E.

Watson, a picturesque lawyer-politician of Georgia whose hatred for the governing aristocracy knew no bounds.[1]   Under the leadership of such men as these the Southern Alliance, well before the election of 1890, had been transformed into a frankly political order, the chief business of which was to capture the machinery of the Democratic Party, in every southern state.   Success in this undertaking, as the leaders well knew, would mean Alliance domination of the South, for there the one-party system insured that candidates once nominated were certain of election.

The enormous effectiveness of Alliance activities was mirrored in the election results.   In at least four northwestern states, Kansas, Nebraska, South Dakota, and Minnesota, third-party candidates won *Alliance* the balance of power, although in no case did they obtain *successes* outright control.   In the South, Alliance gains were even more spectacular.   Alliance candidates for governor were nominated and elected in three states, South Carolina, North Carolina, and Georgia, while in no less than eight states Alliance-controlled legislatures were chosen.   Even in Congress, the evidence of agrarian discontent was emphatically recorded.   Two third-party senators, William A. Peffer of Kansas and James H. Kyle of South Dakota, were on hand for the opening session of the Fifty-Second Congress, while eight third-party representatives from the Northwest voted for Thomas E. Watson of Georgia for Speaker. Watson was the only southern Congressman to admit that he was now a third-party man, but among the southern delegations there sat perhaps thirty or forty Alliance members and many others who were drawn to the Alliance by bonds of sympathy.   Indeed, the *Congressional Directory*, a volume which congressmen regularly compile about themselves, showed that during this period a remarkable number of senators and representatives, regardless of party or section, were at pains to confess their intimate connection with the farm and their deep devotion to farmer interests.[2]

To the third-party men of the Northwest the logical next step was the formation of a new nation-wide party of the people, but to Southerners such a course seemed fraught with the greatest of peril.   The Democratic Party of the South was primarily a symbol of white supremacy. Democratic rule meant white rule.   If the white voters of the South

[1] A model biography of the leading southern Populist is C. V. Woodward, *Tom Watson, Agrarian Rebel* (1938).

[2] Fewer northern than southern studies of Populism have achieved book publication. P. R. Fossum, *The Agrarian Movement in North Dakota* (1925), treats satisfactorily some aspects of the subject.   Elizabeth S. Barr, "The Populist Uprising," in *A Standard History of Kansas and Kansans*, II (1918), edited by W. E. Connelley, is a delightful bit of historical rhetoric.

were divided, Negro voting might become common, and the supremacy of the white race would be jeopardized. Perhaps even the horrors of reconstruction might be repeated. Southern Alliance men preferred, therefore, to work within the framework of the Democratic Party, although there was one great objection to such a course. The southern wing of the party, however strong it might become, could hardly hope to dominate the party as a whole. Through an Alliance-controlled southern Democracy a certain amount of useful state legislation might be achieved, but reforms that depended upon nation-wide action would still be of out reach. The so-called "sub-Treasury plan," for example, to which the Southern Alliance was committed after 1889, could never be put into effect without a law of Congress. This plan, much ridiculed then, would seem less radical to a later generation. It called for national warehouses in which non-perishable farm produce might be stored and upon which the owners might borrow from the United States government as much as eighty per cent of the "local current value" of their deposits in Treasury notes, issued for the purpose by the United States government, and providing incidentally an unpredictable amount of money inflation.

Southern reluctance was insufficient to restrain the third-party ardor of northwestern Alliance men, and at Cincinnati, in May, 1891, a mass *The People's* convention composed mostly of Westerners, but attended by *Party* a few Southerners, formally launched the People's Party as a national organization. The following February in St. Louis a delegate convention representing all the farm orders of the nation tried in vain to achieve organic union, but succeeded in adopting a common platform, the preamble of which, written and read by the versatile Donnelly, reflected with remarkable accuracy the spirit of the agrarian revolt:

> We meet in the midst of a nation brought to the verge of moral, political and material ruin. Corruption dominates the ballot box, the legislatures, the Congress, and touches even the ermine of the bench. The people are demoralized. Many of the States have been compelled to isolate the voters at the polling places in order to prevent universal intimidation or bribery.[1] The newspapers are subsidized or muzzled; public opinion silenced; business prostrated, our homes covered with mortgages, labor impoverished, and the land concentrating in the hands of capitalists.... The fruits of the toil of millions are boldly stolen to build up colossal fortunes, unprecedented in the history of the world, while their possessors despise the republic and endanger liberty. From the same prolific womb of governmental injustice we breed two great classes — paupers and millionaires.

---

[1] This refers to the Australian system of secret voting, recently introduced into the United States, and strongly supported by the Populists. On party problems in general consult M. I. Ostrogorski, *Democracy and the Organization of Political Parties* (2 vols., 1902).

Four months later, at Omaha, Nebraska, the first national nominating convention of the People's Party came together. Amidst scenes of unprecedented enthusiasm the Populists adopted as their own most of the planks of the St. Louis platform, including a slightly revised version of Donnelly's rhetorical preamble. Land, transportation, and finance furnished the principal issues. Believing, as they did, that the value of the gold dollar had been artificially stimulated to the benefit of the creditor class and to the distress of the debtors, the Populists demanded first and foremost an extensive expansion of the currency — in other words, money inflation. The amount of the circulating medium, they contended, whether by direct paper-money issues or by the "free and unlimited coinage of silver at the ratio of sixteen to one," or by both, should "be speedily increased to not less than fifty dollars per capita." As for the transportation issue, they advocated that the government should own and operate the railroads, and also, for good measure, the telegraph and telephone systems of the country. On the subject of public lands they looked faintly in the direction of conservation by demanding the return to the government by "railroads and other corporations" of all lands received "in excess of their actual needs." Alien landownership the Populists also condemned, and among other reforms favorably mentioned in their platform were the sub-Treasury system, the Australian ballot, a graduated income tax, postal savings banks, shorter hours for labor, the initiative and referendum, election of United States senators by direct vote of the people, and a single term for the President and Vice-President. For their candidates the Populists chose James B. Weaver of Iowa,[1] who had fought for the North in the Civil War, to head the ticket, and James G. Field of Virginia, an ex-Confederate, for second place.

The Populists, while predicting a victory of the "people" over the "plutocrats" in 1896, hoped only to make a good showing in 1892. Circumstances came ably to their assistance. The Republi- *Election* cans, in spite of the overwhelming rebuke they had received ` *of 1892* in 1890, had little choice but to renominate the unpopular Harrison and to defend the long list of dubious measures, including the McKinley Act, that were associated with his administration; while the Democrats, convinced that another battle must be fought over the tariff, turned for a third time to Cleveland. Signs of dissension in both old parties were apparent. Three days before the opening of the Republican Convention,

---

[1] The best biography of Weaver is F. E. Haynes, *James Baird Weaver* (1919). Populist flirtations with Walter Q. Gresham, who became Cleveland's Secretary of State, are noted in Matilda Gresham, *Life of Walter Quintin Gresham* (2 vols., 1919).

Blaine had resigned as Secretary of State and had permitted his friends
to work openly, if unavailingly, for his nomination. Cleveland, likewise,
had met with formidable opposition. David B. Hill of New York had
sought in every way to discredit the ex-President and to take the nomination away from him; moreover, among soft-money men of the West
and the South Cleveland's hard-money views aroused the strongest
antagonism.

The Populists went into the campaign as the one party willing to take
a radical stand on the money question. Their free-silver plank was less
a matter of conviction than of expediency, for the views of the original
Populists were derived from the Greenbackers rather than from the
Silverites. Nevertheless, "free silver" furnished the one really exciting
issue of the campaign. On this issue, primarily, several states of the
Rocky Mountain West broke from their Republican moorings and voted
either for the Populists or, because of Populist secessions from the Republican Party, for the Democrats. Thanks in part to deliberate propaganda on the part of the silver interests, Populist campaigners in the
Middle West and in the South found their audiences increasingly interested in the magic of free silver. The "sham battle" over the tariff
went on to its logical conclusion, and, quite as the prophets predicted,
Cleveland defeated Harrison. But, regardless of what might happen
to the Populist Party, it was apparent that the silver issue had a
future.

For the moment the triumph of the Democrats seemed complete.
Cleveland's popular vote was 5,554,414 to Harrison's 5,190,802 and
A Demo- Weaver's 1,027,000; the electoral vote stood; Cleveland,
cratic victory 277; Harrison, 145; and Weaver, 22. For the first time
since the Civil War both houses of Congress as well as the Presidency
were in Democratic hands. The Populists, for all their brave talk, had
failed to make a dent in the "solid South," and the votes they had won
in the West had been obtained in some instances only by co-operation
with the Democrats. The country had again, as in 1890, voted its opposition to the McKinley Tariff; it had again rebuked the Republicans for
their two-faced handling of the money question in the Sherman Silver
Purchase Act; it had denounced anew the partisanship and extravagance
of the Republican pension policy; it had condemned the inadequacy and
ineffectiveness of the Sherman Anti-Trust Act; it had rebuked the President for his wavering attitude toward civil service reform; and it had
shown its impatience with the effort to revive the nightmare of reconstruction by means of a "Force Bill." Significant and interesting was
the fact that the six northwestern states admitted by the Republicans

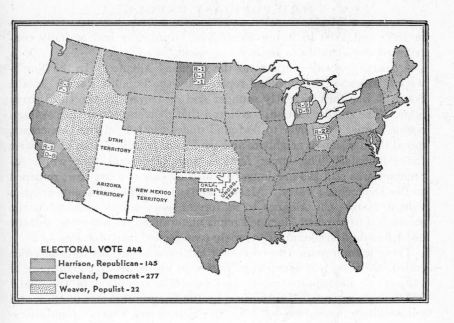

ELECTORAL VOTE 444

- Harrison, Republican - 145
- Cleveland, Democrat - 277
- Weaver, Populist - 22

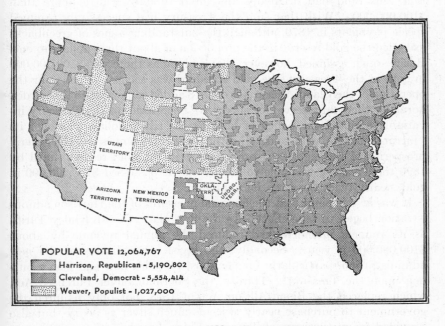

POPULAR VOTE 12,064,767

- Harrison, Republican - 5,190,802
- Cleveland, Democrat - 5,554,414
- Weaver, Populist - 1,027,000

PRESIDENTIAL ELECTION OF 1892, BY STATES AND BY COUNTIES

in 1889 and 1890 to insure Republican supremacy had actually contributed considerably to Republican defeat.

A casualty of the election was the Farmers' Alliance. In the Northwest it was absorbed into and replaced by the Populist Party. In the South it was torn violently asunder and destroyed by the third-party issue. The smaller faction, convinced that deliverance for the southern cotton-farmer was never to be found under the rule of the Democrats, dared the derision of neighbors and the loss of friends to join hands with the Populists. The larger faction, equally certain that white supremacy was still the one issue to which all others must bow, returned to the Democratic Party. Macune and a few of his adherents tried in vain to restore the Alliance to its former non-partisan status, but the scandals that pursued Macune's name undermined his influence, and the order he had done so much to create soon passed into oblivion.

There is some reason to suppose that, even before his term of office ended, Harrison had occasion to rejoice in his defeat. A nightmare of *The gold* his administration had been the condition of the "gold *reserve* reserve." Authorized by the Resumption Act of 1875, and painstakingly assembled by John Sherman during Hayes's administration, this fund had originally amounted to only a little more than $100,000,000. With that sum the Treasury had successfully resumed specie payments in 1879, although the outstanding issues of greenbacks exceeded the gold reserve in the proportion of about three dollars to one. Businessmen assumed, however, that as long as there was $100,000,000 in gold in the Treasury, the gold standard was secure. Each year the operation of the Bland-Allison Act of 1878 added somewhat to the burden borne by the gold reserve, for successive Secretaries of the Treasury invariably adopted the policy of backing the silver dollar, whatever its "intrinsic" value, with gold. But the plentiful revenues and the general prosperity of the eighties steadily increased the gold reserve, until by 1890 the Treasury was able to record that it possessed $190,000,000 in gold, nearly twice the essential minimum.

It was at this point that the financial measures of the Harrison administration began to take effect. In the first place, the McKinley Tariff, as its framers intended, had reduced the annual revenue by about $100,000,000 a year. Secondly, the lavish expenditures of the new administration, particularly for pensions, placed a new and heavy burden upon the Treasury. Thirdly, the Sherman Silver Purchase Act, which replaced the Bland-Allison Act of 1878, not only required the government to purchase nearly twice as much silver as before, but also provided for a new issue of Treasury notes, based on these silver purchases, that all sound-money men agreed must be redeemable in gold rather than in silver. Failure to maintain their parity with gold would mean that the silver standard would succeed the gold standard, and the purchasing power of the American dollar would decline to the commercial value of the silver dollar — a drop of nearly fifty per cent.[1]

Well before the end of the Harrison administration the condition of the Treasury had begun to excite general alarm. By 1892, the Treasury surplus, which recorded the excess of revenues over expenditures, had almost reached the vanishing point. Far more *Condition of the Treasury* significant was the fact that the last two years had witnessed heavy withdrawals of gold. Faith that the government could redeem its greenbacks and Treasury notes in gold was obviously shaken, for gold flowed steadily out of the Treasury and paper flowed in. By January, 1893, the gold reserve had dwindled to only $108,000,000, and the Harrison administration, in order to stave off the inevitable crisis until after March 4, was driven to heroic measures. Late in January, Harrison's Secretary of the Treasury successfully implored the New York banks to exchange $6,000,000 in gold for paper, a sum that kept the gold reserve above the $100,000,000 mark until after Cleveland was inaugurated. But when the Democrats took over the Treasury, they found a gold reserve of only $100,982,410.

By April 21, 1893, within a matter of weeks after the change of government, the gold reserve dropped below the $100,000,000 mark, and the Panic of 1893 was on. Before six months had passed no *Panic of 1893* less than eight thousand business failures, involving liabilities of $285,000,000, were recorded. Four hundred banks, most of them in the West or in the South, closed their doors. Railroads followed each other into receivership in a procession that ended only after 156 companies, among them the Erie, the Union Pacific, and the Northern Pacific, had gone into bankruptcy. Panic conditions lasted throughout the summer, after which the country settled down to the long, hard process of waiting out a depression that was to last four full years.

While the condition of the Treasury, which gave rise to the fear that the government would be unable to maintain the gold standard, undoubtedly ushered in the Panic of 1893, there were other reasons in abundance that must be taken into account in explaining both the panic and the depression. Well to the front was the long-standing agricultural distress of the West and the South. For both sections the be-

[1] W. J. Lauck, *The Causes of the Panic of 1893* (1907), blames the panic mainly upon the currency situation. Compare with F. P. Weberg, *The Background of the Panic of 1893* (1929).

ginning of the depression might better have been set at 1887 than at 1893. The purchasing power of the stricken sections had steadily declined, and in consequence the earnings of all businesses that depended on farm markets or the handling of farm goods had suffered. The eighties, too, had been a period of overexpansion in industry. The great transcontinental railroads, the huge industrial trusts, and the building of the larger cities and the new cities that they had made necessary had drained dry the investment resources of the nation. Furthermore, the depression, far from being a strictly American affair, was of world-wide dimensions. From 1889 on, and particularly after the so-called "Baring panic" of 1890 in England, all Europe had recorded subnormal business conditions; indeed, one reason for the depletion of the American gold reserve was the withdrawal of foreign capital from investment in America in order to bolster up the waning fortunes of European enterprise.

To twentieth-century Americans familiar with the economic activities of the Hoover and Roosevelt administrations, the refusal of Grover Cleveland to regard the problem of business recovery as a direct concern of the government may seem surprising. To Cleveland the depression was a business matter that lay quite outside the realm of politics. He regarded it as his duty, as President, to maintain the historic gold standard if he could, and to keep the government solvent; but beyond that neither he nor the majority he was able to command in Congress dreamed that the government had a duty to perform. Even the radicals of the time — the Populists and the Silverites — confined their demands almost entirely to money inflation of one sort or another. For this attitude Cleveland and his contemporaries are neither to be praised nor censured. They acted as nineteenth-century politicians had always acted. Van Buren, Buchanan, Grant, and Hayes had confronted major depressions during their terms of office, but neither they nor their advisers had conceived of it as the duty of the government to defeat depression and restore prosperity. The business cycle was a strictly business affair.

On the money question, however, Cleveland acted with vigor. Failure to maintain the gold standard would have seemed to him a breach of public faith. Accordingly, he called Congress at once into *Repeal of the Silver Purchase Act* special session and asked it to repeal the obnoxious Sherman Silver Purchase Act, which in his judgment had done so much to deplete the gold reserve. He could hardly have thought of a better way to alienate the West and the South, where silver orators were gaining converts every day. The debtor farmers, to whom the gold standard meant low prices and continued agricultural distress, had no desire whatever to save it; for them the fifty-cent dollar had no terrors. The silver interests of the Far West were even more violently opposed to repeal. What silver needed, they insisted, was a larger rather than a smaller subsidy; better still, "the free and unlimited coinage of silver at the ratio of sixteen to one." Congress at length supported Cleveland in his resolve, but only at the cost of a definite split in the Democratic Party. Enough eastern Republicans joined the eastern Democrats to repeal the Sherman Law, but the confidence of western and southern Democrats in the President they had chosen was sadly shaken.[1]

Cleveland's next move alienated the soft-money men still further. In spite of the fact that silver purchases were discontinued, the drain on the gold reserve continued. By October the amount of gold in the Treasury was less than $82,000,000, and before the end of the year it was down to $68,000,000. Faced by this emergency the President, after some hesitation, authorized his Secretary of the Treasury, John G. Carlisle, to invoke the provisions of the still-unrepealed Resumption Act of 1875, and to buy enough gold to maintain the proper reserve. In January, 1894, an issue of $50,000,000 worth of five per cent bonds brought $58,000,000 in gold into the Treasury, but of this sum $24,000,000 was immediately withdrawn, and before the end of the year one more purchase of gold was necessary — an "endless chain," for in each case the gold was hardly in the Treasury until it was drawn out again.

By February, 1895, with the gold reserve down to $41,000,000 and currency depreciation once more seemingly in sight, the President saved the situation by a deal with the Morgan and the Belmont *Purchases* banking firms, the latter representing the Rothschilds of *of gold* Paris. According to the terms of this unusual agreement the favored firms were permitted to purchase a $62,000,000 issue of thirty-year four per cent bonds at 104½ instead of at their market value of about 111. Thus the bankers were insured an enormous profit. In return for this special consideration, however, the purchasers guaranteed two things, first, to procure half of the needed gold from abroad, and secondly, to use their influence to prevent further withdrawals of gold from the Treasury. This deal, while violently and perhaps justly criticized, did serve to restore confidence, and when some months later the government offered $100,000,000 in four per cent bonds to the highest bidder, the issue was promptly subscribed five times over. After this transaction all

[1] Cleveland's stand on the money question can best be followed in Nevins, *Grover Cleveland*, already cited, and in Robert McElroy, *Grover Cleveland* (2 vols., 1923). Among the financial histories that treat fully of this subject are A. B. Hepburn, *A History of Currency in the United States* (1915); Horace White, *Money and Banking* (new edition, 1914).

fear that the government could not maintain the gold standard speedily vanished. But to the strongly Populistic South and West the maintenance of the gold standard was more an evil than a good, and worse still, the President had attained this undesired end by "selling out" to Wall Street. The depths of Cleveland's unpopularity knew no bounds.

Part of the price that Cleveland paid for maintaining the gold standard was the defeat of his long-cherished plans for a genuine revision downward of the tariff. Of necessity, or so he thought, he had postponed the tariff battle until after the repeal of the Sherman Act. But when that end had been accomplished, his prestige with the silver wing of his party was so impaired that in that quarter his commands were no longer respected. Moreover, the alliance of eastern Democrats and eastern Republicans, originally called into existence against silver, soon found that it could also function effectively on the tariff. The result was a tariff measure, the Wilson-Gorman Act of 1894, so far removed from the party's pledges on the subject that Cleveland called it a "piece of party perfidy," and obstinately refused to sign the bill, although he did permit it to become a law without his signature.

When William L. Wilson of West Virginia, scholarly chairman of the House Ways and Means Committee, introduced the tariff bill into the *Tariff legislation* House, tariff reformers had good reason to congratulate themselves. The Wilson Bill, patterned after the Mills Bill of 1888, proposed to put raw materials, such as lumber, wool, and coal on the free list, in part as compensation to manufacturers for the reduced protection they were to receive, and in part as a means of lowering the prices that consumers would have to pay. Sugar, too, both raw and refined, was to be admitted free, and the expensive sugar bounty was to be abolished. On most factory-made items, such as cotton, woolen, and silken fabrics, crockery, and glassware, the duties were to be materially reduced, although their protective character was by no means destroyed. Fearful that the lowered duties might reduce the revenue below the needs of the government, the framers of the bill heeded the Populist demand for an income tax, and levied a flat two per cent against incomes over four thousand dollars.

As it passed the House, the Wilson Bill was an honest attempt at tariff reduction. In the Senate, however, two eastern Democrats, Brice and Gorman, aided and abetted by log-rolling Democrats from every section, and in particular by the "sugar senators" from Louisiana, joined with the Republicans to attach 633 amendments to the bill, wholly changing its character. The sugar bounty was not revived, but duties that were worth twenty million dollars annually to the Sugar Trust were placed on both raw and refined sugar. Throughout the revised measure the low-tariff principle was all but ignored. Reluctantly the House acquiesced in the wrecking of its work, and the President's attempts at intervention proved unavailing. In general the duties of the Wilson-Gorman Tariff were lower than those of the McKinley Tariff, and not far different from the duties set by the Tariff of 1883. The provision for an income tax, which actually reached the statute books, was declared unconstitutional by the Supreme Court in a five-to-four decision (1895). This was the more remarkable because of the fact that an income tax had been levied and collected during the Civil War without serious question as to its unconstitutionality. Populists were convinced that the action of the Court was just one more evidence of the unholy alliance between business and government that Donnelly had denounced in his famous preamble:

> We have witnessed for more than a quarter of a century the struggles of the two great political parties for power and plunder, while grievous wrongs have been inflicted upon the suffering people. We charge that the controlling influences dominating both these parties have permitted the existing dreadful conditions to develop without serious effort to prevent or restrain them. Neither do they now promise us any substantial reform. They have agreed together to ignore in the coming campaign every issue but one. They propose to drown the outcries of a plundered people with the uproar of a sham battle over the tariff, so that capitalists, corporations, national banks, rings, trusts, watered stock, the demonetization of silver, and the oppressions of the usurers may all be lost sight of. They propose to sacrifice our homes, lives and children on the altar of mammon; to destroy the multitude in order to secure corruption funds from the millionaires. [1]

[1] Chester McA. Destler, *American Radicalism, 1865–1901: Essays and Documents* (1946), contains many thoughtful observations on the nature of American radicalism. Fred A. Shannon, *The Farmer's Last Frontier: Agriculture, 1860–1897* (1945), presents admirably the economic background of frontier Populism. Francis Butler Simkins, *Pitchfork Ben Tillman, South Carolinian* (1944), gives a generally sympathetic picture of a leading southern agrarian. George H. Knoles, *The Presidential Campaign and Election of 1892* (1942), is an excellent monograph.

CHAPTER XII

THE SILVER CRUSADE

THE distress in agriculture that led to the Populist revolt was no more serious than the plight of the city workers during the hard years that *Labor* followed the Panic of 1893. Industrial depression meant *disorders* wholesale unemployment, a condition that state and municipal governments were unable to handle effectively and that the national government looked upon as outside its sphere of activity. One violent strike followed another with appalling frequency, and armies of the unemployed repeatedly marched on Washington. Strangely, however, the farmers and the laborers, although they claimed a common enemy, found difficulty in uniting their forces. The Populists were more than eager to produce a united front and made earnest overtures to the laborers, but only the old and weakened Knights of Labor, struggling valiantly to stave off the day of dissolution, signified any interest in co-operation. The American Federation of Labor, to which increasingly the labor world looked for leadership, adhered tenaciously to its policy of keeping the labor movement free from party politics. It was determined neither to become a political party nor to be absorbed in one. The disappointment of the Populists at the resultant failure of their new People's Party to become a genuine party of all the people was acute.

In 1892 a strike broke out in the steel industry, then centered compactly about Pittsburgh, Pennsylvania, that gave the country a fore-*The Home-* taste of the labor difficulties from which it was to suffer *stead strike* during the depression. The Homestead strike, as this conflict was called, involved on the one hand the Amalgamated Association of Iron and Steel workers, a well-established labor organization that had been formed as early as 1876 by a merger of several smaller craft unions, and on the other hand the Carnegie Steel Company, perhaps the most powerful of the several American steel corporations. Carnegie himself was no labor-baiter, and three years before he had agreed to a satisfactory contract with the union, but at the time trouble broke out in 1892 he had

[260]

gone to Europe, leaving the affairs of the company in the hands of Henry Clay Frick, a man whose detestation of organized labor was open and unconcealed.[1] The chief point at issue between the company and the workers was a proposed reduction in the pay for piece-work. The company argued that such a reduction was justified because more efficient machinery had been installed. The worker who made use of the new tools could turn out more pieces than formerly in a given time without any greater expenditure of energy. Thus, according to the employers, a reduction in the piece-rate could be made without reducing the worker's daily or weekly earnings. The union, however, refused to be persuaded, and held that the real intent of the company was a wage-cut.

When on July 1 the union refused to accept the company's terms, Frick anticipated the strike by closing the Homestead works. Technically, therefore, what followed was the result of a "lockout" rather than a strike. The union at once began to picket the works, while Frick showed that he meant business by surrounding the company's property with a wire fence fifteen feet high and three miles long, and also by ordering three hundred guards from the Pinkerton Detective Agency. The boats which brought the "Pinkertons" to the scene of conflict, however, were immediately attacked by the strikers, and fighting that occurred on July 6, 1892, resulted in numerous deaths and injuries on both sides. The Pinkertons were no match for the enraged strikers, who captured and disarmed their entire force and, after holding them for a day as prisoners of war, ran them out of town. Frick then appealed to the state for protection, and the governor responded by sending enough militia to turn the little mill town of Homestead into an armed camp. The strikers held out for nearly five months, but at length public opinion turned against them and they resumed work on the company's terms. An important factor in alienating the public from the strikers, whose case at first had aroused considerable sympathy, was the mad attack, by Alexander Berkman, a young anarchist, on the life of Frick. Frick, although seriously injured, soon recovered, and Berkman for his crime spent fifteen years in prison.

Of all the many labor disturbances that punctuated the years of depression the Pullman strike of 1894 was by far the most significant. In 1880 George Mortimer Pullman, the inventor and builder *The Pull-* of the Pullman sleeping-car, had established for the benefit *man strike* of his employees the "model town" of Pullman on the outskirts of Chicago. This project carried paternalism to an extraordinary extreme. Model dwellings were built by the company and rented to employees;

[1] George Harvey, *Henry Clay Frick* (1928), throws some light on this subject.

company stores were opened at which Pullman employees were encouraged to buy; a company church, a company school, a company park, and a company theater ministered to the various social needs of the community. The entire village, indeed, was owned and operated by the Pullman Palace Car Company as a business investment — a kind of modern feudalism, so critics were accustomed to say. The situation was changed somewhat in 1889 when the village was annexed to Chicago, but for the most part the property rights of the Pullman Company remained undisturbed.

Pullman had no use for labor unions, but during the first year of the depression organizers of the American Railway Union made rapid headway with his men. This union was the brain-child of Eugene V. Debs (1855–1926), who was later to become the outstanding leader of the Socialist movement in the United States. Debs was born in Terre Haute, Indiana, of French-Alsatian ancestry, and at the time of the Pullman strike was still less than forty years of age. He had worked in the railway shops of his home town when he was a boy of only fourteen, and at sixteen he had become a locomotive fireman. A passionate defender of the underprivileged and devoted to the union idea, he held high office in the Brotherhood of Locomotive Firemen, and for a time edited *The Locomotive Fireman's Magazine*. He became increasingly impatient, however, with the unaggressive attitude of the railway brotherhoods and the American Federation of Labor, with which the brotherhoods co-operated, although they would not join it. Convinced that industrial unions were preferable to trades unions and that railroad men should all be members of one organization, in 1893 he founded the American Railway Union, and such was his persuasiveness that within a year the new union had enrolled one hundred and fifty thousand members.

The Pullman strike was precipitated in the spring of 1894 when the Pullman Company, hard hit by the depression, laid off one third of its *Railroad* men and cut the wages of the rest from thirty to forty per *tie-ups* cent. No reductions, however, were made in the rent charged for company houses nor in the price of goods at the company stores. In protest the men quit work, and with the demand for sleeping-cars at a standstill Pullman showed no disposition to call them back. With their credit withdrawn at the company stores, the strikers were on the verge of starvation when the American Railway Union came to the rescue with relief money and with the threat of a boycott against the hauling of Pullman cars. On June 26 Debs ordered the boycott to be applied on all the western railroads, and "A.R.U." men obeyed by cutting out Pullman cars from their trains and leaving them on side-tracks.

When boycotters were discharged for such acts, the strike became general, and not Pullman cars alone but whole trains stood on side-tracks. From Cincinnati to San Francisco the effects of the strike were felt. Traffic between Chicago and the West was virtually paralyzed and hoodlums who joined the strikers stooped to every sort of violence, as all the accumulated bitterness and resentment of the unemployed multitudes was poured into the strife. Engines were crippled, freight-cars were overturned and looted, loyal employees were driven from their posts.

The railroad operators, faced by this dangerous situation, would normally have been willing to trust the governor of Illinois — the state most seriously involved — to keep order, if necessary by call- *Federal* ing out the militia to aid the civil authorities. But the *troops* governor of Illinois happened to be John P. Altgeld, already notorious among conservatives for his pardoning of the Haymarket anarchists. The operators, therefore, demanded that federal troops be brought in, and when Altgeld took no steps in that direction they appealed directly to the President for aid. Cleveland was in a quandary, for while the Constitution authorized the President to protect a state against domestic violence, it expressly stated that such action was to be taken "on application of the legislature, or of the executive (when the legislature cannot be convened)." The legislature of Illinois was not in session and the governor of the state had issued no call for help, but the President at length decided that he might intervene on the pretext that the Chicago disorders interfered with the free transport of United States mail. By the fourth of July two thousand regulars, including cavalry and field artillery, had moved into the troubled zone. Having arrived there, they exerted themselves not merely to see that the mails were carried, but also to break the strike. Altgeld protested vigorously that Cleveland's action was unconstitutional and demanded the immediate withdrawal of the federal troops, but Cleveland stood his ground. No doubt Altgeld, had he been given time to do so, would have restored order, but it is by no means certain that he would have tried to break the strike.[1]

Governmental action against the strikers was not confined to the use of troops, for the federal courts soon took a hand. Debs, who had assumed direct supervision of the strike, and several other leaders *Use of the* were arrested by federal officers on the charge of conspiracy *injunction* to obstruct the mails, and although released on bail were enjoined by

---

[1] Cleveland's action precipitated a long-drawn-out controversy. The President's case is stated in Grover Cleveland, *The Government in the Chicago Strike of 1894* (1913); but this should be compared with Harry Barnard, *Eagle Forgotten, the Life of John Peter Altgeld* (1938); W. R. Browne, *Altgeld of Illinois* (1924); and Edward Berman, *Labor Disputes and the President of the United States* (1924).

Federal Judges Grosscup and Woods against doing anything to prolong the strike. In direct defiance of this order, Debs urged a group of labor leaders on July 12 to promote a general strike by all the labor organizations of the country. Thereupon he and six others were cited for contempt of court and sentenced to six months in jail. Thus summarily removed from the scene of conflict, Debs was left free to read and to think, and when he emerged from confinement he announced his conversion to socialism.[1] His imprisonment served also to call attention to the fact that the courts were not averse to obtaining results by the use of the injunction that they could not so certainly have obtained had the normal procedure of a jury trial been followed. Criticism of "government by injunction" and of the use of the regular army to break strikes was freely expressed. To many the now familiar Populist charge that a corrupt alliance existed between business and government to suppress the liberties of the people seemed only too well substantiated.

That another view of the duty of government could be taken was shown by Governor Davis H. Waite of Colorado, whom Populists, with *"Bloody Bridles" Waite* Democratic assistance, had elected in 1892. "It is better," he had said, "infinitely better, that blood should flow to the horses' bridles rather than our national liberties should be destroyed." Known thenceforth as "Bloody Bridles" Waite, he did not hesitate to help the striking miners during the so-called "Cripple Creek War" of 1894 instead of giving the customary aid and comfort to the employers. When an army of deputy sheriffs made ready to attack the strikers, Waite called out the entire state militia to preserve the peace, and marched his troops between the opposing forces. Waite was a man of no tact and little judgment, but his attitude, like Altgeld's, gave courage to the forces of labor. Throughout the nineties in Colorado, Idaho, and Montana the Western Federation of Miners battled employers with a degree of violence that bordered on revolution. In May, 1897, the president of this organization urged every union in Colorado and Idaho to arm itself "so that in two years we can hear the inspiring music of the martial tread of 25,000 armed men in the ranks of labor."[2]

Attempts to induce the government to help solve the problem of unemployment by means of work relief, while not entirely unknown, proceeded usually from the minds of men whom the public regarded as "crack-pots." Most famous of these was General Jacob S. Coxey of

[1] McAlister Coleman, *Eugene V. Debs: A Man Unafraid* (1930), and Floy R. Painter, *That Man Debs and His Life Work* (1929), both review fully Debs's connection with the Pullman strike.

[2] Louis Adamic, *Dynamite* (1931). This book recounts, with sympathy, the more violent labor outbreaks from the Civil War to the Great Depression.

Massillon, Ohio, a Greenbacker and a Populist, who advocated that *"Coxey's army"* Congress should issue $500,000,000 in legal-tender notes to be expended at the rate of $20,000,000 a month on the building of good roads. Wages of one dollar and fifty cents per eight-hour day were to be paid to all who needed employment. Coxey also urged that municipalities desirous of making public improvements should be authorized to issue non-interest-bearing bonds equal to half their assessed valuation. These bonds might then be used as security with the Secretary of the Treasury to obtain loans of legal-tender notes to pay for the construction of schools, courthouses, paved streets, and other worthy projects. Both schemes, on the financial side, were highly inflationary in character, but they aimed at a type of governmental activity that in the next great depression became extremely familiar.

In seeking to promote his ideas Coxey hit upon the expedient of presenting, by means of a march of the unemployed on Washington, a "living petition" to Congress. Newspaper men, no less amused by the General's picturesque personality than by his fantastic notions, gave much-needed publicity, and by Easter Sunday, 1894, when the march was scheduled to begin, a motley array of recruits had converged on Massillon. Most of the unemployed walked, but General Coxey, his wife, and his infant son, Legal Tender Coxey, rode in carriages. At the beginning of the march "Coxey's army" consisted of not more than one hundred men, including newspaper reporters, but in spite of continuous desertions its number increased as the march progressed. Many of the men were able to demonstrate that they had had experience in living off the country, but Populists and labor organizations took up the cause of the crusaders and provided them plentifully with supplies. On the first of May, five hundred strong, the army entered Washington determined to lay its demands before a Congress, now thoroughly excited. At the end of Pennsylvania Avenue the marchers met a cordon of police under orders to halt their advance. Several of the leaders, including Coxey, were arrested for disobeying an ordinance to keep off the grass, the army was turned back to its camp, and the speech Coxey had prepared to deliver from the Capitol steps reached the public only through the newspapers. It was an effective document:

> Up these steps the lobbyists of trusts and corporations have passed unchallenged on their way to the Committee rooms, access to which we, the representatives of the toiling wealth producers, have been denied. We stand here today in behalf of millions of toilers whose petitions have been buried in committee rooms, whose prayers have been unresponded to, and whose opportunities for honest, remunerative, productive labor have been

taken away from them by unjust legislation, which protects idlers, speculators, and gamblers.[1]

Coxey's army was not the only organization of its kind to march on
Washington. An army of six hundred men under the command of
Other labor General Lewis G. Fry had set out from Los Angeles six
marches weeks before Coxey's followers reached Washington, and
by the end of May at least two hundred of them had joined Coxey's
camp on the outskirts of that city. Another detachment that had taken
a different route arrived before the end of June. A San Francisco army
under General Charles T. Kelly "bummed" its way twelve hundred
strong to Utah, captured a Union Pacific train of twenty-six boxcars,
and arrived at Council Bluffs, Iowa, April 15. Traveling by foot, by
river steamboat, and by rail the army held together as far as Ohio, where
it was scattered by a succession of adversities, although Kelly and a
handful of the more persistent reached Washington before the summer
was over. Similar movements from the Far West, from the Middle
West, even from New England, made news during the summer of 1894.
But the concentration of so many unemployed in the Washington area
overtaxed the charitable resources of the city and ended inevitably in
starvation and distress. Finally the Commissioners of the District of
Columbia found means to send most of the marchers home, while strag-
glers in Virginia and Maryland were rounded up and either driven across
state boundaries or sent to workhouses.

The acute labor unrest of 1894 drove fear into the hearts of the conservatives, and encouraged the Populists to hope that eventually farmers
and laborers would learn to work together. If only such a union could
be achieved, they believed that the people, not the plutocrats, would
soon rule. But Populist strategy called for union through the agency of
the Populist Party. First the Populists must capture the government,
and then, as rapidly as possible, they must put into effect the numerous
and complicated reforms of their cherished platforms.

As events turned out, whatever union of the working classes was actually accomplished came primarily on the issue of free silver, and more
Rise of the or less without regard for the wishes of party leaders.
silver issue Propaganda from mine-owners in the silver states of the
Far West flooded the country with denunciations of the "crime of 1873"
and with innumerable arguments to prove that only "the free and unlimited coinage of silver at the ratio of sixteen to one" was required to
restore prosperity. *Coin's Financial School*, a little book written by

[1] Donald L. McMurry, *Coxey's Army* (1929), p. 120. This book deals fully with all the
various labor "marches" of the period.

William H. Harvey and published in 1894, set forth in simple language, and seemingly with unanswerable logic, the doctrines of the silverites. "Professor Coin," as the author called himself, purported to run a school in Chicago for financiers, and the lectures he gave on the money question were recorded in the book. Illustrated with numerous cartoons and diagrams, and sometimes reduced to the simplicity of a dialogue between the "Professor" and his students, the book appealed to an enormous audience. Silver orators, such as William Jennings Bryan, knew its arguments by heart and spread them far and wide. Soon countless thousands had come to believe that an international conspiracy to set gold above silver was at the root of the economic distress from which the nation suffered. The restoration of prosperity need not await the enactment of a long and complicated series of reforms. By the simple expedient of restoring silver to its historic status as money, all wrongs would be righted.

> It means work for the thousands who now tramp the streets . . . not knowing where their next meal is coming from. It means food and clothes for the thousands of hungry and ill-clad women and children. . . . It means the restoration of confidence in the business world. It means the re-opening of closed factories, the relighting of fires in darkened furnaces; it means hope instead of despair; comfort in place of suffering; life instead of death.

Unhappily for the plans of the Populists, the silver issue cut across party lines.[1] Silver Republicans in the West and Silver Democrats in both the West and South captured the old party organizations in state after state. Even the Populists themselves, caught up in the silver frenzy, were forced increasingly to ignore all the rest of their policies and to concentrate on "free silver," a panacea rather than a program.

> The dollar of our daddies,
> Of silver coinage free,
> Will make us rich and happy
> Will bring prosperity.

With the silver forces still divided among three parties, the state and congressional elections of 1894 turned upon hard times and the unpopularity of Cleveland. The Democrats were no more respon- *Elections* sible for the depression than the Republicans, if as much so, *of 1894* but it was their misfortune to be in power when the panic broke, and the Republicans drove home the charge that Democratic supremacy and hard times went together. As a result the Republicans obtained a two

---

[1] Among the many contemporary studies of the silver question two may properly be listed: F. W. Taussig, *The Silver Situation in the United States* (1892), and Horace White, *Coin's Financial Fool; or, the Artful Dodger Exposed* (1895).

to one majority in the national House of Representatives, greatly reduced the Democratic majority in the Senate, and captured nearly every state government outside the South. The behavior of the Populists during the campaign tended, if anything, to aid the Republicans. In the West the Populists, unable or unwilling to co-operate with the Democrats as fully as in 1892, tended to avoid fusion and to keep "in the middle of the road"; in the South, they unblushingly joined forces with the Republicans. The total Populist vote, however, was more than forty per cent larger in 1894 than in 1892, and enthusiastic Populists cited the rapid rise of Republicanism before 1860 as evidence of what their party could do by 1896. Leading Republicans held a different view of the situation; some of them boasted openly that in 1896 they could "nominate a rag baby and elect it President."

That the original Republican plan for 1896 did not contemplate a straight-out endorsement of the single gold standard was apparent from the record of the candidate slated for first place on the Republican ticket. William McKinley (1843–1901), author of the McKinley Tariff Bill of 1890, and governor of Ohio from 1891 to 1895, was a tariff expert with no deep convictions on the money question. Indeed, in so far as he had committed himself, he seemed to have taken the silver side. In 1878 he had voted for the Bland-Allison Act, and in 1890, when the Sherman Silver Purchase Act was being formulated, he again advocated special favors for silver. As a compromise candidate, satisfactory to both the silver and the gold factions of the party, he seemed ideal, for his leanings toward silver were nicely balanced by the fact that he was a thoroughgoing party regular who could be trusted not to get out of step with the party leaders. His availability for the Republican nomination in 1896 was further emphasized by his creditable record as a Union officer in the Civil War, by his chivalrous devotion to his invalid wife, by his suave and genial manners, and by his abiding friendship with Marcus Alonzo Hanna, Cleveland industrialist and boss of the Republican Party in Ohio. Hanna had the normal attitude of his class toward tariff protection, but his regard for McKinley was personal no less than political. He early made up his mind that McKinley must be the Republican standard-bearer in 1896, and long before the convention met had rounded up the necessary votes.[1]

The steady drift of the electorate toward the free-silver "heresy" upset the Republican plan for a fence-sitting campaign on the money question.

---

[1] Herbert Croly, *Marcus Alonzo Hanna* (1913), is far superior to any biography of McKinley in its understanding of the forces that shaped McKinley's policies. Thomas Beer, *Hanna* (1929), is also useful.

Southern Democrats, thoroughly frightened by the strength the Populists had shown in 1894, accepted free silver as a means of *The "battle*
winning back the ground they had lost. Western Democrats, *of the*
and frequently also western Republicans, made every effort *standards"*
to outdo the Populists in their devotion to silver. Thirty Democratic
state conventions, all in the West or the South, emphatically endorsed
"the free and unlimited coinage of silver at the ratio of sixteen to one."
Shrewd observers could easily foretell that, in spite of the strenuous
efforts of President Cleveland and the gold-standard Democrats of the
Northeast, the Democratic Party would be forced to include in its platform an uncompromising demand for free silver. Confronted by this
situation, the Republican leaders, Hanna among them, finally determined to commit their party to the single gold standard. They could
not hope by a straddling platform to compete with the unequivocal demands of the Democrats for free silver, and they might, by adhering
steadfastly to gold, win over the dissident Democratic "gold-bugs" to
the support of the Republican ticket. The tariff issue would have to
stand aside. Republicans knew full well, when at St. Louis they nailed
a "sound-money" plank into their platform, that the "battle of the
standards" would dwarf all other party differences to insignificance.

> We are unalterably opposed [this plank read] to every measure calculated
> to debase our currency or impair the credit of our country. We are, there-
> fore, opposed to the free coinage of silver, except by international agreement
> with the leading commercial nations of the world, which we pledge ourselves
> to promote, and until such agreement can be obtained the existing gold
> standard must be preserved. All our silver and paper currency must be
> maintained at parity with gold, and we favor all measures designed to main-
> tain inviolably the obligations of the United States and all our money,
> whether coin or paper, at the present standard, the standard of the most
> enlightened nations of the earth.

The complete conversion of the Republicans to the single gold standard
was not accomplished without a party split. More than one hundred
votes were cast for an amendment, introduced by Senator Henry M.
Teller of Colorado, that favored the "independent coinage of gold and
silver at our mints at the ratio of sixteen parts of silver to one of gold."
When this amendment was rejected, thirty-four delegates, led by Teller,
and including four United States senators and two representatives, left
the hall in protest. That they would join the Democrats in case the latter came out for silver seemed a foregone conclusion. But the Republicans adhered steadfastly to their program, nominated McKinley for
President with Garret A. Hobart of New Jersey for Vice-President, and

[269]

adjourned in the hope that Marcus A. Hanna, their new campaign man ager, could find the money and the means to restore their party to power The action of the Republicans left the Democrats, whose conventior met a few weeks later at Chicago, no logical choice but to endorse free silver. The Democratic National Committee, however, was still in the hands of the men who had helped to nominate Cleveland in 1892, and they made a determined effort to halt the trend toward silver. But when their nominee for temporary chairman, David B. Hill of New York, a "gold-bug," was defeated by Senator John W. Daniel of Virginia, a silverite, 556 to 349, it was apparent that the radicals were in control. The platform they presented and adopted (628 to 301) on the money question bore no trace of compromise.

> We demand the free and unlimited coinage of both silver and gold at the present legal ratio of sixteen to one without waiting for the aid or consent of any other nation. We demand that the standard silver dollar shall be a full legal tender, equally with gold, for all debts, public and private, and we favor such legislation as will prevent for the future the demonetization of any kind of legal tender money by private contract.

The Democrats had produced a platform; they were not long in finding a candidate. Before the convention met, the leading aspirant among the *William* silverites was Richard P. Bland, a congressman from Mis-*Jennings* souri. But Bland's candidacy had awakened little enthusi-*Bryan* asm, and many delegates regretted the constitutional provision that alone would keep them from voting for the far more colorful John P. Altgeld of Illinois, a naturalized citizen of German birth. Among the numerous minor candidates was William Jennings Bryan (1860–1925) of Nebraska, a young man only thirty-six years of age whose reputation for persuasive oratory was already well known.[1] Bryan had served two terms in Congress, 1891 to 1895, and had once attracted nation-wide attention by a powerful speech on the tariff. During the depression, without actually becoming a Populist, he had taken up with most of the Populist doctrines, particularly free silver. As Ignatius Donnelly, the most famous orator of Populism complained, "We put him to school and he wound up by stealing the schoolbooks."

For months before the nominating convention met in 1896, Bryan had been speaking on free silver to western audiences, and had rehearsed many times the ringing phrases that were to bring him fame at Chicago.

---

[1] Unfortunately there is as yet no really good biography of Bryan. Probably the most nearly satisfactory is M. R. Werner, *Bryan* (1929). Paxton Hibben, *The Peerless Leader, William Jennings Bryan* (1929), and J. C. Long, *Bryan, The Great Commoner* (1928), leave much to be desired, but are still superior to W. J. and Mary B. Bryan, *The Memoirs of William Jennings Bryan* (1925).

Fully conscious of his genius as an orator, he knew in his heart that if he could only find the occasion to make the speech he had learned so well the coveted prize would be his. The opportunity came when he was asked to close the debate on a resolution that would have repudiated free silver and commended the Cleveland administration.

> Serene and self-possessed, and with a smile upon his lips, he faced the roaring multitude with a splendid consciousness of power. Before a single word had been uttered by him, the pandemonium sank to an inarticulate murmur, and when he began to speak, even this was hushed to the profoundest silence. . . . He spoke with the utmost deliberation, so that every word was driven home to each hearer's consciousness, and yet with an ever-increasing force, which found fit expression in the wonderful harmony and power of his voice. His sentences rang out, now with an accent of superb disdain, and now with the stirring challenge of a bugle call. . . . The leaderless Democracy of the West was leaderless no more.
>
> The scene enacted in the Convention, as Mr. Bryan finished speaking, was indescribable. Throughout the latter part of his address, a crash of applause had followed every sentence; but now the tumult was like that of a great sea thundering against the dykes. Twenty thousand men and women went mad with an irresistible enthusiasm. The orator had met their mood to the very full. He had found magic words for the feeling which they had been unable to express. And so he had played at will upon their very heartstrings, until the full tide of their emotion was let loose in one tempestuous roar of passion, which seemed to have no end.[1]

Bryan's speech was not a reasoned defense of the silver cause, and was not meant to be. Rather it was a leader's call to action. His closing words, "You shall not press down upon the brow of labor this crown of thorns, you shall not crucify mankind upon a cross of gold," summarized in a sentence all that had gone before. At that moment, had the convention been given the chance, it would doubtless have nominated Bryan by acclamation. When the proper time came, in spite of the fact that more than a hundred and fifty gold Democrats persistently abstained from voting, Bryan obtained the necessary two-thirds majority after only five ballots. For Vice-President the convention chose Arthur Sewall, a wealthy banker and shipbuilder from Maine.

The plight of the Populists when they learned what the Democrats had done was far from pleasant. The Democratic platform had not only appropriated the silver issue; it had denounced with *Plight of the* Populistic fervor the "absorption of wealth by the few," *Populists* and had called for a stricter control of trusts and railroads by the federal government. The Democratic candidate, Bryan, was a Populist in

---

[1] Harry Thurston Peck, *Twenty Years of the Republic* (1907), pp. 498–502. The quoted sentences are interspersed between long excerpts from Bryan's speech.

everything but name. The Populist leaders, confident that both the Republicans and the Democrats would be captured by the "gold-bugs," had set the date of the Populist Convention later than either of the old-party conventions, and had hoped to rally all free-silver men and all reformers to their standard. Now they were faced squarely with the problem of sacrificing their party by endorsing the Democratic nominee or aiding the Republicans by dividing the silver vote. In general western Populists were willing to accept Bryan and join the Democrats, but to southern Populists such a course, involving, as it did, full surrender to a hated enemy, was extremely painful to contemplate. After a heated battle the Populist Convention voted in favor of a compromise. It would name its vice-presidential candidate first on the assumption that a southern Populist would be chosen instead of the wholly unacceptable Sewall. Proponents of the plan argued that the convention might then nominate Bryan for President, if it chose, with the full expectation that the Democrats would withdraw Sewall, accept the Populist nominee for Vice-President, and so emphasize the separateness as well as the temporary fusion of the two parties.

The Populist choice for Vice-President fell on Thomas E. Watson, the fiery Georgian, after which there was no further chance to stop Bryan *The Populist ticket* for first place. Had the Democrats then substituted Watson for Sewall, the Populists could have held up their heads during the campaign. But the Democrats were satisfied that they had won what they wanted, and ignored Watson, who nevertheless remained in the race and campaigned vigorously. The anomaly of the situation led to endless confusion in the balloting, and many Populists voted the Democratic ticket in order to be sure that their ballots would count. The Populist Party, indeed, practically dissolved during the campaign. For the next three presidential elections it continued to put tickets in the field, but after 1896 it was never again a serious factor in American politics.

By repudiating Cleveland [1] and absorbing Populism, the Democrats had placed their party in a position to challenge seriously the Republican *Campaign of 1896* expectation of an easy victory. Bryan as a campaigner was superb. "Probably no man in civil life," observed the New York *Nation*, "had succeeded in inspiring so much terror, without taking life, as Bryan." Between the time of his nomination and election day he traveled eighteen thousand miles and spoke to hundreds of audiences.

[1] The gold wing of the Democratic Party subsequently held a convention and nominated John M. Palmer of Illinois for President and Simon B. Buckner of Kentucky for Vice-President. Cleveland supported this ticket, but like most of the "Gold Democrats" hoped for a Republican victory.

Inspired by the endless vitality of their leader, a host of lesser orators spread the gospel of free silver to every village and crossroads in the country. The Democratic campaign chest, however, was slender, for the only large contributions came from the hard-pressed silver interests of the Far West. It was at this point that the Republicans proved invulnerable. Conceding privately that "the Chicago Convention has changed everything" and that the campaign "will be work and hard work from the start," Hanna, the Republican campaign manager, began an earnest solicitation of funds from all the important business interests that had a financial stake in Republican success. Exactly how much money he and his subordinates collected will never be known, but Hanna later admitted receiving gifts of not less than $3,500,000, a huge sum for the times, and particularly for a lean year. With ample funds at his disposal and more always to be had for the asking, Hanna embarked upon a "campaign of education" well calculated to discredit the reasoning of the silverites. Hundreds of well-paid orators challenged the tenets of Bryan and his underfed volunteers, tons of shrewdly phrased pamphlets exploded the theories of "Professor Coin," batteries of skillful writers provided news and editorials for subsidized newspapers. By staking everything on so dubious an issue as free silver, the Democrats had laid themselves wide open to this kind of attack. No doubt the "bimetallists," as they called themselves, in contrast with the gold "monometallists," were sincere in their conviction that the need for free silver exceeded every other reform in importance, but they found few good economists who would agree with the arguments by which they defended it. Republican pamphleteers dwelt upon the absurdity of trying to maintain two different "yardsticks" with which to measure money, and featured the downright dishonesty involved in paying off valid debts with "fifty-cent" silver dollars. Among the reformers themselves there was much dissent from the free-silver hypothesis and some genuine dismay at the overemphasis it received. Henry Demarest Lloyd, the author of *Wealth Against Commonwealth* (1894), a powerful indictment of the existing economic order, described free silver as a "fake" and called it the "cowbird of the reform movement. It waited until the nest had been built by the sacrifices and labors of others, and then laid its eggs in it, pushing out the others which lie smashed on the ground."

No doubt the Republican propaganda actually won over many free-silverites to Republican views, but not all that Hanna's lieutenants did was strictly educational. Every time-tested device for *Republican tactics* gathering in the votes was utilized — parades led by brass bands, torchlight processions, flaming posters, campaign caps and buttons. As the end drew near, threats were passed out freely. Working-men were told that the election of McKinley would mean high wages and prosperity, but the election of Bryan, the loss of their jobs. Employers were known to reinforce this argument by telling their employees that if Bryan were elected they need not come back to work. Farmers were informed that in case there was a Democratic victory their mortgages would not be renewed. Nor was there any lack of funds among the Republicans on election day to keep on duty a full quota of "workers at the polls." Not among the least of Hanna's shrewd moves was to keep McKinley discreetly in the background. Hanna well knew that in a rough-and-tumble campaign the Republican candidate would have been no match for Bryan. Small delegations were permitted to visit McKinley at his home in Canton, Ohio, and to be charmed by his personality, but they were given no fighting message. McKinley's famous "front-porch" speeches mainly recorded calm confidence; the others could do the fighting. Widely advertised as the "advance agent of Prosperity," he was never once really required to defend the title he had received.

It was a common statement that, if the election had been held in August instead of November, Bryan would have been the victor. No one knows. Possibly a rise in the price of wheat due to a *Election results* short crop abroad, whereas the American crop was abundant, seriously affected the results. However that may be, the Republicans undoubtedly picked up many votes as the campaign neared its close, and in the end they won an overwhelming victory. In general the agricultural South and West supported Bryan, while the industrial Northeast supported McKinley; but McKinley's Northeast extended as far west as Iowa, Minnesota, and North Dakota, while Bryan's solid South and West were broken by such notable Republican exceptions as Maryland, Delaware, West Virginia, Kentucky, California, and Oregon. McKinley received more than seven million popular votes to six and one half million for Bryan, while the electoral vote stood 271 to 176. The real meaning of the election was somewhat obscured by the unfortunate issue on which it had been fought. In actual fact Bryan represented the forces of agriculture, both in the South and in the West, and to a lesser extent the forces of labor. McKinley, on the other hand, was the candidate of northeastern industry, which, ever since the Civil War, had been well-entrenched in the control of the national government and meant to hold its ground. The defeat of Bryan and the downfall of Populism freed the industrial leaders, temporarily at least, from the menace of popular interference with their monopolistic ambitions. Tom Johnson, the perennial mayor of Cleveland, Ohio, described the election

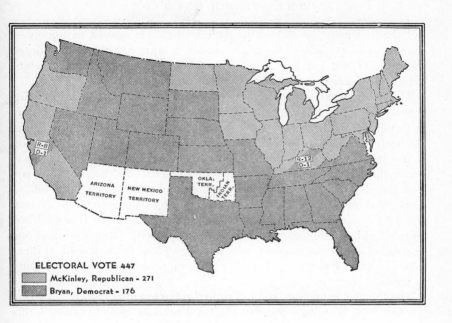

ELECTORAL VOTE 447

- McKinley, Republican - 271
- Bryan, Democrat - 176

R-8
D-1

R-12
D-1

ARIZONA TERRITORY

NEW MEXICO TERRITORY

OKLA. TERR.

INDIAN TERR.

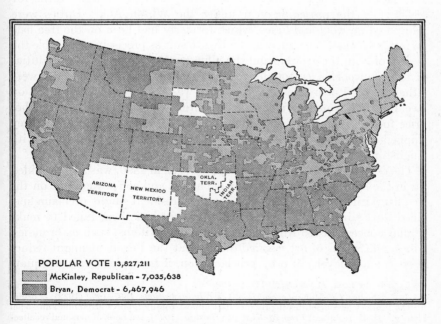

POPULAR VOTE 13,827,211

- McKinley, Republican - 7,035,638
- Bryan, Democrat - 6,467,946

ARIZONA TERRITORY

NEW MEXICO TERRITORY

OKLA. TERR.

INDIAN TERR.

PRESIDENTIAL ELECTION OF 1896, BY STATES AND BY COUNTIES

as "the first great protest of the American people against monopoly — the first great struggle of the masses in our country against the privileged classes. It was not free silver that frightened the plutocrat leaders. What they feared, then, what they fear now, is free men." [1]

McKinley was inaugurated to the accompaniment of brightening economic skies and promptly took the necessary steps to identify Republican policies with the return of prosperity. Congress, being safely Republican in both houses, was called immediately into special session, not, as one might have supposed, to enact a gold-standard law, but rather to revise the tariff along strictly protectionist lines. In the preceding session the Republicans had already framed and presented a tariff bill, so within record time a measure introduced by Representative Nelson Dingley, Jr., of Maine was enacted into law. The rates it established quite outdid all previous efforts at tariff protection. Its purpose, as one inspired observer pointed out, was not to produce revenue and incidentally to afford protection, but rather to afford protection and incidentally to produce revenue.[2]

The Dingley rates were so high as to discourage importation. During the first year they were in force the total revenue collected from tariffs *The Dingley* dropped twenty-five million dollars below the returns for *Tariff* the preceding year under the Wilson Act. Duties were reimposed on wool and hides, which formerly had been on the free list; an intricate sugar schedule was devised to suit as precisely as possible the desires of both the growers and the refiners of sugar; and the high duties of 1890 on woolens, cotton, linen, silk, crockery, and steel products were either restored or increased. So ample was the duty of $7.84 a ton on steel rails that American steel manufacturers were able to charge a higher price for the rails they sold in the United States than for those they shipped to London and sold, presumably at a profit, in competition with English rails.

The establishment of limited reciprocity, as in 1890, was also provided for in the new law. A few items such as tea and coffee were put on the free list with the understanding that the President might proclaim specified duties in force if the nations that exported them failed to make similar concessions to American goods. Other items, such as brandies, wines, and works of art, carried duties that the President might reduce to designated levels, also by proclamation, if he could obtain adequate

---

[1] Tom L. Johnson, *My Story* (1911), p. 109.

[2] J. F. Rhodes, *The McKinley and Roosevelt Administrations, 1897–1909* (1922), is useful for the inside view of politics it presents, but almost totally ignores economic and social history. H. H. Kohlsaat, *From McKinley to Harding* (1923), is a book of personal recollections by "one who knew."

favors in return. Finally, on all tariff-bearing articles, the President might negotiate treaties with foreign nations to scale down the American rates as much as twenty per cent, but all such treaties required ratification by the Senate before they could become effective. By presidential proclamation some minor breaches were made in the high-tariff wall, but the eleven reciprocity treaties negotiated by the administration were all rejected by the Senate.

McKinley's failure to ask Congress for a rigid gold-standard law is not difficult to explain. The Senate, while safely Republican on the tariff, contained too many hold-over silver Senators to be regarded *International bi-metallism* as trustworthy on the money question. McKinley therefore took advantage of the clause in the Republican platform that called for an international conference on bimetallism to substitute diplomacy for legislative action. That he would maintain the gold standard, with or without the sanction of law, was apparent from his choice of a conservative Chicago banker, Lyman J. Gage, as his Secretary of the Treasury. To give plausibility to the negotiations on silver, which were almost certain to fail, McKinley chose as his Secretary of State the aged John Sherman, whose historic connection with American monetary problems made his selection seem ideal. Sherman's memory was known to be failing, but this slight disqualification was more than offset by the fact that his seat in the Senate was coveted by McKinley's friend and patron, Marcus A. Hanna. On April 12, 1897, McKinley named a commission of three ardent bimetallists, headed by Edward O. Wolcott of Colorado, to visit Europe in the interest of international bimetallism. At Paris the commission was received with some show of cordiality, but at London it learned that Great Britain positively would not open her mints to silver on any terms satisfactory to the Americans. The final failure of "international bimetallism," coupled with heavy Republican gains in the election of 1898, enabled Congress at last to pass the long-promised gold-standard law on March 14, 1900.

The close coincidence between the return of prosperity and the return of the Republicans to power furnished a valuable weapon to Republican campaigners for many years to come. It is possible, of *The return of prosperity* course, that the prospect of Republican victory promoted business confidence and led to business expansion. Good times were on the way back, however, even before the election, and it seems reasonable to suppose that the course of events would not have been far different, even if Bryan had been elected. Undoubtedly one reason for the upward surge was an increase in the money supply. It is a curious fact that monetary inflation actually occurred in spite of all the Republicans had done to prevent it, and it occurred in a way they had least expected, by means of an increase in the world's supply of gold. For a quarter of a century before 1890 the amount of new gold mined each year was practically constant. Then a steady increase began which by the end of the nineties had reached spectacular proportions. In the year 1897, approximately twice as much gold was produced as in the year 1890; in 1898 nearly two and one half times as much. The cyanide process by which more gold was extracted from the ore mined, coupled with new discoveries of gold in Australia, South Africa, and the Klondike, accounted for the increase. Bryan was doubtless right when he first began to assert that the amount of gold in existence was inadequate to transact the world's business, but his arguments were less convincing with each succeeding year. Before Bryan became active in politics American business had to overcome the handicap of a steadily appreciating dollar, which meant also steadily diminishing price levels; by the time Bryan began to run for President, the value of the dollar had begun to diminish, and prices were on the rise. American agriculture no less than industry responded to the stimulus of gold inflation, while in the West the drouth at long last came to an end. Good harvests in America were matched by poor harvests abroad and the price of farm produce began to rise. Presently the Spanish-American War, the Philippine Insurrection, and the Boer-British War each added its quota to the boom that had already begun.[1]

[1] E. E. Robinson, *The Presidential Vote, 1896–1932* (1934), is a useful statistical compilation. Matthew Josephson, *The President Makers: The Culture of Politics and Leadership in an Age of Enlightenment, 1896–1919* (1940), is biographic rather than political. Almont Lindsey, *The Pullman Strike* (1942), is the best available account of that labor disturbance. Elmer Ellis, *Henry Moore Teller, Defender of the West* (1941), is an excellent biography of the most eminent Silver Republican.

CHAPTER XIII

THE OLD AMERICAN WAY

BETWEEN 1876, the one-hundredth anniversary of the signing of the Declaration of Independence, and 1889, the one hundredth anniversary of the inauguration of government under the Constitution, the United States became habituated to centennial celebrations. It was a foregone conclusion, therefore, that so available a date as the four hundredth anniversary of the discovery of America by Columbus would not be overlooked. As early as 1890 an act was passed by Congress providing for an exhibition, to be held in 1892, that should commemorate the progress of the nation in art, industry, and agriculture. Rivalry for the honor and profit involved in staging the "Fair" was keen between New York, Washington, St. Louis, and Chicago, but Chicago, with a guaranty of ten million dollars, was the successful bidder.

Great were the preparations that were made for what its promoters were pleased to call the "World's Columbian Exposition." In its behalf the ablest of America's artists, under the general direction of Daniel Hudson Burnham,[1] pooled their talents. Frederick Law Olmsted, the landscape architect who had laid out Central Park, New York; Stanford White, C. F. McKim, R. M. Hunt, and Louis Sullivan, architects; Augustus Saint-Gaudens, Daniel Chester French, Lorado Taft, and Frederick Macmonnies, sculptors; Kenyon Cox, Gari Melchers, and Edwin Blashfield, painters; all these and others contributed of their genius to produce an artistic setting of surpassing beauty for the exhibition. "Look here, old fellows," Saint-Gaudens once told these leaders as they pored together over their plans, "do you realize that this is the greatest meeting of artists since the fifteenth century?" For the site of the Fair ninety acres of Lake Front adjoining the business district of Chicago and six hundred acres in Jackson Park were dedicated. Here, at a cost of twenty-six million dollars, arose a "White City" so breath-takingly beautiful as to win the highest praise,

The Chicago World's Fair

[1] Charles Moore, *Daniel H. Burnham* (1921).

not merely from the multitudes, but also from such professional skeptics and sophisticates as Henry Adams and Charles Eliot Norton. In full revolt against the grotesque architecture of the "General Grant" period, the planners of the White City adhered closely to classical designs — a confession, in a sense, that America had not yet produced a worth-while native architecture. But as a classical reproduction — "what the Romans would have wished to create" — it was superb.

The Fair was dedicated on Columbus day, October 12, 1892, but it was not officially opened until the following spring. In spite of the depression, twelve million visitors entered its gates, and it was a financial success. Its exhibits well revealed the material and artistic achievements of America and the world, for nearly every foreign nation was represented. The Palace of Fine Arts satisfied Americans that they no longer had need to apologize for the work of their sculptors and painters. Buildings devoted in whole or in part to transportation, manufactures, machinery, electricity, mines and mining, agriculture, horticulture, floriculture, and the liberal arts mirrored the remarkable transformations of the age. The Midway Plaisance, with its exotic "villages," its exciting "Streets of Cairo," its enormous "Ferris Wheel," and its innumerable other amusement features, set the pattern for future American playgrounds. Less talked about than they deserved were the numerous "congresses" that accompanied the Fair. Their purpose was to present the most pressing scientific, literary, and religious problems of the times. A fitting climax to the series of religious congresses was a great "parliament of religions" in which Catholics, Protestants, and Jews rubbed shoulders and exchanged ideas with Buddhists, Confucianists, Mohammedans, and representatives of many other religious sects. Out of the Fair and the congresses Americans got a far better understanding of their country and its place in the world than they had ever had before. They went home to imitate its architecture, to seek for beauty in the replanning of their towns and cities, and to dream dreams, not wholly unrealized, of a more abundant life.

Among the World's Fair congresses the one on history attracted comparatively little attention, but at an evening session, on July 12, 1893, *Frederick Jackson Turner* Frederick Jackson Turner, a youthful professor from the University of Wisconsin, read a paper of great importance on "The Significance of the Frontier in American History." [1] Pointing out that "the germ theory of politics" had been sufficiently

[1] This essay, together with other interesting material bearing on the co-called "Turner hypothesis," appears in the latest compilation of Turner essays, *The Early Writings of Frederick Jackson Turner* (1938).

FREDERICK JACKSON TURNER

emphasized, and that the evolution of institutions along the Atlantic coast was, after all, a fairly "familiar phenomenon," he urged historians of the United States to study the West as well as the East.

> American social development has been continually beginning over again on the frontier. This perennial rebirth, this fluidity of American life, this expansion westward with its new opportunities, its continuous touch with the simplicity of primitive society, furnish the forces dominating American character. The true point of view in the history of this nation is not the Atlantic coast, it is the Great West.... What the Mediterranean Sea was to the Greeks, breaking the bonds of custom, offering new experiences, calling out new institutions and activities, that and more, the ever retreating frontier has been to the United States directly, and to the nations of Europe more remotely.

Turner's words were heeded, and soon a veritable cult of the West had sprung up among the writers of American history. Sometimes the American Historical Association, founded in 1884 by scholars of unimpeachable eastern connections, was accurately, if facetiously, described as the "Turner-verein." Turner's disciples outdid their master in claiming significance for the frontier, and they often claimed too much. Nevertheless, it seems clear that the influence of a succession of frontiers had much to do with molding the character of American civilization. Years before, E. L. Godkin, editor of the *Nation*, had recognized this fact in an elaborate review of de Tocqueville's *Democracy in America*. The pioneering element, he wrote,

> spread itself thinly over a vast area of soil, of such extraordinary fertility that a very slight amount of toil expended on it affords returns that might have satisfied even the dreams of Spanish avarice. The result has been very much what we might have concluded, *a priori*, that it would be. A society composed at the period of its formation mainly of young men, coming from all parts of the world in quest of fortune, released from the ordinary restraints of family, church, and public opinion, even of the civil law, naturally and inevitably acquires a certain contempt for authority and impatience of it, and individualism among them develops itself very rapidly. If you place this society, thus constituted, in the midst of a wilderness, where each member of it has to contend, tools in hand, with Nature herself for wealth, or even subsistence, the ties which bind him to his fellows will for a while at least be rarely anything stronger than that of simple contiguity; and the only mutual obligation which this relation suggests strongly is that of rendering assistance occasionally in overcoming material difficulties — in other words, the simplest bond which can unite human beings. Each person is from the necessity of the case so absorbed in his own struggle for existence, that he has seldom occasion or time for the consideration and cultivation of his social relations. He knows nothing of the antecedents of his neighbors, nor they of his. They are not drawn together, in all probability, by a single

memory or association. They have drifted into the same locality, it is true, under the guidance of a common impulse, and this a selfish one. So that the settler gets into the habit of looking at himself as an individual, of contemplating himself and his career separate and apart from the social organization. We do not say that this breeds selfishness — far from that; but it breeds individualism.[1]

Whether Godkin was right or wrong in his explanation of its causes, few will deny the existence among early Americans of a strongly individualistic bent. If, as Godkin held and Turner preached, this *The frontier* emphasis upon individualism proceeded from "the frontier *life* life," then it would seem to follow that the gradual extinction of the frontier would make a difference. Godkin may not have been fully aware of the fact, but by the time he wrote these words the kind of frontier he described was rapidly disappearing. A generation later, when Turner wrote, it was virtually gone. Enormous tracts of unsettled land still existed in the trans-Mississippi West, but most of this land was arid plains or rugged mountains, totally unfitted for the type of agriculture that earlier American pioneers had practiced. Radical changes in methods of farming made possible a long-sustained advance, but by the end of the century the law of diminishing returns had begun to operate. "Free land" still existed in quantities, and settlers who knew no better than to take it could still be found, but for the ordinary farmer who pioneered in the twentieth century the returns were rarely such as might have satisfied "the dreams of Spanish avarice." Rather, they were such as to saddle upon the next generation a vexatious problem of resettlement and relief.

Undoubtedly the diminishing importance of the frontier life had its effect upon the character of American civilization. New forces were now at work that had little to do with the frontier life, except to stifle it. Coincident with the passing of the frontier an economic revolution had occurred that in its transforming influence had affected not only the United States but the whole world besides. Railroads permeated every part of the country, and at both coasts connected with steamship lines that crisscrossed every ocean. Telegraph, telephone, and cable service grew daily more complete. Cheap paper, cheap printing, and cheap postage greatly facilitated the circulation of newspapers, books, periodicals, and advertising literature. Inventions crowded forward in an exciting procession. Big business, equipped and re-equipped with new and then still newer tools, drove little business out of business. New

---

[1] E. L. Godkin, "Aristocratic Opinions of Democracy." in *North American Review*, c, 194–232 (January, 1865).

breeds of immigrants flocked in from the Old World to do the hard work of industry. Labor and capital drew apart with an acute class-consciousness that the frontier life had never known. Before this barrage the individualism of log-cabin, covered-wagon days gave way. For the few it became an instrument with which to exploit the many; for the many it tended, more and more, to become merely a memory.

Whatever the forces that worked together to shape the pattern of American society in the late nineteenth century, undoubtedly the *Uniformity in American Society* economic revolution, aided and abetted by the gradual disappearance of the frontier, played a principal part. Responding to the new impetus, an urbanized industrialized society swept rapidly from East to West.[1] Labor, influenced no less by the influx of European ideas than by the influx of European immigrants, tended to subordinate the welfare of the individual to the welfare of the class. Farmers, transformed by the machine age into petty business men who produced primarily to sell, forsook their individualistic traditions to battle co-operatively for their rights through Granges, Alliances, and even a third political party. With the whole nation open, almost equally, to the operation of the same forces, life in the United States became increasingly standardized. Sectional differences and local idiosyncrasies yielded slowly but surely before an insistent demand for uniformity.

Much has been written to show how the coming of the immigrants in the late nineteenth century brought diversity rather than uniformity to *Immigrant influences* the American people. What is sometimes forgotten is that, in spite of the rising immigrant tide, the native Americans continued to be overwhelmingly in the ascendance. During the thirty years preceding 1900 the percentage of native-born inhabitants remained practically constant, varying through four sets of census figures less than one per cent from an average of eighty-six per cent. It is true, of course, that many native Americans — in 1900 about one fifth of the total population — had at least one immigrant parent; but it is also true, if the matter of ancestry must be fully examined, that all native Americans, except for the Indians, were the descendants of immigrants. Even more to the point is the fact that until the last decade of the nineteenth century the immigrants, numerous as they were, came primarily from the British Isles and Canada, from Germany, and from the Scandinavian countries. In the seventies 82.8 per cent were so classified, in the eighties, 75.6; in the nineties, when the trend from southern and eastern

---

[1] By all odds the best study of the transformation of American life wrought by the economic revolution is A. M. Schlesinger, *The Rise of the City, 1878–1898* (1933).

Europe began in earnest, 41.8. During these three decades some 7,834,412 immigrants entered the United States from Canada or from northwestern Europe, as against only 2,953,714 from southern and eastern Europe. The former, as a rule, were quickly and easily assimilated into the American population; a large proportion of them were English-speaking on their arrival, and practically all of them made haste to imitate the American way of life. Against the winds of uniformity that were blowing, the nineteenth-century immigrants offered as little resistance as the descendants of the Puritans and the Cavaliers.

In a sense the frontier, while it lasted, had had much to do with the increasing homogeneity of the American people. It had been both a melting-pot and a mixing-bowl. Moreover, every part of the United States, at one time or another, had gone through the frontier process, and the experience had everywhere left its mark — more or less the same mark. Just as the child is father to the man, so the primitive society of frontier times bequeathed a number of its most distinctive characteristics to later generations. Such ideals as flowed from the frontier's love of conquest, of individual freedom, and of equality of opportunity lived on into a period when the actual conditions of life belied them. The frontier might have vanished, but the restless search for greener pastures that it had bred survived.[1]

But if the frontier had promoted homogeneity, the passing of the frontier tended to promote it even more. It is not necessary to believe that while the West was young all of the more aggressive *Passing of* and energetic people went West, leaving to the East only a *the frontier* stagnant and unenterprising lot. Nevertheless, with the frontier at the vanishing point, with the railroads offering tempting rates, and with opportunity knocking more boldly in the eastern cities than on the western plains, there occurred in the late nineteenth century a remarkable return of the West upon the East. The enterprising Easterner going west was met by the enterprising Westerner going east. Western ideas got a hearing in the East, just as eastern ideas had all along got a hearing in the West. Western leaders in business, in politics, in the professions appeared in every eastern city. Northerners, too, went south, and Southerners went north. The population was mixed up as never before, and the characteristics of one section became increasingly the characteristics of all.

This strikingly homogeneous nature of American society can perhaps

---

[1] An illuminating interpretation of the rôle of the West in American history is contained in F. L. Paxson, *When the West is Gone* (1930). See also D. R. Fox (editor), *Sources of Culture in the Middle West* (1934).

DENSITY OF POPULATION, 1870

DENSITY OF POPULATION, 1890

DENSITY OF POPULATION, 1910

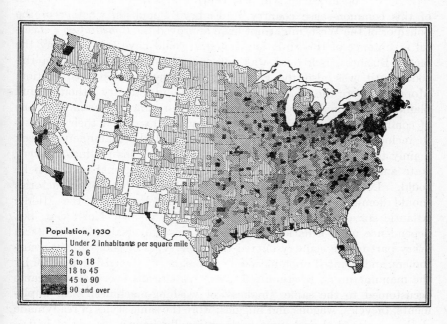

DENSITY OF POPULATION, 1930

be best appreciated when compared with European society during the same period. In Europe only a few hundred miles at most would bring the traveler to a region where the people saluted a different flag, spoke a different language, cherished a different culture. In America, for nearly three thousand miles east and west, and for half that many miles north and south, one met with the same flag, the same language, and essentially the same culture. Minor differences of course endured. New Englanders broadened their *a*'s, did curious things to their *r*'s, and sometimes forgot their final *g*'s. Southerners spoke with a soft and musical drawl that owed something, no doubt, to the influence of a large colored population; certain cities reflected the speech characteristics of a leading immigrant group — Jewish in New York, German in Milwaukee, Swedish in Minneapolis. Only by such trifles as these could the remnants of separate cultural heritages be observed. Far greater differences existed within the compass of the British Isles alone. Americans everywhere tended to talk alike, think alike, act alike.

"After all, business is the biggest thing in this country." So the editor of the Atlanta *Constitution* told his readers on January 8, 1890; *Nation-wide* and for good measure he added, "Politicians may talk, but *business* businessmen will act, control, and dominate the destinies of this common-sense country." Embryo Populists, whether of the South or of the West, might not have approved the *Constitution's* cheerful acceptance of this situation, but few would have tried to deny the fact. Business, moreover, was not only the "biggest thing" in the country, it was also the greatest single agency of standardization. More and more the "princes of commerce and industry" thought and planned in national terms. With revolutionary improvements in means of communication at their disposal, they had expanded their interests to include the whole nation. No longer did the manufacturer seek mainly to reach a local market; he must now sell his product in every state and territory of the Union — beyond the national borders if he could. Local natural resources might determine that cotton-factories should dominate in the South, iron- and steel-works in the Middle Atlantic states, and flour- and grist-mills in the new Northwest, but dependence upon a nation-wide market was universal. Merchants in every part of the country offered the same types of goods to their customers, and counted upon national campaigns of advertising, paid for by the manufacturers, to stimulate sales. Americans everywhere became accustomed to the same "makes" of washing-machines, farm implements, bicycles, wagons and buggies; wore the same styles of readymade clothes; painted their houses with nationally known brands of house-paint; purchased quantities of patent breakfast foods, patent tooth-powder, and patent liniment ("good for man or beast"). Mail-order houses, selling commodities pictured in catalogues at cut-rate prices direct to the trustful purchaser, did a thriving business. Retail prices, in spite of widely divergent transportation costs, varied little from one section of the country to another, and even the methods of doing business became standardized.

Industrialism, of course, meant the growth of cities, but this was a development that spread itself with remarkable uniformity the whole country over. While the Northeast led the way in urbanization, other sections of the country showed themselves excellent imitators. The South during and after reconstruction sought eagerly to crowd itself with factories and cities; as Henry Watterson put it, "The South, having had its bellyful of blood, has gotten a taste of money, and is too busy trying to make more to quarrel with anybody." The West, too, from the time of the Civil War on, tried hard to get rid of its overgreat dependence upon agriculture which made no one rich, and to embrace industry which made riches for at least a few. In 1871 the Milwaukee Chamber of Commerce lamented:

> We are sending our hard lumber east to get it back as furniture and agricultural implements, we ship ores to St. Louis and New York, to pay the cost of bringing it back as shot, type, pipe, sheet lead, white lead, paint, etc., we ship away our wool crop and import cloth, carpets, blankets and other fabrics; we give rags for paper, and hides for boots and harness, and iron-ore for stoves — and our consumers all the while are paying the double costs of this unnecessary transportation.

What this chamber of commerce really wanted for Milwaukee was factories, of whatever kind, and Milwaukee soon got them. So also did every other enterprising western city with good railroad or water connections. In 1870 only 20.9 per cent of the American population lived in places of eight thousand inhabitants or more, whereas in 1900 33.1 per cent were so situated. In the East the percentage of city dwellers ran well above this figure; in the South, the Middle West, and the Far West, well below it. But the trend toward urbanization was national, not sectional, and it affected every part of the country.[1]

The new cities and the rejuvenated old ones showed remarkable similarities. According to James Bryce, "American cities *American* with eight or nine exceptions differ from one another only *cities* herein, that some of them are built more with brick than with wood, and

---

[1] Josiah Strong, *The Twentieth Century City* (1898), is a useful study written from the sociological point of view.

others more with wood than with brick." The checkerboard of "squares" in which William Penn had laid out Philadelphia became the favorite American pattern for city development, and each new "addition" strove valiantly to be exactly like the rest. Pavements rarely kept up with expansion, and while asphalt and brick won increasing popularity, cobblestone, stone block, wood block, and macadam continued in general use. Telephone, telegraph, and electric light poles and wires, all rare or missing in the seventies, became chronic by the nineties, and competed with trees and fences for space at the sides of roads and railroads. Business districts at any given time were everywhere much alike, but each decade saw the height of downtown buildings increase. The first of the skyscrapers, made possible by the use of structural steel and iron, was the ten-storied Home Insurance Building of Chicago, completed in 1885. Thereafter, with one accord, city skylines rose, while traffic congestion increased in spite of the best efforts of horsecars, cable cars, elevated railways, and electric streetcars to keep pace with it. For those who could afford the time and cost of transportation to work, residence districts pushed farther and farther into the surrounding country; for those who could not, apartment houses, tenements, and slum districts were multiplied. Unknown to the cities of the nineteenth century were the long lines of automobiles, the garages, the filling stations, and the motion-picture "palaces" of today. Omnipresent then, but almost obsolete now, were horse-drawn vehicles, livery stables, blacksmith shops, and saloons with shuttered doors. But the uniformity of yesterday is matched only by the uniformity of today.

Behind these externals lay a pattern of life that varied little from city to city. The great majority of city-dwellers were employees of industry or trade, dependent upon wages for their daily bread. From eighty to ninety per cent of them rented the space they lived in. Except in the South, unskilled labor was recruited mainly from the less assimilable immigrant groups, who, at least for a generation, lived in foreign "quarters," and clung tenaciously to their foreign ways. While a few women in the upper strata of society grumbled that the opportunity for "careers" was still in large measure denied them, those on the lower levels suffered no such sorrows. The percentage of women gainfully employed rose from fifteen per cent in 1870 to twenty per cent in 1900. In Philadelphia, by the latter year, one third of the women (counting girls over ten years of age) worked for wages away from their homes. Wherever it could be used to advantage, child labor was ruthlessly exploited — in the cotton-mills of the South, in the sweatshops of the

East, in the packing-plants of the West. The middle classes, who depended upon regular incomes or salaries instead of wages, were for the most part native Americans who had come to the cities from the rural districts. Naturally, most of them retained in the cities the characteristics and customs of country-dwellers, so that American cities in their cultural aspects became, in a sense, merely overgrown country towns. A small fraction of the population enjoyed large incomes, and some of them, particularly the *nouveaux riches*, laid firm foundations for Thorstein Veblen's theory of conspicuous waste.[1]

It would be a mistake, however, to assume that the United States was merely a nation of cities. More than sixty per cent of the people, as late as 1900, still lived in the country, or in towns of less than *Rural* four thousand inhabitants. Practically all of these, and *America* many more besides, depended directly or indirectly upon agriculture for their livelihood. Even the cities, in the last analysis, owed much to the farms, for throughout the nineteenth century an abundant farm demand, restricted from foreign purchases by a protective tariff policy, absorbed the products of the city factories, and spared American manufacturers the necessity of finding in foreign markets an outlet for their goods. For agriculture, as for industry, these were revolutionary years. New tools had to be learned and used, new types of crops had to be raised to suit the city markets, experiments with diversification and standardization had to be carried through, a rising price for farmlands had to be faced. Less and less the American farmer farmed according to ritual; more and more he used his intelligence and the reports of scientific investigators to improve his profits. Caught securely in the meshes of the prevailing economic system, he made every effort to understand it and to bend it to his needs. The farmer movements of the period were not the work of wild-eyed radicals; the farm leaders and a host of well-informed followers based their arguments upon reasoning as sound as that which guided the actions of the prudent industrialist. The interests of the farmers perhaps collided with those of the industrialists, but that did not necessarily make the farm policies radical.

Farm life tended gradually to merge with village life. On Saturdays farmers went to town to trade; on Sundays they went to town to church; on other days when work was not too pressing they went to town, with or without excuses. Retired farmers went to town to live and to be visited by their children, who in many cases were now their tenants. Farm boys and girls went to school in town, got jobs in town, and, when

---

[1] Thorstein Veblen, *The Theory of the Leisure Class* (1899), launched a strong attack on orthodox economic theories with reference to capital and industry.

The size of each state and city is based on population.

A space this size represents 125,000 people.

All cities of 100,000 population or more are shown.

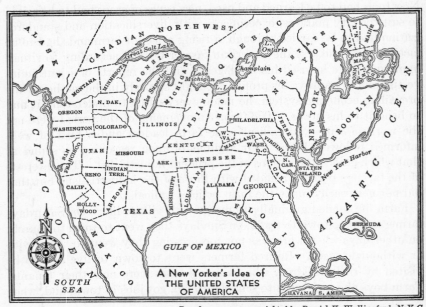

A New Yorker's Idea of
THE UNITED STATES
OF AMERICA

Based on a map copyrighted by Daniel K. Wallingford, N.Y.C.

RELATIVE IMPORTANCE OF CITY AND COUNTRY POPULATIONS

they could, set out with the town boys and girls for the city. Farmers and farm wives borrowed from the town the conveniences that the town had borrowed from the city. Steadily, the extreme isolation of farm life broke down — a process that the rural free delivery of mail, rural telephones, rural electrification, the automobile, and the radio were soon to accelerate immeasurably.

Country towns and villages enjoyed an importance during most of the nineteenth century that they have entirely lost today, and were beginning to lose at its close. As centers of trade for the sur- *Town life* rounding countryside, they could count upon a certain amount of steady business. The stores might be strung along a single "Main Street," or they might surround a central block on which, in county-seats, the courthouse was certain to be located. Only in the business districts of the larger towns were the streets paved, and both horses and drivers took the mud, ruts, and dust philosophically. The dwellings, at least on one side of the inevitable railroad track, were quite commodious, and the yards even more so. Barns and outbuildings were numerous, for many townspeople kept a horse or two, a cow, a pig to butcher in the fall, and some poultry. Room was usually found also for a few fruit trees and a sizable vegetable garden. The incomes of village-dwellers were not large, but they had no need to be.

All the town did deference to the railroad. Incoming passenger trains were met by as many of the inhabitants as were footloose, arrivals and departures were carefully noted, and the town paper was scanned each Wednesday or Thursday to see that no such news was omitted. The station agent was an individual of importance who often asserted his dignity by a superb indifference to the wants of customers. Over the railroad the crops from the surrounding country went to market, over it came the many necessities of life that the farmers and the villagers were unable to produce for themselves. By means of it, and the telegraph line that seemed somehow a part of it, contact with the rest of the world was maintained. Resentment against railroad extortions was rife, especially in the West, and demands for railroad regulation merged into demands for government ownership, but the awe-inspiring importance of the railroad was never forgotten. Not infrequently the railroad companies played leading rôles in local as well as in state and national politics.

Before the automobile age annihilated distance, and while the city still seemed far away, the village had a lively and separate life *Religion* of its own. At the center of this was the church, which gave excuse for and organization to the gregarious instincts of the people.

In the cities the immigrants and the children of immigrants had greatly increased the Catholic and Jewish population, but rural America stood steadfastly by the faith of its Protestant fathers.[1] In every village on a Sunday morning the calm was shattered at regular intervals by the jangling bells of not less than three or four rival denominations. Church services went on all day, and attendance was good: Sunday School at ten o'clock, preaching at eleven o'clock, children's services in the afternoon, young people's meeting at seven o'clock, evening worship with liberal congregational singing at eight o'clock. Weekday services included prayer-meetings on Wednesday or Thursday evening, to which only a handful of the most devout repaired; better-attended meetings of ladies' aid societies, missionary societies, and guilds, all absorbed in money-raising efforts; choir-practice for the faithful, if somewhat storm-tossed, musical contingent; and "protracted meetings," or "revivals," held night after night for several weeks once or twice each year. For these long meetings evangelists who imitated the methods of Moody and Sankey were often called in to aid the local pastors, and with good luck hundreds might be induced to "make their profession of faith." The old emotionalism of the frontier was not quite dead. "Shouting" was not unusual, "conversion" was for many an intensely exciting experience, and preaching reached its climax of success when "not a dry eye was left in the house." A few country churches, each in its mournful setting of tombstones, still managed to survive, as the long rows of teams tied each Sunday to the church's hitch-racks well attested. Farm families, however, preferred increasingly to attend church in town and so the country congregations dwindled.

Theologically speaking, the great problem of the times was the attempt of religion to digest the scientists' doctrine of evolution. For the older

Science vs. religion generation, of whatever denomination, this was asking a great deal. The idea of an infallible Church or an infallible Book had been too long and too steadfastly maintained to be surrendered without a struggle, and heresy charges drove many of the modernists from their pulpits. But the reasonableness of the evolutionary hypothesis could not be lost indefinitely on a world that owed so much to scientific discovery. Prominent clerics, among them Henry Ward Beecher and Lyman Abbott, attempted to reconcile science and

[1] The social history of religion in America has not yet been adequately written. Among the best of the existing treatises are H. K. Rowe, *The History of Religion in the United States* (1924); W. W. Sweet, *The Story of Religions in America* (1930); H. K. Carroll, *The Religious Forces of the United States* (1912). On the subject of revivals, see F. G. Beardsley *A History of American Revivals* (1912); G. C. Loud, *Evangelized America* (1928); and H. C. Weber, *Evangelism* (1929). Thomas Beer, *The Mauve Decade* (1926), is smart and cynical on all aspects of the society of the times.

religion, and the popular defense of evolution made by a Scotchman, Henry Drummond, in his book *Natural Law in the Spiritual World* (1884), profoundly impressed the American reading public.[1] For the most part American thinkers, in the struggle over evolution and the literal interpretation of the Scriptures, merely followed the lead of Europeans; if there was an American contribution to the controversy, it was to the effect that, after all, conduct was far more important than belief. Laymen, a little befuddled by the uproar, called for practical rather than theoretical Christianity, adopted as a part of their creed the temperance efforts of the Woman's Christian Temperance Union and the Anti-Saloon League, gave friendly support to the establishment of institutional churches that could minister to the spirit through the flesh, applauded Jane Addams of Chicago and Lillian D. Wald of New York for their settlement work, and held such agencies of "uplift" as lecture courses and Chautauqua programs to be laudable byproducts of Christianity. As already noted, Christian Science, the first new American religion since Mormonism, went to the logical extreme of asserting the complete control of mind over matter. Thus might the spirit itself minister to the flesh, and religion serve the practical purpose of keeping its devotees well.[2]

Undoubtedly public education played an important part in the standardizing process so characteristic of the times. During these years the public-school system achieved the pattern that with only *Public* slight variations it has maintained ever since. In the rural *education* districts the one-room country school, ungraded but designed to carry its pupils through the equivalent of eight grades in town, still endured. In the towns and villages an eight-grade elementary school, followed by a four-year high school, was the goal most often set and increasingly attained. State-supported normal schools for the training of teachers, a state-supported college of agriculture, and a state-supported university, which might or might not include the college of agriculture, completed the customary picture. Strangely, forty-five states and several territories, in spite of complete freedom to mold their educational systems as they chose, emerged with essentially the same system. Even the content of public education tended to become fixed. In the rural and elementary schools instruction in the "three R's" reigned supreme without much attention to "extras." High schools, in spite of some

---

[1] But see also A. D. White, *A History of the Warfare of Science with Theology in Christendom* (2 vols., 1896).

[2] On Christian Science, see *ante*, p. 109. The growing significance of settlement work is best set forth in Jane Addams, *Forty Years at Hull House* (1935), and Lillian D. Wald, *The House on Henry Street* (1915).

commendable efforts to prepare their graduates for life rather than for college, held steadfastly to a curriculum not far different from that of the old academies they supplanted. Practically all of the colleges and universities took up with the elective system that Charles W. Eliot had introduced at Harvard, but the courses thus offered, cafeteria fashion, differed little from campus to campus. Most of the older generation of instructors had been trained in Germany; most of the younger generation at Harvard or Johns Hopkins, the two universities that had pioneered the way for graduate work in America.[1] At the end of the century scarcely a college student anywhere was more than a single generation removed in his instruction from one or the other of these institutions. Students everywhere, thus exposed to about the same educational diet, tended to get about the same results from their college work and to emerge with strikingly similar points of view. Contacts in college with individuals from other parts of the country helped them to "rub off the rough corners," and still further promoted the cause of standardization. Private institutions, even those under religious leadership, shared almost equally, to the dismay of the orthodox, in the standardizing process. The earnest pursuit of truth for truth's sake, regardless of religious, political, or economic prejudices, met occasional setbacks, but the eloquent defense of academic freedom, made by the Regents of the University of Wisconsin in answer to an attack on Professor Richard T. Ely, the noted economist, raised a banner that institutions of higher learning the whole country over were increasingly willing to defend: "Whatever may be the limitations which trammel inquiry elsewhere, we believe that the great State University of Wisconsin should ever encourage that continual and fearless sifting and winnowing by which alone the truth can be found."[2]

Other evidence of the rapid drift toward standardization in American life may be cited almost at will. Improved means of transportation led to the formation of a host of national organizations, each with its annual meeting attended by delegates from the whole country over. Subjected to the same influences, the delegates carried back home the same ideas. Better means of communication led to the astonishing expansion of the Associated Press and other news-gathering agencies, which furnished identical stories to the readers of hundreds of different news-

---

[1] D. C. Gilman, *The Launching of a University* (1906), tells the story for Johns Hopkins, and Henry James, *Charles W. Eliot* (2 vols., 1930), does a similar service for Harvard. On the University of Chicago, which played a worthy part in stimulating graduate study in the West, see T. W. Goodspeed, *William Rainey Harper, First President of the University of Chicago* (1928).

[2] Richard T. Ely, *Ground Under Our Feet — an Autobiography* (1938).

papers and thus laid the basis for a common reaction. The day when an editor such as Horace Greeley of the New York *Tribune* or Charles A. Dana of the *Sun* expressed his personality through his newspaper had long since passed. Among the new editors Joseph Pulitzer of the New York *World*, and William Randolph Hearst of the San Francisco *Examiner*, did indeed introduce an exaggerated type of sensationalism, but their methods were quickly copied by all except a few of the most conservative journals. Newspapers imitated one another in format as well as in content; they not only read alike; they looked alike. Magazines, even of the popular variety, built up national circulations, and promoted whatever cause they served in a national way. Musical "hits" registered in New York were whistled a few days later by the newsboys in every other American city, and within weeks had reached the country towns. Plays that enjoyed a "run" in New York soon took to the road, and were produced also by the numerous stock companies that flourished in the pre-motion-picture age. Chautauqua circuits of popular lecturers and entertainers were formed to spin around like a top each season until the entire American map had been covered, and all who had ears to hear had heard.

Even sports became nationalized. Baseball, which in any recognizable form had been non-existent before the Civil War, developed during the seventies and eighties into the "great American game," with a complicated system of major and minor leagues that *Sports* every boy and youth in America understood. Football, which was introduced into the United States during the seventies as an adaptation of English Rugby, had by the nineties conquered most of the American colleges and universities. Professional boxing approached the level of respectability when "Gentleman Jim" Corbett won the heavyweight championship in 1892.[1] By this time, too, the bicycle had been tamed, and bicycling had become a fad that women and children as well as men could enjoy. For devotees of the less strenuous life there were such milder activities as lawn-tennis, roller-skating, and croquet. The poor no less than the rich, town- and country-dwellers no less than city-dwellers, found in sports a satisfying refuge from the workaday world, which replaced, in a sense, the excitement once associated with a developing frontier. And, at least for masculine America, the doings recorded on the "sports page" furnished lively topics of conversation when all else failed.

It would, of course, be ridiculous not to concede that striking differ-

[1] A. G. Spalding, *America's National Game* (1911); A. M. Weyand, *American Football* (1926); Alexander Johnston, *Ten — and Out* (1927).

ences as well as striking similarities have always existed, and will always exist, in a nation as vast as the United States. In many ways, no doubt, the differences were more important than the similarities. But the fact remains that by the end of the nineteenth century, American civilization had achieved a distinct pattern, a pattern quite as unique as that possessed by any other nation. Bryce's *American Commonwealth*, which first appeared in 1888, revealed this pattern with all its faults to thinking Americans. Thereupon the book itself became a powerful agency of standardization. Seized upon as a college text and repeatedly reissued, it served for a generation as the mirror with which Americans viewed themselves. Some of the things they saw they liked and meant to keep; others they definitely did not like and meant to change. In part, at least, out of this new comprehension came the heavy rumblings of reform with which the twentieth century opened.[1]

[1] The subject matter of this chapter has recently received considerable attention by historians. Richard Hofstadter, *Social Darwinism in American Thought, 1860–1915* (1944), is a brilliant monograph. A. I. Abell, *The Urban Impact on American Protestantism, 1865–1900* (1943), is illuminating. Sidney Warren, *American Freethought, 1860–1914* (1943), is concerned primarily with the more radical thinkers, such as Ingersoll. Zechariah Chaffee, Jr., *Free Speech in the United States* (1941), is excellent.

The work of American historians is summarized in Michael Kraus, *A History of American History* (1937); and with somewhat greater effort at interpretation in William T. Hutchinson (ed.), *The Marcus W. Jernegan Essays in American Historiography* (1937). H. D. Cater (ed.), *Henry Adams and his Friends* (1947), contains many interesting Adams letters and a biographic introduction. Eric F. Goldman (ed.), *Historiography and Urbanization: Essays in American History in Honor of W. Stull Holt* (1941), is a set of suggestive essays. On newspapers, Philip Kinsley, *The Chicago Tribune: Its First Hundred Years*, Vol. II, *1865–1880* (1945), is written with considerable detachment. J. W. Barrett, *Joseph Pulitzer and his World* (1941), is an appreciative, non-critical biography.

On immigration, Louis Adamic, *A Nation of Nations* (1945), overemphasizes the non-English contribution. Marcus Lee Hansen and John Bartlett Brebner, *The Mingling of the Canadian and American Peoples* (1940), is a story in intermigration.

Miscellaneous: F. R. Dulles, *America Learns to Play: A History of Popular Recreation* (1940); Irving McKee, "*Ben-Hur*" *Wallace* (1947).

CHAPTER XIV

THE DIPLOMATIC FRONT

UNTIL well toward the end of the nineteenth century the foreign policy
of the United States reflected primarily the interest of the American
people in westward expansion.   Washington's doctrine of   *American*
isolation was designed to keep the new nation free from any   *isolation*
European entanglements that might distract its attention from the main
business in hand — the conquest of a continent.   The Monroe Doctrine,
by which European governments were warned to keep out of American
affairs, was merely the converse of the same proposition.   By it the
United States hoped to end for all time the threat of outside interference
with the workings of "manifest destiny."   The War of 1812 and the war
with Mexico were both expansionist wars, and the Civil War was fought,
in considerable part at least, to decide whether the North or the South
should have the advantage in the formation of new western states.   During all these years the United States was busy at home.   It cared little
about the doings of other nations so long as they showed no desire to
block the American policy of expansion.   American political development was self-centered and introspective.   American economic development was a frantic struggle to exploit the rich natural resources that the
continent had divulged, and to satisfy, mainly by domestic production,
the needs of a rapidly growing people.   American diplomacy, especially
during the quarter-century that followed the Civil War, was episodical
and inconsequential.[1]

By the last decade of the nineteenth century a change had set in.   The
era of continental expansion was over, the United States was full grown,
the time-honored frontiering process was fading from the picture.   Good
free lands and good cheap lands were nearing exhaustion.   Population
penetration into the High Plains and the Rocky Mountain plateau all
but eliminated from census maps the zone of uninhabited territory that

[1] J. H. Latané, *A History of American Foreign Policy* (1927), is a good guide to the diplomacy of this period.   On special subjects John Bassett Moore, *The Principles of American Diplomacy* (1918), speaks with authority.

until 1890 had stretched unbroken from the Canadian to the Mexican border. American industry was catching up on its assignment. Already, for many mines and factories, the time had come when the needs of the domestic market could be fully supplied, with a margin left over for sale abroad. American capital had been multiplied many times over, and considerable sums now sought foreign investment. The interest of the United States in itself alone began to give way to an active American interest in the whole wide world. Isolation had lost its charm; increasingly the American government felt called upon to play an important part in international affairs.

James G. Blaine, twice Secretary of State (1881, 1889–92), has often been spoken of as the "harbinger of the new era." This, no doubt, is an *Blaine's* exaggeration, but Blaine did attempt to widen the sphere of *foreign* American influence to include, in fact as well as in theory, all *policy* of the Americas. Toward European nations with an interest in the western hemisphere, but most particularly toward Great Britain, he adopted an uncompromising, almost belligerent, attitude. While serving under Garfield, for example, he made a blustering demand that the British government give up its rights under the Clayton-Bulwer Treaty of 1850 to joint control of any interoceanic canal that should be built. Such a canal, Blaine maintained, must at least in time of war be under strictly American control. This same policy had been proclaimed by President Hayes a few years earlier, but Hayes had been content merely to state the American case; Blaine went much further and tried, in vain as events proved, to force the British to relinquish their claims.[1]

During his second term of office, in the fur-seals controversy, Blaine made another attempt to bluff the British into conceding to the United States a special privilege. "Seward's Folly," as unkind critics called Alaska, had netted at least one valuable resource, the fur-seal industry, for each spring the fur seals gathered at the Pribilof Islands to rear their young and to breed. In 1870 the United States, in order to protect the herds, granted a monopoly on fur-seal fishing to the Alaska Fur Company on condition that it kill only a specified number of "bachelor" seals each year. In the middle eighties Canadian hunters challenged the American monopoly and began to indulge in pelagic sealing, that is, the killing of seals on the high seas. This action brought an immediate protest from the United States, and in 1886 three Canadian sealers were seized by an American revenue cutter, brought to an American port, and condemned. The British government, which still represented Canada in foreign rela-

[1] For Blaine's activities under Garfield, see *ante*, p. 192. Bemis, *American Secretaries of State*, viii, contains a useful article on the later period by J. B. Lockey.

tions, protested vigorously that the seizure of the ships was illegal, and that the American grant of monopolistic fishing rights could not extend beyond the three-mile limit. In spite of these protests the American government continued the seizures, and on March 2, 1889, Congress by law extended the prohibition against the killing of seals "to all the dominions of the United States in the waters of Bering Sea."

The fur-seal controversy, therefore, by the time it reached Blaine was an old story. The new Secretary in a series of dispatches to Lord Salisbury, the British Foreign Minister, upheld with more bril- *The fur-seal* liance than logic the American contention, and in asserting *controversy* that the seals as American property were entitled to American protection wherever they went he came dangerously near conferring upon *ferae naturae* the rights of American citizens. When finally a complete impasse had been reached, both parties agreed to submit the dispute to the arbitration of a commission of seven members, two to be chosen by each side, and three others. The verdict that the commission rendered in 1893 found in favor of the British so far as the question of international rights was concerned, and ordered the United States to pay damages for the ships it had captured and condemned. Restrictive regulations were adopted, however, which forbade pelagic sealing within a zone of sixty miles surrounding the Pribilof Islands, and proclaimed a closed season on sealing from May 1 to July 31 of each year. These measures were difficult of enforcement, and it was not until 1911, when Great Britain, Russia, the United States, and Japan entered into a mutually binding pact on the subject that the danger of extinction of the seal-herds disappeared.[1]

It is possible to discern in Blaine's foreign policy an effort to reserve the Pacific as a region for future American exploitation. Blaine cultivated good relations with Japan, and at the same time *Hawaii* managed to keep friendly with China in spite of the deepening antagonism between the two great Oriental nations. Nor was Blaine displeased at the prospect of the speedy annexation to the United States of Hawaii, for generations the chief stopping-place in the mid-Pacific for vessels bound to Asia. Hawaii, in addition to its advantageous location, was also well adapted to the production of sugar, a fact which had induced Americans to invest millions of dollars in Hawaiian plantations, and had led the American government, as early as 1876, to permit the importation into the United States of Hawaiian sugar, duty free. Japanese subjects had also flocked to Hawaii, and the American planters, spurred on in part by the danger of Japanese aggression and in part by the notorious inefficiency of the Hawaiian government, staged a revolu-

[1] S. B. Stanton, *The Behring Sea Controversy* (1892).

tion in 1893 that forced Queen Liliuokalani, the reigning monarch, off th
throne. All this was done with the knowledge, and perhaps the conni
vance, of the American Minister, John L. Stevens, of Augusta, Maine
a close personal and political friend of James G. Blaine. Indeed, a
a convenient time while the revolution was in progress Stevens summonec
marines from an American warship, ostensibly to protect American live
and property; actually, to insure the success of the revolt. Neither h
nor his superior in Washington ever doubted that Hawaii must becom
a part of the United States. "The Hawaiian pear is now fully ripe,"
Stevens wrote as the revolution triumphed, "and now is the golden hou
for the United States to pluck it." Following this dispatch the Americar
government made all convenient haste to negotiate a treaty of annexa
tion, but when Harrison left office its ratification was still pending in th
United States Senate. President Cleveland, shocked at the part th
American Minister had played in the proceedings, promptly withdrev
the treaty, and so for the next few years the Hawaiian Republic had n
choice but to maintain its separate existence. In 1898, after the retur
of the Republicans to power, the islands were annexed to the Unitec
States by joint resolution of both houses of Congress.[1]

About three thousand miles to the southwest of the Hawaiian Island
lay another archipelago, the Samoan Islands. In 1872 an American se

Samoa captain, noting the convenience of a stopping-place in th
South Seas on the way to New Zealand and Australia, ob
tained from a native chief the right for the United States to establisl
a coaling-station at the fine harbor of Pago Pago on the island of Tutuila
German interests, already active in exploiting the rich copra business o
the islands, from the first resented the activities of the Americans
Nevertheless, the American government in 1878 embodied in a treaty th
sea captain's agreement, and promised the Samoan "king" its goo
offices for the purpose of adjusting satisfactorily his relations with othe
governments. The following year Germany and Great Britain eacl
secured a harbor and commercial privileges in the islands, and thereafte
differences between the numerous overlords of the Samoans grew in
creasingly acute. By 1889, with thirteen ships representing the con
tending powers concentrated in the Samoan harbor of Apia, hostilitie
seemed imminent, but a timely tropical hurricane sank all the ships bu
one, after which Bismarck called a conference in Berlin to settle th
Samoan problem. The Berlin conference unwisely decided upon

---

[1] An excellent study of the movement that led to the annexation of Hawaii is containe
in J. W. Pratt, *Expansionists of 1898* (1936), which is extremely useful for this whole perio
of American history. See also E. J. Carpenter, *America in Hawaii* (1899).

tripartite protectorate for the islands, an agreement more notable for the fact that the United States for once had gone back on its historic policy of no entangling alliances than for any good it did the Samoan Islanders.[1]

Time proved the impossibility of maintaining the Berlin agreement, and in 1899 the three nations agreed to a division of the islands between the United States and Germany. Great Britain was indemnified for her withdrawal by obtaining title to the Gilbert and Solomon Islands which had formerly belonged to Germany — the "Gilbert and Sullivan Islands," as American State Department officials, never very seriously concerned about the whole affair, insisted on calling them. Ultimately the United States saw point to asserting its jurisdiction over dozens of little Pacific islands, some of which were uninhabited and almost totally devoid of vegetation, but which might become useful nonetheless as radio and airplane stations. After the World War the German portion of the Samoan Islands became a mandate of New Zealand.

While Blaine seemed to see in the Pacific an American sphere of influence that must be protected, he was far more interested in his policy of Pan-Americanism than in any other phase of diplomacy. *Pan-Americanism* His dream, borrowed no doubt from Henry Clay whom he admired and imitated, was to induce the Latin-American states of North and South America to enter a kind of informal federation, with the United States, as an interested and friendly "elder sister," at its head. Through such a union Blaine hoped to eliminate wars between the lesser American nations and to promote better commercial relationships between them and the United States. During his first term of office he urged with some success that warring American nations should submit their disputes to the United States for arbitration, and in the fall of 1881, he invited all the independent American nations to attend a conference on arbitration to meet a year later in Washington. But Blaine was soon out of office and his successor, Frederick T. Frelinghuysen, withdrew the invitation on the ground that such a conference might "create jealousy and ill-will" on the part of uninvited, non-American nations.

The idea of a Pan-American conference lived on, in spite of Frelinghuysen's action. When Blaine returned to the State Department in 1889, Congress had authorized just such a conference as he had wished and the invitations had already been extended. It thus fell to Blaine's lot to receive in Washington on October 2, 1889, the representatives of nineteen independent American republics. Nothing could be accom-

---

[1] G. H. Ryden, *The Foreign Policy of the United States in Relation to Samoa* (1933), thoroughly exhausts the subject. F. R. Dulles, *America in the Pacific* (1932), treats both Hawaii and Samoa.

plished on the important subject of arbitration, but the First Pan-American Congress, as this meeting came to be called, made considerable progress in the discussion of such important problems as the standardization of sanitary regulations, the building of an intercontinental railroad, and the adoption of uniform weights and measures, including a common silver coin. One permanent result of the congress was the establishment of an International Bureau of American Republics, with headquarters in Washington. This bureau, supported by the joint contributions of all its members, became a valuable clearing-house for all inter-American information. Later its name was changed to the Pan-American Union, and by the generosity of Andrew Carnegie it was provided with a handsome marble palace in which to carry on its work. The First Pan-American Congress was not meant to be the last, nor was it. A total of four such congresses were held before the World War, and five more have been held since its close, each at a different national capital. Through this agency much has been done to accomplish the ends that Blaine had in mind.

Blaine's efforts to make tariff reciprocity an agency of Pan-Americanism have been noted in another connection.[1] The action that he obtained from Congress in the McKinley Act he deemed wholly unsatisfactory, but under the authority of that measure he and his successor negotiated a number of treaties and won some concessions to American trade. Blaine was almost the first American diplomat to recognize the full importance of selling American manufactured products abroad.

A civil war in Chile temporarily undid most of Blaine's work on behalf of Pan-Americanism. There a struggle broke out between the President, who wished to be a dictator, and the Congressional Party, *Relations with Chile* which sought to uphold the Constitution. The President had the army on his side, and at first it seemed he would win. Then he began to lose. Unfortunately the American Minister to Chile, Patrick Egan, an appointee of Blaine's choosing and a spoilsman, was utterly unfitted for the post he held. Instead of maintaining a strict neutrality, he sided openly with the President and made himself extremely unpopular with the presently victorious Congressional Party. Indeed, Egan, who was certainly no turncoat, did not hesitate to give asylum to the chief officers of the presidential party when their opponents had won. That the attitude of the American government was identical with that of its Minister was inferred by the Chilean revolutionists when the *Itata*, a ship carrying arms to them from a port of the United States, was detained and ultimately seized by an American warship, the *Charleston*.

[1] See *ante*, p. 218.

Later an American court held that the *Itata* had a perfect right to sail and ought not to have been detained. Another incident that put the United States in a bad light was the indiscreet, although unintentional, revelation by an American naval officer of an attempt on the part of the revolutionary forces to make a surprise attack on Santiago.[1]

The supreme catastrophe in Chilean-American relations came when Captain Winfield Scott Schley of the U.S.S. *Baltimore* permitted more than a hundred of his sailors to go ashore at Valparaiso while feeling against the Americans was at its height. As Schley might well have foreseen, the sailors got into trouble and a street battle followed in which two, of them were killed and nineteen wounded. The Chilean government, now in the hands of the former revolutionists, blamed the American sailors for what had happened and, instead of expressing regret for the incident, demanded the recall of Egan as *persona non grata*. Thereupon Blaine, with singular disregard for his policy of Pan-Americanism, supported Harrison in making peremptory demands upon the Chilean government under threat of military measures. Considering the relative strength of the two countries, there was nothing for the Chilean government to do but to back down, and to pay over the $75,000 indemnity that the United States insisted upon. This result was viewed in the United States as a gratifying diplomatic victory, but it was dearly bought. Not Chile alone, but Latin-American nations generally, tended to regard the United States as a bully to be feared rather than a friend to be trusted.

That the aggressive nature of American diplomacy was neither a personal policy of Blaine's nor a party policy of the Republicans was made evident shortly after Harrison left office by Cleveland's handling of the Venezuelan boundary dispute. The boundary line between Venezuela and British Guiana lay in a tropical wilderness and had never been properly delimited. Long a subject of desultory controversy, the subject became really interesting when the news came out that gold had been discovered in the disputed territory. To Cleveland the prospect of the British government enforcing its will upon Venezuela, as the American government had recently enforced its will upon Chile, was extremely disquieting, for he had made up his mind that in case such action resulted in the taking of territory that properly belonged to an American nation the Monroe Doctrine would clearly have been violated. In his message to Congress of 1894, he therefore expressed

The Venezuelan controversy

---

[1] Satisfactory accounts of the difficulties with Chile are contained in H. C. Evans, Jr., *Chile and Its Relations with the United States* (1927), and W. R. Sherman, *The Diplomatic and Commercial Relations of the United States and Chile. 1820–1914* (1926).

his hope that the matter would be arbitrated, and Congress by resolution promptly echoed his sentiments. The English government, however, refused to submit the whole question to arbitration, although pointing out that it had long been willing to arbitrate within certain specified limits. This attitude satisfied neither Cleveland nor his aggressive Secretary of State, Richard Olney, who took the matter up with Lord Salisbury, the British Foreign Minister, in a dispatch of July 20, 1895. "Today," said Olney, "the United States is practically sovereign on this continent, and its fiat is law upon the subjects to which it confines its interposition." Any advance of the British boundary at the expense of Venezuela, Olney claimed, would "greatly embarrass the future relations between this country and Great Britain." [1]

The British answer to this somewhat bombastic pronouncement was withheld until late in November, and from the American point of view was wholly unsatisfactory. To Salisbury the Monroe Doctrine was a mere matter of history which bound no one. There was nothing that the United States could do in Latin America, he insisted, that Great Britain could not do if she wished. Thoroughly angered by the British reply, Cleveland brought the issue to a head in a special message to Congress of December 17, 1895. After restating fully the American case, he asked for an appropriation to pay the expenses of a boundary commission to be appointed by himself, with full authority to determine where the correct boundary lay. "In making these recommendations," he said, "I am fully alive to the responsibility incurred and keenly realize all the consequences that may follow"; in other words, if the British government would not back down, the United States would fight. Cleveland's motives in taking such an uncompromising stand have been the object of much speculation. Some think that he might have wished to take public attention from the troublesome issue of free silver, and perhaps also to rehabilitate with the American public his rapidly failing reputation. He well knew that a long-established tradition, based in considerable part upon American ignorance of foreign affairs, required the American public to "stand by the President" in any dispute with a foreign power. Another, and better justified, view of the situation is that Cleveland, with his typical stubbornness, was merely determined to uphold the Monroe Doctrine, come what might.

Certainly American public opinion "stood by the President," and for a time war seemed imminent. Cleveland obtained the appropriation he

[1] Henry James, *Richard Olney and His Public Service* (1923), is a good biography. On the Venezuelan affair see also A. L. P. Dennis, *Adventures in American Diplomacy, 1896–1906* (1928), and Dexter Perkins, *The Monroe Doctrine, 1867–1907* (1937).

had asked of Congress, and appointed his boundary commission. That war did not come was no fault of the American government or people. More or less to the surprise of all concerned, Lord Salisbury abandoned his truculent attitude and agreed to a treaty of arbitration with Venezuela that satisfied the United States. This treaty, by stipulating that possession for fifty years should give clear title, insured that the British would obtain the greater part of the disputed territory, but the British acceptance of the American demands amounted nonetheless to a virtual acceptance of the American contentions. Indubitably the success of Cleveland's diplomacy added new meaning to the Monroe Doctrine. From this time forward Latin-American nations could count confidently on aid from the United States in their disputes with European nations. While by no means unwilling to accept such aid, they continued nevertheless to mistrust the motives of the "Colossus of the North."

Probably the British government, in giving in to the United States, was not actuated wholly by a desire to keep the peace between the two great English-speaking peoples.[1] It could hardly have overlooked the importance in this connection of events that were transpiring in South Africa. When, in December, 1895, President Paul Kruger of the Transvaal Republic successfully repulsed Doctor Jameson's raid of "outlanders" into Boer territory, the event was followed by a birthday cablegram of congratulations from Wilhelm II of Germany to the Boer leader. Both Boers and British took the Kaiser's message to mean that German assistance for the South African Republics might be forthcoming, and the British government made haste to re-form its diplomatic lines in such a way as to face the new threat. Indeed, from this time forward, with the menace of German imperialism increasingly clear, friendship with the United States became a cardinal policy of British statesmanship. The Monroe Doctrine was strikingly vindicated, but the German Kaiser had played quite as important a part in the proceedings as the American President.

England was not the only European power, however, whose concern with American affairs led to diplomatic difficulties with the United States. Spain still held a remnant of her once great American empire, notably the two islands of Cuba and Puerto Rico just south *Cuba* of the Atlantic seaboard of the United States. Cuba had long been a storm-center in Spanish-American relations. Before the Civil War southern expansionists had coveted the island; after the war Cuban insurrectionists had repeatedly sought to involve the United States in their struggles. For ten years, from 1868 to 1878, the island was in con-

[1] L. M. Gelber, *The Rise of Anglo-American Friendship* (1938).

stant turmoil, and in 1895 another revolt broke out. During the first Cuban insurrection the United States maintained with some difficulty an attitude of neutrality. Since American public opinion, always easily inflamed against the Spanish, had to be placated, the American State Department induced the Spanish government to provide for the gradual emancipation of the Cuban slaves, and to make generous promises with respect to its conduct of Cuban affairs. Danger of intervention was greatest when in 1873 the Spanish seized an American ship, the *Virginius*, which was bringing military aid to the insurgents, or "filibustering," and condemned its crew to death. Although the United States had forbidden all such expeditions by law, the American government held that the Spanish had no right to seize the ship on the high seas, and demanded the return of the ship, a money indemnity, and other reparations. On these points the Spanish gave in, but with obvious reluctance, and not without some evidence of foul play. The *Virginius*, for example, had no sooner been restored to its owners than it sank. Hardest for Americans to forgive was the fact that some members of the *Virginius's* crew were executed before the Spanish order granting a reprieve could reach Cuba.

The Cuban insurrection that began in 1895 came about in no small part as a result of American tariff legislation. The McKinley Act of 1890, which admitted raw sugar free of duty and compensated American growers by a bounty, had enormously stimulated the Cuban sugar industry. Much new foreign capital was poured into Cuban plantations, and for a brief period the island enjoyed unusual prosperity. When, in 1894, the Wilson-Gorman Act again made raw sugar dutiable, Cuban sugar prices declined precipitately, and the era of prosperity vanished as rapidly as it had come. With the American market for other Cuban commodities, notably tobacco, also weakened by the depression, hard times and unemployment provided a convenient setting for insurrection. Even in prosperous times the ordinary Cuban, whose lot as a peon was only a little better than that of a serf, had abundant reason for discontent. Spanish policy discriminated not only in favor of the mother country, but also in favor of the small ruling caste of pure-blood Spaniards in Cuba. The Cuban "native," colored by a strong infusion of Negro blood, did most of the work, while the upper-class whites took most of the profits. Furthermore, the Spanish officials in Cuba were notably inefficient and corrupt.

It is an exaggeration to speak of the disorder in Cuba that broke out in 1895 as a revolution, although citizens of the United States tended to view it in that light. Maximo Gomez, the Cuban leader, was utterly unable to maintain a government, or even to keep an army in the field.

What he promoted was insurrection rather than revolution, and his chief weapon was devastation. Small guerrilla bands, *Nature of* often operating by night rather than by day, destroyed *the Cuban* sugar-mills and laid waste plantations belonging to Spanish *revolt* loyalists. Carrying on at first almost without military equipment, the Cuban *insurrectos* were soon receiving aid from other Cubans who resided in the United States, and from American sympathizers, most of whom thought of Gomez and his guerrillas in terms that might better have been applied to George Washington and the patriot army of 1776. In New York a Cuban junta, which called itself the Cuban government, sold bonds, and with the proceeds bought and shipped arms to the insurrectionary forces.

When ordinary methods of dealing with the insurrection failed, the Spanish government sent General Valeriano Weyler to Cuba with the necessary troops and authority to get results. Soon discovering that the droning peon by day could become the liveliest of bandits by night, Weyler ordered all the people living in troublesome areas to concentrate in certain specified cities where their behavior could be watched. He also constructed a system of wire-entanglements and blockhouses — a "corral" — across the island to separate the western more peaceful end from the mountainous east where the guerrilla bands took refuge. Weyler's policy, pursued so ruthlessly as to win him the sobriquet "Butcher" Weyler, was in a fair way to succeed, but it entailed endless suffering, particularly in the *reconcentrado* camps, where tropical diseases caused thousands of deaths, and starvation was by no means unknown.

Meantime American newspaper correspondents, somewhat put to it for news as lurid as the exciting labor disputes of the depression and the political antics of the Populists, had flocked to Cuba to report the progress of the war. In the results of Weyler's policies they found an abundance of thrilling stories, none of which lost much in the telling. The Hearst newspapers were particularly effective in spreading tales of Spanish atrocities, and William Randolph Hearst later claimed that it cost him three million dollars to bring about American intervention in Cuba.[1] Quite as effective with the public as the privately gathered war news were the reports of Fitzhugh Lee, American consul-general at Havana, and of Senator Redfield Proctor, who made a personal investigation. The situation in Cuba was indubitably bad, and the American public, unaccustomed to the horrors of war, began to feel that the gov-

---

[1] The rôle of the American newspapers in promoting the war with Spain is well set forth in J. E. Wisan, *The Cuban Crisis as Reflected in the New York Press, 1895–1898* (1934). and M. M. Wilkerson, *Public Opinion and the Spanish-American War* (1932).

ernment of the United States should do something about it. Cleveland, however, was determined to keep the peace. He refused to recognize the Cuban insurgents as belligerents, made every effort to prevent filibustering expeditions from leaving the United States, and urged upon the Spanish government the necessity of granting autonomy to Cuba as a means of ending the war.

When McKinley took office he, too, saw the wisdom of settling the Cuban controversy without resort to war. He was fully aware, however, *American* of the inflamed state of American public opinion, and was *opinion on* eager to obtain assurances from the Spanish government *Cuba* that the war in Cuba would speedily be reformed. He therefore lodged a strong protest in Madrid "against the uncivilized and inhuman conduct" of the campaign in Cuba, and maintained vigorously the right of the United States to demand "that a war, conducted almost within sight of our shores and grievously affecting American citizens and their interests throughout the length and breadth of the land, shall at least be conducted according to the military codes of civilization." The Spanish government, while deeply resentful of the American attitude, was genuinely interested in averting war with the United States. Somewhat tardily, because of a change of ministry and the necessity of saving face with the Spanish people, it ordered the abandonment of the *reconcentrado* policy, the recall of Weyler, and the establishment for Cuba of legislative autonomy. By this time, however, autonomy had no charm for the Cuban insurrectionists whose goal was independence, and it thoroughly frightened the Cuban loyalists, who feared for the worst if ever their opponents should be entrusted with power. General Stewart L. Woodford, the American Minister to Spain, thought that Spaniards had no idea of what was meant by autonomy, but he was fully convinced that the Spanish government, if given time, would agree to whatever demands the United States cared to make.

The chance of a peaceful settlement was greatly lessened by the publication on February 9, 1898, of the famous "de Lôme letter." This was *The de* not a state document, as most Americans assumed, but a *Lôme letter* private letter written by Enrique Dupuy de Lôme, the Spanish Minister to the United States, to a personal friend in Cuba. It was stolen from the Havana post-office by an insurgent spy, and was given to the press for the effect it would have on American public opinion. Unfortunately the Spanish Minister had described McKinley as a spineless politician whose efforts to maintain peace were hampered by his eagerness to please the multitude and to keep on good terms with the jingoes in his party. McKinley, deeply offended, immediately instructed

Woodford to ask the Spanish government to recall de Lôme, but the offending minister, a man of really high principles, avoided further humiliation by resigning.[1]

The effect of the incident was all that its perpetrators could have asked. Sentiment in favor of intervention grew by leaps and bounds. Soon McKinley, because he followed only reluctantly along the road to war, was being described by Theodore Roosevelt — usually an accurate barometer of public opinion — as having "no more backbone than a chocolate éclair." On occasion Roosevelt went even further and called the President a "white-livered cur," but, in the eyes of the public, Roosevelt, as well as every other American citizen, was entitled to criticize the President, whereas the Spanish Minister certainly was not.

Meanwhile the American consul-general at Havana, Fitzhugh Lee, had reported with much exaggeration an outbreak of rioting by Spanish loyalists who were outraged at the prospect of autonomy. *The Maine* With this as a pretext the U.S.S. *Maine*, which had already been detached from the Atlantic squadron and stationed at Key West, was ordered to Havana Harbor on a friendly visit. This precautionary measure, designed to insure the protection of American interests in case the trouble should prove serious, was not unusual in such circumstances, and should have excited no opposition, although the *Maine* was a more powerful vessel than the exigencies of the situation required. On February 15, 1898, the *Maine* was destroyed by an explosion that killed two hundred and sixty-six members of the crew and wounded sixty others. Many Americans immediately jumped to the conclusion that the Spanish government was responsible for the act, and throughout the United States the battle-cry, "Remember the *Maine*," began to be heard. Investigations conducted by the American divers within the hull of the sunken ship seemed to confirm the American opinion that the explosion came from the outside, while Spanish divers outside the hull reported the exact reverse. Responsibility for the sinking has never been fixed. That the Spanish government could have promoted such a catastrophe at a time when its officials were making every effort to keep on good terms with the United States seems incredible. Speaker Thomas B. Reed, an opponent of intervention, expressed the opinion that the Cuban rebels had blown up the *Maine* to insure American intervention.

With public excitement in the United States at white heat over the

[1] Events leading up to the Spanish-American War are well chronicled in F. E. Chadwick, *The Relations of the United States and Spain: Diplomacy* (1909), but some new material is presented in Orestes Ferrara, *The Last Spanish War* (1937). See also Bemis, *American Secretaries of State*, IX.

de Lôme incident and the destruction of the *Maine*, only a strong President could have prevented war, and unfortunately de Lôme's description of McKinley was all too accurate. In Spain, too, where American criticisms of Spanish colonial policy and American threats of intervention were alike resented, feeling was quite as tense as in the United States. Both the American and the Spanish governments desired to avert war, but neither felt strong enough to stand out vigorously against public opinion. Probably a referendum on the desirability of war would have carried overwhelmingly in both countries. In each case it was the government that held back and the popular majority that demanded action.

In the United States the Spanish negotiations had long since been taken out of the hands of the aged and infirm Sherman, and lodged with *American* his able assistant, William R. Day, who on April 26, 1898, *negotiations* became Secretary of State. Day's notes, following the *with Spain* sinking of the *Maine*, became increasingly peremptory. On March 27 the United States demanded an immediate armistice, with amnesty to the insurrectionists, the final abolition of the *reconcentrado* policy, the admission of relief from the United States for suffering Cubans as well as Americans (relief for the latter had already been admitted), and negotiations for peace through the President of the United States, who, if the negotiations failed, was to act as arbiter. To have yielded on all these terms without some show of resistance would have caused the overturn of the Spanish government, and might even have endangered the monarchy, so an attempt was made to induce the United States to accept the Pope as a mediator. Woodford cabled frantically that he could "get the peace that you have worked so hard for" if only given time, and McKinley admitted a year later that "if he had been left alone, he could have concluded an arrangement with the Spanish government under which the Spanish troops would have withdrawn from Cuba without a war." Had the President decided to make a firm stand for peace he would have received the cordial support of Marcus A. Hanna and many another leading capitalist who feared the economic unsettlement that war might bring. But McKinley knew that opposition to following the lead of the plutocrats on this, or any other matter, was already rife among the young Republicans, and he believed that only by yielding to the popular clamor for war could he be certain of holding his party together. Finally, on April 9, the Spanish government, in response to a joint peace plea, delivered by the great powers of Europe to both Spain and the United States, ordered the cessation of hostilities in Cuba and gave in to the American contentions on every essential point. To the despair of Woodford, who cabled that he could get whatever Cuban settlement McKinley wanted — autonomy, independence, or cession of the island to the United States — the President on April 11 sent a war message to Congress. Six days later Congress by joint resolution demanded that Spain withdraw from Cuba, and authorized the President to use the military and naval forces of the United States to effect that end. Expressly disclaiming any intent to add Cuba to the United States, the resolution went on to claim that the people of the island were "and of right ought to be free and independent."

The outbreak of hostilities in this "needless war," as James Ford Rhodes, the historian, later described it, did not take place because of the failure of American diplomacy. War came in spite of *A needless* the complete success of American diplomacy, and primarily *war* because the American people wanted to have a war. This unnatural craving was in part a legacy of the Civil War, a struggle which for more than thirty years had colored almost every aspect of American thought and action. Veterans of the Civil War were held in honor because of their war record, and particularly in politics they tended to fare better than the men who had stayed at home. As the old soldiers grew older, they forgot the seamy side of war, and told tall tales of heroics and adventure. Young America, typified by Theodore Roosevelt, had grown to manhood on a steady diet of Civil War glorification. It envied the boys in blue or gray, and felt cheated that it had had no chance to win distinction for itself in war. Older America was likewise out to get its thrill — a vicarious and reassuring thrill. It took pride in the great new nation that it had seen emerge, but its faith was somehow tinctured with doubt. Had the United States really arrived as a nation, or was it only on its way? Perhaps by a baptism of blood the country could prove to itself and to the rest of the world that it was really great. If the United States could win a war, who could deny it the high station among the nations of the world to which it aspired? Years later, Theodore Roosevelt recaptured the atmosphere of 1898 when he mourned apologetically, "It wasn't much of a war, but it was the best war we had." America in the spring of 1898 was ripe for any war, and the country's mood was not to be denied.

CHAPTER XV

THE SPANISH-AMERICAN WAR

BY THE time it was needed for war duty the new steel navy, begun in the early eighties, ranked fifth among the navies of the world, and was re-
Admiral garded with much pride by the American people. More-
Mahan over, its *raison d'être*, not very clear when the first keels were laid, had been made plain by an American naval officer, Captain Alfred Thayer Mahan, whose book, *The Influence of Sea-Power on History, 1660–1783*, published in 1890, had won international acclaim. Mahan argued persuasively that victory for a nation at war ordinarily depended upon its control of the seas. This was especially true in the case of imperialistic powers, with distant colonies and overseas commerce to protect; but it was also true of a nation such as the United States, which had neither a colonial empire nor a large merchant marine. The United States, Mahan maintained, must be prepared in time of war to keep the sea-lanes open for foreign neutral shipping bound to and from American ports. This it could do only if it had strength enough to drive enemy blockaders away from its shores. For such a purpose "capital ships," that is, battleships, were needed, since the lighter vessels, of which before 1890 our navy mainly consisted, would be no match for the capital ships of foreign nations. The United States, to feel perfectly safe, must have a fleet of battleships large enough to deal successfully with any enemy force that any enemy nation might be able to send against it. This did not mean that the United States Navy should be as large or larger than any other navy; it need only be large enough to command the seas adjacent to the American coast.[1]

Influenced undoubtedly by Mahan's ideas, some of which had gained currency even before his book was published, the building of capital ships
The new proceeded rapidly during the early nineties. American
navy heavy industries were increasingly capable of supplying the necessary machinery, ordnance, and armor plate. The trend of Ameri-

---

[1] Harold and Margaret Sprout, *The Rise of American Naval Power, 1776–1918* (1939). Admiral Mahan tells his own story in *From Sail to Steam; Recollections of Naval Life* (1907).

can diplomacy seemed to indicate that the duties of the new navy would not long be confined to strictly national defense; there would be colonies also to consider. The national ego, moreover, demanded for the United States whatever trappings of greatness other nations possessed. If other nations, particularly Great Britain, the likeliest enemy, had battleships, why should the United States lack them? In 1890 Congress authorized the construction of "three seagoing, coast-line battleships designed to carry the heaviest armor and most powerful ordnance," and before war broke out in 1898 the *Indiana*, *Massachusetts*, and *Oregon* had been built to these specifications. In 1892 Mahan published another book, *The Influence of Sea-Power upon the French Revolution and Empire, 1793–1812*, which provided further ammunition for the use of the strongnavy advocates, and in spite of the depression five more battleships were authorized before Cleveland left office. It seemed reasonably certain that their completion, together with the addition of numerous minor and auxiliary craft also authorized, would give to the United States Navy that supremacy in American waters that Mahan's theories demanded.

When President McKinley took office he appointed as Secretary of the Navy John D. Long, a prominent politician from Massachusetts of no known sympathy with the existing strong-navy policy.[1]   *Theodore* McKinley himself seems to have been both uninterested   *Roosevelt* and uninformed on naval matters, but the deficiencies of the President and his naval chief were more than offset by the selection of Theodore Roosevelt to be Assistant Secretary of the Navy. Roosevelt had written a book on sea-power, *The Naval War of 1812* (1882), he was notorious for the lengths to which he carried his strong-navy views, and he was eager for the United States to embark upon a policy of extensive overseas expansion. In office he counteracted by every means in his power the lethargy of his superiors, and tried to make the nation ready for the war he was sure would come. He knew and liked the navy men, and with them, he later recounted,

> I used to hold long consultations, during which we went over and over... everything necessary to do in order to put the navy in trim to strike quick and hard.... Sending an ample quantity of ammunition to the Asiatic squadron and providing it with coal; getting the battleships and the armored cruisers on the Atlantic into one squadron, both to train them in manoeuvering together, and to have them ready to sail against either the Cuban or the Spanish coasts; gathering the torpedo boats into a flotilla for practice; securing ample target exercise, so conducted as to raise the standards of our marksmanship; gathering in the small ships from European and South

[1] John D. Long, *The New American Navy* (2 vols., 1903), shows the evolution of the Secretary's interest in naval preparedness.

American waters; settling on the number and kind of craft needed as auxiliary cruisers — every one of these points was threshed over in conversations with officers who were present in Washington, or in correspondence with officers who, like Captain Mahan, were absent.[1]

When war broke out at last, Roosevelt and the navy men were ready. In the afternoon of February 25, ten days after the *Maine* went down, *Preparations* Roosevelt took advantage of Long's temporary absence from *for war* the Navy Office to put the entire navy on a war footing. The Assistant Secretary, so his superior complained, in one half-day's work had "come very near causing more of an explosion than happened to the *Maine*. . . . The very devil seemed to possess him." But Roosevelt was merely seeking to put the finishing touches on plans conceived long before and already in part carried out. As early as December, 1897, Commodore George Dewey, by Roosevelt's scheming, had been placed in command of the Asiatic Squadron and ordered to the Far East, there to make ready for a clash with the Spanish fleet in the Philippines the moment war should come. Early in 1898 the North Atlantic Squadron had been mobilized off Chesapeake Bay under the command of Captain (later Rear-Admiral) William T. Sampson, whose promotion over the heads of a long list of senior officers was as wholly merited as it was deeply resented. Later the bulk of Sampson's squadron was ordered to Key West, while the uneasy seaboard cities of the Atlantic, suffering from the illusion that a Spanish fleet was about to bombard them, were offered protection by a "North Patrol" under Commodore J. A. Howell off the coast of New England, and a "Flying Squadron" under Commodore W. S. Schley, stationed at Hampton Roads. The new battleship *Oregon*, uselessly located in the northern Pacific, was ordered to make ready at San Francisco for the long voyage around Cape Horn — a voyage that began on March 19 and for two months consumed the interest of the newspaper-reading public. The *Oregon*, after successfully steaming some fourteen thousand miles, finally joined Admiral Sampson's squadron, and participated in the Santiago campaign.

If the navy was well prepared for war, undoubtedly the army was not. The 2134 officers and 26,040 enlisted men of the regular army were distributed throughout the country at numerous army posts, *The Ameri-* tributed throughout the country at numerous army posts, *can army* the location of which bore no ascertainable relationship to the problem of mobilization. Some of these so-called "forts" had once been important when there was an Indian frontier; others had been selected mainly because powerful congressmen coveted the advantages of army building and trade for their constituents. There was no central

[1] Theodore Roosevelt, *The Rough Riders* (new edition, 1919), pp. 2–3.

army planning bureau such as the present general staff, and in the matter of promotions the rule of seniority was seldom broken. At the head of the army was its senior major-general, the sixty-year-old General Nelson A. Miles, whose experience in the Civil and Indian wars was of doubtful value in making ready for the war with Spain. Too many officers, with age rather than efficiency on their side, had grown accustomed to a life of easy routine, and while the soldiers were well-drilled and well-disciplined they were far better prepared for peace than for war. The Secretary of War, General Russell A. Alger, a match-manufacturer from Michigan with a dubious Civil War record, was no great help, and the politicians and bureaucrats who served under him were mostly handicaps. The second line of defense, the organized National Guard of the states, was of uncertain size and merit, but capable of great expansion in case of need. Everyone took it for granted, however, that if a really important war should develop, a volunteer army organized along the lines of the Union army in the Civil War would do the fighting. Unfortunately the army had had no such renaissance as had overtaken the navy during the eighties, nor had it had a Theodore Roosevelt.

Congress, for all its impatience to get on with the war, did little to make ready for the conflict before it came. On March 9, 1898, long after the strained relations between the United States and Spain *War* made war a strong probability, Congress passed a bill *legislation* appropriating fifty million dollars "for national defense and for each and every purpose connected therewith." But the President, to whom discretionary authority was given in the expenditure of this sum, spent it mainly on the navy and on coastal defense. When, later on, Alger's administration of the War Department was severely criticized, the Secretary complained that he had neither the funds nor the authority to prepare for war. Not until late in April, after the war resolutions had been passed, did Congress vote the increases in the army that the imminence of war would seem to have justified long before. It then authorized the increase of the regular army to 62,597 men, and the raising of a volunteer army of 125,000 men. As in the Civil War, each state was to be assigned its quota of troops, and the dual state and national character of the volunteer army was to be preserved.[1] A unique feature of the legislation, however, was the provision that the President might accept directly into the national service three regiments of volunteer cavalry. This provision was included primarily to enable Theodore Roosevelt, who now resigned as Assistant Secretary of the Navy, to lead a regiment into battle. With the help of Captain Leonard Wood, an officer in the

[1] Cf. J. D. Hicks, *The Federal Union* (1937), p. 630.

medical corps, Roosevelt brought together a motley array of ex-cowboys, college athletes, and adventurers to form the "First United States Volunteer Cavalry," or, as they were more generally called, the "Rough Riders." Since Roosevelt had had no military experience whatever, he modestly accepted only a lieutenant-colonelcy, while the command of the regiment went to Wood.

The first blow of the war was struck by Dewey at Manila Bay. A British proclamation of neutrality, issued April 24, made it necessary for
Dewey at Manila Dewey to leave Hongkong, where he had been outfitting his fleet preparatory to the anticipated attack on the Spanish. On the twenty-fifth he left Hongkong for the near-by Chinese port of Mirs Bay, where he would be under no compulsion to observe neutral regulations, and on the twenty-seventh he left Mirs Bay for the Philippines. His squadron consisted of the cruisers *Olympia, Baltimore, Raleigh,* and *Boston;* the gunboats *Concord* and *Petrel;* the revenue cutter *McCulloch;* and two colliers. Wisely disregarding mines that were possibly non-existent, and coast fortifications that were not available for use,[1] Dewey's fleet steamed through the wide entrance of Manila Bay before daybreak on the first of May. In leisurely fashion, with time out for breakfast, Dewey's ships proceeded methodically to the destruction of the Spanish ships, which their commander, Admiral Montojo, who knew full well what was in store for him, had thoughtfully stationed at some distance from the defenses of Manila so that the city might be spared the danger of shell-fire and in shallow water where as many as possible of his men might escape. The Spanish losses in this one-sided battle included three hundred and eighty-one killed, besides numerous wounded, while not an American was killed and only seven or eight were wounded.[2]

It is hard to see what useful purpose was served by the sinking of this decrepit and unseaworthy Spanish squadron. If the war was being fought strictly for the liberation of Cuba, as was claimed, the Spanish ships in the Philippines might well have been ignored, for they could never under any circumstances have reached the Pacific coast of the United States, much less the Atlantic. While Roosevelt and the others responsible for Dewey's presence in the Far East may not have realized

[1] Mark Sullivan, *Our Times,* I, *The Turn of the Century* (1926), p. 316.

[2] The most entertaining account of the war is Walter Millis, *The Martial Spirit* (1931). The book is undocumented, but in the main shows careful use of source material. F. E. Chadwick, *The Relations of the United States and Spain: the Spanish-American War* (1911), is dependable but dull. J. H. Latané, *America as a World Power, 1897–1907* (1907), is the volume covering the period for the *American Nation* series, and C. R. Fish, *The Path of Empire* (1919), for the *Chronicles of America.* On the battle of Manila Bay, see the *Autobiography of George Dewey* (1916).

fully the weakness of the Spanish fleet in the Philippines, it is only reasonable to suppose that they were as much interested in colonial expansion as in setting Cuba free. The American public, without seriously
considering the implications of Dewey's victory, rejoiced immoderately
that a victory had been won. Dewey's name was on everyone's lips —
at last the United States had a war hero. He was immediately raised to
the rank of acting Rear-Admiral, and as soon as Congress could pass the
necessary legislation was made Admiral, a rank held before him by only
two Americans, Farragut and Porter. His name and fame were even
celebrated in hand-hewn verse:

> Oh, dewy was the morning
> Upon the first of May,
> And Dewey was the Admiral,
> Down in Manila Bay,
> And dewy were the Regent's eyes [1]
> Them [sic] orbs of royal blue,
> And dew we feel discouraged?
> I dew not think we dew!

Conqueror that he was, Dewey's position in Manila Bay was by no
means comfortable. The Spanish government, deeply disturbed at what
had happened, prepared to send a superior fleet against him from Spain.
Spanish forces held the city of Manila and Dewey had no troops under
his command with which to dislodge them. Fortunately, or so Dewey
thought, an insurrection against Spanish rule was in progress in the
islands, and he attempted to co-operate with the insurrectionists, even
bringing back their exiled leader, Emilio Aguinaldo. Naturally he lost
no time in urging the American government to send an expeditionary
force to aid him in the capture of Manila, but weeks or even months,
must elapse before American soldiers could reach the Philippines. In
the meantime foreign warships began to drop anchor in Manila Bay,
among them a British squadron and a German squadron, either of which
could have disposed of Dewey's ships almost as easily as he had disposed
of the Spanish. Under the circumstances the American admiral can be
pardoned for the nervousness he exhibited, particularly toward the Germans, whom he and other Americans suspected of coveting the islands
for their country. Dewey considered himself in control of the Bay, and
some sharp exchanges occurred between him and Vice-Admiral Otto von
Diederichs, the German commander, who gave only hesitant obedience
to the American orders. The good offices of the British commander,

[1] Alfonso XIII, King of Spain, was at the time a minor, and the Queen Mother was
Regent.

MANILA BAY   SANTIAGO DE CUBA

Captain Edward Chichester, were sufficient to straighten out the difficulties, but both Dewey and the American public tended to exaggerate the friction and to hold more against the Germans than the facts warranted.[1]

Before the end of July, General Wesley Merritt had come to Dewey's rescue with a force of nearly eleven thousand men. By this time both the Spanish and the Americans were more afraid of the insurgents than they were of each other, and negotiations for the surrender of the city to the Americans, on condition that the insurgents should be kept out, were not difficult to arrange. On August 14, unmindful of the fact that the war had come to an end two days before, the Americans received the official capitulation of the city. Happily bloodshed had been kept at a minimum. American losses against the Spanish in the Philippines amounted altogether to eighteen killed and one hundred and nine wounded, and the Spanish casualty list was not much longer.

After the first stirring news of Dewey's victory at Manila Bay, American attention turned quickly toward the coming conflict between the *Admiral Cervera* Spanish and American fleets in the Atlantic. It was common knowledge that a Spanish squadron under the command of Admiral Pascual Cervera had been collected at the Cape Verde Islands, and that on April 29 it had set sail for the west. Cervera's fleet was notably weak, consisting of only four armored cruisers, which together could not throw as much metal as the American battleship *Oregon,* and six torpedo boat destroyers, only three of which were seaworthy. Its crews were inadequately trained, and it lacked both am-

[1] Jeannette Keim, *Forty Years of German-American Political Relations* (1919); C. E. Schieber, *The Transformation of American Sentiment Toward Germany, 1870–1914* (1923); Bertha A. Reuter, *Anglo-American Relations During the Spanish-American War* (1924).

munition and supplies. Conscious of the immense superiority of Sampson's squadron, Cervera was in despair when ordered to leave for the West Indies, and expressly refused to accept responsibility for what might result. Both he and the Spanish authorities knew full well that his ships were being ordered to their destruction, but the sacrifice was thought necessary as a sop to Spanish public opinion, which demanded that everything possible should be done to win the war.

The day before the battle of Manila Bay, American newspapers reported the sailing of Cervera's fleet. Presumably the voyage to America would occupy about two weeks. Admiral Sampson, under orders to intercept and destroy the enemy before he could take refuge in a Spanish colonial port, made preparations to guard the approaches to Cervera's four most probable destinations — Havana, Cienfuegos, and Santiago in Cuba, and San Juan, in Puerto Rico. Schley, in command of the Flying Squadron, was to patrol the southern coast of Cuba, while Sampson himself, with the rest of the fleet, was to remain north of the island with an eye out for Puerto Rico. The Atlantic seaboard cities, being thus abandoned, set up such loud cries of fright that the Navy Department, although it knew that an American harbor was the last place Cervera would wish to enter, felt obliged to detach some ships for coast-guard duty and to anchor a few obsolete gunboats in full sight of the excited populace.

Cervera proved himself an excellent seaman and succeeded in evading the blockaders. He appeared first on May 13, off the island of Martinique in the Lesser Antilles, and next day touched at the *The Spanish* Dutch island of Curaçao near the coast of Venezuela. All *fleet reaches* this was reported to the Navy Department, which relayed *America* the information at once to Sampson and Schley, but on May 19 the Spanish fleet slipped into the harbor of Santiago unobserved. Not until that same day did Schley leave Key West for his post to the south of Cuba, and Cervera had been at anchor a full week before the Flying Squadron reached the vicinity of Santiago. Even then Schley, although he had been apprised by Sampson of the probable location of the Spanish ships, was sure that they were somewhere else. "The air," he said, "was very clear, and the high mountains back of Santiago could be seen, but nothing else." Accordingly, the commodore decided to return to Key West for coal, and headed westward in spite of specific orders from the Navy Department to stand by at Santiago. His excuse for disobeying orders was that the heavy seas prevented him from taking on coal from the collier he had brought along. Finally better weather accomplished what his superiors had been unable to do, and, with his ships successfully recoaled at sea, he returned to Santiago. There on the morning of May 29 he beheld to his amazement the clear outlines of the *Cristobal Colón*, newest and best of Cervera's cruisers, anchored in full view from the mouth of the harbor. How his scouts could have failed to observe her three days before remains an unsolved mystery.

By the first of June, Admiral Sampson with the full Atlantic fleet, including the *Oregon*, reached Santiago and took command. Had the *Sampson's strategy* United States been willing to score a bloodless victory, Sampson need only have maintained his blockade of Cuba until the Spanish were ready to give up. Cervera was too wise and too humane to risk a battle if he could help it, and the Spanish forces in Cuba, cut off from supplies from the mother country, were helpless. Conscious of the fact that a fleet which could not leave its harbor was no better than a fleet sunk, and mildly concerned lest a tropical hurricane might disperse the American squadron, Sampson decided to block the narrow entrance of Santiago Harbor by sinking an old collier, the *Merrimac*, in the channel. This assignment fell to Lieutenant Richmond Pearson Hobson, who with seven men succeeded in sinking the ship, although not in the proper spot, and the harbor remained open. By a miracle Hobson and his crew escaped unhurt and were taken prisoners by the Spanish. Overnight the youthful officer, although his exploit failed completely to accomplish its purpose, became in the eyes of the American public a hero second only to Dewey himself.

Hobson's failure left the escape of the Spanish fleet a theoretical possibility, and called for some other solution of Sampson's problem. Many people, not knowing that Manila Bay was a sizable body of water with an entrance several miles in width, wondered why Sampson could not do what Dewey had done. As a matter of fact Sampson was under instructions from the Navy Department to take no such risks with his ships. The channel into Santiago Harbor, it was supposed, was defended by mines and by effective batteries; hence any effort to effect an entrance might easily end in disaster. But the Spanish ships showed no disposition to come out and fight, while the American public wanted to get on with the war. The best way through the dilemma seemed to be an expeditionary force that could operate in the rear of the Spanish fortifications, capture them, and thus either force the Spanish fleet to leave or enable the American fleet to enter. Sampson himself, confessing thereby that his squadron was unable to complete the task assigned it, asked for troops.

The War Department, meantime, had been struggling with the problem of how to prepare for war after the war had begun. Its first concern was to make ready the expedition to the Philippines under General Merritt. Troops for this purpose, both regulars and volunteers, *Army activities* were assembled from the western states at San Francisco, and before the end of June their transportation to the Philippines had begun. This venture alone was sufficient to tax the resources of the War Department to the limit, but in addition the possibility of an invasion of Cuba had to be faced. The Spanish garrisons in Cuba amounted, according to the newspapers, to no less than two hundred thousand men, and in actual fact to about eighty thousand men. If, therefore, the island should have to be conquered, foot by foot, a formidable army must be organized. After much preliminary indecision it was agreed that the bulk of the regular army should be concentrated at Tampa, Florida, while the volunteers, including such regiments of the National Guard as were accepted, were to encamp at the Chickamauga National Park, near Chattanooga, Tennessee. Roosevelt's Rough Riders assembled first at San Antonio, Texas, but at the insistence of their politically influential officers were soon transferred to Tampa.

The regular army, fully mobilized for the first time since the Civil War, found the experience mildy exhilarating, but the chaos that accompanied the encampment of the volunteers defied description. Army authorities had supposed that the military equipment previously issued to the National Guard would meet the most pressing needs of the civilian soldiers, but seemingly most of the equipment had evaporated. Whole regiments were turned over by the states to federal service, clad only in rags. Cooks went down in defeat before the rations and cooking equipment with which they were confronted, and occasionally unfortunate detachments had nothing to eat but hardtack. An ultra-democratic provision of the Enlistment Act made West Point graduates ineligible for appointment as officers in the volunteer army; hence, with a few exceptions, the officers were as unfamiliar with their duties as the privates with theirs. Out of the bedlam at Chickamauga an army might eventually emerge, but it would take a long time.

Meditating on this fact, and also on the report of his surgeon-general that from one third to one half of the American troops would surely die of yellow fever if landed on Cuban soil during the summer, *Confusion at Tampa* General Nelson A. Miles had decided upon a deliberate plan of campaign. He would first take Puerto Rico, which would be easy if not very significant, and would land a force of regulars at the eastern end of Cuba to organize the insurgents and assist them against the Spanish. Finally, when the American army was fully prepared, a frontal assault would be made on Havana. But Sampson's obvious need of army assistance led to an unexpected change of plans, and General William R. Shafter, in command at Tampa, was ordered to proceed instead, with the most effective force he could muster, to Santiago. This was far easier said than done, although General Miles rushed to Tampa in person to aid his unwieldy subordinate — General Shafter weighed three hundred pounds — in organizing the expedition. The selection of Tampa as a point of embarkation was absurd. Almost any Atlantic seaport would have been better. Tampa was not adequately served by railroads and lacked the docking facilities necessary to handle so great a rush of activity. "No word can paint the confusion," wrote Theodore Roosevelt, but the impatient politicians at Washington demanded immediate action.

On Tuesday, June 7, Shafter received word that "the President directs you to sail at once with what force you have ready." Powerless to effect an orderly embarkation, Shafter passed out the word that the expedition was to leave next day at daybreak, and that those who wanted to go would have to get aboard the best way they could. Thereupon individual initiative came to the rescue in a great variety of unorthodox ways, and next morning thousands of men, and some equipment, were aboard. Roosevelt's Rough Riders were naturally among the first to take possession of a transport, although, unfortunately, it had been decided that they must leave their horses behind. The ships could not sail on Wednesday, as Shafter had threatened, but by nightfall the semblance of order had been restored. The general believed that he would soon be ready to go.

Then came a telegram from Washington that the expedition was not to sail after all. Rumors were about that some of the Spanish ships were elsewhere than in Santiago Harbor. Only after one of Sampson's officers, Lieutenant Victor Blue, reported that he had counted the Spanish ships from the hills above the harbor, would the navy permit Shafter's expedition to sail. So for a week the men stayed aboard ship at Tampa Bay, broiling in the tropical sun, and cursing their luck. At last, on June 14, the thirty-two transports carrying nearly seventeen thousand men put out to sea, and six days later they appeared off Santiago.

Now a new dilemma faced the expedition. What plan of campaign was it to follow? Where was the landing to be effected, and once the *The expedi-* troops were ashore, what next were they to do? On this *tion to* matter Sampson and Shafter conferred, and, as perhaps *Santiago* both thought, reached an agreement. But, if so, neither had understood the other. Sampson's interpretation of the agreement was that the army should land several miles to the east of the harbor and then proceed westward to attack the lofty *morro* that guarded its entrance. Shafter, however, had no such notion. He would land to the eastward, to be sure, but thereafter he proposed to encircle and capture the city of Santiago which lay some four or five miles inland at the back of the bay. To this plan he steadfastly adhered, whatever Sampson chose to think. With the help of lighters furnished by the fleet, the landing was effected without opposition, although the Spanish, had they chosen to make the effort, could have inflicted severe punishment upon the Americans, and might even have driven them off. By the evening of June 22, some six thousand American troops, including Theodore Roosevelt and the Rough Riders, were safely ashore, but it took until the twenty-fifth to land the entire force.

Shafter's plan of campaign was inaugurated with much impromptu modification on the part of his subordinates. "Fighting Joe" Wheeler, whose service with the Confederate army in the Civil War *Shafter's* had won him a commission as major-general of volunteers, *campaign* was determined that his troops, among whom were the Rough Riders, should be the first to see action. By forced marches, entirely contrary to orders, he managed to engage the Spanish on June 24 at Las Guasimas, an outpost which the enemy had planned to abandon without a fight. Here the Rough Riders had their first baptism of battle, and Roosevelt reported proudly that his regiment had "furnished over half the men and over half the loss." Then followed a week of inaction, while Shafter, himself and many of his command already handicapped by illness, prepared for the final assault on Santiago.[1]

On the evening of June 30 the troops began to move again, and next morning a double attack opened, the lesser drive against a Spanish outpost at El Caney, well to the American right, and the major one against the Spanish entrenchments on San Juan Hill, as the series of high ridges before Santiago was called. It was supposed that the reduction of El Caney would occupy only a short time, and that the troops dispatched against it would be able also to participate in the action against Santiago. But the resistance at El Caney was more stubborn than had been anticipated, and the union of the two forces was delayed until the next day. Meantime the column intended for the assault on San Juan Hill moved forward slowly through a winding tropical road, its whereabouts carefully marked by an observation balloon which, until it was shot down, enabled the Spanish artillery to inflict heavy damage upon the invaders. The Americans, also, had a few batteries, but inasmuch as the American

---

[1] For those with an interest in military detail, the work of Colonel H. H. Sargent, *The Campaign of Santiago de Cuba* (3 vols., 1907), should prove satisfactory. Joseph Wheeler, *The Santiago Campaign* (1899), and John Bigelow, Jr., *Reminiscences of the Santiago Campaign* (1899), are interesting personal accounts.

guns were still dependent on the use of black powder, they, too, provided, whenever they were fired, excellent targets for the Spanish artillerymen. Nevertheless, the Americans, with the Rough Riders in the thick of the fray, reached the hills they meant to attack, charged the Spanish entrenchments, and took them. But it was still a long way to Santiago; there were other and stronger entrenchments to be taken, and the attackers had suffered heavy losses. Next day Shafter began to consider the advisability of withdrawing from the positions he had occupied. Even Roosevelt, now in command of the Rough Riders, was worried. "We are within measurable distance of a terrible military disaster," he wrote to Lodge. "We must have help — thousands of men, batteries, and *food* and ammunition." He might well have added ambulances (of which the whole expedition possessed only three) and medical supplies.

But as events proved the Spanish were even more thoroughly disheartened than the Americans. The army was short of ammunition and *Naval battle* the city was on the verge of famine. Nothing, it seemed, *of Santiago* could halt the American advance. Ultimate surrender was inevitable. Foreseeing this situation, the Spanish authorities in Madrid and Havana had ordered Cervera to take the first opportunity to escape with his squadron from the harbor. In vain the admiral protested that "the absolutely certain result will be the ruin of each and all of the ships and the death of the greater part of the crews." He was told to "avoid comments," and to leave in case the city was about to fall, regardless of consequences. On the evening of July 2, Cervera despairingly ordered his ships to get up steam, and on the morning of July 3 he headed for the open seas, his ships turning sharply to the west one by one and proceeding at full speed along the coast. The moment was opportunely chosen, for Sampson on his flagship the *New York* had moved several miles to the east for a conference with Shafter, while the *Brooklyn*, with Commodore Schley aboard, stood farther out to sea than usual. But the fate of the Spanish ships was sealed. The American ships, after some unfortunate maneuvering by the *Brooklyn*, which forced the *Texas* to reverse her engines in order to avoid being rammed, drew alongside the enemy and began a running fight that ended only when the last Spanish ship was beached or sunk. The American gunfire, despite Roosevelt's efforts as Assistant Secretary of the Navy, was not particularly accurate, for no serious hits were registered on the hulls of the Spanish cruisers. But the decks of these ships were of wood, and the first shells to explode upon them set them afire. One of the Spanish ships, the *Cristobal Colón*, by virtue of her superior speed, would have escaped but for the fact that her supply of good coal gave out, and the coal she then had to use was so poor that she was unable to keep up steam. The Spanish casualties from the fight were nearly four hundred killed and wounded; the American casualties, one killed and one wounded.

For months the battle was fought over again and again by the American public to determine whether the credit for the victory belonged to Sampson, whose flagship reached the scene of action only *Sampson or* as the last Spanish ship was beached, or Schley, who had *Schley?* been on hand all the while, but whose orders to the captains of the squadron had been mainly unnoticed or ignored. As a matter of fact, it was a captains' fight, but Sampson could claim that every captain had his orders from the admiral before the fight began. Ultimately a court of inquiry investigated Schley's conduct both before and during the battle, and came to conclusions somewhat damaging to Schley's reputation; but Dewey, chairman of the inquiry, held that Schley had been in command at Santiago when the Spanish fleet was destroyed.[1]

Sampson's (or was it Schley's?) Fourth-of-July present to the American public was nowhere more appreciated than in the American trenches before Santiago. Shafter, who before the naval victory had considered seriously the wisdom of withdrawing his troops, brightened up perceptibly. To be sure, early on the morning of the third he had dispatched a message to General Toral, the Spanish commander at Santiago, threatening bombardment of the city if it were not immediately surrendered. But Shafter knew full well that this message was only a bluff, and he feared that the Spanish knew it too. Not until Cervera's squadron had been destroyed did he think to inform his superiors in Washington of the demand he had made, and by this time the Spanish had turned it down. Shafter's next demand was on the navy. It was up to the navy, he told Sampson and the authorities back home, to effect an entrance into the harbor. If that were only done, the town would surrender, and further loss of life would be avoided. But Sampson had no notion of risking his precious ships against the Spanish mines and batteries (equipment later discovered to be all but harmless), and complained bitterly that the army was unwilling to "do the part which the proper conduct of war assigns to it." As a matter of fact, General Toral had every intention of surrendering, and merely wished to obtain the best possible terms by prolonging the negotiations. He finally struck a very good bargain, for Shafter agreed that the United States should provide free transportation back to Spain for all the troops under Toral's command. On July 16, the articles of capitulation were signed, and next day the American army took possession of the city. By an oversight not difficult to explain, the

[1] W. S. Schley, *Forty-Five Years Under the Flag* (1904).

naval authorities were ignored during these proceedings as completely as possible.

The Spanish surrender came none too soon, for the tropical climate had begun to tell heavily on the American army. The troops had reached *An army of* Cuba at the height of summer clad in woolen uniforms de-*convalescents* signed for winter wear on the Great Plains. Some of them had thrown away their blankets by day, to learn that they were desperately needed by night. Heavy tropical rains added to the discomfort and perplexity of the situation. Food supplies were uncertain, both as to quantity and quality; the expeditionary force got its first fresh meat on July 22, and the soldiers complained that the canned meat they were served — "embalmed beef," they called it — was an actual menace to health. Sanitary precautions were hopelessly inadequate, and dysentery, malaria, typhoid, and even the dreaded yellow fever began to strike. On July 27, the sick list totaled 4,122, three fourths of which were fever patients. The army, having won its war, now demanded the privilege of returning home, but the Washington authorities were hesitant about ordering such a move because of their belief that to do so would spread disease. Finally Roosevelt wrote a letter, and some of the general officers signed a "round robin," both designed to reveal the situation to the American public through the newspapers. According to the "round robin,"

> The army is disabled by malarial fever to such an extent that its efficiency is destroyed and it is in a condition to be practically entirely destroyed by the epidemic of yellow fever sure to come in the near future. . . . This army must be moved at once or it will perish. . . . Persons responsible for preventing such a move will be responsible for the unnecessary loss of many thousands of lives.

Roosevelt and his colleagues might well have saved themselves the pains, for orders to recall the expedition were issued a few hours before their protests appeared in print. On August 8 the withdrawal of the troops began, with the Rough Riders aboard the first transports to leave. Ultimately the entire force, which had been increased by the time of its departure to about twenty-five thousand men, was brought to Montauk Point, Long Island, and encamped. Four fifths of the returning soldiers were ill — "an army of convalescents." Five hundred and fourteen men had already died of disease — twice as many as were killed in battle — and two hundred and fifty-seven others died after reaching the United States. Roosevelt himself returned, feeling, as he admitted, "disgracefully well."

Meantime similar outbreaks of disease had almost demoralized the

army camps in the United States. At Chickamauga heavy rains flooded
the camp, and soon proved that its location, from the point *Disease in*
of view of sanitation, was all that it should not be. Condi- *the army*
tions were little better at Camp Alger, across the Potomac *camps*
from Washington, or in Florida. Everywhere the usual diseases of filth,
such as dysentery and typhoid, put in an early appearance; indeed, the
germs that laid low the expeditionary force in Cuba seem to have been
taken with the troops from the United States. Total deaths for the war
amounted to about five thousand, but only three hundred and seventy-
nine died in battle or of battle wounds — all the rest died from disease.
All this made lively reading in the newspapers and reflected seriously on
the efficiency of the War Department. Demands for the resignation of
Alger multiplied, and at the harassed Secretary's request a commission
was appointed to investigate the conduct of the department. The
report of the commission, long delayed, was inconclusive in its findings,
but Alger's political usefulness was at an end. Finally, a year after the
war was over, the President found a pretext unrelated to the war upon
which he could ask and obtain his unpopular Secretary's resignation.[1]
To succeed Alger, McKinley chose a man of really extraordinary ability, Elihu Root of New York.

In the final days of the war General Miles at last got off the expedition
to Puerto Rico with which he had planned to start hostilities. Much
had been learned from the mistakes of Shafter's expedition, and the
transportation of troops to Puerto Rico was marked by far fewer blunders. Haste was required, however, for on July 13, three days before the
Miles expedition sailed, the Spanish government had opened negotiations
for peace. But Miles managed to reach his objective before an armistice
could be signed, and thus, with somewhat better grace than if he had not
sailed, the United States could lay claim to the island. The one sharply
disappointing feature of the expedition was its almost total lack of opposition. Casualties of the entire operation amounted to three killed and
about forty wounded.

The Spanish negotiations were made through the French Ambassador
at Washington, Jules Cambon, who was told on July 30 that before the
United States would make peace, Spain must agree to with- *American*
draw from the western hemisphere. Spanish sovereignty *terms*
over Cuba must be relinquished, and all the rest of the Spanish West
Indies, including Puerto Rico, must be ceded to the United States. On
the other side of the world the American government demanded the cession of an island in the Ladrones (midway between Hawaii and the Phil-

[1] R. A. Alger, *The Spanish-American War* (1901), is an attempt at self-vindication.

ippines), and possession of the city, harbor, and bay of Manila, pending determination in the treaty of the "control, disposition, and government" of the Philippines. In view of these somewhat extraordinary territorial demands, the United States promised to waive for the time being "any demand for pecuniary indemnity." On these terms an armistice was signed on August 12, and the war was over. In Cuba, as the Spanish garrisons withdrew, they were replaced by regiments of "immunes" under General Leonard Wood. Many of Wood's soldiers, it developed, were by no means as immune as they should have been, but a bright chapter in the history of American sanitation had begun.

On October 1, 1898, commissioners from the United States and Spain met at Paris to work out the details of the treaty of peace. Probably the thought never occurred to William McKinley that he himself might have a place at the peace table. Indeed, it was a well-established tradition, one which so conventional a President could have had no desire to break, that the President of the United States must not set foot on foreign soil. To head the American delegation, McKinley chose his Secretary of State, William R. Day, but even Day was required to resign his post as Secretary before he left the country. Mindful of the fact that a treaty must be ratified by the United States Senate, McKinley sent along three prominent senators, two Republicans and a Democrat — Cushman K. Davis of Minnesota, chairman of the Senate Committee on Foreign Relations, William P. Frye of Maine, president *pro tempore* of the Senate, and George Gray of Delaware. None of them was expected to resign as senator, and none of them did so. The fifth place on the commission went to a newspaper man, Whitelaw Reid, Republican editor of the New York *Tribune*. McKinley's instructions gave the commissioners no option as to the expulsion of the Spanish Empire from America, but the Spanish delegation argued plausibly that, inasmuch as there was no Cuban government worthy of the name, the island should be ceded direct to the United States, who would thereby become responsible for the Cuban debt. The Americans refused this dubious proffer. They agreed that the United States should occupy the island temporarily, but they successfully insisted that Spain should assume the island's debt.

The most heated dispute between the Spanish and the American delegations was over the Philippine Islands.[1] The Spaniards argued earnestly that the situation in the Orient should be considered as of August 12, when the armistice was signed, instead of August 14, when the city of Manila was officially surrendered to General

Treaty of Paris

[1] J. F. Rippy, *America and the Strife of Europe* (1938), discusses the conditions that led to the acquisition of the Philippines.

Merritt. But the Americans refused to concede this point, and before the end of the month they were instructed by President McKinley to obtain the cession of the entire Philippine Archipelago. To the Spanish, and to many Americans, this demand seemed incredible. The total area of the Philippine Islands was seven thousand square miles greater than that of the British Isles, and the United States had actually occupied only the city of Manila. But McKinley had been watching American opinion closely, and had become convinced that the great majority of the American electorate favored annexation. That there would be trouble from the Filipinos he knew, and it worried him. One evening, after he had sought divine guidance in prayer, he made up his mind. "There is nothing left for us to do," he decided, "but to take all the islands and to educate the Filipinos, and uplift, civilize, and Christianize them and, by God's grace, do the very best we can for them as our fellow men, for whom Christ also died." Already three members of the commission, Davis, Frye, and Reid, had made up their minds the same way, and Day, the chairman, was ready to take Luzon, the large island on which Manila was located. Senator Gray, however, held out for a time that to annex any single part of the islands was a "shameful stepping down from the high moral position" the United States had taken in entering the war.

The President's will prevailed, and the American commissioners told the Spanish delegation what had to be done. The protests were long-drawn-out, and in the end the Spanish won an extraordinary concession. Without exactly explaining why it was to be done, the United States agreed to "pay to Spain the sum of twenty million dollars within three months after the exchange of the ratifications of the present treaty." Ordinarily money payments were demanded of vanquished powers instead of being accorded to them, but, in view of the extensive territorial cessions the United States had obtained, a money indemnity could hardly have been required. The twenty million dollars was variously explained as representing the difference in value between what the United States had actually conquered and what it insisted on taking, or the investment the Spanish government had made in the Philippines, or what it was worth to the United States in satisfaction just to have a war and win it. On December 10, 1898, the treaty was finally signed, and early next month the President submitted it to the Senate for ratification.

For a time there was danger that the necessary two-thirds majority could not be obtained.[1] Led by the resourceful William Jennings Bryan, "anti-imperialists" gave battle the whole country over against so wide

[1] The struggle over ratification is well told in W. S. Holt, *Treaties Defeated by the Senate* (1933).

a departure from American tradition as was involved in the acquisition
Ratification of the Philippines. Not Democrats merely, but many prominent Republicans also, including Senator Hale of Maine
and Senator Hoar of Massachusetts, objected strenuously to the terms
of the treaty, and when the time came voted against ratification.
Speaker Thomas B. Reed was "terribly bitter" in his opposition, and
according to Senator Lodge was "saying all sorts of ugly things about
the Administration and its policy." Ultimately Reed resigned his seat
in the House and retired from politics rather than stand with his party
on such an issue. Andrew Carnegie went to Washington and lobbied
against the treaty. Strange as it may seem, the man who finally saved
the treaty was Bryan. Convinced that free silver would not provide the
Democrats with a winning issue in 1900, he saw in a battle over imperialism the one chance of Democratic success. The proper policy, he maintained, would be to accept the treaty, and then to demand that the Philippines be set free. Without the efforts of Bryan, who conferred in Washington with wavering Democrats and Populists, it seems certain that the
administration would have lost. As it was, ten Democrats and eight
Populists voted with thirty-nine Republicans to give the treaty one more
than the two-thirds majority required for ratification. And so McKinley
had his treaty, and Bryan had his issue.[1]

[1] On the rise of American naval power W. D. Puleston, *Mahan: The Life and Work of Captain Alfred Thayer Mahan, U. S. N.* (1939), throws considerable light. On the early American activities in Hawaii, see H. W. Bradley, *The American Frontier in Hawaii: The Pioneers, 1789–1843* (1942).

THE PACIFIC OCEAN

SOUTH AMERICA

Scale of Miles

0   200   400   600   800

CHAPTER XVI

THE AMERICAN EMPIRE

FROM the Spanish-American War the United States emerged as a world power. It had defeated a European nation in war, and it had added to its possessions regions distant enough and different enough *The United* that none could deny the existence of an American Empire. *States as a* Alaska, the Hawaiian Islands, the Philippines, Puerto Rico, *world* Guam, all these and a number of minor islands, together *power* with the temporary occupation of Cuba, satisfied for the moment the ambitions of the most rabid of expansionists. To some, however, it was only a beginning. Senator Albert J. Beveridge of Indiana, an orator worthy of comparison to William Jennings Bryan, scattered throughout one of his most popular addresses the refrain: "The march of the flag went on!" That anything could ever stop its further progress seemed to him incredible.[1]

Alaska the United States had owned since 1867, but only in the nineties had Americans begun to realize its value. In 1896 gold was discovered in the Klondike, a district in northern Canada *Alaska* adjacent to the Alaskan border that could be reached ordinarily only by crossing the Alaskan panhandle, or by ascending the Yukon River. For the next few years the search for gold in the frozen North produced scenes reminiscent of the gold rush to California. The prosperity and notoriety of the Klondike, short-lived though it proved to be, suggested the possibility of gold in Alaska, and new finds and new rushes came thick and fast. The remote village of Nome, Alaska, for example, swelled in population during the year 1899–1900 to twenty thousand, only to shrink again to insignificance. Here as elsewhere the amount of gold that could be obtained without expensive machinery was negligible, but during the next third of a century the gold taken from Alaskan mines exceeded fifty times over the price the United States had paid Russia for the territory. Other valuable mineral deposits, such as

[1] Claude G. Bowers, *Beveridge and the Progressive Era* (1932), p. 75. This book reveals little of the partisanship so common in Bowers's other historical writings.

[333]

silver, copper, lead, and oil, soon proved that "Seward's Folly" was an extremely profitable investment. Governed at first by army, navy, and treasury officials, Alaska was accorded territorial status by an organic act passed in 1884, and revised in 1913.[1]

The acquisition of Hawaii seemed justified by the sugar the islands could produce, but the value of the former colonies of Spain had yet to be *The new* proved. Cuba, according to the resolution that Congress *possessions* had adopted when the war with Spain broke out, must be set free, but just how this was to be brought about was not entirely clear. Here the United States faced, also, a baffling and expensive problem of sanitation, for the yellow fever and other tropical diseases were taking a heavy toll. Fortunately the Puerto Ricans accepted American sovereignty without visible signs of resentment, but for a long time the cost of American occupation was sure to exceed any possible profits. As for the Philippines, the United States had paid Spain twenty million dollars to get them, and had then added another hundred thousand dollars because the boundary zone outlined by the Treaty of Paris had left out a number of tiny islands that the American commissioners had meant to take. The prospect of returns on this investment seemed discouraging in the extreme, for the Filipinos, unlike the Puerto Ricans, had no notion of accepting American rule without a struggle.

The Philippines, probably unheard of by most Americans before the war, consisted of 7083 islands, of which 1668 were large enough to be *The* named, and 342 were populated. Together they had an *Philippines* area of 115,000 square miles, one fourth of which lay within the island of Luzon, which is approximately the size of Ohio. The Philippine population, which was a mixture of native races and immigrants from the Asiatic mainland, included about seven million Spanish-speaking and Roman Catholic Filipinos, besides perhaps two thirds of a million wild and uncivilized Igorrotes and Moros. Under Spanish rule the islanders had suffered from neglect, exploitation, and oppression, and, when the war between the United States and Spain broke out, Filipino insurgents were seriously challenging Spanish supremacy. The insurrection was immensely aided by Dewey's return of its exiled leader, Emilio Aguinaldo, whose forces, by the time the United States had acquired title to the islands, actually held the upper hand everywhere except in Luzon.

At first the Filipinos had assumed naïvely that the American promise of freedom for Cuba carried with it by implication the promise of freedom

---

[1] Jeannette P. Nichols, *Alaska* (1924); J. M. Callahan, *The Alaska Purchase and Americo-Canadian Relations* (1908).

for the Philippines. Even the terms of the Treaty of Paris did not entirely disabuse their minds, for they knew that powerful opposition to annexation existed in the United States, and they hoped that something would happen to prevent it. But they were soon undeceived. On December 21, 1898, President McKinley asserted pointedly the determination of the United States to extend American sovereignty over the islands, and instructed the War Department to make this attitude clear to the Filipinos. General Elwell S. Otis, who had succeeded General Merritt as military governor of the islands, did not dare publish McKinley's message in its original form, although ordered to do so, but even when softened the President's announcement had a very bad effect. As the debate over ratification proceeded, Aguinaldo and the Filipino leaders lost hope. If they were not merely to exchange Spanish rule for American rule, they must fight. On February 4, 1899, two days before the Senate ratified the treaty, an American outpost exchanged shots with some insurgents and the war in the Philippines was on.

The path of empire was to prove thorny indeed. Hard fighting soon drove the insurgents from their trenches around Manila, but the natives took to the hills and inflicted severe punishment upon the *Revolt in the* troops sent against them. In the first two months of fight- *Philippines* ing the Americans admitted losses of nearly twelve hundred killed and wounded, and before the islanders were pacified these losses had been multiplied many times over. Most prominent of the American victims was General Henry W. Lawton, shot by a Filipino sharpshooter. The insurgent forces under Aguinaldo's command amounted in all to perhaps seventy thousand men, many of whom had seen service with the Spanish and were trained in western methods of warfare. Had their supply of arms been adequate they might have prolonged their resistance almost indefinitely, and even when reduced to the use of their native weapon, the bolo, a long, sharply pointed knife, they were formidable antagonists. Retreating from one tropical fastness to another, and from one island to the next, they kept busy an army of occupation as large as their own. The American officers and men, incensed at the constant losses, fought back with methods not much different from those of "Butcher" Weyler in Cuba. To William Howard Taft, of Ohio, benevolent head of a civilian commission sent to the Philippines in the summer of 1900, the Filipino was a "little brown brother," but to the soldiers who were doing the fighting:

> He may be a brother of Big Bill Taft;
> But he ain't no brother of mine.

In the end, of course, American might won, but not until Aguinaldo had been trapped in a most unchivalrous manner and brought back as a captive to Manila. On October 1, 1901, the complete suppression of the insurrection was formally announced, but the facts did not for many months justify such a statement.

Meantime the people of the United States had had a chance to express themselves at the polls on the issue of "imperialism." Republican suc-
Election of 1900 cesses in the elections of 1898 denoted little more than general satisfaction at the victories won by Americans in the war with Spain, but the presidential election of 1900 was a pitched battle, with the forces favoring annexation of the Philippines lined up solidly on one side, and those opposed on the other. The Republicans, with William McKinley once more their standard-bearer, and with Theodore Roosevelt, the hero of San Juan Hill, as their candidate for Vice-President, rejoiced in the "new and noble responsibility" that had come to the American people, and asserted that "no other course was possible" in the Philippines than the one that had been taken. The Democrats, still under the spell of Bryan's oratory, also renominated their leader of the preceding campaign, but for second place they had no war hero; only the time-worn Vice-President of Cleveland's second administration, Adlai E. Stevenson of Illinois. Bryan himself had been a colonel of Nebraska volunteers, but he had had no such luck with the War Department in obtaining a chance to fight as had the Colonel on the Republican ticket. To Bryan, "imperialism" was the "paramount issue" of the campaign, and the Democratic platform recorded his sentiments:

> We condemn and denounce the Philippine policy of the present Administration. It has embroiled the Republic in an unnecessary war, sacrificed the lives of many of its noblest sons, and placed the United States, previously known and applauded throughout the world as the champion of freedom, in the false and un-American position of crushing with military force the efforts of our former allies to achieve liberty and self-government.
> The Filipinos cannot be citizens without endangering our civilization; they cannot be subjects without imperiling our form of government; and as we are not willing to surrender our civilization, or to convert the Republic into an empire, we favor an immediate declaration of the Nation's purpose to give to the Filipinos, first, a stable form of government; second, independence; and third, protection from outside interference such as has been given for nearly a century to the republics of Central and South America.

Throughout the campaign the debate on imperialism held the center
Imperialism the paramount issue of the stage. The arguments were not new; they had all been used while the Treaty of Paris was before the country. Nor was the decision ever in doubt. McKinley, as the cartoonists so graphically portrayed, always had his "ear to the ground,"

and he knew full well that he had read the public mind aright. Nevertheless, Democratic orators dwelt long upon the inconsistency of a democracy such as the United States fighting to suppress the ambitions of another people to be free. They cast William McKinley in the rôle of George III, and Aguinaldo in that of George Washington. They pointed out the practical difficulties involved. The United States was wholly without experience in the governing of colonies. How could it hope to solve the problems of a distant and alien race? A great navy and a great army would be necessary to protect the new possessions. Once the United States had depended upon the Atlantic Ocean and the Pacific Ocean for its defense. But with Asiatic possessions American military might must be expanded to reach far across the seas.

Republican orators had no difficulty in justifying all that had been done. The Philippines, they claimed, offered an inviting missionary field. The United States had at last an opportunity to extend the blessings of American civilization. The Filipinos were not yet capable of governing themselves; freedom would mean only anarchy and misrule, or perhaps conquest by some predatory commercial nation, such as Germany or France. The United States had become a great power, and it must accept the responsibilities of greatness. Kipling's poem on "The White Man's Burden," published by *McClure's Magazine* in February, 1899, made "good sense":

> Take up the White Man's burden —
> Send forth the best ye breed —
> Go, bind your sons to exile
> To serve your captive's need;
>
> To wait in heavy harness
> On fluttered folk and wild —
> Your new-caught sullen peoples,
> Half devil and half child.

There would be profits, too, from imperialism. American trade in the Orient had grown of late, and with colonial possessions it would continue to grow. Even if the great powers of Europe partitioned China, as seemed likely to happen, the Philippines would more than compensate the United States for whatever losses it suffered in the China trade. "It is God's great purpose," said Senator Beveridge, "made manifest in the instincts of our race, whose present phase is our personal profit, but whose far-off end is the redemption of the world and the christianization of mankind." Besides, how could the United States be a really great nation if it had no colonies? Other great nations had colonies and were engaged in a mad scramble for more. Why should Americans deny themselves the right to boast with the British that the sun could never set on their national flag? [1]

It would be a mistake to assume that imperialism was the only subject debated in the campaign of 1900. The free-silver issue might be dead, *Other issues* as many Democrats privately conceded, but a multitude of voters did not know it. Accordingly Bryan and the Democratic orators repeated the monetary demands of 1896, while the Republicans once more adhered firmly to the gold standard. The tariff, too, could not be entirely ignored, and here again both parties had historic positions to defend. This multiplicity of issues led to numerous complications. Strong advocates of imperialism, or "expansion," as the Republicans preferred to call it, might hold low-tariff or even free-silver views, while the bitterest enemies of an overseas empire might be convinced adherents of protection and the gold standard. Cartoonists made merry with the "hold-your-nose-and-vote" crowd. Some gold-standard men "held their noses" and voted for Bryan because they agreed with him on imperialism; some free-traders "held their noses" and voted for the obnoxious McKinley because they believed in expansion; in a variety of ways the old adage that "politics makes strange bedfellows" was proved to be true. Shrewdly, Republican campaigners turned attention away from these discordant issues all they could, and rang the changes on prosperity. By comparing the hard times of Cleveland's second administration with the good times of the McKinley era they were able to associate prosperity with Republican policies and to blame adversity on the Democrats. Slogans such as "The Full Dinner Pail," and "Let Well Enough Alone," pressed home the point.

In the end McKinley won a more overwhelming victory than in 1896. He had again the advantage of a huge campaign fund, while Bryan's *Re-election* backers had even less to spend than four years before. *of McKinley* Bryan carried only the "solid South," and four silver states, Colorado, Nevada, Idaho, and Montana, while McKinley carried all the rest, including Bryan's home state, Nebraska. The popular vote stood 7,219,525 to 6,358,737 and the electoral vote, 292 to 155. The election was notable for the large number of minor parties that had presidential tickets in the field. The regular Populist organization supported Bryan, but a dissident group, the "Middle-of-the-Road" Populists, nominated Wharton Barker of Pennsylvania for President, and Ignatius Donnelly of Minnesota for Vice-President. Two Socialist tickets, one of them

[1] The imperialist position is well stated in *Selections from the Correspondence of Theodore Roosevelt and Henry Cabot Lodge* (2 vols., 1925); on the other side see George F. Hoar, *Autobiography of Seventy Years* (2 vols., 1903), and R. F. Pettigrew, *Imperial Washington* (1922).

headed by Eugene V. Debs, and a Prohibition ticket, each polled appreciable numbers of votes, while several lesser parties won next to no support at all. In spite of his long list of opponents McKinley received a majority of the popular as well as of the electoral vote. Both houses of Congress were also assured to the Republicans by substantial majorities, and, except in the South, Republican candidates for state office were generally the victors. In so far as an election could decide anything, the country had given its approval to imperialism, the gold standard, and a high protective tariff.

Six months after his second inauguration William McKinley visited the Pan-American Exposition at Buffalo, New York, and on September 5 made a speech in which he emphasized the importance of *Death of* reciprocity as a means of promoting foreign trade. Next *McKinley* day, during a reception, he was shot by an anarchist who had no other motive for his crime, apparently, than his disbelief in government. For a few days the President lingered on, but on September 14 he died, and was succeeded by the youthful Vice-President, Theodore Roosevelt. In a sense it was altogether fitting that the problems of consolidating and administering the new American Empire should fall to Roosevelt, for he, far more than McKinley, was responsible for the adventure into imperialism that the nation had undertaken.

When Roosevelt took office the liberation of Cuba was not yet an accomplished fact, but much progress in that direction had been made. Almost the first concern of the American army of occupation *Occupation* was the sanitation of the island. Under the leadership of *of Cuba* Major William Crawford Gorgas, an army physician, Havana, long a favorite breeding-place for tropical diseases, was scoured into a cleanliness it had never known before. When in spite of these measures a yellow fever epidemic broke out in 1900, a special commission headed by Doctor Walter Reed, went to Cuba to investigate. With the help of Doctor Carlos J. Finley, a Cuban whose "scientific clairvoyance" had enabled him to guess the correct solution, they proved that a mosquito, the stegomyia, was the guilty carrier. Two of the American investigators, Doctor Jesse W. Lazear and Doctor James Carroll, were infected in the course of their experiments, and both lost their lives as a result. Lazear died in a matter of days; Carroll recovered, but was so weakened that he died a few years later. The cause of the epidemic now ascertained, Gorgas went to work to eliminate the offending insect, with such success that before the year 1901 had ended Havana for the first time in "more than one hundred and forty years" was completely clear of yellow fever. General Wood, whose hearty co-operation as governor of Cuba had made possible the successes of Reed and Gorgas, extended American ideas of sanitation as rapidly as possible to the whole island. When the time came for American withdrawal, Cuba was almost as safe a place to live as the United States itself.[1]

Wood's administration also brought to the Cubans a higher degree of governmental efficiency than they had ever known before, and the promise of self-government. As early as June, 1900, municipal elections were ordered, and when critics of Republican imperialism asserted during the campaign of 1900 that McKinley never meant to set Cuba free, the President answered with orders for the election in September of a Cuban constitutional convention. The problem of the suffrage was somewhat perplexing, for a census taken by the Americans indicated that two thirds of the Cubans could neither read nor write, while none of them had ever had any experience with free elections. It was finally decided that voting should be restricted to those who could read and write, or who owned two hundred and fifty dollars in property, or who had served in the army of liberation. In November, 1900, thirty-one delegates were chosen, and by February, 1901, the convention had adopted a constitution closely patterned on the Constitution of the United States.

Quite significantly the Cuban Convention at first ignored the special relationship that the American government had assumed would exist *The Platt* between the United States and the republic it had created. *Amendment* On instructions from Washington, Governor Wood brought this oversight to the attention of the delegates, and indicated clearly the nature of the provisions the United States expected them to adopt. Even more emphatic was the action of Congress, which added to the Army Appropriation Bill of March 2, 1901, a series of eight clauses, known as the Platt Amendment, as follows:

1. That the government of Cuba should never by treaty with a foreign power impair its independence.
2. That it should keep its public debt within its capacity to pay from the ordinary revenues of the island.
3. That the United States should have the right to intervene for the preservation of Cuban independence and the maintenance of a government adequate for the protection of life, property, and individual liberty.
4. That the acts of the American military government during the period of occupation should be validated.
5. That the plans for the sanitation of Cuba already begun should be carried out by the new government.
6. That the Isle of Pines should be omitted from the proposed constitu-

---

[1] Mark Sullivan, *Our Times*, I, contains an admirable chapter on this subject.

tional boundaries of Cuba, and its title settled by treaty with the United States.

7. That Cuba should sell or lease to the United States lands necessary for coaling or naval stations.

8. That all these special provisions should be embodied in a permanent treaty with the United States.

Reluctantly, and under strong pressure from Washington, the Cuban Convention finally included the Platt Amendment as an appendix to the constitution it had drawn, and later on, when the new Cuban government had gone into operation, the treaty contemplated by the eighth clause was mutually ratified. Thus the Platt Amendment had the sanction of American statute law, Cuban constitutional provision, and treaty between the two nations. Obviously Cuba was not intended to be quite free; its status could be described more accurately as that of a protectorate of the United States.

On May 20, 1902, American authority was withdrawn from Cuba, and the government turned over to elected Cuban officials. That the Platt Amendment, particularly the third clause, which gave the United States the right of intervention, was not to become a dead letter was soon demonstrated. In August, 1906, an insurrection, aimed at the overthrow of the regularly elected government, broke out, and after a brief period of patience President Roosevelt sent his Secretary of War, William Howard Taft, to Cuba to "sit on the lid." Unable to effect a reconciliation between the contending factions, Taft, on September 26, 1906, assumed the full governmental authority of the island. For more than two years the American occupation continued, first under Taft and later under Governor Charles E. Magoon,[1] and when finally the United States again withdrew it did so only with a warning to the Cubans from the President of the United States that "if elections become a farce and if the insurrectionary habit becomes confirmed ... it is absolutely out of the question that the island should remain independent"; or, in effect, that if the United States had to intervene again in Cuba it would come to stay. Had Roosevelt remained President indefinitely, this threat might have been made good, but subsequent Presidents were more charitable. On several occasions the United States made use of its right of intervention in Cuba, but the island was not annexed. Under Franklin D. Roosevelt, indeed, the Platt Amendment itself was abrogated by agreement between the two nations, but by this time American

Cuba as a protectorate

---

[1] R. H. Fitzgibbon, *Cuba and the United States, 1900–1935* (1935); D. A. Lockmiller, *Magoon in Cuba* (1938); Carleton Beals, *The Crime of Cuba* (1933).

investments in Cuba had made of the island an economic, if not a political, dependency of the United States.

The constitutional and governmental status of Cuba, which was merely administered by the United States while on its way to freedom, could be regarded as exceptional, but some more or less permanent *modus vivendi* had to be arranged for the other new acquisitions. According to the treaty of cession, "the civil rights and political status of the native inhabitants of the territory... ceded to the United States" were left to the determination of Congress. Did this mean that Congress could do as it pleased without extending the liberties guaranteed by the Constitution to its island possessions, or was the freedom of Congress in this respect as much subject to the Constitution in the new territory as in the old? In other words, as the public phrased the question, Does the Constitution follow the flag?

Congress soon revealed through the various acts by which it provided for the establishment of civil government in the new possessions that it *Status of* had no notion whatever of setting limits to its authority. *dependencies* In the Foraker Act of 1900, for example, which outlined a form of government for Puerto Rico, a tariff was levied against Puerto Rican imports into the United States equal to fifteen per cent of the regular Dingley rates. If Puerto Rico had become a part of the United States this provision was clearly contrary to the constitutional requirements that "all duties, imports, and excises shall be uniform throughout the United States." Obviously, therefore, Congress did not regard the island as a part of the United States in the constitutional sense of the term, nor did the President who signed the law. But what would be the attitude of the federal courts, which since the time of John Marshall had felt free to set aside laws of Congress that in their judgment did not harmonize with the Constitution? [1]

In a series of five-to-four opinions on what came generally to be known as the "insular cases" the Supreme Court decided in 1901 not to interfere *The "in-* with the stand that Congress and the President had taken. *sular cases"* The first of these cases, *De Lima vs. Bidwell*, was brought by an importer of Puerto Rican sugar against the collector of the port of New York who *before* the enactment of the Foraker Act, but *after* the acquisition of Puerto Rico by the United States, had charged the full Dingley duties. In this case the Court held that the money collected must be refunded, for Puerto Rico was no longer foreign territory. In another case, however, *Downes vs. Bidwell*, where the collections had

---

[1] W. F. Willoughby, *Territories and Dependencies of the United States* (1905), is useful on the legal and constitutional side.

been made *after* the passage of the Foraker Act and according to its terms. the Court held that a refund was unnecessary, for Puerto Rico was not exactly a part of the United States. To eight justices these decisions seemed utterly contradictory, for the result was achieved by Mr. Justice Brown changing sides, and voting in the second decision with the four justices who had constituted the minority in the first decision. The reasoning by which he justified this shift of opinion no one but himself seemed to understand. Mr. Justice Harlan, who, together with three of his associates had voted in both cases that the Constitution must follow the flag, dissented from the *Downes vs. Bidwell* decision in vigorous terms.

> I confess that I cannot grasp the thought that Congress, which lives and moves and has its being in the Constitution and is consequently the mere creature of that instrument, can, at its pleasure, legislate or exclude its creator from territories which were acquired only by authority of the Constitution.

Nevertheless Mr. Justice Brown's decision stood. Puerto Rico and the other dependencies, he maintained, were "territory appurtenant — but not a part — of the United States." Two other opinions, the "Fourteen Diamond Rings" case and *Hawaii vs. Mankichi*, applied the same principles to the Philippines and the Hawaiian Islands respectively. The Constitution followed the flag only when and in so far as Congress ordered.

"Mr. Dooley," a mythical Irish-American whose efforts to enlighten his slow-witted contemporary, "Mr. Hennessy," revealed through the newspapers the opinions of a shrewd commentator, Finley Peter Dunne, was much impressed by the decision of "Justice Brown — Fuller, C. J., Gray, J., Harlan, J., Shiras, J., McKenna, J., White, J., Brewer, J., and Peckham, J., dissenting fr'm me an' each other." The Constitution, Mr. Dooley concluded, had no business "to shadow the flag to all th' tough resorts on th' Passyfic Coast."

> "Ye can't make me think th' constitution is goin' thrapezin' around ivrywhere a young leftinant in th' ar'rmy takes it into his head to stick a flagpole. It's too old. It's a home-stayin' constitution with a blue coat and brass buttons on to it, an' it walks with a goold-headed cane. It's old an' it's feeble an' it prefers to set on the front stoop and amuse the childer. It wudden't last a minyit in thim thropical climes."

Then, reflecting on the victory of imperialism at the polls in the election of 1900, Mr. Dooley went on:

> "Some say it laves the flag up in th' air an' some say that's where it laves the constitution. Annyhow, something's in the air. But there's wan thing I'm sure about."

"What's that?" asked Mr. Hennessy.

"That is," said Mr. Dooley, "no matter whether the constitution follows the flag or not, th' Supreme Court follows th' illicition returns."

The thoroughly conservative *Review of Reviews* put the matter much more prosaically. "The decision of the Supreme Court," it pontificated, "means that we are not to be hampered in our serious policies by the ingenious use of logic in the interpretation of an ancient document that was not intended to hamper posterity."

The beginnings of a Philippines policy had been made before the death of McKinley. In 1899 a commission of five, headed by President Schur-
Government of the Philippines man of Cornell University, was sent to make a study of conditions in the islands, and to report back a plan whereby self-government might eventually be established. Impressed by the ignorance of the people and the variety of their races and languages, the commission urged delay in extending the American political system to the islands, but next year McKinley sent a second commission headed by William Howard Taft of Ohio, to make the start. Taft's commission, in spite of some friction with the military authorities, soon took over full legislative and administrative responsibility. It worked out a plan for extending self-government gradually to Philippine municipalities, and divided the islands into provinces, each with an appointive head. On July 1, 1901, under authority of an act of Congress passed the preceding March, Taft became civil governor of the Philippines (governor-general after 1905), while the commission, reinforced shortly afterward by the appointment of three Filipino members, con tinued to act as a legislature. A supreme court, appointed by the President of the United States, completed the familiar picture of three independent departments of government. In 1907 the Filipinos were allowed the privilege of electing an assembly, which became the lower house of the legislature, while the commission served as the upper house.

American rule accomplished much more than the mere pacification and governmental organization of the Philippines. An immediate major problem was the disposition of the so-called "friar lands," some four hundred thousand acres belonging to various Catholic religious orders. These lands had been coveted by the Filipinos, and during the abortive Philippine revolution many of them had been appropriated by rebellious tenants. The friars, however, insisted that their land titles should be defended by the United States. Perplexed by the conflict of religious and temporal rights, Roosevelt in 1902 sent Taft to Rome to negotiate through the Pope for a settlement, and for seven million dollars, the friars agreed to relinquish their claims. Many American Protestants were outraged at this open recognition of papal power, but the government had exchanged a wholly alien problem for one with which it had considerable experience — the disposal of public lands. Probably no other act did so much to reconcile the Filipinos to American rule.[1]

"Dominion over palm and pine" carried with it also certain familiar aspects of American culture. One of the most important transplantations was the American public-school system. In 1898 perhaps five thousand Filipino children were in school; by 1920, over a million. At first American teachers were placed in charge, but adequately trained Filipinos, many of them educated in the United States, were soon available to take over the work. By 1920 the number of American teachers had dwindled to three hundred, and the English language rivaled the Spanish as the most generally understood tongue in the islands. American notions as to sanitation also reached the Philippines. Smallpox and cholera were stamped out, lepers were isolated in colonies and treated instead of being permitted to roam at will, and the infantile death-rate was sharply reduced. Good roads, too, were built, and improved methods of transportation were introduced. Most significant of all, the modified tariff barriers that had at first restricted trade between the Philippines and the United States soon gave way to virtual free trade, thus opening the rich American markets to Philippine sugar, coconut oil, rice, tobacco, and hemp. The result of this favored economic status was a degree of prosperity such as the Philippines had never known before. Whatever their political differences, the economic ties that bound the islands to the United States became closer with each succeeding year. Rich resources in minerals and lumber that might also be sold to American customers were discovered, and plans for their exploitation were laid.

The net political effect of the new prosperity, however, was to make the Filipinos crave independence ever more and more. Both parties in the United States conceded that sometime this goal must be *The road to* reached, and many of the Democrats insisted that it should *independence* have been reached long before. In 1916, while Woodrow Wilson was President and the Democrats controlled Congress, the Jones Act outlined a scheme of self-government for the Philippines that looked definitely in the direction of independence. Both houses of the Philippine legislature were made elective, and the prerogatives of the governor-general were materially reduced. Indeed, the new governor-general, Francis B. Harrison, practically turned over the reins of authority to

[1] Grayson L. Kirk, *Philippine Independence* (1936), is an excellent study of the relations between the Philippines and the United States from 1898 to the enactment of the act of independence. See also Moorfield Storey and M. P. Lichauco, *The Conquest of the Philippines by the United States, 1898–1925* (1926), a strongly anti-imperialistic view.

a council of state dominated by Filipinos, and accepted more or less openly a rôle as perfunctory as that of a governor-general in one of the British Dominions. This steady drift toward independence was interrupted in 1921 when President Harding sent his former rival for the Republican nomination, General Leonard Wood, to be governor-general of the Philippines. No believer in independence, Wood asserted to the full his legal prerogatives, and until the time of his death in 1927 unrest accumulated in the islands at a rapid rate.[1]

Wood's successors were more conciliatory, and by the time the Democrats returned to power in 1933 the movement for Philippine independence was far advanced. Philippine agitators found new and extremely effective allies in the sugar, dairy, and tobacco interests of the United States, who objected to the competition of duty-free Philippine products, and saw in independence for the islands an opportunity to levy the customary high protective tariff rates against them. Pacifists also threw their influence in favor of independence on the ground that Japanese expansion might sometime reach the Philippines, and thus bring on war between Japan and the United States. Since American investments in the islands had been comparatively slight, there was no effective protest against this point of view, and finally, on December 29, 1932, Congress provided in the Hawes-Cutting Act for a ten-year American protectorate over the islands to be followed by independence. Mindful of the chaotic economic and social conditions that would result from the loss of the American markets, President Hoover courageously vetoed the act, but Congress promptly repassed it over his veto. By this time, however, the Filipinos could see that independence was not without its disadvantages, and the Philippine legislature, by failing to call the constitutional convention prescribed by the act, deliberately allowed the measure to lapse. On March 24, 1934, with Franklin D. Roosevelt as President, a new measure, known as the Tydings-McDuffie Act, once more offered independence after ten years, and this time the offer was accepted. All American officials except a high commissioner were withdrawn from the islands, and the two governments were left with the problem of working out within the ten-year limit such plans as might be deemed necessary to prevent the collapse of the Philippine economic system when the special favors granted by the United States should be withdrawn. The future of Philippine foreign relations was also left open for negotiations, with no assurance given that the United States would feel obliged to aid the

---

[1] The work of these two governors may be followed in F. B. Harrison, *The Corner-Stone of Philippine Independence, a Narrative of Seven Years* (1922), and in Hermann Hagedorn, *Leonard Wood* (2 vols., 1931).

islands in maintaining the independence they were at last about to achieve.

The occupation of Puerto Rico [1] involved fewer perplexities than confronted American officials either in the Philippines or in Cuba. The population of the island was less than a million, nearly two *Puerto* thirds of whom were white, and the rest of Negro extraction. *Rico* There had been no revolution and no war damage of consequence. American rule was accepted without enthusiasm, but without protest. Even under the military régime rapid strides were made toward the better sanitation of the island, the building of roads, and the re-ordering of public finance. So smoothly was the transition accomplished that as early as April 12, 1900, Congress passed the Foraker Act establishing a civil government for Puerto Rico, the first to be accorded any of the new possessions. The pattern of government thus set for the dependencies was similar to that of the traditional American territory, but with a few conspicuous differences. Members of the upper house of the legislature, as well as the governor, were appointed by the President and confirmed by the Senate, while only the lower house — the House of Delegates — was elected directly by the people. Both the governor of Puerto Rico and the Congress of the United States had the right to veto any laws passed by the island legislature. Six administrative officers — secretary, attorney-general, treasurer, auditor, commissioner of interior, and commissioner of education — were endowed with ample powers, and were made responsible to the appropriate cabinet members in Washington rather than to the local governor. Residents of the island were not accorded full American citizenship, but were described as citizens of Puerto Rico. During Wilson's first administration most of these anomalies were ironed out. An Act of March 2, 1917, equipped the island with the customary territorial form of government, and declared its citizens to be citizens of the United States. The possibility of statehood has been frequently discussed, but has received little support.

Even more rapidly than in the case of the Philippines, tariff barriers between the United States and Puerto Rico were broken down. Since the summer of 1901 complete freedom of trade has existed, with the result that Puerto Rican shipments to the United States (consisting chiefly of coffee, sugar, fruits, and tobacco) have been multiplied many times over. As in the Philippines, American occupation meant better roads, better schools, better sanitation. Nevertheless, the general level of well-being in the island remains definitely below American standards, and the relative

---

[1] Knowlton Mixer, *Porto Rico* (1926). By an act of Congress, signed May 17, 1932, the name Puerto Rico was officially substituted for Porto Rico.

absence of unrest among the islanders may be attributed more probably to inertia than to satisfaction with American rule.

Prideful Americans recounting the spoils of imperialism were aware also of certain minor possessions above which waved the Stars and *Other* Stripes. Besides Alaska, the Philippines, and Puerto Rico, *possessions* the United States had acquired the Hawaiian Islands, with a population of more than one hundred and fifty thousand and enormous sugar-producing possibilities. Not more than one fifth of the residents of these islands were native Hawaiians; nearly another fifth were Americans; and the remaining three fifths were Asiatics. Here American investments were important, and the wishes of American residents were given careful consideration. On April 30, 1900, by Act of Congress Hawaii was accorded full territorial status. American sovereignty had also been extended to Tutuila, one of the Samoan Islands in the southern Pacific, to Guam, some fifteen hundred miles east of the Philippines, and to numerous tiny uninhabited islets in the Pacific over which no other nation had chosen to raise its flag. With no form of government prescribed by Congress for these acquisitions, they remained under the absolute control of the President as commander-in-chief of the army and navy. Two other tiny colonies came to the United States as a result of the decision to build a canal across the Isthmus of Panama. The Canal Zone, ten miles wide, obtained by treaty with Panama in 1903, came to be inhabited principally by government employees, and was eventually left to the government of Congress, the President, and the national courts. The Virgin Islands, acquired by purchase from Denmark in 1917, were deemed of value for the proper defense of the Canal. To govern the impoverished twenty-five thousand Negroes and mulattoes who inhabited them, the President was authorized to appoint a governor, subject to the approval of the Senate. The Danish code of laws, already in force, was retained.

Quite as the opponents of imperialism had predicted, the necessity of defending this overseas empire led to a rapid expansion of the military *Imperial* might of the United States. Under Elihu Root as Secretary *defense* of War the United States Army underwent a reorganization so thorough that the scandals of inefficiency that marred the prosecution of the war against Spain could not soon be repeated. In keeping with modern practice a general staff was created to take the place of the major-general in command of the army, and to lay plans for the proper defense of the United States and its possessions. By means of the Army War College, established in 1901, and other service schools, an attempt was made also to carry on the military education of officers after they had been commissioned. The size of the army was not greatly increased, but a new militia law, designed to make of the National Guard a more efficient second line of defense, was placed on the statute books in 1903. Even more striking than the reorganization of the army was the rapid expansion of the navy, to which one or two new battleships were added every year.[1] In 1907 President Roosevelt spectacularly advertised the strength of the American Navy by sending a fleet of sixteen battleships, together with the necessary auxiliary craft, on a voyage around the world. Any power critical of American policies — and the President had Japan particularly in mind — might thus see what it would have to deal with should it provoke the United States to war.

Quite as striking a fact as the sudden acquisition of a colonial empire by the United States was the equally sudden subsidence of the imperialistic urge. To Senator Beveridge (unless perchance he too *Decline of* had changed his mind) the rapid loss of interest by Ameri- *imperialism* cans in expansion must have seemed disheartening indeed. The "march of the flag" would not go on. After the first excitement, interest in the newly acquired possessions diminished, and the public showed not the slightest appetite for more. When the United States entered the World War in 1917, one of the certainties, unchallenged by any political party, was that the American nation would not emerge with more colonies. At the Paris Peace Conference the United States, almost alone among the victors, made no demands for territory, and all efforts to saddle the American government with disagreeable mandates came to nought. From the financial point of view colonial empire had proved to be almost a total loss; the Philippines in particular had cost the government huge sums, and had brought in next to nothing by way of profit. This, perhaps, need not have been so; other nations took a heavy toll from their possessions. But neither the American government nor the American people showed great aptitude along this line. Americans with a taste for foreign investments were not lacking, but they made as good profits, if not better, in lands that lay outside the American Empire. Discouraging, too, was the discovery that distant possessions meant involvement in world politics. American isolation was threatened and the danger of war was increased.

Perhaps a distinction might be drawn between possessions in the western hemisphere and elsewhere. Americans while somewhat indifferent toward territorial acquisitions made in the New World, showed little disposition to give them up. They even acquiesced while their government, under one pretext or another, made virtual protectorates for a time

[1] A. T. Mahan, *Lessons of the War with Spain* (1899).

of nations bordering on the Caribbean Sea and adjacent to the Panama Canal. The Philippines, however, were a heavy load to carry, and without huge naval expenditures they were utterly indefensible. At this distant outpost the "march of the flag" seemed destined to stop, and from it a strategic retreat has already been planned.[1]

[1] William H. Haas (ed.), *The American Empire: A Study of the Outlying Territories of the United States* (1940), is an admirable survey. On Alaska, see Victor J. Farrar, *The Annexation of Russian America to the United States* (1937). On the Virgin Islands, see Luther Harris Evans, *The Virgin Islands: From Naval Base to New Deal* (1945); also, J. Antonio Jarvis, *The Virgin Islands and their People* (1944).

Elmer Ellis, *Mr. Dooley's America: A Life of Finley Peter Dunne* (1941), attempts to revive the leading political humorist of the time.

CHAPTER XVII

WORLD POLITICS

THEODORE ROOSEVELT (1858–1919), twenty-sixth President of the United States, was the youngest man ever to have held the Presidency, but in spite of his mere forty-three years he was by no means *Theodore* lacking in political experience.[1] The descendant of a long *Roosevelt* line of well-to-do New York aristocrats, he was brought up in an atmosphere of culture and learning that contrasted sharply with the Lincolnian tradition, so dear to American hearts. He saw Europe as a child, was carefully prepared for college, attended Harvard, graduated with the class of 1880. His education began, he claimed later, "immediately after leaving college," and certainly he soon learned about politics. Unwilling to live the life of a rich man's son, he found occasion in 1881 to run for the legislature, and with the help of the local machine he was elected. For three terms of one year each he represented his district at Albany, and in spite of his youth he gave a good account of himself. In 1884 he attended the national nominating convention at Chicago as chairman of the New York delegation, and worked energetically, but in vain, to prevent the nomination of James G. Blaine. The sudden death of his young wife, together with his deep disappointment at Blaine's triumph, had much to do with Roosevelt's decision to engage in the cattle business far out on the Dakota frontier. The new life was like a tonic; he loved it. "You would be amused to see me," he wrote to his good friend Henry Cabot Lodge, "in my broad sombrero hat, fringed and beaded buckskin shirt, horsehide chaparajos or riding trousers, and cowboy boots, with braided bridle and silver spurs." Roosevelt's

[1] The only adequately critical biography of Roosevelt is H. F. Pringle, *Theodore Roosevelt* (1931).   Most other writers on Roosevelt are content to expound or elaborate the "Roosevelt legend," so ably set forth in Theodore Roosevelt, *An Autobiography* (1913), and J. B. Bishop, *Theodore Roosevelt and His Time Shown in His Own Letters* (2 vols., 1920). Of this type are W. R. Thayer, *Theodore Roosevelt; an Intimate Biography* (1919); L. F. Abbott, *Impressions of Theodore Roosevelt* (1919); and W. D. Lewis, *The Life of Theodore Roosevelt* (1919).

western experience was brief, but it was also deep. He never quite got over it.[1]

Roosevelt spent only a part of his time in the West, he soon remarried, and he was not long out of politics. "With the most genuine reluctance," or so he claimed, he accepted in 1886 the Republican nomination for mayor of New York, and ran third in a three-cornered race. Two years later he campaigned so energetically for Harrison that when the Republicans won he was rewarded by an appointment to the Civil Service Commission, a position that paid only thirty-five hundred dollars a year, and was accounted by the politicians of little consequence. But Roosevelt was not concerned about the salary, and in spite of the efforts of spoilsmen to cripple his work he soon made of civil service reform something more than an idealist's dream. In 1895, after six years with the commission, he accepted an even humbler office, the presidency of the New York police board, and again lifted the office to his own stature. For two years he warred with great earnestness, although with indifferent success, against vice and crime. Having seen with his own eyes how the "other half" lived, he emerged from the experience a convinced social reformer and the idol of such humanitarians as Jacob Riis. He emerged, too, with a habit of mind that was to remain strongly in evidence throughout his career. Both as civil service commissioner and as police commissioner, he had found that those who opposed his views were almost invariably insincere, or dishonest, or worse, while he himself was cast in the rôle of righteousness. Inevitably he became accustomed to thinking of himself as always right, and his opponents, whatever their views, as always wrong.

In spite of his activity in politics Roosevelt found time to make important contributions to the history of the United States. His *Naval War of 1812* (1882) was begun when he was a student in college, and was published two years after his graduation. He contributed two hastily written volumes to the American Statesmen Series, one of them on *Thomas Hart Benton* (1886), a work of considerable merit, and the other, on *Gouverneur Morris* (1888), not as highly esteemed. His best historical work was a four-volume series, *The Winning of the West* (1889–96), which traced from original sources the path of conquest by which the white man won the region from the Appalachians to the Mississippi. Roosevelt was less impressed with the significance of the frontier than with the tales of heroism and adventure in which it abounded, but it is noteworthy that even before Turner he had begun

Roosevelt, the historian

---

[1] Hermann Hagedorn, *Roosevelt in the Bad Lands* (1921), does justice to this phase of Roosevelt's career.

Copyright, Harris and Ewing

THEODORE ROOSEVELT

to write of the West. Possessed of an easy, flowing style, and an adept at story-telling, he might have ranked with Parkman and Prescott had he chosen history instead of politics as his vocation. Drawing heavily on his western experience he wrote, too, for popular consumption such books as his *Hunting Trips of a Ranchman* (1885), and *Ranch Life and the Hunting Trail* (1888).

Roosevelt again won for himself a place in national politics when he campaigned vigorously for McKinley in 1896; his appointment as Assistant Secretary of the Navy was offered and accepted as a fitting reward for service rendered. After his experience in Cuba he was immediately picked up by the Republican machine in New York to head the state ticket in what threatened, because of charges of corruption against the preceding administration, to be a Democratic year. Elected by a slender majority, he enjoyed hugely his work as governor, but was regarded with grave suspicion by Thomas Collier ("Me-Too") Platt, the "Easy Boss" of New York Republicanism. As a means of getting Roosevelt out of the state, Platt favored the nomination of Roosevelt for second place on the national ticket in 1900. Two other hard-boiled politicians, Matthew S. Quay and Boies Penrose, both of Pennsylvania, supported Platt's scheme for the anguish Roosevelt's nomination would give their upstart political rival, Mark Hanna. Soon an insistent national demand for Roosevelt had set in, and the combined protests of McKinley, Hanna, and Roosevelt himself were easily overruled. Roosevelt had stated publicly that "under no circumstances could I or would I accept the nomination for the Vice-Presidency," while Hanna had reminded some of the delegates to the Philadelphia nominating convention that there would be "only one life between this madman and the White House." Henry Cabot Lodge, who believed that Roosevelt should accept the Vice-Presidency if it were offered him, advised him not to go to the Republican nominating convention if he did not wish the nomination. But Roosevelt went, wearing his cowboy hat, and asserting noisily his unwillingness to run. There were those who quoted Shakespeare: He "doth protest too much, methinks." At any rate, he received the vote of every delegate to the convention, except his own, and he accepted the nomination.

Ever spoiling for a fight, he enjoyed the campaign, but with the election over he was prepared to be bored. "I would rather be anything *Elected* than Vice-President," he had once proclaimed, "say a *Vice-Presi-* Professor of History." He decided that he might as well *dent* while away his time by reading law, a study he had once begun and abandoned, and arranged to borrow the necessary books from Mr. Justice White. His labors on the law, which were to include a Saturday afternoon quiz by the same Justice, had not yet begun, however, when he found himself suddenly elevated to the office he had long before set as the goal of his ambition. For good or ill, he was never to take a lawyer's view of the Presidency.

The perfect good taste that characterized Roosevelt's every act in taking over the Presidency did much to allay the fears of those who had considered him only a brash young man. He at once announced that it would be his "aim to continue absolutely unbroken the policies of President McKinley for the peace, prosperity, and honor of our beloved country." Especially reassuring was the decision to retain

McKinley's cabinet, for whatever his faults McKinley had proved him-self to be an able judge of men. Two of the advisers on whom Roosevelt was to depend most, John Hay, Secretary of State, and Elihu Root, Secretary of War, were already in the cabinet, while a third, William Howard Taft, had been picked by McKinley for the difficult task of inaugurating civil government in the Philippines. Roosevelt even sought with some success to appease Mark Hanna, although, as both knew, the gulf between them on most matters of consequence was very wide. It was inevitable that eventually Roosevelt was to be his own President. For the most part McKinley had been content to follow public opinion, but aggressive leadership was an integral part of the Roosevelt personality. Fortunately the new President embodied to a remarkable degree the interests and prejudices of the average American. When he sought to lead there was no dearth of followers.

Better versed in world affairs than his predecessors, Roosevelt tackled with eager enthusiasm the problems of diplomacy that came before his administration. He found European nations far less con- *Europe and* temptuous of the United States than they had been before *America* the Spanish-American War. To show that Germany had only the friendliest of sentiments toward the United States, the Kaiser conferred a medal on Roosevelt, sent his brother, Prince Henry, on a tour of America, invited Roosevelt's charming daughter, Alice, to christen a yacht he had ordered from an American shipyard, and presented a statue of his illustrious antecedent, Frederick the Great, to adorn the new Army War College on the lower Potomac. France, not wishing to be entirely outdone, founded some exchange professorships, and reminded forgetful Americans of the helpful part France had played in the American Revolution by forwarding to the United States a statue of Rocham-beau. Great Britain, openly hopeful of an alliance with the United States, went much further than presents in demonstrating her friend-ship. How to take advantage of all this display of good-will, and yet to escape commitments that might involve the United States in European affairs, taxed to the full the capacities of the new President and his able advisers.

The threat to American isolation involved in the acquisition of the Philippines was very great. The United States, whether it so desired or not, had become an Asiatic power, with a lively interest *The open-* in whatever went on in Asia. But the great powers of Asia, *door policy* with the exception of Japan, were also the great powers of Europe — Great Britain in India, France in French Indo-China, Russia in Siberia, Germany in Shantung, the Netherlands in the East Indies. How could the United States play the part it must in Asiatic affairs, and at the same time avoid that entanglement in European affairs against which Washington and Jefferson had so pointedly warned?

This problem had reached an acute phase even before Roosevelt became President. China was in danger of dismemberment. During the last quarter of the nineteenth century the nations of Europe, in their mad scramble for colonies, had practically completed the partition of Africa. Now they had turned their attention to China as the last of the great "backward" nations as yet unappropriated. "Spheres of influence" were already marked out in which one nation or another had obtained "concessions" for the "development" of a specified region, and in many instances outright ownership was asserted. England, ever since the Opium War of 1842, had held Hongkong; Japan, after a war with China in 1895, assumed control of Korea; Germany, in compensation for the murder in 1897 of two German missionaries, had obtained a ninety-nine-year lease on the port of Kiao-chau and the recognition of Germany's special rights in the whole of Shantung peninsula; France under the terms of a similar lease occupied Kwangchau Bay far down on the southwestern coast; Russia, besides enjoying special privileges in northern Manchuria, had forced from China a twenty-five-year lease on Port Arthur.

All this was a matter of grave concern to the American government, not only because of America's new proximity to China, but also because the new order in the East threatened to destroy lucrative trade that had long existed between China and the United States. In consequence Secretary Hay, as early as September 6, 1899, addressed identical notes to Great Britain, Germany, and Russia, asking them to accept the principle of the "open door" to world trade in China.[1] Each power was invited (1) to respect the trading privileges and vested interests of other nations within its sphere of influence, (2) to allow the Chinese tariff to continue in force and to be collected by Chinese officials in all such spheres, and (3) to avoid discriminations against other foreigners in port dues and railroad rates. Similar notes were sent presently to France, Italy, and Japan. The only favorable reply came from Great Britain, to whom the open door was entirely satisfactory, since in free competition the British could easily hold their own against all newcomers. The other powers professed complete agreement with Hay's suggestions, but each avoided commitments on the ground that it must first know what the others intended to do. Thereupon, by a clever diplomatic

---

[1] Hay's work for the open door is best examined in Tyler Dennett, *John Hay* (1933), but W. R. Thayer, *The Life and Letters of John Hay* (2 vols., 1915), is well worth reading.

stroke, Hay pointed out that, inasmuch as all the powers had agreed to the principles he had enunciated, the United States would now consider them "final and definitive."

Hay's verbal victory for the open door made little difference to the nations bent on exploiting China, and the outbreak among the Chinese in the spring of 1900 of a violent anti-foreigner movement *The Boxer* seemed to play definitely into the exploiters' hands. Under *uprising* the leadership of a Chinese athletic society known as the Boxers, foreigners in China, whether traders, missionaries, or government agents, were subjected to the grossest indignities, and many of them killed. The Chinese government, which was dominated by a tradition-bound and utterly reactionary Empress Dowager, gave more or less open aid and sympathy to the Boxers, even designating the strongly pro-Boxer Prince Tuan as head of the Foreign Office. In Peking, the capital city, foreigners gathered at their embassies for protection, but there was good reason to fear that even the presence of several hundred legation guards might not suffice to hold the marauders in leash. On June 20, 1900, the German Minister ventured through the city streets to deliver an official protest, but was killed by a Chinese soldier in uniform. Thereupon the entire diplomatic corps took refuge in the British Embassy, and by converting it into a veritable fortress prepared to hold out until help should arrive. Military intervention now became a necessity, and informed observers generally took it for granted that the partition of China among the powers would be the inevitable result.

International negotiations in which the United States participated resulted in the sending of a joint expeditionary force of about twenty thousand men from Tientsin to Peking. During the second week of August, 1900, Japanese, Russian, British, American, and French detachments fought their way together to the Chinese capital through a region thickly infested with hostile Boxers. The decision of the United States to take part in the expedition did considerable violence to the American tradition against entangling alliances, but McKinley and Hay believed that only by pursuing such a course could they hope to prevent the dismemberment of China. The arrival of the international army on August 14 brought deliverance to the beleaguered legations.

Meantime Secretary Hay had taken occasion to state the objects of the expedition in terms that suited American policy. What the United States desired, he maintained, was not the partition of *Hay's* China, but a solution that would bring about permanent *diplomacy* safety and peace in the Orient, while at the same time preserving Chinese national integrity and the open door for world trade. In this policy the

British government expressed complete concurrence, and with its assistance Hay succeeded also in bringing Germany to his point of view. Finally an Anglo-German agreement not only endorsed Hay's principles, but also served notice on the other great powers that they might not take advantage of the existing situation to acquire Chinese territory or to establish new trade barriers. This announcement was received with some dismay by France and Russia, but they had no choice but to acquiesce. After extensive negotiations the powers agreed upon a set of twelve joint demands that required principally (1) the punishment of the chief offenders, (2) the settlement of all foreign claims by a money indemnity instead of by land cessions or special privileges, and (3) the adoption of adequate measures for the safety of foreigners in China.[1]

The indemnity required of China, $333,000,000 to be paid in thirty-nine annual installments, was large, but it would have been much larger *The Boxer* had not the United States made every effort to keep it down. *indemnity* The portion awarded to the United States was $24,440,700, but later investigation showed that the original estimates of American losses had been much too high. Accordingly Congress in 1908, on recommendation of President Roosevelt, reduced the obligation to approximately half its original size, and in 1924 remitted also an unpaid balance of $6,000,000. In appreciation of these friendly acts the Chinese government announced that it would devote the first remission to the education of Chinese students in the United States, and the second, to educational and scientific work in China. For many years Chinese students, supported by "Boxer indemnity" money, were a familiar sight on American campuses, and their absorption of western civilization deeply influenced the course of Chinese development. The handling of the indemnity matter, together with Hay's persistent efforts to preserve Chinese national integrity, caused the Chinese for a generation to regard the United States as a kind of moral, if not political, ally.

The withdrawal of the expeditionary forces from China was set for the fall of 1901, and was carried out according to agreement by all the nations except Russia, which maintained a special concentration in Manchuria with a view to exacting further favors from China. It thus became apparent that if the open door were to be kept open, something more effective than moral suasion would have to be used. Had American public opinion been willing to tolerate the idea, which definitely it was not, an Anglo-Japanese-American alliance might then have been formed to preserve the integrity of China and to maintain the open door. At the moment the three nations seemed to possess a community of inter-

[1] Tyler Dennett, *Americans in Eastern Asia* (1922).

ests. Both English and American trade in China was well established, and in free competition would continue to prosper. Japan, recently westernized, and eager to exploit the rich mineral resources and the enormous markets of China, counted on proximity as a sufficient aid to enable her to compete on equal terms with the western powers. It is barely possible that had the three nations joined hands they might have brought enough pressure to bear upon Russia, short of war, to force her to live up to the agreements she had signed. But the United States had no stomach either for alliances or for war, and Hay could only make futile protests and receive empty promises.

The Japanese, however, were determined that if any nation was to obtain special favors in China it must be Japan, and not Russia. Japanese students of western civilization had reached the conclu- *Japan's* sion that the enormous and growing population of Japan *ambitions* could be supported only by the rapid expansion of manufacturing. But Japan lacked the two greatest essentials for a manufacturing nation, coal and iron, both of which China possessed in abundance. Access to these commodities, as well as to Chinese markets for Japanese goods, the Russian advance might eventually block. With the Japanese "life-line" thus endangered, Japanese statesmen made deliberate plans for the expulsion of Russia from Manchuria. On January 30, 1902, Japan signed a treaty of alliance with Great Britain, which recognized the independence of Korea and China, and applied the open-door policy to both. It was further agreed between the two contracting powers that if either should be attacked in defense of its legitimate interests by a single nation, then the other party to the alliance would remain neutral; but if either should be attacked by more than one nation, then the other ally must come to its aid. One advantage of this alliance from the British point of view was that it would permit the withdrawal of British naval units from the Far East for concentration in European waters where the naval might of Germany was on the rise. The fundamental consideration so far as Japan was concerned was that the Japanese army might now drive the Russians out of Manchuria without fear of attack from any other power.

The Russo-Japanese War that broke out in 1904 was soon over. It was fought on Chinese soil, although China, strongly supported in this endeavor by the United States, succeeded in remaining *Russo-* neutral. Naturally American sympathy ran with Japan, *Japanese* for it was the Russians, rather than the Japanese, who had *War* most openly flouted the "open door." Roosevelt even went so far as to send a private warning to France and Germany that if either of them entered the war on the side of Russia he would bring the United States to the aid of Japan. When revolution at home and Japanese victories in the Far East made peace a necessity for the Russians, and financial exhaustion made it equally imperative for the Japanese, Roosevelt sought and obtained assurance from both belligerents that his services as mediator would be well received. Thereupon he officially offered mediation, was accepted, and in the summer of 1905 received the envoys of the warring nations in the United States. On September 5, 1905, a treaty of peace was signed at Portsmouth, New Hampshire, according to which both parties agreed to evacuate Manchuria, and Russia transferred its leases of Chinese ports and territories to Japan. To the intense regret of the Japanese, who desperately needed the money, Russia was not required to pay the six hundred million dollars indemnity the Japanese had demanded, although Japan did obtain, partly by way of compensation, the southern half of the island of Sakhalin. For his services to the cause of peace Roosevelt received the Nobel Peace Prize and the enthusiastic plaudits of his countrymen.[1]

Once the war was over, the friendly relations between Japan and the United States came to an abrupt end. Roosevelt's failure to back *Japan and* Japan's demand for an indemnity was deeply resented by *America* the Japanese, who believed that with his support they might have collected a huge sum. Japanese immigration into the United States, beginning about 1900, was another source of friction. By 1906 the number of Japanese resident in the Pacific states had reached about seventy-five thousand and they had begun to give native Americans strenuous competition as day laborers and market gardeners. They even bought land, and by swarming all over it broke down the land values of neighboring tracts, and then bought still more. Racial antagonism was easily stirred, and in 1906 the San Francisco school board decided on separate schools for Japanese children, a discrimination that was deeply resented in sensitive Japan. Roosevelt also deprecated the San Francisco school order, and used his influence to secure its modification. More important still, he obtained from the Japanese government a "gentlemen's agreement" whereby Japan herself undertook to terminate the flow of Japanese laborers to the United States. Since these emigrants were also present in Hawaii, Mexico, Canada, and the Canal Zone, and at least among the Hawaiian sugar producers were still desired, the Japanese government continued to grant passports to those

[1] A. W. Griswold, *The Far Eastern Policy of the United States* (1938), is an excellent recent summary, which may be supplemented by Tyler Dennett, *Roosevelt and the Russo-Japanese War* (1925), and P. J. Treat, *Diplomatic Relations Between the United States and Japan, 1895–1905* (2 vols., 1938).

territories, but offered no objection to an American prohibition against entrance of Japanese from any of these regions into the United States. The "gentlemen's agreement" sounded far better than it worked, and anti-Japanese feeling on the Pacific coast failed to subside.[1]

An even more serious menace to Japanese-American accord came from the policy Japan had adopted in the Far East. Left to fight alone on behalf of the open door, the Japanese now began to close the door in the face of the rest of the world. What the Japanese desired, it soon became apparent, was the gradual subjection of China's resources to Japan's necessities. Korea, long under Japanese domination, was openly annexed. This need not have surprised Roosevelt, for in 1905, during the peace negotiations, he had privately agreed to it in return for a similar recognition by the Japanese prime minister of American sovereignty over the Philippines. But Manchuria, too, seemed marked for exclusive exploitation by Japan, and how far the new policy would lead none could tell. Japanese apologists began presently to talk of a Monroe Doctrine for Asia, in which Japan would play the same rôle in the Far East that the United States played in America. But the Japanese Monroe Doctrine obviously involved a kind of economic overlordship that the United States had never asserted in the New World. As the Japanese plans unfolded, there was much loose talk of the "yellow peril." Would Japan eventually seek to take the Philippines? Many people in the United States, probably Theodore Roosevelt among them, believed that war with Japan was imminent, and in 1907, with the intention of either heading it off or else bringing it to a head, the President sent the American battle-fleet around the world.

The Root-Takahira Agreement of 1908, which was embodied in an exchange of notes between the American Secretary of State and the Japanese Ambassador to the United States, was a face- *Root-* saving device, designed primarily to prevent a conflict that *Takahira* neither nation wanted. According to this document (1) *Agreement* the two nations asserted a common desire to develop their commerce on the Pacific freely and peacefully; (2) they agreed to maintain "the existing *status quo*" in the Far East, including the open door in China; (3) they stood together in support of the independence and integrity of China; and (4) they promised, in the event of any threat to existing conditions, to consult with each other as to what measures they should take. This polite exchange said all that the United States could ask, but it was utterly unenforceable on Japan, as both governments knew.

[1] These problems are best treated in T. A. Bailey, *Theodore Roosevelt and the Japanese-American Crises* (1934).

The United States, without allies and unwilling to have them, was in reality powerless to defend either the open door or the integrity of China. While the American adventure into Far Eastern diplomacy was meeting with indifferent success, a gratifying record of triumphs was being established in the western hemisphere. Here the United States was close enough to the problems it attacked to have a better understanding of them, and it ordinarily had no such powerful antagonists to deal with as in the Orient. Furthermore, events soon proved that in all matters of consequence the United States could count with certainty on British support.

One of the results of the discovery of gold in the Klondike was a dispute with Canada over the boundaries of Alaska. Only two feasible *The Alaskan* routes to the gold-producing area existed, one by way of the *boundary* Yukon River, and the other across the Alaskan panhandle. *dispute* Distressed because both of these routes ran through American territory, Canadian officials began to examine old maps and treaties, and at length came out with a claim that the boundary line between Canada and the Alaskan panhandle had been incorrectly located, and should be shifted far to the west. The Treaty of 1825 between Great Britain and Russia, which originally fixed this boundary, provided that it was to follow the crest of the mountains parallel to the coast, but was never to be more than ten marine leagues from the shore-line, following its sinuosities. The Canadians claimed that the proper location of the shore-line was not, as had always been supposed, where sea-water left off, but rather along the farthest western reaches of the islands and promontories that skirted the coast. The boundary line could thus jump from peak to peak, giving Canada access to the Pacific at numerous points, particularly Dyea and Skagway, at the head of the trail to the Klondike. There was talk, even, of building a Canadian railroad to some far northern port.

The Canadian plan for a corridor across the Alaskan panhandle was fully presented by the British government, which at that time still represented Canada in foreign affairs. In 1898 an Anglo-American joint high commission sitting at Quebec failed to reach a decision, and the negotiations that followed were long and involved. Finally, in 1903, the United States agreed to a plan of settlement by which it stood no chance to lose. Three commissioners were to be appointed by each side, and decisions could be made only by a majority vote. In appointing the American commissioners, President Roosevelt took care that no one was chosen who might look with favor on the Canadian case, but the British government appointed only two members (both Cana-

THE ALASKAN BOUNDARY DISPUTE

dians) whose minds were already made up, and selected as the third representative Lord Alverstone, Chief Justice of England, who, to all intents and purposes, became sole arbiter. There is no reason to suppose that Lord Alverstone was instructed as to what course he should pursue, or that he needed to be so instructed. The Americans had the better case, and on every important point he so decided. The significant fact is that the British government, by appointing such a man as Alverstone, showed its willingness to see the United States win the decision, even at the cost of extreme resentment on the part of Canada.[1]

Meanwhile the Hay-Pauncefote treaties had presented even stronger evidence of British good-will. The long voyage of the *Oregon* around *The Hay-* Cape Horn, coupled with the acquisition of new possessions *Pauncefote* in the Philippines, had piled up irresistible sentiment in the *treaties* United States for the building of a strictly American interoceanic canal through some part of Central America. Since the terms of the Clayton-Bulwer Treaty still stood in the way, the Senate as early as 1898 asked the President to obtain the desired changes from Great Britain. Contrary to earlier experience, when the matter was broached to the British government no difficulties were encountered, and in 1900 the first Hay-Pauncefote Treaty was signed. This agreement, however, failed to go as far as American sentiment demanded. It provided that the United States might build the canal as an exclusively American project, but it assumed that the canal would remain unfortified and that its neutrality would be internationally guaranteed. As a result the treaty was amended to death in the United States Senate, and a new treaty had to be negotiated.

In the second Hay-Pauncefote Treaty the British government virtually permitted the United States to write its own terms. The Clayton-Bulwer Treaty, which before had been merely revised, was now abrogated, and a new treaty was written to replace it. By its terms the United States was permitted to acquire territory in Central America and to police the canal — a provision that the American government interpreted to mean the right of fortification. Nevertheless, the canal, while strictly American, was to be "free and open to the vessels of commerce and of war of all nations . . . on terms of entire equality," nor were there to be any discriminations "in respect of the conditions or charges of traffic." What the United States appeared to have gained was the right to build a neutral canal and to guarantee its neutrality, but the new treaty satisfied the Senate, which ratified it, as Hay said, "with no

[1] Considerable light is shed on this subject by Allan Nevins, *Henry White; Thirty Years of American Diplomacy* (1930).

DOMINION OF CANADA

Scale of Miles

0   100   200   300   400

opposition, except from the irreclaimable cranks. Seventy-two to six was near enough unanimity." [1]

The significance of this treaty was deeper than most Americans realized. The British government, in granting to the United States a free hand in building the canal, meant to indicate its belief that the friendship between the two nations was permanent and could never be broken. Had the United States been ready to seal the pact by an outright alliance, Great Britain would have been all too willing; as it was she withdrew her fleets from Caribbean waters, and left to the United States the protection of British interests in that region, just as she had turned over some of her Asiatic interests to the protection of Japan after the Anglo-Japanese alliance.[2] American observers felt certain that the United States had won a great diplomatic victory, but the assistance that Great Britain was able to obtain from America during the World War leaves in some doubt the question of which nation showed the greater diplomatic skill.

Anglo-American accord

With the way cleared for the building of the canal, the next question to demand an answer was where to build it. Two apparently feasible routes existed, one through the narrowest portion of the Isthmus of Panama, the other farther to the north through the Republic of Nicaragua. Both routes had strong adherents in the United States, and the task of choosing between them was not an easy one.

The Panama route had been tried before. In the late seventies Ferdinand de Lesseps, the French builder of the Suez Canal, had organized a company for the purpose, and with his previous record of success as a talking point had induced European investors to stake large sums on the project. De Lesseps also hoped to sell stock in the United States, but the insistence of President Hayes that American policy called for a strictly American canal closed the American market to his blandishments. On faith and without sufficient funds he nevertheless went ahead, obtained a concession from the State of Colombia, bought the Panama Railroad, and in 1882 began operations. By 1889 his company was bankrupt and the work of excavation had ceased. Five years later the New Panama Canal Company was formed, ostensibly to finish the canal, but actually to sell out to the United States. The company claimed that the total capital invested in Panama had reached $260,000,000, but about the only thing of value it possessed was its franchise from Colombia, which would not expire until 1904.

The Nicaraguan route was longer, but because advantage could be

[1] Mary W. Williams, *Anglo-American Isthmian Diplomacy, 1815–1915* (1916).
[2] J. H. Latané, *From Isolation to Leadership* (new edition, 1923), p. 121.

taken of Lake Nicaragua and the river which connected it with the
The Isth- Atlantic, many believed that it was more practicable than
mian Canal the shorter, isthmian route. In 1890 an American company,
Commission in which Frederick Billings, builder of the Northern Pacific,
was deeply involved, had begun work in Nicaragua, but after an expenditure of about six million dollars it, too, had gone bankrupt. The
Nicaraguan route nevertheless strongly appealed to Americans, and the
Isthmian Canal Commission, appointed by President McKinley in 1901
to assess the merits of the two routes, reported in its favor. Part of
the reason for this decision was the price of one hundred million dollars
that the New Panama Canal Company wanted for its property and
rights. Forty million dollars, according to the committee, would have
been enough. In accordance with the committee's recommendation,
the House of Representatives passed a bill in 1902 which provided for
the construction of the canal through Nicaragua.

Powerful forces were at work, however, in favor of the Panama route.
They included President Roosevelt, who believed, quite mistakenly as
it turned out, that a sea-level canal could be constructed through
Panama, whereas locks would be a certainty through Nicaragua. They
included also Marcus A. Hanna, who had obtained a contribution of
sixty thousand dollars to the Republican campaign chest in 1900 from
the New Panama Canal Company. Most important of all, they included a resourceful Frenchman, Philippe Bunau-Varilla, leading light
in the New Panama Canal Company, who shuttled back and forth
between Paris and Washington, and his New York lawyer, William
Nelson Cromwell, who presently collected for his services a fee of
eight hundred thousand dollars. Altogether this array of talent proved
too formidable for the Nicaraguan advocates, and on condition that the
New Panama Canal Company should reduce its charges to forty million
dollars the Senate was persuaded to substitute Panama for Nicaragua in
the bill before it. Talk that some senators had hopefully invested along
the Nicaraguan route, supplemented by the timely eruption of Mount
Monotombo, Nicaragua's active volcano, played more or less important
parts in the proceedings. Bunau-Varilla thoughtfully provided for each
senator a Nicaraguan postage stamp on which the volcano was pictured
in full eruption. Finally the House concurred in the Senate's decision,
and the Panama route was officially adopted. Long before this the
New Panama Canal Company had reconciled itself to forty million
dollars as far better than nothing.

It was still necessary for the United States to negotiate a treaty with
Colombia, for the American plan contemplated real or virtual land-

ownership, not merely a permit to build. Secretary Hay, using the threat of the Nicaraguan alternative, drove a sharp bargain with Tomas Herran, the Colombian Representative at Washington. The United States would pay ten million dollars down *Negotiations with Colombia* and an annual quit-rent of two hundred and fifty thousand dollars for control over a strip of land six miles wide from Panama to Colón, but exclusive of those cities. That was all. Furthermore, it was specifically stated that Colombia might not negotiate with the New Panama Canal Company to obtain a portion of the forty million dollars it was to receive from the United States. The United States Senate promptly ratified the treaty, but the Colombian government, which resented both the terms and the manner in which they had been imposed, refused to ratify. No doubt the fact that the New Panama Canal Company's franchise had only a short time to run also entered the Colombian calculations. Once it lapsed, the Colombian government rather than the French stockholders, would be legally entitled to that payment also. As Roosevelt phrased it in a letter to Hay, "They are mad to get hold of the forty million dollars of the Frenchmen."

Just why it should have been a matter of so great concern to Roosevelt whether some unidentified "Frenchman" or Colombia got the money the United States stood ready to pay is not entirely clear. Perhaps the President's insistent desire for haste in getting the work under way was the controlling factor. At any rate he refused to bargain further with Colombia, and privately — but not too privately — admitted that he would "be delighted if Panama were an independent state; or if it made itself so at this moment." The secession of Panama, which had never been overloyal to Colombia and was naturally eager for the canal, had been in Bunau-Varilla's mind all along as a possible way out. Ably assisted by Cromwell, he now showed the liveliest interest in Panama's independence. A future President of Panama was found in the person of Doctor Manuel Amador, a physician employed by the Panama Railroad and Steamship Company, which was owned by the New Panama Canal Company. Amador came to the United States for a conference with Bunau-Varilla, and returned with a constitution for the Republic of Panama, a proclamation of independence, a message to be sent back to Bunau-Varilla asking him, although a French citizen, to become the first Minister from Panama to the United States, and one hundred thousand dollars in cash for preliminary expenses.

Meantime Roosevelt had discovered a treaty of 1846 between the United States and New Granada (which became Colombia in 1863), by which the United States was bound to protect "the right of way or transit across the Isthmus of Panama." To make sure that revolutionary disturbances — should there be a revolution — would not interrupt transit across the isthmus, Roosevelt ordered American naval units to the vicinity of Panama, and instructed them to "prevent the landing of any armed force with hostile intent, either government or insurgent." Since the only possible route by which Colombia could bring troops to Panama was by sea, and since Doctor Amador had bribed those who were already there, the revolution took place on November 3, 1903, without the usual accompaniment of violence and bloodshed. A Colombian gunboat that inconsiderately began next day to drop shells upon the city of Panama was ordered by the American naval commander to desist, and did so. On November 6, at 11.35 A.M. Roosevelt received official word to the effect that the revolution in Panama had been completely successful. On the same day, at 12.31 P.M., Secretary Hay accorded diplomatic recognition to the new republic. "I took Panama," Roosevelt is said to have boasted later, but this statement hardly gives full credit to Bunau-Varilla and Cromwell.

Secession of Panama

With Colombia out of the way and Bunau-Varilla representing Panama, a new treaty, the Hay-Bunau-Varilla Treaty, quickly cleared the way for the beginning of canal construction. The United States was permitted to acquire a zone five miles wide on each side of the canal "as if she were sovereign," and to fortify it at will. Panama was to receive an initial payment of ten million dollars, and two hundred and fifty thousand dollars per year, beginning nine years after date. The independence of Panama was guaranteed by the United States, but the principles of the Platt Amendment, including the right of intervention, were applied to the new republic. Between 1846 and 1903 Panama had been the scene of no less than fifty-three insurrectionary outbursts. There have been none since.[1]

Colombia's deep resentment at the way it had been treated soon became a matter of real concern to the United States. Not only Colombia, but other Latin-American nations, also, saw in Roosevelt's action a precedent that might be used for other imperialistic ventures at their expense. To alleviate the tension, Secretary Root proposed in 1909 a series of three treaties, between the United States and Panama, the United States and Colombia, and Panama and Colombia. By their terms the first ten installments of the two hundred and fifty thousand dollars quit-rent would have been

Colombian resentment

---

[1] The best general treatment of this subject is H. C. Hill, *Roosevelt and the Caribbean* (1927), but see also E. T. Parks, *Colombia and the United States, 1765–1934* (1935); J. F. Rippy, *The Capitalists and Colombia* (1931); W. D. McCain, *The United States and the Republic of Panama* (1937).

assigned to Colombia. But Colombia would have nothing to do with the suggestion. While Taft was President another effort at appeasement was made. Would Colombia accept ten million dollars for a coaling station and any other canal route that might be available through her territory? Colombia would not. Even when the United States suggested informally that the sum might be raised to twenty-five million dollars, Colombia remained obdurate and asked for arbitration, something the United States dare not risk. During Wilson's administration Secretary Bryan negotiated a treaty with Colombia which expressed regrets for what the United States had done, and offered twenty-five million dollars by way of compensation. This proposal, which Colombia was ready to accept, was rejected by the United States Senate, in which sat many of Roosevelt's loyal friends. After Roosevelt's death, with Harding as President, a treaty very similar to the one Bryan had proposed, but with the "regrets" clause somewhat toned down, was ratified by both nations. By that time the fear that European syndicates would be able to monopolize the rich oil resources of Colombia to the exclusion of American firms made the purchase of Colombian good-will a necessity.

The actual building of the canal was an engineering feat of extraordinary magnitude. The impracticability of a sea-level canal was soon discovered and a lock canal, which would cost less to build *Building* both in time and in money, was decided upon. At first sani- *the canal* tation threatened to be an even greater problem than excavation, but the work of Colonel W. C. Gorgas in making the canal zone a fit place in which to live was so well done that trouble from that source was soon practically eliminated. Administrative difficulties arising from the fact that Congress insisted on delegating the control of operations to a commission instead of to an individual hampered work for a while, but Roosevelt at length made Major George W. Goethals, an army engineer, chairman of the commission, and extracted a promise from all other members of the commission never to disagree with the chairman. After that the work proceeded satisfactorily, and on August 15, 1914, the first ocean steamer passed through the canal. The cost of building it ran to $275,000,000, which the government raised by floating bonds, together with another $113,000,000 for fortifications; but receipts during the first fifteen years of operation brought in large enough net earnings to meet in full the interest on the bonds floated. Roosevelt always considered the building of the Panama Canal the greatest achievement of his administration.[1]

[1] J. B. and Farnham Bishop, *Goethals, Genius of the Panama Canal* (1930); M. D. Gorgas and B. J. Hendrick, *William Crawford Gorgas, his Life and Work* (1924).

In 1912 Congress, looking forward to the opening of the canal, passed a law exempting American coastwise shipping from the payment of tolls. *The tolls controversy* This law was signed by President Taft, who was certainly a good lawyer, but was immediately protested by Great Britain on the ground that the tolls exemption violated that clause of the Hay-Pauncefote Treaty which opened the canal to the vessels of "all nations" on terms of "entire equality." The British government offered no objection to the United States returning tolls to American shippers as rebates or subsidies; what it did object to was the prospect that with the exemption in force the rates would be so set as to require foreign shipping to pay the entire cost and upkeep of the canal. American railroad interests, who foresaw the diversion of much transcontinental traffic from the railroads to the new sea route, also had legitimate grounds for complaint, but Congress let the law stand until June, 1914, when President Wilson successfully insisted on its repeal. Although the President at the time stated no other reason for demanding repeal than that diplomatic negotiations of a very delicate nature were involved, it came out later that this was the price he paid to obtain British support for his policy in Mexico.

Before he became President, and with his thoughts on the New York Republican machine, Roosevelt had once quoted an old adage: "Speak *The "Big Stick" policy* softly and carry a big stick, and you will go far." Later this statement was resurrected and fittingly applied to his policy in Latin America. Backed by the new American navy, Roosevelt prepared to enforce the Monroe Doctrine with aggressive determination; some said that he even intended to use it as a cloak for further imperialistic ventures. Certainly he kept persistently in mind the fact that the Panama Canal must be defended at all costs. Because of the canal events in Latin America that in an earlier age might have passed unnoticed now became matters of grave concern.

The Venezuelan incident of 1902 offered the first occasion for the use of the "big stick." The State of Venezuela, which bordered on the Caribbean Sea adjacent to the proposed canal, was in trouble with Great Britain, Germany, and other European nations because of the non-payment of debts owing their citizens. There was a legitimate difference of opinion as to the amounts due, for in some cases no such sums had ever been delivered as were claimed. But the Venezuelan dictator, Cipriano Castro, was a contemptible creature who seemingly had no intention of paying anything if he could avoid it. Finally Great Britain and Germany, mildly supported by Italy, withdrew their legations from Caracas, blockaded five Venezuelan ports, and even seized Venezuelan gunboats. A British bombardment of Puerto Cabello, in return for an alleged insult to the British flag, finally brought Castro to his senses, and he agreed to arbitration, something he had spurned when it had been offered him by Germany the year before. This offer was transmitted by the United States "without comment" to London and Berlin, and was accepted. .The Hague Tribunal finally settled the case, reducing the claims of foreigners against the Venezuelan government from forty million to eight million dollars.

Throughout these proceedings the United States offered no official protest, and accepted seemingly in good faith the assurances of Great Britain and Germany that they meant no violation of the Monroe Doctrine. Aside from transmitting Castro's offer of arbitration, the American government had merely expressed its hope that a peaceful solution could be reached, and had recommended arbitration. It seems evident, however, that certain activities not recorded in the official documents took place behind the scenes. No doubt Roosevelt's version of these events, written in 1916 when he had become an ardent advocate of American entrance into the World War, was exaggerated and inaccurate. He claimed then that Germany, hoping to seize and fortify some Venezuelan harbor, had declined to arbitrate. Only when threatened with Admiral Dewey's fleet, which was assembled near Puerto Rico for maneuvers, was withdrawal and arbitration accomplished. There is other evidence besides his own to prove that Roosevelt had some dramatic interviews with the German Ambassador during this episode, and that he warned Dewey to keep his fleet ready for action. Exactly what happened may never be known, but it is difficult to believe that his version was wholly imagined.

Whatever the truth of this matter, Roosevelt soon reached the conclusion that the United States must itself be prepared to intervene in Latin-American affairs if it wished to be sure of keeping *The Drago* other nations out. In 1902, while the Venezuelan crisis *doctrine* was on, the Argentinian Foreign Minister, Luis M. Drago, expressed the opinion that "the public debt cannot occasion armed intervention nor even the actual occupation of the territory of American nations by a European power." This doctrine had never been maintained by the United States, but its possibilities interested Roosevelt, who soon went ahead to elaborate it in a way Drago had certainly never intended.[1] The Dominican Republic, which occupied the eastern half of the island of Santo Domingo closely adjacent to Cuba, was deeply in debt to

---

[1] The Drago doctrine was later endorsed by the second Hague Conference. See *post*, pp. 377–78.

European creditors, and was in a state of chronic revolution. Fearful that European intervention — probably by Germany, whose motives Roosevelt most mistrusted — might lead to occupation, and eventually, as with the British in Egypt, to virtual possession, Roosevelt as early as May 20, 1904, announced what came to be known as the "Roosevelt corollary" of the Monroe Doctrine. Restated to Congress in December of the same year, it left the world in no doubt whatever as to the meaning of the "big stick" policy:

> If a nation shows that it knows how to act with reasonable efficiency and decency in social and political matters, if it keeps order and pays its obligations, it need fear no interference from the United States. Chronic wrongdoing, or an impotence which results in a general loosening of the ties of civilized society may in America, as elsewhere, ultimately require intervention by some civilized nation, and in the Western Hemisphere the adherence of the United States to the Monroe Doctrine may force the United States, however reluctantly, in flagrant cases of such wrongdoing or impotence, to the exercise of an international police power.

Roosevelt's interpretation of the Monroe Doctrine, as events proved, was applied with rigor only in the Caribbean zone, which guarded the *Caribbean control* eastern approaches to the Panama Canal. Here it supplemented and assisted the defense policy of the United States which maintained that the Caribbean Sea must become as strictly as possible an American lake. Property rights acquired by the United States on the borders of the Caribbean included: (1) Puerto Rico, annexed at the close of the Spanish-American War; (2) the Canal Zone, obtained on terms practically equivalent to annexation; (3) the Virgin Islands, purchased from Denmark in 1916 for twenty-five million dollars, a price utterly out of proportion to their economic value; (4) convenient sites for naval bases at Guantanamo in eastern Cuba, on the Corn Islands off Nicaragua, and elsewhere; and (5) a concession from Nicaragua giving the United States the sole right of constructing a canal through her territory. Cuba and Panama, thanks to the principles of the Platt Amendment, were virtual protectorates of the United States, while the application of the Roosevelt corollary eventually brought Santo Domingo, Haiti, and Nicaragua quite as completely within the American orbit. Other territory in the Caribbean Zone was either in the hands of friendly European nations who made no effort to match the strength of the United States in the region, or of independent Latin-American nations whose conduct was tempered by fear of the "big stick." [1]

[1] Later Caribbean policy can be followed in J. F. Rippy, *Latin America in World Politics* (new edition, 1938); C. L. Jones, *Caribbean Interests of the United States* (1916); C. L. Jones, *The Caribbean Since 1900* (1936); C. L. Jones, *The United States and the Caribbean* (1929).

Affairs in the Dominican Republic, whose government had been appropriately described as "tyranny tempered by assassination," were in such a state by 1904 that Roosevelt deemed American *The Domini-* intervention a necessity. The national debt of the little *can Republic* republic had reached $32,280,000, mostly owing to European creditors. Graft and inefficiency, together with the steady procession of insurrections, had paralyzed the collection of revenues. Pressure from European nations was mounting ominously. Finally the Dominican government, not without a certain amount of diplomatic preparation, asked the United States to take over the administration of its revenues. In 1905 a treaty was negotiated between the two nations, whereby the United States was to establish a kind of receivership for its bankrupt neighbor, to collect its revenues, and to apply fifty-five per cent of the receipts to the liquidation of outstanding obligations. Although American warships had already begun to patrol Dominican waters, and American marines had been landed in Santo Domingo, the United States Senate refused to accept the treaty. Roosevelt, undeterred by this rebuff, induced the Dominican authorities to accept his nominee for collector of customs, and to permit the deposit in a New York bank of all sums not actually needed to carry on the government. European creditors, pleased with the arrangement, agreed to reduce their claims to seventeen million dollars. Two years later the Senate, appeased by some minor modifications of the original treaty, approved the deal, and Roosevelt's extra-legal policy became official. By means of it Roosevelt claimed to have "put the affairs of the island on a better basis than they had been for a century."

Subsequent Presidents made even more complete use of the Roosevelt corollary than did Roosevelt himself. Wilson, although opposed to Roosevelt in politics, used it in 1916 when the Dominican Republic, again plagued by revolutions, threatened to ignore the Treaty of 1907. There could not then have been danger of European intervention, for the World War was on, but there was such an abundance of "chronic wrongdoing" that Wilson suspended the Dominican government altogether, and turned over the administration of the republic's affairs to American naval officers, supported by the marines. The efficiency of the American occupation was attested by the building of good roads, the improvement of sanitation, the promotion of education, the rehabilitation of government finances, and the ruthless suppression of all efforts of the Dominicans to regain their liberties. By 1924, however, this complete denial of the "right of self-determination" that Wilson had so strongly urged in Paris had aroused opposition both within the United

States and throughout Latin America, the importance of whose good-will the United States was at last beginning to appreciate. A local Dominican government was therefore established, and the American military occupation was brought to a close. American control of the customs remained.

Haiti, the Negro Republic that occupied the western half of the island of Santo Domingo, had almost an identical experience with the United States. Overwhelmed by its debts, it was offered *Haiti* in 1914 the same type of financial receivership that Roosevelt had negotiated with the Dominican Republic nearly ten years before. This offer it chose to reject, but when serious rioting broke out in 1915, the United States landed marines at Port-au-Prince, restored order, and forced on the Haitian government the treaty it had previously refused. The treaty was to run for ten years, and for an additional ten years if the United States so desired. American officers, backed by American marines and a native constabulary, soon supplanted the Haitian authorities in the discharge of their duties; and from 1922 to 1930 the Haitian government was entirely suspended, with an American high commissioner in charge. The same forces that led to American withdrawal from the Dominican Republic operated also with reference to Haiti, and in 1930 President Hoover announced plans for the termination in 1936 of American intervention.

While Taft was President an abortive attempt was made to apply the Roosevelt corollary in two Central American republics, Honduras and Nicaragua. Agreements patterned on the Dominican model were negotiated, but failed of ratification. In Nicaragua, however, marines were landed in 1912 to keep order, and they stayed on until 1925. Without benefit of treaty, the United States policed the country, turned its financial affairs over to an American collector, and put its government on a dole. In 1914 the Bryan-Chamorro Treaty regularized what was going on, and for three million dollars the United States obtained an exclusive right to build an interoceanic canal across Nicaragua, together with appropriate leases for naval bases. In 1925 the American troops were ordered out, but a revolution the following year brought them back again. This time they stayed until 1932.

The charge has often been made that the purpose of American inter-vention in the Caribbean Zone was primarily to promote the develop-*"Dollar diplomacy"* ment of American financial interests in that area. It is demonstrable that a great increase in American investments and a somewhat more modest increase in American trade have followed in the wake of governmental policy, but it is hard to believe that either

Roosevelt or any of his successors were seeking merely to open new fields for American enterprise. Undoubtedly the objectives they had most in mind were the defense of the Panama Canal, the protection of American lives and property already in the troubled areas, and the abatement of governmental nuisances that threatened to become international scandals.

The active participation of the United States in world affairs after the Spanish-American War led many thoughtful Americans to wonder if their nation in its new rôle could hope to escape involvements that would lead to war. With possessions as far away as the Philippines and with interests in every part of the globe, the very idea of American isolation seemed a contradiction. How then could peace be maintained? It did not require much logic to deduce that the surest way to keep the United States out of war was to keep war out of the world, and a strong movement for world peace set in.

When in 1899 the Czar of Russia invited the nations having diplomatic representatives in St. Petersburg to participate in a conference on disarmament at The Hague, the United States sent an impos- *The first* ing delegation and took an active part in the proceedings. *Hague* It soon appeared that nothing could be done on the subject *Conference* for which the conference was called, but there was much discussion of methods for avoiding resort to war. Before adjourning, the conference recommended three means for settling disputes without resort to war: (1) through good offices and mediation, which, when offered by a third party to powers at war or about to go to war, must not be considered an unfriendly act; (2) through international commissions of inquiry, for which so many precedents existed, particularly in the relations between Great Britain and the United States; and (3) through submission to a new court of arbitration to be established at The Hague. To this tribunal each member nation might name as many as four qualified judges, and from the list so obtained nations desiring to arbitrate a given case might pick as many or as few judges as they saw fit. They might define, too, the powers of the arbitrators, but they must consider themselves bound to submit in good faith to the award.

The recommendations of the Hague Conference were accepted by every participating power except Turkey, but in no nation with greater enthusiasm than in the United States. Roosevelt promptly hunted up an old and somewhat unimportant controversy with Mexico, the Pious Fund Case, for submission to the Hague Tribunal — its first case. The finding of the Court was promptly accepted by both nations. The dispute that had led to the Venezuelan incident of 1902 was also settled by the Court, to the great satisfaction of Americans, particularly Roosevelt, who had recommended such a course. A few years later Roosevelt made use of the newly proffered freedom to offer mediation in bringing the Russo-Japanese War to a close.

Keyed up to the idea that the United States must play an important part in the preservation of world peace, Roosevelt involved his country deeply in European affairs when he took a stronger part than his knowledge of the facts warranted in the settlement of the Moroccan crisis of 1905–06. He had a low opinion of the Moroccan government, based perhaps on the fact that Raisuli, a Moroccan brigand, had been able, on May 18, 1904, to kidnap an American citizen named Perdicaris in the outskirts of Tangier. A ringing message from the American State Department, "Perdicaris alive or Raisuli dead," got results that might have been achieved less dramatically had 1904 not been an election year. Perdicaris was promptly released. A month before this incident occurred, Great Britain and France had signed a notable agreement whereby Great Britain obtained a free hand in Egypt and France in Morocco. Secret articles, of which Roosevelt knew nothing, provided also for the eventual partition of Morocco between France and Spain, while Italy's consent to the bargain was purchased by granting the Italian government full freedom of action in Tripoli. The German Kaiser, convinced that a policy of "encirclement" was about to exclude Germany from another market, showed his displeasure by a visit to the Sultan in March, 1905, "to make it known that I am determined to do all in my power to safeguard efficaciously the interests of Germany in Morocco."

On the ground that another open door to world trade was about to be closed, the Kaiser asked Roosevelt to use his influence in favor of an *The Algeciras Conference* international conference to settle the Moroccan question. Roosevelt, believing that "France was right on this issue," hesitated to interfere, but finally urged the French government to adopt a "course which would save the Emperor's self-esteem." At the instigation of the Sultan, who willingly did the Kaiser's bidding, a conference, to be held at Algeciras early in 1906, was arranged, and the United States agreed to send delegates. More important still, Roosevelt and his Secretary of State, Root, helped devise the formula for peace which the conference eventually adopted. According to its terms the nations were to respect Morocco's territorial integrity and to guarantee the open door for world trade within its borders. Moroccan finances were to be stabilized by the establishment of an international bank, and most significant of all, order was to be kept by a native police force *jointly supervised by France and Spain.* Heavy pressure was required to bring the Kaiser to accept these terms, and Roosevelt, although he knew full well that he was taking the United States far outside the isolationist rôle, did his share in applying it.[1]

The American delegates in signing the Algeciras Convention stated expressly that the United States assumed no responsibility for the enforcement of its provisions, while the United States Senate, which gave its approval only after prolonged debate, was even more cautious. The part played by the United States in the conference, so the Senate said, was merely for the protection of American lives and property, and entirely "without purpose to depart from the traditional American foreign policy which forbids participation by the United States in the settlement of political questions which are entirely European in their scope." Had the Senate known how thoroughly the American President had violated this rule, it would hardly have ratified at all. Whether Roosevelt's diplomacy did his country any real service or not may well be questioned. He had helped to cement more closely the Anglo-French Entente, and by assisting Great Britain and France to score a victory over Germany he had done little to allay the Kaiser's fears. But undoubtedly his motive had been to preserve world peace.

At a second Hague Conference, held in 1907, the United States made strenuous efforts to commit the nations of the world even more completely to the settlement of their disputes by peaceful means. *The second Hague Conference* The American delegation, headed by Joseph H. Choate, was under instructions to work for the creation of an international court of justice, comparable to the United States Supreme Court, to which cases could be referred for a legal opinion rather than for arbitration. It was well understood that the Hague Tribunal, or any other court of arbitration, must decide cases before it more with a view to their acceptance than to the justice of the decision. The world court proposed by the United States, however, was to be a permanent affair, consisting of fifteen judges who should be guided solely by the law and the precedents. This suggestion failed of adoption partly because only the American delegation had full instructions on the subject, but more because no agreement could be reached on the manner in which judges should be chosen. The great powers insisted that they should each have representatives in the court at all times, and the lesser powers wanted the same privilege. This would have meant forty-four judges. The American suggestion that the problem might be solved by adopting

[1] Alfred Vagts, *Deutschland und die Vereinigten Staaten in der Weltpolitik* (1935), contains an excellent account, but Dennis, *Adventures in American Diplomacy*, and Nevins, *Henry White*, may also be profitably consulted.

the principle of rotation met with little favor, and the project was dropped.

The second Hague Conference spent much of its time in discussing the laws of war, and ultimately submitted its conclusions on many disputed points to the nations of the world for ratification. Although the United States accepted the new regulations in full, other nations either failed to ratify altogether, or else made so many reservations that the Hague conventions could not be regarded as binding upon any power except by its express consent. A supplementary naval conference, held in London the following year, made a similar effort to codify the law of naval warfare. The Declaration of London, which it adopted, also failed of complete ratification. In Great Britain, the most powerful of the naval powers, and the one, therefore, whose approval was most essential, it was defeated by the House of Lords. These two attempts to agree upon what was lawful in time of war were not altogether barren of meaning. They registered in general the progress of world thought on the subject, and nations that observed the new rules had less to apologize for than those that did not.[1]

The second Hague Conference made one really important contribution to the cause of world peace. It proposed a model arbitration treaty, known also as the mondel or world treaty, for all the nations of the world to follow in negotiating treaties with each other. According to this treaty, all disputes must be submitted to the Hague Tribunal for settlement unless they affected the vital interests, the independence, or the honor of the contracting nations.

By this time, as if in premonition of the desperate conflict soon to come, the United States was more engrossed than ever before with the *The peace* idea of world peace. Andrew Carnegie, the ex-steel mag-*movement* nate turned philanthropist, provided an elaborate Peace Palace at The Hague for the use of the Hague Tribunal, and in 1911 established the Carnegie Endowment for International Peace, with ten million dollars to spend for the promotion of the cause. The year before, Edward Ginn, a Boston publisher, had started off the World Peace Foundation on a similar mission with a million-dollar endowment. Successive American Secretaries of State, Hay, Root, Knox, and Bryan, strove earnestly to negotiate treaties of arbitration that would run the gantlet of the United States Senate, which in defense of its prerogatives furnished more opposition than came from outside nations. Under Hay and Root about twenty such treaties were negotiated, and finally rati-

[1] W. I. Hull, *The Two Hague Conferences and their Contributions to International Law* (1908); J. B. Scott, *The Hague Peace Conferences of 1899 and 1907* (2 vols., 1909).

fied on condition that each special agreement made for the settlement of a dispute must also be submitted for the approval of the Senate. President Taft was earnestly devoted to the cause of world peace, and with his backing Secretary Knox negotiated two treaties, with Great Britain and France respectively, that provided for the arbitration of all "justiciable" questions — nearly universal arbitration; but the Senate amended them to death. Secretary Bryan, who had spoken to Chautauqua audiences all over the country on the subject of peace, believed that his appointment was a direct invitation to further the cause. More successful than any of his predecessors, he obtained the ratification of no less than thirty arbitration treaties, most of them based on what newspaper men called the "twenty minutes before you spank" principle. Bryan believed that war, if postponed until the period of acute tension had ended, could be averted. His treaties provided for the arbitration by international commissions of all disputes "of whatever character and nature." While the arbitration proceedings were in progress, the participating nations might neither increase their armament nor resort to war. It is worthy of note that by 1914 Bryan had obtained treaties of this nature with every one of the European nations allied against Germany in the World War, while Germany, Austria, and Turkey had rejected his proposals.[1]

[1] Merle Curti, *Bryan and World Peace* (1931).
On inter-American problems, see J. Fred Rippy, *The Caribbean Danger Zone* (1940), an excellent interpretation of the roots of American policy in this region; also, W. H. Callcott, *The Caribbean Policy of the United States, 1890–1920* (1942). Miles P. DuVal, Jr., *And the Mountains Will Move* (1947), is the story of the building of the Panama Canal. N. J. Padelford, *The Panama Canal in Peace and War* (1942), makes clear the importance of the Canal in American war strategy.
On Canada and the United States, see Charles Callen Tansill, *Canadian-American Relations, 1875–1911* (1943); Lester Burrell Shippee, *Canadian-American Relations, 1849–1874* (1939); P. E. Corbett, *The Settlement of Canadian-American Disputes* (1937).
On the Far East, A. L. P. Dennis, *The Anglo-Japanese Alliance* (1923); M. J. Pao, *The Open Door Doctrine in Relation to China* (1923); Rodman W. Paul, *The Abrogation of the Gentlemen's Agreement* (1936).
Miscellaneous: Gordon C. O'Gara, *Theodore Roosevelt and The Rise of The Modern Navy* (1943); R. H. Heindel, *The American Impact on Great Britain, 1898–1914* (1940), a successful effort to show the influence of American thought abroad; Joseph Schafer, ed., *Memoirs of Jeremiah Curtain* (1940), includes an American view of Tsarist Russia.

"MY POLICIES"

THE aggressive leadership that characterized Roosevelt's handling of foreign affairs was equally evident in the development of his domestic *Roosevelt's* policies. No lawyer, Roosevelt was unimpressed by the *interpreta-* traditional allocation of separate powers to the executive, *tion of the* the legislature, and the judiciary. The President, as the *Presidency* head of the government, was in his judgment meant to lead. If laws were needed to accomplish a purpose that the President deemed useful, then it was his duty to see that the laws were passed. If Congress proved refractory, then the President must use his power and prestige to force it to act. If the courts put obstacles in the way of presidential policies, then the President must have a care to the appointment of more reasonable judges. The Constitution, he later maintained, "must be interpreted, not as a straight-jacket, not as laying the hand of death upon our development, but as an instrument designed for the life and healthy growth of the Nation." The length to which the Constitution might be stretched, so far as Roosevelt was concerned, was shown in his contention that the President might do anything not expressly forbidden by its terms. Facetious critics even attributed to him sympathy with the statement attributed to a favor-seeker, "What's the Constitution between friends?" [1]

Economics was definitely not Roosevelt's principal forte, but he would have been blind indeed if he had not recognized in the emergence of "big business" a problem of fundamental importance to his adminis-tration. By the beginning of the twentieth century "rugged individual-ism" had run riot in the United States. In one industry after another great corporations, successfully claiming the rights of persons before the law, had grown to monopolistic proportions. The total capital of million-

[1] On Roosevelt's domestic policies, see, in addition to the *Autobiography* and Pringle's *Roosevelt*, three excellent general accounts, D. L. Dumond, *America in Our Time: 1896–1946* (1947); Harvey Wish, *Contemporary America: The National Scene Since 1900* (1945); and O. T. Barck, Jr., and N. M. Blake, *Since 1900* (1947).

dollar corporations had increased from $170,000,000 in 1897 to $5,000,·000,000 in 1900, and to $20,500,000,000 in 1904. Railway mergers, such as the one by which E. H. Harriman brought the Union Pacific and the Southern Pacific together in 1900, had become the order of the day. Concentration in industry was effected both by means of "horizontal" combinations, through which several industries of the same kind were united, and by means of "vertical" combinations, through which businesses of allied interests joined forces.

Typical of the "vertical" combinations, or the "integrated" industries, as they were also called, was the United States Steel Corporation, which the financial genius of J. P. Morgan helped knit *Integration* together in 1901. This was the first of America's "billion- *in industry* dollar" corporations; at the beginning of its second year, in April, 1902, its capital stock amounted to $1,384,681,297. It included as a nucleus the Carnegie Steel Company, which in 1900 had alone made profits of $40,000,000, and in addition six or seven other leading steel producers. But the interests of the new corporation went far beyond the mere manufacture of steel. It came to own and operate the iron and coal mines which contributed its original sources of supply. It controlled the railroads that connected with its coal mines, and the steamers on the Great Lakes that brought the iron ore from the mines of northern Minnesota and Michigan. It had its own smelting furnaces to make pig iron, its blast furnaces for the production of steel, and its foundries and rolling mills for the manufacture of machinery, steel rails, armor plate, and other steel commodities. From mine to market every process was completed within the control of this one gigantic corporation.[1]

What happened to steel happened in greater or less degree to tobacco, petroleum, sugar, copper, beef, starch, flour, whiskey, chewing gum, farm implements, and innumerable other commodities. These enormous industries, still called "trusts" in popular parlance, either achieved or closely approached monopoly, and because the public was determined to have what they produced, acquired virtually the privilege of private taxation. To their prosperity nearly every citizen must contribute. Sometimes, because of a high protective tariff, they were able to keep out foreign competition, and to increase correspondingly the toll that the American public had to pay. Among them a close community of interest existed, well symbolized by the interlocking nature of their boards of directors on which the same names appeared again and again. Since

---

[1] Ida M. Tarbell, *The Life of Elbert H. Gary: the Story of Steel* (1925), is surprisingly friendly to the United States Steel Corporation. See also H. L. Wilgus, *The United States Steel Corporation in Its Industrial and Legal Aspects* (1901).

most of the great combinations were arranged by financiers, a few great banking firms, notably J. P. Morgan and Company, the National City Bank of New York, the First National Bank of New York, and Kuhn, Loeb and Company, occupied a more commanding position than ever before in the nation's business structure.[1]

Inevitably under such a system great fortunes became greater, and notable inequalities of wealth appeared. A writer in the *Arena* of August, 1901, claimed that one half the people owned nothing, that one eighth of them owned seven eighths of the wealth, that one per cent of the population owned fifty-four per cent of the wealth, that one family in every hundred could buy out the other ninety-nine with plenty of money to spare, that one two-hundredths of one per cent of the population — four thousand millionaires — had acquired twenty per cent of the nation's total wealth. The accuracies of all such computations could be easily assailed, but they at least drove home a general truth. America, once a land of opportunity, was rapidly becoming a land in which the best opportunities had been cornered for the benefit of the few. "The United States," according to one observer, "is like an enormously rich country overrun by a horde of robber barons, and very inadequately policed by the central government and by certain local vigilance societies."[2]

The trust problem was not new to Roosevelt's day. Industrial combinations much smaller in size had aroused opposition during the *The trust problem* seventies and eighties, both in states and nation. The Grangers had attempted to regulate the railroads by state authority, and the United States, under the terms of the Interstate Commerce Act of 1887, had made feeble beginnings at national regulation. The Sherman Anti-Trust Law of 1890, based also upon the right of Congress to regulate interstate commerce, was passed in response to the demands of an insistent public opinion, and the government made a few attempts to enforce it. The unfriendly attitude of the courts, however, soon made the law a dead letter. In the Knight Case of 1895 the United States Supreme Court held that the establishment of a monopoly in manufactures, however reprehensible, could be dealt with only by the individual states. "Commerce," said the Court, "succeeds to manu-

[1] Carl Hovey, *The Life Story of J. Pierpont Morgan* (1911); Lewis Corey, *The House of Morgan* (1930); H. L. Satterlee, *J. Pierpont Morgan: An Intimate Portrait* (1939).

[2] Caro Lloyd, *Henry Demarest Lloyd* (2 vols., 1912), is a laudatory biography of one of the first to criticize intelligently the existing economic order. Cf. H. D. Lloyd, *Wealth Against Commonwealth* (new edition, 1936). On the distribution of wealth, see National Bureau of Economic Research, Inc., *Income in the United States, Its Amount and Distribution, 1909–1919* (1921).

Courtesy of the Minneapolis Journal

"THE DEAD RETURNED TO LIFE"

facture, and is not a part of it." After that all effort to employ the power of the national government against the trusts was given up, while the states, although endowed with a plenitude of constitutional authority, had already been proved to be too small to cope with nation-wide corporations. During the depression of the nineties, with many of the trusts in trouble, the public was less critical of them than it had been before, and as good times returned the excitement of the Spanish-American War and the new adventure into imperialism kept in obscurity the remarkable transformations that were taking place in the business world. Not until the opening years of the twentieth century did public attention again focus on the trusts.

The new awakening was due in remarkable degree to the work of the "muckrakers," a group of energetic journalists who made *The "Muck-* it their chief concern to discover and exploit in popular *rakers"* articles the seamy side of business behavior.[1] They owed their name to

[1] C. C. Regier, *The Era of the Muckrakers* (1932), is thorough, but not so well written as the wholly pessimistic John Chamberlain, *Farewell to Reform* (1932). On the part played by the popular magazines, see S. S. McClure, *My Autobiography* (1914). The whole period is admirably treated in H. U. Faulkner, *The Quest for Social Justice, 1898–1914* (1931).

Roosevelt, who was by no means unsympathetic with their work, but who compared some of the most sensational of them to the character in *Pilgrim's Progress* "who could look no way but downward with the muckrake in his hands." A vehicle was available for the muckrakers in the popular magazines that the nineties had produced, *McClure's*, the *Cosmopolitan*, *Everybody's*, the *American*, *Pearson's*, *Munsey's*, the *Arena*, and a number of others. These magazines, most of them monthlies, sold for as little as ten or fifteen cents a copy, and aimed to please. When they found in the literature of exposure a sure road to public acceptance they embraced the opportunity with whole-hearted enthusiasm. S. S. McClure, probably the most able and energetic of the publishers, set a good example for the rest by encouraging his writers to do the most painstaking research before they burst into print. Often he kept writers on his payroll for months, or even years, before they were ready to produce the articles he wanted.

Before they had finished, the muckrakers had given the public a very complete, if perhaps a one-sided, view of the methods by which big business operated. Lincoln Steffens, regarded by many as the ablest of them all, wrote a series of articles for *McClure's* on the "Shame of the Cities" that exposed the corrupt alliance between business and politics in nearly every American metropolis. Ida M. Tarbell, also for *McClure's*, wrote a "History of the Standard Oil Company" that left no doubt whatever as to the ruthlessness of the methods by which John D. Rockefeller had built up his monopoly. Thomas Lawson, an ex-stock manipulator, revealed for *Everybody's* a lurid, behind-the-scenes picture of the financial world that shot the magazine's circulation during the period his articles were being published from 197,000 to 735,000. The list of leading muckrakers is not a long one, but it contains some of the most distinguished names in American journalism, and the total output of each writer was remarkably large. Upton Sinclair in a novel, *The Jungle*, set forth the loathsome conditions that existed in the meat-packing industry; Ray Stannard Baker wrote on a wide variety of subjects, including the railroads, and the exploitation of labor by the trusts; Burton J. Hendrick told the inside story of life insurance; David Graham Phillips denounced "The Treason of the Senate," which reflected, or so he claimed, primarily the wishes of the trusts; George Kibbe Turner exhibited at its worst the vice business of Chicago and New York; Charles Edward Russell wrote on the beef trust and numerous other matters; and Samuel Hopkins Adams, on patent medicines and fraud in advertising. Supplementing and often corroborating the findings of the muckrakers were the volumes of the census of 1900, which soon began to appear, and the compendious *Report of the Industrial Commission* (19 vols., 1900–02), an investigating committee set up by Congress in 1898. Unread by the public at large, but of notable perspicacity, were the philosophical treatises of Thorstein Veblen, *The Theory of the Leisure Class* (1899), and *The Theory of Business Enterprise* (1904). Veblen's reasoning provided reformers of the next generation with some of their most cogent arguments against "predatory wealth." [1]

In his first message to Congress of December, 1901, Roosevelt gave warning of his future attitude toward the trusts, but he was not quite ready to essay the rôle of "trust-buster" in which later he *Roosevelt* so willingly allowed himself to be cast. Summarizing accu- *and the* rately the President's message, Mr. Dooley reported: "Th' *trusts* trusts, says he, are heejoous monsthers built up be th' enlightened intherprise iv th' men that have done so much to advance progress in our beloved country, he says. On wan hand I would stamp thim undher fut: on th' other hand not so fast." By February, 1902, however, the President was ready to act, and on his orders the Attorney-General of the United States announced that he would bring suit under the terms of the Sherman Anti-Trust Act to dissolve the Northern Securities Company, through which the year before a merger of three northwestern railroads had been attempted. If the government could induce the United States Supreme Court to support it in this instance, Roosevelt believed that he might later make the Sherman Act a really effective weapon in arresting the trend toward monopoly that had set in. [2]

The Northern Securities Company was a $400,000,000 New Jersey corporation, brought into existence November 13, 1901, primarily to take over controlling portions of the stock of three competing north-western railroads, the Great Northern, the Northern Pacific, and the Chicago, Burlington and Quincy. By resorting to the device of a hold-ing company James J. Hill, the guiding genius in the proceedings, hoped not merely to eliminate competition, but also to develop a well-articu-lated railroad system that could more effectively meet the transporta-tion needs of the whole great region stretching from Lake Michigan to Puget Sound. Naturally he called in J. P. Morgan to work out the necessary financial arrangements, and both believed, on advice of highly competent counsel, that the scheme they had devised was perfectly

---

[1] The number of the leading muckrakers was surprisingly small, and several of them have left important memoirs. Probably the best of these are *The Autobiography of Lincoln Steffens* (2 vols., 1931), and F. C. Howe, *The Confessions of a Reformer* (1925). On Veblen's contribution, see Joseph Dorfman, *Thorstein Veblen and His America* (1934).

[2] Mark Sullivan, *Our Times*, II, *America Finding Herself* (1927), is devoted in considerable part to Roosevelt's activities as President.

legal. For the President's purposes, however, the Northern Securities Company made an admirable target. A local suit for its dissolution, brought in the state courts of Minnesota, had given the nature of the company excellent preliminary advertising, and the fact that the merger so clearly involved interstate commerce would effectively eliminate the argument on which the Supreme Court had based its decision in the Knight case.

The prosecution of the Northern Securities Company moved along slowly — too slowly to suit Roosevelt. The government won a lower-court decision in 1903, and an "Expedition Act," which Attorney General Knox obtained of Congress the same year, enabled the Supreme Court to give speedier attention to the case than otherwise would have been possible. The decision it announced in 1904, except for the five-to-four vote by which it was reached, was all that the President could ask. The Court held that the Northern Securities Company was a violation of free competition within the meaning of the Sherman Act, and must be dissolved.[1] To the surprise of the President, Associate Justice Oliver Wendell Holmes, who had only recently been appointed to the Court, voted with the minority. Before appointing Holmes, Roosevelt had looked carefully into his record and had concluded that his vote could be depended on. But Holmes maintained that there was no more reason to hold the union of two railroads illegal than "a partner-ship between two stage-drivers who have been competitors in driving across a state line." Justice White, also dissenting, insisted that there was a complete parallel between the Knight case and the Northern Securities case and regretted the spectacle of the Supreme Court reversing itself. But Roosevelt was delighted that the "vicious doctrine" of the earlier decision was no longer "an obstacle to obstruct the path-way of justice." "This decision," he boasted in his *Autobiography*, "I caused to be annulled by the Court that had rendered it."

Acclaimed by the public as the "trust-buster," Roosevelt went ahead with other prosecutions. A total of twenty-five indictments were *Other* brought by the Department of Justice during his adminis-*prosecutions* tration, and in a few instances the government scored victories. Perhaps the most notable of them was the dissolution of the "beef trust," which counted among its sins an agreement whereby six tenths of the nation's dealers in fresh meat avoided bidding against one another in the purchase of livestock. Looking backward, both the wisdom of this policy and the interpretation of the law that made it

[1] B. H. Meyer, *A History of the Northern Securities Case* (1906); A. H. Walker, *History of the Sherman Law of the United States of America* (1910).

J. PIERPONT MORGAN

JAMES J. HILL

FOUNDERS
OF THE NORTHERN
SECURITIES COMPANY

possible, may well be doubted. Efforts to dissolve the trusts were often likened to the unscrambling of eggs. Once a community of interest had been established, "gentlemen's agreements" could be used to serve much the same purpose as more formal organization. Effective regulation, as Roosevelt well knew, rather than a futile effort to restore competition, would have been far more to the point, but the President's bes efforts to obtain legislation appropriate for this purpose met with the almost invariable hostility of Congress. Eventually Roosevelt came to distinguish between "good trusts," which showed a proper concern for the welfare of the consumer, and "bad trusts," which sought only selfish ends. The latter he prosecuted, the former he let alone. The Supreme Court, in the rule of reason it adopted in 1911, came to about the same conclusion. Only when the monopolistic actions of trusts "unreasonably" interfered with interstate commerce would the Court hold against them. By allowing itself this wide latitude, the Court was free to ignore mere "bigness," while at the same time punishing the misuse of power that great size made possible.

Roosevelt's efforts to obtain regulatory laws from Congress most nearly approached success with reference to the railroads. The Inter-*Railroad* state Commerce Act of 1887 had taken a step in this direc-*regulation* tion, but its primary purpose after all had been the maintenance of free competition. Even in that sphere the Interstate Commerce Commission, hampered repeatedly by court decisions, had been singularly ineffective, and without a new grant of powers it could never hope to cope with the great mergers that had taken place since its creation. A half-dozen regional systems, capitalized together at more than nine billion dollars, accounted for three fourths of the nation's mileage. They paid good dividends and attracted foreign as well as American investors. The automobile was yet in its infancy, country highways were practically unknown, and in the realm of transportation the railroads reigned supreme. Upon their effectiveness the business of the country depended; without their co-operation the whole economic structure would fall. Conscious of their importance, the railroads were not without a trace of arrogance, and they resented bitterly all efforts of government to bring them to book. "It seems hard," wrote James J. Hill, a typical railroad magnate, "that we should be compelled to fight for our lives against the political adventurers who have never done anything but pose and draw a salary." [1]

Backed by an aroused public opinion that believed more strongly

---

[1] On the struggle between the government and the railroads, see Pyle, *James J. Hill*, already cited, and George Kennan, *E. H. Harriman: A Biography* (1922).

PENNSYLVANIA SYSTEM
1914

Mackinaw

Buffalo Rochester

Chicago

Toledo Cleveland Elmira

Logansport

New York

Keokuk

Cincinnati

Baltimore

St. Louis Washington

Louisville

NEW YORK CENTRAL SYSTEM
1914

Montreal

Mackinaw

Troy

Boston

Detroit

Chicago Cleveland Buffalo

New York

Pittsburgh

Cincinnati

St. Louis

Louisville

Cairo

TWO TYPICAL RAILROAD SYSTEMS

every day that the people's pockets were being picked by the railroads, Roosevelt early in his administration sought regulatory legislation from Congress. The railroads offered no objection when in response to this summons Congress early in 1903 passed the Elkins Act in an effort to curb the rebate evil. The railroads themselves were weary of rebates and saw little to criticize in a statute that merely forbade variations from the published rates. They were more concerned when Roosevelt asked and obtained from Congress the establishment of a new Department of Commerce and Labor which was to include a fact-finding and possibly bothersome Bureau of Corporations. But the full force of their opposition was unleashed when in 1906, with the complete backing of the President, Representative Peter Hepburn of Iowa introduced into the House of Representatives a measure which, if passed, would grant the Interstate Commerce Commission full authority to regulate railroad rates.[1] The bill passed the House by a majority of 346 to 7, but the real test came in the Senate where the "vested interests" were more deeply entrenched. Eventually a compromise was effected. The commission might regulate rates, but its decisions could be appealed to the courts. The contention of Senator La Follette of Wisconsin, that the commission could not hope to set fair rates until the actual value of railroad property had been determined, fell on deaf ears. Roosevelt, La Follette maintained, was ever ready to take the "half-loaf" if he could not easily get more.

Nevertheless, the Hepburn Act added immeasurably to the power and prestige of the Interstate Commerce Commission. No longer did it *The Hep-* have to go to court to enforce an order; now the carrier had *burn Act* either to accept the rates set by the commission or go to court itself. Furthermore, the law also extended the jurisdiction of the commission to include other common carriers, such as express companies, pipe lines, sleeping-car companies, bridges, and ferries; it forbade the granting of free passes; it prohibited railroads from carrying commodities, except for their own use, that they had produced themselves — coal, for example;[2] and it empowered the commission to prescribe a uniform system of bookkeeping for all railroads, a provision of fundamental importance. Owing to the various methods of accounting in use among the railroads, it had been virtually impossible before

---

[1] Roosevelt's original recommendations on the regulation of the railroads were set forth in his message to Congress of 1904. They were also embodied in the Townsend-Esch Bill, which passed the House in 1905 by the vote of 326 to 17, but was not brought to a vote in the Senate.

[2] This provision, it was hoped, would force the railroads to abandon other businesses than railroading, mining in particular. An exception was made in the case of timber.

to arrive at dependable comparative statistics. The new methods, worked out by Professor H. C. Adams, and installed during the next few years, gave the commission almost its first insight into what the railroads were really doing. In order the better to cope with its new duties, the membership of the commission was raised from five to seven. Within a few years, under the operation of the new law, it had not only effected drastic reductions in rates, but it had also won the respect of the public, the courts, and the carriers themselves, who increasingly tended to accept its decisions as final.

The railroads were not the only trusts to feel the force of national regulation. The meat-packers, the food-processors, and the producers of drugs and patent medicines had much to explain when the *Pure Food* muckrakers got through with them. Upton Sinclair's *The* *and Drug* *Jungle* made a deep impression on the public, and on *Act* Roosevelt himself. Muckraking articles in the *Ladies' Home Journal* and in *Collier's* proved conclusively that most of the popular nostrums depended for their effects upon such ingredients as opium or alcohol, that some of them were definitely habit-forming, and that nearly all of them were frauds. Doctor H. W. Wiley, chief chemist of the Department of Agriculture, and Doctor E. F. Ladd, food commissioner of the State of North Dakota, supplied scientific evidence too conclusive to ignore on the use of harmful preservatives and adulterants in the preparation of meats and other food products. Precedent was not altogether lacking in this field for federal regulation. Laws dating back to the eighties required inspection by the Bureau of Animal Industry of all meats destined for export. This legislation had been necessary to quiet the protests of Germany and other European countries whose people were incensed at having been sold American meat unfit for food; such, for example, as trichina-bearing pork. A law of 1906 extended federal inspection to all meats destined for interstate commerce, and a Pure Food and Drug Act, passed the same year, placed some restrictions, but not nearly enough, on the producers of prepared foods and patent medicines. An amendment to this act, passed in 1911, prohibited also the use of misleading labels, but events proved that the gullible public bought about as freely when the unpleasant truth was printed on the label as when it was not. The real root of the difficulty, fraudulent advertising, escaped unscathed. All such regulation, when undertaken by the federal government, depended for its validity upon the powers of Congress over interstate commerce, and the exact line of demarcation between state and national authority could be drawn only by the courts. Roosevelt, annoyed at the existence of this "twilight zone," strongly favored resolving all doubts in favor of the national government.

Always a happy phrase-maker, Roosevelt's insistence on a "square deal" for labor, capital, and the public gave him the advantage of an *The "square* attractive label for his labor policy. Naturally the rapid *deal"* development of industrial concentration aroused the fears of labor, and as the strength of organized capital grew, the strength of organized labor grew also. By 1905 the American Federation of Labor claimed for its affiliates a total membership of two millions, with perhaps six hundred thousand unaffiliated, but co-operating, union members. Under the circumstances a test of strength between labor and capital was almost inevitable.

The last serious strikes in the United States had centered about the Panic of 1893, but the turn of the century threatened to usher in a new and equally tumultuous period of strife. Labor conditions in the United States were probably at their worst in the coal mines of Pennsylvania, West Virginia, Ohio, and Illinois. Wages were low, employment was irregular, accidents were common, and workingmen's compensation was virtually unknown. The conditions of life in the squalid mining villages were depressing in the extreme. The mining companies owned everything. As Gompers said later, children were "brought into the world by the company doctor, lived in a company house or hut, were nurtured by the company store ... laid away in the company graveyard." A steady stream of newly arrived immigrants, eager to work for any price, thronged to the mines, and slowed down the process of unionization. Nevertheless, in 1897, the United Mine Workers staged a successful strike in the central bituminous area, and under the leadership of the youthful John Mitchell they pushed the work of organization so rapidly in the anthracite districts of eastern Pennsylvania that within a few years they were ready to strike again. At Mitchell's call not less than one hundred thousand anthracite coal workers quit work in 1900, and in a legal, orderly way pressed home their demands. Mitchell's discipline over his men kept them sober and serious, and brought public good-will to his side. The real reason that the miners won, however, was that Mark Hanna, preparing to fight a campaign on the slogan, "the full dinner pail," persuaded the operators to concede some of the miners' demands rather than to embarrass him by such compelling evidence of labor unrest. And so the miners scored a partial victory.

After the election was over it was a different story. Hanna, and a good many other capitalists, seemed genuinely to have hoped for an era of conciliation and compromise between capital and labor, but to some of the nation's industrialists the time seemed ripe for a "show-down." When in 1901 the Amalgamated Association of Iron and Steel Workers — the same that had lost the Homestead Strike of 1892 — struck for the recognition of their union, they were crushed within a month. Even the support of Samuel Gompers, head of the American Federation of Labor, was of no avail against United States Steel's ability to close mills affected by the strike and to produce everything it needed in non-union plants. Next year the anthracite coal operators hoped to score an equally telling victory for the "open shop." When the coal miners, never fully satisfied with the agreement of 1900, asked for the recognition of their union, together with a wage increase of twenty per cent, and a nine-hour day, their request was spurned. Thereupon the miners struck, and from May 12 to October 23, at a total cost of perhaps one hundred million dollars to all concerned, they held their lines intact. According to Mark Hanna it looked as if there could be no agreement until "the miners are *starved* to it," but strike funds were collected from other miners, and the day of surrender postponed. Mitchell, as in 1900, kept his men from violence, and won much sympathy for the strikers' cause. President George F. Baer of the Philadelphia and Reading Coal and Iron Company, who spoke for the operators, was far less skillful. In a letter that he carelessly allowed to fall into the hands of the press he revealed his true sentiments. "The rights and interests of the laboring man," he wrote a supposed sympathizer, "will be protected and cared for — not by the labor agitators, but by the Christian men to whom God in His infinite wisdom has given the control of the property interests of the country."

This bald-faced application of the divine-right theory to the holding of property won merited contempt from the public, and as cold weather set in the shortage of coal turned contempt to anger. In New York City the public schools had to be closed for lack of fuel, and the small stocks that dealers had on hand sold for as high as thirty to thirty-five dollars a ton. Roosevelt was outraged, and worried too about the political effect of a coal shortage on the party in power. "The big coal operators," he wrote later, "had banded together and positively refused to take any steps looking toward an accommodation. They knew that the suffering among the miners was great; they were confident that if order were kept, and nothing further done by the government, they would win; and they refused to consider that the public had any rights in the matter." Finally, when Roosevelt called the leaders of both sides to confer with him in Washington on a settlement, both sides attended, but the operators defied even the President of the United States. The attitude of one of them, probably Baer, so enraged Roosevelt, who was confined at the time to a wheel chair because of an injured leg, that he told a reporter: "If it wasn't for the high office I hold I would have taken him by the seat of the breeches and the nape of the neck and chucked him out of that window." The only man to keep his temper at the conference was John Mitchell.[1]

But Roosevelt was not so easily balked. He sent Root to discuss with J. Pierpont Morgan, as another interested observer, a plan of settlement *Presidential* whereby five arbiters were to be appointed, "by the Presi-*intervention* dent or by you," to settle the strike; also, and more important, the means whereby the operators, who at the President's conference had already rejected this idea, were to be forced to accept it. The President's method was simplicity itself, although its constitutionality was far from demonstrable. The governor of Pennsylvania was to request federal troops to keep order. Roosevelt was then to send in a "first-rate general" under orders "to dispossess the operators and run the mines as a receiver." The public should have its coal, and the operators could think things over. This daring plan, which Roosevelt was absolutely determined to carry out if he had to, was kept a close secret from everyone, apparently, except the operators. As Roosevelt no doubt anticipated, it changed their minds quite perceptibly on the matter of arbitration; now they were all for such a settlement as the President had suggested, except that there must be no union man on the commission. A suitable board of arbiters, according to the operators, would be (1) an officer of the engineer corps, (2) a man of experience in mining, (3) a man of prominence, eminent as a sociologist, (4) the federal judge of the eastern district of Pennsylvania, and (5) a mining engineer. Roosevelt was puzzled, for he was convinced that a union man must sit on the board, but finally he saw a way out. A commission of seven, similar in personnel to the one desired by the operators, was arranged, but the "eminent sociologist" that Roosevelt appointed to it was E. E. Clark, head of the Brotherhood of Railway Conductors. Work was resumed at the mines, and in March, 1903, a decision that in the main favored the miners, although stopping short of union recognition, was accepted by both sides. Thus the President had obtained a "square deal" for labor.

Nor was this all. Repeatedly the President recommended to Congress legislation favorable to labor, such as the protection of women and children in industry, limitations on the use of injunctions in labor disputes, and employer's liability laws for workers on interstate railroads. Only the last-mentioned of these recommendations received the favorable

---

[1] Elsie Glück, *John Mitchell, Miner* (1929), gives an account of the strike; see also, Harold Howland, *Theodore Roosevelt and His Times* (1921).

action of Congress, and the first such law, passed in 1906, was annulled by the Supreme Court. A law of April, 1908, met the Court's objections. In general Roosevelt's thinking on the labor problem was not far in advance of his times, but it represented a distinct improvement over the positions taken by his predecessors.

Another policy dear to Roosevelt's heart was the conservation of the nation's natural resources. When he became President, the United States was "somewhat in the position of the man who had unexpectedly lost most of his fortune." Its greatest re- *Conservation* source throughout its history, or so the people had always thought, had been its vast reservoir of public lands. Now the best of these had been used up; although at the turn of the century more than five hundred million acres still remained open to settlement, only a small fraction of this vast area could ever be farmed in the traditional American way. Moreover, even after the lands had passed into private or corporate hands the tendency had been to exploit them rather than to preserve their fertility. Millions of acres, particularly in the East and the South, had been returned, thoroughly despoiled, to nature, or could be farmed only by the constant use of fertilizer. What had happened to the lands had happened also in varying degrees to other natural resources. Four fifths of the nation's forests had been chopped down without thought as to their replacement, and many of those that remained had been acquired by a few large lumber companies bent on using them up. Mineral resources, too, whether of metals, coal, gas, or oil, had been exploited with the utmost wastefulness. Water-power sites, in return for next to nothing, had been allowed to pass into the hands of private companies who had developed their possibilities along profit-making lines, without regard for the destruction of beauty or prevention of floods. By the turn of the century, pessimists were beginning to foretell that the rich resources of the United States would soon be exhausted, and the poverty of the Old World would extend to the New.[1]

Some earnest, but, as events proved, uninspired, prophets were convinced that the United States would not long be able to provide the food necessary for its teeming millions. This dire threat, reinforced by the demand of the West for a land policy more in accordance with the conditions of western life, led to a drastic revision of the federal land laws. Irrigation had long been regarded as the most likely means of making the western lands worth while, and in 1889, on authority of Congress, Major J. W. Powell of the Geological Survey had made a careful survey of

[1] An early and significant study of this subject is C. R. Van Hise, *The Conservation of Natural Resources in the United States* (1910).

irrigation sites throughout the country. Implicit in Powell's findings was the fact that the cost of irrigation ran so far beyond the means of individuals as to demand either co-operative or governmental action. The Carey Act of 1894, passed by Congress in an effort to encourage co-operative enterprise, authorized the gift of irrigable land to the western states on condition that they permit private companies to construct irrigation works upon it and to charge for water-rights. The land itself settlers could purchase from the state at fifty cents an acre, but inasmuch as water-rights in Carey-Act projects cost from thirty to forty dollars an acre plus maintenance, this privilege fell far short of free land. Nevertheless, in Wyoming, Idaho, Montana, Colorado, Arizona, California, New Mexico, and Texas the Carey Act was used to permit the opening of numerous new irrigation tracts. Each state was entitled, if it wished, to as much as a million acres for this purpose.[1]

The Reclamation Act of 1902, sometimes called the Newlands Act in honor of its sponsor, Senator Francis G. Newlands of Nevada, put the *The New-* federal government itself into the business of building the *lands Act* dams, tunnels, flumes, and ditches necessary for irrigation projects. All revenue that came from the sales of public lands was set aside for investment in irrigation. As in the case of the Carey Act, the cost of construction, which amounted to from twenty to thirty dollars per acre, was assessed against the settlers, who were permitted to take twenty-, forty-, or eighty-acre tracts on condition of five years' residence and the cultivation of half their land. Their payments were put into a revolving fund, which was used to build still more irrigation works. Under the terms of this act several million acres of land were eventually made available for agriculture.

Irrigation dams proved to be useful also for the development of water-power, and pointed definitely toward government activity in that field. During Roosevelt's administration the Bureau of Corporations made a study of the water-power resources of the country, and discovered that they were adequate, if properly harnessed, to turn all the wheels of American industry. Hydroelectric corporations, however, such as the General Electric and Westinghouse, had already pre-empted some of the choicest sites, and were after more. In 1903 Roosevelt showed plainly where he stood on this subject by vetoing a law of Congress that would have permitted private construction of a dam and power-plant at Muscle Shoals, Alabama. The "ultimate effect of granting privileges of this kind," the President maintained, "should be considered in a comprehen-

[1] F. H. Newell, *Irrigation in the United States* (1902); W. E. Smythe, *The Conquest of Arid America* (1905); R. P. Teele, *Irrigation in the United States* (1915).

sive way," and a general policy adopted whereby "these valuable rights" would not be practically given away, but would be so disposed of as to "best substantiate the public interest." In many instances, however, the states, rather than the United States, had the disposal of these valuable concessions, and state officials all too frequently proved to be easy marks for the corporations.

The rapid destruction of the national forests had been noted occasionally for a quarter of a century before Roosevelt's time, and in 1891 Congress had passed a Forest Reserve Act under the terms *Forest* of which the President could withdraw timber lands from *reserves* entry. But neither the public nor the Presidents were much interested. Orders by Harrison, Cleveland, and McKinley set aside some 46,828,-449 acres, all told, that were not to be alienated, but no real halt was called in the process of exploitation. Gifford Pinchot, chief of the forestry service, was the man who more than any other was responsible for a change in this situation. Pinchot knew how other nations administered their forests, and he wished to adapt their methods to the forests of the United States. He knew, too, how intimately the destruction of the forests was bound up with other problems of waste, such as soil erosion, the clogging of river channels, and the promotion of floods. As a close friend of Roosevelt's, he was able to enlist the President's enthusiastic aid, and before Roosevelt left office the total amount of forest land withdrawn from entry had been raised to 172,230,233 acres.

Students of conservation were increasingly impressed by the unity of the problem that confronted them. Deforestation and the building of dams, whether for irrigation or for power purposes, might and sometimes did interfere with the navigability of streams, hence the preservation of internal waterways was involved. An Inland Waterways Commission, appointed by Roosevelt in 1907, not only made a survey of the nation's unused water routes, but studied also nearly every aspect of the conservation problem. The assumption that steamboat traffic might be revived to furnish competition for the railroads proved to be a fallacy, but out of the work of the commission came the plan for a national conference on conservation, to which representatives from all sections and from both parties should be invited. On May 13, 1908, at the White House Roosevelt met with an assembly of notables that included state governors, cabinet members, Supreme Court justices, members of Congress, businessmen, and a wide range of experts. For three days he kept the conference in session, and from it he obtained support for such important policies as the protection of the water supply of navigable streams, the control of forest fires, government regulation for the cutting of timber, the granting of surface titles to public lands separate from the right to exploit the minerals that lay below the surface, and the withdrawal from entry of lands bearing coal, oil, natural gas, and phosphate.

Following the work of the conference, Roosevelt, on his own initiative and without legislative authority, appointed a National Conservation Commission of forty-nine members to make a survey of the nation's resources in minerals, waters, forests, and soils. The members of the commission were unpaid, but the President directed that the executive department should give them all possible assistance. Congress, by no means pleased to see an investigating committee created solely by presidential prerogative, did what it could to hamper the work of the commission, but its first report, presented in January, 1909, filled three large volumes and provided much important information. Meantime forty-one state conservation commissions and many more private agencies had begun to supply the nation with more knowledge of its natural resources and how to deal with them than it had ever before had. On Roosevelt's order, the Secretary of the Interior added to the forest lands already withdrawn from entry some eighty million acres of coal lands, a million and a half acres of lands adjacent to water-power sites, and nearly five million acres of phosphate lands.

While the nation in general applauded Roosevelt's efforts to promote conservation, there were many dissident voices. Corporations engaged *Opposition to conservation* in lumbering, mining, the production of hydroelectric power, and other exploitative activities were openly hostile. The representatives of western states, who saw little to admire about a policy that in some of its aspects could serve only to delay western development, asked pointedly, "What's posterity ever done for us?" In consequence, the President's interest in conservation far outran the willingness of Congress to legislate. He failed to obtain a law authorizing the permanent retention by the government of all lands bearing coal, oil, or natural gas, and not until 1920 was this reasonable policy adopted. In 1909, however, Congress did provide for the separate disposal of the agricultural, timber, and mineral resources of the public lands, while a year later it created the Bureau of Mines to discover and disseminate information on the mineral resources of the United States, and the best methods for their development. The Mondell Act of 1909, like the Reclamation Act of 1902, exhibited a side of conservation that pleased the West, for its effect was to promote rather than to retard development. In the interest of dry-farming, by means of which settlers with the aid of a little rain and some subsoil moisture stood a less than fifty-fifty chance to make a living, the Mondell Act permitted homesteaders to take up as

NATIONAL FORESTS AND NATIONAL PARKS

much as three hundred and twenty acres of non-timbered, non-mineral, non-irrigable land. For proving up no residence term was required, only the evidence of successful cultivation.

There was a direct relationship between Roosevelt's policy of governmental interference in the affairs of business and his policy of conservation. In the former he brought businessmen face to face with the specter of effective governmental regulation, in the latter he served notice that in certain spheres, previously left open to private initiative, the government either would act itself or would permit individuals to act only on terms laid down by the government in advance. The day of rampant individualism was almost done. Perhaps the senior Robert M. La Follette, never a very devoted admirer of Roosevelt, had these considerations in mind when he described conservation as Roosevelt's greatest work. According to the Wisconsin senator, Roosevelt deserved unstinted praise "for staying territorial waste" and for saving the things "on which alone a peaceful, progressive and happy race life can be founded."

The Roosevelt era is distinguished hardly less for what went on within the states than for the national achievements by which it is more commonly known. During this period state government was *State* completely revolutionized, and reforms were instigated that *reforms* intimately affected the lives of the people. Among the state governors Roosevelt had many precursors and imitators, each with a vision of reform. They found the state governments almost completely in the control of whatever big business corporations happened to be most powerful in their particular part of the country. Well-oiled party machines in each state did the bidding of the state "boss," and the "boss" in turn did the bidding of the business interests that furnished the oil for his machine. Speaking before the New York Constitutional Convention of 1915, Elihu Root, an excellent authority, remarked:

> Mr. Platt ruled the state; for nigh upon twenty years he ruled it. It was not the governor; it was not the legislature; it was Mr. Platt. And the capital was not here [at Albany]: it was at 49 Broadway. . . . The ruler of the state during the greater part of the forty years of my acquaintance with the state government has not been any man authorized by the constitution or by law. . . . The party leader is elected by no one, accountable to no one, bound by no oath of office, removable by no one. . . . I don't criticize the men of the invisible government. . . . But it is all wrong.

For a reformer to be elected to a governorship under such conditions was in itself a revolution; once in office his only chance of remaining there was to break the power of the machine.

Outstanding among the reform governors was Robert M. La Follette (1855–1925) of Wisconsin, a man whose influence upon the course of political events during his lifetime was more fundamental *Robert M.* than that of many Presidents. "Fighting Bob," as he came *La Follette* to be called, had entered politics, without benefit of machine assistance, soon after his graduation from the University of Wisconsin in 1879.[1] As county prosecutor of Dane County he made an excellent record, and in 1884 was nominated and elected for the first of three successive terms in the national House of Representatives. He was an indefatigable canvasser, delighted in controversy, and developed political speech-making into a fine art. Like many another Republican he was left at home by the election of 1890, and but for a controversy with the all-powerful Senator Philetus Sawyer, who was both a politician and a lumber baron, his ambitions for a career in state politics might easily have been gratified. When the Democrats took over the government of Wisconsin in 1891, they found that for years the Republican state treasurers had made a practice of depositing the state's funds, interest free, in certain favored banks. The new attorney-general promptly brought suit to recover this interest money for the state, and Sawyer, because he had acted as bondsman for the treasurers, came in for his share of the trouble. According to the La Follette version of the story, Sawyer attempted through La Follette to bribe the judge before whom the case was to be tried — a Democratic brother-in-law of La Follette's. Deeply incensed, La Follette made the whole matter public, and helped the state recover the funds of which it had been defrauded.

From that time on La Follette was a crusader for reform. Determined to win the governorship, he was repeatedly denied the nomination in spite of a growing popular sentiment in his favor; not until 1900 was he able to line up a majority of the convention delegates. Elected, and twice re-elected, he forced through reluctant legislatures laws for the more effective taxation of the railroads and other corporations; for the establishment of direct primaries through which the people, not boss-ridden conventions, could select their own candidates for office; for the termination of the free-pass evil by prohibiting state officials from accepting them; and for the conservation of the natural resources of the state in forests and water-power. In his quest of good government he enlisted the aid of experts from the University of Wisconsin, whose new president, Charles R. Van Hise, was his close personal friend and his choice for the office. He was instrumental, also, in the creation of a Legislative Refer-

[1] La Follette's life-history is still best told in his *Autobiography* (1913), but a more objective study of his career is badly needed.

ence Bureau through which legislators might obtain expert advice on the drafting of bills.

The "Wisconsin idea," which was fundamentally to free the state from business domination through venal party bosses and to turn over public *Other* administration to popularly chosen leaders willing to seek *crusaders* the advice of experts, exactly suited the temper of the times.[1] Other governors in other states duplicated in varying degrees the La Follette record in Wisconsin. In Missouri Joseph W. Folk won public attention as circuit attorney by successfully prosecuting the corrupt ring of St. Louis "boodlers" that for years had fattened on municipal graft. As governor for four years after 1905, he sought with moderate success to repeat in the state arena what he had done for his home city. In New York Charles Evans Hughes became a national figure while serving as counsel for a legislative investigating committee that was examining into the methods of the New York life insurance companies. Hughes's sensational disclosures brought about a revolution in the insurance business and led to his election as governor in 1906. Out in California the star of Hiram Johnson began to rise. As early as 1902 he attracted attention as a member of the staff of prosecuting attorneys in charge of some San Francisco "boodling" cases. In 1908 he secured the conviction of Abe Ruef, grafting municipal boss of San Francisco, after Francis J. Heney, the original prosecutor, had been shot in the line of duty. In 1910 Johnson was elected governor, determined above all else to end the domination of the state by the Southern Pacific Railroad.

The roll of reform governors was a long one, including, besides such prominent individuals as A. B. Cummins of Iowa, and John A. Johnson of Minnesota, many lesser lights whose names never became nationally well known. Private individuals, such as William S. U'Ren of Oregon, crusader for "the Oregon system," also took a hand, while the public at large, fully aroused by the revelations of the muckrakers, demanded and obtained results.[2]

The most fundamental of the political reforms effected during these years was the substitution of the direct primary for the convention *The direct* system of making nominations. Under the old system only *primary* a small fraction of the voters, certainly never more than fifteen per cent, attended the original caucuses or "primaries" by which convention delegates were chosen. A large proportion of those who at-

[1] Charles McCarthy, *The Wisconsin Idea* (1912), is the work of an enthusiastic La Follette supporter.

[2] An excellent chapter on reform within the states is contained in D. S. Muzzey, *The United States of America*, II, *From the Civil War* (1933).

tended were local office-holders and aspirants to office. It was thus easy for the machine to secure a working majority of the delegates to almost every convention, and to put through the "slate" of nominees agreed upon by the leaders in advance. The direct primary, however, substituted voting at the polls by secret ballot for the caucus-convention system, and reduced immeasurably the chances of machine manipulation. Within a comparatively short time after the passage in 1903 of the Wisconsin primary law, similar laws had been enacted by nearly every state in the Union. The results were revolutionary. It would be idle to claim that the direct primaries completely eliminated either business domination of government or the power of venal party bosses. But the new laws greatly promoted the possibility of successful popular uprisings against corrupt machines, and because of them in state after state men were elected to office who under the old system would never have had a chance.

The initiative and referendum were twin measures of popular government that might be used as clubs over legislatures unresponsive to the popular will. By these devices laws could be initiated by petition, and voted on by ballot. The use of the referendum for constitutional provisions and for such local legislation as the flotation of bond issues was by no means new, but its application to ordinary law-making, coupled with the power of popular initiative, was decidedly an innovation. The initiative and referendum were first adopted in South Dakota, in 1898, but obtained their best test in Oregon, where from 1902 to 1910 no less than thirty-two measures were referred to the people for a vote. In Oregon, too, the recall, a measure by which faithless officials, on petition of a stipulated number or percentage of the voters, were required to stand for re-election at special elections, was given a thorough trial. Indeed, "the Oregon system" came to be the term most commonly used to describe the new adventures in popular government. Largely because of U'Ren's effective leadership, Oregon had adopted the Australian ballot in 1891, a registration law in 1899, the initiative and referendum law in 1902, the direct primary in 1904, a sweeping corrupt practices act in 1908, and the recall in 1910. "In Oregon," so it was said, "the state government is divided into four departments — the executive, judicial, legislative, and U'Ren — and it is still an open question who exerts the more power." [1] Within a decade nearly twenty states had the initiative and referendum, and nearly a dozen the recall. Acceptance of "the

---

[1] A. H. Eaton, *The Oregon System* (1912). See also E. P. Oberholtzer, *The Referendum in America* (1911), and C. A. Beard (editor), *Documents on the State-Wide Initiative, Referendum and Recall* (1912).

Oregon system" moved in general from west to east, and in the older states often met unyielding opposition.

That even the federal government might be affected by state reforms was proved when preferential primaries were introduced whereby the voters might express their choices for United States senators. *Direct election of senators* These laws assumed that in senatorial elections state legislatures would be guided solely by the popular mandate, and regardless of personal or party considerations would elect the primary winner to the senatorship. The movement for direct election of United States senators dated far back into the nineteenth century, and had won warm support not only from off-color politicians such as the Populists, but from many conservative citizens as well. Four times, in 1894, 1898, 1900, and 1902, the national House of Representatives had supported a constitutional amendment for the direct election of senators, but each time the Senate had refused to concur. Meantime the scandals involved in legislative elections became increasingly more evident. At best state legislation tended to be treated as of secondary importance in years when a senator was to be chosen; at worst open bribery was resorted to by individuals and corporations bent on the success of a candidate friendly to their interests.

Undoubtedly the framers of the Constitution had intended that the upper chamber should represent not merely the individual states, but also the wealth of the nation. They had builded better than they knew. By the twentieth century the United States Senate could be spoken of, not without a semblance of truth, as a "millionaire's club." Men of great wealth aspired to a seat in it as a crowning evidence of success. Corporations with privileges to protect made every effort to secure a senatorship for one of their directors, or at least for one of their attorneys. Party bosses themselves often sought and obtained election to the Senate. The general level of intelligence in the upper chamber therefore was high — has perhaps never been higher — but the senators, so critics insisted, represented the vested interests of the country rather than the people as a whole. Naturally the Senate refused as long as it dared to risk the results of popular election. But the preferential primaries, which eventually were adopted by more than half the states, brought about by indirection the change that the Senate had tried to avoid. Further, as popularly chosen senators took their seats, the opposition to direct election was broken down. By 1912 the Senate submitted to the inevitable and agreed to the Seventeenth Amendment, which a year later became a part of the Constitution.

Reforms in the field of municipal government paralleled, but hardly

equaled, the reforms being made by the states. The Tammany machine
in New York was no worse than many another, only better *Municipal*
advertised. In nearly every city of considerable size crooked *reform*
deals in the awarding of contracts and franchises, open or secret alliances
with commercialized vice, and the protection of favored classes of criminals who paid well for their privileges were only the worst of the sins of
the politicians in charge. As with Tammany Hall, the machine could
count on the support of thousands of voters who received in return for
their ballots a feeling of security. If a worker lost his job, got into
trouble with the law, needed money to meet an emergency, or faced any
personal crisis whatever, he went to his local leader for help, and got it.
To make surer of success at the polls, however, ballot-boxes were stuffed,
returns were falsified, and a thousand irregularities were condoned.
Lincoln Steffens's articles made the "shame of the cities" better known
than ever before, but reformers had already arisen. In Toledo Samuel
M. Jones, better known as "Golden Rule" Jones, made successful war
upon the private-contract system, and advocated the municipal ownership of public utilities. Elected to office in 1897, he was repeatedly re-
elected, and in 1904 was succeeded by his friend and disciple, Brand Whitlock, who continued the good work. In Cleveland Thomas L. Johnson
became mayor in 1901. A convinced "single-taxer," he secured among
other reforms a long-overdue reassessment of property values, municipal
control of the street-car system, and a three-cent fare. Under his régime
Cleveland could claim to be the "best governed city in the United
States," a claim that Milwaukee, under the Socialist leadership of Emil
Seidel and Daniel W. Hoan, was soon to challenge.[1]

To many thoughtful critics the reform of city government could best
be promoted by a change in the system. City administration was
primarily a business affair; why should it be hampered by a form of
government patterned after that of the United States? Why should the
Democrats and the Republicans run opposing tickets for city offices?
What difference did it make whether a candidate for mayor or alderman
believed in a high tariff or a low tariff, in imperialism or in isolation, in
free silver or the single gold standard? In 1901 the city of Galveston,
Texas, which the year before had been destroyed by a tidal wave and was
in desperate need of efficiency in government, tried to obtain it by turning over the whole problem to a commission of five, each of whom would
administer under rules laid down by a majority vote some department of

---

[1] The battle for municipal reform may be followed in Lincoln Steffens, *The Shame of the
Cities* (1904); Fremont Older, *My Own Story* (1925); C. H. Harrison, *Stormy Years* (1935);
F. C. Howe, *The City, the Hope of Democracy* (1905).

city affairs. Soon many other cities were experimenting with the "commission form" of government, and out of it grew an even more reasonable scheme, the "city manager" plan. This system sought to duplicate the methods of the business corporation. The elected board or commission employed a manager, who ran the city with the same freedom of action that was normally accorded a business executive. Soon hundreds of American cities, large or small, were being administered, usually more efficiently than ever before, by commissions and city managers. Thousands, however, adhered to the old systems, and in all too many instances to the old ways.

The reforms of the Roosevelt era in state and city government greatly facilitated the efforts of those who wished to enlist the aid of the law in the improvement of social conditions. No longer so deferential to the rich man's point of view, and unhampered by the constitutional limitations that so restricted the activities of the national government, the states crowded their statute books with laws that had rarely or never been obtainable before. A large part of the new legislation was designed to promote the "square deal" for labor, but other important subjects, particularly the prohibition of the liquor traffic, received careful consideration.

Most important of the new labor legislation, perhaps, was the series of employer's liability, or workmen's compensation, acts that followed *Labor legislation* Maryland's first feeble beginning in this direction in 1902. These laws were designed to reverse the old common-law rule that a workman had to prove negligence on the part of his employer in order to obtain compensation for injuries, and that even this might be insufficient if he himself, or any "fellow-servant," had been guilty of contributory negligence. The new principle, which by 1921 had been accepted in all but six states, was that in hazardous occupations the employer was liable for all injuries that occurred to his employees while they were at work. As a result of the new laws millions of dollars were soon paid out each year in benefits to injured workmen or their families.

Efforts were made also to increase the protection given to women and children in industry. Most of the states eventually adopted laws forbidding in certain types of industry the employment of children under fourteen years of age, while laws for compulsory school attendance accomplished the same purpose in another way. Opposition from the southern textile industries caused some of the southern states to lag either in the enactment or in the enforcement of child-labor laws, and as early as 1906 a movement was begun to give Congress authority over child labor by a constitutional amendment. Such an amendment was actually submitted in 1924, but it failed of ratification. Laws limiting the number of hours per day that women and children might be employed, and fixing minimum-wage schedules that they must be paid, were also enacted by some of the states. Attempts to extend these same principles to employed men met with stronger opposition, but a few successes were recorded. In the whole field of labor legislation the United States lagged far behind European nations. Unemployment insurance and old-age pensions, for example, while common enough elsewhere, were hardly more than talked about in the United States.

Attempts by prohibitionists to do away with the liquor traffic dates far back into the nineteenth century, but the era of successful activity began with the formation of the Anti-Saloon League in 1893. This *Prohibition* organization received the active support of all the evangelical denominations, and was maintained by the funds its agents were permitted to collect at regular church services. Its methods came to be quite as hard-boiled as those of the politicians with whom it had to deal. It knew one test, and only one test, for fitness to hold office. If a man favored the liquor traffic, the Anti-Saloon League was against him; if he opposed the liquor traffic, the Anti-Saloon League was for him. With a budget that by 1903 had reached four hundred thousand dollars a year, the League was in a position to hire hundreds of organizers and to maintain scores of offices. For a generation, under the leadership of Wayne B. Wheeler and William H. Anderson, it made the issue, "wet" or "dry," take precedence over nearly every other issue in state and local politics. As between low license and high license, the League favored high license. As between high license and "local option," whereby a town or county might vote to exclude saloons, it favored local option. As between local option and state-wide prohibition, it favored state-wide prohibition. And as between state-wide prohibition and national prohibition, it favored national prohibition. Never too squeamish about its methods or its political bedfellows, it took what it could get.

It got a great deal. The liquor business was open to attack for all the same reasons that other big businesses were vulnerable, and for many more besides. A veritable barrage of tracts, sermons, orations, and temperance journals set forth its shortcomings with a degree of passionate intolerance reminiscent of the abolitionists. The efforts of brewers, distillers, and wine-makers to obtain business favors from legislatures, county boards, and city councils were skillfully used to classify the liquor interests with the corruptionists. Local liquor dealers' associations were taunted as defenders of lawlessness and vice, and crooked politics was traced with an unerring eye to the door of the saloon. In the South the mistakes of the Negro were blamed upon liquor, and prohibition was demanded as a necessary preliminary to good relations between the races. While Roosevelt was President the successes of the Anti-Saloon League were mainly confined to the rural districts and were obtained by local option, but before he left office four southern states had voted dry, and within the next few years many others, northern as well as southern, were to follow. By the time the World War broke out, nearly half the people of the United States lived in "dry" territory, while in three fourths of its total area the saloon had been outlawed. The ratification of the Eighteenth Amendment to the Constitution in 1919 merely completed a process that had been long under way.[1]

Woman suffrage   Woman suffrage was a companion reform to prohibition. If women obtained the vote, so prohibitionists reasoned, they would with certainty aid the temperance cause. In 1869 the Territory of Wyoming had conferred the suffrage on women, and by 1911 six western states, Wyoming, Colorado, Utah, Idaho, Washington, and California, had accepted the innovation *in toto*, while many other states gave women the right to vote in certain elections. Like the prohibitionists the suffragists hoped to crown their efforts by obtaining an amendment to the Constitution that would end the denial of the suffrage to women, and, while adding state after state to their list of converts, they continued to work on Congress. An outbreak of "militancy," borrowed from Great Britain during the World War, may have had something to do with bringing Congress to yield in 1919. The Nineteenth Amendment became a part of the Constitution in 1920.[2]

The movements for prohibition and woman suffrage carried along in their wake a great variety of reforms designed to promote the public health and happiness. New building codes were devised, and public parks and playgrounds were multiplied. Renewed efforts were made to wipe out gambling and prostitution. Special courts were established to deal with the problem of juvenile delinquency. Divorce laws were relaxed. Legal discriminations against women, aside from the suffrage, were brought near the vanishing point. Most of these laws, like prohibition and the labor codes, depended for their constitutionality upon the "police power"; that is, the right of the state to do whatever might be necessary to promote the health, happiness, and morality of its citizens. Such laws frequently interfered seriously with the full freedom of

[1] J. A. Krout, *The Origins of Prohibition* (1925); E. H. Cherrington, *The Evolution of Prohibition in the United States of America* (1920); Justin Steuart, *Wayne Wheeler, Dry Boss* (1928).

[2] A. M. Schlesinger, *New Viewpoints in American History* (new edition, 1937), contains an admirable chapter on the "rôle of women."

individuals, and led to an enormous amount of litigation. The courts, almost invariably hostile in the beginning, eventually relented, and in nearly every instance granted a grudging approval to the measures that the public desired. [1]

[1] Catherine Drinker Bowen, *Yankee from Olympus: Justice Holmes and His Family* (1944), is an understanding biography of the great jurist. See also Sister Marie Carolyn Klinkhamer, *Edward Douglas White, Chief Justice of the United States* (1943).

Excellent special studies pertinent to his chapter are: Edward A. Fitzpatrick, *McCarthy of Wisconsin* (1944); Winston Allen Flint, *The Progressive Movement in Vermont* (1941); H. L. Hurwitz, *Theodore Roosevelt and Labor in New York State, 1880–1900* (1943); Eric F. Goldman, *Charles J. Bonaparte, Patrician Reformer: His Earlier Career* (1943); John Lombardi, *Labor's Voice in the Cabinet* (1942).

CHAPTER XIX

ROOSEVELT AND TAFT

FEW other Presidents, if indeed any, have enjoyed the popularity while in office that came to Theodore Roosevelt. To a phenomenal degree he *Roosevelt's* exhibited in his personality the traits that the average *popularity* American most admired; the President was the ordinary citizen as he might have looked if seen under a microscope.[1] The typical American loved sports, and the President was a disciple of the "strenuous life." He rode horseback, played tennis, boxed, and hunted. Tales of his prowess continually reached the public — a day's horseback ride over icy roads to prove to his "swivel-chair" generals that the thing could be done; the existence of a "tennis cabinet"; boxing matches in the White House (in one of them the President lost the sight of an eye); and a bear hunt in which the President refused to kill a planted bear — the original "Teddy bear." The typical American sometimes lost his temper and called people names, but none ever did it with greater artistry than the President, who took so many people to task for their truthlessness that the newspapermen gleefully described his victims as the "Ananias Club." Like most Americans, the President was a devoted family man, and stories of his cheerful unconcern when the Roosevelt children rode a pony into the White House elevator, or burst into a cabinet meeting to announce the birth of a new family of guinea-pigs, appealed strongly to every right-thinking American. All Americans liked entertaining, and the President was an indefatigable entertainer. Anyone who interested him was apt to be called to the White House for a luncheon or a dinner to exchange views with the President; only there was often not much of an exchange, for the President loved to talk and did most of the talking. Roosevelt's prominent teeth, his spectacles, his cowboy hat, and his general air of belligerency made him the cartoon-

---

[1] Entertaining sidelights on the Roosevelt personality are contained in A. W. Butt, *Taft and Roosevelt: The Intimate Letters of Archie Butt* (2 vols., 1930). An earlier volume, *The Letters of Archie Butt* (1924), is also useful.

ist's delight, and his knack of clothing his every deed in an aura of righteousness did him no harm.

> T. R. is spanking a Senator,
> T. R. is chasing a bear,
> T. R. is busting an awful Trust,
> And dragging it from its lair.
> They're calling T. R. a lot of things —
> The men in the private car —
> But the day-coach likes exciting folks
> And the day-coach likes T. R.[1]

Not that the public always agreed with Roosevelt; sometimes it disagreed with him violently, and a few people hated him. When the
President advocated uniform marriage and divorce laws for the states, he
was generally applauded, but nothing much was done about it. When
he argued against "race suicide," and urged native Americans to have
more children, he got no results whatever. When he denounced "nature
fakers," whose books of highly imaginary animal lore delighted the
youth of the land, the books continued to be written and read. When
he joined the crusade for simplified spelling, he found adult America
unwilling to sacrifice the spelling-book knowledge it had so painfully
gained, and young America helpless before its elders. But these idiosyncrasies, for the most part, served only to endear the President to the
public. He made friends with the newspapermen, furnished them good
copy, and obtained valuable front-page publicity by making timely
releases. Once the San Francisco earthquake and fire pushed an important presidential document far into the newspapers' insides, but accidents of that kind happened only rarely.

Roosevelt's relations with the public were at their worst in his handling
of the Negro problem. Although his mother came from the South, he
was a thoroughgoing Northerner in his prejudices, and *Roosevelt*
early in his administration he shocked Southern whites by *and the*
inviting Booker T. Washington, the great Negro educator, *Negro*
to have dinner with him at the White House. Southerners *problem*
admired Washington, but they did not dine with him, or with any other
Negro. "How should you address Washington?" ran one story, perhaps
not apocryphal. "Well," said the Southerner, "you can't call such a
man 'Booker,' and I won't call any Negro 'Mister,' so I just call him
'Professor.'" It was a long time before the South could forgive Roose-

---

[1] From *A Book of Americans*, published by Farrar & Rinehart, Inc. Copyright, 1933,
by Rosemary and Stephen Vincent Benét.

DRAWING
THE LINE
IN MISSISSIPPI

Reproduced by permission of C. K. Berryman

THE MISSISSIPPI BEAR HUNT

velt's disregard of the color line. Nor did it like his determination not to distinguish between whites and blacks in appointments to office. Indianola, Mississippi, got a Negro postmistress, and Charleston, South Carolina, a Negro collector. He showed, too, the utmost contempt for the "lily-white" Republican organizations in the South which vied with the Democrats in their determination to keep Negroes out of politics. On the other hand, he was as impetuous as any Southerner in his hand-ling of the "Brownsville affair." Because a few Negro soldiers had been charged with shooting up the town of Brownsville, Texas, while absent from their barracks without leave, three companies of Negro troops were dishonorably discharged from the service. Subsequent investigations seemed to prove that the troops were much more sinned against than sinning, but Roosevelt left office without having admitted his mistake.

Roosevelt's popularity had much to do with the overwhelming victories scored by the Republicans in the four elections (1902, 1904, 1906, 1908) held during his administration, and his renomination *Election* and re-election in 1904 was a great personal triumph. *of 1904* Eager to be President in his own right, Roosevelt was unduly distressed at the tendency of ultra-conservative Republicans to rally around Mark Hanna for the nomination, but Hanna's death in February, 1904, left him a free field. As one observer remarked, he was nominated by acclamation and elected much the same way. Chosen to serve with him as Vice-President was Charles W. Fairbanks, an Indiana conservative. The Democrats, after two disastrous defeats under the leadership of the radical Bryan, chose as their standard-bearer Alton B. Parker, a "safe and sane" New York judge who accepted the nomination on condition that he be left free to support the gold standard. This attempt to commit the party to a definite monetary policy, when all reference to the subject had been discreetly omitted from the platform, contrasted painfully with Bryan's declaration. "You may dispute whether I have fought a good fight, you may dispute whether I have finished my course, but you cannot deny that I have kept the faith." For a moment it seemed that the convention might replace Parker with Bryan, but it did not, and Bryan accorded the nominee his half-hearted support. For second place on the ticket the Democrats chose Henry Gassaway Davis, a rich octogenarian from West Virginia, who was expected to contribute heavily to the Democratic campaign chest, but proved to be a disappointment.

Parker ran a poorer race than Bryan ever had, receiving only 140 electoral votes to Roosevelt's 336. Roosevelt even broke into the border South by carrying Missouri, West Virginia, and one vote in Maryland. "Wall Street," to the disappointment of the Democrats, supported the Republican nominee, largely because businessmen regarded the Republican Party, in spite of Roosevelt, as more dependable than the Democratic. The Republican campaign chest was well filled with corporation contributions, and Parker won only a life membership in the Ananias Club for his charge that these donations were obtained as "blackmail" in return for the suppression of damaging evidence by the Bureau of Corporations, over which George B. Cortelyou, the Republican campaign manager, presided. Elated by the election returns, Roosevelt immediately issued a dramatic statement that he must have regretted later many times. "The wise custom which limits the President to two terms regards the substance and not the form, and under no circumstances will I be a candidate for or accept another nomination." [1]

Roosevelt's second administration came nearest shipwreck in connection with the Panic of 1907, which was the result, so many claimed, *The Panic of 1907* of his unwarranted attacks on business. His prosecutions of the trusts and his attempts to regulate the railroads, hostile critics declared, endangered legitimate profits; the "square deal" encouraged labor to make unreasonable demands; and conservation called a halt to the lucrative exploitation of natural resources. Public confidence in business integrity was indeed somewhat shaken when in April, 1907, Judge Kenesaw Mountain Landis found the Standard Oil Company of New Jersey guilty on 1462 separate counts of obtaining illegal rebates from the Chicago and Alton Railroad, and assessed against it a fine of $29,240,000; nor was confidence wholly restored when a higher court reversed the sentence. Later in the same year the American Sugar Refining Company was proved to have tampered with the scales on which the sugar it imported was weighed, and the government by court action recovered over four million dollars. This, too, was a bit unsettling, both to the public and to business. Roosevelt was sensitive to the criticism that his policies were undermining confidence, but he claimed that the fault lay with business, and not with him. "If trouble comes from having the light turned on," he told a cabinet member, "remember it is not really due to the light, but to the misconduct which is exposed." He came, indeed, to believe that the Panic of 1907 was purely "psychological"; that it had been intentionally produced by "malefactors of great wealth," bent on discrediting his policies.

Undoubtedly an important factor in bringing on the Panic of 1907 was the wholesale multiplication of securities that had taken place in the early years of the century. United States Steel, for example, was capitalized at a sum far in excess of the total capital of the companies it incorporated. These securities were often sold at higher prices than the earning power of the corporations they represented would justify, and eventual disillusionment was sure to come. Another factor was the inelasticity of the currency and of credit. The United States government had no way of providing an extra supply of money to meet an

---

[1] The political history of the period is portrayed without embellishment in F. A. Ogg, *National Progress, 1907–1917* (1918), but with many embellishments in Mark Sullivan, *Our Times*, iii, *Pre-War America* (1930), and iv, *The War Begins, 1909–1914* (1932).

emergency. The total amount of gold and silver, national bank notes, and Treasury notes that composed the money of the country was relatively fixed. If confidence lagged and money was hoarded, there was sure to be a shortage. Much the same thing was true of credit, which was limited primarily by the ability and willingness of a few great New York bankers to lend. Practically every financial institution in the country was connected in one way or another with the Wall Street bankers, and was amenable to discipline by them. They thus constituted a kind of a "money trust" that almost at will could grant or withhold the credit necessary to keep the nation's business moving.

Unmistakable signs of the gathering storm were apparent throughout the early weeks of October, 1907, and on October 22 a run began on the Knickerbocker Trust Company, the third largest in New York, which by noon of October 23 had exhausted its resources in cash. Runs on other New York banks eventually *Roosevelt and the Panic* forced a dozen more to close their doors. On the stock exchange values plunged downward, and call money became practically unobtainable. To help meet the emergency, George B. Cortelyou, Secretary of the Treasury, deposited twenty-five million dollars of Treasury funds with the New York banks, while clearing-house certificates and payroll checks passed freely in lieu of money. The storm was soon over, but it left in its wake a train of wreckage that affected the whole country. Several railroads went into bankruptcy, factories were closed, and men were out of work. The situation was not as serious, however, as it seemed, and by January, 1908, recovery had set in. Roosevelt had done his part, as he thought, by promising the United States Steel Corporation immunity from prosecution so that it could absorb, and save from collapse, the Tennessee Coal and Iron Company. This, Morgan told the President, was necessary to stave off a really major disaster.[1]

Convinced that the panic might have been averted, or at least that its worst effects might have been avoided, had the banking and currency system of the United States been on a sounder footing, Congress in 1908 passed the Aldrich-Vreeland Act which empowered the national banks of the country for a period of six years to issue emergency currency in times of financial stringency. This was but a mere stop-gap. The most important part of the act was to create a National Monetary Commission to investigate the currency systems of the world and to lay plans for a thoroughgoing reform in the American system. The commission reported in 1912, and on the basis of its findings the Federal Reserve Act of 1913 was adopted.

[1] W. F. McCaleb, *Theodore Roosevelt* (1931), is especially satisfactory at this point.

Meantime the end of Roosevelt's administration was fast approaching and the election of 1908 was at hand. In spite of Roosevelt's asser-

Who should succeed Roosevelt? tion of four years before he was accused of wanting to run again, and certainly many of his admirers would have been delighted to see him have a third term. Neverthe-less, Roosevelt had no intention of running again, and to head off the danger that his devotees might draft him, as they had once done for the Vice-Presidency, he decided to work actively for the nomination of another candidate as committed as himself to the Roosevelt policies. This was the more necessary because of the avowed determination of Republican conservatives to capture the nomination for one of their

Copyright, Harris and Ewing

CHARLES EVANS HUGHES

[416]

kind. Leading candidates from the "stand-pat" wing of the Republican Party were Joseph G. Cannon of Illinois, who as Speaker of the House of Representatives had again and again thwarted Roosevelt's plans; Joseph B. Foraker, who as Senator from Ohio had been equally antagonistic; and Charles Warren Fairbanks of Indiana, the Vice-President, whose correct behavior in office deceived no one as to his thoroughgoing dislike for the President's policies. There were rumors that a "slush-fund" was being collected to promote such "favorite son" candidacies and to insure that in the end a reliable conservative would be nominated.

If he were to choose his successor, three possibilities at once presented themselves to Roosevelt's mind. Next to the President himself, Charles Evans Hughes (1862–1948) of New York was the reformers' delight. Before 1905 Hughes was only a brilliant *Hughes* New York lawyer, but his work as investigator of the New York insurance companies catapulted him at once into national fame. What amazed the insurance companies no less than it gratified the public was the way in which Hughes showed himself even more familiar with the intricacies of the insurance business than many of its high-salaried executives. But Hughes sought facts, not publicity. He demonstrated that the insurance companies had speculated freely with their clients' funds, that their methods had been both crooked and wasteful, and that they had never hesitated to mix politics with business. Had he permitted it, he might have been nominated for mayor of New York, but he chose rather to become the Republican candidate for governor in 1906, a prize that the machine dared not deny him. Elected, he became even more distasteful to the professional politicians than they had feared. He made appointments on merit, gave the most "pitiless publicity" to his conduct of official business, forced the legislature to adopt a direct primary law and to prohibit race-track gambling, and risked public disfavor by a judicious veto of a two-cent passenger-rate law that he claimed was unfair to the railroads. But Roosevelt did not like Hughes. He thought the New York governor too uncompromising, too utterly unwilling to play ball with the politicians. Besides, Hughes had never been associated with the Roosevelt policies; how could one be sure that he would maintain them? Might he not instead substitute policies of his own?

Roosevelt believed that of all his lieutenants Elihu Root (1845–1937), his Secretary of State, was the ablest.[1] It was Root who as Secretary of War had welded the American Empire together. It was Root, too,

---

[1] P. C. Jessup, *Elihu Root* (2 vols., 1938), is admirably thorough, and useful for the entire period of Root's political activity.

Brown Brothers

ELIHU ROOT

who had carried forward undimmed the brilliant work of his predecessor, John Hay, in the State Department. Unfortunately, however, there was nothing about Root that appealed strongly to the public. As a lawyer he had served some of the very corporations that Roosevelt's administration had most opposed; nor had he always been scrupulous in his choice of clients. His first large fee came as a result of his work in defense of "Boss" Tweed. Roosevelt was confident that Root, as President, would serve the interests of the United States with the same single-minded devotion that he had shown as a cabinet member, but that was beside the point. Root was politically unavailable.

[418]

The third possibility was William Howard Taft (1857–1930), whose record was happily untarnished by a profitable law practice.[1] The Taft family had long played a prominent rôle in the affairs of Cincinnati, Ohio, and Taft's father, Judge Alphonso Taft, had once been a member of Grant's cabinet. Taft's rise up the political ladder came principally by the appointive route. An honor graduate of Yale, he became successively a judge in the superior court of Ohio, solicitor-general in the federal Department of Justice, federal judge, commissioner to the Philippines and governor-general, and finally Secretary of War. A consistently able administrator and Roosevelt's favorite envoy abroad, he had had what seemed to be an almost ideal training for the Presidency. His personal inclinations lay toward the Supreme Court, but more than once he felt obliged to reject the appointment he craved in the interest of the unfinished business he had in hand. His family was more ambitious for him than he was for himself. His wife wanted him to be President, and so also did his wealthy brother, Charles P. Taft. He was a huge man weighing three hundred and fifty pounds, good-natured and affable, and blessed with an infectious chuckle. The people might like him. Roosevelt certainly did, and as early as 1907 let it be known that he would support Taft for the Republican nomination in 1908. Presidential support can be, and in this case it was, extraordinarily effective, and as a result Taft was nominated on the first ballot by a convention that would have preferred Roosevelt. Second place on the ticket went as a consolation prize to the conservatives, who counted the nominee, James S. Sherman of New York, as one of the most dependable of their number.

The Democrats, disastrously defeated four years before with the conservative Parker, renominated Bryan, who was still young, vigorous, and hopeful. For Vice-President they nominated John W. Kern of Indiana. Bryan as a favorite Chautauqua orator had probably been heard by more Americans than any other man in public life, and his adherents gave him the same unstinted *The Democrats name Bryan* devotion that Henry Clay and James G. Blaine had once commanded. In 1906 Bryan had made a trip around the world, had been well received, and had returned with his self-confidence restored. Ready at last to admit that free silver was a dead issue, he proposed in August, 1906, a new program for curbing the trusts. Corporations should be barred

[1] H. F. Pringle, *The Life and Times of William Howard Taft* (2 vols., 1939), lacks much of the sparkle that makes Pringle's *Roosevelt* so readable, but is an even better study from the point of view of research. On Taft's earlier career, Mrs. W. H. Taft, *Recollections of Full Years* (1914), is very satisfactory. H. S. Duffy, *William Howard Taft* (1930), is far inferior to Pringle.

from contributing to campaign funds, interlocking directorates should be prohibited, and a federal license should be required of all engaged in interstate business. For the railroad problem he reverted to the Populist remedy, government ownership, "not as an immediate issue, but as an ultimate solution of the controversy." The trouble with Bryan's program was that it was so like Roosevelt's; indeed, well before election time Congress had passed and Roosevelt had signed a measure forbidding corporations to contribute toward the election of national officers, while Bryan had temporized still further on the railroad question.

The real issue in the lackadaisical campaign of 1908 was whether Bryan or Taft could be the better trusted to carry out the Roosevelt *Election* policies. In the end Taft won by an electoral vote of 321 *of 1908* to 162. Besides the "solid South" Bryan carried only Nebraska, Colorado, and Nevada, but he at least surpassed Parker's record of four years before. Republican conservatives, looking carefully into Taft's record as a judge, concluded that they had little to fear from Roosevelt's political legatee. Later, not without a show of justice, Bryan complained that the Republicans had enjoyed an unfair advantage in the campaign. Taft the progressive carried the West, while Taft the conservative carried the East. Forty-six states participated in the election of 1908; for in 1907 the majority party in Congress had at last decided that Republican supremacy was well enough established to risk the admission of Oklahoma, an almost certainly Democratic state. A similar offer to admit New Mexico and Arizona as one state failed because of the opposition of Arizona to such a scheme.

The emphasis placed by both the older parties on reform called striking attention to the important rôle that minor parties, in spite of their inability to attract large numbers of voters to their standards, actually played in American politics. In the campaign of 1908 the Populist Party gasped its last, but many of its cherished principles had long since been espoused by Bryan Democracy and Roosevelt Republicanism. William Randolph Hearst's Independence League, formed primarily to advance the political ambitions of its author, furnished more effective opposition to the nomination of Parker by the Democrats in 1904 than came from any other source, and in 1908, as a third party with a ticket of Hearst's choosing, attempted to out-Bryan Bryan and to out-Roosevelt Roosevelt. Prohibition candidates in every election called emphatic attention to the liquor evil, and often induced the older parties, at least in local contests, to support their creed.

Of ever-increasing importance was socialism, which was brought to the United States, mainly by immigrants, far back in the nineteenth century. Not until the late eighties were the conditions of American life sufficiently similar to those of Europe to make socialism seem plausible, even to the least favored of Americans. Then many "Nationalist Clubs," inspired by ideas gleaned from Edward Bellamy's *Looking Backward*, sought to promote socialism, but their views were mildness itself. "We advocate no sudden or ill-considered changes, we make no war upon individuals, we do not censure those who have accumulated fortunes," so the first Nationalist Club maintained. Far more aggressive was Daniel De Leon, an immigrant from the West Indies who believed that all compromise with capitalism served only to postpone the day of deliverance. De Leon revived the old Socialist-Labor Party that had been launched in the seventies, and beginning in 1892 it regularly nominated tickets in national campaigns. Toward the turn of the century De Leon's extreme radicalism led to a split in Socialist ranks, and in 1900 the Social Democratic or, as it was more commonly called, the Socialist Party, for the first time, but by no means the last, nominated Eugene V. Debs for the Presidency. Loyally supported by Morris Hillquit of New York, Victor L. Berger of Milwaukee, and other anti-Leonites, Debs polled 94,864 votes, nearly three times as many as his Socialist-Labor competitor. Four years later the Debs vote was 402,895, and in 1908 it was 420,890. Meantime the Socialist-Labor Party had lost ground rapidly.[1]

The fundamental tenet of the Socialists was the abolition of the capitalist system in order to make way for the ownership by the public of all the means of production and distribution. This end they hoped ultimately to achieve by use of the ballot, rather than by revolution; nor did they "strive to substitute working-class rule for capitalist-class rule, but to free all humanity from class rule and to realize the international brotherhood of man." Pending more fundamental reforms, they were willing to support such halfway measures as public works for the relief of the unemployed, the collective ownership of the railroads, public utilities, and all existing national monopolies; the improvement of the industrial condition of the workers; the extension of inheritance taxes; a graduated income tax; woman suffrage; the initiative and the referendum; the abolition of the doctrine of judicial review; the election of judges by the people for short terms; and the enactment of further measures for general education and the conservation of health. Many so-called socialistic policies had an ancestry quite separate from the Socialist Party, but many others were original and seeped gradually over into the old-party

Socialism in the United States

---

[1] Nathan Fine, *Labor and Farmer Parties in the United States, 1828–1928* (1928), is good on labor. A. E. Morgan, *Edward Bellamy* (1944), is a useful biography.

platforms. The dying Populists conceded that Roosevelt had put more of their principles into effect than they could ever have believed possible without a Populist victory; the Socialists did not mean to die, but some of their views had received the earnest support of Roosevelt, and they hoped for similar favors from Taft.

The Taft administration took office with almost universal good-will. In his inaugural address the new President pledged himself anew to *Taft takes* perpetuate the policies of his predecessor, and in making *office* up his cabinet he chose three of Roosevelt's chief advisers. Philander C. Knox, once Roosevelt's "trust-busting" Attorney-General, but now a Senator from Pennsylvania, became Secretary of State, while George von L. Meyer, Roosevelt's Postmaster-General, took over the Navy Department, and James Wilson stayed on as Secretary of Agriculture. "Never before in our time," said the New York *Tribune*, "has the entry of a new President into office marked so slight a break politically between the present and the past." In order the better to give his successor a free hand, Roosevelt took off immediately on a hunt for big game in Africa, and for a full year was lost to the civilized world. Persistent rumors of a rift between the outgoing and the incoming President were denied by their public behavior, and by a private letter from Taft to Roosevelt just before inauguration. "You and I know that there has not been the slightest difference between us."

Tariff revision had certainly never been one of the Roosevelt policies. Roosevelt had occasionally toyed with the idea, but he had always found some excuse for avoiding an issue fraught with so many political perils. The chief demand for revision came from the middle-western agrarians who had discovered at last that high duties on manufactured articles not only increased the prices of the things they had to buy, but by limiting imports closed to agriculture many foreign markets. From about 1902 on the "Iowa idea," which called insistently for lower duties, had gained momentum. During the campaign there had been much talk of the tariff as the "mother of the trusts," and both parties had pledged themselves to do something about it. The Democratic pledge was the more specific: "We favor immediate revision of the tariff by the reduction of import duties." The Republicans declared themselves "unequivocally for a revision of the tariff by a special session of Congress," but neglected entirely to be unequivocal as to whether they meant revision up or revision down. What they wanted, they said, was "the imposition of such duties as will equal the difference between the cost of production at home and abroad, together with a reasonable profit to American industry." This might, of course, mean anything or nothing

WILLIAM HOWARD TAFT

Brown Brothers

Copyright, Friander

ROBERT M. LA FOLLETTE

just as Congress chose, and Taft was pressed to state whether the Republicans intended merely to revise the tariff or to revise it downward. Not so skilled in evasiveness as the platform-makers, he promised with complete candor that there would be revision downward.

Time was soon to prove that the promise was easier than the performance. Taft called Congress into special session for March 15, and

Payne-Aldrich Tariff on April 9 the Payne Bill, already well formulated when Congress met, passed the House of Representatives by a strict party vote. Reformers were somewhat surprised that the bill, although frankly protectionist, really provided for moderate reductions downward, but everyone knew that the Senate would rewrite the measure throughout. They knew, too, that the Senate was still far less responsive to the public will than the House. In the latter an increasingly large number of members owed their seats to the new direct primaries, but no such transformation had altered the character of the Senate. Only a few states had as yet adopted senatorial primaries, and in any event the six-year term for senators made the upper chamber, quite as the "founding fathers" had intended, extremely resistant to change. The chairman of the Senate Committee on Finance was Nelson W. Aldrich of Rhode Island, a man of brilliant intellect, but a multi-millionaire industrialist whose views on the tariff were the views of his class. Respected and feared by his colleagues, Aldrich was as nearly the political "boss" of the United States as any one man could be.

Aldrich's committee attached hundreds of amendments to the Payne Bill, very few of which reduced duties downward. Some of the new provisions were "jokers," which by changing specific duties to *ad valorem*, or *vice versa*, or in some other unapparent way, covered up cleverly a sharp revision upward. Regardless of intent to deceive, which was the exception rather than the rule, the bill was complicated and needed careful study to be understood; but Aldrich proposed to "railroad" it through the Senate by making it the sole order of business until passed. At this point a little group of middle-western Republican insurgents, led by Senator La Follette of Wisconsin, interrupted Aldrich's plans by a prolonged debate that revealed to the whole country exactly what was going on. La Follette, ably assisted by Dolliver and Cummins of Iowa, Beveridge of Indiana, Bristow of Kansas, Clapp of Minnesota, and a few others, studied the bill by night and debated it by day. They were unable to prevent its passage, but ten of them joined with the Democrats in refusing to vote for it.[1]

[1] This fight is best studied through biographies of the principal actors, N. W. Stephenson, *Nelson W. Aldrich* (1930); La Follette, *Autobiography*; Bowers, *Beveridge*; and Pringle, *Taft*.

Reproduced by special permission of Herbert Johnson

"PLEASE, MR. ALDRICH"

Taft, meantime, had at first encouraged the insurgents, thinking that they might obtain a better bill, but finally, dismayed at the prospect of a split in his party, had joined forces with the conservative *Taft and the* majority. The Payne-Aldrich Bill that emerged from the *tariff* joint House and Senate conference committee was a complete betrayal of Taft's campaign promises, but he signed it nevertheless. It provided for more decreases than increases in duties, but the decreases were rarely on items of significance, and far more duties were left untouched than were changed. The average rate on dutiable goods was about one per cent higher under the new law than under the Dingley Act of 1897. Taft's attitude amazed and disappointed the public, which during the preceding régime had become accustomed to presidential leadership, and had expected him to bring enough pressure to bear on Congress to get what he and the country wanted. But Taft, as an able constitutional lawyer, had more respect for the legislative independence of Congress than Roosevelt had ever had; besides, he was good-humored and peace-loving, whereas Roosevelt was never happier than in the midst of an "elegant row."

[425]

While Taft himself regarded some of the bill, particularly the woolens schedule, as indefensible, there were parts of it that were legitimately entitled to praise. The European system of maximum-minimum rates, which it incorporated, enabled the President to apply a higher schedule of rates against nations discriminating against American trade. A bipartisan tariff board was also established, the duty of which was to study the relative costs of production at home and abroad and to give Congress expert advice as to the rates it should set. Furthermore, a one per cent tax on the net incomes of corporations in excess of five thousand dollars opened up new possibilities both for the production of revenue and for the use of taxation as a means of regulation.

Separately adopted, but related to the tariff by its bearing on national finance, was a resolution submitting to the states a constitutional amendment for the legalization of a federal income tax. Submitted on July 12, 1909, the Sixteenth Amendment was fully ratified and declared in force on February 25, 1913, just before Taft left office.

Taft, painfully aware of his ebbing popularity, sought by a "swing around the circle" to rehabilitate himself with his western critics. In *Taft's Winona address* the fall of 1909 he traveled sixteen thousand miles, and spoke repeatedly to large, but unenthusiastic, audiences. At Winona, Minnesota, he made the strategic blunder of defending the Payne-Aldrich Tariff, insisting that it was the best tariff bill that the Republican Party had ever passed. Had he apologized for it as the best bill he could get, he might have won the sympathy of the West, but his outspoken support of the detested measure convinced his hearers that he was party to the betrayal of his own promises. What chance had the Roosevelt policies for survival under the leadership of such a man?

Circumstances soon made it appear that on the subject of conservation the new President was no more to be trusted than on the tariff. *The Ballinger-Pinchot controversy* Taft's Secretary of the Interior, R. A. Ballinger of Washington, was not unaware of the skepticism common to his section about the retardation of western development for the benefit of generations yet unborn. Nevertheless, his actions in reopening to private exploitation some water-power sites in Montana and Wyoming and in permitting the alienation of certain valuable coal lands in Alaska were undoubtedly due to legal scruple rather than to unconcern about conservation. As President, Roosevelt was accustomed to follow the dictates of his conscience, if no law stood in the way, whereas Ballinger and Taft both felt obliged to seek legal justification for their acts. Ballinger's behavior was vigorously protested during the summer and fall of 1909 by one of his subordinates, Louis R. Glavis, and by the chief of the forestry service, Gifford Pinchot, whose division lay within the Department of Agriculture. Taft, after careful investigation, decided that there was nothing against Ballinger, and dismissed both Glavis and Pinchot from office. In the case of Pinchot, he took action with great reluctance, for Pinchot, as everyone knew, was a close friend of Roosevelt's. Dismissal, however, was an administrative necessity, for Pinchot had violated a rule prohibiting subordinates from corresponding directly with members of Congress by writing Senator Dolliver in defense of Glavis. "There is only one thing for you to do," Senator Root had told the President, "and that you must do at once." But to the ever more hostile public Taft had lined up with the anti-conservationists. Even when Ballinger was frozen out of the cabinet a year later, it made little difference. Taft had been elected to carry out the Roosevelt policies, and he was carrying them out "on a stretcher." [1]

Hard on the heels of the Pinchot-Ballinger controversy came an outburst of insurgency in the House of Representatives. When conservative Republicans in the House had tried to block an investigation of the Interior Department, a group of Republican insurgents had voted with the Democrats in favor of it, and had discovered that with Democratic co-operation they could control the House. This newly found power they now determined to use against the autocratic sway of the Speaker, Joseph G. Cannon of Illinois, an ultra-conservative who consistently and effectively stood in the way of all progressive legislation.[2] From the early days of the republic the Speaker had been permitted to appoint all committees of the House, designating also the chairmen. This privilege gave him enormous power to punish the recalcitrant and to reward the faithful. Also, as dominant member of the Rules Committee, composed of only five members, he followed the precedents of "Czar" Reed in determining the course of legislation; without his consent it was all but impossible even to bring a measure to a vote. Discontent with "Cannonism" had been apparent in the first session after Taft's inauguration, when twelve Republican members voted against Cannon for the speakership, and a still larger number voted with the Democrats against the rules which gave him his power. The tariff battle and the uproar over conservation

Insurgency in the House

---

[1] Gifford Pinchot, *The Fight for Conservation* (1910); Rose M. Stahl, *The Ballinger-Pinchot Controversy* (1926); A. T. Mason, *Bureaucracy Convicts Itself* (1941).

[2] L. W. Busbey, *Uncle Joe Cannon* (1927), is of some value, but a wholly satisfactory life of Cannon has not yet appeared.

brought new recruits to the insurgents, and by March, 1910, they were ready for a new test of strength.

Ably led by Representative George W. Norris of Nebraska, they presented an amendment to the House rules designed to take the ap-

Revision of the House rules pointment of the Rules Committee out of the hands of the Speaker, and to make it elective by the House. With every parliamentary weapon in his power, Cannon and his conservative Republican supporters met the onslaught, and one session lasted continuously for twenty-six hours. But Norris proved to be quite as adroit as the Speaker, and the combination of Democrats and insurgent Republicans held together. On the final vote about forty Republicans joined the Democrats in voting to change the rules. Cannon, acknowledging defeat, offered his resignation as Speaker, but with his powers curtailed he was permitted to keep his post. When the next Congress met, the rules were still further amended. All committees were made elective, with the Ways and Means Committee acting as a committee on committees. The changes wrought were fundamental. No longer could it be said that the Speaker, next to the President, was the most powerful of American officials; moreover, the chief agency for maintaining party discipline in the House was destroyed. More and more members felt free to vote as their consciences or their constituents might direct, regardless of party pressure.

With insurgency rampant both in the Senate and the House, it was obvious that the party split which Taft had sought to avoid had come about. On the one hand were the conservatives led by Aldrich and Cannon, a faction with which the President, willy-nilly, had come to be allied. On the other hand were the insurgents, who stood for popular, not boss, control of the party, and believed that when the direct primary was established in every state their faction would be in the majority rather than in the minority. They stood also for real tariff revision, for genuine conservation, and for the expansion of governmental control over trusts and railroads. For leadership they looked beyond Norris and La Follette to Africa:

> Teddy, come home and blow your horn,
> The sheep's in the meadow, the cow's in the corn.
> The boy you left to 'tend the sheep
> Is under the haystack fast asleep.[1]

On March 14, 1910, the Roosevelt hunting party disbanded at Khartum in the Anglo-Egyptian Sudan. Not without some assistance, Roosevelt had accounted for nine lions, five elephants, thirteen rhinoc-

[1] *Life*, May 26, 1910, quoted in Mark Sullivan, *Our Times*, IV, 441.

Reproduced by special permission of Herbert Johnson

THE COMMON PEOPLE AWAITING T. R.'S RETURN

eroses, seven hippopotamuses, and no less than two hundred and sixty-two other specimens. In Egypt he observed the symptoms of mounting discontent, and two months later in London he told the British either to get out of there or else to stay in and do their duty. In Italy he missed an audience with the Pope because the Holy Father insisted on knowing in advance that Roosevelt would not visit the Methodist mission in Rome; for good measure the ex-President passed up the Methodists also, but he met the King and Queen. In Austria-Hungary he was banqueted by the Emperor; in Germany he helped the Kaiser review his army; in England, as the official representative of the United States at the funeral of Edward VII, he vied for attention with all the assembled royalty, dead and alive. He delivered carefully prepared addresses at the Sorbonne, at Christiania, at Berlin, and at Oxford. And between times he read letters and newspapers from home that featured the Taft betrayal. He had, too, more direct information; Gifford Pinchot had crossed the ocean to meet him on the *White Nile*.

Back in his country home at Oyster Bay, New York, Roosevelt maintained a discreet neutrality. "I shall make no speeches or say anything *Roosevelt's* for two months," he wrote Taft in response to a letter of *return* welcome, "but I shall keep my mind as open as I keep my mouth shut." La Follette called on the ex-President, and reported that he was "very much pleased" with his visit. Roosevelt saw other insurgents, also, but he paid a friendly call on the President at his summer home in Beverly, Massachusetts, and he wrote in the *Outlook*, to which he had become a contributing editor, that the Payne-Aldrich Tariff was a definite improvement over either the Dingley Act or the Wilson Act. As for the dismissal of Pinchot, he had written Lodge from Europe that he was "not yet sure whether Taft could ... have followed any course save the one he did."

Probably Roosevelt wished above all else to heal the breach in the Republican Party, for he knew full well that the alternative was a Democratic victory, not only in the mid-term elections of 1910, but also in 1912, and he sincerely believed that the Democratic Party was incapable of governing the country. It was with party success in view, not the discomfiture of Taft, that in August, 1910, he took the temporary chairmanship of the New York state nominating convention away from Vice-President Sherman, whom the conservatives had favored, and helped in the nomination of a Liberal candidate, Henry L. Stimson, on a Liberal platform for governor. Only by such a course, he believed, could the Republicans hope to hold the party together and maintain their control of the state. He made two speech-making tours, one through the West and another through the South, as he thought in the interest of party harmony and Republican success at the polls. At Osawatomie, Kansas, he gave a name, the New Nationalism, to the principles for which he stood, and to which he believed that he had committed the Republican Party. While the direction of his sympathies was apparent, he made numerous efforts to conciliate the conservatives. With even-handed justice he endorsed Beveridge the insurgent for re-election to the Senate from Indiana, and Warren Gamaliel Harding, a consistent conservative, for the governorship of Ohio. In his address before the New York Convention he praised the accomplishments of the Taft administration in the highest terms, and in September he again called on the President.

All this was of no avail, for the country was in a mood to rebuke the *Elections* Republicans by voting the Democratic ticket. Stimson, *of 1910* Beveridge, and Harding alike went down to defeat, and the House of Representatives fell to the Democrats with 229 members to

161 for the Republicans and one for the Socialists, Victor L. Berger of Milwaukee. The Senate remained Republican by a vote of 51 to 41, but this majority was so slender that the insurgents, of whom there were a dozen or more, by voting with the Democrats, could easily overturn it. The conservative Republicans had thus lost control of both houses of Congress. In the states the trend was equally pronounced. Not only in New York and Ohio, but in such regularly Republican centers as Massachusetts, Connecticut, and New Jersey, the Democrats emerged triumphant.

There can be no doubt that the election was intended as a rebuke to the Taft administration, but in many ways it was undeserved. In reality, Taft had carried out the Roosevelt policies with considerable success. He had secured a revision of the tariff, something that Roosevelt had not even dared to attempt. He had prosecuted the trusts with vigor and persistence; before his administration ended he had brought more than twice as many suits against them as were undertaken by Roosevelt. He had sponsored the Mann-Elkins Act of 1910, which gave the Interstate Commerce Commission jurisdiction over terminals and services of communication by telegraph, telephone, and cable. It also placed upon the carriers the burden of proving the justice of contemplated changes, for under its terms the commission might suspend new rates for ten months, pending investigation. It included, too, a plan that was essentially Taft's own, to create a special Commerce Court, composed of experts in the law of commerce, to which appeals from the decisions of the commission might be made. Taft's services to conservation were similarly notable. He replaced Pinchot by the head of the Yale School of Forestry, who added to the national forests by the purchase of timbered tracts in the Appalachians. Taft also got authority from Congress that Roosevelt lacked to withdraw coal lands from entry, and he was the first President to withdraw oil lands. Other reform measures enacted during the Taft administration, but generally ignored by his critics, included the improvement of the public land laws; the requirement of safety appliances on railroads; the establishment of a Bureau of Mines charged among other things with the duty of studying the welfare of the miners; a postal savings law; a parcels post law; and the separation of the Department of Commerce and Labor into two departments.

Much of Taft's unpopularity may be attributed to his political ineptitude, and much of it merely to hard luck. He got little credit for the reforms of the Mann-Elkins Act, for the measure as finally passed was more radical than he had dared to recommend. His Commerce

Court was well conceived, but it showed too great friendliness for the
Taft's corporations to suit the public, and one of its judges, R. W.
political Archbald, had to be impeached. In 1913 it was abolished.
ineptitude He signed long overdue measures for the admission of
Arizona and New Mexico, but when Arizona included the recall of
judges in her constitution he refused to proclaim its admission until the
obnoxious clause had been taken out. Once in the Union, Arizona
ostentatiously readopted the clause it had been compelled to delete.

Taft even had trouble about his appointments to the Supreme Court.
When Chief Justice Melville W. Fuller died in 1910, Taft promoted
Associate Justice Edward Douglass White of Louisiana to fill the
vacancy. This was a graceful compliment to a hard-working judge
and a political opponent, but White, besides being a Democrat, was a
Roman Catholic, an ex-Confederate, and a conservative. To appoint
him Taft had to overlook the claims of Associate Justice J. M. Harlan
of Kentucky, who was a Republican, a Protestant, a veteran of the Union
army, and a liberal. Altogether President Taft appointed five new
members to the Supreme Court, all able jurists; and his choices included
liberals and conservatives, Democrats and Republicans. But even the
appointment of Charles Evans Hughes in 1910 failed to win the applause
it merited. Some said Hughes should have been made Chief Justice;
others, that the appointment was designed merely to sidetrack a possible
competitor for the Republican nomination in 1912.

Reciprocity with Canada was a favorite Taft policy, and seemingly
quite in line with the views of the tariff reformers. At length, after
Reciprocity persistent effort, he obtained an agreement in 1911 that
with Canada noticeably lessened the trade barriers between the Dominion
and the United States. The proposed schedules, however, reduced the
tariff on agricultural imports into the United States from Canada, and
offended the middle-western insurgents, whose interest in tariff reform
concerned industry more than agriculture. Only with the assistance
of Democratic votes was the President able to obtain the endorsement
of his program in Congress. But this, events proved, was not enough.
Unwisely the President had said in defense of reciprocity that its ultimate result would be to "make Canada only an adjunct of the United
States." Champ Clark, Democratic Speaker of the House and also a
supporter of reciprocity, even looked forward to the time when Canada
would become a part of the United States. All this was too much for
the Canadians, who voted the party out of power that had negotiated
the agreement and refused ratification.[1]

[1] L. E. Ellis, *Reciprocity, 1911; A Study in Canadian-American Relations* (1939).

[432]

In his foreign policy Taft was similarly unsuccessful. His Secretary of State, Knox, sought earnestly to find investment opportunities for American capital abroad. He negotiated treaties with *Taft's for-* Nicaragua and Honduras, by which American investors *eign policy* would have obtained valuable concessions, and he arranged for American bankers to participate in a six-power international loan to the new republic of China. These policies were but the natural fruit of the Roosevelt corollary in the Caribbean zone and of the open-door policy in China, but the frank admission that profits were involved won for Knox's efforts the epithet, "dollar diplomacy." The Central American treaties were defeated, and Taft's successor as President put an end to the proposed American loan to China.[1]

In the last half of the Taft administration, Congress, under the control of the Republican insurgents and the Democrats, did not hesitate to plague the President openly by passing piecemeal revisions of the tariff that he was certain to veto. A new woolens schedule to replace the unspeakable Schedule K, a farmers' free-list bill, and a cotton bill were sent to his desk in quick succession. Very properly the President took the stand that constant tariff tinkering was unsettling to business, and that if the tariff were to be revised at all, it must be revised as a whole, and not bit by bit. His opponents knew all this as well as he did, but they were interested primarily in forcing him to multiply vetoes that would add to his unpopularity.

The original program of the Republican insurgents was not the formation of a new party, but the capture of the party to which they still belonged. This was made clear as early as January 23, *The La* 1911, when a group of them, meeting at Senator La Fol- *Follette* lette's house in Washington, formed the National Progres- *candidacy* sive Republican League. Included in their program were the reforms designed to enable the people to defeat boss rule, such as the direct election of United States senators, direct primaries, the direct election of delegates to national nominating conventions, the initiative, the referendum, and the recall in the states, and a thoroughgoing corrupt practices act. The president of the League was Jonathan Bourne of Oregon, but before the year was over it had warmly endorsed the candidacy of Senator La Follette for the Republican nomination. "La Follette is the logical man," said Cummins of Iowa, and on the assumption that Roosevelt could not be persuaded to accept another nomination, the

---

[1] Scott Nearing and Joseph Freeman, *Dollar Diplomacy* (1925); D. G. Munro, *The Five Republics of Central America* (1918); J. G. Reid, *The Manchu Abdication and the Powers, 1908–1912* (1935).

same sentiment was echoed by many another of the ex-President's admirers.

The motives that led Roosevelt, on February 24, 1912, to throw his "hat in the ring" are not easily explained. It is clear, however, that his personal friendship for Taft had cooled completely. The reasons for this were probably more intimate than the often-noted failure of Taft to keep all of Roosevelt's cabinet, as he may once have intended to do; or even his crediting his rich brother Charley no less than "dear Theodore" with having brought him into office. Roosevelt did not take all of his family to Africa, and some of those who stayed behind seem not to have got along any too well with the Tafts. With the personal relationship between the two men no longer what it once had been, Roosevelt listened with steadily increasing conviction to the charges dinned into his ears that Taft had betrayed his policies. One thing was especially hard to forgive. Roosevelt, during the Panic of 1907, had promised the United States Steel Corporation immunity for its absorption of the Tennessee Coal and Iron Company, but on October 24, 1911, Taft's Attorney-General, Wickersham, had brought suit for the dissolution of the corporation, citing against it the very deal that Roosevelt had approved. Worst of all, Taft had failed to hold the Republican Party together and had paved the way for a Democratic victory.

As for La Follette, there was good reason to fear that he could not win the Republican nomination, or, having won it, that he could not be elected. Roosevelt had studiously avoided committing himself to the La Follette candidacy, and by the end of the year had made up his mind to try for the nomination himself. On February 2, 1912, La Follette showed signs of nervous exhaustion at a dinner in Philadelphia, and on this flimsy pretext most of his followers incontinently deserted to Roosevelt. The formal announcement of the ex-President's candidacy came three weeks later at the prearranged insistence of seven liberal-minded governors. La Follette always believed that Roosevelt had used him as a stalking-horse to find out the trend of public opinion, and when it seemed favorable, had double-crossed him. This charge is impossible to substantiate, but La Follette never forgave Roosevelt, and convinced himself that Roosevelt had cheated him out of a try at the Presidency. Certainly from the day of Roosevelt's entrance into the race the La Follette candidacy was a lost cause.[1]

Roosevelt's "hat in the ring"

---

[1] The best account is George E. Mowry, *Theodore Roosevelt and the Progressive Movement* (1946), but O. K. Davis, *Released for Publication* (1925), and B. P. DeWitt, *The Progressive Movement* (1915), are of some consequence.

It soon developed that Roosevelt had entered the campaign too late. The presidential machine had already lined up many of the submissive southern delegations, and it now made haste to gather in the rest. Elsewhere, in case the old convention system of choosing delegates was in force, the party regulars almost invariably controlled and obediently delivered their delegations to Taft. On the other hand, wherever the new system of preferential primaries existed, Roosevelt generally won; indeed, several states made haste to adopt such laws in order to promote his chances. Roosevelt's greatest blunder during the campaign was his advocacy of the recall of judicial decisions, an idea that went too far to suit many of his liberal friends and caused the conservatives to harden their hearts against him. When the Republican Convention met in Chicago on June 18, it was apparent that the Roosevelt forces were approximately a hundred votes short of a majority. To make up this deficiency, they had brought contests involving about two hundred and fifty seats, some fairly reasonable and others merely for the "moral effect." But the national committee had already turned most of their contests down, and the convention did likewise. The Roosevelt men insisted that the convention, in making such decisions, should debar from voting all delegates whose seats were contested; such a rule would have enabled them to win. The convention decided, quite in accordance with precedent, to disqualify only the particular delegate or delegation that was being voted on, and to accept the ruling of the national committee on the others until it had been reversed. The application of this rule insured Taft's renomination on the first ballot, although 107 delegates voted for Roosevelt, and 344 sat silent in protest. For Vice-President the triumphant regulars renominated Sherman.[1]

Renomination of Taft

Roosevelt, who had come to Chicago to direct his forces, claimed that he was the victim of a "naked theft," but this was true only in the sense that the rank and file of the Republican voters would doubtless have preferred him to Taft. There was nothing irregular or unusual about what had been done. Precisely the same methods had been used with Roosevelt's approval to nominate Taft four years before. Nevertheless, it was obvious, even before the convention met, that Roosevelt was in no mood to accept defeat. If he lost the Republican nomination, he would run anyway. On June 22 he told a rump convention that met in Orchestra Hall, "If you wish me to make the fight, I will make it, even if only one state should support me."

[1] The stand taken by the national committee is explained and defended in Victor Rosewater, *Back Stage in 1912* (1932).

In Democratic circles the contest between Taft and Roosevelt was viewed with ill-concealed joy. It meant a certain Democratic triumph, *The Demo-* and a large number of willing candidates for the presidential *crats name* nomination were soon in evidence. Practically all of them *Wilson* were of the "favorite son" variety, for the long period of Republican rule had given few Democrats a chance to win national reputations. Champ Clark, the Speaker of the House, was the best known of the aspirants, but he represented primarily the claims of Missouri and the West to recognition. Friends of Oscar W. Underwood, a congressman from Alabama, insisted that the time had come when a candidate from the "deep South" should be chosen. Ohio and Indiana, both doubtful states, presented their newly elected governors, Judson Harmon and Thomas R. Marshall, respectively. New Jersey also introduced a new governor, but one with an unusual background — Woodrow Wilson, a professor of political science, turned university president and then politician. When the Democratic Convention met in Baltimore, July 25, 1912, it was evident that only by a long process of elimination could a nomination be achieved. After the tenth ballot it seemed certain that Champ Clark, who had obtained a majority of the votes, but not a two-thirds majority, would be the nominee. But William Jennings Bryan, still the most powerful man in the Democratic Party, switched from Clark to Wilson on the fourteenth ballot. The Tammany delegation from New York had voted for Clark since the tenth ballot, and Bryan's explanation of his conduct was that he could not support anyone who would owe his nomination to Tammany. Cynics insisted that Bryan was only trying to deadlock the convention so that it would again turn to him, but on the forty-sixth ballot it chose Woodrow Wilson. Second place went to Governor Marshall of Indiana.[1]

All eyes now turned to Chicago, where on August 5 the new Progressive Party would meet to select Roosevelt as its standard-bearer. Already *The new* it had a symbol with which to match the Republican ele- *Progressive* phant and the Democratic donkey — the "bull moose." *Party* It was a favorite term with Roosevelt, one he had used as far back as 1900 when he had boasted to Hanna that he was "as strong as a Bull Moose." An enthusiastic audience of twenty thousand people heard the Progressive leader denounce both old parties as "husks, with no real soul within either, divided on artificial lines, boss-ridden and privilege-controlled, each a jumble of incongruous elements, and neither

---

[1] Interesting commentaries on this convention are contained in Champ Clark, *My Quarter Century of American Politics* (2 vols., 1920), and W. J. Bryan, *A Tale of Two Conventions* (1912).

daring to speak out wisely and fearlessly what should be said on the vital issues of the day." For Vice-President the Progressives named Hiram Johnson of California.

On a great variety of issues the new party spoke out. Its trust policy recognized the corporation as "an essential part of modern business," but demanded effective regulation through "a strong federal administrative commission of high standing." It favored giving the Interstate Commerce Commission power to value the physical property of railroads. It urged the development of agricultural credit and co-operation. It advocated an amendment to the Constitution to bring "under effective national jurisdiction those problems which have expanded beyond reach of the individual states." It endorsed, too, all the current reforms such as the direct primary, woman suffrage, an easier way to amend the Constitution, tariff revision downward to reasonable protection, better working conditions in the factories, the prohibition of child labor, the better regulation of labor by women, minimum-wage standards, and an eight-hour day in continuous twenty-four-hour industries. Such pronouncements delighted social workers, such as Jane Addams, and gave the new party a crusading character that well became its leader. With a fervor reminiscent of Populism the Progressive Convention sang "Onward, Christian Soldiers," and quoted Roosevelt's challenge to the Taft forces at Chicago: "We stand at Armageddon and we battle for the Lord."

Roosevelt's decision to assist in the launching of a new political party made no sense whatever from the standpoint of personal ambition. Had he accepted his defeat by the Republican Convention, Taft would almost certainly have lost the election, and in 1916 Roosevelt could hardly have been denied the Republican nomination. A third-party candidacy, as Roosevelt in his thoughtful moments must have known, had not the slightest chance of success. With the Republican vote split, the Democrats were sure to win. But for the moment, at least, Roosevelt seems to have believed the words uttered to the Chicago Convention. The two old parties, in spite of the labored efforts of their platform makers, really stood for about the same things. The difference between them was principally that one "viewed with alarm," while the other "pointed with pride." Could not the present opportunity be utilized to form a genuine party of reform that would some day seize the reins of government? Under his leadership the thing might be done, and he meant to give it a try.

The campaign provided plenty of excitement and the public enjoyed it thoroughly. The presidential nominees spoke freely and with vigor.

[437]

Roosevelt and Taft, throughout the primary contests and on into the *The campaign of 1912* election campaign, belabored each other as only two friends fallen out can do. Wilson proved to be an admirable public speaker, and those who bothered to follow what he said must have realized that his interpretation of the Democratic platform furnished a close approximation of what the Progressives believed they were fighting for. The high point of the campaign was the attempt of an anti-third-term fanatic to assassinate Roosevelt at Milwaukee on October 14. Ever the disciple of the strenuous life, the ex-Rough Rider delivered an address with a bullet in his right lung — probably as delighted to be able to carry on as he must have been uncomfortable. He had always hoped to die in battle; now at last he could claim to have been wounded in action. It was evident throughout the campaign that Progressive strategy was in the hands of the practical politicians, and not the "lunacy fringe" that the movement had attracted. Wherever it could be done the Progressives ran state and local tickets, and they sought with the greatest earnestness to provide the whole intricate mechanism of party organization. Only in this way could a party be created that would endure.

The results of the election were what all astute observers were able to foresee. Wilson, with only 6,286,216 popular votes, fewer than Bryan had obtained in any of his three defeats, carried forty out of the forty-eight states, and amassed a total electoral vote of 435. Roosevelt was second with 4,126,020 popular votes, and eighty-eight electoral votes scattered through six states. Taft, with a popular vote of 3,483,922, obtained only the eight electoral votes of Utah and Vermont. With the Democrats equally victorious in the congressional and the senatorial elections, Wilson was assured a comfortable working majority in both houses of Congress. In most of the state contests the Democrats also scored victories. Those who looked behind the more obvious results made two significant observations. One was that Eugene V. Debs, the hardy perennial of socialism, received 897,000 popular votes, more than twice as many as in 1908; to a large block of voters, it would seem neither Roosevelt nor Wilson went far enough in their liberalism. The other was that in the state and local contests the Progressives made almost no impression whatever. The Democrats and the Republicans had all the offices. This portent was not lost on Roosevelt. "The fight is over," he told a friend. "We are beaten. There is only one thing to do and that is to go back to the Republican Party. You can't hold a party like the Progressive Party together ... there are no loaves and fishes."

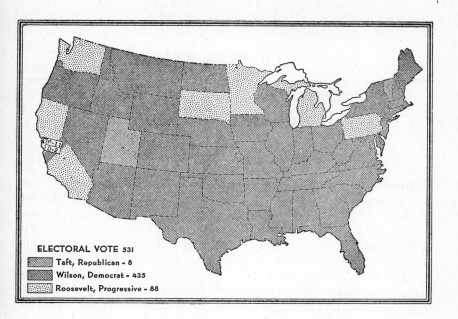

ELECTORAL VOTE 531

Taft, Republican - 8
Wilson, Democrat - 435
Roosevelt, Progressive - 88

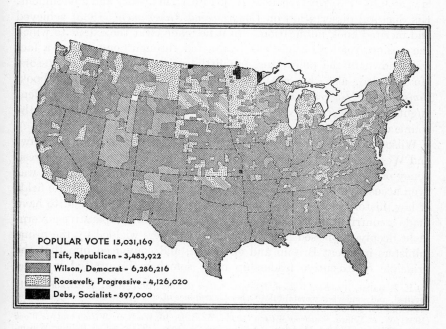

POPULAR VOTE 15,031,169

Taft, Republican - 3,483,922
Wilson, Democrat - 6,286,216
Roosevelt, Progressive - 4,126,020
Debs, Socialist - 897,000

PRESIDENTIAL ELECTION OF 1912, BY STATES AND BY COUNTIES

CHAPTER XX

WOODROW WILSON

WOODROW WILSON (1856–1924), twenty-eighth President of the United States, was born at Staunton, Virginia, of Scotch and Scotch-Irish *Woodrow* lineage.[1] His father, a prominent southern clergyman, was *Wilson* for many years minister of the First Presbyterian Church in Wilmington, North Carolina. Throughout his life Wilson's religious training, with its strongly Calvinistic bent, never forsook him; it was no accident that the protocol of the League of Nations was called a "covenant." Young Wilson, as befitted his father's station in life, was carefully educated, first at Princeton, and then, after a brief bout with the law, at Johns Hopkins, where he took a Ph.D. in history and government. His doctoral dissertation on *Congressional Government* (1885) achieved and merited book publication. In it he made clear the extent to which the business of legislation was transacted through committees, a fact well known to the politicians, but little understood by the professors. He revealed, also, his conviction, elaborated later in another book, *Constitutional Government in the United States* (1908), that the President ought to be the real head of the government, no less in directing the course of legislation than in the enforcement of laws already passed.

Wilson's career led onward through minor positions at Bryn Mawr and Wesleyan to a professorship at Princeton in 1890, and to the presidency of the university in 1902. He wrote well, lectured well, and was even accused of oratorical ability. His books ranged through the fields of law, history, and politics, but only in politics can he be said to have made a contribution to scholarship. His studies in comparative government deeply impressed him with the vast powers wielded by the prime ministers in Great Britain and elsewhere, and convinced him that the principle of executive leadership must somehow be grafted into the

[1] R. S. Baker, *Woodrow Wilson, Life and Letters* (8 vols., 1927–1939), is extraordinarily detailed, and somewhat worshipful. Other biographies of consequence are Josephus Daniels, *Life of Woodrow Wilson* (1924); David Lawrence, *The True Story of Woodrow Wilson* (1924); W. A. White, *Woodrow Wilson* (1924); W. E. Dodd, *Woodrow Wilson and his Work* (1920); Eleanor Wilson McAdoo, *The Woodrow Wilsons* (1937); Edith Bolling Wilson, *My Memoir* (1939).

American system. Roosevelt's expansion of the President's prerogatives were quite in line with Wilson's thinking. "The President," wrote the professor, "is at liberty, both in law and conscience, to be as big a man as he can. His capacity will set the limit."

Until he became president of Princeton, Wilson showed little evidence of the liberalism for which he later became famous. His views were not unlike those of the southern aristocrats who sat in his father's congregations. But the conspicuous lack of democracy that he noted at Princeton led him to insist as president on innovations that would have altered in marked degree the social life and instructional methods of the university. He met opposition, but that served only to bring out a trait in his character that all the world was soon to know; the more he was opposed, the more determined he became to put his principles into effect. The prosperity of Princeton, it developed, depended on the gifts of men who had no interest whatever in the Wilsonian reforms. If there came a difference of opinion between them and the president of the university, then the president must yield or get out. Wilson was not the man to retract his views and chart a different course. When, therefore, in 1910, James Smith, Democratic boss of New Jersey, offered him a nomination for the governorship of the state, he was happy to accept.

Smith had no interest whatever in reform, but reform was in the air, and with a candidate like Wilson to demonstrate that reform ideas had captured the Democratic Party, that party might capture *Wilson as* the state. After the victory there need be no change. *governor* What chance would a mere professor have, whatever his views, in matching wits with political realists? Smith's word would still be law. It fell out for once that the boss had quite misjudged his man. Wilson was elected, but he then put into effect the doctrine of executive leadership he so long had taught. Why were there party bosses? Because the elected leaders failed to use the powers that were rightly theirs. The governor had power; Wilson used it. He could command the attention of the press; Wilson used that too. With the support of public opinion Wilson soon had the legislature doing the governor's bidding, not the party boss's. Smith told it to disregard the nominee of the senatorial primary, James Martine, and to elect James Smith to the United States Senate. But at Wilson's insistence the legislature chose Martine over Smith. On pressure from the governor's office it enacted, too, a number of laws that the Democratic platform had promised, laws to establish employers' liability, to punish corrupt practices, to control the public utilities, and to reform the ballot.

These victories in a state that had long been regarded as the "home of the trusts" made Wilson a marked man, but the honor of having first suggested his name for the Presidency probably goes to Colonel George Harvey, who had called the attention of the Democrats to him as far back as 1906. The list of "original Wilson men" soon grew immoderately, winning a particularly important recruit when another courtesy "Colonel," Edward M. House of Texas, rallied to the standard. House was an adept at back-stage politics. In October, 1911, he brought Wilson to Texas for an address before the State Fair at Dallas, and thereafter his was the chief guiding hand in Wilson's campaign. As a candidate Wilson demonstrated conclusively that he had ideas, and could turn a neat phrase. With almost Rooseveltian pungency he charged that "the government of the United States is at present a foster-child of the special interests," and demanded a "new freedom" for the individual — a freedom that would insure economic no less than political liberty. Although Wilson obviously offered his views on the "New Freedom" as an alternative to Roosevelt's "New Nationalism," the similarities in the ideas of the rival reformers were more in evidence than the differences. Both recognized that by all odds the most important problem government had to face was its relationship with business, and both insisted that the power of government must be used to protect the rights of the ordinary citizen. But whereas Roosevelt placed his emphasis upon the expansion of national powers, Wilson placed his upon the protection of individual freedom.

Having achieved the Presidency, Wilson was determined to be the prime-minister type of President. With this end in view he included in his cabinet as Secretary of State the man whose influence *Wilson and* with the rank and file of the Democratic Party was still *Bryan* second to none, William Jennings Bryan. Wilson suffered from no illusions as to Bryan's fitness for the post assigned him, and once, years before, he had expressed the wish that Bryan might be "knocked into a cocked hat." But it was Bryan, more than Harvey or House or anyone else, who had made Wilson President, and Bryan, if left outside the Wilson *entourage*, had the power to cause the new administration endless trouble. Without Bryan's assistance Wilson could not hope to solidify his control over the Democratic majority in Congress, and no post save the highest would befit a man who had three times been a candidate for the Presidency.[1]

The necessity of maintaining political cohesion shared about equally with the quest for administrative ability in determining Wilson's other

[1] Decidedly the best history of the Wilson administration is F. L. Paxson, *American Democracy and the World War*, I, 1913–1917 (1936); II, 1917–1918 (1939).

WOODROW WILSON

cabinet selections. Aside from Bryan the cabinet contained no names familiar to the public at large. William Gibbs McAdoo of New York, Secretary of the Treasury, had helped Wilson win the nomination, and without being a banker he had an expert's knowledge of finance. Albert Sidney Burleson, a long-time congressman from Texas, brought to the office of Postmaster-General the understanding touch of the professional politician. For the Navy Department expediency directed the choice of a Bryan-like editor from North Carolina, Josephus Daniels, whose inexperience in naval matters was offset by the appointment as Assistant Secretary of Franklin Delano Roosevelt, a young man from New York with a good name who knew about ships.[1] More important than most of the cabinet members were Colonel House, whose rôle of unofficial adviser to the President gave him extraordinary power, and Joseph P. Tumulty, the President's faithful private secretary, a shrewd and practical politician upon whose natural talents Wilson relied in solving his patronage problems.

The President, Wilson once had said, "has no means of compelling Congress except through public opinion." That he meant to use this *Wilson to* power to the full was apparent in his inaugural address in *Congress* which he took pains to itemize, not so much for the benefit of Congress as for the benefit of the people, "the things that ought to be altered." Among them he listed:

A tariff which cuts us off from our proper part in the commerce of the world, violates the just principles of taxation, and makes the Government a facile instrument in the hands of private interests;

A banking and currency system based upon the necessity of the Government to sell its bonds fifty years ago and perfectly adapted to concentrating cash and restricting credits;

An industrial system which, take it on all sides, financial as well as administrative, holds capital in leading strings, restricts the liberties and limits the opportunities of labor, and exploits without renewing or conserving the natural resources of the country;

A body of agricultural activities never yet given the efficiency of great business undertakings or served as it should be through the instrumentality of science taken directly to the farm, or afforded the facilities of credit best suited to its practical needs;

Watercourses undeveloped, waste places unreclaimed, forests untended, fast disappearing without plan or prospect of renewal, unguarded waste heaps at every mine.

---

[1] Wilson's cabinet proved to be particularly fruitful in memoirs. In addition to Bryan's *Memoirs*, it produced W. G. McAdoo, *Crowded Years* (1931); D. F. Houston, *Eight Years with Wilson's Cabinet* (2 vols., 1926); W. C. Redfield, *With Congress and Cabinet* (1924); A. W. Lane and L. H. Wall, *The Letters of Franklin K. Lane, Personal and Political* (1922); Josephus Daniels, *Our Navy at War* (1922).

To make a beginning on the presidential program by passing a new tariff law, Congress was summoned into special session for April 7. Much to everyone's astonishment, the President opened the session in person, and for the first time since the administration of John Adams the two houses of Congress, sitting jointly, listened to a presidential message. It was a clever stroke of politics; according to an unconfirmed rumor Theodore Roosevelt was said to have remarked, "Why didn't I think of that?" The appearance of the President before Congress was an event. Senators and representatives, their families and friends, and all others who could crowd into the galleries were present. It was news, and all the newspapers played it up. Last, but by no means least, the message was short and to the point. Practically every newspaper in the country carried its entire text, and many of them found space for all of it on the front page. "We must abolish everything that bears even the semblance of privilege or of any kind of artificial advantage," the people read approvingly, and then awaited the action of Congress.

Wilson had other strings to his bow. If the Democratic *débâcle* of 1894 on the tariff were not to be repeated, some means must be found for holding willful members to the party's promises. With the President's approval recourse was had to the party caucus, through which the majority of the majority settled all matters in dispute and achieved party unity. Frequently the President himself essayed the rôle of party whip, on occasion he even appeared at the Capitol to direct strategy and to reason with the recalcitrant. Nor did Wilson hesitate, whenever it seemed necessary, to appeal to the public over the heads of Congress. Lobbyists descended upon Washington as they always do when a tariff bill is being framed, and Wilson gave notice to the people through the press that "Washington has seldom seen so numerous, so industrious, or so insidious a lobby." Only by an aroused public opinion, he declared, could it be checked or destroyed. An aroused public opinion came promptly to the rescue. Soon the lobbyists, investigated by Congress and denounced by the press, were more embarrassed than embarrassing. There was also the patronage. Wilson kept himself as clear of such mundane matters as possible, but evidence was quickly available to prove that senators and representatives who supported the administration had much less trouble getting offices for the "deserving Democrats" they favored than those whose votes were in doubt. Guided through the House by Representative Oscar W. Underwood of Alabama and through the Senate by Senator F. M. Simmons of North Carolina, the tariff measure took six months to frame, but at last, on October 3, it received the President's signature.

The Underwood-Simmons Tariff

The Underwood-Simmons Tariff was neither a free-trade measure nor a low-tariff measure, and was not meant to be either. Its schedules of duties, however, were on the average about ten per cent lower than those of the Payne-Aldrich Tariff, and it placed a hundred new items, mostly raw materials or foodstuffs, on the free list. While a total of nine hundred and fifty-eight items were reduced, only eighty, mainly chemicals, carried increased duties, and only three hundred and seven were unchanged. More significant than their framers knew were the income-tax provisions which, thanks to the recent adoption of the Sixteenth Amendment, could be included in the act. One per cent was charged against all incomes in excess of $3000, or, in the case of married couples, $4000; while on incomes above $20,000 a surtax, beginning with an additional one per cent, was gradually stepped up to a maximum of six per cent on incomes above $500,000. At the time the Underwood-Simmons Bill became a law the possibilities of the income tax were only faintly realized, but within a few years it became the chief reliance of the federal government for revenue. As for the tariff schedules of the act, they were in force less than a year when their natural effect was nullified by the outbreak of war in Europe. What they might have done for business and for the revenue had times remained normal will never be known, but during the abnormal years they were in force they fell far short of providing the government with the revenue it needed. Indeed, the wartime demand for American goods that set in proved to be a greater stimulus to American industry than the highest possible tariff rates could ever have provided.

Congress was not yet finished with its work on the tariff when Wilson, by means of another short, strikingly phrased address, presented the second major item on his program of reform — a new banking and currency system. The need for legislation on this subject was universally recognized. From 1908 to 1912 the National Monetary Commission, chosen by the Republicans and headed by Senator Aldrich, one of the most conservative men in public life, studied minutely, with the aid of numerous experts, the banking and currency systems of the world, their history and operation. Forced to report in 1912 soon after the Democrats had captured the House, it revealed clearly the faults of the existing system, and recommended as a cure the establishment of what would have amounted to a third Bank of the United States. During the second half of the Taft administration the Democratic majority in the House of Representatives undertook a similar, although far less scholarly, investigation, with A. P. Pujo of Louisiana as head of the committee in charge. Among the many promi-

Banking and currency reform

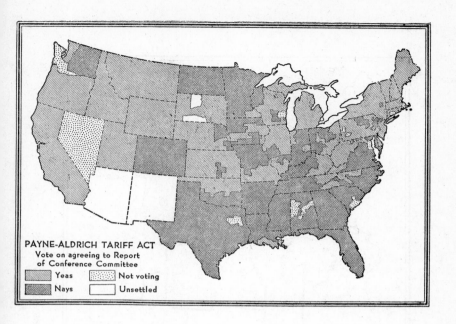

PAYNE-ALDRICH TARIFF ACT
Vote on agreeing to Report
of Conference Committee

Yeas Not voting

Nays Unsettled

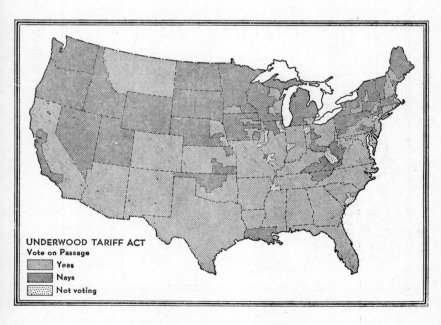

UNDERWOOD TARIFF ACT
Vote on Passage

Yeas

Nays

Not voting

TARIFF LEGISLATION, 1909–13

THE FEDERAL RESERVE DISTRICTS

Boundaries of Federal Reserve Districts
Boundaries of Federal Reserve Branch Territories
⊙ Federal Reserve Bank Cities
● Federal Reserve Branch Cities
○ Federal Reserve Bank Agency

nent financiers called before the Pujo Committee was J. Pierpont Morgan, whose arrogance was undisturbed by the questions he was asked, but whose answers failed to shake the conviction of the committee and the public that a "money trust," controlled by the whims of a few great bankers, actually existed. The Pujo Committee could not agree with the Aldrich Commission that there must be one great central bank. The ghosts of Andrew Jackson and the doctrine of states' rights prevented that. But it could agree that the situation demanded immediate attention.[1]

The Federal Reserve System was the solution which the Democratic majority worked out, in close co-operation with the President, for the dilemma that it faced. Complete centralization, however *The Federal* desirable from the economic point of view, was politically *Reserve* impossible, and a plan of organization that was both finan- *System* cially sound and at the same time would win the support of Bryan and the Populist wing of the Democratic Party had to be devised. To avoid the historic formula of a central bank with sectional branches, the framers of the new system hit upon the expedient of creating a series of sectional banks, held together only by a Federal Reserve Board. This board, which Wilson thought of as analogous to the Interstate Commerce Commission, was to consist of seven members, two of whom, the Secretary of the Treasury and the Comptroller of the Currency, were to be members *ex officio*, while the others (increased to six in 1922) were to be appointed by the President and confirmed by the Senate for ten-year terms. One of the non-political members was to be designated governor of the board. It took six months to work out the details of the Federal Reserve System and to obtain the support necessary for its adoption by both houses of Congress. In the House Carter Glass of Virginia bore the brunt of the battle, and in the Senate, Robert L. Owen of Oklahoma. More than once Congress was ready to postpone the task, and only pressure from the President prevented adjournment. Finally, on December 23, 1913, Wilson affixed his signature to the new law.

The Glass-Owen Federal Reserve Act provided for the division of the United States into not less than eight nor more than twelve districts, each of which would contain some natural metropolitan center in which a Federal Reserve Bank would be established.[2] In each district a

---

[1] Louis D. Brandeis, *Other People's Money* (1914), draws upon the findings of the Pujo Committee to set forth the facts about the existing system of finance.

[2] The drafting of this new financial map of the United States was wisely left by Congress to a special organizing committee that included the Secretary of the Treasury, the Secretary of Agriculture, and the Comptroller of the Currency. Twelve districts were created, and within them the banks were located as follows: First, Boston; Second, New York;

Federal Reserve Association was to be formed to which all national banks must belong and all other banks might belong. Each member bank was required to subscribe six per cent of its capital and surplus to the capital of the Federal Reserve Bank, whose governing board should consist of six members chosen by the member banks, and three by the Federal Reserve Board. The new banks were not to do business with individuals, but as strictly "bankers' banks" they received on deposit the reserves of member banks, rediscounted their commercial and agricultural paper, and granted them loans with governmental securities as collateral. The law also provided for a new type of currency, Federal Reserve notes, which the banks might issue upon their rediscounted paper, provided only that they must maintain a gold reserve of forty per cent. These notes were to constitute obligations on the United States and were to be redeemable in gold. Since they would vary in quantity according to the needs of business, it was believed that they would effectively overcome the inelasticity of the currency from which the country so long had suffered. The United States two per cent bonds upon which the old national bank currency had been issued were to be retired at the rate of $25,000,000 per year.

The Federal Reserve System was carefully devised to end the lack of co-operation between banks in time of crisis. In effect it pooled the credit resources of each district and provided a means whereby the strength of all the banks might be mobilized to sustain any one. Further, on order of the Federal Reserve Board the several regional banks were required to discount paper for each other, so that an abundance of credit available in any given part of the country could promptly be directed to whatever district or districts might be threatened with a shortage.[1]

Other provisions of the act did away with the old Independent Treasury system, or the Sub-Treasury, in which since the forties the funds of the United States had been sequestered, and provided instead that the government might use the Federal Reserve Banks as depositories. These banks might also buy and sell gold and both foreign and

Third, Philadelphia; Fourth, Cleveland; Fifth, Richmond; Sixth, Atlanta; Seventh, Chicago; Eighth, St. Louis; Ninth, Minneapolis; Tenth, Kansas City; Eleventh, Dallas; Twelfth, San Francisco. The assignment of two Federal Reserve Banks to the State of Missouri aroused considerable criticism, particularly from residents of Denver, who felt that the Kansas City bank should have been theirs. There were those, too, who observed that a third Bank of the United States could hardly have done more violence to the doctrine of states' rights than the establishment of twelve regional banks rather than one for each state.

[1] The literature of this subject is immense, but for the historical student H. P. Willis, *The Federal Reserve* (1915), and P. M. Warburg, *The Federal Reserve System* (2 vols., 1930), will prove satisfactory. Carter Glass, *An Adventure in Constructive Finance* (1927), throws light on the origin of the law.

domestic bills of exchange. A number of special restrictions were included to guard against the danger of speculative inflation.

When the Federal Reserve System was first proposed, the bankers of the country were extremely suspicious of it, and the fact that Bryan supported it, however necessary that may have been politically, was well calculated to exaggerate their fears. But before the measure reached final passage, the bankers had begun to see its advantages, and within a short time the best of them were enthusiastic in its praise. While it is a fact that, at the time the Great Depression began, only about one third of the banks of the country were members of the Federal Reserve, it is an even more striking fact that by that time the combined assets of the member banks accounted for more than four fifths of the nation's banking resources.

When Wilson appeared before Congress on January 20, 1914, to direct attention to the trust problem he found himself in a far more advantageous position than either Taft or Roosevelt had *The trust* occupied when attempting to deal with the same subject. *problem* In Roosevelt's time the seriousness of the situation was barely being recognized, and an angry public could think of nothing better to do than to punish somebody. "Malefactors of great wealth" should land in jail, and fines such as Judge Landis had imposed against the Standard Oil Company should be made to stick. Roosevelt, seizing the Sherman Anti-Trust Act as the only weapon available, bludgeoned about with it, but did little good. Taft, loyal to his campaign promises, carried out the Roosevelt policy even after the public had begun to realize its ineffectiveness. Hampered as he was by a rift within his party and lacking in political flair, he could have done little more had he tried. But by Wilson's time the nature of modern business had been better studied, and information was available that Wilson's predecessors had lacked. The Bureau of Corporations established in Roosevelt's time had begun to bear fruit. Economics had elbowed its way to the front in the colleges and universities as the most significant of the social studies. The Federal Reserve Act was possible only because of the elaborate research that had preceded it; but other businesses also had been studied and the time was ripe for the adoption of a policy based on an intelligent understanding of the conditions under which they must operate. Wilson had better control, too, of his party than either Roosevelt or Taft had ever had of theirs. He was a master strategist; besides, as a representative from Georgia blurted out, the Democratic majority had no choice but to "support the Administration or be turned into the wilderness for forty years more."

The platforms of the three major parties all pointed in much the same way on the trust problem. Only the Progressives openly admitted that *Party pledges on the trusts* the concentration of modern business in corporate hands was "both inevitable and necessary," and only the Democrats grew rhetorical in their denunciation of monopoly. All agreed that there were certain business practices which, as the Republican platform phrased it, were "abhorrent to the common sense of justice." Among these practices the Democrats listed the formation of holding companies, interlocking directorates, stock-watering, discrimination in price, and "the control by any one corporation of so large a proportion of any industry as to make it a menace to competitive conditions." The Progressives denounced the monopoly of natural resources, stock-watering, unfair competition and unfair privileges, and "sinister influences on the public agencies of state and nation." As a remedy for such practices the Democrats seemingly had little more to offer than the restoration of competitive conditions by the enactment of drastic anti-trust laws, but the Republicans suggested that the enforcement and administration of laws governing interstate enterprises be placed in the hands of a "federal trade commission," while the Progressives urged for the same purpose "the establishment of a strong administrative commission of high standing." With less ingenuity than is ordinarily required of platform-makers, the various trust planks in the three platforms could have been welded into one harmonious whole.

In his message to Congress on the subject Wilson pointed the way to some such synthesis. He was genuinely eager to prevent the formation of monopolies, but as a means to accomplish this and other worthy ends he particularly stressed the necessity of defining and prohibiting unfair practices. He had no desire to undermine business confidence, but he did insist that business methods be subject to governmental inspection. His Attorney-General, James C. McReynolds, whose reputation had been made as a "trust-busting" prosecutor, was already exhibiting a willingness to avoid anti-trust suits by showing the corporations how they could comply with the law; nor had he heeded the demand for criminal prosecutions, so insistently repeated in the Democratic platform. In addition to the cataloguing of unfair practices, Wilson also urged upon Congress the creation of a new commission with power to enforce the law.

Before the mid-term election of 1914, Congress, after much travail, had enacted two significant measures, the Clayton Anti-Trust Act and the Federal Trade Commission Act.[1] On the latter there was the less

[1] O. W. Knauth, *The Policy of the United States Toward Industrial Monopoly* (1914);

[452]

disagreement, and it reached the statute books by September 26. The new commission was to consist of five members, appointed by *Trust* the President for seven-year terms subject to confirmation *legislation* by the Senate, and was to be bipartisan. It absorbed the duties, organization, and personnel of the Bureau of Corporations which it supplanted, but it had far greater powers. It might investigate the origin and management of corporations, and it might issue "cease and desist" orders enforceable through the courts against such "unfair methods of competition in commerce" as it might discover. On the understanding that the findings of the commission as to fact were final and conclusive, appeals from its orders were allowed to the Federal Court of Appeals, and thence to the United States Supreme Court. It was not due to an oversight that penalties for violations of the orders of the commission were omitted. The intent was first to establish what was fair and lawful. If in spite of the evidence produced by the commission disobedience should be persisted in, prosecutions could be undertaken for violation of the Sherman Act and its various amendments. To the list of dubious corporate practices already proscribed, the Clayton Act, which became a law on October 15, added the following: any discrimination in prices that tended to produce a monopoly; the acquisition by any corporation of the whole or a part of the stock of a competing concern; the existence of interlocking directorates among million-dollar corporations that were or had been competitors; and exclusive contracts that obligated a dealer not to handle the products of other manufacturers.

The Wilson administration may be credited with considerable success in its efforts to reach agreements with business as to what was fair and what was not. The Federal Trade Commission issued *Administra-* hundreds of "cease and desist" orders, and they were *tion of the* usually obeyed. The Department of Justice, continuing *Anti-Trust* Attorney-General McReynolds's policy even after his ele- *Acts* vation to the Supreme Court in 1914, brought fewer suits for dissolution than had been attempted under Roosevelt or Taft, and scored its greatest victories in inducing corporations to accept "consent decrees." In this fashion the government came to terms with the International Harvester Company, the Corn Products Refining Company, and the packers' trust. It continued the prosecution begun during the Taft administration against the United States Steel Corporation, but in 1920, with only seven justices participating, the Supreme Court by a four-to-three vote ruled against the government. The Steel Corporation, according to the

G. C. Henderson, *The Federal Trade Commission* (1924); F. A. Fetter, *The Masquerade of Monopoly* (1931).

Court, was not a monopoly; it had abandoned the practice of joining with competitors to fix prices; it was not engaged in any unfair practices; and it could not be punished for its size alone. As to the absorption of the Tennessee Coal and Iron Company, the Court called attention to the fact that the President of the United States had given his consent to the transaction.

Beyond a doubt Wilson's trust policy was adversely affected by the entrance of the United States into the World War. While that struggle was on, there was little attempt to enforce the restrictions of the Clayton Act, and after the Republicans returned to power in 1921, there was little desire to enforce them.

The attitude that the Wilson administration meant to take toward labor was clearly revealed by the incorporation of what labor called its *A "Magna* "Magna Charta" in the Clayton Act. Section 6 of the act *Charta" for* specifically exempted labor and agricultural corporations *Labor* from prosecution under the terms of the anti-trust laws, while section 20 limited the use of the injunction in labor disputes, prescribed trials by jury in contempt cases, and legalized such labor weapons as strikes, picketing, peaceable assembly, boycotts, and the collection of strike benefits. The framers of the Sherman Anti-Trust Act had probably not meant to extend its provisions to labor unions, and a clause so stating had been considered for inclusion in it. Nevertheless, when in 1902 the Hatters' Union, seeking to force the firm of D. E. Loewe and Company of Danbury, Connecticut, to adopt the closed shop, instituted a nation-wide boycott against Loewe products, the manufacturer brought suit for damages against the union under the terms of the Sherman Act. For years the case was in litigation, but in 1908 the Supreme Court ruled that a combination of labor unions attempting to boycott a dealer's goods was a combination in restraint of trade, and that the injured party might collect three times the eighty thousand dollars he was deemed to have been damaged. This amount, plus costs, the union actually had to pay, and until the passage of the Clayton Act interstate boycotting was too dangerous a weapon to be used. Judicial obstacles had been placed in the way of nearly every other labor practice also, and "government by injunction" had become a truism. The provisions of the Clayton Act were therefore hailed as a great boon to labor, and they were successfully enforced as long as Wilson was President. During the reactionary years of the twenties many of these guaranties were interpreted away by the courts.

Apart from the Clayton Act the record of the Wilson administration was also such as to inspire the confidence of labor. The creation of the

Department of Labor under a law signed by Taft just before he left office
enabled Wilson to select the first Secretary of Labor. His *The Depart-*
choice fell upon William B. Wilson of Pennsylvania, a man *ment of*
who had risen from the ranks in the United Mine Workers *Labor*
and whose appointment was urged by the American Federation of Labor.
Under the sympathetic guidance of the new Secretary the Children's
Bureau, with Julia C. Lathrop at its head, sought to extend to the nation
at least as good advice on the care of its youth as the Department of
Agriculture had long made available to farmers in the case of livestock.
In September, 1916, Congress, spurred on by the revelations of the
Bureau, passed the Keating-Owen Child Labor Bill, which prohibited
the labor of children under fourteen years of age in the production of
goods intended for interstate commerce, but the Supreme Court held
that the measure was unconstitutional. When an attempt to accomplish
the same purpose by use of the taxing power met a similar fate, Congress
sought, also in vain, to secure by an amendment to the Constitution the
power it lacked. During the Wilson administration the Department of
Labor made a persistent effort to deal more effectively with the problem
of unemployment. It greatly expanded its employment service, and it
proved to be particularly helpful in finding work for newly arrived immigrants.

The La Follette Seamen's Act, while not directly sponsored by the
Wilson administration, was passed by Congress in 1915, and signed by
the President. The sinking in 1912 of the White Star steamship
Titanic, the largest ocean liner in the world, had revealed the carelessness
characteristic of the shipping interests, and had paved the way for the
revolutionary legislation demanded by Andrew Furuseth, head of the
Seamen's Union. The La Follette Act bettered the physical conditions
required for crews, and ended the tyrannical control over their men that
sea captains had exercised since the days of Captain Bligh. Contrary to
previous practice, a seaman might now demand half the wages due him
when he wanted it, and he was no longer at the mercy of the consular
courts if he deserted at a foreign port. Maritime interests claimed that
the act placed them at a serious disadvantage in competition with foreign
shipping which had not been forced to make such expensive reforms, but
during the World War there was an abundance of business for all.

Such measures of appeasement as the American Federation of Labor
was able to offer and the Wilson administration to accept fell far short
of the goal set by a small but tempestuous group of extreme *The I.W.W.*
radicals. A number of these extremists, recruited largely
from the Western Federation of Miners, formed in 1905 an organization

known as the Industrial Workers of the World, and commonly called the "I.W.W." or the "Wobblies." [1] In a short time the "Wobblies" became essentially a union of the unskilled migratory laborers who, when they chanced to be employed, did the hard work of the western mines, the lumber camps, and the harvest fields. Under existing conditions they saw no chance whatever for living wages and permanency of employment. Like the European syndicalists they believed that the only effective remedy for the ills from which they suffered was the destruction of capitalism, and the methods they used in pursuit of this aim amounted in effect to war. Their outstanding leader was William D. Haywood, whom public opinion held responsible for the murder in 1905 of ex-Governor Frank Steunenberg of Idaho, although the best efforts of William E. Borah, a rising young Boise lawyer, were insufficient to procure conviction. After a long career of violence in the West, the "Wobblies" came East in 1912 to participate in the textile strikes at Lawrence, Massachusetts, Paterson, New Jersey, and elsewhere. Their frankly revolutionary objectives and their warlike methods resulted in the passage of criminal syndicalist laws by sixteen states which seriously crippled their activities, and in 1918 the United States government completed their destruction by bringing to trial some one hundred and thirteen I.W.W. leaders, including Haywood. Most of the accused were convicted and given long jail sentences. Haywood fled to Russia, which was fast becoming the Mecca of radicals.

Other evidences of radicalism in the labor movement were not difficult to find. When Wilson became President the furor over the bombing in *Mooney and* 1911 of the building which housed the Los Angeles *Times,* *Billings* a rabidly anti-union newspaper, had barely died down. Two brothers named McNamara were accused of the crime, and in spite of generous labor contributions to their defense, they ultimately confessed, and were sentenced, while thirty-eight labor leaders were later convicted as their accomplices. In 1916, during a San Francisco preparedness parade, a bomb exploded killing a number of people. Thomas Mooney and Warren K. Billings, two radical labor leaders, were indicted for the crime, and were convicted on what was later proved to be perjured testimony. Exiles to the United States from Russia who returned to participate in the Communist Revolution carried the tale of these convictions with them, and the incident thus obtained international prominence. California courts, however, consistently refused to set aside the verdict by which the accused men had been convicted, and

---

[1] J. G. Brooks, *American Syndicalism; the I.W.W.* (1913); P. F. Brissenden, *The I.W.W.: A Study in American Syndicalism* (1919).

while the sentence was commuted from death to life imprisonment, not until 1939 was a governor willing to take the political risk of pardoning the prisoners.

The existence of extreme radicalism in the labor movement was generally attributed to the presence in the United States of foreign agitators whom the lax immigration laws had permitted to enter the country. Partly on this account public opinion seemed to demand that some means of restricting immigration should be found. Data not previously available had been collected *Movement for immigration restriction* by an Immigration Commission, created in 1907, and the figures of the census of 1910 were also revealing. In the first fourteen years of the twentieth century about thirteen million immigrants were admitted into the United States, and of this number more than four fifths were from southern and eastern Europe. Perhaps half of the newcomers, after having earned the stake they came for, went back home, but the rest stayed on to swell what threatened to become a permanently unassimilable element in the American population. To cut down on this influx a literacy test had been proposed as far back as Cleveland's administration, and had passed Congress only to be vetoed by the President. Under Taft the same thing happened, and twice under Wilson. Passed by Congress in 1917 over Wilson's veto, the law provided that "all aliens over sixteen years of age, physically capable of reading, who cannot read the English language or some other language or dialect" should be denied admission. The real purpose of the law was not so much to discriminate against the illiterate as to limit the number of immigrants from southern and eastern Europe, where illiteracy was common. Candidates for admission from the northern and western countries of Europe were expected to have little difficulty in passing the test. Wilson's veto message was based upon the ground that the literacy test proved nothing more than lack of opportunity, but the President, like his predecessors, was no doubt influenced by the offense such a measure would give to many American voters of foreign extraction.

In his inaugural address Wilson had given prominent mention to the needs of agriculture, and had particularly stressed the need of rural credits. Increasingly the methods of farming in the United States called for heavier investments, both in land and in machinery. The competition of free lands had ceased to keep down the price per acre of the farmer's investment, and the capital outlay required to enter the farming business in the new era had become almost prohibitive. Even for farmers who owned or inherited their land the cost of essential machinery and livestock led inevitably to a mortgage, and the rates charged by the local bankers and investment companies were by no means nominal. Taxes, too, mounted with the increasing valuation of land, and the toll paid for transportation and other handling charges left only the faintest margin between the cost of production and the farmer's receipts. The existence of unrest among the farmers, particularly in the Middle West, was revealed by the rapid growth of such farm orders as the American Society of Equity and the Farmers' Union, and the threat that the farmers might implement their grievances through political action was evident in the solid farmer support that the La Follette organization obtained in Wisconsin, and the activity of the National Non-Partisan League after 1915 in North Dakota and adjacent states.

The Federal Reserve Act authorized short-term loans up to six months on farm mortgages, but the need for long-term loans, by means of which the purchase of farmlands could be financed, grew steadily more insistent. After two years' consideration of the problem Congress finally agreed to the Federal Farm Loan Act of 1916. The purpose of this measure, according to its enacting clause, was "to provide capital for agricultural development, to create standard forms of investment based upon farm mortgage, and to equalize rates of interest upon farm loans." The Federal Farm Loan System which the act set up was patterned closely upon the Federal Reserve System.[1] A central board consisting of the Secretary of the Treasury and four appointive members was given general control over a dozen Federal Farm Land Banks operating in as many districts. Each of these banks was to be capitalized at not less than seven hundred and fifty thousand dollars, to which private individuals were invited to subscribe; but whatever sums less than the stipulated minimum were not raised in this way the government was obligated to supply. Farmers desiring to borrow money might then form themselves into co-operative farm loan associations in which each borrower took five dollars' worth of stock for each hundred dollars he wished to borrow. With their resources thus united, farm borrowers might obtain loans up to fifty per cent of the appraised value of their land, and an additional twenty per cent on its permanent improvements. Interest rates were kept at from five to six per cent, and provision was made for amortization over a period of thirty-three years. Out of deference to the wishes of private moneylenders, who objected to the government monopolizing the business of supplying rural credits, the law provided also for the establishment of joint-stock land banks, privately financed, except that their bonds were to be tax exempt. These banks might lend directly to individuals on farm mortgage security. The importance of the Federal

[1] W. S. Holt, *The Federal Farm Loan Bureau* (1924).

Farm Loan Act is attested by the fact that by 1930 the two types of banks it established had together lent over two billion dollars to the American farmers.

Before the exigencies of war halted the course of domestic reform the Wilson administration inaugurated another notable policy. Gifts from the federal government to aid the states in such matters as *"Dollar-* education and internal improvements were almost as old as *matching"* the Constitution, but throughout the nineteenth century these gifts had been made primarily in the form of land or the receipts from land sales. By the time Wilson became President this source of supply had so nearly approached exhaustion that some new form of subsidy had to be found. It was discovered in the form of the heavy receipts that came in, or could be made to come in, from the income tax. This revenue, it fell out, was collected from a comparatively small fraction of the total population, most of whom lived in the Northeast. But there was no gainsaying the fact that the earnings from which the income tax was paid were drawn from all over the nation. Coupled with the demand for better educational facilities and better transportation in the larger, poorer, and less densely populated states of the West and the South was the belief that in some fashion the government should attempt to redistribute among all the states the heavy earnings that were being piled up in the industrial areas of the Northeast. Southern and western votes on behalf of such a policy were easily accumulated, and the South and the West controlled the Democratic Party.

The new type of federal grants in aid of education began in 1914 with the passage of the Smith-Lever Act, which provided that the United States should match, dollar for dollar, the contributions of such states as chose to co-operate in a program of agricultural extension. The supervision of this work was left to the Department of Agriculture, working through the land-grant colleges. This measure was followed in 1917 by the Smith-Hughes Act, which appropriated funds, again on a dollar-matching basis, for education in commercial, industrial, and domestic-science subjects in schools of less than college grade. A board of vocational education, created by the act, was given the right to pass on the merits of the projects for which the various states proposed to use their allotments. The impetus which these acts gave to agricultural and vocational education, supplemented by the work of the Bureau of Education, the Children's Bureau, and other federal agencies, was felt in a steadily mounting number of the nation's high schools. Talk began in educational circles of the need for a federal Department of Education with a seat in the cabinet, but opponents of the idea argued that federal

control over the educational policies of the states must not be carrie
too far.[1]

The Federal Highways Act of 1916 carried the dollar-matching prin
ciple into the field of road-building. The automobile, which was at firs

Federal Highways Act condemned because it tore up the roads, soon led to a de
mand for better roads that completely overtaxed the re
sources of the states. It was only natural in such an emer
gency to turn to the federal government for aid, and Democrats wh
could remember well Jackson's war on the Bank soon demonstrated tha
they had quite forgotten his Maysville veto. Aid was needed for a
Lincoln Highway, just marked out from coast to coast, for a Dixie High
way from Lakes to Gulf, and for a half a hundred other projects. Yield
ing to the general pressure, Congress appropriated five million dollars the
first year for distribution among the states. Size, population, and exist
ing mail routes were all to be taken into consideration in determining the
amounts allotted to each. Moreover, every dollar contributed by the
federal government must be matched by a dollar from the state which
received it, and federal control must be accepted in all such dollar-
matching expenditures. When Congress made this first appropriation
it knew little of the cost of road-building, but it soon found out a great
deal. Nor could the process it had begun be ended until a complete set
of federal highways, connecting every important center with every
other, had been built.

Viewing the manifold activities into which under Democratic auspices
the national government had plunged, historically minded individuals

Wilsonian vs. Jeffer- sonian democracy could not fail to note the contrasts between Jeffersonian and
Wilsonian democracy. The Jeffersonian ideal, so Jefferson
himself had said, was "a wise and frugal government which
shall restrain men from injuring one another, shall leave
them otherwise free to regulate their own pursuits of industry and improvement, and shall not take from labor the bread it has earned. This
is the sum of good government." However the Wilsonian ideal might
be described, it could hardly be reconciled with the dictum, "the less
government the better." With Hamiltonian thoroughness the professed disciples of Jefferson had devised a great national banking system
that so far forgot states' rights as to divide the United States into twelve
districts instead of forty-eight; in their attempts to "restrain men from
injuring one another," they had left industry only a closely circum-

[1] On the origin and expansion of federal activities, see W. L. Wanlass, *The United States Department of Agriculture* (1920); J. A. H. Keith and W. C. Bagley, *The Nation and the Schools* (1920); W. S. Holt, *The Bureau of Public Roads* (1923).

THE FEDERAL HIGHWAYS SYSTEM

scribed area in which to regulate its own pursuits; in protecting the rights of labor they had limited the freedom of individuals to a degree that Jefferson could scarcely have imagined; and in taking thought for the public welfare they had assumed for government paternalistic privileges far more sweeping than any he had fought. Fortunately historical consistency is often better honored in the breach than in the observance. It is no discredit to Wilson that in a new age he reversed the tenets of the founder of his party. States' rights and *laissez faire* in an era of rapidly expanding national organization would have been anachronisms. Only through a policy of enlightened nationalism could the Democrats of Wilson's time hope to find the "new freedom" which their leader had promised.[1]

[1] William Diamond, *The Economic Thought of Woodrow Wilson* (1943); H. C. F. Bell, *Woodrow Wilson and the People* (1945); Arthur S. Link, *Wilson: The Road to the White House* (1947).

Wilsonian precepts found hearty support in the legal activities of Louis D. Brandeis, whom Wilson made an Associate Justice of the Supreme Court in 1916. On Brandeis' earlier career, see H. L. Staples and A. T. Mason, *Brandeis and the Fall of a Railroad Empire* (1947). See also Josephus Daniels, *The Wilson Era: Years of Peace, 1910–1917* (1944).

CHAPTER XXI

WILSON'S FOREIGN POLICY

IT WAS APPARENT that Wilson in taking over the Presidency had little expectation of becoming a diplomat. His administration was organized with a view to domestic reform, a policy which extended even to his choice of Secretary of State, and neither in his inaugural address nor in his first message to Congress did he so much as mention foreign affairs. He was aware of impending difficulties between the United States and Mexico, but there is no evidence to show that this prospect caused him much concern. The imminence of a general war in Europe was as completely hidden from him as from other Americans.

Beginning in 1910, Mexico was in the throes of revolution. The old President, Porfirio Diaz, who for more than a third of a century had ruled as a military dictator, had at last been confronted with a revolt beyond his ability to suppress. From the point of view of outside investors Diaz had been a good ruler. By generous concessions he had encouraged foreign capital to develop the rich resources of his country, its railroads, mines, oil fields, public utilities, rubber and coffee plantations, and ranches. By 1912, so President Taft believed, American investments in Mexico had reached a total of not less than a billion dollars, while other huge sums came from European nations, particularly Great Britain, Germany, and France. Naturally such heavy investments did not come unaccompanied, and the number of foreign agents resident in Mexico was very great — at least forty thousand from the United States alone. Under Diaz order was strictly kept, and foreigners had no more reason to be afraid than if they had remained at home.[1]

Discontent with the Diaz régime was slow to develop, for the Mexican masses were ignorant and inarticulate, and Diaz had the guns. Diaz's

---

[1] Carleton Beals, *Porfirio Diaz, Dictator of Mexico* (1932), presents the essential facts in excellent form. Interesting sidelights on the Mexican situation are contained in Edith O'Shaughnessy, *Intimate Pages of Mexican History* (1920).

policies, however, were as burdensome on Mexicans as they were helpful to foreigners. Political liberty was unknown in the republic, and active opposition to the President amounted to flirtation with sudden death. Nevertheless, as Diaz grew old his power began to wane, and some even of those who had long supported him joined forces with Francisco Madero, a sincere liberal, who in November, 1910, had raised the banner of revolt in northern Mexico. In less than six months Diaz was forced to resign and flee the country, whereupon Madero triumphantly assumed the Presidency. But Madero's devotion to constitutional principles annoyed those who wished merely for a younger Diaz, and in February, 1913, by a typically Latin-American *coup d'état*, Madero was arrested and murdered, and Victoriano Huerta, the man most responsible for the crime, took over the reins of authority.

This was the situation that confronted Wilson when he took office. Deeply shocked by Huerta's behavior, the American President at once *The fall* announced that he could show "no sympathy with those who *of Huerta* seek to seize the power of government to advance their own personal interests or ambitions." Wilson's refusal to recognize Huerta as the President of Mexico left that country in an uproar, with counter-revolutionists active in nearly every section. When John Lind of Minnesota, whom Wilson sent on a special mission to treat with the various warring factions, failed to secure either the elimination of Huerta or the union of the forces opposing him, Wilson merely committed the American government to the policy of "watchful waiting," hoping that eventually Huerta would fall. Unfortunately, however, Huerta's régime was viewed with favor by most European nations, and with their encouragement and recognition it lasted on. Finally Wilson, fearful that munitions from a German ship were about to be landed for Huerta at Vera Cruz, ordered the navy to occupy that port, and on April 22, 1914, with considerable loss of life, the order was carried into effect. Three months later, Huerta gave up, and his leading opponent, Venustiano Carranza, took his place.

With Carranza posing as a "constitutionalist" and the rightful succes-sor of Madero, the United States was able to withdraw from Mexico, and *Carranza* resume full diplomatic relations with the Mexican govern-ment. Arms that Carranza was permitted to purchase in the United States helped the new President to restore order, much to the disgust of other revolutionary factions to whom American manufacturers were forbidden to sell. Carranza's chief opponent, Francisco Villa, vented his rage at the United States for this affront by twice crossing the international border in 1916, and murdering American citizens upon

American soil. With the consent of Carranza an American military expedition under the command of General John J. Pershing advanced into Mexico in search of Villa, but it failed to catch him, and was presently withdrawn at Carranza's insistence.

With a semblance of order restored, Carranza proclaimed a new constitution in 1917 which was both anti-foreign and anti-clerical. It proposed to break up the great landed estates for distribution among the people and made many other provisions for the welfare of the working classes; it asserted that the nation had an imprescriptible title to the oil and mineral deposits within its borders; it limited land-ownership and concessionary rights to Mexicans; it ended the union of church and state, declared church edifices national property, and secularized the administration of all educational and benevolent institutions. From this time forward the relations between the United States and Mexico hinged upon the effectiveness with which the anti-foreign provisions of the Constitution of 1917 were enforced. Some Mexican Presidents, such as Obregon, who succeeded Carranza in 1923, treated American investors with considerable generosity, whereas others, such as Calles, whose ascendancy lasted for ten years beginning in 1924, were hard to handle. Wilson's policy toward Mexico was much criticized, but in spite of much insistence on military intervention, it at least stopped short of actual war, and it probably saved the Mexicans from another reactionary régime such as they had suffered from with Diaz.[1]

Constitution of 1917

Keeping out of war with Mexico became a matter of secondary importance for Americans after the outbreak of the World War in the late summer of 1914. To say that such a development was a shock to the American people is a gross understatement. They could hardly believe the news they read. For years, in spite of the great earnestness with which they pursued the cause of world peace, they had taken it for granted that a general European war was impossible. The risks involved in such a conflict for all participants were too appalling. The international ramifications of capital formed too intricate a pattern; one great nation could not attack another without attacking itself. Little nations might fight each other, or a large nation might chastise a small one, but that the greatest and most enlightened nations of the world should fly at one another's throats seemed totally incredible.

War in Europe

Faced by the horrendous fact, the American public, mainly through

[1] Satisfactory discussions of American policy toward Mexico are given in J. F. Rippy, *The United States and Mexico* (new edition, 1931); J. M. Callahan, *American Foreign Policy in Mexican Relations* (1932); G. M. Stephenson, *John Lind of Minnesota* (1935); Harold Nicolson, *Dwight Morrow* (1935).

newspapers, went to school again and brushed up on its European his-
The balance- tory. Europe, it appeared, had depended for years on a
of-power "balance of power" to keep the peace. On the one side
system were Germany, Austria, and Italy, whose agreements as to
military co-operation dated back to the days of Bismarck; on the
other were Great Britain, France, and Russia, ancient enemies whom
the rise of modern Germany had driven together. France and Russia had
been allies since 1891, but the *entente* that bound Great Britain to France
dated no farther back then 1904, while the agreement between Great
Britain and Russia came as late as 1907. Each set of partners made
every effort to line up the lesser nations of Europe on its side. Some, like
Switzerland, Belgium, the Netherlands, and the Scandinavian countries,
maintained a rigid aloofness, but others more or less unofficially chose
sides. The Triple Alliance, as the combination led by Germany was generally called, could count with some certainty on the support of Bulgaria and Turkey, while the Triple Entente, led by Great Britain, was on
friendly terms with Spain and Portugal, and hoped for support from
some of the Balkan nations.[1]

Imperial rivalry, Americans learned, was another part of the picture.
England, France, and Russia had old established empires to which they
Imperial had added liberally in the last quarter of the nineteenth
rivalry century. Germany, too, wanted a "place in the sun," but
she had entered the competition too late to obtain the share of spoils
to which she felt herself, as a great nation, entitled. She had a few
colonies, but they were definitely second-rate. The Triple Entente,
she believed, was created only to draw a "ring of iron" about her that
would prevent the legitimate fulfillment of her desires. Imperial rivalry
went further, however, than the mere acquisition of colonies. In the
development of backward nations lay an equally inviting field. Rivalry
for concessions in China, in Persia, in Morocco, in Turkey, in the Balkans,
everywhere that money could be invested and profits taken, was acute,
with sometimes one nation ahead and sometimes another.

In no region was the atmosphere more tense than in the Balkans and
the Near East. Here, in addition to the ever-present activities of the
The Balkans British and the Germans, the Austrians, the Italians, and
the Russians all claimed special interests based on proximity,
while the Russian government, as a cloak for its ambition to secure free
access to the Mediterranean, essayed the additional rôle of protector to

---

[1] Two of the best works (not entirely in agreement) on the background of the World
War are S. B. Fay, *The Origins of the World War* (2 vols., 1928), and B. E. Schmitt, *The
Coming of the War* (2 vols., 1930).

Greek Orthodox Christians wherever they might be found. In 1908 Austria had annexed Bosnia and Herzegovina, two Serbian provinces handed her for administration in 1878 after the Russo-Turkish War; [1] in 1911 Italy had fought a war with Turkey to justify her conquest of Tripoli; and in 1912-13 two wars had been fought among the little Balkan countries themselves, as a result of which both Turkey and Bulgaria had lost much territory to Greece, Serbia, and Rumania. America did not know it, but for months before the war broke out the Balkan situation had European diplomats all on edge.

Another factor in the situation was the exaggerated nationalism that the nineteenth century had bequeathed to the twentieth. Anthropologists were able to prove conclusively that most European *Nationalism* nations, certainly all the great powers, were peopled by mongrel breeds, with no faintest title to racial purity, but nationalism owed more to a common language and history than to race. Each nation prided itself upon its cultural heritage, perverted its history to make its glories seem greater, and aroused the patriotism of its people to the highest possible pitch. It became, therefore, a matter of national pride to draw within the boundaries of any given nation all who spoke its language or shared its culture. France looked forward to the time when Alsace-Lorraine, taken from her by Germany in 1871, should be again a part of France; Italy dreamed of drawing *Italia irredenta* within her borders; nearly every Balkan nation claimed a part of every other; subject nations like the Poles and the Czechs longed to be free. Austria-Hungary, a polyglot of nationalities, was every neighbor's envy.

All this was bad enough, but the dangers of the situation were compounded again and again by the rampant militarism and navalism that affected every European nation. Universal military training had long been a policy of all the great powers of Europe except Great Britain, and most of the lesser ones. Huge standing armies made every nation an armed camp, with preparedness a national watchword. The insular character of the British Isles saved Great Britain from the necessity of keeping pace in land armament with her rivals on the Continent, but she prided herself upon her navy, which she meant to keep overwhelmingly stronger than any other. Germany's challenge to British supremacy on the high seas — German naval officers toasted "the day" when they would meet the British navy — not only aroused Great Britain to new building, but also led her to abandon her position of "splendid isolation,"

[1] Russia had protested, but had been compelled to withdraw her objection when warned that an attack upon Austria-Hungary would lead to a war with Germany also. She promised Serbia, however, that she would not yield in such a fashion again.

[467]

and to seek allies. On this account she had ended her ages-old rivalries with France and Russia, had made an alliance with Japan, and had sought with great earnestness to win the friendship of the United States.

In Europe the danger that war might break out at any moment was fully realized by the well-informed, and a few Americans understood
House's the situation. Among them was Colonel House, the inti-
"great mate adviser of the President, who in the spring of 1914
adventure" undertook what he called "the great adventure," a trip to Europe to promote the reduction of land and naval armament. House visited the Kaiser and talked with him for half an hour, established close connections with Sir Edward Grey and others in England, and had a try at Paris only to be frustrated there by the customary cabinet crisis. Everywhere he found "militarism run stark mad," but the British told him they were ready to talk reduction, and he so reported to the Kaiser. On June 28, 1914, shortly before he sailed for the United States, he learned that the heir to the Austrian throne, the Archduke Franz Ferdinand, and his wife had been assassinated at Sarajevo, in the province of Bosnia, but neither House nor his English hosts appeared to realize that this somewhat commonplace Balkan incident would lead to war. But war came nevertheless by the time House reached home. His "great adventure" was undertaken too late.[1]

The incidents which led actually to the outbreak of war seemed trifling to Americans. The assassination of the Austrian heir-apparent, it ap-
Immediate peared, was the work of some superpatriotic young Bosnian
causes of Serbs who disliked the Archduke's plan for making the "dual
the war monarchy" of Austria and Hungary into a "triple mon-
archy" which would extend to the Slavs in the empire a right of participation comparable to that enjoyed by the Austrians and the Magyars. Should such a plan succeed, the creation of a greater Serbia might be long delayed, and it was with this thought in mind that the fatal shots were fired. Naturally the Austrian government took a serious view of the situation, the more so because it claimed, probably with good reason, that the Serbian government had guilty knowledge of the plot and had made no effort to prevent its execution. On the assumption that Serbian officials were in reality responsible for what had happened, the Austrian government decided upon punitive measures against its diminutive neighbor, and on July 5 obtained the German Kaiser's permission to

---

[1] Charles Seymour, editor, *The Intimate Papers of Colonel House* (4 vols., 1926–28), provide a running commentary upon all the principal undertakings of the Wilson administration.

go ahead. On July 23 an Austrian ultimatum was delivered to Serbia, which was purposely made so strong as to prevent complete acceptance, and when the Serbian reply proved "evasive" Austria began to mobilize for war.

The ramifications of the European network of alliances now came quickly into play. Russia, in her rôle of protector to all Greek-Orthodox nations, professed to fear that Austria's real intention was annexation rather than punishment, and supported Serbia's plea that the affair should be settled by the Hague Tribunal. Some such settlement was also strongly urged by Great Britain, France, and Italy, but Austria remained obdurate, while Germany, although bending every effort to localize the affair, refused to abandon her ally. On July 28, Austria declared war on Serbia, and on the following day Russia began mobilization. At this point the German Kaiser telegraphed frantically to his kinsman, the Czar, to use his influence for peace, and the Czar ordered that mobilization should be confined strictly to the Austrian frontier. But the Russian military leaders easily persuaded the Czar to reverse himself, and on July 30 he gave the command for general mobilization. Thereupon the German government delivered an ultimatum to Russia, requiring the cessation of mobilization within twelve hours. When this demand fell on deaf ears, Germany on August 1 declared war.

France was the ally of Russia, and Germany now demanded to know in eighteen hours what France intended to do. Bound by her treaty with Russia, and ready to have a try at getting back Alsace-Lorraine, France replied that she would consult her own interests. Thereupon, on August 3, Germany declared war upon France and began at once to move troops toward the Belgian frontier. The German plan of campaign was to avoid the heavily fortified Franco-German frontier, demand passage through Belgium, and by speedy action outflank and destroy the French army before the anticipated Russian invasion of eastern Germany could do any vital damage — a plan that failed, for the Belgians resisted valiantly and the French re-formed their lines and eventually held the invaders at bay. Because the Belgians resisted, Germany, although bound by treaty to protect Belgian neutrality, declared war on Belgium. England, meantime, had been debating her obligations to France, which might mean less than aid in time of war, but the attack on Belgium, whose neutrality she, too, was pledged to defend, decided her. On August 5 she declared war on Germany.

The breath-taking speed with which Europe thus plunged into the abyss of war left Americans aghast. The American course, however, was clear. Neutrality, since the days of George Washington, had become an American tradition. The only exception to the rule had been the *American neutrality* War of 1812, an unconfessed blunder that no one expected to see repeated. On August 4 the President issued the first of a series of proclamations of neutrality by means of which the American State Department struggled to keep abreast of the rapidly spreading war. Two weeks later he urged the American public to be "neutral in fact as well as in name during these days that are to try men's souls. We must be impartial in thought as well as in action." Wilson's neutral course and the frenzied efforts of the government to bring stranded American tourists back from Europe met with universal approval. This was Europe's war, not America's, and with the help of a sizable army of war correspondents the American public prepared to stand by and watch while the fire burned itself out.[1]

But neutrality in thought and deed soon proved to be easier preached than practiced. Popular sympathy from the very outbreak of the war *Sympathy for the Allies* ran heavily in favor of the "Allies," as the nations opposed to Germany and Austria were called, and against the Central Powers. Austria and Germany had issued the first declarations of war; they were apparently the aggressors. Germany was the one nation which seemed wholly prepared for war. Her violation of her treaty with Belgium, called by one German diplomat a "scrap of paper," was hard to forgive. The ruthless progress of German troops through Belgium and northern France produced a deep feeling of sympathy for the under-dogs in the fight. Also, a certain amount of cultural solidarity between the English-speaking peoples came steadily to the fore. Not only Great Britain but the whole British Empire, including Canada, the near neighbor of the United States, was fighting with the Allies. Thus the war was in no small part a contest between the civilization that stemmed from England on the one side, and the German *Kultur* on the other.

American sympathy did not all run with the Allies. The large German element in the American population, ably led by the German-language *German- Americans* press, sympathized whole-heartedly with the Fatherland, and believed that the war was a British-led conspiracy to dismember and destroy Germany. Immigrants and the descendants of immigrants from the other Central Powers (eventually Turkey and Bulgaria joined Germany and Austria) tended also to be guided by sentiments imported from the Old World. The large American popu-

[1] The best single volume on this period of American history is Paxson's *Pre-War Years*, already cited. It may be supplemented on the strictly diplomatic side by Charles Seymour, *American Diplomacy During the World War* (1934).

lation of Irish descent was traditionally anti-British, and sometimes the hatred of Irish-Americans for England made them pro-German. In view of the strong minority sentiment these elements represented, neutrality seemed all the more essential as an American policy. Americans, it seemed, possessed a double loyalty; they were loyal to the United States, but they were loyal also to the country from which they or their ancestors had come.[1]

But there were problems of neutrality and a law of neutrality. Once, a century before, these problems and the American interpretation of the law which they involved had brought the United States into a European war; although most Americans thought of the War of 1812 as a mere continuation of the American Revolution, and were utterly unaware of the lessons it taught. Nevertheless, the similarities between the conditions that existed before 1812 and after 1914 were striking. In both cases the British navy commanded the high seas; in both cases the war meant an abnormal demand for American goods and American shipping; in both cases American neutral rights were frequently violated by both sides; and in both cases, as matters turned out, the United States was eventually drawn into the war.

International law was at least as old as Hugo Grotius, whose book, *De jure belli ac pacis*, was published in 1625. Its rules had nothing more behind them than custom and the common consent of sovereign states. There was a law of peace that was rarely broken, and a law of war that was rarely kept. Invariably in time of war disputes broke out as to what the law really was, and how it should be construed. The rights of neutrals were particularly subject to debate. In general, Great Britain, who expected always to control the seas, was inclined to interpret neutral rights as narrowly as possible, whereas the United States, whose policy was permanent neutrality, and most other nations whose navies were inferior to the British, exaggerated the privileges of neutrals all they could. Attempts to obtain agreement on the meaning of the rules or to amend them met with no success. Neither the code of land warfare adopted by the Second Hague Conference, nor the Declaration of London with respect to naval warfare, was fully ratified. Promptly on the outbreak of the war Wilson asked the belligerents to adhere to the Declaration of London, and the Central Powers agreed to do so if the Allies would bind themselves similarly. But the British feared the limitations on sea-power contained in

International law and the war

---

[1] This problem with respect to the Germans has been well studied in Carl Wittke, *German-Americans and the World War* (1936), and C. J. Child, *The German-Americans in Politics, 1914–1917* (1939).

the new rules and refused to accept them. The United States, therefore, in defending its neutrality had nothing better to depend upon than the jumbled mass of precedents and opinions that had accumulated from the time of Grotius on down. Many of these rules were utterly unrelated to the conditions of modern warfare, but obsolete as they were, they were the only rules that existed.[1]

It was immediately apparent that the British had no notion of allowing the vast amount of American goods and shipping that soon took to the seas to proceed about its business as if there had been no war. This trade represented not merely, or mostly, the ordinary exports of the United States to Europe, but rather millions of dollars' worth of goods that were shipped purely in response to the wartime needs of the belligerents. The products of American farms and factories were earnestly coveted by both sides, and the United States, recovering from a business panic that the outbreak of war had precipitated, was eager to sell. All this was entirely satisfactory to the British, with the single important exception that they were determined to prevent anything of value to the Central Powers from reaching its destination. American goods might flow freely to the Allies, but not to their enemies. To accomplish their purpose the British had only to make use of their naval strength, but, unlike the Germans, they did what they could to reconcile wartime necessities with the existing rules of international law. For authority in dealing with neutral trade, they invoked three well-recognized belligerent rights: (1) the stoppage of trade in contraband goods, (2) the doctrine of continuous voyages, and (3) the blockade.

In each instance, however, British policy tread heavily on neutral toes. The British definition of contraband — that is, goods that might be of *Relations* direct (absolute contraband) or indirect (conditional contra-*with Great* band) use to the enemy — was so generous as to include *Britain* every commodity that the Central Powers might wish to import. This, the American State Department claimed, was going too far. Further, British ships inspected trade between the United States and such neutrals as bordered on Germany, or on any of her partners, to make sure that none of it was ultimately intended for the enemy. If that was deemed to be the case, the trip was regarded as one continuous voyage which might be interrupted anywhere in its progress. This, too, was protested, although in the American Civil War the United

[1] Alice M. Morrissey, *The American Defense of Neutral Rights, 1914–1917* (1939), is an excellent study of the problems in international law presented by the war. It should be compared with Edwin Borchard and W. P. Lage, *Neutrality for the United States* (1937), which takes the ground that the United States was not wholly neutral. An older but still useful study is J. W. Garner, *International Law and the World War* (1920).

States had done practically the same thing to prevent British commodities from reaching the South. Finally, a Ministry of Blockade was set up, which took good care that all shipping found anywhere on the high seas was carefully scrutinized to prevent the Central Powers obtaining anything that the British did not wish them to have. Such a blockade, the United States maintained, was illegal. It was enforced at long distance; it was applied against neutral as well as against belligerent coasts; and it was unenforceable against the countries that bordered on the Baltic Sea, because there the German navy, not the British, was supreme. But the British, while admitting that their methods might be somewhat unusual, argued that they were living up to the spirit, if not the letter, of the law.

The list of protests lodged by the United States against Great Britain included also vigorous denunciations of the British practice of taking neutral ships to Allied ports to be searched. The old rules contemplated search on the high seas, but with modern shipping such a practice was difficult, and after submarine warfare began, extremely dangerous. Sometimes American ships were held up for months at Allied ports. The British practice of searching American mail, both to and from Europe, also drew fire. The British held that American mail pouches, even when consigned to neutral countries, often contained things of value intended for the enemy, and they proposed also to know what information was going into and coming out of Germany. Exports from the Central Powers were given as scant courtesy as imports, and for long periods American industry was shut off from supplies obtainable only from Germany, such as dyestuffs, drugs, and sugar-beet seeds.[1]

The American case against the British for their violations of neutrality was fully and conscientiously stated by the American State Department, but that was all. Probably the original intent was to collect damages after the war for proved violations, much as had been done after the Civil War. In private most American officials agreed that what the British were doing they must do to win, and that a British victory was to the best interests of the United States. Furthermore, American shippers soon grew accustomed to the British regulations, and by conforming to them escaped difficulty. Seized cargoes were usually paid for, but as time went on few cargoes were sent that were in any danger of being seized. Allied demands alone were sufficient to absorb all the surplus goods the United States could produce; indeed, war orders soon turned what might otherwise have been a depression into a boom. Other neu-

[1] Wilson's foreign policy as a whole is well considered in Harley Notter, *The Origins of the Foreign Policy of Woodrow Wilson* (1937), and E. E. Robinson and V. J. West, *The Foreign Policy of Woodrow Wilson* (1917). Much useful information is scattered through the various volumes of Baker's *Woodrow Wilson*, beginning with volume IV.

trals, such as Denmark and Holland, also acquiesced in the British regulations. Since the British rules occasioned no loss of life and practically no loss of property, and since for every market closed at least two new ones were opened, the American public had little heart to object.[1]

The close community of interests that thus developed between the United States and the Allies was an object of great concern to the *Relations* Germans, who were seriously handicapped by their inability *with Germany* to trade with America, and scarcely less to many German sympathizers in the United States itself. Some of the latter, including Senator William J. Stone of Missouri, chairman of the Senate Committee on Foreign Relations, favored a complete embargo on the sale outside the national borders of military supplies, particularly ammunition, but the State Department maintained with unimpeachable logic that such trade was not a violation of neutrality. If Germany could not buy in the United States, it was the fault of the British navy, not of the American government. The German Foreign Office was frantic with rage. It not only lodged frequent and vehement protests against American acquiescence in British trade regulations, but it also encouraged the sabotage by German agents of such American industries as were aiding the Allies. For proved complicity in such plots the Austrian ambassador, Constantin Dumba, and several attachés of the German embassy, including Franz von Papen, were ordered to leave the United States.[2]

Germany's most effective means of retaliation against the pressure of Allied sea-power proved to be the submarine, a type of craft her engineers *Submarine* had brought to extraordinary efficiency. On February 4, *warfare* 1915, in protest against the British stoppage of food shipments to Germany, the German government declared a "war zone" about the British Isles, and announced its intention to sink on sight every enemy merchantman within the area described. The United States was warned to keep American shipping out of the danger zone lest by mistake American ships and lives might be lost. Against this new type of warfare the American government lodged an immediate protest. Its illegality was obvious even to the German government, which defended it only on the ground of retaliation for allegedly illegal actions by the Allies, and the willingness of neutrals to acquiesce in them. The war-zone decree could not be defended as a blockade, for a blockade, to be binding on neutral nations, must effectively stop a major part of the shipping plying to and from the blockaded ports, whereas German sub-

---

[1] B. J. Hendrick, *Life and Letters of Walter Hines Page* (3 vols., 1922–25); *War Memoirs of Robert Lansing, Secretary of State* (1935).
[2] Constantin Dumba, *Memoirs of a Diplomat* (1932).

marines could not possibly hope to intercept more than an occasional ship. Visit and search by a submarine to ascertain the character of the ship and the nature of its cargo would be a virtual impossibility. Sinking on sight defied all the rules that required the attacking warship to provide for the safety of non-combatant passengers and crews. Reciting the evidence as to the illegality of the war-zone decree, Wilson's note of protest declared that the United States was "reluctant to believe" that the warfare contemplated would ever be carried into effect, and warned that in case American ships or lives were lost the German government would be held to a "strict accountability."

The threat to American neutrality posed by the submarine blockade led Wilson to dispatch Colonel House to Europe on a "quest for peace." House cherished the chimerical hope that he might persuade *The* the British to give up their blockade and the Germans their *Lusitania* submarine attacks on merchantmen — the very weapons by which the two leading contenders hoped to win the war. Naturally his "quest" was fruitless, and on May 7, 1915, the British passenger liner, *Lusitania*, on which he had sailed to Europe a few weeks before, was torpedoed without warning and sunk off the Irish coast on her way to England. More than eleven hundred persons lost their lives, including one hundred and twenty-four Americans. The sinking was a perfectly clear violation of neutral rights. Warning had not been given by a shot across the ship's bow, or in any other manner prescribed by sea usage. The fact that an advertisement in a New York paper had warned passengers of what might happen if they sailed on the *Lusitania* proved merely that the act was premeditated; no known rule of international law provided for a newspaper warning, and the advertisement was generally regarded as a hoax. The fact that the *Lusitania* carried ammunition designed for Allied use was equally irrelevant. The Germans had a perfect right to capture and confiscate the ship, even to sink it, but according to the existing rules they must first find out by a search what its cargo contained, and make satisfactory provision for the safety of non-combatants.

American opinion on the *Lusitania* disaster was not entirely unanimous. The sinking was vigorously condemned, and frequently the old battle-cry, "Remember the *Maine*," was raised. Theodore Roosevelt, the most bitter of the anti-German leaders in the United States, described the attack on the *Lusitania* as an "act of piracy," and demanded immediate war. There were many who agreed with him, particularly along the Atlantic seaboard where the importance of keeping open the sea lanes to Europe was the more keenly felt, but in the West and the South there was a tendency to ask why American citizens needed to venture into the danger zone. Should the American government not prevent such incidents in the future by prohibiting its nationals from sailing on belligerent merchant ships, or on ships carrying munitions? Bryan himself took this attitude, which Easterners called "provincial," and he would have been willing even to submit the *Lusitania* incident to arbitration. He signed the first note of protest that Wilson wrote, but the next one was too much for him, and he resigned from the cabinet rather than be party to a policy which in his judgment might easily lead to war. The same sentiment appeared in Congress, where only the vigorous intervention of the President prevented the passage of resolutions, sponsored in the House by McLemore of Texas and in the Senate by Gore of Oklahoma, forbidding American citizens to travel on belligerent merchantmen, except at their own peril.

The *Lusitania* incident led to a diplomatic correspondence between the United States and Germany that lasted all through the summer of *Germany* 1915.[1] Wilson's statement, made in a public address just *backs down* before his first note was sent, "There is such a thing as a man being too proud to fight," seemed to betoken an attitude of weakness, but in three successive notes he argued the case with Germany, taking stronger ground each time. The submarine, he held, used as Germany was using it, was an illegal weapon, and any repetition of the *Lusitania* offense would be regarded as a "deliberately unfriendly" act. This was a threat of war, as the German ambassador to the United States, Count von Bernstorff, well knew, but the offense was repeated on August 19, when the *Arabic* was sunk with the loss of two American lives. Thereupon von Bernstorff, acting on his own initiative, promised the American State Department, in writing, that liners would not be sunk "without warning and without safety to the lives of noncombatants, provided that the liners do not try to escape or offer resistance." Eventually the German government agreed to back up Bernstorff's words with deeds. Wilson had scored a signal diplomatic triumph, but he had won his victory only by the threat of war. When, either by accident or intent, a few more sinkings occurred, notably the *Sussex*, on March 24, 1916, Wilson in a spectacular appearance before Congress renewed his threat and forced from the German government a reiteration of its promises. German insistence that the United States should also force the Allies to give up their illegal practices, Wilson refused to consider as in any way pertinent to the problem. For nine

[1] J. H. von Bernstorff, *My Three Years in America* (1920). The experiences of the American ambassador to Germany are recounted in J. W. Gerard, *My Four Years in Germany* (1920).

months, whether because it feared the United States or because it had discovered a need for more and better submarines, the German government kept its promise.

In part, at least, to implement his threats, Wilson now put himself at the head of a strong demand for military preparedness that, in spite of much "pacifist" protest, was sweeping the country. On *Preparedness* the very day that he dispatched his third *Lusitania* note he authorized the Army and Navy Departments to draft plans for the strengthening of the national defenses, and in his annual message to Congress of December, 1915, he called emphatic attention to these proposals. Early in 1916 he toured the country to speak for preparedness, and on Flag Day, June 14, he led a preparedness parade down Pennsylvania Avenue. His determination to make the United States ready for war was strengthened by the failure of another House mission to Europe, this time in order to offer the Allies a "plan to compel peace." The idea was that Wilson, with Allied foreknowledge, should demand the cessation of hostilities and a conference of the belligerents to discuss peace terms. If the proposals of the Allies — to be agreed upon in consultation with the United States — were not accepted by Germany, then the United States would "probably" join the Allied war effort. Wilson's use of the word "probably," as an afterthought, no doubt wrecked the plan, and the war went on. It was Wilson's fear that if the war should continue the United States would be drawn into it that had led him to accept House's scheme in the first place; now with the failure of the plan the President was even more fearful of war and determined to be ready for it.[1]

The battle of Jutland, fought May 31–June 1, 1916, gave Americans a rude jolt. In that engagement the German High-Seas Fleet boldly challenged the British Grand Fleet in the North Sea and inflicted such serious damage upon it as to serve warning that British command of the seas might soon be threatened. Already the Chicago *Tribune*, persistent champion of a foreign policy based on national self-interest, had warned its readers of the dire consequences to the United States in case the British fleet should be destroyed. "British naval supremacy," it pointed out editorially, "has been the stable factor in world diplomacy for so many years that all but diplomats are inclined to forget it." Americans were reminded that the Monroe Doctrine had been "largely built upon it" and that even the Oriental policies of the United States "had to look to it for sanction." If the British fleet were annihilated,

[1] F. L. Huidekoper, *The Military Unpreparedness of the United States* (1915), was among the books much quoted by preparedness advocates.

every item of American foreign policy "would have to be scrutinized in the light of unknown conditions," and the nation's future might be gravely imperiled. To forestall such a calamity, many Americans, including apparently some of the makers of *Tribune* policy, were ready to form a definite alliance with Great Britain and enter the war.[1]

Opposition to preparedness in Congress now lost ground steadily, for even those who were unwilling to concede that the British navy was the first line of defense for the United States were not unaware of the dangers to America that might flow from German control of the seas. A National Defense Act which authorized the increase of the standing army to 175,000, and the National Guard to 450,000, became law early in June. Even more important was the Naval Appropriation Act, passed two months later, which provided for the immediate construction of four dreadnoughts and four battle cruisers. The total appropriation carried in this measure ran to $313,000,000, the largest sum Congress had ever voted at any one time for naval purposes. Three capital ships, the *Nevada*, the *Oklahoma*, and the *Pennsylvania*, had just been completed. As two further means of promoting the national defense, Congress created (1) a Council of National Defense, to consist of six Cabinet officers and seven unpaid civilian experts, and (2) a United States Shipping Board, which might build, or otherwise acquire, and operate a fleet of merchantmen. The nation was preparing for war as it had never prepared for war before. And there were few who could ask seriously, "What war?"

The campaign and election of 1916 occurred during the months immediately following Wilson's diplomatic victory over Germany. That *Election of 1916* he would be a candidate to succeed himself in spite of the fact that the platform on which he was elected opposed a second term was universally taken for granted. Wilson was the leader of his party. Even the defection of Bryan gave the President no cause for alarm, for by the time Bryan quit the cabinet Wilson had wholly eclipsed him. The congressional elections of 1914 had found most of the Progressives back in the Republican fold, but the Democrats emerged triumphant in a straight-out two-party contest. The reason for this, everyone knew, was Woodrow Wilson. When the Democratic Convention met in St. Louis June 14, it had nothing to do but to renominate both Wilson and his running-mate of four years before, Thomas R. Marshall of Indiana, by acclamation, and to record in its platform

---

[1] Chicago *Tribune*, March 14, 1916, and May 11, 1916. "Isolation, splendid or sordid, is not possible in our age. If the war has taught us nothing else, it has carried that lesson to the uttermost parts of the earth for those who will think." *Ibid.*, December 18, 1915.

complete approval of every action the administration had taken.

In a shrewd effort to unite all forces opposed to Wilson, the Republicans turned for their candidate to Associate Justice Charles Evans Hughes of the United States Supreme Court. With the discretion permitted to justices, Hughes had not openly taken sides for or against Germany, for or against intervention in Mexico, for or against preparedness. Nor had he been involved in any way in the disastrous split of four years before. His background as governor of New York was satisfying to the Progressive wing of the party, and his decisions as associate justice had caused the conservatives no alarm. Hughes's availability was so obvious that the Republicans, meeting at Chicago, June 7, named him on the first ballot, although he had done nothing to advance his candidacy and had not even said that he would accept the nomination. All fell out as planned. Roosevelt, by declining a Progressive nomination and supporting Hughes, dealt a deathblow to the party he had founded. Pro-Germans who thought Wilson had been unfair to Germany, anti-Germans who condemned his soft treatment of wanton aggressors, pacifists who were for peace with everybody at whatever price, war advocates who demanded, sometimes in the same breath, intervention in both Mexico and Europe, all rallied to the Republican standard. The day Hughes resigned from the Supreme Court to accept the proffered nomination he might have been elected, for then all factions could have claimed him as their own.

As the campaign progressed, the President's chances improved. His followers proclaimed truthfully that he had "kept us out of war," forgetting, perhaps, that he had a threat out that might draw the nation in. Many Progressives who had supported Roosevelt in 1912 were ready to change their allegiance to Wilson, for under his dynamic leadership a spectacular and comprehensive program of domestic reform had been achieved. Wilson got the "breaks" of the campaign. When a "hyphenate" American, Jeremiah A. O'Leary, whose object was to induce Irish-Americans and German-Americans to vote the Republican ticket, sent a long telegram to Wilson denouncing him for unfairness to Germany, the President's reply was tart: "I would feel deeply mortified to have you or anybody like you vote for me. Since you have access to many disloyal Americans and I have not, I will ask you to convey this message to them."

Hughes, on the other hand, was obliged to conduct a campaign of carping criticism, while not being free to take sides on anything. He had only one stroke of luck. The four great railway brotherhoods chose the Labor Day immediately preceding the election as a desirable time

to strike for recognition of the basic eight-hour day and time and a
The Adamson Act half for overtime. Such a strike in an age when there was virtually no such thing as transportation by trucks would have throttled business and seriously hampered the President's efforts to speed up preparedness. Faced by this emergency, Wilson asked Congress to prevent the strike by enacting into law the demands of the brotherhoods. Congress obeyed with the passage of the Adamson Act, which became a law on September 1. Here Hughes had ample ground for criticism, and he made the most of it, but when he was asked if he would favor the repeal of the law, he could only reply, "You can't repeal a surrender."

The night of election day it appeared certain that Hughes had won. He had carried the East almost solidly, including the State of New York.
Wilson's narrow victory He had carried also every state in the Old Northwest except Ohio. But the returns from the South and the farther West told a different story. The solid South was conceded to the Democrats, but nothing of the kind was expected from such dependable Republican centers as Kansas and California. Nevertheless Wilson carried every state west of the Mississippi except Minnesota, Iowa, South Dakota, and Oregon, which he lost by slender margins. In the electoral college the vote stood 277 to 254, the closest division since 1876, but the popular vote gave Wilson a lead of 9,129,606 to 8,538,221. Again the Democrats captured both houses of Congress. Significantly the protest vote of nearly a million that had been cast for Eugene V. Debs, the Socialist candidate in 1912, dropped to 585,113 for Allen Benson, in 1916.[1]

Deeply impressed by the popularity of the slogan, "He kept us out of war," Wilson made another attempt shortly after the election to
Wilson's bid for peace bring the war to an end. In a note released December 20, 1916, he asked the fighting powers for "an avowal of their respective views" as to terms upon which the war might be concluded. Both sides, he observed, claimed to be fighting for "virtually the same" things, the rights of small nations and security for themselves. Perhaps if they would state their war aims more precisely, the differences between them would not be too great for statesmanship to bridge. Anticipating Wilson's offer, and with the military situation running strongly in their favor, the German authorities had already let it be known on December 12 that they were willing to enter a peace conference. They thus made Wilson's call for a statement of war aims

[1] The story of this campaign and much other information pertinent to an understanding of the period is in Mark Sullivan, *Our Times*, v, *Over Here, 1914–1918* (1933).

appear to be a reinforcement of their offer. The Allies indignantly rejected the idea of treating with a victorious Germany, but, although deeply offended that Wilson should have made a move for peace at a time when Germany was winning, they replied at length to his inquiry. Peace, they said, must carry with it the restitution of conquered territories, full reparations for damages done, and guaranties that nothing of the kind would happen again. The Germans, however, refused in any way to divulge their peace aims, reserving for themselves full freedom of action at the council table.

Reading these replies, it seemed to Wilson that there could be no hope of a lasting peace if either side were permitted to have its way. On January 22, 1917, in an address before the Senate he began to argue the case for a "peace without victory," hoping that eventually the warring nations would heed the wisdom of his words. Such a peace as the victor might impose upon the vanquished, he said, "would be accepted in humiliation, under duress, at an intolerable sacrifice, and would leave a sting, a resentment, a bitter memory upon which terms of peace would rest, not permanently, but only as upon quicksand. Only a peace between equals can last." He even outlined the terms of what he thought would constitute a just peace: equality of rights for small and great nations; universal recognition of the principle that governments derive their just powers from the consent of the governed; the right of every great people to have an outlet to the sea; the freedom of the seas "in law and in fact"; the limitation of armaments; and the avoidance by all nations of entangling alliances. Already he had made known his belief that there must be a league to enforce peace, and he told the Senate that if such a peace as he had outlined could be made the United States must do its part to maintain it.

These were brave words and true words, but before they were spoken the German government had already decided upon the policy which was to rob them of their effect. Convinced by the German ad- *The submarine again* miralty that unrestricted submarine warfare would speedily destroy enough shipping to isolate Great Britain and force her to sue for peace, the German government announced on January 31, 1917, that its submarines would sink on sight all ships found within specified war zones, whether neutral or belligerent. Its promise to the United States not to sink without warning and without making provision for the safety of non-combatants it withdrew on the ground that the United States had failed to stop the illegal practices of the Allies. Wilson had no choice now but to break off diplomatic relations with Germany, and this he promptly did.

For a time it seemed that the President was seeking a formula short of outright war to resolve the situation. Harking back to the undeclared naval war between France and the United States in 1798, he spoke of "armed neutrality," and asked Congress to grant him authority to provide American merchantmen with guns for their defense. A "little group of willful men," as the President called them, filibustered this measure to death, but the needed authority was found in an unrepealed law of 1797, and the merchantmen were armed. It was clear that if either the United States or Germany struck a blow there would be war. Wilson professed to believe that the Germans would never carry out their threats, but on March 18 German submarines sank three ships with loss of American lives. Thereupon Wilson called Congress into special session for April 2, and on the evening of that day read his call to arms. Everything else had been tried, he claimed, and now the only recourse was war. The President disclaimed any desire to fight against the German people, and distinguished carefully between them and their government. That government, however, had challenged the security of democracy throughout the world. The United States was glad to fight it, he said,

> for the ultimate peace of the world and for the liberation of its peoples, the German peoples included: for the rights of nations great and small and the privilege of men everywhere to choose their way of life and of óbedience. The world must be made safe for democracy. Its peace must be planted upon the tested foundations of political liberty.

The response of Congress to the President's eloquent appeal was not unanimous, but it was overwhelming enough to be convincing. On *Congress declares war* April 4 the Senate passed the war resolution by a vote of 82 to 6, and on April 6 the House concurred by a vote of 373 to 50. Diplomatic relations with Austria-Hungary were promptly broken, but war was not declared until December 7. Against Germany's other allies, Turkey and Bulgaria, the United States issued no declarations of war. Claiming that the war against Germany was being fought on behalf of neutral rights generally, the United States urged other neutrals also to join in the crusade. As a result Cuba, Panama, Siam, Liberia, China, and Brazil entered the war on the Allied side, and several other nations broke off diplomatic relations. Long before, Japan and Portugal had joined in order to fulfill their alliances with Great Britain, while Italy by generous promises and Greece by threats had also been brought into the Allied camp. Thus the war became in fact as well as in name a World War.

It is extremely difficult to catalogue all the factors that worked together to draw the United States into the war. Undoubtedly the diplomatic impasse over submarine warfare did in fact precipitate *Why* hostilities, and he who says that the United States would *America* have entered the war even if illegal sinkings had not been *fought* resumed says far more than he can prove. But undoubtedly there were other considerations at work to influence the American people, such, for example, as British propaganda. But British propaganda was not necessary to convince the United States that the Central Powers were the aggressors, and that the rape of Belgium was a crime. The bulk of the American people took sides in August, 1914, and never wavered in their loyalties throughout the entire period of neutrality. But the British did present their case with skill, and they persuaded many Americans that a German victory would mean the beginning of the end for civilization.[1]

There was also an economic side to the picture which it is difficult to state without overemphasis. Most Americans were only faintly aware of it, but the facts were clear. The United States in the fall *Economic* of 1914 escaped a depression only by virtue of war orders. *factors* These purchases were entirely legal, even when they were of contraband, and were so described by the American State Department. On loans to the Allies by American citizens to pay for war purchases, however, the State Department pursued a shifting course. At first it said that such loans were inconsistent with American neutrality, then it attempted to draw a distinction between loans and credits, but finally in August, 1915, it sanctioned both. By that time American prosperity was more closely bound up than ever with war orders, and without more loans there was the gravest danger that the orders would stop. With the spring of 1917 the Allies had too nearly exhausted their credit in the United States for comfort; already they owed American moneylenders over a billion dollars, and the limit for the sale of their securities had almost been reached. There was point to the argument of the American ambassador to Great Britain, Walter Hines Page, that direct loans from the United States were now necessary, both to avert a panic in the United States, and to save the Allied cause from collapse.

An indication of how completely American economy was geared to the war was given when the German submarine threat of January, 1917, precipitated a sudden stoppage of shipments from Atlantic ports. Thoroughly frightened by the German sinkings, neutral shipping refused

[1] H. C. Peterson, *Propaganda for War* (1939), examines closely the effects of British propaganda in America. It should be compared with J. P. Jones and P. M. Hollister, *The German Secret Service in America* (1918), and H. D. Lasswell, *Propaganda Technique in the World War* (1927).

to put to sea. Belligerent merchantmen continued to come and go, but they were utterly unable to handle the traffic that cluttered the docks and warehouses of the eastern seaboard, and tied up the railroads with unloaded freight as far west as Pittsburgh. Out of the transportation snarl a food and fuel shortage developed in some metropolitan areas; from the lower East Side in New York City, quite in the best revolutionary tradition, there was a march of angry women on the City Hall demanding food. Without American shipping to move American goods overseas, the United States faced economic collapse. And Great Britain faced the loss of the war.

In the spring of 1917 the Germans seemed to have victory within their grasp. German offensives, particularly in the East, had been overwhelmingly successful; Allied offensives were invariably followed by "strategic retreats." Nearly all of Belgium and a large share of northern France lay in German hands. The Russians had lost most of Poland, while Rumania was no sooner in the war on the Allied side than her army was defeated and her territory occupied. Much of Serbia had long since been overrun. With Austria, Bulgaria, and Turkey completely subservient to the German will, the long-dreamed-of *Mitteleuropa* had become a fact. Germany had lost her colonies, and she was beginning to suffer from the Allied blockade, but with the assistance of the submarine she had good reason to believe that her road to victory was clear. From its inception unrestricted submarine warfare took a terrific toll. For weeks one ship out of every four that left British ports failed to return. Neutral shipping tended more and more to stay out of the war-zone. Even if the British navy remained afloat, Great Britain could be starved into submission.

That the United States was ready to rally to the Allied cause whenever such action should be necessary to prevent a German triumph seems far *Fear of a* clearer today than it did at the time. Perhaps the Ameri- *German* cans would have been willing to accept the "peace without *victory* victory" that Wilson advocated, provided that it left British sea-power in command of the eastern Atlantic. Whether they were ready to admit it to themselves or not, Americans knew that they dare not take the risk of the exchange of a friendly power on the Atlantic for an unfriendly power. For a full century the American government had depended upon the friendly support of the British navy to guard the sea-lanes of the Atlantic. That navy alone had maintained the Monroe Doctrine when there was no American navy worthy of the name to assume the task. Anglo-American accord had made possible the location of most of the new American navy in the Pacific, where the threat of

Japanese aggression was all too plain. Germany had long been restive under the restraints of the Monroe Doctrine, and had cast jealous eyes upon Latin-America as a field for colonial expansion. If she drove the British navy from the Atlantic, what would be her next move? As if to provide an unequivocal answer to this question, intercepted dispatches that the British secret service had turned over to the American government revealed on March 1, 1917, that Alfred Zimmermann, the German Foreign Minister, had offered Mexico the states of Texas, New Mexico, and Arizona, together with liberal financial aid, if Mexico would join Germany, in the event of war between Germany and the United States. Further, the President of Mexico was to urge Japan to shift to the side of the Central Powers, presumably in return for what spoils Japan might desire at the expense of the United States. After the news of the "Zimmermann plot" reached the public, a speedy declaration of war on Germany was inevitable.

In explaining why war had to come, the Chicago *Tribune*, two days after Congress had acted, stated the case with admirable clarity:

> So long as it seemed certain that Great Britain would retain control of the sea, the United States found merely an emotional interest in the war, regarding it as merely a question of European maps and European power. . . . The new naval weapon, the submarine, is effective. Great Britain's destiny is in doubt. . . . It is possible . . . that control of the seas would pass from the British. . . . It will comfort most Americans to know that the nation is doing what is needed for the guarding of the present and the guarantee of the future American republic.[1]

In reality, the United States went to war in 1917 less because of German violations of international law, or Allied indebtedness to American producers, or the subtlety of British propaganda than because of the threat to American national interests that would have been implicit in German supremacy in the Atlantic. As a recent observer points out:

> The United States took up arms in the last analysis because it seemed likely that without American intervention the scepter of the Atlantic would pass from the hands of English-speaking peoples into those of a stranger. Of England the Americans had no genuine fears; the stranger might provoke them into a far more terrible war — with perhaps the Continent and a subdued Britain behind him — to settle the ascendancy of the Atlantic Ocean, and, beyond that, this Western Hemisphere.[2]

[1] Quoted from Warren Jenkins, "The Foreign Policy of the Chicago *Tribune*, 1914–1917" (unpublished Ph.D. thesis, University of Wisconsin, 1942).

[2] Forrest Davis, *The Atlantic System: The Story of Anglo-American Control of the Seas* (1941), p. 245. By permission of Reynal and Hitchcock, Inc., publishers.

Wilson's argument that "we entered the war as the disinterested champions of right" was a rationalization. The United States entered *The defense of the Atlantic* the war because she dared not do otherwise. But Wilson touched a magic chord when he said, "The world must be made safe for democracy." With Russia in the throes of a democratic revolution a fair case could be made for the assertion that the war was a conflict between autocracies and democracies. With autocratic rulers free to build up military machines and to declare war at will, the peace-loving democracies were at a serious disadvantage. As long as autocracy was enthroned among the great nations of the world, a lasting peace could never be made. Thus the war became not only a war to make the world safe for democracy, but also a "war to end war." With these emotional overtones — afterthoughts though they may have been — ringing in their ears, the American people went to war in a mood of the highest idealism. They fought for the survival of democracy and for peace on earth.[1]

[1] Most of the books written on the entry of the United States into the First World War are highly controversial. Newton D. Baker, *Why We Went to War* (1936), blamed the submarine primarily. See, also, for a similar point of view Charles Seymour, *American Neutrality, 1914–1917* (1935), and *Woodrow Wilson and the World War* (1921). Criticism of the American policy was first effectively stated in C. H. Grattan, *Why We Fought* (1929). The case against American entrance into the war was carried further by Walter Millis, *Road to War: America, 1914–17* (1935), and C. C. Tansill, *America Goes to War* (1938). The Second World War, with its indifference to neutral rights, seemed to indicate that the reasons for American entrance lay much deeper than the earlier controversialists had believed.

CHAPTER XXII

THE FIRST WORLD WAR

BEFORE the entrance of the United States into the war most Americans had taken it for granted that geographic conditions would limit American participation primarily to naval and financial aid. A succession of missions to Washington from the Allied governments soon proved that the Allies needed everything — money, ships, supplies, men — if the Central Powers were ever to be defeated. Nor could they wait. The United States must act quickly, and avoid mistakes.

Most of all the Allies needed men, and the plans of the General Staff for raising an army in leisurely fashion were immediately speeded up. Convinced that the principle of volunteering, upon which *The American army* both Great Britain and the United States had relied mainly in earlier wars, had been proved by England's recent experiences to be inadequate, the military leaders persuaded Congress to approve in May, 1917, a Selective Service Act. This measure required all men between the ages of twenty-one and thirty (later eighteen and forty-five) to register for military service. The registrants were then divided by local civilian boards into five classes, the first of which consisted of able-bodied, unmarried men, without dependents. The 2,810,296 men actually selected for service during the war came from this group alone. An elaborate lottery system determined the order in which they were called. Not all of the American army, however, was raised by the draft. The combined strength of the regular army and the National Guard stood at about 750,000 men when the Selective Service Act went into operation, and from this pool of trained and partially trained men the military leaders drew heavily in creating the various units that composed the new National Army. By the end of the war the continuous transfer of individuals and units from one division to another had broken down fairly completely distinctions as to origin. For the training of the men thirty-two camps and cantonments, mainly located in the South, were hastily constructed.

Almost as difficult as the problem of obtaining the men was the problem of supplying the army with competent officers. For the higher
Officer training ranks, officers of the regular army and the National Guard were promoted, but for the lower grades the army depended upon the graduates of hastily organized officers' training camps from which "ninety-day wonders" were soon being turned out in profusion. At first only volunteers of excellent promise were accepted for officer training, but later candidates selected on merit from among the drafted men were also given a chance to earn commissions. Political appoint-ments, such as had disgraced the formation of the Civil War armies, both North and South, were deliberately avoided. This decision was a great disappointment to Theodore Roosevelt, who had aspired to emulate his performance in the Spanish-American War, and lead a division of volunteers to France. The war, he complained, was a "very exclusive war," and his hatred for Wilson, already burning brightly, flamed up anew after his rejection.

The problem of financing the war would have been great had the United States had only her own expenditures to consider, but she had
Financing the war also to finance her Allies in considerable part. Economists urged a "pay-as-you-go" system, with taxation of wartime profits and earnings furnishing most of the revenue, but such a system was a practical impossibility. For one thing, money was needed immediately, and newly devised taxes would take months, or even years, to produce the needed funds. Congress therefore resorted to loans, as well as taxes. The first loan act, which became law on April 24, authorized the borrowing of five billion dollars, and subsequent credits were voted as needed. Five huge bond issues were floated, the first four known as "Liberty Loans," and the last, which was offered after the fighting had ended, as the "Victory Loan." The total amounts so subscribed reached $21,448,120,300, and drew upon the savings of over sixty-five million individuals. Each loan was accompanied by a great "drive," in which every conceivable device was used to induce both those who had the means and those who had not to subscribe. The bonds were issued in denominations as low as fifty and one hundred dollars, and the purchase of such a bond, on the installment plan if need be, was made almost a test of loyalty. "Four-minute men" harangued theater, church, and school audiences on the iniquities of the Germans and the necessity of the war. Individuals who were suspected of being "pro-German" were compelled to prove their patriotism by particularly generous contributions; if they did not, their houses might be decorated with yellow paint, or they might even be subjected to rough handling.

Corporations with large payrolls put pressure upon their employees to subscribe. Thrift stamps and war-savings certificates were devised to tap even the savings of the children. Unfortunately the securities marketed by the government were negotiable, and because the government refused to buy them back ahead of dates set for maturity they depreciated materially in value. Speculators thus made excellent profits; worse still, the bonds, unlike the non-transferable bonds issued during the Second World War, served to promote rather than to restrict inflation. Prices rose rapidly, and without serious attempt on the part of the government to hold them down.[1]

The income tax, with its surtax feature, offered an easy means of expanding the national revenue. The Revenue Act of 1916 had already doubled the normal income tax, but the War Revenue Act of 1917 doubled it again, bringing it to four per cent, and taxed incomes as low as a thousand dollars. The graduated surtax and the tax on corporation earnings were also raised, and a new graduated excess profits tax took from twenty to sixty per cent of such business earnings as exceeded the average for the years 1911–1913. The excise taxes on liquor and tobacco were steeply increased, and a host of "nuisance taxes" introduced — on railroad and sleeping-car tickets, on theater tickets and club dues, on telephone and telegraph messages, and on numerous other "luxuries." Postage rates went up, the ordinary letter rate from two to three cents. These were the beginning, and still higher taxes were written into the Revenue Acts of 1918 and 1919. Altogether the United States raised a total of $11,280,000,000 from taxation, nearly one third the amount spent or lent during the same period. The total expenditures from April, 1917, to October, 1919, aggregated $35,413,000,000, of which $9,406,000,000 was lent to the Allies.

The contribution of the American people to the cost of the war included also millions of dollars expended for private benevolence. Probably the Red Cross, with its emphasis on medical care and *Private* hospitalization, was most appreciated by soldiers and public *benevolence* alike. Its first drive for funds, held immediately after the flotation of the First Liberty Loan, netted over $100,000,000, and subsequent drives brought in other huge sums. The Young Men's Christian Association, the Knights of Columbus, the United Hebrew Charities, and the Salvation Army also solicited contributions for wartime activities, and spent lavishly in their efforts to make life in the army camps and

[1] J. H. Hollander, *War Borrowing* (1919); E. L. Bogart, *Direct and Indirect Costs of the Great World War* (new edition, 1920); J. M. Clark, *The Costs of the World War to the American People* (1931).

overseas more bearable. Besides all this, women's organizations knitted socks, prepared bandages, and provided numerous other items of consequence to the soldier's comfort. Undoubtedly the benevolent agencies did much to substitute harmless amusements for the traditional resort of the soldier to intoxication and immorality, and they sought also to bolster up army morale. The "Y" suffered much criticism, mainly because it accepted the task of vending such supplies as candy and cigarettes, instead of confining its efforts more exclusively to straight-out gifts.[1] Nearly all of the work supported by benevolence had to be done; if private agencies had not undertaken it, the government itself would have been obliged to do so. So valuable did this work seem that the government encouraged all drives for funds by benevolent societies while the war was on. Gifts to churches, colleges, hospitals, and endowment funds, whether directly concerned in the war or not, at least cultivated the important habit of giving.

In general the government itself took care of the dependents of soldiers, and made what provision it could to prevent the men who fought

War risk insurance   the war from becoming objects of charity in the future. By rigorous examinations it kept out of the service all those who might reasonably be expected to break under the physical and mental strain of war. Men who had families dependent on them for support were given deferred classification, which amounted in effect to exemption from the draft. The Bureau of War Risk Insurance, established originally in 1914 to write marine insurance, was enlarged in October, 1917, so as to permit it to assume for the military forces of the United States the obligations ordinarily associated with employers' liability. A soldier who had dependents was obliged to allot a part of his pay to his family, and to this sum the government, in accordance with a prescribed schedule, added more. If a soldier died in service, his widow received seventy-five dollars a month until remarriage. If he were disabled, he received compensation commensurate with the degree of his disability. If he were maimed in such a way as to need re-education, the government accepted the responsibility for that also, and charged the Federal Board for Vocational Education with the duty of providing the necessary training. And for all who would take it the government offered an insurance policy of from one to ten thousand dollars, at cost, the premiums to be deducted from the soldier's pay. By 1919 over four and a half million such policies had been written, representing an aggregate of thirty-eight billion dollars. The pay of the American private was thirty dollars a month, the highest in the world, and it was supposed that

[1] Katherine Mayo, *That Damn Y* (1920).

the insurance system adopted by the government would forestall the customary drive for pensions at the end of the war. This hope, as events proved, was vain.

The raising of huge armies, the flotation of unprecedentedly large loans, and the ruthless expansion of taxation were tasks that in a democracy would have been impossible but for the support of a *Public* thoroughly aroused public opinion. When war was declared *opinion on* in 1917, it is reasonable to suppose that the action was ap- *the war* proved by a majority of the people as well as by a majority of Congress. But the popular majority was by no means so overwhelming as the vote in Congress indicated; indeed, many a congressman would have voted the other way had he dared. Most of those who doubted the wisdom of American entrance into the war were sympathetic with the Allied cause and ripe for conversion, but a small minority, composed of pro-Germans, Socialists, and pacifists, were bitterly opposed. Many of them were in complete agreement with Senator La Follette, who in casting his vote against the war resolution maintained, "I say Germany has been patient with us," or with Morris Hillquit, the Socialist, who asserted, "The country has been violently, needlessly, and criminally involved in war." It was essential, if the sacrifices necessary to win the war were to be borne, that public opinion should support the government with virtual unanimity. Partly with this end in view the President, on April 14, 1917, designated the Secretaries of State, War, and Navy as a Committee on Public Information, charged with the duty of publishing the facts about the war. As the executive officer directly responsible for carrying on the work he named George Creel, a well-known and energetic journalist.[1]

Creel's task was both to disseminate the news and to "sell" the war to the people. He had no commission to act as censor; only in so far as military men and the Allies were able to exercise control of *The Creel* the news were the facts suppressed. But he could spread *Committee* and interpret what news there was, and that he meant to do. Gathering about himself as able a group of journalists and historians as he could find, and adding artists, actors, photographers, and linguists as needed, he began to release a spectacular barrage of information and propaganda. Through the *Official Bulletin*, published daily beginning May 10, 1917, he told what was going on with little attempt to distort,

---

[1] George Creel, *The War, the World, and Wilson* (1920), *How We Advertised America* (1920), and *Rebel at Large: Recollections of Fifty Crowded Years* (1947), J. R. Mock and Cedric Larson, *Words that Won the War* (1939); G. G. Bruntz, *Allied Propaganda and the Collapse of the German Empire in 1918* (1938).

and set an example in the treatment of war news that most of the newspapers of the country followed. But he never forgot that a part of his mission was to convince all Americans, and if he could the whole wide world besides, that the American case for war against Germany was unimpeachable. Through "Red, White, and Blue" books, compiled by its historians, the C.P.I. told the public the things it needed to know: *How the War Came to America; The War Message and the Facts Behind It; The President's Flag Day Speech; German War Practices; Why Working Men Support the War; The War Cyclopedia; Conquest and Kultur; The German War Code; The Government of Germany.* Ready-made editorials were distributed by the million to overworked country editors, who ran them gratefully and believed what they said. Foreign-language newspapers were objects of special solicitude, and soon got the idea as to what they were expected to print. Speech-making material for the seventy-five thousand four-minute men and other orators was ladled out with a free hand; motion pictures taught similar lessons to those who lacked either the mind or the will to read; strikingly designed posters helped along the various "drives" by which the war was to be won. Unfortunately, talking pictures and the radio were not yet available; had they been the imagination palls at the thought of the uses the C.P.I. would have made of them.

The net effect of this propaganda was to convince Americans more deeply than ever that only by winning the war could the "world be made *Restrictions* safe for democracy"; only by a "war to end war" could a *on civil* lasting peace be achieved. The war became a holy crusade, *liberties* and those who dared oppose it were given short shrift. It was in response to this opinion rather than because there was any longer reason to fear the minority that the drastic Sedition Act of May 16, 1918, was added to the milder Espionage Act of June 15, 1917. Freedom of speech and of the press meant little in wartime, as the Supreme Court quickly explained. Said Mr. Justice Holmes, voicing a unanimous opinion: "When a nation is at war many things that might be said in time of peace are such a hindrance to its effort that their utterance will not be endured so long as men fight, and that no court could regard them as protected by any constitutional right." Long prison sentences were meted out to prominent critics of the war, including Eugene V. Debs, four times the Socialist candidate for President, and Victor L. Berger, Socialist congressman from Milwaukee. Berger's newspaper, the Milwaukee *Leader*, and the even more outspoken New York *Masses*, a Socialist monthly, lost their second-class mailing privileges. Hundreds of conscientious objectors were sent to jail.

Neither the political nor the economic organization of the United States was fitted to meet the emergencies of war, and drastic changes had to be effected in both.[1] Fortunately the defense measures of 1916 had provided for a planning board known as the Council of National Defense. The six members of this council were cabinet officers with an abundance of other work to do, but they were expected to follow the recommendations of an Advisory Commission of seven civilians, also provided for in the law. Headed by Daniel Willard, president of the Baltimore and Ohio Railroad, and assisted by as many "dollar-a-year" volunteers as it could use, the Advisory Commission soon became what Professor Paxson has aptly called a "civilian general staff." Largely through the plans it devised, the government of the United States was reorganized for wartime efficiency, while industry, agriculture, labor, and every other form of American economic life were forced to operate with the single-minded purpose of winning the war. Temporarily the United States ceased to be a democracy, and the freedom of the individual was sacrificed to the larger necessity of a military victory. New and powerful administrative agencies, responsible only to the President, told the people of the nation what they might and might not do, and what they had to do.

Council of National Defense

Before the war was over, six great wartime agencies had taken over the chief responsibility for adjusting American economic life to the necessities of the war. The oldest of these was the United States Shipping Board, which had been created the year before the war broke out. Through its Emergency Fleet Corporation it struggled valiantly, and with considerable success, to build ships faster than the submarines could sink them. A second agency, the Food Administration, had as its responsibility the supply of food, both for soldiers and for non-combatants, overseas. As Food Administrator, Herbert Hoover preached the "gospel of the clean plate," persuaded the American people to accept "wheatless" and "meatless" days, and encouraged all who could to plant "war-gardens." More important still, Hoover's Grain Corporation set high prices for wheat that led to a remarkable expansion of the nation's wheat acreage, with a corresponding increase in production. A Fuel Administration dealt similarly with the pressing coal and oil problem; a Railroad Administration took over all the railroads of the country and operated them as if they were a single system; a War Trade Board licensed foreign trade and took care that American commodities did not reach the enemy; and a War Industries

The wartime government

[1] W. F. Willoughby, *Government Organization in War Time and After* (1919), is a survey of the federal civil agencies created for the prosecution of the war.

Board, most powerful of all, took full command of American production. Under Bernard Baruch as chairman, the W.I.B. told manufacturers at will what materials they could use, and what materials they must save. It could order them to undertake totally new endeavors. It could determine priorities, and so give or withhold both the raw materials and the transportation upon which every manufacturer depended. It could standardize products, and with the President's approval it could, and did, fix prices. Of great assistance in working out the orders of the War Industries Board was the War Finance Corporation, which, operating with a half-billion dollar revolving fund granted by Congress and such other sums as it could borrow, lent to business that needed encouragement, while restraining vigorously all non-essential demands for capital.[1]

Long before the war was won, the government of the United States was exercising powers that in ordinary times would have been deemed incompatible with democracy. The six great "war boards" — Shipping, Food, Fuel, Railroads, War Trade, and War Industries — owed responsibility for their acts to the President alone. Beginning in March, 1918, the heads of these boards met with him weekly as a kind of war cabinet. Such legislation as they required, Congress ordinarily felt obliged to supply. The most sweeping of these grants was contained in the Overman Act, signed May 20, 1918, by which the President, until six months after the war should end, was given free rein "to utilize, co-ordinate, or consolidate any executive or administrative commissions, bureaus, agencies, offices, or officers" at will; to create new agencies and abolish old ones, and to utilize funds voted for any purpose in whatever way he deemed that purpose best served. One critic of the bill suggested ironically an amendment: "If any power, constitutional or not, has been inadvertently omitted from this bill, it is hereby granted in full." Working closely together under the President, and assured of support by state councils of defense locally maintained, the war boards all but supplanted the ordinary civil authorities. The amount of grumbling that accompanied the resulting regimentation of American life was surprisingly small. The nation took pride in the fact that a democracy could make war efficiently, even if in the process it had to sacrifice many traditional liberties. The tyranny that existed, people well understood, was of their own creation, and could be destroyed when the war was over.

[1] B. M. Baruch, *American Industry in the War: A Report of the War Industries Board* (1921). Benedict Crowell and R. F. Wilson, editors, *How America Went to War* (6 vols., 1921), is an account from official sources of the nation's various war activities, and is admirably complete. Two volumes are devoted to *The Armies of Industry*. See also Arthur Bullard, *Mobilizing America* (1917), and Frederick Palmer, *Newton D. Baker: America at War* (2 vols., 1931). The best single volume on American participation in the war is F. L. Paxson, *American Democracy and the World War*, II, *America at War, 1917–1918* (1939).

The support of organized labor for the war was greatly promoted by the earnest efforts of Samuel Gompers, one of the seven members of the Advisory Commission, whose insistence that the war must not be used to depreciate wages or labor standards became a governmental policy. *Labor and the war* Indeed, the draft, which took many men out of the labor market, and the cessation of immigration, which cut off an historic source of supply, led to a labor scarcity that drove wages to unprecedented heights. By 1918 the average worker was earning nearly twice as much as in 1914, and even allowing for the mounting costs of living he was fully twenty per cent better off than he had been when hostilities began. High wages and steady employment meant also prosperity for the labor unions, whose membership shot upward during the war by no less than thirty-seven per cent. To facilitate the mobility of labor the government greatly expanded the United States Employment Service of the Labor Department, and to fill labor shortage it encouraged the use of women in industry. Labor disputes were kept at a minimum. A War Labor Conference Board, created early in 1918, laid down the rules that should govern the relationship of capital and labor, and a National War Labor Board, under the co-chairmanship of William Howard Taft and Frank P. Walsh, acted as a court of last resort in the settlement of labor disputes. The formulation of labor policies in the new war industries was handed over to a War Labor Policies Board of which Felix Frankfurter became chairman.[1]

Inevitably every American came to feel keenly the effects of the war. The Federal Reserve System stood up admirably under the unexpected burdens it had to shoulder, but the huge bond issues and expanding business they supported made for cheap money and currency inflation. In theory the gold standard was maintained, but gold did not circulate and dollars bought less and less. Salaried employees had greater difficulty than laborers in obtaining the wage increases necessary to meet the rising cost of living, and some of them suffered acutely. Women not only invaded industry, but they were also increasingly in evidence in business and the professions. For the most part the educational system of the country carried on as usual, although higher education was hard hit by enlistments, and, after the service age was lowered from twenty-one to eighteen, by the draft. In an effort to combine education and military training the Students' Army Training Corps was established in practically all the colleges during the fall of 1918. Young men of draft age were allowed to continue their studies in uniform and at the expense

[1] John Steuben, *Labor in Wartime* (1940); Samuel Gompers, *American Labor and the War* (1919).

of the government, while learning the art of war from army officers. The compensation paid the colleges by the government for the use of their facilities saved many of them from financial collapse, but as an educational experiment the S.A.T.C. was a failure.[1] With many of the nation's physicians mobilized for war, the influenza epidemic of 1918 became a serious plague. The "flu," indeed, baffled medical science, and took a heavy toll both in the cantonments and among civilians.

The "home front"   Undoubtedly the most unlovely feature of the "home front" was the ugly intolerance bred by the war. Americans of foreign extraction suffered from it more acutely than any others, especially when they had been "pro-German" in the period of neutrality. Most of the acts of intolerance were not the acts of the government, but of the people. The German language, which before the war had been more widely taught in America than any other foreign language, was all but eliminated from the public schools, and suffered from drastic restrictions in the colleges. Printing, preaching, teaching, even talking in the German language were treated as if criminal offenses, and were sometimes made so. Musicians of German origin, such as Frederick Stock and Fritz Kreisler, were publicly humiliated. Honorary degrees granted to Germans before the war were revoked by the universities that had granted them. All aliens and all citizens of recent alien origin were made to feel their inferiority to the so-called "native Americans." It was as Wilson himself had said on the eve of war: "Once lead this people into war and they'll forget there ever was such a thing as tolerance. To fight you must be brutal and ruthless, and the spirit of ruthless brutality will enter into every fiber of our national life, infecting Congress, the courts, the policemen on the beat." Conformity, as the President had foreseen, became the only true virtue, and the man who refused to conform had to pay a severe penalty. Perhaps the nation would never in any other mood have endured the sacrifices of war.

For actual combat duty the navy preceded the army to Europe by many months. Indeed, Rear-Admiral William S. Sims, who was chosen *The navy in the war* for overseas command, was in London before the United States entered the war, and by May 4 the first detachment of American destroyers had crossed the Atlantic. Ultimately three hundred warships, large and small, and seventy-five thousand officers and men were serving in the overseas detachments of the American navy. Their activities extended from the vicinity of the British Isles to the Mediterranean. No doubt these reinforcements were partly

---

[1] P. R. Kolbe, *The Colleges in War Time and After* (1919); Lewis Paul Todd, *War-time Relations of the Federal Government and the Public Schools, 1917–1918* (1945).

responsible for the fact that the experiment of Jutland was not repeated. The American naval forces made no effort to operate separately, but became to all intents and purposes a part of the British Grand Fleet. American ships were used, among other things, to enforce the very rules of blockade against which the United States as a neutral had protested so vigorously.[1]

The greatest single concern of the combined navies when the United States entered the war was the defeat of the submarine. This was eventually accomplished by a variety of means. American insistence had much to do with the laying of a mine barrage across the opening of the North Sea, between the Orkney Islands and the coast of Norway. This, and a similar mine barrage across the Straits of Dover, seriously crippled submarine activities. Cruising destroyers, armed with improved means of detection, also hunted down the "U-boats," and sank them with depth-charges. By the end of the war about half the German submarine flotilla had been destroyed. American ships likewise played a leading rôle in convoying merchantmen and troop-ships through the danger zone, thereby cheating the submarines of their prey.[2]

The frantic pleas of the Allies for American troops in France led the General Staff to revise its plans with respect to the training of the American army. It was decided that troops would have to be sent overseas only partly trained and partly equipped. The rest of the work could be done over there. Mainly as an earnest of good intentions General John J. Pershing was ordered to France in May, 1917, as head of the American Expeditionary Forces, and next month the first of the American detachments began to arrive. The American plan called for more than the mere transporting of troops. Already the facilities of France and her allies were being taxed to the limit to support their own armies, and the American contingent must be a help, not a burden. Ten thousand tons of wheat reached France in advance of the troops it was supposed to sustain, and, to make way for the coming of further detachments of the A.E.F., harbors had to be dredged, docks constructed, debarkation depots created, railroads made over, freight-yards laid out, telegraph and telephone lines erected, hospitals, barracks, and warehouses put together. All this was done by American labor on the American plan, and for the most part with American materials, although

The A.E.F.

---

[1] W. S. Sims and B. J. Kendrick, *The Victory at Sea* (1920); Louis Guichard, *The Naval Blockade, 1914–1918* (1930); Elting E. Morison, *Admiral Sims and the Modern American Navy* (1942); R. G. Albion and Jennie Barnes Pope, *Sea Lanes in Wartime* (1942); T. A. Bailey, *The Policy of the United States toward the Neutrals, 1917–1918* (1942).

[2] T. G. Frothingham, *Naval History of the World War*, III, *The United States in the War, 1917–1918* (1926).

American sawmills sometimes condescended to turn European logs into lumber. Over five million tons of supplies were sent abroad by the United States before the armistice was signed. As to man-power, the American records show that 2,079,880 men were transported overseas. Not all of these were fighting men, but from them Pershing netted forty-two combat divisions.

From the first General Pershing, who had himself written the orders under which he operated, insisted upon the creation of a separate American army. This did not please the Allies, who wished to use the American troops as replacements, to be brigaded with French or British units. But Pershing was convinced that three years of defensive fighting had unfitted the Allied armies for effective offensive tactics, and finally forced the Allied leaders to give in. The American army thus became a wholly independent unit, and in October, 1917, began to take over a quiet sector of the battle line. When in March, 1918, however, Russia made a separate peace and the Germans began a great *Friedensturm*, designed to end the war in the West, Pershing did not hesitate to lend troops to the hard-pressed French. In the summer fighting before Paris, especially at Château-Thierry early in June, the Americans gave a good account of themselves. Surprised and pleased, Marshal Foch, now Allied commander-in-chief, saw the point to Pershing's insistence, and co-operated cheerfully in the creation of a separate American command. Pershing was never able to supply from American sources all the *matériel* of war necessary for the operations of a complete army. The ordnance, the tanks, and the airplanes he used were in considerable part of Allied manufacture.[1] But the men were all Americans, and they did Pershing's bidding, subject only to the supreme command of Foch. Before the war ended, American troops held one fourth of the battle line, more even than the British.

Pershing's first action as an independent commander was the reduction of the Saint-Mihiel salient, where the German line protruded sharply *The Saint-Mihiel salient* across the Meuse River southeast of Verdun. With some French assistance, but following his own plans, he attacked both flanks of the salient and in two days' time had it completely straightened out. Half a million American troops participated in the battle; they suffered seven thousand casualties, and took sixteen thousand German prisoners. Had they been permitted to do so the Americans would gladly have pushed ahead toward Metz, across the German frontier, but no farther away than they had already come.

[1] Charles De Forest Chandler, *How Our Army Grew Wings: Airmen and Aircraft before 1914* (1943).

PRINCIPAL FRENCH PORTS AND RAILROADS
USED BY AMERICAN EXPEDITIONARY FORCES

⊚ GENERAL HEADQUARTERS   ⊚ H.Q. SERVICES OF SUPPLY
⊘ PRINCIPAL PORTS   ⊕ SECONDARY PORTS   ⊙ IMPORTANT TOWNS
▄▄▄ MAIN LINES   ▬▬ SECOND LINES   ▭▭ THIRD LINES   ∼∼∼ OTHER LINES
NOTE: LARGE NUMBERS INDICATE SUBDIVISIONS OF THE BASE SECTION
INTER.=INTERMEDIATE SECTION   **ADV.** = ADVANCE SECTION

Map drawn from Pershing, *Final Report* (1919), Plate 8

Metz was a key city in the German defenses, and had it fallen the war might have ended in September rather than in November. Pershing was ready with his plans, but Haig, who headed the British forces, favored a different strategy, and Foch listened to Haig instead of Pershing. The American army was shifted to the westward, and directed down the Meuse River and through the Argonne Forest toward Sedan. The war ended before Sedan was taken, but by November 11, Pershing explained later, the American troops "had cut the enemy's main line of communications, and nothing but surrender or an armistice could save his army from complete disaster." [1]

The advance of the American army in the Meuse-Argonne was only a part of the larger campaign by which Foch smashed his way to victory *The Meuse-* through the supposedly impregnable Hindenburg Line, be-*Argonne* hind which the Germans had taken refuge. Three other major offensives, the Ypres-Lys, the Somme, and the Oise-Aisne, preceded and accompanied the American drive. With the Allied forces acting for once in complete co-ordination, an Allied drive was begun north of Saloniki against Bulgaria, another against the Turks in Palestine, and a third against the Austrians in Italy. Everywhere the Allied arms were successful. Before the end of September, Bulgaria was out of the war; Turkey quit in October; Austria surrendered early in November; on November 11 Germany, too, with her armies everywhere in full retreat, gave up the fight.

American participation in the war was not wholly confined to the fighting in France. In July, 1918, an American regiment was sent to Italy, and in October two American divisions were lent to the French for use in Belgium. More debatable was the part played by American troops in Allied maneuvers against Bolshevist Russia. Without authority of a declaration of war against Russia, five thousand Americans fought with the Allies in the Archangel–Murmansk campaign that lasted from September, 1918, to May, 1919; while ten thousand Americans joined an Allied expedition to Vladivostok and eastern Siberia that lasted until January, 1920. [2]

The United States watched with tremendous interest the revolutionary experiment in Russia. As soon as possible after the overthrow of the Czar in March, 1917, an American mission headed by Elihu Root, former

---

[1] J. J. Pershing, *My Experiences in the World War* (2 vols., 1931), is straightforward and realistic, but far less charitable toward the general's civilian superiors than they were toward him. David Lloyd George, *War Memoirs* (6 vols., 1933–37), gives much attention to American participation.

[2] John Cudahy, *Archangel: The American War with Russia* (1924); W. S. Graves, *America's Siberian Adventure, 1918–1920* (1931); L. I. Strakhovsky, *The Origins of American Intervention in North Russia*, 1918 (1937).

Secretary of State, and Hugh L. Scott, chief of staff of the United States Army, was sent to Petrograd to help the new gov- *The Russian* ernment to a good start, and to encourage it in the continued *Revolution* prosecution of the war against Germany. But the wheel of revolution in Russia turned rapidly to the left, and before the end of the year Nicolai Lenin and Leon Trotsky, leaders of the most extreme advocates of Communism, the Bolshevists, had climbed to power with the assistance of German gold, and on the promise to the Russian people of peace. Late in December, 1917, at Brest-Litovsk, they agreed to close out the war on German terms.[1] Finland had declared its independence in July, 1917, and when the Treaty of Brest-Litovsk was finally signed in March, 1918, Poland, Lithuania, and the Ukraine were also separated from Russia, preparatory to leisurely German assimilation. It was clear from this peace that Germany at the moment, whatever her original intent, was engaged in a war of conquest. Should the fighting on the western front end in a German victory, it seemed reasonable to suppose that similar terms would be imposed upon the rest of the Allies. The defection of Russia thus was a tremendous help to Germany, and the repudiation by the Bolshevists of their foreign debts by no means improved the feelings of the Allies. Naturally they wished to bring to power in Russia a government that would resume the war against Germany and agree to meet its financial obligations. The military activities on Russian soil, in which the United States participated, were parts of the ill-fated Allied projects for bringing about these results.

The military contribution that the United States made to the winning of the war was not inconsiderable.[2] An army of 3,500,000 men was raised, of whom 1,400,000 saw active service overseas. Had *America's* the hostilities lasted over into 1919, as the Allied plans an- *contribution* ticipated, the American activities would have assumed a still *to victory* more impressive character. As it was, the "Yanks" captured 44,000 prisoners, took 1400 guns, and brought down 755 enemy airplanes. The American contribution in the air was somewhat of a disappoint-

---

[1] This was a preliminary agreement. The final treaty was signed three months later.
[2] L. P. Ayres, *The War with Germany* (1919), is a valuable statistical study. T. G. Frothingham, *The American Reinforcement in the World War* (1927), is a clear and satisfactory account. J. B. McMaster, *The United States in the World War* (2 vols., 1918–20), and J. S. Bassett, *Our War with Germany* (1919), are full, but disappointingly dull. Other useful accounts are R. J. Beamish and F. A. March, *America's Part in the World War* (1919); Shipley Thomas, *The History of the A.E.F.* (1920), Frederick Palmer, *America in France* (1918); Hunter Liggett, *Commanding an American Army: Recollections of the World War* (1925); R. L. Bullard, *Personalities and Reminiscences of the War* (1925). J. G. Harbord, *The American Army in France, 1917–1919* (1936), wrote from the vantage-point of a high-ranking participant. The Meuse-Argonne is the subject of Frederick Palmer, *Our Greatest Battle* (1919).

ment. In spite of the earnest activities of the Aircraft Production Board, and the creation of the new "Liberty engine," "the eyes of the army went aloft in foreign planes." But 11,000 aviators had been trained by the time of the armistice, and 4300 of them were in France. American casualties, considering the short period of time Pershing's troops were engaged, were heavy — heavier, probably, than in corresponding French and British units where the troops were better trained and the utmost effort was made to hold down losses in man-power. But the total number of deaths suffered by the American army from all causes were under 125,000 and of these less than half were battle deaths. Compared with the 1,700,000 battle deaths suffered by the Russians, the 1,600,000 by the Germans, the 1,385,000 by the French, the 900,000 by the British, and the 800,000 by the Austrians, the American losses seemed inconsequential, but they were sustained during only about six months of actual fighting, while for the European belligerents the war lasted over four years. Excellent health precautions practically eliminated such filth diseases as dysentery and typhoid, from which so many American soldiers had died in previous wars, and skillful surgery and hospitalization returned five sixths of those wounded to their regiments. The worst scourge came from the influenza, which took as heavy a toll among civilians as among soldiers.

But it would be quite unfair to judge the part that the United States played in the war wholly from the military angle. The American troops *The will* came to Europe with a will to win, and their coming bol- *to win* stered up enormously the morale of the war-wearied Allies. Confidence in victory was standard equipment for all Americans, and it was systematically whipped up at every training camp, both in the United States and in Europe. It was a singing war, with tunes and verses inspired by cocksureness. The men went to camp, embarked and disembarked, marched and relaxed to "It's a long way to Tipperary," "Over There," and a dozen similar "hits." The American "doughboy" refused even to be depressed by the petty vexations of army life. He made fun of them in the stories passed along by word of mouth, and in the *Stars and Stripes*, a newspaper that the soldiers of the A.E.F. themselves edited in a style that combined the best and the worst of the college daily and the American sports page. Punctilious officers saw themselves as privates saw them in cartoons and comic strips drawn by professionals. The unlimited assurance with which the American army tackled its task impressed even the Germans.

There was much else for which the United States could claim credit. Pershing was quick to point out that the Allies needed above all else a unified command. "When one was attacking, the other was usually standing still." American insistence, together with the grave *Unity of* threat of German victory as a result of the *Friedensturm*, *command* helped pave the way for the assumption of supreme com- *and supply* mand by Marshal Foch. The American genius for business organization led to another almost equally important reform — a unified system of supply.[1] The American idea was that all resources — shipping, food, munitions, and other supplies — should be pooled, and drawn upon as needed. To accomplish this end much inertia had to be overcome, but before the war was over a remarkable transformation had been wrought. For this change much credit was due to General Charles G. Dawes, Pershing's purchasing agent. Last, but not at all least came the ideal of a peace so even-handed in its justice toward all nations, great and small, victor and vanquished, that the causes of war would be forever abolished. Six thousand years of history proclaimed the illusiveness of such a hope, but the eloquent arguments of the American President made the hope itself a reality. Long before the entrance of the United States into the war, Wilson had been urging such a settlement, and before its close his preachments had gained an almost miraculous ascendancy over world opinion. What he stated in general terms every nation translated into the specific terms its national aspirations demanded. A "peace of justice" meant something quite different to each people, but in every case it meant something worth fighting for. And if this war should be indeed the war that would end all war, the goal was doubly worth the effort. Wilson's idealism became a two-edged sword. On the one hand it provided the Allies with a unified purpose in the war; on the other it tended to break down enemy morale. Why fight against a peace of justice?

Wilson's interest in a peace of justice had been stated clearly in his "peace without victory" speech of January, 1917. After the entrance of the United States into the war, he modified his stand only *The debate* by insisting on a complete victory over the autocratic rulers *on war aims* of the Central Powers, but for the *people* of Germany and of her allies, as distinguished from their *governments*, he still adhered to generous terms. When Pope Benedict XV urged a negotiated peace in August, 1917, Wilson in reply drew this distinction clearly. The United States, he said, wished neither punitive damages, nor the dismemberment of empires, nor the establishment of exclusive economic leagues after the war, but the autocratic rulers must go. That his ideas comported illy

---

[1] Johnson Hagood, *The Services of Supply: A Memoir of the Great War* (1927); C. G. Dawes, *A Journal of the Great War* (2 vols., 1921).

with the network of semi-secret treaties on the post-war world that the Allies had agreed to among themselves, the President must have known. These treaties planned a victor's peace rather than a peace of justice, but Wilson seemed to believe that the popularity of his views with the masses in all countries would bring the Allied governments eventually to his program. As a matter of fact, Lloyd George, the British Prime Minister, while fully aware of his country's commitments, echoed the President faithfully, although Clemenceau, the French Premier, admitted frankly, "My war aim is to conquer."

Wilson gave classic statement to his views in a speech delivered before Congress in January, 1918. If the world were to become "a fit and safe place to live in," the peace should embody these "Fourteen Points":

1. Open covenants of peace openly arrived at.
2. Freedom of navigation upon the seas, alike in peace and in war.
3. Equality of trade conditions among all nations consenting to the peace.
4. Guaranties that national armaments will be reduced.
5. The adjustment of colonial claims in the interests of the populations concerned.
6. The evacuation of all Russian territory.
7. Belgium must be evacuated and restored.
8. French territory should be freed and restored, and the wrong of Alsace-Lorraine should be righted.
9. Readjustment of Italian frontiers along clearly recognizable lines of nationality.
10. The peoples of Austria-Hungary should be accorded opportunity for autonomous development.
11. Rumania, Serbia, and Montenegro should be evacuated and restored, and Serbia secured in access to the sea.
12. The Turkish portions of the Ottoman Empire should be assured a secure sovereignty, but other nationalities under Turkish rule should have autonomy.
13. An independent Polish state with free and secure access to the sea.
14. A general association of nations for mutual guaranties of political independence and territorial integrity.

Wilson's program was not the product merely of his own thinking. In the main, it was suggested to him by the "Inquiry," a group of scholars drawn together by Colonel House to provide the American State Department with the specific data it would need at the peace conference. It was never formally accepted by the Allies as their own. Wilson spoke for himself and for the government he headed, but he could not speak officially for the nations he usually referred to as the "Associates" of the United States in the war.

The German government in repeated state papers showed that it had no interest whatever in the type of peace Wilson sought. Its real answer to the Fourteen Points was the Treaty of Brest-Litovsk *German* with Russia in March, 1918. This treaty sheared off from *aspirations* Russia over 300,000 square miles of territory, with a population of 56,000,000 people. It took away one third of Russia's railway mileage, seventy-three per cent of her total iron output, eighty-nine per cent of her coal production, five thousand factories, mills, distilleries, and refineries. By a supplementary agreement signed in August, 1918, Germany exacted also an indemnity of six billion marks. There is no reason to suppose that the terms of this treaty were unpopular with the people of Germany. Probably the people, no less than the government, were ready for a peace of violence, similar to the Treaty of Brest-Litovsk, against the western nations. Wilson's Fourteen Points were described by one German writer as a "real symphony of a will to no peace." It was only in defeat that either the German government or the German people began to show an interest in a "just peace."

The German defeat, when it came, was thoroughgoing and complete in a strictly military sense. Later on the German people were persuaded to believe that they had laid down their arms in the hope of *Defeat of* a just peace when they might have fought on indefinitely. *Germany* But they were badly beaten, and their commanding officers knew it. Their allies had been knocked out, one by one. Their supposedly impregnable Hindenburg Line had cracked. Their submarine campaign had failed. Their services of supply were breaking down. The morale of their troops, in full retreat, was declining. Revolution, born less of Wilson's promises than of military disaster, was in the air. Ludendorff and Hindenburg informed the German Emperor in September that all was lost, and that peace must be made at once. Ludendorff had a nervous breakdown. It was the hopelessness of the military situation and the certainty of Allied victory that led the German government, like a drowning man grasping at a straw, to ask Wilson for an armistice on the basis of the Fourteen Points. It was the impending collapse of the military front, and not merely unrest at home, that forced Germany to sue for peace.[1]

The negotiations for an armistice were begun early in October, 1918,

[1] "The charge that Wilson purposely betrayed us over the Fourteen Points acquired greater prominence from the fact that a legend was fostered in Germany to the effect that we laid down our weapons in reliance on the Fourteen Points. This legend is a flat falsification of history, as everyone knows who then took any part in the negotiations. We had to lay down our arms because the Supreme Command insisted that we should do so in order to avoid a catastrophe, and then we invoked Wilson's help with an appeal to the Fourteen Points." *Memoirs of Count Bernstorff* (1936), p. 136.

by a new German Chancellor, Prince Max of Baden, reputedly a liberal, who professed to Wilson that he spoke "in the name of the German government and the German people." Even so, the pre-armistice negotiations were long drawn out. Wilson's Fourteen Points were accepted by the Allied leaders only after elaborate interpretations and amendments, to all of which the Germans were obliged, because of the military situation, to consent. Among other things, Wilson's second point, the "freedom of the seas," was ruled out altogether at the insistence of the British, while with reference to invaded territories, it was expressly stipulated that full compensation must be made for all damage done "by land, by sea, and from the air." When the German envoys signed the armistice they knew, therefore, that they were obtaining substantially less than the Fourteen Points, but they knew also that failure to sign meant only the substitution of unconditional surrender for what was left of the Wilson program. Even so, the armistice was not actually signed until the German fleet at Kiel had mutinied rather than put to sea for a final test of strength, the Kaiser himself had been forced to abdicate, and leaders who owed no allegiance to the former "autocratic rulers" were in complete control. With the signing of the armistice, November 11, 1918, the war came to an end.

The armistice

The military terms of the armistice revealed still further the extremity of the German collapse. No nation with the faintest hope of victory could have accepted them. The German army must retire to the left bank of the Rhine, surrendering huge stores of military supplies and railroad equipment; the bridgeheads at Cologne, Coblenz, and Mainz must be occupied by Allied troops; Allied prisoners of war and deported inhabitants of occupied territory must be returned without reciprocity; the German submarines and battle fleet must be taken to a neutral or Allied port for internment (the Germans took their ships to Scapa Flow as required, but ultimately scuttled them); and the predatory treaties of Brest-Litovsk and Bucharest, with Russia and Rumania respectively, must be cancelled. The Allies on their part were at liberty to requisition such German property as their armies of occupation might need, and to maintain the blockade of Germany that they had set up during the war. All this the German leaders knew and agreed to when they signed the armistice. Alone among the Allied commanders, General Pershing had opposed any armistice at all. He believed that only by a knockout blow delivered on German soil could the German people be made to realize the completeness of their defeat.

Military terms of the armistice

Wilson, meantime, had suffered a disastrous political setback at home.

In the mid-term elections of 1918 the Republicans won the House of Representatives by a majority of twenty votes, and the *Election* Senate by a majority of two. Wilson himself had contrib- *of 1918* uted to the Democratic defeat by an appeal on October 25 for a Democratic majority in Congress through which alone, he maintained, he could hope to carry on his policies. The Republicans skillfully turned this statement into a charge that they had not supported the war, and undoubtedly gained many votes as a result. But the Wilson administration had already accumulated about all the enmity it could hope to carry; every European nation that participated in the war had already had at least one change of government since it began. Wilson's propaganda for an early peace and a just peace had small appeal for the "bitter-enders," who with Theodore Roosevelt at their head blamed the President for his delay in getting into the war, and made fun of his note-writing and idealism. But the fact that he had led the country into the war at all was equally offensive to the pacifists and the German-Americans. To critics of his war policy were added those who disliked the liberal legislation of his first administration, his surrender to labor in the Adamson Act, and his attitude toward Mexico. Most important of all, the Republican politicians after six long years of separation from the spoils of office were alert to every opening that would facilitate their return to power, and directed their campaign with skill.

The logical place for the making of the treaty of peace, as had so often been the case after previous wars, proved to be Paris. Unwisely, perhaps, Wilson chose to represent the United States in person at the Conference, and to take along with him a delegation that would in no way interfere with his wishes.[1] So many experts, however, some of whom had been active in Colonel House's "Inquiry," accompanied the official delegates, that a large liner, the *George Washington*, was required to transport them all to Europe. The President's party reached France December 13, 1918, but the Paris Peace Conference did not actually convene until January 18, 1919. In the meantime Wilson paid official visits to Paris, London, and Rome, and inspected some of the battlefields of the war. Everywhere he was received with the most whole-hearted enthusiasm on the part of the people, and with every show of hospitality on the part of the heads of the Allied governments, although many of them regretted the necessity of having to deal with him personally.

The Paris Peace Conference was an extraordinary gathering. All the

[1] The other members of the American delegation were Robert Lansing, Secretary of State; Colonel House, the President's intimate friend; General Tasker H. Bliss, a military adviser; and Henry White, a Republican who had long since retired from active political life.

Allies were represented, including such non-participating belligerents as
China and Brazil, but the Germans for good reason were
denied any voice whatever in the proceedings. It was clear
that the problem of reconciling conflicting Allied opinions
would be a serious enough task without the presence of a German
delegation ready to take every advantage of Allied disagreements. The
Conference, of course, was too large to carry on the actual negotiations,
and met only for plenary sessions to confirm what had already been
agreed upon behind the scenes. All matters of consequence were settled by the "Big Four," Clemenceau of France, Lloyd George of England, Orlando of Italy, and Wilson of the United States. Of this group,
Wilson was still committed in principle to the Fourteen Points, although
some of his points had been seriously modified in the pre-armistice
negotiations. But Clemenceau, Lloyd George, and Orlando considered
themselves bound primarily by the secret treaties which the Allies
had negotiated with each other early in the war. These treaties promised France Alsace-Lorraine, the Saar Basin, and an independent government for the rest of German territory west of the Rhine. Great
Britain was to receive most of the German colonies, and a free hand in
Egypt, Persia, and Mesopotamia. Italy was assured her *Italia Irredenta*
— the Trentino, the southern Tyrol, and control of the Adriatic. Rumania had been assigned Transylvania and other territorial acquisitions.
Japan was to succeed Germany in Shantung and in the islands of the
northern Pacific. Russia, whose withdrawal from the war had forfeited
her claims, was to have been given Constantinople and the Dardanelles.
To the Allies these terms signified a just and lasting peace, and they proposed to obtain them as nearly as they might.[1]

The Paris Peace Conference

Wilson had hoped that the influence of an aroused world opinion
would enable him to persuade the Allies to forget their harsh terms, and
to accept more literally his Fourteen Points program. In
the end he won only a compromise. Compared with the
infamous Treaty of Brest-Litovsk that Germany had forced upon
Russia only the year before, the Treaty of Versailles was extremely
moderate; but compared with what Wilson had hoped to get, it left
much to be desired. When delegates from the new German republic
agreed to this treaty on June 28, they surrendered Alsace-Lorraine to

The Treaty of Versailles

---

[1] E. M. House and Charles Seymour, editors, *What Really Happened at Paris* (1921);
Robert Lansing, *The Big Four and Others of the Peace Conference* (1921); Frederick Palmer,
Bliss, Peacemaker: The Life and Letters of General Tasker H. Bliss (1934); H. W. V. Temper-
ley, editor, *A History of the Peace Conference of Paris* (1924); C. H. Haskins and R. H.
Lord, *Some Problems of the Peace Conference* (1920); B. M. Baruch, *The Making of the
Reparation and Economic Sections of the Treaty* (1920); J. M. Keynes, *The Economic Con-
sequences of the Peace* (1919).

France; gave generous blocks of territory including a corridor to the sea along the Vistula to Poland; and ceded border rectifications to Belgium and Denmark. The German colonies were all taken away, and handed over to the Allied countries, not for outright annexation, to be sure, but under a League of Nations mandate system that in practice amounted to nearly the same thing. The Saar Basin, Germany's richest coal-mining area, was turned over to French exploitation for a period of fifteen years, during which time it was to be under the political control of an international commission; at the end of the stipulated period the people of the Saar might decide by plebiscite whether the region should be returned to Germany, continued under international control, or ceded to France. Reparations for the damages done by the German armies had been agreed to in the pre-armistice terms, but the Conference was unable to fix upon the amount due, and left this to be decided by a Reparations Commission after peace was restored.[1] In some ways harder for the Germans to bear than the reparations bill (most of which was never paid anyway) was the assertion in the treaty that their country and her allies were responsible "for causing all the loss and damage to which the Allied and Associated governments have been subjected as a consequence of the war." This "war-guilt" clause, they maintained, quite indefensibly placed full blame upon the Central Powers for the outbreak of war in 1914.

The Treaty of Versailles also provided for the complete disarmament of Germany. Her standing army was reduced to one hundred thousand men and conscription was abolished; frontier fortifications not in Allied hands were to be razed; the manufacture, importation, or exportation of war materials was virtually prohibited; and the German navy was reduced to insignificance. The treaty promised, however, that the Allies would themselves soon take steps toward disarmament, a promise that was only in part fulfilled. Nor did Germany remain long unarmed.

Harsh as these terms were, they did not satisfy Clemenceau, who conceded even this much only on condition that there be a separate alliance between Great Britain, the United States, and France to repel jointly any future attacks on France. Wilson consented to the alliance, but the Senate, as he should have foreseen, refused to accept so forthright a departure from the American tradition

The League of Nations

---

[1] In May, 1921, the Commission set the German bill for damages at about thirty-three billion dollars, well beyond the ability of Germany to pay. In 1922, on the ground that Germany had defaulted in her payments, the French seized the Ruhr Valley coal fields. Finally, after several fruitless efforts to solve the problem by international agreement, Germany under Hitler openly repudiated her obligations, and the Allies were unwilling to fight about it. France relinquished the Ruhr in 1925. Ten years later, the Saar voted by an overwhelming majority for reunion with Germany.

of non-intervention in European affairs. Wilson pinned his hope for future peace, however, less on the proposed alliance than upon the League of Nations, which by his persistent efforts the Allies were at length induced to include in the Treaty of Versailles. Through this organization, he hoped, many of the injustices of the treaty could be righted later on, when wartime fevers should have abated. The Covenant of the League described three principal agencies: (1) a permanent Secretariat with headquarters established presently at Geneva, Switzerland; (2) a Council of nine members (later enlarged), to consist of one representative from each of the great powers, France, Great Britain, Italy, Japan, and the United States, and four others to be chosen by the Assembly; (3) an Assembly in which every member nation was to have a representative and a vote. The members of the League agreed by the famous Article X "to respect and preserve as against external aggression the territorial integrity and existing political independence" of all other members, and to recognize the right of every member nation to bring problems that might disturb the peace to the attention of the Assembly or the Council. Peace was to be achieved primarily by arbitration or adjudication, and the establishment of a permanent court of international justice was contemplated; but disputes not so adjusted must be submitted for settlement either to the Council or to the Assembly. Against nations making illegal war the Council might impose drastic economic sanctions, and in case it deemed military measures necessary to check aggressors it might make appropriate recommendations to members of the League.[1]

The Treaty of Versailles was only one of many treaties that taken together may properly be called the Peace of Paris. Wilson's tenth *The Peace* point had expressly stated that he wished to see the place *of Paris* of Austria-Hungary among nations "safeguarded and assured," but the disintegration of that unhappy power had been so complete that its resurrection as one nation was beyond the realm of possibility. Each of the many national groups that composed the old Empire was now determined to be free, except, possibly, German-Austria, which would have preferred union with Germany. But the Treaty of Saint-Germain, signed September 10, 1919, warned the new "Republic of Austria" to "abstain from any act which might directly or indirectly or by any means whatever compromise her independence."

[1] R. S. Baker, *Woodrow Wilson and World Settlement* (3 vols., 1922), is friendly to Wilson, and invaluable for a study of the Peace Conference. It may be compared with David Lloyd George, *Memoirs of the Peace Conference* (2 vols., 1939). See also J. T. Shotwell, *At the Paris Peace Conference* (1937); and D. H. Miller, *The Drafting of the Covenant* (2 vols., 1928).

[510]

This action was taken partly in order to prevent Germany from being strengthened by the addition of so many Austrians, and partly to prevent the new state of Czechoslovakia from being nearly encircled by Germany. The Treaty of Trianon with Hungary was not signed until June 4, 1920. It cut down the domain of the old Magyar kingdom to an irreducible minimum. The Treaty of Neuilly with Bulgaria, signed November 27, 1919, trimmed off in similar fashion the borders of Germany's smallest ally, and the Treaty of Sèvres with Turkey, signed August 10, 1920, left little non-Turkish territory to the Turks.

Through these and numerous supplementary treaties the "Balkanization" of central Europe was completed. The states that had aided the Allies were rewarded by territorial gains; those that had supported the Central Powers were punished by territorial losses. Numerous new states appeared on the map of Europe: Finland, Estonia, Latvia, Lithuania, Poland, Czechoslovakia, Yugoslavia, Albania. Everywhere the problem of "minorities" threatened the permanence of peace, for boundary lines that would separate every nationality from every other simply could not be drawn. Even the victors were not wholly satisfied. During the Peace Conference Wilson had insisted that the Italians were not entitled to Fiume on the eastern coast of the Adriatic, and as a result the Italian delegation had left the Conference. Ultimately they came back, and by a *coup* Italy obtained the coveted port later on. But the Italians never forgave Wilson, although he consented to the inclusion within Italian borders of several hundred thousand Austrian Germans in the Trentino. This, like many another such decision, was condoned on the ground that it was necessary to provide the nation concerned with a defensible frontier. By the time these treaties were written, Wilson must have realized that in much of Europe "clearly recognizable lines of nationality" simply did not exist. Even less attainable was the hope seemingly cherished by each of these little states of achieving economic self-sufficiency.

The seeds of future wars were thus strewed plentifully about, but Wilson hoped that through the League of Nations their growth might be prevented. Unfortunately, he was soon to discover that *The Senate* for this innovation he was unable to win the support of his *and* own government. All those forces that had worked to dis- *the treaty* credit him in the election of 1918 now made ready to destroy his latest handiwork, the Treaty of Versailles, and the League of Nations it established. The election had given the Senate to the Republicans by the narrowest possible margin, and Henry Cabot Lodge of Massachusetts, whose hatred for Wilson knew no bounds, had become chairman

[511]

of the Senate Committee on Foreign Relations, to which the treaty must be referred. Once, when Wilson had returned to Washington during the Peace Conference, Lodge and his followers had made their attitude clear, but Wilson felt sure that he could carry the people with him. It was his theory of government that the people, if thoroughly aroused, would and could force their rulers to heed the popular will. The Senate might prefer not to ratify the treaty, but in the end it would have to give in.

But Wilson overlooked the lengths to which his opponents were willing to go in their determination to discredit him. He was probably right in his assumption that the American people were for the time being ready to accept the treaty, including the plan for world co-operation implicit in the League of Nations Covenant. Indeed, only a few "bitter-enders," such as La Follette of Wisconsin, Reed of Missouri, and Johnson of California, were willing to go the whole length of outright rejection. The anti-Wilson forces pursued far shrewder tactics. Instead of voting to kill the treaty, they proposed to attach to it a series of reservations, or interpretations, most of which were directed against the League of Nations rather than the injustices of the treaty, and in reality meant comparatively little. But each reservation was well calculated to arouse the President's ire. If the opposition could make the reservations just strong enough to be sure that Wilson would reject them, and not so strong as to offend the public, they could not only insure the failure of the treaty, but could put the blame for its failure upon Wilson himself. The discrediting of the President and his following would thus be complete and devastating.

In the midst of the fight on the treaty, Wilson attempted to take his case to the people on an extensive speaking tour — had the radio *Wilson's* then been available this hot summer trip, which completely *collapse* sapped his vitality, would not have been necessary. Already badly shattered by an attack of influenza in Paris, and never robust, he broke down physically under the strain, and was obliged to return to Washington. There he suffered a paralytic stroke that for a time practically eliminated him as a factor in the government.[1] The Senate did not hesitate to score a victory over its fallen foe. With fifteen reservations to outmatch by one Wilson's Fourteen Points, the major-ity stood ready to ratify, but the minority, staunchly loyal to Wilson, declined to accept the reservations, although it was well known that the leading European powers would have preferred ratification with

---

[1] Much responsibility devolved on his second wife, Mrs. Edith Bolling Wilson, whom he had married in December, 1915, after the death of the first Mrs. Wilson in August, 1914. On the problem of the succession, see C. M. Thomas, *Thomas Riley Marshall* (1939).

the reservations to no ratification at all. Many votes were taken, and the treaty was twice before the Senate. On the final vote, March 20, 1920, the Senate was ready to accept the treaty by a vote of forty-nine to thirty-five, with the encumbering reservations attached. This was less than the necessary two thirds, but a change of seven votes would have meant ratification. Among those voting against the treaty were some of the President's closest adherents, Democratic regulars who were willing to accept the treaty precisely as it stood, but in no other form. Thus the treaty failed with an overwhelming majority of the Senate favoring its adoption, although some wanted it with reservations, and others only without reservations. Many observers believed that if Wilson had been well a compromise could have been reached, but others insisted that the reservations were designed to kill the treaty, and would have been made stronger had they been acceptable to the President. What would have transpired had Wilson followed the advice of House to resign the Presidency and leave the battle to Vice-President Marshall may only be surmised. By this time the friendship between the President and his former intimate had cooled, and House's letter was never answered. Himself a casualty of the war he had helped to make, Wilson could not yet understand the thoroughgoing nature of his defeat. From the news that filtered into his sick-room he continued to believe that the American people, who were now in reality drifting rapidly back into isolationism, were still with him. When Congress by joint resolution sought to declare the war with Germany at an end, he interposed his veto, charging that such a course would amount to an "ineffaceable stain upon the gallantry and honor of the United States." The election of 1920, he maintained, must be made a "solemn referendum" to decide whether the American people would accept or reject the obligations of the treaty and the League.

Looking backward from the vantage-point of a Second World War, it would seem that the United States, by its half-hearted refusal to support the League of Nations, destroyed whatever chance there was to prevent another general war. Had the American nation shown itself willing to accept the responsibilities of world leadership, it is possible that the return to international anarchy which marked the next two decades might have been forestalled. Conceivably, also, the mistakes and the injustices of the treaty, of which there were many, might have been ironed out through instrumentalities provided for in the League. But when the richest and most powerful of all the nations refused to co-operate in any effective way for the maintenance of peace, the possibility of another world war became a certainty. During the fight on the League, Wilson had recorded his conviction that, in case his efforts failed, the war would have to be fought all over again. What might have happened can never be known, but a generation later the war that Wilson predicted came to pass.[1]

[1] D. F. Fleming, *The United States and the League of Nations, 1918–1920* (1932), is a comprehensive treatment of this subject. H. C. Lodge, *The Senate and the League of Nations* (1925), is bitterly hostile to the League, and to Wilson personally. R. J. Bartlett, *The League to Enforce Peace* (1944), follows the organization from its beginning to its end. T. A. Bailey, *Woodrow Wilson and the Lost Peace* (1944), and *Woodrow Wilson and the Great Betrayal* (1945), are brilliantly written, but place on Wilson's shoulders an undue share of the blame for the defects of the peace and the failure of the Senate to ratify. Ray Stannard Baker, *American Chronicle* (1945), gives a much fairer picture. See also Josephus Daniels, *Years of War and After, 1917–1923* (1946); and A. M. Arnett, *Claude Kitchen and the Wilson War Policies* (1937).

THE SEARCH FOR NORMALCY

WITH the government disorganized as a result of the partial incapacity of the President, and with the United States still technically at war with Germany, the American people turned with relief from the *The Election* pressing problems of reconstruction to the excitement of a *of 1920* presidential campaign. The death of Theodore Roosevelt in 1919 removed the logical Republican candidate from the scene, but the Roosevelt following found in General Leonard Wood an admirable successor to the Roosevelt tradition. Wood had been on intimate terms with Roosevelt from the days of the Rough Riders, and had, like Roosevelt, been left at home during the World War. Wood's military ability was not open to question, and he did admirable duty in training troops for overseas service, but Wilson regarded him as troublesome and insubordinate while Pershing was definitely determined not to have him around. Wood's nomination was opposed by the politicians, who looked upon him as an interloper, and by many others who, mindful of the unhappy experience with General Grant, objected to the elevation of a regular army officer to the Presidency. To treat that high office as a consolation prize seemed also inappropriate. Wood nevertheless obtained an early lead over all other aspirants, and for a time it looked as if his nomination could not be prevented.[1]

Others who were willing to answer the call of duty if it came included Senator Hiram Johnson of California, Roosevelt's running-mate in the Progressive campaign of 1912, and an irreconcilable during the fight on the Treaty of Versailles; Governor Frank O. Lowden of Illinois, the successful businessman in politics; Senator Warren G. Harding of Ohio, an amiable Senate regular who had been permanent chairman of the Republican nominating convention in 1916; and Herbert Hoover, Food Administrator during the World War. Of all these men Hoover was by far the ablest, and was generally so recognized, but before the war he

---

[1] J. C. Malin, *The United States After the World War* (1930), is an excellent guide to political happenings of the twenties. At this point, also, the admirable work of L. M. Hacker, *American Problems of Today* (1938), becomes useful.

had spent much time outside the United States, and he was out of touch with American politics. Closely identified with the Wilson administration and a supporter of the League of Nations, he even seemed uncertain as to whether he wished to be considered for the Republican or the Democratic nomination; and as long as that uncertainty existed his candidacy could not be treated lightly by either party. When he finally announced that he was a Republican, his chance of obtaining a nomination vanished. The Democrats could not name him, and since that was so the Republicans need not. His chief support came from the women he had taught to "hooverize," from the college professors, and from the *Saturday Evening Post.* Altogether they netted him only nine and one-half votes on the first ballot.

The presidential primaries that had figured so conspicuously in the Taft-Roosevelt contest of 1912 were brought again into prominence in *Nomination of Harding* 1920. Wood's friends included many men of wealth who spent generously to promote his candidacy, and the relationship between these heavy expenditures and the large number of delegates pledged to Wood received much unpleasant publicity. Lowden also had means at his disposal, and the number of votes he could count upon was next to Wood's. Johnson attached a considerable block of liberals and isolationists, but Harding's candidacy had failed to arouse enthusiasm outside his own state, and very little even there. Nevertheless, the Republican Convention, which met in Chicago on June 8, nominated Harding on the tenth ballot. Party leaders were convinced that any Republican could win, and were weary of "supermen" in the White House. They wanted, and obtained, an ordinary politician whom they could control. Harding was personally likable, looked the part of a President, and was untroubled by any deep-seated convictions. For Vice-President the convention would gladly have chosen Johnson, but he refused to be considered. The party leaders then decided on Lenroot of Wisconsin, but the delegates got out of hand and nominated the almost forgotten favorite son of Massachusetts, Calvin Coolidge. The platform made an effort to compromise on the League of Nations, but it was regarded as satisfactory by Johnson, the intransigeant.[1]

The Democratic Convention met at San Francisco on June 28. There is some reason to believe that Wilson himself, although not a candidate, *Cox and Roosevelt* wished the opportunity to decline a complimentary nomination, but the convention contented itself with approving his administration and advocating unqualified ratification for the Treaty

---

[1] The most complete study of the nomination of Harding is in Mark Sullivan, *Our Times,* VI, *The Twenties* (1935).

and the League. With Hoover out of the picture, a three-cornered contest developed between William G. McAdoo, the President's son-in-law, A. Mitchell Palmer, the Attorney-General, and James M. Cox, Governor of Ohio. McAdoo made no effort to secure the nomination, perhaps because he could foresee nothing better than defeat and held hopes for 1924. Branded as the "crown prince," his position at best was difficult. Palmer as Alien Property Custodian had been involved in many unpleasant dealings with foreigners in the United States, and when he became Attorney-General in 1919 he conducted a "red hunt" that resulted in the wholesale deportation of aliens suspected of radical tendencies. In December, 1919, an American steamship, the *Buford*, returned two hundred and forty-nine such aliens to Russia. Palmer's intemperate attitude toward labor and political agitators cost him much liberal support, and tended to obscure his good record as a prosecutor of profiteers. Cox was finally nominated by the Democrats on the forty-fourth ballot, mainly, as in the case of Harding, because he was satisfactory to the professional politicians. His nomination was regarded as a defeat for Wilson, since he was in no way connected with the Wilson administration, but for Vice-President the convention chose Franklin D. Roosevelt, Wilson's Assistant Secretary of the Navy.

Until they met with the President, Cox and Roosevelt were ready to ignore the "solemn referendum" on the League of Nations, and wage their campaign on issues that had a wider popular appeal. *The "solemn referendum"* But Wilson's earnestness changed their minds and they stood steadfastly on his record. Harding had been a reservationist in the Senate, but during the campaign he hedged so successfully that such League advocates as Hughes, Root, and Taft came earnestly to his support, while the Johnson-Borah irreconcilables thought he shared their views. His naturally befuddled mind, and his unusual command of obscure English, provided an excellent concealment for his views, if, indeed, he had any. The "league to elect Harding" was united on little else, for it contained pro-League and anti-League Republicans, anti-Wilson Democrats, "hyphenates" who hated Wilson for all he had done or had failed to do for the nations they had left, liberals who denounced the "white terror" under Palmer, and millions who had suffered from what they had begun to suspect was a needless war. Cox bore the Democratic label and stood on the Wilson record. On that account he was defeated. The American people held no brief for Harding, but he was the only alternative, and they elected him, as one journalist observed, "by disgust." His popular majority was nearly seven millions, and in the electoral college he received 404 votes to Cox's 127. He was assured,

[517]

Courtesy of the Dallas News

HARDING'S PLATFORM ON THE LEAGUE

also, of a Congress that would be overwhelmingly Republican in both houses.

Warren Gamaliel Harding (1865–1923) was a prominent citizen of Marion, Ohio, a typical middle-western town of some thirty thousand inhabitants. Most of his education he obtained as editor *Harding* and proprietor of the Marion *Daily Star*. From his youth up he had supported Republican principles through thick and thin, and

[518]

he presently became recognized as one of the small group of leaders who directed the course of Republican policies in Ohio. He made the nominating speech for Taft against Roosevelt in the convention of 1912, and in 1914 he won both nomination and election to the United States Senate. He was a genial good fellow, well liked by his neighbors, and thoroughly imbued with the common man's vanities and prejudices. He knew that he was no intellectual giant, but prided himself on his ability to "get along with" people, and took comfort in the thought that as President he could command the judgment of the "best minds" in the party. His most devoted political friend was Harry M. Daugherty, another Ohio machine politician, whose knowledge of the seamy side of politics was unexcelled. Daugherty's greatest ambition was realized when, as Harding's campaign manager, he piloted his candidate to victory at the Chicago Convention.

In forming his cabinet Harding hit upon some of the best minds in the party, and some of the worst. He was persuaded to forego his desire to appoint Senator Albert B. Fall of New Mexico as Secretary of State, for Fall was an insistent advocate of intervention in Mexico, and chose instead the distinguished ex-jurist Charles Evans Hughes, Republican nominee in 1916. But Fall was a crony whom Harding liked, and into the cabinet he went as Secretary of the Interior, although he happened to be also a rabid anti-conservationist. For Secretary of the Treasury Harding finally decided upon Andrew W. Mellon of Pittsburgh, one of the two or three richest men in the United States; and by a stroke of luck he was able to persuade Hoover to become Secretary of Commerce. The rest of the cabinet was mediocre or worse. Daugherty, who had won no laurels as a lawyer, was made Attorney-General, and Edwin Denby of Michigan, a man whose chief qualification for the position seems to have been that he had once been a member of the marines, was made Secretary of the Navy.

The "best minds"

In his other appointments Harding showed the same inability to distinguish between good and bad. He made ex-President Taft Chief Justice of the Supreme Court when opportunity offered, a graceful and deserved compliment, but he turned over the newly organized Veterans' Bureau to a rogue named Charles R. Forbes who eventually landed in a federal prison. In general, the new President regarded political offices as the lawful spoils of victory, and to members of the unsavory "Ohio gang" that followed him to Washington went many choice plums.[1]

Whatever he might have meant by the ambiguities he uttered during

[1] S. H. Adams, *Incredible Era: The Life and Times of Warren Gamaliel Harding* (1939).

[519]

the campaign, Harding interpreted his election as a mandate against *Separate peace with Germany* American participation in the League of Nations. The Treaty of Versailles, therefore, which embodied the Covenant, could not be ratified. Following the resolution of July 2, 1921, by which Congress declared the war at an end, negotiations with Germany led to a treaty signed August 25, 1921, whereby the United States obtained all the advantages of the Treaty of Versailles, and none of the responsibilities.

The let-down from Wilsonian idealism with which the Harding Administration took office was broken somewhat by the International Conference on Limitation of Armaments that the new President called to meet in Washington on Armistice Day, November 11, 1921. The program of naval expansion begun by the United States, Great Britain, and Japan during the war, had developed at its close into an unhealthy and expensive rivalry that threatened to continue indefinitely. Senator Borah was most prominent among the advocates of limitation, and Harding's invitation was issued in no small part as the result of Borah's insistence. Every possible device was employed to build up the Conference as the Republican counterpart of the Wilsonian program. It was persistently spoken of as the "Peace Conference," although it was nothing of the kind, and a great to-do was made over its opening. At eleven o'clock on the appointed day the whole nation paused in commemoration of the restoration of peace, while at the Arlington National Cemetery the body of an unknown American soldier was ceremoniously interred.[1]

Next day, after the formal welcome by President Harding was over, Secretary Hughes presented a program of naval reduction so drastic as *The Washington Conference* to startle the Conference. Exhibiting a knowledge of detail that was in itself amazing, he advocated that the naval strength of the great powers should be fixed at stipulated ratios, that naval tonnage in excess of specified maxima should be scrapped, and that no new ships should be constructed for a period of ten years. In the end five powers, the United States, the British Empire, Japan, France, and Italy, agreed to limit their strength in capital ships to total tonnages that bore to each other roughly the ratios of 5:5:3:1.7:1.7, respectively. Unfortunately this agreement left unsolved the important problem of lesser craft. Some critics said that the elimination of capital ships was inconsequential, since the battle of Jutland had proved that they were no longer of value. But the limi-

---

[1] The atmosphere of the Conference is well captured in Mark Sullivan, *The Great Adventure at Washington* (1922). Certain behind-the-scenes activities, not often written about, appear in H. O. Yardley, *The American Black Chamber* (1931), an exciting story of the work accomplished by the cryptographic bureau.

tations adopted at least resulted in tremendous budgetary savings for the nations concerned, and naval experts generally refused to concede that dreadnoughts and battle-cruisers were obsolete. In 1927, at the suggestion of President Coolidge, a conference met at Geneva to discuss the limitation of auxiliary ships, but failed to reach an agreement. In 1930 at London, a conference called by President Hoover fared somewhat better. Some limitations were imposed on the building of lesser craft, Japan was appeased by a more generous quota, and the naval holiday was extended to 1936. But Japan served notice in 1934 that after 1936 she would no longer be bound by any limitations, and after that date the race for naval supremacy was vigorously renewed.[1]

The Washington Conference resulted in the drafting of two other noteworthy treaties, one signed by four powers, and the other by nine. The Four-Power Pact, agreed to by the United States, the *The Four-* British Empire, France, and Japan, paved the way for the *Power Pact* abrogation of the Anglo-Japanese Alliance, which had become distasteful to both Great Britain and the United States. The new pact proposed to preserve the peace in the Pacific by pledging the contracting powers mutually to respect one another's rights "in relation to their insular possessions and insular dominions in the region," and to refer to a joint conference such disputes as might cause trouble. The four powers also bound themselves to "communicate with one another fully and frankly" on the action to be taken in case their rights were "threatened by the aggressive action of any other power." Had the pact ever been taken seriously, as it was not, it might have constituted almost as decisive a departure from the American doctrine of isolation as if the United States had entered the League of Nations. Closely connected with it was Article XIX of the Treaty on Naval Limitation which bound the United States, the British Empire, and Japan to maintain the *status quo* with respect to "fortifications and naval bases in the Pacific."

The Nine-Power Treaty related to "principles and policies to be followed in matters concerning China," and was signed by the United States, Belgium, the British Empire, China, France, Italy, *The Nine-* Japan, the Netherlands, and Portugal. The situation in *Power Pact* the Far East had changed materially as a result of the World War. In 1915 Japan had in effect repudiated the doctrine of the open door by presenting to China twenty-one notorious demands for special privileges, many of which China was forced to concede. In 1917, by the Lansing-

---

[1] Useful accounts of the Conference are given in R. L. Buell, *The Washington Conference* (1922), and Yamato Ichihashi, *The Washington Conference and After* (1928). For a brief treatment, see Griswold, *Far Eastern Policy of the United States.*

Ishii Agreement, Japan once more gave lip-service to the open door, but won from the United States recognition "that territorial propinquity creates special relations between countries." At the Paris Peace Conference, Japan insisted on being awarded the German concessions in Shantung, although the Japanese delegates promised Wilson that Japan would eventually withdraw from the peninsula, which, at least in a military sense, she did. Japan was also given a mandate over the German island of Yap in the northern Pacific. The purpose of the Nine-Power Pact was to reconcile this situation, as nearly as possible, with the open door for world trade in China and the integrity of the Chinese Republic. In words the new treaty seemed to administer a strong rebuff to Japanese policy, for it pledged the signatory powers to respect Chinese sovereignty, to aid China in maintaining an effective government, to use their influence in favor of "equal opportunity for the commerce and industry of all nations" in China, and to "refrain from taking advantage of conditions in China to seek special rights." But Japan was soon violating all these pledges with impunity, and the treaty provided no means whereby an offending power could be restrained. Minor agreements not written into the Nine-Power Treaty adjusted the Shantung controversy, settled the status of the island of Yap, provided for the study of extraterritoriality in China, and dealt with several other problems of Far Eastern relations.[1]

The Washington Conference was not the only Republican effort to promote world peace. The idea of a permanent court of international *The World Court* justice had been advocated by the American delegation to the Second Hague Conference in 1907, and was far more closely identified with Republican than with Democratic policy. When, therefore, under Article XIV of the League of Nations Covenant, plans were drawn in 1922 for such a court, there seemed no good reason why a Republican administration should not give the new institution its blessing. Indeed, Elihu Root, respected elder statesman of the Republican Party, had assisted in drafting the World Court protocol, and John Bassett Moore, America's foremost authority on international law, was slated for a place on its bench of eleven (later fifteen) judges. The only difficulty in the way of American participation seemed to lie in the fact that the judges were to be chosen by the Council and Assembly of the League of Nations, but it was proposed that for this purpose only the United States might have a voice in the proceedings. Certain that public

[1] On the Far Eastern situation, consult Eleanor Tupper and G. E. McReynolds, *Japan in American Public Opinion* (1937); F. R. Dulles, *Forty Years of American-Japanese Relations* (1937); and D. F. Fleming, *The United States and World Organization, 1920–1933* (1938).

opinion was "overwhelmingly in favor of participation," President Harding urged American adherence to the Court, only to be rebuffed by the Senate, in which the irreconcilables were able to prevent any action whatever being taken. Extreme isolationists professed to fear that adherence to the Court would be only the entering wedge to further involvement in world affairs, and the still-embittered critics of "Wilsonism" would have nothing to do with anything even remotely connected with the League. Harding was not the last American President to advocate the adherence of the United States to the World Court.[1] Coolidge, Hoover, and Roosevelt all urged the Senate to ratify its protocol, but they all failed to get results. In spite of non-participation by the United States, an American judge has always sat on the court. Moore was succeeded by Charles Evans Hughes in 1928; Hughes, by Frank B. Kellogg in 1930; Kellogg, by Manley O. Hudson in 1936.

"The war will last a hundred years," ran a soldier saying, "five years of fighting and ninety-five of winding up the barbed wire." No doubt Harding, when he told a Boston audience in May, 1920, that *Demobilization* "America's present need is not heroics but healing, not nostrums but normalcy," was thinking vaguely of the barbed wire that would have to be rolled up before reconstruction could be considered complete. When he took office as President the crippled Wilson administration had been searching for a year and a half to find the road back to normalcy. Demobilization of the American war machine had been pushed forward with the utmost speed, although the homesick American soldiers remained in Europe long enough to change the words incorrectly attributed to Pershing, "La Fayette, we are here," to "La Fayette, we are still here." But sending the army home wound up only a little of the barbed wire. If pre-war conditions were to be restored, the wartime government must be scrapped and an economic machine that had been geared relentlessly to the high speeds of war must be slowed down to the tempo of peace. To these ends Congress whittled away the special wartime powers of the President, abolished as rapidly as it dared the war agencies it had so recently created, laid plans for the early return of the railroads to their owners, and sought in various ways to get the government out of business as completely and as speedily as possible.

The impossibility of turning the clock back to pre-war days was well illustrated by the problem of the railroads. The experience with a centralized railroad administration had demonstrated the folly of unrestrained competition, and the railroad unions, which had prospered

[1] M. O. Hudson, *The Permanent Court of International Justice and the Question of American Participation* (1925).

under government operation, even wished to see the wartime system made permanent. Realizing that the country was in no mood for such a settlement, the unions, with considerable public support, turned instead to the so-called "Plumb plan," which contemplated government purchase of the railroads, but their operation as a unit by a board of directors on which representatives of the public, the operating officials, and the workmen should sit. But all such socialistic schemes fell before the conservative reaction that gripped the nation at the close of the war.

The Esch-Cummins Transportation Act of 1920, which Congress finally adopted, made no such compromise with socialism as the unions desired, but it did break much new ground. Some of its terms turned out to be quite unworkable, but others were of lasting importance.[1] Consolidation ceased to be a crime, and was definitely promoted by a clause which instructed the Interstate Commerce Commission to lay plans for reducing the number of railroad systems in operation, even at the cost, if need be, of ignoring the various anti-trust laws. Under this grant of power the commission presently proposed to consolidate all the railroads of the country into nineteen systems, but objections from the railroads themselves defeated the plan, and only a few such combinations were effected. The act sought also to resolve all conflicts between state and national regulatory authorities in favor of the national government. The Interstate Commerce Commission was given a free hand in dealing with such discriminations against interstate commerce as arose from intrastate regulations, a grant of power that ultimately reduced almost to insignificance the authority of the states over the railroads. "Commerce is a unit and does not regard state lines," said Chief Justice Taft, in holding that the law was not an improper invasion of state prerogatives. Other useful provisions of the act gave the commission authority to rule on what new securities the roads might issue, and how the money so obtained should be spent; also, it permitted the consolidation of the four great express companies of the nation into one American Railway Express Company.

Certain well-advertised features of the law proved to be less important than had been anticipated. In response to a long-continued demand *Railway legislation* the commission was authorized to proceed with the evaluation of railroad property, and to set such rates as would be fair to patrons and would bring the stockholders a reasonable return on

[1] Rogers MacVeagh, *The Transportation Act, 1920: Its Sources, History, and Text* (1923); D. P. Locklin, *Economics of Transportation* (1938); H. G. Moulton and associates, *The American Transportation Problem* (1933).

their investment. Much difficulty was encountered in determining the rules by which evaluation should proceed. The commission sought to base its estimates upon reproduction costs as of 1914, believing that these figures would furnish a close approximation of "actual original costs," but the Supreme Court in the O'Fallon decision of 1929 held that the evaluation should be based upon current reproduction costs — a much higher figure. Another provision that led to trouble was the so-called "recapture clause," according to which the better-paying systems were required to pay half their profits in excess of six per cent into a reserve fund for their own use, and the other half into a contingent fund from which the commission might make loans to the weaker roads. By implication this clause set six per cent as "a fair return," but neither the roads nor the public was satisfied with the arrangement. Eventually the "recapture clause" was repealed, and the impounded funds returned to the roads that had earned them. The act also contained elaborate provisions for the establishment of a Railroad Labor Board of nine members, three representing labor; three, the employers; and three, the public. Through this body, it was hoped, all labor disputes might be amicably adjusted. The board permitted generous pay increases in 1921 and the commission allowed the railroads to meet the increased cost of operation by charging higher rates. But the board failed to stop a shopmen's strike in 1922, and in 1926 it was replaced by a Federal Board of Mediation which had no authority to act except on invitation of one or the other of the parties to a dispute.

The railroads, events proved, would have had a new world to face even if there had been no war. For three quarters of a century they had held an easy supremacy in transportation, but they were now compelled increasingly to compete for business with motor trucks, passenger buses, and automobiles, to say nothing of airplanes, pipe lines, and water transportation, particularly coastwise traffic by way of the Panama Canal. It cannot be said that in meeting the new conditions the railroads showed either forethought or resourcefulness. They tended rather to complain bitterly about the "unfair competition" they were compelled to face and to run to the government for help. For them times had greatly changed since the days of the Grangers when all they had asked was to be let alone.

Another post-war legacy almost as perplexing as the railroads was the disposal of the great fleet of merchantmen that the government had acquired during the war. In this instance there was no *The mer-* prospect of returning the property to former owners, for *chant marine* the American merchant marine of pre-war days had been relatively inconsequential. The government itself had built or otherwise acquired its ships for special wartime service. It might operate them, to be sure, in time of peace the same as in time of war, but the prejudice against government ownership was strong, and growing stronger. An important complication was the realization that shipping was an absolute essential in time of war; should war come again to America it ought not to be found so short of ships.[1]

The Jones Merchant Marine Act of 1920 was the first effort of Congress to deal with the shipping problem. By the terms of this act the Shipping Board and its subsidiary, now called the Merchant Fleet Corporation, were continued, with authority to operate the ships as long as necessary, to lay out new shipping lanes for American commerce, and to turn over the ships and the routes to private companies as fast as American purchasers could be found. To induce private capital to invest in shipping, the Merchant Fleet Corporation was provided with a revolving fund of twenty-five million dollars from which it could make liberal loans to private operators. The ships themselves were offered for sale at bargain rates. Two hundred wooden ships, for example, brought little more than the building of a single vessel had cost the government. Special favors to American shipping interests included preferential tariffs on goods imported in American bottoms, a monopoly on all trade with the American colonies, and liberal contracts for carrying the mails. All this was insufficient to tempt many American investors into the shipping business, and hundreds of ships rotted or rusted at their docks.

Finally, by the Jones-White Act of 1928 Congress offered new and still more generous inducements, with somewhat better results. Shipbuilders could borrow three fourths of the costs of construction from the government, and by way of subsidy operators could obtain mail contracts that ran for long periods and bore no important relationship to the cost of carrying the mails. Even so, the Fleet Corporation failed to extract itself completely from the shipping business, and throughout the Great Depression, with foreign trade languishing, the American merchant marine fell far short of the goals that had been set for it.

An anticipated result of any war is the problem of the returned soldier. For those who might sustain injuries from the war the government had made generous provision in 1917 through the Bureau of War Risk Insurance, and when the war was over these provisions were still further liberalized. In 1921 all problems pertaining to service men were turned

---

[1] E. W. Zimmermann, *Zimmermann on Ocean Shipping* (1921); National Industrial Conference Board, *The American Merchant Marine Problem* (1929); D. H. Smith and P. V. Betters, *The United States Shipping Board* (1931); P. M. Zeis, *American Shipping Policy* (1938).

over to a Veterans' Bureau, which built and administered hospitals, supervised rehabilitation activities, and ruled on claims for compensation. Its work cost the government on an average a half billion dollars a year.

But the demand for aid did not end with the men who had sustained injuries or illnesses traceable to the war. Veterans who had suffered no disability found frequently that the jobs they had once *The veter-* held had been given to others, while the task of getting and *ans' bonus* holding new jobs was by no means easy. They observed, too, that the men of their age who had stayed at home had made a good start in the world, while the returned soldier found himself two years behind in the competition. Furthermore, the high wartime wages and salaries earned by civilians contrasted sharply with the dollar a day paid to the soldiers. To tide them over the period of unemployment following their return to civil life, the government had paid a small discharge bonus to the soldiers, and to this a number of the states added small sums. But many veterans soon convinced themselves that the United States still owed them something by way of "adjusted compensation." This plea the American Legion, which was founded in 1919 and soon emerged as the leading organization of veterans, pushed earnestly upon Congress, and in 1922 a bill that would have granted fifty dollars for each month of service to every veteran of the war failed of enactment only because of a presidential veto. But the Legion continued its pressure and in 1924 succeeded in marshaling a large enough majority in Congress to override the President's opposition. As passed the law took the form of a grant of paid-up insurance to fall due twenty years later. The amount owing each soldier was computed on the basis of a dollar and a quarter for each day overseas, and a dollar for each day in service at home. On an average the policies ran to more than one thousand dollars each, and against his policy each veteran was permitted to borrow up to 22.5 per cent of its face value. Altogether this "bonus bill," as its opponents insisted on calling it, added about three and one half billion dollars to the total cost of the war.[1]

The colossal expenditures of the war called striking attention to one of the anomalies of the American system of government. Since the found- ing of the republic, Congress had been content to make such *Budget* appropriations and to levy such taxes as it saw fit, hoping, *reform* but not consciously planning, that expenditures and receipts would

---

[1] Katherine Mayo, *Soldiers, What Next!* (1934); Roger Burlingame, *Peace Veterans* (1932); National Industrial Conference Board, *The World War Veterans and the Federal Treasury* (1932).

[527]

somehow cancel each other. Government bureaus asked largely of Congress and sometimes duplicated activities. In both houses numerous committees had authority to recommend expenditures, and each was free to act without reference to what any other committee was doing. The need for a planned national budget had long been apparent. As far back as 1911 President Taft had appointed a Commission on Economy and Efficiency that had recommended the adoption of a budget system. President Taft was unable to induce Congress to accept such an innovation, but at the end of the war the demand for economy at last moved Congress to act. Before the end of the Wilson administration a bill providing that a national budget should be drafted each year under the supervision of the President had passed both the House and the Senate, only to be vetoed by Wilson. Wilson had no objection to the budget system; on the contrary he believed in it. But he resented a clause in the proposed law which made it impossible for the President to remove the comptroller, an officer charged with the responsibility of auditing all expenditures to see if they were being made in harmony with the law, and to be appointed for a fifteen-year term. Provision for such an arrangement, Wilson believed, was unconstitutional, and might well produce — did indeed produce under the second Roosevelt — a situation in which the President and the comptroller could not agree.[1]

When Harding became President he called Congress into special session to consider among other pressing problems the establishment of a budget system. In June, 1921, the Budget Act became a law, although the provision to which Wilson had objected was retained. As director of the budget, the President named Charles G. Dawes, a Chicago banker whose talents had been proved by his work as agent for the A.E.F. in France. All regular expenditures came within the scrutiny of the director, who made every effort to eliminate duplications and to pare down requests to reasonable dimensions. Estimates so obtained were then submitted to Congress, where in each house a single Committee on Appropriations determined the final recommendations. That the work of Dawes and his successors resulted in considerable savings there could be little doubt.

A second problem of the special session was to deal with wartime taxation. With the war at an end an insistent outcry had been raised *Financial* against the high taxes being collected to support it. In *legislation* spite of the fact that the public debt had mounted to over twenty-four billion dollars, Secretary Mellon believed that the revenues

[1] W. F. Willoughby, *The Problem of a National Budget* (1918); *The National Budget System* (1927); *Financial Condition and Operations of the National Government, 1921–30* (1931).

were excessive and ought to be reduced, and the Revenue Act of 1921 followed his recommendations in part. The act repealed the excess-profits tax, but in reducing the surtax rates cut the maximum rates only from sixty-five to fifty per cent, whereas Mellon had urged an initial cut to forty per cent, and an ultimate cut to thirty-three per cent. Other adjustments he found even less satisfactory. The tax on corporation incomes, for example, was raised from ten per cent to twelve and one half per cent. Urged on by representatives from the western farmers, who pointed to the distress that post-war deflation had brought to agriculture, the special session enacted also an Emergency Tariff Act. The new law was designed merely as a stopgap to last until a more permanent revision could be made. It raised the tariff on wheat in order to protect northwestern farmers against Canadian importation, and gave added protection to such other farm products as meat, wool, and sugar. The dumping of foreign goods in the United States was also strictly prohibited, and an embargo was laid on German dyestuffs.

The thoroughgoing tariff revision upward historically associated with a Republican triumph was effected by the Fordney-McCumber Act, signed September 19, 1922.[1] The new law raised tariff rates to the highest levels yet known. Not content with approximating the heavily protective schedules of the Payne-Aldrich Tariff, it provided that *ad valorem* duties might be charged either on the foreign or on the American valuation of the goods, whichever happened to be the higher. Thus, by following the normally higher American valuation, the tariff charges could be spectacularly increased without a corresponding increase in the rates. The act gave lip-service to the rule that the tariff was designed merely to equalize the cost of production at home and abroad, established a Tariff Commission with power to suggest such changes to the President as its investigations might warrant, and authorized the President to shift the rates as much as fifty per cent up or down. This provision for flexibility proved to be more important in theory than in fact. Neither President Harding nor President Coolidge felt obliged to follow the recommendations of the commission, and in a six-year period only five reductions were ordered, on mill feed, bobwhite quail, paint-brush handles, phenol, and cresylic acid. Thirty-two changes upward were recorded, including certain dairy products, chemicals, and pig iron. Among the recommendations of the commission that were pigeonholed was one advocating a reduction in the rates on sugar.

The search for normalcy led paradoxically to the shattering of one of

---

[1] The latest edition of Taussig's *Tariff History* contains a satisfactory account of this legislation.

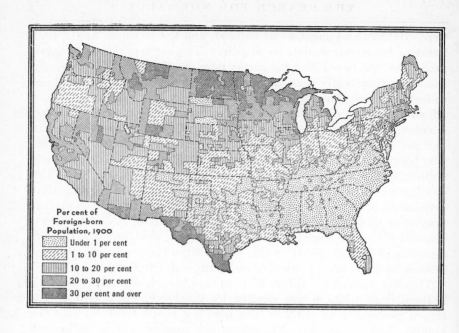

Per cent of
Foreign-born
Population, 1900

Under 1 per cent
1 to 10 per cent
10 to 20 per cent
20 to 30 per cent
30 per cent and over

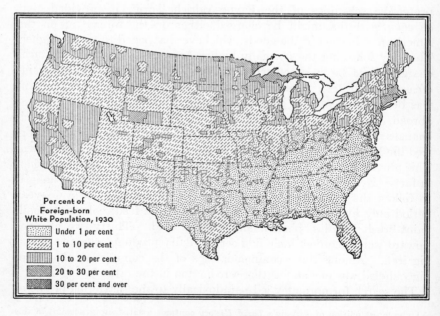

Per cent of
Foreign-born
White Population, 1930

Under 1 per cent
1 to 10 per cent
10 to 20 per cent
20 to 30 per cent
30 per cent and over

FOREIGN-BORN POPULATION IN THE UNITED STATES, 1900–1930

America's oldest and most cherished traditions — a hearty welcome to immigrants. Premonitions of the coming change were apparent in May, 1917, when Congress passed over Wilson's veto the same provision for a literacy test that he had defeated two years before. But the cessation of hostilities soon proved conclusively that something more drastic than a literacy test would be necessary if the distressed multitudes of Europe were to be prevented from seeking refuge in America. In the year ending June 30, 1921, over eight hundred thousand immigrants came to the United States, and in spite of the attempted restriction nearly two thirds of them came from the countries of southern and eastern Europe. Confronted by this situation, Congress in 1921 passed an Emergency Immigration Act that assigned to each nation an immigrant quota consisting of not more than three per cent of the number of its nationals resident in the United States according to the census of 1910. Immigrants from other American nations were exempted from the quota system, but in 1922 an amendment required that all aliens resident in an American country must have lived there not less than five years before being freed from the quota restrictions. *Restrictions on immigration*

The law of 1921 was meant merely as a temporary stopgap while the details of the new immigration policy were being worked out, and in 1924 Congress passed another immigration act. This time the quota was set at two per cent of the nationals resident in the United States in 1890, thereby reducing still further the numbers eligible for admission, particularly from southern and eastern Europe. The law also provided that after July 1, 1927, the number of quota immigrants was to be limited to one hundred and fifty thousand, while quotas were to be based upon "national origins," the same to be determined from a study of the census of 1920. The difficulty in determining the national origins of the American people completely baffled the committee of cabinet members (the Secretaries of State, Commerce, and Labor) charged with that duty, and not until 1929 were its half-hearted recommendations put into effect. Whatever their imperfections, the new quotas insured that an overwhelming proportion of the thin trickle of immigrants permitted to enter the United States originated in those countries that had first contributed to its settlement. Great Britain and northern Ireland, for example, were permitted to send 65,721 immigrants annually, while the Italian quota was only 5802. The special favors shown to citizens of other American nations led at first to a heavy immigration from Mexico, but immigration officials soon put a stop to this by refusing entrance to Mexican laborers on the ground that they were likely to become public charges. The census of 1930 revealed that the proportion of foreigners resident in the United States had indeed ceased to increase.[1]

While the Harding administration under the leadership of Secretary Hughes was adjusting the United States to the new world order, and *The Harding* while Congress under conservative domination was trying *scandals* to legislate the way back to normalcy, a host of political termites had invaded the structure of government. Their presence was in no small part due to the foolish search for mediocrity that had obsessed the Republican leaders when they looked about for an accommodating nominee in 1920. They wanted a man in the White House who could be managed, one who could be trusted not to exhibit any of the distressing qualities of independence that had characterized Theodore Roosevelt and Woodrow Wilson. What they failed to foresee was that a man weak enough to have no troublesome ideas of his own might turn out to be putty in the hands of others than the self-appointed leaders of the party. Harding's cronies, many of them Ohio friends of earlier days, came with him to Washington. They were still his friends, and he still trusted them. Perhaps the President was inspired by his office to adopt a higher code of political ethics than he had ever recognized before, but his associates had experienced no such change of heart. To them victory meant spoils in a very literal sense, and the greater the victory the greater the spoils.

Harry M. Daugherty, the Attorney-General, was Harding's closest political adviser; between his office and the White House there was a *Daugherty* private wire that was used many times each day. Equally *and Miller* close to Daugherty on the other side was Jess Smith, a member of the "Ohio gang" whose influence professional lobbyists and fixers soon knew to be for sale. Smith's abilities were better suited to the atmosphere of a courthouse ring than to the fast company he was keeping in Washington, and he soon became frightened by his involvements. Told by Daugherty that Harding wished him to leave Washington, and fearful of the consequences whether he left or stayed, he committed suicide. Ultimately it came out that in a single case he had taken fifty thousand dollars to arrange a favorable settlement before the Alien Property Custodian, Thomas W. Miller, another of Daugherty's friends. Miller was also a crook, and had to be dismissed from office; in 1927 he was jailed on conviction of having taken a bribe. Daugherty was cleverer and far more circumspect than his henchmen, but his close as-

[1] R. L. Garis, *Immigration Restriction* (1927); Manuel Gamio, *Mexican Immigration to the United States* (1930).

sociation with dubious characters made him suspect, and his resignation was required the year after Coolidge became President. When brought to trial for having conspired to "defraud the United States," he was not convicted because the jury disagreed. During the trial he refused to answer questions on the ground that the testimony he would be obliged to give might tend to incriminate him. He also left room for the inference that if he were compelled to testify what he would have to say might reflect seriously upon Harding, although no financial wrongdoing was ever traced directly to the President.[1]

Another set of scandals involved the work of the Veterans' Bureau, at the head of which Harding had placed Charles R. Forbes, a chance acquaintance whom he had met on a trip to Honolulu. Forbes was soon making deals with contractors in the building of hospitals and the purchase and sale of supplies that meant great personal gains for himself, but heavy losses for the government. Daugherty was not responsible for the Forbes appointment, and reported the rumor of irregularities to Harding, who arranged that Forbes should go abroad, and then resign. But a Senate investigating committee was soon hot on Forbes's trail, and the suicide of his closest adviser, Charles F. Cramer, heightened suspicions. In 1925 Forbes was convicted of defrauding the government, and sentenced to a term in a federal prison.

But the worst scandals of the Harding administration involved another member of the cabinet, Albert B. Fall, Secretary of the Interior, who accepted generous bribes for facilitating the transfer *Fall and the* of the naval oil reserves at Teapot Dome, Wyoming, and *oil men* Elk Hills, California, to the Sinclair and Doheny oil interests, respectively. These reserves were under the control of the Secretary of the Navy, Edwin Denby, but Fall easily persuaded that amiable and incompetent individual to consent to their transfer to the Interior Department. Wholly unsuspecting, Harding signed the transfer, while Theodore Roosevelt, Jr., Assistant Secretary of the Navy, missed the opportunity of a lifetime by failing to discover and denounce the fraud that was being perpetrated. Once Fall had the coveted reserves in his hands, he signed contracts permitting the favored oil interests to exploit them. On the assumption that borderline borings were draining the government's oil away, he made a reasonable case that the navy was better off to accept a percentage of the oil taken out than to leave its fields unopened, but he found difficulty later in explaining why competitive bids were avoided

[1] Satisfactory accounts of the Harding scandals are contained in Mark Sullivan's *Our Times*, vi, and in F. L. Allen, *Only Yesterday* (1931), "an informal history of the nineteen-twenties." On the oil scandal see, also, M. E. Ravage, *The Story of Teapot Dome* (1924).

and why the whole affair was kept secret as long as possible. Again a senatorial investigation, demanded in a resolution introduced by Senator La Follette and conducted by Senator Thomas J. Walsh of Montana, brought out the facts. Fall's attitude had evidently been affected by a "loan" of one hundred thousand dollars from Doheny and several times that amount from Sinclair. Several years later civil suits in the federal courts resulted in the cancellation of the Doheny lease because of "fraud and corruption," and the Sinclair lease because of "collusion and conspiracy." Criminal prosecutions were less successful. Fall was finally tried and convicted in 1929 of taking a bribe, was fined one hundred thousand dollars, and was sentenced to a year in jail, but the adage, "You can't convict a million dollars," seemed fully demonstrated when the two multi-millionaires, Harry F. Sinclair and Edward L. Doheny, won acquittals. Sinclair, however, was compelled to serve two short jail sentences for contempt, one for having refused to answer questions put to him by a Senate investigating committee, and the other for having employed detectives to shadow jurors during the course of one of his trials.

Harding never knew the whole truth about the scandals that were to label his administration as the most corrupt since General Grant's, but *Death of* he knew enough by the summer of 1923 to feel sick at heart. *Harding* In search of rest and solace he decided on a trip to Alaska, but the speech-making and traveling tired him out physically and failed to ease his mind. When he spoke at Seattle on the return trip, July 27, he was ill; six days later in San Francisco, on August 2, he was dead. Shocked by the suddenness of his passing, and not yet fully aware of his shortcomings, the country made a fine pageant of his funeral, but there was little real grief. He had failed completely during his brief term of office to capture the public imagination, and the yearnings for normalcy which he shared with the people had been only faintly realized. Even among those responsible for his nomination in 1920 there was a feeling that his death was perhaps a blessing, for shrewd prognosticators believed that the Republican Party, with Harding as its nominee, would have had little chance for success in the campaign of 1924.[1]

[1] On the Harding period the best general account is F. L. Paxson, *Post-war Years: Normalcy, 1918–1923* (1948). H. M. Robinson, *Fantastic Interim* (1943), is entertaining, but highly colored. Karl Schriftgiesser, *The Gentleman from Massachusetts: Henry Cabot Lodge* (1944), is a severe indictment. M. R. Werner, *Privileged Characters* (1935), and John Ise, *The United States Oil Policy* (1926), deal with the oil scandals. C. L. Hoag, *Preface to Preparedness: The Washington Disarmament Conference and Public Opinion* (1941), emphasizes the influence of the public opinion on diplomacy. Harold and Margaret Sprout, *Toward a New Order of Sea Power: American Naval Policy and the World Scene, 1918–1922* (1940), stresses the significance of seapower. See also H. M. Vinacke, *A History of the Far East in Modern Times* (1944); Dorothy Borg, *American Policy and the Chinese Revolution, 1925–1928* (1947); D. F. Fleming, *The United States and the World Court* (1945).

CHAPTER XXIV

THE ROAD TO PROSPERITY

To THE SURPRISE of the pessimists, the inflated prosperity that the World War brought to the United States lasted on for about a year and a half after the return of peace. Prices held up amaz- *Post-war* ingly, and the demand for goods seemed insatiable. To a *prosperity* very great extent this condition was due to an orgy of buying on the part of the American public. During the war the people had "hooverized," not only upon supplies needed for the armies at the front, but to some extent also upon nearly every other type of consumer goods. With the war ended, savings need no longer be invested in Liberty bonds; they could be spent, and they were spent. Indeed, many who during the war had followed the advice of the government not to dispose of their bonds regarded the return of peace as an invitation to exchange them for coveted luxuries. Soldiers mustered out of service usually spent their discharge bonuses and back pay before settling down to work. Even the foreign market held up. The war-ravaged countries of Europe needed American materials for the work of rehabilitation and American foodstuffs to feed their peoples. They bought freely also of South America, China, and Japan, and thus indirectly stimulated purchases from these quarters in the United States. American exports during 1919 were about a billion dollars higher than in any previous year of American history. Manufacturers found that to continue their high wartime profits they need turn only to the production of goods for civilians instead of for soldiers. Farmers were convinced that the market for American foodstuffs in Europe had become a permanent fixture, and that their prosperity was guaranteed for all time.[1]

[1] Most of the textbooks in American economic history give satisfactory accounts of the business conditions that followed the war. Among the best of them are F. A. Shannon, *Economic History of the People of the United States* (1934); H. U. Faulkner, *American Economic History* (new edition, 1931); E. L. Bogart, *Economic History of the American People* (1938); E. C. Kirkland, *A History of American Economic Life* (1932). A flood of detail is available in the report of the Conference on Unemployment, *Recent Economic Changes in the United States* (2 vols., 1929).

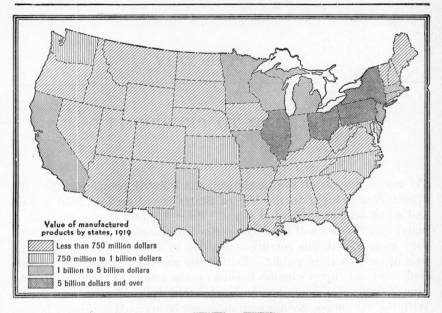

Value of manufactured
products by states, 1919

Less than 750 million dollars
750 million to 1 billion dollars
1 billion to 5 billion dollars
5 billion dollars and over

DISTRIBUTION OF FACTORY OUTPUT, 1919

The optimism of the nation's food producers, whipped up systematically by the real estate men and the country bankers who stood to make
The real heavy profits every time a farm changed hands, developed
estate boom throughout most of the Middle West into a thoroughgoing
speculative boom. The price of wheat, guaranteed by the government
for an eighteen-month period after September 2, 1918, at $2.26 a bushel,
rose by the spring of 1920 to more than three dollars. At the same time
corn sold for over two dollars a bushel, with other farm prices equally
inflated. Naturally land prices went up, but sales were soon being made
less because of the earning power of the land than because of the profits
that were to be made by selling it at abnormally high figures. The land
boom reached its climax in Iowa, where land worth from eighty to a
hundred dollars an acre before the war sold during 1919 and early 1920
for from two hundred to four hundred dollars an acre. During the year
that ended in March, 1920, the sale price of Iowa farms increased on an
average sixty-three dollars per acre, or about thirty-two per cent. Most
purchases were made possible only by heavy mortgages, but money for
the purpose was available seemingly in an unending stream at the
country banks, whose swollen deposits reflected the prosperity of their

[536]

customers. Farm purchases included also electrical equipment, agricultural machinery, motor cars, and blooded livestock, all bought on the installment plan in the hope of future profits. Farmhouses were increasingly modernized, and for the first time in American history a large class of country dwellers lived under conditions that closely approximated the advantages of the city.

The prosperity of farm and factory extended also in varying degrees to the workers, but tended if anything to promote rather than to restrain industrial conflict. Organized labor had been greatly *Strikes* strengthened by the war, which raised wages to unprece- *of 1919* dented heights, steadied employment, and added to the unions many new, if somewhat undisciplined, members. The restraints imposed upon labor by the patriotic desire of all classes to win the war were removed by the return of peace, and the mounting cost of living gave rise to the charge that wages, high as they were, had not risen correspondingly. Furthermore, the long period of prosperity had unfitted labor psychologically to accept such readjustments as the restoration of peacetime conditions made inevitable. During the year 1919 strike after strike broke out, among the most notable being a general strike in Seattle that was calmed down only by the intervention of outside labor leaders, a strike in the steel industry that lasted for months before its failure was admitted, and a series of strikes among the coal miners and the textile workers.[1]

The presence of many radicals among the strike leaders did much to give labor a black eye with the public, and to pave the way for an hysterical outburst against the "reds." The Department *"Red"* of Justice under both Palmer and Daugherty waged vigor- *baiting.* ous war against the radicals, and sent many of them back to the lands from which they had come, or to jail.[2] With the blood-lust of wartime not yet fully abated, state and local governments sometimes showed even less restraint. The two most notable victims of this rage were Nicola Sacco and Bartolomeo Vanzetti, two Italian workmen who were convicted of a double murder that occurred in South Braintree, Massachusetts, on April 15, 1920. Many competent investigators believed that these convictions were obtained less because of the evidence, which was wholly circumstantial, than because of the records of the two men as radicals, but a prolonged nation-wide effort failed to save them from

---

[1] V. W. Lanfear, *Business Fluctuations and the American Labor Movement, 1915–1922* (1924); Selig Perlman and Philip Taft, *History of Labor in the United States, 1896–1932* (Commons, *History of Labor in the United States,* IV, *Labor Movements*); Interchurch World Movement, *Report on the Steel Strike of 1919* (1920).

[2] Jane P. Clark, *Deportation of Aliens from the United States to Europe* (1931).

execution.[1]   That some real danger from radicalism did exist seemed evident from the explosion of a bomb in Wall Street just before noon on September 16, 1920.   Thirty-eight persons were killed and hundreds were wounded, but the perpetrators of the crime were never discovered.   An equally unlovely aspect of the post-war hysteria was the rise of the Ku Klux Klan, a modern imitation of the secret order that according *The Ku*   to tradition had played so important a part in saving the *Klux Klan*   South from the excesses of the carpet-baggers.   Founded by William J. Simmons of Atlanta, Georgia, the new order sought to enlist under its banner every type of "one-hundred-per-cent American" prejudice, and thanks in considerable part to the hatreds engendered by the World War its organizers soon began to meet with success.   The Klan was ardently fundamentalist in religion and politics, denounced everything savoring of radicalism, and prided itself upon being at one and the same time anti-Negro, anti-Semite, anti-foreigner, and anti-Catholic.   The Negro, according to many southern whites, had been spoiled by the high wages he had been permitted to earn during the war, and by the stories of racial equality that colored veterans had brought back from France.   He needed to be "put in his place."   Sometimes these sentiments were echoed by the white residents of the northern towns and cities that had imported colored labor from the South during the war.   The Jews were denounced as un-American radicals, as conscienceless profiteers, and just as Jews.   Recent immigrants and the children of immigrants, particularly in case they chanced not to be of "Nordic" blood, were accused of a desire to undermine and destroy American institutions.   Besides, this was not their country, and why should they be here?   Catholics were baited as half-hearted Americans who set their religion above their patriotism, and owed allegiance to a foreign potentate, the Pope.   By 1920 Klan lodges were attracting attention throughout the South and the West; Klan members marched in white hoods and shrouds through village streets, burned "fiery crosses" on conspicuous hillsides, at best made themselves thoroughly ridiculous, and at worst committed insufferable nuisances.   In extreme cases individuals who had drawn the wrath of the order were beaten, tarred and feathered, or even killed.   Membership in the Klan was a closely guarded secret, as well became an order that sometimes took the law into its own hands.   The fading of prosperity served only to add new fuel to the fire, and for several years the Klan continued to increase in numbers.   An exposé of the moral and financial irregularities of the Klan leaders, made by the New York *World* in the fall of 1921 and followed by a still more

[1] Felix Frankfurter. *The Case of Sacco and Vanzetti* (1927).

damaging congressional investigation, failed to check the growth of the Klan, which got a new "Imperial Wizard," and by the middle of the decade counted perhaps four million members.[1]

A premonition that the post-war prosperity might not last appeared as early as October, 1919, when the stock market broke badly, but there was little real distress until the summer of 1920. Undoubt- *A business* edly the most important cause of the decline which then set *decline* in was the failure of Europe to continue its generous purchases of American goods. This was due in part to the unexpectedly rapid recovery of European agriculture, but there were other factors also. For months after the signing of the armistice the government of the United States continued the policy of lending to its associates in the war, but by 1920, confessing its inability to "assume the burdens of all the earth," it was making no new loans. Foreign exchange, influenced by the enormous debts owing the United States, dropped precipitately; in February, 1920, the English pound was worth only about three dollars, the French and Belgian francs only seven or eight cents each, and the German mark only two or three cents. European purchasers found it practically impossible to pay the prices demanded for American goods, the more so because of the high American tariff, raised still higher in 1921, which interfered seriously with their desire to exchange what they could produce for what they needed to buy. The American public itself added to the general distress by indulging in a "buyers' strike" against the abnormally high retail prices that were being charged. Aimed mainly at luxuries, the "strike" fell with particular force upon silk, which within a seven-month period fell from $18.40 a pound to $5.81. The resulting prostration of the silk industry in Japan lessened, in turn, the ability of the Japanese to buy American cotton.

The years 1920 and 1921 saw a general slackening in nearly every field of business. Retailers and wholesalers who had bought at high prices found their shelves stocked with goods that no one wished to buy. Manufacturers who had made heavy purchases of high-priced raw materials were confronted by wholesale cancellations of orders. Railroad earnings went down, and banks were forced to contract their loans. Stocks and bonds slumped disastrously, and speculators were particularly hard hit. A total of 8881 business failures, with liabilities of $295,121,805, occurred in 1920, and 19,652, involving $755,777,685, in 1921. With nearly three and a half million men out of work the country faced for the first time in many years a serious problem of unemployment.

[1] J. M. Mecklin, *The Ku Klux Klan* (1924).

The suffering in agriculture was even more acute than in industry. The European market upon which American farm prosperity had come to depend seemed irretrievably lost.[1] European purchasers had not merely cut down on their buying; they had turned to other sources of supply. During the war half the British imports of fresh beef, for example, had come from the United States, but by 1923 this proportion had declined to only five per cent. Meat and wheat from the Argentine, from Canada, from Australia, and from Russia supplied the European market, leaving the American farmer high and dry. When at the end of May, 1920, the government guaranty on the price of wheat was removed, a steady fall in all farm prices began that within a year had brought wheat down to a dollar a bushel, and corn to the lowest figure in twenty-five years. Cotton-growers fared quite as badly as the growers of food crops. By 1919 the price of cotton had risen to thirty-eight cents, and the extraordinary wartime demands had led to the opening of vast quantities of new cotton land in the Southwest. But by 1920 the price of cotton was only eighteen cents, and it kept on going down until before the end of the decade it sold for as little as seven cents. Cotton from Egypt and India had begun to wrest from the American South the world supremacy in its greatest crop that it had held unchallenged for a hundred years.

The depression in agriculture

Even the American market failed the farmers. The war had done much to change the food habits of Americans, and while the "wheatless" and "meatless" requirements of the Food Administration were soon gladly forgotten, less wheat and less meat were consumed in proportion to other foods. Health preachments took another toll; Americans generally, and American women in particular, were cutting down on their surplus weight. In the first quarter of the twentieth century the per capita consumption of wheat flour declined twenty per cent, of corn meal and rye flour sixty per cent, of barley — no longer in demand for the manufacture of beer — ninety per cent. Excepting only pork and dairy products, the American per capita consumption of animal foods showed also a sharp decline. Moreover, lands devoted to growing crops had increased during the war decade by nearly fifty million acres, while better machinery and better methods of farming had tended to increase the yield per acre. But the rate of increase in the American population was slowing down; immigration was restricted by law to a small fraction of those who wished to come; and the size of American families showed a marked tendency to decline. To add to the confusion in agriculture, mechanized farming, together with the use of trucks and automobiles

[1] E. G. Nourse, *American Agriculture and the European Market* (1924).

AGRICULTURAL PRODUCTION IN THE UNITED STATES, 1919

in towns and cities, had cut down heavily upon the production of horses and mules, and upon the food crops, such as oats, used to maintain them. Thus still more acres were freed for the production of still more human food for a market that did not exist.

The American farmer soon realized that with his mortgage payments wholly out of proportion to his income, with taxes boosted sky-high to *Bank* correspond with the new land values, and with the cost of *failures* labor, machinery, and transportation still approximating wartime levels, his day of prosperity was done. He tried to borrow at the country banks whose easy lending policy had played so large a part in his undoing, only to find that the banks themselves were in trouble. Not content to lend from their own resources alone, they had borrowed heavily from the Federal Reserve Banks, which until 1920 had made little effort to check credit expansion. But in that year the Federal Reserve Board decided to take such measures as might be necessary to bring credit under more effective control. The discount rate was raised, and banks that had overreached themselves struggled frantically to collect enough loans to meet their obligations. Failures among the western country banks became increasingly common, some of them the fault of farmers who were determined to hold their crops until prices should rise, whether they could meet their debts to the banks or not. Farm mortgages were frequently foreclosed, but there was comparatively little retreat from the land. Farmers who had lost their property rights stayed on as tenants, and mortgage-holders often preferred the postponement of payments to foreclosure. Thus, in spite of the low prices farm yields tended to increase. During the three years that followed the disastrous break of 1920, production levels in nine basic field crops maintained or surpassed the levels of the preceding three years.

As in previous periods of agricultural distress, the farmers most seriously affected by the hard times showed a strong disposition to work *Farmer* through farmer organizations for the redress of grievances. *organiza-* The old Grange, although more active in the Northeast *tions* than in the states of the Middle West where its fame had once been greatest, showed renewed vitality. The American Society of Equity, founded in Indiana in 1902, and its subsidiary, the Equity Co-operative Exchange, enjoyed the support of numerous grain-growers all the way from Wisconsin to Montana. In the same region the Farmers' Union, also dating back to 1902, but of Texas origin, developed its greatest strength. More national in scope was the American Farm Bureau Federation, an unforeseen by-product of the Smith-Lever Act of 1914. The purpose of this measure was to encourage agricultural

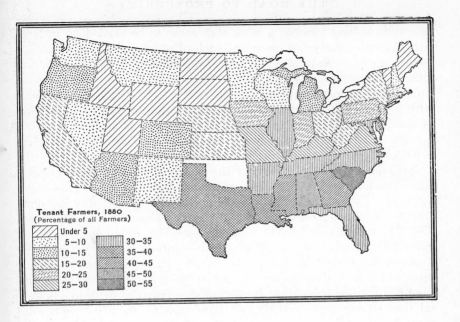

Tenant Farmers, 1880
(Percentage of all Farmers)

	Under 5		
	5—10		30—35
	10—15		35—40
	15—20		40—45
	20—25		45—50
	25—30		50—55

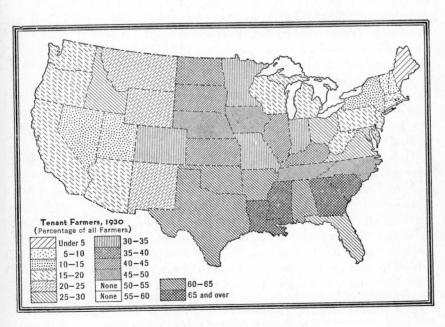

Tenant Farmers, 1930
(Percentage of all Farmers)

	Under 5		30—35
	5—10		35—40
	10—15		40—45
	15—20		45—50
	20—25	None	50—55
	25—30	None	55—60
			60—65
			65 and over

INCREASE IN FARM TENANCY

education among farmers, a work that came to be carried on in large part through county farm bureaus, each of which was provided with a county agent. Naturally the local bureaus soon joined together in state organizations, and by 1920 the American Farm Bureau Federation provided a national capstone for the edifice. By September 1, 1921, with forty-six states participating, the Federation claimed a membership of nearly a million farmers. Derided by the less favored farm orders because of its close connection with the government, it was nonetheless capable of expressing with vigor the farmers' point of view.[1]

Quite in a class by itself was the National Non-Partisan League, which spread from North Dakota as a center into a dozen northwestern

The Non-Partisan League states. Although the American Society of Equity had done much to prepare the way for the League, the organization that took form in 1915 was essentially the brain-child of one man, Arthur C. Townley, a gifted promoter only thirty-five years of age. Townley had been a member of the Socialist Party, and the experiment upon which he wished to embark was essentially one in state socialism. First he proposed to weld the farmers of the state together into a powerful dues-paying organization, and then through their votes to seize control of the state government and through it to accomplish his reforms. Most of the League program was as old as Populism, but it still had an irresistible appeal for the North Dakota wheat farmer: (1) the state ownership of terminal elevators, flour-mills, packing-houses, and cold-storage plants; (2) state inspection of grain and grain dockage; (3) the exemption of farm improvements from taxation; (4) state hail insurance on the acreage tax basis; and (5) rural credit banks operated at cost. The object of these reforms was primarily to eliminate the profits of the middlemen, and thus to save for the farmer a greater proportion of the wealth that he produced.

Townley's experiment opened auspiciously, for the harvests of 1915 were good, and the farmers were able to pay the high dues that the League exacted. A weekly newspaper, the *Non-Partisan Leader*, kept up a constant barrage of League propaganda, and high-pressure organizers traveled all over the state in automobiles recruiting members. When little more than a year old, the League went into the Republican primaries, nominated most of its candidates for state office, including the governorship, and elected them. Two years later it won majorities in the state legislature, and began to pass the laws it had promised. Before

---

[1] B. H. Hibbard, *Marketing Agricultural Products* (1921), contains a good account of the principal farm orders, and much else of value on the agricultural situation. See also Edward Wiest, *Agricultural Organization in the United States* (1923).

Courtesy of the Non-Partisan Leader

THE USELESS MIDDLEMAN

its ascendancy came to an end, it had provided for a state-owned elevator and a state-owned flour-mill, and had made a beginning on the rest of its program. But it encountered the unflinching opposition of capital, both from within and from without the state, and it had constant trouble with the courts. By 1921, when the League-dominated governor, Lynn J. Frazier, was defeated in a recall election, it was on the defensive. Meantime League organizers had spread their gospel across the state border into Minnesota. Unable to capture the Republican machinery, they made common cause with organized labor, and set up a Farmer-Labor Party, which in 1920 won strong support, although it failed to elect its ticket. From this time forward, both in North Dakota and Minnesota, and to a lesser extent in many other northwestern states also, the League furnished a convenient rallying center for the forces of agrarian discontent.[1]

With the exception of the Non-Partisan League, the farmer organizations generally emphasized co-operative marketing as the best means of
Co-operative solving the problem of low prices. Through their influence
marketing many selling associations were formed, some of which succeeded remarkably well, but many of which failed. Most influential among the promoters of co-operative selling was Aaron Sapiro, a shrewd California lawyer who before he became general counsel for the American Farm Bureau Federation in 1923 had already helped organize co-operatives among the producers of tobacco, wheat, broom-corn, milk, potatoes, and many other commodities. The success of a co-operative depended in large part upon its ability to enforce among its members an ironclad contract for the prevention of private sales. Enabling legislation was therefore required of the states, and although a few states had satisfactory laws on the subject, in most instances they had yet to be obtained. Sapiro's ideas were finally incorporated into a standard Co-operative Marketing Act, which was adopted by Kentucky in 1922 and thereafter, with sundry variations, in nearly every state. Probably the most consistently successful of the co-operatives was the California Fruit Growers' Association, which over a long period was able to dominate the market for western citrus fruits, and to set substantially what prices it chose. Co-operatives that dealt in such widely produced commodities as wheat, livestock, and cotton obtained far less satisfactory results.[2]

In their quest for agricultural prosperity the farm organizations naturally did not overlook the possibility of aid from the federal government.
The Farm In May, 1921, on the suggestion of Grey Silver, head of
Bloc in the American Farm Bureau Federation, the creation of a
Congress "Farm Bloc" in both houses of Congress was undertaken.
In the Senate the Bloc came to consist of fourteen Republicans and twelve Democrats, all from the West or the South, and led for a time by Senator Kenyon of Iowa, then by Senator Capper of Kansas. In the House the membership of the Bloc was less clearly defined, but its exist-

---

[1] The Non-Partisan League has attracted many writers, but the definitive work on this subject is yet to come. Andrew A. Bruce, *Non-Partisan League* (1921), which is hostile to the League, should be compared with H. E. Gaston, *The Nonpartisan League* (1920), and C. E. Russell, *The Story of the Nonpartisan League* (1920), which are somewhat friendly. See also A. S. Tostlebe, *The Bank of North Dakota* (1924).

[2] H. H. Bakken and M. A. Schaars, *The Economics of Co-operative Marketing* (1937).

ence was nonetheless real. For three or four years the Farm Bloc held together, and during this period it exerted a powerful influence upon the course of legislation.

Most of the measures promoted by the Bloc had as their purpose either the easement of rural credits or the promotion of co-operative marketing. A bill sponsored by Senator Norris of Nebraska would have created a gigantic government-owned corporation, with power to build warehouses, and to buy, sell, and export farm products with a view to the stabilization of prices. But the administration regarded this measure as sheer socialism, and persuaded the Farm Bloc to accept instead an extension of the life of the War Finance Corporation, which was given a hundred million dollars to lend to the producers, sellers, and exporters of farm products. Of greater permanent importance was the Intermediate Credits Act of 1923, which the Farm Bloc successfully pushed through Congress. Twelve intermediate credit banks were to be established in the same cities and under the same control as the Federal Land Banks, but as distinct corporations. Each bank was to have a capital of five million dollars, and was empowered to discount agricultural paper from commercial firms for terms not less than six months nor more than three years. This measure met the needs of such farmers as the growers of livestock, for example, whose business required credit for a longer period than the Federal Reserve Banks were permitted to give, but not for the long terms available under the Federal Farm Loan Act of 1916. The Intermediate Banks were also authorized to lend to co-operatives, and to the exporters of agricultural produce. Still another measure designed to have a salutary effect upon rural credits added a "dirt farmer" to the membership of the Federal Reserve Board.[1]

Pressure from the Farm Bloc brought the enactment of a number of laws which farm leaders hoped would promote the more profitable marketing of farm produce. After a hot fight in which opponents of the bill insisted that an attempt was being made to raise the price of cattle by legislation, Congress prohibited packing-houses from discriminating among those from whom they purchased, and from seeking to control or manipulate the prices they paid. Enforcement of these regulations was vested in the office of the Secretary of Agriculture, whose authority extended to the examination of the packer's books. Even more significant was the Capper-Volstead Act of 1922, known frequently as the "Magna Charta of Co-operative Marketing." Mindful of the many protests against the jailing of co-operative members for combination in

[1] Arthur Capper, *The Agricultural Bloc* (1922); Clara Eliot, *The Farmers' Campaign for Credit* (1927).

restraint of trade, Congress now exempted co-operative associations from the restrictions of the anti-trust laws, and set forth the conditions undei which they might engage in interstate commerce. By another act an attempt was made to prevent gambling in futures. As originally passed, this law rested upon the taxing power of Congress, and was invalidated by the Supreme Court. Repassed as an exercise of the interstate commerce power, it was sustained.

While Congress under the compulsion of the Farm Bloc was making valiant, if more or less fruitless, efforts to come to the aid of agriculture, *Calvin* the executive branch of the government was doing a far *Coolidge* better job of extending a helping hand to business. In this respect the policies of Harding and his successor Calvin Coolidge (1872–1933) were one. Nominating conventions often choose their presidential candidate to represent one wing of his party, and the Vice-President another; this, indeed, was the intention of the manipulators who awarded the Republican nomination to Harding. But the nomination of Coolidge was a political accident that threw the Vice-Presidency to a man whose economic prejudices corresponded precisely with those of his predecessor. A Vermonter by birth, Coolidge attended Amherst College, studied law, and began to practice in 1897 at Northampton, Massachusetts. Always a dependable regular, he climbed aboard the political escalator in 1899 when he became a councilman; by 1901 he was city solicitor; by 1904 clerk of courts; by 1907 a member of the legislature; by 1910 mayor of Northampton; by 1912 a member of the state senate; by 1916 lieutenant-governor; and by 1919 governor.[1]

Throughout his long career of office-holding Coolidge had done little to excite either opposition or approval. He was conscientious in the discharge of his duties, abstemious of spoken words, utterly uninterested in trouble-making reforms. His most publicized act came in 1919 during the Boston police strike, when he somewhat belatedly called out the state militia to keep order. His telegram on this occasion to President Gompers of the American Federation of Labor well illustrated his gift for making commonplace statements sound significant: "There is no right to strike against the public safety by anybody, anywhere, anytime." Woodrow Wilson was one of the many to congratulate Coolidge upon his stand, thus contributing to the volume of publicity that was soon to transform him from an obscure governor of Massachusetts into the Republican nominee for the Vice-Presidency. After the inaugura-

[1] W. A. White, *Calvin Coolidge: The Man Who Is President* (1925); *Masks in a Pageant* (1928); and *A Puritan in Babylon: The Story of Calvin Coolidge* (1938), furnish perhaps the fairest estimates of Coolidge.

tion Harding broke a precedent by inviting Coolidge to sit in on cabinet meetings, but the Vice-President interpreted his rôle as that of the silent observer merely, and took little part in the proceedings. As presiding officer of the Senate he had no chance to distinguish himself, but some articles he found time to write for the *Delineator* on "Enemies of the Republic" featured the dangers that American college women were encountering from "red" propaganda, and made him faintly ridiculous.

Coolidge as President accepted the Harding cabinet, making changes reluctantly and only under heavy pressure, and carried forward the work of the Harding administration without any perceptible change in direction. Fortunately he brought with him to his high office no faintest trace of corruption, and he had never been the kind of person who attracted to himself a "gang." Gradually the corruptionists who had saddled themselves upon Harding were eliminated, and the Republican leaders began to congratulate themselves on having escaped so successfully from the consequences of the Harding scandals. If Coolidge could be "built up" to presidential proportions, perhaps the defeat they had foreseen in 1924 could be avoided. Unimpressive in appearance and given to long lapses into silence, the new President was conspicuously lacking in glamor — a former President's daughter was reported to have wagered that he had been "weaned on a pickle." But his unalloyed conservatism made him friends in influential circles, and before many months in spite of his handicaps he had become one of the most popular of American Presidents.

The Harding-Coolidge formula for business recovery was never precisely stated in a political document, but it soon became fully apparent. First of all came economy in federal expenditures, a policy *The recovery* that under Harding was tolerated as a political necessity, *program —* but under Coolidge accurately reflected the presidential *economy* state of mind. Budget directors took their duties seriously, and the normal peace-time disbursements of the national government, if not actually reduced, were given little opportunity to expand. Considerable saving was accomplished by cutting down on the naval and military appropriations, but all such gains were seriously discounted by the mounting bill for pensions and veterans' relief. Nevertheless, whereas expenditures due to war had absorbed ninety-four per cent of the national budget in 1920, they accounted for only eighty-six per cent in 1924. It is worth noting in this connection that throughout the early twenties state and local expenditures mounted even more rapidly than federal spending declined. It is difficult to believe, therefore, that there was the direct relationship between "Coolidge economy" and the return of prosperity that Republican politicians were wont to claim. After 1925 even federal expenditures began to mount again.

A second item in the recovery program was the reduction of taxes, particularly those that "penalized success" by robbing business of its *Reduction* "legitimate profits." Not content with the repeal of the *of taxes* excess-profits tax and the surtax reductions contained in the Revenue Law of 1921, Mellon pressed Congress at every opportunity for further reductions:

> High rates [he maintained] tend to destroy individual initiative and seriously impede the development of productive business. Taxpayers subject to the higher rates cannot afford for example to invest in American railroads or industries or embark on new enterprises in the face of taxes taking away 50 per cent or more of any return that may be realized. These taxpayers are withdrawing their capital from productive business and investing it instead in tax exempt securities and adopting other lawful methods of avoiding the realization of taxable income. The result is to stop business transactions that would normally go through and to discourage men of wealth taking the risks incidental to developing and opening new businesses. Ways will always be found to avoid taxes so destructive in their nature and the only way to save the situation is to put taxes on a reasonable basis.

Mellon was unable to persuade Congress to reduce the maximum surtax as rapidly as he had hoped, but in the Revenue Act of 1924 the rate was brought down from fifty to forty per cent, and two years later to twenty per cent. Other reductions did away with most of the wartime excise taxes, radically reduced the normal income tax rates, modified the estate tax, and abolished the gift tax. In 1921 a man with a million-dollar income paid a federal tax of $663,000; by 1926, with the Mellon reductions in force, he paid less than $200,000. Unhappily a considerable proportion of the funds thus released for private use seems to have gone into highly speculative investments. Had the tax rates been permitted to remain at the wartime levels, it seems reasonable to suppose that the liquidation of the national debt might have proceeded even more rapidly than it did, and that the speculative craze of the later twenties might have been avoided. As it was, Mellon was able to lower the obligations of the United States during the decade of the twenties from about twenty-four billion to about sixteen billion dollars.[1]

A third item in the Republican recovery program was the systematic elimination of the government from competition with private business. The Transportation Act of 1920, although passed before Wilson left office, was essentially a Republican measure, and in full accord with the

---

[1] Mellon's policies are critically examined in Harvey O'Connor, *Mellon's Millions* (1933), the extremely unfriendly "biography of a fortune."

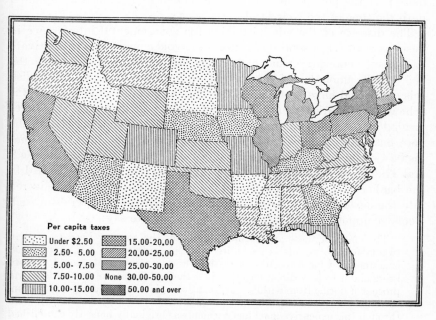

FEDERAL INCOME AND PROFITS TAXES, 1928

policies adopted during the Harding-Coolidge régime. The same may be said of the frantic efforts of the Shipping Board to dispose of government owned ships. But the most striking case in point was the refusal of the administration to countenance any plan for the effective governmental operation of the Muscle Shoals power development in Alabama, begun during the World War to aid in the production of nitrates. In a single stretch of thirty-seven miles the Tennessee River falls one hundred and thirty-four feet. To make use of this power the government planned a series of dams and two nitrate plants. One of the nitrate plants was in operation by 1918, but the great Wilson Dam was not completed until 1925, when the wartime need for nitrates had long passed. To Senator Norris of Nebraska and others who were undismayed by the prospect of a government-owned business, the Muscle Shoals development seemed to offer an ideal opportunity for the production of cheap power, but Congress was persuaded to offer the whole property for sale. The only bidder was Henry Ford, whose terms involved so heavy a loss to the government that they could not be accepted. A small trickle of power was leased to the Alabama Power Company for distribution in the surrounding territory, but for the most part the potentialities of this development remained unexploited until the time of the New Deal.

Government withdrawal from business

The distaste of the administration for governmental interference in business went far beyond these efforts to avoid competition with private enterprise, and called also for a drastic reduction in the amount of federal regulation. Legislation to accomplish this end would have been difficult to obtain, but the same purpose was achieved by indirect means. One by one the great regulatory bodies created by preceding administrations were packed with the friends of the very businesses they were supposed to regulate. The Interstate Commerce Commission was in effect handed over to the railroads, the Federal Trade Commission to the trusts, and the Federal Reserve Board to the bankers. For good measure the Tariff Commission was delivered into the custody of the protectionists. In criticism of a series of such Coolidge appointments, Senator Norris had this to say:

Restraints on regulation

> The effect of these appointments is to set the country back more than twenty-five years. It is an indirect but positive repeal of Congressional enactments, which no Administration, however powerful, would dare to bring about by any direct means. It is the nullification of federal law by a process of boring from within. If trusts, combinations, and big business are to run the government, why not permit them to do it directly rather than through this expensive machinery which was originally honestly established for the protection of the people of the country against monopoly and control?

Not content merely with removing in so far as possible all discouraging checks to private enterprise, the administration in a great variety of ways gave business direct and substantial aid. For the *Government aids to business* shipping business and the new aircraft industry it provided generous subsidies. For all businesses that might stand a chance to profit from tariff protection, it kept the tariffs high. For those with a taste for foreign investment, the State Department promised to lend a hand by denouncing bad foreign securities, and whether because of this, or in spite of it, American capital sped abroad in a seemingly endless stream. For the better promotion of foreign trade the Department of Commerce extensively and expensively reorganized its foreign service. For the benefit of domestic producers the Bureau of Standards offered elaborate facilities for testing, and recommended standard types in all sorts of manufactured articles from building-bricks to automobile tires. Secretary Hoover, as head of a commission to study waste in industry, brought in numerous suggestions bearing upon business efficiency. His work as head of the Department of Commerce was generally credited with having "elevated a relatively unimportant cabinet position to one of major rank." The *Detroit News* enthusiastically credited his activities with having ended the "threat to our prosperity."

Finally, the return of the Republicans to power was accompanied by a drastic change in the attitude of the national government toward labor. Appointments to the federal courts, whose decisions on the *The disciplining of labor* legality of many labor policies remained of fundamental importance, went with but rare exception to dependable conservatives. To Harding in his brief term of office fell the selection of four members of the United States Supreme Court, and the men he chose, Taft, Sutherland, Butler, and Sanford, were all traditionalists of the old school. Less apparent, but hardly less important, was the careful attention given by Daugherty as Attorney-General to the records of all proposed appointees to the lower courts and to subordinate positions in the Department of Justice. Before he left office in 1924 he was thus able to make an indelible imprint upon the administration of justice in the United States. Characteristic of the stiffening attitude of the courts toward labor was the sweeping injunction he obtained when a strike of the railroad shopmen seriously disrupted interstate commerce. From Federal Judge J. H. Wilkerson of Chicago, a Harding appointee, Daugherty obtained a temporary injunction that forbade every conceivable type of strike activity. "Not merely violence but picketing of all sorts, strike meetings, statements to the public, the use of union funds to carry on the strike, and the use of any means of communication by the

leaders to direct it," all fell under the ban of the court. The fact that
this injunction was sustained on appeal demonstrated the hollowness of
the hope that the Clayton Anti-Trust Act had furnished an enduring
"Magna Charta for Labor." [1]

Whether because of the administration's policies, as their defenders
claimed, or in spite of them, as a few critics contended, the recovery of
Business business from the depression that had gripped the country
recovery when Harding was inaugurated was phenomenal. By the
time Coolidge became President the tide had turned, and when the
campaign of 1924 had to be faced the Republicans could count on prosperity as their best talking point. Steady gains were reported in iron
and steel, in the automobile industry, in the building trades, and among
wholesalers and retailers. Dividends that had vanished during the depression were resumed by a large number of corporations in 1923 and
1924, while occasional stock dividends demonstrated still more conclusively that times had changed. Even the railroads began to increase their earnings, and all signs pointed to brightening economic
skies.

Of fundamental consequence in the new business vitality was the rapid
rise of the automobile industry, which was still in its infancy before the
The automo- war, but during the twenties multiplied its output again and
bile industry again. Between 1920 and 1925 the annual production of
motor vehicles in the United States doubled, while the number of automobiles in actual use almost quadrupled. The growth of the automobile
industry meant a corresponding prosperity for the manufacturers upon
whom it depended for iron and steel, for fabrics, plate-glass, and tires;
it brought into existence an unending number of new establishments for
"sales and service"; it was the making of the oil industry, from oil well
to filling station; it provided the wages and profits to promote a building
boom that extended all the way from the humble dwelling-houses of the
workers to the magnificent skyscrapers where the industrial leaders had
their offices. The success of the automobile industry was made possible
largely by the mass-production methods popularized by Henry Ford, and
generally adopted. Ingenious machines fashioned standard parts and
assembled them into cars with a maximum of speed and a minimum of
human labor. The completed product was then offered to the public
at a low price, on easy installments, with profits for manufacturer and
dealer dependent primarily upon a large volume of business. Even the

[1] Felix Frankfurter and Nathan Greene, *The Labor Injunction* (1930), is the leading authority on this subject, but see also E. E. Witte, *The Government in Labor Disputes* (1932), and
A. T. Mason, *Organized Labor and the Law* (1925).

GEOGRAPHICAL DISTRIBUTION OF PRODUCTS IN THE UNITED STATES

foreign market could sometimes be tapped, for the efficiency of mass production in American factories offset the lower wages paid abroad.[1]

But automobiles were not the only products of the factory to be manufactured and sold in the Ford way. Phonographs and radios, household *Installment* and office equipment, furnaces and plumbing, electrical sup- *buying* plies, and a thousand miscellaneous items were similarly made available for the multitudes. American purchasers found themselves able to buy for a small payment down and for many similar payments in the months or years to come a host of luxuries that in an earlier age the ordinary citizen could never have hoped to own. Money was even left over for amusements, and "motion-picture palaces" provided low-priced theatricals not for just a few Americans but for all of them. Naturally this more abundant life came to be closely associated with Republican policies, for the Republicans were in power when it arrived, and they cheerfully admitted their responsibility for bringing it to pass. In Coolidge, the accidental occupant of the White House, the public came to recognize a kind of personification of the new prosperity, and in spite of his conspicuous lack of charm his popularity rose to unbelievable heights. Long before the time set for the Republican nominating convention of 1924 it was a foregone conclusion that he would be the nominee.

Discontent with the blessings of Coolidge prosperity was nevertheless rife among two powerful elements of American society, the farmers and *Farmer and* laborers. With the farmers the hard times that had begun *labor dis-* in 1920 continued, to the complete discomfiture of those *content* theorists who held that without agricultural recovery there could be no business recovery. With the laborers the return of good times meant prosperity also for the unions, and a determination to share more fully in the long profits that industry was beginning to take. The example of Russia, where a workers' commonwealth seemed well on the way to success, was not without its psychological effect. Imperfections in the American industrial system, such, for example, as technological unemployment, were not difficult to detect. The research bureaus that every enlightened employer maintained, aided and abetted by the research activities of the government and the universities, produced new machines and new processes that threw thousands out of work. Often those who lost their jobs found new types of employment, but often also they did not. In spite of the unparalleled prosperity there were literally millions of men out of work all the time. Might there not be a

[1] T. N. Carver, *The Present Economic Revolution in the United States* (1925); R. G. Tugwell, *Industry's Coming of Age* (1927); Stuart Chase, *The Tragedy of Waste* (1925), *Men and Machines* (1929), and *Prosperity: Fact or Myth* (1929).

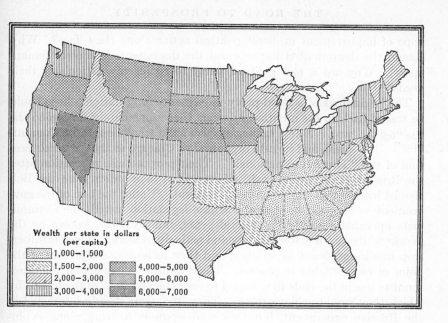

Wealth per state in dollars
(per capita)
- 1,000—1,500
- 1,500—2,000
- 2,000—3,000
- 3,000—4,000
- 4,000—5,000
- 5,000—6,000
- 6,000—7,000

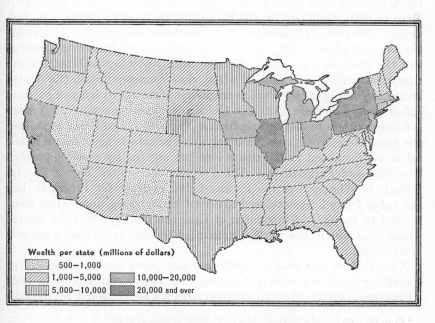

Wealth per state (millions of dollars)
- 500—1,000
- 1,000—5,000
- 5,000—10,000
- 10,000—20,000
- 20,000 and over

CONCENTRATION OF WEALTH, 1922

hope of improvement in direct political action along class lines? Why should the discontented farmers and the discontented laborers remain apart? Why not a new political party to represent particularly their needs? [1]

The beginnings of a third-party movement along national lines could be traced back to the months and years that immediately succeeded the war. A few extremists went the whole length of Commu-

The "left wing"

nism, and in 1919 organized at Chicago as the American section of the "Third International." Their purpose was revolution after the Russian pattern, and their willingness to take orders from the Bolshevist leaders was, and remained, apparent. Under the ban of the government as long as the special wartime legislation lasted, the Communists operated covertly for several years, but by 1924, known as the Workers' Party, they were openly and actively at work. Their membership was insignificant in number, and they in no sense represented the point of view of labor in general. The Socialists differed from the Communists less in the ends they hoped to see achieved than in the means by which they would achieve them. They, too, were deeply interested in the Russian experiment, but they were content to work along evolutionary rather than revolutionary lines. In the election of 1920, with Debs as their candidate for the fifth time, they polled nearly a million votes. Debs was in federal prison at the time, under sentence for violation of the Espionage Act. He was later pardoned by President Harding. But the prospect for a really effective third party lay with neither the Communists nor the Socialists, whose close connection with Old World radicalism deeply offended the average American, but with a new Farmer-Labor Party, which in 1920 at a Chicago convention sought with some success to fuse into one organization a National Labor Party organized the year before, Townley's National Non-Partisan League, and a handful of old-fashioned 1912 Progressives represented by a self-appointed Committee of Forty-Eight. The Progressives wanted Robert M. La Follette of Wisconsin as the Farmer-Labor nominee for President, but the Labor Party leaders refused to accept him, and the nomination went instead to Parley P. Christensen of Utah, an unknown western lawyer whose total vote in the election amounted to little more than a quarter of a million.

Nevertheless, the work of building a new party that could hope for something more than merely a protest vote went steadily on. In 1922 a Conference for Progressive Political Action was sponsored by the rail-

---

[1] F. E. Haynes, *Social Politics in the United States* (1924). See also Haynes, *Third Party Movements Since the Civil War*, and Fine, *Labor and Farmer Parties in the United States*.

[558]

road unions, whose members could not forget the advantages they had enjoyed under governmental operation, and saw little pro- *Conference* spect of change under either Republican or Democratic lead- *for Progres-* ership. The C.P.P.A. sought support not only from the *sive Political* *Action* groups that had formed the Farmer-Labor Party of 1920, but also from the Socialist Party, and from organized labor in general. It established a Committee of Fifteen which took an active part in the congressional campaign of 1922, claimed some credit for the rebuke which the election returns administered to Republican policies, and rejoiced in the re-election of La Follette to the Senate, together with the astounding victories of such other liberals as Henrik Shipstead of Minnesota, Lynn Frazier of North Dakota, Smith W. Brookhart of Iowa, Burton K. Wheeler of Montana, and R. B. Howell of Nebraska. Numbers of congressmen who had voted for the Esch-Cummins Act were defeated, while most of those who had opposed it survived. According to *Labor*, a railroad union journal, the election

> wasn't a "Democratic landslide," but it was a Progressive triumph, such a victory as the Progressives have not won in this country in many a day. It was gloriously non-partisan. Party lines were smashed and labor displayed its political strength in a manner unparalleled in the history of the country. ... La Follette was the outstanding winner and Washington is already talking of him as a most formidable presidential possibility in 1924.

Activities of the C.P.P.A. following the elections of 1922 led directly toward the nomination of an independent ticket, although until 1924 the cloak of non-partisanship was maintained. That La Follette would be the third-party standard-bearer if he would accept the nomination was increasingly apparent, and when the C.P.P.A. Convention met in Cleveland, July 4, 1924, he was not only nominated, but was allowed to write his own platform and to name his own running mate. For Vice-President his choice fell upon Burton K. Wheeler, Democratic senator from Montana, and for a platform he suggested a program only a little more socialistic than the Progressive platform of 1912.

Eager "to break the power of the private monopoly system over the economic and political life of the American people," La Follette demanded such standard reforms as the public ownership of the rail- *The La* roads and certain natural resources including water-power, *Follette* coal, oil, ores, and timber lands; the reduction of taxes on *candidacy* small incomes, with high surtaxes, inheritance taxes, and excess-profits taxes for the rich; a constitutional amendment to limit the right of the Supreme Court to set aside the laws of Congress; restrictions on the use of injunctions by the courts; and a series of relief measures for the farmers. A few days after the meeting of the C.P.P.A., the Socialist Convention, by a vote of 106 to 17, decided to support La Follette, and a little later the American Federation of Labor also gave him its blessing. When the Farmer-Labor Party virtually eliminated itself from the political scene, a "united front" of all the left-wing forces was obtained, except for the Communists, whose offer of support La Follette rejected.

It is possible that the Democrats, by nominating a liberal candidate and adopting a liberal program, might have forestalled the appearance *Democratic* of a third-party ticket. The Harding scandals were theirs *dissensions* to capitalize upon as well as the unrest in farm and labor circles, but unfortunately they found themselves rent asunder by a factional fight over the Ku Klux Klan. This order, like its predecessors the Know-Nothing Party and the A.P.A., had carried its program of racial and religious discrimination into politics, and in the rural states of the South and the West where the native-born Protestant population was dominant had scored telling victories. In Oklahoma an anti-Klan governor was impeached and removed from office; in most of the states of the Southwest, particularly Texas, Louisiana, and Arkansas, the Klan held the balance of power; in Indiana, Ohio, Kansas, Missouri, Colorado, and elsewhere it was too strong to be ignored. The Klan was no respecter of parties and counted Republicans as well as Democrats among its members, but it proved to be a far greater menace to the Democrats than to the Republicans. To win the election the Democratic Party required not only the support of rural voters in the South and the West, but full co-operation from the Democratic city machines, many of which, like Tammany in New York, were dominated by Catholics of recent immigrant origin. The bonds that held these two widely separated elements together were weak at best. Country Democrats, not always without reason, suspected city Democrats of every kind of iniquity; city Democrats were as contemptuous as they were ignorant of the problems of rural-life. The two factions were diametrically opposed on the prohibition issue; the city Democracy was aggressively wet, while the country Democracy was fanatically dry. There were other confusing cross-currents. In the South, for example, the Democratic leaders were usually conservative on problems involving industry and finance, while in the West the legacy of Bryanism was still strong. "A Democrat would rather fight another Democrat than a Republican any day," ran a familiar saying, in which there was more than a modicum of truth.[1]

When the Democratic nominating convention met in Madison Square

[1] For a clear understanding of these political cross-currents, and much else that is unique about American life, André Siegfried, *America Comes of Age* (1927), is invaluable.

Garden, New York, on June 24, a large block of delegates from the eastern city-dominated states were determined to draw *Davis and* blood. In Alfred E. Smith, brilliant Roman Catholic gov- *Bryan* ernor of New York, who had worked his way up from the "sidewalks of New York" through the Tammany organization, they had a candidate for the nomination of whom they could justly be proud. They had also a plank, that expressly denounced the Klan, ready for insertion in the platform. When the platform committee discreetly refused to tempt defeat by openly insulting the Klan, the anti-Klan delegates carried the fight to the floor of the convention, only to see their resolution lost by a majority of four and one half votes. In the balloting for nominations the Klan forces threw their support to William G. McAdoo, who by no means shared their views, but was neither a Catholic nor in any intimate way identified with city machines. With the two-thirds rule still in effect neither Smith nor McAdoo could be nominated, and on the one hundred and third ballot the convention turned to John W. Davis of West Virginia and New York, a brilliant but conservative lawyer whose connection with the firm of J. P. Morgan and Company completely disqualified him in the eyes of labor and the western liberals. To offset this blunder the convention made another. For Vice-President it chose Governor Charles W. Bryan of Nebraska, brother of William Jennings Bryan, a man who had nothing but his name to recommend him for the post, but whose name alone was sufficient to alienate the eastern conservatives. With such a ticket, nominated after such a fight, the Democrats had no slightest chance of winning the election. They had done everything necessary "to snatch defeat from the very jaws of victory."

Meantime the Republicans, meeting at Cleveland on June 10, had completed their ticket by nominating Charles G. Dawes for Vice-President, and by adopting a platform highly complimentary to *Coolidge* the policies which they claimed were responsible for the re- *and Dawes* turn of prosperity. They were able to succeed, where the Democrats had failed, in keeping the Klan issue in abeyance, and they gave becoming lip-service to the enforcement of prohibition. During the campaign Republican speakers more or less ignored the Democrats, whose candidate for the Presidency would have better graced the Republican ticket than the far less able Coolidge, and centered their fire upon the Progressives, who had laid themselves open to attack along two lines. A few inadequately informed third-party men had claimed that La Follette might win enough electoral votes to throw the election into the House, where the even division between the parties might enable the Progressives to determine the choice. A little study of political history would have demonstrated the extreme improbability of such a result, but Republican campaigners made much of the threat to prosperity that a long-drawn-out contest in the House would involve, and urged with good effect that the voters must choose between "Coolidge or chaos." La Follette's attack on the courts, particularly his insistence that the power of the Supreme Court to invalidate congressional legislation should be limited, provided another good talking point. With the independence of the judiciary threatened, the principal safeguard of constitutional government would be removed, or so Republican orators claimed, leaving racial and religious minorities at the mercy of the majority. La Follette's war record, the threat of socialism, and the supposed un-Americanism of a three-party system all came in for denunciation at the hands of both old parties. But the chief advantage enjoyed by the Republicans over their adversaries was the abundant prosperity which engulfed the country. Agriculture, to be sure, was not yet able to share equally with industry in the profits that were being taken, but even the price of wheat and corn rose obligingly during election year.

The election was a Coolidge landslide. In the popular vote the Republican ticket won a plurality of more than seven million, and a majority *The Coolidge* of about two and a half million. The electoral college gave *landslide* Coolidge 382 votes, Davis 136, and La Follette 13. All of the Davis vote came from the South and La Follette carried only his own state, Wisconsin. Congress was safely Republican in both houses, and by much wider margins than after the elections of 1922.

The defeat was a crushing blow to Progressive hopes, although in reality the third-party ticket had done extremely well. La Follette polled a total of nearly five million votes and ran ahead of Davis in eleven western states. Seven far western and three southern border states gave the Progressive and Democratic tickets together more votes than went to Coolidge and Dawes. But the forces that had combined to support La Follette had looked upon his candidacy as a kind of trial balloon. If it seemed to point the way to ultimate victory, they would proceed with the organization of a new third party all along the line; if not, they would drop the project altogether. There had been no attempt during the campaign to set up state and local third-party tickets; Progressives were encouraged merely to vote for the men on other tickets whose views best represented their own. After the overwhelming triumph of Coolidge, further effort seemed futile and was not undertaken. La Follette himself, full of years and worn out by the strenuous campaign he had made, died a few months later. His son, Robert M. La Follette, Jr., elected to his father's seat in the Senate, took office as a Republican.

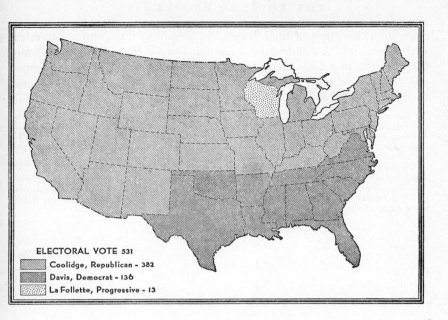

ELECTORAL VOTE 531

Coolidge, Republican - 382
Davis, Democrat - 136
La Follette, Progressive - 13

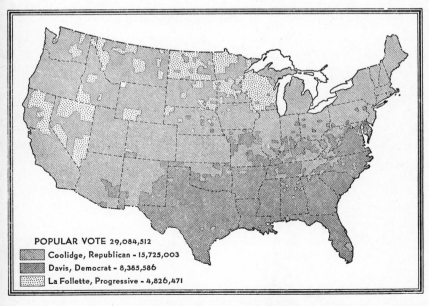

POPULAR VOTE 29,084,512

Coolidge, Republican - 15,725,003
Davis, Democrat - 8,385,586
La Follette, Progressive - 4,826,471

PRESIDENTIAL ELECTION OF 1924 BY STATES AND BY COUNTIES

Surveying the wreck of their hopes, the discouraged reformers lamented with Jeremiah: "A wonderful and horrible thing is committed in the land; the prophets prophesy falsely, and the priests bear rule by their means; and my people love to have it so: and what will ye do in the end thereof?"[1]

[1] Jeremiah, v, 30, 31. K. C. MacKay, *The Progressive Movement of 1924* (1947), is a careful study of the La Follette campaign. C. M. Fuess, *Calvin Coolidge, the Man from Vermont* (1940), is an excellent biography. James E. Lawrence, ed., *Fighting Liberal: The Autobiography of George W. Norris* (1945), is the not very illuminating memoir of a tired old man. Far more significant is *The Autobiography of William Allen White* (1946).

On the red-baiting tendencies of the period, see G. L. Joughin and E. M. Morgan, *The Legacy of Sacco and Vanzetti* (1948). On the Negro, Gunnar Myrdal, *An American Dilemma: The Negro Problem and Modern Democracy* (2 vols., 1944), is a study of unusual excellence and objectivity. See also Bernard H. Nelson, *The Fourteenth Amendment and the Negro since 1920* (1946).

CHAPTER XXV

THE ROAD TO DEPRESSION

IN SPITE of the continuing devotion of most Americans to the doctrine of isolation, evidence that the United States must play a leading rôle in international affairs accumulated rapidly during the *America* twenties. As a result of the war, the American nation had *and the* enormously expanded its industrial plant; it had discovered *world* unsuspected possibilities by way of agricultural production; it had accumulated out of its profits huge sums for new investment. Moreover, if the high speed to which its economic machine had been geared were to be maintained, the country must import many materials which it could not produce, such as rubber, silk, nickel, and tin, and many others which it could produce only in limited quantities, such as sugar, wool, hides, and nitrates. What the United States really needed was a peaceful and friendly world generally committed to the open door. That American statesmen of the twenties failed to achieve this goal should have occasioned no surprise. They were faced at home by a sentimental regard for political isolation and a deep-rooted belief in the protective tariff system; they were faced abroad by the jealousies and hatreds engendered by the war and the peace, feelings compounded so far as they concerned the United States by the conviction that the American people had escaped most of the war's ravages, but had taken most of its profits.

Among the most perplexing of the problems before the American government during the twenties was the collection of the loans by which the United States had so largely financed the Allied cause after 1917, and the work of reconstruction after the war was over. To the American people these intergovernmental loans seemed no different from the loans of one individual to another, and their repayment was regarded as a matter of simple honesty. Europeans took a somewhat different view of the situation. The war, they argued, was a common endeavor, in which each nation had given all that it had to give. The United States had entered the conflict late, and its casualty list was short; why should

[565]

it begrudge the dollars it had spent? Why should it not forgive its debtors, especially since American prosperity so far outstripped anything European nations could boast? Moreover, most of the money lent had been expended in the United States, and goods rather than gold had been sent abroad. Was it fair to ask European nations to pay back gold that they had never seen; indeed, half the world's supply of gold was already in the United States. Nor could European nations hope to build up large balances in America by the shipment of goods; the high American tariff forestalled that. To the war-heated imaginations of European critics "Uncle Sam" became "Uncle Shylock," and hostile feeling ran high.

Nevertheless, in 1922 Congress created a World War Foreign Debt Commission which opened negotiations with the various Allied nations, and ultimately succeeded in reaching refunding agreements with fifteen of them.[1] American policy called for settlements in accordance with ability to pay; hence the interest charges ranged from as low as four tenths of one per cent in the case of Italy to the normal three and three tenths per cent required of Great Britain and the more solvent states. The British settlement was effected as early as June, 1923, and the others during the next few years. Opposition to repayment reached its maximum in France, where the costly work of reparation threatened to bankrupt the government, but an agreement was signed in April, 1926, which set the interest rate at one and six tenths per cent, and allowed a period of sixty-two years for payment. The grand total of all the funded debts was fixed at more than eleven and one half billion dollars, with three fourths of the amount owing by Great Britain (4.6 billions), France (4.02 billions), and Italy (2.04 billions). Repayments by December 31, 1930, amounted to about two and one half billion dollars, of which more than seventy per cent came from Great Britain. Next year, following the Hoover moratorium, a few nations met their obligations, but thereafter payments from all nations except Finland virtually ceased.

Russia alone among the European nations that had borrowed from the United States refused to consider the funding of her debt. The Soviets, in keeping with their views on capitalism, repudiated all financial obligations incurred by preceding Russian governments, and denied the claims for indemnification lodged by foreigners whose property had been confiscated or destroyed during the revolutions of 1917. On this account, and also because of the persistent Communist propaganda carried on by

[1] A brief statement of the war debts problem is available in B. H. Williams, *Economic Foreign Policy of the United States* (1929). For fuller accounts consult National Industrial Conference Board, *The Inter-Ally Debts and the United States* (1925); H. G. Moulton and Leo Pasvolsky, *World War Debt Settlement* (1926); and *War Debts and World Prosperity* (1932).

Russian agents in the United States, the American government long refused to accord recognition to the Soviet government, although no attempt was made to prevent American firms from trading with Russia at their own risk.

Inevitably the problem of war debts became closely intertwined with the problem of German reparations. If Germany could meet her obligations to the Allies, then the Allies could make their payments to the United States. Any connection between these *Reparations* two problems was vigorously denied by the American government, but its existence in fact if not in theory was abundantly clear. The difficulties experienced by Germany in paying the extortionate sums required by the Reparations Commission in 1921 led to two efforts at readjustment, one in 1924, and another in 1929. It was significant that in each case the commission of experts entrusted with the negotiations was headed by an American, in the first instance by Charles G. Dawes, and in the second by Owen D. Young. The Dawes Plan reduced the sums required from Germany each year, arranged for a foreign loan to support the Germany monetary system, and required French withdrawal from the Ruhr. For four years, in large part by borrowing in the United States, Germany was able to meet the new payments, but by 1928 she was again in trouble. The Young Plan proposed another set of annuities to run for a period of fifty-nine years, the capitalized value of which would amount to only about ten billion dollars, approximately the sum due from the Allies to the United States. Further, it stipulated that additional reductions might be made proportional to any readjustments in the inter-Allied war debts; in other words, if the United States would reduce its demands, the Allies would also reduce theirs. But the Young Plan, too, overtaxed the resources of Germany, and after 1931 all reparation payments were discontinued. Altogether Germany had paid the Allies about four and one half billion dollars, more than half of which had been borrowed from American investors.[1]

The search for a means to insure world peace went on insistently throughout the period of Coolidge prosperity. Unfortunately the organizations most actively concerned with the problems were *The quest* in complete disagreement as to the best means to promote *for peace* the cause they held so dear. Peace-lovers of the Wilson school kept up the fight for American entrance into the League as the surest way to prevent the outbreak of war. They rejoiced when representatives of the United States, at first unofficially, but later on terms of entire equality, sat in on the non-political discussions of League committees, such, for

[1] Karl Bergmann, *History of Reparations* (1927).

example, as the conference on the opium traffic. Ultimately, they asserted, the United States could no longer ignore the obligations of membership. Others who still saw in the League nothing more than a convenient instrument for enforcement of an unjust peace urged that the United States should give its full support to the World Court. Still others, perhaps with greater faith than wisdom, believed that the peace could best be maintained by a simple declaration on the part of every nation that it would not resort to war. Chief leader of the third group, whose panacea was labeled the "outlawry of war," was Senator William E. Borah of Idaho. Most American politicians, including the President, were inclined to regard the "outlawry" scheme as impractical, and possibly contrary to the Constitution of the United States which specifically gave Congress the right to declare war, but a pact signed by seven European nations at Locarno in 1925 seemed to indicate a certain willingness on their part to flirt with the idea. By that document Germany, Belgium, France, Great Britain, and Italy undertook mutually to guarantee the peace of western Europe, and Germany agreed to arbitrate her disputes with France, Belgium, Poland, and Czechoslovakia. Further, the signatory powers agreed not to attack each other, not to invade each other's territory, and not to resort to war against each other, except for purposes of defense or in response to their obligations under the League of Nations, to which, it was decided, Germany must be admitted.

Hailed as at least a partial renunciation of the "right to make war," the Pact of Locarno stimulated the "outlawry" advocates in the United States to renewed endeavors. The United States, they pointed out, stood now almost alone in its resistance to every plan for world peace. They were soon aided by Aristide Briand, French foreign minister, who on April 6, 1927 — tenth anniversary of the entrance of the United States into the World War — urged a treaty between France and the United States similar to those agreed upon by the European nations at Locarno. What Briand really had in mind was to replace the Root Arbitration Treaty of 1908, which was due to expire in 1928, with a stronger one, but "outlawry" enthusiasts were quick to seize the opportunity he had given them. They persuaded the Secretary of State, Frank B. Kellogg of Minnesota, who had succeeded Hughes in 1925, to expand the scope of the negotiations. Replying to Briand, Kellogg said:

> It has occurred to me that the two governments, instead of contenting themselves with a bilateral declaration of the nature suggested by M. Briand, might make a more signal contribution to world peace by joining in an effort to obtain the adherence of all the principal Powers of the world to a declaration renouncing war as an instrument of national policy.

Kellogg's proposal resulted in prolonged negotiations which led finally to the signing at Paris, on August 27, 1928, of a general *The Kellogg-* treaty along the lines he had proposed.[1] The representa- *Briand Pact* tives of fifteen nations, including Japan, Italy, and Germany, affixed their signatures to a document which contained the following clauses:

> I. The High Contracting Parties solemnly declare in the names of their respective peoples that they condemn recourse to war for the solution of international controversies, and renounce it as an instrument of national policy in their relations with one another.
>
> II. The High Contracting Parties agree that the settlement or solution of all disputes or conflicts of whatever nature or of whatever origin they may be, which may arise among them, shall never be sought except by pacific means.

Ultimately sixty-two nations gave their adherence to the Kellogg Pact; but the futility of all such declarations, unless buttressed by a firm desire to live up to them, was soon demonstrated by the attacks of Japan on China, Italy on Ethiopia, and Germany on Poland, Denmark, Norway, the Netherlands, Belgium, and Luxemburg. The pact may, indeed, have lulled into a sense of security nations that might otherwise have been better prepared for the assaults of their predatory neighbors. Nevertheless, European statesmen saw significance in the willingness of the United States to co-operate at last, however faintly, in the effort to maintain world peace, but the customary Senate reservations revealed the microscopic nature of the involvement. Although the Senate ratified the treaty with only one dissenting vote, it insisted that there could be no curtailment of America's right of self-defense, that no obligations had been assumed which were incompatible with the Monroe Doctrine, and that the United States was not bound to take action against states that broke the treaty. Kellogg did the best he could to make the pact to which he had given his name a success. He negotiated supplementary treaties of arbitration with such nations as would consent to them, and took particular pains to make arbitration compulsory between the United States and other American nations.

The contradiction that existed between the American doctrine of isolation and economic realities was well illustrated by the agricultural problem that confronted the United States throughout the *American* decade of the twenties. The Republican formula for re- *agriculture* covery worked well for a while in industry, but it failed to achieve results

---

[1] D. H. Miller, *The Peace Pact of Paris* (1928); J. T. Shotwell, *War as an Instrument of National Policy* (1929); David Bryn-Jones, *Frank B. Kellogg* (1937).

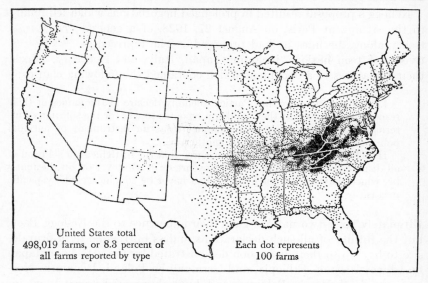

SELF-SUFFICING FARMS IN THE UNITED STATES
This type of farm indicates a lower standard of living than the commercial farm.

for the farmer primarily because the price of his principal products depended upon world-wide conditions of supply and demand. The United States produced far more wheat, for example, than it could possibly consume at home, and must sell its surplus abroad in competition with all the other wheat-producing nations. Thus the price of wheat in the United States depended upon the price of wheat on the world market; American prices differed from world prices only in the cost of transportation to a given foreign port. Manufacturers when confronted by a similar situation either reduced their output, or sometimes, with the help of the protective tariff, sold their excess product abroad at a loss, while keeping the American price high. But the farmer was able neither to control his surplus nor to take advantage of the tariff. As an individualist, each farmer raised what crops he chose, and sold to whomever he wished, while his wisest calculations might be completely upset by the weather. Nor could he without nation-wide organization maintain a two-price system, such as monopolistic industries found easily possible. With but few exceptions the high tariff rates on farm products did him no good. The price brought by the exportable surplus, and not the duties on mythical imports, set the price for whatever he had to sell.

With the experts in the United States Department of Agriculture, the economists in the agricultural colleges, and the businessmen whose prosperity depended upon farm sales all pointing to the export- *The Mc-* able surplus as the chief cause of the farmers' woes, it is not *Nary-* surprising that plans for its more advantageous disposal *Haugen Bill* were soon forthcoming. Of these the most publicized was embodied in the McNary-Haugen Bill, which was introduced into Congress as early as 1924. Its authorship could be traced directly to George N. Peek, president of the Moline Plow Company, and Hugh S. Johnson, his assistant and general counsel, who had both discovered that for their organization, at least, there could be no prosperity until the farmer was able to buy. What their measure was designed to do was to make the agricultural tariff effective by establishing a two-price system for American farm produce, one a tariff-protected price for the American market, and the other, the world price for the foreign market. A government agency should be established which during emergencies would buy up any given surplus at a price based upon pre-war averages, thus setting a higher price in the United States than existed abroad. The surplus might then be held for disposal until a lean year, or it might be sold to foreign buyers for whatever it would bring. In the latter case, the loss sustained was to be charged back against American producers by an equalization fee, but their net returns, it was believed, would be far higher than under existing conditions. "If it is a wise policy to protect industry in the East," they argued, "it must be equally wise to protect agriculture in the West."[1]

The McNary-Haugen Bill, in one form or another, was repeatedly before Congress during the Coolidge administration. It won the ardent support of nearly all the farm organizations, and of the Secretary of Agriculture, Henry C. Wallace, whose death in 1924, however, enabled the President to replace him with a man of less pronounced views. Twice, in 1924 and in 1926, the bill was voted down, largely because it failed to recognize the needs of the southern farmer, but in 1927, with the list of commodities to which it applied including cotton and tobacco along with wheat and corn, it passed the Senate by a vote of 51 to 43, and the House by a vote of 214 to 178. The opposition to "McNary-Haugenism" of President Coolidge and his cabinet, particularly the Secretary of Commerce, Herbert Hoover, had long been known, so that the veto message

[1] James E. Boyle, *Farm Relief: A Brief on the McNary-Haugen Plan* (1928); G. N. Peek and Samuel Crowther, *Why Quit Our Own* (1936); J. D. Black, *Agricultural Reform in the United States* (1929); Wilson Gee, *The Place of Agriculture in American Life* (1930); B. H. Hibbard, *Effects of the Great War upon Agriculture in the United States and Great Britain* (1919).

by which the measure was defeated occasioned little surprise. Next year the farmers again mobilized their strength, and pushed the bill through Congress by still more substantial majorities. But they met another veto, and they fell short of the two-thirds majority necessary to enact the measure without the President's consent. Opponents of the bill argued throughout the debates that the plan was "economically unsound." If it were adopted, the whole population would have to pay higher prices for food, while the farmer's certainty of good returns would invite ever larger and larger crops until the system itself would in time break down. They pointed, too, to the difficulties that would have been encountered in "dumping" the American surplus abroad at a time when many foreign nations were making every effort to build up their economic self-sufficiency.

As an alternative to the McNary-Haugen idea the Grange offered the export debenture plan, a somewhat simpler system for raising the price level of American farm products. Export bounties equal to one half the existing tariff rates on specified agricultural commodities — wheat, corn, rice, cotton, tobacco, swine, and cattle — were to be paid by the United States in the form of "debentures," which, in turn, would be receivable for customs. On the presumption that these debentures would be purchased at a discount by importers, proponents of the plan argued that the bounty to the farmers would come directly out of the protective tariff. No less than the McNary-Haugen Bill, the export debenture plan would serve to "get the farmers up on stilts" along with the manufacturers, whose high prices the tariff guaranteed. To forestall overexpansion it was proposed that a federal farm board be created with power to reduce or even to abolish the debentures in proportion as crop yields went up. But "sound economists" were as much opposed to the debenture as to the McNary-Haugen plan, while the farmers were less certain that it would work. Several times it was brought before Congress, but invariably it was voted down.

The export debenture plan

With farm prices believed to be well below the cost of production, the demand for farm relief threatened to become a principal issue in the presidential campaign of 1928. Would the President, in spite of the third-term tradition, seek re-election? Still the idol of the world of industry and finance, Coolidge's popularity seemed definitely on the wane in the Middle West; the flattery he received elsewhere for his "courage" in vetoing the McNary-Haugen Bill of 1927 was not echoed by farmers who compared the low prices they received for what they had to sell with the high tariff-protected prices they must pay for the things they had to

CALVIN COOLIDGE

HERBERT HOOVER

buy. Perhaps to regain western support the President that same year spent the summer vacation on a fishing trip in South Dakota. "He who, until last year, never threw a line into a stream — unless it was the muddy pool of politics. He who, posing as a farmer, has never been out of political office since maturity." It was difficult to see in this move anything other than a bid for renomination and re-election, but on August 2, 1927, Coolidge announced cryptically, "I do not choose to run for President in 1928." Whether he feared the opposition of the farmers, or wished merely to be drafted, may never be known. But he was taken at his word, and other aspirants for the Republican nomination immediately made their candidacies known.[1]

By the time the Republicans met in convention at Kansas City, June 12, 1928, it was evident that their candidate for President would be *Nomination* Herbert Hoover. This was a great disappointment to the *of Hoover* middle-western farmers who would have preferred Lowden of Illinois, a firm believer in the McNary-Haugen idea. But efforts to display their strength by means of "processions of Fords" to Kansas City failed to secure either the nomination of Lowden or the endorsement of the agricultural program for which he stood. When the convention went on record against McNary-Haugenism by a vote of 817 to 267, Lowden withdrew his candidacy, leaving Hoover virtually a clear field. Hoover had learned a great deal about politics since 1920 when his friends had mustered only thirteen votes for him in the nominating convention. He was not beloved by the politicians, for he was not one of them, and they questioned their ability to control him, but he had built up a strong personal following that the politicians dared not ignore. Hoover, more than any other man except Coolidge, was identified in the public mind with the exuberant prosperity that the country as a whole — the farmers excepted — had come to enjoy. He was popular with the masses precisely because he was not a politician. He was the best vote-getter in sight, and on that account the politicians dared not repeat the slight of 1920. On the eve of the convention Vare of Pennsylvania, a political boss of the old school, came out for Hoover, and Mellon, the Secretary of the Treasury, echoed the same sentiments. After these declarations the battle was over, and Hoover was nominated on the first ballot. For his running-mate, as a gesture of good-will toward the unhappy middle-western farmers, the convention chose Senator Charles Curtis of Kansas.

The Republican platform said little of the future, but it recited with gusto the accomplishments of the Coolidge administration, and credited

[1] Calvin Coolidge, *Autobiography* (1929).

it with the prosperity which the country enjoyed. Economy had been "raised to the dignity of a principle of government"; debt reduction and tax reduction had both been achieved; the protective tariff, "as vital to American agriculture as it is to American manufacturing," had been maintained; foreign debts had been adjusted and foreign trade promoted and expanded; the outlawry of war had been accomplished; the prohibition amendment had been loyally supported. As a substitute for the McNary-Haugen plan the platform offered a program known to have the support of the Republican nominee, a federal farm board which through stabilization corporations should attempt to push farm prices to higher levels. On the subject of labor, its declarations were somewhat hazy, although it admitted that the over-free use of injunctions in labor disputes presented "a serious question for legislation."

The Democratic nomination had also been decided in advance. Of the two leading contenders for the honor in 1924, McAdoo had been eliminated by the disclosure that he had received large fees *Smith and* from the oil interests, a reflection upon his judgment rather *Robinson* than upon his honesty. Furthermore, leaders of the conservative South and the radical West had resigned themselves to the necessity of allowing the city machines for once to name their candidate, and to find out by bitter experience whether he could win or not. Meeting in a southern city — Houston, Texas — for the first time since the Civil War, the southern and western delegates swallowed their misgivings and permitted the nomination of Smith on the first ballot, knowing full well that, as a Catholic, a wet, and a Tammany man, he was sure to have an uphill fight. For Vice-President the Democrats presented Senator Joseph T. Robinson of Arkansas, a Protestant and a dry from a state that had no large cities within its borders. But no one was deceived. The ticket of Smith and Robinson, despite its "one-hundred-per-cent American" names, represented primarily the descendants of recent immigrants who made up the bulk of the voting population in all the great cities of the East.

In view of their nomination of Smith, the Democrats had little need for a platform, for it was a certainty that their candidate would be their platform. They took occasion, however, to denounce the Republican record of corruption under Harding, to pledge a reform in banking that would prevent speculation, and to promise for agriculture equality with other industries. Perhaps in part because of the close relationship between tariff protection and the various plans of farm relief before the country, the Democrats retreated from their historic low-tariff position,

HIS SUCCESS IS ESSENTIAL To OURS!

SOMETHIN'S GOTTA BE DONE FOR HIM!

Courtesy of Clifford Berryman

WHAT A GRAND AND GLORIOUS FEELING!

and in language that might well have been borrowed from the Republicans urged tariff rates to equal the "actual differences between the cost of production at home and abroad." Toward labor they showed the greatest friendliness, denouncing the injunction evil, urging the construction of public works during times of unemployment, and emphasizing the protection of women and children in industry. On the Eighteenth Amendment, they declared for enforcement, but, as they had clearly foreseen, their candidate came out flatly for repeal. He also went beyond the commitments of the platform to give his whole-hearted endorsement to the McNary-Haugen plan for farm relief, including the equalization fee.

The two candidates for the Presidency afforded an unusual contrast. Herbert Hoover (1874–   ) was born at West Branch, Iowa, the son

Hoover of Quaker parents. Left an orphan at an early age, he worked his way through college, and ultimately graduated in mining engineering at Leland Stanford University. In pursuit of his specialty he saw much of the world — Mexico, Canada, Australia, India, China, and Russia — and as a promoter he amassed a modest fortune. Living in England at the outbreak of the World War, he was a natural choice to head overseas relief work, and served as chairman, first of the American Relief Commission, and later of the Commission for the Relief

[576]

of Belgium. In these offices, as Food Administrator during American participation in the World War, and as Secretary of Commerce he had demonstrated repeatedly his extraordinary ability as an administrator. His life-history was the typical American success story; with variations it could be made to fit the hopes of every normal American youth.

Alfred Emanuel Smith (1873–1944) had a background more unusual in a presidential candidate. He was born in an East-Side New York tenement, the son of humble working-class parents of Irish descent. He was perhaps no poorer than Hoover, but quite out of keeping with the American tradition he rose from the city side-walks rather than from the country cornfields. He attended parochial school, but never went to college. Thrust into politics as a birthright, he accepted without hesitation the rule of Tammany, and as an organization Democrat played the political game honestly according to the established rules. Once he was rewarded for faithful service by being made sheriff of New York County, a position that carried with it many lucrative fees, but most of the offices he held were not very remunerative. His career was crowned by his election for four terms as governor of New York. Liberal-minded, and devoted to the interests of the working classes from which he sprang, he displayed a rare genius for political administration and achieved noteworthy results in spite of constant opposition from a Republican controlled legislature.[1]

Smith

The development of the radio placed a new burden upon presidential candidates. No longer could they escape the limelight by a "front-porch" campaign. The public wanted to hear them and if possible also to see them. Smith yielded to the new technique, and toured the country extensively, speaking at various points before nation-wide hook-ups. With radio broadcasting still in its infancy, he failed to make a good impression. He spoke from notes rather than from manuscript, and, while fascinating enough to the audience before him, he was often in-audible or inarticulate to the listeners-in. Moreover, his New York accent and his occasional mispronunciations caused much unfavorable comment. Hoover, on the other hand, although a far less effective public speaker, poured what he had to say directly into the microphone, and it came out better than it went in. His pronunciation was no better than Smith's, but it was the kind that most Americans were themselves accustomed to use, and so gave little offense.

[1] Of the Smith biographies the best is H. F. Pringle, *Alfred E. Smith: A Critical Study* (1927). See also A. E. Smith, *Up to Now: An Autobiography* (1929). These accounts may be contrasted with the antagonistic W. H. Allen, *Al Smith's Tammany Hall* (1928), and M. R. Werner, *Tammany Hall* (1928). On the election in general see R. V. Peel and T. C. Donnelly, *The 1928 Campaign* (1931).

Ignoring his opponent, and scarcely admitting that he was conducting a campaign, Hoover gave a new dignity to the doctrines in which Republicans had long believed, but had not quite known how to defend. Convinced that in the American system of capitalism, with its constantly turning factory wheels, its high wage scales, and its widespread ownership, lay the key to permanent prosperity, he was vehemently opposed to anything savoring of socialism. Equality of opportunity was a priceless heritage that must be maintained at all costs, and strictly by traditional means. Individual enterprise, unhampered by governmental interference, had built the American nation, and through the same effective leadership the problems of the future could best be solved.

> We in America today are nearer to the final triumph over poverty than ever before in the history of any land. The poorhouse is vanishing from among us. We have not reached the goal, but given a chance to go forward with the policies of the last eight years, we shall soon with the help of God be in sight of the day when poverty will be banished from this nation.[1]

Hoover's triumphant victory at the polls in November was due primarily to four factors: (1) the belief which he assiduously cultivated *Hoover's* that the continuance of Republican rule meant the con- *victory* tinuance of prosperity; (2) the prejudice of rural America against the Tammany background of a corrupt machine based on immigrant votes from which Smith had risen; (3) the deep-seated opposition of many American Protestants to the elevation of a Catholic to the Presidency; and (4) the determination of the evangelical churches to retain prohibition, which Smith denounced, but Hoover called a "noble experiment." "Hoover Democrats," voting the Republican ticket in large numbers, shattered the solid South; for the first time since reconstruction the Republicans carried Virginia, North Carolina, Tennessee, Florida, and Texas. Smith also lost his own state, New York, and every western and border state. The electoral vote stood 444 to 87, and the popular vote 21,392,190 to 15,016,443. Naturally the Hoover landslide carried with it overwhelming Republican majorities in Congress and in some of the states. The heavy protest vote that had been cast for La Follette four years before had dwindled to a mere quarter of a million votes for Norman Thomas, the Socialist candidate.

The Hoover administration was certain to encounter difficulties even if it had been blessed with good times. The new President was funda-

---

[1] Hoover's well-reasoned restatement of the Republican creed is available in two widely distributed books, Herbert Hoover, *American Individualism* (1923), and *The New Day* (1928). The latter consisted of his campaign addresses in 1928. The same philosophy, oriented with reference to the New Deal, Hoover defended further in *The Challenge to Liberty* (1934), and *The American Road* (1938).

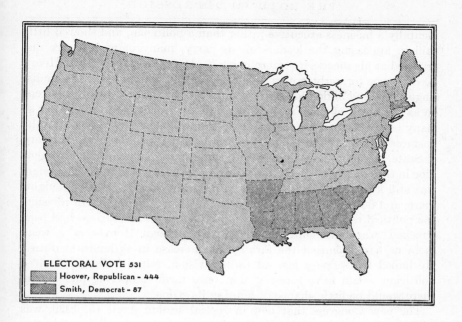

ELECTORAL VOTE 531
Hoover, Republican - 444
Smith, Democrat - 87

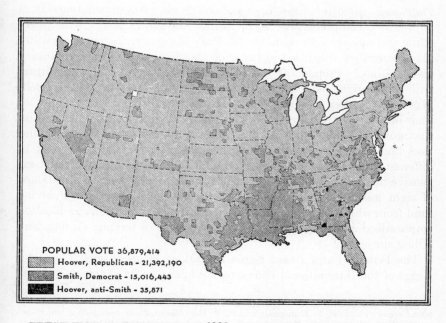

POPULAR VOTE 36,879,414
Hoover, Republican - 21,392,190
Smith, Democrat - 15,016,443
Hoover, anti-Smith - 35,871

PRESIDENTIAL ELECTION OF 1928, BY STATES AND BY COUNTIES

mentally a business executive rather than a politician, and showed little skill in appeasing the leaders of his party, many of whom were disgruntled at his success in "muscling in." His cabinet, headed by Henry L. Stimson, formerly governor-general of the Philippines, was undistinguished, and added little to his political strength. Mellon was kept on as Secretary of the Treasury less because Hoover wanted him, or so many believed, than because of the esteem in which he was held by the business interests of the country; all the others, including the Secretary of State, were virtually unknown to the general public. The insurgent bloc in the Senate, while reduced in numbers as a result of the campaign, was still strong and troublesome. Prohibition was sure to be a nightmare, and farm relief a perpetual despair. Furthermore, tariff revision, the political reef upon which many preceding administrations had been wrecked, was imminent. During the campaign Hoover in a weak moment had promised the farmers an increase in agricultural duties. He hoped to escape a general tariff revision, but a more experienced politician would have foreseen that once tariff tampering had begun, there would be little chance of limiting its scope.

The new Congress that met in special session April 15, 1929, was willing to go along with Hoover on the subject of farm relief, and in two *The Federal* months' time had embodied his recommendations in a *Farm Board* comprehensive Agricultural Marketing Act. The pricefixing and subsidy features of the McNary-Haugen and export debenture plans were now discarded in favor of an effort to stimulate voluntary co-operation. Proponents of the measure believed that agriculture, with appropriate federal encouragement, would be able to save itself. Working together through co-operatives, the farmers could apply to their business the same principles of orderly production and distribution that governed the activities of a prudent manufacturer. They could thus find means to curtail production whenever necessary, to shift to different crops as demands changed, and to eliminate wasteful and expensive methods of marketing. The act created a Federal Farm Board of eight members, and provided it with a half-billion-dollar revolving fund from which it could lend to co-operatives, and to such stabilization corporations as it might set up for the purpose of buying, storing, and selling surpluses.[1]

The Federal Farm Board began operations at once, with Alexander Legge of the International Harvester Company as its chairman. In its

[1] E. R. A. Seligman, *The Economics of Farm Relief* (1929); Bernhard Ostrolenk, *The Surplus Farmer* (1932); E. F. Dummeier and R. B. Heflebower, *Economics with Applications to Agriculture* (1934); E. G. Nourse and associates, *America's Capacity to Produce* (1934).

efforts to stimulate the formation of co-operatives it was entirely successful, and loans for this purpose during the first year of its operation amounted to over $165,000,000. There is no reason to doubt that these activities contributed significantly to the orderly marketing of nearly every type of crop produced in the United States. Much sound advice was also distributed as to the curtailment of production in crops where the market was glutted, although other governmental agencies, particularly the Department of Agriculture and the agricultural colleges, considerably confused the situation by explaining to the farmers how more and more of the same commodities might be grown on less but better soil.

With respect to wheat and cotton it soon became apparent that something far more drastic than co-operative marketing was necessary if the rapid downward trend of prices was to be stopped. *Stabilization* Accordingly, in 1930, a Grain Stabilization Corporation and *activities* a Cotton Stabilization Corporation were set up, each with authority to buy in the open market in order to raise prices. As long as governmental purchases continued, the effect on the price of wheat and cotton was good, but after a year or two the Stabilization Corporations found themselves in possession of vast stores of produce that they were unable to market. In June, 1931, the Grain Corporation, with an unmarketed and seemingly unmarketable supply of 257,000,000 bushels of wheat on its hands, ceased its purchases, and the next month the price of wheat dropped to fifty-seven cents. Meantime, the Cotton Corporation, after purchasing the carry-over from two successive seasons, had accumulated three and a quarter million bales of cotton in its warehouses, and was also forced to acknowledge defeat. In 1932 the price of cotton dropped to as low as five cents a pound. The following year the Federal Farm Board ended its brief career with total losses set at about $184,000,000. No doubt it also had much to its credit, but its tangible benefits were difficult to discover or assess.[1]

Meantime, Congress had plunged eagerly into the revision of the tariff that Hoover had promised. For months before the special session of Congress convened, the House Ways and Means Com- *The Hawley-* mittee had been holding hearings, and on May 7, 1929, its *Smoot* chairman, Willis C. Hawley of Oregon, introduced a bill *Tariff* that did not far exceed the limited recommendations of the President.

---

[1] The activities of the Hoover administration are covered intimately and defended in two difficult books, W. S. Myers and W. H. Newton, *The Hoover Administration: A Documented Narrative* (1936), and R. L. Wilbur and A. M. Hyde, *The Hoover Policies* (1937). A very different point of view is presented in R. G. Tugwell, *Mr. Hoover's Economic Policy* (1932); see also W. S. Myers, *The Foreign Policies of Herbert Hoover, 1929–1933* (1940).

But a log-rolling generosity at once developed which resulted in the amendment of the original bill to suit the demands of practically every congressman with a constituency to conciliate. As it passed the House later in the month, the Hawley Bill was already a general revision of the tariff with a scale of duties far higher than those of the record-breaking Fordney-McCumber Act of 1922. The Senate Finance Committee, headed by Reed Smoot of Utah, altered the bill in detail, but not greatly in principle. When the Senate debate opened, insurgency developed, and for a time it seemed that a coalition of Democrats and independent Republicans might bring about some important readjustments. Unfortunately a succession of deals with individual members of the coalition weakened the opposition and made possible the retention of the extremely high rates. Some of the supposedly most intransigent insurgents were induced to vote for increases that they would otherwise have opposed in order to obtain in return increases that pressure groups among their constituents earnestly desired. Such insurgents as could not be bought off tried to improve the measure by including within it the export debenture plan for the relief of agriculture, and a flexible schedule clause which would have given Congress rather than the President authority to act on changes recommended by the Tariff Commission; but ultimately, largely because of pressure from the President, both provisions were stricken out. The Hawley-Smoot Tariff, as it came from the conference committee, accepted in the main the higher rates proposed by either house, and raised the general level of protection by about seven per cent. In the Senate the final vote was 44 to 42. Five Democrats, from Louisiana (sugar), Florida (fruit), and Wyoming (wool), voted with the majority, while eleven Republicans and one Farmer-Laborite voted against it.

In spite of a rising volume of criticism directed against the measure, Hoover gave it his signature. It was not what he had wished, and he did not disguise his disappointment; but neither did he heed the petition of more than a thousand American economists who explained cogently the pressing need for a presidential veto. According to this "round robin," which was signed by practically all the leading economists of the country, the Hawley-Smoot Tariff was certain (1) to raise prices for the American consumer; (2) to encourage wasteful and unnecessary concerns to remain in business; (3) to limit the exportation of American products, both from farm and factory, by restricting imports, (4) to yield no benefits to the farmers whose prices were fixed by what the exportable surplus would bring; and (5) to insure reprisals from foreign countries whose trade would be adversely affected. Probably all of

Acme

HENRY FORD

these predictions came true, but on the last there was no room for doubt. While the bill was under consideration, protests against its passage were registered by trade associations in nearly every European country, and immediately after its passage reprisals set in. One of the first came from Canada, which promptly increased the rates on most of its important imports from the United States, and others came thick and fast. In 1932 Great Britain, whose devotion to free trade had long been slipping, veered completely over to the protective tariff policy. For the establishment of these higher trade barriers in the face of world-wide depression the United States bore a leading responsibility.[1]

Long before the passage of the Hawley-Smoot Tariff the Great De-

[1] J. M. Jones, *Tariff Retaliation* (1934).

[583]

pression had begun. It was preceded, quite in the fashion of many *Background* previous depressions, by a prolonged period of speculation, *of the Great* this time mainly in the stocks and bonds of business cor-*Depression* porations. The prosperity of the twenties was to a remarkable extent corporation prosperity. Few individuals owned great businesses; Henry Ford was an outstanding exception. Most "big businesses" were jointly owned by hundreds or thousands of stockholders, whose investments might vary from a hundred-dollar share to values running far into the millions. Throughout the prosperous twenties the multiplication of stocks went on with ever-increasing tempo, and into such investments multitudes of individuals placed their savings, great and small. The fact that American business was actually owned by millions of investors was regarded with satisfaction by President Hoover and others as proof of its essential democracy, but any careful examina tion of corporation statistics was apt to prove that a comparatively small number of investors owned the greater part of the stock. Moreover, the direction of a given industry lay inevitably with the few insiders represented on boards of directors. In a sense the control of business was less democratic than ever before. With investments so widely diffused, the individual with a three per cent holding might be as powerful as the majority stockholder of an earlier age.

While many of those who purchased stocks were genuinely interested in obtaining sound investments, many others operated only as specula-*Stock* tors, buying when prices were low, and selling when they *speculation* rose. Most small purchasers bought "on margin," depositing only enough money with their brokers to cover the probable range of fluctuation. They were sure to encounter difficulties if their guesses went wrong. This speculative demand for stocks was to a great extent responsible for the generally high price-level to which securities rose during the later twenties. More frequently than not the actual earning power of a given stock was far too low to justify the prices at which it sold; valuations equal to twenty-five times the interest returns were by no means uncommon. Optimists refused to be alarmed at the situation, and insisted that the high prices paid for American securities were merely an evidence of the healthy condition of American enterprise. Investors had faith, and were willing to back it with their dollars, in the soundness of American business. Even the Federal Reserve Board, at least indirectly, supported the speculation, for it allowed loans to corporations ostensibly interested in programs of expansion, only to see the funds so obtained quickly passed along to the speculators. Between September, 1927, and September, 1929, borrowings for speculation on the

New York Stock Exchange rose from three and one third to eight and one half billion dollars. Prices of stocks, in the language of one misguided observer, soared upward to "what looks like a permanently high plateau." An issue never known to pay a dividend climbed steadily from forty dollars to four hundred and fifty dollars a share.

In the midst of all this madness a few warning voices pointed out that the business cycle might not be as obsolete as many seemed to believe, and that a crisis was probably close at hand. Too much of the country's credit was being diverted into stock-exchange loans, and industry as a result of the easy money was being tempted to overexpand. Who was to buy all the goods that producers could make and sell? Already the building boom that had characterized the earlier twenties was on the decline, automobile sales were off, and oil production far exceeded the demand. But these wise protests were brushed aside by optimists in high places who counseled against selling America short, and assured investors that all was well. Two days before the market crashed, Charles E. Mitchell, president of the National City Bank of New York, asserted unequivocally: "I know of nothing fundamentally wrong with the stock market or with the underlying business and credit structures."

The stock-market collapse came in October, 1929, when English interest rates were raised to six and one half per cent in order to bring home needed capital that had been attracted to the United *Panic* States by the high speculative profits. As a result many *of 1929* European holdings were thrown on the market, and prices began to sag. Frightened at the prospect, and no longer able to borrow at will, American speculators also began to unload. On Thursday, October 24, 1929, 12,800,000 shares changed hands, and until October 29, when the sales reached 16,410,030 shares, the frantic selling continued. During the month of October the value of stocks listed on the New York Stock Exchange declined from eighty-seven billion to fifty-five billion dollars, or about thirty-seven per cent. And this, it developed, was only the beginning. In spite of repeated assurances from high authorities, both in government and finance, that prosperity lay "just around the corner," no less than nine similar declines to "new low levels" were recorded within the next three years. By the first of March, 1933, the value of all stocks listed on the New York Stock Exchange was set at only nineteen billion dollars, less than one fifth the inflated figures of October 1, 1929.

In spite of optimistic efforts to maintain that the stock-market collapse was purely a paper loss which would not seriously undermine the fundamental soundness of American business, it was soon evident that a period of unparalleled depression had begun. Prices dropped sharply; foreign trade fell off; factories curtailed production, or in many cases closed their doors never to reopen them; real estate values (but not mortgages) declined; new construction, except on governmental works, practically ceased; banks went under; worst of all, wages were cut drastically and unemployment figures began to mount. By the end of 1930 about six or seven million workers were out of jobs; two years later the number had doubled. Nor was the United States alone in its distress. No longer able to secure American loans, foreign nations fell likewise into the abyss of depression; indeed, many of them, like Germany, had not far to fall. Once again the isolationist-minded people of the United States were to learn by experience that whatever seriously affected one great nation was bound to affect all.

Efforts to account for the plunge from prosperity to adversity soon demonstrated conclusively that no one factor alone, but only a great *Causes of* number of factors working together, could have produced *the depres-* such startling results. Economists were also able to reach *sion* substantial agreement as to the principal causes of the depression, although they were by no means in harmony as to the degree of responsibility to be assigned to each cause.[1] Among other disturbing influences they cited the following:

1. Agricultural overexpansion, both in the United States and elsewhere. American farmers produced more wheat, cotton, corn, livestock, *Agricultural* and other commodities than they could sell at satisfactory *overexpan-* prices, and to some extent the same condition existed in *sion* much of the rest of the world. Agricultural surpluses piled up at home and abroad with devastating effect on the price of each new crop. Farm purchases steadily declined, for the farmers had less and less with which to buy. Payments on the heavy mortgage burden assumed in more prosperous times still further curtailed the farmers' buying power, and drove many of them to tenancy.

2. Industrial overexpansion. The American industrial plant had been overbuilt during the period of the boom, and could not be operated at *Industrial* maximum capacity. There were too many factories, and *overexpan-* too much machinery. American industry was geared to *sion* produce far more than it could sell. Automobiles, for example, had been turned out in steadily increasing numbers during the

---

[1] The analysis of causes given in Brookings Institution, *The Recovery Problem in the United States* (1936), may be compared with the similar attempt in Hacker, *American Problems of Today.* See also W. Z. Ripley, *Main Street and Wall Street* (1927); W. B. Donham, *Business Adrift* (1931); Fred A. Shannon, *America's Economic Growth* (1940); and, for a popular account, G. V. Seldes, *The Years of the Locust: America, 1929–1932* (1933).

twenties to supply a new market. But the time came when every American family that could afford to own an automobile (and many who could not) had one or sometimes more than one. With twenty-six and one half million motor cars in operation by 1929, the market for automobiles was confined largely to replacements. The same condition existed in the housing industry. Rapid building during the twenties had overexpanded the lumber industry and others concerned with the production of building materials. But the time came when all the people who could afford to build new houses had built them, and plants that had once flourished stood idle.

3. The increasing effectiveness of machines. Ingenious labor-saving devices made possible greater production with comparatively less labor. Fewer and fewer men produced more and more goods. *Labor-saving* "Technological unemployment" might not be permanent, *machines* but at least the men who were thrown out of work by the new machines had to seek other jobs, and they sometimes failed to find them. Thus the buying power of labor was diminished. The new machines might make more goods, but whose wages were to pay for them? Introduction of these labor-saving devices might well have been paralleled by increased wages, a shortening of the labor day and the labor week, and a diminishing use of women and children in industry. But only occasionally were such accompaniments recorded.

4. Capital surpluses were too high; as a prominent banker, Frank A. Vanderlip, expressed it, "Capital kept too much and labor did not have enough to buy its share of things." [1] This was the more *Capital* easily possible because of the monopolistic nature of much *surpluses* American business, which so greatly facilitated the control of prices. Throughout the boom years the tendency of business was to take too long profits, and to reinvest the capital thus accumulated in order to produce still more goods, which in return might produce still more profits. A wider distribution of earnings, particularly if paid out in the form of higher wages, might well have stimulated purchasing power and diminished the danger of ultimate collapse.

5. The overexpansion of credit, both for productive and consumptive purposes. Money was plentiful and cheap throughout the twenties, and the policy of the Federal Reserve Board was definitely *Over-* to keep it so. It was too easy to borrow, whether for busi- *expansion* ness expansion, for speculation, or for the satisfaction of *of credit* personal desires. There was too much installment buying, and too much

[1] Quoted by L. M. Hacker and B. B. Kendrick, *The United States Since 1865* (1932), p. 729.

of the national income was diverted into interest payments. In keeping with the speculative spirit of the time, purchasers cheerfully mortgaged their futures to obtain goods that would often be consumed before they could be paid for.

6. International trade was out of balance. European nations, with their economies badly shattered by the war, had depended mainly on *Decline of* funds borrowed from American investors to pay for imports *international* and to stabilize foreign exchange. The only way they *trade* might have repaid these obligations was by shipping goods to the United States. But the Fordney-McCumber Act of 1922, followed by the Hawley-Smoot Act of 1930, definitely forestalled any such possibility. The debtor nations of Europe in self-defense were obliged to adopt high-tariff policies, and by various other expedients to stimulate whatever industries were necessary to cut down their reliance on foreign goods. During the years of 1922–27 the production of British-made automobiles, for example, was increased from forty-nine per cent of the domestic supply to eighty-six per cent. Thus the United States, blindly committed to the protective principles of an earlier age, stood to lose both its export business and a good share of the money by which this business had been sustained. Many manufacturers understood the situation, and did their best to prevent the adoption of tariffs that in the long run were certain to bring disaster, but most Americans were slow to recognize that international trade was a "two-way street," and were quite unprepared for the collapse that followed the withdrawal of American credits.

7. Political unrest throughout the world, particularly in Europe, Asia, and South America, added to the difficulties in the way of a sustained *Political* prosperity. The intergovernmental debts, whether funded *unrest* or not, constituted a continuing threat both to trade and to international good feelings. The reparations problem remained unsettled. Most countries were overburdened with governmental debts, and few national budgets were in balance. Agitation for independence was chronic in India, the designs of Japan toward China were abundantly clear, and warfare soon broke out between Bolivia and Paraguay over the Chaco. Altogether the international skies seemed dark, and the prospects of a return to "normalcy" as far away as ever. [1]

---

[1] George Soule, *Prosperity Decade* (1947), treats of the period 1917–1929 from the economic point of view. Frank Graham, *Al Smith, American: An Informal Biography* (1945), is a good re-evaluation of an outstanding character of the period. John E. Stoner, *S. O. Levinson and the Pact of Paris: A Study in the Techniques of Influence* (1942), is informing on the "outlawry of war" movement.

CHAPTER XXVI

THE NEW AMERICAN WAY

IT SEEMS PROBABLE that the automobile effected a greater change in the American way of life than ever proceeded from any other single cause.[1] The civilization of the nineteenth century remained to the *The auto-* end a "horse-and-buggy" affair; the civilization of the *mobile* twentieth century was soon geared to the automobile. Starting from insignificance during the later nineties, the automobile industry by the time of the Great Depression outranked all others in importance, even steel. The new system of mass production at low cost which it introduced put motor transportation within the financial reach of nearly every American family; by 1929 twenty-six and one half million motor cars of one kind or another were registered in the United States. The requirements of automobile travelers stimulated a movement for good roads, one significant result of which was to bring the city closer to the country, and the country to the city. With good roads available family vacations could be taken far from home, and every summer huge armies of tourists took to the road. Because the owner of an automobile might live a considerable distance from his work, suburban developments expanded as never before. Buses and trucks took over the short-haul traffic of streetcars and railroads. Hazards to life and health increased as traffic speeded up, and automobile accidents soon provided one of the commonest causes of death or injury. Crime was made easy, for the automobile assured law-breakers of a ready means of escape. Thousands of pleasure-bent children and youths at large on the roads increased the worries of parents, and drove the chaperon out of business. As a visiting senator from Hawaii complained, there were always "too many people in too many cars in too much of a hurry going in too many different directions to nowhere for nothing."

---

[1] The best study of American society during the twenties is P. W. Slosson, *The Great Crusade and After, 1914–1928* (1930). C. A. Beard and Mary R. Beard, *America in Mid-passage* (1939), which also features social history, begins where their *Rise of American Civilization* leaves off. Much useful material is contained in the President's Research Committee on Social Trends, *Recent Social Trends in the United States* (2 vols., 1933).

[589]

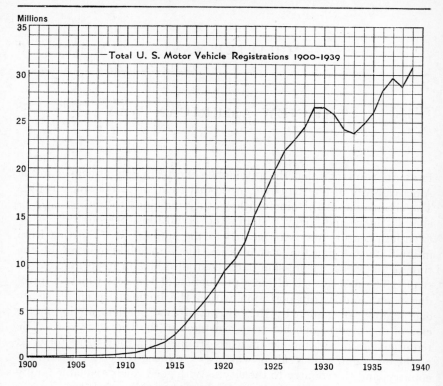

AUTOMOBILES IN USE 1900-1939

"The saga of the motor car" was intimately connected with the life-history of Henry Ford, whose dream of a good low-cost car was realized *Henry* in an incredibly short time. Beginning at Detroit as early *Ford* as 1893, Ford was making a fairly dependable car by the turn of the century, and by 1914 had produced a half-million of his famous "Model T." It was an unsightly car, designed for service and not for beauty, but it would run and it was cheap. Ford's methods of production were even more important than the car he built, for he used standardized, interchangeable parts, and by means of a "production line," along which each workman did his one assigned task and no other, he brought the process of manufacturing to a new level of efficiency. Other producers gave him competition, particularly the General Motors Corporation, which was established by William C. Durant as early as 1908. But for a long time Ford held the upper hand in the

[590]

1771 — The Cugnot Steam Wagon

1889 — Serpollet (Steam)

1893 — Haynes

1906 — Stanley Steamer

1910 — Oldsmobile

Modern Sedan

EVOLUTION OF THE AUTOMOBILE

small-car field, and not until 1927 would he retool his plants in order to produce a better-looking car, the "Model A." Meantime, cars of every size and price had found their market, although three great companies, the Ford, the General Motors, and the Chrysler-Dodge companies controlled all together about four fifths of the motor-car industry. Almost alone among manufacturers Ford continued to own and operate his own company, and consistently refused to impair his complete control by selling stock to outsiders. He paid high wages, but had little use for labor unions, and demanded the complete loyalty of his employees.[1]

Second only to the automobile in their revolutionary results were the "movies," or as they were more properly called, motion pictures. This *The* "*movies*" new form of amusement was the gift of America's greatest inventor, Thomas A. Edison, who had worked out most of the essential principles of the process before 1900. But the earliest movies were of interest merely because of their scientific novelty, and not because they presented pictures worth seeing. Prize-fights, parades, street crowds, and news events provided the material for the first reels, which were shown sometimes in connection with vaudeville performances, and sometimes as independent "nickel shows" in abandoned store buildings, Chautauqua tents, or other improvised quarters. But improvements were gradually introduced, and producers soon learned to unfold a story on the screen that the public would like to watch. After a period in which they imitated too closely the legitimate theater, they learned at last to suit the action to the techniques they were able to employ. The showing in 1915 of the *Birth of a Nation* marked the beginning of a new era in which the "silent drama" carried everything before it. This picture, based upon Thomas Dixon's *The Clansman*, set forth effectively the agonies endured by the South during reconstruction. It was cheered by packed houses in North and South alike, and revealed clearly the profit possibilities of the new industry. With interest assured, elaborate motion-picture theaters appeared in every town and city, the price of admission was raised, and in southern California, where the sun shone dependably a good share of the year, the making of motion pictures became a major occupation. Film artists, such as Charlie Chaplin, Douglas Fairbanks, and Mary Pickford, were soon better known than politicians, and magazines devoted exclusively to the doings of the movie colony began to appear on most of the newsstands.

The movies had just succeeded in outgrowing their early crudities when the invention of talking pictures forced them to start all over

[1] Henry Ford, *My Life and Work* (1922); S. T. Bushnell, *The Truth About Henry Ford* (1922); H. L. Barber, *Story of the Automobile* (1917).

again.   In October, 1927, Al Jolson's success in *The Jazz Singer* proved that sound effects had come to stay, and within two *Talking* years' time the movies had everywhere been converted into *pictures* "talkies."   The change eliminated scores of actors whose voices were unsuited to sound transmission, but it also served to open the profession to artists of the legitimate stage who had formerly regarded the screen performances with unconcealed contempt.   Many competent artists passed back and forth freely from one medium to another, while successful plays on the legitimate stage were often reproduced in the movies. One of the best received of these was *The Barretts of Wimpole Street*, by Rudolph Bezier, in which the screen star, Norma Shearer, imitated closely the admirable acting of Katherine Cornell, America's greatest actress, on the legitimate stage.   While many inferior pictures were made, the public tended more and more to become conscious of good acting, and to demand it as a matter of course.   With the increasing perfection of sound instruments, musical plays grew rapidly in favor, paving the way for the successes of such singing artists as Jeanette MacDonald and Deanna Durbin.   Walt Disney's *Silly Symphonies* introduced a new technique, the animated cartoon, which won many a well-earned laugh, and graduated eventually into the wholly admirable *Snow White and the Seven Dwarfs*.   The invention of technicolor gave great vitality to the films that employed it, but was less generally used than had been anticipated.   It attained a high degree of perfection in Margaret Mitchell's *Gone with the Wind*, starring Clark Gable and Vivien Leigh, which was produced in 1939.   In general American pictures were preferred not only in the United States, but in many foreign countries also, but the popularity of such British films as *The Private Life of Henry VIII*, in which Charles Laughton played the title-rôle, showed that American producers could not safely ignore British competition.

The significance of the movies in American life was difficult to assess, but hard to overemphasize.   Practically everyone, of high or low degree, attended the motion-picture shows with more or less regu- *Influence of* larity, and for the rising generation the lessons they taught *the movies* were doubtless far more effective than the precepts of the schoolroom. The suggestions of the screen as to styles, manners, taste in furniture and art, and even morals, did not go unnoticed.   It seems reasonable to suppose, for example, that there was some causal relationship between the popularity of the *Birth of a Nation* and the subsequent revival of the Ku Klux Klan.   Pictures featuring the careers of criminals may also have accounted for numerous juvenile delinquencies, while such feminine fashions as the universal use of cosmetics probably owed at least as much to Hollywood as to Paris. Since the same movies were shown everywhere, they tended to emphasize strongly the national tendency toward uniformity. Probably the well-modulated voices and correct speaking of the film artists did far more than the high-school teachers of English to make young Americans talk better and talk alike. Whether the morals of movie actors and actresses were above or below the average for the country as a whole would be difficult to prove, but the interest of stage stars in publicity, whatever the cost, made their doings generally known, and they may have had imitators. Censorship of pictures, sometimes effective but often of little consequence, was established in nearly every state, but producers learned mainly by trial and error what would be well received and what would not. As a kind of supreme arbiter in all matters of public relations, the picture industry chose Will H. Hays, who resigned as Postmaster-General under Harding to accept the assignment.[1]

Another new influence upon American life was furnished by the radio. Wireless telegraphy and telephony were known before the outbreak of *Radio* the first World War, but during that struggle they proved to be of such tremendous military value that revolutionary improvements were made within a few years' time. After the war radio "fans," whose interest was primarily that of amateur scientists, bought millions of dollars' worth of equipment, and counted with joy the number of distant stations they could hear. By 1920 the manufacturers of radio supplies were beginning to furnish programs as a means of promoting the use of what they had to sell, and from this practice the institution of radio broadcasting developed. The pioneer station in this endeavor was KDKA of Pittsburgh, which among other things successfully broadcast the returns of the election of 1920. Soon many broadcasting stations, generously supported by advertisers, were competing for control of the air, and to prevent complete chaos Secretary Hoover maintained an informal system of licensing in the Commerce Department. When in 1926 the Attorney-General ruled that the Secretary of Commerce was exceeding his legal authority, the resulting confusion led Congress to establish next year a Federal Radio Commission of five members with the right to license broadcasting stations, and to determine the power, wave-lengths, and hours of operation to be allotted to each. Presently chains of stations, linked together at first as "stunts" but later because of the advantages observed, formed nation-wide net-

[1] Alice M. Mitchell, *Children and Movies* (1929); H. B. Franklin, *Sound Motion Pictures* (1929); W. M. Seabury, *The Public and the Motion Picture Industry* (1926); Federal Council of the Churches of Christ in America, *The Public Relations of the Motion Picture Industry* (1931).

[594]

Clear
Regional
Local

RADIO BROADCASTING STATIONS IN THE UNITED STATES

works over which the same program could be transmitted to every receiving set in the country. Steady improvements by what speedily became one of America's biggest businesses soon enabled listeners also to hear and enjoy broadcasts by short wave from abroad.[1]

The influence of the radio on American society is as difficult to assess as the influence of motion pictures. It furnished a new weapon for the use of advertisers, who found that through broadcasting they could reach an audience that was hardly touched by the billboards, the newspapers, and the periodicals. Experts were soon able to chart with accuracy the effects of a new program or a change of hour upon the sales volume of those who paid for time on the air. It introduced a new form of dramatic art which must appeal only to the ear, as the first movies had appealed only to the eye. Such comedians as Amos 'n' Andy, whose black-face make-up had to be imagined, and Charlie McCarthy, a ventriloquist's creation, became fireside favorites. It stimulated interest in music, including good music, and the type of broadcasts heard during the Ford Hour, the General Motors Hour, and the RCA Magic Key Hour made millions of ordinary citizens familiar with the works of the great composers. It provided also a powerful means for swaying public opinion. During election years candidates for President could argue their cases with the whole nation as an audience; radio orators such as Father Coughlin could build up nation-wide followings; and promoters of almost any cause, good or bad, could get a hearing for a price. News bulletins, usually timed to appear after the newspapers carrying the same items were on the streets, acquainted the listener with what was going on in the world, and a host of able commentators interpreted the news. Crises in diplomacy, such as those that preceded the outbreak of the second World War, were followed by the whole American people with an intensity of interest that newsprint seemed powerless to evoke. Television was soon a laboratory possibility, but many technical and financial considerations barred it from general use.

Less immediately effective upon the lives of individuals, but fraught with great potentialities, was the airplane. As early as 1903 Orville and *The airplane* Wilbur Wright had made successful flights with power-driven planes at Kitty Hawk, North Carolina, and an incredulous world was soon convinced that the thing could be done. When war broke out in 1914, aviation was still in its infancy, but the importance of aircraft, at first for scouting purposes and later for use in actual combat, led to revolutionary improvements in design and construction.

[1] Paul Schubert, *The Electric Word: The Rise of the Radio* (1928); Federal Council of the Churches of Christ in America, *Broadcasting and the Public* (1938).

[596]

1896 — Lilienthal Glider

1894 – 1903
Langley (Power)

1903 — Wright Brothers
(Glider)

1917 — Lawson Air Liner

1927 — Lindbergh
(Spirit of St. Louis)

Modern Trans-Atlantic Liner

EVOLUTION OF THE AIRPLANE

Among other things American inventors pooled their knowledge to produce the new "Liberty motor," an admirable engine, but the war was over before it could be turned out in large enough numbers to have had any important effect on the result. After the war "gypsy" fliers, who made a precarious living by taking passengers up in the air for the thrill they would get, kept the public conscious of the airplane, and prepared the way for its use in commercial transportation. "Stunt fliers" also revealed its possibilities, particularly for long-distance flights. The Atlantic was crossed by way of the Azores as early as May, 1919; from Newfoundland to Ireland in June of the same year; and from Great Britain to New York by a British dirigible the following July. But the achievement that most caught the country's fancy was the solo flight of Charles A. Lindbergh, a youthful aviator who took off from Roosevelt Field, Long Island, on May 20, 1927, and thirty-three hours later landed successfully in the vicinity of Paris.[1] By order of President Coolidge Lindbergh was brought home on a warship, and rose immediately to the status of the nation's greatest hero. The fact that he was not the first to fly the Atlantic, and that two other Americans, Clarence D. Chamberlain and C. A. Lewis, flying from the same field on July 4 for Berlin, got within a hundred miles of their destination, in no wise diminished Lindbergh's fame. Later in the month Commander Richard E. Byrd at the head of a party of four also flew to Europe, and two army aviators reached Honolulu from California, while in June, 1931, Wiley Post flew around the world in less than eight days' time.

The development of commercial aviation in the United States did not begin in earnest until several years after the signing of the armistice, *Air mail* although the government early gave its assistance by air-mail contracts.[2] By 1924 a regular mail service had been established between New York and San Francisco, and four years later there were as many as forty-eight airways in the United States, covering twenty thousand miles, and serving three hundred and fifty-five cities. Most of these lines depended upon government mail contracts for their profits, and regarded the incidental carrying of passengers or freight as somewhat of a nuisance. When Hoover became President in 1929 his Postmaster-General, Walter Folger Brown, resolved to remedy this situation. The government subsidies were paid, he believed, not merely for carrying the mail, but also to encourage the development of a new

---

[1] C. A. Lindbergh, "*We*" (1927), is the story of this flight. On the development of the airplane see Mark Sullivan, *Our Times*, II, and Faulkner, *Quest for Social Justice*.

[2] The slow progress of commercial aviation in the United States is evident from W. J. Davis, *The World's Wings* (1927).

and useful means of transportation which might incidentally serve the country well in time of war. Brown wrote new contracts, which, by abandoning the "per pound" basis for carrying the mail in favor of the "space-mile" principle, placed a premium on the building of larger planes. He also used his discretionary power in the awarding of contracts in such a way as to eliminate the small operators, whose ability to develop the industry was obviously less than that of the well-established and adequately financed lines.

As a result of Brown's policy American aviation was able to survive the blows it suffered from the Depression. Many "little fellows" went under, but great systems developed which brought transportation by air into common use, and placed American airplanes among the wonders of the world. Passenger comfort became a matter of first importance, and sufficient private business was obtained by the air lines to make possible the gradual reduction of governmental subsidies. It was inevitable, however, that the success of the large, government-aided operators should arouse the jealousy of their less favored competitors, and bitter complaints were poured into the receptive ears of James Farley, who became Postmaster-General after the election of 1932. Convinced that collusion had existed between his predecessor and the various successful bidders, Farley cancelled all domestic air-mail contracts by an order of February 19, 1934, and for two weeks the country was without any air-mail service whatever. Then the President ordered the army air corps to take over the task of carrying the mails, but the army pilots were unaccustomed to the highly specialized type of flying required, and in quick succession a dozen of them lost their lives. As speedily as possible, new air-mail legislation was rushed through Congress, and new contracts were let to commercial companies, but the government's change of policy resulted, to say the least, in much temporary confusion. By the Mead-McKellar Air-Mail Act of 1935 the Interstate Commerce Commission was given power to raise or lower rates of payment under existing mail contracts, an innovation that served somewhat to emancipate the air lines from the complete control of the Post-Office Department.

Regardless of its difficulties with the government the aviation industry was soon expanding with great rapidity. A six-cents letter rate, introduced June 1, 1934, greatly increased the volume of mail *Passenger* carried by air, and helped the companies recover much of *travel by* the loss suffered from the cancellation of contracts. Steady *airplane* improvements in airplane design and in safety and cheapness of service made the public more "air-minded" with each succeeding year. By

AMERICAN AIRWAYS

Boston
New York
Washington
Pittsburgh
Detroit
Jacksonville
Atlanta
Miami
New Orleans
St. Louis
Chicago
Minneapolis St. Paul
Fargo
Dallas
Omaha
Kansas City
Ft. Worth
Brownsville
Denver
Albuquerque
Billings
Salt Lake City
Seattle
San Francisco
Los Angeles

PACSTROM CO., N.Y.

RATES OF TRAVEL

the end of 1939 the nation's seventeen scheduled air lines reported that during the year their pilots had flown a total of 81,700,000 miles and had carried 1,900,000 passengers. During this period only two fatal accidents had occurred, in which only nine passengers were killed — one death for each 82,000,000 passenger miles. World transport services, also extensively organized, was seriously affected by the outbreak of war in the fall of 1939, but the extensive use of airplanes by the belligerents, particularly by the Germans, introduced a new era in military aviation. The United States, along with France and Great Britain, came quickly to realize that the airplane as a weapon of war was indispensable. Thousands of orders, both from the American and from foreign governments, led to a period of more intense activity among the airplane builders of the United States than had ever been known before.

The automobile, the movies, the radio, and the airplane were but the more visible symbols of a highly mechanized age. The gadgets of science had invaded every phase of American life. The farmer no *A mechan-* longer followed a plow, but drove a tractor. The most *ized age* humble of physicians must surround himself with thousands of dollars' worth of expensive equipment. Alert industrialists expected to retool their plants at frequent intervals. School buildings must be elaborately provided with the machines necessary for vocational training. Ordinary citizens took a thousand things for granted that their ancestors would have regarded as miracles; central heating, running water, sanitary plumbing, gas for cooking, electric energy for lighting and a dozen other household purposes; direct telephone connections with the outside world. Thoughtful observers sometimes wondered about the effect of all these "improvements" upon the people who depended upon them. Was the resourcefulness of the individual being undermined? Was overreliance upon machines softening the fabric of American character? Whatever the answers, there were few to advocate that the new machines be scrapped, and the older and harder ways revived.[1]

To inheritors of the Puritan tradition there was much about the changing American scene that was alarming. Among most of the Protestant denominations church-going had declined precipitately. A few popular city preachers held their congregations, but in the country towns the competition of the automobile, the movies, the radio, and the golf links had proved impossible to meet. The younger generation made open sport of the old morality; styles in feminine apparel left little to the imagination; and flippancy in speech and manners became almost a national obsession. Fundamentalism was in full retreat. The action of several southern legislatures during the twenties in prohibiting the teaching of evolution was more in the nature of a confession of defeat than a call to action. William Jennings Bryan, by aiding the prosecution at Dayton, Tennessee, of a young man who had disobeyed the law, was generally thought to have made himself and his cause ridiculous. But the greatest blow that the evangelical churches suffered was the failure of prohibition. Effectively organized through the Anti-Saloon League, the church people had won state after state to the temperance cause, and when the Eighteenth Amendment was adopted in January, 1920, they had rejoiced almost as immoderately as over the signing of the armistice. Less than fourteen years later they looked on with despair while the Twenty-First Amendment recalled the Eighteenth, and the "noble experiment" came to an end.[2]

[1] The literature of pessimism as applied to this period is painfully voluminous. Samples worth citing are J. T. Adams, *Our Business Civilization* (1929); Walter Lippmann, *A Preface to Morals* (1929); F. R. Kent, *Political Behavior* (1928); H. E. Stearns, editor, *Civilization in the United States: An Inquiry by Thirty Americans* (1922); M. A. Hallgren, *Seeds of Revolt* (1933). The nearest approach to a scientific study of the social scene is presented in R. S. and H. M. Lynd, *Middletown* (1929), and *Middletown in Transition* (1937).

[2] Charles Merz, *The Dry Decade* (1931), is a good popular account of prohibition. It may be compared with the Federal Council of the Churches of Christ in America, *The Prohibition Situation* (1925).

[602]

The rock on which prohibition foundered was enforcement. It was one thing to outlaw the existing liquor traffic, but quite another to prevent its replacement by illicit vendors of liquor who profited from breaking the law. The Eighteenth Amendment made no great change in the national appetite for strong drink, and a large minority of the population felt outraged that any such attack on personal liberty had been made. This was particularly true of the city populations in which the immigrant element constituted so important a part. Others who had never drunk before were impelled out of sheer perversity to do what the law forbade. Americans from colonial times on down had never felt obliged to obey a law that they did not like; indeed, many argued that the only way to defeat an obnoxious law was to prove that it could not be enforced. Thus a market for liquor still existed, and to supply it a whole new industry came into being. The ways of the "moonshiners," who since the days of the Whiskey Rebellion had hidden their stills in the mountains to avoid the payment of revenue, were extensively imitated; "rum-runners" brought a steady stream of cargoes from abroad to unpatrolled sections of the American coast; heavily laden smugglers crossed the border from Mexico and from Canada; chemical formulae, sometimes dependable and sometimes not, were used to "renovate" industrial liquor by the removal of denaturants; private citizens set up toy stills, manufactured "homebrew" and "bathtub gin," turned the pure unfermented juice of the grape into more or less palatable wine. *Prohibition*

The Volstead Act, by which Congress (over Wilson's veto) defined intoxicating beverages as those containing as much as one half of one per cent alcohol and created the machinery for enforcement, imposed upon federal officials an almost impossible task. *Problems of enforcement* "Bootleggers" had already gained valuable experience in the states where prohibition had preceded the Eighteenth Amendment. They knew how easily the problem of distribution could be solved by automobiles and trucks, and they were past-masters of the art of bribery and deception. Against these experts the Prohibition Bureau, which until 1927 was outside the civil service, mobilized a miscellaneous army of petty politicians and their friends. Furthermore, the entrance of the national government into the field of enforcement led the states to relax their efforts; wet states in many instances repealed the limitations they had once placed on liquor dealers, while dry states cheerfully resigned to federal agents the task of matching wits with the bootleggers. The United States Department of Justice found itself suddenly swamped with a type of business it had never known before, and prohibition cases clogged the federal courts. Thirty-five hundred civil cases and sixty-five thousand criminal cases were brought within a period of less than two years.

Soon the illicit liquor business was one of the nation's biggest and most profitable. Since it operated wholly outside the law, all restraints *The boot-* were eliminated, and competitors traded bloody blows. *leggers* Backed by dependable gangs of thugs, the "big shots" fought furiously for the enormous profits of monopoly, and in each large city a well-recognized king of the underworld emerged, to whom, while his reign lasted, the whole business paid tribute. Deaths among the gangsters were numerous, but trials for these murders were rare and convictions still rarer. The gang leaders, successfully defended by highly paid criminal lawyers known as "mouthpieces," not only sneered openly at the prohibition agents, but systematically instituted one new "racket" after another. Gambling, prostitution, the trade in narcotics, and other illegal activities came naturally within the orbit of the "racketeers," but even the most legitimate of businesses were not immune. Restaurant keepers, cleaners and dyers, laundrymen, garage owners, anyone who took in cash might at a moment's notice be compelled to pay heavily for "protection" against these selfsame protectors. Failure to meet the racketeers' demands meant smashed windows, flattened tires, burned delivery trucks, bombed stores, and for the most obdurate sudden death. Labor unions were invaded for the chance to graft from membership dues, and in altogether too many instances city governments paid more attention to the demands of the racketeers than to the welfare of the citizens. Racketeering was at its worst in Chicago and New York, but few large cities escaped its ravages, and the whole nation paid tribute, directly or indirectly, to the gangsters.

With conditions fast becoming unbearable, a Law Enforcement Commission of eleven members was appointed by President Hoover in 1929 *The Wicker-* to conduct an investigation. Headed by George W. Wicker-*sham Com-* sham, formerly Attorney-General under Taft, the commis-*mission* sion took its duties seriously, but when it reported in 1931 it was still undecided. Its findings of fact seemed to recognize the hopelessness of adequate enforcement, but a majority of the commissioners recommended that the prohibition experiment be continued.[1] In the summer of 1932 President Hoover, in spite of the impending campaign, admitted that some changes in the existing system would have to be made, while the Democratic platform went the whole length of demand-

---

[1] Report of the National Commission on Law Observance and Enforcement, Seventy-First Congress, third session, *House Document* no. 722 (serial 9361).

ing repeal. Following the triumphant Democratic victory at the polls, Congress acted even before the new administration could take office. In February, 1933, the repeal amendment was submitted, and by the end of the year it was a part of the Constitution.

The end of prohibition, however, did not mean the end of racketeering, for by this time the gangsters were deeply entrenched in all sorts of rackets. One of the most amazing of these was the "snatch racket," which in May, 1932, claimed its most famous victim when the infant son of Charles A. Lindbergh was kidnaped for ransom by a lone operator, and killed. As the profits of bootlegging disappeared, criminals turned instead to kidnaping, bank burglaries, and other bold crimes, and in an alarming number of instances easily made good their escape. Finally Congress, by a series of "crime control" acts passed in the spring of 1934, faced squarely the responsibility of the federal government in bringing the situation under control. By the terms of these laws criminals who crossed state lines during the course of their exploits were made liable to drastic penalties (for kidnapers, death), and the Investigation Division of the Federal Department of Justice, headed by J. Edgar Hoover and known later as the Federal Bureau of Investigation, was given great freedom of action in enforcement. At the end of the year Hoover's agents had accounted by death for a dozen of the country's most notorious criminals, and had brought many others to justice. State officers, forced to compare results with the effective "G-men," also began to take their duties seriously. Early in 1935 the kidnaper of the Lindbergh baby was convicted and sentenced in New Jersey. That same year Thomas E. Dewey was made special prosecutor to conduct a drive against organized crime in New York, and achieved such conspicuous success that in 1937 he was given a popular mandate to continue the work as district attorney of New York County. When other evidence failed, racketeers were sometimes convicted for federal income-tax evasion. This had happened to "Scarface Al" Capone, the underworld ruler of Chicago, as far back as 1931, and his long imprisonment at Alcatraz, the escape-proof federal penitentiary located on an island in San Francisco Bay, served as a continual warning to would-be imitators. Toward the close of the decade there was reason to hope that at last the era of unrestrained lawlessness had approached its end.[1]

Racketeering

[1] M. A. Kavanagh, *The Criminal and his Allies* (1928), and R. W. Child, *Battling the Criminal* (1926), are somewhat sensational in character. R. B. Fosdick, *American Police Systems* (1920), and A. A. Bruce, *The Administration of Criminal Justice in Illinois* (1929), are more dependable. Of particular interest because of its author's position is J. Edgar Hoover, *Persons in Hiding* (1938).

If young America embraced lawlessness, it was not because its education had been neglected. Compulsory school attendance up to sixteen *Educational* or even eighteen years of age was required by law in most *trends* states, and was well enforced by public opinion. School buildings were elaborately equipped, not only with teaching paraphernalia, but also with auditoriums, gymnasiums, swimming pools, and such other facilities as might contribute to well-rounded lives on the part of the pupils. Bus service made possible the elimination of the weaker country schools, and the establishment, especially for the higher grades, of well-appointed consolidated systems. New principles of education, emanating chiefly from Teachers College, Columbia, revolutionized the methods of teaching, and emphasized the need of "education for life." The influence of John Dewey, who insisted that the chief end and aim of schooling should be the development of socially useful adults, permeated nearly every classroom.[1] Preparation for college played a diminishing rôle in high-school curriculums, where a host of young people who had no interest in nor aptitude for a college course must be kept occupied. Vocational education and manual training flourished as never before. For the most part primary and secondary education in the United States meant public education, although many private schools existed, particularly in the East. Toward the end of the twenties the annual bill for education in the United States approached three billion dollars.

Higher education flourished in spite of the indifference toward it exhibited in many of the lower schools. During that part of the *Colleges and* twentieth century which preceded the outbreak of the *universities* World War the number of students enrolled in colleges and universities increased from about 114,000 to nearly a quarter of a million. The years of American participation in the war diminished somewhat the rate of acceleration, but after the war was over, the rise began again, and until 1929 continued at about the rate of an additional quarter of a million every five years. Junior colleges were provided in many states so that the first two years of a college course could be obtained by great numbers of students without the necessity of leaving home. State teachers' colleges, designed to provide the proper "teacher training" for those whose duty it would be to put the new principles of education into effect, also multiplied amazingly. Graduate schools, with courses leading to the master's or the doctor's degree, appeared in all the larger universities, and the Ph.D. degree became almost as essential for the

---

[1] John Dewey, *The School and Society* (1899), and *Democracy and Education* (1916), state clearly the author's thesis that social utility should be the principal aim of education.

aspirant to a college instructorship as the teacher's certificate to the beginner in the public schools.[1]

In spite of their steady flow of customers the institutions of higher education in the United States were subjected to endless criticism. The elective system by which students were permitted to collect a hodge-podge of relatively unrelated courses toward a baccalaureate degree was denounced as warmly as in the days of President Eliot. To some observers the dominance of sports and society on college campuses constituted the principal shortcoming of higher education; others were disagreeably impressed by the ages-old tendency of youth to flirt with radical ideas. Probably most college students expected as a result of their educational endeavors to get a better job than would otherwise have been open to them. Many "bread-and-butter" courses aided them in this ambition, but wise employers recognized that a four years' residence in a stimulating environment was in itself a valuable experience. The advent of the depression at first cut down materially on college and university enrollments, but not many institutions actually went under, and the students soon returned. It should be noted that college faculties were for the most part concerned not merely with instruction, but also with research. A large proportion of the discoveries in pure science, and a still larger proportion of the exploratory ventures in other fields, were the contributions of university professors. To a considerable extent on this account, most of the great foundations for philanthropy, such, for examples, as those established by Rockefeller and Carnegie, continued their interest in higher education.

Perhaps the most successful of the achievements that stemmed from the educational world lay in the realm of science and health. The diagnosis of deep-seated disease, and sometimes the cure *Scientific* also, received an enormous impetus from the steady im- *achievements* provement in X-ray technique; the discoveries of bacteriologists sent such dread diseases as diphtheria into the discard along with typhoid and malaria, and tremendously reduced the toll taken by most of the contagions from which children suffered; the significance of vitamins in food was carefully explored and the results made available to the public; the employment of blood transfusions was greatly facilitated by the proper attention to blood-matching; and the use of sulfanilamide practically eliminated death from streptococcic infections. In making these and a thousand other advances, the scientific world worked together

[1] E. H. Wilkins, *The Changing College* (1927); R. L. Kelly, *Tendencies in College Administration* (1925); J. E. Kirkpatrick, *The American College and Its Rulers* (1926); R. C. Angell, *The Campus* (1928).

Millions

PREDICTED CHANGES IN AGE COMPOSITION OF
THE AMERICAN POPULATION

This chart assumes medium fertility, medium mortality, and no immigration. (From
Problems of a Changing Population (Washington, National Resources Committee, 1938.)

without regard for international barriers, but to the sum total of advancement American investigators contributed an honorable part, while in the United States more than in most nations the results of medical knowledge were made immediately available to the masses. Hospital facilities were provided for those who could pay for them, and in most instances also for those who could not. Rising standards in medical education meant better physicians, and the attention to health given in the schools bore significant results. Americans lived longer. Between 1901 and 1927 the average life expectancy in the United States rose from forty-nine to fifty-nine years. The increasing number of deaths from such diseases as cancer and heart ailments proved merely that more people were living long enough to die from the afflictions of old age.[1]

[1] Among the more popular books on scientific subjects are R. T. Young, *Biology in America* (1922); Julius Stieglitz, *Chemistry in Medicine* (1928); L. I. Dublin, *Health and Wealth* (1928).

The World War of 1914–18 served in a general way to mark the beginning of a new era in American literature. Mark Twain died in 1910 and William Dean Howells in 1920. With their passing the *American literature* generation of writers that dated from the period of the Civil War and reconstruction had practically disappeared. The new generation was deeply influenced by the social conflicts that developed out of the machine age, conflicts that the world's descent into war served so greatly to accentuate. In the novel they found their best medium of expression, and in their desire to be true to reality they sometimes overshot the mark. Some of them, like Frank Norris, in *The Octopus* (1910), and Winston Churchill in *Coniston* (1906), both of whom were impressed by the overweening power of the railroads, wrote with the muckraker's hope of reform. Others, like Jack London, in *The War of the Classes* (1905) and *The Iron Heel* (1910), saw no hope for society except in revolution. Still others were content to set forth what they saw, and to present no solution. The plight of the underdog particularly fascinated Theodore Dreiser, whose hapless characters in *An American Tragedy* (1925) might well have been copied from the crime columns of the daily newspapers, and probably were.

The search for realism led to many re-examinations of the American past, none more fruitful than those pertaining to the frontier. Hamlin Garland's autobiographic *A Son of the Middle Border* (1917) recaptured much of the harshness of the pioneer environment, but only as an old man recounts experiences from which he emerged as a great success. Willa Cather in *O Pioneers* (1913) and *My Ántonia* (1918) strove also to strip away the glamor that had attached itself to the frontier, and in accomplishing her task displayed literary craftsmanship of a high order. James Boyd in *Drums* (1925) and *Long Hunt* (1930) did a similar, but less notably excellent, service for an earlier age. O. E. Rölvaag's *Giants in the Earth* (1927) told with stark realism the bitter struggle of the immigrant farmer against the bleak Northwest, while Mari Sandoz's *Old Jules* (1935) varied the scene to fit the conflict fought by another immigrant, the author's father, against the semi-arid, treeless plains. Ellen Glasgow, writing of the post-Civil-War South instead of the frontier, portrayed in a long series of volumes from the *Battle Ground* (1902) to *Vein of Iron* (1935) the decay of the old southern society, while Margaret Mitchell, exploiting in *Gone with the Wind* (1936) another phase of the same theme, revealed the soul-searing methods by which the New South was built.

Most American writers, however, preferred the theme of the present, and in dealing with the setting that lay about them none showed greater

proficiency than Sinclair Lewis. Thoroughly out of patience with
Sinclair the selfish commercialism that was exhibited in every phase
Lewis of American life, Lewis satirized the rundown country town
in *Main Street* (1920), the growing city and its prosperous "realtors" in
Babbitt (1922), the medical profession in *Arrowsmith* (1925), the evangelical clergy in *Elmer Gantry* (1927), and the American merchant princess
in *Dodsworth* (1929). What Sinclair Lewis sought to do through fiction,
Henry L. Mencken attempted in the field of criticism, first as a writer
for the *Baltimore Sun*, but after 1924 as editor of an ultra-smart magazine *The American Mercury*, which for several years was the favorite
diet of all who sought to appear sophisticated. Mencken's particular
delight was to bait the prohibitionists, whose cant and sophistry he
found it easy to expose. But neither Lewis nor Mencken was willing
to approve an attack by revolution on the social system he criticized,
and they soon lost caste with the radicals who had at first hailed them
as prophets.

American verse of merit, for the first time since the days of Bryant
and Whitman, was again being written. Most of it, too, was deeply
Poetry critical of society. Edgar Lee Masters in his *Spoon River
Anthology* (1915) recited with telling irony the aimless life-
histories of the people whose gravestones might be seen in any village
cemetery. Vachel Lindsay in *The Congo and Other Poems* (1919) at
once startled the literary world with his unusual verse forms and turned
attention toward the American Negro as a theme for exploitation.
Robert Frost in *North of Boston* (1914) and *New Hampshire* (1923) dealt
sympathetically, but in utter realism, with the peculiarities of rural New
Englanders. John G. Neihardt in *The Song of Hugh Glass* (1915), *The
Song of Three Friends* (1919), and *The Song of the Indian Wars* (1925)
attempted with considerable success an epic of the frontier. Stephen
Vincent Benét in *John Brown's Body* (1928) and *A Book of Americans*
(1933) wrote good history in vivid verse. Carl Sandburg in *The People
Yes* (1936) described in homespun language the drab daily deeds of
ordinary men, and dripped "corrosive sublimate" upon "formalities,
conventionalities, 'stuffed shirtfronts,' the high proprieties of the high." [1]

The United States produced also a few good playwrights. Foremost
among them was Eugene O'Neill, whose long series of dramatic successes

[1] Beard and Beard, *America in Midpassage*, II, 680. On American poetry, see Amy
Lowell, *Tendencies in Modern American Poetry* (1917) and J. L. Lowes, *Convention and
Revolt in Poetry* (1919); on the novel, A. H. Quinn, *American Fiction* (1936), and F. L.
Pattee, *The New American Literature, 1890–1930* (1930). Granville Hicks, *The Great Tradition* (1933), is a left-wing view. On literature in general see W. P. Trent and others, *The
Cambridge History of American Literature* (3 vols., 1936), III.

WILLIAM DEAN HOWELLS MARK TWAIN

SINCLAIR LEWIS EUGENE O'NEILL

FOUR MEN OF LETTERS

included *Emperor Jones* (1921), *Desire Under the Elms* (1924), *Marco*
Plays and *Millions* (1924), *The Great God Brown* (1925), *Strange Inter-*
playwrights *lude* (1927), *Mourning Becomes Electra* (1931), *Ah, Wilder-*
ness! (1932), and *Days Without End* (1933). O'Neill's plays exploited
complex psychological themes, and sometimes dwelt almost morbidly
upon the problems of sex. Of the many other less gifted but extremely
able American playwrights perhaps Maxwell Anderson and Elmer Rice
are most worthy of mention. Anderson in *What Price Glory* (1924)
brought home with tremendous effectiveness the grim realities of war,
including the artistic nature of military profanity, and in *Both Your*
Houses (1933) skillfully satirized the national capital in the throes of the
New Deal. Rice, in such plays as *On Trial* (1914), *For the Defense* (1919),
and *Counsellor-at-Law* (1931), dealt understandingly with legal complications, but rose to new heights in his *Judgment Day* (1934) which courageously faced the conflicting ideologies of the international scene. In
spite of strenuous competition from the movies the legitimate stage maintained its hold upon New York and Chicago audiences, while many of
the more popular plays took to the road and were shown all over the
country. Stock companies generally succumbed, but amateur theatricals, particularly those sponsored by the schools and colleges, flourished
as never before.

American art, while far from barren in such fields as painting and
sculpture, reached its highest peak in architecture. The possibilities
Architecture of the skyscraper were not fully realized until designers gave
up the attempt to embroider their buildings with irrelevant
decorations, and began to emphasize vertical lines and related masses.
In 1916 New York city furnished an unexpected boon to builders when
it legislated the "set-back" into existence in order to insure that some
daylight should reach the city streets. This furnished an opportunity
to introduce variety into architectural designs that led to notable improvements, but the skyscraper was still not without its limitations.
This became abundantly apparent when William F. Lamb's Empire
State Building raised the New York skyline, perhaps for the last time,
to a new altitude. Aside from the discovery that the building provided more office space than tenants could readily be induced to take,
the physical difficulties involved in getting so many people into and out
of so large a building, and back and forth from their homes to their work,
indicated clearly the desirability of smaller buildings more widely dis-
persed. Public buildings offered another opportunity for significant
architectural innovations. Outstanding among these was the state
capitol at Lincoln, Nebraska, designed by Bertram Goodhue. Called

Mathison Aerial Survey

THE NEW YORK SKYLINE

by enthusiasts the most beautiful building in America, it broke the monotony of the Nebraska prairie with an imposing shaft which, unlike the customary dome, provided at the same time an abundance of well-lighted office space. Its decorations, generous with color and bold in design, told in well-thought-out symbolism the history of western civilization and its impact upon the Indian culture of the plains.

In domestic architecture many influences were at work, and much mere experimentation was in evidence. At once novel and practical were the designs of Frank Lloyd Wright whose house on the Wisconsin River, Taliesin, was extensively copied by himself and many mere imitators. But Wright's first principle was that a building must harmonize with its natural surroundings, and "be made to grow easily from its site." [1]

Of tremendous interest in revealing the trend away from traditional-

[1] Frank Lloyd Wright, *An Autobiography* (1932).

ism in architecture toward the new ideal of "functionalism" was the
Century of Century of Progress Exposition which opened in Chicago
Progress during the spring of 1933, just forty years after Chicago's
Exposition earlier world's fair had first startled the nation. From an
architectural point of view the two expositions could hardly have stood
in greater contrast. Visitors of 1893 saw a dream of classical beauty
done in the purest white; visitors of 1933 saw huge, shapeless structures,
painted with the boldest colors, and suggestive of nothing they had ever
seen before. Only after night when the floodlights were loosed could
the ordinary observer see a setting worthy of admiration. But the
buildings, windowless and curiously shaped as they were, served well the
purposes for which they were built, a lesson that was by no means lost
on the millions who saw them. Soon "modernistic" structures appeared
all over the nation as architects vied with one another in the effort to
make an honest adjustment of their materials to the needs they were
meant to serve. The location of the Exposition also taught a lesson.
The land on which it stood was all "made land," dredged up from the
bottom of Lake Michigan to provide a wide approach to the waterfront.
After the fair was over the entire area was to be made into a city park,
and still more dredged-up land was to facilitate the construction of an
elaborate system of automobile highways bordering upon the lake.
City planning had made much progress since 1893, and the example of
Chicago in taking better advantage of its natural setting was followed
by many other cities. The Fair, in spite of the hard times, was no less
successful financially than its predecessor of forty years before, and
was held over for the following year.

Six years later two other American cities, San Francisco and New
York, held fairs. The setting for the Golden Gate Exposition was a
World's four-hundred-acre man-made island in San Francisco Bay,
Fairs of and its purpose was to show how completely civilized west-
1939 ern America and the Pacific Basin had become. The
buildings essayed a blend of Mayan, Incan, Malayan, and other Pacific
forms that registered a marked advance over the architectural innovations exhibited at Chicago. In New York the "World of Tomorrow"
was the principal theme of the most elaborate fair ever staged in America.
The exposition grounds occupied nearly two square miles of territory in
Flushing Meadows, at the very heart of Greater New York, and the
project involved an expenditure of over one hundred and fifty million
dollars. The buildings showed that the search for architectural innovations had by no means ceased, but the garish colors and angular lines of
the Century of Progress were much toned down. Both the Golden Gate

TWO EXAMPLES OF MODERN ARCHITECTURE: THE NEBRASKA
STATE CAPITOL, THE SEATTLE ART MUSEUM

Exposition and the World of Tomorrow were reopened the succeeding year, but in spite of large attendances neither was able to duplicate the financial success of the Century of Progress.

These three world's fairs, quite apart from the revolt they registered against architectural traditions, made significant contributions to American life. The millions who visited them came away with a better understanding of the intricate processes by which the scientific advancement of their age had been attained, and with a conviction that the wonders of the future would far surpass anything they had yet seen. They learned much, too, about the rest of the world that schoolroom lessons in geography could never have taught them, and in consequence were better prepared for the era of international change so soon to burst upon them. And whether they traveled to the East or to the West or to both, by automobile or by streamlined train or by airplane, they could hardly fail to observe the limitless resources with which their country was blessed, and the anachronism of poverty and unemployment in a land so rich.[1]

[1] F. L. Allen, *Since Yesterday* (1940), is a worthy successor to *Only Yesterday*. D. W. Brogan, *The American Character* (1944), and Graham Hutton, *Midwest at Noon* (1946), are the observations of highly intelligent British travelers. Simeon Strunsky, *The Living Tradition: Change in America* (1939), features the social aspects of history. John Gunther, *Inside U.S.A.* (1947), is an interesting journalistic travelogue. Howard Mumford Jones, *Ideas in America* (1944), and E. E. Robinson, *The New United States* (1946), contain stimulating essays of a general nature.

Jeremiah Milbank, Jr., *The First Century of Flight in America: An Introductory Survey* (1943), and Fred C. Kelly, *The Wright Brothers* (1943), are good popular accounts. Henry Ladd Smith, *Airways: The History of Commercial Aviation in the United States* (1942), shows the similarity between early railroad and early aviation organization.

Darrell Garwood, *Artist in Iowa: A Life of Grant Wood* (1944), is interesting. A. H. Quinn, *History of the American Drama from the Civil War to the Present Day* (1936), includes a chapter on the playwrights of the 1930's.

Richard H. Shryock, *American Medical Research, Past and Present* (1947), and Helen Clapesattle, *The Doctors Mayo* (1941), give good pictures of the rise of modern medicine.

Howard K. Beale, *A History of Freedom of Teaching in American Schools* (1941), and *Are American Teachers Free?* (1936), are unduly pessimistic.

CHAPTER XXVII

THE NEW DEAL BEGINS

IN A SENSE Herbert Hoover rather than Franklin D. Roosevelt inaugurated the New Deal. While the Hoover policies in some respects contrasted markedly with the Roosevelt policies, it was not Roosevelt, but Hoover, who first accepted as a governmental responsibility the task of defeating the depression. Hoover *Hoover begins the New Deal* was not the only American President to face such a crisis; many of his predecessors, notably Van Buren, Grant, and Cleveland, had been depression Presidents. But none of these had regarded the elimination of hard times as a problem of government. The government merely took care of itself the best it could while the lean years lasted, and left to business the task of fighting its own way back to recovery. Whenever bankruptcies and reorganizations had reduced the debt totals to a point where business could again carry on profitably, the upward turn began. Had this normal course of liquidation been permitted after 1929, it is possible that the railroads, the life insurance companies, the building and loan associations, the savings banks, and nearly every other important type of American business might have gone down in the crash. The whole capitalistic system of economy was endangered. Fully aware of the gravity of the situation, Hoover set himself resolutely against so ruthless a collapse and took personal charge of the fight to prevent it.[1]

For a time the President directed his efforts mainly toward obtaining the voluntary co-operation of business and labor leaders in measures of self-help. At a series of conferences in Washington he talked against the curtailment of buying power that must inevitably follow the reduction of payrolls, and urged that "the first shock" of the depression "must fall on profits and not on wages." He insisted that wage scales ought not for the moment to be lowered at all, and that when reductions became unavoidable they should be made only in proportion as the cost

[1] W. S. Myers, editor, *State Papers and Other Public Writings of Herbert Hoover* (2 vols., 1934), furnishes a complete documentary record of the Hoover administration. Also useful is T. G. Joslin, *Hoover — Off the Record* (1934).

of living went down. He hoped that expenditures for construction would not be curtailed, and succeeded in committing many industries to a policy of expansion in spite of the unsettled economic conditions. But "business as usual" soon proved to be a difficult formula for executives to maintain in the face of declining receipts and mounting inventories. Sometimes efforts were made to "spread the work" by lessening the number of hours per week permitted each individual, but in spite of good intentions wages did go down and unemployment figures began to mount.

Hoover was quite as much interested as Roosevelt later became in providing public works to take up the slack of depression unemployment. *Public* As early as January, 1930, he was asking Congress to in-*works* crease by huge sums its appropriations for public buildings, for the improvement of rivers and harbors, and for public roads. He was also deeply interested in a long-standing project for the building of a great dam across the Colorado River below the Grand Canyon. By this means water could be stored up for irrigation and power purposes, the Imperial Valley of California could be protected from danger of overflow, and the city of Los Angeles could be assured an adequate water supply. Called at first the Hoover Dam, the project was renamed the Boulder Dam during the next administration, but the actual work of construction began while Hoover was President, and with his full consent and co-operation. When finished it raised the water level of the Colorado River by nearly six hundred feet, and was regarded as one of the greatest engineering achievements of all time. Actual expenditures for public works during Hoover's four years in office reached a total of more than two and a quarter billion dollars, and had much to do with unbalancing the national budget, a condition which Roosevelt at first criticized, but later adopted as one of the primary essentials to recovery. Hoover was distressed that so many different governmental agencies were carrying on building operations, and recommended in his annual message to Congress of December 8, 1931, that all such operations should "be consolidated into an independent establishment under the President to be known as the Public Works Administration directed by a public works administrator." But the actual establishment of the "PWA" awaited the legislative enactments of the Roosevelt régime.

While thus in complete sympathy with indirect aid for the unemployed, Hoover was convinced that the responsibility for direct relief *Relief* must be left as fully as possible in the hands of states, *policies* municipalities, and voluntary agencies. He feared that **federal appropriations might rob local authorities of the incentive to do** what they could, and he was convinced that the appropriation of the huge sums it would necessitate would not only serve further to unbalance the budget, but would also stimulate unfortunately the "pork-barrel" instincts of Congress. Under the urging of a voluntary "President's Emergency Relief Organization," every locality in the country made a desperate effort to "take care of its own," but an abundance of evidence soon accumulated that national aid could not be avoided indefinitely. Some states were far harder hit than others, and correspondingly less able to shoulder the heavy burdens of relief. In the mining districts of West Virginia, for example, the economic props dropped almost completely from under many communities, while in the ordinarily prosperous states of the lower Mississippi Valley a drouth of unprecedented severity during the summer of 1930 produced near-famine conditions. It was apparent that only the national government had the resources in taxes and credit with which to meet these emergencies. By the spring of 1932 the President, with the help of the Red Cross and local committees set up by his Emergency Relief Organization, was using the wheat and cotton surpluses of the Federal Farm Board for relief; when that means proved inadequate he secured from Congress an appropriation of three hundred million dollars to be lent to such states as were no longer able to finance their relief expenditures. Throughout his administration the distribution of all relief grants remained in the hands of local nonpartisan committees on a strictly decentralized basis. The fact that this work was done without building up a "paid bureaucracy" of federal employees seemed to Hoover a matter of great importance, but before he left office the demand for precisely the type of organization he deplored had reached impressive proportions.[1]

Loans to the states for relief and loans for a great variety of other purposes were made through the instrumentality of a Reconstruction Finance Corporation, established by Congress early in 1932 *The RFC* at President Hoover's suggestion. The necessity of direct governmental loans to prevent the further collapse of business became apparent when a National Credit Corporation, also sponsored by Hoover, failed to mobilize resources sufficient to meet existing needs. The RFC, with Charles G. Dawes of Chicago as its first president, lent freely to banks, agricultural credit corporations, life insurance companies, and other financial organizations, and also to the hard-pressed railroads. Many bankruptcies were thus forestalled or delayed, and the President was able only with difficulty to restrain Congress from per-

---

[1] Hoover's policies may be followed best in Myers and Newton, *The Hoover Administration*, and in Wilbur and Hyde, *The Hoover Policies*.

mitting RFC loans "for any conceivable purpose on any conceivable security for anybody who wants money." With his approval Congress extended the scope of the corporation to include loans to states for relief, to public and private agencies for construction work, and to prospective purchasers of agricultural commodities, both at home and abroad. Unfortunately, Congress did much to defeat the purpose of RFC loans to financial institutions by insisting on full publicity for all such transactions. Many banks thus lost face with their depositors, and were subjected to runs that in some cases caused them to close their doors. A large loan to the Chicago bank in which Dawes was interested convinced many critics that favoritism played an important part in obtaining RFC credits, but the loan was made after Dawes had severed his connections with the RFC, and over his protest. Loans actually disbursed before Hoover left office amounted to nearly two billion dollars.

New Dealers complained later that the chief trouble with the RFC during Hoover's administration was that it poured money into the financial structure "at the top instead of at the bottom." Businesses to which it lent were able to meet the most pressing of their obligations, but their earning power was not materially improved. Some of them, because of their unsound management and overcapitalization, might better have been permitted to fail. What was really needed, these critics maintained, was a restoration of the purchasing power of needy individuals. However this may have been, it seems evident that the lending policy of the Hoover régime was the direct lineal ancestor of the pump-priming activities that so notably characterized Roosevelt's efforts to deal with the depression.

Another Hoover policy with a definitely New-Dealish flavor was embodied in the Home Loan Bank Act of July 22, 1932. Under its terms *The Home Loan Banks* a series of Home Loan Banks were established to discount home mortgages, and thus to provide home-owners with a service similar to that rendered by the Federal Reserve Banks in the commercial field. Building and loan associations, savings banks, insurance companies, and other dealers in home mortgages were eligible for membership in the system. Unfortunately the Home Loan Banks were not established until after thousands of home-owners had already lost their property, but when at last the banks began to operate they were able to cut down materially on foreclosures and to promote some new building. After Roosevelt became President they were permitted to continue in operation, and by 1937 they counted over four thousand mortgage-holding organizations, with loans of over a billion dollars, among their members.

While Hoover was willing to ease the credit situation of the country in a great variety of ways, he was determined to maintain the gold standard and opposed with vigor a mounting demand for *The Bonus* money inflation. This inflationary idea reached Congress *Bill* by way of a plan for veterans' relief. Early in 1931 Congress voted over the President's veto to permit veterans to borrow from the government as much as fifty per cent of the face value of their bonus certificates, instead of the twenty-two per cent originally authorized. This imposed upon the Treasury a cash outlay of between one and two billion dollars at a time when the government was already facing a deficit, and in spite of the fact that not more than one fifth of the veterans were in real need. But agitators soon began to insist that the veterans had been only half paid, and that if the government could not afford to pay them in any other way it should authorize an issue of fiat money. This proposal was embodied in the Patman Bonus Bill, which passed the House on July 15, 1932, under pressure of a "Bonus Expeditionary Force" of about eleven thousand men, mostly unemployed veterans, who had assembled in and near Washington to collect what they insisted was due them. Ultimately the Senate rejected the Patman bill, but the BEF stayed on ominously. Congress then provided the President with funds to pay the way home for legitimate veterans, and by this means about half the number were induced to leave. The rest were driven from their camps and ejected from the District by the United States Army. Hoover claimed that in this action the military authorities exceeded their orders, but the incident was widely exploited as evidence of his heartlessness. By 1932, however, annual expenditures on behalf of World War Veterans had mounted to $860,000,000.[1]

The attempts of Hoover's Federal Farm Board to deal with the depressed condition of agriculture have already been recounted.[2] In addition to its activities, credits were extended through the *Relief for* RFC to the banks upon which the farmers depended, and *agriculture* to drouth-stricken sections for the purchase of such necessities as feed for livestock and seed. Hoover also negotiated a treaty with Canada for the building of a Great Lakes–St. Lawrence seaway which, when and if completed, would presumably reduce the cost of transporting middle-western crops to foreign markets. Had he remained in office he was ready to organize a "land-use" program, which would aim to divert lands from unprofitable to profitable use, and to end "the cultivation of lands the chief return of which is the poverty and misery of

[1] W. W. Waters, *B.E.F.: The Whole Story of the Bonus Army* (1933).
[2] See *ante*, p. 580.

those who live upon them." But all his plans and efforts paled into insignificance before the hard fact that farm prices refused to rise, and in many instances sank to lower figures than had been known for decades. In Iowa a Farmers' Holiday Association under the leadership of Milo Reno attempted to use the technique of the strike against production at a loss. Farmer picket-lines intercepted milk trucks on their way to market and dumped their contents into ditches. Sometimes, also, grim groups of farmers prevented foreclosure sales by force, or excluded from them all legitimate purchasers so that they themselves might bid in the mortgaged property at nominal sums and return it to its owner.

Not all of the actions taken by the Hoover administration in its efforts to deal with the depression were concerned with internal affairs. When in March, 1931, France refused to permit Germany and Austria to unite in a customs union, a train of events was set in motion which led to the almost complete collapse of European finance. Until that time the depression had remained primarily an American affair, but from then on its world-wide character was abundantly apparent. The finances of central Europe sank first, but eventually every European nation was affected, including Great Britain, which in September, 1931, was forced to abandon the gold standard. American investors in foreign securities, particularly those of Germany, were hard hit, and American trade with Europe was more drastically curtailed than ever before.

Believing that the huge burden of intergovernmental debts constituted one of the chief impediments to world trade, and therefore to world *Hoover's* recovery, Hoover in June, 1931, advocated a moratorium *moratorium* for one year on both the principal and interest of all such obligations. This action was deeply resented by France, who wished to continue her collections from Germany, and it was far from popular in the United States; but in due time it was accepted by the fifteen governments involved and went into effect. At the Lausanne Conference of 1932 the European powers attempted to solve the debt riddle for all time by granting Germany a three-year moratorium on reparations, and by establishing a new low figure, $714,000,000, as the amount to be paid. All this, however, was contingent upon the willingness of the United States to cancel its war debts. Many American businessmen, believing that private debts from abroad could be more readily collected if the public debt were out of the way, favored cancellation, but neither Hoover nor his successor, Roosevelt, conceded this point. Reparation payments were never resumed by Germany, and when the moratorium ended in 1932 only six governments, Great Britain, Czecho-slovakia, Italy, Finland, Latvia, and Lithuania, met their obligations to the United States. The next year all these nations, except Finland, made only small token payments, and after that no payments at all. The attitude of Finland, which paid in full every year, even after its territory was invaded by Russia in the winter of 1939–40, won much acclaim in the United States, but the sums involved were small. In 1934 Congress passed the Johnson Act, which prohibited Americans from purchasing the securities of any nation in default on its debt to the United States. By this time the debts in fact, if not in law, had ceased to be, and their restraining influence upon the course of international trade could not have been great.

The effect of the depression upon the political fortunes of Herbert Hoover and the party he represented was bound to be disastrous. More and more the tendency grew to hold the President personally *Elections* responsible for the economic difficulties from which the *of 1930* country suffered. His efforts to restrain the government from embarking upon a program of direct relief were cited as evidence to prove that he cared little about the sufferings of the unemployed, but much about the tax burden on the well-to-do. His nomination of Charles Evans Hughes to succeed Taft as Chief Justice was criticized as a move to strengthen the conservative majority on the Supreme Court, and was opposed by twenty-six senators, many of them Republicans. His nomination of John J. Parker of North Carolina as Associate Justice was defeated on the same ground. The mid-term elections of 1930, although held before there was any real comprehension of the seriousness of the economic situation, indicated clearly that the administration had lost the confidence of the country. The new Senate was almost evenly divided between Democrats and Republicans, but among the latter there were perhaps a dozen insurgents whose denunciations of Hoover often exceeded the fiercest outbursts of the Democrats. In the House an overwhelming Republican majority was turned into a minority, and a Democratic Speaker, John N. Garner of Texas, was chosen. In spite of frequent protestations that they had no intention of hampering the President in his efforts to deal with the depression, the Democrats, both in and out of Congress, were not unmindful of their opportunity to return to power, and gave the administration only the most temperate co-operation.[1]

---

[1] Hoover's political record was the subject of numerous ephemeral biographies; for example, W. W. Liggett, *The Rise of Herbert Hoover* (1932); Clement Wood, *Herbert Clark Hoover: An American Tragedy* (1932); Herbert Corey, *The Truth About Hoover* (1932).

When the time came for the presidential campaign of 1932, the Republicans had no choice but to stand on their record. Meeting at *Presidential* Chicago on June 14, they renominated both Hoover and *nominations* Curtis, and gave unstinted praise to the policies that had *of 1932* guided the country through the past four years. By this time the breakdown of prohibition was generally conceded, and the Republican platform promised to submit a repeal amendment, although leaving individual members of the party free to decide for themselves whether to support it or not. Interest centered on the Democratic Convention, which met later in the month, also in Chicago. Its nominee most careful observers believed to be certain of victory. Among the more prominent aspirants for the honor were Speaker Garner, to whom William Randolph Hearst had given his blessing; Alfred E. Smith, the unsuccessful nominee of four years before; Newton D. Baker, Secretary of War under Wilson; Governor Albert Ritchie of Maryland; and Governor Franklin D. Roosevelt of New York. It soon developed that the active pre-convention work of James A. Farley, Roosevelt's campaign manager, had given the New York governor a commanding lead over all the rest, and after the third ballot a deal with the Garner forces resulted in the ticket of Roosevelt and Garner. The Democratic platform denounced the Republicans for their policy of "economic isolation," accused them of favoritism to monopolies, and held their administration of the government strictly responsible for "a state of financial distress unprecedented in peace times." By way of remedy the Democrats promised among other things a competitive tariff for revenue, reciprocal trading agreements, more adequate relief for the unemployed, effective assistance to agriculture, the regulation of stock exchanges, the repeal of prohibition, the reform of the banking system, and "an immediate and drastic reduction of governmental expenditures." [1]

In Franklin D. Roosevelt (1882–1945), the Democrats had a candidate whose picturesque career rivaled that of his distant relative, Theodore *Franklin* Roosevelt. Born to a comfortable fortune, as the other *D. Roosevelt* Roosevelt had been also, he was a graduate of Groton and Harvard, had been frequently abroad, spoke French almost as fluently as English, and had acquired at least an elementary knowledge of the law. In 1905 he had married his sixth cousin, Eleanor Roosevelt, a favorite niece of the President's; and, like the other Roosevelts, they became the parents of a large and versatile family. Young Roosevelt, although a Democrat by birthright, never disguised his admiration for

---

[1] A useful handbook on the campaign is R. V. Peel and T. C. Donnelly, *The 1932 Campaign* (1935).

FRANKLIN D. ROOSEVELT

the President whose name he bore, and tended consciously or unconsciously to pattern after him. In 1910 he was a member of the New York legislature, and won the undying enmity of the Tammany machine by his fight against its candidate for the United States Senate, William F. Sheehan. Partly because his name was Roosevelt, and partly because he knew about ships, he became Assistant Secretary of the Navy under Woodrow Wilson, a post of great responsibility which he filled with ability during the World War. In 1920 he was the unsuccessful Democratic candidate for Vice-President, and after the campaign made preparations for a business career.

The transformation of Roosevelt from a retired minor politician to a dynamic leader of men began when he was laid low in August, 1921, by an attack of infantile paralysis that left him hopelessly crippled in both legs. By an unsurpassed exhibition of will power he fought his way back to health and even learned to walk again, although not without need of firm support. Utterly unconquered in spirit, he read widely, corresponded with the leaders of the Democratic Party, and dedicated himself to its rebuilding along liberal lines. In 1928, although he was not sure that his recovery was sufficiently complete to warrant it, he consented to run for governor of New York, largely because Alfred E. Smith, his close personal and political friend, believed that Roosevelt's name on the Democratic ticket would help his own chances of carrying the state. To the surprise of all concerned, Roosevelt ran far better than Smith and survived the Hoover landslide. As governor for only four years, and that in the midst of the depression, he inaugurated few policies of note, but his ability to deal adroitly with all matters affecting human nature, his unfailing good humor, and his consuming interest in new ideas made him a marked man. He alone of all the candidates for the Democratic nomination afforded any real contrast to Hoover. Just what he might do as President no one, perhaps not even he himself, could be quite sure. But the fear that he would use his remarkable powers of leadership to promote untried and unorthodox policies led conservative Democrats to oppose his nomination with every weapon at their command. To their dismay he had the votes. Alfred E. Smith, although once Roosevelt's friend, stood out to the end against him, and after the nomination gave him only the most grudging support.[1]

At the outset of the campaign Hoover really seemed to think that he

---

[1] The definitive analysis of Roosevelt's character lies far in the future, but Emil Ludwig, *Roosevelt* (1938), is at least worth reading. Eleanor Roosevelt, *This is My Story* (1937), is informative only on the purely personal side.

had a chance to win. He even turned over the work of campaigning to subordinates, and refused for weeks at a time to be drawn *The cam-* away from his desk in Washington. But Roosevelt, al- *paign* though convinced that only the gravest misstep could prevent a Democratic victory, launched a slashing attack. Unwilling to await the normal formalities of notification, he flew to Chicago in order to accept the nomination in person before the Democratic Convention adjourned. It was here that he first promised the country a "New Deal," and throughout the campaign he made the need for new men and new measures his central theme. He drew about himself a "brain trust" of "bright young men," including Raymond Moley, Rexford G. Tugwell, and Adolph A. Berle, Jr., who helped him formulate his plans and work up his addresses. He made campaign speeches the country over, traveling in all some twenty-five thousand miles before the day of election. He excoriated the Hoover administration with telling effect:

> I sum up the history of the present administration in four sentences: First, it encouraged speculation through its false economic policies; second, it attempted to minimize the crash and misled people as to its gravity; third, it erroneously charged the cause to other nations of the world; and finally, it refused to recognize and correct the evils at home which had brought it forth; it delayed relief, it forgot reform.

On the precise measures by which the New Deal meant to do the things that the Hoover administration had left undone, Roosevelt was studiously vague, but he left no doubt as to his interest in reform, in experiment, and in the "forgotten man."

Driven to defend himself by the Roosevelt onslaught, and at last fully aware of his diminishing chances, Hoover also took the stump. He assured the country anew that the depression was beginning to lift, and he pointed with considerable pride to the various measures his administration had taken to speed the return of prosperity. To deal with the international aspects of the situation he promised American participation in a World Economic Congress, already called, through which the stabilization of currencies was to be achieved and the way paved for a recovery in world trade. During the early months of the campaign there were some indications that the tide had turned, and that prosperity really was "just around the corner," as the President seemed to think. But before election day the downward trend began anew, and with this development the Republicans saw their last faint hope disappear. The audiences that Hoover faced during the closing days of the campaign saw before them a broken and defeated man, and his voice over the radio sounded tired and weak. Roosevelt, on the other hand, impressed the public everywhere with his confidence and charm, and as a radio speaker his technique was unsurpassed.

The certainty of a Roosevelt landslide was recognized well before the election. Besides the solid South that any Democratic candidate could *The Demo-* normally expect to carry, there appeared to be in the making *cratic land-* an equally solid West. Such insurgent Republicans as *slide* Norris of Nebraska, La Follette of Wisconsin, Johnson of California, and Cutting of New Mexico came out openly for Roosevelt, and millions of ordinary voters prepared to cast a Democratic ballot for the first time in their lives. In the industrial centers of the East the forces of discontent also played into Roosevelt's hands. When the vote was counted, it was apparent that Hoover had been as badly defeated by Roosevelt as four years before Smith had been defeated by Hoover. The electoral vote stood 472 to 59, and the popular vote, 22,809,638 to 15,758,901. Hoover carried only six states, Maine, New Hampshire, Vermont, Connecticut, Delaware, and Pennsylvania. Both houses of Congress were as overwhelmingly Democratic as they had been Republican four years before, and in the states the Democratic landslide carried into office many candidates who had regarded their names on the party ticket as either a courtesy or a joke. In general, the dissatisfied elements of society supported Roosevelt, but the existence of a small more radical minority was revealed by the vote of 884,781 for Norman Thomas, the Socialist candidate, and 102,991 for William Z. Foster, the Communist.[1]

According to the Republican version, it was the prospect of Roosevelt's election, climaxed by the election itself, which gave the final blow *The "lame-* to business confidence, and caused the very bottom to drop *duck"* out of the depression. Worst of all, the discredited Hoover *amendment* administration, together with the Congress that had been elected in 1930, must remain in office for nearly four months; until March 4, 1933, the New Deal that the election had demanded could not be dealt. Foreseeing just such a situation, Senator George W. Norris of Nebraska had for years been pressing upon Congress an amendment to the Constitution which would do away with the "lame-duck" session of Congress after the election, and would permit the newly chosen President, Vice-President, and members of Congress to take office in January instead of in March. Finally in March, 1932, the Norris proposal was submitted to the states for adoption, and on February 6, 1933, it was proclaimed in effect as the Twentieth Amendment to the Constitution. But its adoption came too late to save Hoover and the "lame-duck"

[1] E. E. Robinson, *The Presidential Vote, 1896–1932* (1934), is a useful compilation of election statistics.

Congress that assembled in December, 1932, from the embarrassment of having to deal with a crisis after they had been discredited by a vote of no confidence.

How to meet the pressing problems before him under such a handicap gave Hoover much concern. He might have followed the course that President Wilson was said to have had in mind should *Hoover and* Hughes have won the election of 1916. The President *Roosevelt* could have appointed the President-elect Secretary of State, after which both the President and the Vice-President could have resigned. According to the law the Presidency would then have devolved upon the newly chosen head of the cabinet. Probably a procedure so out of keeping with American tradition was possible only in theory, and it was certainly given little, if any, consideration. But Hoover did hope to secure the co-operation of the President-elect in deciding important matters of state. On two occasions he invited Roosevelt to confer with him at the White House on the war debts question, which Great Britain and most of the other nations concerned were determined to reopen at once. On both occasions Roosevelt accepted the President's invitation, but he refused to commit his administration in advance to anything more specific than a willingness to discuss war debts and other economic problems with a British representative soon after March 4. Hoover tried also to induce Roosevelt to join with him in an effort to check the spread of bank failures during February, 1933, a condition which privately the President attributed to "the breakdown of public confidence in the new administration now coming in." What Hoover really wanted was a statement from Roosevelt that he would not countenance money inflation, an unbalanced budget, or the flotation of loans so heavy as to impair the credit of the government. In view of the later policies of the Roosevelt administration it is not surprising that the President-elect side-stepped this suggestion. As Hoover himself admitted, it would have meant the "abandonment of ninety per cent of the so-called New Deal." Congress, too, now more responsive to the wishes of Roosevelt than to the pleas of the President, turned down the latter's recommendations for reduced expenditures and new taxes to balance the budget, for a complete reorganization of the executive departments, and for such reforms in the nation's financial system as, he believed, would put an end to bank failures.

Whether it was fair or not to blame the banking crisis that had developed upon an administration that had not yet taken office, *The banking* there could be no doubt as to the gravity of the situation. *crisis* Unemployment was at its worst during the winter of 1932–33, with the number of men out of work estimated at anywhere from thirteen million to seventeen million. Production in one great industry after another dropped to almost negligible proportions. Fear that the financial structure of the country was endangered showed in the mounting totals of gold exported and of gold and currency hoarded; by the middle of February each item had grown to about fifteen million dollars a day. In Detroit, where the drastic curtailment of automobile production had created a peculiarly difficult situation, the banks held on grimly, but by Lincoln's Birthday they were near the breaking point. Loaded down with frozen assets and drained of their deposits by frightened customers, they escaped collapse only when the governor of the state on his own authority extended the holiday period by eight days, and then obtained from the legislature the right to prolong it if need be still further. With the Michigan banks suspended, the panic spread to one state after another, and nearly every state executive declared a long bank holiday. Meantime, President Hoover, unable to secure any co-operation from the President-elect, watched helplessly while the financial machinery of the nation came virtually to a standstill. When Roosevelt took office the zero hour had seemingly been reached.

Whatever unwillingness he might have shown to accept responsibility before he took office, the new President showed no such hesitation after *Roosevelt's* March 4, 1933. His cabinet included none of the great *cabinet* names — Owen D. Young, Newton D. Baker, John W. Davis, Alfred E. Smith, and the like — pressed upon him by those who doubted his ability, and showed his evident determination to be his own master. Cordell Hull of Tennessee, the Secretary of State, was a dependable party wheel-horse devoted to the now almost forgotten low-tariff views of the party. William H. Woodin, the Secretary of the Treasury, was a New York banker who had always been regarded as a Republican; because of ill-health he was soon replaced by a personal friend of the President's, Henry Morgenthau, Jr., also of New York. Two other ex-Republicans were included, Harold L. Ickes of Illinois, the Secretary of the Interior, and Henry A. Wallace of Iowa, the Secretary of Agriculture. Both were previously unknown to national politics, although Wallace succeeded to the post his father had held in the Harding administration. James A. Farley, now national chairman of the Democratic Party, became Postmaster-General and chief dispenser of the patronage. For the first time a woman, Frances Perkins (Mrs. Paul Wilson), the new Secretary of Labor, received a cabinet assignment, to the considerable distaste of organized labor, which had tried in vain to dictate a different choice. The one really outstanding figure that the

President had meant to include in his official family, Thomas J. Walsh of Montana, who had been slated for the attorney-generalship, died a few days before inauguration. All observers agreed that the President's private "brain trust" would have much more to do with the shaping of his policies than the somewhat nondescript cabinet he had constructed.[1]

But there was no lack of presidential leadership. In his inaugural address the President alluded to the possibility that the "need for undelayed action" might call for a "temporary departure" *The Emer-* from the "normal balance of executive and legislative *gency Bank-* authority." He was ready, if need be, to ask Congress for *ing Act* "the one remaining instrument to meet the crisis — broad executive power to wage a war against the emergency as great as the power that would be given me if we were in fact invaded by a foreign foe." The next day after the inauguration the President closed every bank in the country, and by the time he had assembled Congress in special session on March 9 he had ready for instant passage an Emergency Banking Act. Breaking all known records, the law received the President's signature before the day was over. This measure authorized the Secretary of the Treasury to call in all gold, whether in the shape of coin, bullion, or gold certificates; it provided for the examination and reopening of all banks deemed sound, and for a system of "conservators" to take charge of all others; and it authorized an extensive issue of emergency currency to be used if necessary in halting runs. By March 13, such banks as federal examiners found solvent began to reopen, and the government's guaranty of their stability proved sufficient to restore public confidence. Only fifteen million dollars' worth of the new emergency currency had to be used, and millions of dollars that the banks had paid out during the crisis to anxious depositors began to flow back. Some three thousand banks, scattered throughout the country, were either reopened under conservators or were not reopened at all, but there was no longer any reason to doubt the essential soundness of the banking structure, and business proceeded as usual.

Before the end of March the President had pressed three other emergency measures through Congress. The first of these was an Economy Act by which he hoped to accomplish the "immediate and *The Econ-* drastic reduction of government expenditures," promised by *omy Act* the Democratic platform, and repeatedly described by Roosevelt during his campaign as a fundamental necessity to recovery. The national

---

[1] Dumond, *America in Our Time, 1896–1946,* is especially full on the first four years of the New Deal. The active part played by the President himself is apparent from *The Public Papers and Addresses of Franklin D. Roosevelt* (5 vols., 1938).

debt had mounted rapidly during the Hoover administration, from $17,343,850,202 when he took office to $20,937,350,964, when he retired. This meant an increase of $3,593,500,762 during the four years, nearly three fourths of which was due to expenditures undertaken during Hoover's last year to promote recovery and to provide relief. Whatever he might have thought during the campaign, the President now recognized the necessity of stupendous expenditures for relief, but he advocated a double-entry system of accounting by which emergency expenditures should be separated from ordinary expenditures, and budget-balancing confined strictly to the latter. The Economy Act, signed on March 20, authorized the President to cut salaries as much as fifteen per cent, to reduce payments to veterans, especially for non-service-connected disabilities, and to reorganize administrative agencies with economy in mind. Under its terms Roosevelt saved $125,000,000 on salaries and $300,000,000 on pensions in spite of the violent outcries of office-holders and ex-soldiers. Never before in the history of the country had pension payments been reduced, and as events were soon to prove they were not now reduced for long. Naturally many critics found fault with Roosevelt's plan for maintaining both a balanced and an unbalanced budget, but the public as a whole accepted his theory that the depression, like a war, must be fought to a finish, regardless of the emergency expenditures involved.[1]

The Beer Act, passed on March 22, was heralded as a revenue measure, although in reality its chief purpose was to break down as far as was constitutionally possible the effectiveness of the Prohibition Amendment. The rigid one half of one per cent alcoholic content by which an intoxicating beverage had been previously defined was changed to three and two tenths by weight, and appropriate taxes were levied on the manufacture of beer and wine in such states as might permit it. The revenues derived from this measure were inconsequential, but the process of repeal went on with the greatest of speed. For this purpose the "lame-duck" session of Congress that had just ended had submitted a Twenty-First Amendment to the Constitution, with the proviso that it should be ratified by special state conventions, instead of in the customary way by the action of state legislatures. Thus each state was able to vote directly on the question of repeal. It was soon apparent what the verdict would be, but not until December 6, 1933, did the Twenty-First Amendment become a part of the Constitution.

The Beer Act

The third of these emergency measures, signed March 31, 1933, was

[1] L. M. Hacker, *A Short History of the New Deal* (1934), furnishes an excellent summary of governmental activities during Roosevelt's first year.

a pet project of the President's, to which he had alluded early in his campaign. It created a Civilian Conservation Corps, the purpose of which was to establish reforestation camps in every *The CCC* part of the country to provide work for unmarried young men between the ages of eighteen and twenty-five who were without employment. The CCC soon had more than a quarter of a million youths at work under army officers clearing forests, planting trees, improving roads, preventing floods, and performing other equally useful tasks. Enlistments were for one year. The men received a dollar a day each in addition to medical care and maintenance, but were required to allot twenty-five dollars a month to dependents or relatives. Some observers saw in the move a surreptitious effort to strengthen the United States Army, but in general the CCC more than justified the President's hopes. Thousands of young men who had roamed the city streets searching in vain for jobs, or with too frequent success for trouble, thus found something worthwhile to do. Most of them were immensely improved in health and morale as a result of their experience, and there was no dearth of volunteers. By 1935 the original enrollment had been doubled, and the country had come to regard the CCC less as an emergency measure of relief than as a permanent American institution.

During the few weeks necessary to push these measures to enactment, the President had demonstrated ably his capacity for leadership. Relying as he must on the support of public opinion, he showed *Presidential* an unerring sense of the dramatic. Whether in a radio *leadership* appeal to the nation or in a personally delivered message to Congress, he never failed to time his pronouncements exactly and irresistibly right. He held frequent conferences with the representatives of the press, took them freely into his confidence, made them like him, and obtained through them a steady stream of favorable publicity. Like Theodore Roosevelt and Woodrow Wilson before him, he had no scruples as to the constitutional right of the Executive to direct the course of legislation. His energetic "brain-trusters," sometimes without much help from congressional committees, drafted the laws that Congress was called upon to pass. Whenever he could he used the same tactics on legislators that he used on newspapermen, but he was entirely capable of sterner measures. Farley, his patronage broker, kept books on every congressman, and it was an open secret that those who voted with the President could hope to have their recommendations for appointments honored, while those who voted against him could not. The President knew, too, that the best time to get his program through was while the country still regarded the steps taken as essential to meet an emergency, and while

Acme

THE SEAT OF GOVERNMENT

congressmen, with their hunger for patronage unappeased, were unwilling to interrupt the "honeymoon" period with which each new administration begins. To forestall long debates over bothersome details he frequently induced Congress to delegate much discretionary authority to the President himself, or to some executive officer. Thus many of the New Deal measures were passed in more or less skeleton form, with the details to be filled in later by the President and his advisers. Operating in this hasty fashion the special session of Congress enacted into law within a hundred days the principal policies of the New Deal.

The Emergency Banking Act foretold at the very outset the direction in which the New Deal was to go. With the whole financial system in a *Direction of* state of collapse, the President might have turned toward *the New* the left, with social revolution somewhat after the Russian *Deal* pattern as his goal. Had he directed Congress to nationalize the banking system, a long step toward the state ownership and administration of all industry and finance would have been taken. He might also have turned to the right, toward what, in contrast with communism, was currently called fascism, and drew its inspiration from the exploits of Mussolini in Italy. His goal then would have been to preserve the private profit system at the expense, if need be, of democracy.

But neither communism nor fascism had any deep rooting in America, and one seemed as likely as the other to develop into an irresponsible dictatorship. There is no evidence that Roosevelt considered either way. What he proposed was a middle course, more in line with American precedents. The business of the nation should be left in private hands, but controls should be set up by the government to prevent the ever-recurring booms and crises from which capitalism had suffered so long. Extreme individualism had already been limited by extensive governmental regulation; what Roosevelt had in mind was to extend regulation to the point where it would result in a planned economy. The powers of government would be amplified, but the rights of the individual would not be destroyed. In addition to this interest in permanent reform, the President was determined also to make more adequate provision for the relief of the unemployed, and to promote by every means at his disposal the restoration of a normal business prosperity.[1]

Very early in his administration the President was called upon to decide whether he could achieve these objectives and at the same time carry on a program of international co-operation. Apparently he at first thought that the two were not incompatible. He accepted, seemingly without reservation, the commitments of his predecessor with respect to American participation in the World Economic Conference to be held in London during the summer of 1933 He received cordially the British Prime Minister, J. Ramsay McDonald, who visited Washington in April to discuss plans for the conference, and a little later he gave equally friendly audiences to the special emissaries of France, Italy, Germany, and Japan. He even showed some disposition to extend the scope of the conference to include the revision of war debts, and he appointed as head of the American delegation the Secretary of State, Cordell Hull, whose devotion to tariff reduction and the reopening of world trade amounted almost to a religion. The conference opened auspiciously on June 12, and in spite of much jockeying for position on the part of participants, its sessions seemed by no means destined to futility. Within two weeks Roosevelt proclaimed publicly his belief that its duty was to "establish order in place of the present chaos by a stabilization of currencies, by freeing the flow of world trade, and by international action to raise price-levels."

The London Economics Conference

---

[1] From its very inception the New Deal produced a host of interpreters and critics whose writings, for the most part, are best forgotten. Samples representing various points of view are as follows: C. A. Beard and G. H. E. Smith, *The Future Comes* (1934); E. K. Lindley, *The Roosevelt Revolution: First Phase* (1933); H. A. Wallace, *America Must Choose* (1934); William MacDonald, *The Menace of Recovery* (1934); Walter Lippmann, *The Method of Freedom* (1934); Norman Thomas, *After the New Deal, What?* (1936).

But for reasons not entirely clear the President soon changed his mind. Early in July he cut the ground completely from under Secretary Hull by renouncing any considerable interest in the stabilization of currencies, and by asserting his determination to seek recovery in America through the establishment of a "sound internal economic system." Whatever the motives that led the President to this decision, it was a fact that the program of legislation he had pushed through Congress was based on the assumption that the United States must "go it alone." For the moment international co-operation was to be side-tracked and economic isolation given a trial. Since American assistance was fundamental in the development of any world program, there was nothing left for the London Conference to do but to wind up its affairs and go home. To the surprise of most observers Secretary Hull resisted the temptation to resign from the cabinet, while Raymond Moley, the "brain-truster" who was credited with bringing about Roosevelt's change of front, soon lost favor with the President and returned to private life. [1]

[1] Dixon Wecter, *The Age of the Great Depression, 1929–1941* (1948), treats of the social aspects of the New Deal. Broadus Mitchell, *Depression Decade* (1948), emphasizes the economic policies of the first two Roosevelt administrations. Frances Perkins, *The Roosevelt I Knew* (1946), is perhaps the best reminiscence to come from any of Roosevelt's close advisers. G. W. Johnson, *Roosevelt: Dictator or Democrat?* (1941), is a friendly estimate. P. L. Kleinsorge, *The Boulder Canyon Project: Historical and Economic Aspects* (1941), is a scientific survey. A. G. Mezerik, *The Revolt of South and West* (1946), shows the antagonism to eastern domination.

CHAPTER XXVIII

THE NEW DEAL IN OPERATION

IT WAS soon apparent that the New Deal had set itself the triple task of relief, recovery, and reform. The legislation of the "hundred days," hastily conceived as it was, all pointed toward one or more *The three* of these objectives. Inconsistencies were frequent; relief *R's* sometimes got in the way of recovery, and recovery in the way of reform. But occasionally, also, reform measures promoted recovery, and recovery almost always helped solve the problem of relief. Whatever their contradictions and interactions, the three goals remained constant, and they were never long forgotten. From time to time changes based on experience, or even on political expediency, appeared, but they were invariably defended as merely a better way of accomplishing what the New Deal had set out to do.

In the matter of relief the New Deal amplified and extended what the Hoover administration had already begun. Through a Federal Emergency Relief Administration, created May 22, 1933, un- *Relief —* returnable contributions instead of RFC loans were made *FERA* available to the states for relief purposes.[1] Out of an appropriation of half a billion dollars fifty per cent was to be allotted on the basis of one dollar of federal funds for every three dollars of local money, while the remainder was to be used for direct grants to states whose relief needs exceeded their financial resources. In actual fact only three states were able to meet as much as half the cost of their relief load, and many contributed less than ten per cent. The law permitted local authorities to provide either work relief or an outright dole, but since in practice the dole was far more economical than "made work," it was used unsparingly. In February, 1934, Congress appropriated $950,000,000 more for the use of the FERA, and by the end of the year about one sixth of the

---

[1] Most of the literature provoked by the New Deal is both controversial and ephemeral, and in matters of opinion is not to be taken too seriously. With respect to unemployment and relief, the following may be found useful: Harry L. Hopkins, *Spending to Save; The Complete Story of Relief* (1936); Nels Anderson, *The Right to Work* (1938); Grace Adams, *Workers on Relief* (1939).

population of the country was on relief. Of this number fully ninety per cent were dependent on the dole. Additional aid to the needy was given through the Federal Surplus Commodities Commission of the Department of Agriculture, created in October, 1933, which spent thirty million dollars during the first year of its existence in buying surplus farm products for distribution through local relief organizations. One of the most difficult of the relief problems was the army of transients which roamed the country. Since these men possessed no legal residence, local authorities were hesitant to accept responsibility for them, but transient camps were established which took care of many of them, while others were induced to join the CCC. Of some assistance also was the United States Employment Service, established during the "hundred days" by the Wagner Act to co-ordinate all local, state, and national employment agencies into one comprehensive system. Before long the amount of "panhandling" on the city streets was materially reduced.

At the head of the FERA was Harry L. Hopkins, a professional social worker who had been in charge of relief activities in New York while *The CWA* Roosevelt was governor. Hopkins believed emphatically in work relief as preferable to the dole for psychological reasons. What most people wanted was neither charity nor public support. Provided with a dole a man tended to become a pauper; but provided with a job he retained his self-respect and might become again a useful member of society. With this principle in mind the President established the Civil Works Administration in October, 1933, as a branch of the FERA, to provide emergency jobs for workers who might otherwise have to spend the winter on relief. The CWA actually gave the first employment they had had for years to millions of men, but the work provided was of indifferent merit, and the haste with which the organization was set up led to an unknown amount of graft and favoritism. Meant merely as a temporary expedient, the CWA was discontinued the following spring. It had demonstrated, however, that the unemployed were eager for work; also, that whatever money was paid out in this fashion was quickly spent, and tended to stimulate business recovery all along the line. Altogether the CWA cost the government about $845,000,000.

In one respect the relief activities of the government proved to be enormously disappointing. The relief rolls somehow failed to shorten, and for the most part tended even to lengthen. People who had savings to rely upon in the earlier years of the depression saw their savings dwindle and disappear until they had no recourse except to seek relief. Private charities broke down in the face of burdens too stupendous.

Young men came of age and sought for jobs that were not to be found. Newly devised machinery threw more men out of work. Year after year there seemed to be no really significant falling-off in the relief rolls, while there were at any time other millions of unemployed men who had not yet exhausted their savings or who were helped out by solvent friends or relatives.

Federal relief workers thus became convinced that the situation they faced could hardly be deemed a mere emergency; or, if so called, that the emergency would not be short-lived.   In harmony with *Work relief* these views, the new Relief Act of April 8, 1935, called upon *— WPA* the government not only to provide relief, but also to provide "work relief, and to increase employment by providing useful projects."   For this purpose a total of nearly five billion dollars was appropriated on the understanding that federal relief officials would help devise work projects, would prescribe rules for the selection of workers, and would regulate the conditions of labor.   The relief program met immediate opposition from two sources: chamber of commerce groups who for reasons of economy to the taxpayer preferred the dole to the far more expensive work projects, and the labor leaders, who feared the adoption of low wage schedules that might break down the prevailing rates of pay on private work.   Nevertheless, the new program was put into effect during the summer of 1935.   The FERA handed over to a new Works Progress Administration, established in July under the direction of the energetic Hopkins, the task of providing work for all employables.   It was hoped that all unemployables, such as the aged, the blind, dependent children, and the like, could be returned to the care of the states, with such federal assistance as the new Social Security Act would make available.[1]

The trifling projects sometimes sponsored by the FERA, the CWA, and in its earlier months the WPA, gave rise to the derisive epithet, "boondoggling," a term often used indiscriminately to describe all made work.   As time went on, the nature of the projects undertaken was much improved.   The ideal which the WPA set for itself but never fully attained was to provide the unemployed with the kind of work they were best fitted to do.   For the unskilled laborers, who constituted the great majority of the relief workers, jobs were found in connection with such projects as the construction of country roads and city streets, the improvement of parks and playgrounds, and the building of flood-control or irrigation dams.   Carpenters, plasterers, masons, plumbers, and other skilled laborers were used to erect or repair schoolhouses, libraries, city halls, courthouses, and other public buildings.   Even the "white-collar"

[1] See *post*, p. 667.

[639]

classes were not neglected, and projects were devised to aid artists, writers, actors, musicians, architects, and many others possessed of more or less professional abilities. Among the projects undertaken were several of great interest to historians, such as the surveys of historical records, and of national, state, and local archives. There were indeed few aspects of American life that were not in some way affected by the activities of the WPA. Supplementary to its program was the work of the National Youth Administration through which needy high-school and college students were enabled to earn small sums for non-instructional assistance to their teachers, while equally needy young people who were not in school were provided with useful part-time jobs. NYA workers earned on an average more than fifteen dollars each per month.[1]

The sums spent on work relief during the two Roosevelt administrations ran far into the billions, and the number of workers aided far into the millions. Efforts were made to cut down on WPA activities whenever an upward trend in business was indicated, but all such reductions met the violent protests of discharged workers, most of whom found it impossible to obtain other employment. WPA wage scales were adjusted as nearly as possible to fit local circumstances. Unskilled laborers earned on an average fifty dollars a month, and white-collar workers considerably more. The hours of work required per week likewise varied, but they were never excessive. Labor unions, armed with the same formidable lists of rights and grievances with which they confronted private employers, soon put in their appearance, and professional radicals found in the WPA a happy hunting ground. In 1939 the federal theater project, although it was almost able to pay its own way, had to be discontinued because of persistent accusations that it was being used to spread radical propaganda.[2]

Undoubtedly the substitution of work relief through the WPA for the dole system that might have been developed by the FERA was an ex-

WPA results tremely expensive proposition, but the nation got something for its investment. Scarcely a community could be found that had not benefited by repaired or even newly constructed public buildings, improved streets and highways, new or renovated parks and playgrounds, together with dozens of other more or less permanent contributions to the convenience and comfort of the public. WPA artists decorated public buildings with murals that revealed much hitherto hidden talent, writers devised guidebooks that served well the needs of the states and localities whose places of interest they charted, while

[1] Betty and E. K. Lindley, *A New Deal for Youth* (1938), tells the story of the NYA.
[2] Willson Whitman, *Bread and Circuses* (1937) is an account of the WPA theater project.

other white-collar workers indexed newspapers, located historical documents, classified and rearranged archives, and did a countless number of other useful chores. More and more the conviction grew that the WPA, or some organization like it, would have a permanent place in American life. If private industry could not fully employ the talents of the whole population, was it not the duty of the state to fill the gap?

Undoubtedly the original intent of the New Deal was to bring about a degree of business recovery that would provide normal employment for all who were capable of earning a living. To this end *Recovery —* the RFC, which had been established during Hoover's *RFC loans* administration, was continued, with the added function of lending to private industry as well as to financial institutions, railroads, and public agencies. All such loans were to be made on a strictly business basis, with the expectation of repayment. The easement of credit that the RFC provided was eagerly accepted by the business world, and its loans soon totaled many billions of dollars. Money lent to financial corporations, such as banks, building and loan associations, insurance and mortgage companies, was almost invariably soon repaid, but loans to railroads, industrial enterprises, and public agencies came back slowly. Nevertheless, of the seven and one half billion dollars lent by the RFC to December 31, 1939, over seventy-seven per cent had been repaid.

To supplement its lending policy the government proposed to stimulate industry still further by a program of direct spending. This was to be accomplished mainly through a Public Works Adminis- *Public* tration, for the use of which the hundred days' session of *works —* Congress appropriated $3,300,000,000. It was supposed *PWA* that the erection of public buildings and other such construction projects would provide much new business for the heavy industries in particular, and less directly for business in general. This, rather than work relief, was the main purpose of the PWA, although the reduction of unemployment was anticipated as an important by-product of its activities. Contractors, however, were not required to select their employees from relief rolls. At the head of the PWA the President placed his Secretary of the Interior, Harold L. Ickes, whose determination to get value received for all the assignments he made considerably slowed down the pump-priming aspects of his organization. The Administrator ruled out all boondoggling activities, and required detailed plans before the spending process could begin. Since architects' drawings for large buildings took many months to complete, after which contracts still had to be let and materials assembled, Ickes's policy inevitably resulted in interminable delays. Furthermore, a large proportion of the projects were undertaken in collaboration with state or local governments which were required to contribute the major part of the cost of construction in the form of bonds delivered to the PWA. In many instances this meant difficulty and delay because of constitutional limits on indebtedness and referendum requirements on the issuing of bonds.[1]

The PWA found no difficulty in obtaining an abundance of acceptable projects upon which to expend its funds, but the program was too slow in developing to give business the "shot in the arm" that had been expected. On this account some of the PWA funds were diverted to CWA and other spending agencies, while new appropriations for public works went mainly to WPA. The business recession of 1937–38 served, however, to revive the PWA, and with plans by this time available in abundance it was able to give much immediate aid to industry. By the end of 1939 it had sponsored projects in all but three counties within the United States at an estimated cost of only a little less than six billion dollars. Federal PWA expenditures centered chiefly upon the improvement of waterways and harbors (including dams for flood control and irrigation purposes), the construction of federal-aid highways, and the building of post-offices, courthouses, warehouses, and such other structures as were needed for federal purposes. Large sums were also used for the building of naval and coast-guard vessels, and for the improvement of army camps, aviation fields, and national parks. Non-federal expenditures made possible hundreds of new municipal waterworks, sewerage, and electric lights systems, innumerable public office buildings and hospitals, and schoolhouses of every description from kindergarten to university. While these improvements were constantly criticized as "spending money that we haven't got for buildings that we can't afford," the PWA investments undoubtedly did much to keep the wheels of industry turning and to make jobs for men who otherwise might have been unemployed. Also, with but few exceptions, the structures erected served a useful social purpose.

Quite the most ambitious of the New Deal efforts to restore prosperity was the National Recovery Administration, authorized June 16, 1933, under the terms of the National Industrial Recovery Act.

The NRA   The NRA was the principal New Deal answer to those who demanded a planned economy. Its purpose was to facilitate the cooperation of all American employers in a gigantic effort to shorten working hours, raise wages, and increase employment. Whatever anti-trust legislation barred the way to reasonable group understandings was swept

[1] H. L. Ickes, *Back to Work: The Story of PWA* (1935); A. D. Gayer, *Public Works in Prosperity and Depression* (1935); J. F. Isakoff, *The Public Works Administration* (1938).

aside. Just as the War Industries Board had promoted the smooth functioning of American business during the World War, so now the NRA was to enable industry to pull together in a joint battle against the depression.

Roosevelt's appointment of Brigadier-General Hugh S. Johnson (retired) as chief administrator of the NRA served still further to emphasize the kinship of the new policy with the regimentation of industry that had been accomplished during the World War. Johnson had been closely associated with Baruch in the work of the War Industries Board, and his activities as head of the NRA strongly reflected his earlier experience. He revived the methods of popular appeal that had proved effective during the war, and sought to instill in the public mind the conviction that support of the NRA was a patriotic duty. He furnished a handsome emblem, the Blue Eagle, to be displayed by all business houses that agreed to follow NRA regulations and by all householders who pledged themselves to buy only from Blue Eagle firms. And he used his limitless energy to induce manufacturers, mine operators, common carriers, utility corporations, merchants, and every other type of business men in the country to devise "codes of fair competition" by which, group by group, they agreed to standardize their behavior.[1]

At first Johnson's efforts were crowned with conspicuous success. His vigorous and colorful personality won for him a degree of popularity that for a time rivaled even the President's; next to the President he was certainly the most conspicuous figure in *NRA codes* American life. Within a matter of months he was able to secure from the representatives of perhaps ninety-five per cent of the business interests of the country the adoption of satisfactory codes, which, when approved by the President, were invested with the full force of law. For all businesses not organized under their own code authorities the President issued a "blanket" code, which abolished child labor, fixed a thirty-five-hour week for ordinary labor and a forty-hour week in white-collar jobs, and established minimum-wage scales of forty cents an hour for the former and from twelve to fifteen dollars a week for the latter. The privately negotiated codes varied considerably, depending upon the type of industry they were designed to fit, but in addition to the prohibition of child labor and the establishment of maximum hours and minimum wages, they usually made elaborate provision for the control of prices and sales practices, and the limitation of production.

[1] H. S. Johnson, *The Blue Eagle from Egg to Earth* (1935); L. S. Lyon and others, *The National Recovery Administration* (1935); C. L. Dearing and others, *ABC of the NRA* (1934).

The NRA assumed that the best way to revive business was to increase purchasing power, and that this could best be accomplished by means of higher wages and re-employment. But inasmuch as employers very generally felt obliged to balance their increased labor costs with increased prices the net effect was somewhat disappointing. Furthermore, difficulties in enforcement soon began to appear that made the problems of prohibition pale into insignificance. "Chiselers" who displayed the Blue Eagle, but ignored the rules, put the honestly intentioned dealer at a serious disadvantage. Wartime methods of compulsion were lacking, and the hope that the code authorities set up by each business group could secure the obedience of all members proved illusive. A few important establishments refused entirely to co-operate. Henry Ford increased wages, but subscribed to no code. Montgomery Ward and Company neglected to pay the dues required of retailers to cover the cost of code administration. Furthermore, the Federal Department of Justice soon found that it could not depend with certainty upon the support of the courts.

But the most discouraging problems of the NRA flowed from the labor provisions included in Section 7(a) of the National Industrial Recovery Act, which stated:

(1) That employees shall have the right to organize and bargain collectively through representatives of their own choosing, and shall be free from the interference, restraint, or coercion of employers of labor, or their agents, in the designation of such representatives or in self-organization or in other concerted activities for the purpose of collective bargaining or other mutual aid or protection;

(2) That no employee and no one seeking employment shall be required as a condition of employment to join any company union or to refrain from joining, organizing, or assisting a labor organization of his own choosing; and

(3) That employers shall comply with the maximum hours of labor, minimum rates of pay, and other conditions of employment approved or prescribed by the President.

These provisions were hailed with delight by labor leaders, who recruited their depression-torn ranks with great rapidity, and stood guard militantly against every tendency on the part of employers to turn the codes to the disadvantage of the workers. To aid in the settlement of such disputes as might crop up, the President established a National Labor Board, headed by Senator Robert F. Wagner of New York, which successfully mediated thousands of grievances, but was compelled to rely mainly upon moral authority to enforce its decisions. Particularly vexing was the failure of the National Industrial Recovery Act to specify whether company unions might participate in collective bargaining, and whether a union that represented a majority of the workers in a given industry might be construed to represent the minority as well. In the summer of 1934 Congress replaced the NLB with a more powerful National Labor Relations Board, which strongly supported the most extreme contentions of labor. By this time industry was in full revolt against the NRA in general and Section 7(a) in particular, and the real or fancied grievances it furnished led to one violent strike after another. A strike of longshoremen that began in the ports of the Pacific coast early in May developed into a general strike throughout the San Francisco area. It was broken in July only after a corps of vigilantes had raided the strikers' offices and had seized their leaders. In September a strike in the textile industries kept half a million men out of work for nearly a month, but ended in an almost complete victory for the employers. These, together with many less extensive outbreaks, marked the year as one of the most disturbed in the whole history of American industrial relations. Johnson held labor mainly responsible for the turn events had taken, and in a speech delivered in New York, September 14, 1934, openly denounced the textile workers for having broken faith with him. Ten days later he resigned.[1]

Bereft of Johnson's dynamic leadership, and no longer able to count on the full support of either industry or labor, the NRA played a steadily diminishing rôle in American economic life. By law the organization was due to expire after two years unless given *End of NRA* a longer lease of life by Congress. It lasted on in reorganized form under the guidance of Donald R. Richberg until May, 1935, when a decision of the United States Supreme Court gave it the *coup de grâce*. In the so-called Schechter case the Court held that Congress had overstepped constitutional limits both in delegating "legislative authority to the President to exercise an unfettered discretion," and in presuming that the interstate commerce clause applied to "all enterprises and transactions which could be said to have an indirect effect upon interstate commerce." As for the contention that exceptional powers were necessary to meet a pressing emergency, the Court held that the Constitution had been designed no less for emergencies than for ordinary conditions. The President was deeply incensed at the stand the Court had taken, but he bowed to its authority and the whole NRA organization was rapidly dismantled.

Efforts to salvage some of the gains attributed to the NRA were not entirely lacking. At the insistence of the administration the Guffey-

[1] C. R. Daugherty, *Labor Under the NRA* (1934).

Snyder Act was passed in August, 1935, to promote the stabilization of conditions in the bituminous coal industry. This measure seemed to the President so important that he told the House Ways and Means Committee: "I hope your committee will not permit doubts as to the constitutionality, however reasonable, to block the suggested legislation." But a five-to-four decision of the Supreme Court in May, 1936, invalidated the law, and returned the soft-coal business to its customary chaos. Another measure, the Wagner-Connery Labor Relations Act, was designed to soften the blow sustained by labor in the loss of Section 7(a). The new act stated that the policy of the United States was to protect the rights of laborers to organize and to bargain collectively with employers through representatives of their own choosing. A new National Labor Relations Board, also of three members, which replaced the NLRB of the year before, was authorized to halt unfair practices on the part of employers and to seek enforcement for its orders through the federal courts. The new NLRB successfully ran the gantlet of the Supreme Court, although the board's right to interfere where the process of manufacture was strictly local in character was sustained by a bare majority. In 1938 Congress took steps also toward the re-establishment throughout the country of minimum wages and maximum hours and the abolition of child labor. By the Wages and Hours Act it laid down rules that a wages and hours division of the Department of Labor was expected to enforce.

One result of the labor turmoil that characterized these years of change and experiment was the division of organized labor itself into *The labor split — CIO* two competing camps. The American Federation of Labor, led since 1924 by William Green, adhered consistently to the Gompers policy of co-operating with capital as long as wages and working conditions remained satisfactory. With the capitalistic system as such it refused to quarrel, provided only that labor obtained a reasonable reward for the work it was called upon to do. Furthermore, the A.F. of L. still set much store by the crafts union type of organization, and opposed with vigor all attempts to organize into one union all the workers in a given industry, regardless of their skills or their lack of skills. The Federation, so its critics complained, had thus lost touch with the problems of the ordinary worker. After the destruction of the NRA in 1935, John L. Lewis, militant head of the United Mine Workers, took the lead in the formation of a Committee for Industrial Organization, the purpose of which was to promote the unionization of industries as units, and not in accordance with specified trades or skills. In this endeavor he was officially opposed by the A.F. of L., but, with the support

[646]

of his own and several other powerful unions, he sent organizers into many of the great mass-production industries, such as automobiles, steel, textiles, rubber, aluminum, plate-glass, and furniture. In most instances the CIO plan of organization seemed to meet a long-felt need; old unions took on new life, and new unions were founded as needed. For co-operating with Lewis in this work ten unions were suspended in 1936 by the A.F. of L., and as a result the CIO assumed a permanent character that its prime movers had not at first intended. Claiming to represent a membership of nearly four million workers as against the five million of the A.F. of L., the CIO changed its name in November, 1938, to the Congress of Industrial Organizations, adopted a constitution after the A.F. of L. model, and elected Lewis as its first president.[1]

The methods by which the CIO had risen to such great importance involved among other things the use of a weapon new to American labor history, the "sit-down" strike. Workers instead of first leaving the factories, and then picketing them to prevent *The "sit-down"* the employment of "scabs," simply retained in idleness the posts they ordinarily held, and forcibly resisted removal. This technique was successfully employed in CIO strikes against two great automobile companies, General Motors and the Chrysler Corporation. In both instances, with the assistance of Governor Frank Murphy of Michigan, agreements were finally reached to vacate the plants on condition that the CIO union should be recognized as the bargaining agent for its members, while later negotiations won other concessions. The United States Steel Corporation, long the despair of labor leaders, did not await the coming conflict, but in March, 1937, accorded the CIO Steel Workers' Organizing Committee full bargaining authority for all its membership. Most of the other so-called "Big Steel" companies also capitulated, but "Little Steel," led by T. M. Girdler of the Republic Steel Corporation, fought back. Strikes that began in May, 1937, spread rapidly through Pennsylvania, Ohio, and Illinois, and were accompanied by much disorder. But the timely action of employers prevented "sit-down" strikes, and without this weapon the strikers lost. Moreover, the public had become thoroughly weary of labor conflict, and was disposed to blame the violence that accompanied CIO strikes on communist agitators. William Green, the A.F. of L. leader, complained bitterly that the CIO methods were discrediting the whole labor movement. Even when the police brutally shot down a number of picketers at the Republic

---

[1] J. R. Walsh, *C.I.O., Industrial Unionism in Action* (1937); Benjamin Stolberg, *Story of the CIO* (1938); Edward Levinson, *Labor on the March* (1938); Herbert Harris, *Labor's Civil War* (1940).

Steel Works in South Chicago, there was little effective protest. Parallel to the New Deal program for industry and labor was an equally comprehensive plan for the rehabilitation of agriculture. Strik-
The AAA ing out along what the President himself called "a new and untrod path," the Agricultural Adjustment Act of May 12, 1933, sought a remedy for the chronic overproduction that had for so long kept American farm prices down. Frankly recognizing that the foreign market could not be depended upon, the framers of the act proposed to restrict the American output, if need be, to what the United States alone could consume. By careful supervision of production, prices were to be brought back to the average levels of the five years preceding the World War. To accomplish these ends an Agricultural Adjustment Administration was set up with authority to buy and hold surpluses, and to contract with the producers of specified basic commodities for whatever co-operation might be needed to insure crop control. Since the farmers were to be paid generously for their co-operation, agriculture stood to receive a double subsidy, one by way of direct money payments on the basis of the contracts signed, and the other through higher prices for crops harvested. The cost involved in the crop-restriction program was to be met by a tax levied against the processors of farm produce, who in turn would pass the burden along to the consumers. The farmer, if this elaborate scheme of economic planning worked, would find himself at last on a parity with other economic groups. Basic commodities at first brought within the scope of the act were cotton, wheat, corn, hogs, rice, tobacco, and milk, but a year later the list was greatly lengthened.[1]

The AAA was organized within the Department of Agriculture, and operated under the watchful and sympathetic supervision of Secretary
Cotton control Wallace. It experimented first with cotton, and in the summer of 1933 succeeded in persuading about three fourths of the cotton-growers of the country to sign contracts reducing their cotton acreage by about one third. Since the planting had already been done, this meant that much growing cotton had to be plowed under. Cash payments for obedience to the government's orders amounted to from seven to twenty dollars per acre. To offset this expense a tax of four cents a pound was levied on cotton processed by manufacturers. The results from the farmers' point of view were good, for benefit payments amounted to about two hundred million dollars, while the price of cotton climbed from five and one half to nine and one half cents a

[1] E. G. Nourse and others, *Three Years of the Agricultural Adjustment Administration* (1937); E. G. Nourse, *Marketing Agreements under the AAA* (1935).

[648]

pound. It was clear, however, that the amount of cotton produced had not declined in proper proportion to the acreage taken out of cultivation. Farmers generally plowed under their poorest stands, and generously fertilized the rest. Accordingly, a Cotton Control Act was passed April 21, 1934, which enabled the AAA to assign definite quotas for states, counties, and individual farmers throughout the cotton-growing area. For those who produced beyond their quotas a penalty tax of five cents a pound or more was collected at the gins. By these means the cotton crops of 1934 and 1935 were held down to approximately ten million bales instead of the fourteen million average of the preceding five years. Much the same plan was carried out, with equally noteworthy effect, among tobacco-growers.

The AAA made no effort during its first season to reduce the plantings of wheat and corn, but bad weather conditions kept down production of both commodities to subnormal levels, and prices were *Wheat,* better than usual. In 1934 an attempt was made to reduce *corn, and* wheat acreage by fifteen per cent, corn acreage by twenty *hogs* per cent, and hog production by twenty-five per cent. Benefit payments for the estimated reductions were to be made at the rate of twenty-eight cents per bushel for wheat, thirty cents per bushel for corn, and five dollars per head for hogs. The processing taxes assessed to meet these expenditures were fixed at thirty cents per bushel on wheat, five cents per bushel on corn, and $2.25 per hundredweight on hogs. A devastating drouth that extended over almost all the grain-growing states during the summer of 1934 gave more aid than was desired to the crop-reduction program, and obliged the AAA to join with other governmental agencies in providing direct drouth relief. So complete was the drouth in some of the western states that many farmers had nothing to live on except the money they received from the government under their crop-reduction contracts; furthermore, the windstorms that swept ceaselessly through the western "dust bowl" threatened to render much land permanently useless. Nevertheless, the AAA continued its crop-reduction program in 1935, and claimed for its activities an important influence in striking a better balance between supply and demand. Other farm products to which the program was extended included sugar, rice, rye, cattle, and dairy products.

Caustic criticism of so vast an undertaking was inevitable. Crop reductions, at a time when drouth conditions threatened the country with actual shortages, were difficult to defend, and in many instances had to be modified. But some actions had been taken, such as the purchase and slaughter of thousands of young pigs and sows, that could

HISTORIC POSTAGE STAMPS

Since 1893 United States postage stamps have not been used merely for carrying the mail, but also for commemorating historic events, and — more recently — for advertising. The Alaska stamp is one of four commemorating the territories of the United States; the Ohio marks the completion of the locks to make that stream navigable all year. The Chicago Century of Progress and other World's Fair stamps advertise these events. The Panama Canal stamp above commemorates the twenty-

h anniversary of the opening of the Canal; the one on this page celebrates the opening.
e others are self-explanatory.

not be reconsidered. Farmers whose lifelong habits had been based upon growing more and more found it difficult to adjust themselves to an economy of growing less and less. They signed the contracts and accepted the benefit payments because they needed the money, but they resented the system. Processors complained bitterly at the heavy taxation forced upon them, and found themselves seriously handicapped in competing for markets outside the United States. Consumers paid steeply increased prices for nearly everything that came from the farm.

In spite of these criticisms the country was hardly prepared for the drastic action of the United States Supreme Court which announced *The AAA* January 6, 1936, in a six-to-three decision, that the Agri-*invalidated* cultural Adjustment Act was unconstitutional. In an opinion read by Justice Roberts the Court held that there was nothing in the Constitution to justify federal control of agricultural production, and that, in attempting to deal with the strictly local business of farming, Congress had invaded a right reserved to the states. Since the processing taxes and benefit payments existed only as means to an illegal end, the Court held that they, too, were invalid. The implications of this decision worried the minority of the Court, which in a dissenting opinion read by Justice Stone warned the majority that "courts are not the only agency of government that must be assumed to have capacity to govern." Nor could agricultural economists quite understand how farming could be classified as a strictly local business when most farm prices, if unregulated, would depend upon nation-wide and even upon world-wide conditions.

In wrecking the AAA the Supreme Court did not destroy the entire New Deal structure for dealing with agriculture. Since not less than *Rural credits* two out of every five American farms were mortgaged, *— FCA* many of them, as matters stood, for far more than they were worth, the importance of rural credits was obvious. In June, 1933, President Roosevelt, acting on authority of Congress, sought to eliminate unnecessary duplication of effort by consolidating under the control of a new Farm Credit Administration every federal agency in the United States that had anything to do with agricultural credits. Included in the reorganization was the Federal Farm Loan Board, which governed the banks that dealt in long and intermediate term credits to farmers, the Federal Farm Board established during Hoover's administration, and certain rural credits functions that had previously been connected with the Reconstruction Finance Corporation and the Department of Agriculture. With the help of such supplementary legislation as experience proved to be desirable, the FCA by 1934 was lending at

[652]

the rate, on an average, of five million dollars a day. Much of this credit was used to refinance mortgages that might otherwise have been foreclosed, but loans for production and for marketing were also supplied. Frequently the new government loans were for less than the face of the old mortgage, but creditors gladly accepted the loss involved rather than take over the mortgaged property. Some loans were made also to buy back property that had been lost through foreclosure proceedings.

As a further check on the trend toward tenancy the Frazier-Lemke Bankruptcy Act of June, 1934, prohibited creditors from holding fore-closure sales for a period of five years, provided that the farmers concerned could pay what government officials regarded as a reasonable rental on their property. This law was too much for the Supreme Court, which invalidated it as a taking of private property without due process of law, but a new measure, the Frazier-Lemke Moratorium Act of August, 1935, which accomplished much the same purpose, was sustained. This second act delayed foreclosure proceedings for a three-year period, provided a court of law would give its approval, both to the propriety of the delay and to the adequacy of the rental to be paid.

Spurred on by the acute agricultural distress that accompanied drouth conditions, the New Deal in April, 1935, added to its rapidly lengthening list of alphabetical agencies still another, the Resettlement *The RA* Administration. Headed at first by Rexford G. Tugwell, *and FSA* a college professor with a strong belief in the necessity of economic planning, the RA took over and greatly expanded the work of rural rehabilitation already begun by the FERA and other governmental agencies. Outright grants for subsistence needs and loans secured by crop liens for the purchase of seed, tools, fertilizer, and other essentials were made to hard-pressed farmers; millions of acres of marginal and submarginal land that ought never to have been cultivated were bought by the government for reforestation, conversion into grazing land, or other conservational use; the resettlement in "healthy rural communities" of dispossessed farmers who were unable to find adequate opportunities for themselves was attempted; and work on a few "green-belt" suburban communities, designed "to provide low-rental houses for low-income groups," was begun. The RA found much difficulty in inducing farmers to leave their lands, however undesirable they might be, and its resettlement activities soon turned out to be of minor importance. In view of this fact, in 1937 it was renamed the Farm Security Administration, and turned its attention chiefly to making loans to competent farm tenants, share-croppers, and farm laborers to enable them to become farm owners. It experimented, also, with the establishment of rural village communities from which as centers co-operative farming might be carried on; but so alien a system found little response among American farmers.

The hostility of the Supreme Court was sufficient to put an end to the NRA, which had begun to break down anyway, but the critical condition of agriculture required that some substitute be found immediately for the AAA. As a stopgap measure, designed mainly to save the situation until something better could be devised, Congress enacted in February, 1936, the Soil Conservation and Domestic Allotment Act. Instead of the control of production at which the AAA had aimed, the primary objective of the new act was to be soil conservation. The all-important payments to farmers were to be continued, but henceforth they were to be made in return for co-operation with the government in an elaborate program for the promotion of soil fertility, the prevention of erosion, and the more economic use of farm land. By placing restrictions on the planting of soil-depleting crops, some effort was made to hold down the production of such basic commodities as cotton, wheat, and corn, but by 1937 the cotton yield reached the startlingly high figure of 18,945,028 bales, while most other crops showed a wide margin over the nation's ability to consume. Furthermore, there was no longer a processing tax to meet the cost of the benefit payments, and the money had to come directly out of the Treasury. Mindful of the tender susceptibilities of the Supreme Court, Congress provided that state agencies should eventually be given a conspicuous part in carrying on the new program.

Finally in 1938 Congress enacted a new Agricultural Adjustment Act as "the Nation's well-matured answer" to the needs of the American *The new* farmer. It retained the soil-conservation and benefit-*AAA* payment features of the preceding program; it made provision in five key crops, wheat, cotton, corn, tobacco, and rice, for the limitation of acreage allotments in accordance with probable needs; it authorized the making of storage loans as a means of holding agricultural surpluses off the market; and it sanctioned resort to marketing quotas in emergencies, provided that two thirds of the growers of the commodity concerned recorded their approval in a referendum vote. All this was a part of an elaborate effort to raise the income of farmers to "parity," that is, to the same ratio with the incomes of other groups that had existed in the five years prior to 1914; to make doubly sure of this goal the sum of $212,000,000 was appropriated in 1939 for "parity payments" to help bridge the gap between current prices and "parity prices." For the benefit of wheat-growers, a Federal Crop Insurance Corporation was established in the Department of Agriculture from which guaranties could be obtained to the amount of fifty or seventy-five per cent of normal yields. Payments of losses and premiums were to be made either in wheat or in its cash equivalent.

Although participation in the AAA program was kept on a purely voluntary basis, the generous subsidies offered were hard for farmers to resist. About five and a quarter million agricultural producers, working through three thousand county conservation associations and many more subordinate committees, took part in the 1939 program. Nearly three fourths of the crop land of the nation was involved. In accordance with the wishes of Secretary Wallace, an "ever normal granary" was promoted by loans on warehoused surpluses which amounted approximately to nine cents per pound on cotton, sixty cents per bushel on wheat, and fifty-seven cents per bushel on corn. By this device it was hoped that both producer and consumer would be protected against shortages and price fluctuations. The marketing quota provisions of the act were also promptly invoked to protect the prices of cotton and of several types of tobacco, while nearly one hundred and seventy thousand wheat-growers, some of them in drouth-threatened areas where there was little prospect of a crop, took out federal crop insurance. The cost of all this to the government exceeded half a billion dollars a year.

While the New Deal measures served undoubtedly to increase farm incomes, they left many of the fundamental problems of American agriculture still unsolved. Wheat surpluses threatened to *Wheat surpluses* remain permanent in spite of every effort to turn the activities of wheat farmers into other lines. Against a normal domestic consumption of 650,000,000 bushels of wheat, American farmers produced 932,000,000 bushels in 1938 and 755,000,000 in 1939. The lower figure for 1939 was due less to the activities of the AAA than to drouth conditions on the western plains, and since the average wheat production during the ten-year period that ended in 1937 was about 753,000,000 bushels, it was evident that not much progress had been made toward crop control. Meantime the world supply of wheat had mounted to the highest figure on record, and the struggle to find export outlets became correspondingly strenuous. Hopes that the outbreak of war in Europe might greatly stimulate the demand for American wheat were unrealized as late as the spring of 1940, when the successes of the German arms in Flanders led to a drop of thirty cents in July futures on the Chicago market. And what was true of wheat was true in greater or lesser degree of most basic American food crops.

[655]

The plight of cotton was even more distressing, for American cotton-growers needed to dispose of a full half of their normal crop abroad.[1]

The plight of cotton Cotton had long since ceased to be an American monopoly, but during the thirties the speed with which the rest of the world had begun to achieve its independence of the American product took on a tremendous acceleration. This was due in part to the trend of the times toward national self-sufficiency, but the American habit of reducing cotton acreage after each low-price season led British importers to encourage the development of new sources of supply in Latin America, Egypt, and India. When the AAA first began to operate, about forty-five per cent of the cotton used abroad was American cotton; five years later the proportion had dropped to twenty-three per cent. During the cotton year ending July 31, 1939, American cotton exports amounted to only 3,362,000 bales, the smallest figure since 1882. Meantime, in spite of frantic efforts on the part of the AAA to cut production, the 1939 cotton carry-over had mounted to more than thirteen million bales, an increase since the year before of over eleven per cent, and an all-time high. Moreover, the greater part of this excess cotton was stored in government warehouses as collateral for loans, and could not be disposed of except with the consent of the owners. The amount of American cotton actually available for immediate sale was thus small enough to insure a maximum amount of foreign competition. The outbreak of hostilities in Europe led to some heartening export activity during the late summer and fall of 1939, but the next spring the threat of a speedy German victory served, as in the case of wheat, to undermine confidence. The panic that hit the American markets in May, 1940, lowered the price of July futures by about ten per cent.

The effect of the New Deal measures upon the social organization of the deep South was far more revolutionary than had been foreseen. Re-

Social changes in the South ductions in the cotton acreage meant that thousands of share-croppers were left without land to work, while AAA benefit payments enabled landlords to purchase the machin. ery necessary to throw still other thousands off the land. Former share, croppers dropped to the status of agricultural day laborers, with at best only seasonal employment, and with frequent to constant dependence on relief. These conditions, greatly augmented in the southwestern dust bowl by the persistent drouths, raised up an army of wanderers who roamed the West in "jallopies," searching endlessly for employment. Far out into the Southwest, through New Mexico and Arizona to Cali-

[1] H. I. Richards, *Cotton and the AAA* (1936). Cotton and many other southern problems are well discussed in Jonathan Daniels, *A Southerner Discovers the South* (1938).

fornia, the blight of cotton-growing extended, and wherever it went the poverty-stricken cotton hand went with it. All over the South the need for diversified farming was as apparent as it was difficult to promote, while with "normalcy" forever fading into the future, the gains that industry was able to make over agriculture were slight.[1]

In many of the New Deal measures the reform motive stood out clearly. This was certainly true of the monetary policy, which, as the President told the World Economic Conference of 1933, was designed to provide "the kind of dollar which, a generation hence, will have the same purchasing and debt-paying power as the dollar value we hope to attain in the near future." In other words, *Reform — the currency* while the President was ready to cheapen the dollar as a means of promoting recovery and facilitating the payment of debts, he set as his ultimate goal the old Populistic ideal of a dollar that could be depended upon not to fluctuate in value. To the dismay of many conservative economists, he promptly took the United States off the gold standard, secured from Congress a Gold Repeal Resolution which invalidated the gold clauses employed in so many public and private contracts, and prepared to experiment with a managed currency. Gold exports were forbidden; gold coin, gold bullion, and gold certificates were taken out of circulation; and a price fixed by the government was paid for all gold newly mined in the United States or offered for sale from abroad. Finally, under authority of the Gold Reserve Act of January 30, 1934, the amount of gold in the standard dollar was reduced to 59.06 per cent of its former content.[2]

While the President's program for raising prices by cheapening the dollar met at first with some success, the net results proved to be far less significant than he had hoped or his critics had feared. The new dollars, regardless of their theoretical value as expressed in terms of gold, bought almost as much as the old dollars, and the President, although permitted by law to reduce the former gold content by as much as fifty per cent, made no further move toward devaluation. Under the terms of a new Silver Purchase Act, signed June 19, 1934, he did, however, begin the purchase of silver, ostensibly to increase the supply of silver in the national monetary stocks until it had reached a value equal to one fourth the total amount. But this policy in practice turned out to be little more than a generous bounty to the silver producers of the

---

[1] C. S. Johnson and others, *The Collapse of Cotton Tenancy* (1935).

[2] H. G. Moulton, *Financial Organization and the Economic System* (1938); W. R. Burgess, *Reserve Banks and the Money Market* (1936); A. D. Gayer, editor, *The Lessons of Monetary Experience* (1937).

country, who were thereby assured a market for their output at a figure far in excess of the current world price. Unhappily, none of these measures provided any reasonable assurance that the purchasing power of the dollar would or could be stabilized.

That the President had no intention of risking any extensive currency inflation was evident from his failure to issue the three billion dollars of fiat money authorized by the so-called Thomas Amendment to the Agricultural Adjustment Act of 1933; also, from his veto of the Soldiers' Bonus Bill of 1935, which proposed to pay off in the same type of currency all outstanding adjusted compensation certificates. The next year a similar Bonus Bill was passed over the President's veto, but without the inflationary feature. Some economists believed that the huge sums of gold and silver acquired by the government under its new monetary policy constituted in themselves a potential threat of inflation. By January 1, 1940, the United States had in its possession over seventeen billion dollars' worth of gold and about two billion dollars' worth of silver as against a total amount of currency in circulation of less than eight billions (a sum well above the Populist goal of fifty dollars per capita). But the government's riches were tightly guarded, and played no greater part in determining currency values than the Federal Reserve authorities chose to permit. After 1936 about one third of the gold supply was transferred to Fort Knox, a newly constructed depository in the hills of Kentucky.

Roosevelt opposes inflation

In order to prevent the recurrence of such an epidemic of bank failures as had ushered in the Roosevelt administration, Congress made repeated changes in the national banking system. The Glass-Steagall Act of 1933 responded to a strong popular demand by creating a Federal Deposit Insurance Corporation through which deposits up to $2500 might be immediately guaranteed, and still larger sums after six months' time. Further, the act provided for divorcement of commercial and investment banking, permitted national banks to establish branch banks in states that accorded that privilege to state banks, gave the Federal Reserve Board the right to place severe restrictions upon banks that lent too freely for speculative purposes, forbade loans from their own banks to the executive officers of Federal Reserve Banks, and expanded the Federal Reserve System to include industrial and savings banks. Two years later another banking act greatly strengthened the control of the national government over the whole Federal Reserve System. The old Federal Reserve Board was replaced by a board of governors of seven members, all to be appointed directly

The Glass-Steagall Act

[658]

by the President for terms of fourteen years each. The powers of the new board included a veto over selections for chief executive officers made by the various Federal Reserve Banks, practically complete control over the expansion and contraction of bank credits, and the right to raise the reserve requirements of member banks.

Also included within the list of the Roosevelt reforms was an attempt to deal with the problems of speculative investments. A Federal Securities Act, signed on May 27, 1933, insisted that the vendors of securities must be made to tell the public the truth about *The SEC* what they had to sell, and imposed heavy penalties for the interstate circulation of fraudulent advertising, through the mails or otherwise. The next year another act established the Securities and Exchange Commission to take over from the Federal Trade Commission the administration of these regulations. While it was beyond the power of the SEC to guarantee the purchasers of securities against loss, it could and did compel the disclosure of such information as might enable investors to form intelligent opinions of their own. The SEC was authorized also to license stock exchanges, and to regulate their practices in such a way as to stimulate legitimate trading and to discourage mere gambling.[1]

Under the terms of the Public Utilities Act of 1935 the SEC obtained a special grant of power with respect to the activities of public utility holding companies. During the prosperous twenties the holding company device had been carried to unreasonable extremes, partly to enable favored financial groups to exercise monopolistic control over a given area, and partly to multiply securities for sale to a gullible public. Holding companies were pyramided one upon another in topheavy edifices that at best were likely to siphon off the profits of operating companies into the pockets of a few insiders, and at worst were ready to topple over of their own weight the moment anything went wrong. Of the latter type was the utility empire of Samuel Insull, which collapsed in 1932 leaving thousands of investors ruined. There were many who favored a "death sentence" for all utility holding companies, but Congress was content merely to bring them under the regulatory authority of the SEC, and to limit their operations "to a single integrated public-utility system." Much litigation followed the attempt of the SEC to set up its controls in the utility field, but as time went on recognition of its powers tended to grow.

Partly to promote recovery, but partly also with a view to reform, the

[1] R. L. Weissman, *The New Wall Street* (1939), tells of the changes wrought by the new legislation.

New Deal instituted drastic changes in the control of transportation. *Railroad co-ordination* The railroads in particular required attention, for the competition of automobiles, trucks, and pipe lines, with such inevitable loss of business as accompanied the depression, had brought them to the very brink of ruin. Railroad equipment was run down or worn out, roadbeds needed reworking, and the cost of operation all too frequently exceeded the passenger fares and freight charges taken in. Hampering regulations required maintenance of service that was no longer necessary, and habits of competition prevented long-overdue retrenchments. To meet this situation two extreme measures were commonly discussed. One was for the government itself to take over and administer the railroads as it had done during the war, perhaps even purchasing them outright; the other was to put the railroads through the "wringer" of ruthless bankruptcy proceedings, and thus to reduce their indebtedness to a point commensurate with their earning capacity.

The New Deal was unwilling to seize either horn of this dilemma. On the one hand, it was a matter of common knowledge that government operation of the railroads had been tolerated by the public during the war merely as an emergency measure, and that government ownership could be attained only by the purchase of railroad property at a highly fictitious valuation. On the other hand, it was also known that railroad securities in large amounts were held by insurance companies, savings banks, and other institutional investors whose collapse would serve only to extend the scope of the depression and deepen the general gloom. As a kind of compromise Congress passed, and on June 16, 1933, the President approved, an Emergency Railroad Transportation Act, which provided for a federal co-ordinator of transportation whose duty was to eliminate wasteful competition, to co-ordinate train service, and to effect needed economies.[1]

As federal co-ordinator the President appointed Joseph B. Eastman, a believer in government ownership who nevertheless exerted himself to the utmost to make the existing system work. At his suggestion the western lines cut their passenger fares to two cents a mile, with such satisfactory results to their incomes that in 1936 the Interstate Commerce Commission made the rate change general. In 1938, however, an increase was allowed to two and one half cents, but early in 1940 the ICC restored the two-cent rate. RFC loans were used freely to buy new railroad equipment, and to permit improvements in service. It was in

---

[1] H. G. Moulton and others, *The American Transportation Problem* (1933). See also the reports of J. B. Eastman, Federal Co-ordinator of Transportation, in Seventy-Third Congress, second session, *Senate Document* no. 152 (serial 9790), and Seventy-Fourth Congress, first session, *House Document* no. 89 (serial 9920).

this way that many of the roads obtained the funds to experiment with streamlined, air-conditioned trains, drawn by Diesel-electric or steam-electric locomotives. Thanks to the comforts so provided, a fair proportion of the traveling public was won back from automobile to railroad transportation, at least for long distances, and the profits to the railroads were good. Motor buses and trucks engaged in interstate traffic were brought under the control of the ICC by an act of August, 1935, and with business in general, except during the recession of 1937–38, on the upgrade, the financial condition of the railroads slowly improved. By 1939 the net operating income of all Class I railroads in the United States was $588,800,000 as against only $334,325,000 in 1932.

With respect to ocean-going means of transportation the New Deal frankly accepted the theory that a strong merchant marine was an essential part of the national defense program. The Mer- *The merchant* chant Marine Act of 1936 declared: (1) that the United *marine* States should have shipping adequate to maintain its normal flow of water-borne commerce "at all times"; (2) that this shipping should be "capable of serving as a naval and military auxiliary in time of war"; (3) that it should be owned so far as possible by American citizens and operated under the American flag; (4) that it should be "composed of the best-equipped, safest, and most suitable types of vessels." The act supplanted the old Shipping Board and its subsidiary Merchant Fleet Corporation with a new Maritime Commission, one duty of which was to determine the ocean lanes in which American ships should ply, and another, to work out, in full co-operation with the Navy Department, a "long-range program for replacements and additions to the American merchant marine." The old system of subsidies by means of mail contracts now gave way to a new system whereby government assistance was so computed as to equalize the cost of construction and operation under foreign and American auspices, with further payments, if necessary, to offset foreign subsidies by an American equivalent. Also, the commission itself, provided the President approved, might build and operate ships. When private building, in spite of the subsidies offered, failed to achieve adequate results, the commission availed itself of this privilege, and in 1938 began a program of construction designed to provide fifty new ships each year for a period of ten years. During the recession of 1937–38 it bought many ships from private companies that had come to grief, and in 1939 it instituted with the consent of Congress a "turn-in and build" program which enabled American shipowners to receive a generous allowance toward new ships by turning over to the commission ships not less than seventeen years old. The result of these various measures was to make the year 1939 the busiest in the annals of American shipbuilding since the first World War. Altogether the year witnessed the construction of over 471,000 gross tons of shipping, and as it closed fifty-nine new ships were being built. When the second World War broke out, the total American tonnage was two thirds as great as the British, and far in excess of any other. It was also vastly improved in serviceability.[1]

Social workers who knew well the faulty housing conditions from which many underprivileged Americans suffered were quick to urge *The housing* governmental assistance for home-building as one of the *problem* best means of promoting both recovery and reform. Coupled with this problem, also, was the need of saving large numbers of home-owners from losing their property through mortgage foreclosures. To meet these needs government credit was for a time extended through the Home Owners' Loan Corporation, the purpose of which was to refinance home mortgages, and through Federal Savings and Loan Associations, locally established, which provided funds for new building. By June, 1936, when its lending ceased, the HOLC had acquired mortgages totaling three billion dollars and had helped at least a million home-owners. Another agency, the Federal Housing Administration, established in 1934, undertook to insure home mortgages of which it approved up to eighty (later ninety) per cent of the appraised value of the property involved. This left to private capital the business of providing the money, but the FHA took most of the risk.

Far more revolutionary in character was the National Housing Act of 1937 under which a United States Housing Authority was established *National* to aid local communities in remedying their "shortage of *Housing* decent, safe, and sanitary dwellings for families of low in-*Act of 1937* come." For this purpose an initial appropriation of eight hundred million dollars was made. That the program aimed specifically at slum clearance was evident from the stipulation that for each new building made possible by federal money there must be an equivalent destruction or improvement of inadequate housing. As a result of USHA activities, nineteen low-rent apartment houses had been constructed by the end of 1939 in thirteen different cities, and loans of more than a half-billion dollars for the use of 155 communities had been approved. USHA buildings cost on an average less than $3000 per family unit, with monthly rentals varying from $11.45 in the South to $15.80 in the North. The program looked forward to the ultimate

---

[1] National Industrial Conference Board, *The American Merchant Marine Problem* (1929); P. M. Zeis, *American Shipping Policy* (1938).

removal of 640,000 persons from "sub-standard living conditions to new low-rent homes." [1]

The conservation of hydroelectric power, and its use in the interest of the people as a whole rather than for the benefit of privately owned utility companies, was another reform dear to the hearts of most New Dealers. Ever since the presidency of Theo- *The TVA* dore Roosevelt efforts had been made to prevent the unrestrained private exploitation of the nation's resources in water-power. Water-power sites had been freely withdrawn from entry, and in 1920 a Federal Water-Power Commission, consisting of the Secretaries of War, Interior, and Agriculture, had been given the right to license and regulate all water-power projects that could be reached by federal authority. The duties of the commission soon proved to be too heavy for the three busy Secretaries, and in 1930 a Federal Power Commission of five appointive members was created with responsibilities analogous to those of the Interstate Commerce Commission. The New Deal, however, wished to go much farther than mere regulation, and to experiment with actual ownership and operation by the government. Effectively guided in all that concerned this subject by Senator George W. Norris of Nebraska, it singled out the Tennessee Valley for its first great project. This region, ramifying into seven different states — Tennessee, Kentucky, Alabama, Mississippi, Virginia, North Carolina, and Georgia — and embracing within its boundaries some forty thousand square miles, seemed to offer an ideal testing ground for the various New Deal theories on social and economic planning. It counted among its residents a high proportion of the underprivileged classes whose status cheap power was expected to benefit; and it possessed vast natural resources, most of which were either inadequately exploited or were being allowed to degenerate. Since the government had already spent huge sums upon the Muscle Shoals development, it was believed that here, if anywhere, results might speedily be obtained.

In May, 1933, Congress authorized the President to appoint a board of three directors, known as the Tennessee Valley Authority, into whose hands control of the mighty project was to be placed. The TVA was authorized to construct dams for the improvement of navigation and the control of floods; to develop new forms of fertilizer and to promote their use; to build and operate hydroelectric plants and to distribute the power they generated; and to take such other steps as it might see fit to promote the agricultural and industrial development of the region

---

[1] L. W. Post, *The Challenge of Housing* (1938); M. W. Straus and Talbot Wegg, *Housing Comes of Age* (1938); William Ebenstein, *The Law of Public Housing* (1940).

1 Cushman
2 Tieton
3 Grand Coulee
4 Booneville
5 McKay
6 Owyhee
7 Arrow Rock
8 Shasta
9 Kennett
10 Don Pedro
11 Exchequer
12 Friant
13 Boulder
14 Parker
15 Lake Pleasant
16 Bartlett
17 Roosevelt
18 Mormon Flat
19 Stewart Mtn.
20 Horse Mesa
21 Coolidge
22 Elephant Butte
23 Alamagordo
24 Conchas
25 Sheesman
26 Taylor Park
27 Seminoe
28 Alcova
29 Shoshone
30 Fort Peck
31 Belle Fourche
32 Kentucky
33 Pickwick Ldg.
34 Wilson
35 Wheeler
36 Guntersville
37 Chickamauga
38 Hiwassee
39 Watts Bar
40 Coulter Shoals
41 Norris
42 Tygart R.

IRRIGATION AND POWER DEVELOPMENT IN THE UNITED STATES

Scale of Miles

0 10 20 30 40 50

THE TENNESSEE VALLEY AUTHORITY

involved. The TVA was quickly organized, and with the Muscle Shoals plant as a starting-point was soon able to supply cheap electric power to a limited area. With the help of PWA funds it pushed rapidly the construction of six new dams; the greatest of which, the Norris Dam, was completed in 1936. By 1940 TVA power was being generated at four dams, and was being used both to carry forward new construction and to provide cheap power for residential and commercial consumers. By June, 1939, according to TVA estimates, the Authority was serving about 180,000 customers, either directly or indirectly, and its acquisition later in the year of facilities belonging to the Tennessee Electric Power Company added perhaps 150,000 more.

Because the TVA was a government-owned enterprise, operating in direct competition with private business, it met with the most determined *Opposition* opposition. TVA rates were supposedly based upon the cost *to TVA* of production, but TVA officials, by charging off a large part of their costs to flood and navigation control, were able to devise a "yardstick" for measuring rates that to private companies seemed impossibly low. With this point of view the TVA chairman, Arthur E. Morgan, was disposed to agree, and for months he fought a losing battle with the other two members of the board, who were able as the majority to determine its policies. Eventually, after Morgan had refused a request from the President to substantiate his charges, he was removed from office, and the policy favored by his colleagues was continued. Opponents of the TVA also hoped in vain for aid from the courts. Did Congress have the right to permit the TVA to build transmission lines and distribute power under the guise of flood and navigation control? Were the TVA dams so built as to facilitate flood control, or was that a mere subterfuge, with their real purpose being the generation of power? In February, 1936, the Supreme Court upheld the sale of power from the Wilson Dam, built long before the TVA took charge, and three years later it refused to approve an injunction sought by private companies to prevent TVA from distributing power in competition with them. Neither decision ruled finally on the constitutionality of TVA activities as a whole, but the friendly support of the Court seemed assured.[1]

The work undertaken by the TVA spread as time went on into a great variety of fields. It carried on an elaborate program for the con-*Varieties of* trol of water on the land, and the consequent checking of *TVA* erosion; it produced great quantities of fertilizer, and tested *endeavor* its effectiveness in most of the states of the Union; it experimented with low-cost housing for the benefit of its employees; it pro-

[1] J. F. Carter, *The Future is Ours* (1939), is an optimistic view of the TVA development.

moted actively the use of the Tennessee River for commercial navigation: it extended the advantages of electricity to many farmers through a program of rural electrification; and it co-operated generously with local authorities in providing public health services, particularly with a view to checking the ravages of malaria and tuberculosis. These contributions to the general welfare were not invariably appreciated by the people they were meant to help, but the evidence seemed conclusive that the conditions of life in the Tennessee Valley had been enormously improved by the work of the TVA. Other hydroelectric developments under the New Deal, such as the Grand Coulee and Bonneville Dams on the Columbia, Boulder Dam on the Colorado, and Fort Peck Dam on the upper Missouri, were not accompanied by the extensive program of social betterment promoted by the TVA, but they were all intended to provide whatever benefits to society might accrue from the existence of an unlimited flow of cheap power.

Probably the most revolutionary of all the New Deal undertakings lay in the field of social security. By an act passed August 14, 1935, Congress established a Social Security Board, the business *Social* of which was to provide for or promote old-age annuities, *security* unemployment insurance, and more adequate care for the needy, the dependent, and the disabled. The necessity of some such legislation seemed abundantly apparent. Medical efficiency and a better understanding of health requirements had promoted longevity, while employers tended more and more to keep down the average age of the men on their payrolls. Technological unemployment and business readjustments were certain, even in the best of times, to throw many people out of work, and all the frantic efforts of the New Deal had failed utterly to provide complete re-employment. The aged, confronted by what looked to be a hopeless situation, listened with respect to such fantastic demands as those of Doctor F. E. Townsend of California, who urged a two per cent transaction tax to provide pensions up to two hundred dollars per month for everyone over sixty who would quit work and spend the money as fast as it came in. The unemployed looked with equal favor upon the program urged by Congressman Ernest Lundeen of Minnesota, who advocated payments of not less than ten dollars per week to all jobless persons over eighteen years of age. The discontented generally were ready to be impressed by the blandishments of Huey P. Long, a political trickster who, first as governor of Louisiana and later as United States Senator, promoted the organization of a "Share-the-Wealth Society," which set as its goal an income of not less than five thousand dollars a year for every American family. With so many

[667]

political quacks making headway, it seemed essential that the government should take immediate steps to provide a workable system of social security.

The Social Security Act was said to be "the most complex measure ever considered by Congress." (1) By the familiar dollar-matching device it enabled the federal government to assist the states in the care of "unemployables." It particularly encouraged state provision for old-age pensions, for the care of dependent children, and for aid to the needy blind. (2) Further, it authorized grants to promote through state agencies the rehabilitation of the physically disabled, the care of mothers and children, and the improvement of the public health. Its most notable provisions, however, set up (3) an elaborate federal-state system of unemployment compensation, and (4) a strictly federal system of old-age insurance.[1]

The plan for unemployment compensation required each state desirous of co-operating with the federal government to establish for the *Unemployment compensation* purpose an appropriate administrative agency. Because of the widely divergent conditions that existed in different parts of the nation, the states were permitted a considerable amount of latitude in suiting their regulations to local requirements. Funds for the support of the program were provided by a federal tax on payrolls. For the year 1936 the employers of eight or more persons were required to pay into the federal Treasury the equivalent of one per cent of the wages paid to all employees on their pay rolls as long as twenty weeks; the second year the tax was to be two per cent; thereafter, three per cent. Toward this tax, however, employers were permitted to credit all payments up to ninety per cent of the federal tax made toward the support of a federally approved state unemployment system. The cost of authorized state administration was met by federal grants, but all state unemployment funds had to be deposited in the United States Treasury for investment in federal obligations.

By the summer of 1937 every state in the Union, together with the District of Columbia, Alaska, and Hawaii, had complied with the requirements of the Social Security Act, and the next year the payment of benefits began. Although the law excluded from its operation all government employees, farm laborers, domestic servants, casual workers, and the employees of charitable organizations, probably half the working population of the country came under its protection. In 1939

---

[1] P. H. Douglas, *Social Security in the United States* (1936), contains the text of the Social Security Act. See also Abraham Epstein, *Insecurity, a Challenge to America* (new edition, 1938), and I. M. Rubinow, *The Quest for Security* (1934).

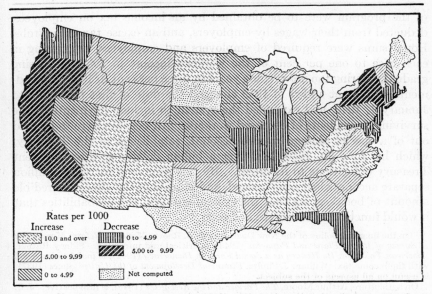

Rates per 1000

Increase

- 10.0 and over
- 5.00 to 9.99
- 0 to 4.99

Decrease

- 0 to 4.99
- 5.00 to 9.99
- Not computed

RATES OF NATURAL INCREASE IN THE AMERICAN POPULATION
(Based on Census of 1930)

the SSB took over the United States Employment Service, and thereafter attempted to co-ordinate job insurance with job placement. Anyone thrown out of work was required to register at his local employment office, which must try to help him find another job. If, after a specified waiting period, he remained unemployed, benefit payments were authorized. These payments, in practice, amounted to from five to fifteen dollars a week, and lasted on until the worker had either exhausted all his wage credits, or had reached the maximum period permitted by law, usually three or four months; provided, of course, that in the meantime he had failed to find another job.

The plan for old-age insurance included in the Social Security Act looked forward to the payment of monthly benefits to qualified workers in industry and commerce who retired from employment at *Old-age* the age of sixty-five. The same groups were excepted from *insurance* its operation as were denied the advantages of unemployment compensation. Payments of from fifteen to eighty dollars a month, depending upon the total amount of wages earned by the beneficiary after 1936, were to begin on January 1, 1942, and were to continue until the time of death, with lump-sum settlements payable to the estates of those who died before reaching the age of sixty-five. Funds for the carrying-out

[669]

of the program were to be obtained by an income tax on employees, deducted from their wages by employers, and an excise tax on payrolls. Equal sums were required of employers and employees, amounting in each case to one per cent of the worker's income in 1937, and rising gradually during the intervening years to three per cent in 1949. Amendments to the act added in 1939 changed the date of first payments to January 1, 1940, and expanded the system to include payments to the surviving dependents of deceased workers. All benefits were to be paid out of a special old-age reserve account, established in the Treasury, which by June 30, 1939, had over a billion dollars in three per cent Treasury obligations to its credit. By this time over forty-five million separate accounts had been opened, and in spite of the almost incredible amount of bookkeeping that the system entailed, the probabilities that it would function smoothly seemed good. [1]

[1] On the financial policy of the New Deal, Joseph E. Reeve, *Monetary Reform Movements: A Survey of Recent Plans and Panaceas* (1943), is critical and informing. Sidney Ratner, *American Taxation: Its History as a Social Force in Democracy* (1942), is mainly concerned with the income tax. William J. Shultz, *Financial Development of the United States* (1937), is useful on all aspects of the subject.

On agriculture, Arthur Moore, *The Farmer and the Rest of Us* (1945), is provocative. J. S. Davis, *On Agricultural Policy, 1926–1938* (1939), is severely critical of the New Deal. Henry A. Wallace, *New Frontiers* (1934), defends the policies he inaugurated.

Miscellaneous: Herbert Harris, *Labor's Civil War* (1940), treats of the break between the A.F. of L. and the C.I.O. D. E. Lilienthal, *TVA; Democracy on the March* (1944), states the objectives and achievements of the T.V.A. C. F. Roos, *N.R.A. Economic Planning* (1937), gives a good account of the short-lived N.R.A. Oliver La Farge (ed.), *The Changing Indian* (1942), shows the effect of the Indian Reorganization Act of 1934. J. G. Frederick, *The New Deal: A People's Capitalism* (1944), is Democratic campaign literature.

POLITICS, AT HOME AND ABROAD

To some observers the term "Roosevelt Revolution" seemed a reasonable equivalent for what was more generally called the New Deal. Certainly the President himself was actively at the center *The "Roose-* of all the governmental changes that went on. On one *velt Revolu-* occasion he likened himself to the quarterback on a football *tion"* team whose business it was to choose the plays and call the signals. That his endless vitality accounted for the persistent drive of his administration and that he personally made most of the decisions on policy were matters of general knowledge. The New Deal without Roosevelt would not have been the New Deal at all. Also, there was much that was revolutionary about what had been done. Dozens of new agencies were at work that had virtually no precedents for their existence in the history of American government. By means of them the nation carried the regulation of business to lengths never before attempted in time of peace; it made an effort to tell the farmers what they might and what they might not raise; it sought with energy and persistence to better the lot of labor; it lent money where the bankers refused to lend; it even went directly into business itself. But the Roosevelt Revolution, if so it may be called, was after all a very temperate affair. Like the Jefferson Revolution of 1800, and the Jackson Revolution of 1828, it left more unchanged than it changed. Compared with the Bolshevik Revolution which turned Russia upside down, or the Nazi Revolution which transformed Germany from a half-hearted republic into a totalitarian state, it was hardly a revolution at all. Private enterprise was retained and encouraged; personal liberty was in no wise endangered; and elections were still held.[1]

Whether or not the New Deal should properly be described as a revo-

[1] E. K. Lindley, *Half Way with Roosevelt* (1936), is a sympathetic appraisal of the first Roosevelt administration. See also Earle Looker, *The American Way, Franklin Roosevelt in Action* (1933); W. F. Ogburn, editor, *Social Change and the New Deal* (1934); S. C. Wallace, *The New Deal in Action* (1934).

lution, a large number of Americans were perfectly certain that they did not like it. Business managers complained that private enterprise was being stifled by governmental regimentation and that individual liberty, at least for the business corporation, was being seriously curtailed. Labor too, they said, was being spoiled, both by the easygoing methods of such public agencies as the WPA and by the persistent governmental favoritism shown to organized labor. Since private capital could not readily be induced to take risks under existing conditions, the activities of the government would inevitably tend to increase; in time private business might have to retire altogether and let the government run everything.

Critics of the New Deal also viewed with alarm the mounting size of the national debt. The economies effected in the early days of the *The national* Roosevelt régime did not last long, and taxation sufficient *debt* to meet the rising tide of New Deal expenditures was politically inexpedient. The government therefore resorted to wholesale borrowing, and with investors uncertain as to the future of private enterprise, the appetite of the public for government bonds seemed insatiable. But how long could the nation thus continue to live on its fat? On June 30, 1933, the national debt was about twenty-two and one half billion dollars. On January 1, 1940, it was over forty-two billion, and was fast approaching the forty-five-billion-dollar debt limit set by Section 21 of the Second Liberty Bond Act, a sum which the public had become accustomed to regard as the highest reasonable maximum. But the ease with which the German armies overran their western opponents in the spring of 1940 led to an expensive preparedness program, and the debt limit had to be raised again.[1]

The most unsavory of the anti-Roosevelt epithets were saved for the President himself and the bureaucracy he headed. Roosevelt was un-*Roosevelt* doubtedly one of the most popular of American Presidents, *haters* but he was also one of the most cordially hated. Himself a man of means, he was denounced bitterly as a "traitor to his class," who, in order to curry favor with the masses, stood ready to destroy his own kind. He was accused, too, of building up a powerful federal bureaucracy, the business of which was not only to man the various governmental agencies, but also to keep the Democratic Party in power. One of the reasons why Congress had been so easily persuaded to pass the laws that the President wanted was that in most instances new appointees were to be exempted from the usual requirements of civil

[1] H. L. Lutz, *Public Finance* (1936); Twentieth Century Fund, *Facing the Tax Problem* (1937).

"IT'S ALL PART OF A GREAT BIG PLAN"

service examinations. Such a policy meant an amazing number of offices for "deserving Democrats," and a nation-wide machine of such magnitude as to make the best efforts of Andrew Jackson and his intimates seem petty indeed. Eventually the President extended the civil service regulations to include a large proportion of the newly created offices, but thousands of dependable partisans were at the same time "blanketed in" to permanent positions.[1]

Not all of those who opposed Roosevelt were opponents of a revolutionary program. To many radicals the Roosevelt Revolution had not gone nearly far enough. Among these could be counted the eccentric and thoroughly corrupt Huey P. Long of Louisiana, who aspired to extend the borders of the dictatorship he had established in his home state. Long was ready, judging from his performance in Louisiana, to outspend Roosevelt, and he gave the impression that he was also more than willing to despoil the rich in the interest of the poor.[2] No less openly hostile was Father Coughlin, a Roman Catholic priest of Detroit with unorthodox views on the money question and a penchant for Jew-

G. S. Claire, *Administocracy* (1934).
[2] Carleton Beals, *The Story of Huey P. Long* (1935).

[673]

baiting. Father Coughlin established a National Union for Social Justice in the name of which he propagated his views every week by radio. Many Socialists and Communists, while convinced that Roosevelt's program was far too moderate, thought of it as an entering wedge for their doctrines, and for a time showed more friendliness for the New Deal than most of its other supporters wished. The Communists in particular, acting on orders from the Kremlin to maintain a "popular front" of all liberals, gave Roosevelt their open support. This attitude ended abruptly, however, when Hitler and Stalin made common cause in 1939. Since Roosevelt was known to be an ardent protagonist of the western democracies, the Communists, whose duty it was to continue their obedience to Stalin at all costs, had no choice but to substitute denunciations for their former commendations.

By 1934, when the state and congressional elections gave the country its first opportunity to return a verdict on the New Deal, the Republi-
Elections of 1934
cans had not sufficiently recovered from their rout of two years before to furnish much opposition. The Democrats again won by a landslide. Two years later, however, with a modicum of recovery seemingly assured, the Republicans took heart and prepared to fight. Such improvement in business conditions as had come to pass, they maintained, was due less to the New Deal than to the courageous conservatism of the Supreme Court, which had stricken down both the NRA and the AAA, and in numerous other decisions had revealed its opposition to the Roosevelt policies. The downward trend of business during the winter of 1932–33, culminating in the bank panic of 1933, they explained as only the natural result of fear on the part of business, fear as to what Roosevelt intended to do. The Hoover administration, according to this version of events, had already almost defeated the depression, and had Hoover been re-elected, normal times would long since have returned. Aided by the American Liberty League, founded in 1934 by leading Republican industrialists, and openly supported by Alfred E. Smith and many other conservative Democrats, the opponents of Roosevelt entered the campaign of 1936 with high hopes of success.[1]

The Democrats, now more completely under the domination of an outstanding leader than at any time since the ascendancy of William
Campaign of 1936
Jennings Bryan, met in convention at Philadelphia, June 23, to renominate Roosevelt and Garner, and to endorse the New Deal. Annoyance with the attitude of the Supreme Court was

[1] Among the many vigorous assaults on Roosevelt two of the most telling were J. P. Warburg, *Hell Bent for Election* (1935), and *Still Hell Bent* (1936). But Warburg finally supported Roosevelt for re-election. On the other side see J. P. Kennedy, *I'm for Roosevelt* (1936).

[674]

apparent, but the Democratic leaders showed little desire to make the Court the principal issue of the campaign. The Republicans, however, were determined to force the fighting along this line. Meeting in Cleveland, June 9, they pointedly denounced the President for his usurpation of congressional authority, his indifference to the rights of the states, and his willingness to ride rough-shod over the Constitution as interpreted by the Supreme Court. The great dilemma of the Republicans was their lack of "presidential timber." The two New Deal landslides had carried down practically every outstanding Republican to defeat. Of those who survived, the three best known were United States Senator Arthur H. Vandenberg of Michigan, Senator William E. Borah of Idaho, and Governor Alfred M. Landon of Kansas. Since Borah's sporadic radicalism made him an impossible leader for a strictly conservative cause, and since Vandenberg was only passively interested, the choice of the convention fell, almost by default, upon Landon. The Vice-Presidential nomination went to Colonel Frank Knox, owner and publisher of the Chicago *Daily News*.[1]

Three minor parties also entered candidates: The Socialists, Norman Thomas; the Communists, Earl Browder; and a new Union Party, William Lemke, Republican congressman from North Dakota. Thomas fought a valiant and honorable campaign, in which he criticized the New Deal for its halfway measures, and the Republicans for their devotion to reaction; Browder, on the other hand, made little effort to conceal his hope for a New Deal victory. Lemke tried to wear the mantle of the La Follette Progressives who had gone down to defeat in 1924, but he won little support. In general the left-wing forces, including many normally Socialist or Communist voters, were solidly united behind Roosevelt. John L. Lewis, leader of the CIO, earnestly supported the President, and the CIO contributed heavily to his campaign chest.

While Landon, for a Republican, was in reality outstandingly liberal, and while the Republican platform by no means called for the complete rejection of all the New Deal policies, the campaign inevi- *The new* tably impressed the voters as a contest between the forces *political* of reaction, who wished to return to the ways of bygone *division* years, and the forces of liberalism, who were willing to experiment in an effort to find a better way. It was evident that the "vertical" line of cleavage between the parties, so characteristic of nineteenth-century American politics, had given way to a "horizontal" division, which

[1] Campaign biographies are of little significance, but they appear regularly every four years. Frederick Palmer, *This Man Landon* (1936), sets forth the virtues of the Republican candidate. It may be supplemented by W. A. White, *What It's All About* (1936), and A. M. Landon, *America at the Crossroads* (1936).

placed the more-favored economic groups in the Republican column and the less-favored elements in the Democratic. This was revealed with some clarity by the campaign contributions, which for the Republicans amounted to about nine million dollars, and for the Democrats to about five and one half million dollars. The great trouble with such a contest, from the Republican point of view, was that the lower classes had the votes. Thousands of citizens whose only means of support had been the relief payments or the made work of New Deal agencies saw little reason to exchange such small favors for the more rugged individualism promised by Republican campaign orators. Farmers whose antecedents were Republican were conscious of the fact that the benefit payments they received were quite as definitely Democratic. The country might be heading for disaster, as the Republicans claimed, but the personal prospects of a great host of voters seemed to hinge on Democratic success. All this, according to the Republican version, amounted to little less than wholesale bribery by the use of public funds. Under these circumstances the only possible result of the contest was another Democratic landslide.

The situation was not helped by the nature of Landon's campaign. As a radio orator he was extremely inept, and in comparison with the *Straw votes* President's finely modulated periods his utterances sounded schoolboyish. He offended the labor leaders by his rash attacks, and lost far more votes than he gained by coming out boldly against the Social Security Act. His audiences proved to be lukewarm or even hostile, while the President received an ovation everywhere he spoke. Straw ballots taken to discover the trend of public opinion predicted, with one notable exception, an easy Democratic victory. The *Literary Digest*, which had successfully foretold the result in every presidential campaign since 1916, depended upon the distribution of millions of postcard ballots to voters whose names appeared in telephone books and in similar lists. From its returns Landon appeared far in the lead except in the South, but the fact that a majority of those who voted in the poll had favored Hoover in 1932 caused many observers to discount its findings. What it really proved was that more Republicans than Democrats got their names in print, or at least took the trouble to fill out and return the postcard ballots. Thereafter forecasters tended to follow the "sampling" methods, used, for example, in the Gallup poll, which sought to ascertain the sentiments of a reasonable cross-section of the nation's voters.

The Democratic landslide of 1936 exceeded the expectations of all the most seasoned observers, with the exception of James A. Farley,

the Democratic campaign manager, who accurately predicted that the
Republicans would carry only two states, Maine and Ver- *Election*
mont. The electoral vote stood 523 for Roosevelt to 8 *results*
for Landon, and the popular vote 27,750,000 to 16,680,000. Not since
James Monroe was re-elected in 1820 with but a single opposing electoral
vote had an American election been so one-sided. Another significant
aspect of the voting was the waning strength of the left-wing minor
parties. The new Union Party polled only 892,000 votes, the Socialists
187,000, and the Communists 80,000. Undoubtedly much of this falling-
off was due to the satisfaction felt by radicals with the direction the New
Deal had taken. In both houses of Congress the Democratic majorities
became so large as to threaten dissension. In the House the Democrats
won 328 seats out of 435, and in the Senate 77 out of 96.

This overwhelming victory no doubt furnished in part the explanation for an attack on the Supreme Court that the President launched
shortly after his second inauguration. Before the election he had not
hesitated to express his irritation with decisions that were based upon
precedents set in "horse-and-buggy days," but he had studiously re-
frained from attacking the Court during the campaign. Now, with
sixty per cent of the nation's voters behind him, what might have been
hazardous before seemed safe enough. That the Court majority was
bitterly hostile to the New Deal seemed obvious. Out of nine important
decisions involving New Deal measures, only twice did the government
score victories, and in one of these, the law invalidating gold clauses in
contracts, the majority was only five to four. Not a single member of
the Court had been appointed by Roosevelt; only Andrew Johnson of
all the Presidents since the Civil War had served so long without being
privileged to choose at least one justice. Of the nine members of the
Court, six were more than seventy years of age, and of these six, five
were fairly consistently conservative. That some of these veterans
were determined to retain their seats until Roosevelt was out of office
seemed at least a reasonable inference. With a "second New Deal" in
the making to replace the measures voided by the Supreme Court, the
President decided on a course of action which, he believed, would prevent
any similar disaster in the future.

There were two ways in which reform of the Court could be effected:
(1) by an amendment to the Constitution, which might either require
retirement at a given age or set limits to the doctrine of *Roosevelt*
judicial review; (2) by a law of Congress to provide for an *attacks the*
increase in the number of justices, thus permitting the *Court*
President to "pack" the Supreme Court with new appointees of less

conservative views. The President chose the latter alternative, probably because it seemed to permit of speedier action, but he coupled with it an ingenious provision for calling attention to the advanced age of some of the justices. The measure he urged on Congress would have set the age of seventy for the voluntary retirement of Supreme Court justices, and for each member of the Court who reached that age and failed to retire the President might appoint an additional justice until a maximum Court of fifteen members had been reached. The measure also provided for an extensive reorganization of the lower federal courts with a view to expediting business and increasing efficiency.[1]

Probably the President was quite unprepared for the furor that his "court-packing" bill evoked. Many Democrats, both in and out of Congress, professed to believe with the Republicans that the last safeguard of American liberty was endangered, and that what the President aspired to create was a dictatorship, pure and simple. In the Senate, where the administration forces chose to stage the initial contest, Burton K. Wheeler of Montana, an ardent New Dealer in every other respect, led the opposition with infinite resourcefulness. Wheeler held no brief for the Court as constituted, but whatever change was to be made, he held, should be made by constitutional amendment. In the end the President for the first time on a matter of major importance failed to carry Congress with him. Astutely led by Chief Justice Hughes, the Court itself took a major part in the proceedings; by a series of decisions favorable to the New Deal, it reminded older citizens of Mr. Dooley's famous observation, "The Supreme Court follows the illiction returns," and materially weakened the President's case. Probably also at Hughes's suggestion, Justice Willis Van Devanter, senior member of the Court in point of service and a pronounced conservative, announced his determination to take speedy advantage of the act which Congress passed March 1, 1937, granting full pay to retiring justices over seventy years of age. Finally, the sudden death of Senator Joseph Robinson, administration floor leader in charge of the Court bill, put an end to the President's hopes. Congress passed a bill which instituted some of the reforms Roosevelt had called for in the lower courts, but it left the Supreme Court intact.

Nevertheless the President soon got what he wanted most, a court

---

[1] The powers exercised by the Supreme Court produced an immense amount of contro versial literature. Among the many books worthy of note are Charles Warren, *Congress, the Constitution, and the Supreme Court* (1935); E. S. Corwin, *The Twilight of the Supreme Court* (1934), and *Court Over Constitution* (1938); Morris L. Ernst, *The Ultimate Power* (1937); Irving Brant, *Storm Over the Constitution* (1936); Walter Lippmann, *The Supreme Court. Independent or Controlled?* (1937).

less conservative in character, which would no longer stand in the way of New Deal objectives. Had he been less impatient, he *The new* might have obtained the same result with far less bitterness *Supreme* and party dissension. The fight well illustrated two out- *Court* standing features of the American constitutional system: (1) the difficulties involved whenever one department of the government attempts to dominate another; and (2) the inability of any department, including even the Supreme Court, to resist indefinitely the popular will. When Justice Van Devanter resigned, the President chose as his successor Senator Hugo L. Black of Alabama, a man less learned in the law than he was loyal to the principles of the New Deal. When, after the appointment had been confirmed by the Senate, the country learned that the new justice had once been a member of the Ku Klux Klan, a loud demand for his resignation broke forth. But Black refused to resign, publicly admitted his membership in the Klan as a youthful indiscretion, and settled down under excellent tutelage to acquaint himself more intimately with the law. Before the end of his second term Roosevelt made four more appointments to the Supreme Court, Stanley F. Reed of Kentucky, his able Solicitor-General; Felix Frankfurter, of the Harvard Law School; William O. Douglas, recently of the Yale Law School; and Frank Murphy, formerly Governor of Michigan and for a short time Attorney-General in the Roosevelt cabinet. Each of these men was adequately learned in the law, but judges of the lower federal courts and of the state courts were quick to note that the Supreme Court could no longer count within its membership a single man who had risen to the position he held by virtue of judicial experience. Partly on this account, and partly because the new court was evidently determined not to thwart the New Deal, they bemoaned the fact that a hard-working judge might follow consistently opinions handed down by the Supreme Court itself, and still see his judgments reversed.

The Supreme Court fight was barely ended when a downward trend in business, called by Democrats a recession and by Republicans a new depression, provided the administration with another major *The reces-* problem. The slump came unheralded, and caught New *sion of 1937* Dealers along with everyone else unawares. It was caused in no small part by the attempt of the national government beginning in 1937 to curtail expenditures, a fact which supported the argument of Roosevelt's opponents that there had been no real recovery all along, but only a continuous process of pump-priming. New Dealers, on the other hand, charged that capital itself had gone on strike, and that business contraction in the interest of maintaining high price-levels was a principal cause of the trouble. Whatever the merit of these contentions, the administration moved rapidly to halt the decline. The Board of Governors of the Federal Reserve System promptly reversed the deflationary policy it had been pursuing since the summer of 1936, and the "second New Deal," at which Congress had balked while the Court battle went on, was promptly instituted. This included much additional pump-priming, particularly through the WPA, the PWA, the RFC, and the USHA; the creation of a new AAA, already described, for the revival of agriculture; and somewhat belatedly (1939) a wide grant of power to the President to reorganize the federal departments of government in the interest of greater efficiency. The conviction that methods of price control had been devised in monopolistic industries led also to an attempt to enforce the moribund anti-trust laws. Since the days of the ill-starred NRA these regulations had been more or less in abatement, but the President now chose Thurman W. Arnold of the Yale Law School to be Assistant Attorney-General, and charged him with the duty of making them live again. Arnold was well but most unfavorably known to the business world for the caustic criticisms contained in his book, the *Folklore of Capitalism* (1937). Important results were expected also from a National Economic Committee (better known as the Monopoly Investigation), authorized by Congress in June, 1938, and headed by Senator Joseph O'Mahoney of Wyoming. The business of this committee was to inquire into the existence of monopolistic practices in the United States and their effect upon business conditions. It was composed of three senators, three representatives, and six experts from as many executive departments.

Well before the time for the mid-term elections of 1938, the recession seemed to be at an end and business was again on the upgrade. But the *Party politics* electorate was left in a far more critical mood toward the New Deal than it had ever exhibited before. With considerable logic the Republicans could argue that the country after over five years of spending was still on the relief basis, and that whatever prosperity existed was dependent on the continued outpouring of public funds. Once more the battle-cry was raised that business must be freed if any real recovery was to be expected. The fight on the Supreme Court had also injured the Democratic chances, partly because so many voters of both parties had opposed the President's course, and partly because of the internal dissensions that the Court fight had engendered. This situation was greatly intensified by the President's attempt to "purge" the party of a selected group of senators and representatives who had frequently opposed his policies. Among those so proscribed were Senators W. F. George of Georgia, Millard E. Tydings of Maryland, and E. D. ("Cotton Ed") Smith of South Carolina, and Representative John J. O'Connor of New York, all of whom, except the last mentioned, were triumphantly renominated and re-elected. Republican gains were also spectacular, and included seventy-nine seats in the House and eight in the Senate. Many states that had abandoned the Republican column in recent elections also returned to their former allegiance, electing Republican governors, or legislatures, or both. Noteworthy among these changes were Pennsylvania, Massachusetts, and Connecticut in the East, and Michigan, Wisconsin, and Minnesota in the West.

Particularly surprising was the blow dealt what had seemed to be a promising third-party movement in the Northwest. For eight years the Farmer-Labor Party in Minnesota, ably led by Governor *Third-party* Floyd B. Olson until his death in 1936, and after that by *misfortunes* Governor Elmer A. Benson, had dominated the government of the state, while in Wisconsin the Progressives, equally well captained by Governor Philip F. La Follette, a son of "old Bob" and a brother of "young Bob," had won handily in the elections of 1934 and 1936. Plans were under way for a union of forces, and Governor La Follette had already launched a movement for the transformation of his local state party into a nationwide organization. If, as at times seemed likely, the Democratic Party should turn conservative or split, the Progressive Party might function as a welcome home to the New Deal radicals. But in Minnesota a little known and extremely youthful Republican named Harold E. Stassen defeated Benson, while in Wisconsin a Milwaukee industrialist, Julius P. Heil, defeated La Follette. In both states the Democratic organization was all but extinct, and the third parties continued as the chief opponents of the Republicans; but the prospect that they would ever unite to become the nucleus of a new nation-wide left-wing party seemed remote indeed.[1]

By this time foreign affairs had come to play a much more significant rôle in American policy than had been anticipated when the New Deal first was instituted. After the collapse of the London *The Hull* Economic Conference of 1933, the United States had shown *trade pacts* an evident determination to "go it alone," regardless of what might happen to the rest of the world, but Secretary Hull worked quietly, and as events proved effectively, in the opposite direction. Hull was convinced that the surest road to recovery, both for the United States and

---

[1] An excellent state history, brought down to the present, is W. F. Raney, *Wisconsin, a Story of Progress* (1940). See also J. S. McGrath and J. J. Delmont, *Floyd Björnsterne Olson* (1937).

for the rest of the world, lay in the revival of international trade, something that could never happen as long as high tariff barriers blocked the way. He believed, too, that the free movement of goods throughout the world was an essential preliminary to the establishment of anything bordering upon permanent peace. To reduce the high tariffs, which so effectively excluded American goods from foreign markets, he advocated the negotiation of a series of reciprocal trade agreements. By this means the nations with which the United States wished to trade might be induced to lower their tariff barriers in return for equivalent American reductions. Furthermore, the "most favored nation" clause that had been written into so many treaties between the United States and foreign powers would operate to extend indefinitely the scope of any changes effected. This system had certain definite advantages over the old-fashioned general tariff revision. In the first place, bargains could be struck with foreign nations by which the United States might hope to gain as well as to give; secondly, the log-rolling proclivities of Congress, which had defeated so many efforts to lower the tariff, might be avoided.

Not until June, 1934, did Congress get around to the passage of the Trade Agreements Act necessary to enable Secretary Hull to carry his program into effect. That measure delegated to the President the right for a three-year period to negotiate agreements with other countries for the mutual lowering of tariff rates. Without so much as referring the matter back to Congress for its consent, he might lower American duties by as much as fifty per cent, provided only that the American free list be not disturbed, one way or the other. Under this grant of authority, which was renewed in 1937 and again in 1940, Secretary Hull went promptly to work, and in five years' time had concluded more than twenty treaties, among which were particularly sweeping agreements with Canada and Great Britain. Perhaps three fifths of the exports and imports of the United States were affected by these treaties. A large number of agreements were negotiated with Latin-American countries, whose good-will toward the United States was thereby considerably increased. American farmers, particularly those of the Middle West, quite generally opposed the treaties on the ground that American agricultural interests were being sacrificed for the benefit of industry. It was true that some of the treaties did facilitate the importation of foreign foodstuffs, but Secretary Hull and the Trade Agreements Committee of specialists, upon whom he relied for technical advice, were convinced that whatever stimulated American industry increased the buying power of American labor, and so aided the farmer indirectly, probably far more than the limited importations of foreign farm products harmed him.[1]

The deep-seated interest in securing the friendship of Latin-America that had long characterized American foreign policy was continued and intensified under Roosevelt. Hoover as President-elect *The "good* had made a "good-will tour" of eleven Latin-American *neighbor"* republics, and as President had worked steadily toward the *policy* withdrawal of American troops from occupied areas.[2] Roosevelt speedily let it be known that his policy toward Latin America was likewise to be that of the "good neighbor." He sent Secretary Hull to the seventh Pan-American Conference, held in Montevideo, and cordially approved the doctrine on which the Conference agreed, that "no state has the right to intervene in the internal or external affairs of another." Presently, in 1936, he journeyed seven thousand miles by sea to Buenos Aires in order to open a special Inter-American Conference for Peace, and told delegates that non-American states seeking "to commit acts of aggression against us will find a Hemisphere wholly prepared to consult together for our mutual safety and our mutual good."

A practical demonstration of how the "good neighbor policy" might be expected to operate was given in the case of Cuba, which dared at last to attempt the overthrow by revolution of its current *Cuba* dictator, Guerardo Machado. The depression which began in 1929 became particularly acute in Cuba after the passage in 1930 of the Hawley-Smoot Tariff, which increased the rates on sugar imported into the United States. Machado, a thoroughgoing tyrant who had maintained himself in office since 1924, should normally have been one of the first casualties of the depression and well deserved the honor. But American investors in Cuban securities liked him, for he consistently made the interest payments due on the huge sums that the Cuban government had borrowed in the United States.[3] Out of deference to their wishes the Hoover administration had so strongly supported Machado that the Cubans, fearing American intervention even more than they feared Machado's tyranny, dared not revolt. When Roosevelt became President, he let it be known that Machado could expect no further backing from the American government, and as a result the dictator was promptly driven from office. Unhappily, however, the government which succeeded him lasted only three weeks, when another revolution

---

[1] H. J. Tasca, *Reciprocal Trade Policy of the United States* (1938); Carl Kreider, *The Anglo-American Trade Agreement: A Study of British and American Commercial Policies* (1943).
[2] See *ante*, p. 374.
[3] Carleton Beals, *Crime of Cuba*, abundantly emphasizes the sins of American capital. See also H. F. Guggenheim, *The United States and Cuba* (1934).

occurred. Undoubtedly American pressure was applied from this time forward to insure the establishment of an orderly and competent government in the island, but no American troops were landed, and American interests were watched over exclusively by recognized diplomatic agents. For the first time since the Spanish-American war a serious revolutionary outbreak in Cuba came to an end without the customary military intervention by the United States. Furthermore, on May 29, 1934, a treaty between the United States and Cuba formally released the latter from the terms of the Platt Amendment, which for a generation had rankled in Cuban breasts. That same year a reciprocal trade treaty materially reduced the tariff on Cuban exports to the United States and checked the decline of Cuban-American trade.

Other evidence that the "big stick" policy was really at an end accumulated rapidly. By an agreement reached in August, 1934, the financial receivership which the United States maintained in Haiti was greatly liberalized, and the last detachment of American marines was ordered to leave the republic. About the same time negotiations were begun with Panama to abolish the special privileges that that nation had been forced to accord the United States, and after a long delay this, too, was accomplished. Even the drastic action taken by Mexico in 1936, which ordered the expropriation of all foreign-owned oil property within Mexican borders, led only to relatively mild expostulations from Secretary Hull, who, after all efforts to settle the controversy through diplomatic channels had failed, requested merely that it be submitted to arbitration.[1]

The Roosevelt administration also made a systematic effort to draw Canada more closely into the fraternity of American nations. This was *Canada* somewhat facilitated by the greater independence which Canada enjoyed, after the World War, within the British Empire, particularly by the fact that the United States and Canada had exchanged ministers since 1927 and were able to carry on their diplomatic relations directly instead of by way of London. Roosevelt was no more successful than Hoover in obtaining Senate ratification for the St. Lawrence Waterway Treaty, negotiated in 1932 to make possible a deep-sea channel from the Gulf of St. Lawrence to the Great Lakes, but on a visit to Canada in 1938 he reminded his hearers that the Monroe Doctrine applied as much to the territory north of the United States as to the territory south of it. "I give you assurance," he said, "that

---

[1] Nathaniel and Sylvia Weyl, *The Reconquest of Mexico: The Years of Lázaro Cárdenas* (1939), is wholly sympathetic with the Cárdenas program. On Panama see W. L. McCain, *The United States and the Republic of Panama* (1937).

the people of the United States will not stand idly by if the domination of Canadian soil is threatened by any other empire." [1]

The decline of "Yankee imperialism" in the Americas was paralleled across the Pacific by the progress of the Philippine Islands toward complete independence.   In accordance with the *The Philippines* Tydings-McDuffie Act of 1934 the Islands had become an autonomous Commonwealth, with a President of their own choosing, Manuel Quezon, and an elective National Assembly.   Except for control over foreign relations and a few other specified restrictions, the Philippine nationalists had thus obtained practically all the liberty they had ever sought, but they were still far from happy.   They knew full well that the economic prosperity of the Islands had been built upon freedom of trade with the United States, a privilege that was now to be gradually withdrawn.   They knew also that independence would carry with it the obligation of self-defense.   Fully alive to this need, President Quezon in 1935 asked and obtained from President Roosevelt the services of General Douglas MacArthur, Chief-of-Staff of the United States Army.   First as military adviser to the Philippine government, and then as Field Marshal of the Philippine army, MacArthur made it his aim to create a native constabulary strong enough to hold any foreign invader at bay, pending the anticipated assistance of the United States Navy.   The date set for full independence was July 4, 1946, and the date was met.   But in the meantime the tumultuous events of the Second World War had come and gone.

[1] J. M. Callahan, *American Foreign Policy in Canadian Relations* (1937).   On other subjects treated in this chapter, see E. E. Robinson, *The Presidential Vote, 1936* (1940), a supplement to the author's earlier volume, *The Presidential Vote, 1896–1932* (1934); R. H. Jackson, *The Struggle for Judicial Supremacy* (1941), which gives the background for Roosevelt's attack on the Court; S. J. Konefsky, *Chief Justice Stone and the Supreme Court* (1945); A. T. Mason, *Brandeis: A Free Man's Life* (1946). On Hull's diplomatic activities, see *The Memoirs of Cordell Hull* (2 vols., 1948); H. B. Hinton, *Cordell Hull: A Biography* (1942); J. M. Letiche, *Riciprocal Trade Agreements in World Economy* (1948).

CHAPTER XXX

THE DISINTEGRATION OF PEACE

DURING the two decades that followed the First World War Americans who had enthusiastically supported that struggle, in order "to make the world safe for democracy," suffered many disappointments. The failure of the United States to accept responsibility for anything that happened outside its borders was in itself disillusioning, and perhaps to some extent also a cause of the world's rapid descent into international discord. But quite as distressing was the discovery, as the years wore on, that democracy, both in Europe and in Asia, was on the wane; that dictatorships of such magnitude as modern times had never known before were being born; that the arbitrary will of autocrats to war, against which Wilson had hoped the League of Nations would insure the world, was present in an increasingly aggravated form. The League of Nations, in spite of American failure to participate in its counsels, was duly organized, but its weakness in the face of the appalling problems that confronted it soon became painfully apparent. What the League might have been had the United States chosen to be its leading member, the world can never know. But the strength it was able to muster, without American assistance, was insufficient to stem the tide that led to war.[1]

The first of the great European nations to undergo drastic revolutionary change was Russia. The Czar had abdicated in March, 1917, and *The Russian Revolution* had transferred his powers to a provisional government of liberal democrats, headed by Alexander Kerensky. But the real revolution began only in October, 1917, when the "Bolshevists," or extreme Communists, under the leadership of Nikolai Lenin and Leon Trotsky, undertook to establish their long-envisioned dictatorship of the proletariat. They made peace with Germany at the price of the infamous Treaty of Brest-Litovsk, and then fought off with

---

[1] Two excellent compendiums of post-World War history are: W. C. Langsam, *The World Since 1914* (6th edition, 1948) and F. P. Chambers, C. P. Grant, and C. C. Bayley, *This Age of Conflict* (1943). See also Winston S. Churchill, *The Second World War*, Vol. I, *The Gathering Storm* (1948).

incredible success numerous uprisings against their authority, both from within and without. By the end of 1922, they had formed a large portion of the territory left to Russia into a Union of Soviet Socialist Republics, with the expectation that eventually non-Russian as well as Russian countries would wish to join up.

The official guide of Bolshevist conduct was the *Communist Manifesto*, published in 1848 by Karl Marx and Friedrich Engels. In harmony with the Marxian ideal, the Bolshevist leaders sought to establish a classless society. The land and all large-scale industry was nationalized; only personal property was left in the hands of individuals. Such agencies of production as mines and factories were taken over by the state, and the government gradually assumed responsibility for the distribution of goods. Ideally there was only one employer, the government; and, while most labor was free, on occasion armies of "forced labor" were recruited for work in the forests or on the roads and railroads. Labor became the duty of every citizen; the "parasitic" classes of capitalist society who lived from past earnings or the earnings of others were to be no more. As the new order was set up, the old order was destroyed. The old bureaucracy, the professional classes, landowners, property-minded members of the upper and middle classes, whether great or small, were driven into exile or mercilessly liquidated. Slowly, but with inexorable certainty, the revolution penetrated even to the most remote country districts. "Collectivist" farms tended increasingly to replace the old peasant holdings, and well-to-do "kulaks" who resisted disappeared. The Russia that grew up was thus composed in large part of those who could be benefited by the new régime; the favored few who had prospered during the old régime had been eliminated.

In theory the Soviet system was extremely democratic, but practice and theory were sometimes unrelated. From the first, thousands of local "soviets," or committees each composed of workers or peasants, participated in governmental affairs, even selecting by indirect means a Congress of Soviets, supreme over all. Ultimately, under the Constitution of 1936, citizens of the "USSR" chose members to a Soviet of the Union according to electoral areas, on the basis of one deputy for each 300,000 of the population. But, since only the Communist Party was tolerated, an inner circle of party leaders managed somehow to win practically all the higher offices. Party membership was rigorously restricted; in 1939 party members numbered only about a million and a half, all true and tested believers in the Marxian dogma, as interpreted by the leader of the Communist Party, originally Lenin, and some years after his death in 1924, Josef Stalin. The Soviet Union was thus ruled in fact, if not in name, by a small group of Communists, often called the "Politburo," of whom Stalin was the chief. Whoever or whatever the state officials, all real authority was vested in the man, or the group, who could control the Communist Party.[1]

The original Communist policy was that national revolution was only the prelude to world revolution. With this goal in mind, an organization known as the Third International,[2] or Comintern, was founded in 1919 by Lenin, with headquarters in Moscow. Theoretically, at least, the Comintern was not a part of the Russian government, but was wholly separate from it, a kind of supreme authority for Communists throughout the world. From this central agency revolutionary propaganda was dispensed, and to it professional revolutionaries operating outside Russia looked for guidance and support. But as time went on the Russian government showed far more concern for internal national interests than for overthrowing the capitalist system elsewhere. Particularly was this true after the accession of Stalin to power. Trotsky, a believer in immediate world revolution, was exiled, while three successive "five-year plans" were undertaken to make Russia self-sustaining, and able to defend herself in case of war. The Comintern continued to exist, but since the Russian Communist Party had the largest number of dues-paying members, it reflected accurately the policies of the Russian government. Finally, in June, 1943, presumably on orders from Stalin, the Comintern was abolished altogether.

Foreign as the Russian system was to the "American way of life," it was no more difficult for Americans to comprehend than the "Fascist" *Mussolini's* dictatorship in Italy that Benito Mussolini had set up in *rise in Italy* the years following 1922. Parliamentary government had never worked especially well in Italy, and in the face of the bewildering problems of the post-war era it threatened to break down altogether. Fear that in this event a Bolshevist revolution such as had overcome Russia might take place in Italy gave Mussolini his chance. His party, the Fascisti, although originally shot through with socialistic doctrines, had become "rightist" in character, and longed now for the opportunity to give Italy a strong government that could restrain the radicals and maintain order. Born to command, and with a personality almost irresistible to the Italian temperament, Mussolini had gathered into his following the sons of property-holders whose

---

[1] M. T. Florinsky, *Toward an Understanding of the U.S.S.R.* (1939).

[2] The First International was the work of Karl Marx and lasted from 1864 to 1876; the Second International was a Socialist organization that began in 1889, and was opposed by the Third International. A Fourth International was formed by the followers of Trotsky after his break with Stalin in 1929.

fear of socialism was only too well grounded, ex-veterans of the First World War who resented the aspersions cast on Italy's war record, and patriotic young bloods generally to whom his program of direct action against radicals strongly appealed. Organized Fascist bands, or "squadrists," called also "Black Shirts" from the garb they affected, paraded the streets in force, beat up the "reds," wrecked workers' clubs, and broke up strikes. By the summer of 1922 their strength was estimated at three hundred thousand.

It was well known that Mussolini was now prepared to seize authority, and late in October, 1922, his adherents began their famous "march on Rome." But to avert violence, the King made Mussolini Premier, and the Black Shirts went home without the bloody fighting they had expected. Thereafter parliamentary government in any normal sense did not last long. Non-Fascist members of the Cabinet were dropped, opposition parties were disbanded, and the whole government down to the most minor offices was thoroughly "fascistized." Personal liberty disappeared, the press was rigidly controlled, courts ruled as they knew they must. A Fascist militia, composed of the most dependable elements of the Black Shirts, gave the color of legality to "squadrist" attacks on individuals known to be critical of "Il Duce." Thus, Fascism in Italy, like Communism in Russia, became a weapon through which the will of the dictator became supreme. The young Fascist who revised Descartes' *cogito, ergo sum,* to read, "I never think, therefore I am," had the spirit of Fascism in a nutshell.[1]

Fascist ideology set great store by the grandeur of ancient Rome. The party designation was derived from the word *fasces,* Latin designation for the bundle of rods surrounding a battle-axe that lictors once carried as symbols of authority before kings, *Fascism* consuls, praetors, and emperors. What ancient Rome was, united and powerful, feared and respected, Fascist Italy aspired to become. Nationalism was exalted and stimulated by pride in the old Roman past. The Roman salute of the uplifted arm was revived, and every aspect of the Roman legend held in veneration. Fascism also idealized physical energy and force. It glorified all the warlike attributes, esteemed virility and efficiency, called for discipline and the will to conquer. Like ancient Rome, modern Italy must have the strength to expand its borders, and the right to boast of empire. Thickly spread over all Fascist activities was a heavy layer of theatricals and pageantry; Fascist pomposity and pretense always approached the very verge of the ridiculous. In political organization, Fascism experimented with the teachings of

[1] H. W. Schneider, *Making the Fascist State* (1928).

the national syndicalists, and in the "corporative state" claimed to have achieved a new governmental principle. Representation was based no longer upon political or geographic units, but upon organized economic interests, syndicates of employers as well as of employees. For the Fascists had no quarrel with capitalism; they meant to protect it, not to destroy it. And yet, the state must always be regarded as supreme; "nothing for the individual, all for Italy," was the motto of every believer. Only in this spirit could "the moral and material greatness of the Italian people" be achieved.[1]

Whatever may be said of its contradictory philosophic concepts, Fascism as personified in Mussolini did provide Italy with a government strong enough to govern. The Fascists despised democracy as outmoded, and too soft to confront the rigors of the twentieth century. Italian democracy had invited this criticism, but Mussolini's government was effective. The Duce soon had the national budget in balance, he launched public works that not only appealed to the national pride but helped also with the problem of unemployment, he stimulated both agricultural and industrial development, he put an end to labor strife, encouraged education, promoted foreign trade, developed natural resources, built up the army and navy, stimulated "air-mindedness," and to the everlasting joy of tourists "made the railroads run on time."

The third great dictatorship to make its appearance in Europe came in Germany. There the roots of democracy had never driven deep, and *Hitler's rise in Germany* the Weimar Republic, established at the close of the first World War, had the additional disadvantages to overcome of having agreed to the hated Treaty of Versailles, and of having permitted the nation to descend into a catastrophic currency inflation. Disgust with the new régime was evident in the elections of 1925, when the voters selected as President one of the outstanding heroes of the old Germany, Field Marshal Paul von Hindenburg. By this time the land was filled with revolutionaries, some of whom wished to follow the example of Communist Russia, while others favored rather the precepts of Fascist Italy. Noisiest among the latter was Adolf Hitler, an Austrian-born German with a talent for soapbox oratory who was a member of the German Workers' Party, later renamed National Socialist. The "Nazis," as these agitators were called, adopted the Fascist salute, chose the swastika as their emblem, organized a black-shirted bodyguard for the Nazi leaders, sent forth brownshirted Storm Troopers to break up Communist meetings, made ready with small pretense at concealment to overthrow the existing democratic

[1] Herman Finer, *Mussolini's Italy* (1935).

régime. A premature effort at revolution was made in 1923 at Munich. Its chief significance was the fact that it landed Hitler in jail, where he found time to write his dreams of a Nazi-dominated world into a book, *Mein Kampf*, thereafter the law and the gospel for all his followers.

Quite as hostile as the Nazis toward the democratic experiment in Germany was the army, organized after the war as the *Reichswehr* under General Hans von Seekt. This force, according to the Treaty of Versailles, was supposed to number only a hundred thousand men, but in actual fact it was probably much larger. Led by the ablest and most conservative elements in the old imperial army, the *Reichswehr* was quickly welded into a center of reactionary sentiment, where Social Democrats were unwelcome, even in the ranks, and where longing for the good old authoritarian days was outspokenly apparent. That the *Reichswehr* was intended as merely a nucleus around which to build a much larger army as soon as possible became clearer with each passing year. Its leaders tolerated, and perhaps even connived at, the training of numerous bands of irregular soldiery, "free corps" adventurers such as Hitler's, which in time of stress could be absorbed into the national military forces. As a result of this policy, Germany, far from being disarmed, as the Treaty of Versailles contemplated, had probably as many as two million men under arms by 1930, a formidable beginning for complete remilitarization. Army officers were sent to Russia for training in the new military techniques, airplane and submarine factories were located outside Germany's borders, and industrial plants designed to be transformed overnight into war plants were operated within Germany itself. To restore German faith in military leadership, the public was fed on the "stab-in-the-back" legend, according to which Germany had never really suffered military defeat, but had been forced to make peace because of disloyalty on the home front, disloyalty that was ascribed mainly to Social Democrats, Communists, and Jews.[1]

The ends sought by the Nazis and the army thus came to have much in common, and military leaders were able to view the rise of Hitler with considerable equanimity. To his support the Nazi spellbinder drew nearly all of the discontented elements of society for whom Communism had slight appeal — the white-collar workers, hard hit by the chronic hard times; small shopkeepers whose businesses were threatened by chain stores and trusts; discouraged peasants fearful of a Communist revolution; members of the professional classes who blamed Jewish competition for all their own shortcomings; unemployed intellectuals, particularly in and from the universities, for whom the existing economic

[1] Hans Ernest Fried, *The Guilt of the German Army* (1942).

system held little of promise; youth in search of adventure and a future; women intoxicated by the highly charged emotionalism of Hitler's appeal. All these, however, would hardly have been sufficient to install Hitler in power; it was the financial support of the great industrialists, who thought of the Nazis as a means of heading off the Communists, that insured the success of the movement.

As long as the Republic lasted, the Nazis were unable to command a majority of the Reichstag, but their growing strength was recognized by President Hindenburg in February, 1933, when he made Hitler his Chancellor. Within a few months the last vestige of democracy was wiped out, and the Nazification of the state was complete. Henceforth Hitler was the only "Führer," and a powerful secret police suppressed the slightest show of criticism. Germany, like Russia and Italy, had become a dictatorship. Just as Communism was what Stalin said it was, and Fascism was what Mussolini said it was, so now Naziism was what Hitler said it was. All three governments were totalitarian; in every instance the individual existed for the state, not the state for the individual.[1]

The Nazi ideology, like the Fascist, was less noted for common sense and consistency than for its wholesale appeal to the prejudices that *Naziism* Hitler found about him. The Nazis adopted in full the army theory that Germany had been betrayed in 1918, not defeated, and demanded the complete overthrow of the Versailles settlement. This was held to be Germany's due, not merely because of injustices in the treaty, but because Germans, as members of the master race, had superior rights. Raceism, more than anything else, was basic in the Nazi philosophy. The "Nordic," or "Aryan," races, among whom the Germans were held to be the only really pure strain, were born to command; all other races, Latin, Slav, Semite, Negro, Oriental, were born merely to take orders. Racial purity was supremely important, mixtures with "impure" blood an intolerable affront to the race. The Jewish race, of all races, was the most reprehensible. It was both parasitic and unassimilable, the source of most of the woes of the world. Acting on these principles, the most fiendish persecutions of the Jews were ordered by the Nazis on the slightest pretexts.

Blood-brother of raceism was German nationalism, for through the activities of the German nation the German race found expression. As nationalism was good, internationalism was the quintessence of evil. All organizations of an international nature were therefore suspect; Communism, which looked forward to world revolution, was the worst

[1] F. L. Schuman, *The Nazi Dictatorship* (1936); William L. Shirer, *Berlin Diary* (1941).

of all, but such international institutions as the Roman Catholic Church, the Masonic order, and the League of Nations came likewise under the ban. Furthermore, the German nation must have room to grow — *Lebensraum*. To fulfill its mission it must expand its borders to include the "heartland" of the European continent. Nazi-infected pseudo-scientists, calling their work geopolitics, drew ample boundaries for the greater, self-sufficient Germany that must come. To fill out these boundaries, and so accomplish the mission of the race, Hitler demanded an increase in the German birth rate — there should be two hundred and fifty million Germans instead of only eighty million. The German colonies, too, must be returned, and German mastery recognized throughout the world.

While the safety of democracy in Europe and America was being thus imperiled, news of alarming developments came also out of Asia. Although the government of Japan had been changed late *The rise* in the nineteenth century to harmonize somewhat with *of Fascism* Occidental practices, the theory of popular sovereignty had *in Japan* always been effectively excluded. The state was in a sense a theocracy, for the Emperor was worshipped as the Son of Heaven, and such privileges of government as were extended to the people were held to be merely gifts emanating from the divine will. In actual practice the Emperor was at the mercy of a small group of "elder statesmen" and privy councilors, whose advice he dare not reject. Following the form, if not the spirit, of the British constitution, a two-house Diet existed, the House of Peers and the House of Representatives, but the Cabinet was responsible to the Emperor rather than to the Diet, and a peculiarly independent status was assigned to the ministers of War and Navy. Invariably these men were selected from among the highest-ranking active officers of the branches concerned, and they were responsible for their acts, neither to the Diet nor to the Cabinet, but only to the Emperor himself.

During the First World War, Japan had enjoyed an unusual prosperity. Her military contribution to the defeat of the Central Powers had been comparatively slight, but she had profited greatly from the sale of war goods to the Allies, and from the use they made of her excellent fleet of merchantmen. After the war, American purchases of Japanese silk long staved off economic disaster, but the Great Depression cut down American buying power and seriously imperiled Japanese prosperity. This situation played directly into the hands of the nation's powerful military leaders, who had long maintained that Japan need only essay the rôle of conqueror to get whatever she needed. In taking such a stand, they had the support of a carefully nurtured mythology, according to which the Japanese people were a superior race, destined to rule the world. War would bring plunder, and was thus an end in itself, but the military leaders had much civilian support for the theory that Japanese expansion was an economic necessity.[1]

First on the calling list of the Japanese war lords was Manchuria.[2] This region, it was argued, if fully exploited by Japan, would provide the nation with the raw resources and the manufacturing outlet that it needed. Japanese bankers and industrialists were already entrenched in Manchuria, and they were eager for the security that conquest would bring them. After Manchuria there were other worlds to conquer — as much of the rest of China as might be needed to keep that still unformed nation subject to the Japanese will, and, if the times broke aright, the white man's dominions in all eastern Asia and the Indies. Various terms were used to cloak the Japanese designs. For a time emphasis was laid on the similarity between Japanese ambitions in the Far East and the ambitions of the United States in the Americas. Japan wanted merely a "Monroe Doctrine for Asia." But the "New Order," or the "Co-Prosperity Sphere," that Japanese spokesmen soon began to talk about for eastern Asia exceeded the wildest dreams of American imperialists. What the Japanese leaders really wanted was to make their neighbors their slaves.[3]

The Manchurian "incident" of 1931 was the beginning of a procession of events that led directly toward the Second World War. On the faintest pretexts, Japanese troops occupied large sections of Manchuria, organized it into the satellite state of Manchukuo, and set a puppet Emperor, Henry Pu-yi, on its throne. Because this act of aggression constituted a direct violation of the Kellogg-Briand Peace Pact, the United States, through Secretary of State Henry L. Stimson, refused to recognize Manchukuo's government, but the Stimson policy had no effect on Japanese expansionists. When the British-dominated League of Nations voiced mild disapproval, Japan gave notice of her intent to withdraw from the League (March 27, 1933). Only the Chinese did anything really effective about the matter. Through a nation-wide boycott on Japanese goods, the Chinese people inflicted notable punishment upon Japanese industry. China, next to the United States, had been Japan's best customer, but in the months following the occupation of Manchuria sales of Japanese goods to China fell off by as

Manchukuo

[1] Joseph C. Grew, *Report from Tokyo* (1942).
[2] Owen Lattimore, *Manchuria, Cradle of Conflict* (1935).
[3] The background of the Far-Eastern situation is well set forth in H. S. Quigley and G. H. Blakeslee, *The Far East: An International Survey* (1939).

much as two thirds. Wholesale discriminations against Japanese business interests in China became also the order of the day.

Another result of the Japanese aggressions was to unite the faction-torn Chinese for self-defense. Even the deeply antagonistic Nationalists under Chiang Kai-shek and the Communists under *The Chinese* Chang Hsueh-liang found ways of co-operating, with Chiang *"incident"* Kai-shek as Generalissimo. When, therefore, the Japanese decided in 1937 to prosecute an undeclared war against China, their troops were confronted by organized opposition. But the Chinese were no match for the well-trained and well-supplied Japanese armies, who took territory almost at will, and eventually had under their control most of the Chinese seacoast and much of the adjacent interior. While the Japanese refused to admit that the China "incident" was a war, the League of Nations seemed to regard it as such, and after much delay recommended that the various member nations extend what aid they could to China. Over the Burma Road, which by 1938 American-trained engineers had completed with the use of Chinese coolie labor, China was able to import some useful war materials, and eventually both the British and the American governments extended credits to China. At all times the Japanese invaders were at pains to visit their wrath upon British and American residents and business interests in the military area. An incident of the war was the destruction on December 12, 1937, by Japanese bombers, of an American gunboat, the *Panay*. The act was deliberate and intended, but the American public was apathetic and the apologies of the Japanese government were accepted.[1]

Meantime, the "robber" nations of Europe were also on the march. In 1935, Mussolini began a war of conquest against Ethiopia, with the avowed intent of adding that backward African kingdom to his empire. This venture was so fraught with peril for the *Ethiopia* peace of Europe that for a time it seemed as if the League of Nations might employ effective economic "sanctions" to prevent it. If Italy could be kept from obtaining oil, it appeared that the war could not go on. But the League finally backed down. It applied sanctions, but not the oil sanctions that alone were well calculated to achieve results. Perhaps the reason for this weak attitude lay in the fact that the British navy, upon which the main brunt of enforcing the sanctions would have fallen, was inadequately prepared for war. Whatever the reasons, the League of Nations as a means of keeping the peace of the world became a farce from this time forward. Mussolini went ahead, practi-

[1] Claude A. Buss, *War and Diplomacy in Eastern Asia* (1941).

cally unimpeded, with his plan of conquest, drove the Ethiopian monarch, Haile Selassie, into exile, and on May 9, 1936, announced that the Italian King had also assumed the title of Emperor.

Inflated with one victory, Mussolini soon sought another. When in 1936 a revolt broke out in Spain against the democratic government *The Spanish* of the Spanish Republic, Mussolini sent his "legions" to *Civil War* the aid of the revolutionary leader, General Francisco Franco, whose Fascist tendencies were unmistakable. Aid for Franco came also from Germany, and a little help for the "Loyalists," as the government forces were called, came from Russia. The civil war in Spain was widely recognized as a dress rehearsal for the coming world war, but the democratic nations were unwilling to do anything effective for the hard-pressed Loyalists, who, after a bitter and bloody struggle, lost out. In General Franco, the new dictator of Spain, both Hitler and Mussolini recognized a kindred spirit and a potential ally.

Only those who wished to be deceived could believe that Hitler's rise to power in Germany would not still further unsettle the peace of Europe. The same year that Hitler became Chancellor — *Appeasement* 1933 — Germany gave notice of her withdrawal from the League of Nations; two years later, after the plebiscite required by the Treaty of Versailles, she took back the Saar Basin; next year, in 1936, German troops reoccupied and remilitarized the Rhineland; two years after that, early in 1938, they occupied Austria, and added that formerly independent state to Hitler's "Third Reich." The portion of German *Lebensraum* next coveted by Hitler was Czechoslovakia, which Germany now almost completely surrounded, but the Führer chose at first to demand only the Sudetenland, a strip along the Czecho-German border mainly inhabited by Germans. To retain this region, which was essential to her defense, Czechoslovakia was ready to fight, but she was held back by nations she had thought were her friends, France and England. Among the people of the western democracies pacifism had become a passion; they simply would not have another war. Probably, therefore, their governments were quite in accord with public opinion when they proposed to keep Germany at peace by a policy of "appeasement." After extensive preliminary threats by Hitler and concessions by the western democracies, Prime Minister Chamberlain of Great Britain and Premier Daladier of France met with Hitler and Mussolini at Munich in September, 1938, to find a solution short of war. They found it by demanding that Czechoslovakia yield to Hitler's demands, and as a result German troops marched into the Sudetenland.[1] Then in March,

[1] John F. Kennedy, *Why England Slept* (1940).

1939, Czecho-Slovakia itself, as the sadly mangled state was renamed, was occupied by Hitler, and most of its territory added to the Reich. Not to be outdone, Mussolini the very next month transported an army across the Adriatic and took possession of Albania. To diminutive Victor Emmanuel III went another title, King of Albania.

By this time a bond of friendship had been formed between Hitler and Mussolini, a bond that quite clearly was meant also to include Japan. The objection of all three nations to the spread of *Rome-Berlin* Communism found expression in the Anti-Comintern Pact *Axis* signed between Germany and Japan in 1936, and adhered to by Italy in 1937. Then in May, 1939, immediately following the Czechoslovakian and Albanian incidents, Germany and Italy concluded also a ten-year military alliance — the "Rome-Berlin Axis." The agreement pledged that if either of the two powers should become involved in war, the other would come to its aid "with all its military forces, on land, sea, and in the air." Rumor had it that the next expansionist effort of the Axis Powers would be to acquire Tunisia for Italy.

What Mussolini had done in the Balkans, Great Britain and France were prepared to discount, but Hitler's extinction of Czechoslovakia, in complete disregard of his promise that the Sudetenland *End of* would be his final conquest, brought appeasement to an end. *appeasement* "If it is so easy to discover good reasons for ignoring assurances so solemnly and repeatedly given," said Chamberlain, "what reliance can be placed upon any other assurances that come from the same source?" That Hitler intended to press on with his program of expansion was clear to all. From Lithuania he demanded, and received, Memel. From Poland he demanded under threat of war consent to the restoration of the free city of Danzig to the Reich, and to the building of a strictly German highway and railroad across the Polish Corridor. Only a few years before, Hitler had signed a non-aggression pact with Poland, but by this time evidence of the worthlessness of his pledges was so overwhelming that these new demands occasioned little surprise. With British and French opinion now unwilling to support further appeasement, Prime Minister Chamberlain, with the full support of the French government as well as his own, promised the Polish government all possible aid in case the independence of Poland should be threatened. Similar guarantees were soon given Greece and Rumania, and an Anglo-Turkish pact provided for mutual assistance "in the event of aggression leading to war in the Mediterranean area." France, also, began to patch up her differences with Turkey over Syria, and even the United States showed concern. President Roosevelt, in a message of

Roosevelt   Hitler   Mussolini

Courtesy of David Low

"WARMONGER"

April 16, 1939, to the Axis dictators, asked them for assurance that they would not invade thirty named states. The recipients of the message treated it with ridicule, but they were unable to prove conclusively that their neighbors were not afraid of them.

Throughout these proceedings the great enigma had been Russia. That the signers of the Anti-Comintern Pact had anything but contempt
The Russian- for the Soviet system could hardly be doubted; they made
German it plain on every possible occasion that they intended to
accord destroy it. But the western democracies had also had their suspicions of Russia; was not the Comintern as much dedicated to their destruction as to that of the Axis Powers? During the negotiations that preceded Munich, Russia had been deliberately slighted. In that conference, which decided the fate of Czechoslovakia, one of Russia's near neighbors, no Russian had been permitted a voice. Talk was rife that the western democracies were deliberately building up Nazi Germany as a counterweight to Soviet Russia, and that a war to the death between Germany and Russia was the real objective of British and French diplomacy. However this may have been, both Great Britain and France were by March, 1939, extremely eager for Russian collaboration, and a special British envoy was sent to Russia to negotiate an Anglo-Soviet pact. Throughout the summer of 1939, while Hitler breathed out

more and more threatenings against Poland, these negotiations continued, but without results. Certain that nothing could drive such bitter enemies as Hitler and Stalin together, editorial writers and news commentators believed that the delay was over Russian insistence on a free hand in dealing with the Baltic countries, and speculated on just how much of what he wanted Stalin would be able to obtain. Then, to the amazement of the whole world, came the announcement that Russia and Germany had agreed late in August, first, to a commercial pact according to which German manufactured goods were to be exchanged for Russian raw materials, and then to a non-agression pact which declared that each nation would respect the territory and sovereignty of the other. Thus reinforced, Hitler went ahead in a three weeks' blitzkrieg to conquer two thirds of Poland, leaving the rest of that unhappy country to Russia.

In response to the frantic demands of Poland, Great Britain and France, on September 5, declared war on Germany, but they were able to do nothing whatever to restrain the Nazi drive. Both *The Second* nations mobilized fully; the British re-established the block- *World War* ade they had found so effective in the First World War, and the French manned their much-touted Maginot Line. But for more than half a year there was little real fighting, and the situation could be described

Courtesy of David Low

RENDEZVOUS

with some propriety as a "phony war." During most of this period the spotlight was upon Russia rather than Germany, for Stalin took quick advantage of the opportunity presented him to seek a restoration of the old Russian frontiers along the Baltic. With only the slightest diplomatic preparation, his troops took over Latvia, Lithuania, and Estonia. His efforts to overrun Finland, however, were met with stiff resistance, for the Finns were determined to retain their independence at all costs. From December, 1939, to March, 1940, the Russo-Finnish War went on, and the tenacity with which the Finns defended their borders against the vastly superior foe excited the amazement and admiration of the whole world. For her act of aggression Russia was expelled from the League of Nations, to which she had been admitted five years before, and war materials both from the ,Allied nations and from the Scandinavian countries were rushed in great quantity to the Finnish armies. Plans were even laid for the sending of an Allied expeditionary force to help the Finns, but before this could be done the Russians had begun to win, and the Finnish government made peace. By the terms agreed upon, the Finnish boundaries were "rectified," but the independence of Finland was left intact.

In April, 1940, the "phony war" in the West came to a sudden end. That month Hitler's armies overran Denmark and Norway, the former *The fall of* without resistance, and the latter in spite of all the help *France* that Allied ships and Allied troops could give. In May the Nazi blitzkrieg struck Belgium and Holland with devastating fury, and by the end of June it had brought, not them alone, but France also, to surrender. Two weeks before France confessed defeat, Mussolini forced an unwilling Italy into the war on Hitler's side, while such of the lesser nations of Europe as had not yet been conquered made every effort to curry favor with the victorious Third Reich. To most observers the invasion of England appeared imminent. The army that the British had landed on the Continent was able, almost by a miracle, to withdraw at Dunkirk, but it had lost practically all its equipment, and appeared to be easy prey for the conquering foe. Only the royal air and naval forces blocked the way. Fully mindful of this fact, the British navy took prompt action to keep as many French warships as possible out of Hitler's hands. The French squadron at Oran in North Africa was attacked by British units on July 3 and in large part destroyed, while a similar squadron at Alexandria was persuaded to remain immobilized.

In desperate but still defiant mood, the British nation and empire battened down to carry on the war alone. "I have nothing to offer," said the new Prime Minister, Winston Churchill, "but blood, toil, tears, and sweat." As if to help redeem this pledge the *England* German *Luftwaffe* began an aerial bombardment of Britain in August, 1940, that destroyed large sections of London as well as many other British cities, and lasted on through the entire fall and winter. From fallen France, now ready to concede a German victory, there came few brave words or deeds. After the surrender to Germany, a government more subject to Hitler than to the will of the French people was set up at Vichy, with southeastern France and the overseas empire, theoretically at least, under its control. The Chief-of-State, aged Marshal Pétain, struggled with only slight success to maintain the fiction of French independence. As for the other conquered countries, most of them established exile governments in London, where also a faction of "Free French," under the leadership of General Charles de Gaulle, refused to recognize that the Vichy government really represented France.[1]

The steady disintegration of peace in Europe during the first six years of the Roosevelt administration had forced the American people, much against their wishes, to think seriously about what course their government should pursue in case another great war should break out. Many Americans, after reflecting on the results of the "war to end war" which they had entered in 1917, were convinced that the proper course of conduct for the United States was to maintain its neutrality, come what might. Undoubtedly this sentiment was greatly strengthened by the findings of a Senate committee, headed by Senator Gerald P. Nye of North Dakota, which in 1934 began to examine into the unsavory record of the munitions industries during and after the last war.[2] Extreme isolationists began to demand insistently that Congress enact neutrality laws so strict as to preclude all possibility of American involvement in case war again broke out in Europe.

Opposed to this point of view were the believers in "collective security" who argued that the world had become too small for any nation so large and influential as the United States to remain aloof *"Collective* from what was going on. If war came it might easily engulf *security"* the United States, regardless of any laws Congress might pass, or of the will of the American people for peace. Even if the United States failed to take part in a general war, it would still be intimately affected. Normal lines of trade would be broken up; the basis for a new world

[1] Francis T. Miller, *History of World War II* (1945), is an early effort to put the whole story together. Walter Phelps Hall, *Iron out of Calvary: An Interpretative History of the Second World War* (1946), is probably the best single volume on the subject yet to appear.
[2] H. C. Engelbrecht and F. C. Hanighen, *Merchants of Death* (1934), is a popular exposé of the activities of the munitions-makers.

depression more calamitous than any ever known before would be laid; disease germs as destructive as those which in 1918 spread the influenza to every nation, neutral or belligerent, would be unleashed; and in a thousand other ways the United States would feel the impact of hostilities. The proper course, therefore, was to prevent war. Let the United States join with peace-loving nations to curb aggressors and to compel peace. Mere negative neutrality was not enough. War must be prevented.

As early as 1933, when Hitler rose to power in Germany and began his program of rearmament, Roosevelt made it clear that, whatever other Americans might think, the President of the United States leaned strongly in the direction of collective security. In an address to the nations of the world issued May 16, 1933, the day before Hitler was to make what was expected to be a warlike statement to the Reichstag, Roosevelt urged the adoption of the MacDonald plan for the elimination of weapons designed primarily for aggressive warfare. "Modern weapons of offense," he pointed out with admirable prescience, "are vastly stronger than modern weapons of defense. Frontier forts, trenches, wire entanglements, coast defenses — in a word, fixed fortifications — are no longer impregnable to the attack of war planes, heavy mobile artillery, land battleships called tanks, and poison gas." If the nations would agree not to possess or use these weapons, then the "frontiers and independence of every nation" would become secure. A few days later Norman H. Davis, American representative at the fruitless Geneva conference on disarmament, told the delegates that, provided only a satisfactory treaty could be arranged, the United States would be willing to consult with the other nations in case of a threat to peace. Further, should any disciplinary measures be undertaken against an aggressor nation, the United States "would refrain from any action tending to defeat such collective effort," that is, from insisting on its rights as a neutral. A good definition of an aggressor nation, Davis suggested, was one "whose troops are found on alien soil in violation of treaties." [1]

The disarmament conference died a lingering death, and many Americans were relieved that Roosevelt was not obliged to live up to the pledges he had made. [2] The President nevertheless showed repeatedly that he had not changed his mind. His classic utterance on the subject, aimed apparently at Japan and

A quarantine of aggressors?

---

[1] The subsequent fate of such nations as Austria, Czechoslovakia, Poland, Finland, Norway, Denmark, Belgium, and Holland led one observer to amend this definition as follows: "An aggressor nation is a little nation that has something that a big nation wants."

[2] J. W. Wheeler-Bennett, *The Pipe-Dream of Peace: The Story of the Collapse of Disarmament* (1935).

Italy for their operations respectively in China and Ethiopia, came on October 5, 1937, during an address delivered in Chicago:

> It seems to be unfortunately true that the epidemic of world lawlessness is spreading. When an epidemic of physical disease starts to spread, the community approves and joins in a quarantine of the patients in order to protect the health of the community against the spread of the disease. . . . War is a contagion, whether it be declared or undeclared. It can engulf states and peoples remote from the original scene of hostilities. We are determined to keep out of war, yet we cannot insure ourselves against the disastrous effects of war and the dangers of involvement. . . . There must be positive endeavors to preserve peace. America hates war. America hopes for peace. Therefore, America actively engages in the search for peace.

The American search for peace did not stand in the way of active naval expansion, particularly after the breakdown of all plans for disarmament seemed assured. In January, 1938, the President *Naval* asked Congress to appropriate a billion dollars for naval *expansion* defense, and after some delay and debate Congress acquiesced. From the point of view of those who believed in collective security the navy was necessary if the United States was to have any influence in restraining "warmongers," while from the point of view of the isolationists it was necessary to defend American borders against a warmongering world.

Probably the advocates of collective security were only a small minority in the United States, and Roosevelt found it expedient from time to time to tone down or disavow the sentiments he *Neutrality* undoubtedly felt. In this instance Congress, rather than *legislation* the President, represented the dominant public opinion. By a series of neutrality laws it attempted to legislate into oblivion all possible opportunities for the United States to be drawn into a non-American conflict. The first of these acts, passed in 1935 during the Italian attack on Ethiopia, required the President to impose an embargo upon the shipment of arms to belligerent nations, and authorized him to prohibit Americans from traveling upon the ships of belligerents. The second act, passed the following year, maintained these provisions, and added a prohibition against the flotation of loans in the United States by any non-American belligerent. The third act, more comprehensive than the rest, became law in May, 1937. It, too, included the preceding legislation on neutrality and imposed additional restrictions. American merchant ships might not carry munitions to belligerents nor arm themselves against attack. Certain discretionary powers were also bestowed upon the President. He might forbid American ships to transport commodities of any kind to a belligerent nation; he might require all shipments to be made on a strictly "cash-and-carry" basis; and he might exclude enemy warships, submarines, and armed merchantmen from the use of American ports. These acts went far toward eliminating all the alleged causes of conflict that had led the United States to enter the World War in 1917. By them notice was pointedly served upon European nations that the American people were no longer willing to defend the principles of neutrality for which they once had fought.

While the President found these laws somewhat unpalatable, he showed considerable facility in adapting them to his views on foreign policy. He recognized the existence of a state of war between Italy and Ethiopia, and declared the embargo on arms in force. This was advantageous to Ethiopia, which could not have purchased arms in America in any event, and an intended handicap to Italy, which might have done so. But since Japan had not declared war against China, he refused to recognize the hostilities in the Orient as war, presumably in order to enable the Chinese to continue their purchases of American munitions. In the case of Spain, where civil war existed, but with the Italians and Germans helping the insurgents and the Russians helping the loyalists, he applied the embargo, much to the discomfiture of the loyalists, who had the money with which to buy. Finally, impressed by the near-certainty of a general war, the President asked Congress early in 1939 to modify the Neutrality Act of 1937 by removing the mandatory feature of the embargo on arms and armaments. It was his idea that the American government should be left free to follow traditional practice on this subject. But Congress was recalcitrant, and the President's efforts to amend the Act resulted only in a promise that neutrality legislation would be the first order of business at the next session of Congress.

Roosevelt urges changes

Meanwhile the darkening war-clouds in Europe led Roosevelt to renewed emphasis upon "continental solidarity" and "hemispheric defense." When the eighth Pan-American Conference met in Lima, December 10, 1938, the United States was acutely conscious of the inroads being made by German and Italian propaganda in Latin-American states, and sought to unite the twenty-one republics of the New World in a common defense against "aggressor nations." The agreement which Secretary Hull was able to obtain was not nearly as binding as the American government had hoped, but it affirmed that the peoples of America still had faith in "absolute adherence to the principles of international law," and that they would work together to defend the peace of the continent. When war actually broke

"Continental solidarity"

out, delegates from the various American republics met at Panama, October 1, 1939, to consider a common policy of neutrality. After several days' deliberation they issued a declaration which asserted that the "waters adjacent to the American continent" must be "free from the commission of any hostile act by any non-American belligerent nation." Two months later an engagement between German and British naval units off the mouth of the River Plate demonstrated conclusively that something stronger than words would be required to keep the war far removed from American shores. In the spring of 1940 the assistance which Hitler's armies received from Nazi sympathizers in Norway, the Netherlands, Belgium, and France led to a new wave of excitement throughout the Americas. Was there a "fifth column"[1] in each American nation ready to betray it to some European invader? Fear that some such situation might indeed exist led many Latin-American governments to affirm more earnestly than ever before their desire to coöperate fully with the United States.

The occupation of the Dutch West Indies by the Allies after the defeat of the Netherlands brought no protest from the United States, but when France was compelled to sue for peace notice was promptly served on Germany that the United States under the terms of the Monroe Doctrine could permit no transfer of American colonies from one European nation to another. This contention was scornfully rejected by Germany, which insisted that the United States had no right to advance such an argument unless willing on its part to keep entirely aloof from European affairs. The surliness of the Nazi reply, coupled with the fact that after the French surrender British and French warships seemed to be on the verge of a clash in American waters, led the President to advocate that the Pan-American Conference scheduled to meet in Havana on July 20 should adopt a new rule for territorial readjustments in the American hemisphere. On behalf of the United States he formally renounced all territorial aspirations, and he urged that the twenty-one American republics should act together, each having equal voice, in determining what post-war rearrangements would be permitted in the New World. He suggested further that the system he favored for the Americas might well be applied in other continents also. Instead of Asia for the Japanese and Europe for the Germans, let each of the nations of Asia have an equal voice in Asiatic affairs, and each of the nations of Europe an equal voice in European affairs.

---

[1] This term was first used by General Mola, the commander of the Spanish insurgents, in his campaign against Madrid. Four columns, he announced, were marching on the city, and they would be joined by a secret "fifth column" from within the city itself.

Neither Europe nor Asia was in position to heed the President's advice, but at the Havana Conference the patient diplomacy of Secretary *Act of* Hull bore significant fruit. An Act of Havana was adopted *Havana* which forbade the transfer of any European colony to another non-American power, and stated that if any such transfer were attempted the colony in question would pass immediately under the joint control of the American states. To provide for the government of the colony a committee of twenty-one, to consist of one member for each American nation, might be summoned at will by any of the participating nations, and as an assurance against impotence this committee was to be considered fully constituted "from the date of the appointment of two thirds of its members." Furthermore, actions might be taken with the approval of two thirds of the members present, while a special emergency declaration gave the United States the support for the Monroe Doctrine from the other American nations that it long had craved:

> If the necessity for emergency action be deemed so urgent as to make it impossible to await action of the committee, any of the American republics, individually or jointly with others, shall have the right to act in a manner required for its defense or the defense of the continent.

In spite of these apparent successes, it was obvious that many obstacles blocked the way toward any real union of the Americas. Culturally the English-speaking peoples of North America were infinitely farther removed from the Latin-Americans than the latter were from the peoples of southwestern Europe. Economic interests tended also to bind Latin America to Europe rather than to the United States, for Europe could provide a market for Latin-American goods, whereas the United States already had too much of what the other Latin-American nations wished to sell. In respect to government, too, the same pattern persisted. Dictatorships were the rule rather than the exception in Latin America, and democracy was only a thin veneer. Even in the matter of geography "hemispheric solidarity" was far less significant than it sounded, for South America lay entirely to the east of North America, and much of it was closer to the Old World than to the United States. The one important bond of union that Roosevelt could count on was fear.

Roosevelt's idea of American solidarity included Canada no less than Latin America. Fortunately his efforts to bring the two great English-speaking nations of North America together had the advantage of many ties, both in blood and history, that were lacking in dealing with the other Americas. By 1940 Roosevelt and the Canadian Prime Minister Mackenzie King were in close conference at Ogdenburg, New York, on how to promote measures of joint defense. In spite of the fact that the

United States was a neutral, while Canada was a belligerent, the heads of the two governments solemnly agreed that a Permanent Board on Defense should be set up, to consist of four or five members from each country, the business of which would be to "commence immediate studies relating to sea, land, and air . . . defense of the north half of the Western Hemisphere." As head of the United States delegation, the President appointed Mayor Fiorello H. La Guardia of New York, a former Congressman who had distinguished himself as a member of the United States air service during the First World War. On both sides of the border this declaration was hailed as the practical equivalent of a military alliance.

In the Far East, while the United States seemed by no means unwilling to escape from the defense of the Philippines, the American Secretary of State, Cordell Hull, repeatedly made it clear that his nation *The* had no intention of recognizing any new order imposed on *Far East* China by force of arms; and on July 26, 1939, he startled the Japanese government by abrogating the commercial treaty between Japan and the United States that had existed since 1911. This move was generally believed to anticipate an embargo on American munitions shipments to Japan, but no such action was taken, and the conquest of China went on. In the summer of 1940, however, the United States forbade the export to any foreign country without license of essential war materials such as heavy scrap-iron and petroleum, and on September 27 it followed this announcement with a complete embargo on the shipment of iron and steel scrap, except to Great Britain and the nations of the western hemisphere. Within a few hours this blow was countered by the revelation that a joint "economic, political, and military" alliance, aimed primarily at the United States, had been formed by Germany, Italy, and Japan. Predictions were rife that the next move in the diplomatic chess game would be an agreement between the United States and Great Britain whereby the American battle fleet might be assured the right to use the great British naval base at Singapore, but in actual fact events took a very different turn.[1]

It was the European scene, however, far more than the Asiatic, which cast a fateful spell over the American people. The sudden fall of France, and the desperate peril of Britain aroused their deepest *American* fears. American thinking had all along been predicated *fears* upon the assumption that the British navy was unbeatable, and that

---

[1] J. C. Grew, *Ten Years in Japan* (1944), recounts the events that led up to the attack on Pearl Harbor. See also T. A. Bisson, *American Policy in the Far East, 1931–1940* (1940); and H. L. Stimson, *The Far Eastern Crisis: Recollections and Observations* (1936).

whatever happened in Europe the Atlantic Ocean would remain in friendly hands. But now the danger of a complete German victory had to be faced. Suppose Hitler succeeded in sinking the British navy, or worse still, in capturing it? Would he then be content to rule in France and let America alone? What would be his attitude toward Latin America? Heretofore British economic interests and American national policy had coincided in relation to the Americas. The Monroe Doctrine had been possible no less because American sea-power stood back of it than because the British, too, gave it tacit support. Would the United States eventually have to fight Hitler alone? And whether the war came to the New World or not, what would international relations be like with the democracy-hating dictatorships supreme in Europe, Asia, and Africa? [1]

[1] This concern found full expression in William E. Dodd, Jr., and Martha Dodd, eds., *Ambassador Dodd's Diary, 1933–1938* (1940).

CHAPTER XXXI

THE UNITED STATES IN THE
SECOND WORLD WAR

FROM the very beginning of the war in Europe, President Roosevelt had used his influence to further the cause of the Allies. Immediately following the German attack on Poland, he convened Con- *Amendments* gress in special session on September 21, and asked for a *to the Neu-* revised Neutrality Act that would permit the United States *trality Act* to sell arms, ammunition, and implements of war to such nations as were able to pay for them in cash and to carry them away in foreign-registered ships. American public opinion was overwhelmingly with the Allies, and the President made no effort to conceal his hope that the control of the seas enjoyed by England and France would enable them to buy freely from across the Atlantic. Early in November, Congress acceded to the President's request, but in ending the embargo on munitions it made every effort to insure the United States against outright participation in the war. The prohibition on loans to belligerents was continued, American ships were barred from carrying passengers or materials to belligerent shores; and travel by American citizens on the vessels of belligerents was specifically forbidden. One result of the failure of the United States to defend its traditional rights as a neutral was that the minor neutral nations were left without a champion and helpless before the superior might of their predatory neighbors. Hundreds of neutral ships went down as German submarine warfare assumed at once the unrestricted character that it had attained in the preceding war only after more than two years of fighting, and at the cost of American participation on the Allied side.

Even after the fall of France and the British withdrawal from the Continent, a surprisingly large number of Americans were ready to take their chances on a Hitlerian victory. To them the consider- *Isolationists* ation of chief importance was that, come what might in *vs. Inter-* Europe, the United States must keep out of the war. Since *ventionists* there was no danger whatever of American involvement on the German side, they concentrated their attacks on those who wished to show in any tangible way the partiality that most Americans felt for the beleaguered British. Chief among the advocates of an adamant "isolationism" were Senator Burton K. Wheeler, of Montana, who had broken with the Roosevelt administration over the Supreme Court issue; Colonel Charles A. Lindbergh, the aviator, whose father had suffered much persecution as an opponent of the First World War; William Randolph Hearst and his editorial writers for the Hearst newspapers; Colonel Robert R. McCormick, of the *Chicago Tribune*; the two La Follette brothers, of Wisconsin; Representative Hamilton Fish, of New York; and Senator Gerald P. Nye, of North Dakota. They were aided by a powerful and well-financed organization, attractively named the "America First Committee," which left no stone unturned to discredit all would-be "interventionists." Actually, very few Americans were prepared to advocate outright military intervention, but among those who were unable to look with complacency upon the final triumph of Hitler, all possible aid for the Allies "short of war" became an increasingly popular slogan. A "Committee to Defend America by Aiding the Allies" was headed for a time by the venerable William Allen White, of Kansas, but in general the "interventionists" lacked both the leaders and the funds to make their propaganda fully effective. They took comfort, however, in the fact that they had on their side the President of the United States. It was he who had persuaded Congress to permit the shipment of American-made munitions to the enemies of Germany and Italy; furthermore, he had deliberately turned back to the manufacturers as supposedly outmoded such military items as airplanes, knowing full well that they would promptly be shipped to the Allies.

It is not surprising, considering the unparalleled situation they faced, that the American people began to look with critical eye at their de-

Preparedness fenses. Naval preparedness, they well knew, had long been regarded with considerable favor, but no attempt had been made to build up separate Atlantic and Pacific squadrons. The United States possessed a fleet approximately equal to the British navy, and still, or so the American public fondly believed, somewhat superior to the Japanese. But American strategists had never faced the possibility of an attack in the Atlantic and Pacific at the same time. They had assumed always that the Panama Canal would enable American ships to shuttle back and forth as needed from one ocean to another. Now, with Japan determined to push its "new order" to unpredictable lengths in the Pacific, and with the plainly visible threat of German domination in the Atlantic, the country awoke with a start from its pleasant dream of security. Even the Panama Canal was vulnerable, if only an enemy nation could obtain a near-by American base for aircraft operation. The success of the German methods of land warfare had also to be taken into account. While the rest of the world had struggled ineffectively with the problems of peace, the German nation had prepared for war. Under the complete domination of the Nazi hierarchy its people had been disciplined and trained, both physically and psychologically, for the supreme effort that lay before them. Autocratic rulers had demanded and obtained perfect co-ordination of military might, on land, by sea, and in the air, regardless of all hamstringing traditions. German scientists had turned their remarkable talents to the improvement of the weapons of warfare found most useful in the last war, and had conducted a ceaseless search for new ways to strengthen the nation's fighting power. While other nations had failed miserably to solve their problems of unemployment, Germany had devoted herself so intensely to the quantity production of war machines as to produce a chronic labor shortage.

The various battles by which the Nazi victories were won proved the potency of the new weapons, and the hopeless inadequacy of the old. The United States was particularly lacking in the equip- *Lessons from* ment necessary for mechanized warfare. If British and *the Nazi* American sea-power should be overcome, the military in- *victories* vasion of North America was no more an impossibility than it had been during the American Revolution or the War of 1812. Indeed, Canada, the northern neighbor of the United States, was already at war, and Winston Churchill, the fighting British Prime Minister who had succeeded Chamberlain after the British *débâcle* in Norway, had promised, in case the British Isles were overcome, to move the British government to the "Empire beyond the seas," and from there to "carry on the struggle until, in God's good time, the New World, with all its power and might, steps forth to the rescue and liberation of the Old." Should Germany attempt to invade Canada, the Monroe Doctrine would automatically bring the United States into the war, and should a German invasion prove successful, the undefended border between the United States and its northern neighbor might not be the boon it had always seemed. To meet even a minor mechanized invasion, existing methods and weapons would be well-nigh helpless.

Under these circumstances it seemed clear to most Americans, "isolationists" and "interventionists" alike, that the least the United States could do was to arm to the teeth with all possible speed. *The defense* But even this minimum necessity met vigorous opposition. *program* Professional pacifists, among whom the most prominent were Socialists,

Communists, and members of the liberal Protestant clergy, joined forces with other extreme advocates of neutrality to denounce preparedness as merely a prelude to war. Nevertheless, Congress early in June, 1940 appropriated by decisive majorities more than three billion dollars for the national defense, and made clear its intention of adding whatever other sums might be regarded as necessary. By the end of September total appropriations for defense purposes had reached the astounding figure of thirteen billion dollars. To facilitate further large-scale borrowing, the national debt limit was raised to forty-nine billion dollars the first, but not the last, such increase. Additional income and excise taxes were also voted, in defiance of the tradition that new taxes were not to be thought of in an election year.

Appropriating the money, however, was quite a different thing from actual rearmament. At best, according to the *Army and Navy Journal*, the United States would still be "a year and a half hence, far behind the fighting forces of the European nations." Plans had yet to be formulated for adjusting the nation's productive plant to the manufacture of the necessary tanks and other mechanized equipment, and for raising and training the essential man-power. To furnish political supervision over the activities of Army and Navy, the President broke precedents right and left by making Henry L. Stimson, formerly Secretary of State under Herbert Hoover, his Secretary of War, and Frank Knox, Republican Vice-Presidential candidate in 1936, his Secretary of the Navy. To put the nation on a war footing, so far as industry was concerned, he set up a National Defense Advisory Commission of seven members, headed by William S. Knudsen, president of the General Motors Corporation, and Edward R. Stettinius, Jr., chairman of the board of the United States Steel Corporation. When production bottlenecks and labor difficulties proved too difficult for the commission to handle, the President tried again, creating this time an Office of Production Management, with Knudsen as director-general, and Sidney Hillman as a representative of labor, associate director-general. Continuing complications were attributed by most critics to the President's unwillingness to place the whole problem of production under one-man control.

Unwilling to risk the delay involved in raising an army by volunteering, the President urged Congress to adopt a Selective Service Act comparable to the conscription measure of 1917. This plan met with the most determined opposition, but by the middle of September, 1940, preparedness leaders in Congress were able to score a complete victory. The new measure required all men between the ages of twenty-one and thirty-five inclusive to register for a year of military training, and on

October 16 approximately seventeen million citizens presented them-selves for the draft. From this number the Army planned to call into service during the first year about eight hundred thousand men, and to replace them with a similar number each succeeding year. Each class, at the end of its period of training, was to remain subject to recall for emergency service during a ten-year period. Congress might also at any time declare the nation in peril, and hold the men in training under arms indefinitely. As the nation's peril increased, the terms of the draft law were stiffened. The first class called had not yet completed its year of training when, on August 18, 1941, Congress authorized the President to hold all draftees in service for as much as eighteen months beyond the period for which they had been called originally. Four months later the requirement of registration was extended to include all men from eight-een to sixty-four years of age, with service liability limited to those from twenty to forty-five.[1] Meantime the National Guard, as the nation's second line of defense, had long since been called into service.

While the United States was still at peace, it seemed to many Ameri-cans that the best possible insurance against the troubles that a Nazi victory was sure to bring would be more effective measures "short of war" to help along the British war-effort. When it became known that the British navy was perilously short of destroyers, whereas the United States was not, a strong demand set in for selling outmoded American destroyers to the British, just as previ-ously military airplanes had been sold to the Allies. Although specific legislation seemed to bar the way to any such action, the President was advised by Attorney-General Jackson that his powers as Commander-in-Chief of the Army and Navy would permit him to exchange obsolete destroyers for such naval bases as he might deem essential to the de-fense of the United States. Accordingly, the President announced early in September that the United States had leased from the British govern-ment for a period of ninety-nine years eight bases, one each in New-foundland, Bermuda, the Bahamas, Jamaica, St. Lucia, Trinidad, An-tigua, and British Guiana. When these advanced positions were fully equipped, it was supposed that the Atlantic coast line of the United States, as well as the Panama Canal, would be completely safeguarded against attack from the east. In return for this "dismemberment of the British Empire," as the Axis Powers chose to term the deal, fifty

Measures "short of war"

[1] The decision to induct eighteen- and nineteen-year-old boys was reached reluctantly in November, 1942, after the United States had been at war for nearly a year. There-after volunteering, which had been encouraged before, was stopped, and not only the Army but the Navy and the Marine Corps as well, were obliged to depend upon the draft for additional man-power.

American destroyers were soon turned over to British crews. That the hard-pressed British, now fighting gamely against incessant attacks from the air as well as the constant threat of invasion by sea, could count on further aid from the United States when the need arose seemed evident.

With foreign relations at so critical a stage, and with the necessity of speeding up the national defense program so obvious, many observers *The presi-* regarded the necessity of holding a presidential election in *dential cam-* 1940 as almost a calamity. In nations such as Great Brit-*paign* ain, where the parliamentary system of government was in operation, an election could be postponed, but in the United States the Constitution was inexorable on this point; the election had to be held.

But, as events proved, this was no ordinary election. Shattering all precedents, the Democrats renominated Roosevelt for a third term, and chose Henry A. Wallace of Iowa, Secretary of Agriculture, as his running-mate. The Republicans, convinced that the leading contenders for their nomination lacked the popular appeal necessary to defeat the President, turned to an ex-Democrat and a businessman, Wendell L. Willkie of Indiana, with Senator Charles L. McNary of Oregon as vice-presidential candidate. Both conventions adopted platforms, the Democrats praising and the Republicans castigating the New Deal. But the platforms, as everyone knew, meant only what the candidates chose to make them mean. Roosevelt's record was not to be concealed, but where did Willkie stand on the issues of the day? Already he had made it clear that on many matters he saw eye to eye with the President, and as the campaign developed, it became evident that almost the only question at issue was whether Roosevelt or Willkie, limited, of course, by the parties they represented, would be the better fitted to carry on the New Deal policies, both foreign and domestic. Willkie made a splendid campaign, stressing that in a democracy no one man should be considered indispensable, but the voters preferred in the crisis to stand by the President. About fifty million voters went to the polls, the largest number in American history. Of these nearly fifty-five per cent voted for Roosevelt, who carried 38 states with 449 electoral votes, while Willkie carried only 10 states with 82 electoral votes. Both houses of Congress and a majority of the state governments remained safely Democratic.

The most obvious conclusion to be drawn from the election, one that foreign powers were quick to point out, was that Roosevelt's policy with *The Lend-* reference to the European war had received the emphatic *Lease Act* endorsement of the American people. Thus fortified, the President reasserted his determination to give all possible aid to Britain, and set "four freedoms" as the American goal for the post-war world — freedom of speech, freedom of religion, freedom from want, freedom from fear. He also submitted to Congress a plan whereby the government of the United States should lend, lease, or otherwise transfer to the nations resisting aggressors such military equipment as American factories were able to produce and the American government to acquire. This measure, which amounted almost to a declaration of partial war, was fought for weeks by the isolationists in and out of Congress, but it ultimately passed both houses by decisive, nonpartisan majorities, and on March 13, 1941, received the President's signature. Among other Republicans to give the Lend-Lease Act hearty support was Wendell Willkie, whose relations with the President had become almost cordial. When Willkie decided to pay a visit to England, he conferred first with Roosevelt, and took a letter from him to be delivered in person to Prime Minister Churchill.

Other actions that left no doubt as to exactly where the United States stood on the war were soon coming thick and fast. Huge appropriations were rushed through Congress for the purchase of lend-lease materials needed by the British. Axis, Danish, and French ships in American ports were seized, and crews deemed guilty of sabotaging their ships were arrested. An executive agreement, reached April 10, 1941, between Secretary of State Hull and the Danish minister to Washington (who had refused to co-operate with his Nazi-dominated government), gave the United States permission to make military use of the island of Greenland. Amidst steadily mounting tension, the President during the next few weeks turned over fifty sorely needed tankers to the British government, closed the Axis consulates in the United States and deported their personnel, and, following the sinking in the South Atlantic of an American merchantman, the *Robin Moor*, proclaimed a state of "unlimited national emergency." The last pretense of American neutrality had all but evaporated.

Meantime Hitler, after a winter of diplomatic preparation, made ready in the spring of 1941 to march his armies southward into the Balkans. Acting under irresistible pressure, Hungary, Rumania, and Bulgaria agreed to receive his troops and co-operate with his régime. The government of Yugoslavia was like-minded, but the Yugoslav army revolted at the orders it was given, and staged a plucky but hopeless struggle against the invaders. Next the Greeks, whom Mussolini had been seeking in vain to conquer since the fall of 1940, were overwhelmed, and the little British army sent to their aid from Egypt was expelled in tattered fragments. For a time the British held Crete, but by the first of June an airborne Nazi invasion had forced them back on

Africa. There the British commander, General Sir Archibald Wavel had recently pushed the Italians far to the westward along the coast c Libya, but whatever chance he might have had to expel them fror Africa altogether he lost with the collapse of the ill-fated Greek venture The hold of the British on the eastern Mediterranean seemed tenuou indeed. To anticipate a possible Nazi thrust through Turkey or Pales tine toward the oil fields of Iraq and Iran, British and "Free French forces, early in June, occupied Syria, but their chances of resisting a Naz attack in force seemed slender indeed.

Then, to the amazement of all the world, Hitler on June 22, 1941, witl Hungary, Rumania, and Finland as allies, attacked Russia. His ex *Hitler at-* planation of this astounding reversal of policy was tha *tacks Russia* Russia was about to attack him, but there is little or n evidence to support such a theory. On the contrary, ever since the Nazi-Communist pacts of 1939, Russia had sought desperately to avoic giving offense to Germany. The Russian dictator, Stalin, had, to be sure, kept his army mobilized, and as subsequent events proved he had made astonishing strides with preparedness. But he had encouraged Communists outside Russia to harass in every possible way the Allied war effort, and had seemed in all respects willing to play the rôle of non-belligerent assistant to Hitler. The new adherent to the anti-Nazi cause was received, however, with every show of cordiality. From Churchill came the prompt announcement: "Any man or state who fights against Naziism will have our aid. Any man or state who marches with Hitler is our foe." And from Roosevelt came the assurance that supplies would soon be flowing from the United States to Russia under the terms of the Lend-Lease Act. To the surprise of most experts, the Russians offered sustained military resistance to the invading armies. The Germans and their allies took much territory, but the collapse that they had expected failed to materialize. In the winter of 1941–42, the Russian armies for several months even held the offensive, and regained some of the ground they had lost.

With Russia, a totalitarian nation, fighting on the Allied side, the question of "war aims," so much discussed during the First World War, *The Atlantic* attracted increasing attention, particularly in the United *Charter* States. In part to answer this question, and in part to give dramatic emphasis to the solidarity of Anglo-American opinion, President Roosevelt and Prime Minister Churchill met at an undisclosed point in the Atlantic, and on August 14, 1941, issued over their joint signatures the so-called "Atlantic Charter." This document disclaimed for Great Britain and the United States any desire for territorial, or other, aggrandizement, or for any territorial changes not in accord with the wishes of the people concerned. It asserted the right of all peoples to choose the form of government under which they wished to live, and promised to promote equal access for all states, "great or small, victor or vanquished," to the raw materials of the world. Other objectives named were improved labor standards, economic advancement, and social security, freedom from fear and want, the unhindered use of the high seas, and the disarmament of aggressor nations as a step toward the abandonment of the use of force in international relations. In many ways the Atlantic Charter was reminiscent of Wilson's Fourteen Points, as it was no doubt meant to be, but it was couched in general terms, and lacked the specific statements of war aims that characterized the earlier document.

By this time the increasing tempo of submarine attacks had brought the "Battle of the Atlantic" to a crisis. Since a substantial number of the freighters being sunk carried lend-lease materials, many Americans demanded that the United States join with Great Britain in convoying merchant fleets overseas. A step in this direction had seemingly been taken when on July 7 the President had announced that units of the United States Navy had arrived in Iceland to supplement, and ultimately to replace, the British forces already there. But Roosevelt seemed reluctant to start a "shooting war," and ordered merely that American ships and aircraft should "patrol" the western Atlantic in order to advise the British as to the whereabouts of Axis craft. The effectiveness of these patrols brought speedy Axis retaliation. Eight American freighters had already been sunk when, on September 4, 1941, the American destroyer *Greer* was attacked, but not hit, while trailing a German submarine. Thereupon the President ordered destroyers to shoot submarines "on sight." In mid-October another destroyer, the *Kearny*, was hit, and eleven of her crew were killed. That same month, the *Reuben James* was torpedoed and sunk, with the loss of seventy-six of her crew. After these attacks, Congress, by a measure signed November 17, authorized the arming of American merchant ships, and freed them from the remaining restrictions of the neutrality laws, which thus far had kept them outside "combat zones." Complete participation by the United States in the war seemed close at hand.

The final dénouement, however, came from an unexpected quarter. The collapse of France had given Japan another opportunity to press on toward her goal of military and economic domination of all eastern Asia. From the subject French government, set up at Vichy after the surrender to Germany with the aged Marshal Pétain as Chief-of-State, the Japanese had obtained the right in 1940 to occupy the northern part of French Indo-China, and on July 23, 1941, they were given permission to take over the rest of the former French dependency. Japanese troops pouring into this area posed a grave threat, not only to the Philippine Islands, but also to the British and Dutch possessions in the Far East. In protest, therefore, the American government on July 24 froze all Japanese assets in the United States, an action which the Dutch and British governments quickly paralleled. During the protracted discussions which followed, the United States proposed a settlement based on the following principles: (1) respect for the territorial integrity and sovereignty of all nations; (2) non-interference in the internal affairs of other countries; (3) equality of commercial and other opportunities; and (4) non-disturbance of the *status quo* in the Pacific except by peaceful means. Finally, when these principles were spurned, the United States demanded assurance from the Japanese government that it intended to withdraw its troops from China and French Indo-China. A few weeks later, on November 15, a Japanese envoy, Saburo Kurusu, arrived ostentatiously by airplane in the United States with what purported to be new Japanese proposals. "We must all pull together for peace," Kurusu told American reporters.

But the Kurusu mission was only a blind, for the course Japan meant to follow had already been decided. On the early morning of December *Pearl* 7, while the peace conversations at Washington were still in *Harbor* progress, a Japanese carrier-borne air force of one hundred and five airplanes attacked the great American naval base at Pearl Harbor, in Hawaii. So complete was the surprise that most American aircraft were destroyed on the ground, leaving the American battle fleet at the mercy of the treacherous foe. Nineteen of the eighty-six American ships in the harbor were seriously hit, five great capital ships were either sunk or otherwise put out of action, and casualties to personnel reached 4575 killed, wounded, or missing. So complete was the catastrophe that the American government delayed an entire year before making public the full details. Had the Japanese brought with them troops to effect a landing, they might with ease have taken the whole of the Hawaiian Islands.

The day after Pearl Harbor was attacked, Congress, with only one dissenting vote, recognized the existence of a state of war between the United States and Japan, while Japan issued its overdue declaration of war against the United States and the British Empire. When a few days later Germany and Italy, in conformity with their commitments to Japan, declared war against the United States, Congress, by a unani-

mous vote in both houses, responded with similar declarations against
the Axis powers in Europe. Thus the total war that most Americans
had hoped so earnestly to avoid became a fact at last. As in the First
World War, many other American nations were soon involved in the
conflict. Some of them, notably Mexico and Brazil, went the whole
length of declaring war, while others were content to show their "good-
neighborliness" by measures "short of war." Eventually every
American power severed diplomatic relations with the Axis. Even the
Argentine declared war in 1945.

For many months the war in the Pacific went badly for the United
Nations, as the Allies now began to call themselves. The attack on
Pearl Harbor was followed immediately by attacks on the Philippine
Islands, Wake Island, Guam, Hong Kong, British Malaya, and Thai-
land. The Thai government offered practically no resistance, Guam fell
on December 11, Wake Island, December 24, and Hong Kong on Christmas Day. In the Philippines General MacArthur, whose forces during
the last phases of the dispute with Japan had been somewhat augmented
by troops from the United States, made a valiant stand on the Bataan
peninsula and the island of Corregidor. But the assistance from the
United States Navy on which his campaign was predicated was not forthcoming, and in the end the Japanese won by sheer force of numbers.
Bataan capitulated in April, and Corregidor in May. Well before the
end came, General MacArthur, in response to an insistent demand from
both the United States and Australia, left the Philippines by stealth to
take command of the United Nations forces in Australia. Meantime
Japanese troops overran Malaya, captured the great British base at
Singapore, conquered Burma, and except for a few precarious footholds
forced the United Nations completely out of the East Indies. With the
Burma Road closed, aid to China decreased to next to nothing, and the
Allies fell back upon India and Australia as bases of operation. To add
to the general gloom, German submarines operating off the Atlantic
coastline and in the Caribbean sank hundreds of American freighters,
and produced an acute gasoline and fuel-oil shortage along the Atlantic
seaboard.

Stung to desperation by the unbroken procession of defeats, the people
of the United States settled down with determination to create a war
machine adequate to cope with their enemies. Early in 1942 a War
Production Board headed by Donald M. Nelson, formerly an executive
of Sears, Roebuck and Company, gave the country the one-man economic leadership that critics of the President had long demanded. Plans
were laid to replace with home-manufactured synthetic products the na-

tion's rubber supply, lost to the Japanese with the fall of Malaya and the East Indies. Low speed-limits for automobile traffic, as well as tire- and gasoline-rationing, were accepted as necessary evils. The army expanded its numbers with all possible speed, and before the year was over announced an ultimate goal of eight million men in uniform. American troops poured overseas, a million strong by the end of the year, to England and northern Ireland, to Australia and New Zealand, to East Africa and Egypt. A new highway was built through Canada to Alaska, and the tiny outposts seized by the Japanese in the Aleutians were subjected to constant air bombardment. Factories turned from the making of peacetime goods to build tanks, and supply other army needs; shipyards increased their capacity, and more than made good the losses sustained by both battle and merchant fleets. Labor, with but relatively few exceptions, forgot its internal conflicts, and carried on with only infrequent resort to strikes. Food conservation, including the rationing of such items as sugar and coffee, provided a steady flow of lend-lease foodstuffs

"IT'S A LIE, WE'RE NOT RETREATING—
JUST ADVANCING BACKWARD!"

[720]

abroad, while caring adequately for army and civilian needs, both overseas and at home. Taxes rose to heights Americans had never deemed possible before, but the people nevertheless responded cordially to the plea that they invest at least ten per cent of their incomes in war bonds.

Well before the end of the year the tide of battle had begun to turn. In the Pacific the forces of the United Nations had chalked up a series of costly but important naval victories — in the Coral Sea, off Midway, and in the Solomon Islands. The initiative seemed definitely to have passed from the Japanese to the Allies on August 7, when the marines took Tulagi harbor and the air-field on Guadalcanal Island. Heartening news came also from Russia, where for a second year the coming of winter found the army ready to take the offensive, and from Egypt, where the Axis forces, after a spectacular recovery that threatened for a time to overwhelm Cairo and Alexandria, were thrown back once again in precipitate retreat. Still disappointed in the progress made, the American people gave the Roosevelt administration a stinging rebuke on election day, November 3, by reducing substantially the Democratic majorities in both House and Senate, and by overthrowing Democratic control in many of the states.

Four days later, but on November 8, North African time, came the news that a huge Anglo-American armada had landed troops in French Morocco and Algeria, with the avowed intention of occupying the entire North African seacoast of the French Empire, *Invasion of North Africa* both Mediterranean and Atlantic. This daring operation had been planned during a meeting of Churchill and Roosevelt in Washington the preceding June, but the secret was well kept, and the Axis Powers were seemingly taken completely by surprise. Thanks to the fact that an Allied "fifth column" had carefully prepared the way for the attack, General Dwight D. Eisenhower, in supreme command of operations on land, got his troops ashore with a minimum of opposition. Although Marshal Pétain's Vichy government, to which North Africa professed to be loyal politically, ordered resistance, there was little serious fighting except at Casablanca and Oran.

The Allies had planned to use General Henri Honoré Giraud, who had escaped from German imprisonment, as head of the French government in North Africa, but by chance Admiral Jean François Darlan, Vichyite commander of the French Navy, happened to be in Algeria at the time the invasion occurred. When Darlan's authority was found to be great and his cooperation available, he was assigned the rôle intended for Giraud, only to be removed from the scene by assassination, December 24, 1942. Thereupon Giraud took over, in accordance with the original

Air Line
or
Great Circle Distances
in the Pacific

Japan and dominated areas

Naval bases

Allied plan, but his leadership, as well as Darlan's before him, was strongly contested by General Charles de Gaulle, head of the "Free French" government in London. At a meeting held in January, 1943, at Casablanca, Churchill and Roosevelt brought Giraud and de Gaulle together, and for a time both French leaders had seats on a governing council. Unfortunately this scheme worked badly, and in the end the Allied governments were obliged to permit the elimination of Giraud. As for the Vichy government in France, it became progressively more and more subject to German control. The southeastern half of France, which up to the time of the North-African invasion had not been occupied by German troops, was quickly taken over, and the remnant of the French fleet at Toulon was obliged to scuttle itself to escape capture by German land forces.

Obviously the Allied governments had hoped that their African conquests would extend to Tunisia before that colony could be occupied by the Axis, but in this they were disappointed because of bad weather, long lines of communication, and prompt antici- *Tunisia* pation of their action by the Axis authorities. The final struggle did not come until May, 1943, when the British Eighth Army under General Sir Bernard Law Montgomery closed in from the east, and British, French, and American troops from the west. All of Tunisia, including the cities of Tunis and Bizerte, was quickly occupied by the victorious Allied troops, who, during the final phases of the struggle, took well over two hundred thousand prisoners. Before the collapse, General Erwin Rommel, famed commander of the Africa Corps, had escaped to Europe, but practically all the troops he left behind were either killed or captured.

The next great goal of Allied endeavor was Sicily, which Eisenhower's forces invaded on July 10, 1943, and conquered in less than six weeks. Before this task was completed, King Victor Emmanuel, assisted by elements in the fascist grand council, forced *Italy* Mussolini out of power, and set up a new government under Marshal Pietro Badoglio as premier. Badoglio's aim was peace, but the Italian peninsula was invaded before he accepted Eisenhower's terms of unconditional surrender and turned over the entire Italian navy to the Allies. Stiff German resistance held the Allies back many months in Italy, but at length, on June 4, 1944, Rome was taken. Thereupon the King, although keeping his title, turned over his duties to his son, Humbert, and a new cabinet headed by a non-Fascist, Ivanoe Bonomi, replaced the Badoglio government. The chief strategic purpose of the North African and Italian campaign was to clear the Mediterranean of enemy seapower, and this end was fully accomplished. By the fall of 1944, with

Italy recognized as a "co-belligerent," Allied arms had reached the valley of the Po.

The long-awaited "second front" was launched from England across the channel to the coast of Normandy, June 6, 1944. To conduct this *The second front* campaign Eisenhower and Montgomery were transferred from Italy. Despite great weather difficulties and the lack of a harbor, the invasion was completely successful, and the reconquest of France began. On August 24–25, Paris was occupied by Allied troops amidst riotous demonstrations of joy by its inhabitants. To reinforce the Channel invaders, another expedition landed August 15 on the Mediterranean coast of France, and worked its way northward with extraordinary rapidity. By November, 1944, nearly all of France and Belgium had been freed, part of the Netherlands had been cleared of enemy troops, and Allied armies were fighting on German soil. Somewhat tardily, the British and American governments recognized de Gaulle's "Free French" committee as the provisional government of France. For Belgium and the Netherlands, governments-in-exile, long since functioning in England, had only to be transferred to the Continent.

In the air and on the seas the German situation grew steadily more desperate. The attempt of the *Luftwaffe* to bomb the British into submission had not only failed completely; it had brought *On the sea and in the air* devastating retaliation. While the Germans were able to make only "nuisance" raids over England, British bombers and American flying fortresses attacked German, German-held, and Italian cities by night and day. Harbor installations, airfields, war factories, railway yards, power plants, bridges, and dams — every conceivable type of construction that might aid the Axis war effort was subjected to the most merciless bombing. After the Allied landings on the French coast had been effected, a German secret weapon, the robot bomb, did considerable execution among the civilian population of southern England, but it failed completely to halt the invasion. On the high seas, where German submarines had taken a discouragingly high toll, new devices for detecting and destroying them diminished drastically their sinkings and all but eliminated them as a factor in the war. Lend-lease supplies flowed in a steady stream to Russia, while communications with the British Isles and the Mediterranean approached peace-time conditions.

Meantime on the eastern front the Germans had suffered equally *The eastern front* devastating reverses. Their second great drive into Russia, made in 1942, stalled completely at Stalingrad. Thereafter the Russians took the offensive, and in one overwhelming display of strength after another drove the Germans from their soil. By the fall of 1944 they had freed also three German satellite states, Bulgaria, Rumania, and Finland, each of which, like Italy, joined the Allies in the war against Germany. Much of Poland had also been occupied, and Russian troops had invaded Hungary, Yugoslavia, Czechoslovakia, and East Prussia. By the end of the year, British troops were far along with the re-conquest of Greece, and "Partisan" forces under Marshal Tito in Yugoslavia were giving great aid in the liberation of their country. The utter hopelessness of the German situation seemed plain to all except the Nazi leaders.

Many optimists, including even General Eisenhower, had dreamed of victory in 1944, but as winter set in, the Allied campaigns, both eastern and western, slowed down to a halt. To make matters *The German* worse, the Germans, under General Karl von Rundstedt, *counter-* launched on December 17 a terrific and utterly unantici- *attack* pated counterattack in the Belgium-Luxembourg sector. So spectacular were the initial German gains that for a time it looked as if the important harbor of Antwerp, recently opened to Allied shipping, would be cut off. But as the old year ended and the new year began, the Allied command, mainly through the efforts of General George S. Patton's Third American Army, brought the German drive to a standstill, and regained the initiative. Before January was over, all the ground lost by the Allies had been retaken, and the battle of Germany had begun in earnest.[1]

The time had now come for the careful synchronization of Allied activities on the eastern and the western fronts. In the eastern theater, the Russians delayed their customary winter offensive until *Conquest of* January 12, 1945. Then they struck out so forcefully with *Germany* five huge armies that the German defenses were smashed all the way from the Baltic to the Carpathians. By the end of February, Russian troops, after clearing the Germans from most of Poland, and from much of Hungary and Czechoslovakia as well, stood on German soil only thirty-one miles from Berlin. In the west, Eisenhower had planned the destruction of the German armies facing him before they could retreat across the Rhine, and to a remarkable extent he was able to

[1] The most satisfactory accounts of American participation in the war are still to be found in official publications. George C. Marshall, *Biennial Report of the Chief of Staff of the United States Army* (1941, 1943, 1945), gives the best running account of the war. See also H. A. DeWeerd (ed.), *Selected Speeches and Statements of General of the Army George C. Marshall* (1945). Much helpful information is readily available in the annuals of the various encyclopaedias, *Britannica Book of the Year, The Americana Annual, Collier's Year Book,* and *The New International Year Book.* H. C. Butcher, *My Three Years with Eisenhower* (1946) is the diary of a favored observer. On the pre-war period, *Peace and War, United States Foreign Policy, 1931-1941* (1943), presents the American case in documentary detail. More informal, but semi-official, is Forrest Davis and E. K. Lindley, *How War Came* (1942).

accomplish this feat. His principal attack was somewhat delayed by the von Rundstedt offensive, but the month of February saw him in full action, with his American, British, Canadian, and French troops fighting in admirable co-ordination. Before March was many days old, Allied troops had penetrated into nearly every stronghold of the famed West-wall, doing untold military damage, and taking prisoners by the hundreds of thousands. Many Germans succeeded in withdrawing across the Rhine, but on March 7, owing to the failure of the retreating forces to destroy a bridge at Remagen, they were followed by American soldiers in considerable numbers. The Remagen bridge soon collapsed, but from newly established bridgeheads Allied forces in great strength pushed forward through the very heart of the Reich. The "scorched-earth" policy that the Nazi leaders had ordered, together with the persistent bombing of German cities and the wholesale devastation incidental to military operations, left Germany a scene of incredible ruin.

By the last week of April the eastern and western invaders of Germany had met on the banks of the Elbe, and the end was in sight. Victorious *"V-E Day"* Russian armies occupied Rumania, Bulgaria, Austria, and Hungary. The German armies that had long stalled the Allied advance in northern Italy began to crumble, then surrendered. Italian "partisans" caught and executed the hapless Mussolini, leaving his body and that of his mistress to the studied insults of a Milanese mob. The Russians fought their way street by street through the rubble of Berlin, and took possession of what was left of the stricken city. Hitler himself committed suicide, following a weird marriage ceremony in which he made his mistress his wife. Shortly after, Admiral Karl Doenitz, upon whom Hitler had directed that his mantle should fall, notified the Allies that Germany was ready to surrender, and on May 8, 1945, the Allied victory in Europe, "V–E Day," was officially proclaimed.

By this time Allied might had also made itself dominant in the Pacific. There, in mid-November, 1942, the Japanese tried to oust the Americans from Guadalcanal, but failed, in large part because of naval defeats administered by American squadrons operating under the *The Pacific* command of Admiral William F. Halsey. Japanese efforts to push across New Guinea to Port Moresby in order to strike at Australia were also frustrated. After that, the bitter fighting necessary to clear the way back to the Philippines could begin. By this time the American Navy had recovered from the losses sustained at Pearl Harbor, and with each succeeding month its strength increased enormously. Up in the cold and fog of the Aleutians, where since June, 1942, the

Japanese had held two American islands, Kiska and Attu, the Americans struck at Attu, May 11, 1943, and before the end of the month had conquered the island. When Americans and Canadians landed on Kiska in August, they found that the Japanese had already departed. The next great effort of the American Navy was to drive the Japanese from the islands of the mid-Pacific. In November, 1943, marine and army forces successfully invaded several atolls in the Gilberts, among them Tarawa, where the fighting was particularly bloody. Kwajalein in the Marshalls was taken early in 1944.

It was now plain that the strategy of Admiral Chester W. Nimitz, commander-in-chief of the Pacific fleet, called for a direct advance across the Pacific to Asiatic waters. No effort was made to clear every island occupied by the Japanese, but important bases, together with air fields that could dominate wide stretches of ocean, were taken and strongly held. By June, 1944, the advance had reached Saipan in the Marianas, fifteen hundred miles from Tokyo and sixteen hundred miles from Manila. Frightened by the approaching danger, the Japanese sent carrier-based planes to attack the American ships off Saipan, but the attackers suffered heavily, while American planes in turn sought out the fleet from which the enemy planes had come and inflicted heavy damage upon it. The bloody but successful conquest of Saipan was followed in the next month by the occupation of Guam and Tinian, the former an American island held by the Japanese since the beginning of the war. Bomber attacks could now be made from these bases, as well as from China, upon Formosa and the Japanese homeland, and the exploit of the *Hornet*, which had sent its planes in April, 1942, to attack Tokyo, was repeated by land-based planes from Saipan, November 23, 1944. From this time on, the destruction of Japanese cities and industrial targets proceeded mercilessly.

In order to shorten the bombing range to Japan, two more islands were assaulted and taken by American land and naval forces early in 1945. The first, Iwo Jima, a tiny islet in the volcano group midway between Guam and Tokyo, was only five miles long by three wide, but it provided the Japanese with three air fields and a radar station. Enemy intelligence was thus able to detect flights of Tokyo-bound American planes and to flash the news to the homeland of *Iwo Jima* their approach. So great was the nuisance value of this island that on February 19, after weeks of preparatory bombing, two divisions of marines, supported by a prodigious show of naval force, undertook its conquest. The fighting was terrific, for the Japanese had expected the attack, and had crowded the island with a maximum of men and armor.

[727]

For a full month the battle lasted, and American casualties mounted to twenty thousand, but the coveted terrain was won.

The last major amphibious operation in the advance on Japan began on Easter Sunday, April 1, when Okinawa, largest island in the Ryukyus, *Okinawa* situated only three hundred and seventy miles from Japan proper, was invaded. Fourteen hundred ships and upwards of one hundred thousand American soldiers and marines participated in the action. At first, resistance was light, and the Americans got ashore easily, but in southern Okinawa, toward which the Japanese retreated, the enemy staged a desperate and unexpectedly prolonged resistance. While the land engagement was in progress, a Japanese naval squadron sent perhaps five hundred planes to attack the American ships standing offshore, but most of the attackers were intercepted and shot down, while the Japanese naval units from which they operated were soon discovered and put out of action. During this engagement Japanese *Kamikaze*, specially trained pilots who deliberately sought to smash their bomb-laden planes into the American ships, first made their appearance in large numbers. Enough of them succeeded in their suicidal missions to inflict serious losses, both in ships and in personnel, upon the American fleet; but, despite this setback and persistent *Kamikaze* harassment thereafter, the battle of Okinawa went on to its inexorable end. By the middle of June, the Americans were in complete control of the island, and the doom of Japan was sealed. American bombers, operating, not only from convenient air fields, but also from the decks of a host of task-force carriers, now burned and blasted the Japanese islands at will.

Meantime, the campaign of MacArthur, who had promised to return from Australia to the Philippines, had made similarly notable strides. *MacArthur's* MacArthur's strategy, depending always on the careful co-*return to the* ordination of land, sea, and air forces, was to bomb furiously *Philippines* and by-pass the principal Japanese bases, and by "leap-frog" tactics to land at unexpected, and sometimes undefended, points along the route he must clear. By January, 1944, he had begun to advance in this fashion along the northern shores of New Guinea, and well before the end of the year he was ready to make the last long jump to the Philippines. On October 20, he landed in person with a large army of invasion on the island of Leyte, and began the reconquest he had promised. To defend MacArthur's movements, a heavy naval concentration under Admiral Halsey was obliged to fight one of the greatest sea-actions of history, for the Japanese at last decided that they must risk a major portion of their fleet. In the waters adjacent to Leyte, beginning on October 25, the Americans fought off the Japanese in a series of complicated and extensive actions so costly to the enemy as to reduce the Japanese Navy, the Americans claimed, to "fifth-rate" status.

After the battle of Leyte Gulf, organized resistance on Leyte and on the neighboring island of Samar disintegrated slowly but surely. By the end of the year, MacArthur had also landed troops on Mindoro Island, preparatory to his main attack, which he had reserved for Luzon. In January, 1945, with the aid of planes operating from Mindoro air-fields, he put ashore a formidable force at Lingayen Gulf, and began the fateful march to Manila. Japanese resistance was light at first, but the approaches to the capital were stubbornly defended, and not until February 3 were American troops able to enter it. After that, the Japanese staged within the city a gruesomely effective last-ditch fight that lasted for weeks. Bitter fighting also continued elsewhere on Luzon, and the American reconquest of the island was hardly complete at the end of June, when it was officially announced by General MacArthur. Meantime Mindanao, the next largest of the Philippine Archipelago, as well as certain lesser islands, had been successfully invaded, and Japanese hopes were waning fast. Stiff fighting continued, however, in many of the islands until the end of the war.

While the war in the Pacific was thus being planned and fought, Allied forces were doing what little they could to hold the Japanese from further conquests on the mainland of Asia. The task *The Asiatic* could hardly have been more difficult. With India as a *mainland* base, some Allied aid to the Chinese was soon being flown in over the Himalayas, but it was never enough. Bad relations between the government of Chiang Kai-shek and the armed communist bands that con-trolled much of North China added to the turmoil from which that unhappy nation suffered. Meager American air forces, operating under General Joseph W. Stilwell, gave great aid to Chiang's armies, but in spite of their best efforts Japanese troops were able to penetrate into Chinese territory about as far as they cared to go.

Perhaps Stilwell scored his principal triumph in clearing the Japanese from northern Burma so that a new route from India to China, the Ledo Road, could be opened. Using American-trained Chinese troops, he was nearing the completion of this task when, in the fall of 1944, he was relieved of his command and recalled to the United States. Personal differences with Chiang Kai-shek over the training and disposition of Chinese troops were said to account for this strange action. Under Stilwell's successor, General David I. Sultan, American engineers went on with the construction of the road, and in January, 1945, the first motor caravan crossed it all the way from India to China. Allied successes farther to the south in Burma, under the leadership of Lord Louis Mountbatten, were also heartening, but in spite of the achievements in Burma the war ended with the Japanese still in control of their principal gains on the mainland of Asia.

Nevertheless, the Japanese will to continue the war had not much longer to go. Far-cruising American submarines, joining their successes *The atomic* to those of American surface forces, helped to drive the *bomb* Japanese Navy and merchant marine almost completely from the seas. In consequence, connections between the home islands and the overexpanded "Co-Prosperity Sphere" broke down. On occasion American task forces maneuvered close to the Japanese shore, and lobbed their shells into coastal installations. *Kamikaze* attacks became more numerous and daring, and they took a heavy toll of American lives and shipping, but the "softening-up process" preliminary to invasion went on. Early in August, the climax was reached with the dropping of an atomic bomb on Hiroshima, a military point of some importance that until then had escaped the activities of American airmen. Shortly thereafter, a similar bomb was dropped on Nagasaki. The results obtained were cataclysmic — a single bomb was as devastating to an enemy city as the concentrated action of a thousand ordinary bombers equipped with full loads of ordinary explosives. The development of the atomic bomb was the result of co-operative efforts by numerous American, British, and Canadian scientists, who, with the full backing of their governments, had pooled their talents in a successful effort to split the atom. The cost of their experiments to the American people alone probably reached two billion dollars, but the bomb that the scientists produced undoubtedly served to shorten the war materially. It served also to make the peoples of the world realize, fully perhaps for the first time, how totally catastrophic another World War would be.

For some months it had been known to the British and American chiefs of state that Russia intended eventually to enter the war against Japan. With the end so nearly in sight, the Russian government found it inexpedient to delay longer, and on August 9, following a formal declara-*Japanese* tion of war, issued the day before, Russian troops began to *surrender* advance against light opposition into Manchuria. Faced by this new threat, and assured by the President of the United States that only surrender could save Japanese civilization from total annihilation by the further use of atomic bombs, the Japanese gave up. As early as August 10, the Japanese news agency, Domei, broadcast that

Japan was willing to accept the terms of unconditional surrender, as defined by the Allies at Potsdam, Germany, the preceding month, provided only that Emperor Hirohito's sovereignty would not be questioned. The President of the United States, replying for the Allies, stated the willingness of the nations at war with Japan to retain the Emperor for the time being, on condition that he take orders from an Allied Supreme Commander, to be resident in Japan. This offer the Japanese government accepted, and by August 14 the world knew for sure that the war was over. Not for several days, however, did a Japanese delegation appear, as required, in Manila to arrange for the formal surrender, and not until September 1, when delegates from the principal Allies, with General MacArthur representing the United Nations, received a delegation of Japanese officials aboard the battleship *Missouri* in Tokyo Bay, were the documents of surrender actually signed. Thereafter the occupation of Japan by American forces proceeded rapidly, and the American commander, General MacArthur, began to give orders to the Emperor of Japan. September 2, 1945, was officially designated VJ Day by the President, but by this time the chief celebrations were over.[1]

The solidarity of the "home front" during the years of American participation in the Second World War was virtually unbroken. The Japanese attack on Pearl Harbor, followed as it was by declarations of war against the United States by both *The "Home Front"* Germany and Italy, left little room for opposition to the war, and even the isolationists accepted hostilities as a necessary evil. There was some smoldering gossip to the effect that Roosevelt had deliberately connived at the Pearl Harbor attack, but only the most bitter of the "Roosevelt-haters" gave credence to such talk.[2] Few Americans of German descent had ever had much to say in favor of Hitler, and those few took the stand they did mainly because of pathological quirks of character rather than

---

[1] An immense literature on the history of the Second World War is beginning to unfold. Kent R. Greenfield (ed.), *United States Army in World War II* (4 vols., 1947–49), begins an official War Department series for the Ground Forces that may run to a hundred volumes. W. F. Craven and J. L. Cate (eds.), *The Army Air Forces in World War II* (1948), begins a similar series for the Air Forces. S. E. Morison, *History of United States Naval Operations in World War II* (3 vols., 1947–48), unlike the preceding volumes, begins a one-man synthesis. D. S. Ballantine, *U. S. Naval Logistics in the Second World War* (1947), is concise and critical. John R. Deane, *The Strange Alliance: The Story of our Efforts at Wartime Cooperation with Russia* (1947), is semi-official. Walter Karig and Welbourn Kelley, *Battle Report* (1944), is a detailed story of the Pacific war to the end of 1943. E. M. Zacharias, *Secret Missions: The Story of an Intelligence Officer* (1947), sheds light on the disintegration of the Japanese will to fight. James A. Field, Jr., *The Japanese at Leyte Gulf* (1947), attempts to show what the Japanese were trying to do in this greatest sea-battle of all time.

[2] George Morgenstern, *Pearl Harbor, The Story of the Secret War* (1947), places all the blame for the Japanese attack on the Roosevelt administration. More credible is the painstaking account by Walter Millis, *This Is Pearl!* (1947).

because they were German. A small but sometimes noisy collection of these "Bundists" existed in nearly every large population center before American involvement in the war, but after hostilities started they were rarely heard from. Many Americans of Italian descent had been proud of Mussolini in his earlier days, but they had viewed with misgivings his Ethiopian adventure, and had regarded his subservience to Hitler with deep chagrin. They believed, probably quite correctly, that the great majority of Italians in Italy had no stomach for the war, and wished themselves out of it. The Japanese of the Pacific Coast and in Hawaii, as an identifiable racial group, were regarded with much suspicion, although throughout the war not one of them was ever found guilty of an act of sabotage or espionage.

Dissident political groups also caused little trouble. Anti-war sentiment among Communists during the period of neutrality was violent and outspoken until after the German declaration of war on Russia. Thereupon the Communists became ardent supporters of the Allied cause, although they had once branded it as wholly imperialistic and unworthy. When the United States entered the war, American Communists gave their government consistent support. This was especially important on the labor front, for during the three-and-one-half years of American participation in the war strikes in unions where Communists or "fellow-travelers" were in control all but disappeared. Socialists quite generally followed the lead of Norman Thomas in denouncing the war, but they were few in number, and what they said made little difference. There was the usual sprinkling of conscientious objectors, particularly among the minor evangelical sects, but their influence, likewise, was slight, and was for the most part ignored.

Undoubtedly the worst outbreak of intolerance during the war had as its victims the members of the Japanese race in Hawaii and on the Pacific *The Japanese* Coast. "Americans of Japanese Ancestry" (AJA's) were *in Hawaii* divided into two main groups, the first generation, or *Issei*, who were born in Japan and were therefore ineligible to citizenship, and the second generation, or *Nisei*, who were American born, and by virtue of the Fourteenth Amendment, American citizens. In addition there were a few of the third generation, or *Sansei*. In the Hawaiian Islands the number of AJA's amounted to approximately one third of the total population, and grave fear was expressed as to what they would do in case of a Japanese invasion. There was talk that they should all be interned, and perhaps even be sent to the mainland, but since any such action would have totally disrupted the sugar-pineapple plantation economy upon which the economic life of the Islands depended, the

Hawaiian Japanese were allowed to remain in their homes. But the political rights of Hawaiian citizens, regardless of race or color, were almost totally obliterated. After Pearl Harbor martial law was declared in the Islands, and for the duration of the war the normal procedures of democratic civilian government were suspended. Army officers assumed the duties of civilian officials, including judges and police magistrates, and enforced the most stringent military regulations upon the entire population. The complete docility of the Hawaiian Japanese became apparent at once; they stayed loyally at their work, and in every type of defense activity they outdid themselves to prove their patriotism. After the Battle of Midway, with the war moving ever farther and farther away, civilian government might have been restored with safety, but military rule continued until the very end. Regulations that might have been necessary with the war near at hand were enforced with ruthless military efficiency long after the reasons for their adoption had disappeared. Only with the greatest of difficulty did the Hawaiians obtain the restoration of their normal rights of self-government at the end of the war. This unhappy experience with military rule led the residents of the Islands to voice an insistent demand for statehood when the war was over. With statehood, they reasoned, the extinction of civilian rights and civilian government would be more difficult, should there be another war. But they were destined to disappointment. While the House of Representatives passed the bill which would have made Hawaii the forty-ninth state, the measure died when the Senate failed to act on it.[1]

In California the situation was different due to the fact that the Japanese constituted only a small fraction of the population, by all estimates well under two per cent. But a great outcry was raised *The Japanese in California* that acts of espionage and sabotage could be prevented only by removing all the Japanese, aliens and citizens alike, from the immediate vicinity of the Pacific Coast. Finally, under military orders, the Japanese were herded together in "relocation camps," located at a considerable distance into the interior. The camps themselves were hastily thrown together, and conditions in them were far from satisfactory. Nevertheless, only a few minor outbreaks occurred, and on the whole the Japanese "evacuees" conducted themselves well. As early as December, 1944, it became evident that the Courts would soon free the Japanese if the Army did not, so as soon as the

---

[1] Three interesting books deal effectively with the Hawaiian situation: S. D. Porteus, *And Blow Not the Trumpet, A Prelude to Peril* (1947); T. B. Clark, *Hawaii, the 49th State* (1947); A. W. Lind, *Hawaii's Japanese* (1946)..

fighting was over they were allowed to return to their homes. Unfortunately, in many instances they had no homes to go to, and had lost their businesses and property. Some of them scattered throughout the country rather than to try to resume life along the Pacific Coast, but the majority preferred their pre-war environment, and in spite of sporadic cases of violence against them, were soon absorbed into the post-war economic boom that overtook the Pacific states. The superb record of the AJA's who fought in the American army during the war left most of those who had had any part in the persecution of the Japanese considerably shame-faced.[1]

Except for the mistreatment of the Japanese, there were fewer evidences of intolerance during the Second than during the First World War. Occasional arrests and imprisonments were made, usually as a result of the activities of J. Edgar Hoover's Federal Bureau of Investigation (FBI); a few inconsequential newspapers were barred from the mails; some would-be saboteurs were brought to book; between three and four thousand enemy aliens were interned. But an attempted mass-trial of twenty-eight individuals accused of sympathy with the Nazis became somewhat farcical, and ended in a mistrial, with most of the accused escaping further difficulty. The so-called Dies Committee, created by the House of Representatives to investigate un-American activities, was less important than its name would seem to indicate. Actually, it took little interest in either pro-Nazis or pro-fascists, but concentrated primarily upon the exposure of "subversive" left-wing activities. The ardor with which Communists and fellow-travelers supported the war, however, left the Committee with little of importance to do. Its principal efforts were seemingly directed toward trying to confuse political liberals and labor leaders with Communists.

Perhaps the American people inherited a somewhat lighter burden of intolerance from the Second than from the First World War but the cost in dollars, lives, and social dislocations was very much heavier. Expenditures by the United States on the Second World War reached about three hundred billion dollars, more than eight times the amount spent on the First World War. The cost in lives was about 375,000, three times as many as in the First World War, although fewer in proportion to the amount of fighting done. Better training before battle action helped keep down the casualty lists, and greater medical efficiency not only prevented any such calamity as came from the "flu" in the First World

---

[1] W. S. Tsuchida, *Wear It Proudly* (1947), recounts the war-time experiences of an American Japanese. Dorothy Thomas, *The Spoilage* (1946), tells the drab story of Japanese internment.

War, but also returned to service a surprisingly large proportion of the nearly 700,000 wounded. The demand for war-workers drew great numbers of civilians from the small towns and country to factory cities, and especially to the seaboard, where ship-building on the assembly-line principle reached an amazingly high level of productivity. Many of the labor migrants, as in the First World War, were Negroes who left the South with little expectation of returning. The Pacific Coast, especially the state of California, gained rapidly in population from all sources; at the end of the war California, with nearly ten million people instead of its pre-war seven, had replaced Illinois as third most populous state in the Union, and was threatening the position of Pennsylvania as second. Cities everywhere, but particularly on the Pacific Coast, suffered from acute shortages in housing, water-supply, electric power, telephone service, and other similar necessities.

The cost of the war, as was more or less inevitable, had to be met in large part by borrowing. As a result the national debt mounted during the war to about two hundred and sixty billion dollars, *Cost of* more than five times as much as it had been at the time *the war* of Pearl Harbor. Experience with war loans during the First World War and with deficit financing during the New Deal had built up a body of practice that made the flotation of loans a relatively easy matter. Bonds of every size and nature were devised to appeal to every variety of purchaser. The public was urged to invest in them at all times, and not merely during "drives," as in the First World War. Pay-roll deductions to aid in the acquisition of bonds were given every encouragement, and found many takers. Nevertheless, to speed up sales, there were no less than eight special "drives," each with a tremendous fanfare of advertising appeal. An earnest effort was made to tap the savings of the small investor, and the total sale of "E" bonds, a large proportion of which were in denominations as low as $25, reached about forty billion dollars. Unlike the bonds of the First World War, which were transferable and were frequently sold at a discount by hard-pressed investors, the new series were non-transferable, and were redeemable by the government on demand; thus purchasers who had over-bought, or who found that for any reason they could not hold their bonds, were guaranteed against the heavy losses that in the previous war had overtaken buyers of "Liberty Bonds."

Congress wisely did what it could to insure that a maximum amount of the war expenditures should come from taxation rather than from borrowing. As a result, approximately forty per cent of the cost of the war was paid for out of tax collections, a substantially larger proportion than came from tax sources during the First World War. The income tax, which was so designed as to take something from nearly everyone, and nearly everything from some who were in the higher brackets, was the principal source of revenue. Single persons with incomes above $500, and married persons with incomes of above $1200, paid a basic six per cent, with an additional thirteen per cent on the first two thousand dollars of taxable income, and steeply rising rates on each additional two thousand dollars. The rate on income in excess of $200,000 reached eighty-two per cent. To make sure that small incomes did not escape, the taxes were collected after July 1, 1943, as income was earned, instead of at the end of each year, while employers were required to withhold and pay the government at regular intervals the assessments against their employees. Corporation taxes, excess profits taxes, and all sorts of excise, or "nuisance," taxes on luxury and near-luxury items added greatly to the revenue. A Tax Simplification Act, passed in May, 1944, made the calculation of income taxes somewhat less difficult for many in the lower brackets, but it was not intended to reduce the rates. Furthermore, every citizen knew full well that the war would leave an enduring legacy of high taxation, one that might well plague many generations to come.[1]

[1] On the 1940 elections, C. A. M. Ewing, *Presidential Elections from Abraham Lincoln to Franklin D. Roosevelt* (1940), is a useful statistical story. C. W. Stein, *The Third Term Tradition* (1943) ends with the election of 1940. J. A. Farley, *Jim Farley's Story: The Roosevelt Years* (1948), gives much attention to Roosevelt's third nomination. On the movement for aid to the Allies, see Walter Johnson, *William Allen White's America* (1947).

On the home front, John Dos Passos, *State of the Nation* (1944), is thoughtful. Ralph Barton Perry, *Puritanism and Democracy* (1944), seeks to identify the American cause in World War II with the American tradition. Donald M. Nelson, *Arsenal of Democracy: The Story of American War Production* (1946), explains in considerable part why the United States won. E. R. Stettinius, Jr., *Lend-Lease, Weapon for Victory* (1944), is commendably straightforward. Elliott Roosevelt, *As He Saw It* (1946), is strongly anti-Churchill and pro-Stalin.

On the diplomatic front, Allan Nevins and L. M. Hacker, *The United States and Its Place in World Affairs, 1918–43* (1943), is excellent on all aspects of the subject. Wendell Willkie, *One World* (1943), shows the high hopes of the war period, largely unrealized. Walter Johnson, *The Battle against Isolation* (1944), is an excellent summary. Dexter Perkins, *America and Two Wars* (1944), treats of the diplomacy of involvement. Herbert Hoover and Hugh Gibson, *The Problems of Lasting Peace* (1942), is suggestive.

CHAPTER XXXII

POST-WAR PROBLEMS

NEARLY a year before the end of the war, the people of the United States had been obliged to hold a presidential election. To many Americans the necessity of observing this constitutional requirement seemed even more unfortunate in 1944 than in *Election of 1944* 1940. The war was going well, and its successful prosecution had in most minds a long priority over domestic politics. But the Constitution still being what it was, the election had to be held, the first war-time election in the United States since 1864. Except for the existence of war, there is little reason to suppose that Roosevelt would, or could, have run for a fourth term, but the need of his continued leadership during the crisis was, for those who trusted him, a sufficient reason for retaining him as the Democratic candidate. He was nominated with little opposition by the Democratic convention, but the Democratic city bosses joined forces with the Southern conservatives to oust Henry A. Wallace, the idealistic New-Dealer, as Vice-Presidential candidate in favor of Senator Harry S. Truman, of Missouri, an inconspicuous regular whose chief service to his country had been made as head of a Senate Committee on the investigation of the national defense program. The Republicans had expected a hard-fought campaign for the nomination between Governor Dewey, of New York, and Wendell Willkie, with some third candidate, possibly Governor John W. Bricker, of Ohio, the probable nominee. But when, early in the campaign, Willkie was decisively defeated in the Wisconsin primary, he withdrew, and the nomination went to Dewey on the first ballot, with only one opposing vote. Before election time, Willkie died of a heart attack. For Vice-President the Convention turned enthusiastically to Bricker.

The campaign which followed, like the campaign which preceded it, was notable for the wide range of agreement between the two candidates. Both of them endorsed, in the main, the social legislation of the New Deal. Both urged some kind of international organization after the war for the maintenance of peace. Dewey even went so far as to approve the findings of the Dumbarton Oaks Conference at Washington, in which just before the campaign the leading Allies had drawn tentative plans for an organization to preserve peace — plans strongly reminiscent of Wilson's League of Nations. What the campaign lacked in issues, it made up in personalities. In a series of well-delivered speeches Dewey charged the President with failing to prepare the country for war, claimed that the administration was composed of tired, corrupt, and quarrelsome old men, pointed with concern at the support the Communists were giving Roosevelt, and urged insistently that it was time for a change. Roosevelt, in turn, capitalized on the willingness of the Republicans to accept so much of the New Deal program, noted the successes in the war that had been won under his leadership, questioned the devotion to international co-operation of the many pre-Pearl Harbor isolationists who supported Dewey, and implied that it was no time for a change.

For the fourth time Roosevelt won a decisive victory. The President led in thirty-six states with 432 electoral votes, while Dewey led in twelve states with only 99 electoral votes. The Democrats also retained their majority in the Senate, greatly improved it in the House, and won a majority of the governorships. The voting was closer, however, than these figures indicate. Roosevelt's popular majority, a little more than three million votes, was the slenderest given any successful candidate for the Presidency since Wilson's second election in 1916. Aside from registering the confidence of the majority in Roosevelt's military leadership, the election demonstrated clearly that the American people were far more ready than they had been twenty-five years earlier to accept for the United States an important rôle in international affairs. Isolationism might rise again, but for the moment that historic American policy seemed dead indeed. The discriminating defeat of numerous outstanding isolationists and ex-isolationists, such, for example, as Representative Fish, of New York, and Senator Nye, of North Dakota, made certain that the new Congress would be receptive to any plan of post-war co-operation that seemed to offer a reasonable hope of world peace.[1]

During the campaign of 1944, the health of President Roosevelt had *Death of Roosevelt* become a matter of considerable concern to the American public. From photographs and moving pictures it was apparent that the cares of office had greatly aged the President. The lines on

[1] E. E. Robinson, *They Voted for Roosevelt, The Presidential Vote, 1932–1944* (1947), shows the results of the election of 1944. Richard Hofstadter, *The American Political Tradition and the Men Who Made It* (1948), has an interesting chapter on Roosevelt.

his face had deepened, he had lost weight, and he was noticeably less willing to exert himself to stand or walk. He suffered much from colds and bronchial infections, and was frequently obliged to take extended rests. So much was said on the subject that his personal physician publicly denied, almost too insistently, that the President was ill, while Roosevelt himself, in spite of an earlier promise not to "campaign in the usual partisan sense," took to the stump during the month of October, and gave a half-dozen full-length political speeches. He even braved a heavy downpour of rain to ride in an open car throughout a long campaign parade in New York City, and emerged seemingly none the worse for his experience. Apparently the country was convinced that he was capable of carrying on, or so the election returns seemed to show, but on April 12, 1945, he died suddenly at his winter home in Warm Springs, Georgia, of what his physicians called a massive cerebral hemorrhage.

Roosevelt was succeeded, of course, by Vice-President Harry S. Truman (1884–   ), whom the Democratic convention of 1944 had preferred to the far more prominent Wallace. As Roosevelt was the perfect embodiment of the extraordinary American, so *Truman* Truman, to an almost uncanny degree, was the typical ordinary American. He was a small-town product from Missouri, utterly undistinguished in appearance. He spoke with a flat Middle-Western accent, played the piano a little, belonged to the Lions' Club and the Baptist Church. He had never attended college, but had served acceptably as a National Guard officer in the First World War. He had worked on a farm in his youth, lost money keeping store, gone into politics because he needed a job. As a regular organization Democrat, he was not above accepting a county judgeship at the hands of "Boss" Pendergast, an unblushing corruptionist who controlled the destinies of the Democratic Party in Kansas City, and aspired to control the State. In Missouri a county judge is an administrative officer, comparable to a county commissioner in many other states; Truman was neither a lawyer nor a "judge" in the usual sense. But he had under his control the expenditure of huge sums of money, particularly in the construction of highways and public buildings, and no faintest suspicion of dishonesty ever attached to any of his acts. At Pendergast's suggestion, he was nominated for the Senate in 1934, won as any other Democrat might have won that year, and in 1940 was renominated and re-elected. His emergence as a fearless and non-partisan senatorial investigator, one who was willing on occasion even to point out the shortcomings of the President, gave him much favorable publicity, but it was generally assumed that he had reached the zenith of his career. But when Wallace was passed by, Truman, partly because he was almost the only Middle-Westerner available, won the unexpected and unsolicited nomination that a few months later was to make him President.

The first great concern of the new President was to carry through to a successful conclusion the United Nations Conference on International Organization, already called by the United States, Great Britain, Russia, and China to meet in San Francisco, April 25, 1945. Roosevelt had earnestly promoted the holding of this conference before the war came to an end, and had promised to open it in person. Obviously, his hope was to utilize the habit of co-operation that had developed among the Allies in time of war as a foundation upon which to build a permanent world organization, designed to keep the peace in the future. He was eager, also, to avoid the complications that had embarrassed the similar efforts of Woodrow Wilson, when that President had sought in his day to create a League of Nations and to write a treaty of peace at the same time.

The unity of effort that the Allies, now commonly called the United Nations, had achieved in the war was truly remarkable. No longer *Allied unity* could it be said, as during the First World War, that when one Ally advanced, the others were sure to be standing still. Close co-ordination of policy, both in military and in diplomatic activities, was apparent on every hand. This fortunate development was due in considerable part to the frequent conferences held by heads of states, their foreign ministers, and their military advisers. As early as August, 1942, Prime Minister Churchill visited Stalin in Moscow, with the American Ambassador to Russia representing the United States. Stalin was then pressing hard for a second front in France, something he long failed to obtain, but this conference was only the beginning of a series. After the invasion of North Africa, Churchill and Roosevelt, as already noted, met at Casablanca, North Africa, in January, 1943, to lay further plans. They conferred with de Gaulle and Giraud, and they had hoped that Stalin and Chiang Kai-shek would join them, but each of the latter two claimed that it was impossible for him to leave his own country at that time. Out of this conference came much undisclosed planning, and the announcement that only by "unconditional surrender" could the Axis nations obtain peace. At a conference of foreign ministers, held in Moscow during October, 1943, definite plans were laid for the second front in France, and for some kind of world organization to follow the war. Next came a conference of Churchill, Roosevelt, and Chiang Kai-shek in Cairo during mid-November, 1943, and immediately thereafter the first meeting of both Churchill and Roosevelt with Stalin, at Teheran.

So complete were the plans worked out at the Cairo and Teheran meetings that more than a year elapsed before the conferees got together again. Then, early in January, 1945, the "Big Three," Churchill, Roosevelt, and Stalin, accompanied by large retinues of "top-drawer" military and governmental advisers, met at Yalta in the Crimea. The Yalta Conference not only reached agreements on the "timing, scope, and co-ordination of new and even more powerful blows" against Germany, but authorized also the call that brought the Conference of the United Nations to San Francisco the following April.

Undoubtedly the decisions of the Yalta Conference must go down in history as among the most significant ever to have been made by heads of state in modern times. The key to the future, as all the *The Yalta* world knew, lay mainly in the hands of the Russian leaders. *decisions* Would they in time of peace continue the co-operative attitude they had shown in time of war, or would they return to the original Bolshevik program, and make their goal the ultimate destruction, by whatever means they could employ, of every government that refused to follow the Communist party line? President Roosevelt, like Wilson before him, believed that the only pathway to world peace was through the establishment of a world organization of friendly states, and, again like Wilson, he was willing to concede a great deal to achieve what appeared to be an absolutely essential objective.[1] He was deeply concerned by the fact that the Soviet leaders were obviously intent on welding all eastern Europe into a Russian sphere of influence, but he could think of no better way to deal with the problems this would present than through an effective world organization, of which Russia must be a member.

It was in this mood that Roosevelt gave in during the Yalta Conference to Stalin's demand for what amounted to three Russian votes in the proposed United Nations organization. On the pretext *Concessions* that Russia had given to the various Soviet republics con- *by Roosevelt* trol over their military establishments and foreign relations, Stalin insisted that Byelorussia (White Russia) and the Ukraine, as well as the Soviet Union itself, should be regarded as separate members of the United Nations. Probably at the time the President made this concession he had in mind asking for a similar voting advantage for the United States, but he found no support for the idea at home, and he soon abandoned it. As a further gesture of conciliation to Russia, Roosevelt agreed to the principle of a great-power veto on all important

---

[1] The pro-Russian attitude of the Administration during the war is shown in Joseph E. Davies, *Mission to Moscow* (1941). The ideas of this book were also presented to the public in film version.

acts of the Security Council, a provision which he believed would also promote ratification of the United Nations charter by the United States Senate. But the concessions to Russia went much further than this. Stalin was determined to extend the Russian frontiers, both in Europe and in Asia, and on these points also the President gave in. As to the European boundary settlements, Roosevelt conceded to Russia the right to annex all of eastern Poland, and to Poland the right to make compensatory annexations at the expense of Germany. With reference to the Far East, in direct contradiction of pledges he had once made Chiang Kai-shek, he agreed to provisions that would make Russia dominant in Manchuria at the close of the war, and, in addition, he promised the Soviets the right to annex the southern half of Sakalin and the Kuril Islands.

In return for all this Roosevelt believed that he had obtained important pledges from Stalin. As to Poland, Russia agreed that the "provis-
Concessions by Stalin ional government which is now functioning in Poland should be reorganized on a broader democratic basis with the inclusion of democratic leaders from Poland itself and from Poles abroad." A similar agreement was reached, and for similar reasons, with regard to Yugoslavia. Undoubtedly both the British and the American negotiators hoped that these agreements would result in Polish and Yugoslavian governments entirely free from Russian domination; they could hardly have foreseen the complete lack of good faith with which the Russians would treat their promises. Furthermore, they thought they had won full assurance of Russian co-operation in the creation and maintenance of a peace-time United Nations. As for the Far East, Stalin promised again — he had said the same thing to Cordell Hull in 1943 — that "in two or three months after Germany has surrendered and the war in Europe has terminated the Soviet Union shall enter the war against Japan."[1]

In the light of subsequent events, much criticism has been leveled at Roosevelt for his part in the Yalta decisions. It is well to remember,

---

[1] The text of the Yalta Agreement and many other pertinent documents appear in Louise W. Holborn, editor, *War and Peace Aims of the United Nations*, 1939–1945 (2 vols., 1943–48). What happened behind the scenes at Yalta is still a matter of heated dispute. An anti-Roosevelt version by William O. Bullitt, "How We Won the War and Lost the Peace," in *Life*, XXV, 83–97 (August 30, 1948), 88–103 (September 6, 1948), received wide attention, but is less convincing than the account by Rear Admiral Ellis M. Zacharias, "The Inside Story of Yalta," *United Nations World*, III, 12–18 (January, 1949). See also Philip E. Mosely, "The Berlin Deadlock," *American Perspective*, II, 331–339 (December 1948); and Rudolph A. Winnacker, "Yalta — Another Munich?" *Virginia Quarterly Review*, XXIV, 521–537 (Autumn, 1948.) There is also a chapter on the subject in Robert E. Sherwood, *Roosevelt and Hopkins* (1948).

however, that these criticisms developed long after the event, in an atmosphere of victory achieved; whereas the actual *Military considera-tions* agreements were made several months before the war was fully won, and at a time when the Russians were seemingly in a far stronger military position than were their western allies. When the Yalta Conference convened, Russian troops were already far into Germany, with their advance units on the Oder River, fifty miles from Berlin, whereas on the western front, the ground lost by the disastrous and frightening "Battle of the Bulge" had just been recovered, and Allied troops were only beginning to enter Germany. At this same time Russian occupation forces held eastern Czechoslovakia and most of Hungary in their grasp, and Tito's Russophile Partisans were driving the Germans out of Yugoslavia, whereas the Anglo-American invasion of Italy seemed hopelessly stalled in the Apennines. In the Far East, the war against Japan was by no means won, and Roosevelt's military advisers were deeply pessimistic. The atomic bomb had not yet been tested, and its possible usefulness as a military weapon had to be discounted completely. According to the American Secretary of War, Henry L. Stimson, the Joint Chiefs of Staff estimated that to defeat Japan they "would be faced with the enormous task of destroying five million men and five thousand suicide air craft." They still believed that the Japanese homeland would have to be invaded directly, and judging from such operations as Okinawa and Saipan, they figured that the cost of victory would be not less than "a million casualties to American forces alone," while "the major fighting would not end until the latter part of 1946 at the earliest." Furthermore, many of the troops that would be needed for this campaign were still fighting in Europe, and would not be released until the final defeat of Germany.

Roosevelt's concessions to Russia at Yalta should be measured against this background. His military advisers wanted the fullest Russian co-operation, both in the East and in the West, and they had little concern for the political results of such concessions as might be necessary to obtain their objectives. It seemed merely realistic to give the Russians what they would be able to take in Europe anyway, whether the concessions were made or not. As for what was promised the Russians in Asia, the Joint Chiefs of Staff were not thinking in terms of the post-war world, but in terms of how to achieve victory. In conceding what he did Roosevelt was merely yielding, as a civilian commander, to the insistent demands of his military experts.[1]

The Yalta Conference also ratified a plan which had been in process

[1] See note on page 742.

of development ever since Teheran for the eventual dismemberment of
Dismember- Germany into four zones of military occupation, one each
ment of for the British, American, Russian, and French forces.
Germany Berlin, the capital, although located deep in the Russian
zone, was to be an international area under joint four-power control.
There is no reliable evidence to support the frequently-made assertion
that Roosevelt, either at the time of Yalta, or at any other time, conceded to Russian troops the honor of occupying Berlin in advance of the
troops of other nations. The American advance was indeed halted when
it might easily have reached Berlin far ahead of the Russians, but General
Eisenhower took full responsibility for this decision, and justified it on
military grounds. Military rather than political considerations seem
also to account for the fact that American armies, which might have captured Prague, the Czechoslovakian capital, were stopped in their tracks,
thus giving the Russians both the honor and the advantage of taking
another capital city.

Meantime plans for the San Francisco Conference had long since
been laid. Knowing full well that any plan of world co-operation, in
Dumbarton order to succeed, must have the support of the four most
Oaks powerful Allies — Great Britain, the United States, Russia,
and China — representatives of those powers met at Dumbarton Oaks
in Washington during the fall of 1944, and issued a set of tentative proposals. The Dumbarton Oaks plan foreshadowed a United Nations
Charter, which would be similar in many respects to the Covenant of the
League of Nations, but with conspicuous differences. The new plan contained nothing comparable to the famous "Article X" that had done so
much to defeat the League of Nations for ratification by the United
States Senate; it gave greater authority to the smaller Security Council
(representing five great powers and six selected others) and less to the
larger Assembly, thereby eliminating a principal cause for delay and in-
decisiveness in the actions of the League; it made more feasible the use
of force against would-be aggressors, and put less trust in disarmament;
it proposed as an integral part of the plan a Permanent Court of International Justice; and it presumed that the Charter, unlike the Covenant,
would be entirely separate from any treaty of peace.[1]

Invited to the Conference at San Francisco were all of the nations,

---

[1] Among the numerous books that undoubtedly helped shape American thinking on
foreign policy are Walter Lippmann, *U. S. Foreign Policy* (1943), and *U. S. War Aims*
(1944); Sumner Welles, *The Time for Decision* (1944); Forrest Davis, *The Atlantic System*
(1941), a study of Anglo-American co-operation; and Carl Becker, *How New Will the Better
World Be?* (1944). C. A. Beard, *American Foreign Policy in the Making, 1932–1940*
(1946), comes to the defense of the isolationist attitude.

now numbering upwards of fifty, that had joined in the hostilities against the Axis powers. At the Conference the smaller nations took an active and important part in the proceedings, and greatly influenced the results, although none of the fundamentals of the *The San* Dumbarton Oaks proposals was altered. Least palatable *Francisco* to the small nations was the insistence by Russia, agreed *Conference* to by Churchill and Roosevelt at Yalta, that all of the five great powers (including France) must concur in important decisions of the Security Council. This left each of the nations so favored free from any effective restraint on its military or diplomatic activities. Optimists could only hope that the rule of self-restraint would be stronger than the rule of law. Whatever the faults and virtues of the Charter, it was widely ratified, and in the United States Senate met only negligible opposition.

In line with the general spirit of world co-operation exhibited at Dumbarton Oaks and San Francisco was a series of important international agreements already reached on a wide variety of subjects. *Other* At Bretton Woods in New Hampshire, a conference held *Conferences* in July, 1944, proposed an International Bank for Reconstruction and Development, and a parallel organization to maintain stability in the exchange values of national currencies. Somewhat earlier, a United Nations Relief and Rehabilitation Administration (UNRRA), a Food and Agriculture Organization of the United Nations, and a Provisional International Civil Aviation Organization had been set up. Much still remained to be done before these efforts could become truly effective, but at least in the United States the hope was strong that the United Nations would be able to act effectively in time of peace no less than in time of war. If the three great Allies were ready to show the restraint necessary to keep the peace among themselves, it was evident that by acting together they could keep other nations at peace. Many observers professed to believe, also, that the lesser nations, as time went on, would achieve a steadily growing recognition in the councils of the United Nations.

Some of the more immediate problems of peace were settled by the "Big Three" in a meeting held at Potsdam near Berlin during the month of July, 1945. On this occasion President Truman *The Potsdam* represented the United States, with his new Secretary of *Conference* State, James F. Byrnes, of South Carolina, taking an important part in the proceedings.[1] The British delegation was at first headed, as usual, by

---

[1] Cordell Hull had retired on account of illness in November, 1944, and had been succeeded by Edward R. Stettinius, Jr., who as Secretary of State had headed the American delegation during the San Francisco Conference.

Churchill, but before the conference ended, the results of Britain's first general election since 1935 became known, and Churchill's place was taken by a new Prime Minister, Clement R. Attlee, leader of the Labor Party. Thus, when the Potsdam Conference ended, Stalin was the only member of the old war-time triumvirate to remain in power. The new "Big Three" laid down at Potsdam the political and economic principles that were to govern the treatment of Germany in the initial period of control. Supreme power was vested in an Allied Control Council, composed of American, British, Russian, and French generals. In accordance with the Teheran and Yalta decisions, the conquered Reich was to be divided into four zones of military occupation, one for each of the four nations mentioned, and Berlin, the capital, was to be similarly partitioned. From this conference came also the ultimatum to Japan, in conformity with which that nation surrendered.

As even the most casual student of American history might have predicted, the first concern of the American people after the fighting of the *Demobiliza-* Second World War had come to an end was to "bring the *tion* boys home." It had been so after every war in which the United States had ever fought. To most members of the armed forces the surrender of Germany and Japan meant not only that the war had come to an end, it meant also that the time of their deliverance was near, a subject upon which they began to speak their minds freely. At home, their wives and mothers, their fathers and children, vied with one another in putting pressure on Congress to implement the common desire. It had been a long war, and many of the American participants had been in uniform four or five years, some even longer. With the victory won, why should they not be released?

Speedy demobilization was not without its hazards, as thoughtful observers, both within and without the government, well knew. The United States would need large numbers of troops for occupation duty in the conquered countries; furthermore, the existence of a well-trained army and a powerful navy would undoubtedly give the nation great diplomatic strength during the impending sparring among the Allies for a peace settlement. But neither the civilian nor the military leaders were able to stand out against the insistence of the public. Shortly after VE Day a plan was announced whereby all service personnel would be discharged in accordance with an elaborate point system, based on such factors as length of service, length of time overseas, battle stars and decorations, and family responsibilities. As long as the war with Japan lasted, reason could be found for holding down the pace of demobilization, but with the arrival of VJ Day discharges were stepped up to the full limit of transportation capacity. In response to a determined demand "to get the boys home for Christmas," service discharges during the single month of December, 1945, reached a total of over a million and a half.

Under the so-called "G.I. Bill of Rights," signed June 22, 1944, discharged veterans were entitled to unemployment compensation at the rate of $20 per week for a period of one year, with certain *G.I.* compensatory allowances for veterans who obtained em- *Benefits* ployment, but at less than $100 a month. Veterans might also obtain government-guaranteed loans of as much as $2000 for the purpose of buying homes or starting up in business. Also, veterans who wished to continue their college education or to obtain "job-training" might receive for as long a period as four years up to $500 a year for books and tuition, and $50 a month for living expenses, or, if married, $75 a month. As inflationary prices began to prevail, these allowances were raised, first to $65 and $90 respectively, and then to $75 and $105, with an additional allowance of $15 for married veterans with two or more dependents. While many veterans joined the "52–20 Club," and drew their unemployment benefits for a full year, the great majority either found employment, or went back to school. College enrolments, as a result, soon rose to startling figures.

This rapid disintegration of the armed forces, while politically expedient, was quite out of keeping with the naval and military requirements of the nation. The Navy could not safely permit *The peace-* crews to abandon ship the minute an American port was *time draft* reached, nor could the Army withdraw every soldier immediately from its far flung overseas bases. Besides, the obligations of occupation in Germany, Austria, Italy and Japan had to be considered. Nevertheless, the announcement in January, 1946, of a less liberal policy of discharges was greeted by near-riots on the part of homesick servicemen all over the world and by a deluge of protests from the home front. There was much opposition to the idea of a peacetime draft, but it was soon evident that the only way to meet the situation was by substituting new draftees for the men who had fought the war. In consequence, Congress reluctantly extended, first for forty-five days and then for a full year, the life of the Selective Service Law, which by the terms of its enactment had been scheduled to expire on May 15, 1946. Changes in the law exempted from the draft eighteen-year olds, fathers, and veterans who had served for six months in the United States or for any length of time overseas. The law also provided that the Army might retain only 1,550,000 men until July 1, 1947, and after that only 1,070,000 men, while the Navy personnel, including the Marine Corps, might not exceed 664,000 men. In actual practice an increase in voluntary enlistments, due mainly to higher rates of pay prescribed by Congress, led to the discontinuance of the draft in September, 1946. By the end of the year the strength of United States military personnel had dropped to 670,000 men for the Army, 395,000 for the Navy, and 83,700 for the Marine Corps.[1]

Next in importance to demobilization, as the public saw it, was "reconversion," meaning the restoration of the nation's business to its normal peace-time behavior. The American people had
Reconversion submitted to many restraints during the war. Through such agencies as the War Production Board (WPB) and the Office of Price Administration (OPA), the national government had made the most drastic conversion to a war economy. Factories that had once produced goods exclusively for civilian consumption were required to change over to the production of war goods. The manufacture of automobiles, for example, together with the sale of new cars, came to an abrupt end in January, 1942, and thereafter the automobile industry was obliged to devote all its facilities to war production. Whole new factories had to be constructed, as in the airplane industry, and existing plants had to be re-tooled to meet the new needs. "Priorities" became a life and death matter to businesses, as one essential commodity after another was withdrawn from general use, and allocated to whatever war production demands were currently uppermost. To hold down the cost of living, rent increases were banned, and an elaborate system of price controls, designed to freeze prices at approximately the levels reached during the early months of the war, gradually came to affect nearly every item of merchandise that could be bought or sold. The rationing of fuel oil and gasoline, begun early in the war, was continued relentlessly, while such articles as sugar, butter, meat, coffee, and canned goods could not be purchased without the use of bothersome rationing stamps, of which no one ever seemed to have nearly enough.

The reconversion problem that was sure to come with peace had led Congress in 1944 to change the Office of War Mobilization into an Office of War Mobilization and Reconversion, and to center in this agency national leadership of the return to normal conditions. Operating successively under such able directors as James F. Byrnes, later Secretary of State, Fred M. Vinson, later Chief Justice of the United States, John W Snyder, later Secretary of the Treasury, and John Roy Steelman, specia

[1] The danger of war with Russia, which developed in 1947–48, led to a strong deman« for universal military training, but Congress refused to go that far. When enlistment failed to meet the required quotas, Congress in 1948 passed a new selective service law and the draft was resumed for a short period.

assistant to the President, the OWMR discharged its obligations with fair effectiveness. The production of civilian goods started to climb, returning veterans and dislocated war workers found new jobs, and profits, both in business and agriculture, continued good.

But there were breakers ahead, particularly in the bad relations that developed between labor and management. Strikes multiplied alarmingly. Workers demanded compensation in hourly rates for *Labor* the loss of wages they had suffered when extra pay for over- *troubles* time, dependably present throughout the war, was no longer available. Management, struggling with the problem of wholesale cancellation of government contracts and the expense of re-tooling and re-conditioning war plants, was unwilling to settle on terms satisfactory to the unions. A strike in General Motors that affected 180,000 workers began in November, 1945, and lasted on until March, 1946. Two hundred thousand electrical workers and 750,000 steel workers quit their jobs in January, 1946. By the end of that month it was estimated that throughout the nation not less than 1,650,000 workers were on strike, while one set of strikes was no sooner settled than others appeared. In April, 400,000 United Mine Workers, led by John L. Lewis, went on strike. Worse still, on May 23 two of the great railroad brotherhoods, disregarding the fact that the government had seized the lines a few days before, tied up the entire railroad system of the nation. Faced by this emergency, the President asked Congress for drastic legislation, and announced by radio that he would use the army, if necessary, to operate the roads unless the strikers were back on the job the next day. With public opinion strongly on his side, the President's ultimatum worked, and the railroad strike was called off. As a result of the various strikes, new wage schedules, involving increases of about 18.5 cents per hour, or between seventeen and eighteen per cent, were worked out for most major industries. Before the end of 1948 a second and a third round of similar wage increases had occurred.

Higher wages, whether justifiably or otherwise, resulted in higher prices, and pushed along the pronounced trend toward inflation that had set in immediately after the war came to an end. Price *Inflation* controls had been accepted as necessary evils as long as the war lasted, but with the fighting finished the public echoed the impatience of business men for a return to "business as usual." Yielding a little to this mood, President Truman ended gasoline rationing shortly after VJ Day. On articles that were still rationed or carried price ceilings, the public, no longer restrained by the necessity of winning the war, began to patronize the black markets in an ever increasing volume. The need

[749]

of continued price controls was well stated by Chester Bowles, head of the OPA, but the people were in no mood to listen. According to Bowles' argument, shared by most economists, the great back-log of purchasing power built up during the war, if turned loose in free competition for the limited amount of goods available, would produce a violent inflation of prices. Such a development, Bowles warned, might lead to another boom comparable to the overexpansion of the 1920's, and another collapse, as in 1929. But the National Association of Manufacturers argued just the other way around. The removal of price controls, according to its elaborate propaganda, was the best way to fight inflation. With price controls off prices might rise temporarily, said the NAM, but the higher prices would lead to the production of a greater volume of goods, and when the supply caught up with the demand prices would come down again.

Whatever the merits of the argument, the people were tired of government restraint on their everyday living, and the end of controls drew near. In June, 1946, just three days before OPA was to expire by statute limitation, Congress passed a bill extending its life, but with such hampering modifications that President Truman, in angry frustration, vetoed the measure. For three weeks all controls were off, and the price ceiling soared upward nearly twenty-five per cent, as against a rise of only a little more than thirteen per cent in the three years preceding. Then Congress passed, and the President signed, a bill not unlike the one just vetoed. Its hollowness was soon apparent. The law was not meant to be effective on most articles, and the attempt to enforce rigid limitations failed utterly. Meats, for example, all but disappeared from legitimate markets. Finally the harassed President, weary of trying to hold the line against such odds, announced by radio on October 14 that all price ceilings, except on rents, would have to go. The results seemed to bear out Bowles' predictions. By the end of the year the consumers' price index was 55.5 per cent higher than in August, 1939, and 31.7 per cent higher than in December, 1945. And prices had only just begun to rise, for with each round of wage increases there came inevitably a round of price increases.

Undoubtedly President Truman had had an eye to the mid-term elections to be held in November, 1946, when he gave up his efforts to hold *Elections* down inflation. But his gesture was one of despair, and it *of 1946* did him no good. Regardless of the merits of the case, the Democratic party had to bear the blame for all the post-war ills from which the people suffered. The Democratic Congress and the Democratic President had been at cross purposes in their efforts to head off inflation, and inflation had come. They had been no less at odds on how to handle the labor problem, for the President had vetoed the Case Federal Mediation Bill, in which Congress, in response, it had supposed, to the President's demands, had proposed stern measures for dealing with strikes. Administration efforts to deal with the housing shortage, which returning veterans found so acute, failed also to produce satisfactory results. Taxes remained high and the budget went unbalanced. Capitalizing on the dissensions of the Democrats and the discontent of the public, the Republicans won the Congressional elections by a landslide, 241 Republicans to 188 Democrats in the House, and 51 Republicans to 45 Democrats in the Senate. State and local elections showed a similarly strong Republican trend, and the Republicans looked forward confidently to a complete sweep in 1948.

If a Democratic Congress and a Democratic President could not get along together, there was even less to hope from a Democratic President and a Republican Congress. The rift between the two be- *The Eightieth* came apparent soon after the Eightieth Congress convened, *Congress* in January, 1947. Determined to reduce taxes and to make a record for economy, the Republican majority promptly attacked President Truman's recommendations for continued expenditures after the New Deal fashion, and for the retention of taxes at the high war-time levels. Not without some misgivings Congress stood ready to make substantial cuts, both on expenditures and on taxation, but the President fought back. He could not restore appropriations that Congress had lopped off, but he could, and did, veto the tax reduction bill that Congress passed. According to the President, the lower tax rates would have added more fuel to the fires of inflation and at the same time would have failed to give relief where relief was most needed. The House sustained the veto by the slender margin of two votes. The high tax rates were anything but popular, but at the end of the year the President had the consolation of being able to show a balanced budget.

An even worse breach between the legislative and executive branches of the government came with the passage of the Taft-Hartley Labor-Management Relations Act, which made substantial amend- *The Taft-* ments to the Wagner-Connery Act of 1935. In an effort to *Hartley Act* force labor unions to accept full responsibility for their acts, as management claimed that it was required to do, the new law permitted employers to sue unions for breach of contract and for damages due to jurisdictional strikes. The law also prohibited the closed shop, which forbade the hiring of any but union men, and permitted the union shop, in which all employees must join the union after being hired, only under specified conditions. Strikes and lockouts had to await a sixty day "cooling-off" period; unions might not make contributions to political campaign funds and must account publicly for their financial expenditures; they might no longer claim from management the "check-off" of union dues without the consent of the individuals concerned; and their officers, in order to seek the assistance of the National Labor Relations Board, must swear that they were not Communists. The Taft-Hartley Act was exceedingly distasteful to labor spokesmen, and was denounced by President Truman in a veto message of unparalleled severity. But the bill repassed both houses of Congress by overwhelming majorities, and late in June, 1947, it became law over the President's veto.

Meantime in international affairs the hope that the victorious Allies would be able to work together successfully in the pursuit of peace had *The pursuit* been all but blasted. In accordance with a decision of the *of peace* Potsdam Conference, peace treaties with Italy, Finland, Hungary, Bulgaria, and Rumania were to precede any final agreements on Germany and Austria. But the best efforts of the United States, Great Britain, and France to draft these treaties continually ran afoul of endless bickering on the part of the Russian negotiators. To begin with, the task of negotiating treaties with the five minor powers was turned over to a Council of Foreign Ministers representing not only the "Big Three," but China and France as well. At the first meeting of this Council, held in London during September, 1945, it was decided that the actual work of treaty drafting was to be done by the ministers of the nations that had signed the appropriate armistices. Thus the representatives of four nations, the United States, Great Britain, the Soviet Union, and France, were to draft the treaty with Italy; three nations, the United States, Great Britain, and the Soviet Union, the treaties with Rumania, Bulgaria, and Hungary; and two nations, Great Britain and the Soviet Union, the treaty with Finland. But the meeting finally broke up over Russian insistence that the participation of China and France in the discussions should be more rigorously limited. Objections came also from the minor Allies, who resented the high-handed assumption of all authority by the Great Powers. Finally at a conference of the "Big Three," Byrnes, representing the United States, Bevin, the United Kingdom, and Molotov, the Soviet Union, held in Moscow, December, 1945, it was agreed that China should withdraw altogether from participation in the Council's debates, while French participation should be limited strictly to Italian matters. Also, largely on Byrnes' insistence, a general peace conference was scheduled to meet May 1, 1946, in Paris, which was to include, besides the members of the Council, representatives from all the European Allies, from the British Commonwealths and India, from Brazil, Ethiopia, the Ukraine, and Byelorussia — twenty one nations in all. The Conference might discuss the draft treaties, and might suggest changes, but the right to make amendments was reserved to the Council of Foreign Ministers.

By this time most American observers had come to the conclusion that the Soviet government had returned to its original policy of world revolution, and that in the peace negotiations its delegates had this goal constantly in view. The Russians, it seemed *Soviet policy* evident, far preferred the continuation of political and economic chaos in the countries concerned to any peace terms that might embarrass them in their plans for the expansion of Communism. Every month of delay in the establishment of normal governments compounded the chaos and played into the hands of the Russian propagandists. In each of the former German satellites, local Communist groups, acting on orders from Moscow, were busily preparing the way for the establishment of Communist control whenever peace should be concluded. The longer the delay and the greater the disorder, the better were their chances of success. Hence, the Russian delegates, both in the Council of Foreign Ministers and at the Paris Peace Conference, exhausted every pretext for prolonging the deliberations. Sensing finally that Roosevelt's policy of conciliation had failed, Byrnes and his colleagues, with strong British and French backing, stood their ground with such firmness against the Russian bickering that they were accused by Russian sympathizers of shifting to a "get-tough-with Russia" attitude. Chief among their critics in the United States was Henry Wallace, who had become Secretary of Commerce in President Roosevelt's cabinet after the election of 1944, and had been retained by President Truman. In a speech delivered in New York, September 12, 1946, which Wallace claimed the President himself had read in advance and had endorsed, the Secretary urged that the United States return to the Roosevelt policy of giving Russia a free hand in eastern Europe, and abandon its newly adopted attitude of "toughness." But President Truman, after some hesitation, dismissed Wallace from his cabinet, and gave the Byrnes policy his full support.[1]

The ordeal of negotiation finally shifted from Paris to New York, where the Council of Foreign Ministers met from November 4 to December 12, 1946; then back again to Paris, where the five *Minor peace* treaties were officially signed, February 10, 1947. The *treaties* war-making potential of all the five satellite nations was reduced to

[1] James F. Byrnes, *Speaking Frankly* (1947), lives up to the promise of its title.

insignificance, heavy reparations were assessed against them, and all except Bulgaria were obliged to make extensive territorial readjustments. Italy, once Germany's closest associate, ceded land to France, Greece, Albania, and Yugoslavia, and turned over the administration of her colonies to the four principal Allies. Even before the end of the war she had been forced to give back their freedom to her two conquered provinces, Ethiopia and Albania. In the final negotiations, the city of Trieste, long a stumbling block to agreement, became also a free territory, with a governor to be chosen and paid by the Security Council of the United Nations. Among the Allied powers the principal gainer from these treaties was Yugoslavia, a nation in which the Communists under Marshall Tito had already achieved complete control. Yugoslavia's territorial holdings were greatly enhanced, her reparations bill topped the Allied list, and her right to arm remained unrestricted. Undoubtedly the Soviet negotiators intended that in this powerful Russian satellite they would have a strategic springboard for their expected jump to full control of the Mediterranean.

The restoration of peaceful relations with the minor enemy states had proved to be difficult, but with Germany and "liberated" Austria *Germany and* the task remained for years a total impossibility. In the *Austria* first place, no steps could be taken toward a final settlement until the long-drawn-out negotiations with the minor powers had come to an end. And, secondly, the plans devised for temporary government, particularly in Germany, were so unworkable as to insure a maximum of ill-feeling and disagreement among the occupying powers. The government of Germany as a whole was to rest in the hands of an Allied Control Council composed of the four high commanding officers of the four zones of occupation, while the subdivided city of Berlin was to be ruled by a *Kommandatura*, consisting of the four local commandants, aided by their technical staffs. All decisions, whether for the nation as a whole or for the capital city only, required the unanimous consent of the representatives of all four occupying powers. It was decreed further that Germany should be administered as "a single economic unit," with uniformity of treatment to all Germans everywhere in Germany, regardless of the zone in which they happened to live. As if to make sure that this incredible plan could never be made to work the western democracies neither asked nor received from Russia guarantees of uninterrupted access to Berlin, although the only way they could reach the city was through the Russian zone.

The system designed for the occupation of Austria was hardly less complicated, but unlike Germany, where the national government had

ZONES OF OCCUPATION: GERMANY, AUSTRIA, BERLIN

totally disappeared, Austria had a government of her own through which the occupying forces could operate. This government had been established with full Russian cognizance, just before the end of hostilities, but it was a multi-party, not a merely Communist affair, and it eventually won recognition from the three great western democracies as well as from Russia. The occupying forces adopted the same cumbersome division into four zones both for the nation as a whole and for Vienna, the capital city, that they had devised for use in Germany. When it became apparent that the Austrian government had no intention of surrendering to Communist domination, the Russians showed their irritation in many ways, most particularly by refusing to co-operate with the other Allies in the making of a treaty of peace; but no such friction developed between the western Allies and Russia in Austria as was soon to mar all efforts to restore normal conditions in Germany. Unlike the trustful western powers who had depended on Russian good-will to insure their access to Berlin, the Russians had obtained formal consent from the other powers to their maintenance of "communication lines" with Austria through both Hungary and Rumania. This gave the Russian government the opportunity to keep military forces, not only in Austria, but in the two neighboring states also, even after a treaty of peace with them had been signed and ratified.

The occupation of Germany presented an interminable procession of virtually insoluble problems. The defeated nation had to be fully dis-*Occupation* armed, and its military potential destroyed; "denazified" *of Germany* local governments had to be instituted; a reliable German police force had to be created; the rubble of war had to be cleaned up, and new housing provided; education had to be revamped in such a way as to eliminate the last vestige of Nazi propaganda; hundreds of thousands of "displaced persons" had to be cared for; the shattered remnants of the nation's economic life had to be collected together, and made the basis for a genuine recovery. All this, moreover, had to be done principally through the instrumentality of a joint military occupation, and by unanimous consent of the representatives of four mutually suspicious Allies. Perhaps the greatest miracle of all was that the Allied Control Council actually reached agreement on about fifty major measures, and as many minor directives, during its first sixteen months of existence.

Not among the least of the problems that confronted the Allies was *Trials of war* the necessity of delivering on a promise they had reiterated, *criminals* time and again during the period of hostilities, to bring to trial those Germans who were principally responsible for the war, and for the inhumanities practiced during it. They could not reach Hitler, Himmler, Goebbels, and Ley, for these four had committed suicide rather than face Allied retribution. But more than a score of other leading Nazis, including Göring, were brought to trial before an international military tribunal at Nuremburg, November 20, 1945. Serving as one of the judges was a former Attorney-General of the United States, Francis Biddle, and as one of the leading prosecutors, a Justice of the United States Supreme Court, Robert H. Jackson. The proceedings dragged on interminably, but thanks in no small part to the patience and persistence of Justice Jackson, the whole sordid record of the Nazi leaders was fully revealed. Many critics of the trial denied that the heads of a conquered enemy state could be legally held accountable for their acts by an international tribunal. But Justice Jackson argued that Germany had been party to the Kellogg-Briand Peace Pact of 1928, which formally renounced war as an instrument of national policy, and had in other international agreements gone on record in opposition to what its Nazi leaders had done. He held further that the trial and conviction of the German war criminals by an international tribunal would set a valuable precedent, one which future heads of state would not regard lightly when tempted to resort to war.[1] After ten months of hearings, the court held all but three of the defendants guilty as charged, sentenced eleven of them to be hanged, and eight others to serve long prison terms. Göring managed to commit suicide before his sentence could be carried out, but on October 16, 1946, the other ten who had been condemned to die were executed. Later on many less notable criminals were also brought to trial, usually for incredible war atrocities, and a large number of death sentences were carried out. In these proceedings "denazified" German courts eventually took a considerable part.

The trial of the Nazi criminals was about the last evidence of full cooperation between Russia and the western democracies over Germany. At the Paris meeting of the Council of Foreign Ministers *Russian intransigence* during April and May of 1946 the United States had urged the making of a treaty of peace with Germany, but the Russians refused, insisting that they needed more time to study the situation. Nor would the Russians sign a treaty with other members of the Big Four, proposed by the United States, guaranteeing for a twenty-five year period the demilitarization and disarmament of Germany. Equally futile, as far as Russia was concerned, was the effort of the United States, at the close of the same meeting, to induce the four

[1] R. H. Jackson, *The Nürnberg Case* (1947), and *The Case Against the Nazi War Criminals* (1947). See also Sheldon Glueck, *The Nuremberg Trial and Aggressive War* (1947).

nations occupying Germany to maintain economic unity in administration. Only Great Britain showed an interest in this proposition, a fact of considerable importance, since in December, 1946, the United States and Great Britain agreed to the gradual economic unification of their zones — the beginning of "Bizonia."

It soon became evident that in the months following the Potsdam agreement Russian policy had shifted. At the time of the Potsdam conference all the great powers, Russia included, had wished to keep Germany decentralized, as the best available means of preventing the revival of the nation's military might. All had agreed to the removal of such industrial plants from Germany as might serve a military end, and many such plants had been removed, particularly for shipment to Russia. But the Russians soon found that they were unable to use their booty effectively — sometimes they could not even put the dismantled plants together again. They therefore made up their minds that the best thing for them to do was to turn Germany into "a high-powered industrial state," with the capacity for production that the Russians themselves lacked, but with a political system that would insure German subordination to Russia. In short, what the Russians wanted was a centralized Germany under Communist control, able and willing to pay Russian reparations, and they would settle for nothing less. Meantime, the Russians continued to rob their zone of occupation of everything of value, including the agricultural commodities that had once been used to supply the more industrialized sections of western Germany.

Struggling against odds to keep their sections together economically, the British and American "Bizonia" was soon turned into a British, American, and French "Trizonia," with the consequent division of Germany into two separate states becoming each day more clearly defined. The break between East and West approached finality in March, 1948, when the Russians refused all further participation in the work of the Allied Control Council, and thus destroyed almost the last vestige of unity among the occupying powers.

On the other side of the world, in eastern Asia, the road to peace was quite as long and tortuous as in Europe. China had gained much "face" *China* during the war.[1] She had become one of the five principal Allies, with great-power status in the Security Council of the United Nations, and the same privilege of vetoing unacceptable measures that had been accorded to the other four. Also, the United States and Great Britain, as early as 1943, had relinquished their claims to extraterritorial rights and privileges in China, special favors that had

[1] F. R. Dulles, *China and America: The Story of their Relations since 1784* (1946).

long been regarded by the Chinese government as humiliating in the extreme. Further, the Chinese record of resistance to Japan, both before and after Pearl Harbor, had won not only the admiration of the entire Allied world, but also a succession of loans and other aids from the United States. Nevertheless, the end of the war, instead of bringing peace to China, brought only the beginning of a war to the death between the Nationalist government of Chiang Kai-shek and an increasingly powerful Communist faction which, with the covert backing of the Russian government, operated with great effectiveness throughout northern China. Viewed in broad perspective, the contest in China appeared to be only another manifestation of the Russian program for spreading Communism, and with it Russian domination, throughout the entire world.

In an effort to restore peace in China the government of the United States, in December, 1945, sent General George C. Marshall, Chief of Staff of the United States Army throughout the war, on a *Marshall's* special mission to China, under orders to bring the warring *mission to* factions together into one government. But Chiang Kai- *China* shek, much as he desired to please the United States, was utterly unwilling to take any Communists into his government. Marshall did arrange an armistice, however, in January, 1946, but it was of use primarily to the Communists. Russia had agreed to withdraw her forces from Manchuria, but she had no intention of allowing the prize she had seized to fall into the hands of the Nationalist government. Instead, Russian policy called for turning Manchuria over to the Chinese Communists as fast as they were able to occupy it, and for arming them with captured Japanese munitions. Thus, when the armistice was broken a few months later, the Chinese Communists were stronger than they had ever been before. Marshall struggled on for nearly a year in search of a formula that would satisfy both parties, and bring peace, but he was obliged eventually to confess his failure and return to the United States. He held no brief for the Communists, but he was dismayed by the almost hopeless corruption and inefficiency of the Nationalist government, and by the unbridled inflation it had promoted. On his recommendation the United States adopted a "plague-on-both-your-houses" attitude toward the Nationalists and the Communists, withdrew most of its troops from China, cut down aid to Chiang's government to a thin trickle, and gave up all further efforts at mediation. As the war continued, the Communists gained ground steadily. By the spring of 1949 they had not only succeeded the Russians in control of Manchuria, but also had pushed steadily southward until they were able to cross the Yangtze-kiang River. Meantime, Chiang Kai-shek, after failing to hold the invaders at bay, had resigned his office, and had retired to Formosa. Not only were the Nationalists obliged to witness the fall of Peiping and Nanking; they could not even prevent the investment and capture of Shanghai. That all China would soon fall to the victorious Communists was the common prediction.

In Korea, as in China, the pathway to peace encountered almost insuperable obstacles. At the Cairo Conference of 1943, Roosevelt,

Korea Churchill, and Chiang Kai-shek had pledged themselves to establish an independent Korea, but at the end of the war the United States and Russia divided that unhappy nation between them at the thirty-eighth parallel for purposes of military occupation, the Russians taking the northern half of the country, and the Americans the southern half. During the Moscow Conference of December, 1945, the American and Russian representatives agreed to the establishment of a native Korean government under a four-power trusteeship of the United States, Great Britain, the Soviet Union, and China, but the mutual distrust of each other's motives on the part of the two occupying powers prevented the implementation of this agreement. Russian interpretation of the Moscow pact would have assured the establishment of a Soviet Republic in Korea; American interpretation, the exact reverse. With each passing month, the economic separation of the country became more rigid, and, in spite of a very earnest Korean spirit of nationalism, the hope of eventual unity, more remote. Finally, during the summer of 1948, two Korean governments appeared, one for each section, each claiming to be the rightful government of all Korea. In the Russian zone a Korean Peoples' Republic, modeled on the Soviet pattern, depended for its existence on the backing of Russia and a Russian trained Korean "red army" of about 125,000 men. In the American zone, a Republic of Korea based on a Constitution drawn up by a Korean Assembly, had the support of the United States, and a small American-trained Korean constabulary of perhaps 26,000 men. Here, as elsewhere in the world, the tension between the United States and the Soviet Union was great, with an unstable peace at the mercy of the slightest incident.

With conditions on the Asiatic mainland so far from satisfactory Americans congratulated themselves that developments in Japan had

Japan turned out somewhat better than expected. The decision to retain the Emperor, and for that matter most of the essential features of the Japanese government, had proved to be a master stroke. Pleased with this concession, the people of Japan accepted the

American occupation as at least a necessary evil, co-operated willingly with the American authorities, and strove in every way to regain the good-will of their former enemies. Furthermore, since the victory over Japan had been so completely won by the United States, it was only natural that military occupation should be primarily in American hands, and under American command. Thus Japan escaped the complications that arose in Germany from the partition of the nation among a number of conquerors, all of whom were determined to play a prominent part in governmental affairs. Compared with Germany, the situation in Japan, at least during the first months of American occupation, was simplicity itself. MacArthur gave the orders, and the Japanese government carried them out.[1]

* It was not long, however, before protests from such nations as Great Britain and Australia, no less than from Russia, led the United States to concede to the other Allies a voice in the disposal of Japanese affairs. At the Moscow Conference of December, 1945, it was agreed that a Far Eastern Commission should be created, to be composed of one representative from each of the eleven Pacific powers that had fought against Japan — the United States, the United Kingdom, the Soviet Union, China, France, the Netherlands, Canada, Australia, New Zealand, India, and the new Philippine Republic. Of these powers, the first four might exercise the right of veto. The Commission was to meet in Washington, under the chairmanship of the American member, in order to formulate policies for the carrying out of the Japanese terms of surrender, and to review such directives as might be issued for the guidance of the Supreme Commander, or by him. In addition to the Far Eastern Commission in Washington there was to be also an Allied Council in Tokyo with four members, one each from the United States, the British Commonwealth (United Kingdom, Australia, New Zealand, India), the Soviet Union, and China. The Allied Council had little more than advisory authority, although on some matters of first importance the opposition of one of its members could force the Supreme Commander to refer an impending order to the Far Eastern Commission for approval. To emphasize the international character of the occupation, the American forces in Japan were now joined by a small number of troops from the British Commonwealth. China, also, was to have sent a contingent, but the Chiang government was never able to spare any of its fighting forces for occupa-

---

[1] Masses of data on the occupation of Japan are presented in *Summation No. 1 of Non-Military Activities in Japan and Korea* (September–October, 1945), and similar subsequent publications, issued by the General Headquarters Supreme Commander for the Allied Powers.

tion duty. Russia, too, was invited to send troops to Japan, but pointedly refused to do so.

In spite of all this display of international co-operation, the Japanese occupation still remained primarily an American affair. Under Mac-

Japanese war trials Arthur's efficient leadership every effort was made to demilitarize Japan and to destroy the ruling clique which had led the nation into war. Before the Americans took over, many of the war-time Japanese leaders had committed suicide, but in due time ex-Premier Hideki Tojo, and some twenty-seven others, were brought to trial under conditions analagous to those which ruled at Nuremberg, in Germany. Eventually, Tojo and six others were given death sentences and executed, while long terms of imprisonment were meted out to most of the remaining defendants.

Efforts were made, also, to revive and extend whatever democratic political institutions Japan had known before the war. A representative

Reforms in Japan diet, elected in April, 1946, under the observation of the occupation authorities, drew up a new constitution which renounced war as an instrument of national policy, denied the divinity of the Emperor, stripped his office of all real power, adopted a western-style bill of rights, and instituted responsible government with the legislative authority vested in a bicameral parliament, the lower house of which could, if necessary, override the opposition of the upper house. In the economic sphere, efforts were made to break up large landed estates in the interest of a wider distribution of holdings, to dissolve the large industrial and banking corporations that had lent their support to the war, to develop labor organizations after the western pattern, and to institute extensive educational reforms. But all these measures failed dismally to restore normal economic conditions in Japan. The cost of living soared to wildly inflationary heights; housing, clothing, and food shortages were disastrously apparent; and all efforts to revive international trade proved unavailing. Indeed, far down into 1949 the very survival of the nation seemed to depend upon the steady importation of un-paid-for supplies from the United States.

In the summer of 1947 the United States urged that the eleven powers represented on the Far Eastern Commission should make a start toward the drafting of a treaty of peace with Japan. According to the American plan, decisions should be reached by a two-thirds majority of the powers, and the treaty thus drafted should be submitted to a general peace conference, in which all the states at war with Japan should participate. But the American peace plan failed, primarily because of opposition from Russia and China, both of whom insisted that the unanimous consent of the Big Four should be required for every decision. And so, with no prospect of a formal treaty of peace in sight, Japan dragged miserably along through its fourth year of occupation.

In the Philippine Islands the United States undertook to deliver on its long-standing promise, under the Tydings-McDuffie Act, of independence on July 4, 1946. This was the more difficult be- *The* cause of the enormous destruction that the war had wrought, *Philippines* not only in Manila, which was at least fifty per cent destroyed, but to an equal or lesser extent throughout the Islands. In spite of all the obstacles to be overcome, however, General MacArthur, in February, 1945, turned over to President Sergio Osmeña full responsibility for Philippine civil administration. Osmeña had been the Philippine Vice-President, but had succeeded to the presidency on the death of Manuel Quezon in August, 1944, only to be supplanted in turn by Manuel Roxas as a result of the presidential elections of April, 1946.[1] It was obvious to most observers that independence, much as it was prized by the Filipinos, might become a hazard to the United States, as well as to the Islanders themselves, without adequate means of defense. The American Congress therefore passed a Philippines Military Assistance Act, the purpose of which was to create and maintain an effective Philippine army. At American insistence sites in the Philippines were also turned over to the United States for military and naval bases. Further, the American government could not ignore the responsibility that it had incurred by reason of the close economic ties that had so long bound the Philippines to the United States. Would it be reasonable or right to cut the Islands loose from the connections in America upon which their prosperity had so long depended? After much debate, Congress in 1946 finally passed a Philippine Trade Act which provided for an eight year period of free trade on a quota basis, to be followed by the gradual imposition of tariff duties over a twenty year period, with an additional five per cent of the regular duties to be charged each year until the full amount should be reached.

It was clear, too, that the United States was under moral obligation to aid the Philippine government in the heroic task of rebuilding its ruined cities and restoring its shattered economy. To these ends Congress paralleled the Trade Act with a Philippine Rehabilitation Act, which appropriated a total of $720,000,000 to compensate the Philippine government and the owners of private property in the Islands for the damages they had suffered. And, as a final gesture of good-will, a Fili-

[1] President Roxas died April 15, 1948, and was succeeded by the Vice-President, Elpidio Quirino.

INTERNATIONAL
AIR ROUTES

pino Naturalization Act established for the Philippine Islands a quota similar to that permitted to other nationals entering the United States.

The internal problems of the Philippine Republic were by no means settled with independence and the various agreements with the United States. The old sugar-coconut-tobacco economy of the pre- *The* war period, which had profited the landlord-merchant class *Hukbalahap* a great deal, but the ordinary peasant, very little, had been shattered by the war. Many of the peasants were loath to go back to it, and insisted on radical agrarian reforms. A left-wing organization of extremists known as the Hukbalahap played heavily on this spirit of discontent, and under the leadership of Luis Taruc broke forth into open revolt. Evidence that the Hukbalahap were not averse to revolution after the Communist pattern strengthened the government in its opposition to the movement, but the prospect of peace seemingly depended upon the willingness of the Philippine authorities to undertake the reforms that the peasants desired.

Although events in the rest of the Asiatic theater were seemingly of little consequence to the United States, the American people had begun to understand that anything which happened anywhere in the world might concern them eventually. They therefore viewed with more than passing interest post-war developments in the Asiatic empires of European nations. It was apparent that most of the colonial peoples had no intention whatever of going back to the old system of subservience to white domination. They had seen the white man defeated and humiliated, and although they had little use for their Japanese conquerors, they had lost their awe and fear of the Europeans. What they wanted when the Japanese were driven out was self-rule such as the United States unhesitatingly granted to the Philippines.

In recognizing this new spirit among colonial peoples, Great Britain was not far behind the United States. American criticism of British colonial policy had always been extremely vocal, but it was *India,* considerably allayed by the decision of the British Labor *Burma,* Government to grant both India and Burma whatever de- *Malaya* gree of independence they might choose. In India, the task was far less how to get the British to leave than how to get the Hindus and Moslems in India to agree on a plan of self-government. At length a divided India was agreed upon, with a Dominion of India dominated by the Hindus, and a Dominion of Pakistan dominated by the Moslems. For Hindu India, an Englishman, Earl Mountbattan of Burma became governor-general, but for Pakistan, the outstanding Moslem leader, Mohammed Ali Jinnah, was named at his own insistence. Independence

[765]

day for India was set for August 15, 1947, at which time all British power was relinquished, and native responsibility began. In Burma there was less internal friction than in India, but the Burmese leaders insisted upon, and obtained, complete independence, rather than dominion status, and the transfer of power to them came early in 1948. The new native government showed little ability to keep order, and the country was soon in the throes of Civil War. In Malaya post-war political reorganization was less drastic, but two new governmental units were set up, the Malayan Union, which brought together into a federation states that had previously been governed separately, and the colony of Singapore. Considerable progress was made toward the establishment of a common Malayan citizenship.

Unfortunately, the willingness of the United States and Great Britain to grant home rule to their dependencies was not fully shared by other *Indo-China and Indonesia* European nations who had possessions in the Orient. In Indo-China the French at first recognized a native provisional government for what was called the Viet Nam Republic, but differences developed that resulted in open warfare between French and Indo-Chinese forces. By the end of 1947, the French government had crowded as many as 100,000 French troops into Indo-China, and all hope of an amicable settlement seemed lost. In the populous Dutch East Indies, the returning European overlords confronted an equally determined independence movement. At first the Dutch authorities were reluctant to make extensive concessions to the revolutionists, but sharp and effective fighting on the part of the revolting Javanese brought a change of heart. Eventually a United States of Indonesia was agreed upon, to take over all local government in 1949. But before the agreement could be implemented, fighting broke out again between the Dutch and the natives. For a time intervention by the Security Council of the United Nations brought hostilities to an end. By January, 1948, the principles of a new agreement had been worked out, with the United States of Indonesia accepting equal status with the Netherlands under the Dutch crown in a Netherlands-Indonesian Union. But late in that same year the conflict was resumed.

The great significance that citizens of the United States had learned during the war to attach to events in Europe and Asia served in a way *Latin America* to detract from their interest in the other Americas. Before the war the "good neighbor" policy had seemed to be a matter of fundamental importance in international relations; the end of the war left it no less important, perhaps, but far less in the news. Just before the meeting at San Francisco which resulted in the formation of the United Nations, an Inter-American Conference on Problems of War and Peace had met in Mexico City, and had adopted the Act of Chapultepec, a kind of substitute for the Monroe Doctrine. The Act declared that anything calculated to disturb the peace in the Americas was a matter of common concern to every American nation and a cause for consultation; further, the Act also asserted that aggression by a non-American power against any American nation was to be regarded by all as an attack on all. In other words, instead of the United States, unilaterally, pledging itself to defend the Americas, as under the Monroe Doctrine, now all of the various American nations agreed among themselves to accept joint responsibility for their common defense. This same determination to act collectively against aggressors was written into the Treaty of Rio de Janeiro, ratified by the United States Senate in December, 1947.

The one nation with which the United States found it most difficult to be good-neighborly was the Argentine. Friction between the two countries was long-standing, and proceeded in no small *The* part from the desire of the Argentine to exert the same kind *Argentine* of leadership in South America that the United States exercised for the Americas as a whole. Economically the two nations were rivals, each with practically the same agricultural exports to sell. Furthermore, business men from the United States after the First World War had given their nation a bad reputation with the Argentine people, a reputation which the inept diplomatic representatives sent out from Washington did little to redeem. To make matters worse, the policy of the United States toward the Argentine seemed built on shifting sands. When, during the closing years of the war, the wheel of revolution turned up an army colonel, Juan Domingo Perón, as the strong man behind the Argentine government, the United States criticized his pro-fascist tendencies with the greatest of bluntness, then with great inconsistency championed successfully the admission of the Argentine to the United Nations, then as a means of preventing the election of Perón to the Argentine presidency, issued a "Blue Book" describing his pro-Axis record, then, when he was elected in spite of, or perhaps because of, this propaganda, switched again to trying to get along with him.

Whatever the inconsistencies of Washington diplomacy, it became clear as time went on that the principal objective of United States policy in the Western Hemisphere was to unite all the American *Truman to* nations against Communism, rather than against fascism, *Mexico* as during the war. By an Inter-American Military Co-operation Act, passed in May, 1946, the President of the United States was permitted

[767]

to extend military aid and advice to the other American nations, and in a sense to try to organize them for defense. As a gesture of good-will President Truman, in March, 1947, visited Mexico City as the guest of the Mexican government, the first President of the United States to make such a trip. His visit was well received, and was followed by a similar visit by the Mexican President, Miguel Alemán, to Washington.

Unfortunately the United States made little effort to revive the economic life of Latin America, which the dislocations of the war had left badly shattered. Inflation was the rule, and the avid demand for manufactured goods from the United States tended to increase rather than diminish the difficulties, for the Latin-American nations had not the goods to send to the United States in payment for what they wished to buy. Inevitably they blamed the "Colossus of the North" for many of the ills from which they suffered.

CHAPTER XXXIII

ONE WORLD—OR TWO?

For most Americans the chief hope of holding the world together lay in the United Nations. The process of putting the San Francisco Charter into effect began at London, January 10, 1946, when the General Assembly, widely-heralded as the "town-meeting *The United Nations* of the world," began its first session. Although each member nation was entitled to only one vote in the Assembly, it might have as many as five delegates, so the United States sent five of its most distinguished citizens as its first representatives — Secretary of State James F. Byrnes, Former-Secretary of State Edward R. Stettinius, Jr., United States Senators Tom Connally and Arthur H. Vandenberg, and Mrs. Anna Eleanor Roosevelt, the widow of Franklin D. Roosevelt. For its first President the Assembly chose Paul-Henri Spaak of Belgium. Then, as the Charter required, it proceeded with the election of the six non-permanent members of the Security Council. Aside from this and certain other elective functions, the Assembly was supposed to be primarily a deliberative body, less important because of the power it exercised than because of the forum it provided for the discussion of world problems. Its sessions were ordinarily to occur only annually for short periods of time each, but in 1946 it met for a second time at Flushing Meadows, Long Island, and chose New York City as the permanent headquarters of the United Nations. An offer of $8,500,000 by John D. Rockefeller, Jr., for the purchase of a six block tract along the East River in Manhattan determined that the United Nations would eventually have a skyscraper capital in the heart of the great American metropolis.

Unlike the Assembly, the Security Council, with its five permanent members (the United States, the Soviet Union, the United Kingdom, France, and China) and its six members elected by the *Organization* Assembly, was supposed to remain in continuous session. For the first non-permanent members of the Council, the Assembly chose Egypt, Mexico, the Netherlands, Australia, Brazil, and Poland. The first three of these six had terms of one year only, thereafter three

[769]

new members were to be chosen each year for two-year terms, and were to be ineligible for immediate re-election. The presidency of the Council rotated among member nations, each serving for a month at a time. The Security Council held its first meeting in London, January 18. On its recommendation the Assembly chose Trigve Halfdan Lie, a Norwegian Labor Party leader, as the first Secretary-General of the United Nations. After the initial sessions in London, the Council held most of its meetings in New York, first at Hunter College, and later at Lake Success, Long Island; then, late in 1948, in Paris.

It soon became apparent that the Security Council, under existing regulations, could never become the effective instrument that at least *The Security* some of the framers of the United Nations Charter had *Council* hoped. The chief difficulty lay in the provision which permitted each great power to veto any important action that might be proposed. According to the Charter, decisions by the Council could be taken only with the concurrence of seven members, and even this vote would be insufficient unless every one of the five great powers voted with the majority. But few of those who accepted this provision could have foreseen the ruthlessness with which one nation, Russia, would exercise the veto power. During the first three years of the life of the United Nations the Russian veto was interposed no less than thirty times. In practice Russian use of the veto power made the United Nations almost as ineffective after the Second World War as the failure of the United States to ratify the Treaty of Versailles made the League of Nations ineffective after the First World War. In each instance the international organization continued in existence, but in each instance, also, its usefulness was almost fatally impaired.

In spite of the discouraging effect of the constant Russian vetoes, the United Nations completed most of the machinery for world co-operation that had been authorized by the San Francisco Charter, and accomplished what it could.

1. The Economic and Social Council, composed of eighteen members to be chosen by the General Assembly, six each year for three-year *Economic* terms, was duly constituted, and met persistently following *and Social* its first session in London, January 23, 1946. The Council *Council* set up a wide variety of commissions to advise it, and through which to operate, some of them, such as the Commission on Narcotic Drugs, designed to take over the work formerly done by comparable bodies of the now defunct League of Nations. Especially commendatory was the work of a Sub-Commission on Reconstruction of Devastated Areas, which made a comprehensive report on eight war-torn

nations, and suggested appropriate international action. The Economic and Security Council did not originate the United Nations Educational Scientific and Cultural Organization but it reached an agreement with it, which gave UNESCO, as it was generally called, the blessing of United Nations sponsorship.

2. In addition to the Economic and Social Council, the United Nations also set up a Trusteeship Council of twelve members, six of whom represented nations actually in charge of "trust terri- *The Trustee-* tories," and six of whom represented other nations. The *ship Council* Trusteeship Council had somewhat shadowy supervisory authority over existing mandates, and over territory detached from a defeated nation, except that "strategic areas" were to be directly under the Security Council. In the latter category came the former Japanese mandates in the Marshall, Mariana, and Caroline islands, which were handed over to the United States for administration.

3. The Security Council also selected, in conjunction with the Assembly, the fifteen judges of the International Court of Justice. This Court received its first case in 1947, when a British charge that *International* illegally-sown Yugoslavia mines had damaged two British *Court of* destroyers in the Corfu Channel was referred to it for *Justice* settlement.

4. A Military Staff Committee, to be composed of the chiefs of staff of the five great powers, or their representatives, was supposed to advise the Security Council on the means by which armed force *Military* might be used to carry out United Nations decisions, but *Staff* the chronic failure of this Committee to reach agreements *Committee* robbed the Security Council completely of military weapons.

5. The constant inability of the Security Council to reach decisions, due to the impasse between the United States and Russia, threw more and more responsibility upon the General Assembly, which *The "Little* could at least debate matters freely. For this purpose its *Assembly"* short, supposedly annual, sessions proved inadequate, so on motion of the United States an Interim Committee, sometimes called the "Little Assembly," was created. This consisted of one representative from each member nation, and its decisions, although in no way binding on anyone, could be reached by a two-thirds vote. It was promptly boycotted by Russia and her satellites, but its usefulness as a reflector of world opinion was so great that it seemed likely to become a permanent institution.[1]

[1] Vera Micheles Dean, *The Four Cornerstones of Peace* (1946), gives the genesis of the United Nations organization. Floyd A. Cave, and associates, *The Origins and Consequences of World War II* (1948), treats fully of efforts to make the United Nations effective.

The United Nations, in spite of its seeming impotence, had some significant accomplishments to its credit. The government of Iran, in January,

Iran, 1946, protested against the continued occupation of Iranian
Indonesia territory by Russian troops, and charged the Soviet government with interference in Iranian internal affairs. The charge was heatedly denied by the Russian representative on the Security Council, and for a time he withdrew from its sessions. The quarrel ended, without United Nations action, when the Russian government recalled its troops from Iran, but the evidence that the overwhelming majority of the Council sympathized with Iran may have had some influence in modifying the Russian attitude. The Ukraine, one of the three Russian Soviet Republics given separate representation in the United Nations, next charged that Japanese troops were being used to suppress a native revolt in Indonesia, and moved that the United Nations institute an investigation. This motion was voted down, but the continued disorders in Indonesia soon had that subject before the Council again, and in August, 1947, the Council voted to send a "Good Offices Committee" of three to Indonesia to arrange a settlement. But the results, as noted, were inconclusive.[1]

United Nations efforts at mediation were often far less successful. In the dispute between Greece and her neighbors, the "UN" failed com-

Greece pletely to achieve a settlement. The Ukraine first brought the problem of Greece before the Council, in January, 1946, charging that the continued presence of British troops in Greece constituted a threat to the peace of the Balkans. This the Greeks not only denied, but they also hurled back a countercharge to the effect that Albania, Bulgaria, and Yugoslavia were directly supporting the Communist guerrillas along the Greek border who were trying to overthrow the Greek government. The Security Council then voted to send a United Nations Commission to Greece on another mission of investigation. The majority of this Commission came to the conclusion that the Greek charges were true, but the minority, consisting of the Russian and Polish representatives, held the exact opposite. When the Commission reported its findings to the Security Council in the summer of 1947 Russia used the veto to prevent action being taken in accordance with the wishes of the majority. The Council then helplessly turned the Balkan situation over to the Assembly for further investigation.

The Security Council was equally ineffective in taking action with respect to the Franco régime in Spain, which the Polish representative declared to be a threat to world peace. A majority opinion admitted

[1] See p. 766.

the potential threat of Spanish fascism, but noted the absence of any aggressive act, and recommended only that if the Spanish *Spain,* government did not change its spots in due time, the mem- *Trieste* bers of the United Nations should withdraw their representatives from Madrid. This mild action ran afoul of the usual Russian veto. Russian intransigence also prevented the Security Council from appointing a governor for Trieste, as it was supposed to do under the terms of the Italian treaty. The net result was that Trieste remained under Anglo-American control.

Infinitely perplexing likewise was the Arab-Jewish contest for the control of Palestine, which by the year 1947 reached the United Nations. The Zionist movement for the creation in Palestine of a *Palestine* Jewish national state received a tremendous impetus after the war by the arrival of thousands of Jewish refugees from the European war zones. Arab opposition to Zionism, plus the problem of accepting such large numbers of "displaced persons," posed a serious problem for the British government, which held a mandate over Palestine dating back to the year 1922. The United States was also involved, not only because of the sentimental interest of many American Jews in Zionism, but also because of the possession by such neighboring Arab states as Iran, Iraq, and Saudi Arabia of great oil resources which American companies were either exploiting or hoped to exploit. It was hazardous politically to offend Jewish voters in the United States, and it might be hazardous economically to run the risk of offending the intensely anti-Jewish Arab Kings. An Anglo-American Committee of Inquiry, appointed in 1945, reported in April, 1946, that the British should admit into Palestine 100,000 of the refugee Jews from Central Europe who had suffered at the hands of the Nazis, but that instead of setting-up an independent Palestinian state, either Jewish or Arab, the British mandate should be continued until a United Nations trusteeship could be devised. This report pleased neither Arabs, Jews, nor British, although President Truman approved it for the United States.

With violence between Arabs and Jews on the increase, the British government requested that the General Assembly of the United Nations study the problem further. As a result, the Assembly appointed a Special Committee on Palestine in May, 1947, which, three months later, brought in an elaborate report. In this document the majority proposed the partition of Palestine into three states, one dominantly Arab and one dominantly Jewish, but with the City of Jerusalem independent of both, and all three bound together in a single economic union. This report, after prolonged debate, was adopted, strangely enough with the United States and the Soviet Union both supporting it, but it served only to feed the flames of conflict in Palestine, and its intense unpopularity with the Arabs led the United States virtually to go back on the stand it had taken.

The British, however, had resolved to withdraw from Palestine, and in May, 1948, the British High Commissioner actually took his departure. *The new* Thereupon the Jews proclaimed the independent state of *State of* Israel, as of midnight, May 14–15, 1948. The new state *Israel* received immediate recognition by the United States and the Soviet Union, but its Arab neighbors promptly attacked it with what little military might they could muster. In the fighting that followed, the Jews, in spite of their inferiority in numbers, showed remarkable ability to defend themselves, and it seemed evident that the Arabs could not destroy the new "Israel." Obviously this war in the Holy Land was one that the United Nations could not overlook, but instead of taking any direct action to end the fighting the General Assembly merely authorized the five great powers to send a mediator to Palestine. For this task the powers chose Count Bernadotte of Sweden, who quickly achieved a truce, only to be assassinated by Jewish extremists who opposed partition, and wished the war to continue until the Jewish state should include all of Palestine. Despite this untoward incident, and much irregular fighting, a workable settlement of the problem was eventually arranged, largely through the efforts of Count Bernadotte's American successor, Dr. Ralph Bunche.

The seeming agreement between the United States and Russia over Palestine deceived no one. By this time it was apparent that these two *The control* great powers stood in deadly antagonism to each other. *of atomic* This was shown in a variety of ways, but perhaps most con- *energy* clusively in the divergent attitudes of the two nations with reference to the control of atomic energy. Tests undertaken in July, 1946, by the United States Navy at Bikini Island demonstrated beyond a shadow of a doubt that the new atomic bomb was not merely another piece of ordnance, it was a cataclysm. A small number of bombs, strategically placed, could destroy a whole metropolitan area, and make it uninhabitable for years to come. A considerable number of bombs could paralyze an entire nation. A third world war, with atomic weapons in use by both sides, would mean the end of civilization.[1]

Even before the Bikini tests, in January, 1946, the General Assembly of the United Nations had established an Atomic Energy Commission to investigate the entire problem, and to make recommendations for the

[1] David Bradley, *No Place to Hide* (1948), gives the results of the Bikini tests.

control of atomic energy by international means, but a seemingly incurable difference of opinion developed between the Russian and the American points of view. The American plan, framed by a commission headed by Bernard M. Baruch, called for the creation of an International Atomic Development Authority with full power to control the use of atomic energy everywhere in the world, particularly with a view to preventing it from being turned to warlike ends. This Agency was to have unrestricted privileges of inspection in all nations, and its actions were not to be subject to the usual veto power of the United Nations. Over against the American plan, the Russians proposed merely an international agreement to abandon atomic warfare, with each nation free to enforce the agreement for itself. Furthermore, the veto power was to remain inviolate. As a part of the American plan, the United States offered to surrender its stock-pile of atomic bombs whenever international control should be set up, but the Russians called for the destruction of the American bombs as a prelude to any agreement. Ultimately the Russians grudgingly conceded the necessity of international control and inspection, but they were unyielding in their insistence on the other items of their program, and nothing was accomplished. The United States, with its long lead in the development of atomic energy, could hardly give up its advantages without full assurance that some effective means had been devised to restrict the atomic activities of a potential enemy.

Within the United States, Congress, meantime, had set up a five-man commission with exclusive authority over the development of atomic energy, and under civilian rather than army or navy control. As chairman of the commission, President Truman appointed David E. Lilienthal, for many years the efficient head of TVA. Under Lilienthal's leadership, American scientists continued their efforts to unlock the secrets of nuclear energy, and to make their findings of use for peaceful as well as for warlike purposes.

With the increasingly tense situation between Russia and the United States, the idea of "One World," which had seemed so sure of achievement during the war, became each succeeding month a *The* dimmer hope. When in May, 1943, the Comintern had *Cominform* been dissolved "as the directing center of the international working-class movement," the Soviet-inspired announcement had strongly advocated a "working-class movement of each separate country, working within the framework of its own country." This statement had been widely hailed as the end of the old Communist plan to promote world revolution, and the beginning of a new policy based on the principle of "live, and let live," the principle on which the new United Nations was to be built. But in September, 1947, Communist representatives from Russia and her satellites, augmented by a few others from France and Italy, met in Warsaw to establish a Communist Information Bureau, or Cominform, the purpose of which was to "coordinate the activity of communist parties on foundations of mutual agreement," that is, to provide one leadership for Communist propaganda everywhere in the world. It was clear that the old policy of world revolution had been resumed, and that the Russian leaders were bent on creating "One World," to be sure, but one Communist world.

Both before and after the Warsaw Manifesto was issued, its words were matched with deeds. Wherever the Red Army controlled, either *The "iron curtain"* by direct occupation or by the heavy shadow it cast across an international border, free governments disappeared. By one means or another Communist minorities, backed by Moscow, took over the governments of Poland, Yugoslavia, Bulgaria, Rumania, Hungary, and finally even Czechoslovakia. Intercourse between these countries and the outside world became ever more difficult. The Russian zones in Germany and Austria were separated by heavy Red Army patrols from other zones of occupation, and under the guise of reparations were stripped of their resources. In Russian-occupied Austria, everything that the Nazis had stolen was defined as German property, and was taken over by the Russians. Much else went on of which only rumors got through to the West. From the Baltic to the Adriatic an "iron curtain" had descended, back of which the Soviet leaders could in safety and in secrecy consolidate their gains, and lay their plans for others.

The immediate objectives of the plotters were not long disguised. In Italy and France, Communist minorities were galvanized into action, with the control of the Italian and French governments, by fair means or foul, as their objectives. The government of Turkey was told that it must either cede territory to Russia, and permit the Russian government to establish military bases that would command the Dardanelles, or else take a consistently pro-Russian line such as its neighbors to the North had done. Most revealing of all, Greek Communist guerrillas were given every aid and comfort by neighboring Communist states in their effort to overthrow the existing non-Communist Greek government. If Russia could only draw Greece within her orbit, she could out-flank the Dardanelles and Suez, and challenge the Anglo-American line of communications with the Far East, much as Germany had done before her.

It was this Greek situation that finally led the United States to take a positive stand against the Russian program of aggression. When the British government, in line with its general policy of re- *The Truman* trenchment, announced that it could no longer afford to *Doctrine* maintain a garrison in Greece, and would withdraw its troops from that nation, the United States had a momentous decision to make. Either it must somehow take the place the British were vacating, or it must stand idly by while Russian-backed Communists went through the now familiar process of destroying the liberties of one more "liberated" country. The government of Greece had little to recommend it, but it was anti-Communist, and at least subject to improvement. If the Communists came in, then down would come the iron curtain, and the rule of force for an indefinite period would completely take the place of the rule of law and reason. Faced by this situation the President of the United States sent a message to Congress, March 12, 1947, calling for American aid both to Greece and to Turkey. His message, marking as it did a milestone in the history of American foreign policy, was promptly called the Truman Doctrine. The world was confronted with two ways of life, the President pointed out, one based on majority rule, with generous guarantees for the freedom of the individual, and the other "based upon the will of a minority forcibly imposed upon the majority." [1]

> I believe that it must be the policy of the United States to support free peoples who are resisting attempted subjugation by armed minorities or by outside pressure.
> I believe that we must assist free peoples to work out their own destinies in their own way.
> I believe that our help should be primarily through economic and financial aid which is essential to economic stability and orderly political processes.

To give strength to his words, the President recommended that Congress appropriate $300,000,000 for aid to Greece and $100,000,000 for aid to Turkey.

The Truman Doctrine aroused much discussion in the United States, and a small minority, headed by Henry Wallace, denounced it unsparingly. Others regretted that the United States had acted unilaterally instead of through the United Nations. To reassure this faction, Senator Vandenberg introduced, and both houses of Congress accepted, an amendment requiring the President to discontinue American aid in the event that the Security Council of the United Nations should at any time hold it to be unnecessary or unwise. On this issue the United

---

[1] Ruhl J. Bartlett, ed., *The Record of American Diplomacy: Documents and Readings in the History of American Foreign Relations* (1947), p. 728. This compilation includes valuable sections on war-time diplomacy and the United Nations.

States would waive its veto privilege. So amended the appropriation passed, and with the funds thus made available the United States began at once to ship military and economic supplies to the nations concerned. To administer the American expenditures in Greece, the President chose a Republican, ex-Governor Dwight Griswold of Nebraska.

By this time American foreign policy had achieved a definitely bipartisan nature. The American delegates to the United Nations con-
The biparti- tained members of both parties, with Senator Vandenburg,
san foreign a Republican, quite as important a representative of the
policy United States as any Democrat. The American member of the Security Council was another Republican, ex-Senator Warren R. Austin of Vermont, who had succeeded former Secretary of State Stettinius to that important United Nations post in January, 1947. That same month, after the resignation of Secretary Byrnes for reasons of health, the President chose as Byrnes' successor former Chief-of-Staff George C. Marshall, who had never been in politics and never expected to be. Possibly Marshall was technically a Democrat, but he was as nearly a non-party man as the President could have chosen. One of Secretary Marshall's principal advisers, almost certain to be present in all overseas conferences, was John Foster Dulles, a Republican who was very close to Governor Thomas E. Dewey of New York, and was generally thought to be Dewey's choice for Secretary of State. With the Russian menace looming ever larger, it thus appeared that the Truman Administration had discarded party politics in foreign affairs, and that party leaders generally had decided that partisanship must stop at the water's edge.

The Truman Doctrine was quickly supplemented by what was sometimes called the Marshall Plan, and sometimes the European Recovery
The Plan. It seemed clear that the United States could not
Marshall hope to achieve much success in the "containment of Com-
Plan — munism" if it reserved its aid until a given nation was just
ERP about ready to go down, or if it helped only one or two of the weakest nations at a time. Europe as a whole needed to be put on its feet economically. If that could be done, perhaps the Communist drive could be stopped in its tracks. It was with some such thoughts as these in mind that Secretary Marshall, in an address delivered at Harvard University, June 5, 1947, called upon European nations first to get together on what they could do to help themselves, and then to state in concrete terms what additional aid they would need from the United States. If they could demonstrate a determination to co-operate for their own good, and would give assurance that the aid they received

would be used for the economic benefit of Europe as a whole, the United States would help what it could. The Marshall Plan was enthusiastically received throughout all western Europe, but Russia and her satellites, to whom it was also open, held aloof.

As a matter of fact, the European Recovery Plan (ERP) was by no means the first contribution of the United States toward the rehabilitation of the war-torn world. Lend-lease activities, which *Background* began March, 1941, and lasted on until terminated by *of ERP* President Truman in August, 1945, had funnelled some $48,500,000,000 worth of American assistance into the economies of the various Allied nations in return for reverse lend-lease valued at only $7,800,000,000. In the post-war settlements, adoption of the principle that goods used up in the war effort should not be paid for reduced to millions rather than billions the obligation of the Allies to the United States; also, provisions for the repayment of these sums were made exceptionally generous, avoiding as completely as possible all actual transfers of cash. Except for a few minor nations, practically all the recipients of lend-lease aid, outside of the Russian orbit, had arranged settlements by the end of 1946, but the Soviet Union, in spite of an agreement in the spring of 1947 to negotiate, steadily refused to come to terms. The extent to which lend-lease aided the Allies in meeting their post-war problems cannot be measured, but it must have been considerable. As for Great Britain, her economy had been so closely geared to lend-lease that Congress, after lengthy consideration of the problem, voted late in 1945 to lend the British government $3,750,000,000 over a five-year period, and an additional $650,000,000 to cover the British obligation to the United States under the lend-lease agreement. The interest charged on the British loan was to be only two per cent, less than it cost the United States to borrow the money from its own people, and even this interest was to be waived when too detrimental to British exchange. Repayments of the principal were to be made in fifty equal installments, beginning in 1951.

American aid to recovery had also included substantial contributions to the United Nations Relief and Rehabilitation Administration (UNRRA), the purpose of which was to bring relief to the *UNRRA* victims of war in any area under control of the United Nations. The creation of this organization was the result primarily of American promotion, and dated back to an Allied conference held in Washington as early as 1943. The policies of UNRRA were set by a Council in which each member state was represented, but a central committee of nine — the five great powers and four others — was empowered to make emergency decisions. Administration was in the hands of a director-general and staff, the latter numbering by 1946 approximately 12,000 persons. During its lifetime UNRRA had successively three directors-general, all Americans, Governor Herbert H. Lehman of New York, Mayor Fiorello La Guardia of New York City, and Major-General Lowell W. Rooks of the United States Army. It obtained its funds from its more than forty member nations, each of which agreed on two occasions, first in March, 1944, and again in December, 1945, to contribute one per cent of its national income to the UNRRA treasury. Collections, however, were sometimes difficult, or even impossible. It was obvious from the start that the major contributions toward UNRRA would come from the United States; in actual fact 72 per cent of its funds came from this source, while 90 per cent of the food and other supplies it distributed came from American firms and factories.

During the summer and fall of 1945 UNRRA gave substantial aid to millions of starvation-threatened people in Greece, Yugoslavia, Czecho-

Dissatisfaction with UNRRA slovakia, Poland, Italy, Austria, China, and the Philippines. It also undertook to look out for the needs of the hundreds of thousands of displaced persons in the western zones of Germany and Austria, and in Italy. By 1946 other nations such as Albania, Byelorussia, the Ukraine, Finland, Hungary, and Ethiopia were sharing the benefits of UNRRA. Undoubtedly its operations were of tremendous assistance to the nations it touched, but many Americans, including high officials of the State Department, soon became acutely dissatisfied with UNRRA operations. They charged that in many instances UNRRA supplies were used by governments that received them "to feed their political supporters and starve their political enemies." In Yugoslavia, for example, there could be no doubt that Tito, the Communist dictator, had so distributed these contributions as to strengthen the hold of his régime upon his people. There were also charges of graft and maladministration, notably with respect to China, where the Chiang government seemed unable to keep UNRRA supplies out of the hands of black market operators. Further, the question was constantly raised, were countries that received aid doing all they could do to help themselves? Or were they counting on a permanent dole, mainly to be contributed by the United States? By the end of 1946 UNRRA had lost the support of the American government, and was doomed. The policy of the American State Department called for more self-help on the part of the nations concerned, and strictly American, rather than international, control of any aid given. "It is our position," said Secretary Byrnes, "that whatever the United States does in the way of relief should be done by the United States unilaterally. We want to give aid as the United States and not as a member of an international organization."

Thus, in a sense, the Marshall Plan grew out of American experience with post-war relief. The problem that confronted the United States was not how to avoid giving American aid, but rather how *Russia* to avoid having American money and supplies used to build *rejects* up hostility to the nation that provided them. The United *ERP* States was not even averse to aid for Russia and her satellites. All of them were definitely within the scope of the American offer. But the American idea was that the various nations of Europe should plan and work together for joint recovery, and it was primarily because of this condition that the Russians withdrew. If all Europe, acting as one economic unit, or any substantial part of it outside Russian domination, should begin to prosper, the chance for the spread of the Russian system would go. Communism needed despair and hopelessness as the soil from which to grow. The Marshall Plan offered the prospect of recovery instead. So, when the customary three power conference of foreign ministers, Ernest Bevin of Great Britain, Georges Bidault of France, and V. M. Molotov of Russia, met at Paris late in June, 1947, to consider the American offer, Molotov claimed that it would infringe on the sovereignty of the lesser states, and refused to have anything to do with it. Bevin and Bidault then called a conference of twenty-two European states to discuss the subject, excluding Russia and Spain, but not excluding the Russian satellites. All but the Russian-dominated nations of eastern Europe accepted the invitation, and of these Czechoslovakia at first accepted, then, on direct orders from Moscow, cancelled its acceptance.

Meeting at Paris in July, the sixteen nations that wished to take advantage of Marshall's offer appointed a Committee of European Economic Co-operation, consisting of one member from each *Congress* nation, to draw up the necessary program. Two months *supports* later this Committee reported various ways and means by *ERP* which the member-nations could help themselves, but estimated that to meet unavoidable deficits they would have to have from the United States within a four-year period the gigantic sum of $19,330,000,000. Scaled down by American scrutiny to $17,000,000,000 the sum was still so huge as to confront the Truman Administration with a tremendous task in obtaining from Congress the necessary appropriations. But public sentiment rallied to the support of "ERP," and at a special session held in November, 1947, "interim" aid of over half a billion dollars was voted to France, Italy, and Austria, with an additional $18,000,000 for China. Then the following April Congress voted $5,300,000,000 to carry the program through the coming year. The President's request for a pledge of $17,000,000,000 over a four-year period was modified to an annual appropriation, with further grants to be dependent upon the success of the program, but the evident intent of the bipartisan majority that pushed the plan through Congress was to continue the appropriations only if conditions in Europe would justify such action. To administer ERP Congress set up an Economic Co-operation Administration (ECA), at the head of which the President appointed Paul G. Hoffman, a Republican business executive from Indiana. Armed with ample funds, and backed by the good-will of the overwhelming majority of the American people, ERP went rapidly to work on the "containment" of the Russian system behind the Russian-imposed iron curtain. The hope was that in due time the sixteen co-operating nations would be sufficiently prosperous to have no further need of outside aid, and no further fear of a Communist revolution.

Evidence that ERP had made a deep impression on European minds was not long in coming. In their eagerness to obtain American aid the *European reaction* governments of France and Italy had made bold to eliminate all Communists from their cabinets, actions which led to prolonged strikes and violence on the part of the Communist-dominated unions. But the non-Communist governments stood their ground, and in both countries eventually got the upper hand. The Italian elections of April 18–19 were particularly significant. Italian Communists made the mistake of thinking that they could win in a free election, only to discover when the election was over that they had been voted down by overwhelming majorities, about 70 per cent of the electorate against them to only about 30 per cent for their "Popular Front." In France strikes and repeated cabinet crises at first crippled the efforts of the government to promote recovery, but in a political way strengthened the rightist movement headed by General de Gaulle rather than the Communists. But by the spring of 1949, the effect of American aid had so improved the economic life of both Italy and France that something akin to normal conditions seemed in sight, while progress toward economic unity in the low countries, Belgium, the Netherlands, and Luxembourg (Benelux), was heartening. Marshall's resignation as Secretary of State, which came in January, 1949, because of failing health, brought in a new Secretary, Dean Acheson, but no change of policy on the part of the United States.

As American aid began to give visible proof that it was really promoting recovery, the North Atlantic nations that felt themselves in peril from Russian aggression began also to draw together in a *The North* military way. First Great Britain and France joined with *Atlantic* the Benelux countries to create a regional system of col- *Treaty* lective defense, a course of action authorized by the United Nations charter. When the United States indicated its willingness to enter such an organization, negotiations began which ended on March 15, 1949, with the signing of the North Atlantic Treaty by twelve nations — Belgium, Canada, Denmark, France, Great Britain, Iceland, Italy, Luxembourg, the Netherlands, Norway, Portugal, and the United States. According to this pact, "armed attack against one or more" of the member nations was to "be considered an attack against them all." Further, the clear implication was that the United States would help its overseas partners to re-arm.

But the Russians were by no means idle. The establishment of the Cominform in September, 1947, was apparently meant, at least in part, as an offset to the Truman Doctrine and the Marshall Plan. *Russian* Then in February, 1948, with complete Russian support and *aggressions* connivance, the Communists seized power in Czechoslovakia, where until that time a middle-of-the-road multi-party government had been permitted to exist. Efforts were also made to discipline the Communist dictator of Yugoslavia, Marshal Tito, whom the Comintern in June, 1948, accused of deviation from the party line. But Tito, although fully cognizant of the hazards of his course, stood his ground, and refused to be erased. Just what this internal dissension meant the western world was unable to fathom, but it was evident that the solidarity of the eastern bloc of nations in opposition to the West remained unshaken. This was registered clearly when an international conference on the control of the Danube River met in Belgrade July 30, 1948. At every opportunity the seven Communist states of eastern Europe, including Yugoslavia, voted solidly against the three western powers, the United States, Great Britain, and France, to exclude all non-Danubian powers from a voice in the control of the river, and thus in effect to make Russia its mistress.

But the outstanding action taken by Russia to show her displeasure with the western world was with reference to Germany. When in the summer of 1948, despairing of ever reaching any further agreements on German affairs with the Russian authorities, the western occupation powers announced their intention of establishing a native German government for Trizonia, the intense displeasure of the Soviets was at once apparent. Russian policy called for a united Communist Germany, nothing less, with Berlin as its capital, and Russian promotion of discord and inefficiency in the four-power government had clearly been designed with that end in view. The three occupation authorities, as a step toward the union they contemplated, also issued a new currency to be used in common throughout western Germany, and in the western-occupied portion of Berlin. On the pretext that this currency reform would "place Berlin's economy and her working population in an untenable situation which only can be solved by Berlin's close connection with the eastern part of Germany," the Soviet authorities laid down a blockade against the movement of supplies from the West into Berlin, whether by rail, highway, or canal. Since there were some two millions of people in the western-occupied section of the city whose lives might depend on the continued importation of food from the West, it seemed clear that the Soviet intent was to force the western powers out of Berlin by the threat of wholesale starvation. With the western powers eliminated, nothing further would stand in the way of the Russians taking over the entire capital city — an important step toward their goal of a united Communist Germany under Russian control.

The answer of the western powers to this new Soviet approach could hardly have been anticipated by the Russians. The air-lanes to Berlin *The Air-Lift* were still open, and the western powers at once undertook to fly in the supplies necessary to feed the beleaguered Germans. Both British and American planes were used on the "Air-Lift," which within a matter of days developed an amazing efficiency. New air-fields were opened up, and soon coal to keep the people warm and even to keep the factories going was reaching Berlin by air. Hundreds of air-planes were brought from the United States to participate in the operation, and both British and American military pilots got a superb training that the Russians could hardly have overlooked. Even dense fogs and winter weather failed to stop the steady movement across the Russian zone of the all-essential cargoes. General Lucius D. Clay, the United States Military Governor in Germany, stated clearly the American position with reference to Berlin when he said "They can't drive us out by any action short of war." The Russians, however, did everything else they could think of. They withdrew their representative from the *Kommandatura*, set up a separate police in their section of Berlin, excluded the personnel of the lawful city government from the City Hall, which was within their area, and installed a German Communist of their own choosing as mayor. But in spite of all this, month after month, in good weather or bad, the air-lift continued. Eventually it was bringing to Berlin more tons of freight per day than the railroads had brought in during their normal operation. Furthermore, the Allies, in retaliation against the blockade of Berlin, established a counter-blockade on goods from Trizonia to the Russian zone of Germany, a devastating blow to the Eastern German economy.

One of the most notable results of the air-lift was the change in attitude on the part of the Germans toward the western occupational authorities. Armies of occupation are rarely popular, nor do they often *Divided* deserve to be, and dislike of their conquerors by the Ger- *Berlin* mans, whether in the East or in the West, was intense.[1] But the air-lift did much to make friends among the Germans for all who participated in it, particularly for the Americans, who bore so large a proportion of the expense, and furnished so many of the planes. With this assurance that they were not to be abandoned, the German leaders went promptly to work on the development of a constitution for the 45,000,000 Germans living in the western occupational zones. The only requirements laid on them were (1) that the new constitution be democratic, (2) that it be based on the federal principle, and (3) that civil liberties be fully guaranteed. Nor need the new constitution be regarded as merely designed for that portion of Germany under western control. If and when the Russians should permit, there would be no bar on the states in eastern Germany joining the new government. In Berlin itself, although the failure of the air-lift would mean dire retribution for all who had supported the western powers, the people in the city's western zones rallied strongly to the support of their deliverers. Eventually a divided city with two separate governments emerged. In the Russian sector, as already noted, the Communists took over, but in the western zones, at a free election held late in the year, which the Russians had urged the people to boycott, well over eighty per cent of the voters came out to register their support of anti-Communist candidates.

Meantime the western powers had exerted themselves in every possible way to induce the Russian government to accept a compromise settlement. In August, 1948, their ministers in Moscow opened *Efforts to* direct negotiations on the subject, and seemingly reached *compromise* an agreement that in return for western concession of an exclusively Russian-controlled currency in Berlin, the embargo should be lifted. But in Berlin, due to the obduracy of the Russian member of the *Kommandatura*, the implementation of this agreement broke down completely. Finally, in September, the western powers referred the whole matter to the Security Council of the United Nations, charging that it

[1] Julian Bach, *America's Germany: An Account of the Occupation* (1946); S. K. Padover, *Experiment in Germany: The Story of an American Intelligence Officer* (1946).

amounted to a threat to world peace. But here, too, every effort at agreement failed. During these proceedings, which were held in Paris, President Truman conceived the idea of sending a special mission to Moscow, headed by Chief Justice Frederick M. Vinson, but Secretary Marshall held that any such action would be an unwarranted snub for the Security Council, and the plan was abandoned. It was generally believed that the Russians no less than the western powers would have been glad to find some face-saving way out of the situation, but the trade barriers were maintained for nearly a year.

Finally, in the spring of 1949, the Russian leaders changed their tactics. Negotiations at Lake Success, New York, between a member of *End of the* the Russian delegation, Yakov Malik, and a representative *Air-Lift* of the United States Department of State, Philip Jessup, showed that the Russians were now willing to lift their blockade, if at the same time the western powers would end their counter-blockade and agree to a meeting of the Council of Foreign Ministers to discuss the whole German question. Since the western powers had been willing to accept such a settlement all along, the deal was quickly closed. All blockades were lifted May 12, 1949, and the meeting of the Council of Foreign Ministers began on May 23. Meantime, the West German constitutional convention had finished its work, and had submitted for approval of the eleven West German states its plan for a "Federal Republic of Germany." That the Russians hoped to forestall the actual establishment of such a republic was evident, but neither the western powers nor the people of Trizonia seemed disposed to alter their course.

Tension over the Berlin situation and the air-lift was heightened by the fact that 1948 was an election year in the United States. Would the *Election of* two political parties split on the foreign issue? Could *1948* Russia count on dissension in the United States as her ally in the program of expansion she had cut out for herself? It was apparent from the beginning of the campaign that most of the leaders on both sides, Republicans no less than Democrats, were determined that the bipartisan foreign policy to which they had subscribed must not be abandoned. So evident was this, that Henry Wallace early announced that he would head a third party movement in opposition to the "get-tough-with-Russia" program, which, he claimed, would eventually lead the two nations to war. In Wallace's opinion, the old Roosevelt policy of generously conceding to Russia practically everything she wanted was still the only correct policy, and he denounced the Truman administration roundly for abandoning it. He held, further, that on domestic affairs Truman had yielded to the conservatives, and he called for a revival of the New Deal philosophy of the first two Roosevelt administrations. He persuaded Senator Glen H. Taylor of Idaho to join his ticket as Vice-Presidential candidate, and with the enthusiastic cooperation of Communist and "fellow-traveler" leaders a so-called Progressive convention, held in Philadelphia late in the summer, ratified these two self-nominations. Russian sympathy for the Wallace movement was warmly and officially expressed, and the Russian leaders seemed to think that Wallace's candidacy would strike a responsive chord in American hearts.[1]

Both Republicans and Democrats held their conventions in Philadelphia, also, the Republicans in June and the Democrats in July. The Republicans felt certain of victory, for they had won the *Conventions* mid-term elections of 1946, and they were sure that the *and candidates* Wallace candidacy would cut in heavily on the Democratic vote. For a time it looked as if a strong public demand might force the Republicans to nominate General Dwight D. Eisenhower, but the popular war leader accepted instead the presidency of Columbia University, and removed himself from consideration in no uncertain terms. This left Governor Thomas E. Dewey of New York, Senator Robert A. Taft of Ohio, and ex-Governor Harold E. Stassen of Minnesota as the principal candidates. Taft appealed strongly to the old-line conservatives, and Stassen to the younger, more liberal-minded element in the party. But Dewey took pains not to offend either side unduly, and lined up the votes. He was nominated on the second ballot, and at his suggestion the convention chose Governor Earl Warren of California as his running-mate. The Republican platform, while by no means ready to abandon all the social gains made during the Roosevelt era, urged that greater responsibility should be given to the states in such matters as housing, conservation, public health, and security for the aged. It favored also "minimum" governmental controls over business, and lauded the American free enterprise system as the "mainspring of material well-being and political freedom." On the moot labor problem, it pledged the party to protect "both workers and employers against coercion and exploitation." The conservatism of these pronouncements was thinly veiled, and reflected well the point of view of the Republican majority in the Eightieth Congress.

The Democrats had little hope of victory. Some of them were so certain of Truman's defeat that they imitated the Republicans in trying to induce Eisenhower to accept their nomination, with precisely the

[1] W. B. Hesseltine, *The Rise and Fall of Third Parties from Anti-Masonry to Wallace* (1948).

same result. The more disgruntled then tried to rally around Justice
Democratic William O. Douglas of the Supreme Court, but they could
discourage- not induce him to help them. President Truman was thus
ment practically unopposed when the convention met, and was
nominated without serious opposition. The Convention experienced
some difficulty in finding anyone of prominence willing to accept second
place on a ticket that seemed certain of defeat, but at length it chose
Senator Alben Barkley of Kentucky, the venerable leader of the Democratic minority in the Senate. The chief excitement in the Democratic
convention came from a successful effort, led by Mayor Hubert Humphrey of Minneapolis, to write into the platform a plank calling on
Congress to support the President "in guaranteeing these basic and
fundamental rights: (1) The right of full and equal political participation, (2) the right of equal opportunity of employment, (3) the right of
security of person, and (4) the right of equal treatment in the services
and defense of our nation." This action was resented deeply by many
southern delegates whose states used the poll-tax and other devices,
some legal and some extra-legal, to discriminate against the Negroes,
but the platform as finally adopted carried the drastic civil rights plank.
It also denounced unsparingly the record of the Eightieth Congress,
called for the repeal of the Taft-Hartley Act, advocated an extension of
social security benefits and an increase in the minimum wage from 40
cents an hour to 75 cents, urged more adequate federal legislation on
housing, and promised strong federal support of farm prices.

On foreign policy the two platforms were in fundamental agreement.
Both supported the United Nations warmly, while condemning the
The truce on intemperate use of the veto by Russia. Both stood loyally
foreign by the foreign aid program, although the Republicans
policy wished to be more generous to China than the Democrats
had been. Both favored full recognition of the new Jewish state of
Israel. Both accepted the policy of reciprocal trade agreements as a
means of regulating the tariff. When Candidate Dewey criticized the
Democratic platform for claiming that the Democrats had originated
the bipartisan foreign policy, President Truman countered by appointing
Dewey's intimate friend and adviser, John Foster Dulles, as one of the
United States representatives to the third session of the United Nations
General Assembly, which was to open on September 24 in Paris.

As the campaign got under way all signs pointed to the certainty of
The Republican victory. Republican chances were increased
Dixiecrats when the extreme states-rights faction of the Demo-
cratic Party, which had taken such offense at the Civil Rights plank in

their party's platform, held a rump convention at Birmingham, Alabama, and nominated a separate States' Rights Democrat or "Dixiecrat" ticket, consisting of Governor J. Strom Thurmond of South Carolina for President and Governor Fielding Wright of Mississippi for Vice-President. It was apparent that this ticket would carry at least three or four states in the Lower South. All of the various public opinion polls predicted with extreme confidence the election of Dewey. Sixty-five per cent of the newspapers of the country supported the Republican candidates. Dewey himself campaigned as if he were a sure winner, avoiding controversial issues, and scarcely recognizing the existence of an opposition.

Truman, on the other hand, conducted a vigorous campaign, almost unaided. He called a special session of the Republican dominated Eightieth Congress to meet in September, right after the nominations,

"Look, No Hands!"

Dorman H. Smith for NEA Service, Inc.

[789]

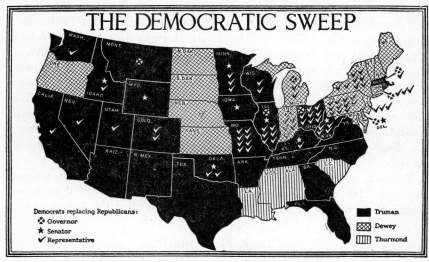

THE DEMOCRATIC SWEEP

Democrats replacing Republicans:
✪ Governor
★ Senator
✔ Representative

■ Truman
▨ Dewey
▥ Thurmond

TIME Map by V. Puglisi, Courtesy of TIME, Copyright Time Inc., 1948

Truman and asked it to put through legislation to halt rising prices, to meet the housing crisis, to protect civil rights, and to take various other steps called for by both platforms. When it adjourned without acting on his suggestions, he toured the country condemning it for its failure to deliver on promises in the Republican platform, and branded it as the worst Congress the nation had ever had. As the campaign wore on, it became apparent that the crowds were coming to hear the President, but were not coming to hear Dewey. Wallace also lost ground as the President hammered home the gains that labor had won and might still expect to win from the Democrats, and pointed out the losses it had suffered, and would continue to suffer, if the Republicans won. But most observers discounted the results of the Truman campaign. People came out just to see a President, they said, and to hear his intemperate remarks. The Wallace vote might not be as heavy as expected, but it would be heavy enough to insure Dewey's victory.

The election results were probably the greatest political upset in all American history. With 49,363,798 voters coming to the polls, more *Another Democratic landslide* than in any other election except 1940, the Republicans went down to a resounding defeat. Truman failed to capture a majority of all votes cast for President, but his share amounted to 49.5 per cent of the total to Dewey's 45.1 per cent, and 5.4 per cent for all others. The Wallace vote, due in considerable part to the consistency with which Wallace's speeches during the campaign followed the Communist party line, reached only a little over a million, less than 2.5 per cent. In the electoral college, the vote stood Truman 303, Dewey 189, Thurmond 39, Wallace 0. One elector in Tennessee, although chosen on the Truman ticket, voted for Thurmond, otherwise Truman's vote would have been one more, and Thurmond's one less. In the Congressional and State elections the Democratic victory was even more decisive; indeed, 683,382 more voters cast their ballots for state, county, and local candidates than cast their votes for President. Since, in these elections, well over fifty per cent of the total number of voters cast Democratic rather than Republican ballots, both houses of Congress were overwhelmingly Democratic, and Democratic governors were chosen in most of the states.

Looking backward, it was easier to explain why Truman won than it had been to foresee his victory. The forces of labor had rallied to his standard, and had quietly, but efficiently, got out the labor vote. Middle western farmers in historically Republican states such as Iowa and Minnesota had voted Democratic because they feared that price supports for agricultural commodities might disappear under Republican rule. The housewives of the nation, harassed by inflationary prices on every purchase they made, remembered Truman's unsuccessful struggle to maintain price ceilings, and the assurances of conservative Republicans that if price ceilings were removed self-regulation would eventually bring prices down. Furthermore, many local Democratic candidates greatly appealed to the voters, and helped the national ticket along. In Minnesota, for example, the young and popular Mayor Humphrey easily defeated his Republican opponent in the race for senator. In Illinois, Paul Douglas and Adlai E. Stevenson, candidates for senator and governor, respectively, and both dependable Democratic liberals, quite overwhelmed their old-guard Republican opponents. So it was to a great extent throughout the nation. As for the two presidential candidates, Dewey's best efforts failed to convince the voters that he was not cold and calculating, while Truman, for all his lack of dignity, at least proved himself to be thoroughly human and in touch with the common man. Most of all, the election showed that the American people were not yet ready to turn their backs on the New Deal. As Truman so effectively pointed out, that was exactly what the Eightieth Congress had tried to do, and what might be expected from the Republicans, if they succeeded in winning both the executive and the legislative branches of the government. In a sense, as many observers pointed out, the election of 1948 was the fifth straight victory for Franklin D. Roosevelt.

In spite of the spectacular Democratic triumph, the "Fair Deal" program that Truman submitted to the Eighty-first Congress failed of complete acceptance. The President's efforts to establish equality of civil rights in the South by means of federal anti-poll tax and anti-lynching laws, and provisions to insure equal job rights for all, met death at the hands of a southern Democratic filibuster. The Republicans, aided by conservative Democrats, saved the Taft-Hartley Act from repeal. The President's ambitious and expensive plans for social security expansion, which included federal aid to schools, a public welfare department in the cabinet, and compulsory national health insurance, lost out. So also did his recommendation that means be found to raise four billion dollars in additional revenue in order to balance the budget, a proposition that the Republican minority insisted would, if carried out, seriously imperil the business life of the nation. The opponents of the President made much of the trend toward "stateism," and the "welfare state," that they professed to see in the "Fair Deal," and predicted the direst results if it should succeed.

The "Fair Deal"

Nevertheless the President found it possible to praise the Eighty-first Congress on its adjournment in October, 1949, for its "rather remarkable record of achievement." It had continued rent control to July, 1950, and had voted $2,734,000,000 for slum clearance and low-rent housing. It had balked at a new method of aiding agriculture by direct subsidies, submitted by Secretary of Agriculture Charles F. Brannan, but had agreed to maintain high farm price supports and to provide adequate storage facilities for surplus crops. It had also followed the President's recommendation that minimum wages be raised from forty to seventy-five cents per hour. But it was in the field of foreign affairs that it had given Truman his greatest victories. The Hull program of reciprocal trade agreements was continued. The Marshall Plan for economic aid to Europe was maintained at the cost of $5,809,990,000. The North Atlantic Treaty was duly ratified, and, when it became known that Russia had mastered the secret of the atomic bomb, a total of $1,314,010,000 was appropriated to provide military assistance to the new Allies of the United States. Furthermore, Congress also provided the unprecedented sum of over fifteen billion dollars for national peacetime defense. Investigations into an unfortunate quarrel within the newly-created Department of National Defense over the role of the Navy in future wars marred the closing weeks of the session, but, even so, when the first session of the Eighty-first Congress finally adjourned, it had served notice on any potential enemy that the United States was emphatically on guard.

LIST OF BOOKS CITED

(With page references to original citations in the text.)

Abbott, L. F. *Impressions of Theodore Roosevelt.* 1919. 351 n.

Abell, A. E. *The Urban Impact on American Protestantism, 1865–1900.* 1943. 298 n.

Adamic, Louis. *Dynamite, the Story of Class Violence in America.* 1931. 264 n.

—— *A Nation of Nations.* 1945. 298 n.

Adams, C. F., Jr. *Charles Francis Adams.* 1900. 57 n.

—— *Railroads. Their Origin and Problems.* 1893. 169 n.

Adams, E. D. *Great Britain and the American Civil War.* 2 vols. 1925. 56 n.

Adams, Grace. *Workers on Relief.* 1939. 637 n.

Adams, J. T. *Our Business Civilization.* 1929. 602 n.

Adams, S. H. *Incredible Era. The Life and Times of Warren Gamaliel Harding.* 1939. 519 n.

Addams, Jane. *Forty Years at Hull House.* 1935. 295 n.

Albion, R. A., and Pope, J. B. *Sea Lanes in Wartime; the American Experience, 1775–1942.* 1942. 497 n.

Alexander, D. S. *Four Famous New Yorkers; the Political Careers of Cleveland, Platt, Hill, and Roosevelt.* 1923. 212 n.

Alger, R. A. *The Spanish-American War.* 1901. 329 n.

Allen, F. J. *The Shoe Industry.* 1916. 71 n.

Allen, F. L. *Only Yesterday.* 1931. 533 n., 616 n.

—— *Since Yesterday.* 1940. 616 n.

Allen, W. H. *Al Smith's Tammany Hall.* 1928. 577 n.

Alter, J. C. *James Bridger.* 1925. 127 n.

Anderson, Nels. *The Right to Work.* 1938. 637 n.

Andrews, E. B. *The United States in Our Own Time.* 1903. 205 n.

Angell, R. C. *The Campus.* 1928. 607 n.

Armes, Ethel. *The Story of Coal and Iron in Alabama.* 1910. 224 n.

Arnett, A. M. *Claude Kitchin and the Wilson War Policies.* 1937. 514 n.

—— *The Populist Movement in Georgia* (Columbia University, *Studies in History, Economics and Public Law*, CIV). 1922. 247 n.

Arnold, B. W. *History of the Tobacco Industry in Virginia from 1860 to 1894* (Johns Hopkins University, *Studies in Historical and Political Science*, Series XV, 1–2). 1897. 11 n., 224 n.

Asbury, Herbert. *The Gangs of New York; an Informal History of the Underworld.* 1928. 84 n.

Ayres, L. P. *The War with Germany, a Statistical Summary.* 1919. 501 n.

[i]

Babcock, K. C. *The Scandinavian Element in the United States.* 1914. 74 n.
Bach, Julian. *America's Germany: An Account of the Occupation.* 1946. 785 n.
Bailey, T. A. *A Diplomatic History of the American People.* 1940. 56 n.
———— *The Policy of the United States toward the Neutrals, 1917–1918.* 1942. 497 n.
———— *Theodore Roosevelt and the Japanese-American Crises.* 1934. 361 n.
———— *Woodrow Wilson and the Great Betrayal.* 1945. 514 n.
———— *Woodrow Wilson and the Lost Peace.* 1944. 514 n.
Baker, N. D. *Why We Went to War.* 1936. 486 n.
Baker, R. S. *American Chronicle: The Autobiography of Ray Stannard Baker.* 1945. 514 n.
———— *Woodrow Wilson and World Settlement.* 3 vols. 1922. 510 n.
———— *Woodrow Wilson, Life and Letters.* 8 vols. 1927–39. 440 n., 473 n.
Bakken, H. H., and Schaars, M. A. *The Economics of Co-operative Marketing.* 1937. 546 n.
Balch, Emily G. *Our Slavic Fellow Citizens.* 1910. 74 n.
Ballantine, D. S. *U.S. Naval Logistics in the Second World War.* 1947. 731 n.
Bancroft, Frederic. *The Life of William H. Seward.* 1900. 32 n.
Bancroft, H. H. *History of Nevada, Colorado, and Wyoming, 1540–1888* (1890). 118 n.
Banks, E. M. *Economics of Land Tenure in Georgia* (Columbia University, *Studies in History, Economics and Public Law,* XXIII). 1905. 228 n.
Barber, H. L. *Story of the Automobile.* 1917. 592 n.
Barck, O. T., Jr., and Blake, M. M. *Since 1900.* 1947. 380 n.
Barclay, T. S. *The Liberal Republican Movement in Missouri, 1865–1871.* 1926. 50 n.
Barnard, Harry. *Eagle Forgotten; the Life of John Peter Altgeld.* 1938. 263 n
Barnes, J. A. *John G. Carlisle, Financial Statesman.* 1931. 200 n.
Barr, Elizabeth S. "The Populist Uprising." In W. E. Connelley, ed., *A Standard History of Kansas and Kansans,* II. 1918. 249 n.
Barrett, D. C. *The Greenbacks and Resumption of Specie Payments (Harvard Economic Studies,* XXXVI). 1931. 149 n.
Barrett, J. W. *Joseph Pulitzer and his World.* 1941. 298 n.
Barrows, C. L. *William M. Evarts, Lawyer, Diplomat, Statesman.* 1941. 163 n.
Bartlett, R. J. *The League to Enforce Peace.* 1944. 514 n.
————, ed. *The Record of American Diplomacy: Documents and Readings in the History of American Foreign Relations.* 1947. 777 n.
Baruch, B. M. *American Industry in the War: A Report of the War Industries Board.* 1921. 494 n.
Bassett, J. S. *Our War with Germany.* 1919. 501 n.
Beale, H. K. *Are American Teachers Free? An Analysis of the Restraints upon the Freedom of Teaching in American Schools.* 1926. 616 n.
———— *The Critical Year; A Study of Andrew Johnson and Reconstruction.* 1930. 27 n.
———— *A History of Freedom of Teaching in American Schools.* 1941. 616 n.
Beals, Carleton. *The Crime of Cuba.* 1933. 341 n., 683 n.
———— *Porfirio Diaz, Dictator of Mexico.* 1932. 463 n.
———— *The Story of Huey P. Long.* 1935. 673 n.

[ii]

Beamish, R. J., and March, F. A. *America's Part in the World War.* 1919. 501 n.

Beard, C. A. *American Foreign Policy in the Making, 1932–1940.* 1946. 744 n.

——, ed. *Documents on the State-Wide Initiative, Referendum and Recall.* 1912. 403 n.

Beard, C. A., and Mary R. *America in Midpassage.* 1939. 589 n., 610 n.

—— *The Rise of American Civilization.* 2 vols. 1927. 25 n., 589 n.

Beard, C. A., and Smith, G. H. E. *The Future Comes.* 1934. 635 n.

Beard, Mary R. *The American Labor Movement.* 1931. 181 n.

Beardsley, F. G. *A History of American Revivals.* 1912. 109 n., 294 n.

Becker, C. L. *Cornell University: Founders and the Founding.* 1943. 114 n.

—— *How New Will the Better World Be?* 1944. 744 n.

Beer, Thomas. *Hanna.* 1929. 268 n.

—— *The Mauve Decade.* 1926. 294 n.

Bell, H. C. F. *Woodrow Wilson and the People.* 1945. 462 n.

Bemis, S. F. *A Diplomatic History of the United States.* 1936. 56 n.

Bemis, S. F., ed. *The American Secretaries of State and Their Diplomacy.* 10 vols. 1927–29. 57 n., 300 n., 311 n.

Benét, Rosemary and Stephen Vincent. *A Book of Americans.* 1933. 411 n.

Bergmann, Karl. *History of Reparations.* 1927. 567 n.

Berman, Edward. *Labor Disputes and the President of the United States* (Columbia University, *Studies in History, Economics and Public Law,* CXI). 1924. 263 n.

Bernstorff, J. H. von. *Memoirs of Count Bernstorff.* 1936. 505 n.

—— *My Three Years in America.* 1920. 476 n.

Bigelow, John. *The Life of Samuel J. Tilden.* 2 vols. 1895. 140 n.

Bigelow, John, Jr. *Reminiscences of the Santiago Campaign.* 1899. 325 n.

Binkley, W. E. *American Political Parties: Their Natural History.* 1943. 220 n.

Bishop, J. B. *Theodore Roosevelt and His Time Shown in His Own Letters.* 2 vols. 1920. 351 n.

Bishop, J. B., and Bishop, Farnham. *Goethals, Genius of the Panama Canal.* 1930. 369 n.

Bisson, T. A. *American Policy in the Far East, 1931–1940.* 1940. 708 n.

Black, J. D. *Agricultural Reform in the United States.* 1929. 571 n.

Blaine, J. G. *Twenty Years in Congress.* 2 vols. 1884–86. 192 n.

Blegen, T. C. *Building Minnesota.* 1938. 125 n.

—— *Norwegian Migration to America, 1825–1860.* 1931. 74 n.

Blegen, T. C., and Ruud, M. B. *Norwegian Emigrant Songs and Ballads.* 1936. 74 n.

Bogart, E. L. *Direct and Indirect Costs of the Great World War.* 1920. 489 n.

—— *Economic History of the American People.* 1938. 535 n.

Borchard, Edwin, and Lage, W. P. *Neutrality for the United States.* 1937. 472 n.

Borg, Dorothy. *American Policy and the Chinese Revolution, 1925–1928.* 1947. 534 n.

Bowen, C. D. *Yankee from Olympus: Justice Holmes and his Family.* 1944. 409 n.

Bowers, C. G. *Beveridge and the Progressive Era.* 1932. 333 n., 423 n.

Bowers, C. G. *The Tragic Era; the Revolution after Lincoln.* 1929. 14 n.
Boyd, W. K. *The Story of Durham.* 1925. 224 n.
Boyle, J. E. *Farm Relief: A Brief on the McNary-Haugen Plan.* 1928. 571 n.
Bradford, Gamaliel. *D. L. Moody, a Worker in Souls.* 1927. 109 n.
Bradley, David. *No Place to Hide.* 1948. 774 n.
Bradley, H. W. *The American Frontier in Hawaii: The Pioneers, 1789–1843.* 1942. 332 n.
Branch, E. D. *The Cowboy and His Interpreters.* 1926. 132 n.
——— *The Hunting of the Buffalo.* 1929. 131 n.
——— *Westward; the Romance of the American Frontier.* 1930. 117 n.
Brandeis, L. D. *Other People's Money.* 1914. 449 n.
Brant, Irving. *Storm Over the Constitution.* 1936. 678 n.
Brawley, B. G. *A Social History of the American Negro.* 1921. 6 n.
Briggs, H. E. *Frontiers of the Northwest.* 1940. 231 n.
Brissenden, P. F. *The I.W.W.: A Study in American Syndicalism.* 1919. 456 n.
Brogan, D. W. *The American Character.* 1944. 616 n.
Brookings Institution. *The Recovery Problem in the United States.* 1936. 586 n.
Brooks, J. G. *American Syndicalism; the I.W.W.* 1913. 456 n.
Brooks, R. P. *The Agrarian Revolution in Georgia, 1865–1912* (University of Wisconsin, *Bulletin*, History series, Vol. III, no. 3). 1914. 11 n.
Brooks, Van Wyck. *New England: Indian Summer, 1865–1915.* 1940. 114 n.
Brown, W. G. *The Lower South in American History.* 1902. 47 n.
Browne, W. R. *Altgeld of Illinois.* 1924. 263 n.
Bruce, A. A. *The Administration of Criminal Justice in Illinois.* 1929. 605 n.
——— *Non-Partisan League.* 1921. 546 n.
Bruce, P. A. *Rise of the New South (History of North America, XVII).* 1905. 221 n.
Bruntz, G. G. *Allied Propaganda and the Collapse of the German Empire in 1918.* 1938. 491 n.
Bryan, W. J. *A Tale of Two Conventions.* 1912. 436 n.
Bryan, W. J. and Mary B. *The Memoirs of William Jennings Bryan.* 1925. 270 n.
Bryce, James. *The American Commonwealth.* 2 vols. 1924. 158 n.
Bryn-Jones, David. *Frank B. Kellogg.* 1937. 569 n.
Buck, P. H. *The Road to Reunion.* 1937. 22 n.
Buck, S. J. *The Agrarian Crusade (Chronicles of America, XLV).* 1920. 93 n.
——— *The Granger Movement (Harvard Historical Studies, XIX).* 1913. 93 n.
Buell, R. L. *The Washington Conference.* 1922. 521 n.
Bullard, Arthur. *Mobilizing America.* 1917. 494 n.
Bullard, R. L. *Personalities and Reminiscences of the War.* 1925. 501 n.
Burgess, J. W. *Reconstruction and the Constitution, 1866–1876.* 1902. 12 n.
Burgess, W. R. *The Reserve Banks and the Money Market.* 1936. 657 n.
Burlingame, M. G. *The Montana Frontier.* 1942. 138 n.
Burlingame, Roger. *Peace Veterans.* 1932. 527 n.
Busbey, L. W. *Uncle Joe Cannon.* 1927. 427 n.
Bushnell, Sarah T. *The Truth About Henry Ford.* 1922. 592 n.
Buss, C. A. *War and Diplomacy in Eastern Asia.* 1941. 695 n.

Butcher, H. C. *My Three Years with Eisenhower.* 1946. 725 n.

Butt, A. W. *The Letters of Archie Butt.* 1924. 410 n.

────── *Taft and Roosevelt: The Intimate Letters of Archie Butt.* 2 vols. 1930. 410 n.

Byars, W. V. *An American Commoner, the Life and Times of Richard Parker Bland.* 1900. 152 n.

Byrne, P. E. *Soldiers of the Plains.* 1926. 128 n.

Byrnes, J. F. *Speaking Frankly.* 1947. 753 n.

Caldwell, R. G. *James A. Garfield.* 1931. 191 n.

Callahan, J. M. *The Alaska Purchase and Americo-Canadian Relations* (West Virginia University, *Studies in American History,* nos. 2–3). 1908. 334 n.

────── *American Foreign Policy in Canadian Relations.* 1937. 685 n.

────── *American Foreign Policy in Mexican Relations.* 1932. 465 n.

Callcott, W. H. *The Caribbean Policy of the United States, 1890–1920.* 1942. 379 n.

Capper, Arthur. *The Agricultural Bloc.* 1922. 547 n.

Carman, H. J., David, Henry, and Guthrie, P. N., eds. *The Path I Trod: The Autobiography of Terence V. Powderly.* 1940. 190 n.

Carnegie, Andrew. *Autobiography of Andrew Carnegie.* 1920. 63 n.

Carpenter, E. J. *America in Hawaii.* 1899. 302 n.

Carroll, H. K. *The Religious Forces of the United States Enumerated, Classified, and Described.* 1912. 294 n.

Carter, J. F. *The Future Is Ours.* 1939. 666 n.

Carver, T. N. *The Present Economic Revolution in the United States.* 1925. 556 n.

Cary, Edward. *George William Curtis.* 1894. 91 n.

Cash, W. J. *The Mind of the South.* 1941. 244 n.

Caskey, W. M. *Secession and Restoration in Louisiana.* 1938. 18 n.

Casson, H N. *The History of the Telephone.* 1910. 173 n.

Cater, H. D., ed. *Henry Adams and his Friends.* 1947. 298 n.

Cave, Floyd A., and others. *The Origins and Consequences of World War II.* 1948. 771 n.

Chadsey, C. E. *The Struggle Between President Johnson and Congress over Reconstruction.* 1896. 30 n.

Chadwick, F. E. *The Relations of the United States and Spain: Diplomacy.* 1909. 311 n.

────── *The Relations of the United States and Spain: the Spanish-American War.* 1911. 318 n.

Chafee, Zechariah, Jr. *Free Speech in the United States.* 1941. 298 n.

Chamberlain, John. *Farewell to Reform.* 1932. 383 n.

Chambers, F. P., Grant, C. P., and Bayley, C. C. *This Age of Conflict.* 1943. 686 n.

Chandler, A. N. *Land Title Origins: A Tale of Force and Fraud.* 1945. 244 n.

Chandler, C. DeF. *How our Army Grew Wings: Airmen and Aircraft before 1914.* 1943. 498 n.

Chase, Stuart. *Men and Machines.* 1929. 556 n.

────── *Prosperity: Fact or Myth.* 1929. 556 n.

────── *The Tragedy of Waste.* 1925. 556 n.

Cherrington, E. H. *The Evolution of Prohibition in the United States of America.* 1920. 408 n.

Child, C. J. *The German-Americans in Politics, 1914–1917.* 1939. 471 n.

Child, R. W. *Battling the Criminal.* 1926. 605 n.

Churchill, W. S. *The Second World War.* 2 vols. 1948–49. 686 n.

Claire, G. S. *Administocracy; the Recovery Laws and Their Enforcement.* 1934. 673 n.

Clapesattle, Helen. *The Doctors Mayo.* 1941. 616 n.

Clark, Badger. *Sun and Saddle Leather.* 1936. 138 n.

Clark, Champ. *My Quarter Century of American Politics.* 2 vols. 1920. 436 n.

Clark, D. E. *The West in American History.* 1937. 121 n.

Clark, J. B. *Populism in Alabama.* 1927. 247 n.

Clark, J. M. *The Costs of the World War to the American People.* 1931. 489 n.

Clark, J. S. *The Life and Letters of John Fiske.* 2 vols. 1917. 103 n.

Clark, Jane P. *Deportation of Aliens from the United States to Europe* (Columbia University, *Studies in History, Economics and Public Law*, no. 351). 1931. 537 n.

Clark, M. R., and Simon, S. F. *The Labor Movement in America.* 1938. 190 n.

Clark, T. B. *Hawaii, the Forty-ninth State.* 1947. 733 n.

Clark, T. D. Pills, Petticoats and Plows: The Southern Country Store. 1944. 244 n.

Clemen, R. A. *The American Livestock and Meat Industry.* 1923. 68 n.

Cleveland, Grover. *The Government in the Chicago Strike of 1894.* 1913. 263 n.

Cochran, T. C., and Miller, William. *The Age of Enterprise: A Social History of Industrial America.* 1942. 81 n.

Cole, A. C. *A Hundred Years of Mount Holyoke College.* 1940. 104 n.

Cole, A. H. *The American Wool Manufacture.* 2 vols. 1926. 71 n.

Coleman, C. H. *The Election of 1868.* (Columbia University, *Studies in History, Economics and Public Law*, no. 392). 1933. 40 n.

Coleman, J. W. *The Molly Maguire Riots.* 1936. 154 n.

Coleman, McAlister. *Eugene V. Debs. A Man Unafraid.* 1930. 264 n.

Commager, H. S., ed. *Documents of American History.* 1934. 21 n.

Commons, J. R. *Races and Immigrants in America.* 1907. 74 n.

Commons, J. R., and associates. *History of Labor in the United States.* 4 vols. 1918–35. 152 n., 537 n.

Conference on Unemployment. *Recent Economic Changes in the United States.* 2 vols. 1929. 535 n.

Cook, J. H. *Fifty Years on the Old Frontier.* 1923. 132 n.

Coolidge, Calvin. *The Autobiography of Calvin Coolidge.* 1929. 574 n.

Coolidge, L. A. *Ulysses S. Grant.* 1917. 43 n.

Coolidge, Mary R. *Chinese Immigration.* 1909. 156 n.

Copeland, M. T. *The Cotton Manufacturing Industry of the United States* (*Harvard Economics Studies*, VIII). 1912. 71 n.

Corbett, P. E. *The Settlement of Canadian-American Disputes.* 1937. 379 n.

Corey, Herbert. *The Truth about Hoover.* 1932. 623 n.

Corey, Lewis. *The House of Morgan.* 1930. 382 n.

Corwin, E. S. *Court over Constitution.* 1938. 678 n.

—— *The Twilight of the Supreme Court.* 1934. 678 n.

[vi]

Coulter, E. M. *The Civil War and Readjustment in Kentucky.* 1926. 36 n.
——— *The South during Reconstruction, 1865–1877.* 1947. 39 n.
Craven, W. F., and Cate, J. L., eds. *The Army Air Forces in World War II.* Vol. I. 1948. 731 n.
Crawford, J. B. *The Crédit Mobilier of America.* 1880. 53 n.
Creel, George. *How We Advertised America.* 1920. 491 n.
——— *Rebel at Large: Recollections of Fifty Crowded Years.* 1947. 491 n.
——— *The War, the World, and Wilson.* 1920. 491 n.
Croly, Herbert. *Marcus Alonzo Hanna.* 1913. 268 n.
Cross, I. B. *A History of the Labor Movement in California.* 1935. 163 n.
Crowell, Benedict, and Wilson, R. F., eds. *How America Went to War.* 6 vols. 1921. 494 n.
Cubberley, E. P. *Public Education in the United States.* 1934. 96 n.
Cudahy, John. *Archangel: The American War with Russia.* 1924. 500 n.
Cullom, Shelby M. *Report of the Committee on Interstate Commerce* (49 Cong., 1 sess., *S. Rep.* no. 46 — serial 2356). 1886. 172 n.
Curti, Merle. *Bryan and World Peace* (Smith College, *Studies in History,* XVI). 1931. 379 n.
Current, R. N. *Old Thad Stevens: A Story of Ambition.* 1942. 39 n.
Custer, G. A. *My Life on the Plains.* 1874. 128 n.

Dabney, Virginius. *Below the Potomac: A Book about the New South.* 1942. 244 n.
Daggett, Stuart. *Chapters on the History of the Southern Pacific.* 1922. 166 n.
Dakin, E. F. *Mrs. Eddy.* 1930. 110 n.
Dale, E. E. *Cherokee Cavaliers; Forty Years of Cherokee History.* 1939. 130 n.
——— *The Range Cattle Industry.* 1930. 136 n.
Daniels, Jonathan. *A Southerner Discovers the South.* 1938. 244 n., 656 n.
Daniels, Josephus. *The Life of Woodrow Wilson.* 1924. 440 n.
——— *Our Navy at War.* 1922. 444 n.
——— *The Wilson Era: Years of Peace, 1910–1917.* 1944. 462 n.
——— *The Wilson Era: Years of War and After, 1917–1923.* 1946. 514 n.
Daugherty, C. R. *Labor Under the NRA.* 1934. 645 n.
David, Henry. *The History of the Haymarket Affair.* 1936. 184 n.
Davie, M. R. *World Immigration, with Special Reference to the United States.* 1936. 188 n.
Davies, J. E. *Mission to Moscow.* 1941. 741 n.
Davis, Forrest. *The Atlantic System: The Story of Anglo-American Control of the Seas.* 1941. 485 n., 744 n.
Davis, Forrest, and Lindley, E. K. *How War Came.* 1942. 725 n.
Davis, J. P. *The Union Pacific Railway.* 1894. 75 n.
Davis, J. S. *On Agricultural Policy, 1926–1938.* 1939. 670 n.
Davis, Jerome. *The Russian Immigrant.* 1922. 189 n.
Davis, O. K. *Released for Publication; Some Inside Political History of Theodore Roosevelt and His Times.* 1925. 434 n.
Davis, Susan L. *Authentic History, Ku Klux Klan, 1865–1877.* 1924. 47 n.
Davis, W. J. *The World's Wings.* 1927. 598 n.
Davis, W. W. *The Civil War and Reconstruction in Florida* (Columbia University, *Studies in History, Economics and Public Law,* LIII). 1913. 36 n.

Dawes, C. G.   *A Journal of the Great War.*   2 vols.   1921.   503 n.

Dean, Vera M.   *The Four Cornerstones of Peace.*   1946.   771 n.

Deane, J. R.   *The Strange Alliance: The Story of our Efforts at Wartime Cooperation with Russia.*   1947.   731 n.

Dearing, C. L., and others.   *ABC of the NRA.*   1934.   643 n.

Debo, Angie.   *Prairie City: The Story of an American Community.*   1944.   244 n.

——— *Tulsa: From Creek Town to Oil Capital.*   1943.   244 n.

Dennett, Tyler.   *Americans in Eastern Asia.*   1922.   358 n.

——— *John Hay: from Poetry to Politics.*   1933.   356 n.

——— *Roosevelt and the Russo-Japanese War.*   1925.   360 n.

Dennis, A. L. P.   *Adventures in American Diplomacy, 1896–1906.*   1928.   306 n., 377 n.

——— *The Anglo-Japanese Alliance.*   1923.   379 n.

Destler, C. McA.   *American Radicalism, 1865–1901: Essays and Documents.*   1946.   259 n.

De Voto, Bernard.   *Mark Twain's America.*   1932.   106 n.

De Weerd, H. A., ed.   *Selected Speeches and Statements of General of the Army George C. Marshall.*   1945.   725 n.

Dewey, D. R.   *Financial History of the United States.*   12th ed.   1936.   59 n.

——— *National Problems, 1885–1897 (American Nation, XXIV).*   1907.   213 n.

Dewey, George.   *Autobiography of George Dewey.*   1916.   318 n.

Dewey, John.   *Democracy and Education.*   1916.   606 n.

——— *The School and Society.*   1899.   606 n.

De Witt, B. P.   *The Progressive Movement.*   1915.   434 n.

Dewitt, D. M.   *The Impeachment and Trial of Andrew Johnson.*   1903.   32 n.

Dexter, E. G.   *A History of Education in the United States.*   1904.   96 n.

Diamond, William.   *The Economic Thought of Woodrow Wilson.*   1943.   462 n.

Dick, Everett.   *The Sod-House Frontier, 1854–1890.*   1937.   231 n.

——— *Vanguards of the Frontier.*   1941.   138 n.

Dodd, W. E.   *Woodrow Wilson and His Work.*   1920.   440 n.

Dodd, W. E., Jr., and Dodd, Martha, eds.   *Ambassador Dodd's Diary, 1933–1938.*   1941.   708 n.

Dodge, G. M.   *How We Built the Union Pacific Railway.*   1910.   75 n.

Donaldson, Thomas.   *The Public Domain.*   1884.   236 n.

Donham, W. B.   *Business Adrift.*   1931.   586 n.

Dorfman, Joseph.   *Thorstein Veblen and His America.*   1934.   385 n.

Dos Passos, John.   *State of the Nation.*   1944.   736 n.

Douglas, P. H.   *Social Security in the United States.*   1936.   668 n.

Dublin, L. I.   *Health and Wealth.*   1928.   608 n.

Du Bois, W. E. B.   *Black Reconstruction.*   1935.   6 n.

Duffy, H. S.   *William Howard Taft.*   1930.   419 n.

Dulles, F. R.   *America in the Pacific.*   1932.   303 n.

——— *America Learns to Play: A History of Popular Recreation, 1607–1940.*   1940.   298 n.

——— *China and America: The Story of their Relations since 1784.*   1946.   758 n.

——— *Forty Years of American-Japanese Relations.*   1937.   522 n.

Dumba, Constantin.   *Memoirs of a Diplomat.*   1932.   474 n.

Dumke, G. S.   *The Boom of the Eighties in Southern California.*   1944.   244 n.

Dummeier, E. F., and Heflebower, R. B. *Economics with Applications to Agriculture.* 1934. 580 n.

Dumond, D. L. *America in our Time; 1896–1946.* 1947. 380 n., 631 n.

Dunn, A. W. *From Harrison to Harding.* 2 vols. 1922. 213 n.

Dunning, W. A. *Essays on the Civil War and Reconstruction.* 1904. 12 n.

—— *Reconstruction, Political and Economic, 1865–1877 (American Nation,* XXII). 1907. 2 n.

DuVal, M. P., Jr. *And the Mountains will Move: The Story of the Building of the Panama Canal.* 1947. 379 n.

Dyer, Brainerd. *The Public Career of William M. Evarts.* 1933. 163 n.

Dyer, F. L., and Martin, T. C. *Edison, His Life and Inventions.* 1929. 174 n.

Earhart, Mary. *Frances Willard: From Prayers to Politics.* 1944. 114 n.

Eastman, J. B. *Report of Federal Coordinator of Transportation* (74 Cong., 1 sess., *H. Doc.* no. 89 — serial 9920). 1934. 660 n.

—— *Report of Federal Coordinator of Transportation on Regulation of Transportation Agencies* (73 Cong., 1 sess., *S. Doc.* no. 152 — serial 9790). 1933. 660 n.

Easum, C. V. *The Americanization of Carl Schurz.* 1929. 92 n.

Eaton, A. H. *The Oregon System.* 1912. 403 n.

Ebenstein, William. *The Law of Public Housing.* 1940. 663 n.

Eckenrode, H. J. *The Political History of Virginia During Reconstruction* (Johns Hopkins University, *Studies in Historical and Political Science,* Series XXII, nos. 6, 7, 8). 1904. 16 n.

—— *Rutherford B. Hayes, Statesman of Reunion.* 1930. 143 n.

Eddy, Sherwood. *A Century with Youth: A History of the Y.M.C.A. from 1844 to 1944.* 1944. 114 n.

Eggleston, Edward. *The Hoosier Schoolmaster.* New ed. 1928. 96 n.

Eliot, C. W. *A Late Harvest.* 1924. 101 n.

Eliot, Clara. *The Farmers' Campaign for Credit.* 1927. 547 n.

Ellis, Elmer. *Henry Morse Teller, Defender of the West.* 1941. 278 n.

—— *Mr. Dooley's America: A Life of Finley Peter Dunne.* 1941. 350 n.

Ellis, L. E. *Reciprocity, 1911; A Study in Canadian-American Relations.* 1939. 432 n.

Ely, R. T. *Ground Under Our Feet — an Autobiography.* 1938. 296 n.

Engelbrecht, H. C., and Hanighen, F. C. *Merchants of Death.* 1934. 701 n.

Epstein, Abraham. *Insecurity, a Challenge to America.* 1938. 668 n.

Ernst, Morris L. *The Ultimate Power.* 1937. 678 n.

Evans, H. C., Jr. *Chile and Its Relations with the United States.* 1927. 305 n.

Evans, H. O. *Iron Pioneer. Henry W. Oliver.* 1942. 81 n.

Evans, L. H. *The Virgin Islands: From Naval Base to New Deal.* 1945. 350 n.

Ewing, C. A. M. *Presidential Elections from Abraham Lincoln to Franklin D. Roosevelt.* 1940. 736 n.

Farley, J. A. *Jim Farley's Story: The Roosevelt Years.* 1948. 736 n.

Farrar, V. J. *The Annexation of Russian America to the United States.* 1937. 350 n.

Faulkner, H. U. *American Economic History.* 1931. 535 n.

—— *The Quest for Social Justice, 1898–1914 (History of American Life,* XI). 1931. 383 n., 598 n.

Fay, S. B. *The Origins of the World War.* 2 vols. 1928. 466 n.

Federal Council of the Churches of Christ in America. *Broadcasting and the Public.* 1938. 596 n.

—— *The Prohibition Situation.* 1925. 602 n.

—— *The Public Relations of the Motion Picture Industry.* 1931. 594 n.

Ferleger, H. R. *David A. Wells and the American Revenue System, 1865–1870.* 1942. 58 n.

Ferrara, Orestes. *The Last Spanish War.* 1937. 311 n.

Fetter, F. A. *The Masquerade of Monopoly.* 1931. 453 n.

Ficklen, J. R. *History of Reconstruction in Louisiana* (Johns Hopkins University, *Studies in Historical and Political Science,* Series XXVIII, no. 1). 1910. 16 n.

Field, J. A., Jr. *The Japanese at Leyte Gulf.* 1947. 731 n.

Fine, Nathan. *Labor and Farmer Parties in the United States, 1828–1928.* 1928. 421 n., 558 n.

Finer, Herman. *Mussolini's Italy.* 1935. 690 n.

Fish, C. R. *The Civil Service and the Patronage* (*Harvard Historical Studies,* XI) 1905. 195 n.

—— *The Path of Empire* (*Chronicles of America,* XLVI). 1919. 318 n.

—— *The Restoration of the Southern Railroads* (University of Wisconsin, *Studies in the Social Sciences and History,* no. 2). 1919. 8 n.

Fitzgibbon, R. H. *Cuba and the United States, 1900–1935.* 1935. 341 n.

Fitzpatrick, Edward A. *McCarthy of Wisconsin.* 1944. 409 n.

Flack, H. E. *The Adoption of the Fourteenth Amendment* (Johns Hopkins University, *Studies in Historical and Political Science.* Extra vol. XXVI). 1908. 24 n.

Fleming, D. F. *The United States and the League of Nations, 1918–1920.* 1932. 514 n.

—— *The United States and World Organization, 1920–1933.* 1938. 522 n.

—— *The United States and the World Court.* 1945. 534 n.

Fleming, W. L. *Civil War and Reconstruction in Alabama.* 1905. 36 n.

—— *The Sequel of Appomattox* (*Chronicles of America,* XXXII). 1919. 2 n.

——, ed. *Documentary History of Reconstruction.* 2 vols. 1906–07. 12 n.

Flick, A. C. *Samuel Jones Tilden.* 1939. 140 n.

Flint, W. A. *The Progressive Movement in Vermont.* 1941. 409 n.

Florinsky, M. T. *Toward an Understanding of the U.S.S.R.* 1939. 688 n.

Flynn, J. T. *God's Gold; the Story of Rockefeller and His Times.* 1932. 176 n.

Foerster, R. F. *The Italian Emigration of Our Times* (*Harvard Economic Studies,* XX). 1919. 189 n.

Folwell, W. W. *A History of Minnesota.* 4 vols. 1921–30. 125 n.

Ford, H. J. *The Cleveland Era* (*Chronicles of America,* XLIV). 1921. 211 n.

Ford, Henry. *My Life and Work.* 1922. 592 n.

Fosdick, R. B. *American Police Systems.* 1920. 605 n.

Fossum, P. R. *The Agrarian Movement in North Dakota* (Johns Hopkins University, *Studies in Historical and Political Science,* XLIII). 1925. 249 n.

Fox, D. R., ed. *Sources of Culture in the Middle West.* 1934. 285 n.

Frankfurter, Felix. *The Case of Sacco and Vanzetti.* 1927. 538 n.

—— and Greene, Nathan. *The Labor Injunction.* 1930. 554 n.

Franklin, Fabian. *The Life of Daniel Coit Gilman.* 1910. 98 n.

[x]

Franklin, H. B.   *Sound Motion Pictures.*   1929.   594 n.
Franklin, J. H.   *From Slavery to Freedom.*   1947.   39 n.
Frederick, J. G.   *The New Deal: A People's Capitalism.*   1944.   670 n.
Frederick, J. V.   *Ben Holladay, the Stagecoach King.*   1940.   138 n.
French, J. C.   *A History of the University Founded by Johns Hopkins.*   1946.   114 n.
Fried, H. E.   *The Guilt of the German Army.*   1942.   691 n.
Fritz, P. S.   *Colorado, The Centennial State.*   1941.   138 n.
Frothingham, T. G.   *The American Reinforcement in the World War.*   1927.   501 n.
——— *The Naval History of the World War.*   3 vols.   1924–26.   497 n.
Fuess, C. M.   *Calvin Coolidge, the Man from Vermont.*   1940.   564 n.
Fuller, R. H.   *Jubilee Jim; the Life of Colonel James Fisk, Jr.*   1928.   83 n.

Gamio, Manuel.   *Mexican Immigration to the United States.*   1930.   532 n.
Gardiner, Dorothy.   *West of the River.*   1941.   138 n.
Gardiner, J. H.   *Harvard.*   1915.   101 n.
Garis, R. L.   *Immigration Restriction.*   1927.   532 n.
Garner, J. W.   *International Law and the World War.*   1920.   472 n.
——— *Reconstruction in Mississippi.*   1901.   36 n.
Garwood, Darrell.   *Artist in Iowa: A Life of Grant Wood.*   1944.   616 n.
Gaston, H. E.   *The Nonpartisan League.*   1920.   546 n.
Gates, P. W.   *The Wisconsin Pine Lands of Cornell University: A Study in Land Policy and Absentee Ownership.*   1943.   114 n.
Gayer, A. D.   *Public Works in Prosperity and Depression.*   1935.   642 n.
———, ed.   *The Lessons of Monetary Experience.*   1937.   657 n.
Gee, Wilson.   *The Place of Agriculture in American Life.*   1930.   571 n.
Geiger, G. R.   *The Philosophy of Henry George.*   1933.   241 n.
Gelber, L. M.   *The Rise of Anglo-American Friendship.*   1938.   307 n.
Gerard, J. W.   *My Four Years in Germany.*   1920.   476 n.
Giddens, P. H.   *The Beginnings of the Petroleum Industry: Sources and Bibliography.*   1941.   81 n.
——— *The Birth of the Oil Industry.*   1938.   81 n.
Gilman, D. C.   *The Launching of a University.*   1906.   296 n.
Glass, Carter.   *An Adventure in Constructive Finance.*   1927.   450 n.
Glasscock, C. B.   *The Big Bonanza; the Story of the Comstock Lode.*   1931.   118 n.
Glasson, W. H.   *Federal Military Pensions in the United States.*   1918.   207 n.
Gluck, Elsie.   *John Mitchell, Miner.*   1929.   394 n.
Glueck, Sheldon.   *The Nuremberg Trial and Aggressive War.*   1947.   757 n.
Godkin, E. L.   "Aristocratic Opinions of Democracy."   In *North American Review,* C (January, 1865).   283 n.
Goldman, E. F.   *Charles J. Bonaparte, Patrician Reformer: His Earlier Career.*   1943.   409 n.
———, ed.   *Historiography and Urbanization: Essays in American History in Honor of W. Stull Holt.*   1941.   298 n.
Gompers, Samuel.   *American Labor and the War.*   1919.   495 n.
——— *Seventy Years of Life and Labor.*   2 vols.   1925.   186 n.
Goodspeed, T. W.   *William Rainey Harper, First President of the University of Chicago.*   1928.   296 n.

[xi]

Gorgas, M. D., and Hendrick, B. J. *William Crawford Gorgas, His Life and Work.* 1924. 369 n.

Grady, H. W. *The New South.* 1890. 222 n.

Graham, Frank. *Al Smith, American: An Informal Biography.* 1945. 534 n.

Grattan, C. H. *Why We Fought.* 1929. 486 n.

Graves, W. S. *America's Siberian Adventure, 1918–1920.* ·1931. 500 n.

Greeley, Horace. *Recollections of a Busy Life.* 1930. 50 n.

Greenfield, K. R., ed. *United States Army in World War II.* 4 vols. 1947–49. 731 n.

Greenslet, Ferris. *The Lowells and their Seven Worlds.* 1946. 114 n.

Gresham, Matilda. *Life of Walter Quintin Gresham.* 2 vols. 1919. 251 n.

Grew, J. C. *Report from Tokyo.* 1942. 694 n.

———— *Ten Years in Japan.* 1944. **707 n.**

Grinnell, G. B. *The Cheyenne Indians: Their History and Ways of Life.* 2 vols. 1923. 126 n.

———— *The Fighting Cheyennes.* 1915. 126 n.

Griswold, A. W. *The Far Eastern Policy of the United States.* 1938. 360 n., 521 n.

Guggenheim, H. F. *The United States and Cuba.* 1934. 683 n.

Guichard, Louis. *The Naval Blockade, 1914–1918.* 1930. 497 n.

Gunther, John. *Inside U.S.A.* 1947. 636 n.

Haas, W. H., ed. *The American Empire: A Study of the Outlying Territories of the United States.* 1940. 350 n.

Hacker, L. M. *American Problems of Today.* 1938. 515 n., 586 n.

———— *A Short History of the New Deal.* 1934. 632 n.

Hacker, L. M., and Kendrick, B. B. *The United States Since 1865.* 1932. 587 n.

Hafen, Le Roy R. *Colorado, the Story of a Western Commonwealth.* 1933. 118 n.

Hafen, LeR. R., and Rister, C. C. *Western America: The Exploration, Settlement, and Development of the Region beyond the Mississippi.* 1941. 138 n.

Hagedorn, Hermann. *Leonard Wood.* 2 vols. 1931. 346 n.

———— *Roosevelt in the Bad Lands.* 1921. 352 n.

Hagood, Johnson. *The Services of Supply: A Memoir of the Great War.* 1927. 503 n.

Haight, Elizabeth H., and Taylor, J. M. *Vassar.* 1915. 101 n.

Hall, C. R. *Andrew Johnson, Military Governor of Tennessee.* 1916. 15 n.

Hall, W. P. *Iron out of Calvary: An Interpretative History of the Second World War.* 1946. 701 n.

Hallgren, M. A. *Seeds of Revolt.* 1933. 602 n.

Hamilton, J. G. de R. *Reconstruction in North Carolina.* (Columbia University, *Studies in History, Economics and Public Law,* LVIII). 1914. 36 n.

Hamilton, P. J. *The Reconstruction Period (History of North America, XVI).* 1906. 12 n.

Hammond, M. B. *The Cotton Industry.* 1897. 11 n., 229 n.

Haney, L. H. *A Congressional History of Railways in the United States* (University of Wisconsin, *Bulletin,* Economics and Political Science Series, III, no. 2 VI, no. 1). 2 vols. 1908–10. 170 n.

Hansen, M. L., and Brebner, J. B. *The Mingling of the Canadian and American Peoples.* 1940. 298 n.

Harbord, J. G. *The American Army in France, 1917–1919.* 1936. 501 n.

Harris, Herbert. *Labor's Civil War.* 1940. 647 n., 670 n.

Harrison, C. H. *Stormy Years.* 1935. 405 n.

Harrison, F. B. *The Corner-Stone of Philippine Independence, a Narrative of Seven Years.* 1922. 346 n.

Hart, A. B. *Salmon Portland Chase.* 1917. 41 n.

Harvey, George. *Henry Clay Frick.* 1928. 261 n.

Harvey, R. H. *Samuel Gompers.* 1935. 186 n.

Haskins, C. H., and Lord, R. H. *Some Problems of the Peace Conference.* 1920. 508 n.

Haworth, P. L. *The Hayes-Tilden Disputed Presidential Election of 1876.* 1906. 143 n.

Haynes, F. E. *James Baird Weaver.* 1919. 251 n.

—— *Social Politics in the United States.* 1924. 558 n.

—— *Third Party Movements Since the Civil War, with Special Reference to Iowa.* 1916. 149 n., 558 n.

Heck, F. H. *The Civil War Veteran in Minnesota Life and Politics.* 1941. 220 n.

Hedges, J. B. *Henry Villard and the Railways of the Northwest.* 1930. 164 n.

Heindel, R. H. *The American Impact on Great Britain, 1898–1914.* 1940. 379 n.

Henderson, G. C. *The Federal Trade Commission.* 1924. 453 n.

Hendrick, B. J. *The Age of Big Business (Chronicles of America, XXXIX).* 1920. 175 n.

—— *Life and Letters of Walter Hines Page.* 3 vols. 1922–25. 474 n.

Hepburn, A. B. *A History of Currency in the United States.* 1915. 257 n.

Hesseltine, W. B. *A History of the South, 1607–1936.* 1936. 221 n.

—— *The Rise and Fall of Third Parties from Anti-Masonry to Wallace.* 1948. 787 n.

—— *Ulysses S. Grant, Politician.* 1935. 43 n.

Hibbard, B. H. *A History of the Public Land Policies.* 1924. 236 n.

—— *Effects of the Great War upon Agriculture in the United States and Great Britain* (Carnegie Endowment for International Peace, *Economic Studies*, no. 11). 1919. 571 n.

—— *Marketing Agricultural Products.* 1921. 544 n.

Hibben, Paxton. *The Peerless Leader, William Jennings Bryan.* 1929. 270 n.

Hicks, Granville. *The Great Tradition.* 1933. 610 n.

Hicks, J. D. *The Federal Union.* 1937. 317 n.

—— *The Populist Revolt.* 1931. 245 n.

Hill, H. C. *Roosevelt and the Caribbean.* 1927. 368 n.

Hinton, H. B. *Cordell Hull: A Biography.* 1942. 685 n.

Hoag, C. L. *Preface to Preparedness: The Washington Disarmament Conference and Public Opinion.* 1941. 534 n.

Hoar, G. F. *Autobiography of Seventy Years.* 2 vols. 1903. 338 n.

Hofstadter, Richard. *The American Political Tradition and the Men who Made It.* 1948. 738 n.

—— *Social Darwinism in American Thought, 1860–1915.* 1944. 298 n.

Hollander, J. H. *War Borrowing.* 1919. 489 n.
Holborn, Louise W., ed. *War and Peace Aims of the United Nations, 1939–45.* 2 vols. 1943–1948. 742 n.
Holt, Rackham. *George Washington Carver: An American Biography.* 1943. 114 n.
Holt, W. S. *The Bureau of Public Roads.* 1923. 460 n.
—— *The Federal Farm Loan Bureau.* 1924. 458 n.
—— *Treaties Defeated by the Senate.* 1933. 331 n.
Hoover, Herbert. *American Individualism.* 1923. 578 n.
—— *The American Road.* 1938. 578 n.
—— *The Challenge to Liberty.* 1934. 578 n.
—— *The New Day.* 1928. 578 n.
—— *The State Papers and Other Public Writings of Herbert Hoover.* Edited by W. S. Myers. 2 vols. 1934. 617 n.
Hoover, Herbert, and Gibson, Hugh. *The Problems of Lasting Peace.* 1942. 736 n.
Hoover, J. E. *Persons in Hiding.* 1938. 605 n.
Hopkins, H. L. *Spending to Save; the Complete Story of Relief.* 1936. 637 n.
Horn, S. F. *Invisible Empire: The Story of the Ku Klux Klan, 1866–1871.* 1939. 47 n.
Hough, Emerson. *The Passing of the Frontier (Chronicles of America, XXVI).* 1921. 121 n.
—— *The Story of the Cowboy.* 1897. 132 n.
House, E. M. *The Intimate Papers of Colonel House.* Edited by Charles Seymour. 4 vols. 1926–28. 468 n.
House, E. M., and Seymour, Charles, eds. *What Really Happened at Paris.* 1921. 508 n.
Houston, D. F. *Eight Years with Wilson's Cabinet.* 2 vols. 1926. 444 n.
Hovey, Carl. *The Life Story of J. Pierpont Morgan.* 1911. 382 n.
Howard, J. K. *Montana: High, Wide and Handsome.* 1943. 138 n.
Howe, F. C. *The City, the Hope of Democracy.* 1905. 405 n.
—— *The Confessions of a Reformer.* 1925. 385 n.
Howe, G. F. *Chester A. Arthur.* 1934. 195 n.
Howells, W. D. *Years of My Youth.* 1916. 108 n.
Howland, Harold. *Theodore Roosevelt and His Times (Chronicles of America, XLVII).* 1921. 394 n.
Hudson, M. O. *The Permanent Court of International Justice and the Question of American Participation.* 1925. 523 n.
Hütter, J. P. *La Question de la Monnaie d'Argent aux États-Unis des Origines à 1900.* 1938. 151 n.
—— *L'Incidence Économique de la Frappe de Monnaie d'Argent aux États-Unis de 1878 à 1893.* 1938. 217 n.
Huidekoper, F. L. *The Military Unpreparedness of the United States.* 1915. 477 n.
Hull, Cordell. *The Memoirs of Cordell Hull.* 2 vols. 1948. 685 n.
Hull, W. I. *The Two Hague Conferences and Their Contributions to International Law.* 1908. 378 n.
Humphrey, S. K. *Following the Prairie Frontier.* 1931. 236 n.

Hurwitz, H. L. *Theodore Roosevelt and Labor in New York State, 1880–1900*. 1943. 409 n.

Husband, Joseph. *The Story of the Pullman Car*. 1917. 80 n.

Hutchinson, W. T. *Cyrus Hall McCormick: Harvest, 1856–1884*. 1935. 177 n.

———, ed. *The Marcus W. Jernegan Essays in American Historiography*. 1937. 298 n.

Hutton, Graham. *Midwest at Noon*. 1946. 636 n.

Ichihashi, Yamato. *The Washington Conference and After*. 1928. 521 n.

Ickes, H. L. *Back to Work: The Story of the PWA*. 1935. 642 n.

Iles, George. *Leading American Inventors*. 1912. 175 n.

Institute of American Meat Packers. *The Packing Industry*. 1924. 68 n.

Interchurch World Movement. *Report on the Steel Strike of 1919*. 1920. 537 n.

Isakoff, J. F. *The Public Works Administration* (University of Illinois, *Studies in the Social Sciences*, XXXVI). 1938. 642 n.

Ise, John. *United States Forest Policy*. 1920. 114 n.

——— *The United States Oil Policy*. 1926. 536 n.

Jacobstein, Meyer. *The Tobacco Industry in the United States*. (Columbia University, *Studies in History, Economics and Public Law*, XXVI, no. 3). 1907. 11 n.

Jackson, R. H. *The Case Against the Nazi War Criminals*. 1946. 757 n.

——— *The Nürnberg Case*. 1947. 757 n.

——— *The Struggle for Judicial Supremacy: A Study of a Crisis in American Power Politics*. 1941. 685 n.

James, Henry. *Charles W. Eliot*. 2 vols. 1930. 296 n.

——— *Richard Olney and His Public Service*. 1923. 306 n.

Jarvis, J. A. *The Virgin Islands and their People*. 1944. 350 n.

Jenkins, J. W. *James B. Duke*. 1927. 224 n.

Jenkins, Warren. "The Foreign Policy of the Chicago *Tribune*, 1914–1917." Unpublished Ph.D. Thesis, University of Wisconsin, 1942. 485 n.

Jenks, J. W., and Clark, W. E. *The Trust Problem*. 1929. 175 n.

——— and Lauck, W. J. *The Immigration Problem*. 1926. 188 n.

Jessup, P. C. *Elihu Root*. 2 vols. 1938. 417 n.

Johnson, Allen, and Malone, Dumas, eds. *Dictionary of American Biography*. 20 vols. 1928–36. 20 n.

Johnson, C. S. *The Negro in American Civilization*. 1930. 38 n.

——— and others. *The Collapse of Cotton Tenancy*. 1935. 657 n.

Johnson, E. R. *American Railway Transportation*. 1912. 170 n.

Johnson, G. W. *Roosevelt: Dictator or Democrat?* 1941. 636 n.

Johnson, H. S. *The Blue Eagle from Egg to Earth*. 1935. 643 n.

Johnson, T. L. *My Story*. 1911. 276 n.

Johnson, Walter. *The Battle Against Isolation*. 1944. 736 n.

——— *William Allen White's America*. 1947. 736 n.

Johnston, Alexander. *Ten — and Out! The Complete Story of the Prize Ring in America*. 1927. 297 n.

Jones, C. L. *Caribbean Interests of the United States*. 1916. 372 n.

——— *The Caribbean Since 1900*. 1936. 372 n.

——— *The United States and the Caribbean*. 1929. 372 n.

Jones, Eliot. *The Trust Problem in the United States.* 1921. 178 n.
Jones, H. M. *Ideas in America.* 1944. 616 n.
Jones, J. M. *Tariff Retaliation.* 1934. 583 n.
Jones, J. P., and Hollister, P. M. *The German Secret Service in America.* 1918. 483 n.
Joseph, Samuel. *Jewish Immigration to the United States from 1881 to 1910.* 1914. 189 n.
Josephson, Matthew. *The Politicos, 1865–1896.* 1938. 139 n.
—— *The President Makers: The Culture of Politics and Leadership in an Age of Enlightenment, 1896–1919.* 1940. 278 n.
—— *The Robber Barons; the Great American Capitalists, 1861–1901.* 1934. 67 n.
Joslin, T. G. *Hoover — Off the Record.* 1934. 617 n.
Joughin, G. L., and Morgan, E. M. *The Legacy of Sacco and Vanzetti.* 1948. 564 n.

Karig, Walter, and Kelley, Welbourn. *Battle Report.* 1944. 731 n.
Kavanagh, M. A. *The Criminal and His Allies.* 1928. 605 n.
Keim, Jeannette. *Forty Years of German-American Political Relations.* 1919. 320 n.
Keith, J. A. H., and Bagley, W. C. *The Nation and the Schools.* 1920. 460 n.
Kelly, F. C. *The Wright Brothers.* 1943. 616 n.
Kelly, R. L. *Tendencies in College Administration.* 1925. 607 n.
Kendrick, B. B. *The Journal of the Joint Committee of Fifteen on Reconstruction* (Columbia University, *Studies in History, Economics and Public Law,* LXII, whole no. 150). 1914. 24 n.
Kennan, George. *E. H. Harriman: A Biography.* 1922. 388 n.
Kennedy, J. F. *Why England Slept.* 1940. 696 n.
Kennedy, J. P. *I'm for Roosevelt.* 1936. 674 n.
Kent, F. R. *Political Behavior.* 1928. 602 n.
Keppel, F. P. *Columbia.* 1914. 101 n.
Kinsley, Philip. *The Chicago Tribune: Its First Hundred Years.* Vol. II, 1865–1880. 1945. 298 n.
Kirk, G. L. *Philippine Independence.* 1936. 345 n.
Kirkland, E. C. *A History of American Economic Life.* 1932. 535 n.
Kirkpatrick, J. E. *The American College and Its Rulers.* 1926. 607 n.
Kleinsorge, P. L. *The Boulder Canyon Project: Historical and Economic Aspects.* 1941. 636 n.
Klinkhamer, Sister M. C. *Edward Douglas White, Chief Justice of the United States.* 1943. 409 n.
Knauth, O. W. *The Policy of the United States Toward Industrial Monopoly* (Columbia University, *Studies in History, Economics and Public Law,* LVI). 1914. 452 n.
Knight, E. W. *The Influence of Reconstruction on Education in the South.* 1913. 39 n.
—— *Public Education in the South.* 1922. 97 n.
Knoles, G. H. *The Presidential Campaign and Election of 1892.* 1942. 259 n.
Kohlsaat, H. H. *From McKinley to Harding.* 1923. 276 n.
Kolbe, P. R. *The Colleges in War Time and After.* 1919. 496 n.

Konefsky, S. J.   *Chief Justice Stone and the Supreme Court.*   1945.   685 n.

Kraus, Michael.   *A History of American History.*   1937.   298 n.

Kreider, Carl.   *The Anglo-American Trade Agreement: A Study of British and American Commercial Policies, 1934–1939.*   1943.   683 n.

Krout, J. A.   *The Origins of Prohibition.*   1925.   408 n.

Kuhlmann, C. B.   *The Development of the Flour-milling Industry in the United States.*   1929.   70 n.

La Farge, Oliver, ed.   *The Changing Indian.*   1942.   670 n.

La Follette, Robert M.   *La Follette's Autobiography.*   1913.   401 n., 423 n.

Landon, A. M.   *America at the Crossroads.*   1936.   675 n.

Lane, Anne W., and Wall, Louise H.   *The Letters of Franklin K. Lane, Personal and Political.*   1922.   444 n.

Lanfear, V. W.   *Business Fluctuations and the American Labor Movement, 1915–1922* (Columbia University, *Studies in History, Economics and Public Law,* no. 247).   1924.   537 n.

Langford, N. P.   *Vigilante Days and Ways.*   1912.   123 n.

Langsam, W. C.   *The World Since 1914.*   6th ed.   1948.   686 n.

Lansing, Robert.   *The Big Four and Others of the Peace Conference.*   1921.   508 n.

——— *War Memoirs of Robert Lansing, Secretary of State.*   1935.   474 n.

Larson, Henrietta M.   *Jay Cooke: Private Banker* (*Harvard Studies in Business History,* II).   1936.   59 n.

Lasswell, H. D.   *Propaganda Technique in the World War.*   1927.   483 n.

Latané, J. H.   *America as a World Power, 1897–1907* (*American Nation,* XXV).   1907.   318 n.

——— *From Isolation to Leadership.*   1923.   365 n.

——— *A History of American Foreign Policy.*   1927.   299 n.

Lattimore, Owen.   *Manchuria, Cradle of Conflict.*   1935.   694 n.

Lauck, W. J.   *The Causes of the Panic of 1893.*   1907.   255 n.

Laughlin, J. L.   *The History of Bimetallism in the United States.*   1892.   149 n.

Lawrence, David.   *The True Story of Woodrow Wilson.*   1924.   440 n.

Lawrence, J. E., ed.   *Fighting Liberal: The Autobiography of George W. Norris.*   1945.   564 n.

Leech, Harper, and Carroll, John.   *Armour and his Times.*   1938.   81 n.

Lester, J. C., and Wilson, D. L.   *Ku Klux Klan, Its Origin, Growth and Disbandment.*   1905.   47 n.

Letiche, J. M.   *Reciprocal Trade Agreements in World Economy.*   1948.   685 n.

Leupp, F. E.   *The Indian and His Problem.*   1910.   128 n.

Levinson, Edward.   *Labor on the March.*   1938.   647 n.

Lewis, Oscar.   *The Big Four; the Story of Huntington, Stanford, Hopkins, and Crocker.*   1938.   75 n.

Lewis, W. D.   *The Life of Theodore Roosevelt.*   1919.   351 n.

Liggett, Hunter.   *Commanding an American Army: Recollections of the World War.*   1925.   501 n.

Liggett, W. W.   *The Rise of Herbert Hoover.*   1932.   623 n.

Lilienthal, D. E.   *TVA; Democracy on the March.*   1944.   670 n.

Lind, A. W.   *Hawaii's Japanese.*   1946.   733 n.

Lindbergh, C. A.   *"We."*   1927.   598 n.

Lindley, Betty and E. K.   *A New Deal for Youth.*   1938.   640 n.

Lindley, E. K. *Half Way with Roosevelt.* 1936. 671 n.
———— *The Roosevelt Revolution: First Phase.* 1933. 635 n.
Lindsay, Charles. *The Big Horn Basin* (University of Nebraska, *University Studies*, XXVIII–XXIX). 1932. 137 n.
Lindsey, Almont. *The Pullman Strike.* 1942. 278 n.
Link, A. S. *Wilson: The Road to the White House.* 1947. 462 n.
Lippmann, Walter. *The Method of Freedom.* 1934. 635 n.
———— *A Preface to Morals.* 1929. 602 n.
———— *The Supreme Court, Independent or Controlled?* 1937. 678 n.
———— *U.S. Foreign Policy.* 1943. 744 n.
———— *U.S. War Aims.* 1944. 744 n.
Lloyd, Caro. *Henry Demarest Lloyd.* 2 vols. 1912. 382 n.
Lloyd, H. D. *Wealth Against Commonwealth.* 1936. 382 n.
Lloyd George, David. *Memoirs of the Peace Conference.* 2 vols. 1939. 510 n.
———— *War Memoirs.* 6 vols. 1933–37. 500 n.
Locklin, D. P. *Economics of Transportation.* 1938. 524 n.
Lockmiller, D. A. *Magoon in Cuba.* 1938. 341 n.
Lodge, H. C. *The Senate and the League of Nations.* 1925. 514 n.
Lomax, J. A. *Cowboy Songs and Other Frontier Ballads.* 1910. 138 n.
———— *Songs of the Cattle Trail and Cow Camp.* 1919. 138 n.
Lombardi, John. *Labor's Voice in the Cabinet: A History of the Department of Labor from Its Origin to 1921.* 1942. 409 n.
Long, J. C. *Bryan, The Great Commoner.* 1928. 270 n.
Long, J. D. *The New American Navy.* 2 vols. 1903. 315 n.
Lonn, Ella. *Reconstruction in Louisiana after 1868.* 1918. 36 n.
Looker, Earle. *The American Way, Franklin Roosevelt in Action.* 1933. 671 n.
Lorwin, L. L. *The American Federation of Labor.* 1933. 186 n.
Loud, G. C. *Evangelized America.* 1928. 294 n.
Lowell, Amy. *Tendencies in Modern American Poetry.* 1917. 610 n.
Lowes, J. L. *Convention and Revolt in Poetry.* 1919. 610 n.
Ludwig, Emil. *Roosevelt.* 1938. 626 n.
Lutz, H. L. *Public Finance.* 1936. 672 n.
Lynch, D. T. *"Boss" Tweed; the Story of a Grim Generation.* 1927. 89 n.
Lynd, R. S. and Helen M. *Middletown.* 1929. 602 n.
———— *Middletown in Transition.* 1937. 602 n.
Lyon, L. S., and others. *The National Recovery Administration.* 1935. 643 n.

McAdoo, Eleanor Wilson. *The Woodrow Wilsons.* 1937. 440 n.
McAdoo, W. G. *Crowded Years.* 1931. 444 n.
McCain, W. D. *The United States and the Republic of Panama.* 1937. 368 n., 784 n.
McCaleb, W. F. *Theodore Roosevelt.* 1931. 415 n.
McCall, S. W. *Life of Thomas Brackett Reed.* 1914. 214 n.
———— *Thaddeus Stevens.* 1899. 19 n.
McCarthy, C. H. *Lincoln's Plan of Reconstruction.* 1901. 12 n.
McCarthy, Charles. *The Wisconsin Idea.* 1912. 402 n.
McClure, S. S. *My Autobiography.* 1914. 383 n.
McCulloch, Hugh. *Men and Measures of Half a Century.* 1888. 41 n.
MacDonald, William. *The Menace of Recovery.* 1934. 635 n.

McElroy, Robert. *Grover Cleveland.* 2 vols. 1923. 257 n.

McGinty, G. W. *Louisiana Redeemed: The Overthrow of Carpetbag Rule, 1876–1880.* 1941. 58 n.

McGrath, J. S., and Delmont, J. J. *Floyd Björnsterne Olson; Minnesota's Greatest Liberal Governor.* 1937. 681 n.

Mack, E. M. *Nevada: A History of the State from the Earliest Times through the Civil War.* 1936. 138 n.

MacKay, K. C. *The Progressive Movement of 1924.* 1947. 564 n.

McKee, Irving. *"Ben-Hur" Wallace.* 1947. 298 n.

Mackenzie, Catherine. *Alexander Graham Bell, the Man Who Contracted Space.* 1928. 173 n.

MacLaren, Malcolm. *The Rise of the Electrical Industry during the Nineteenth Century.* 1943. 190 n.

McMaster, J. B. *The United States in the World War.* 2 vols. 1918–20. 501 n.

McMurry, D. L. *Coxey's Army.* 1929. 266 n.

MacVeagh, Rogers. *The Transportation Act, 1920: Its Sources, History, and Text.* 1923. 524 n.

McVey, F. L. *The Populist Movement* (American Economic Association, *Economic Studies*, I). 1896. 245 n.

Mahan, A. T. *From Sail to Steam; Recollections of Naval Life.* 1907. 314 n.

—— *Lessons of the War with Spain.* 1899. 349 n.

Malin, J. C. *The United States after the World War.* 1930. 515 n.

—— *Winter Wheat in the Golden Belt of Kansas: A Study in Adaptation to Subhumid Geographical Environment.* 1944. 244 n.

Marshall, G. C. *Biennial Report of the Chief of Staff of the United States Army.* 1941–45. 725 n.

Marshall, James. *Santa Fe: The Railroad that Built an Empire.* 1945. 190 n.

Martin, R. C. *The People's Party in Texas* (University of Texas, *Bulletin*, no. 3308). 1933. 247 n.

Mason, A. T. *Brandeis: A Free Man's Life.* 1946. 685 n.

—— *Bureaucracy Convicts Itself: The Ballinger-Pinchot Controversy of 1910.* 1941. 427 n.

—— *Organized Labor and the Law.* 1925. 554 n.

Mayo, Katherine. *Soldiers, What Next!* 1934. 527 n.

—— *That Damn Y.* 1920. 490 n.

Mecklin, J. M. *The Ku Klux Klan.* 1924. 539 n.

Merz, Charles. *The Dry Decade.* 1931. 602 n.

Meyer, B. H. *A History of the Northern Securities Case* (University of Wisconsin, *Bulletin*, Economics and Political Science Series, I). 1906. 386 n.

Mezerik, A. G. *The Revolt of the South and West.* 1946. 636 n.

Milbank, Jeremiah, Jr. *The First Century of Flight in America: An Introductory Survey.* 1943. 616 n.

Miles, N. A. *Serving the Republic.* 1911. 128 n.

Miller, D. H. *The Drafting of the Covenant.* 2 vols. 1928. 510 n.

—— *The Peace Pact of Paris.* 1928. 569 n.

Miller, F. T. *History of World War II.* 1945. 701 n.

Millis, Walter. *The Martial Spirit; a Study of Our War with Spain.* 1931. 318 n.

—— *Road to War: America, 1914–17.* 1935. 486 n.

Millis, Walter. *This is Pearl! The United States and Japan—1941*. 1947. 731 n.
Milmine, Georgine. *The Life of Mary Baker G. Eddy and the History of Christian Science*. 1909. 110 n.
Milton, G. F. *The Age of Hate; Andrew Johnson and the Radicals*. 1930. 14 n.
Mitchell, Alice M. *Children and Movies*. 1929. 594 n.
Mitchell, Broadus. *Depression Decade*. 1947. 636 n.
——— *The Rise of the Cotton Mills in the South*. 1921. 223 n.
Mitchell, Broadus, and Mitchell, G. S. *The Industrial Revolution in the South*. 1930. 223 n.
Mitchell, W. C. *A History of the Greenbacks*. 1903. 43 n.
Mixer, Knowlton. *Porto Rico*. 1926. 347 n.
Mock, J. R., and Larson, Cedric. *Words That Won the War*. 1939. 491 n.
Montague, G. H. *The Rise and Progress of the Standard Oil Company*. 1903. 67 n.
Moody, John. *The Masters of Capital (Chronicles of America, XLI)*. 1921. 175 n.
——— *The Railroad Builders (Chronicles of America, XXXVIII)*. 1919. 77 n.
——— *The Truth About the Trusts*. 1904. 178 n.
Moore, Arthur. *The Farmer and the Rest of Us*. 1945. 670 n.
Moore, Charles. *Daniel H. Burnham*. 1921. 279 n.
Moore, J. B. *The Principles of American Diplomacy*. 1918. 299 n.
Morgan, A. E. *Edward Bellamy*. 1944. 421 n.
Morgenstern, George. *Pearl Harbor: The Story of the Secret War*. 1947. 731 n.
Morison, E. E. *Admiral Sims and the Modern American Navy*. 1942. 497 n.
Morison, S. E. *History of U.S. Naval Operations in World War II*. 3 vols. 1947–48. 731 n.
Morrissey, Alice M. *The American Defense of Neutral Rights, 1914–1917*. 1939. 472 n.
Moulton, H. G. *Financial Organization and the Economic System*. 1938. 657 n.
Moulton, H. G., and others. *The American Transportation Problem*. 1933. 524 n., 660 n.
Moulton, H. G., and Pasvolsky, Leo. *War Debts and World Prosperity*. 1932. 566 n.
——— *World War Debt Settlement*. 1926. 566 n.
Mowry, George E. *Theodore Roosevelt and the Progressive Movement*. 1946. 434 n.
Munro, D. G. *The Five Republics of Central America*. 1918. 433 n.
Muzzey, D. S. *James G. Blaine*. 1934. 192 n.
——— *The United States of America*. 2 vols. 1933. 402 n.
Myers, Gustavus. *History of the Great American Fortunes*. 3 vols. 1910. 83 n.
Myers, W. S. *The Foreign Policies of Herbert Hoover, 1929–1933*. 1940. 581 n.
———, ed. *State Papers and Other Public Writings of Herbert Hoover*. 2 vols. 1934. 617 n.
Myers, W. S., and Newton, W. H. *The Hoover Administration: A Documented Narrative*. 1936. 581 n., 619 n.
Myrdal, Gunnar. *An American Dilemma: The Negro Problem and Modern Democracy*. 2 vols. 1944. 564 n.

National Bureau of Economic Research, Inc. *Income in the United States, Its Amount and Distribution, 1909–1919.* 1921. 382 n.
National Industrial Conference Board. *The American Merchant Marine Problem.* 1929. 526 n., 662 n.
—— *The Inter-Ally Debts and the United States.* 1925. 566 n.
—— *The World War Veterans and the Federal Treasury.* 1932. 527 n.
Nearing, Scott, and Freeman, Joseph. *Dollar Diplomacy.* 1925. 433 n.
Nelson, B. H. *The Fourteenth Amendment and the Negro Since 1920.* 1946. 564 n.
Nelson, D. M. *Arsenal of Democracy: The Story of American War Production.* 1946. 736 n.
Nevins, Allan. *Abram S. Hewitt, with Some Account of Peter Cooper.* 1935. 62 n.
—— *The Emergence of Modern America, 1865–1878 (History of American Life, VIII).* 1927. 60 n.
—— *Grover Cleveland: a Study in Courage.* 1932. 203 n., 257 n.
—— *Hamilton Fish: The Inner History of the Grant Administration.* 1936. 55 n.
—— *Henry White; Thirty Years of American Diplomacy.* 1930. 364 n., 377 n.
—— *John D. Rockefeller.* 2 vols. 1940. 81 n.
——, ed. *Letters of Grover Cleveland, 1850–1908.* 1933. 203 n.
——, ed. *Selected Writings of Abram S. Hewitt.* 1937. 62 n.
Nevins, Allan, and Hacker, L. M. *The United States and Its Place in World Affairs, 1918–43.* 1943. 736 n.
Newell, F. H. *Irrigation in the United States.* 1902. 396 n.
Nichols, Jeannette P. *Alaska.* 1924. 334 n.
Nicolson, Harold. *Dwight Morrow.* 1935. 465 n.
Nixon, R. B. *Henry W. Grady, Spokesman of the New South.* 1943. 244 n.
Nordhoff, Charles. *The Cotton States in the Spring and Summer of 1875.* 1876. 38 n.
Notter, Harley. *The Origins of the Foreign Policy of Woodrow Wilson.* 1937. 473 n.
Nourse, E. G. *American Agriculture and the European Market.* 1924. 540 n.
—— *Marketing Agreements under the A.A.A.* 1935. 648 n.
——, and associates. *America's Capacity to Produce.* 1934. 580 n.
—— *Three Years of the Agricultural Adjustment Administration.* 1937. 648 n.
Nowlin, W. F. *The Negro in American National Politics.* 1931. 38 n.
Noyes, A. D. *Forty Years of American Finance.* 1909. 147 n.

Oberholtzer, E. P. *A History of the United States Since the Civil War.* 5 vols. 1917–37. 2 n., 89 n., 155 n., 156 n.
—— *Jay Cooke, Financier of the Civil War.* 2 vols. 1907. 59 n.
—— *The Referendum in America.* 1911. 403 n.
O'Connor, Harvey. *Mellon's Millions.* 1933. 550 n.
O'Gara, Gordon C. *Theodore Roosevelt and the Rise of the Modern Navy.* 1943. 379 n.
Ogburn, W. F., ed. *Social Change and the New Deal.* 1934. 671 n.
Ogden, Rollo, ed. *Life and Letters of Edwin Lawrence Godkin.* 2 vols. 1907. 90 n.

Ogg, F. A. *National Progress, 1907–1917 (American Nation, XXVII).* 1918. 414 n.

Ogle, R. H. *Federal Control of the Western Apaches, 1848–1886.* 1940. 138 n.

Olcott, C. S. *The Life of William McKinley.* 2 vols. 1916. 217 n.

Older, Fremont. *My Own Story.* 1925. 405 n.

Oliver, J. W. *History of the Civil War Military Pensions* (University of Wisconsin, *Bulletin*, History Series, IV). 1917. 207 n.

Olson, J. C. *J. Sterling Morton.* 1942. 244 n.

Orcutt, W. D. *Burrows of Michigan and the Republican Party.* 2 vols. 1917. 210 n.

Orth, S. P. *The Armies of Labor (Chronicles of America, XL).* 1919. 181 n.

────── *The Boss and the Machine (Chronicles of America, XLIII).* 1919. 211 n.

────── *Our Foreigners (Chronicles of America, XXV).* 1920. 74 n.

Osgood, E. S. *The Day of the Cattleman.* 1929. 136 n.

O'Shaughnessy, Edith. *Intimate Pages of Mexican History.* 1920. 463 n.

Ostrogorski, M. I. *Democracy and the Organization of Political Parties.* 2 vols. 1902. 250 n.

Ostrolenk, Bernhard. *The Surplus Farmer.* 1932. 580 n.

Otken, C. H. *The Ills of the South.* 1894. 229 n.

Overton, R. C. *Burlington West: A Colonization History of the Burlington Railroad.* 1941. 190 n.

Padelford, N. J. *The Panama Canal in Peace and War.* 1942. 379 n.

Padover, S. K. *Experiment in Germany: The Story of an American Intelligence Officer.* 1946. 785 n.

Paine, A. B. *Mark Twain: a Biography.* 3 vols. 1912. 106 n.

────── *A Short Life of Mark Twain.* 1920. 106 n.

────── *Thomas Nast, His Period and His Pictures.* 1904. 89 n.

Painter, Floy R. *That Man Debs and His Life Work.* 1929. 264 n.

Palmer, Frederick. *America in France.* 1918. 501 n.

────── *Bliss, Peacemaker: The Life and Letters of General Tasker Howard Bliss.* 1934. 508 n.

────── *Newton D. Baker: America at War.* 2 vols. 1931. 494 n.

────── *Our Greatest Battle.* 1919. 501 n.

────── *This Man Landon.* 1936. 675 n.

Pao, M. J. *The Open Door Doctrine in Relation to China.* 1923. 379 n.

Parish, J. C. *The Persistence of the Westward Movement and Other Essays.* 1943. 244 n.

Parks, E. T. *Colombia and the United States, 1765–1934.* 1935. 368 n.

Pattee, F. L. *A History of American Literature Since 1870.* 1915. 108 n.

────── *The New American Literature, 1890–1930.* 1930. 610 n.

Patton, J. W. *Unionism and Reconstruction in Tennessee, 1860–1869.* 1934. 16 n.

Paul, R. W. *The Abrogation of the Gentlemen's Agreement.* 1936. 379 n.

Paxson, F. L. *American Democracy and the World War.* 2 vols. 1936–39. 442 n., 470 n., 494 n.

────── *History of the American Frontier, 1763–1893.* 1924. 117 n.

────── *The Last American Frontier.* 1910. 121 n.

────── *Postwar Years: Normalcy, 1918–1923.* 1948. 534 n.

Paxson, F. L.   *Recent History of the United States.*   1937.   104 n.
——— *When the West Is Gone.*   1930.   285 n.
Peake, O. B.   *The Colorado Range Cattle Industry.*   1937.   138 n.
Peck, H. T.   *Twenty Years of the Republic, 1885–1905.*   1907.   205 n., 271 n.
Peck, M. G.   *Carrie Chapman Catt: A Biography.*   1944.   114 n.
Peek, G. N., and Crowther, Samuel.   *Why Quit Our Own.*   1936.   571 n.
Peel, R. V., and Donnelly, T. C.   *The 1928 Campaign.*   1931.   577 n.
——— *The 1932 Campaign.*   1935.   624 n.
Peirce, P. S.   *The Freedmen's Bureau* (University of Iowa, *Studies in Sociology, Economics, Politics and History,* III, no. 1).   1904.   7 n.
Pelzer, Louis.   *The Cattlemen's Frontier.*   1936.   138 n.
Perkins, Dexter.   *America and Two Wars.*   1944.   736 n.
——— *The Monroe Doctrine, 1867–1907.*   1937.   306 n.
Perkins, Frances.   *The Roosevelt I Knew.*   1946.   636 n.
Perlman, Selig.   *A History of Trade Unionism in the United States.*   1922.   180 n.
Perry, R. B.   *Puritanism and Democracy.*   1944.   736 n.
Pershing, J. J.   *My Experiences in the World War.*   2 vols.   1931.   500 n.
Peterson, H. C.   *Propaganda for War.*   1939.   483 n.
Pettigrew, R. F.   *Imperial Washington.*   1922.   338 n.
Phelps, Mary M.   *Kate Chase, Dominant Daughter; the Life Story of a Brilliant Woman and Her Famous Father.*   1935.   41 n.
Pierce, E. L.   *Memoir and Letters of Charles Sumner.*   4 vols.   1877–93.   20 n.
Pike, J. S.   *The Prostrate State: South Carolina under Negro Government.*   1935.   38 n.
Pinchot, Gifford.   *The Fight for Conservation.*   1910.   427 n.
Pomeroy, E. S.   *The Territories and the United States, 1861–1890: Studies in Colonial Administration.*   1947.   244 n.
Porteus, S. D.   *And Blow not the Trumpet, a Prelude to Peril.*   1947.   733 n.
Post, L. W.   *The Challenge of Housing.*   1938.   663 n.
Potwin, M. A.   *Cotton Mill People of the Piedmont* (Columbia University, *Studies in History, Economics and Public Law,* no. 291).   1927.   225 n.
Powderly, T. V.   *Thirty Years of Labor.*   1889.   181 n.
Powell, L. P.   *Mary Baker Eddy.*   1930.   110 n.
Pratt, J. W.   *Expansionists of 1898.*   1936.   302 n.
President's Research Committee on Social Trends.   *Recent Social Trends in the United States.*   2 vols.   1933.   589 n.
Pringle, H. F.   *Alfred E. Smith: A Critical Study.*   1927.   577 n.
——— *The Life and Times of William Howard Taft.*   2 vols.   1939.   419 n., 423 n., 434 n.
——— *Theodore Roosevelt.*   1931.   351 n., 380 n., 434 n.
Puleston, W. D.   *Mahan: The Life and Work of Captain Alfred Thayer Mahan, U.S.N.*   1939.   332 n.
Pyle, J. G.   *The Life of James J. Hill.*   2 vols.   1917.   168 n., 388 n.
Pyre, J. F. A.   *Wisconsin.*   1920.   101 n.

Qualey, C. C.   *Norwegian Settlement in the United States.*   1938.   74 n.
Quick, Herbert.   *One Man's Life; an Autobiography.*   1925.   96 n.
Quiett, G. C.   *Pay Dirt, a Panorama of American Gold Rushes.*   1936.   120 n.
——— *They Built the West.*   1934.   77 n.

Quigley, H. S., and Blakeslee, G. H.   *The Far East: An International Survey.*
1939.   694 n.

Quinn, A. H.   *American Fiction.*   1936.   610 n.

—————— *History of the American Drama from the Civil War to the Present Day.*
1936.   636 n.

Ramsdell, C. W.   *Reconstruction in Texas* (Columbia University, *Studies in
History, Economics and Public Law*, XXXVI).   1910.   36 n.

Randall, J. G.   *The Civil War and Reconstruction.*   1937.   2 n.

Raney, W. F.   *Wisconsin, a Story of Progress.*   1940.   681 n.

Raper, A. F. and Reid, I. DeA.   *Sharecroppers All.*   1941.   244 n.

Ratner, Sidney.   *American Taxation: Its History as a Social Force in Democracy.*
1942.   670 n.

Rauch, Basil.   *The History of the New Deal, 1933–1938.*   1944.   631 n.

Ravage, M. E.   *The Story of Teapot Dome.*   1924.   533 n.

Redfield, W. C.   *With Congress and Cabinet.*   1924.   444 n.

Reeve, J. E.   *Monetary Reform Movements: A Survey of Recent Plans and Panaceas.*   1943.   670 n.

Regier, C. C.   *The Era of the Muckrakers.*   1932.   383 n.

Reid, J. G.   *The Manchu Abdication and the Powers, 1908–1912.*   1935.   433 n.

Reuter, Bertha A.   *Anglo-American Relations During the Spanish-American War.*
1924.   320 n.

Rhodes, J. F.   *History of the United States from the Compromise of 1850.*   9 vols.
1900–28.   12 n., 89 n., 155 n.

—————— *The McKinley and Roosevelt Administrations, 1897–1909.*   1922.   276 n.

Richards, H. I.   *Cotton and the A.A.A.*   1936.   656 n.

Richardson, L. B.   *William E. Chandler, Republican.*   1940.   163 n.

Riegel, R. E.   *America Moves West.*   1930.   117 n.

—————— *The Story of the Western Railroads.*   1926.   77 n.

Ripley, W. Z.   *Main Street and Wall Street.*   1927.   586 n.

—————— *Railroads: Finance and Organization.*   1915.   172 n.

—————— *Railroads: Rates and Regulation.*   1912.   172 n.

—————— *Trusts, Pools, and Corporations.*   1916.   178 n.

Rippy, J. F.   *America and the Strife of Europe.*   1938.   330 n.

—————— *The Capitalists and Colombia.*   1931.   368 n.

—————— *The Caribbean Danger Zone.*   1940.   379 n.

—————— *Latin America in World Politics.*   1938.   372 n.

—————— *The United States and Mexico.*   1931.   465 n.

Rister, C. C.   *Border Command: General Phil Sheridan in the West.*   1944.
138 n.

—————— *Land Hunger: David L. Payne and the Oklahoma Boomers.*   1942.   244 n.

—————— *Southern Plainsmen.*   1938.   244 n.

Robinson, E. E.   *The New United States.*   1946.   636 n.

—————— *The Presidential Vote, 1896–1932.*   1934.   278 n., 628 n.

—————— *The Presidential Vote, 1936.*   1940.   685 n.

—————— *They Voted for Roosevelt: the Presidential Vote, 1932–1944.*   1947.
738 n.

Robinson, E. E., and West, V. J.   *The Foreign Policy of Woodrow Wilson.*   1917.
473 n.

Robinson, H. M. *Fantastic Interim.* 1943. 534 n.
Robinson, W. A. *Thomas B. Reed, Parliamentarian.* 1930. 214 n.
Rollins, P. A. *The Cowboy.* 1922. 132 n.
Roos, C. F. *N.R.A. Economic Planning.* 1937. 670 n.
Roosevelt, Eleanor. *This is My Story.* 1937. 626 n.
Roosevelt, Elliott. *As He Saw It.* 1946. 736 n.
Roosevelt, F. D. *The Public Papers and Addresses of Franklin D. Roosevelt.* 5 vols. 1938; 4 vols., 1941. 661 n.
Roosevelt, Theodore. *The Rough Riders.* 1919. 316 n.
—— *Theodore Roosevelt; an Autobiography.* 1913. 351 n., 380 n.
Roosevelt, Theodore, and Lodge, H. C. *Selections from the Correspondence of Theodore Roosevelt and Henry Cabot Lodge, 1884–1918.* 2 vols. 1925. 338 n.
Rosewater, Victor. *Backstage in 1912.* 1932. 435 n.
Ross, E. D. *Democracy's College: The Land-Grant Movement in the Formative Stage.* 1942. 114 n.
—— *The Liberal Republican Movement.* 1919. 50 n.
Rowe, H. K. *The History of Religion in the United States.* 1924. 294 n.
Rubinow, I. M. *The Quest for Security.* 1934. 668 n.
Russell, C. E. *Blaine of Maine: His Life and Times.* 1931. 201 n.
—— *The Story of the Nonpartisan League.* 1920. 546 n.
Ryden, G. H. *The Foreign Policy of the United States in Relation to Samoa.* 1933. 303 n.

Sabin, E. L. *Building the Pacific Railway.* 1919. 75 n.
Sageser, A. B. *The First Two Decades of the Pendleton Act* (University of Nebraska, *University Studies,* XXXIV–XXXV). 1934. 195 n.
Sargent, H. H. *The Campaign of Santiago de Cuba.* 3 vols. 1907. 325 n.
Satterlee, H. L. *J. Pierpont Morgan: An Intimate Portrait.* 1939. 382 n.
Schafer, Joseph. *Carl Schurz, Militant Liberal.* 1930. 92 n.
——, ed. *Memoirs of Jeremiah Curtin.* 1940. 379 n.
Schieber, C. E. *The Transformation of American Sentiment Toward Germany, 1870–1914.* 1923. 320 n.
Schlesinger, A. M. *New Viewpoints in American History.* 1937. 408 n.
—— *The Rise of the City, 1878–1898* (*History of American Life,* X). 1933. 284 n.
Schley, W. S. *Forty-Five Years Under the Flag.* 1904. 327 n.
Schmidt, L. B., and Ross, E. D., eds. *Readings in the Economic History of American Agriculture.* 1925. 236 n.
Schmitt, B. E. *The Coming of the War.* 2 vols. 1930. 466 n.
Schmitt, M. F., ed. *General George Crook: His Autobiography.* 1946. 138 n.
Schneider, H. W. *Making the Fascist State.* 1928. 689 n.
Schriftgiesser, Karl. *The Gentleman from Massachusetts: Henry Cabot Lodge.* 1944. 534 n.
Schubert, Paul. *The Electric Word: The Rise of the Radio.* 1928. 596 n.
Schuman, F. L. *The Nazi Dictatorship.* 1936. 692 n.
Schurz, Carl. *The Reminiscences of Carl Schurz.* 3 vols. 1907–08. 3 n.
—— *Speeches, Correspondence and Political Papers of Carl Schurz.* Edited by Frederic Bancroft 6 vols. 1913. 22 n.

[xxv]

LIST OF BOOKS CITED

Scott, J. B.   *The Hague Peace Conferences of 1899 and 1907.*   2 vols.   1909. 378 n.

Seabury, W. M.   *The Public and the Motion Picture Industry.*   1926.   594 n.

Seitz, D. C.   *The Dreadful Decade.*   1926.   82 n.

Seldes, G. V.   *The Years of the Locust: America, 1929–1932.*   1933.   586 n.

Seligman, E. R. A.   *The Economics of Farm Relief.*   1929.   580 n.

Seward, G. F.   *Chinese Immigration in its Social and Economical Aspects.*   1881. 156 n.

Seymour, Charles.   *American Diplomacy During the World War.*   1934.   470 n.

—— *American Neutrality, 1914–1917.*   1935.   486 n.

—— *Woodrow Wilson and the World War* (*Chronicles of America*, XLVIII). 1921.   486 n.

Seymour, Flora W.   *The Story of the Red Man.*   1929.   128 n.

Shannon, F. A.   *America's Economic Growth.*   1940.   586 n.

—— *Economic History of the American People.*   1934.   535 n.

—— *The Farmer's Last Frontier: Agriculture, 1860–1897.*   1945.   259 n.

Sharp, F. C., and Fox, P. G.   *Business Ethics; Studies in Fair Competition.* 1937.   85 n.

Sheldon, W. D.   *Populism in the Old Dominion.*   1935.   247 n.

Sherman, John.   *Recollections of Forty Years.*   2 vols.   1895.   147 n.

Sherman, W. R.   *The Diplomatic and Commercial Relations of the United States and Chile, 1820–1914.*   1926.   305 n.

Sherwood, R. E.   *Roosevelt and Hopkins.*   1948.   742 n.

Shinn, C. H.   *Mining Camps: A Study in American Frontier Government* (1885). 120 n.

—— *The Story of the Mine.*   1901.   118 n.

Shippee, L. B.   *Canadian-American Relations, 1849–1874.*   1939.   379 n.

Shirer, W. L.   *Berlin Diary.*   1941.   692 n.

Shotwell, J. T.   *At the Paris Peace Conference.*   1937.   510 n.

—— *War as an Instrument of National Policy and Its Renunciation in the Pact of Paris.*   1929.   569 n.

Shryock, R. H.   *American Medical Research Past and Present.*   1947. 616 n.

Shultz, W. J.   *Financial Development of the United States.*   1937.   670 n.

Siegfried, André.   *America Comes of Age.*   1927.   560 n.

Simkins, F. B.   *Pitchfork Ben Tillman, South Carolinian.*   1944.   259 n.

—— *The South Old and New: A History, 1820–1947.*   1947.   39 n.

—— *The Tillman Movement in South Carolina.*   1926.   247 n.

Simkins, F. B., and Woody, R. H.   *South Carolina during Reconstruction.*   1932. 36 n.

Sims, W. S., and Hendrick, B. J.   *The Victory at Sea.*   1920.   497 n.

Sinclair, W. A.   *The Aftermath of Slavery.*   1905.   47 n.

Slosson, P. W.   *The Great Crusade and After, 1914–1928.*   1930.   589 n.

Smalley, E. V.   *History of the Northern Pacific Railroad.*   1883.   164 n.

Smith, A. D. H.   *Commodore Vanderbilt.*   1927.   86 n.

Smith, A. E.   *Up to Now: An Autobiography.*   1929.   577 n.

Smith, C. H.   *The Coming of the Russian Mennonites.*   1927.   236 n.

Smith, D. H., and Betters, P. V.   *The United States Shipping Board.*   1931. 526 n.

Smith, H. L. *Airways: The History of Commercial Aviation in the United States.*
1942. 616 n.
Smith, J. R. *The Story of Iron and Steel.* 1908. 61 n.
Smith, T. C. *Life and Letters of James Abram Garfield.* 1925. 191 n.
Smythe, W. E. *The Conquest of Arid America.* 1905. 396 n.
Somers, Robert. *The Southern States Since the War, 1870–1871.* 1871. 3 n.
Soule, George. *Prosperity Decade.* 1947. 588 n.
Spalding, A. G. *America's National Game.* 1911. 297 n.
Sprout, Harold and Margaret. *The Rise of American Naval Power, 1776–1918.*
1939. 314 n.
────── *Toward a New Order of Sea Power: American Naval Policy and the World
Scene, 1918–1922.* 1940. 534 n.
Stahl, Rose M. *The Ballinger-Pinchot Controversy* (Smith College, *Studies in
History*, XI). 1926. 427 n.
Stanton, Elizabeth Cady, and others. *History of Woman Suffrage.* 6 vols.
1881–1922. 112 n.
Stanton, S. B. *The Behring Sea Controversy.* 1892. 301 n.
Stanwood, Edward. *American Tariff Controversies in the Nineteenth Century.*
2 vols. 1903. 200 n.
────── *A History of the Presidency.* 2 vols. 1916. 42 n.
Staples, T. S. *Reconstruction in Arkansas, 1862–1874* (Columbia University,
Studies in History, Economics and Public Law, CIX, whole no, 245). 1923.
16 n.
Stearns, H. E. ed. *Civilization in the United States: An Inquiry by Thirty
Americans.* 1922. 602 n.
Steffens, Lincoln. *The Autobiography of Lincoln Steffens.* 2 vols. 1931. 385 n.
────── *The Shame of the Cities.* 1904. 405 n.
Stein, C. W. *The Third Term Tradition: Its Rise and Collapse in American
Politics.* 1943. 736 n.
Steinman, D. B. *The Builders of the Bridge: The Story of John Roebling and his
Son.* 1945. 81 n.
Stephenson, G. M. *A History of American Immigration, 1920–1924.* 1926.
74 n.
────── *John Lind of Minnesota.* 1935. 465 n.
Stephenson, N. W. *Nelson W. Aldrich: A Leader in American Politics.* 1930.
423 n.
Stettinius, E. R., Jr. *Lend-Lease, Weapon for Victory.* 1944. 736 n.
Steuart, Justin. *Wayne Wheeler, Dry Boss.* 1928. 408 n.
Steuben, John. *Labor in Wartime.* 1940. 495 n.
Stewart, W. M. *Reminiscences.* 1908. 118 n.
Stieglitz, Julius. *Chemistry in Medicine.* 1928. 608 n.
Stimson, H. L. *The Far Eastern Crisis: Recollections and Observations.* 1936.
708 n.
Stolberg, Benjamin. *The Story of the CIO.* 1938. 647 n.
Stoner, J. E. *S. O. Levinson and the Pact of Paris: A Study in Techniques of In-
fluence.* 1942. 588 n.
Storey, Moorfield. *Charles Sumner.* 1900. 20 n.
Storey, Moorfield, and Lichauco, M. P. *The Conquest of the Philippines by the
United States, 1898–1925.* 1926. 345 n.

LIST OF BOOKS CITED

Strachey, Ray. *Frances Willard: Her Life and Work.* 1912. 110 n.
Strakhovsky, L. I. *The Origins of American Intervention in North Russia, 1918.* 1937. 500 n.
Straus, M. W., and Wegg, Talbot. *Housing Comes of Age.* 1938. 663 n.
Strong, Josiah. *The Twentieth Century City.* 1898. 289 n.
Strunsky, Simeon. *The Living Tradition: Change and America.* 1939. 616 n.
Stryker, L. P. *Andrew Johnson; a Study in Courage.* 1929. 14 n.
Sullivan, Mark. *The Great Adventure at Washington.* 1922. 520 n.
—— *Our Times; the United States, 1900–1925.* 6 vols. 1926–35. 242 n., 318 n., 340 n., 385 n., 414 n., 428 n., 480 n., 516 n., 533 n., 598 n.
Sweet, W. W. *The Story of Religions in America.* 1930. 294 n.
Swint, H. L. *The Northern Teacher in the South, 1862–1870.* 1941. 18 n.
Swisher, C. B. *American Constitutional Development.* 1943. 190 n.

Taft, Helen H. (Mrs. William Howard). *Recollections of Full Years.* 1914. 419 n.
Tansill, C. C. *America Goes to War.* 1938. 486 n.
—— *Canadian-American Relations, 1875–1911.* 1943. 379 n.
—— *The Congressional Career of Thomas Francis Bayard, 1869–1885.* 1946. 220 n.
—— *The Foreign Policy of Thomas F. Bayard, 1885–1897.* 1940. 220 n.
Tarbell, Ida M. *The History of the Standard Oil Company.* 2 vols. 1904. 67 n.
—— *The Life of Elbert H. Gary: the Story of Steel.* 1925. 381 n.
—— *The Nationalizing of Business, 1878–1898 (History of American Life, IX).* 1936. 174 n., 238 n.
—— *The Tariff in Our Times.* 1911. 200 n.
Tasca, H. J. *The Reciprocal Trade Policy of the United States.* 1938. 683 n.
Taussig, F. W. *The Silver Situation in the United States.* 1892. 267 n.
—— *The Tariff History of the United States.* 1931. 200 n., 529 n.
Taylor, A. A. *The Negro in South Carolina During the Reconstruction.* 1924. 6 n.
—— *The Negro in the Reconstruction of Virginia.* 1926. 38 n.
Teele, R. P. *Irrigation in the United States.* 1915. 396 n.
Temperley, H. W. V., ed. *A History of the Peace Conference of Paris.* 1924. 508 n.
Thayer, W. R. *The Life and Letters of John Hay.* 2 vols. 1915. 356 n.
—— *Theodore Roosevelt; an Intimate Biography.* 1919. 351 n.
Thomas, C. M. *Thomas Riley Marshall.* 1939. 512 n.
Thomas, Dorothy. *The Spoilage.* 1946. 734 n.
Thomas, H. C. *The Return of the Democratic Party to Power in 1884 (Columbia University, Studies in History, Economics and Public Law, LXXXIX).* 1919. 205 n.
Thomas, Norman. *After the New Deal, What?* 1936. 635 n.
Thomas, Shipley. *The History of the A. E. F.* 1920. 501 n.
Thomas, William I., and Znaniecki, Florian, *The Polish Peasant in Europe and America.* 5 vols. 1918–1920. 189 n.
Thompson, C. Mildred. *Reconstruction in Georgia, Economic, Social, Political, 1866–1872 (Columbia University, Studies in History, Economics and Public Law, LXIV).* 1915. 36 n.

Thompson, Holland.   *The Age of Invention* (*Chronicles of America*, XXXVII).
    1921.   175 n.
——— *From the Cotton Field to the Cotton Mill.*   1906.   223 n.
——— *The New South* (*Chronicles of America*, XLII).   1919.   221 n.
Thompson, J. W.   *A History of Livestock Raising in the United States.*   1942.
    138 n.
Thompson, Slason.   *A Short History of American Railways.*   1925.   170 n.
Thwing, C. F.   *The American and the German University.*   1928.   102 n.
——— *A History of Higher Education in America.*   1906.   98 n.
Todd, Helen.   *A Man Named Grant.*   1940.   43 n.
Todd, L. P.   *Wartime Relations of the Federal Government and the Public Schools,*
    1917–1918.   1945.   496 n.
Tostlebe, A. S.   *The Bank of North Dakota* (Columbia University, *Studies in*
    History, Economics and Public Law, CXIV).   1924.   546 n.
Treat, P. J.   *Diplomatic Relations Between the United States and Japan, 1895–*
    1905.   2 vols.   1938.   360 n.
Trent, W. P., and others.   *The Cambridge History of American Literature.*   3
    vols.   1936.   610 n.
Trimble, W. J.   *The Mining Advance into the Inland Empire* (University of
    Wisconsin, *Bulletin,* History Series, vol. III).   1914.   119 n.
Tsuchida, W. S.   *Wear it Proudly.*   1947.   734 n.
Tugwell, R. G.   *Industry's Coming of Age.*   1927.   556 n.
——— *Mr. Hoover's Economic Policy.*   1932.   581 n.
Tupper, Eleanor, and McReynolds, G. E.   *Japan in American Public Opinion.*
    1937.   522 n.
Turner, F. J.   *The Early Writings of Frederick Jackson Turner.*   1938.   280 n.
Twain, Mark.   *Roughing It.*   1872.   118 n.
Twentieth Century Fund.   *Facing the Tax Problem.*   1937.   672 n.
Tyler, Alice F.   *The Foreign Policy of James G. Blaine.*   1927.   192 n.

Vagts, Alfred.   *Deutschland und die Vereinigten Staaten in der Weltpolitik.*   2
    vols.   1935.   377 n.
Vance, R. B.   *Human Factors in Cotton Culture.*   1929.   227 n.
——— *Human Geography of the South.*   1932.   227 n.
Van Hise, C. R.   *The Conservation of Natural Resources in the United States.*
    1910.   395 n.
Veblen, Thorstein.   *The Theory of the Leisure Class.*   1899.   291 n.
Vestal, Stanley.   *Kit Carson.*   1928.   127 n.
——— *Mountain Men.*   1937.   127 n.
——— *Sitting Bull.*   1932.   128 n.
Viles, Jonas.   *The University of Missouri.*   1939.   101 n.
Villard, Henry.   *Memoirs of Henry Villard.*   2 vols.   1904.   164 n.
Vinacke, H. M.   *A History of the Far East in Modern Times.*   1944.   534 n.

Wald, Lillian D.   *The House on Henry Street.*   1915.   295 n.
Walker, A. H.   *History of the Sherman Law of the United States of America.*
    1910.   386 n.
Wallace, H. A.   *America Must Choose.*   1934.   635 n.
——— *New Frontiers.*   1934.   670 n.

Wallace, S. C. *The New Deal in Action.* 1934. 671 n.
Walsh, J. R. *C.I.O., Industrial Unionism in Action.* 1937. 647 n.
Wanlass, W. L. *The United States Department of Agriculture.* 1920. 460 n.
Warburg, J. P. *Hell Bent for Election.* 1935. 674 n.
——— *Still Hell Bent.* 1936. 674 n.
Warburg, P. M. *The Federal Reserve System.* 2 vols. 1930. 450 n.
Ware, N. J. *The Labor Movement in the United States, 1860–1895.* 1929. 181 n.
Warren, Charles. *Congress, the Constitution, and the Supreme Court.* 1935. 678 n.
——— *The Supreme Court in United States History.* 2 vols. 1937. 46 n.
Warren, Sidney. *American Freethought, 1860–1914.* 1943. 298 n.
Washington, Booker T. *Up From Slavery; an Autobiography.* 1937. 105 n.
Waters, W. W. *B.E.F.: The Whole Story of the Bonus Army.* 1933. 621 n.
Webb, W. P. *Divided We Stand.* 1937. 179 n.
——— *The Great Plains.* 1936. 115 n.
——— *The Texas Rangers.* 1935. 131 n.
Weber, H. C. *Evangelism.* 1929. 294 n.
Weberg, F. P. *The Background of the Panic of 1893.* 1929. 255 n.
Webster, Laura J. *The Operation of the Freedmen's Bureau in South Carolina* (Smith College, *Studies in History*, vol. I, no. 2–3). 1916. 7 n.
Wecter, Dixon. *The Age of the Great Depression, 1929–1941* (*History of American Life*, XIII). 1948. 636 n.
Weissman, R. L. *The New Wall Street.* 1939. 659 n.
Welles, Gideon. *Diary of Gideon Welles, Secretary of the Navy Under Lincoln and Johnson.* 3 vols. 1911. 32 n.
Welles, Sumner. *The Time for Decision.* 1944. 744 n.
Werner, M. R. *Bryan.* 1929. 270 n.
——— *Privileged Characters.* 1935. 534 n.
——— *Tammany Hall.* 1928. 89 n., 577 n.
Weyand, A. M. *American Football.* 1926. 297 n.
Weyl, Nathaniel and Sylvia. *The Reconquest of Mexico: The Years of Lázaro Cárdenas.* 1939. 684 n.
Wharton, V. L. *The Negro in Mississippi, 1865–1890.* 1947. 18 n.
Wheeler, Joseph. *The Santiago Campaign.* 1899. 325 n.
Wheeler-Bennett, J. W. *The Pipe-Dream of Peace: The Story of the Collapse of Disarmament.* 1935. 702 n.
White, A. D. *A History of the Warfare of Science with Theology in Christendom.* 2 vols. 1896. 295 n.
White, Bouck. *The Book of Daniel Drew.* New ed. 1937. 86 n.
White, Horace. *Coin's Financial Fool; or, the Artful Dodger Exposed.* 1895. 267 n.
——— *The Life of Lyman Trumbull.* 1913. 32 n.
——— *Money and Banking Illustrated by American History.* 1914. 257 n.
White, W. A. *The Autobiography of William Allen White.* 1946. 594 n.
——— *Calvin Coolidge: The Man Who is President.* 1925. 548 n.
——— *Masks in a Pageant.* 1928. 548 n.
——— *A Puritan in Babylon: The Story of Calvin Coolidge.* 1938. 548 n.
——— *What It's All About.* 1936. 675 n.
——— *Woodrow Wilson.* 1924. 440 n.

Whitman, Willson. *Bread and Circuses.* 1937. 640 n.
Wickersham, George W. *Report of the National Commission on Law Observance and Enforcement* (71 Cong., 3 sess., *H. Doc.* no. 722 — serial 9361). 1931. 604 n.
Wiest, Edward. *Agricultural Organization in the United States* (University of Kentucky, *Studies in Economics and Sociology,* II). 1923. 544 n.
Wilbur, R. L., and Hyde, A. M. *The Hoover Policies.* 1937. 581 n., 619 n.
Wildman, M. S. *Money Inflation in the United States.* 1905. 43 n.
Wilgus, H. L. *A Study of the United States Steel Corporation in Its Industrial and Legal Aspects.* 1901. 381 n.
Wilkerson, M. M. *Public Opinion and the Spanish-American War* (Louisiana State University, *Studies,* no. 8). 1932. 309 n.
Wilkins, E. H. *The Changing College.* 1927. 607 n.
Willard, Frances E. *Glimpses of Fifty Years.* 1889. 110 n.
Williams, B. H. *Economic Foreign Policy of the United States.* 1929. 566 n.
Williams, C. R. *The Life of Rutherford Birchard Hayes.* 2 vols. 1914. 143 n.
Williams, G. W. *History of the Negro Race in America from 1619 to 1880.* 2 vols. 1882. 6 n.
Williams, Mary W. *Anglo-American Isthmian Diplomacy, 1815–1915.* 1916. 365 n.
Willis, H. P. *The Federal Reserve.* 1915. 450 n.
Willkie, Wendell. *One World.* 1943. 736 n.
Willoughby, W. F. *Financial Condition and Operations of the National Government, 1921–30.* 1931. 528 n.
—— *Government Organization in War Time and After.* 1919. 493 n.
—— *The National Budget System.* 1927. 528 n.
—— *The Problem of a National Budget.* 1918. 528 n.
—— *Territories and Dependencies of the United States.* 1905. 342 n.
Wilson, Edith Bolling. *My Memoir.* 1939. 440 n.
Winkler, J. K. *Incredible Carnegie: the Life of Andrew Carnegie.* 1931. 63 n.
—— *Tobacco Tycoon: The Story of James Buchanan Duke.* 1942. 81 n.
Winston, R. W. *Andrew Johnson, Plebeian and Patriot.* 1928. 14 n.
Winther, O. O. *The Great Northwest.* 1947. 138 n.
Wisan, J. E. *The Cuban Crisis as Reflected in the New York Press, 1895–1898* (Columbia University, *Studies in History, Economics and Public Law,* no. 403). 1934. 309 n.
Wish, Harvey. *Contemporary America: The National Scene since 1900.* 1945. 380 n.
Witte, E. E. *The Government in Labor Disputes.* 1932. 554 n.
Wittke, Carl. *German-Americans and the World War.* 1936. 471 n.
—— *We Who Built America, the Saga of the Immigrant.* 1940. 74 n.
Woestemeyer, Ina Faye, and Gambrill, J. M. *The Westward Movement.* 1939. 118 n.
Wood, Clement. *Herbert Clark Hoover: An American Tragedy.* 1932. 623 n.
Woodburn, J. A. *The Life of Thaddeus Stevens.* 1913. 19 n.
Woodley, T. F. *Thaddeus Stevens.* 1934. 19 n.
Woodward, C. V. *Tom Watson, Agrarian Rebel.* 1938. 249 n.
Woodward, W. E. *Meet General Grant.* 1928. 43 n.
Wright, F. L. *An Autobiography.* 1932. 613 n.

Yardley, H. O.   *The American Black Chamber.*   1931.   520 n.
Yellen, Samuel.   *American Labor Struggles.*   1936.   183 n.
Young, R. T.   *Biology in America.*   1922.   608 n.

Zacharias, E. M.   *Secret Missions: The Story of an Intelligence Officer.* 1947. 731 n.
Zeis, P. M.   *American Shipping Policy.*   1938.   526 n., 662 n.
Zimmermann, E. W.   *Zimmermann on Ocean Shipping.*   1921.   526 n.

INDEX

Abbott, Lyman, on evolution, 294
Abilene, Kansas, cow-town, 132
Acheson, Dean, becomes Secretary of State, 782
Act of Chapultepec, modifies Monroe Doctrine, 767
Act of Havana, forbids transfer of European colonies in America, 706
Adams, Charles Francis, favored for Liberal Republican nomination, 51
Adams, H. C., works out bookkeeping system for railroads, 391
Adams, Henry, approves Chicago Fair (1893), 280
Adams, Samuel Hopkins, muckraker, 384
Adamson Act, denounced by Hughes, 480
Addams, Jane, settlement worker, 295; supports Progressive Party (1912), 437
Adjusted compensation. *See* Bonus bill
Advertising, aided by half-tone process, 174; stimulates nation-wide business, 288; frauds in, 391; motion-pictures, 594; radio, 596; restrictions under Federal Securities Act, 659
Agricultural Adjustment Administration (AAA), purposes of, 648; ended by Supreme Court, 652; under new Agricultural Adjustment Act (1938), 654; Thomas Amendment (1933), 658; during recession of 1937–38, 680
Agricultural Marketing Act, of 1929, 580
Agriculture, disadvantages of, 60; exhibits at Philadelphia Centennial, 114; in the South, 226; common interest of West and South, 242; before Panic of 1893, 256; represented by Bryan, 274; revolution in, 291; need for government credits, 457; war prosperity, 535; depression in, 540; efforts to rehabilitate, 547; continued depression in, 556, 569; McNary-Haugen Bill, 571; export debenture plan, 572; farm relief under Hoover, 580; overexpansion of, 586; drouth of 1930, 619; RFC loans for, 621; under AAA 648; FCA loans for, 652
Aguinaldo, Emilio, Filipino leader, 319; successes of, 334; capture of, 335
Air-lift, supplies Berlin, 784; efforts to end, 785
Airplanes, in World War I, 501; compete with railroads, 525; production of, 553; improvements in, 596; use in air-mail, 598; Mead-McKellar Act, 599; military weapon, 601; in World War II, 711; Japanese use at Pearl Harbor, 718
Alabama, reconstruction constitution, 35; cotton industry in, 223; iron mines in, 224
Alabama claims, 56; settlement, 57
Alaska, fur-seal industry, 300; gold in, 333;

government of, 334; dispute over boundary, 362; highway to, 720
Albania, taken by Italy, 697; post-war settlement, 754
Aldrich, Nelson W., tariff activities in 1890, 217; in 1909, 423; heads monetary commission, 446
Aldrich-Vreeland Act, on banking and currency, 415
Aleutians, Japanese in, 726
Algeciras Conference, U.S. participation in, 376; U.S. Senate on, 377
Alger, Russell A., Secretary of War, 317; resigns, 329
Alliance. *See* Farmers' Alliance
Allied Control Council, governs Germany, 754; early agreements, 756
Allison, W. B., on silver coinage, 152; on tariff, 210
Alsace-Lorraine, coveted by France, 467; to be returned, 508
Altgeld, John P., pardons anarchists, 184; during Pullman strike, 263; Democratic leader, 270
Alverstone, Lord, arbitrates Alaskan boundary dispute, 364
Amador, Manuel, Panama revolutionist, 367; bribes Colombian troops, 368
Amendments to U.S. Constitution, Thirteenth, 21; Fourteenth, 24; Fifteenth, 36; Sixteenth, 426; Seventeenth, 404; Eighteenth, 408; Nineteenth, 408; Twentieth, 628; Twenty-first, 602, 605
American Expeditionary Force, sent to France, 497; numbers of, 498; in Italy, 500; battle losses, 502
American Farm Bureau Federation, origins, 542; work of, 544
American Federation of Labor, founded, 185; policies of, 186; growth of, 188; refuses to support Populists, 260; unsatisfactory to Debs, 262; growth of, 392; endorses La Follette, 560; opposes industrial unions, 646
American Legion, favors bonus bill, 527
American Liberty League, opposes New Deal, 674
American Missionary Association, work in South, 8
American neutrality, during World War I (1914), 473, 474; legislation on, 703; during second World War, 705
American Protective Association (A.P.A.), program of, 560
American Railway Union, organizes Pullman employees, 262
American Society of Equity, farmer organization, 458; origins of, 542
Ames, Oakes, Crédit Mobilier agent, 53

INDEX

Amnesty Act, 1872, 49
Ananias Club, formed by Theodore Roosevelt, 410
Anderson, Maxwell, playwright, 612
Anderson, William H., Anti-Saloon League leader, 407
Angell, James B., president of University of Michigan, 98
Anglo-Japanese Alliance, formed, 359; ended, 521
Anthony, Susan B., suffragist, 112
Anthracite Coal Strike (1902), outbreak of, 393; intervention by Theodore Roosevelt, 394
Anti-Monopoly party, activities, 94
Anti-Saloon League, church support of, 295; activities of, 407, 602
Apache Indians, discourage prospectors, 120; campaigns against, 128
Arabic, sunk by submarines, 476
Arapaho Indians, on warpath, 125; Sand Creek massacre, 126; settlement in Indian Territory, 127
Arbeiter Zeitung, anarchist newspaper, 183
Archangel-Murmansk campaign, American part in, 500
Archbald, Judge R. W., impeached, 432
Architecture, Chicago World's Fair, 279; skyscrapers, 290; recent trends in, 612; World's Fairs of 1933 and 1939, 614
Argentine, the, severs relations with Axis, 719; post-war friction with U.S., 767
Arizona, created a territory, 119; transient labor problem in, 656
Arkansas, under Lincoln's plan of reconstruction, 12; readmitted, 36; Klan activities in, 560
Armed neutrality, plans for (1917), 482
Armistice (1918), terms of, 506
Armour, Philip, meat packer, 68
Army of the United States, in the South, 8; partial withdrawal, 21; under second congressional plan, 30, 32, 36; used against Fenians, 56; used against Indians, 124, 129; used in strikes of 1877, 155; used in Pullman strike, 263; before Spanish-American War, 316; increases in, 317; mobilization, 323; Santiago campaign, 325; an "army of convalescents," 328; reorganized, 348; in Boxer uprising, 357; increases of 1916, 478; in war with Germany, 487; the A.E.F. 497; contribution to allied victory, 501; preparedness program of 1940, 710; in Philippines, 719; in Africa, 721; in Italy, 723; in Europe, 725; on Pacific Islands, 727; demobilization, 746; post-war strength, 747
Arnold, Thurman W., Assistant Attorney-General, 680
Arrears of Pension Act, passed in 1879, 207
Arthur, Chester Alan, collector of the port of New York, 147; removed by Hayes, 147; named for Vice-President, 161; becomes President, 194; sketch of, 195; urges tariff reform, 199; breaks with Conkling, 200
Asia, American interest in, 355; unrest in, 588; World War II, 694; post-war, 765
Associated Press, news-gathering agency, 296

Atchison, Topeka and Santa Fe Railroad, chartered, 78; connections with Southern Pacific, 165
Atlanta, Ga., after the war, 4; scene of cotton expositions, 222
Atlantic and Pacific Railroad, chartered, 78; grant absorbed by Santa Fe, 165
Atlantic Charter, signed, 716
Atomic bomb, use at Hiroshima and Nagasaki, 730; Bikini tests, 774; American proposals for international control, 775
Attlee, Clement R., becomes British Prime Minister, 746
Austin, Warren R., U.S. member of Security Council, 778
Australia, becomes Allied base, 719
Australian ballot, furthered by election of 1888, 211; supported by Populists, 250 n., 251; adopted in Oregon, 403
Austria, created separate state, 510; post-war government, 754
Austria-Hungary, at war with U.S., 482; defeated, 500
Automobile, requires road improvement, 460; stimulant to business recovery, 554; widespread ownership of, 587; effect on American life, 589

Badoglio, Pietro, Italian premier, 723
Baer, George F., leads coal operators, 393
Baker, Newton D., candidate for Democratic nomination (1932), 624
Baker, Ray Stannard, muckraker, 384
Ballinger-Pinchot controversy, origins of, 426
Baltimore and Ohio Railroad, growth of, 166
Bancroft, George, writes Johnson's first message, 18
Banks, failures in 1870's, 86; in 1890's, 255; leading banking firms, 382; Federal Reserve System, 449; failures in early 1920's, 539, 542; RFC loans to, 620; crisis of 1933, 630; Emergency Banking Act, 631; Glass-Steagall Act (1933), 658
Baring panic, in England, 256
Barker, Wharton, Mid-Road Populist nominee, 338
Barkley, Alben, candidate for Vice-President (1948), 788; elected, 790
Barnard, Frederick A. P., president of Columbia, 97
Baruch, Bernard, heads War Industries Board, 494; on atomic energy, 775
Bascom, John, president University of Wisconsin, 98
Baseball, national sport, 297
Bayard, Thomas F., Secretary of State, 205
Beecher, Henry Ward, trial of, 85; on revivalism, 109; on evolution, 294
Beer Act, passed in 1933, 632
Belgium, attacked by Germany (1914), 469; attacked by Germany (1940), 700; liberation of, 724; progress toward recovery, 782
Belknap, William W., accepts bribe, 55
Bell, Alexander Graham, invents telephone, 173
Bellamy, Edward, *Looking Backward*, 421
Benedict XV, Pope, peace message of, 503
Benelux, economic union of low countries, 782

Benét, Stephen Vincent, writings of, 610
Benson, Allen, Socialist nominee (1916), 480
Benson, Elmer A., governor of Minnesota, 681
Berger, Victor L., Socialist leader, 421; elected to Congress, 431; imprisoned, 492
Berkman, Alexander, attack on Frick, 261
Berle, Adolph A., Jr., Roosevelt braintruster, 627
Berlin, taken by Russians, 744; post-war government of, 754; supplied by air-lift, 784
Bernadotte, Count, seeks Palestine settlement, 774
Bernstorff, Count Johann von, on submarine sinkings, 476
Bessemer, Henry, discovers "air-boiling" process, 61
Beveridge, Albert J., imperialistic views, 333, on Philippines, 337
Bevin, Ernest, British foreign secretary, 752; attends conference on Marshall Plan, 781
Bezier, Rudolph, *The Barretts of Wimpole Street*, 593
Bicycle, increasing use of, 297
Bidault, Georges, French foreign minister, 781
"Big Four," at Paris Peace Conference, 508
Big Stick Policy, adopted by Theodore Roosevelt, 370; elaborated, 372
Billings, Frederick, Northern Pacific president, 164; deposed by Villard, 165; interested in Nicaraguan canal route, 366
Billings, Warren K., conviction of, 456; pardoned, 457
Billion Dollar Congress, under Harrison, 219
Bimetallism, in campaign of 1896, 273; international conference on, 277
Bingham, John A., on Fourteenth Amendment, 24
Birmingham, Ala., development of, 224
Birth of a Nation, motion picture success, 592; influence of, 593
Bissell, George H., efforts to refine petroleum, 63
Black, Hugo L., appointed to Supreme Court, 679
Black Beauty, by Anna Sewell, 112
Black codes, instituted in the South, 21
"Black counties," during reconstruction, 33
"Black Friday," during gold conspiracy, 53
Black Hills Gold Rush, 123, 128
Black Kettle, at Fort Lyons, 126
"Blacklists," used by employers, 153; by trusts, 177
Blaine, James G., desires Republican nomination, 140; heads "Half-Breeds," 160; Secretary of State under Garfield, 192, 193; sketch of, 192; nominated for President, 201; plagued by Mulligan letters, 202; passed over for Harrison, 211; made Secretary of State by Harrison, 212; interest in reciprocity, 218; resigns from cabinet, 292; on Clayton-Bulwer Treaty, 300; on fur-seal controversy, 300; on Hawaiian annexation, 301; on Samoa, 302; on Pan-Americanism, 303; relations with Chile, 304
Blair, Francis P., Jr., nominated for Vice-President, 42

Bland, Richard P., advocates free silver, 152; candidate for Democratic nomination (1896), 270
Bland-Allison Act, passed, 152; fails to cheapen silver, 216; burden on the gold reserve, 254
Blashfield, Edwin, painter, 279
Bliss, Tasker N., member Peace Commission, 507 n.
Blockade, British rules of, 472; by German submarines, 474; German suffering from, 484; in World War II, 699
Blue, Victor, reconnoiters Santiago Bay, 324
Blue Eagle, NRA emblem, 643
Bolivia, war with Paraguay, 588
Bolshevists, win control in Russia, 501
"Bonapartism," charged against Grant, 162
Bonus bill, provides "adjusted compensation," 527; paid in advance of date due, 658
Bonus Expeditionary Force, descends on Washington, 621
"Boondoggling," in relief projects, 639
"Bootleggers," activities of, 603; gangsterism among, 604
Borah, William E., prosecutes Haywood, 456; supports Harding, 517; urges conference on limitation of armaments, 520; advocates outlawry of war, 568; considered for presidential nomination (1936), 675
Boston, fire of 1872, 80; slums, 82; literary pretensions, 107; police strike, 548
Boulder Dam, construction of, 618
"Bourbons," leaders of southern Democracy, 161; favor industrialization, 222; legalize crop-lien system, 228; dependence upon "black counties," 231; attacked by Macune, 248
Bourne, Jonathan, president National Progressive Republican League, 433
Boutwell, G. S., Secretary of the Treasury, 44
Bowles, Chester, heads OPA, 750
Boxer uprising, in China, 357; settlement following, 358
Boxing, American interest in, 297
Boycotts. *See* Strikes
Boyd, James, writings of, 609
Bozeman Trail, attempts to open, 126
Brady, Thomas J., in star-route frauds, 195
Bragg, E. S., favors Cleveland, 203
Brazil, at war with Germany, 482; included in Paris Peace Conference, 508; enters World War II, 719
Brest-Litovsk, Treaty of, between Russia and Germany, 501, 686; German answer to the Fourteen Points, 505; cancelled, 506
Bretton Woods Conference, on world finance, 745
Briand, Aristide, peace pact, 568
Bricker, John W., candidate for Vice-President, 737
Bridger, Jim, plainsman, 127
Bristow, Benjamin H., uncovers "Whiskey Ring," 54; seeks Republican nomination, 140
British Guiana, dispute with Venezuela, 305
British Isles. *See* Great Britain, Ireland
Brookhart, Smith W., elected to U.S. Senate, 559
Brooklyn Bridge, erected, 80

[xxxv]

Brooks, Phillips, preacher, 109
Browder, Earl, Communist candidate, 675
Brown, B. Gratz, candidate for governor, 50; for Vice-President, 51
Brown, Walter F., Postmaster-General, 598; air-mail contracts, 599
Brownsville affair, 412
Bryan, Charles W., nominee for Vice-President (1924), 561
Bryan, William Jennings, aspires to Democratic nomination (1896), 270; speech before convention, 271; nominated, 271; defeated, 274; heads anti-imperialists, 331; saves Treaty of Paris from defeat, 332; renominated in 1900, 336; negotiates treaty with Colombia, 369; with Nicaragua, 374; supports Parker, 413; third race for the presidency, 419; helps nominate Wilson, 436; becomes Secretary of State, 442; supports Federal Reserve system, 451; resigns from Cabinet, 476; eclipsed by Wilson, 478; opposes doctrine of evolution, 602
Bryan-Chamorro treaty, between U.S. and Nicaragua, 374
Bryce, James, opinion of the Nation, 90; publishes American Commonwealth, 298
Bryn Mawr, opens, 104
Budget reform, need for, 527; Budget Act, 528
Buffaloes, attack stage-coaches, 121; killing of, 130
Bulgaria, fights with Germany, 470, 482; defeated, 500; treaty of Neuilly, 511; in World War II, 725; peace negotiations, 752; treaty terms, 754; Communist control of, 776
Bulge, Battle of the, German counter-attack, 725; effect on Yalta Conference, 743
Bull moose, Progressive symbol, 436
Bunau-Varilla, Philippe, Panama canal intrigues, 366; plans revolution, 367; minister to U.S., 368
Bunche, Dr. Ralph, achieves Palestine settlement, 774
Burchard, Samuel, helps defeat Blaine, 204
Bureau of Corporations, established, 390; studies water-power sites, 396; charged with political activity, 413; contribution of, 451; absorbed into Federal Trade Commission, 453
Bureau of Mines, established, 398, 431
Bureau of Standards, service to business, 553
Bureaucracy, Hoover's efforts to avoid, 619 fostered by the New Deal, 672
Burke Act, amends Dawes Act, 130
Burleson, Albert S., Postmaster-General, 444
Burlingame Treaty, with China, 159
Burlington and Missouri River Railroad, chartered, 78; western extension, 166
Burnham, Daniel H., plans Chicago World's Fair (1893), 279
Business, ethics after Civil War, 84; large-scale character, 85; bankruptcies, 86; trend toward consolidation, 172; evidences of monopoly, 175; organization of trusts, 177; importance in American life, 288; development of "big business," 380; integration in industry, 381; unfair practices condemned, 452; failures in 1920's, 539;

government aids to, 553; recovery under Coolidge, 554; installment buying, 556; under NRA, 643; hostility to the New Deal, 672. See also Corporations, Industry
Butler, Benjamin F., favors "Salary Grab" Act, 54; Greenback candidate in 1884, 205
Butterfield, John, wins mail contract, 121
"Buyers' strike," in 1921, 539
Burma, in World War II, 730; post-war independence, 765
Burma Road, opened, 695; closed, 719
Byrnes, James F., Secretary of State, 745; OWMR director, 748; member Council of Foreign Ministers, 752; supported by Truman, 753; delegate to United Nations, 769; resignation, 778
Byrd, Richard E., explorer, 598

Cable, George W., writings of, 108
Cables, transoceanic service, 172
"Calamity Jane," western character, 123
Cairo Conference, during World War II, 740
California, mining in, 115; Kearneyism in, 156; grants suffrage to women, 408; votes for Wilson in 1916, 480; Fruit Growers' Association, 546; transient labor problem, 656; population increase, 735
Cambon, Jules, French ambassador to U.S., 329
Canada, Fenian disturbances, 56; Pacific railroad, 166; emigration to U.S., 284; fur-seal controversy, 300; gold in Klondike, 333; Alaskan boundary dispute, 362; proposed reciprocity with U.S., 432; tariff reprisals, 583; St. Lawrence Seaway, 621; reciprocal trade treaty with U.S., 682; joint-defense plans, 685; strengthened ties with U.S., 706; danger of invasion, 711; highway to Alaska, 720
Canal Zone, government of, 348; part in Caribbean control, 372
Cannon, Joseph G., Speaker of the House, 427; offers to resign, 428
Capone, "Scarface Al," conviction of, 605
Capper-Volstead Act, to promote co-operative marketing, 547
Carey Act, to promote irrigation, 396
Caribbean Zone, special U.S. interests in, 372; U.S. efforts to control, 370, 433
Carleton, J. H., Union officer, 119
Carlisle, John G., elected speaker, 200; Secretary of the Treasury, 257
Carnegie, Andrew, sketch of, 62; philanthropies, 98; attitude toward labor, 260; builds home for Pan-American Union, 304; opposes annexation of Philippines, 332; builds Hague Peace Palace, 378; sells out to United States Steel, 381
"Carpet-bag rule," instituted, 35; opposition to, 36; corruption of, 38; contributions of, 39; excesses under Grant, 47; during election of 1876, 142; ended, 146
Carranza, Venustiano, Mexican revolutionary, 464
Carrington, H. B., builds Fort Kearny, 127
Carroll, Dr. James, experiments on yellow fever, 339
Cary, Samuel F., Greenback nominee for Vice-President, 141

Casablanca Conference, during African invasion, 740
Case Federal Mediation Bill, vetoed by Truman, 751
Castro, Cipriano, Venezuelan dictator, 370
Cather, Willa, writings of, 609
Catholic church. *See* Roman Catholic church
Cattle industry, beginnings, 131; expansion into Northwest, 134; nature of, 136
Centennial Exposition, at Philadelphia, 113
Central Pacific Railroad, charter, 75; construction difficulties, 76; completed, 78
Century of Progress Exposition, at Chicago, 614
Cervera, Pascual, commands Spanish Atlantic squadron, 320; evades American fleet, 321; reaches Santiago, 321; ordered to escape, 326
Chaco, warfare in, 588
Chamberlain, Clarence D., aviator, 598
Chaplin, Charlie, motion picture star, 592
Charleston, S.C., war devastation, 3; given Negro collector, 412
Chase, Salmon P., Chief Justice, 41; Presidential ambitions, 42; legal tender cases, 45; aspires to Liberal Republican nomination, 51
Château-Thierry, American troops used at, 498
Chautauqua movement, supported by the churches, 295; nature of, 297
Chesapeake and Ohio Railroad, connections west and south, 78
Cheyenne Indians, on warpath, 125; Sand Creek massacre, 126; settlement in Indian Territory, 127
Cheyenne, Wyoming, center of cattle industry, 134
Chiang Kai-shek, Chinese leader, 695; differences with Stilwell, 729; at Cairo Conference, 740; defeats by Communists, 759; resigns, 760
Chicago, packing center, 68; fire of 1871, 80; Haymarket Riot in, 183; during Pullman strike, 263; holds World's Fair (1893), 279; Century of Progress Exposition, 614
Chicago and Northwestern Railroad, chartered, 78; western extension, 166
Chicago, Rock Island and Pacific Railroad, chartered, 78; western extension, 166
Chichester, Edward, British commander in Manila Bay, 320
Chief Joseph, Nez Percés leader, 128
Child labor, during seventies, 82; in southern mills, 225; general use of, 290; efforts to regulate, 394, 406; constitutional amendment submitted, 407; Supreme Court on, 455
Children's Bureau, established, 455; work of, 459
Chile, Civil War in, 304; relations with the United States, 305
China, danger of dismemberment, 356; Boxer uprising in, 357; at war with Germany, 482; included in Paris Peace Conference, 508; boycotts Japanese goods, 694; war with Japan, 695; U.S. policy toward, 704, 707; U.S. military operations in, 729; representation in Council of Foreign Ministers, 752; post-war status, 758; Marshall's mission to, 759; opposes treaty with Japan, 762
Chinese, used on Central Pacific, 77; problem of in California, 156; Exclusion Act, 159
Chisholm Trail, route of Long Drive, 132; pushed farther west, 134
Chivington massacre, 126
Choate, Joseph H., at second Hague Conference, 377
Christensen, Parley P., Farmer-Labor nominee (1920), 558
Christian Science, founded, 109; doctrines of, 295
Christianity. *See* Religion
Chrysler-Dodge company, automobile manufacturers, 592; yields to "sit-down" strike, 647
Churches. *See* Religion
Churchill, Winston, British Prime Minister, 701; promises death struggle, 711; signs Atlantic Charter with Roosevelt, 716; Casablanca Conference, 723; at Moscow, Teheran, and Cairo, 740
Churchill, Winston, *Coniston*, 609
Cincinnati, Ohio, Liberal Republican convention in, 51; center of "pork-packing" industry, 68
"Cipher dispatches," in election of 1876, 143
Cities, growth of, 289; government of, 405; city manager plan, 406; city planning, 614
Civil Rights Bill, passed by Congress, 23; passed over Johnson's veto, 24
Civil service reform, urged on Congress, 45; indifference of Grant toward, 50; demanded by Liberal Republicans, 51; attempted by Hayes, 146; Flanagan on, 162; favored by Arthur, 195; Pendleton Act, 196; Cleveland's record on, 205; Harrison's record on, 213; undermined by New Deal, 673
Civil Works Administration (CWA), established, 638
Civilian Conservation Corps (CCC), created, 633
Clapp, Moses E., insurgent senator, 423
Clark, Champ, on Canadian reciprocity, 432; candidate for Democratic nomination (1912), 436
Clark, E. E., "eminent sociologist," 394
Clark, William A., fortune of, 122
Clarkson, J. S., removals of postmasters, 213
Clay, Lucius D., U.S. military governor in Germany, 784
Clayton Anti-Trust Act, terms of, 453; "Magna Charta for Labor," 454; labor injunctions, 554
Clayton-Bulwer Treaty, Blaine's efforts to modify, 194, 300; abrogated, 364
Clemenceau, Georges, war aim, 504; member "Big Four," 508
Clemens, Samuel Langhorne, sketch of, 106; writings, 107; death of, 609
Cleveland, Grover, elected governor of New York, 201; favored by Mugwumps, 202; nominated for President, 203; elected President, 205; on civil service reform, 205; on pensions, 207; battleflag order, 207; tariff message, 208; re-

nominated, 211; defeated for re-election, in 1888, 212; re-elected in 1892, 252; attitude toward the depression, 256; intervention in Pullman strike, 263; prevents annexation of Hawaii, 302; in Venezuelan boundary dispute, 305; efforts to avoid war with Spain, 310

Cleveland, Ohio, center of oil industry, 67

"Closed shop," favored by A.F. of L., 186

Coal industry, in the New South, 224; in northern states, 392; in Alaska, 426

Co-education, beginnings of, 104

Coin's Financial School, influence of, 266

Colfax, Schuyler, nominated for Vice-President, 40; in Crèdit Mobilier scandal, 53

Collective security, advocated in U.S., 689, 701; defended by F. D. Roosevelt, 702; attacked by isolationists, 709

Colombia, grants concession to de Lesseps company, 365; proposed Hay-Herran treaty with U.S., 367; later relations with U.S., 368, 369

Colorado, beginnings, 117; admission, 118; Cripple Creek War, 264; votes for Bryan in 1900, 338; grants suffrage to women, 408; votes for Bryan in 1908, 420; Klan activities in, 560

Colored Alliance, affiliate of Southern Alliance, 247

Columbia, S.C., after the war, 4

Cominform, revives Communist propaganda for world revolution, 776

Comintern, Third International, 688; opposed by Axis, 697; supposed abolition of, 775

Commerce. *See* Foreign Trade

Commerce, Department of, under Coolidge, 553

Commerce and Labor, Department of, established, 186, 390; divided, 431

Commerce Court, created, 431; abolished, 432

Commission for the Relief of Belgium, headed by Hoover, 577

Commission form of city government, spread of, 406

Commissioner of Education, office established, 96

Committee for Industrial Organization (CIO), formation of, 646; introduces "sitdown" strike, 647

Committee of Forty-Eight, seeks to form third party, 558

Committee on Public Information, constituted, 491

Communist Manifesto, principles of, 687

Communist Party, organized in the U.S., 558; inspired by Russia, 566; blamed for labor outbreaks, 647; "popular front" activities, 674; record in World War II, 732; troubles with Dies Committee, 734; Taft-Hartley Act, 752; supports Wallace (1948), 791

Comstock Lode, discovered, 118; riches of, 119; effect on value of silver, 151

Conference for Progressive Political Action, formed, 558; activities of, 559

Congress for Industrial Organization, adopts constitution, 647. *See* Committee for Industrial Organization

Conkling, Roscoe, on Fourteenth Amendment, 24; "boss" of New York, 140; heads Stalwarts, 160; urges third term for Grant, 161; resigns and seeks re-election, 194

Connally, Tom, delegate to United Nations, 769

Connecticut, divorce laws, 84; Democratic gains in (1910), 431; votes for Hoover (1932), 628; Republican gains in (1938), 681

Connolly, Richard B., member Tweed Ring, 88

Connor, P. E., campaign against Sioux, 126

Conscription Act, of 1917, 487; of 1940, 712

Conservation, favored by Populists, 251; urged by Theodore Roosevelt, 395; conference on, 397; National Conservation Commission, 398

Constitution of the United States, on method of counting electoral votes, 142; on territories and dependencies, 342; Roosevelt's interpretation of, 380; "twilight zone" between state and national authority, 391; on nature of the Senate, 404

Constitutions, state, during reconstruction, 34; provisions in Missouri, 50; California constitution of 1877, 158; constitutional convention in New York, 400; provisions for popular government, 403

Continental solidarity, emphasized at Lima Conference, 704; difficulties in the way of, 706

Continuous voyages, British interpretation of, 472

Contraband, British practices regarding, 472

Contract and Finance Company, in construction of Central Pacific, 77

Convict labor, used to build the "New South," 222

Cooke, Jay, financial activities, 59

Cooley, Thomas M., heads Interstate Commerce Commission, 172

Coolidge, Calvin, nominated for Vice-President, 516; urges adherence to World Court, 523; ignores Tariff Commission, 529; sketch of, 548; becomes President, 549; economy program, 549; appointees of, 552; growing popularity of, 556; re-election, 562; refusal to run in 1928, 574

Cooper, Peter, steel manufacturer, 62; Greenback nominee for President, 141

Co-operative Marketing Act, adopted by Kentucky, 546

Co-operatives, during Granger movement, 95; favored by Knights of Labor, 182; sponsored by Farmers' Alliances, 246, 247; failure of Texas Exchange, 248; promoted by farmer organizations (1920's), 546; exempted from anti-trust laws, 548; encouraged by Hoover, 580

Copper mines, in Montana, 119; in the Southwest, 120

Corbett, "Gentleman Jim," boxer, 297

Corn Islands, site for naval base, 372

Cornell, Ezra, endows Cornell University, 98; locates lands, 99

Cornell, Katherine, actress, 593

Corporations, methods of finance, 85; special privileges of, 170; use of due process clause, 179; power over labor, 180; increasing size of, 380; concern over establishment of Bureau of Corporations, 390; opposition to conservation, 398; control state governments, 400; attacked by La Follette, 401; efforts to control U.S. Senate, 404; tend to overcapitalize, 414; necessity conceded by Progressives, 452; efforts to regulate, 453; wartime taxation of, 489; during prosperity of 1920's, 584; liberties curtailed by the New Deal, 672. *See also* Business, Industry

Corral system, in Cuba, 309

Corregidor, surrender by U.S., 719

Corrupt practices act, favored by Progressive Republicans, 433; enacted in New Jersey, 441

Cortelyou, George B., heads Bureau of Corporations, 413; Secretary of the Treasury, 415

Cotton, seizures after Civil War, 5; culture of, 10; world demand for, 221; southern manufacture of, 222; utilization of cottonseed, 223; methods of production, 226; one-crop evil, 229; low price of, 540; cooperative marketing of, 546; efforts to stabilize price of, 581; under AAA, 648; Cotton Control Act, 646; declining market for, 656

Coughlin, Father Charles E., radio orator, 596; anti-Roosevelt views, 673

Council of Foreign Ministers, conducts peace negotiations, 752; signs minor treaties, 753; fails to make peace with Germany, 757; renews discussion of the German question, 786

Council of National Defense, created, 478; activities of, 493

Country stores, in post-war South, 10; crop-lien system, 227

Cowboys, characteristics, 132

Cox, James M., Democratic nominee for President (1920), 517

Cox, Kenyon, painter, 279

Coxey, Jacob S., leads march on Washington, 265

Cramer, Charles F., adviser of Forbes, 533

Crazy Horse, Sioux leader, 128

Crédit Mobilier of America, purpose of, 53; activities, 77

Creel, George, heads Committee on Public Information, 491

Crime of 1873, committed, 150; denunciations of, 266

Crimean Conference. *See* Yalta Conference

Cripple Creek War, in Colorado, 264

Crocker, Charles, builder of Central Pacific, 77

Cromwell, William, counsel for New Panama Canal Company, 366; aids Bunau-Varilla, 367

Crop-lien system, in the South, 10, 227

Cuba, seizure of the *Virginius*, 308; insurrection in 1895, 308; nature of the Cuban revolt, 309; Spanish efforts to suppress, 309; American protests, 310; the de Lôme letter, 310; popular demand for intervention, 312; war in, 320; surrender to U.S., 330; promised freedom, 334; sanitary measures in, 339; Platt Amendment, 340; American authority withdrawn, 341;

virtual protectorate of U.S., 372; declares war on Germany, 482; revolution in, 683

Cullom, Shelby M., heads committee to investigate railroads, 171

Cummins, A. B., governor of Iowa, 402; insurgency of, 423

Currency. *See* Money question

Curtis, Charles, nominated for Vice-President, 574; elected, 578; defeated for re-election, 624

Curtis, G. W., Editor *Harper's Weekly*, 44; heads Civil Service Commission, 45; favors re-election of Grant, 52; sketch of, 91; opposes Blaine in 1884, 201; supports Cleveland, 203

Custer, George A., Washita massacre, 126; Custer massacre, 128

Cutting, Bronson, supports Roosevelt (1932), 628

Czechoslovakia, created a state, 511; absorbed by Hitler, 696; occupied by Russians, 725; American advance halted, 744; Communist control of, 776; rejects Marshall Plan, 781; Communists seize government, 783

Czechs, emigration to United States, 73, 189

Dakota Territory, growth of, 237; drouth in, 238

Dana, Charles A., editor, 297

Danbury Hatters' Case, significance of, 454

Daniel, John W., temporary chairman Democratic convention (1896), 270

Daniels, Josephus, Secretary of the Navy, 444

Danube navigation, conference on, 783

Darlan, Jean François, assassination of, 721

Daugherty, Harry M., Attorney-General under Harding, 519; intimacy with Harding, 532; brought to trial, 533; prosecutes "reds," 537; influences Harding appointments, 553

Davis, Cushman K., member peace delegation (1898), 330

Davis, David, *Ex parte Milligan*, 37; aspires to Liberal Republican nomination, 51; elected to U.S. Senate, 143

Davis, Henry Gassaway, Democratic candidate for Vice-President (1904), 413

Davis, John W., Democratic nominee for President (1924), 561

Davis, Norman H., at Geneva conference, 702

De Gaulle, Charles, "Free French" leader, 701; opposes Giraud, 723; at Casablanca, 740; heads rightist movement, 782

Dawes, Charles G., promotes unified system of supply for Allies in the First World War, 503; named Director of the Budget by President Harding, 528; Republican nominee for Vice-President (1924), 561; elected Vice-President, 562; Dawes Plan for reparations for Germany, 567; heads RFC, 619

Dawes, H. L., on tariff reform, 198

Dawes Act, granting Indians lands in severalty, 129

Day, William R., Secretary of State, 312; heads peace delegation, 330

Deadwood, Black Hills mining town, 123

Debs, Eugene V., sketch of, 262; defies court injunction, 264; Socialist candidate for President (1900), 339; in later campaigns, 421; large vote for in 1912, 438; imprisoned, 492; polls heavy vote in 1920, 558

Debt, Confederate, unpaid, 4; demand for repudiation, 16; in Fourteenth Amendment, 26

Debt, United States, Republicans favor payment, 41; in coin or equivalent, 45; reduced by Mellon, 550; increased under Hoover, 632; increased by the New Deal, 672; debt limit raised, 712; mounts during World War II, 735

Declaration of London, fails of ratification, 378; not binding in the World War (1914), 471

Delaware, votes for Hoover (1932), 628

De Leon, Daniel, Socialist leader, 421

De Lesseps, Ferdinand, forms Panama Canal Company, 365

De Lima vs. Bidwell, 342

De Lôme letter, publication of, 310

Demobilization. See Army of the United States

Democratic party, supports Johnson, 23; feared by industrialists, 27; joined by southern whites, 35; convention of 1868, 42; supports Greeley in 1872, 52; gains during seventies, 139; in election of 1876, 141; dissensions in, 161; on tariff reform, 199, 200, 209; one-party system in the South, 229; Alliance influence in, 249, 250; splits on money question, 257; drift toward free silver, 269; turns conservative in 1904, 413; victories in 1910, 431; returns to power (1913), 445; re-elects Wilson, 480; loses House of Representatives (1918), 507; dissensions over Klan issue, 560; splits over Smith in 1928, 575, 578; returned to power, 628; committed to experimentation, 675; reverses in 1946, 750; platform of 1948, 788; wins election, 790

Denby, Edwin, transfers naval oil reserves to Interior Department, 533

Denmark, attacked by Germany, 700

Densmore, James, promotes typewriter, 174

Denver and Rio Grande Railroad, construction of, 166

Dependents' Pension Act, passed, 216

Depressions, after 1873, 59; effect on business, 164; after 1893, 255; after 1919, 539; after 1929, 586

Desert Land Act, for sale of government land, 234

Destroyer-naval bases deal, 713

Dewey, George, sent to Asiatic waters, 316; battle of Manila Bay, 318; made Rear-Admiral, 319; position in Manila Bay, 319

Dewey, John, educational philosophy, 606

Dewey, Thomas E., New York prosecutor, 605; wins Republican nomination in 1944, 737; favors bipartisan foreign policy, 778; renominated in 1948, 787; defeated, 790

Diaz, Porfirio, Dictator of Mexico, 463; resigns, 464

Diederichs, Otto von, German commander in Manila Bay, 319

Dies Committee, investigates un-American activities, 734

Dingley Tariff, terms of, 276

Diplomacy. See Foreign policy

Dixiecrats, in campaign of 1948, 788

Direct primaries, established in Wisconsin, 401; elsewhere, 402; preferential primaries in senatorial elections, 404; favored by insurgents, 428, 433; in presidential nominations (1912), 435; (1920), 516.

Disney, Walt, popularizes animated cartoons, 593

Disputed election of 1876, 142

Dix, Dorothea L., reformer, 112

Doctrine of Isolation, defined, 299; threats to, 355; ignored by Theodore Roosevelt, 377; by Woodrow Wilson, 509; contradicted by League of Nations, 510; violated by Harding's Four-Power Pact, 521; undermined by economic developments, 565; contradicts economic realities, 569; affected by depression conditions, 586

Doheny, Edward L., involved in oil scandals, 534

Dollar diplomacy, in Caribbean zone, 374; in the Far East, 433

"Dollar-matching," in educational grants, 459; for good roads, 460

Dolliver, Jonathan P., insurgent senator, 423; correspondence with Pinchot, 427

Dominican Republic, indebtedness of, 371; U.S. intervention in, 373

Donnelly, Ignatius, Populist orator, 248; presents Alliance platform, 250; on Bryan, 270; nominated for Vice-President (1900), 338

Dorsey, Stephen W., involved in star-route frauds, 195

Douglas, Paul, elected senator, 791

Douglas, Stephen A., monument unveiled, 27

Douglas, William O., appointed to Supreme Court, 679; refuses to run for President, 788

Downes vs. Bidwell, 342

Draft, of 1917, 487; of 1940, 712; post-war draft, 747, 748 n.

Drago Doctrine, asserted, 371

Drake, Edwin, bores for oil, 64

Dreiser, Theodore, An American Tragedy, 609

Drew, Daniel, business practices, 85

Drummond, Henry, on evolution, 295

Dry-farming, efforts to promote, 398

Due process of law, in Fourteenth Amendment, 24; in Granger cases, 94; used by corporations, 179

Dulles, John Foster, State Department adviser, 778; delegate to United Nations, 788

Dumba, Constantin, sabotage activities, 474

Dumbarton Oaks Conference, plans for United Nations organization, 738, 744

Dunkirk, British withdrawal from, 700

Dunne, Finley Peter, creator of "Mr. Dooley," 343; on Roosevelt's attitude toward the trusts, 385

Durant, William C., founds General Motors, 590

Durbin, Deanna, screen star, 593

Dutch East Indies, conquered by Japanese, 719; post-war struggle for independence, 766. See also Indonesia

Dutch West Indies, occupied by Allies, 705
Dyea, coveted by Canada, 362

Eads, James B., bridge-builder, 80
Eastman, Joseph B., Railroad Co-ordinator, 660
Eaton, Dorman B., Civil Service Commissioner, 196
Economic revolution, progress of, 60; accelerated by Civil War, 68; new industries, 71; effect on education, 100; railroads' contribution to, 172; effect on American society, 283, 284. *See also* Business, Corporations, Industry
Economy Act, signed by F. D. Roosevelt, 631
Eddy, Mary Baker G., author of *Science and Health*, 109
Edison, Thomas A., sketch of, 173; inventor of motion pictures, 592
Edmunds, George F., candidate for Republican nomination (1880), 161; favored by Independents in 1884, 201
Education, provisions for in reconstruction constitutions, 34; advances during the seventies, 95; high schools, 96; universities, 97; Morrill Act, 99; law schools, 102; women's colleges, 104; public education, 295; in Philippines, 345; federal grants in aid of, 459; during World War, 495; recent developments in, 606; criticisms of higher education, 607
Egan, Patrick, American minister to Chile, 304; recall demanded by Chile, 305
Eggleston, Edward, writings of, 108
Eighteenth Amendment, adopted, 408
Eightieth Congress, record, 751; denounced by Truman, 790
Eisenhower, Dwight D., commands in Africa, 721; transferred to England, 724; conquest of Germany, 725; halts American advance, 744; refuses to be candidate for President, 787
El Caney, engagement at, 325
Elections, of 1866, 26; of 1868, 40, 87; of 1870, 48; of 1872, 52; of 1874, 139; of 1876, 141; of 1878, 149; of 1880, 163; of 1882, 196; of 1884, 205; of 1886, 209; of 1888, 212; of 1890, 220, 249; of 1892, 252; of 1894, 267; of 1896, 274; of 1898, 277, 336; of 1900, 338; of 1902, 413; of 1904, 413; of 1906, 413; of 1908, 413, 420; of 1910, 430; of 1912, 438; of 1914, 478; of 1916, 478; of 1918, 507; of 1920, 517; of 1922, 559; of 1924, 562; of 1928, 578; of 1930, 623; of 1932, 628; of 1934, 674; of 1936, 677; of 1938, 681; of 1940, 714; of 1942, 721; of 1944, 737; of 1946, 750; of 1948, 786
Electoral Commission, in election of 1876, 143
Electric lighting, comes into use, 174
Elgin, Ill., watch-making center, 71
Eliot, Charles W., made president of Harvard, 97; experiments with elective system, 100; improves medical education, 102; influence of, 296; elective system criticized, 607
Elk Hills, oil scandal, 533
Elkins Act, forbids rebates, 390
Ely, Richard T., economist, 296

Emergency Banking Act, signed by Roosevelt, 631; indicates nature of New Deal, 634
Emergency Fleet Corporation, operations of, 493
Emergency Immigration Act (1921), terms of, 531
Emergency Railroad Transportation Act, 660
Emergency Relief Organization, set up by Hoover, 619
Emergency Tariff Act, terms of, 529
Employers' liability laws, advocated by Theodore Roosevelt, 394; passed by the states, 406
"Endless chain," gold purchases under Cleveland, 257
Enforcement Acts, against Ku Klux Klan, 48
Engels, Friedrich, associate of Marx, 687
England. *See* Great Britain
English, William H., candidate for Vice-President, 162
Equity Co-operative Exchange, subsidiary of American Society of Equity, 542
Erie Railroad, western connections, 78; stock manipulations by Daniel Drew, 86; growth of, 166; bankruptcy of, 255
Esch-Cummins Act, terms of, 534; designed to take government out of business, 550
Espionage Act, limits personal liberty, 492
Ethiopia, attacked by Italy, 695; U.S. policy toward, 704
European Recovery Plan, proposed by Marshall, 778; accepted by sixteen nations, 781; effect on Europe, 782
Evans, John, governor of Colorado, 126
"Ever-normal granary," promoted by Secretary Wallace, 655
Evolution, scientific doctrine of, 294; controversy over, 295; increasing acceptance of, 602
Ex parte Milligan, 37
Expedition Act, speeds consideration of Northern Securities case, 386
Export debenture plan, for relief of agriculture, 572; attempted inclusion in Hawley-Smoot Tariff, 582
Express companies, in the Far West, 121; American Railway Express Co., 524

Fairbanks, Charles W., elected Vice-President (1904), 413
Fairbanks, Douglas, motion picture star, 592
Fall, Albert B., Secretary of the Interior under Harding, 519; accepts bribes from oil interests, 533; convicted, 534
Far Eastern Commission, advises on government of Japan, 761
Farley, James A., cancels air-mail contracts, 599; Roosevelt's campaign manager (1932), 624; Postmaster-General, 630; as patronage broker, 633; predicts Democratic landslide (1936), 676
Farm Bloc, formed, 546
Farm Credit Administration (FCA), handles rural credits, 652
Farm orders, Grangers, 93; Farmers' alliances, 245; American Society of Equity, 458; Farmers' Union, 458; National Non-Partisan League, 458; during 1920's, 542

Farm Security Administration (FSA), New Deal agency, 653
Farmer-Labor Party, in Minnesota, 545; in campaign of 1920, 558; during 1930's, 681
Farmers' Alliance, members in Congress, 220; beginnings of, 245; seeks union of all farm orders, 250; decline of, 254
Farmers' Declaration of Independence, Granger document, 94
Farmers' Holiday Association, attempts strike, 622
Farmers' Mutual Benefit Association, farm order, 245
Farmers' Union, growth of, 458, 542
Fascism, under Mussolini in Italy, 688; feared in Latin America, 704; overthrown in Italy, 723
Federal Board of Mediation, replaces Railroad Labor Board, 525
Federal Bureau of Investigation, wars on racketeers, 605; activities in World War II, 734
Federal Crop Insurance Corporation, New Deal agency, 654
Federal Deposit Insurance Corporation (FDIC), New Deal agency, 658
Federal Elections Bill, championed by Lodge, 219; unpopularity of, 220
Federal Emergency Relief Administration (FERA), created, 637
Federal Farm Board, created, 580; discontinued, 581; surpluses used for relief, 619; absorbed into FCA, 652
Federal Farm Loan Board, created, 458; merged in FCA, 652
Federal Highways Act, passed in 1916, 460; resulting good roads, 589
Federal Housing Administration (FHA), New Deal agency, 662
Federal Land Banks, created, 458; duties extended, 547
Federal Power Commission, activities of, 663
Federal Radio Commission, licenses broadcasting stations, 594
Federal Reserve System, established, 449; described, 450; shoulders war burdens, 495; permits credit expansion, 542; governing board expanded, 547; under Coolidge, 553; supports stock speculation, 584, 587; Glass-Steagall Act, 658; during recession of 1937–38, 680
Federal Securities Act, New Deal measure, 659
Federal Surplus Commodities Commission, distributes farm products, 638
Federal Trade Commission, created, 453; under Coolidge, 552
Federal Water-Power Commission, activities of, 663
"Fellow-servant" doctrine, abrogated in the states, 406
Fenian Movement, affects Canadian relations, 56
Fertilizers, manufactured in the South, 224
Fetterman massacre, in Wyoming, 127
Field, Cyrus W., lays transatlantic cable, 173
Field, James G., candidate for Vice-President, 251
Fifteenth Amendment, adopted, 36

"Fifth column" activities, feared in America, 705
Filibustering, during Cuban insurrection, 308; Cleveland's efforts to prevent, 310
Finland, pays war debt to U.S., 566, 623; attacked by Russia, 700; allied with Germany, 716; aids Allies, 725; peace negotiations, 752
Finley, Dr. Carlos J., blames mosquitoes for yellow fever, 339
Fish, Hamilton (b. 1808), Secretary of State, 44; negotiates Treaty of Washington, 57
Fish, Hamilton (b. 1888), isolationist views, 710; defeated for re-election, 738
Fisheries, dispute with Great Britain over, 57
Fisk, James, in gold conspiracy, 52; extravagance, 83; railroad activities, 86
Fisk University, Negro college, 104
Fiske, John, philosopher, 103
Five Civilized Tribes, holdings reduced, 127
Flagler, H. M., oil refiner, 67
"Floaters," in Indiana politics, 211
Florida, in election of 1876, 142; end of carpet-bag rule, 145
Flour-milling, beginnings of, 69; roller process, 70; organization of the industry, 381
Foch, Ferdinand, in supreme command, 498
Folger, William J., defeated for governor of New York, 201, 203
Folk, Joseph W., St. Louis prosecutor, 402
Food Administration, established, 493; effect on American food habits, 540
Football, conquers colleges, 297
Foraker Act, provides government for Puerto Rico, 342
Forbes, Charles R., heads Veterans' Bureau, 519; found guilty of fraud, 533
Force Bill, championed by Lodge, 219; unpopularity of, 220
Ford, Henry, bids for Muscle Shoals, 552; production methods, 554, 590; refuses to co-operate with NRA, 644
Fordney-McCumber Act, terms of, 529; effect of, 588
Foreign policy of U.S., during Grant's administration, 55; Treaty of Washington, 57; widening scope of, 299; under Blaine, 300; in the Pacific, 301; Pan-Americanism, 303; Venezuelan Controversy, 305; relations with Spain, 310; peace with Spain, 329; open-door policy, 356; Alaskan boundary dispute, 362; Hay-Pauncefote treaties, 364; Hay-Herran Treaty, 367; Hay-Bunau-Varilla Treaty, 368; Venezuelan incident (1902), 371; Caribbean control, 372; "dollar diplomacy," 374; American neutrality (1914), 470; Lusitania, 475; War with Germany, 482; Paris Peace Conference, 507; neutrality legislation, 703; continental solidarity, 704; the Far East, 707; changes in neutrality laws, 708; measures "short of war," 713; the Atlantic Charter, 716; war with Japan, Germany and Italy, 718
Foreign trade, stimulated by Department of Commerce, 553; increasing importance of, 565; unbalanced condition of, 588
Forests, destruction of, 395; beginning of conservation, 397

Fort Benton, Montana, reached by steamboats, 119
Fort C. F. Smith, constructed, 127
Fort Kearney, on Oregon Trail, 124
Fort Kearny, on Bozeman Trail, 127
Fort Knox, gold depository, 658
Fort Laramie, on Oregon Trail, 124
Fort Yuma, railroad through, 165
"Forty acres and a mule," freedmen's ambition, 8, 10
Foster, William Z., Communist candidate, 628
Four-Power Pact, on Pacific affairs, 521
Fourteen Diamond Rings Case, on Philippine tariff policy, 343
Fourteen Points, statement of, 504; altered in pre-armistice negotiations, 506; disregarded in Treaty of Versailles, 510
Fourteenth Amendment, submitted, 24; due process clause, 179
France, founds exchange professorships, 355; interests in China, 356; agrees to Boxer settlement, 358; part in Algeciras conference, 376; investments in Mexico, 463; European allies, 466; danger of defeat, 484; war debts settlement, 566; rejects Austro-German customs union, 622; Munich deal, 698; declares war on Germany, 699; fall of (1940), 700; "Free French" vs. Vichy government, 701; allows Japanese to take French Indo-China, 718; during North African invasion, 723; liberation of, 724; cessions from Italy, 754; Communist reverses, 782
Franco, Francisco, Spanish dictator, 696; regime investigated by UN, 772
Frankfurter, Felix, heads War Labor Policies Board, 495; becomes Associate Justice, 679
Frazier, Lynn J., governor of North Dakota, 545; elected to U.S. Senate, 559; sponsors Frazier-Lemke Act, 653
Free lands, as "safety valve," 82; rapid use of, 239; "passing of," 241, 283
Free passes, given by railroads, 177; attacked by Western Rural, 246; attacked by La Follette, 401
Free silver. See Silver as currency
Freedmen's Aid Society, work with Negroes, 9
Freedmen's Bureau, established, 7; activities, 7, 10; proposed bill to continue, 22; bill vetoed by Johnson, 23; passed over Johnson's veto, 24
Freedom of the seas, omitted from armistice terms, 506
Freighting, in the Far West, 120, 122
Frelinghuysen, Frederick T., Secretary of State, 303
French, Daniel Chester, sculptor, 279
French Indo-China, invaded by Japanese, 718; post-war conflict, 766
Friar lands, in Philippines, 344
Frick, Henry Clay, heads Carnegie Steel Company, 261; attacked by Alexander Berkman, 261
Frontier, significance of, 280; disappearance of, 284; influence of, 285
Frost, Robert, writings of, 610
Fry, Lewis G., leads march of the unemployed, 266

Frye, William R., member peace delegation (1898), 330
Fuel Administration, organized, 493
"Full Dinner Pail," as campaign issue, 338
Fuller, Melville W., Chief Justice, 432
Fur-seals controversy, Blaine's part in, 300; settlement of, 301
Furuseth, Andrew, heads Seamen's Union, 455
"Fusion," between Populists and Republicans, 268

G.I. Bill of Rights, becomes law, 747
Gage, Lyman P., Secretary of the Treasury, 277
Gallup poll, follows sampling method, 676
Galveston, Tex., after Civil War, 4; commission plan of government, 405
Gambling, during 1870's, 84; in the mining West, 120; efforts to wipe out, 408
Garfield, James A., nominated for President, 161; elected, 163; sketch of, 191; death of, 192
Garland, Hamlin, A Son of the Middle Border, 609
Garner, John N., elected Speaker, 623; elected Vice-President, 628; re-elected, 677
General Motors Corporation, established in 1908, 590; yields to "sit-down" strike, 647
General Staff, established for U.S. Army, 348; plans for raising an army, 487; revises plans for war in France, 497
Gentlemen's agreement, between U.S. and Japan, 360
Geneva Conference (1933), fails to achieve disarmament, 702
George, Henry, Progress and Poverty, 239; single tax theories, 241
George, Milton, founds Farmers' Alliance (northern), 246
George, W. F., opposed by Roosevelt, 681
George Washington, carries American peace delegation to Europe, 507
Georgia, readmitted, 36; cotton industry in, 223; shortage of banking facilities in, 227; Alliance successes in, 249; in TVA area, 663
German-Americans, attitude during the first World War, 470; oppose Wilson's re-election, 479; compelled to buy bonds, 488; persecution of, 496
Germany, emigration from to United States, 72, 189, 284; interests in Samoa, 302; friendly attitude toward U.S., 355; interests in China, 356; endorses open-door policy, 358; differences with Venezuela (1902), 370; possible interests in Dominican Republic, 372; efforts to safeguard interests in Morocco, 376; protests against American pork, 391; investments in Mexico, 463; allies of, 466; declarations of war (1914), 469; offers negotiated peace (1916), 480; inaugurates unrestricted submarine warfare, 481; at war with U.S., 482; makes peace with Russia, 498; plans for conquest, 505; complete defeat of, 500, 505; revolution in, 506; accepts responsibility for war losses, 508; disarmament of,

508; Harding signs separate peace with, 520; reparations problem, 567; signs Kellogg-Briand Peace Pact, 569; Lausanne settlement, 622; Hitler's rise in, 690; expansion of, 696; accord with Italy, 697; accord with Russia, 698; attacks Poland, 699; overruns western Europe (1940), 700; aerial attack on Britain, 701; successful war methods, 711; campaigns in the Balkans, 715; attacks Russia, 716; declares war on U.S., 718; uses robot bomb, 724; conquest of, 725; Yalta decisions on, 744; post-war government, 754; problems of occupation, 756; trials of war criminals, 757; Bizonia and Trizonia, 758; Russian policy in, 783; air-lift to Berlin, 784; constitution for western Germany, 785

Geronimo, Apache chieftain, 128
"Ghost Dancers," among Dakota Indians, 129
Gilbert and Solomon Islands, awarded to Great Britain, 303
Gilman, Daniel Coit, president of Johns Hopkins, 98
Ginn, Edward, establishes World Peace Foundation, 378
Girard, Stephen, philanthropist, 98
Giraud, Henri Honoré, assumes French command in Africa, 721; at Casablanca, 740
Girdler, T. M., heads Republic Steel Corporation, 647
Glasgow, Ellen, writings of, 609
Glass, Carter, frames Federal Reserve Act, 449; sponsors Glass-Steagall Act, 658
Glavis, Louis R., dismissed from office, 427
Godkin, E. L., editor New York Nation, 44; sketch of, 90; on significance of the frontier, 282
Goethals, George W., builds Panama Canal, 369
Gold conspiracy, by Fisk and Gould, 52
Gold Democrats, in campaign of 1896, 272 n.
Gold reserve, accumulated by Sherman, 147; strained by Sherman Silver Purchase Act, 217; decline of under Harrison, 254; reasons for depletion, 256; gold purchases under Cleveland, 257; under Federal Reserve System, 450; Gold Reserve Act, 657
Gold standard, advocated by Republicans, 269, 273; enacted into law, 277; supported by Parker (1904), 413; during World War I, 495; maintained by Hoover, 621; abandoned by Great Britain, 622; abandoned by U.S., 657
"Golden Spike Special," celebrates completion of Northern Pacific, 165
Gomez, Maximo, Cuban leader, 308
Gompers, Samuel, sketch of, 186; on conditions in coal industry, 392; supports war policy, 495
"Good neighbor" policy, under F. D. Roosevelt, 683
Goodhue, Bertram, architect, 612
Gore, Thomas P., on American neutrality, 476
Gorgas, William C., begins sanitation of Havana, 339; sanitation of Canal Zone, 369
Göring, Hermann Wilhelm, suicide of, 757

Gough, John B., temperance reformer, 110
Gould, Jay, in Gold conspiracy, 52; relations with Grant, 53; railroad activities, 86; unpopularity of, 183
Graduate schools, established in America, 102; multiplication of, 606
Grady, Henry W., preaches southern industrialization, 222
Grain Corporation, during World War I, 493
Grain Stabilization Corporation, activities of, 581
Grand Army of the Republic, works for pensions, 207; opposes Cleveland, 212; expands in New West, 242
Grand Rapids, Mich., furniture center, 224
Grandfather clause, in southern constitutions, 219
Grange, origins of, 93; legislation against railroads, 94; co-operatives, 95; in California, 157, 158; effects of, 169; survivals of, 542; favors export debenture plan, 572
Grant, U.S., report on the South, 22; favored by the Radicals, 28; named Secretary of War, 31; nominated for President, 40; elected, 43; chooses cabinet, 44; enforces Ku Klux Act, 48; re-elected, 52; part in gold conspiracy, 53; desires to annex Santo Domingo, 55; entertained by Fisk, 83; third-term movement, 161
Gray, George, member peace delegation (1898), 330; opposes annexation of the Philippines, 331
Great American Desert, myth of, 231, 238
Great Britain, emigration to U.S., 72, 73, 189, 284; interests in Samoa, 302; Venezuelan boundary dispute with U.S., 306; policy toward U.S., 307; naval rivalry with, 315; efforts to secure alliance with U.S., 355; interests in China, 356; co-operates with U.S., 358; alliance with Japan, 359; Alaskan boundary settlement, 362; Hay-Pauncefote treaties with U.S., 364; differences with Venezuela (1902), 370; part in Algeciras Conference, 376; investments in Mexico, 463; European Allies, 466; declares war on Germany (1914), 469; views on neutral rights, 471; successful propaganda in U.S., 483; injured by submarine, 484; war aims of, 504; part in secret treaties, 508; immigrant quota to U.S., 531; declining imports from U.S., 540; war debt funded, 566; change to high tariff policy, 583; abandons gold standard, 622; reciprocal trade treaty with U.S., 682; Munich deal with Germany, 696; seeks alliance with Russia, 698; declares war on Germany (1939), 699; withdraws troops from Dunkirk, 700; obtains American destroyers, 713; defeats in Asia, 719; base for second front, 724; German occupation, 744; election of 1945, 746; efforts for peace, 752; Bizonia and Trizonia, 758; new colonial policy, 765; troops in Greece, 772; Palestine mandate, 773; withdrawal from Palestine, 774; American loan, 779
Great Depression, background of, 584; Panic of 1929, 585; causes of, 586
Great Northern Railroad, constructed, 166; success of, 168
Greece, in World War I, 482; in World War

II, 715; cessions from Italy, 754; United Nations investigation, 772; Communist efforts to control, 776; the Truman Doctrine, 777

Greeley, Horace, opposes "Grantism," 50; Liberal Republican nominee, 51; accepted by Democrats, 52; defeated, 52; death, 52; comments on Pike's Peak Gold Rush, 117; on tariff protection, 198; influence of, 297

Green, William, heads A.F. of L., 646; opposes CIO methods, 647

Greenbacks, efforts to call in, 45; effect on business, 60; Greenback Party, 141; rise to parity with gold, 148; in election of 1878, 149; celebrated in song, 149; in election of 1880, 163

Greenland, military use by U.S., 715

Grey, Sir Edward, British foreign minister, 468

Griswold, Dwight, American aid administrator in Greece, 778

Grotius, Hugo, on International Law, 471

Guadalcanal Island, fighting in, 726

Guam, acquired by U.S., 333; government of, 348; in World War II, 719

Guantanamo, site for naval base, 372

Guffey-Snyder Act, invalidated, 646

Hague Conferences, first, 375; second, 377, 471

Hague Tribunal, established, 375; limitations of, 377

Haig, Douglas, British commander in France, 500

Hailie Selassie, Ethiopian monarch, 696

Haiti, U.S. intervention in, 374; withdrawal from, 684

"Half-Breeds," in Republican Party, 160

Hall, A. Oakey, member Tweed Ring, 88

Halsey, William F., naval commander, 726; Battle of Leyte Gulf, 728

Hampton Normal and Agricultural Institute, for Negroes, 105

Hancock, W. S., during reconstruction, 33; Democratic candidate for President, 162; defeated, 163

Hanna, Marcus A., Republican "boss" of Ohio, 268; supports McKinley for President, 268; campaign manager, 270; collects campaign fund, 273; aspires to seat in U.S. Senate, 277; opposes war with Spain, 312; opposes Theodore Roosevelt for Vice-President, 354; secures campaign contribution from New Panama Canal Company, 366; urges conciliation upon mine operators, 392; death of, 413

Harding, Warren G., seeks Republican nomination (1920), 515; nominated, 516; elected, 517; sketch of, 519; urges adherence to World Court, 523; favors budget reform, 528; on tariff reduction, 529; weakness of, 532; death of, 534; appointees to Supreme Court, 553; pardons Debs, 558

Harkness, E. S., philanthropies, 98

Harkness, S. V., oil refiner, 67

Harlan, Justice J. M., on insular decisions, 342; passed over for promotion by Taft, 432

Harmon, Judson, governor of Ohio, 436

Harper's Weekly, edited by G. W. Curtis, 44,

91; denounces Tweed Ring, 89; prints Mulligan letters, 202

Harriman, E. H., promotes railway merger, 381

Harrison, Benjamin, nominated for President, 211; elected, 212; sketch of, 213; on civil service reform, 213; defeated for reelection, 252

Harrison, Francis B., governor-general of the Philippines, 345

Hart, A. B., criticizes disposition of the public lands, 239

Harte, Bret, writings, 107

Harvard University, endowment, 98; medical school, 101; law school, 102; graduate school, 102, 296

Harvey, Col. George, original Wilson man, 442

Harvey, William H., author *Coin's Financial School*, 267

Havana Conference, promotes continental solidarity, 706

Hawaii, movement for annexation of, 301; annexation accomplished, 302; value to U.S., 334; government of, 348; attacked by Japanese, 718; Americans of Japanese ancestry in, 732; seeks statehood, 733

Hawaii vs. Mankichi, 343

Hawes-Cutting Act, authorizes Philippine independence, 346

Hawley-Smoot Tariff, opposed by American economists, 582; reprisals by foreign countries, 583; effect of, 588; on Cuba, 683

Hay, John, Secretary of State, 355; advocates open door in China, 356; Hay-Pauncefote treaties, 364; Hay-Herran Treaty, 367; Hay-Bunau-Varilla Treaty, 368

Hayes, John L., heads civilian tariff commission, 199

Hayes, R. B., nominated for President, 140; declared elected, 143; sketch of, 145; withdraws troops from South, 146; opposes Chinese exclusion, 159; favors American canal, 365

Haymarket riot, in Chicago, 183

Hays, Will H., resigns as Postmaster-General, 594

Haywood, William D., I.W.W. leader, 456

Hearst, William R., editor, 297; favors war with Spain, 309; forms Independence League, 420; favors Garner for President (1932), 624; isolationism, 710

Heil, Julius P., governor of Wisconsin, 681

Hemispheric defense, approved by F. D. Roosevelt, 683; by Lima Conference, 704; at Havana Conference, 705

Hendrick, Burton J., muckraker, 384

Hendricks, Thomas A., candidate for Vice-President, 141, 203

Heney, Francis J., California prosecutor, 402

Hepburn Act, to regulate railroad rates, 390

Hepburn committee, investigates railroads, 171

Hepburn vs. Griswold, 45

Herran, Tomas, negotiates treaty with Hay, 367

Hewitt, Abram S., introduces open-hearth process, 62

Hickok, "Wild Bill," western hero, 123

High schools, established, 96; recent improvements in, 606
High Point, N.C., furniture center, 224
Hill, Benjamin H., senator from Georgia, 222
Hill, David B., Democratic governor of New York, 212; seeks presidential nomination (1892), 252; defeated for temporary chairman (1896), 270
Hill, James J., builds Great Northern, 166; sketch of, 168; forms Northern Securities Company, 385; opposition to regulation, 388
Hillman, Sidney, co-head of preparedness commission, 712
Hillquit, Morris, Socialist leader, 421; opposes war with Germany, 491
Hiroshima, atomic bombing of, 730
Hitler, Adolf, Nazi leader, 690; *Mein Kampf*, 691; rise to power, 692; aggressions of, 696; deal with Stalin, 699. *See* Germany
Hoan, Daniel W., Milwaukee Socialist, 405
Hoar, George F., anti-imperialist, 332
Hobart, Garret A., candidate for Vice-President, 269
Hobson, Richmond P., sinks *Merrimac*, 322
Holladay, Ben, western express magnate, 121
Holley, Alexander L., uses Bessemer process, 60
Holmes, Dr. Oliver Wendell, service to medicine, 102
Holmes, Justice Oliver Wendell, dissents from Northern Securities decision, 386; upholds wartime limitations on liberty, 492
Home Insurance Building, first American skyscraper, 290
Home Loan Banks, established under Hoover, 620
Home Owners' Loan Corporation (HOLC), New Deal agency, 662
Home Rule for South. *See* Reconstruction
Homestead Act, in settlement of West, 233, 241
Homestead Strike, outbreak of, 260; issues of, 261
Honduras, proposed treaty with U.S., 374, 433
Hookworm disease, in the South, 226
Hoover, Herbert, Food Administrator, 493; seeks Republican nomination (1920), 515; urges adherence to World Court, 523; as Secretary of Commerce, 553; opposes McNary-Haugen Bill, 571; nominated for President, 574; sketch of, 576; defends Republican principles, 578; institutes radio licensing system, 594; policy toward depression, 617; interest in public works, 618; criticism of, 623; re-nominated, 624; campaign for re-election, 627; efforts to obtain Roosevelt's co-operation, 629; good-will tour of Latin America, 683
Hoover, J. Edgar, heads Federal Bureau of investigation, 605; activities in World War II, 734
Hopkins, Harry L., heads FERA, 638
Hopkins, Johns, endows university, 98
Hopkins, Mark, president of Williams, 191
Hopkins, Mark, railroad magnate, 77

Hornet, attacks Tokyo by air, 727
House, Col. Edward M., favors Wilson for Democratic nomination (1912), 442; his "great adventure," 468; his "quest for peace," 475; "plan to compel peace," 477; starts the Inquiry, 504; on Peace Commission, 507; advises Wilson to resign, 513
Housing problem, confronted by the New Deal, 662
Houston, Texas, entertains Democratic convention (1928), 575
Howard, O. O., heads Freedmen's Bureau, 7; promotes establishment of Howard University, 104
Howard University, Negro college, 104
Howell, J. A., commands North Patrol, 316
Howell, R. W., elected to U.S. Senate, 559
Howells, William Dean, writings, 108; death of, 609
Hudson, Manley O., elected to World Court, 523
Huerta, Victoriano, overthrows Madero, 464
Hughes, Charles Evans, elected governor of New York, 402; sketch of, 417; appointed Associate Justice, 432; nominated for President, 479; supports Harding (1920), 517; becomes Secretary of State, 519; opens Washington Conference, 520; elected to World Court, 523; appointed Chief Justice, 623; opposes court-packing plan, 678
Hull, Cordell, becomes Secretary of State, 630; attends World Economic Conference, 635; promotes trade treaties, 682; at Lima Conference, 704; at Havana Conference, 706; refuses to recognize Japanese conquests in China, 707; negotiates concerning Greenland, 731; promised Russian entrance into World War II by Stalin, 742; resigns, 745 n.
Humanitarian reform, in seventies, 108; progress of, 112
Humphrey, Hubert, urges Civil Rights plank, 788; elected senator, 791
Hungary, Treaty of Trianon, 511; entered by Russian troops, 725; peace negotiations, 752; Russian forces in, 756; Communist control of, 776
Hunt, R. M., architect, 279
Hunt, William H., begins new navy, 209
Huntington, Collis P., railroad magnate, 77
Hydroelectric power, private exploitation of, 396; withdrawals of water-power sites, 398; sites opened by Ballinger, 426; other New Deal developments, 667
Hyphenate Americans, denounced by Wilson, 479; support Harding, 517

Iceland, United States Navy in, 717
Ickes, Harold L., Secretary of the Interior, 630; heads PWA, 641
Idaho, created a territory, 118; admitted as a state, 214; labor violence in, 264; votes for Bryan in 1900, 338; grants suffrage to women, 408
Igorrotes, Philippine savages, 334
Illinois, Granger laws in, 93; during Pullman strike, 263; coal industry in, 392; CIO strikes in, 647
Immigration, desired by South, 10; fur-

nishes labor supply for North, 60; after Civil War, 72; statistics of, 73: growth of, 188; change in character of, 189; demands for restriction, 190; fostered by railroads, 236; Americanization of immigrants, 284; Japanese to California, 360; furnishes coal-miners, 392; promotes radicalism, 457; Old World sympathies of immigrants, 470; cessation during World War, 495; decline in, 531; restrictions on, 531; opposition to, 538; hinders prohibition, 603

Impeachment, of President Johnson, 32; of Secretary Belknap, 55; of Judge Archbald, 453

Imperialism, urged by Beveridge, 333; in campaign of 1900, 336; defended by Republicans, 337; approved by the electorate, 339; subsidence of interest in, 349

Income tax, advocated by Populists, 251; enacted in Wilson-German Act, 258; declared unconstitutional by Supreme Court, 259; authorized by Sixteenth Amendment, 426; assessed, 446; use during first World War, 489; reductions after the war, 529; during second World War, 736

Independence League, in campaign of 1908, 420

India, agitation for independence in, 588; becomes Allied base, 719; operations from, 729; British grant independence, 765

Indiana, divorce laws, 84; "floaters" in elections, 211; Klan activities in, 560

Indians, attack stage-coaches, 121; breakdown of old policy toward, 124; Sioux outbreak in Minnesota, 125; Arapaho and Cheyenne, 125; Sand Creek massacre, 126; study of by Congress, 127; councils with, 127; pauperization, 128; Custer massacre, 128; lands in severalty, 129; education of children, 130

Indonesia, United Nations investigation, 772

Industrial unions, favored by Debs, 262; by CIO, 646

Industrial Workers of the World, radical labor union, 456

Industry, advantage over agriculture, 60; steel, 61; oil, 63; stimulated by Civil War, 67; meat-packing, 68; flour-milling, 70; revolutionary developments in, 71; monopolistic tendencies of, 85; affected by Granger decisions, 94; concentrations in, 172, 175, 177; growth in the South, 222; supremacy in national life, 242; over-expansion during eighties, 256; favored by McKinley, 274; integration in, 381; efforts to restore competition, 388; attitude toward labor, 393; government regulation, 400; depression of early 1920's, 539; methods of, 554; enormous expansion of, 565, 586; opposes NRA, 645; O'Mahoney investigation of, 680; preparedness activities of, 712; war activities of, 735; reconversion, 748. See also Business, Corporations.

Inflation, after World War II, 749

Influenza, ravages during World War, 496, 502

Ingersoll, Robert G., on Blaine, 201

Initiative and referendum, use of, 403;

favored by Progressive Republicans, 433

Injunctions, use during Pullman strike, 264; limitations favored by Theodore Roosevelt, 394; restrictions set by Clayton Act, 454, 554; revival under Harding, 553

Inland Waterways Commission, surveys water routes, 397

Inquiry, The, under Colonel House, 504

Installment buying, growth of, 556, 587

Insular cases, decided by Supreme Court, 342

Insull, Samuel, utilities magnate, 659

Insurance companies, failures, 86; investigated by Hughes, 417

Insurgency, in the Senate, 423; in the House, 427; the insurgent program, 433; during Hoover's administration, 580

Intemperance, during 1870's, 84; efforts of reformers, 110

Interlocking directorates, become common, 381; Bryan favors prohibition of, 420

Intermediate Credits Act, farm relief measure, 547

International Civil Aviation Conference, held in U.S., 745

International Law, attempts to codify, 378; history of, 471

Interstate Commerce Commission, established, 172; attempts to regulate railroads, 382, 388; powers increased by Hepburn Act, 390; by Mann-Elkins Act, 431; by Esch-Cummins Act, 524; under Coolidge, 552; regulates air-mail contracts, 599; establishes two-cent passenger rate, 660; powers extended to motor buses and trucks, 661

Interventionists, favor collective security, 701

Iowa, Granger laws, 94; "Iowa idea," 422; votes for Wilson (1916), 480; boom in farm lands, 536

Irish-Americans, in Fenian movement, 56; new arrivals, 72; employed on Union Pacific, 76; influence in politics, 161; opposition to Wilson, 479

Iron mines, in the South, 224; in Minnesota and Michigan, 381

"Ironclad oath," in second Congressional plan, 30

Irons, Martin, strike leader, 183

Irrigation, introduced into Colorado, 117; water shortage in California, 157; under Desert Land Act, 234; survey of irrigation sites, 396

Isolation. See Doctrine of Isolation

Isolationism, advocated in United States, 701, 709

Isthmian Canal Commission, appointed by McKinley, 366

Italy, emigration from to U.S., 73, 189; differences with Venezuela (1902), 370; war with Turkey, 467; Italia irredenta, 467, 508; in World War I, 482; dispute over Fiume, 511; immigrant quota to U.S., 531; war debt funded, 566; signs Kellogg-Briand Peace Pact, 569; fascism in, 634, 688; attacks Ethiopia, 695; absorbs Albania, 697; alliance with Japan, 707; invaded and defeated, 723; peace negotiations, 752; treaty of peace, 754; Communists in, 782

Itata incident, in Chilean relations, 304
Iwo Jima, attacked by Americans, 727

Jackson, Helen Hunt, criticizes Indian policy, 129
Jackson, Robert H., approves legality of destroyer deal, 713; prosecutes war criminals, 757
James, Henry, writings of, 108
James, Jesse, bandit, 84
Jameson's raid, effect on British policy, 307
Japan, good relations with U.S., 301; ambitions in the Philippines, 346; war with China (1895), 356; participates in suppression of Boxers, 357; interest in alliance with U.S., 358; ambitions in the Orient, 359; war with Russia, 359; hostility toward U.S., 360; immigration from to U.S., 360; abandons open-door policy, 361; at war with Germany, 462; participates in Washington Conference, 520; relations with China, 521; violation of pledges, 522; signs Kellogg-Briand Peace Pact, 569; designs on China, 588; aggressions in China, 694; U.S. abrogates commercial treaty with, 707; alliance with Germany and Italy, 707; takes French Indo-China, 718; attacks U.S. at Pearl Harbor, 718; victories, 719; defeats, 721, 727; surrender, 731; American occupation, 760; failure to obtain peace treaty, 762
Japanese, immigration to U.S., 360; in Hawaii, 732; treatment during World War II, 733
Jay Cooke and Company, failure of, 59
Jefferson, Territory of, 117
Jenckes, T. A., civil service reformer, 44
Jessup, Philip, U.S. Ambassador-at-large, 786
Jewett, Sarah Orne, writings of, 108
Jews, emigration to United States, 189; denounced by modern Ku Klux Klan, 538
Johns Hopkins University, opens, 98; graduate school, 102, 296
Johnson, Andrew, sketch of, 14; relations with Radicals, 15; plan of reconstruction, 16; first message to Congress, 18; vetoes Freedmen's Bureau Bill, 23; his Washington's Birthday speech, 23; vetoes Civil Rights Bill, 23; in election of 1866, 27; drinking habits, 28 n.; impeachment trial, 32; opposes Fenians, 56; elected to U.S. Senate, 139
Johnson, Hiram, elected governor of California, 402; Progressive nominee for Vice-President, 437; opposes Treaty of Versailles, 512; seeks Republican nomination (1920), 515; supports Harding, 517; supports Roosevelt (1932), 628
Johnson, Hugh S., promotes McNary-Haugen idea, 571; heads NRA, 643; resigns, 645
Johnson, John A., governor of Minnesota, 402
Johnson, Reverdy, minister to England, 56
Johnson, Tom L., on meaning of election of 1896, 274; mayor of Cleveland, 405
Johnson Act, prohibits foreign loans in U.S., 623

Joint-stock land banks, Wilson measure, 458
Jolson, Al, success in *The Jazz Singer*, 593
Jones, Samuel M., Toledo reformer, 405
Jones Act, for government of Philippines, 345
Jones Merchant Marine Act (1920), terms of, 526
Jones-White Act, to stimulate ship-building, 526
Judah, Theodore D., Central Pacific engineer, 76
Jutland, battle of, significance, 477; lessons of, 520

Kamikaze, Japanese suicide planes, 730
Kansas, grant to Santa Fe Railroad, 165; migration to, 236; mortgage problem in, 237; Farmers' Alliance in, 246; Populist revivalism in, 248; Alliance successes in, 249; votes for Wilson (1916), 480; Klan activities in, 560
Kansas City, packing center, 69; real estate boom in, 238
Kansas Pacific Railroad, chartered, 78
Kearney, Denis, Sand-lot leader, 157
Keating-Owen Child Labor Act, invalidated by Supreme Court, 455
Kelley, Oliver Hudson, founds Patrons of Husbandry, 93
Kellogg, Frank B., elected to World Court, 523; proposes peace pact, 568; Kellogg-Briand Pact ratified, 569
Kelly, Charles T., leads march of the unemployed, 266
Kelly, William, discovers "fuel-less" process, 62
Kentucky, in TVA area, 663
Kenyon, William S., heads Farm Bloc, 546
Kern, John W., nominated for Vice-President (1908), 419
Kidnaping, frequency of, 605
Kier, Samuel M., sells "rock oil," 63
Kindergarten idea, introduced, 96
Kipling, Rudyard, on the white man's burden, 337
Klondike, gold from, 278; routes to, 333
Knickerbocker Trust Company, failure of, 415
Knight case, renders Anti-Trust legislation innocuous, 180, 382
Knights of Labor, organized, 181; growth of, 182; blamed for Haymarket riot, 184; decline of, 185; joins forces with Populists, 260
Knights of the White Camellia, reconstruction organization, 47
Knox, Frank, Republican nominee for Vice-President (1936), 675; Secretary of the Navy under F. D. Roosevelt, 712
Knox, Philander C., negotiates arbitration treaties, 379; prosecutes Northern Securities Company, 386; Secretary of State under Taft, 422; accused of "dollar diplomacy," 433
Knudsen, William S., heads preparedness commission, 712
Kommandatura, government of Berlin, 754; Russian withdrawal from, 784
Korea, annexed by Japan, 361; after World War II, 760

Ku Klux Klan, during reconstruction, 47; Ku Klux Act (1871), 48; investigation of, 49; prosecution of, 52; twentieth century revival of, 538; splits Democratic party, 560; deadlocks New York convention (1924), 561

Kurusu, Saburo, mission to U.S., 718

Kyle, James H., Populist senator, 249

Labor, Department of, created, 431; war work of, 495

Labor Reform Party, in election of 1872, 153, 181

Labor, unrest in the seventies, 152; early trades unions, 153; growth of labor organization, 180; Knights of Labor, 181; American Federation of Labor, 185; influenced by immigrants, 189; favors tariff protection in 1888, 212; conditions of in the South, 225; following Panic of 1893, 260; increasing class-consciousness of, 284; Roosevelt's square deal for, 392; labor legislation, 406; Clayton Act, 454; the I.W.W., 455; conditions during first World War, 495; strikes of 1919, 537; disciplining of, 553; discontent of, 556; under NRA, 644; the CIO, 646; "sit-down" strikes, 647; in World War II, 720; post-war strikes, 749

La Croix, Edmond N., "new process" milling, 70

Ladd, Dr. E. E., on food adulteration, 391

Ladrones, U.S. demands an island in, 329

La Follette, Philip F., governor of Wisconsin, 710

La Follette, Robert M., Sr., on railroad regulation, 390; on conservation, 400; sketch of, 401; on Payne-Aldrich Tariff, 423; calls on Theodore Roosevelt, 430; candidate for Republican nomination for President, 433; apparent breakdown, 434; sponsors Seamen's Act, 455; opposes war with Germany, 491; opposes Treaty of Versailles, 512; demands investigation of oil scandals, 534; urged for Farmer-Labor nomination (1920), 558; Progressive nominee for President (1924), 559; campaign, 561; death, 562

La Follette, Robert M., Jr., elected to U.S. Senate, 562; supports Roosevelt (1932), 628; isolationism, 710

La Guardia, Fiorello H., heads U.S. defense delegation, 707; director-general of UNRRA, 780

Lamb, William F., architect, 612

Land ownership, in the South, 11; alien ownership condemned by Populists, 251

Land policy of U.S., grants to railroads, 75; Morrill Act, 99; criticisms of, 170, 231; grants and sales to citizens, 233; passing of free land, 241; wasteful character of, 395; revisions of, 398; grants for education and transportation, 459

Landis, Kenesaw Mountain, fines Standard Oil, 414

Landon, Alfred M., Republican nominee for President (1936), 675; radio ineptitude, 676

Langdell, G. C., dean of Harvard-Law School, 102

Lansing, Robert, on Peace Commission, 507 n.

Lansing-Ishii Agreement, between U.S. and Japan, 521

Las Gausimas, engagement at, 325

Lathrop, Julia C., heads Children's Bureau, 455

Latin-America, distrust of the U.S., 305; affected by Venezuelan boundary dispute, 307; offended by Roosevelt's recognition of Panama, 368; "big stick" policy, 370; opposes Dominican policy of U.S., 374; grows more cotton, 656; reciprocal trade treaties with U.S., 682; "good neighbor" policy, 683; "continental solidarity," 704; U.S. concern over, 706; supports U.S. in World War II, 719; post-war relations with U.S., 766

Laughton, Charles, screen actor, 593

Lausanne Conference, on reparations, 622

Law Enforcement Commission, appointed by Hoover, 604

Lawlessness, in border states, 84; in Far West, 122; during 1920's, 604

Lawson, Thomas, muckraker, 384

Lawton, Henry W., killed by Filipinos, 335

Lazear, Dr. Jesse W., experiments on yellow fever, 339

League of Nations, early advocated by Wilson, 481; in Fourteen Points, 504; included in Treaty of Versailles, 510; "solemn referendum" on (1920), 517; advocates of in U.S., 567; weakness of, 686; on Ethiopian war, 695; Germany withdraws from, 696; Russia expelled from, 700; contrasts with United Nations, 744

Lease, Mary Elizabeth, Populist orator, 248

Ledo Road, building of, 729

Lee, Fitzhugh, American consul-general at Havana, 309

Legal-tender cases, decided by Supreme Court, 45

Legge, Alexander, chairman Federal Farm Board, 580

Lemke, William, Union Party nominee (1936), 675

Lend-Lease Act, passed by Congress, 714

Lenin, Nicolai, Russian leader, 501, 686

"Let Well Enough Alone," as campaign issue, 338

Lewis, C. A., aviator, 598

Lewis, John L., heads CIO, 646; supports Roosevelt for re-election (1936), 675; strike of 1946, 749

Lewis, Sinclair, writings of, 610

Leyte Gulf, naval battle of, 728

Liberal Republicans, origins, 50; nominate Greeley, 51; defeated, 52; Republican efforts to please, 140

Liberty loans, methods of flotation, 488

Liberty motor, use during World War, 598

Lie, Trigve Halfdan, Secretary-General of United Nations, 770

Lilienthal, David E., heads commission to develop atomic energy, 775

Liliuokalani, Queen of Hawaii, 302

Lima Conference, promotes Pan-American accord, 704

Limitation of Armaments, Washington Conference, 520; Geneva Conference, 521; London Conference, 521

Lincoln, Abraham, plan of reconstruction, 12; death of, 14

Lind, John, mission to Mexico, 464

Lindbergh, Charles A., flies across Atlantic, 598; his son kidnaped, 605; isolationism, 710

Lindsay, Vachel, writings of, 610

Linotype, invention of, 175

Liquor interests, during 1870's, 84; oppose temperance reformers, 110; attacked by Anti-Saloon League, 407

Literacy test, for immigrants, advocated, 190, 457; vetoed by Wilson, 531

Literary Digest poll, predicts Landon's election, 676

Little Crow, Sioux leader, 125

Little Rock and Fort Smith Railroad, aided by Blaine, 202

Lloyd, Henry Demarest, attacks Standard Oil Company, 175; deplores emphasis on free silver, 273

Lloyd George, David, states British war aims, 504; member "Big Four," 508

Lobbyists, called "third house," 177; activities during passage of tariff of 1883, 199; aid in framing Allison Bill, 210; denounced by Wilson, 445

Locarno, Pact of, signed by European powers, 568

Lodge, Henry Cabot, on elective system in education, 100; opposes Blaine, 201; champions Force Bill, 219; advises Roosevelt, 354; Chairman Senate Committee on Foreign Relations, 511

Logan, John A., nominated for Vice-President, 201

"Log-rolling," during passage of tariff of 1883, 199

London, Jack, radical views of, 609

Long, Huey P., "Share the Wealth Society," 667; ready to outspend Roosevelt, 673

Long, John D., Secretary of the Navy, 315; on Theodore Roosevelt, 316

Long drive, supplies livestock to packers, 69; history of, 132

Los Angeles, bombing of *Times* plant, 456; water supply of, 618

Louisiana, under Lincoln's plan of reconstruction, 12; under carpet-bag rule, 38; lottery, 84; in election of 1876, 142; withdrawal of Federal troops, 146; "sugar" senators from, 258; Klan activities in, 560

Lowden, Frank O., seeks Republican nomination (1920), 515; loses to Hoover (1928), 574

Lowell, James Russell, lines on Boss Tweed, 89

Lumbering, in the New South, 224

Lundeen, Ernest, on unemployment relief, 667

Lusitania, sinking of, 475

Luxembourg, progress toward recovery, 782

Luzon, in Philippines, 331; importance of, 334

Lynn, Mass., leads in shoe manufacture, 71

McAdoo, William Gibbs, Secretary of the Treasury, 444; considered for Democratic nomination (1920), 517; seeks nomination in 1924, 561; eliminated in 1928, 575

MacArthur, Douglas, creates Philippine army, 685; leaves Philippines, 719; returns, 728; receives Japanese surrender, 731; supreme commander in Japan, 761

McClellan, George B., as promoter, 85

McClure, S. S., magazine publisher, 384

McCormick, Rob't R., isolationist views, 710

McCosh, James, president of Princeton, 98; opposes elective system, 100

McCulloch, Hugh, attempts to reduce greenback circulation, 60

McDonald, J. Ramsey, visits United States, 635

MacDonald, Jeanette, screen star, 593

McGuffey readers, continued use of, 96

Machado, Guerardo, Cuban dictator, 683

McKim, C. F., architect, 279

McKinley, William, frames tariff bill, 217; Republican candidate for President in 1896, 268; "front porch" campaign, 274; becomes President, 276; efforts to obtain bimetallism, 277; efforts to avert war with Spain, 310; yields to popular demand for war, 313; appoints peace delegation, 330; asserts sovereignty over Philippines, 335; renominated, 336; re-elected, 338; death of, 339

McKinley Tariff, becomes law, 217; provisions of, 218; unpopularity of, 220; effect on Cuba, 308

McLemore-Gore resolutions, to warn Americans from belligerent ships, 476

Macmonnies, Frederick, sculptor, 279

McNary, Charles L., Republican candidate for Vice-President (1940), 714

McNary-Haugen Bill, passes both Houses of Congress, 571; vetoed by President Coolidge, 572; endorsed in principle by Smith, 576

McParlan, James, detective, 154

McReynolds, James C., Attorney-General under Wilson, 452; appointed to Supreme Court, 453

Macune, C. W., Alliance leader, 246; political activities, 248; tries to save the Alliance, 254

Madero, Francisco, leads Mexican revolution, 464

Magazines, used by muckrakers, 384

Magoon, Charles E., military governor of Cuba, 341

Mahan, Alfred T., on influence of sea-power, 314, 315

Maine, laws on prohibition, 110; votes for Hoover (1932), 628; votes for Landon (1936), 677

Maine, second-class battleship, 209; destruction at Havana, 311

Malaya, occupied by Japanese, 719; postwar government, 766

Manchuria, becomes Manchukuo, 694; conquered by Russians, 730; Yalta decisions on, 742; Chinese Communists in, 759

Manila, surrendered to U.S., 320, 330; fighting near, 335; in World War II, 729

Manila Bay, Battle of, 318

Mankato, Minn., scene of Indian executions, 125

Mann-Elkins Act, increases powers of Interstate Commerce Commission, 431
Manufacturing, beginnings in the South, 9; prosperity in the North, 60; in the "New South," 222; nation-wide markets for, 288. See Business, Corporations, Industry
Maritime Commission, in charge of merchant marine, 661
Marsh, O. C., paleontologist, 103
Marshall, George C., mission to China, 759; Secretary of State, 778
Marshall, Thomas R., nominated for Vice-President (1912), 436; elected, 438; renominated, 478; re-elected, 480; refuses to supplant Wilson, 513
Marshall Plan. See European Recovery Plan
Martine, James, elected U.S. Senator, 441
Marx, Karl, political theories of, 687
Maryland, enacts employer's liability law, 406
Massachusetts, abandons prohibition, 110; Democratic gains (1910), 431; Republican gains (1938), 681
Masters, Edgar Lee, writings of, 610
"Mavericks," branding practice, 136
Mead-McKellar Air Mail Act, regulates airmail contracts, 599
Medicine, education in, 101; in the mining West, 120; recent improvements in, 607
Melchers, Gari, painter, 279
Mellon, Andrew W., becomes Secretary of the Treasury, 519; favors reduction of taxes, 528; reduces national debt, 550; supports Hoover for Republican nomination, 574; continued in office, 580
Mencken, Henry L., writings of, 610
Merchant marine, under U.S. Shipping Board, 478; after the World War, 525; Merchant Fleet Corporation, 526; Maritime Commission, 661
Merrimac, sunk in Santiago Harbor, 322
Merritt, Wesley, commands American expedition to Philippines, 320, 323; succeeded by Otis, 335
Metz, goal of the American army, 498
Meuse–Argonne, battle of, 500
Mexican Central Railroad, completed, 166
Mexico, under Diaz, 463; Revolution of 1910–11, 463; "watchful waiting," 464; Constitution of 1917, 465; sought by Germany as an ally, 485; immigration from to U.S., 531; diplomatic relations with, 684; enters World War II, 719
Meyer, George von L., Secretary of the Navy, 422
Michigan, iron mines, 62; banking crisis in (1933), 630; Republican gains in (1938), 681
"Middle of the Road" Populists, in elections of 1894, 268
Miles, Nelson A., Indian campaigns, 128; commands U.S. army, 317; plans for war with Spain, 323; conquest of Puerto Rico, 329
Militarists, seek defeat of Wilson, 479
Military tribunals, doubtful legality, 37
Mill villages, in the South, 225
Miller, Joaquin, writings, 108

Miller, Thomas W., Alien Property Custodian, 532
Milling industry. See Flour-milling
Mills, Roger Q., introduces tariff bill, 209
Milwaukee, packing center, 68; desire for industries, 289
Minimum-wage schedules, in the states, 407
Mining booms, in Colorado, 117; in Nevada, 118; in the Northwest, 118; in the Southwest, 119; social conditions in mining towns, 120; social inheritance from, 124
Minnesota, flour-milling in, 70; Granger laws, 94; Indian cessions in, 124; Sioux uprising in, 125; Farmers' Alliance in, 246, 249; votes for Hughes (1916), 480; Farmer-Labor Party in, 546; Republican gains in (1938), 681
Mississippi, rejects carpet-bag constitution, 35; readmitted, 36; in TVA area, 663
Missouri, in Liberal Republican movement, 50; votes for Roosevelt (1904), 413; Klan activities in, 560
Missouri Pacific Railroad, chartered, 78; western extension, 166; strike on, 182
Mitchell, Charles E., president National City Bank, 385
Mitchell, John, leads United Mine Workers, 392, 393
Mitchell, Margaret, Gone With the Wind, 593; portrays the New South, 609
Mobile, Ala., after the war, 4
Moley, Raymond, Roosevelt brain truster, 627; loses favor with Roosevelt, 636
Moline, Ill., farm-implement center, 71
"Molly Maguires," society of coal miners, 154
Molotov, V. M., Russian foreign minister, 752; rejects Marshall Plan, 781
Mondell Act, to promote dry-farming, 398
Money question, greenback currency, 45, 60; resumption, 147; appreciating value of the dollar, 148; silver question, 149; Bland-Allison Act, 153; affected by the tariff, 208; Populist stand on, 251; in campaign of 1892, 252; the gold reserve, 254; Cleveland on, 256; gold purchases, 257; demands for free silver, 267; in campaign of 1896, 273; gold standard law, 277; increase in gold supply, 278; inelasticity of the currency, 414; the "money trust," 415; banking and currency reform, 446; Federal Reserve System, 449; depression demand for inflation, 621; New Deal reforms, 657. See also Inflation
"Mongrel Tariff" of 1883, enacted, 199
Monotype, invention of, 175
Monroe Doctrine, defined, 299; involved in Venezuelan boundary dispute, 305; vindicated by Cleveland, 307; in Venezuelan incident of 1902, 371; Roosevelt corollary, 372; the Atlantic System, 484; cited in ratifying Kellogg-Briand Pact, 569; invoked against Germany, 705; supported by Latin-America, 706; dependence on British sea-power, 710; post-World War II modifications, 767
Montana, beginnings, 119; admitted to the Union, 214; labor violence in, 264
Montgomery, Bernard Law, serves under Eisenhower, 724

Moody, Dwight L., evangelist, 109
Mooney, Thomas, conviction of, 456; pardoned, 457
Moore, John Bassett, elected to World Court, 522
Moratorium on intergovernmental debts, advocated by Hoover, 622
Morgan, Arthur E., TVA chairman, 666
Morgan, J. P., Cleveland's deal with, 257; helps form United States Steel Corporation, 381; importance as banker, 382; helps form Northern Securities Company, 385; consulted by Theodore Roosevelt, 394; advice concerning Tennessee Coal and Iron Company, 415; testifies before Pujo Committee, 449
Morgan, Lewis H., anthropologist, 103
Morgenthau, Henry, Jr., Secretary of the Treasury, 630
Moroccan crisis of 1905, U.S. intervention in, 376
Moros, Philippine savages, 334
Morrill Act, land grant, 99; stimulus to agricultural education, 101; aids engineering, 101
Morris, Nelson, Chicago meat packer, 69
Morrison, W. R., introduces tariff-reform bill, 200, 208
Mortgage problem, in the New West, 237; in the 1920's, 542; as a cause of depression, 586
Morton, Levi P., nominated for Vice-President, 211
Morton, Oliver P., desires Republican nomination, 140
Motion pictures, invented by Edison, 592; the "talkies," 593
Mountbatten, Lord Louis, British commander in Asia, 730; becomes governor-general of India, 765
Muckrakers, journalistic exploits of, 383
Mugwumps, oppose Blaine, 202
"Mulligan letters," damage Blaine's reputation, 140; in campaign of 1884, 201
Munich deal, over Czechoslovakia, 696
Municipal government, home rule for cities, 158; Lincoln Steffens on, 384; reforms attempted, 405; influenced by racketeers, 604
Munn vs. Illinois, 94
Murphy, Frank, governor of Michigan, 647; appointed to Supreme Court, 679
Muscle Shoals, private exploitation vetoed by Theodore Roosevelt, 396; World War development of, 552; TVA activity, 663
Music, stimulated by radio, 599
Mussolini, Benito, Italian leader, 688. See Italy

Nagasaki, atomic bombing of, 730
Nasby, Petroleum V., lampoons Johnson, 28
Nast, Thomas, cartoons on Johnson, 28; on Greeley, 52; on Tweed Ring, 89; in Harper's Weekly, 91
Nation (New York), edited by Godkin, 90; explains defeat of Blaine, 205; on Bryan, 272
National Association of Manufacturers, on inflation, 750
National banking system, begins to func-

tion, 60; loans, 80; dependence on government bonds, 209; inadequacy in the South, 227. See Banks
National Conservation Commission, appointed by Roosevelt, 398
National Credit Corporation, sponsored by Hoover, 619
National debt. See Debt, United States
National Defense Act (1916), terms of, 478
National Defense Advisory Commission, created, 712
National Farmers' Alliance. See Farmers' Alliance
National Guard, on eve of Spanish-American War, 317; lack of equipment, 323; reorganized, 349; increases of 1916, 478; called up, 713
National Housing Act (1937), 662
National Industrial Recovery Act, becomes law, 642; labor clauses of, 644; invalidated by Supreme Court, 645
National Labor Board, established, 644
National Labor Party (1919), organized, 558
National Labor Reform Convention, 1872, 51
National Labor Relations Board, created, 645; revised, 646; discriminations against Communists, 752
National Labor Union, formed at Baltimore, 153, 181
National Monetary Commission, established, 415; reports, 445
National Non-Partisan League, in North Dakota, 458; activities of, 544; opposition to, 545; in national politics, 558
National Progressive Republican League, formed by the insurgents, 433
National Recovery Administration (NRA), purposes of, 642
National Socialism (Naziism), in Germany, 690
National War Labor Board, created, 495
National Youth Administration (NYA), New Deal agency, 640
Navy of the U.S., steel construction begun, 209; need for, 314; new construction authorized, 315; placed on war footing, 316; during Spanish-American War, 318, 326; expansion of, 349; sails around the world, 361; increases of 1916, 478; in World War I, 496; expansion program (1938), 703; preparedness program (1940), 710; acquires naval bases, 713; in Iceland, 717; at Pearl Harbor, 718; Pacific operations, 726; problems of demobilization, 747
Nebraska, migration to, 236; Farmers' Alliance in, 246, 249; votes against Bryan in 1900, 338; votes for Bryan in 1908, 420
Needles, California, railroad pass, 165
Negro suffrage, contemplated by Johnson, 16, 17; favored by Sumner, 21; in Fourteenth Amendment, 25; in second Congressional plan, 30; in practice, 33; Fifteenth Amendment, 36; in Republican platform of 1868, 40; favored by Chase, 41; discouraged, 49; circumvented by legislation, 219; fear of during Populist period, 250
Negroes, after Civil War, 6; Freedmen's

Bureau, 7; as soldiers, 8; churches and schools, 9; plans for emigration, 10; labor systems, 10; conflicts with whites, 22; race riots, 27; Union League, 33; in reconstruction conventions, 34; as office-holders, 38; not to blame for reconstruction excesses, 39; Negro militia, 47; vote for Grant, 52; education of, 97, 104; vocational schools for, 105; intimidated during election of 1876, 143; legally disfranchised, 219; in southern industry, 225; diseases among, 226; tenancy among, 227; join Colored Alliance, 247; in prohibition crusade, 408; treatment by Theodore Roosevelt, 412; persecuted by modern Ku Klux Klan, 538; in World War II, 735

Neihardt, John G., writings of, 610

Nelson, Donald M., heads War Production Board, 719

"Nesters," invade cattle country, 136

Netherlands, The, attacked by Germany, 700; status of Dutch West Indies, 705; liberation of, 724; Netherlands-Indonesian Union, 766; progress toward recovery, 782

Neutrality. See American neutrality

Neutrality Acts (1930's), abandon U.S. neutral rights, 703; amended, 709

Nevada, mining boom, 118; statehood, 118; decline of, 119; votes for Bryan in 1900, 338; in 1908, 420

New Deal, record on civil service, 197; anticipated by Hoover, 617; promised by Roosevelt, 627; direction of, 634; relief measures of, 637; recovery measures of, 611; reform measures of, 657; Roosevelt's part in, 671

New Freedom, demanded by Wilson, 442

New Hampshire, votes for Hoover (1932), 628

New Jersey, Democratic victory in (1910), 431

New Mexico, mineral resources, 119; seeks admission to the Union, 214; plan for union with Arizona, 420; transient labor problem in, 656

New Nationalism, advocated by Theodore Roosevelt, 430, 442

New Panama Canal Company, formed, 365; efforts to sell out to U.S., 366; protected in Hay-Herran Treaty, 367

New South, name given the post-war industrialized South, 221; diversification of industries, 224

New Ulm, Minn., scene of Indian uprising, 125

New West, defined, 231; settlement of, 236; boom in, 237; drouth in, 239

New York Central Railroad, growth of, 166

New York City, slums, 82; Tammany control of, 87; suffering during coal strike (1902), 393; World of Tomorrow Exposition, 614

New York State, in election of 1888, 212; chooses Theodore Roosevelt as governor, 354; Democratic gains (1910), 431; votes for Hughes (1916), 480

New York Stock Exchange, during Gold Conspiracy, 53; after failure of Jay Cooke, 59, 81; during Panic of 1907, 415; in 1929, 585

New York Times, denounces Tweed Ring, 89; questions Tilden victory, 141

New York Tribune, opposes Radicals, 51

New York World, exposes modern Ku Klux Klan, 538

Newcomb, Simon, astronomer, 103

Newlands, F. G., introduces Reclamation Act, 396

Newlands Act, for irrigation, 396

Newspapers, character of, 297; on Cuban insurrection, 309

Nicaragua, proposed canal route through, 365; route favored by Isthmian Canal Commission, 366; concedes U.S. sole right to build canal through, 372; U.S. intervention in, 374; Knox negotiates treaty with, 433

Nimitz, Chester W., Pacific naval commander, 727

Nine-Power Pact, on the Far East, 521

Nineteenth Amendment, ratified, 408

Nome, Alaska, gold rush to, 333

Non-Partisan Leader, farm journal, 544

Non-Partisan League. See National Non-Partisan League

Normal schools, improve method of instruction, 96

"Normalcy," sought by Harding, 523

Norris, Frank, The Octopus, 609

Norris, George W., leads House insurgents, 428; sponsors farm marketing bill, 547; interest in Muscle Shoals, 552; on Coolidge appointments, 552; supports Roosevelt (1932), 628; urges "Lame Duck" amendment, 628; on federal water-power, 663

North Atlantic Treaty, to head off Russian aggression, 783

North Carolina, cotton industry in, 223; tobacco industry in, 224; Alliance successes in, 249; in TVA area, 663

North Dakota, admitted to the Union, 214; Farmers' Alliance in, 246; Non-Partisan League in, 544

Northern Pacific Railroad, backed by Jay Cooke, 59; charter, 78; revived in 1878, 164; completed, 165

Northern Securities Company, attacked by Roosevelt, 385; ordered to dissolve, 386

Norton, Charles Eliot, approves Chicago Fair (1893), 280

Norway, emigration from to U.S., 72; overrun by Nazis, 700; signs North Atlantic Treaty, 783

Nye, Gerald P., munitions investigation, 701; isolationism, 710; defeated for re-election, 738

O'Connor, John J., opposed by Roosevelt, 681

O'Conor, Charles, prosecutes Tweed Ring, 89

O'Fallon decision, on railroad evaluation, 525

Office of Price Administration, activities of, 748; efforts to avert inflation, 750

Office of Production Management, during World War II, 712

Office of War Mobilization, activities of, 748

Officer training, during World War I, 488

Official Bulletin, World War publication, 491

Ogden, Utah, meeting point of Union and Central Pacific, 75

Ohio, "Ohio idea," 42, 45, 149; oil fields in, 65; coal industry in, 392; Democratic gains in (1910), 431; votes for Wilson (1916), 480; "Ohio gang," 519; Klan activities in, 560; CIO strikes in, 647

Oil industry, early uses of petroleum, 63; organization of, 67, 176, 381; stimulated by automobile, 554

Okinawa, taken by Americans, 728

Oklahoma, opened to settlement, 231; admitted to the Union, 420; anti-Klan governor impeached, 560

Old-age pensions, in the states, 407; Townsend plan, 667; New Deal legislation, 668

Olmsted, Frederick Law, landscape architect, 279

Olney, Richard, Secretary of State, 306

Olson, Floyd B., governor of Minnesota, 681

Omaha, Nebr., packing center, 69; Union Pacific terminal, 75; freighting center, 122; real estate boom in, 238; Populist convention in, 251

O'Mahoney, Joseph, heads Monopoly Investigation, 680

Omnibus bill, admits northwestern states, 214

One-crop evil, in the South, 229

One-party system, in the South, 229

O'Neill, Eugene, playwright, 610

Open-door policy, advocated by Hay, 356; leads to "dollar diplomacy," 433; reaffirmed at Washington Conference, 522; violated by Japan, 694

Open shop, strike issue, 393; in Taft-Hartley Act, 751

Orlando, Vittorio, member "Big Four," 508

Oregon, electoral vote disputed (1876), 142; "Oregon system," 402; adopts initiative and referendum, 403; votes for Hughes (1916), 480

Oregon Railroad and Navigation Company, controlled by Villard, 164

Oregon, U.S.S., ordered to Atlantic, 316; joins Sampson's squadron, 322

Otis, Elwell S., military governor of the Philippines, 335

Outlawry of war, advocated by Borah, 568

Overland Mail, in Far West, 121

Overman Act, expands powers of the President, 494

Owen, Robert L., helps frame Federal Reserve Act, 449

Pacifists, oppose program of preparedness, 477; oppose Wilson for re-election, 479; divided counsels among, 567

Packing industry, beginnings, 68; criticized by Sinclair, 384; dissolution of the beef trust, 386; comes to terms with U.S. government, 453; laws to regulate, 547

Page, Walter Hines, American Ambassador to Great Britain, 483

Pago Pago, American coaling station, 302

Painting, exhibits at Philadelphia Centennial, 113; at Chicago World's Fair (1893), 280; WPA art projects, 640

Palestine, Arab-Jewish contest, 773; independent state of Israel created, 774

Palmer, A. Mitchell, candidate for Democratic nomination (1920), 517; prosecution of "reds," 537

Panama, railroad through, 365; plans for revolution in, 367; revolution accomplished, 368; virtual protectorate of U.S., 372; declares war on Germany, 482; U.S. gives up special privileges, 684

Panama Canal, advocated by James G. Blaine, 192; diplomatic preparations for, 364; proposed route of, 365; building of, 369; tolls controversy, 370; vulnerable, 710

Pan-Americanism, advocated by James G. Blaine, 192, 303; hampered by Civil War in Chile, 304; promoted by F. D. Roosevelt, 683, 706

Panay, destroyed by Japanese, 695

Panics, of 1873, 59, 80, 157; of 1893, 255; of 1907, 414; of 1919, 539; of 1929, 585

Papen, Franz von, sabotage activities in U.S., 474

Paraguay, war with Bolivia, 588

Paris Peace Conference (1919), nature of, 507; the secret treaties, 508; resulting treaties, 510; awards to Japan, 522; (1946), considers minor treaties, 752

Parker, Alton B., Democratic nominee (1904), 413

Parker, John J., refused confirmation as Associate Justice, 623

Parliament of religions, at Chicago Fair (1893), 280

Patman Bonus Bill, passes House, 621

Patrons of Husbandry, founded, 93

Patrons of Industry, farm order, 245

Patton, George S., commands Third American Army, 725

Payne, H. B., seeks Senate seat, 177

Payne-Aldrich Tariff, formulated, 423; signed by Taft, 425; establishes Tariff Board, 426; praised by Theodore Roosevelt, 430

Peabody, George, philanthropy, 9, 105

"Peace without victory," urged by Wilson, 481

Pearl Harbor, attacked by Japanese, 718; responsibility for, 731

Peek, George N., on farm relief, 571

Peffer, William A., Populist senator, 249

Peik vs. the Chicago and Northwestern Railroad, 94

Peirce, Benjamin, mathematician, 103

Pellagra, common in the South, 226

Pendleton, George H., sponsors "Ohio idea," 42; introduces measure for civil service reform, 196

Pennsylvania, steel industry in, 62; oil borings, 64; coal industry in, 392; votes for Hoover (1932), 628; CIO strikes in, 647; Republican gains in, 681

Pennsylvania Railroad, connections with the West, 87; growth of, 166

Penrose, Boies, favors Theodore Roosevelt for Vice-President, 354

Pensions, "pauper" pension bill, 207; Dependents' Pension Bill, 216; expenditures for, 216; mounting bill for, 549

People's Party. *See* Populist Party

"Perdicaris alive or Raisuli dead," Roosevelt demand on Morocco, 376

Perkins, Frances, Secretary of Labor, 630
Permanent Court of International Justice, in United Nations Charter, 744; organized, 771. *See also* World Court
Perón, Juan Domingo, Argentine dictator, 767
Pershing, John J., expedition into Mexico, 465; sent to France, 497; insists on separate American army, 498; favors unified command, 503; opposes armistice, 506
Pétain, Henri, becomes French Chief-of-State, 701; orders resistance to Allies in Africa, 721
Petersburg, Va., war devastation, 3
Philadelphia, Centennial Exposition in, 113; furnishes pattern for city development, 290
Philanthropy, toward South, 9; in education, 98; to promote peace, 378
Philippine Islands, coveted by Americans, 319; in armistice terms, 330; acquired by U.S., 331; description of, 334; revolt in, 335; pacified, 336; government of, 344; social conditions in, 345; progress toward independence, 685; taken by Japan, 719; retaken by U.S., 728; given independence, 763; troubles with Hukbalahap, 765
Phillips, David Graham, muckraker, 384
Photography, improvements in, 175
Pickford, Mary, motion-picture star, 592
Pike's Peak Gold Rush, 117
Pillsbury, C. A., Minneapolis miller, 70
Pinchot, Gifford, chief of the forestry service, 397; dispute with Ballinger, 427; meets Roosevelt in Egypt, 430
"Pinkertons," used in Homestead strike, 261
Pious Fund Case, settled by Hague Tribunal, 375
Pittsburgh, Pa., center of oil industry, 67; during railroad strikes of 1877, 155
Platt, Thomas C., resigns as U.S. Senator, 194; boss of New York, 354
Platt Amendment, on relations between U.S. and Cuba, 340; paralleled in relations with Panama, 368; abrogated, 684
Plumb plan, for railroad operation, 524
Plummer, Henry, western bad-man, 122
Poland, Polish emigration to U.S., 73, 189; Treaty of Brest-Litovsk, 501; in Peace of Paris, 511; object of German aggression, 697; overrun by German troops, 699; entered by Russians, 725; Yalta decisions on, 742; Communist control of, 776
"Police power," importance in social legislation, 408
Politburo, Soviet governing body, 688
Polk, Col. L. L., Alliance leader, 248
Pomeroy, Samuel C., attempted bribery for, 92
Pony Express, in Far West, 121
Populist Party, members in Congress, 220; origins of, 245, 247; Cincinnati convention, 250; Omaha convention, 251; in election of 1892, 252; sympathy with marches of the unemployed, 265; increasing emphasis on free silver, 267; in campaign of 1894, 268; convention of 1896, 272; decline of, 272; supports Bryan in 1900, 338; last campaign of, 420
Pork-barrel legislation, bill vetoed by Ar-thur, 200; opposed by Cleveland, 209; passed under Harrison, 219
Porter, Noah, president of Yale, 98
Post, Wiley, aviator, 598
Postal rates, reduced, 175
Potsdam Conference, attended by Truman, 745; decisions, 746
Powderly, Terence V., leads Knights of Labor, 181
Powell, J. W., geologist, 103; surveys irrigation sites, 395
Pre-emption Act, used in settling West, 233
Preparedness program, under Wilson, 477; under F. D. Roosevelt, 710
Pribilof Islands, breeding-place for fur-seals, 300
Primaries. *See* Direct primaries
Priority right, western rule of law, 123
Proctor, Redfield, on Cuban insurrection, 309
Progressive Party, of 1912, 437; of 1924, 558; in Wisconsin during 1930's, 681
Prohibition, early laws repealed, 84; Prohibition Party, 110; in election of 1884, 205; Anti-Saloon League, 407; becomes nationwide, 408; in campaign of 1908, 420; in election of 1928, 578; repealed, 602; problems of enforcement, 603; party platforms on (1932), 624
Propaganda in the United States, by British, 483; by Committee on Public Information, 491
Prospectors, comb the West, 115
Prosperity, returns in 1879, 159; in 1897, 276; as campaign issue in 1900, 338; during and after World War, 535; promised by Hoover, 627; sought by New Deal, 637, 680
Prostitution, during 1870's, 84; efforts to wipe out, 408
Public Utilities Act, to regulate holding companies, 659
Public Works Administration (PWA), recommended by Hoover, 618; established under Roosevelt, 641; "pump-priming" aspects, 642; during recession of 1937–38, 680
Puerto Cabello, Venezuela, bombarded by British, 371
Puerto Rico, Miles's plan to conquer, 323; conquest effected, 329; accepts rule of U.S., 334; government of, 342, 347; part in Caribbean control, 372
Pujo, A. P., investigates "money trust," 446
Pulitzer, Joseph, editor, 297
Pullman, George M., builds sleeping-car, 80; establishes "model town" of Pullman, 261; precipitates Pullman strike, 262
Pure Food and Drug Act, 391

Quay, Matthew, Republican campaign manager in 1884, 211; favors Theodore Roosevelt for Vice-President, 354
Quezon, Manuel, President of the Philippines, 685; death of, 763

Race suicide, deplored by Theodore Roosevelt, 411
Racketeering, during prohibition era, 604; after prohibition, 605

Radcliffe College, opens, 104
Radical Republicans, relief at death of Lincoln, 14; support of Johnson, 15; break with Johnson, 22; control joint committee on reconstruction, 24; in election of 1806, 26; control Congress, 28; supported by Grant, 47
Radio, in campaign of 1928, 577; influence on American life, 594; in campaign of 1936, 676
Railroads, in the South, 8, 9; new construction, 74, 78; during Panic of 1873, 80; Granger laws, 93; low rates to Philadelphia Centennial, 113; strikes of 1877, 154; building resumed, 164; trend toward consolidation, 168; criticisms of, 169; regulatory commissions, 171; Interstate Commerce Commission, 172; in the New West, 231; land sales, 233; western grievances against, 244; Populist stand on, 251; after Panic of 1893, 255; during Pullman strike, 263; importance to country towns, 293; mergers of, 388; Hepburn Act, 390; attacked by La Follette, 401; bankruptcies in 1907, 415; Bryan's views on, 420; during World War, 493; return to private operation, 524; Railroad Labor Board, 525; under New Deal, 660
Randall, Samuel J., Speaker of the House, 199; defeated for re-election, 200
Rawlins, J. A., Secretary of War, 44; death, 55
Rebates, obtained by Standard Oil, 176; forbidden by Elkins Act, 390
Recall, adopted in Oregon, 403; favored by Progressive Republicans, 433; applied to judicial decisions, 435
"Recapture clause," in Transportation Act of 1920, 525
Recession of 1937, causes of, 679
Reciprocity, included in McKinley Tariff, 218; in Dingley Tariff, 276; Blaine's efforts on, 304; favored by McKinley, 339; reciprocity with Canada proposed, 432; promoted by Cordell Hull, 682; with Cuba, 684
Reclamation Act, for irrigation, 396
Reconcentrado camps, in Cuba, 309
Reconstruction, defined, 2; Lincoln's plan for, 12; Johnson's plan for, 16; Joint Committee on, 19; Congressional plans for, 24, 30; Third Reconstruction Act, 32; registration of voters, 33; Fourth Reconstruction Act, 36; elections in the South, 37; Republican victories, 43; leads to solid South, 49; scandals of, 87; end of, 146
Reconstruction Finance Corporation (RFC), established by Hoover, 619; extends credits to agriculture, 621; lends to private industry, 641; to railroads, 660; during recession of 1937–38, 680
Reconversion, after World War II, 748
Recovery program, under Harding and Coolidge, 549; under the New Deal, 641; the NRA, 642; the AAA, 648; the FCA, 652; the RA and FSA, 653; the new AAA, 654
Red Cloud, leads western Sioux, 127
Red Cross, subscription drives, 489; during drouth of 1930, 619

"Red hunt," conducted by Palmer, 517; victims of the rage, 537
Red, White, and Blue books, published by the C.P.I., 422
Reed, James A., opposes Treaty of Versailles, 512
Reed, Stanley F., appointed to Supreme Court, 679
Reed, Thomas B., Speaker of the House, 214; Reed's rules, 215; views on sinking of the Maine, 311; opposes annexation of Philippines, 332; end of Reed's rules, 427
Reed, Dr. Walter, investigates yellow fever in Cuba, 339
Referendum. See Initiative and referendum
Reform measures (New Deal), currency, 657; banking, 658; the SEC, 659; railroad co-ordination, 660; merchant marine, 661; housing, 662; TVA, 663; social security, 667
Refrigerator car, perfected by Swift, 69
Regulation of Industry. See Business, Corporations, Industry
Reid, Whitelaw, member peace delegation (1898), 330
Relief, Hoover's policy toward, 618; demanded for veterans, 621; the CCC, 633; the FERA, 637; the CWA, 638; the WPA, 639; the NYA, 640; a permanent problem, 667
Religion, revivals of 1870's, 109; among immigrants, 189; "parliament of religions" at Chicago Fair (1893), 280; in rural America, 293; conflict with evolution, 294; emphasis on the practical, 295; decline in church-going, 602
Remsen, Ira, president Johns Hopkins University, 103
Reno, Milo, leads Farmers' Holiday Association, 622
Reparations problem, original settlement, 509; Dawes Plan, 567; Young Plan, 567; payments discontinued by Germany, 622
Report of the Industrial Commission, influence of, 385
Republican Party, opposition to Johnson, 23; on Negro suffrage, 30; convention of 1868, 40; re-nominates Grant, 51; losses during seventies, 139; in election of 1876, 141; the G.O.P., 160; nominations of 1880, 161; lack of program, 162; led by James G. Blaine, 192; on tariff problem, 198, 210; campaign fund in 1888, 211; rebuked for tariff policy, 220; favors gold standard, 269; in the South, 412; insurgency during Taft's administration, 428; split by Roosevelt, 435; in election of 1918, 507; returns to power (1920), 520; recovery program of, 549; failure with agriculture, 569; loses power, 628; attacks New Deal, 675; gains after World War II, 751; record of Eightieth Congress, 787; defeat in 1948, 790
Reservation system, for Indians, 127
Resettlement Administration (RA), New Deal agency, 653
Resumption of specie payments, planned, 147; accomplished, 148
Revenue Act of 1921, reduces taxes, 529; reductions deemed inadequate by Mellon, 550

Revenue Act of 1924, reduces surtax, 550
Review of Reviews, on Insular cases, 344
Revivals. *See* Religion
Rhodes, James Ford, on Spanish-American War, 313
Rice, Elmer, playwright, 612
Rice culture, in Louisiana, 11
Richberg, Daniel R., heads NRA, 645
Riis, Jacob, humanitarian, 352
Ritchie, Albert, candidate for Democratic nomination (1932), 624
River traffic, in the South, 4
Robinson, Joseph T., Democratic nominee for Vice-President, 575; death of, 678
Rockefeller, John D., sketch of, 67; philanthropies, 98; plans monopoly, 176; heads Standard Oil Trust, 177; criticized by Tarbell, 384
Rockefeller Foundation, attacks hookworm disease, 226; interest in higher education, 607
Roebling, John A., bridge-builder, 80
Rölvaag, O. E., *Giants in the Earth*, 609
Roman Catholic Church, insulted by Burchard, 204; strength in American cities, 294; in Philippine Islands, 334, 344; opposed by modern Ku Klux Klan, 538; in election of 1928, 578
Rome-Berlin Axis, creation of, 697; extended to Tokyo, 707
Rommel, Erwin, German commander in Africa, 723
Roosevelt, Anna Eleanor, delegate to United Nations, 769
Roosevelt, Franklin D., record on civil service, 197; on relations with Cuba, 341; Assistant Secretary of the Navy, 444; nominated for Vice-President (1920), 517; urges U.S. adherence to World Court, 523; sketch of, 624; elected governor of New York, 626; elected President, 628; political skill, 633; the "Roosevelt Revolution," 671; renominated, 674; re-elected, 677; proposed court-packing bill, 678; good neighbor policy, 683; message to Hitler, 698; proposes "quarantine of aggressors," 703; seeks defense agreement with Canada, 706; urges amendment of the Neutrality Acts, 709; preparedness program, 712; nominated for third term, 714; Lend-Lease Act, 715; Atlantic Charter, 716; Casablanca Conference, 723, 740; accused of connivance at war, 731; nominated for fourth term, 737; death of, 739
Roosevelt, Theodore, opposition to Blaine, 201; civil service commissioner, 213; on Spanish-American War, 313; Assistant Secretary of the Navy, 315; organizes Rough Riders, 318; nominated for Vice-President (1900), 336; elected, 338; becomes President, 339; warns Cubans against disorder, 341; sketch of, 351; early political career, 352; retains McKinley's cabinet, 355; mediates in Russo-Japanese War, 360; on San Francisco school order, 360; favors Panama Canal route, 366; "big stick" policy, 370; Venezuelan incident of 1902, 371; "Roosevelt corollary," 372; interpretation of the presidency, 380; on muckrakers, 384; on the trusts, 385;

popularity of, 410; handling of Negro problem, 411; statement on third term, 414; hunting trip to Africa, 422; expedition disbanded, 428; lectures British on Egypt, 429; tours Europe, 429; in elections of 1910, 430; candidate for Republican nomination (1912), 434; defeated by Taft, 435; nominated by Progressives, 437; attempt to assassinate, 438; on *Lusitania* sinking, 475; declines Progressive nomination (1916), 479; heads "bitterenders," 507
Roosevelt, Theodore, Jr., Assistant Secretary of the Navy, 533
Roosevelt corollary, announced, 372; used by other Presidents, 373
Root, Elihu, on Negro suffrage, 220; chosen Secretary of War, 329; reorganizes U.S. Army, 348; negotiations with Japan, 361; attempts to conciliate Colombia, 368; helps devise formula for Algeciras Conference, 376; negotiates arbitration treaties, 378; consults Morgan for Roosevelt, 394; on invisible government, 400; sketch of, 417; mission to Russia, 500; supports Harding (1920), 517; supports World Court, 522
Root-Takahira Agreement, between Japan and U.S., 361
Rough Riders, assembled by Roosevelt and Wood, 318; transferred to Tampa, 323; embark for Santiago, 324; see fighting, 325, 326; leave Cuba, 328
Ruef, Abe, San Francisco grafter, 402
Rules Committee, in House of Representatives, 427; powers limited, 428
"Rum, Romanism, and rebellion," in campaign of 1884, 204
Rumania, emigration from to U.S., 73, 189; in World War I, 484; in World War II, 725; peace negotiations, 752; Russian forces in, 756; Communist control of, 776
Rural credits, short- and long-term, 458; intermediate, 547; under FCA, 652
Rural life, character of, 291; increasing comforts of, 293
Russell, Charles Edward, muckraker, 384
Russell, Majors, and Waddell, freighters, 121
Russia, interests in China, 356; agrees to Boxer settlement, 358; war with Japan, 359; European allies, 466; interests in the Balkans, 466; mobilization (1914), 469; revolution in, 486, 686; makes peace with Germany, 498; repudiates war debts, 501; influence on American labor, 556; refuses to fund war debt, 566; U.S. refuses to recognize, 567; under Bolshevist rule, 687; supports Hitler, 698; expansion of, 700; war with Finland (1939–40), 700; attacked by Germany, 716; Stalingrad defense, 724; gains made at Yalta, 741; postwar change of policy, 753; opposes treaty with Japan, 762; prevents agreement on control of atomic energy, 775; UNRRA aid to, 780; rejects ERP, 781; Berlin blockade, 783
"Rustling," by cattle-thieves, 136

Sacco, Nicola, convicted of murder, 537

Sackville-West, Sir Lionel, favors re-election of Cleveland, 212
"Safety-valve" theory, evaluated, 241
Saint-Gaudens, Augustus, sculptor, 279
St. John, John P., Prohibitionist candidate for President, 205
St. Joseph, Mo., packing center, 69
St. Lawrence Waterway, promoted by Hoover, 621; by F. D. Roosevelt, 684
Saint-Mihiel salient, reduced by Pershing's army, 498
Saipan, taken by Americans, 727
"Salary Grab" Act, during Grant's administration, 54
Salisbury, Lord, on fur-seal controversy, 301; on Venezuelan boundary dispute, 306; views on Monroe Doctrine, 306; revises attitude toward United States, 307
Saloons, during 1870's, 84; in the mining West, 120. See Anti-Saloon League, Prohibition
Salvation Army, activities of, 109; during World War, 489
Samoan Islands, American interests in, 302; division of, 303
Sampson, William T., commands North Atlantic squadron, 316; prepares to meet the Spanish, 321; confers with Shafter, 324, 326; Sampson or Schley? 327
San Francisco, Kearneyism in, 157; earthquake and fire, 411; Golden Gate Exposition, 614
San Francisco Conference, United Nations charter, 745
San Juan Hill, Battle of, 325, 326
Sanborn, John D., contract with Treasury, 54
Sandburg, Carl, The People Yes, 610
Sand Creek massacre, in Colorado, 126
"Sand-Lotters," in San Francisco, 157
Sandoz, Mari, Old Jules, 609
Sankey, Ira D., revivalist, 109
Santiago de Cuba, reached by Cervera, 321; army advance on, 324; naval battle near, 326; surrender of, 327
Santo Domingo, Grant's efforts to annex, 55. See Dominican Republic
Sapiro, Aaron, promotes co-operative marketing, 546
Sato, Shosuke, criticizes land policy, 239
Sawyer, Philetus, controversy with La Follette, 401
"Scalawags," in reconstruction conventions, 34
Scandinavians, enter United States, 72, 189; easy assimilation of, 284
Schechter case, invalidates NRA, 645
Schenck, Robert C., as promoter, 85
Schley, Winfield S., blunders in Chile, 305; commands Flying Squadron, 316; operations in Cuban waters, 321; Sampson or Schley? 327
Schofield, J. M., as Secretary of War, 32; in charge of Virginia, 33
Schurz, Carl, on results of Sherman's march, 2; on Charleston, S.C., 3; report on conditions in the South, 22; Senator from Missouri, 44; a Liberal Republican, 50; presides over Liberal Convention, 51; sketch of, 91; in Hayes cabinet, 146; opposes Blaine in 1884, 201

Scott, Hugh L., heads mission to Russia, 501
Scranton, Pa., during strikes of 1877, 156
Seattle, Wash., general strike in, 537
Secret Treaties, among the Allies, 504; terms of, 508
Securities and Exchange Commission (SEC), New Deal agency, 659
Sedition Act, during World War I, 492
Seidel, Emil, Milwaukee Socialist, 405
Selective Service Act, passed in 1917, 487; in 1940, 712
"Senatorial courtesy," rule of, 147
Seventeenth Amendment, adopted, 404
Sewall, Arthur, Democratic nominee for Vice-President (1896), 271
Seymour, Horatio, nominated for President, 42; defeated, 43
Shafter, William A., ordered to Santiago, 324; plan of campaign, 325; considers withdrawal, 326; obtains surrender of Santiago, 327
Shantung, awarded to Japan, 522
Share system, in the South, 10, 227; effect of New Deal on, 656
Shaw University, Negro college, 104
Shearer, Norma, screen star, 593
Sheep-raising, in the Great Plains, 137
Shenandoah Valley, war devastation, 3
Sheridan, P. H., in charge of Louisiana and Texas, 32
Sherman, James S., nominated for Vice-President (1908), 419; in New York state convention (1910), 430; renominated in 1912, 435
Sherman, John, Secretary of Treasury, 146; accumulates gold reserve, 147; desires Republican nomination (1880), 161; connection with Sherman Anti-Trust Act, 179; as Secretary of State, 277
Sherman Anti-Trust Act, passed, 179, 216; difficulty of enforcement, 180, 382; Roosevelt's efforts to enforce, 385; applied to labor unions, 454
Sherman Silver Purchase Act, enacted, 216; burden on the gold reserve, 254; repeal demanded by Cleveland, 256
Shipstead, Henrik, elected to U.S. Senate, 559
Shoales, Charles L., invents typewriter, 174
Silliman, Benjamin, Jr., report on refinement of petroleum, 64
Silver, Grey, heads American Farm Bureau Federation, 546
Silver as currency, history of, 149; early legislation on, 150; declining use of, 151; favored by soft-money advocates, 152; Bland-Allison Act, 153; Sherman Silver Purchase Act, 216; as campaign issue in 1892, 252; demands for free coinage, 257, 266; in campaign of 1900, 338; Silver Purchase Act (1934), 657
Silver Republicans, numerous in the West, 267
Simmons, F. M., supports Underwood-Simmons Tariff, 445
Simmons, William J., founder of modern Ku Klux Klan, 538
Simpson, "Sockless" Jerry, Populist orator, 248
Sims, William S., commands U.S. Navy, 496

Sinclair, Harry F., involved in oil scandals, 534

Sinclair, Upton, criticizes meat-packing industry, 384

Single tax, advocated by Henry George, 241; by Tom Johnson, 405

Sioux (Minnesota), uprising of, 124; defeat of, 125

Sioux (western), on war-path, 127; leave Dakota reserve, 128; Custer massacre, 128

Sioux City, Ia., packing center, 69

"Sit-down" strike, used by CIO, 647

Sitting Bull, Sioux leader, 128; death of, 129; part in killing of the buffalo, 131

Sixteenth Amendment, adopted, 426

Skagway, coveted by Canada, 362

Skyscrapers, earliest, 290; later characteristics of, 612

Slovaks, emigration to United States, 73, 189

Slums, in 1870's, 82; fostered by immigration, 189; due to city crowding, 290

Smith, Alfred E., seeks Democratic nomination, 561; nominated in 1928, 575; sketch of, 577; loses nomination to Roosevelt (1932), 624; opposes New Deal, 674

Smith, Donald A., completes Canadian Pacific, 166; associated with J. J. Hill, 168

Smith, E. D., opposed by Roosevelt, 681

Smith, James, "boss" of New Jersey, 441

Smith, Jess, member of the "Ohio gang," 532

Smith, Sophia, founds Smith College, 104

Smith-Hughes Act, aids high-school education, 459

Smith-Lever Act, for agricultural extension, 459; leads to American Farm Bureau Federation, 542

Smithsonian Institution, surveys Grand Canyon, 103

Smoot, Reed, supports Hawley-Smoot Tariff, 582

Snyder, John W., OWMR director, 748

Social legislation, in the states, 407, 408; favored by Progressive Party (1912), 437; under the New Deal, 667

Social Security Act, New Deal measure, 668; opposed by Landon, 676

Socialist Party, nominates candidates in 1900, 338; history of, 421; vote in 1916, 491; opposition to war with Germany, 492; differs from Communists, 558; supports La Follette in 1924, 560; friendliness toward New Deal, 674; during World War II, 732

Socialist-Labor Party, revived by De Leon, 421

"Sod-house frontier," rapid disappearance of, 236

Soft-money ideas, Ohio idea, 42, 45; among western and southern debtors, 148; free silver, 151

Soil Conservation and Domestic Allotment Act, 654

Soldiers' Bonus Bill (1935), vetoed by Roosevelt, 658

Solid South, emerges, 49; in election of 1876, 141; end of carpet-bag rule, 146; challenged by Force Bill, 219; undented by Populists, 252; votes for Bryan in 1900, 338; broken by Roosevelt (1904), 413;

carried by Bryan (1908), 420; votes for Wilson (1916), 480

South, problems of, 1; conditions in, 2; transportation system, 4; losses from war, 4; from confiscation, 5; from death, 5; national policy toward, 6; need of outside capital, 9; plans for reconstruction, 24, 30; under carpet-bag rule, 35, 47; Ku Klux activities, 48; educational handicaps, 97; home rule, 146; the "new South," 221; labor conditions in, 225; agriculture in, 226; on protective tariff, 244; spread of silver heresy in, 269; on Smith candidacy (1928), 575; effect of New Deal measures on, 656

South America, unrest in, 588. See also Latin America

South Carolina, under carpet-bag rule, 38; and Ku Klux Act, 48; education in, 97; in election of 1876, 142; withdrawal of Federal troops, 146; cotton industry in, 223; Alliance successes in, 249

South Dakota, admitted to the Union, 214; Farmers' Alliance in, 246, 249; adopts initiative and referendum, 403; votes for Hughes (1916), 480; selected by Coolidge for vacation (1927), 574

Southern Pacific of Kentucky, railroad holding company, 165

Southern Pacific Railroad, unpopularity in California, 157; transcontinental connections, 165; merger with Union Pacific, 381; attacked by Hiram Johnson, 402

Southern Railway System, begun, 166

Spaak, Paul-Henri, President United Nations Assembly, 769

Spain, relations with U.S., 307; the *Virginius* affair, 308; sentiment for war with U.S., 312; peace treaty with U.S., 331; civil war in, 696; policy toward, 704; investigated by U.N., 772

Speculation, in western lands, 238, 536; in corporation securities, 584

Spencer, Herbert, views popularized by Fiske, 103

Spheres of influence, marked out in China, 356

Spies, August, anarchist editor, 183; tried, 184

Spoils system, used by Grant, 44, 50; leads to scandals, 87; denounced by Godkin, 90; denounced by Hayes, 145; under Harding, 519, 532

Sprague, Kate Chase, Washington hostess, 42

"Square deal" for labor, Theodore Roosevelt on, 392; in the states, 406

Stage-coaches, in the Far West, 120, 121

Stalin, Josef, Russian leader, 687; abolishes Comintern, 688; deal with Hitler, 699; seeks old Russian frontiers, 700; conferences with Churchill and Roosevelt, 740

"Stalwarts," in Republican Party, 160

Standard Oil Company, founded, 67; growth of, 176; prosecution of, 180; criticized by Tarbell, 384; fined by Judge Landis, 414

Stanford, Leland, railroad magnate, 77

Stanton, Edwin M., Johnson's efforts to remove, 31; resigns, 32

Stanton, Elizabeth Cady, suffragist, 112

Star-route frauds, uncovered, 195

Stassen, Harold E., governor of Minnesota, 681; candidate for Republican nomination (1948), 787

Steamboating, as seen by Mark Twain, 106; on upper Missouri, 119; possibility of revival, 397

Steel, romance of, 61; Bessemer and open-hearth processes, 62; organization of the steel business, 381. *See also* United States Steel Corporation

Steelman, John Roy, OWMR director, 748

Steffens, Lincoln, muckraker, 384; advertises municipal corruption, 405

Stephens, Alexander H., on conditions in the South, 3

Stephens, Uriah S., founds Knights of Labor, 181

Stettinius, Edward R., Jr., Secretary of State, 712; at San Francisco Conference, 745 n.; heads U.S. delegation to United Nations, 769

Steunenberg, Gov. Frank, murder of, 456

Stevens, John L., American minister to Hawaii, 302

Stevens, Thaddeus, sketch of, 19; his "conquered provinces" theory, 20; condemned by Johnson, 23; on Fourteenth Amendment, 25; favors impeachment of Johnson, 31; on Grant, 40; death of, 43

Stevenson, Adlai E. (b. 1835), nominated for Vice-President, 336

Stevenson, Adlai E. (b. 1900), elected senator from Illinois, 791

Stilwell, Joseph W., activities in China, 729

Stimson, Henry L., candidate for governor of New York, 430; Secretary of State under Hoover, 580; opposes Japanese aggressions in China, 694; Secretary of War under Roosevelt, 712; decision to use atomic bomb, 743

Stock Exchange. *See* New York Stock Exchange

Stokes, Edward S., killer of Jim Fisk, 83

Stone, William J., favors munitions embargo, 474

Straight University, Negro college, 104

Strikes, on railroads in 1877, 154; during 1885 and 1886, 182; Haymarket riot, 183; supported by A.F. of L., 186; Homestead strike, 261; Pullman strike, 262; among coal miners, 392; I.W.W.'s in, 456; strikes of 1919, 537; Boston police strike, 548; under NRA, 645; "sit-down" strikes, 647

Students' Army Training Corps, during World War I, 495

Submarine warfare, practiced by Germany, 474; abandoned for nine months, 476; how defeated, 497; success in World War II, 709; operations off U.S., 719

Sub-Treasury plan, for national warehouses, 250; favored by Populists, 251

Sub-Treasury system, for treasury receipts, 208; abolished, 450

Sugar industry, in Louisiana, 11; sugar bounty (1890), 218; Sugar Trust, 180; aided by Wilson-German Tariff, 258; charges against, 414

Sullivan, Louis, architect, 279

Sumner, Charles, sketch of, 20; his "state-suicide" theory, 20; condemned by Johnson, 23; opposes annexation of Santo Domingo, 55; on *Alabama* claims, 56

Sumner, William Graham, on protective tariff, 197

Supreme Court of the United States, on reconstruction, 37; number of justices reduced by Congress, 37; Legal-Tender cases, 45; increased in size, 46; decision in Knight case, 180, 382; invalidates income tax, 259; insular cases, 342; dissolves Northern Securities Company, 386; invalidates child labor law, 395; attacked by Theodore Roosevelt, 435; decision in Danbury Hatters' case, 454; O'Fallon decision, 525; Harding's appointments to, 553; powers attacked by La Follette, 562; invalidates NRA, 645; invalidates Guffey-Snyder Act, 646; invalidates AAA, 652; invalidates Frazier-Lemke Act, 653; on TVA, 666; opposition to Roosevelt policies, 674; attacked by Roosevelt, 677; decisions friendly to the New Deal, 678; reconstituted by Roosevelt, 679

Surplus, in U.S. Treasury, 160; decline of, 255

Sussex, attacked by German submarine, 476

Sweden, emigration from to United States, 72

Sweeny, Peter B., member Tweed Ring, 88

Swift, Gustavus F., Chicago meat-packer, 69

Taft, Charles P., brother of William Howard, 419

Taft, Lorado, sculptor, 279

Taft, Robert A., seeks Republican nomination (1948), 787

Taft, William Howard, heads commission to Philippines, 335; sits on the lid in Cuba, 341; becomes Civil Governor of the Philippines, 344; Secretary of War, 419; becomes President, 422; signs Payne-Aldrich Tariff, 425; defends it, 426; dismisses Pinchot, 427; accomplishments as President, 431; break with Roosevelt, 434; renominated in 1912, 435; defeated, 438; heads National War Labor Board, 495; supports Harding (1920), 517; becomes Chief Justice, 519; opinion on intrastate commerce, 524; interest in budget reform, 528

Taft-Hartley Labor-Management Relations Act, becomes law, 751; issue in 1948, 788

Tammany Society, political activities, 87; opposes Cleveland, 203; operations well known, 405; favors Champ Clark in 1912, 436; importance to Democratic Party, 560; supports Smith, 575

Tampa, Fla., troop concentration center, 323

Tanner, James, as commissioner of pensions, 213

Tarbell, Ida M., on Standard Oil, 384

Tariff, reductions of 1872, 46; attitude of Liberal Republicans toward, 51; in campaign of 1880, 163; criticisms of, 197; protectionist arguments, 198; revisions of 1883, 199; attitude of the parties on, 200; attacked by Cleveland, 208; Mills Bill, 209; McKinley Act, 217; attitude of southern farmers toward, 244; Wilson-

Gorman Act, 258; Dingley Act, 276; effect on Cuba, 308; as campaign issue (1900), 338; on Puerto Rican sugar, 342; "Iowa idea," 422; Payne-Aldrich Act, 423; reductions attempted, 433; Underwood-Simmons Act, 445; Emergency Tariff Act (1921), 529; Fordney-McCumber Act, 529; designed to aid business, 553; revision promised by Hoover, 580; Hawley-Smoot Tariff, 582; Hull reciprocal trade treaties, 682

Tariff Commission, established by Fordney-McCumber Act, 529; under Coolidge, 552

Taussig, Frank W., on protective tariff, 198

Taxation, reduction in excises, 46; reforms in Wisconsin, 401; wartime taxation, 488; post-war reductions, 529; Mellon's policy on, 550; in World War II, 712, 721; Tax Simplification Act, 736; Republican efforts to reduce, 751

Taylor, Glen H., candidate for Vice-President, 787; defeated, 791

Teachers College, Columbia, influence of, 606

Teapot Dome, oil scandal, 533

Technicolor, in motion pictures, 593

Technological unemployment, growth of, 556, 587

Teheran Conference, during World War II, 740

Telegraph, to Pacific, 121; use in business, 172

Telephone, invention of, 173

Television, a laboratory possibility, 596

Teller, Henry M., bolts Republican Party, 269

Tenancy, among freedmen, 10; among southern whites, 11, 227; attempts to check trend toward, 653

Tennessee, war devastation, 3; under Lincoln's plan of reconstruction, 12, 15; restored rights as a state, 26; industry in, 223; iron mines in, 224; in TVA area, 663

Tennessee Coal and Iron Company, absorbed by U.S. Steel, 415, 454

Tennessee Valley Authority (TVA), created, 663; opposition to, 666

Tenure of Office Act, passed, 28; invoked against Johnson, 31; declared unconstitutional, 32

Texas, national banks in, 227; land grants to railroads, 233 n.; Farmers' Alliance in, 246; Klan activities in, 560

Texas and Pacific Railroad, chartered, 78; absorbed by Southern Pacific, 165; strike on, 182

Texas vs. White, 37

Theater, in Deadwood, D.T., 123; in New York and Chicago, 612; federal theater project, 640

Third-party movements, common in American politics, 245; in election of 1900, 338; in 1908, 420; during 1920's, 558; during 1930's, 681; in 1948, 786

Thomas, Norman, Socialist candidate for President, 578, 628, 675; opposition to World War II, 732

Thompson, J. Edgar, employs Carnegie, 63, 78

Thrift stamps, supplement Liberty Loans, 489

Thurman, Allen G., nominated for Vice-President, 211

Thurmond, J. Strom, Dixiecrat candidate for President, 789; defeated, 791

Tilden, Samuel J., prosecutes Tweed Ring, 89; sketch of, 140; candidate for President, 141; too old for another nomination, 162

Tillman, Benjamin F., Alliance leader, 248

Timber and Stone Act, amends government land policy, 234

Timber Culture Act, amends government land policy, 234

Titanic, sinking of, 455

Tito, Marshal, Yugoslav leader, 725; strengthens Communism, 754; break with Moscow, 783

Titusville, Pennsylvania, scene of first oil well, 64

Tobacco industry, in upper South, 11; growth of, 224; organization of, 381

Tojo, Hideki, trial and execution, 762

Tokyo, bombed by Americans, 727; occupied, 731; post-war government, 761

Toral, José, Spanish commander at Santiago, 327

Town life, importance in nineteenth century, 293

Townley, Arthur C., founds Non-Partisan League, 544

Townsend, Dr. F. E., on old age pensions, 667

Trade. See Foreign trade

Trade Agreements Act, to promote reciprocity, 682

Transportation Act of 1920. See Esch-Cummins Act

Treaty of Neuilly, between Bulgaria and the Allies, 511

Treaty of Paris (1898), American instructions, 330; terms of, 331; ratification of 332

Treaty of Portsmouth, ends Russo-Japanese War, 360

Treaty of Rio de Janeiro, provides for all-American defense, 767

Treaty of Saint-Germain, between Austria and the Allies, 510

Treaty of Sèvres, between Turkey and the Allies, 511

Treaty of Trianon, between Hungary and the Allies, 511

Treaty of Versailles, terms of, 508; consideration by U.S. Senate, 512; Senate reservations, 512; defeat of, 513; rejected by Harding, 520

Treaty of Washington, between U.S. and Great Britain, 57

Trieste, World War II settlement, 754; U.N. failure to appoint governor, 773

Trotsky, Leon, Russian leader, 501, 686

Truman, Harry S., nominated for Vice-President, 737; becomes President, 739; ends gasoline rationing, 749; vetoes OPA extension, 750; opposes tax reduction, 751; dismisses Wallace from Cabinet, 753; visits Mexico City, 768; approves proposed Palestine settlement, 773; the Truman Doctrine, 777; nominated for President (1948), 788; elected, 790

Trumbull, Lyman, Liberal Republican, 51
Trusts, Standard Oil Trust, 176; general resort to, 177; advantages of, 178; growth of, 381; early attempts to regulate, 382; Wilson's efforts to control, 451; campaign promises of 1912, 452; legislation on, 453
Tuberculosis, common among Negroes, 226
Tugwell, Rexford G., Roosevelt brain-truster, 627; heads RA, 653
Tumulty, Joseph P., private secretary to Wilson, 444
Tunisia, Allied campaign in, 723
Turkey, fights with Germany, 482; defeated, 500; American aid to, 777
Turner, Frederick Jackson, on significance of the frontier, 280
Turner, George Kibbe, muckraker, 384
Tutuila, American interests in, 302; acquisition of, 348
Twain, Mark. See Samuel Langhorne Clemens
Tweed Ring, compared with carpet-bag rule, 39; activities, 88; death of Tweed, 89
Twentieth Amendment, adopted, 628
Twenty-first Amendment, recalls the Eighteenth, 602, 605, 632
"Twilight zone," between state and national authority, 391
"Two-thirds rule," deadlocks Democratic Convention (1924), 561
Tydings, Millard E., opposed by Roosevelt, 681
Tydings-McDuffie Act, for independence of the Philippines, 346; carried out, 763
Typewriter, invented, 174

Underwood, Oscar W., candidate for Democratic nomination (1912), 436; supports Underwood-Simmons Tariff, 445
Unemployment, in 1870's, 82; after Panic of 1893, 260; during Panic of 1907, 415; Wilson's efforts to reduce, 455; after the World War, 539; affected by technological improvements, 556; during 1930's, 586, 587, 618; after election of 1932, 629; reduced by CWA, 638; by PWA, 642; permanent nature of, 667; Social Security Act, 668
Uniformity, in American life, 284; accentuated by movies, 594
Union League, work with Negroes, 33; opposed by Ku Klux Klan, 47; works for Grant, 52
Union of Soviet Socialist Republics (USSR), see Russia
Union Pacific Railroad, relations with Crédit Mobilier, 53; charter, 75; labor problem, 76; completed, 78; gauge, 80; bankruptcy of, 255; merger with Southern Pacific, 381
Union Party, nominates Johnson for Vice-President, 15; taken seriously by Johnson, 17; in election of 1866, 26
United Confederate Veterans, formed, 242
United Hebrew Charities, wartime activities, 489
United Mine Workers, strikes of, 392, 749
United Nations, Dumbarton Oaks Conference, 738; San Francisco Conference, 740; the Yalta decisions, 741; first meeting of

General Assembly, 769; Security Council, 770; Economic and Social Council, 770; Trusteeship Council, 771; International Court of Justice, 771; Military Staff Committee, 771; Little Assembly, 771; business before, 772; efforts to end air-lift, 785
United Nations Relief and Rehabilitation Administration (UNRRA), established, 745; activities, 779
United States Army. See Army of the United States
United States Employment Service, during World War I, 495; under New Deal, 638
United States Housing Authority (USHA), New Deal agency, 662; during recession of 1937–38, 680
United States Navy. See Navy
United States Shipping Board, created, 478; activities of, 493; the new merchant marine, 525; efforts to sell ships, 552; supplanted by Maritime Commission, 661
United States Steel Corporation, formed, 381; capitalization of, 414; absorbs Tennessee Coal and Iron Company, 415; suit for dissolution brought under Taft, 434; decision for defendant, 453; reaches agreement with CIO, 647
United States Supreme Court. See Supreme Court
U'Ren, William S., Oregon reformer, 402; promotes "Oregon system," 403
Utah, establishes woman suffrage, 112, 408; prosperity of, 120

V–E Day, officially proclaimed, 726
V–J Day, officially proclaimed, 731
Vail, Theodore N., promotes telephone, 173
Van Devanter, Willis, resigns from Supreme Court, 678
Van Hise, Charles R., university president, 401
Vandenberg, Arthur H., presidential candidate, 675; delegate to United Nations, 769; supports Truman Doctrine, 777
Vanderbilt, Cornelius, railroad activities, 78, 86; endows Vanderbilt University, 98; as railroad consolidator, 168
Vanderlip, Frank D., on causes of the Great Depression, 587
Vanzetti, Bartolomeo, convicted of murder, 537
Vassar College, opens, 103
Veblen, Thorstein, theory of conspicuous waste, 291; books by, 385
Venezuela, boundary dispute, 305; incident of 1902, 370; settlement of the incident, 371, 375
Vera Cruz, occupied on Wilson's order, 464
Vermont, votes for Hoover (1932), 628; votes for Landon (1936), 677
Veterans' Bureau, headed by Forbes, 519; duties of, 527; scandals in, 533; expenditures for veterans, 621
Vichy government, activities, 717, 721
Vienna, post-war occupation, 756
Vigilantes, in Montana, 122
Villa, Francisco, Mexican bandit, 464
Villard, Henry, railroad operations, 164; completes Northern Pacific, 165

Vinson, Fred M., OWMR director, 748; proposed mission to Russia, 786

Virgin Islands, acquired from Denmark, 348; part in Caribbean control, 372

Virginia, loyal government recognized, 12; industry in, 223; in TVA area, 663

Virginius affair, during first Cuban insurrection, 308

Visit and search, British practice, 473; German practice, 475. *See also* American neutrality

Vladivostok expedition, American part in, 500

Vocational Education, Federal Board of, work of rehabilitation, 490

Volstead Act, for prohibition enforcement, 603; amended, 632

Volunteer army. *See* Army of the United States

Wabash decision, amends Granger doctrine, 171

Wade, Benjamin, congratulates Johnson, 15

Wade-Davis Bill, pocket-vetoed by Lincoln, 13

Wages and Hours Act, New Deal measure, 666

Wagner, Robert F., heads National Labor Board, 644

Wagner Act, establishes U.S. employment service, 638

Wagner-Connery Labor Relations Act, New Deal measure, 646; succeeded by Taft-Hartley Act, 751

Waite, Davis H., governor of Colorado, 264

Wald, Lillian D., settlement worker, 295

Wall Street, supports T. Roosevelt (1904), 413; bomb explosion in (1920), 538

Wallace, Henry A., Secretary of Agriculture under F. D. Roosevelt, 630; supervises AAA, 648; promotes "ever normal granary," 655; Democratic nominee for Vice-President, 714; defeated for renomination, 737; pro-Russian attitude, 753; candidate for President, 786; poor showing, 791

Wallace, Henry C., Secretary of Agriculture under Harding, supports McNary-Haugen Bill, 571

Walsh, Frank P., heads National War Labor Board, 495

Walsh, Thomas J., investigates oil scandals, 534; death of, 631

Wanamaker, John, Postmaster-General under Harrison, 213; predicts higher prices due to tariff, 219

War aims, statements of, 481, 503; Wilson's Fourteen Points, 504; Central Powers, 505

War Boards, enumerated, 494; abolished, 523

War criminals, trials of, in Germany, 757; in Japan, 762

War Debts, owing to U.S. citizens, 483; owing to U.S. government, 488; American expectation of repayment, 565; funding negotiations, 566; cancellation advocated, 622; payments to U.S. discontinued except by Finland, 623; subject of Hoover-Roosevelt Conference, 629; Roosevelt's attitude toward, 635

War Finance Corporation, furnishes credit to business, 494; life extended after the war, 547

War Industries Board, functions of, 493

War Labor Conference Board, created, 495

War Labor Policies Board, created, 495

War Production Board, established, 719; activities of, 748

War Risk Insurance, Bureau of, established, 490; succeeded by Veterans Bureau, 526

War-savings certificates, supplement Liberty Loans, 489

War Trade Board, functions of, 493

Warmoth, H. C., governor of Louisiana, 38

Warren, Earl, candidate for Vice-President, 787

Wartime finance, loans to the Allies, 483; Liberty Loans, 488; taxation, 488; in World War II, 721; cost of the war, 735; inflation, 749

Warsaw Manifesto, establishes Cominform, 776

Washburn, C. C., Minneapolis miller, 70

Washburne, E. B., Secretary of State, 44; resigns to become minister to France, 44; desires Republican nomination, 161

Washington, Booker T., heads Tuskegee Institute, 105; dines with Theodore Roosevelt, 411

Washington, admitted to the Union, 214; grants suffrage to women, 408

Washington Conference, on limitation of armaments, 520

"Watchful waiting," Wilson's policy toward Mexico, 464

Water-power. *See* Hydroelectric power

Watson, Thomas E., Populist leader, 248; candidate for Speaker, 249; candidate for Vice-President (1896), 272

Watterson, Henry, writes Democratic platform of 1880, 163; on southern industrialism, 289

Weaver, James B., Greenback candidate for President in 1880, 163; Populist orator, 248; Populist candidate for President in 1892, 251

Webb, W. P., on the Great Plains, 115

Wedemeyer, A. C., activities in China, 729

Wellesley, college for women, 104

Wells, D. A., made special commissioner of the revenue, 46; advocates lower tariffs, 197

Wells, Fargo, and Company, express firm, 121; served the Black Hills, 123

West Virginia, oil fields in, 65; coal industry in, 392; votes for Roosevelt (1904), 413; relief burden in, 619

Western Rural, farm journal, 246

Westinghouse, George, demonstrates airbrake, 80

Weyler, Valeriano, Spanish commander in Cuba, 309

Wheat, declining price of, 540; co-operative marketing of, 546; rising price during campaign of 1924, 562; exportable surplus, 570; grain stabilization corporation, 581; crop insurance for, 654; continuing surpluses of, 655

Wheeler, Burton K., elected to U.S. Senate, 559; Progressive nominee for Vice-President, 559; opposes court-packing plan, 678; isolationism, 710

Wheeler, "Fighting Joe," in Santiago campaign, 325

Wheeler, Wayne B., Anti-Saloon League leader, 407

Wheeler, William A., nominated for Vice-President, 140

"Whiskey Ring," Grant scandal, 54

White, Andrew D., president of Cornell, 98

White, Henry, on Peace Commission (1919), 507 n.

White, Justice Edward D., dissents from Northern Securities decision, 386; made Chief Justice by Taft, 432

White, Stanford, architect, 279

White, William Allen, heads Committee to Defend America, 710

"White counties," in the South, 33

Whitlock, Brand, Toledo reformer, 405

Whitman, Walt, Leaves of Grass, 105

Whitney, William C., Secretary of the Navy, 209

Wickersham, G. W., Attorney-General under Taft, 434; heads Law Enforcement Commission, 604

Wiley, Dr. H. W., on food adulteration, 391

Wilhelm II of Germany, congratulates Kruger, 307; sends Prince Henry to U.S., 355; visits Sultan of Morocco, 376; receives Col. House, 468; abdication of, 506

Wilkerson, Judge J. H., grants labor injunction, 553

Willard, Daniel, heads Advisory Commission, 493

Willard, Frances E., founds W.C.T.U., 110

Willkie, Wendell L., Republican nominee for President (1940), 714; death, 737

Wilson, James, Secretary of Agriculture, 422

Wilson, William B., Secretary of Labor, 455

Wilson, William L., introduces tariff measure, 258

Wilson, Woodrow, on Panama tolls controversy, 370; intervention in Dominican Republic, 373; nominated for President (1912), 436; sketch of, 440; as governor of New Jersey, 441; legislative program, 444; personal messages to Congress, 445; departures from the Jeffersonian tradition, 460; Mexican policy, 464; proclaims American neutrality (1914), 470; Lusitania correspondence, 476; Sussex note, 476; favors preparedness, 477; renominated, 478; re-elected, 480; asks for statements of war aims, 480; asks for war with Germany, 482; demands war to end war, 486; on wartime intolerance, 496; urges a "just peace," 503; his reply to the Pope, 503; the Fourteen Points, 504; election of 1918, 507; heads American peace delegation, 507; Senate efforts to discredit, 512; collapse of, 512; ignores House's advice to resign, 513; opinions on budget reform, 528; congratulatory telegram to Coolidge, 548; plan to resign in 1916, 629

Wilson Dam, on Tennessee River, 552

Wilson-Gorman Tariff, becomes law, 258; provisions of, 259; effect on Cuba, 308

Windom, William, heads committee to investigate railroads, 171

Winona, address, by President Taft, 426

Wirz, Henry, execution of, 37

Wisconsin, Granger laws, 94; University of, 101; under Robert M. La Follette, Sr., 401; "Wisconsin Idea," 402; Republican gains in (1938), 681

Wolcott, Edward O., heads committee on international bimetallism, 277

Woman suffrage, demands for, 110; Nineteenth Amendment, 408; endorsed by Progressive Party, 437

Women in industry, employment of, 82; numbers of, 290; protection for demanded by Roosevelt, 394; state laws respecting, 408; activities during World War I, 495

Women's Christian Temperance Union, founded, 110; church support of, 295

Women's colleges, growth of, 104

Wood, Leonard, helps raise Rough Riders, 318; commands "immunes" in Cuba, 330; extends sanitation in Cuba, 340; governor-general of the Philippines, 346; seeks Republican nomination (1920), 515

Woodford, Stewart L., minister to Spain, 310; seeks to avert war, 312

Woodin, William H., Secretary of the Treasury, 630

Work relief, under CWA, 638; under PWA, 639

Worker's Party (1924), name used by Communists, 558

Workingmen's Party, formed in California, 157; wins special election, 158

Workmen's compensation. See Employers' liability laws

Works Progress Administration (WPA), New Deal agency, 639; during recession of 1937–38, 680

World Court, favored by U.S. at second Hague Conference, 377; contemplated by League of Nations Covenant, 510; organized, 522; participation by United States defeated, 523; American sentiment for, 568. See also Permanent Court of International Justice

World Economic Congress, advocated by Hoover, 627; Roosevelt sends delegation to, 635; wrecked by Roosevelt, 636

World Peace Foundation, established, 378

World War Foreign Debt Commission, negotiations of, 566

World War I, outbreak of, 465; immediate causes of, 468; American neutrality, 470; importance to U.S. of allied trade, 472; U.S. declares war on Germany and Austria-Hungary, 482; reasons for American intervention, 483; American participation in, 501; American losses, 502; unified system of supply, 503; armistice terms, 506

World War II, outbreak of, 699; German successes, 700; U.S. measures "short of war," 713; Lend-Lease Act, 714; Atlantic Charter, 716; U.S. at war, 718; Japanese victories, 719; Pacific operations, 721; invasion of North Africa, 721; Tunisia and Italy, 723; second front in France, 724; V–E Day, 726; Pacific victories, 727; V–J Day, 731; the "home front," 731; war losses, 734; cost, 735

World's Fairs, Philadelphia, 113; Chicago (1893), 279; Chicago (1933), 614; New York, 614; San Francisco, 614
Wounded Knee, Battle of, with Sioux Indians, 129
Wright, Fielding, Dixiecrat candidate for Vice-President, 789; defeated, 791
Wright, Frank Lloyd, architect, 613
Wright, Orville and Wilbur, aviators, 596
Wyoming, adopts woman suffrage, 112, 408; Wyoming Stock-Growers' Association, 136; admitted to the Union, 214

Yale University, confers first Ph.D., 102
Yalta Conference, concessions to Russia, 741
Yap, awarded to Japan, 522
"Yellow dog" contracts, opposed by A.F. of L., 186

Yellow fever, among troops in Cuba, 328; investigations into, 339
Yellow peril, talk of, 331
Young, Brigham, Mormon leader, 120
Young, Owen D., helps draft plan for German reparations, 567
Young Men's Christian Association, work of, 109; wartime activities, 489
Young Women's Christian Association, work of, 109
Yugoslavia, created a state, 511; partisan forces in, 725; Yalta decisions on, 742; gains from World War II, 754; Communist control of, 776; use of UNRRA aid, 780; break with Russia, 783

Zimmermann Plot, influence in U.S., 485